THE
LAW
OF THE
POOR

CHANDLER PUBLICATIONS IN
POLITICAL SCIENCE
VICTOR JONES, EDITOR

The Editors of California Law Review
who participated in the production
of this symposium are:

Contents

Preface JACOBUS TEN BROEK vii

Introduction MICHAEL E. TIGAR xi

The American Welfare System J. M. WEDEMEYER AND
    PERCY MOORE 2

The Children of Leviathan: Psychoanalytic Speculations
    Concerning Welfare and Punitive Sanctions
    BERNARD L. DIAMOND 33

Welfare from Below: Recipients' Views of the Public
    Welfare System SCOTT BRIAR 46

Race, Poverty, and the Law LOREN MILLER 62

Privacy, Poverty, and the Constitution ALBERT M. BENDICH 83

Unconstitutional Conditions: Welfare Benefits with Strings
    Attached ROBERT M. O'NEIL 119

Controlling Official Behavior in Welfare Administration
    JOEL F. HANDLER 155

Vagrancy Concepts in Welfare Law MARGARET K. ROSENHEIM 187

The Constitutionality of Residence Tests for General and
    Categorical Assistance Programs BERNARD EVANS HARVITH 243

Public Housing and the Poor: An Overview
    LAWRENCE M. FRIEDMAN 318

Protecting the Interests of the Indigent Tenant: Two
    Approaches CARL SCHIER 346

Juvenile Courts, Family Courts, and the Poor Man
    MONRAD G. PAULSEN 370

Poverty and the Law of Child Custody HERMA HILL KAY AND
    IRVING PHILIPS 393

Guardianship or "Permanent Placement of Children"
    HASSELTINE B. TAYLOR 417

Family Law and Welfare Policies: The Case for "Dual Systems"
THOMAS P. LEWIS AND ROBERT J. LEVY   424

Dual Systems of Family Law: A Comment WALTER O. WEYRAUCH   457

Reimbursement of Counsel Fees and the Great Society
ALBERT A. EHRENZWEIG   468

The German System of Legal Aid: An Alternative Approach
PHILIP A. STOHR   477

The Disabled and the Law of Welfare JACOBUS TEN BROEK
AND FLOYD W. MATSON   485

The Right to Live in the World: The Disabled in the Law
of Torts JACOBUS TEN BROEK   517

Mental Health Services for the Poor HENRY WEIHOFEN   596

Marriage and Legitimacy in Mexican Culture: Mexico
and California WOODROW BORAH AND SHERBURNE F. COOK   622

The Urban Law Program of the University of Detroit
School of Law NORMAN L. MILLER AND JAMES C. DAGGITT   685

Preface

THIS SYMPOSIUM is the product of a project organized in the fall of 1965 and brought to completion in the spring of 1966. The purpose of the symposium and project is reasonably ambitious: to provide a critical review of the rules and procedures, doctrines and presuppositions of the law applicable to the poor, primarily as that law is found in welfare codes, statutes, ordinances, programs, and administration, but as it is found in a limited number of other areas as well. We thus hope to share in the initial steps currently under way: (1) in exploring the scope and nature of the law applicable to the poor; (2) in bringing awareness of the importance and extent of this field of law to the legal profession, law schools, and social scientists generally; (3) in providing a foundation of thought, analysis, and scholarship for the use of the legal profession and the courts in deciding cases and for the use of legislators and welfare planners.

Because the law applicable to the poor, as thus defined, proves to be, today, no less than in earlier times, in large measure a special law, consisting of rules and procedures applicable to the poor as a distinct class, we have come to speak of it as the law of the poor.

The overall task of review is far from completed. Many topics are untouched. Many elements of similarity and of difference between the law of the poor and the law of the rest of the community remain to be investigated and publicized. Only a beginning has been made in determining the extent to which the Constitution and wise social policy require the abolition of the law of the poor and the means of bringing about the legal as well as the social, economic, and political integration of the poor into the life of the community.

Studies of the substantive law, it seems to us, are a necessary concomitant of the efforts to bring the law to the poor through making legal services available to them, efforts such as those of the national conferences and other activities of the Department of Health, Education and Welfare, and the Office of Economic Opportunity, and the recent decisions of the United States Supreme Court laying down various requirements of counsel and records in the case of indigent defendants.

The procedures of the project may be briefly stated. First, the prospective authors and the potential topics had to be brought together, a process which often required some modification of both. The papers were completed, multilithed, and distributed to all the authors and selected critics in advance of a three-day conference at the University of California, Berkeley. It was thus possible to devote the conference to presentation of critiques of the papers and to general discussion among the authors rather than to reading the papers. Following the conference, the authors had another month in which they might revise their papers in the light of the criticism and discussion before finally submitting them for publication. The editors of the *California Law Review* joined in the conference, thus getting a preview of the articles, the help of commentary of other contributors in the field, and a preliminary opportunity for discussion with the authors.

The valuable duty of critic-discussant at the conference was performed by: Jerome E. Carlin, Assistant Professor and Resident Sociologist, Center for the Study of Law and Society, University of California, Berkeley; Barbara Curran, Research Attorney, American Bar Foundation; Caleb Foote, Professor of Law and Criminology, University of California, Berkeley; Harold Horowitz, Professor of Law, University of California at Los Angeles; Paul Jacobs, Journalist and Research Analyst, Center for the Study of Law and Society, University of California, Berkeley; Marvin E. Larson, Director, Kansas State Department of Social Welfare; Frank C. Newman, Dean, School of Law, University of California, Berkeley; Edward V. Sparer, Legal Director, Center on Social Welfare Policy and Law, Columbia University School of Social Work; Olive Stone, Senior Reader in Law, London School of Economics and Political Science; Arvo Van Alstyne, Professor of Law, University of California at Los Angeles; Walter O. Weyrauch, Professor of Law, University of Florida and Visiting Research Lawyer, Social Science Project, Space Sciences Laboratory, University of California, Berkeley.

A word must be said about sponsorship and support. The Center for the Study of Law and Society, an interdisciplinary enterprise on the Berkeley campus, undertook the role of official sponsor early in the conception of the project, provided back-up support while funds were being sought, contributed the services of its Vice-Chairman, Sheldon Messinger, as associate project director, and otherwise made its staff and facilities available. Principal financing of the project came in the form of a grant from the California State Department of Social Welfare and that department also gave active support in other respects. The National Federation of the Blind provided a fund of knowledge and experience in the field of welfare and welfare law, and, through its Berkeley office, typing, secretarial, multilithing, and other services.

The editors of the *Californa Law Review* have been collaborators from the beginning. Theirs has been the arduous task of the editorial work, a task performed with ability, industry, and distinction.

*Jacobus tenBroek**

---

* A.B., 1934, M.A., 1935, LL.B., 1938, J.S.D., 1940, University of California, Berkeley; S.J.D., 1947, Harvard University; D. Litt., 1956, Findlay College; LL.D., 1964, Parsons College. Project Director, Conference on the Law of the Poor; Professor of Political Science, University of California, Berkeley.

Introduction

There is a logic to the order in which the articles in this symposium appear. The first group of articles deals with general and recurrent problems in the law of the poor. Later articles deal with special problems such as housing, legal services, family law, and so forth.

I

GENERAL PROBLEMS

The first article, "The American Welfare System," is coauthored by the Director of the California State Department of Social Welfare, John Wedemeyer. The article provides a framework for much of the discussion in the later contributions, and describes the statutory and administrative parameters of American welfare law.

The next two articles, by Dr. Bernard Diamond and Professor Scott Briar, view welfare law from two nonlegal perspectives. Dr. Diamond's article projects certain psychoanalytical insights into a discussion of the purposes and practices of American welfare law. Professor Briar reports the findings of a study of welfare recipients' attitudes toward the conditions upon application for and receipt of benefits; the study reveals that at this point the recipients may comprise the group least sensitive to incursions upon their privacy and freedom of action.

Judge Loren Miller's article, "Race, Poverty, and the Law," discusses another problem which cuts across the law of the poor: the connection between color and low income. Professor Albert Bendich argues for a radical restructuring of the American welfare system to guarantee the "right of privacy"; his article, "Privacy, Poverty, and the Constitution," attacks not only existing conditions which attach to the receipt of welfare benefits, but also the inadequacy of the grants themselves. Professor Bendich argues that inadequate welfare grants prevent recipients from purchasing shelter, food, and other rudimentary necessities that are preconditions to enjoying a "right of privacy."

Professor Robert M. O'Neil discusses "Unconstitutional Conditions: Welfare Benefits with Strings Attached." Drawing on recent cases in analogous fields as well as precedent in welfare law, he examines conditions such as loyalty oaths, demands that the recipient of a benefit order his social life in a particular way, and so forth.

Professor Joel Handler focuses upon the great discretion lodged in the lower levels of welfare law decision-making. Though he recognizes and sympathizes with the current moves to ensure reviewability of welfare administrator decisions, and to provide substantive standards for review, Professor Handler is pessimistic as to the prospects for reforming the basic social worker-client relationship through techniques of administrative law.

Professor Margaret Rosenheim's article discusses the recurrence of vagrancy concepts in welfare law. She finds the social stigma which attached in medieval times to the vagrant, and to his alleged characteristics of wandering, idleness, and profligacy, reflected in conditions attached to many modern welfare programs.

Professor Bernard Harvith attacks at length the residence tests which condition much of the public assistance in the United States today. His attack focuses upon both the general assistance programs, which are funded by states, and the categorical assistance programs, which are federally-supported under authorizations permitting states to impose residence tests for qualification.

II
SPECIAL AREAS
A. Housing and the Poor

Professor Lawrence Friedman's article, "Public Housing and the Poor: An Overview," concentrates principally upon federally-assisted project housing. Professor Friedman's critique is directed at both the ideology and the administration of public housing programs since 1937.

Carl Schier's discussion, "Protecting the Indigent Tenant: Two Approaches," argues for an extension of warranty concepts to increase the landlord's obligation to provide habitable shelter, and proposes a statutory lease as a means of securing tenant protection.

B. Family Law

Professor Monrad Paulsen's article, "Juvenile Courts, Family Courts, and the Poor Man," draws heavily on Professor Paulsen's observations of the New York Family Court. He is on the whole approving of the family court concept, but finds that in practice the courts are a mechanism for dispensing unequal justice.

Professor Herma Hill Kay and Dr. Irving Phillips deal with child custody in the family law of the poor. They focus upon the values courts apply in deciding to make a custody award, and upon the pressures exerted by welfare law systems upon child custody. Hasseltine Taylor's article proposes that the system of guardian and ward, with ancient lineage in Anglo-American law, be used to solve some problems of permanent care for children.

As a final contribution to the section on family law, we have included a discussion of the theory and practice of "dual systems of family law." Professor tenBroek first enunciated the theory that the family law of

California (and by implication of all the fifty states) applies different rules to the rich and the poor and suggested that aspects of this dual system might fall afoul of the equal protection clause. In this symposium, Professors Robert Levy and Thomas Lewis make a "case for dual systems," pointing out that not every rule of unequal application is for that reason unconstitutionally discriminatory. They point to examples of rules which in their view justifiably fall unevenly upon the rich and the poor. Professor Walter O. Weyrauch summarizes the tenBroek theory and provides a critique of it and of the Levy-Lewis position.

C. Legal Services

The problem of legal services for the poor has been treated in many law reviews, bar journals, judicial opinions, and legislative reports. In this symposium, we have tried to hew to the substantive aspects of the law of the poor, except where we believed that something could be said that has not already been inserted into the dialogue about lawyers and poverty. The two articles on legal services have this merit. Professor Albert Ehrenzweig draws upon his experience as judge, practicing attorney, and law teacher in Europe and the United States to propose that American jurisdictions adopt the European system of awarding counsel fees to the winning party in a lawsuit. He feels that such a system would encourage the poor to litigate claims small in amount.

Philip Stohr describes the West German system of legal aid to the civil litigant, *Armenrecht*. This system provides for appointment of counsel for the civil plaintiff or defendant as a matter of right.

D. The Physically Disabled

The physically disabled are the subject of two sets of rules in American law. The first set of rules provides welfare benefits, hospital and medical services for the indigent, vocational rehabilitation and counselling—these rules are a part of the American welfare system. The second set of rules is really a set of exceptions—or refusal to create exceptions—to rules of civil liability and civil right.

Professors Jacobus tenBroek and Floyd Matson have written on "The Disabled and the Law of Welfare." Professor tenBroek has contributed an article on the physically disabled in the law of torts.

E. Mental Handicap

The field of mental health services for the poor is dealt with by Professor Henry Weihofen, who also points up procedural problems in coercing citizens to use such services. Professor Weihofen also makes brief mention of tort and criminal law problems of the mentally handicapped.

F. Phenomena of Cultural Carryover

Professors Sherburne Cook and Woodrow Borah have contributed a study of family patterns in Mexican-American families receiving welfare. Their research indicates that many of the same patterns are a part of Mexican culture, traceable to medieval Spanish canon and secular law. Their data is limited and justifies only a tentative statement of their hypothesis, which is that much conduct thought to be endemic to "the poor" may in fact reflect patterns of behavior endemic to cultural groups which tend to be at the lower end of the socio-economic scale.

G. The Law Schools and Poverty

Dean Norman Miller and James C. Daggitt have written of the University of Detroit School of Law Urban Law Program. Combining teaching and research with provision of legal services to the poor, the program may suggest that the law schools can do much more than they have in this field. Miller and Daggitt point out that the changing complexion of American life, and the increasing recognition of the problems of the poor, bring new legal concepts into importance for legal study and research.

*Michael E. Tigar***

** B.A., 1962, LL.B., 1966, University of California, Berkeley. Editor-in-Chief, California Law Review, 1965-66.

THE
LAW
OF THE
POOR

The American Welfare System

J. M. Wedemeyer* and *Percy Moore***

I

THE STATUTORY FRAMEWORK

THIS ARTICLE MAINLY DISCUSSES the American system of welfare represented by the interrelated federal and state statutes and administrative practices and relations developed pursuant to the Social Security Act of 1935.[1] This rather narrow approach is not chosen to discount the very substantial body of related welfare law encompassed in other statutes. It is based, rather, upon two premises: First, the programs and administrative relationships established under the Social Security Act have come to be recognized generally as *the* public welfare program, and hence to have a certain connotation to the ordinary citizen; second, and more importantly, the 1935 enactments represent the sharpest break with previously existing patterns of welfare administration that we have experienced.

A. Antecedent Welfare Operations

Until about the middle of the nineteenth century, welfare consisted primarily of various forms of poor relief administered and financed under private auspices or by local cities or counties under laws which placed a vaguely defined responsibility upon the legal subdivision. Generally, there were no standards as to either content or amount of aid, no concept of right, and qualification for relief rested upon complete destitution and lack of any relatives to charge with support. The concept of welfare was characterized by frequent transporting of the poor back to their place of legal settlement, vagrancy practices, and methods designed to deter people from seeking help. Courts seldom considered the rights of the person in need. Court procedures frequently resembled criminal prosecutions rather than expressions of humanitarian concern. Such solicitude as was expressed tended to be mostly for communities or individuals who had gratuitously assumed some cost of maintaining an indigent person. Cases frequently dealt with recovery of costs from reluctant relatives or from jurisdictions believed to be responsible as the place of legal settlement.[2]

---

* Director, California Department of Social Welfare.

** Staff Assistant to the Director, California Department of Social Welfare.

[1] 49 Stat. 620 (1935), as amended, 42 U.S.C. §§ 301-1394 (1964), as amended, 42 U.S.C. §§ 302-1396d (Supp. I, 1965).

[2] See generally LEYENDECKER, PROBLEMS AND POLICY IN PUBLIC ASSISTANCE 21-51 (1955);

The current vestige of practice characteristic of this era generally is found in the category of General Relief, or General Assistance, frequently administered with many of the typical attitudes, and often under state statutes and local ordinances, which date back to this period.

Particularly during the last half of the nineteenth century, rather extensive development of special provisions for certain groups of dependent or needy people began to appear, and along with this, though relatively late in the game, came provisions for some minimum standard of care enforced through governmental supervisory and inspection bodies. At first these provisions tended largely to be concerned with children— the provisions usually applying to orphanages or institutions. There was no uniform pattern of public support for these institutions so that they operated as privately financed organizations, as partially or totally subsidized private facilities, or as public institutions.

This was followed by development of similar facilities and programs for other persons or groups recognized as having a particular claim on the public largesse—such as the blind, the aged, the mentally ill, the mentally retarded. These piecemeal statutory developments represented a growing recognition that the basic poor relief provisions and the increased and indiscriminate use of the "poorhouse" or almshouse were inadequate.

Leyendecker characterizes the developments during the last half of the nineteenth century and up to the depression years as the growth of "preferential assistance."[3] Preferential assistance was the result of a growing belief that "while the poor as a class were [to be] generally distrusted . . . some poor persons were 'worthy' in that their poverty was 'no fault of their own,' or because there seemed to be evidence that they had the capacity for 'moral regeneration.' . . . [T]he almshouse with its deterrent and punitive features would be the only recourse of all others who professed to be in need."[4]

The programs which emerged from this pre-depression period and the concepts and attitudes which accompanied them provided the prototypes both for elements of the Social Security Act and for many other specialized programs which must equally be considered part of the functioning welfare system of the United States. Most of these developments emerged during the first three decades of the current century. They may be characterized in three main ways: first, the immediate antecedents of the categorical public assistance provisions of the Social Security Act;

Riesenfeld, *The Formative Era of American Public Assistance Law*, 43 CALIF L. REV. 175, 200-33 (1955).

[3] LEYENDECKER, *op. cit. supra* note 2, at 52-57.

[4] *Id.* at 46.

second, the beginning of the variety of special service programs, many stimulated by some form of limited federal grant-in-aid; and third, the beginnings of social insurance programs in the states and other countries.

The forerunners of categorical assistance programs consisted of laws enacted in a number of jurisdictions providing for noncontributory "pensions" to the blind, the aged, veterans, and widows or other women with children deprived of the father's support. Most state laws clearly retained many of the conditions that reflected concern for worthiness—factors which conditioned any concept of right.[5] Nevertheless the popular designation of the benefits as "pensions" carried connotations that had not existed previously. The designation was controversial, and many social service leaders of the times opposed it, calling it unwarranted.[6]

Most of the "pension" legislation enacted by states was permissive; that is, local jurisdictions could make such grants, but usually were not required to do so. Funding was strictly local, depending upon property taxes. While the state laws set some standards, much as to eligibility and benefits was left to local inclination. In the few instances where special financing was provided, the provisions were far from adequate.[7]

Because of the above factors, in 1934 the Mother's Pension programs were actually operative in fewer than half the jurisdictions covered by the permissive statutes, and less than one-fourth of the estimated needy families were being served.[8]

Special service programs provided for the areas of education and rehabilitation rather than for basic support of dependent persons. Vocational rehabilitation was one such program, with federal financial support beginning in 1920.[9] Various programs for child welfare and for maternal and child health had been stimulated by the first White House Conference on Children.[10] The Social Security Act, though not basically affecting the form and substance of some of these health and welfare programs,

---

[5] "The preferential character of the proposed programs was reflected in provisions that pensions should be restricted to 'worthy' persons, that is, widows who were of 'good moral character,' aged persons who had not been tramps or failed to support their families. Ex-criminals and beggars were to be excluded." *Id.* at 53.

[6] ABBOTT, FROM RELIEF TO SOCIAL SECURITY 267-69 (1941). Among the opponents, according to Abbott, former Chief of the United States Children's Bureau, were such social work leaders as Edward T. Devine, Mary Richmond, and Frederic Almy.

[7] As an extreme example, North Dakota provided a special tax levy that, in 1934, prorated among the old-age pensioners, yielded an average "pension" of sixty-nine cents a month. SOCIAL SECURITY BD., SOCIAL SECURITY IN AMERICA 136 (1937).

[8] *Id.* at 233, 241.

[9] 41 Stat. 735 (1920), as amended, 29 U.S.C. §§ 31-42 (1964), as amended, 29 U.S.C. §§ 31-42 (Supp. I, 1965).

[10] Held in 1909 upon the call of President Theodore Roosevelt. See 1960 WHITE HOUSE CONFERENCE ON CHILDREN AND YOUTH, PROCEEDINGS 2 (1960).

provided increased financial support for what had largely been token operations. Locally, probation and parole programs developed along with the initial interest in juvenile courts.

Developments in "social insurances" afforded some basis for the major expansion undertaken by the Social Security Act. Workmen's compensation laws had developed in many states. A number of retirement programs had developed, including the Federal Civil Service Retirement System.[11]

These three areas of "preferential assistance" have grown, both in conjunction with and independent of the Social Security program, and form what may vaguely be described as the "welfare system." They afford the major means we have for working with people with special problems of dependency, health, or social adjustment. That they form an organized and coordinated system that is generally available or accessible is debatable. They have, however, formed a basis for some measure of relief from economic misfortune and its related difficulties.

B. The Social Security Program

The Social Security program was not conceived as a comprehensive or integrated public welfare system. It established a series of methods to supplement the traditional ownership, employment, and wage system for distributing income to certain disadvantaged persons—an economic security system. It fell short of being an integrated, coordinated system to promote individual and collective welfare by enhancing opportunities for individual achievement.[12] Attention of the designers appears to have been focused upon bringing certain large dependent groups into a different socio-economic relationship to the self-supporting public, based on assumptions as to the appropriate place of these groups vis-à-vis the labor market, rather than upon accomplishing any substantial economic status change for individuals based on increasing their capacity for social or economic achievement.

Four main areas of concern led to enactment of the Social Security

---

[11] 41 Stat. 614 (1920), as amended, 5 U.S.C. §§ 2251-68 (1964), as amended, 5 U.S.C. §§ 2251-68 (Supp. I, 1965).

[12] Cohen, *Factors Influencing the Content of Federal Public Welfare Legislation*, in NATIONAL CONFERENCE OF SOCIAL WORK, THE SOCIAL WELFARE FORUM, 1954, at 199-215 (1954). Cohen discusses the skepticism with which Congress regarded such ideas, when, as late as 1949, they refused to enact proposals to add specific authorization for services "designed to help families and individuals become self-supporting, to keep families together in their own homes, and to reduce the need for institutional care." *Id.* at 212-13. However, earlier similar services for the blind had been authorized. He cites some belief that the effort was regarded as being promoted more for professional enhancement than in the interest of possible beneficiaries. *Id.* at 213-14.

Act in 1935:[13] (1) employment opportunities and protections for wage earners; (2) retirement benefits; (3) expansion of special service programs; and (4) federal support for categories of dependent persons.

1. Employment Opportunities and Protections for Wage Earners

Although the act contained no specific provision for employment opportunities, the subject was cited as of first importance. Sublime faith in the economic system's ability to utilize all able-bodied persons led the framers of the program to do little more than point out the need to buttress the private sector with substantial provisions for public works.[14]

In the fiscal year 1939-40, when old age insurance benefits were started, expenditures under social insurance programs came to one-fifth of that year's income-maintenance outlays of 5.2 billion dollars.[15] Almost seventy per cent of that 5.2 billion went for public aid alone, including almost forty-eight per cent for work relief programs.[16]

That employment was often interrupted by seasonal and cyclical changes, threatening the security of many, was recognized. There were specific recommendations for compulsory, federally-supported, state-operated programs of unemployment compensation.[17] The necessity for close cooperation between such an unemployment insurance program and the employment services featured in the statute had much to do

---

[13] COMM. ON ECONOMIC SECURITY, REPORT TO THE PRESIDENT *passim* (1935). See generally SOCIAL SECURITY BD., *op. cit. supra* note 7 *passim*.

[14] There was little particular reference to problems of technological displacement or obsolescence in most of the reports, although by 1940 there was some concern that in many respects foreshadowed current worries. See, *e.g.*, H.R. Doc. No. 850, 76th Cong., 3d Sess. *passim* (1940). Public works were spoken of as the major resource for the use of manpower—slum clearance, public roads, fabricating, consumer goods, flood control, river and harbor improvement, public buildings. One House committee, however, stated: "The number of men and women who are thrown out of work because particular technical developments render their special skill or trade 'obsolete' may constitute only a small percentage of our total unemployed but their individual problems are the most acute . . . . [T]o change his occupation . . . is certainly no easy task for a man whose whole background of training and experience has been in one field." *Id.* at 83.

"In another portion, Representative Landis of Indiana filed a minority statement as part of the report of the Committee on Youth and Unemployment in which he stated: "[T]he principal cause of unemployment and low national income today is that the young people of our Nation are leaving school without being prepared for definite jobs. . . . Probably our whole system would collapse without some workers who offer unskilled manpower of the strictly brawn type. But we have too many laborers who are untrained and unskilled." *Id.* at 97.

[15] SOCIAL SECURITY ADMINISTRATION, U. S. DEP'T OF HEALTH, EDUC. & WELFARE, SOCIAL SECURITY PROGRAMS IN THE UNITED STATES 6-7 (1964).

[16] *Id.* at 6.

[17] SOCIAL SECURITY BD., *op. cit. supra* note 7, at 92-96.

with shaping the nature of the employment services. The act contained a minimum of standards and intentionally left to the states a major amount of freedom to shape their own statutes.[18]

Aside from technical matters, the prescribed standards dealt with: (a) administrative methods reasonably calculated to insure full payment of compensation when due; (b) opportunity for a fair hearing; (c) payment through public employment offices and cooperation with federal agencies concerned with employment; (d) provisions to guarantee that persons would not be denied compensation for refusing to take a job involved in a labor dispute or under less favorable conditions of work and pay than generally prevail in the community.[19]

Unemployment compensation, administered under the Secretary of Labor since 1949, has had increasing public acceptance. Because the program operates under varying state laws and involves conditions of disqualification, there continues to be a tendency to regard it as a form of "welfare," with the traditional associations of worthiness and suspicion. This confusion has persisted in spite of the fact that benefits are not based on a means test. It may be stimulated by the fact that for many wage-earners there is a sequential pattern of reliance upon unemployment benefits and welfare benefits. Some persons concurrently utilize both systems because their unemployment benefits fall far short of providing the minimum needs as measured for public assistance.[20]

Unemployment compensation programs generally exclude from coverage agricultural workers, family workers, domestic servants in private homes, the self-employed, state and local government employees, most employees of nonprofit organizations operated for religious, charitable, or educational purposes, and employees of private firms with fewer than four employees in twenty weeks of a year. These exclusions, especially among farm and other low-wage employees, generate part of the public assistance caseload. Nevertheless, about four out of five wage and salary workers were covered by the unemployment compensation program in an average week in 1963.

---

[18] H.R. REP. No. 615, 74th Cong., 1st Sess. 8-9 (1935); S. REP. No. 628, 74th Cong., 1st Sess. 13 (1935).

[19] *Id.* at 34, 46-47.

[20] In most states, the wage replacement formula is designed to compensate about fifty per cent of the weekly wage. In December 1963 the average weekly benefit for total unemployment was about thirty-six per cent of the average weekly wage in covered employment. SOCIAL SECURITY ADMINISTRATION, *op. cit. supra* note 15, at 23. Public assistance, therefore, provides a form of supplement to unemployment compensation allowance for many families.

2. Retirement Benefits

A national retirement system for the aged was accomplished in the Social Security Act by establishing a compulsory, contributory system of annuities,[21] financed through taxes imposed upon both employee and employer[22] and administered by the federal government.[23] In 1939 this system was substantially changed to a family program by providing additional benefits to dependent members of the wage-earner's family after his retirement and survivor's benefits after his death.[24] Beginning in 1956 the system was broadened to provide benefits to disabled workers.[25] At the end of 1963, of about nineteen million beneficiaries, eleven million were retired or disabled wage-earners, three million were dependent spouses, two million were widows or dependent widowers, and 2.6 million were children.[26]

By fiscal 1963-64, Old Age, Survivors, and Disability Insurance and Unemployment Compensation outlays accounted for more than three-fourths of all income-maintenance expenditures.[27] Public assistance expenditures, which accounted for about twenty-two per cent of the outlays in 1940,[28] accounted for only twelve per cent in 1964.[29]

Improvements in the Old Age, Survivors, and Disability Insurance (OASDI) program have proceeded under direct federal administration with comparatively little controversy. The absence of a means test, as such, has avoided many of the issues associated with public assistance. OASDI has close relationships to, but lacks popular identification with public assistance.

It is important to note, however, that while coverage has been expanded and benefits upgraded, substantial numbers of OASDI beneficiaries in all classifications receive supplemental payments from public assistance programs to enable them to meet their minimum maintenance expenses. In California, for example, about seventy per cent of the individuals receiving state Old Age Security grants under the public assistance program also receive OASDI benefits.[30]

---

[21] 49 Stat. 622 (1935), as amended, 42 U.S.C. §§ 401-25 (1964), as amended, 42 U.S.C. §§ 401-27 (Supp. I, 1965).

[22] Social Security Act of 1935, ch. 531, §§ 801, 802, 49 Stat. 636.

[23] 49 Stat. 635 (1935), as amended, 42 U.S.C. §§ 902-06 (1964), as amended, 42 U.S.C. § 907 (Supp. I, 1965).

[24] Social Security Act Amendments of 1939, ch. 666, § 201, 53 Stat. 1363.

[25] 70 Stat. 815 (1956), as amended, 42 U.S.C. §§ 423, 425 (1964), as amended, 42 U.S.C. §§ 423-25 (Supp. I, 1965).

[26] SOCIAL SECURITY ADMINISTRATION, op. cit. supra note 15, at 9.

[27] Id. at 6.

[28] Ibid.

[29] Ibid.

[30] Data compiled by the Division of Research and Statistics, California State Depart-

3. Special Service Programs

Special services were expanded through increased federal support of the state programs referred to earlier—vocational rehabilitation,[31] child welfare services,[32] child and maternal health[33] (including a new provision for care and service to crippled children[34]). These programs involved some new aspects of administration and administrative relationships but did not enjoy the same support and financial commitment that the employment and retirement titles did.

4. Special Categories of Dependent Persons

Federal support of state-administered programs for special categories of dependent persons was provided by including in the act a system of "non-contributory pensions" for the aged[35] and for mothers of dependent children.[36] A comparable provision for the blind[37] was added by the Senate, although it was not in the recommendations to the President or in the House adopted bill.[38]

C. Summary

The American welfare system thus can be described as a series of provisions in each state for: (1) federally aided public assistance to specified categories of needy people; these provisions are known generally as "Old Age Assistance," "Aid to the Blind," "Aid to the Disabled,"[39] and "Aid to Families with Dependent Children" (including, since 1961, families in need because the parent is unemployed[40]); (2) a residual

---

ment of Social Welfare, for the annual report to the Department of Health, Education, and Welfare, on concurrent receipt of OASDI (unpublished, Feb. 1966).

[31] Social Security Act of 1935, ch. 531, § 531, 49 Stat. 633.

[32] 49 Stat. 633 (1935), as amended, 42 U.S.C. §§ 721-29a (1964), as amended, 42 U.S.C. §§ 721-29-1 (Supp. I, 1965).

[33] 49 Stat. 629 (1935), as amended, 42 U.S.C. §§ 701-05 (1964), as amended, 42 U.S.C. §§ 701-04 (Supp. I, 1965).

[34] 49 Stat. 631 (1935), as amended, 42 U.S.C. §§ 711-15 (1964), as amended, 42 U.S.C. §§ 711-14 (Supp. I, 1965).

[35] 49 Stat. 620 (1935), as amended, 42 U.S.C. §§ 301-06 (1964), as amended, 42 U.S.C. §§ 302-06 (Supp. I, 1965).

[36] 49 Stat. 627 (1935), as amended, 42 U.S.C. §§ 601-09 (1964), as amended, 42 U.S.C. §§ 602-06 (Supp. I, 1965).

[37] 49 Stat. 645 (1935), as amended, 42 U.S.C. §§ 1201-06 (1964), as amended, 42 U.S.C. §§ 1202-06 (Supp. I, 1965).

[38] H.R. REP. No. 628, 74th Cong., 1st Sess. (1935).

[39] Added by 64 Stat. 555 (1950), as amended, 42 U.S.C. §§ 1351-55 (1964), as amended, 42 U.S.C. §§ 1352-55 (Supp. I, 1965).

[40] 75 Stat. 75 (1961), as amended, 42 U.S.C. § 607 (1964). The name of the program was changed in 1962. See Public Welfare Amendments of 1962, § 104(a)(3), 76 Stat. 185. Prior to that, and still in some state legislation, the program was designated "Aid to Dependent Children" (in some states, "Aid to Needy Children"). In the same year a single

program, financed locally or by the state or in some combination, called "General Assistance," "General Relief," or some similar designation; plus (3) associated programs such as "Child Welfare," special state categories (for example, California's Aid to Potentially Self-Supporting Blind[41]), and other local or state programs such as those for licensing facilities for crippled children, probation service, vocational rehabilitation, and the care of children and aged.

The system is administered either by a state department or by local departments under the supervision of a state department. The degree of supervision over local operations may vary between federally aided programs and those established solely by the state. For example, in California the State Department of Social Welfare exercises no standard setting, supervisory, or financial functions with respect to General Assistance. In a few states General Assistance is administered completely separately from federally assisted programs.

II

HOW THE SYSTEM FUNCTIONS

A. Organization and Structure

Federal public welfare functions under the Social Security Act are carried out by the Welfare Administration in the Department of Health, Education, and Welfare, headed by a Commissioner, and within that organization by the Bureau of Family Services with respect to public assistance and by the Children's Bureau for child welfare. The functions of program planning and development, formulating of standards, and deciding whether state plans qualify, are exercised by the professional and technical staff of the bureaus in Washington.

Bureau representatives are stationed in regional offices of the Department to provide field consultation and assistance to states and for performing most of the related field work. The regional staff members are responsible to the Washington bureaus but work under the Regional Director, who is responsible to the Secretary of the Department of Health, Education, and Welfare.

Accounting and auditing, merit system operations, and similar technical functions are carried out under other bureaus of the Department. Regional offices also include representatives of the United States Public Health Service, the Office of Education, Vocational Rehabilitation, and other branches of the Federal Department.

---

category of aid was created for adults, 76 Stat. 197, as amended, 42 U.S.C. §§ 1381-82 (1964), as amended, 42 U.S.C. § 1382 (Supp. I, 1965), which has received increasing acceptance among the states.

[41] CAL. WELFARE & INST'NS CODE §§ 13000-102.

State public welfare functions are ordinarily carried out by a state department or commission established under state law, responsible for administering the program or supervising its administration by local authorities. As of 1964, twenty-eight state programs were state-administered and twenty-two state-supervised. The three territorial programs and the District of Columbia were classified as "state" administered.[42]

The responsibilities of state departments frequently go beyond those required by the Social Security Act. The department may be in charge of such other major operations as mental health, corrections, parole and probation, and various institutions of a medical or custodial character,[43] or it may only supervise closely associated services, such as licensing, adoptions, or other specialties not specifically within the Social Security Act framework.

The difference between state-administered and state-supervised systems is one of relationship rather than structure. There is universally a headquarters staff that is responsible for overall program planning and direction, state plan development and maintenance, relationships and negotiations with federal authorities, and program evaluation. There is a field staff responsible for keeping local operations in conformance with standards and goals. In some states, the field staff are located in district offices.[44] In others, they function as extensions of program or technical bureaus or as a field division, headquartered in the state central office.

Local offices are, of course, a universal necessity. Under a state-administered system, there is greater flexibility in establishing offices so as to secure optimal effectiveness considering the staff resources and the distribution of the risk population. When the program is administered as a part of a local jurisdiction—usually a county—many additional problems are posed. The problems range from that of smaller organizational units than may be desirable to ones of complex conflicts over methods, philosophies, and goals. Usually under such systems the local unit operates as a part of a local governmental structure responsible to the local governmental body, either directly or through a board or commission. Fiscal and budget operations must conform to local arrangements and usually differ from one jurisdiction to another. Ordinarily, state-supervised plans involve local sharing of costs. Arrangements as to state-local division of costs vary between states and sometimes within states as between purpose or programs.[45] In California, for example, the county

---

42 See BUREAU OF FAMILY SERVICES, U.S. DEP'T OF HEALTH, EDUC. & WELFARE, CHARACTERISTICS OF STATE PUBLIC ASSISTANCE PLANS *passim* (Public Assistance Rep. No. 50, 1964).

43 *E.g.*, N.J. STAT. ANN. § 30:1-7 (1964); WIS. STAT. ANN. § 46.03 (1957, Supp. 1966).

44 *E.g.*, California and New York.

45 See BUREAU OF FAMILY SERVICES, *op. cit. supra* note 42 *passim*.

share of costs of aid given varies by program from one-seventh of the nonfederal remainder of the cost of Old Age Assistance[46] to 32.5 per cent of the nonfederal cost of Aid to Families with Dependent Children.[47] Also, California provides no share of the nonfederal cost of administration.[48] For programs not encompassed in the public assistance titles of the Social Security Act, state funds may or may not be provided to the locality. When the local administration is responsible to the local legislative body—which is accustomed to determining the policy within its jurisdiction—there is much opportunity for sharp conflicts, competitive interests, and major disagreements over statewide policies. Under these circumstances, personnel in the local units may find themselves severely circumscribed or having to meet additional local criteria and conditions.

Internally, organization of local administrations generally follows similar patterns regardless of the state relationship. Such differences as do exist tend to reflect size and complexity of the operation more than basic differences in organizational concepts. Usually there is a "direct operations" or case-carrying staff responsible for findings and decisions about applicants and recipients and for the agency's relationships with such persons vis-à-vis benefits and services. The staff functions under one or more levels of supervisory personnel, depending on the size and complexity of the agency. The staff is ordinarily organized and assigned under concepts of social work operations, whether or not they have any particular training or background in social casework.[49] They may be divided into units responsible for particular categorical groupings—aged, blind, disabled, for example, or in some instances by specialty or function—for example, intake, child welfare, and licensing. Casework personnel in larger organizations may be backed up by a number of specialty units or assignments—for example, special units for fraud investigation or for establishing property or relatives' support resources, homemaker or out-of-home care arrangements and placement, medical social services, vocational and physical rehabilitation, and training.

Generally, the time and effort of local "direct operations" personnel have been pre-empted by requiring them to keep a system of elaborate cost control devices. These devices consist of investigatory procedures designed to assure down to the last cent the validity of each individual eligibility determination and to ascertain that each penny of the recip-

---

46 CAL. WELFARE & INST'NS CODE § 15201.

47 CAL. WELFARE & INST'NS CODE § 15200.

48 CAL. WELFARE & INST'NS CODE §§ 15150, 15151.

49 In 1960 it was reported that public assistance agencies had "only 2% of qualified social workers among their caseworkers and about 15% in addition with partial social work training." Advisory Council on Public Assistance, *Report on Findings and Recommendations*, S. Doc. No. 93, 86th Cong. 2d Sess. 28-29 (1960).

ient's is considered in computing the grant. This pre-emption of case-workers' time has been coupled with a lack of organized service resources—other than those available through the native competence, ability, or general knowledge of the caseworker. Agency personnel generally lack specific formal training in direct services work, and other public and private agencies are not attuned to the needs and characteristics of the dependent population. These factors have combined to make the welfare system a method for assuring the continued existence of individuals at a level which effectively precludes much constructive achievement rather than a program of planned support geared to accomplishing a set of social and personal goals.

The 1962 amendments[50] to the Social Security Act provide concepts and fiscal support for administrative efforts to enhance positive achievement. Fortunately, since the passage of the amendments, many favorable shifts are occurring. The added impetus given by the Economic Opportunity Act of 1964[51] has had a stimulating effect both in the immediate welfare system and among the related agencies. Progress is apparent in isolated instances but will be slow and is apt to be disappointing to the public, since it often is measurable only in terms of individuals rather than in significant trends. The hard fact remains that now, as when the Social Security Act was adopted in 1935, self-support independent of public aid cannot be a realistic goal for many nor an immediate goal for most. Providing a reasonable level of maintenance in such a way as to encourage preparation to use future opportunity will remain the basic service that can be provided. The manner in which this service is conducted will largely condition the degree of future dependence of the handicapped, the disabled, and the children and their "able-bodied" parents.

B. Supervisory Methods

In general, the processes of supervision between the Federal Department and state departments are comparable to those between state departments and the local branches. The following discussion surveys the commonly used methods.

1. Standard-Setting

Standard-setting is the process of formulating and enunciating standards having to do with benefits, procedures, and operations. Standards consist of: (a) required practice or provisions stated as "requirements"

---

[50] Public Welfare Amendments of 1962, § 101(a), 76 Stat. 173 (codified in scattered sections of 42 U.S.C.).

[51] 78 Stat. 508, 42 U.S.C. §§ 2701-981 (1964), as amended, 42 U.S.C. §§ 2713-967 (Supp. I, 1965).

or regulations; (b) recommended practice or policy regarded as desirable but not mandatory; (c) guides that define processes thought to be constructive ways of exercising responsibility or carrying out various functions, or that define criteria as to facts or evidence to be weighed in arriving at decisions. These three types may be separately set forth or combined in some form of handbook or manual.

The Federal Department in setting standards has used "implied" as well as specific requirements in the Social Security Act; but for the most part it has moved slowly and preferred to define standards "in terms of relatively flexible 'principles' instead of detailed methods or practices. Thus, the Bureau . . . does not apply detailed rules and regulations to state administrative methods comparable to those used by the national administrators of unemployment compensation grants. . . . The policy . . . does not, however, satisfy the need in definition of requirements for clear and distinct rules. . . . Under pressure from state and national sources, the Bureau . . . has turned increasingly to the use of more objective criteria for measuring state conformity . . . . [I]t has gradually felt it necessary, if not desirable, to 'spell out' methods of practices that the states must adopt in order to qualify for funds."[52]

Perhaps recognizing that a program's goals can be compromised or circumvented by the way the program is administered, the Federal Department has tended to concentrate on methodology rather than results. This has led to criticisms by state administrators that the Federal Department has become too engrossed in administrative detail for which state authorities are responsible. States would prefer more definition of desired results and designation of criteria for measuring results than is now set forth. State administrators believe that they could be held responsible for achieving specified results expressed in "people" terms and for planning and executing such operations as may be necessary to achieve those results.

Perhaps one factor that has slowed the application of mandatory federal requirements has been the difficulty states have had in securing judicial review of controversies with the Federal Department. A recent enactment may provide this judicial review and afford the Secretary of the Department a better opportunity for standard-setting by freeing him from being the court of last resort.[53]

The lack of definite federal standards has left to the states a significant role in standard-setting and establishing supervisory mechanism. What in effect has become the standard has tended to be, in terms of

---

[52] RAUP, INTERGOVERNMENTAL RELATIONS IN SOCIAL WELFARE 50-51 (1952).
[53] 79 Stat. 419, 42 U.S.C. § 1316 (Supp. I, 1965).

"people results," the lowest level of performance, process, benefit, or practice reflected among the state plans negotiated with and accepted by the Federal Department.

Even what constitutes a state plan has been quite indefinite. In essence, it has consisted of little more than a requirement that the state "submit for approval whatever materials are conceivably pertinent to the national conditions for grants. In practice this has included laws, administrative orders made in accordance with the laws, opinions of the attorney general, judicial decisions, manuals for state or local welfare staffs, annual reports, administrative bulletins, and administrative organization charts. For merit system plans, it has included all compensation and classification plans."[54]

The concept that plans consist of statutory and operational detail rather than formulated goals and methods by which they may be achieved has been extremely confusing to those with whom state administrators must work. It certainly has not led to public understanding or to best relationships with legislators and control agencies. It has also tended to obscure for the poor what they may appropriately expect of the welfare system. There is some evidence that this concept of state plan is changing and that there may be positive developments that focus on purpose and results. For example, in the amendments of 1962[55] and of 1965[56] emphasis is placed on long-term goals and their achievement.

State standards for guidance of local operations tend to be much more definite than those of the Federal Department for the states. Their adequacy and their application with equity may be open to question but, for the most part, they provide a more specific guide for local operations. This is, of course, a necessity for state-administered plans. As to the state-supervised plans, many of the same criticisms of state standards exist that have been noted with respect to the federal standards.

2. Field Consultation

Field consultation is performed on a regular basis in the Federal Department through regional representatives and technical staff and in the states by various arrangements for field representatives or consultants. State representatives are sometimes assigned on a general basis and sometimes as technical specialists. Consultants provide an important avenue of interpretation, advice, and aid to local administrations, and serve as liaison between headquarters and local personnel. In both

---

54 RAUP, *op. cit. supra* note 52, at 57.
55 76 Stat. 173 (1962) (codified in scattered sections of 42 U.S.C.).
56 79 Stat. 286 (1965) (codified in scattered sections of 42 U.S.C.).

the federal and state systems, such personnel commonly are not delegated final authority, this being reserved in many respects to headquarters personnel. Field personnel commonly function in a sort of "middleman" role.[57] They are extremely important in maintaining good relationships and in planning program substance.

Local administrations range in size from one man to thousands of employees. Each size requires a different type of help from field personnel. The larger local administrations often command among their own employees persons of considerably more technical competence and experience than does the state administration in its field staff. The Federal Department has similar problems as between state departments of differing size and complexity.

3. Administrative Reviews

The Federal Department and most states maintain some pattern of administrative review of state and local operations. The patterns vary from periodic specific evaluative assessments made by a field representative to rather broad studies performed by teams of technical and administrative specialists. One former weakness of evaluative procedures was that for the most part they were confined to a review of records and documents, even with case reviews. This deficiency has been substantially corrected by the "quality control" system discussed below. Administrative review now tends to focus on operations and organization rather than on cases.

4. Budget Estimates and Review

Most states maintain some system of budgetary review and approval. States are required to submit periodic estimates to the Federal Department. In state-supervised systems, such as California's, much of the budgetary control may be exercised by the local governing organization. Greater authority and responsibility tends to rest at the level that provides the least funds.

5. Expenditure Reports and Other Statistics

Federal and state agencies require caseload and expenditure reports as part of an extensive reporting system designed to reflect the quality and quantity of local operations. A chronic complaint of operating levels is the heavy amount of paperwork involved. The entire area of data accumulation is receiving major attention in many quarters.[58]

---

[57] RAUP, op. cit. supra note 52, at 64-65, 71-72.

[58] See, e.g., LOCKHEED MISSILES & SPACE Co., CALIFORNIA STATEWIDE INFORMATION SYSTEM STUDY—FINAL REPORT (1965).

6. *Fiscal Audit*

Audits of lower departmental operations are required and carried out by both state and federal departments. They are usually carried out on a test-check basis, believed to be sufficient to test the integrity of fiscal transactions. Common practice is to deduct questioned items from amounts claimed unless the validity of the item can be established. Serious departures indicated by test-check findings may be followed up with audit operations in depth, and corrective action may be required.

7. *Quality Control*

A rather recent development in federal-state-local relationships and supervisory practices has been the federal requirement that states maintain a statewide test check sufficient to demonstrate the validity of case decisions. This requirement was imposed following the rather extensive congressional inquiry in 1961-62 into the question of welfare fraud. It is a logical extension of the "case-review" discussed above, but utilizes methods designed to correct some of the deficiencies of that system. For example, it requires interviews with recipients as well as record review.

When conducted at a level which satisfies only federal requirements, this operation has little value for state supervision of local practices. However, it is capable of expansion to provide both state and local administrators with comparative data as between local operations. Such data was formerly unobtainable, except through occasional studies. The methodology of quality control is still in a developmental state. Its scope is limited largely to testing the validity of eligibility and grant determinations. Its applicability to testing the quality of services to and relationships with the recipient and risk population is a potential yet to be explored.

8. *Enforcement of Personnel Standards*

The nearly universal use of merit employment systems throughout the welfare system is generally regarded as assuring high standards of performance. The imposition of civil service standards was an early source of controversy and was not required until 1939.[59] The enforcement of merit system practices has absorbed a tremendous amount of effort and has detracted more attention from the development of staffing, performance, and workload standards than is desirable in view of the shortage of trained personnel. Only since 1962 has the Federal Department insisted

---

[59] *E.g.*, Social Security Act Amendments of 1939, ch. 666, § 101, 53 Stat. 1360.

on state effort along developmental lines. Without major attention in these areas, future enforcement will continue to emphasize technical observance of merit system procedures rather than solid performance.

9. Fair Hearings

The appeal, or fair hearing, process has not been extensively used in many jurisdictions and in others may be seriously compromised by the imposition of "pre-hearing processes." It has, when used, provided an opportunity for individuals to secure modification of actions of local officials and provided a base for examining the policies and standards underlying those decisions.

Generally, the fair hearing process has had extensive use in those jurisdictions where individuals were supported through organizations or outside sources operating in the interest of special groups. For example, in California fair hearings have been a major tool of the California League of Senior Citizens. In the state of Washington, the Washington Pension Union effectively used fair hearings to influence policy during 1940-50.

The main shortcomings of the fair hearing process appear to be two. First, the prosecution of an appeal demands a degree of security, awareness, tenacity, and ability which few dependent people have. The same factors which compel the dependent person to avoid controversy in settling grievances make him avoid this avenue. He may create more immediate problems than he would face by accepting the initial decision. Second, there is an administrative tendency to use the existing policy to justify the action rather than to use the situation to question the policy. In most states the authority responsible for the decision on appeal is the same authority responsible for the basic policy.

10. Enforcement of Conformity

Both the federal government and the state may withhold funds when there is failure to conform to standards and requirements. There is, of course, great reluctance to employ this device because of the widespread impact on the lives of individuals, particularly in those states where federal funds provide up to three-fourths of the total expenditure. That fact also has made it reasonably effective where it has been threatened or employed. More often, reliance is placed upon negotiation and other forms of enforcement, such as exceptions to certain cases or expenditures. Amendments in 1965 giving states the right to judicial review[60] may encourage use of the stronger measure but they may also prolong the nonconformity.

---

[60] 79 Stat. 286, 42 U.S.C. § 1316 (Supp. I, 1965).

Under state-administered systems, the actions to enforce conformity by local units are usually not distinct from the ordinary administrative sanctions—dismissal or discipline, for example. State-supervised systems, such as California's, have problems comparable to the Federal Department; thus compliance is usually achieved through negotiation without resort to the ultimate sanctions. Such states commonly employ the system of exceptions, and some, by law, may withdraw state support. This withdrawal of support from a local jurisdiction includes withdrawal of federal funds, creating a dangerous situation for the state as a whole, since one of the basic federal requirements—that of statewide effectiveness of programs—is not then met. California, which has withdrawn funds upon occasion, has successfully limited the withdrawal to administrative funds.

Resort to the courts to compel compliance through injunctions, mandamus, or certiorari has been commonly available to state supervisory agencies. In addition, provisions sometimes exist by which the state authority can assume or "take over" local authority and responsibility for as long as is necessary.

III

WELFARE PRINCIPLES

The Social Security Administration in 1950 described social welfare in the United States "as encompassing the development and administration of (1) social insurance, (2) social assistance, and (3) other social services designed to strengthen family life and to provide care and protection for special groups such as children, the aged, and mentally, socially, or physically handicapped persons."[61]

This definition, useful for certain purposes, is narrow and misleading. Its emphasis on methodology and its use of the term, "social services," tends to raise more questions than it answers. It reflects more the standpoint of the administrator than of the citizen user. It appears to exclude those functions vital to individual welfare that do not come within the scope of whatever is read into the term "social services." Nevertheless it would probably be accepted as accurate by most now engaged in "welfare" practice.

Friedlander's definition goes so far to the other extreme that it is difficult to see either the object persons or the methodology:

> Social welfare is the organized system of welfare services and institutions designed to aid individuals and groups to attain satisfying standards of life and health. It aims at personal and social relationships

---

[61] BUREAU OF PUBLIC ASSISTANCE, SOCIAL SECURITY ADMINISTRATION, SOCIAL WELFARE ADMINISTRATION IN THE UNITED STATES OF AMERICA 1 (1950).

which permit individuals the development of their full capacities and the promotion of their well-being in harmony with the needs of the community.[62]

It is difficult to identify any particular public service or element of private and public social and economic life that would not come within this definition. It does have more clarity as to purpose and result than the former. However, it still reflects the concept that welfare services are those things done by the community in carrying out some obligations toward others —of doing for. It carries little hint of entitlement.

Current trends underscore the need for redefinition along the following lines: The welfare system comprises those specialized benefits, personal services, or applications of general public services which disadvantaged persons may use to resolve problems that restrict their enjoyment of opportunities for maintenance or participation in society to a level substantially below that realized by the average citizen.

Such a definition avoids associating the system with one specific discipline, provides a purpose related to the user, and avoids begging the question of right to use. Many would argue that such a definition ignores those needs that all persons have in common or may face at some time. The fact remains that it is relatively easier for a group of people to organize those things which they need in common. Individuals, if not able to solve their problems with their own resources, would fall within the definition. Major difficulty usually occurs when the available methods and resources are either unusable by or unavailable to the disadvantaged individual, and some special effort or program is required. The special arrangement commonly becomes suspect in the eyes of the public.

Whatever the specific program content at different times, "welfare" in America has dealt primarily with those who were regarded to be misfits or relics of the common social and economic system. It has represented a form of legal obligation to provide in some manner for at least those who "through no fault of their own" had no other recourse but complete destitution.

A. Congressional Purpose—The Social Security Act

The inclusion of federally aided categories in the Social Security Act is generally regarded as a turning point in the American welfare system —a marked departure from the practices under poor relief. Most social workers and many others attribute this turn to the legislative endorsement of new principles for administration and to the statutory adoption of new standards and methods. A case is made that public assistance and

---

[62] FRIEDLANDER, INTRODUCTION TO SOCIAL WELFARE 4 (1955).

poor relief are completely distinct. Vasey, for example, claims that unlike poor relief, "public assistance places much more emphasis on the dignity and rights of the individual recipients . . . and attaches more importance to how people are treated and assisted."[63]

Cohen, on the other hand, commenting upon some aspects of Aid to Dependent Children, points out that many important details which we regard as "fundamental, underlying, basic principles" of the program were matters of compromise or resulted from congressional desire to have standards and definitions consistent with those established for Old Age Assistance.[64]

The framers of the Social Security Act were concerned primarily with the unemployed and the aged. The main elements of the act dealt with unemployment compensation and the compulsory retirement system. Old-Age Assistance was an almost mandatory interim arrangement due to the phasing arrangements of the retirement system. Having formulated the concepts for operating the retirement benefit program, it was natural that there be some carry-over to the categorical assistance programs. The treatment given the categories, both in the preparatory recommendations and in the congressional consideration, seems to have been at a comparatively low key. So similarities in statutory detail were probably not matters of basic design. It appears likely that Congress desired to rock the boat no more than was necessary to justify the use of federal funds and to encourage the states to extend coverage to people who were then being cared for at federal expense.[65] The Senate report, for example, clearly indicates that there would be no major disturbance of state practice with regard to "worthiness": "The limitations of subsection (b) [of Section 2, Old Age Assistance] do not prevent the state from imposing other eligibility requirements (as to means, moral character, etc.) if they wish to do so."[66] Almost identical wording was repeated with respect to Aid to Dependent Children. Similar language was used in the House report.[67]

The extent to which practice under the Federal Emergency Relief Administration varied from the poor law practice was evidently intended. The report of the Committee on Economic Security indicates, however, that thinking was geared more to ideas of "humane treatment" than to conscious concepts of rights. It was apparently thought that families under

---

63 VASEY, GOVERNMENT AND SOCIAL WELFARE 140 (1958).

64 Cohen, *Factors Influencing the Content of Federal Public Welfare Legislation*, in NATIONAL CONFERENCE OF SOCIAL WORK, THE SOCIAL WELFARE FORUM, 1954, at 199, 215 (1954).

65 Primarily under the Federal Emergency Relief Act of 1933, ch. 30, 48 Stat. 55.

66 S. REP. No. 628, 74th Cong., 1st Sess. 29, 35-36 (1935).

67 H.R. REP. No. 615, 74th Cong., 1st Sess. 18, 24 (1935).

state programs could best be assisted through the tried procedures of social case work, with its individualized treatment. Further, the Committee stated, "While the standards of relief administration have been so greatly improved in these last years of stress and strain, the old poor laws remain on the statute books of nearly all states. . . . The Federal Government should insist as a condition of any grants-in-aid that standard relief practice shall be used . . . to preserve the gains that have been made."[68]

Aid to Dependent Children was then, as it has remained since, the stepchild of the welfare system. So little importance was attached to it by the congressional framers that Edwin Witte, the Chairman of the Committee on Economic Security, is quoted as saying, "Nothing would have been done on this subject if it had not been included in the report of the Committee."[69]

In other respects, the Social Security Act indicated that Congress had little intent of providing the same basic assurances to families as were given to other categories of recipients. A less favorable federal sharing formula was provided (one-third[70] as compared to one-half[71]), and increases in federal contributions for Aid to Dependent Children have consistently been less than for the aged, blind, and disabled.

There was clear indication that categorical programs were to be controlled and guided primarily by local fiscal commitment rather than by concepts of need and basic entitlements—a characteristic that has persisted throughout the history of the programs. The Senate added to the House-adopted bill an additional statement of purpose—that of providing funds to enable each state to furnish assistance only "as far as practicable under the conditions in such State."[72] This statement replaced one relating to the provision of adequate standards of care.

The Congress was in some respects, however, more liberal than its advisors and the drafters of the bill. An open-end appropriation, like that for the aged, was substituted for the proposed closed-end appropriation.[73] Framers of the original proposal had assumed that, if necessary, funds would be prorated among the states. They also assumed that there would be waiting lists of eligible persons. The 1950 amendments went further by adding the requirement that state plans furnish aid "with reasonable promptness to all eligible individuals."[74] The amendment has been at-

---

[68] COMM. ON ECONOMIC SECURITY, REPORT TO THE PRESIDENT 44-45 (1935).

[69] Cohen, *supra* note 64, at 204.

[70] Social Security Act of 1935, ch. 531, § 403(a), 49 Stat. 628.

[71] *E.g.*, Social Security Act of 1935, ch. 531, § 3(a), 49 Stat. 621 (Old Age Assistance); § 1003(a), 49 Stat. 646 (Aid to the Blind).

[72] Social Security Act of 1935, ch. 531, 49 Stat. 620.

[73] Cohen, *supra* note 64, at 205.

[74] 64 Stat. 550 (1950), 42 U.S.C. § 601(a)(9) (1964).

tributed "to the strong feeling of 'equity' " in the mind of lawyer members of Congress and to the belief that waiting lists could give rise to undesirable discrimination and preferences.[75]

The federal commitment was to a hope for progress within each state based upon the availability of supplemental federal financing rather than to a set of clearly formulated national goals related to quality of services, quality of benefits, and measurable results for individuals.

B. Achievements Under the Act

The achievements of the welfare system, though far from satisfying to many, have afforded a marked contrast in some respects to the poor law and to the administration of General Assistance under extensions of poor law principles. What has accounted for this?

Perhaps the most important contribution to a different aura was the entrance of the federal government into a role of continuing direct responsibility for the care of needy people. The law established the individual's immediate welfare as a matter of national concern entitled to consideration in the deployment of national resources. Cracking four hundred years of complete relegation of the poor to the largesse of their most immediate neighbors was bound to have psychological consequences as significant as the fiscal.

Another important element was the series of requirements imposed upon states as conditions for receiving federal grants-in-aid.[76] The number

---

[75] Cohen, *supra* note 64, at 209.

[76] Aside from the special requirements imposed under 1965 amendments pertaining to medical assistance under a new title, 79 Stat. 344, 42 U.S.C. § 1396(a) (Supp. I, 1965), the requirements include:

1. Statewide operation;
2. State financial participation;
3. Administration by or under a single state agency whose requirements are mandatory upon local agencies;
4. Proper and efficient methods of administration including maintenance of personnel standards on a merit basis;*
5. Protections against release of information about individuals;*
6. Opportunity for anyone to apply and have determination of eligibility made promptly;*
7. Opportunity for hearing and adjudication of grievances;
8. Submission of reports as required by the Federal Department;
9. Consideration of any income and resources (with some exceptions);*
10. Maintenance of standards for institutions;*
11. Notice to law enforcement officers in case of abandoned or deserted children;*
12. Prohibition of concurrent aid under separate programs;*
13. Freedom of choice as to source of eye examination in determining blindness;*
14. Description of services provided;*
15. Development of plan for service to each child;*
16. Limits on imposition of residence restrictions;

* Added since passage of the Social Security Act in 1935.

of requirements, relatively few in the original act, has been almost doubled by amendments. The requirements vary between categories; there are differences as to specificity and ease of interpretation, with most lacking objective criteria.[77] Some are expressed negatively and others positively. But regardless of the rationalizations and interpretations advanced by their legislative authors, they have left much room for achievement through administrative procedures.

Four of these standards warrant comment as affording the sharpest contrast with poor law practice and tending to have the greatest impact on individuals and how they fare under the program.

First, the requirement that the program be in effect in all political subdivisions and be administered by or under a single state agency whose rules, regulations, and standards are mandatory on local administrative authorities was probably designed as little more than assurance that there be programs available everywhere. Geographic coverage rather than quality of care appears to have been the primary goal. Although the framers disliked imposing federal standards, they did desire a strong state standard-setting role.

The limited objectives of the framers and their reluctant delegation of authority to the Federal Department has not prevented steady progress toward standardization of practice under requirements imposed by the Federal Department. Raup, for example, in describing the evolution which has occurred quotes former Commissioner Arthur Altmeyer as testifying repeatedly in 1949 in hearings before the United States House Ways and Means Committee that, " 'We require the states, of course, . . . to establish statewide standards for determining needs.' The legal grounds for the requirements, according to Commissioner Altmeyer, are *implied* in three requirements of the Social Security Act—those for 'statewide' operation of the plan, for financial participation by the state, and for fair hearings: 'The law calls for a state plan, and not a county-by-county series of plans. The law calls for state financial participation. The law calls for the giving to any applicant who feels aggrieved what the law calls a fair hearing. We believe that it is implicit in all of these provisions . . . that the Social Security Act contemplated that people equally in need under a State plan should be treated consistently.' "[78]

The federal interpretation of these requirements has been to increas-

---

17. Limits on imposition of age restrictions;
18. Limits on imposition of citizenship requirements;
19. Limitations on payment of benefits except in money (see text at pages 349-50 *infra*).

[77] See RAUP, *op. cit. supra* note 52, at 49-54.
[78] *Id.* at 50.

ingly assure "that assistance and other services provided by law and by the state plan will be available to the same extent and under similar circumstances to all eligible persons regardless of the locality in which they live."[79] Achievement leaves much to be desired, but substantial standardization has occurred, more within states than among them.

Second, the requirement that the state plan must provide opportunity for anyone wishing to do so to apply for assistance or service and to have the application acted upon with reasonable promptness was not added until 1950.[80] Its deferred addition is eloquent testimony to the persistence of poor law practices. The intervening period saw considerable conflict over whether the right to file and receive prompt attention was essential in developing proper and efficient administration. The issue has not been resolved. There continue to be those who believe efficient and proper administration is measurable only in immediate dollar outlays and those who see it in terms of equal access to benefits and services. Much remains to be done along this line.

Third, the requirement that benefits must be provided in the form of money payments, unrestricted as to the particular way in which the individual chooses to apply them towards his needs, is stated only obliquely in the act. It is not directly mentioned as a condition for state plan approval. During the early years it was rigidly followed. The only deviation until very recently was with respect to medical care, for which vendor payments were permitted. This principle was in sharp contrast to usual practice under the poor laws, which had already been substantially modified under the Emergency Relief programs. "The poor law was administered in accordance with the belief that the recipient must not be considered competent to manage his own affairs."[81]

Federal authorities never contended that money payments were appropriate for every individual. It was maintained that federal aid was intended for those who were competent to manage their own affairs properly or who, under appropriate state law, had guardians or other persons entitled to act in their behalf. The care of incompetent individuals, such as those in custodial institutions, remained a residual responsibility of the state without federal aid. This approach, however, has become less tenable as states have indicated their reluctance to continue accepting the cost of residual responsibility, and have become committed to the idea that the cost of caring for the poor is properly a responsibility to be

[79] Bureau of Family Services, U.S. Dep't of Health, Educ. & Welfare, The State Agency's Responsibility for Local Operations 4 (1964).

[80] E.g., 64 Stat. 548 (1950), as amended, 42 U.S.C. § 302 (1964).

[81] Vasey, op. cit. supra note 63, at 143.

shared by the federal government. Thus the issue has shifted from one of whether "incompetents" should be included to one of *how* they can be included without violating the basic principle of money payments.

The principle has always been under attack, mainly in connection with Aid to Dependent Children, where it is inextricably involved with efforts to control family use of inadequate benefits and with public distrust of welfare recipients. While it was probably a carry-over from the concept as applied to the aged in the initial provisions of the act, Congress has been amazingly constant in resisting substantial change. Cohen, for example, quotes Senator Milliken as saying in 1950 to persons advocating modification, "We want to make the acceptance of assistance as consistent with human dignity as possible. . . . Now, when you commence to set up a detailed category of what he must spend his money for—[it] . . . can be carried to a point where most people would say that it is not American."[82]

There have been important modifications in recent amending legislation.[83] Most people, at least nominally, acknowledge the overall principle of money payment and personal management as sound. Yet it is questionable that the recent modifications will satisfy those who have persistently sought modification. The fact that alternative payment methods consume more personnel and administrative time, particularly if coupled with standards for utilization and accompanying service, provides little assurance that erosion of this principle will not continue.

Fourth, the opportunity for a fair hearing before the state agency for any claimant whose claim is denied or is not acted upon with reasonable promptness is of major importance. This requirement is discussed above as a method of supervision.[84]

At least two requirements added since the original act generate problems inconsistent with recent rehabilitative objectives and lend themselves to discriminatory practices.

First, state plans must provide that in determining need all income and resources of a person or family must be taken into consideration. Superficially this seems closely related to the matter of uniform treatment. In actual practice, it has tended to negate motivation of recipients toward independence, to provide many of the most frustrating administrative

---

[82] Cohen, *supra* note 64, at 210-11.

[83] Third party payment provisions were added to title IV, Aid to Families with Dependent Children, 76 Stat. 189, 42 U.S.C. § 606(b)(2) (1964), in 1962, and to title I, Old Age Assistance, 79 Stat. 356, 415, 42 U.S.C. § 306(a) (Supp. I, 1965); title X, Aid to the Blind, 79 Stat. 358, 416, 42 U.S.C. § 1206 (Supp. I, 1965); and title XIV, Aid to the Permanently and Totally Disabled, 79 Stat. 358, 417, 42 U.S.C. § 1355 (Supp. I, 1965), in 1965.

[84] See page 342 *supra*.

and supervisory problems in defining criteria for eligibility, and to keep open many avenues of procrastination and restrictive and discriminatory practice. It has tended to sacrifice the sound planning and providing of minimum security and welfare for recipients to those considerations relating to the smallest immediate cash outlay possible. Further, the present accuracy of measurements of needs is dubious at best—few states are able to provide any measure approaching a standard of adequacy.

Second, the plan for aid to dependent children must provide for prompt notice to law enforcement officials when aid is granted to a child deserted or abandoned by his parent. Though enacted as an aid to enforce the absent parent's responsibility to support, the lack of uniform practice among prosecuting attorneys, the persistent confusion of the function with that of fraud prosecutions, and the general inability of dependent persons to defend themselves in the face of investigations by law enforcement officers have created a multitude of opportunities for discriminatory and abusive treatment.[85]

Though offering many sharp contrasts to poor law practice, the principles enunciated in the federal law are obviously not, nor were they apparently intended to be, comprehensive assurances of either a certain level of benefits and services or a particular manner in which recipients are to be regarded. Vast areas of discretion are left to the states. State statutory provisions in sharp or direct conflict with federal requirements have almost universally been modified, but short of this the extent to which principles have been given effective expression has been largely a matter of degree, varying state by state, and frequently from time to time, depending upon local issues and attitudes. In almost every state there are variations between local jurisdictions which in some instances are almost as great as the variations between states.[86] Such differences, even measured only in monetary terms without regard to the more subtle aspects of relationships to recipients, may be greater in those states in which county rather than state authorities administer the program—the so-called "state-supervised" programs.

Thus while the expanded potential for financing and the conditions attached to receipt of federal funds are important influences, as Vasey has pointed out, "how they are enforced or promoted and the pattern and quality of administrative relations among the participating levels of government may be equally or more important . . . ."[87]

---

[85] For a full discussion of this subject, see tenBroek, *California's Dual System of Family Law*, 17 Stan. L. Rev. 659-71 (1965).

[86] See text accompanying note 89 *infra*.

[87] Vasey, *op. cit. supra* note 63, at 321.

C. Implications for the Future

There can be little question that the welfare system has alleviated to a very marked degree the most onerous conditions and methods by which needs of the poor were earlier met. That it has produced any definitive solutions for providing economic security to either the communities or the recipients is being severely challenged, at least partly on the basis that the arrangement is not sufficiently systematized because: (1) It lacks specific objectives and fails to focus on the risk population; (2) it fails to take into account the conditions that create welfare problems; and (3) it does not command the necessary means for appropriate action.

Recent considerations of this matter by the California State Social Welfare Board clearly indicate that concepts of the "welfare system" must be broadened to include not only the functions of the nominal "welfare agencies," but also many functions performed by other public organizations not particularly identified by the public as such agencies. These functions include education, health, employment, housing and code enforcement, mental health, and correctional or law-enforcement organizations. Thus the above criticisms apply in some degree to all those agencies which in fact form the "welfare family of agencies."

As described for the California State Social Welfare Board in a recent document,[88] a "welfare system" needs:

1. To be directed toward the specific risk population encompassing:

a. The unemployed and marginally employed—those who, because of recurrent unemployment, seasonal unemployment, or low wages, do not receive a year-round income sufficient to support themselves and their families at a subsistence level;

b. Families without breadwinners, for whatever reason, with incomes below the subsistence level;

c. The disabled, whether from age or other reason, with incomes below the subsistence level.

2. To take into account and be geared to specific risk conditions limiting employability, specifically:

a. Low-grade skills;

b. Low-grade education;

c. Limitations on ability to take advantage of resources for improving skills or education (for example, lack of transportation, lack of child care, lack of counseling);

---

[88] Cal. State Social Welfare Bd., A Proposal to Apply Systems Analysis Methods to California's Welfare Program, Jan. 1966 (unpublished).

d. Low motivation, particularly pervasive feelings of being excluded, not being cared about, or being cut off.

3. To command the means of creative and pertinent action, including:

a. Support, including supplemental income up to some common level of subsistence on a consistent basis and related to annual income, and the buttressing of skill-raising, education-raising, and motivation-raising results;

b. The establishment and articulated use of all employment, training, educational, counseling, casework, and supporting social services;

c. Administrative and management practices under which the use of personnel, the efficiency of paperwork, the costs and fiscal limits, and the articulation of the public welfare role with those roles of other departments which are in fact part of the total welfare system, are designed, used, and evaluated in terms of people-centered results—that is, their impact and efficiency in modifying the risk factors and enhancing the capabilities and achievement of those within the risk population.

The welfare system has not yet produced a system for like treatment of individuals in like circumstances—in terms of benefits, qualifying conditions, or treatment. In benefits, for example, assistance for the aged ranged from a state-wide average of as low as thirty-nine dollars per month to 122 dollars in September 1965—a variation of over three hundred per cent.[89] In the family program, average benefits ranged from a low of about thirty-seven dollars per family to more than 237 dollars.[90] Recipient rates also vary substantially, indicating varying eligibility criteria. In September 1965, New York and California, with nearly equal populations, had 56,972 old age assistance recipients and 273,316 respectively.[91] Within states, variations, often marked, are found. For example, in California, in which aid standards are set by the state department, average monthly benefits to the disabled during the quarter ended June 30, 1965, varied by county from 71.45 to almost 112.89 dollars.[92] In the family program, the average payment per person varied from about 37.99 dollars

---

[89] BUREAU OF FAMILY SERVICES, U.S. DEP'T OF HEALTH, EDUC. & WELFARE, ADVANCE RELEASE OF STATISTICS ON PUBLIC ASSISTANCE, Table 3 (Sept. 1965).

[90] Id. at Table 7.

[91] Id. at Table 3.

[92] CAL. STATE DEP'T OF SOCIAL WELFARE, PUBLIC WELFARE IN CALIFORNIA, Table 2 (Statistical Series PA 3-72, Sept. 1965).

to almost 56.97 dollars.[93] Such differences remain largely unexplained, let alone justified.

With respect to adequacy of benefits there are marked differences throughout the country between categories as well as between states and localities. The adult categories, particularly the aged, tend to fare much better than families. This subject was extensively explored by the Advisory Council on Public Assistance in 1959. Staff reports pointed out that not only did most states provide inadequate benefits according to their own standards of need,[94] but, more importantly, in the AFDC program only one state's standard met the U.S. Department of Agriculture standards for measuring needs of low income families.[95]

Inequities of this magnitude in the tangible aspects of how people are treated strongly suggest the existence of equally great differences in the way that welfare organizations relate to the needy individuals attempting to utilize the programs. Much remains to be done to systematize and humanize the "system" and to make it the kind of institution that conforms to the American ideal of public service.

One of the factors most frequently cited by state and local jurisdictions to rationalize the inequities is their inability to finance the needed programs. This article does not elaborate the problems or systems of financing. Suffice it to say that the base provisions for federal sharing, which have steadily increased, have been changed more frequently than any other portion of the act. The principle of equalization, a prime justification for federal financing in many fields, was not an initial requirement of the act. Recent changes have moved in this direction but no firm conditions have yet been attached to federal financing. Thus the inadequacies and inequities known to exist in many of the states in which the Federal Department makes its largest proportionate investment must be attributed to the lack of federal standards. Federal financing in these states has reached the level of eighty per cent.

In those states in which local levies provide the contribution of the local jurisdiction—largely the state-supervised systems—slight progress has been made towards state-wide equalization. The total amount thus financed is often extremely small, but since the level of total expenditure within the state is often determined by the local share, local attitudes—reflecting among other things a reluctance to contribute and local competition with other purposes considered more directly in the interest of

---

93 *Id.* at Table 2A.

94 Advisory Council on Public Assistance, *Report on Findings and Recommendations*, S. Doc. No. 93, 86th Cong., 2d Sess. 18-19 (1960).

95 *Id.* at 54-68.

local voters—provide powerful incentives for every form of restrictive practice.

The lack of equalization could well be the major factor, whether at the federal-state or the state-county level, behind the failure to achieve equity in the administration of the programs. Failure to correct this deficiency could well contribute to the continuation of the present inadequacy and ineffectiveness of standards and administrative performance.

The implications of the Economic Opportunity Act of 1964[96] to the conventional welfare system are still unclear. Some titles of the act are direct descendents of work relief and conservation programs of the depression years. Title V of the act applies specifically to persons receiving public assistance and provides one hundred per cent federal financing for programs intended to upgrade employment skills. Many local communities have been unable to constructively use available funds due to the general lack of supportive services in the community. The unavailability of adequate, inexpensive child care facilities, for example, hampers the involvement of significant numbers of mothers in training programs of any kind. The inability to finance needed medical care services for adults in the family program is another hindrance to participation. The slums and ghettos of the inner city where poverty is most impacted have been found to be graveyards when it comes to adequate public services.

Many local communities have very mixed feelings about training programs within the welfare system. Some are reluctant to attempt to train more people for an overcrowded local labor market. Some groups prefer a reservoir of untrained labor to meet peak seasonal demands. Popular attitudes about the "undeserving" poor, who are equated with the family program recipients, tend to dampen local support. In many instances, local training programs have been little more than work relief projects thinly disguised as work conditioning experiences. Such subterfuges have tended to make the training aspects of the program appear punitive rather than helpful. Serious questions, as yet unanswered, have arisen as to the efficacy of training programs within the framework of the welfare system, especially when those programs are under local auspices.

Title II of the Economic Opportunity Act is only indirectly related to the conventional welfare system, yet it represents the most dramatic challenge to traditional attitudes about the poor. This title provides ninety per cent federal funding for programs sponsored by local communities in their efforts to combat poverty. The programs are to be put

---

[96] 78 Stat. 508, 42 U.S.C. 2701-981 (1964), as amended, 42 U.S.C. §§ 2713-967 (Supp. I, 1965).

together by representative boards and the act specifies that these boards are to include "maximum feasible participation of the poor"—not "doing for" but "doing with." The statutory interpretation by the Office of Economic Opportunity has led to considerable political turmoil.[97] There is no denying that the law has granted to the poor the right to participate in the decision-making process as it affects them and the communities in which they live. There is also no denying that the poor have had to put up quite a fight to stay on the inside.

This conflict, which has been concentrated in the major urban centers, has had an effect on the welfare system, although judgments about the effect would be premature. The people on welfare live within the target areas of the act because they are maintained in poverty. Many have grievances against the welfare system as well as other parts of the community structure. The neighborhood councils and boards provide forums for the coalescing of opinion and the breeding of remedial action. In many instances, representatives of the welfare system participate on these councils and gain added insights into how they are perceived by the people they think they are helping. Even more important, the poor, including those on public assistance, are becoming organized and articulate. To the extent that they are successful, programs, including public assistance, will be modified to meet their more insistent demands. Perhaps then the professional managers of many of the public systems will know what they are to do and how they are to do it.

---

[97] See generally Comment, 75 YALE L.J. 599 (1966).

The Children of Leviathan: Psychoanalytic Speculations Concerning Welfare Law and Punitive Sanctions

*Bernard L. Diamond**

THE ENGRAVED TITLEPAGE of the first edition of Hobbes' *Leviathan*, published in 1651, portrays the State as a giant man, looming over the countryside. On close inspection, this giant may be seen to be the synthesis of a multitude of individual human beings. But in the aggregate, the Leviathan is simply a giant replica of its tiny human components.

The temptation is very great to anthropomorphize a political entity like the State or a social institution like the Law. If such social organizations are but gigantic replications of the individual, numerous inferences and deductions can be made about their structure and function. The natural laws of human biology automatically apply, and one may predict the course of the social institution in history according to the same rules with which one predicts the lifetime course of the human. Thus, governments, social institutions, indeed, whole cultures undergo an autonomous biological development—birth, childhood, maturity, old age, and death and dissolution in the same inevitable sequence as is predestined for the individual organism.

Having succumbed to the basic temptation of anthropomorphism in form and structure, it is very easy to progress to the next stage: the assumption of identity of pathology between the individual creature and the social aggregation, function, or institution. Medicine, particularly psychiatry, is adept in supplying the vocabulary for such anthropomorphisms. We speak glibly of "sick" and of "healthy" economies; because schizophrenia is a disease of the mind characterized by fragmentation and internal division of the ego, so a nation divided against itself is "schizophrenic." The complex maneuverings of national foreign policies are described in terms appropriate to the sparring of two maladjusted adolescents. It is a sad fact that such anthropomorphisms are not recognized as mere metaphors and analogies but are used by people everywhere, including some scholars and politicians, as the basis for comprehension, appraisal, prediction, and manipulation of social and cultural structures.

Psychoanalysis, much more than other schools of psychiatry, is par-

* A.B., 1935, M.D., 1939, University of California. Professor of Law and of Criminology, University of California, Berkeley.

ticularly enticing in its potential applicability to social entities. Psychoanalysis is concerned with the most basic of all human psychological forces: sex and aggression, love and hate. Psychoanalysis is preoccupied with the origin, growth and development, and ultimate expression of these deep human drives. Sex and aggression are conceived of as innate biological forces which undergo an incredibly varied series of transformations before they manifest themselves in their adult mature forms. Detrimental influences, both intra and extrapsychic, affect the development and vicissitudes of these biological drives. If the noxious influences are not overcome, psychopathology results. The symptoms of the resultant psychopathological states are explainable as consequences of the dynamic interaction of the pathological drives and the defenses of the ego. In short, the psychodynamic mechanisms explain and account for the manifestations of psychical disease, and these same mechanisms provide the means for the remedial process through the techniques of psychoanalytic therapy.

There have been many attempts to apply psychoanalytic theories and clinical knowledge to social problems. The most famous is, of course, Freud's small monograph, *Civilization and Its Discontents*, first published in 1929. Freud rather casually presents a number of admittedly speculative ideas as to the inherent opposition of culture and social organization to the instinctual gratification (happiness) of the individual. Throughout the essay, Freud is unabashedly anthropomorphic in his analogies between the development and pathology of society and that of the individual. He states: "[W]e . . . have recognized the evolution of culture as a special process, comparable to the normal growth of an individual to maturity . . . ."[1] Again: "The analogy between the process of cultural evolution and the path of individual development may be carried further in an important respect."[2] He follows with: "Another point of agreement is that the cultural super-ego, just like that of an individual, sets up high ideals and standards, and that failure to fulfill them is punished by both with 'anxiety of conscience.' "[3] Finally, Freud concludes with his social diagnosis: "If the evolution of civilization has such a far-reaching similarity with the development of an individual, and if the same methods are employed in both, would not the diagnosis be justified that many systems of civilization—or epochs of it—possibly even the whole of humanity—have become 'neurotic' under the pressure of the civilizing trends?"[4]

---

[1] FREUD, CIVILIZATION AND ITS DISCONTENTS 64 (Riviere transl. 1930).
[2] *Id.* at 136.
[3] *Id.* at 137.
[4] *Id.* at 141.

Freud's mild and undogmatic little essay immediately became the focal point of bitter controversy. To the psychoanalyst, Freud's excursion into sociology was taken to grant unrestricted license to diagnose all that ails society as if whole cultures were but individual patients on the analytic couch. To others, the discovery that there existed other biological responses related to social development of animals, such as "territoriality," or evidence (of which there is a good deal) that aggression is not necessarily biologically innate in all living creatures as Freud postulated, provided the grounds for a triumphant denunciation of all psychoanalytic theory and method.

One ludicrous consequence of taking Freud's book so seriously was the total banishment of all psychoanalytic theory and practice from Soviet Russian psychiatry. Freud expressed some pessimistic predictions that he did not expect that even the utopian Marxist society with its abolition of private property would eliminate all problems of aggression and individual unhappiness from the world.[5] Such views were sufficient to label psychoanalysis as anti-Marxist and exclude a whole discipline of psychological knowledge from a major portion of the civilized world.

It is unfortunate that all concerned with these subsequent bitter conflicts did not pay more attention to Freud's warning. He emphatically cautions:

> But it behoves us to be very careful, not to forget that after all we are dealing only with analogies, and that it is dangerous, not only with men but also with concepts, to drag them out of the region where they originated and have matured. The diagnosis of collective neuroses, moreover, will be confronted by a special difficulty. In the neurosis of an individual we can use as a starting-point the contrast presented to us between the patient and his environment which we assume to be "normal." No such background as this would be available for any society similarly affected; it would have to be supplied in some other way. And with regard to any therapeutic application of our knowledge, what would be the use of the most acute analysis of social neuroses, since no one possesses power to compel the community to adopt the therapy?[6]

Social institutions cannot be properly diagnosed as simply collective obsessional neuroses, nor can it be reasonably expected that psychoanalytic insight will result in desirable social change. Nevertheless, I think that certain aspects of psychoanalytic methodology—certain ways of looking at and investigating human problems—have a most fruitful application to the understanding of social issues. With full awareness of Freud's warning that we are only dealing with analogies, I shall apply

---

[5] *Id.* at 88-91.
[6] *Id.* at 141-42.

certain psychoanalytic methods of reasoning to some of the problems included in this symposium.

Jacobus tenBroek has recently published an extraordinarily exhaustive and scholarly analysis of California's dual system of family law.[7] tenBroek traces our present conflicted, inconsistent, punitive, and discriminatory welfare laws to their origin in the Elizabethan Poor Law of 1601.[8] He fully documents the close relationship between criminal sanctions and welfare aid to the poor. He describes in detail how society, as soon as it assumed the burden of providing welfare aid through governmental channels, accompanied this aid with punitive sanctions, usually of a highly discriminatory character. Thus today, our society relieves the misery of the poor and dependent with its right hand and takes away security with its left hand through imposition of criminal or other punitive sanctions contingent upon grants of such welfare aid. How can one explain this ambivalent attitude towards the poor? What can possibly explain this monstrous contradiction of social morality?

tenBroek's explanation is simple and direct:

> Today in California, no less than in Elizabethan England, the family law of the poor derives its particular content and special nature from the central concept of the poor law system: public provision for the care and support of the poor. He who pays the bill can attach conditions, related or unrelated to the purpose of the grant, and almost always does. . . . The basic motive, thus, once the original step is taken, is fiscal and economic: to conserve public funds to the fullest extent possible consistent with the original undertaking. Although this fundamental motive from time to time has been augmented by the punitive, the moralistic, the political, and restrained by the humane and the rehabilitative, it has been determinative in molding the character and fixing the features of the law of the poor in general and the family law of the poor in particular.[9]

As a psychoanalyst, I find it difficult to accept tenBroek's economic motive as the basic dynamic force behind the malignant social symptom of ambivalence towards the poor and dependent. I find it hard to believe that concern over money alone can cause, in tenBroek's words, "Californians to associate welfare with punitive, repressive, discriminatory, exclusionary goals as well as with relief and rehabilitation.[10] More is required to explain this phenomenon. For as tenBroek says, "When problems of poverty are handled under the police powers of the Constitu-

---

[7] tenBroek, *California's Dual System of Family Law: Its Origin, Development, and Present Status* (pts. 1-3), 16 STAN. L. REV. 257, 900; 17 STAN. L. REV. 614 (1964-65).

[8] 43 Eliz. 1, c. 2 (1601).

[9] tenBroek, *California's Dual System of Family Law: Its Origin, Development, and Present Status*, 17 STAN. L. REV. 614, 676-77 (1965).

[10] *Id.* at 680.

tion, poverty comes to be equated with disease, immorality, and disorder. Indeed, historically these were inseparable conditions."[11]

When a psychoanalyst attempts to analyze a neurotic symptom, he follows a definite chain of reasoning utilizing certain assumptions which are basic to the psychoanalytic theory of neurosis: (1) He assumes that the symptoms have meaning and purpose, no matter what their apparent irrationality and seeming lack of sensible purpose; that the symptoms, no matter how contradictory, confused, paradoxical, or inconsistent, bear a primitive, symbolic, and always meaningful relationship to the infantile conflict out of which the symptoms developed. (2) That the symptoms accomplish specific benefits for the patient, despite the pain and suffering which result. In other words, in the psychic economy of the personality, the symptoms show a net profit. (3) That the benefit or profit to the patient which is derived from the symptoms is of two orders: secondary gain, which is the conscious, or easily made conscious, contemporary motive for the symptoms; and primary gain, which is the deeper, infantile, unconscious, and repressed motive. (4) That because of the primary gain, there is an investment of energy (cathexis) in the formation of a symptom which impels the patient to resist giving up the symptom, even when the secondary gain has diminished.

If one analyzes the present day welfare laws *as if* they were symptoms of a social neurosis, utilizing assumptions analogous to those described above for the comprehension of the neurotic symptoms of an individual, one can immediately make some speculative inferences. The validity of these inferences is, of course, not at all established. But they should be considered and may, perhaps, provide clues to further social and historical research.

The intensely ambivalent quality of the social attitudes behind our welfare laws indicates that these attitudes arise out of very old (that is, culturally infantile) conflicts concerned with primitive emotions and fears. The obvious emotions are love and hate. Thus society simultaneously loves and hates its poor, its dependent, and its disabled. The emotion of love requires that the poor and weak be protected, nurtured, and provided for, as if they were helpless children. Failure to do so would cause collective guilt which would prevent those who have from enjoying what they have, knowing that others have not. Our love for the poor arises out of guilt rather than compassion. Our acts of charity, both as individuals and as the collective family of the state, are thus primarily for our benefit rather than for the benefit of the recipient. tenBroek is quite right in stating, "They [welfare programs] are designed

---

[11] *Ibid.*

to safeguard health, safety, morals, and well-being of the fortunate rather than directly to improve the lot of the unfortunate."[12]

The concurrent hatred implies fear—deep, primitive, unconscious fear—that the very existence of the poor and weak in society threatens the existence of that society. Punitive sanctions must then be applied to control those whom one fears, to make certain that they do not grow and prosper and gain the strength to fulfill their threat of usurpation of power. As the individual most fears death and annihilation, so society most fears anarchy and revolution. The poor and dependent, as a class, become endowed with magical, destructive powers totally out of proportion to reality. They become sacrificial recipients of scapegoated sins, but at the same time they are tabooed objects who cannot be destroyed without dire consequences.

The poor and the disabled are thus like the insane, idiots, and children (and, in some societies, slaves and women) in being nonpersons. Nonpersons may be understood as those individuals in any society who, as a class, are defined differently in their social functions, privileges, and opportunities than those who are predominant in the society. A nonperson may occasionally be given special consideration (such as the relief from criminal responsibility for the insane), but in most instances the nonperson is sharply cut off from the major benefits to be derived from the society. Particularly, the nonperson is not allowed the privilege of having a say (in the sense of wielding power) over his own destiny or that of the society in which he lives. Yet he is not extruded from society, but must be retained, cared for, and nurtured.

There seems to be no historical precedent against exploitation of the nonperson for the benefit of the more potent members of society. In fact, such exploitation of nonpersons, be they insane, children, poor, or crippled, has been a constant feature of most societies. But their direct destruction has been tabooed except in a very few, atypical cultures (for example, Nazi Germany).

In a recent paper by Platt and myself,[13] we have shown that from ancient times, the social and legal atttitudes toward the criminal responsibility of the insane have been closely associated with deep-seated attitudes towards the child, who is regarded simultaneously as a helpless being to be loved and nurtured and as a wild beast to be curbed and tamed. We were able to demonstrate that the current tests of criminal responsibility of the insane are derived from tests earlier applied to the child. The historical correctness of this legal association of both the

---

[12] *Id.* at 681.

[13] Platt & Diamond, *The Origins and Development of the "Wild Beast" Concept of Mental Illness and Its Relation to Theories of Criminal Responsibility*, 1 J. OF THE HISTORY OF THE BEHAVIORAL SCIENCES 355 (1965).

insane and the child with the ambivalent attributes of the feared wild beast and the loved, helpless infant is amply documented.

In a second paper,[14] we trace the familiar "right and wrong" test of criminal responsibility back to its ultimate mythological source in the story of Genesis, where the ingestion of the fruit of the tree of the knowledge of good and evil transforms the child-like and innocent (hence, nonperson) Adam and Eve into mortal, sinful human beings.

Professor tenBroek's extensive documentation[15] of the development of our system of family and welfare law seems, in my opinion, to support a similar ambivalent position in society of the poor, the blind, the disabled, and the dependent, so that they, like the insane and children, are nonpersons.

Psychoanalytic theory of neurosis postulates the Oedipal conflict as the focal point, the critical period, in the development of the child. Failure to resolve the Oedipal conflict in socially acceptable patterns leads to residues of infantile sexual conflicts which persist into adulthood and force the development of neurotic ego defenses which are then expressed in symptom formation. The Oedipal conflict presupposes a state of ambivalent conflict between parent and child. The sexual instinct for propagation of the race demands that the young be loved and provided for. But the growth and development of each child also competitively threatens the survival of the parent. Each father is the potential victim of his own son. Freud speculated that the origin of this universal Oedipal phase of childhood development derives from dimly perceived racial memories of some universal prehistoric society where the sons literally did rise up and slay their fathers.[16]

Freud's theory of primitive society has never been substantiated by anthropological research, and the universality of the Oedipal conflict in all cultures at all times is certainly open to question. But there is ample clinical evidence to demonstrate that ambivalent attitudes of love and hate between parent and child are exceedingly wide-spread in a large variety of cultures, and that, at least in our western culture, these attitudes are at the root of subsequent neurotic conflict and symptom formation.

Viewed in this light, and carrying psychoanalytic speculation farther, all nonpersons—children, the poor, the disabled, the disenfranchised, the discriminated against minority, the criminal, the sinful, the slave (real or economic), and in some instances the woman—symbolically represent the child in a large-scale Oedipal struggle with the potent and socially

---

[14] Platt & Diamond, *The Origins of the "Right and Wrong" Test and Its Subsequent Development in the United States*, 54 CALIF. L. REV. (1966) (to be published).

[15] tenBroek, *supra* note 7.

[16] FREUD, TOTEM AND TABOO *passim* (Brill transl. 1918).

integrated members of society who collectively symbolize the father. This Leviathan father replicates on the larger social scale the intensely ambivalent attitudes towards society's children—the varied types of nonpersons—that the individual father has towards his own child. The law thus becomes the formal expression of this collective Oedipal neurosis.

What might be the "neurotic" benefits, real or imagined, concealed within the legally formalized, ambivalent attitudes towards the socially incapacitated? How does society profit from treating its welfare recipients simultaneously with aid and with punishment? Here, I speculate, there must be achieved a delicate balance between acceptance and rejection. Clearly, if society were simply to reject, to allow its poor and disabled to starve, to be completely cast out from the community, it would mean the complete renunciation of our most ancient Judaeo-Christian ideals of morality and civilized behavior: "Am I my brother's keeper?"[17] and "[T]hou shalt love they neighbour as thyself"[18] from the Old Testament, and "Therefore all things whatsoever ye would that men should do to you, do ye even so to them"[19] from the New Testament. It would be impossible to even conceive of such total renunciation of traditional ideals if it were not for the brutal fact that we have experienced within our own lifetime such naked examples in totalitarian societies. But barring such extraordinary historical exceptions, a peaceful, civilized society must, individually and collectively, incorporate attitudes of compassion, nurture, and love towards its less fortunate members. One might even postulate that there exists in the collective, social mind an inner drive towards the utopian welfare state analogous to the instinctual inner drive of the individual psyche. Such a trend has certainly been a deep and ancient social ideal.

There exist, however, strong forces in opposition. If the welfare state is one ideal, individual responsibility, initiative, and competition represent another. This ideal, too, is deep and ancient, and it takes many forms: from the early theological concept of free will to the modern economic doctrine of free enterprise. Man is a responsible, free agent, answerable to God and mankind for his actions. If he fails in his social obligations, either through sinfulness, poverty, or disability, it is his own doing. He must not only suffer the consequences of his deviancy, but he must be punished as a moral lesson for those who have not yet failed or who might be tempted to renounce their social obligations.

The ideal of individual responsibility and initiative favors the strong

---

17 *Genesis* 4:9 (King James).

18 *Leviticus* 19:18 (King James). The passage also appears in the New Testament. *Matthew* 22:39 (King James).

19 *Matthew* 7:12 (King James).

and the powerful: those that have, as against those that have not. It implies a Darwinian struggle for social survival: a struggle to the death between the fit and the unfit. The nonperson, be he poor, disabled, criminal, insane, or simply a child, is the inevitable enemy of the person. The nonperson threatens the very existence of the person. He is unconciously perceived to threaten the person's possessions, his powers, and his values—even his ultimate survival.

It seems that our traditional welfare laws and policies achieve an insecure balance of forces. They are ordinarily effective in maintaining the *status quo*, but the balance is always precarious in two senses: (1) Those that have not—the nonpersons—may at any moment rise up and take what they need from those that have (thus, revolution and anarchy); and (2) the ranks of those that have may desert to the enemy. That is, those that have may regard conformity to society's mores and the renunciation of their individual gratifications too high a price for the social benefits they are supposed to achieve. They may come to regard the ideal of individual responsibility and self-reliance as a fraud and a hoax whose practical benefits may never materialize or whose goals are too arduous to aspire towards.

Viewed in this light, compassion towards the nonperson and literal application of the Biblical injunctions is very dangerous. It threatens revolution at its worst; it undermines the value systems of the establishment at its best.

The solution—a typically neurotic one, in my opinion—is to compromise by both giving to and oppressing the nonpersons. Our society, through its welfare policies, is compassionate towards them. It provides aid and nurture, but only to the degree that it ensures that they remain nonpersons. Nonpersons must not be allowed to suffer to the point where they might be tempted to reverse the social order. At the same time they must be constantly reminded, through the infliction of punitive sanctions and discriminatory exclusions, that they are nonpersons. They must be living examples to all who might be tempted to renounce their social obligations and join the ranks. All valid persons in society must be constantly reminded that desertion to the enemy means only humiliation, misery, pain, and suffering.

The secondary gain of this neurotic compromise is, as tenBroek describes,[20] economic. The financial cost of society's institutionalized charity and compassion is kept to a reasonable minimum.

But beneath this superficial and quite consciously intended economic motivation, there must exist a more powerful, unconscious conflict of

---

[20] tenBroek, *supra* note 9, at 676.

forces which is concerned with the very existence of the social order. These forces, arising out of the infancy of our social development, elicit defensive compromises which make sense only when viewed in a historical perspective. The primary gain of the social neurosis is to hold these conflicting forces in check, to maintain the balance, and to avoid the annihilation of the social order and its accompanying value systems. In this sense, we have the Oedipal struggle between parent and child on the grand scale of the Leviathan.

Psychoanalytic therapy is based on the major assumption that the neurotic symptom is archaic. The symptom is thought of as a defense of the ego against threatening emotional forces (for example, castration fear) which were very real and immediate during the early developmental period of the child. The erection of the neurotic ego defenses, no matter how disabling or how painful, was an urgent and necessary process at the time of their original construction. The ego, in its youthful instability, does not possess the strength nor the rationality to defend itself in less pathological ways when confronted with overwhelming conflict. The child has not yet learned all of the tricks, strategies, and techniques of the adult for getting out from under oppressive emotional conflict with minimum expense to one's self and with minimum loss of self-esteem. These are modes of adaptation which are available only to the mature adult who has acquired them through a long process of trial-and-error learning.

However, the neurotic defenses of the child's immature ego become autonomous and persist long after the need for them is urgent and necessary. The neurotic defenses make no allowance for the otherwise growing strength of the ego as the child develops into the adolescent and adult. It is probable that the very existence of certain types of neurotic defenses deprives the growing ego, no matter how strong, from acquiring the necessary skill and learning experience to utilize more normal means of coping with emotional adversity—especially with anxiety and fear arising out of internal sexual and aggressive impulses. In other words, the neurotic ego defense protects the child, but it also impedes further emotional development and the acquisition of more effective defenses suitable to the stronger ego of the adult. The neurotic adult is, therefore, utilizing defense mechanisms which are designed to protect against the dangers of a past age. The neurotic symptoms are compromises in a struggle that may have little relevance to the external realities of the adult's world. They impede and constrict the functioning of the adult ego so that the significant struggles of the real world are neglected or evaded.

A neurotic defense is like the high wall around a medieval city. The wall originally was necessary: It defined the boundaries of the city, it gave the city a sense of solidarity and substance as an integrated social unit, and it protected against the outside marauders who were enemies of the city. But as the city grows, it outstrips its boundaries; its enemies in the surrounding countryside have long since disappeared, or perhaps been incorporated into the city. Now the wall serves only to strangle traffic, to create slums, and to impede further growth. Yet the wall is there; adaptations to its existence have been made. Certain elements of the city have a vested interest in the existence of the wall. It would be expensive to tear it down, and there would be disputes as to what should occupy the land upon which it stood. Further, the wall, as archaic and useless as it may be, gives a certain character to the city; it is an important part of the city's identity. To tear the wall down would change the very nature of the city.

So it is with neurotic symptoms. And so it is, I believe, with "neurotic" social defenses. The immature society—economically insecure, unstable in government, with the threat of anarchy and revolution very real, and whose ideological values and social ideals are only tentatively formed and incompletely accepted—such a society can be excused for its irrational welfare policies.

Elizabethan Poor Law of 1601[21] was undoubtedly appropriate to the English society of the time. It is not so appropriate to a rich, powerful, secure, and mature nation such as the United States. We, as a nation, are strong enough in our economic and social development to permit us to relinquish our ambivalent attitudes toward the recipients of our welfare aid. Our democratic social order is no longer vulnerable to sudden overturn. Our affluence is so great that no amount of sharing of the wealth is going to allow the have-not nonpersons—our social children—to overthrow those who have and those who belong. The valid persons of our society need not fear the corruption of their ideals and ideologies by the outsiders. It is not necessary that aid to the families of needy children be accompanied by discriminatory, punitive sanctions and harsh moral regulations to save us from "creeping socialism." It is not necessary to fear that poverty programs will destroy our system of free enterprise or that welfare assistance to the unemployed aged given in a manner which enhances, rather than degrades, the sense of individual worth and dignity will corrupt our ideal of individual responsibility and initiative. Our national ego is strong, and we can afford to give up our social neuroses.

Nevertheless, resistance to improvement is to be expected. Social

---

21 43 Eliz. 1, c. 2 (1601).

neuroses are as heavily cathected as are individual neuroses. They represent too much of an emotional investment to be easily relinquished; they represent too large a component of our social identity. Thus each new recommendation to diminish the punitive ambivalence of our welfare policies will be met with extremist fears of socialism, communism, subversion, and destruction of our moral values and our ideals of individual responsibility.

The extremist will demand that with every dollar of welfare aid, there must also go a measure of social degradation, of restriction of personal freedom, and of punitive sanctions. He will threaten that it is subversive to do otherwise. Such an attitude must be exposed as the social paranoia that it is and as a neurotic resistance against the development of the mature society in which all may participate with individual dignity.

By now, the reader can perceive that I have done precisely what I warned against earlier: that is, fully anthropomorphized social attitudes and the legal expression of those attitudes as if they were the neurotic symptoms of an individual. Such psychoanalytic speculations are not intended as historical or scientific facts, but rather as a speculative, conceptual framework on which to order a wide diversity of social and historical information concerning a collection of highly disparate classes of individuals whose common denominator is that they occupy a marginal position in society and are the recipients of highly ambivalent social attitudes.

The interesting possibility exists, however, that the goal to be achieved is independent of the theoretical conceptualizations which serve to define the goal. A psychoanalyst might define our present social welfare dilemma as if it were a neurotic sickness. Sociologists, lawyers, or welfare specialists might prefer a completely different theoretical orientation. Certainly, the Marxist would prefer his own theories. And the conservative, rugged individualist Republican would have a different framework in which to structure his view of these matters.

But could there not be a consensual agreement among all that the goal is inherent in the very nature of man and his culture? The goal of the child is to grow up—to become an adult, a valid member of a social group with authentic relationships to others of that group. Social institutions, including the criminal law and family law, should facilitate this process and further the integration of the adult-to-be with his individual family, his community, his nation, and most of all, the family of all mankind.

The goal of social welfare legislation can be similarly defined. Its purpose is to make persons out of nonpersons. To transform Leviathan's children into adults; to validate them as full participating members of the social order, with all the rights, privileges, benefits, and obligations that accompany full citizenship. Anything short of that goal must be regarded as a failure.

Welfare From Below: Recipients' Views of the Public Welfare System[†]

*Scott Briar**

> I think the Welfare Department is too soft, too lenient. They don't
> make investigations to see how the welfare money is being spent. If
> the workers went to the house more often they would be able to tell
> if people are cheating. They could go to the home anytime they want
> to, day or night. If the person isn't guilty, then they shouldn't care
> when the worker comes.

T HESE ARE NOT THE WORDS of an irate taxpayer or public official concerned about the rising costs of public welfare programs. On the
contrary, this statement was made by a poorly educated welfare recipient
living in the Negro ghetto of an industrial city. But the importance of
this statement is that these views are not atypical of the opinions expressed by the more than ninety welfare recipients interviewed in the
study reported in this article.

In the growing body of literature on what has been called "the law
of the poor,"[1] little attention has been paid to the conceptions held by
the poor themselves about their relationship to the law and to legal and
quasi-legal institutions. This omission is partly due to the lack of systematic data on this subject, a lack which is only beginning to be remedied.[2] Another explanation, one which partly accounts both for the
inattention to the conceptions of law held by the poor and for the lack
of research on the subject, is found in two assumptions which appear
in some of the recent literature[3] on the law of the poor: (1) that one of
the basic *social* problems in this area is the lack of legal services; and (2)

† This article is based on research supported by Grant No. 230 E-5-141, Welfare Administration, U.S. Department of Health, Education, and Welfare and in part by a grant from
the California State Department of Social Welfare to the Social Welfare Research Projects
Office, School of Social Welfare, University of California. The author acknowledges the assistance of Miss Mildred Alexander in the development of the interview schedule used in this
research and the contribution of Mrs. Naomi Streshinsky to all stages of the work reported
here.

* D.S.W., 1961, Columbia University; Associate Professor, School of Social Welfare, and
Research Associate, Social Welfare Research Projects Office and Center for the Study of Law
and Society, University of California, Berkeley.

1 *E.g.,* U.S. DEP'T OF HEALTH, EDUC. & WELFARE, THE EXTENSION OF LEGAL SERVICES
TO THE POOR (1964); Carlin & Howard, *Legal Representation and Class Justice,* 12 U.C.L.A.L.
REV. 381 (1965).

2 See, *e.g.,* Zeitz, *Survey of Negro Attitudes Toward Law,* 19 RUTGERS L. REV. 288
(1965).

3 See, *e.g.,* THE EXTENSION OF LEGAL SERVICES TO THE POOR, *op. cit. supra* note 1, *passim.*

that if legal services are provided, the poor will use them. The former assumption is well supported, but the validity of the second is in doubt.

While some programs designed to extend legal services to the poor have reported success, others have not, for reasons which appear to be due in part to the attitudes of potential users among the poor. An example is Sparer's description of the problems arising because of the sentiments and attitudes held by potential users of the Mobilization for Youth Legal Services Unit; for example, he notes that "they felt too unsure of themselves to argue with—or insist upon anything with [officials] . . . ."[4]

Thus one reason for conducting studies in this area is that knowledge about the views of law held by the poor may be useful in designing effective programs for extending legal services to them. Second, such research may shed light on the effects of the legal order on the persons directly affected. The experiences of the poor may be particularly instructive in this regard since the poor are more likely than others to be directly affected by certain major legal institutions, particularly the police, the courts, and the correction agencies.

This article attempts to contribute to both of the above aims by describing the findings of a study concerned in part with welfare recipients' views of the welfare agency. It should be emphasized that welfare recipients constitute only a portion of the population living in poverty,[5] and therefore the findings reported here cannot be generalized to the nonwelfare poor. The welfare poor tend to be more impoverished and to be afflicted by other problems to a greater extent than the nonwelfare poor.[6] Most important, the welfare poor live dependent on the operations of an institution, the public welfare agency, established to administer welfare legislation.

---

[4] Sparer, *Education on New York's Lower East Side*, in THE EXTENSION OF LEGAL SERVICES, *op. cit. supra* note 1, at 123.

[5] Estimates of the proportion of the poor who are welfare recipients vary, partly as a function of the definition of poverty. Morgan *et al.* estimate that twenty-three per cent of all poor families receive public assistance. MORGAN, DAVID, COHEN & BRAZER, INCOME AND WELFARE IN THE UNITED STATES 216 (1962).

[6] There have been few systematic studies of the differences between welfare and nonwelfare poor. Robert Stone, of the Institute of Social Science Research, San Francisco State College, in a study still in process, attempted to find a matching, nonwelfare sample for comparison to a sample of AFDC-U, CAL. WELFARE & INST'NS CODE §§ 11201, 11250, families. After much effort, he had to settle for a nonwelfare group which, although it was otherwise comparable, had a higher average income than the AFDC-U sample. Sydney Bernard found that the essential difference between welfare applicants and nonapplicants in a homogeneous low-income neighborhood was that the nonapplicants had more financial resources of various sorts available to them than the applicants. Bernard, The Economic and Social Adjustment of Low-Income Female-Headed Families, May, 1964 (unpublished, Florence Heller Graduate School for Advanced Studies in Social Welfare, Brandeis University).

I

THE STUDY

The study reported here is part of a continuing project concerning the impact of public welfare policies and operations on family life. As part of the exploratory phase of this project, intensive interviews were conducted with more than one hundred recipients of AFDC-U[7] (the program which provides aid to intact families with dependent children in which the father is unemployed).[8] These interviews, which ranged in length from three to six hours extending over two to three sessions, probed systematically and in depth each recipient's experiences with the agency, his conceptions of the agency and its operations, his perceptions of his rights and obligations vis-à-vis the agency, his attitude towards certain welfare policies and issues, and the effects of recipient status on his family life.[9]

The findings presented in this article are based primarily on interviews conducted with a systematically selected sample of ninety-two AFDC-U recipients, consisting of forty-six married couples heading family units in recent receipt of AFDC-U funds. Since the husbands and wives were interviewed separately (using the same interview schedule), and since the husband and wife in the same family frequently differed in their responses to questions about the agency and their separate experiences with it, the data are reported for individuals rather than families.[10]

The recipients were selected from the official rolls of the county welfare department in inverse order of date of application, beginning with the most recent applicant prior to July 1, 1965. A quota sampling procedure was used to yield an equal number of recipients in each of the three major ethnic groups in the county studied; thus the sample includes thirty Caucasian (fifteen families), thirty Negro (fifteen families), and

---

[7] CAL. WELFARE & INST'NS CODE §§ 11201, 11250.

[8] The author acknowledges the assistance of the following graduate students at the University of California, Berkeley, in conducting some of these interviews: Arlene Brasher, Archie Hanlan, Susan Reed, Hezekiah Singleton, and Arabella Springer.

[9] A structured schedule was used in these interviews to insure that comparable data were collected from the respondents. So far as possible, responses were pre-coded (on the basis of pre-test interviews). In addition, all interviews were tape recorded so that each recipient's free responses also would be available for analysis.

[10] There are several reasons for treating the forty-six couples as ninety-two individual recipients in the presentation of findings. As noted in the text, the husband and wife in each family were interviewed separately, and their views of the recipient experience frequently differed (although the *distribution* of responses for husbands and wives as groups *typically* do not differ substantially) so that it is not possible to speak of a "family" response. The sample, however, is not and should not be construed as consisting of ninety-two independent recipients; rather it is a cohort of husbands and wives receiving AFDC-U.

thirty-two Mexican-American (sixteen families) AFDC-U recipients.[11] In many instances the *distribution* of responses obtained from these three groups are, in effect, identical; consequently, findings are reported for the total sample, except where significant or systematic differences among the three ethnic groups were found.

In a study of this sort the question of response validity always must be considered. Did the recipients report their "true" beliefs and opinions, or did they say what they thought the interviewers wanted to hear? Important as these questions are, they are difficult to answer categorically. Nevertheless, in this study there are a number of reasons for believing that the responses obtained reflect the recipients' own opinions. First, in approaching recipients, interviewers identified themselves as being with the University of California and took great pains to make clear that the study was not connected with the welfare department. Second, recipients frequently made comments about the welfare agency and their experiences with it that they would have been unlikely to make had they believed the agency would have access to their responses. Third, Negro recipients were interviewed by a Negro interviewer, and Spanish-speaking interviewers were used with the Mexican-American recipients. Fourth, the interviewers spent from three to seven hours (in more than one session) with each respondent. Fifth, the dominant responses reported herein were contrary to what the interviewers privately had hoped and wanted to hear; the responses revealed a state of affairs which was a source of frustration to the interviewers and which made it necessary to caution the interviewers to check their desires to educate and inform the recipients about their "rights." Finally, the most convincing test of validity is the extent to which the responses obtained are consistent with other known beliefs and behaviors of the group studied; this aspect is considered following presentation of the findings.

The welfare department in the county in which this research was conducted has acquired a reputation both locally and nationally for its progressiveness. Thus the recipients interviewed in this study are somewhat atypical in that their welfare experiences have been with a department which is unusual in the degree of its commitment to a professional and client-oriented approach to welfare services. It is not known, however, to what extent or in what respect recipients' perceptions of the welfare

---

[11] The actual proportions of these three groups in the AFDC-U population in the county studied, as of July 1964, were: Caucasian, 50.3%; Mexican-American, 10.8%; and Negro, 38.9%. CALIFORNIA STATE DEP'T OF SOCIAL WELFARE, RESEARCH AND STATISTICS. Comparison of the study sample with known characteristics (for example, family size, age, education, and usual occupation of the unemployed parent) of the AFDC-U population in the community studied revealed no great differences between the two groups.

system vary in relation to the character of the welfare department—these questions require further research.

It should be noted that the AFDC-U family is a recent phenomenon in public welfare programs—in California the program did not begin until February 1964. Prior to that time, intact family units with dependent children in need of public assistance had two options: (1) general assistance, or "relief," which is dependent on county funds, provides extremely low benefits, and for all practical purposes is unavailable in many localities and difficult to obtain in many others; and (2) separation of husband and wife so that the mother and the children could become eligible for benefits under the AFDC program.[12] Thus the AFDC-U program provides assistance to a portion of the "able-bodied poor," one of the groups for which society traditionally has been most reluctant to provide stable financial assistance—partly out of fear that to do so would undermine their incentive to seek gainful employment.[13]

II

THE VIEW FROM BELOW

A. On the Edge of Disaster: Becoming a Welfare Recipient

The typical AFDC-U recipient-father,[14] when he appears with his wife at the welfare agency to apply for aid, has only about ten dollars left in his pocket, has been out of work for three weeks or more, and has three or four children (five or six if he is Mexican-American) to feed and care for. He is comparatively young (thirty to thirty-five), and when he last worked was earning less than four hundred dollars per month in a job requiring few skills. His wife is not employed, and for a while they got by on unemployment compensation or with the help of small loans and gifts from friends and relatives, but these resources are exhausted. Moreover, given his usual income, he is deeply in debt (thirty-nine percent have debts in excess of one thousand dollars) and is worried about how he will meet his monthly payments as well as feed, clothe, and house his family.

He is not a stranger to this city. Chances are that he has lived in this community for ten years or more—though he moved to his present ad-

---

12 Cal. Stats. 1955, ch. 1956, § 1, at 3586.

13 Part of the political support for the AFDC-U program in California came from groups that hoped this program would: (1) curb "immorality" among AFDC recipients, and (2) remove an incentive for the unemployed father to desert his family.

14 It should be emphasized that the composite picture of the recipient presented in this paper is limited to the sample interviewed in this study. No wider generality can be claimed at this stage in the research. Consequently, whenever a finding is reported about "recipients" the qualifying phrase "in this sample" is implied.

dress less than two years ago—and he has lived in the state over fifteen years. He has not applied for welfare aid before (sixty per cent in this sample had not), and he was reluctant to do so. But his friends and relatives, and finally his wife, have urged him to go to the welfare department, and eventually he agreed.

When applicants arrive at the welfare department—or Social Service Department as it is called in this county—they first meet the receptionist. She asks them some factual questions (for example, "What is your name?" "Where do you live?" "Have you ever applied for aid here before?") and then directs them to the waiting room. In this room—light, windowless, but reasonably pleasant—an applicant may begin to experience the sense of estrangement evident in the responses of most recipients interviewed. As one father described it, "I looked around [the waiting room] and saw a bunch of old people and Negroes—I felt I should be someplace else."

But few recipients were this sensitive and perceptive about their personal reactions to the experience of becoming and being a welfare recipient. For most, this sense of estrangement is expressed in a less subtle way: Our respondents almost never (and most respondents never) referred to welfare recipients as "we" but as "they." This characteristic estrangement—also manifest in a tendency to view oneself as an atypical recipient, a self-conception which seemed to be held by nearly all the recipients interviewed[15]—reflects the desire of these recipients to dissociate themselves from the image they have of other recipients. Our respondents expressed opinions about other public welfare recipients which usually have been associated primarily with conservative, anti-welfare groups. For example, fifty-eight per cent of the recipients interviewed believe that more than twenty-five per cent of all welfare recipients remain on welfare longer than necessary, and nearly one-half believe that over twenty-five per cent of all recipients "cheat" the welfare department.[16]

In addition, the recipients seemed to use their own situations as a standard for evaluating the claims of other recipients. For example, each recipient regarded as justifiable his own reason for seeking welfare

---

[15] Few clear exceptions to this generalization were found. One was a woman in a small group of persons (not included in the data reported in this paper) whose applications for aid were denied. This woman had previously been a welfare recipient and had re-applied for aid. Subsequent to denial of her re-application, she became a community organizer in an OEO project. When interviewed, she spoke of welfare recipients as "we."

[16] A report of a fifteen-month survey of welfare fraud conducted by the California State Department of Social Welfare and released in December 1965 found that established fraud amounted to a "fraction of 1/30th of 1 per cent of the total Aid to Families of Dependent Children caseload." California State Dep't of Social Welfare, News Release, Dec. 10, 1965.

assistance, but often judged other reasons depending on their similarity to his own situation. Thus in response to specific questions asking whether a person would be justified in requesting assistance under various specified conditions, Mexican-American recipients (a number of whom were farm laborers) were more likely to say that a farm laborer is justified in requesting aid during the off-season than were Negro and Caucasian recipients. Negro and Caucasian recipients were more likely to say that recipients should not be expected to take farm labor jobs than were Mexican-American recipients. And the Mexican-American and Negro recipients were much more apt than were Caucasians to say that a man is justified in requesting welfare assistance if he cannot find work because of discrimination.

B. Welfare Assistance: A Right or Charity?

Returning to the typical (or, more accurately, composite) recipient couple that we followed into the waiting room of the welfare office, after a wait of from one-half to two hours[17] a lady (the intake social worker) appears, takes them into an office in the inner recesses of the building, and begins the application interview. What are the recipients' expectations of this situation? What are their conceptions of the request they are making?

Welfare assistance under federally assisted programs such as AFDC-U is a right in that entitlement is defined by statute and not by the arbitrary (however well-motivated) decision of a charitable organization. If a family meets the statutory requirements the agency is obligated to grant their claim for assistance.[18]

While this conception of the federal assistance programs is held by the soical workers in the department studied, our findings suggest that few recipients regard welfare assistance as a right. One indicator, though a rather marginal one, is that none of the recipients interviewed could define "AFDC-U." Thirteen per cent gave a partially correct definition (for example, "Aid to Families of Dependent Children—Universal"), but seventy-eight per cent said they had no idea what the term meant.[19]

---

[17] It must be emphasized that throughout this section, we are attempting to present experiences as they were perceived by the recipients. Actually, in the agency studied, applicants rarely have to wait more than thirty to forty-five minutes to see the intake social worker.

[18] See generally Reich, *The New Property*, 73 YALE L.J. 733 (1964); Taylor, *The Nature of the Right to Public Assistance*, 36 SOCIAL SERVICE REV. 265 (1962).

[19] Another indicator of this sort is the difficulty we encountered, in the pre-test stage of this study, in wording questions asking whether a person in certain specified situations is entitled by law to receive aid. This concept of entitlement proved to be exceedingly elusive for recipients. After trying various wordings, we finally settled for "Is he [the person in the specified situation] legally entitled to aid?" It still was necessary, however, to explain the

A better, more direct indicator is the manner in which the recipients refer to the aid and whose property it is. The statement of one recipient defending the social worker's close scrutiny of recipients' lives characterizes the attitudes of most recipients: "You are going to them for money . . . *they* are supporting you." A more convincing piece of evidence, because it is quantifiable and less anecdotal, is the recipients' perceptions of who has control over the assistance grant once it is given. Asked whether the social worker has a right to know how the aid money is spent, sixty-six per cent said yes. (Responses of two recipients typify this view: "The social worker's job is to find out that the money is being spent right," and, "They [the social workers] are supposed to know all about a person on welfare.") Asked what the agency would do if the social worker found that aid funds were not being spent properly, seventy per cent of the recipients said that aid would be terminated. And asked whether in their opinion aid *should* be cut off under these circumstances, seventy-six per cent of the recipients said yes. In the eyes of these recipients, "the new property"—Reich's term for the property to which people are entitled by virtue of government benefits[20]—belongs to the welfare agency.

Thus the stance these recipients adopt toward the welfare agency is not that of a rights-bearing citizen claiming benefits to which he is entitled by law but that of a suppliant seeking, in the words of a number of recipients, "a little help to tide us over until we can get back on our feet again." Moreover, the "little help" they sought was modest indeed. Of those recipients who were able to specify the amount of aid they expected when they applied for assistance, sixty-four per cent said they expected to receive less than one hundred dollars. Since over fifty per cent of the recipients actually were given aid in excess of one hundred dollars, it is not surprising that most recipients were satisfied with the amount they received and that only seventeen per cent reported that the amount of aid granted was less than they had expected.

C. *Agency Decision-Making*

For most recipients, decision-making in the welfare department is a mysterious process, one which they do not understand and one which—as they conceive of it—is not visible to them. According to their descriptions of the application interview, the worker asked a great many questions, many designed to find out if they were telling the truth: "They have to check on what you say, so they have to ask all these questions. They

---

meaning of this question to many recipients, and it was not always clear that recipients were able to distinguish between what the person was legally entitled to receive and what the agency would in fact "give" him.

[20] Reich, *supra* note 18.

can't just give money to anybody who walks in and says they need it, or they would be in trouble. If she'd given it on my word, she'd been a fool."

In the application interview, the social worker also begins the complicated task of calculating the "budget," a crucial step in the determination of need and of the amount of aid, if any, to which the applicant is entitled. This process is difficult for the staff to master and harder still to interpret to applicants.[21] In the words of one recipient: The intake worker "sat there and figured and figured a whole bunch of things. All the time she was figuring, I wasn't paying any attention." "Why weren't you paying attention?" "Because I felt uncomfortable being there."

The next stage in the application process is deciding whether the recipient is eligible for aid. Actually, this stage—within the agency—involves a number of steps and may follow one of several different pathways, but these complexities need not concern us here. As the recipients perceived it, *a* decision was made—yes or no. The recipients were asked who made the decision; their responses are presented in Table I.

TABLE I

THE LOCUS OF AID DECISIONS AS PERCEIVED BY RECIPIENTS

	Number	Per Cent
Social worker and someone else	48	52
Social worker, on his own	27	29
Other	7	8
Don't know	10	11
Totals	92	100

Table I indicates that recipients divide into two major groups in their responses. The larger group believes that someone other than the worker is involved in the decision to grant aid: "The social worker just helps you fill out the papers—how much family you have, and so on. Then she gives the forms to her boss who says yes or no whether you can get aid." The second group attributes to the social worker the authority to make this decision: "The worker has the right to decide if there is need for aid."

Regardless of the recipient's belief about who makes the decision, it may be of little significance insofar as his view of the legal status of his request for aid is concerned. Compare, for example, the following two statements, representing the two groups of recipients:

---

[21] As part of this research, we observed a number of application interviews. Although the research observers were trained, experienced social workers, even they found the budgeting process difficult to follow at points. To fully understand the steps involved, the recipient had to be able first to understand interpretations by the worker which might include technical terms such as "participation maximum" and second to comprehend anomalies such as the discrepancy between the amount the worker has calculated and has told the applicant is his *minimum need* and the lesser amount the agency will grant him.

Worker, on his own:
> The worker decided herself. She is very experienced and knows from experience how much a family needs. She is smart and all out to help the needy.

Worker and someone else:
> There is someone she [the social worker] has to confer with, a committee or something that agrees. Well, they're the ones—I guess they vote on it or something like that and they say who gets it and who don't.

In either event, the decision is one over which the recipients appear to feel they have—or apparently even expect to have—little control.

In view of these and other findings presented earlier, it is hardly surprising that forty-six per cent of the recipients report that they were not told about their rights on welfare and that sixty per cent said they were not informed about the right to appeal. The point is not whether they were told about these rights—our observations indicate that many, if not most, of these recipients probably were given this information by the social worker—but rather that this information probably is not particularly meaningful and useful to a person who sees himself as a suppliant, and therefore it may be ignored or soon forgotten. An example of their lack of a clear conception of the appeal procedure is seen in the recipients' responses to a question asking to whom a recipient should appeal if he disagrees with a decision made about his case by the welfare department.[22] These responses are presented in Table II. As the data in this

TABLE II
RECIPIENTS' PERCEPTIONS OF THE PERSON TO WHOM AN APPEAL SHOULD BE MADE

	Number	Per Cent
Don't know	28	30
"Person in Sacramento"	15	16
"Head of the Welfare Department"	13	14
Social worker's supervisor	8	10
"Person in —" (city in which the central administrative offices for the county welfare department are located)	7	7
Social worker	6	7
District attorney	4	4
Other	11	12
Totals	92	100

table indicate, nearly one-third of the recipients did not know where to appeal, the remainder lacked a consistent conception about where to

---

22 Actually, initiation of the appeal procedure is relatively simple for the recipient. He simply writes or calls a field office of the State Department of Social Welfare. And as noted in the text, most, if not all, recipients are told that such a procedure is available and also are given a brochure which includes information about the opportunity to appeal.

initiate an appeal, and very few considered appealing to a resource outside the welfare system. The "other" category, which includes a variety
of responses (for example, "State Personnel Board"), does include a few
recipients who said they would see an attorney; but as one of these respondents said, "I'd go to a lawyer, though I don't know what he
could do."

D. The Welfare Department—A Benevolent Autocracy

The recipients' vague, diffuse, and limited conceptions of their own
rights and of the welfare department's obligations to them contrast
sharply with the well-crystallized views most of them have of the welfare
agency's rights and of their own obligations to the agency. Some evidence
to this point is presented earlier, namely the findings showing that most
respondents believe that social workers have a right to know how recipients spend the aid money and, further, that aid would and should be
terminated if not spent properly.

The agency, however, also is seen as having legitimate authority over
recipients extending considerably beyond the surveillance of aid expenditures. This can be illustrated first by further examination of the agency's
authority over the management of money. We asked a series of questions
on this subject, including a set addressed to the following situation:
"Suppose the social worker suggests that a couple on welfare come in
once a week for budget counseling." The questions and the responses
obtained are given in Table III.

TABLE III
RECIPIENTS' OPINIONS ABOUT BUDGET COUNSELING

Suppose the social worker suggests that a couple on welfare come in once a week for budget counseling:	Yes No. %	No No. %	Don't Know No. %	Other No. %	Totals No. %
1. Would they have to come in?	57 (61)	24 (27)	11 (12)	– —	92 (100)
2. Would their aid be cut off if they refused to come in?	55 (60)	22 (24)	14 (15)	1 (1)	92 (100)
3. Should the couple be expected to come in?	88 (95)	4 (5)	— —	– —	92 (100)

As Table III indicates, not only did most recipients believe that the
agency could make budget counseling a compulsory condition for receiving aid, they were virtually unanimous in their belief that couples *should*
be expected to come in if the worker suggests such counseling.

Similar sets of questions were asked about areas of agency authority
less directly related to management of the aid grant. For example, if the

social worker suggests that a recipient see a psychiatrist, seventy-six per cent of the respondents said that the recipient should be expected to go and sixty-six per cent said he must go in order to continue receiving aid. But the recipients perceived some limits to the range of the welfare agency's authority. While sixty-seven per cent of the recipients said that a recipient should go if the social worker suggests marital counseling, only twenty per cent believed that a recipient's aid would be cut off if he refused to follow this suggestion.

However, the findings which most dramatically indicate the extent of authority these recipients confer on the agency and which best illuminate their reasons for granting the agency extensive authority over their lives are those obtained in response to a series of questions about the use of night visits as a means of checking on recipients.[23] These questions and the recipients' responses to them are shown in Table IV.

TABLE IV
RECIPIENTS' OPINIONS ABOUT NIGHT SEARCHES BY THE WELFARE DEPARTMENT

	Yes No. %	No No. %	Don't Know No. %	Other No. %	Totals No. %
1. Should the welfare department make night visits?	63 (69)	24 (26)	3 (3)	2 (2)	92 (100)
2. Does the recipient have a right to refuse to let the worker come into his home at night?	46 (50)	40 (43)	5 (5)	1 (1)	92 (100)
3. Are there any other times when the recipient has a right to refuse to let the worker enter his home?	34 (37)	49 (53)	6 (7)	3 (3)	92 (100)
4. Is there a law that says you can refuse entry to your home to anyone who does not have a search warrant?	53 (87)	5 (8)	3 (5)	– —	61ᵃ (100)
5. (If yes to #4) Does this law apply to welfare recipients?	35 (66)	9 (17)	9 (17)	– —	53ᵃ (100)

ᵃ These two questions were added to the schedule after the first 31 interviews had been completed.

---

[23] For a penetrating analysis of the legal aspects and constitutionality of this practice see Reich, *Midnight Welfare Searches and the Social Security Act*, 72 YALE L.J. 1347 (1963).

As the data presented in Table IV indicate, over two-thirds of the recipients favor night searches by the welfare department. The reasons the recipients gave for favoring this practice are anticipated by findings reported earlier: (1) The agency has a right to know how aid funds are spent; and (2) many recipients cheat or continue to accept aid after they no longer need it.

However, the data of greater interest in this table concern the recipients' views about a recipient's right to refuse entry to the social worker at night. Nearly ninety per cent of the respondents say that there are laws which give a person the right to refuse entry to anyone who does not have a search warrant, and over two-thirds believe that these laws apply to welfare recipients. Yet only one-half the respondents say that a welfare recipient has a right to refuse entry to the social worker on a night visit. How can the seeming inconsistency in these findings be explained? Why (as further analysis of these data not reported here reveal) do a substantial proportion of the recipients who say that there is a law that permits the recipient to refuse entry to the worker at night also say that the recipient has no right to invoke this law? Analysis of the recipients' responses to these questions reveals a common theme: The recipient has an *obligation* to let the worker come into his home at any time because the welfare agency is supporting him: "You are going to them for money. They got the right to go and look in your house without no questions—they're supporting you." And this theme appears in the statements of those recipients who said that the recipient does have a right to refuse entry at night: "According to the criminal law, they [the recipients] do have the right, yes—I don't think it's right, but they do have that right." "All people have the right not to let someone enter their home if they don't want them to. But in the case of the social worker, one ought to let her in." In other words, most recipients favored the practice of night visits—they tend to differ only over the necessity for the agency to obtain a search warrant.

CONCLUSION

Before considering the meaning and significance of these findings, the limitations of the research should be noted. The welfare recipients interviewed in this study were drawn from one aid program as administered in one locality. It is not known to what extent these findings hold for recipients of other public assistance programs[24] or for recipients in other

---

[24] In collaboration with Irving Piliavin, Associate Professor, School of Social Welfare, University of California, Berkeley, the author currently is conducting a study designed to collect data comparable to that reported in this article from samples of recipients in other categorical aid programs.

communities in which, among other things, the character of the public welfare agency may be quite different. Nevertheless there is reason to believe that some of the findings may have wide generality.

For one thing, the conservative (in the sense that assistance is perceived as a privilege rather than a right) views expressed by these recipients on certain welfare issues are not surprising. The prevalence of political and social conservatism and of submissive attitudes toward authority among persons in low-income groups has been documented in a number of studies.[25] Moreover, while social workers and others concerned with promoting the expansion of welfare programs have long advocated that public assistance should be provided on a basis of entitlement rather than privilege, public welfare recipients have had few opportunities to be exposed to this view.

For these are people with limited education and limited access to the publications and forums in which this view is expressed. Nor are more than a few recipients exposed to organizations which attempt to inform them of their rights and of the welfare agency's obligations to them—in fact, few such organizations exist.[26] In view of these conditions, only if these recipients had expressed a welfare ideology markedly different from the views reported here would there have been reason to suspect that this group of recipients is atypical.[27]

Secondly, although public welfare departments differ greatly in many ways (including the service orientations of the social work staff and the liberality of assistance grants), certain characteristics are common to many of them: the elaborate complexity of determining eligibility and especially of budgeting (including both the determination of need and of the amount of assistance to which the recipient is entitled); the low visibility, for the recipient, of agency decision-making processes and of appeal opportunities and procedures; the comparative powerlessness, from the recipient's viewpoint, of the line social worker—the person with whom he must deal—in the decisions made about his assistance grant; the linkage of financial assistance to other services so that the aid recipient also automatically becomes a client who, at least partly at the discretion of the agency, may become the object of other services (for example,

---

[25] See, *e.g.*, BERELSON & STEINER, HUMAN BEHAVIOR: AN INVENTORY OF SCIENTIFIC FINDINGS 572-73 (1964).

[26] See Brager & Specht, *Mobilizing the Poor for Social Action*, 1965 SOCIAL WELFARE F. 197.

[27] It should be emphasized that the recipients interviewed were not all of one mind on welfare issues. In this article, we present the dominant and modal responses obtained from the sample studied. The characteristics of those recipients who expressed divergent opinions—for example, the small group who did *not* favor night visits—will be examined in subsequent reports by the author.

counseling and psychiatric treatment); and review and surveillance of recipient's expenditure of aid funds beyond that necessary to establish eligibility and detect possible fraud.

Our findings suggest that the presence of these characteristics—common to many public welfare agencies—serves to reinforce and thereby perpetuate recipients' conceptions of themselves as suppliants rather than rights-bearing citizens. Moreover, the presence of these characteristics may obliterate the effects on recipients of the distinctive attributes of specific welfare departments. Thus the dimension which has received the most attention in comparative studies of welfare agencies, namely the extent to which staff are committed to a professional versus a bureaucratic service-orientation,[28] may, in the presence of the other characteristics enumerated above, have little effect on recipients' conceptions of their rights. In a paradoxical way, commitment to a professional orientation by public welfare workers may, *when the above characteristics are also present in the agency,* reinforce the suppliant role. For the practices of the welfare agency together with the beliefs about public welfare which many recipients hold when they go to the agency appear to evoke a sense of obligation[29] to the agency; this sense may be accentuated if the agency is benign and the social worker is kind, sympathetic, and understanding.

These considerations suggest that to the extent that one objective of public welfare programs is to help recipients become "responsible citizens"—an aim presumably shared by both proponents and critics of more liberal welfare programs—the public welfare agency must be organized and operated in such a way that it at least does not generate or reinforce attitudes of submissiveness and suppliance on the part of the recipients. More than that, however, these considerations imply that public welfare agencies—because of their strategic position vis-à-vis the poor— could become positive instruments for the inculcation in recipients of a conception of themselves as rights-bearing citizens, with all of the benefits this may have for increasing self-confidence and hope among these people.[30] To accomplish this would appear to require, at the very least: radical simplification of the eligibility and budgeting processes so that they are comprehensible to recipients with limited education; high visibility of agency decision-making in individual cases to reduce its apparent arbitrariness (from the recipient's viewpoint) and to make accessible to the recipient the information necessary to understand and review

---

[28] See, *e.g.*, BLAU & SCOTT, FORMAL ORGANIZATIONS 60-74 (1962).

[29] For an insightful theoretical discussion of the sense of obligation incurred in donor-donee relationships, see Gouldner, *The Norm of Reciprocity: A Preliminary Statement*, 25 AMERICAN SOCIOLOGICAL REV. 161 (1960).

[30] See generally Cahn & Cahn, *The War on Poverty: A Civilian Perspective*, 73 YALE L.J. 1317 (1964).

agency decisions affecting his claim; high visibility and accessibility of appeal procedures; and a redefinition of the social worker's role away from that of an instrument of agency rules and regulations towards one of an advocate who, because he is informed and knowledgeable about the applicant's rights and the agency's obligations, can assist the applicant to secure the maximum benefits to which he is entitled. For as Edgar and Jean Cahn have stated, "Law is made not merely through statutes and legislative programs, but also through modes of official behavior."[31] The mode of official behavior necessary to inculcate in recipients a conception of themselves as rights-bearing citizens is one which provides them with "the means and the effective power wherewith to criticize, to shape, and even to challenge the actions or proposed actions of officials."[32] This perspective, if implemented in the public welfare agency, has the potential of becoming the agency's most effective means of enhancing the dignity and self-respect of the persons it seeks to serve.

[31] *Id.* at 1333.
[32] *Id.* at 1330.

Race, Poverty, and the Law

*Loren Miller**

THE PROUDEST BOAST of American lawyers is that all men stand equal before the law. The boast is a noble and useful one even if it isn't quite borne out by the facts. Too much of that equality is of the kind described by Anatole France when he said that the laws of his country were fair: They forbade both rich men and poor men from sleeping under bridges on rainy nights. Recent events in the South have brought the realization that all men aren't equal before the law in some southern courtrooms and have occasioned soul searching to find out whether persons of differing economic circumstances are always equal before the law.

Senator Robert F. Kennedy, former Attorney General, insists that the "poor man looks upon the law as an enemy . . . . For him the law is always taking something away."[1] Nicholas deB. Katzenbach, present Attorney General, puts it that, "To us, laws and regulations are protections and guides, established for our benefit, and for us to use. But to the poor, they are a hostile maze, established as harassment, at all costs to be avoided."[2]

Racial identity, particularly for Negroes, has always been as troublesome a factor as poverty in the quest for equality before the law. Most Negroes, the overwhelming majority, are poor. The poor Negro has trouble on his hands when he seeks to surmount the twin obstacles of race and poverty and attain that equality guaranteed alike by federal and state constitutions and ingrained in American hopes.

One of the biggest obstacles to a frank national confrontation of this problem is the general American reluctance to admit that the original Constitution condoned and permitted discrimination against Negroes and that there was a great leeway for racial discrimination under late nineteenth- and early twentieth-century construction of the Civil War amendments. Racial inequality before the law affects all Negroes, no matter what their economic status or station in life. Jim Crow laws catch the affluent as well as the impoverished Negro in their nets. To complicate the matter, few persons believe that the Negro is entitled to full equality. Working class suburban cities and towns voted against a 1964 Fair Housing law in Los Angeles County, California in about the same proportion as middle-class and upper middle-class suburbs.[3] An analysis of a

---

* Judge, Municipal Ct., Los Angeles.

1 Address by Robert F. Kennedy, Law Day, University of Chicago, May 1, 1964, cited in WALD, LAW AND POVERTY: 1965, at 6 n.13 (1965).

2 WALD, *op. cit. supra* note 1, at 6 n.14.

3 Hite, Los Angeles County Vote on Proposition 14 by Cities, 1964.

vote in Berkeley, California, showed a majority of white citizens with college degrees or better education opposed that city's fair housing ordinance.[4] Large law firms have always drawn the same color lines against ambitious young Negro lawyers as have other employers.[5]

I

HISTORICAL PERSPECTIVES

Most persons would deny vigorously that they entertain racial prejudices in any degree. Their denials are not contrived fictions; they are believed by those who utter them. Americans simply have a double standard of judgment as to rights of white persons as contrasted to those of Negroes. To them, white persons are born vested with that vast array of rights and privileges vaguely thought of as natural rights. Negroes, on the other hand, are regarded as entitled to such rights as the white majority grants them. It is commonly said that Negroes must "earn" the rights they would enjoy. That attitude is deeply rooted in our history.

Heeding the admonition of James Madison that it would be "wrong to admit, in the constitution, that there could be property in man,"[6] the Constitution makers fashioned a document that makes no mention of slaves, slavery, or race. Yet that great instrument protected slavery in the states where the institution existed, provided for the return of escaped slaves to their masters,[7] devised a formula for counting slaves in the apportionment of members of Congress,[8] prohibited Congress from taxing slavery out of existence,[9] and preserved the African slave trade for twenty years.[10] The slave trade and taxing clauses could not even be amended before 1808.[11] The Founding Fathers heeded Madison's advice so well that the layman cannot identify the articles dealing with slavery without the aid of an historian.[12] In fact, few lawyers can turn the trick.

Every Fourth of July and every Bill of Rights Week, orators shout

---

[4] An unpublished survey taken in 1962 by California Research Associates showed that of a sampling of 368 Berkeley voters, 201 opposed a fair housing ordinance and 167 favored it. About 58% of white college graduates opposed the measure.

[5] A casual check will show no Negro lawyers in any of California's top law firms. These firms deny discrimination, of course. All nonemployers of Negroes also deny discrimination. All give the same reason for the nonemployment of Negroes: Merit alone is the only test used!

[6] LIVERMORE, NEGROES AS CITIZENS, AS SLAVES AND AS SOLDIERS 65 (1862).

[7] U.S. CONST. art. IV, § 2, cl. 3.

[8] U.S. CONST. art. I, § 2, cl. 3.

[9] U.S. CONST. art. I, § 9, cl. 4.

[10] U.S. CONST. art. I, § 9, cl. 1.

[11] U.S. CONST. art. V.

[12] MILLER, THE PETITIONERS 18-28 (1966).

themselves hoarse and teachers exhaust themselves telling Americans, adults and children, that the original Constitution and the Bill of Rights protected the rights and liberties of *all* Americans. This bit of pleasant folklore is arrived at by taking all the language of the Constitution at face value. In truth, the equalitarian guarantees explicit and implicit in the Constitution and amplified in the Bill of Rights offered absolutely no protection to the approximately 700,000 persons held in slavery at the birth of the nation and, as the Supreme Court was to hold later, little more protection for the some 60,000 free Negroes of the North and South. The Constitution, Chief Justice Roger B. Taney said in the *Dred Scott* case, decided in 1857, was made by and for white men.[13] Negroes, he elaborated, "were not intended to be included, under the word 'citizens' in the Constitution, and can therefore claim none of the rights and privileges which that instrument provides for and secures to citizens of the United States."[14] He went further to say that free Negroes were "not even in the minds of the framers of the Constitution when they were conferring special rights and privileges upon the citizens of a State in every other part of the Union."[15] Citizenship extended to Negroes by some states, he said, did not and could not confer national citizenship on them. Distinguishing state citizenship from national citizenship, the Court held that the states were in entire control of civil rights,[16] and that the citizen of a state must look to the state for protection of those rights.

Of course, the Chief Justice's construction of the Constitution ran directly counter to that contended for by anti-slavery lawyers and theoreticians, but his was the practical construction put upon the document prior to and at the time of the decision. A portion of the hue and cry raised against the majority opinion in the *Dred Scott* case was the normal reaction of men who wince and cry out in pain, real or simulated, when their deeds are described in apposite language. The interpretation of the Constitution advocated by Chief Justice Taney as regards the rights of Negroes, free and slave, prior to the Civil War has had enormous consequences for the nation.

The most important principles that suffused the Constitution and undergirded stability for the political institutions created by it were the dignity of the individual and the inviolability of the rights and privileges recognized in that instrument and protected against governmental in-

---

13 Dred Scott v. Sandford, 60 U.S. (19 How.) 393 (1857).

14 *Id.* at 404.

15 *Id.* at 411-12.

16 See *id.* at 405.

fringement. Those principles demanded that every man be treated as, and function as, an individual, as a *person*, in constitutional language. By such reckoning no person had group identity in the eyes of the law; he was neither Jew nor Gentile, Catholic nor Protestant, rich nor poor. He was a person, and as such he could claim the rights, privileges, and protections of the Constitution and the Bill of Rights.

The Constitution vindicated those principles for white Americans, but recognition and protection of slavery inflicted a mortal wound as far as the Negro was concerned. For the word slave was for all practical intents and purposes synonymous with the appellation Negro. The Constitution as construed and as applied imposed legal disabilities on the slave; he was stripped of his individual dignity simply because of his race and stood not as a *person* but as a slave before the law of the land. The slave existed beyond the pale of the protections of the original Constitution and the Bill of Rights. He was a stranger in a strange land; his status as a Negro was itself an invidious classification.

Nor did the freeborn or emancipated Negro escape the disabilities laid on his slave kinsman. The existence of Negro slavery was an ever present reminder that every free Negro was a *freedman*, not a *free man*, to whom rights or privileges might be extended or denied at will. Again, such an attitude ran counter to the beliefs and theories of anti-slavery lawyers and theorists; again, it was the practical construction upon which northern and southern states acted as they enacted laws barring free Negroes from schools, places of public accommodation, the ballot box, and other facilities open to white Americans.

In spite of theory, and from the earliest days, there were classifications of white men based on economic distinctions which impaired equality before the law assumed to be the birthright of free men. The right to vote or hold office often depended upon property qualifications;[17] the debtor could be imprisoned; the appellant in a criminal trial might be denied a transcript of his hearing unless he could pay for it;[18] a poor defendant could be forced to trial without a lawyer;[19] a litigant desirous of a jury trial in a civil matter might be required to deposit costs.[20] The vagabond, the roamer, the idle, the beggar might be denominated a

---

[17] See EMERSON & HABER, POLITICAL & CIVIL RIGHTS IN THE UNITED STATES 138-41 (2d ed. 1958).

[18] See, *e.g.*, Estabrook v. King, 119 F.2d 607 (8th Cir. 1941). *Contra*, Griffin v. Illinois, 351 U.S. 12 (1956).

[19] See Betts v. Brady, 316 U.S. 455 (1942), overruled in Gideon v. Wainwright, 372 U.S. 335 (1963).

[20] See, *e.g.*, CAL. CODE CIV. PROC. §§ 671(5), (6), (7).

vagrant and penalized because of his status—indeed, he still faces that possibility in many states.[21]

It is only in these latter days—very latter days—that some Americans have come to see that economic classification of a citizen may be disabling even where it is not specifically condemned by the Constitution. Most Americans are still blinded to a full realization of the importance of that fact by the belief that has so long sustained the nation that ours is an equalitarian society in which only the lack of ambition, thrift, and desire keep some in poverty. Deep in their hearts, a majority of Americans believe that any man can find a job if he has a mind to do so, that with a job he can save money, buy a home, and ultimately become a middle-class member of the affluent society. Within that context they nurse the belief that an economic classification is temporary and hence permissible—they hope that the penalties poverty exacts may even spur ambition. By that same token, they are uncomfortable over the fact that the individual cannot shed his race or vanquish his color as he can his poverty, and they are happy to say, and hear their judges say, that racial classification is suspect.[22]

In a constitutional sense, racial classification as a device to impose disabilities is worse than suspect: It is forbidden by the Civil War amendments, or at least it was forbidden until the Supreme Court revised the meanings of those amendments. The precise purpose of the amendments was to abolish all invidious racial distinctions tolerated by the original Constitution, as interpreted by the Supreme Court, and to provide a new constitutional basis for congressional action to establish equality whenever states or individuals were laggard or insisted on imposing racial disabilities.[23]

After the ratification of the thirteenth amendment in 1865, Congress enacted the first Civil Rights Act of 1866[24] in response to the threats of the Black Codes[25] to reduce Negroes to semi-slavery. Congress codified the sweeping legislative command for equality as contained in the 1866

---

[21] See Hicks v. Dist. of Columbia, 383 U.S. 252 (1966) (dissenting opinion). Vagrancy laws in some Southern States are fashioned to penalize what are believed to be shortcomings of Negroes, and were formerly used to further peonage. See STEPHENSON, RACE DISTINCTIONS IN AMERICAN LAW 58, 275 (1910).

[22] See Bolling v. Sharpe, 347 U.S. 497 (1954); see also Korematsu v. United States, 323 U.S. 214, 216 (1944).

[23] See generally HARRIS, THE QUEST FOR EQUALITY, ch. 2 (1960); tenBROEK, EQUAL UNDER LAW (rev. ed. 1965).

[24] Ch. 31, 14 Stat. 27 (1866).

[25] E.g., Miss. Laws 1865, ch. 4, § 1 (restrictions on free Negroes' right to purchase and inherit real property); see Supplemental Brief for the United States as amicus curiae, pp. 45-48, Griffin v. Maryland, 378 U.S. 130 (1964); McPHERSON, POLITICAL HISTORY OF THE UNITED STATES DURING THE PERIOD OF RECONSTRUCTION 29-44 (1871).

Civil Rights Act in the constitutional shorthand of the fourteenth amendment, ratified in 1868. In 1870 it proposed and secured ratification of the
fifteenth amendment. Each of the amendments provides that Congress
shall have power to enforce the provisions by appropriate legislation.
Congress exercised its newly established power in the sweeping and
searching Reconstruction legislation that culminated in the Civil Rights
Act of 1875.[26] "[H]ereafter," said Charles Sumner, "there shall be no
such word as 'black' or 'white,' but that we shall speak only of citizens
and men."[27]

Then the Supreme Court took over. In *The Slaughter-house Cases*,[28]
it restored the *Dred Scott* doctrine that there are two categories of citizenship, national and state, and gutted the privileges and immunities clause
of the fourteenth amendment of all meaning. In *United States v. Cruikshank*,[29] it restored control of civil rights to the states. In *United States v.
Reese*,[30] it severely restricted the scope and reach of the fifteenth amendment. In the *Civil Rights Cases*,[31] it further cabined the meaning of the
fourteenth amendment with its ruling that Congress could not proscribe
an individual's discriminatory conduct. In *Virginia v. Rives*,[32] it validated
the indictments and verdicts of all-white juries in the absence of specific
objections and proof by a Negro defendant of systematic and purposeful
racial exclusion, and thus it set up a rule which allowed extensive discrimination in jury selection. In *Williams v. Mississippi*,[33] and later in *Giles v.
Harris*[34] and *Giles v. Teasley*,[35] it gave its blessing to state constitutional
and statutory provisions deliberately and professedly designed to circumscribe the franchise. In *Plessy v. Ferguson*,[36] it approved a state's racial
classification, undertaken to establish the separate-but-equal rule in the
use of state facilities or public utilities. In *Berea College v. Kentucky*,[37]
it approved state statutes proscribing interracial association for innocent
purposes. In *Gong Lum v. Rice*,[38] it approved separate schools. In

---

[26] Ch. 114, 18 Stat. 336 (1875). The Civil Rights Act of 1875 was the final civil rights
law of the Reconstruction era. There was no similar legislation until 1957. 71 Stat. 634
(1957), as amended, 5 U.S.C. § 295, 28 U.S.C. §§ 1343, 1861, 42 U.S.C. §§ 1971, 1975-75e,
1995 (1964).

[27] 2 Cong. Rec. 948 (1874).

[28] 83 U.S. (16 Wall.) 36 (1873).

[29] 92 U.S. 542 (1875).

[30] 92 U.S. 214 (1875).

[31] 109 U.S. 3 (1883).

[32] 100 U.S. 313 (1879).

[33] 170 U.S. 213 (1898).

[34] 189 U.S. 475 (1903).

[35] 193 U.S. 146 (1904).

[36] 163 U.S. 537 (1896).

[37] 211 U.S. 45 (1908) (education at an integrated school).

[38] 275 U.S. 78 (1927).

Corrigan v. Buckley,[39] it validated racial restrictive covenants and by indirection approved judicial enforcement of such agreements. In *Grovey v. Townsend*,[40] it decided that state political parties could exclude Negroes from primary elections.

It is important to realize that prior to the Civil War amendments, the degradation of the Negro as tolerated by the Court after the addition of those amendments was consistent with constitutional theory and practice. The long list of disabilities just recited would have excited no opposition from pre-Civil War lawyers except from anti-slavery theoreticians. Chief Justice Taney's statement in the *Dred Scott* case that a Negro had no "rights which the white man was bound to respect" was a trifle too sweeping, but it is literally true that a Negro had no civil rights except those conferred on him by white men. The obvious and often expressed aim of the framers of the Civil War amendments was to confer those rights on Negroes through the Constitution and to obviate the power of white Americans to dole out such rights as they chose.[41] Their view of the way to achieve that end was to vest the same rights in Negroes as were vested in white persons.

Those rights were conceived of as the natural rights of man as a member of the body politic. The Negro was made a citizen and hence vested with the same rights as a free born white man. His rights were a part of his birthright. None could take them from him because he was now a free man. None could detract from them. Among free born men vested with natural rights, race and skin color were to be an irrelevance. If any state trenched on these rights, there was a remedy, but, as Senator Oliver P. Morton of Indiana pointed out, that "remedy . . . was expressly not left to the courts. The remedy was legislative because in each case the amendment itself provided that it shall be enforced by legislation on the part of Congress."[42]

The Supreme Court, however, had its own notions as to its power. It ignored the congressional fiat and interpreted the amended Constitution in the light of precedents that were based on the implicit concept of its original interpretation of the Constitution that the Negro, free or slave, lacked the full attributes of citizenship.

The net result of the Court's post Civil War decisions was to return Negroes to a modified second class citizenship of the kind that obtained

---

[39] 271 U.S. 323 (1926).

[40] 295 U.S. 45 (1935). *But cf.* Nixon v. Condon, 286 U.S. 73 (1932); Nixon v. Herndon, 273 U.S. 536 (1927).

[41] See HARRIS, *op. cit. supra* note 23; MILLER, *op. cit. supra* note 12, at 85-101; TEN-BROEK, *op. cit. supra* note 23.

[42] MILLER, *op. cit. supra* note 12, at 97, 438 n.20.

prior to the Civil War and to resurrect the dictum of the *Dred Scott* case that "the unhappy black race were separated from the white by indelible marks . . . ."[43] This separatism was said to be based upon racial instinct as the Court noted in the *Plessy* case: It intoned that "legislation is powerless to eradicate racial instincts or to abolish distinctions based upon physical differences . . . ."[44] Social Darwinism had been assimilated to the amended Constitution; the William Graham Sumner dogma that law-ways cannot change folkways[45] had become constitutional doctrine. Fortunately, the Court has repudiated most of the holdings that have just been cited, but they were the law of the land during the critical and formative years from the early 1870's to the middle 1930's, and during that sixty-year period were among the prime factors in institutionalizing racial segregation and discrimination.

As the first Justice John Marshall Harlan observed in his dissent in the *Civil Rights Cases*, the majority opinion in that case postulated a basis for establishing a color caste system with one "class of human beings in practical subjection to another class with power in the latter to dole out to the former just such privileges as they may choose to grant."[46] That, of course, is precisely what happened, with white Americans doling out to Negroes "just such privileges as they [chose] . . . to grant." Or as he put it in the *Plessy* case, "we have yet, in some of the States, a dominant race—a superior class of citizens, which assumes to regulate the enjoyment of civil rights . . . upon the basis of race."[47]

The belief that whites retain the "power . . . to dole out" to Negroes "just such privileges as they may choose to grant" flourishes in contemporary society; it finds expression in the vulgar judgment that "Negroes are moving too fast" or "asking too much" in their demand for civil rights; in a Supreme Court decision postponing the enjoyment of an admittedly vested and, therefore, *personal and present* constitutional right until recalcitrant schoolboards bestow it on its possessors with "all deliberate speed"; and in the enactment of a California constitutional provision protecting the right of white persons to discriminate in the sale or rental of real property. Because few white Americans subscribe to the proposition that Negroes are born with the same rights which they believe inhere in white Americans, most of them, even persons of goodwill, accept the popular judgment that it is quite proper for the majority to "regulate the enjoyment of civil rights . . . upon the basis of race"

---

43 Dred Scott v. Sandford, 60 U.S. (19 How.) 393, 410 (1857).
44 Plessy v. Ferguson, 163 U.S. 537, 551 (1896).
45 SUMNER, FOLKWAYS *passim* (1906).
46 109 U.S. 3, 62 (1883).
47 Plessy v. Ferguson, 163 U.S. 537, 560 (1896) (dissenting opinion).

until that mythical day when the "hearts and minds of men," even the most backward, have changed and all racial prejudices have disappeared.

These historical facts with their intrusions into current thinking must be borne in mind and assessed if a discussion of race, poverty, and the law is to be invested with substance and realism. It must also be borne in mind that racial classification has rarely been benign in purpose or intent in American law. Rather, it has been a means of enforcing restrictions or restraints.[48]

Despite the restrictive interpretations put upon them, the Civil War amendments have always been construed to prohibit discriminatory racial legislation by the states or their political subdivisions and to interdict imposition or support of racial disabilities by the executive and judicial branches[49] of state government. Even separate but equal legislation or administrative practices made elaborate bows in the direction of equality by proscribing white use of "Negro" facilities as well as Negro use of "white" facilities,[50] with the courts finally arriving at the curious conclusion that where interracial association was proscribed, the equal protection clause of the fourteenth amendment was served by imposing the same penalty on both the white and Negro offender.[51] Troublesome questions often arose as to the equality of separate facilities, but the courts assuaged the constitutional conscience of the nation with the doctrine of substantial equality in which, for example, a one-room ungraded school for Negroes was said to be "substantially equal" to a ten-room graded school for whites,[52] or a wooden railway car with no running water or air conditioning was said to be "substantially equal" to Pullman accommodations.[53] The command for equality, the courts said, did not require the furnishing of identical facilities.

Where the separate but equal concept could not be applied but the desire to restrict Negro participation was present, every effort was made to posit desired restrictions on permissible classifications which would encompass as many Negroes as possible while netting a small number

---

[48] See Sedler, *School Segregation in the North and West: Legal Aspects*, 7 St. Louis U.L.J. 228 (1963).

[49] See Shelley v. Kraemer, 334 U.S. 1, 14-18 (1948).

[50] See, *e.g.*, the elaborate racial zoning laws invalidated in Buchanan v. Warley, 245 U.S. 60 (1917).

[51] Pace v. Alabama, 106 U.S. 583 (1882).

[52] See Lowery v. Board of Graded School Trustees, 140 N.C. 25, 52 S.E. 267 (1905); *cf.* Daviess County Bd. of Educ. v. Johnson, 179 Ky. 34, 39, 200 S.W. 313, 314 (1918).

[53] See practices averred to in Mitchell v. United States, 313 U.S. 80, 96 (1940); McCabe v. Atchison, T. & S.F. Ry., 186 F. 966, 970 (8th Cir. 1911), *aff'd on other grounds*, 235 U.S. 151 (1914).

of white persons.[54] Because poverty has always been one of the hallmarks of Negro life in the United States, economic classification has proved very useful.[55] Thus Negro voting was circumscribed by requiring a poll tax payment as a prerequisite for voting.[56] Property qualifications were imposed as a condition of jury service in some Southern States.[57] When Mississippi led the southern revolt that disfranchised Negroes in the late nineteenth century, it "swept the circle of expedients" by classifying as ineligible persons convicted of such crimes as vagrancy, assault, and like offenses of the poor.[58] Finally, the Southern States hit upon classification of illiterates and those lacking ability to read, understand, and explain state and federal constitutions as persons unfit to exercise the suffrage[59]— the illiterate and the lacking in understanding were, of course, the poor. These fair-on-their-face laws were enforced in such a discriminatory manner as to disfranchise almost the entire southern Negro population— a practice that gained nation-wide acquiescence and drew approval from the Great Commoner, William Jennings Bryan.[60]

II

POVERTY AND RACE

Any economic classification that affects the poor as a group will include a disproportionate number of Negroes simply because a disproportionate number of Negroes live below the poverty line in American life.[61] If disabilities attend economic classification, Negroes will be disadvantaged, no matter how nondiscriminatory the legislation may appear to be. Fair-on-their-face statutes, such as a levy of a poll tax as a condition of voting, will not vary that result. Uniform bail schedules lay a heavier burden on the poor than on the well-to-do and inevitably leave a dispro-

---

[54] Guinn v. United States, 238 U.S. 347 (1915) (all persons eligible to vote prior to January 1, 1866, and their descendants, entitled to vote; all others must pass literacy test); Williams v. Mississippi, 170 U.S. 213 (1898) (literacy tests for voting and jury duty).

[55] It is no secret that welfare payments in most Southern States are kept low out of a desire not to "coddle" or "spoil" Negroes.

[56] See Harper v. Virginia State Bd. of Elections, 86 Sup. Ct. 1079 (1966), overruling Breedlove v. Suttles, 302 U.S. 277 (1937); 1 EMERSON & HABER, POLITICAL AND CIVIL RIGHTS IN THE UNITED STATES 168-76 (2d ed. 1958). But see, KEY, SOUTHERN POLITICS 617-18 (1949).

[57] Property qualifications as to the right to vote were almost universal at the time of the adoption of the Constitution.

[58] Brief for American Civil Liberties Union, amicus curiae, p. 70, United States v. Mississippi, 380 U.S. 128 (1965) (citing Ratcliff v. Beale, 74 Miss. 297, 20 So. 865 (1896)).

[59] Id. at 77. Miss. Const. § 244 (1890).

[60] "The white man in the South has disfranchised the Negro in self-protection, and there is not a white man in the North who would not have done the same under the same circumstances." Speech by William Jennings Bryan, Cooper Union, N.Y., 1908.

[61] Address by President Lyndon B. Johnson, Howard University, June 4, 1965.

portionate number of Negroes in custody. The same hardship results from use of a uniform fine schedule for traffic violations and other misdemeanors. Laws which penalize owners who are unable to secure and maintain public liability and property damage insurance on their automobiles hit the poor hard and fall with a heavy hand on proportionately more Negroes than whites. There are many situations in which classification does not seem to rest on poverty but in which economics intrudes. Thus it has been said that the application of juvenile delinquency statutes is "heavily weighted against the poor family."[62] There, again, the disproportionate amount of poverty in the Negro ghettos operates to disadvantage the Negro youngster. Of course, the same observation may be made of the application of criminal statutes to the adult.

The preponderant number of Negroes caught in these legal nets is almost invariably pointed to by the unknowing or by the hostile to "prove" Negro criminality, or irresponsibility, or inferiority. In their proper turn, such attitudes serve to persuade law enforcement administrators that rights and privileges ought to be doled out rather sparingly to Negroes to prevent them from "going too fast" or "demanding too much" in the way of privileges they are believed to be ill-equipped to exercise. The result is a difference in the quality of law enforcement as between white persons and Negroes, particularly as far as the poor are concerned, a difference that is reflected in the almost universal hostility of the poor Negro to law enforcement officials. The poor Negro sees that his friends and neighbors, indeed, members of his own family are more often caught in the toils of the law than the white person, that the burdens of the law's penalties are more onerous for them, and that law enforcement officials can misuse him at their whim. In his own shorthand, he describes all of these inequities as "police brutality." And just as the unobservant white person lays the Negro's shortcomings to race without weighing economic and other factors, so the Negro poor tend to lay all of their ills to what they regard as racial prejudice. It is in this atmosphere that welfare laws operate and are administered.

A. The Negro Poor Under Welfare

Welfare legislation and its administration are critical in Negro life because so many Negroes are affected—again, because a disproportionate number of them fall into those categories of the poor for whom assistance is designed and necessary. Provision for welfare is an almost exclusively legislative function with legislators having almost free rein. There is comparatively little case law on the subject, but there is a welter

---

[62] WALD, LAW AND POVERTY: 1965, at 10-11 (1965).

of administrative rules and regulations, most of them designed by the administrators to win legislative favor and approbation. The legislature which pays the piper calls the tune.

Welfare legislation in American states traces back to Elizabethan poor laws with overlays of humanitarianism, enlightened flashes of public conscience, weak and wavering realization that a nation as rich as the United States can well afford an adequate standard of living for all of its citizens, and that failure to nurture the young and care for the ill and the aged is costly public policy. Nevertheless, the ill, the handicapped, the aged, the jobless (after unemployment benefits are exhausted), the deserted mother, the fatherless child are often treated as beggars and mendicants at best or as rogues, vagabonds, and vagrants at worst. The welfare administrator who keeps as many applicants as possible out of benefits is in a fair way to win the approbation of his community and of its establishment. All too often, rules are administered to exclude apparently qualified applicants, and every effort to utilize existing regulations in such a manner as to obtain benefits is branded as "fraud." A Los Angeles superior court judge who could find no legal fault in utilization of some of the rules in order to maximize benefits fell back on the charge of "moral fraud" on the part of some beneficiaries. Current mores condone, even honor, the rich taxpayer whose lawyers and accountants find loopholes in the law that enable him to avoid income tax payments, but the welfare recipient who finds a loophole that enables her to increase aid to her children is an object of public wrath. The taxpayer is entitled to whatever savings he can effect; the welfare recipient is not "entitled" to aid provided for him.

Undergirding popular attitudes toward the needy poor is the premise that the poor are the authors of their own woes and ills, and are sponging on the rest of society. The hope is that if sponging can be made as disagreeable as possible, they will do as others have done, and are doing, and earn their keep in the sweat of their own brows. The public insists on maintaining a close watch over them and continually demands more stringent local control so that doles can be kept a shade below local standards.[63]

Community hostility toward welfare recipients is heightened by administrative sub-classification of these poor on ethnic lines. When such racial classifications are made, it is at once discovered that the Negro ratio is high, considerably higher than the population ratio.[64]

---

[63] This attitude rests on the belief that by reducing the lot of the welfare recipient to disagreeable poverty, we will force him to find one of the jobs assumed to be available to those who want to work.

[64] See e.g., Los Angeles District Attorney, Report to the Governor's Commission on the

The discovery looses a great clamor even though it is well known that Negro unemployment hovers around two to three times that of white workmen[65] and that what is described as employment for Negroes is all too often marginal work that requires supplemental aid or assistance. Given the almost pathological American preoccupation with race and the demand for racial explanations for every social ill involving Negroes, it is not surprising that it is somewhat widely believed that a high percentage of Negroes prefer relief to steady jobs. By way of proof, examples are constantly dredged up of the Negro who prefers drawing seventy-five dollars per week on relief to accepting a dead-end job that would pay him $58.45 weekly.

The current horrific example of supposed racial exploitation of public assistance is the Aid to Families with Dependent Children (AFDC) program.[66] In the classic case, aid was furnished for the children where the father was absent, although now help may be given where the father is unemployed.[67] The father may be absent because of death, desertion, or incarceration, or because there has been no formal marriage. Lack of formal marriage makes the child illegitimate according to old and built-in notions of morality, and illegitimacy is one of the oldest and most disabling of legal classifications, tainting both mother and child.[68] To the everlasting surprise of everybody—and nobody—the slightest inquiry uncovers the fact that illegitimacy is higher among Negroes as such than among the general population,[69] in a nation which has been trying to destroy the Negro family for the past three hundred years.

Under slavery there were neither valid marriages nor Negro families; the Negro woman was simply a brood mare used to produce as many valuable slave children as possible. The succeeding plantation and sharecropping systems placed a high value on a large number of children who could help in cropping; the law made no effort to fix responsibility for support on the father or fathers of the woman's children. White men (ordinarily the privileged members of society) who fathered a great many of the illegitimate children of Negro women had no legal re-

---

Los Angeles Riot 15, Oct. 28, 1965, reprinted in the Los Angeles Daily Journal, Dec. 7, 1965, pt. 3.

[65] Address by President Lyndon B. Johnson, Howard University, June 4, 1965. See also YOUNG, TO BE EQUAL, ch. 3 (1964).

[66] 49 Stat. 627 (1935), as amended, 42 U.S.C. §§ 601-09 (1964), as amended, 42 U.S.C. §§ 602-06 (Supp. I, 1965).

[67] 75 Stat. 75 (1961), 42 U.S.C. § 607 (1964), amending 49 Stat. 627 (1935).

[68] The bastard child is held in low esteem; the mother of the bastard is held up to ridicule and shame. The bastard rarely inherits from the father and is subject to all manner of legal disabilities.

[69] 1 VITAL STATISTICS OF THE UNITED STATES 1962, p. 1-18, table 1-21.

sponsibility whatever. In an increasingly urban society, the Negro woman could, and can, find a job where the Negro male could not, and cannot, and she has thus been assured of family primacy. Until quite recently when aid to the Negro family became a burden on the white taxpayer, urban law enforcement authorities, north or south, made very little effort to compel the putative father to support his children. White fathers are still not compelled to support their illegitimate Negro children in southern or border states.

Public knowledge of the imbalance of Negroes on welfare rolls depends on the keeping and dissemination of racial statistics by welfare administrators. There is, however, no more legal warrant for the keeping and dissemination of these statistics, as such, than there is for compilation and distribution of religious data on recipients of old age assistance or aid to dependent children, and the fact that the figures are kept and so widely distributed is testimony to deeply rooted beliefs that race is a telling factor in human conduct. What has happened is that the social work establishment has created a racial classification within the economic classification required by law to determine eligibility. This is not to say that racial statistics should never be kept by state agencies; there are times when such figures can be justified as an aid to identification. My own view is that the Constitution is color-blind when discrimination is practiced against persons because of their race, but color-conscious when persons have special needs as a result of prior racial discrimination.[70] There is, however, no evidence that the color-consciousness exhibited by social work agencies has been utilized to correct the disabilities of Negro recipients that arise as a result of racial discrimination.

Racial statistics are so badly kept that they are useless and meaningless. Illegitimate children of a Negro mother and a white father are classified as Negroes, and illegitimate children of a white mother and a Negro father are likewise denominated as Negroes, in conformity with the blood theories of Nazis and white supremacists. Statistical comparisons are invidious since all Negroes are lumped in together and matched against all white persons—the illegitimacy rate in the Negro slum is, in effect, compared with the illegitimacy rate in the upper-class white suburb. Nobody has tried to make a comparison between such rates among the Negro middle class and its white prototype. Nobody compares the Negro slum with the white slum. Current comparisons are as true and as meaningless as the similarly true and meaningless statement that American Negroes suffer less from beri-beri and leprosy than their remote African cousins.

---

[70] An example of such need is in Sedler, *supra* note 48.

One of the presumably unintended results of administrative racial classification of welfare recipients has been to arouse legislative hopes that a permissible social classification can be found to reach the constitutionally impermissible end of racial discrimination. Thus the Louisiana legislature enacted a statute lopping off or curtailing assistance to dependent children when the mother had an additional illegitimate child.[71] Legislators were frank in saying that the laws were aimed at Negro families. Of course some whites would have been caught in the net, but the success of Southern States in administering fair-on-their-face statutes in voting and other areas leads to the suspicion that errant white mothers had little to fear. Federal intervention was necessary to scotch some of these schemes.[72] No such bald attempts at discrimination are apt to occur in Northern States where Negroes have access to the ballot box, but undoubtedly the constant harping on racial imbalance in welfare rolls persuades legislators to keep benefits at a minimum. Nor can there be any doubt that the figures incite white public opinion and help to preserve and create racial stereotypes.

In 1960 at the height of a campaign to disfranchise Negroes, Louisiana denied the vote to persons who had "lived with another in 'common law' marriage,"[73] persons who had "given birth to an illegitimate child,"[74] and persons who had acknowledged themselves to be the "father of an illegitimate child"[75] within five years preceding the passage of the law. The obvious intent was to deprive Negroes of the vote through penalizing them for social conduct believed to be more common among them than the general population. The belief was that public opinion was so inflamed against illegitimacy among Negroes that such a measure would enlist wide support and ultimately win judicial approbation. The state's long success in administering other apparently fair statutes in such a manner as to include Negroes and exclude white persons doubtless encouraged belief that few white offenders would be affected.

Welfare administrators are intimidated by the very figures they keep and cite. All too many of them adopt the attitude that it is their

---

[71] La. Acts 1960, No. 251, § 1.

[72] U.S. DEP'T OF HEALTH, EDUC. & WELFARE, STATE LETTER No. 452 (Jan. 17, 1961), issued after the Social Security Administration was unable to declare the Louisiana statute not in conformity with the federal requirements. Social Security Administration, U.S. Dep't of Health, Educ. & Welfare, Decision of Commissioner of Social Security in the Matter of the Conformity of the Louisiana Plan for Aid to Dependent Children Under Title IV of the Social Security Act, Jan. 16, 1961, p. 7.

[73] LA. CONST. art. viii, § 1(c)(4).

[74] LA. CONST. art. viii, § 1(c)(5).

[75] LA. CONST. art. viii, § 1(c)(6).

function to limit the number of recipients by technical interpretation of rules and regulations. Sometimes they achieve their end by making application for and acceptance of welfare benefits as difficult as possible. In Los Angeles prior to the recent riot, Watts residents had to make their applications and apply for welfare adjustments in adjoining lily-white suburbs which were difficult and expensive to reach. In other situations, the very concept of fairness may be made to serve discriminatory ends: Discretionary budget figures may be set in areas of Negro occupancy at exactly the same as those in other areas although transportation, food costs, and rents are higher in the protected sellers market sheltered by the ghetto. Every administrator knows about the hue and cry against excessive numbers of Negroes on welfare rolls, and it is not at all remarkable that not a few foresee advancement if they can reduce that disparity.

The McCone Commission investigating the Los Angeles riots suggested that some California relief recipients may have migrated to the state because relief payments are higher than in other states.[76] The between-the-lines inference was that southern Negroes may leave that section for California to take advantage of the state's relatively liberal payments to dependent children. Politicians took the cue and converted the suggestion to an accusation with the connotation that there was something reprehensible in such migration. Of course, Europe's poverty stricken streamed to the United States by the millions in the late nineteenth and early twentieth centuries with the almost certain knowledge that if they failed to find employment they would certainly secure a far higher measure of charity than in their homelands. The prime motivation for the migration of a Mississippi sharecropper to Los Angeles or San Francisco is to find employment which is disappearing in his home state before onrushing mechanical farm implements. The knowledge, if he has it, that California will give him more assistance for his children if he can establish residence and is unable to find a job is certainly no deterrent factor in his decision to migrate. Just why it should be is never made plain. The curious idea that he should remain in Mississippi where he is jobless and where his dependent children must subsist at a starvation level presupposes that he ought to prefer a state which denies him almost every conceivable citizenship right over one where his rights are held in higher esteem. Very few people who urge him to make that judgment would make it themselves—even if it meant some relief for a California taxpayer. Citizenship is national and a citizen has an absolute

---

[76] CAL. GOVERNOR'S COMM'N ON THE LOS ANGELES RIOTS, VIOLENCE IN THE CITY—END OR BEGINNING 69-71 (1965).

right to move from one state to another. That right cannot be denied or curtailed because he is an indigent person.[77]

B. The Law and The Poor

Undoubtedly the poor have failed to secure the fullest measure of their legal rights because they have not been able to afford the services of lawyers. The very paucity of judicial precedents and the lack of decisions construing the rights of welfare recipients testify to the fact that their cause has seldom been presented to the courts. Welfare administrators have been left free to interpret the legislative command almost at will. Such appeals as have been taken have generally been decided by lay persons within the concerned agency. It is only in recent years that there has been any attempt to invoke constitutional safeguards against intrusions on the rights of the welfare recipient—indeed, there has been little realization that he has any "rights." He has been regarded as a beggar and, as everybody knows, beggars can't be choosers.

It took almost two decades of Supreme Court litigation to establish the very simple fact that a poor man accused of serious crime is entitled to a lawyer as a matter of right.[78] The nation is still pretty well satisfied with a bail system under which a presumptively innocent person may lose his job, his home, and his family while he remains in jail in default of what is thought of as "reasonable bail," even when there is reason to believe that he would appear for trial if released on his own recognizance. At best, uniform bail schedules are uniform for the affluent and the poverty stricken defendant under the pretext that uniformity in application means equal protection of the law. At worst—and circumstances are ordinarily at their worst in misdemeanor courts where the poor appear most often—bail may be set at the caprice of the magistrate who often becomes panic stricken in the face of public sentiment in a crisis.

When arrests mounted in the Los Angeles riot, all bail was increased over the uniform schedule, and for a panic stricken moment there was a serious suggestion that rioters be held without bail even where there was no proof or charge of homicide. The effect of the increase was to burden the poor defendant with an additional bondsman's fee of from one hundred to three hundred dollars or to make sure of incarceration during which he ran the risk of losing his job. Many defendants later released or held on only minor charges did lose their jobs.

---

[77] See Edwards v. California, 314 U.S. 160 (1941) (concurring opinion).
[78] Gideon v. Wainwright, 372 U.S. 335 (1963).

Bail may also be used to work direct racial discrimination. Southern courts often hold Negro misdemeanants to high bail in civil rights disturbances and release white offenders on very low bail.

There is a much larger body of precedential law in the area of civil rights of racial minorities than in those areas where poverty lies at the root of conflict with the law. Most civil rights law has been accumulated in the past forty years since the NAACP entered the field in a planned and orderly way.[79] However, only a small portion of present civil rights law pertains to the problems that grow out of the Negro's economic status, as such; emphasis has been on use of public accommodations, attendance at schools, segregation in transportation, and like questions. Indeed, as the Urban League's Whitney Young has suggested, there is some danger that the Negro may wind up with a mouthful of civil rights living in a hovel on an empty belly.[80]

There is a need for an orderly and well conceived program to meet the legal needs of the poor and, of equal importance, to put them on a legal parity with the affluent members of our society. At the same time, care must be exercised to see that today's poor can become tomorrow's affluent and that legal safeguards designed to protect their current status do not hinder or hamper such progress.

Some equalitarian notions are going to have to be re-examined. For example, there has to be a facing up to the fact that the one hundred dollar bail and the one hundred dollar fine of the uniform bail and fine schedules do not fall with equal impact on the ten thousand dollar a year junior executive and the four hundred dollar a month father of a family of five, even if both have violated the same statute in exactly the same manner. The public defender system is an excellent device in the quest for justice for the underprivileged—if the public defender is given staff and funds that will enable him to match skill and wits with the public prosecutor. Welfare recipients need counsel, perhaps as a class, as laws, rules, and regulations become ever more complicated. The social worker can no longer serve as counsel as she did in the days of direct handouts. The slum tenant and the preyed-upon installment buyer need lawyers.

The poor person who bears the burden of unpopular ethnic identification in our society is doubly put upon in all too many situations. He is poor and black in a world attuned to the needs and interests of the affluent and the white. His is not entirely an economic problem; nor is it entirely a racial issue. It is both and it must be dealt with simultaneously

---

[79] MILLER, THE PETITIONERS 252-62 (1966).
[80] YOUNG, TO BE EQUAL 53-54 (1964).

at both levels. The Negro's classic civil rights problems may be safely left to the civil rights organizations. What needs attention, and badly, is that complex of problems, which becomes one problem, arising out of the Negro's economic status and classification as intertwined with and complicated by racial classification. Americans have lived in a fictional "separate but equal" world so long that they tend to talk and think in racial terms. Social workers and legislators talk about "Negro" illegitimacy, for example. Of course, there is no such thing. There are many factors that affect the rate of births out of wedlock. Poverty is one of those factors. It makes formal divorce too costly for the poor; it makes access to birth control information difficult; moreover, it actually keeps the mother and the unwanted child together and the necessity for securing public assistance makes illegitimacy highly visible and the subject of conversation. My own preliminary studies on the basis of census data indicate that the illegitimate birth rate varies little as between racial groups within the same income range. There is every probability that the same thing is true as respects juvenile delinquency and crime rates.

There are, however, other figures which show wide disparities between Negroes and whites in the same economic groupings. President Johnson cited statistics in June 1965, showing that thirty-five years ago the unemployment rate for white job seekers was about the same as that for Negroes but that the present rate for Negroes is roughly twice that of whites; that the relative income of Negro working men to white workers is on the decline; that the median income for the Negro family as compared to white families has declined some four per cent in the past half-dozen years; and that the number of white families living in poverty has declined about twenty-seven per cent since 1947 while the number of Negro families has dropped only about three per cent. There is what he called a widening gulf between the two racial groups.[81] These figures reflect the increasing alienation of the Negro poor from American society and the striking failure of the welfare state to close the gap that has existed between whites and Negroes since the days of slavery.

Legislation which is effective in relieving the burdens of the poor will inevitably assist a disproportionately large number of Negroes for the reason already observed that a proportionately large number of Negroes fall within poverty classifications. That is all to the good in the effort to vanquish poverty on the widest possible scale. But such assistance could well leave untouched the gap that now exists between the

---

[81] Address by President Lyndon B. Johnson, Howard University, June 4, 1965.

two racial groups. There is a rising demand for compensatory measures to close that gap.

The critical question is whether the color-blind constitution which equalitarians have always demanded will tolerate such compensatory measures. Some assail the very suggestion as a proposal for discrimination in reverse or a new kind of Jim Crow directed against white persons.[82] This is no place to consider the inquiry in exhaustive detail, but the short answer is that the command of the fourteenth amendment is a command for equality. "It is clear," says Jacobus tenBroek in a study of the fourteenth amendment, "that the demand for equal protection cannot be a demand that laws apply universally to all persons. The legislature . . . must impose special burdens upon, or grant special benefits to, special groups or classes of individuals. Classification determines the range of persons to be affected by the special burden or benefit of a law not applicable to all persons."[83] It is plain that the command for equality voiced in the fourteenth amendment can be effective only after corrective measures have been taken to eradicate the inequality resulting from past discrimination. The framers of the fourteenth amendment, who were most insistent that the Constitution as amended was color-blind, had no constitutional qualms about enactment of remedial legislation such as the Freedmen's Bureau Acts,[84] which were designed to assist Negroes and newly freed slaves. It seems then that compensatory legislation designed to benefit Negroes as a class is constitutionally permissible.

In a realistic sense, current poverty legislation is compensatory. The poor are classified as such, and beneficial laws—or what are thought of as beneficial laws—are enacted to enable them to overcome handicaps and facilitate their entrance into the affluent society. Such classification earns no strictures and arouses no constitutional doubts because it is viewed as benign and as compatible with the American thinking that everybody is entitled to an even chance in life—nobody is to be ill-fed, or ill-clothed, or ill-housed. Many persons who boggle at similarly benign racial classification designed to relieve Negroes *as Negroes* misread the real meaning of the equalitarian dictate of the amended Constitution: The fourteenth amendment was designed to cure the ills of omission as well as commission, and Congress has power to legislate in either sphere. Poverty legislation cannot effectively aid the Negro poor until disparities between the white poor and the Negro poor are erased.

---

[82] *But see* YOUNG, *op. cit. supra* note 80, at 32.
[83] TENBROEK, EQUAL UNDER LAW 21 (rev. ed. 1965).
[84] Ch. 135, 15 Stat. 83 (1868); ch. 200, 14 Stat. 173 (1866); ch. 90, 13 Stat. 507 (1865).

As the President has put it: "You do not take a person who, for years, has been hobbled by chains and liberate him, bring him up to the starting line of a race and say, 'You are free to compete with all the others,' and still justly believe that you have been completely fair." He added that "it is not enough just to open the gates of opportunity. All of our citizens must have the ability to walk through those gates."[85] That is true of all the poor who seek equality in the affluent society; it is doubly true for the poor Negro who must surmount two hurdles to find equality in that society.

In historical perspective it is apparent that the Negro's long attempt to attain what he calls first class citizenship has been, and is, an attempt to be dealt with as an individual, as a *person* in constitutional terms, when he seeks a job, or tries to buy a home, or votes in a local, state, or federal election, or eats in a restaurant, or reads a book in a public library, or joins the Air Force, or attends school, or even swims in the ocean. The problem of how to make constitutional guarantees meaningful and fruitful is the problem inherent in an inquiry into race, poverty, and the law. There are no sure guidelines; in fact, the issues are not yet clearly defined. What has been said here is only an introduction. The road to solution lies through uncharted constitutional territory.

---

[85] Address by President Lyndon B. Johnson, Howard University, June 4, 1965.

Privacy, Poverty, and the Constitution

Albert M. Bendich*

*We are coming to recognize that the legal assistance we have given
some poor men has been only a beginning . . . . [W]e are coming to
recognize how fundamental is the role of law in providing every man
membership—and not merely existence—in our society . . . . The scales
are now tipped against the poor . . . . The solution is not charity, but
justice.[1]*

ARTICLE 22 OF THE UNIVERSAL DECLARATION OF HUMAN RIGHTS provides that "everyone, as a member of society has the right to social
security and is entitled to realization . . . of the economic, social and
cultural rights indispensable for his dignity and the free development of
his personality."

In our own society, the constitutional guarantee of privacy has increasingly come to be thought of as protecting dignity and free development of personality. And the pattern of Supreme Court decisions has
recently begun to suggest that the first, fourth, fifth, and ninth amendments are to be seen as parts of an integrated framework guaranteeing
various aspects of the "privacy" or "dignity" or "freedom" of the individual.[2]

The "economic, social and cultural rights" which the Universal Declaration of Human Rights expressly describes as being indispensable to
dignity and free development of personality are largely assumed in our
society to be made available in ways that do not require their legal
provision.

The war on poverty, however, has focused attention on the fact that
the indispensable conditions of privacy, dignity, and freedom are lacking
for millions of Americans. Thus, while the Constitution's guarantees presuppose the existence of these indispensable conditions,[2a] their actual non-
existence tends to reduce the guarantees themselves to mere suppositions.

Poverty is thus simultaneously a condition which deprives individuals
of freedom and dignity and undermines the most fundamental constitutional guarantees. But, if poverty is at war with the Constitution, the
Constitution is equally at war with poverty. It is the central thesis of

---

* A.B., 1950; M.A., 1952; LL.B., 1955; University of California, Berkeley. Associate
Professor of Speech, University of California, Berkeley; Member, California Bar.

1 Address by Attorney General Nicholas deB. Katzenbach to the National Conference on
Law and Poverty, Washington D.C., June 24, 1965, pp. 1, 4.

2 See, *e.g.*, Griswold v. Connecticut, 381 U.S. 479, 484 (1965).

2a Thus, *e.g.*, the fourth amendment's guarantee of freedom from unreasonable searches
and seizures ("The right of the people to be secure in their persons, houses, papers and
effects") presupposes, *inter alia*, that *persons* have houses.

this paper that persons in our society have a constitutional right to privacy and to the conditions which are indispensable to its realization. By reasoning similar to that by which we have recently come to understand that the guarantee of due process requires a lawyer to be provided for persons too poor to engage private counsel, because a defense attorney is an indispensable aspect of justice in a criminal trial, this paper works its way to conclusions requiring, as matters of constitutional entitlement, provision of the minimal necessaries of "membership—and not merely existence—in our society." For the millions of Americans who are poverty-stricken, this approach means invoking the whole range of fundamental rights and principles, which have hitherto been as inaccessible to them as if they had lived in some other time and place, and insisting that the Constitution be taken seriously not only for the privileged but for the underprivileged as well. The ultimate conclusion, therefore, is that the war against poverty is not a war to rescue the poor so much as it is a war to defend the constitutional principles of freedom, dignity, and equality. It is not a matter of charity, but of justice.

I

PRIVACY

A. Background

"The right to be let alone," Justice Brandeis wrote, is "the most comprehensive of rights and the right most valued by civilized men."[3] Justice Douglas added that the "right to be let alone is indeed the beginning of all freedom."[4] And the Supreme Court has held that "the right of privacy is a fundamental personal right, 'emanating from the totality of the constitutional scheme under which we live.' "[5]

We can appreciate the significance of the right to privacy in several ways; perhaps the simplest is to try to imagine what life under total official scrutiny would be like. Here we are indebted to George Orwell for his image of "Big Brother." The painful details—the spies, human and mechanical, the suspicion, the fear, the feelings of exposure, helplessness —add up to a portrait of inhuman tyranny. It is these details and this picture against which the right to privacy is designed to protect us.

But the right to privacy has a positive as well as a negative function. Historically, the right to privacy is intimately tied up with the nurturing of independence of mind and spirit. It is part of the process of civilization struggling to overcome tyranny and oppression. It is related most intimately to the development of the first amendment freedoms: conscience,

---

[3] Olmstead v. United States, 277 U.S. 438, 478 (1928) (dissenting opinion).

[4] Public Util. Comm'n v. Pollak, 343 U.S. 451, 467 (1952) (dissenting opinion).

[5] Griswold v. Connecticut, 381 U.S. 479, 494 (1965) (Goldberg, J., concurring).

speech, press, assembly, petition. But, basically, the right to privacy grew up as part of the ongoing struggle for the freedom and dignity of the individual, his right to determine his own destiny, to think and choose for himself, and to join in association with free and equal fellow citizens in shaping and working to reach common social and political ends.

Early in the process of these struggles, it was discovered that freedom from intrusion, security of one's person, house, papers, and effects from uninvited scrutiny, from unreasonable searches and seizures, was basic to freedom and dignity: that if the people were to be masters, they must not be treated as servants; that free men were independent men—not suppliants, and not beggars; but indeed rulers and choosers.

These are some of the reasons underlying James Otis' denunciation in 1761 of the hated writs of assistance (general warrant pursuant to which the King's agents could at their pleasure conduct exploratory searches of men's homes for evidence of contraband) as "the worst instrument of arbitrary power," and as placing the "liberty of every man in the hands of every petty officer." John Adams, after he became President, said of Otis' speech: "then and there the child Independence was born."[6]

General warrants had been a tool of the Star Chamber, under the repressive regimes of the Tudors[7] and the Stuarts,[8] for the searching out of dissenters and the literature of dissent. Men like Wilkes and Lilburne were whipped and tortured because of their opinions and writings which, because they questioned or did not agree with state policy, were deemed criminal and styled "seditious libels." Out of the struggles of this period, as part of the growing understanding of the sort of procedures which were

---

[6] TUDOR, LIFE OF JAMES OTIS 61, 66 (1823), quoted by Justice Frankfurter in Frank v. Maryland, 359 U.S. 360, 364 (1959).

[7] A Star Chamber decree of 1586 provided "that it shall be lawful . . . to make search in all workhouses, shops, warehouses of printers, booksellers, bookbinders or where they shall have reasonable cause of suspicion . . . ." The books thus seized were to be inspected by ecclesiastical officers who were to decide whether they should be burnt. The Tudor censorship employed these powers "to suppress both Catholic and Puritan dissenting literature." Marcus v. Search Warrant, 367 U.S. 717, 725 (1961). See also SIEBERT, FREEDOM OF THE PRESS IN ENGLAND, 1476-1776, at 83, 85-86, 97 (1952).

[8] In Stanford v. Texas, 379 U.S. 476, 482 (1965), Justice Stewart, speaking for a unanimous Court, said: "But while the Fourth Amendment was most immediately the product of contemporary revulsion against a regime of writs of assistance, its roots go far deeper. Its adoption in the Constitution of this new nation reflected the culmination in England a few years earlier of a struggle against oppression which had endured for centuries. The story of that struggle has been fully chronicled in the pages of this Court's reports [see Marcus v. Search Warrant, 367 U.S. 717, 724-29 (1960); Frank v. Maryland, 359 U.S. 360, 363-66 (1958) (dissenting opinion). See also Boyd v. United States, 116 U.S. 616 (1885)] and it would be a needless exercise in pedantry to review again the detailed history of the use of general warrants as instruments of oppression from the time of the Tudors, through the Star Chamber, the Long Parliament, the Restoration, and beyond." See also HANSON, GOVERNMENT AND THE PRESS, 1695-1763 (1936).

necessary to protect and assist the development of freedom of speech and other aspects of political freedom, the English law developed the privilege against self-incrimination, to protect the privacy of a person's thoughts against the destructive prying of inquisitors, and the requirement of special as opposed to general warrants, safeguarding the privacy of a person's body, house, papers, and effects.[9]

Thus the zone of independence, dignity, and privacy was widened. These achievements symbolized the presence among the people of a certain new authority, a certain new power and freedom; it also signified a certain new limit to the authority of the state. It removed certain subjects and certain areas from the possibility of official scrutiny. To be one's own master in these categories was to be no man's slave and to preclude the attitudes of mastery and servility appropriate to slavishness. In this realm, no man was to be beholden to any other, no man was to be dependent on another; "charity" was therefore inconsistent with the emergence of democratic concepts of the relation between the state and the individual. These were the principles which "privacy" implied, nurtured, and protected.

Later, these English achievements were partially embodied in the guarantees of the fifth and fourth amendments of our Bill of Rights. But Otis had wanted no more than to have such established rights of Englishmen as these extended to the Colonists when, in his famous speech denouncing writs of assistance, he said: "A man is as secure in his house as a prince in his castle. This is the privilege of the House and it obtains if a man be deeply in debt or if civil process be served against him. Only for felonies may an officer break and enter—and then by special, not general warrant. For general warrants there is only the precedent of the Star Chamber . . . ."[10]

As we know, it required a revolution before Americans could begin to enjoy some of the great rights which had been won in the preceding centuries in England. And after the revolution, a Constitution and Bill

---

[9] "In 1765, in England, what is properly called the great case of *Entick v. Carrington*, 19 Howell's State Trials, col. 1029, announced the principle of English law which became part of the Bill of Rights and whose basic protection has become embedded in the concept of due process of law. It was there decided that English law did not allow officers of the Crown to break into a citizen's home, under cover of a general executive warrant, to search for evidence of the utterance of libel. Among the reasons given for that decision were these: 'It is very certain that the law obligeth no man to accuse himself; because the necessary means of compelling self-accusation, falling upon the innocent as well as the guilty, would be both cruel and unjust; and it should seem, that search for evidence is disallowed upon the same principle. There too the innocen would be confounded with the guilty.' *Id.* at col. 1073," quoted by Justice Frankfurter in Frank v. Maryland, 359 U.S. 360, 363 (1959).

[10] BOWEN, JOHN ADAMS AND THE AMERICAN REVOLUTION 215 (1950), quoted in BARTH, THE PRICE OF LIBERTY, 71-72 (1961).

of Rights—building upon, incorporating, and extending these great rights —had to be hammered out and ratified before the country could be said to have consolidated its drive for independence.

Of course, consolidation did not mean that the principles implicit in the revolution were fully realized. Slavery, poverty, illiteracy, racial and sexual discrimination, property qualifications[11]—all these and other in-consistent attitudes, conditions, and practices co-existed with the prin-ciples of justice, freedom, equality, dignity, privacy, and democracy. Such attitudes, conditions, and practices sapped the vitality of the revolutionary principles just as the latter militated against slavery and social and sexual discrimination. But the history of the struggles for freedom of the press, for freedom from unreasonable searches and seizures, for freedom from torture and inquisition, for freedom from taxation without representation, for freedom from the quartering of troops upon a peacetime civilian popu-lation, for freedom from the oppression of all arbitrary discrimination— the history of these struggles "was, of course, part of the intellectual matrix within which our constitutional fabric was shaped."[12] And that history makes unmistakably clear the intimate relation and interdepen-dence of the first, fourth, and fifth amendments to the Constitution, and displays a pattern designed for "safeguarding not only privacy and pro-tection against self-incrimination but 'conscience and human dignity and freedom of expression as well.' "[13] From this perspective, the character-ization of the right to privacy as "the most comprehensive of rights,"[14] "the beginning of all freedom,"[15] "the right most valued by civilized men,"[16] and a "fundamental personal right emanating from the totality of the constitutional scheme under which we live,"[17] appears entirely appropriate.

In the past decade and a half, we have had occasion to review this history and its meaning with particular frequency and immediacy because of the accelerated and intensified assaults upon these great principles and rights generated in part by the paranoia of the cold war years, and, in part, reflecting the growth of a corporate, managerial, bureaucratized society. With the proliferation of loyalty oaths, legislative investigating committees, security checks by public and private employers, the con-sequent suspicions which were created and aroused, and the potent new

---

[11] *Cf.* Harper v. Virginia State Bd. of Elections, 86 Sup. Ct. 1079 (1966).

[12] Marcus v. Search Warrant, 367 U.S. 717, 729 (1961).

[13] Stanford v. Texas, 379 U.S. 476, 485 (1965), quoting Justice Douglas' dissenting opin-ion in Frank v. Maryland, 359 U.S. 360, 376 (1959).

[14] Olmstead v. United States, 277 U.S. 438, 478 (1928) (dissenting opinion).

[15] Public Util. Comm'n v. Pollak, 343 U.S. 451, 467 (1952) (dissenting opinion).

[16] Olmstead v. United States, 277 U.S. 438, 478 (1928) (dissenting opinion).

[17] Poe v. Ullman, 367 U.S. 497, 521 (1960) (Douglas, J., dissenting).

techniques for ferreting out information which the psychologists and the electronic engineers developed and made available, it became imperative that the various meanings of privacy and the reasons for its development as a summation of various fundamental rights of free and civilized people be reviewed, relearned, and meaningfully reasserted in the changed context of an oligopolistic and welfare as opposed to a *laissez faire* society.[18]

In this age of masses, concentration, and experts, it has become evident that the rhetorical formulas of political freedom must rest upon the substantive ground of individual dignity, nurtured and protected by individual rights, if our professed intention to build the great society is to be regarded seriously, not as cynical politicians' talk. Repeatedly, and in the most varied ways, recent experience has shown that without privacy for family life, without security in the home to allow for and nourish the development of a sense of self, without a feeling of personal security (a sense of freedom from fears of injury or reprisal for thinking and speaking honestly, acting autonomously) necessary to the development of independent opinions and the courage to stand by them, there could be no such thing as a free people. Self-government, as we rediscovered, presupposes self-respecting individuals; self-respecting individuals presuppose self-managing, freely choosing, independent individuals committed to respecting the rights of others. The concept of a free society was shown to be inseparable from the dignity of its constituents. Thus, as we learned, the constitutional doctrine summing up and symbolizing many of these values—"guaranteeing" them—is the "right to privacy."

In this regard it is important to return to the context of Justice Brandeis' statement, quoted at the beginning, about the right of privacy:

---

[18] The old frontier was lost. Seemingly, the virtues of the Jeffersonian yeomanry, independence, autonomy—the virtues which the Bill of Rights had been framed to protect—were being lost too. Instead of a yeomanry of sturdy individuals, a lonely crowd; instead of self governing persons, other directed masses. In the face of onslaughts upon people and the values of the first, fourth, and fifth amendments such as the investigation by legislative committees of political thoughts, associations, reading habits; the growth of conspiracy concepts matching the growth of managerial power in the few to direct and control the many; the development of "security" consciousness both politically and industrially; the drive for conformity reflected in such conditions as corporate scrutiny of the qualities of junior executives' wives, and psychological inquisitions into their souls (to which William Whyte responded with the advice: "cheat-respect yourself"!, WHYTE, ORGANIZATION MAN 405-10 (1956))— in the face of such onslaughts upon privacy it is not surprising to find Americans generally so insensitive to invasions of the right. And, of course, the poor, who have historically been the most oppressed and deprived, have suffered the most vicious, and the least noticed, invasions of privacy. (No one advises the poor to "cheat." And in a recent best seller, PACKARD, NAKED SOCIETY 275-76 (1964), dealing with privacy, a mere sixteen lines is devoted to the poor; and they take note of only the most superficial invasions of privacy.) Perhaps, for that reason, the vindication of their rights may redeem us all.

"The makers of our constitution," he said,

> undertook to secure conditions favorable to the pursuit of happiness. They recognized the significance of man's spiritual nature, of his feelings and of his intellect. They knew that only a part of the pain, pleasure, and satisfactions of life are to be found in material things. They sought to protect Americans in their beliefs, their thoughts, their emotions and their sensations. They conferred as against the Government, the right to be let alone—the most comprehensive of rights and the right most valued by civilized men.[19]

B. The Right To Be Let Alone

The right to be "let alone," as a phrase, is not of course to be taken literally. It requires little reflection to perceive that persons do not construe their dignity, independence, or privacy as being threatened when firemen arrive to put out a blaze. Indeed, to be "let alone" in such circumstances could very well preclude dignity, independence, and privacy as efficiently as "the midnight knock on the door." In the same way, it is clear that for the government to leave persons alone in other areas of life might be equally destructive of their independence, dignity, and privacy. For example, should the government leave persons under unlawful, violent physical attack alone, or should it go to their assistance? Is it violative of, compatible with, or a prerequisite to dignity, independence, and privacy for the government to furnish financial assistance to those who would otherwise be destitute? Obviously, it is a governmental obligation to protect citizens against violent physical attack. Is there not a similar obligation to protect citizens against destructive and violent economic change? Against the ravages of planned or at least controllable economic change? Is there not an obligation to protect persons against ignorance by providing schools?[20] Can persons in our society achieve independence or dignity or privacy without some minimal income, some minimal housing, some minimal education? If it is only government action which can assure minimal economic and social security and if government by a policy of avoidance and inaction deprives persons of these necessities, does it not violate the guarantee of due process as well as equal protection? Do these guarantees not *require* the welfare state to *provide* welfare? Indeed, in this post *laissez faire* age, does not the "totality of the constitutional

---

[19] Olmstead v. United States, 277 U.S. 438, 478 (1928) (dissenting opinion).

[20] In Brown v. Board of Educ., 347 U.S. 483, 493 (1954), a unanimous Supreme Court declared: "Today, education is perhaps the most important function of state and local governments. Compulsory school attendance laws and the great expenditures for education both demonstrate our recognition of the importance of education to our democratic society. It is required in the performance of our most basic public responsibilities, even service in the armed forces. It is the very foundation of good citizenship."

scheme under which we live" require the provision of at least the minimal prerequisites of meaningful membership in the society?[21]

C. Privacy and Poverty

As a matter of abstract consideration it seems clear that poverty and privacy are intimately and inversely related. If the essence of the right to privacy is in that pattern of rights making for meaningful freedom of choice in the context of our society, it requires little reflection to perceive that nutritional or cultural starvation constitutes a form of compulsion or constraint rather incompatible with such freedom. This is implicit in the popular phrase "beggars can't be choosers." Indeed, the concept of a man's home being his castle, for purposes of security and privacy, presupposes not only the existence of a house but also that the man will be able to enter, leave, and provision it in such a way that it is not his prison or dungeon. Solitary confinement though it may confer solitude, is not our concept of "the right most valued by civilized men." The concept of a "home" presupposes that its inhabitants will not be under economic seige. But, historically, the poorhouse (during the very period of the development of the concept of privacy) was a prison rather than a home; and that history is shockingly modern.[22]

In England, contemporaneously with the development of the concept of the security of the home, poor men were not only beseiged by the effects of such economic forces and policies as the shift from feudal to capitalist

---

21 *Cf.* Burton v. Wilmington Parking Authority, 365 U.S. 715, 725 (1961): "[N]o state may effectively abdicate its responsibilities by either ignoring them or by merely failing to discharge them . . . . By its inaction . . . the State has not only made itself a party to the refusal of service, but has elected to place its power, property, and prestige behind the admitted discrimination."

22 "In 1824 after a public uproar and an official investigation, the state [New York] initiated a system of county poorhouses, and within a decade fifty counties had erected such institutions. Outdoor relief was virtually abolished; all poor were to be sent to the poorhouse 'unless the sickness of the pauper prevent.' All vagrants if 'proper objects for such relief' were to be sent there unless 'notorious offenders.' At the discretion of the justice of the peace with the concurrence of the superintendent, disorderly persons might also be sent there instead of to jail. The justice's warrant need only state 'generally, that such person has been convicted of being a disorderly person without more particular specification of the offense.' Children under fifteen found begging were also to be sent to the poorhouse until able to support themselves. Vagrants and disorderly persons were to be kept at hard labor, and all other inmates were to labor to the extent of their ability. The superintendents of the poorhouses, with the consent of a majority of the judges of the county court, were empowered to establish 'such prudential rules . . . for the well ordering of the same, and the employment, relief, management and government of the persons therein placed . . . and the correction of the refractory, disobedient and disorderly, by solitary confinement therein, and feeding them on bread and water only, as they shall deem expedient." tenBroek, *California's Dual System of Family Law: Its Origin, Development, and Present Status*, 16 STAN. L. REV. 257, 296-97 (1964). Attempted escape from the poorhouse "resulted in solitary confinement and bread and water." *Id.* at 298.

relations, and the attendant enclosure movement, but were literally driven from their homes and reduced to the status of "vagrants," "paupers," and "rogues."[23] Nor, of course, was this process limited to England or to the sixteenth or seventeenth centuries. In 1776 Pitt said: "The poorest man may, in his cottage, bid defiance to all the forces of the crown. It may be frail; its roof may shake; the wind may blow through it; the storm may enter; but the King of England may not enter; all his force dare not cross the threshold of the ruined tenement."[24]

He spoke in terms of apparent universal application. But he obviously was not speaking of the destitute. The poorest man in Pitt's rhetoric at least had a cottage. But, as we know, large numbers of unfortunate persons had no shelter at all, from either wind or storm, let alone the King's men who seized them and placed them in orphanages, asylums, workhouses, poorhouses, jails, or saw to it that they became indentured servants. Within a few years of the enactment of the Elizabethan poor laws, in 1601, Shakespeare wrote "King Lear" in 1605-06. It is surely not accidental that Lear in the great storm scene in Act IV, Scene IV, before the hovel on the heath, addresses the *unsheltered* poor:

> You houseless poverty . . .
> Poor naked wretches, wheresoe'er you are,
> That bide the pelting of this pitiless storm,
> How shall your houseless heads and unfed sides,
> Your looped and windowed raggedness, defend you
> From seasons such as these? O, I have ta'en
> Too little care of this! Take physic, pomp;
> Expose thyself to feel what wretches feel,
> That thou mayst shake the superflux to them,
> And show the heavens more just.[25]

II

POVERTY AND THE CONSTITUTION

A. Early Developments

The poverty-stricken constituted an exception not only to the ideals of English freedom but also to the protections of the Bill of Rights. That

---

[23] See, *e.g.*, HILL, PURITANISM AND REVOLUTION, 219-27 (1964). "The vagabond class was drawn largely from evicted peasants: they were helpless in the new world of capitalist insecurity unless they had skilled labor power to sell." *Id.* at 227. "The problem set by vagabondage and vagrancy was to force men who had been deprived of their independent means of livelihood to enter into 'free' contracts to work for a capitalist employer, and to accustom them to the habit of steady work throughout the year. A new pattern of social discipline had to be imposed. . . . Poor relief must be associated with, and subordinate to, the imposition of the new discipline: houses of correction, family means tests, the apprenticing of pauper children to a trade, whether they or their parents wished it or not." *Id.* at 222.

[24] Frank v. Maryland, 359 U.S. 360, 378-79 (1959) (dissenting opinion).

[25] SHAKESPEARE, KING LEAR, Act IV, Scene IV.

document though framed in a rhetoric of universal application, did not in practice or contemporary expectation apply universally. Part of the process of understanding the constitutional position of the poor today thus requires becoming acquainted with the historically antecedent attitudes and practices, which helped to condition their present position, and with all those forces, circumstances, and conditions, which make for the gaps between our ideals in word and our lives in fact.

In America, the poverty-stricken, those denominated "vagrants," "vagabonds," "paupers," and "rogues" were deemed in law to be in themselves, offensive. Such persons offended by their mere existence; they constituted a "moral pestilence"; their very being was a form of "contraband." In the Articles of Confederation they had been classified together with fugitives from justice.[26] Under the common law and the laws of the several states, they could be seized and jailed or otherwise denied freedom available to others.[27] They could hardly be said, therefore, to have enjoyed a right to privacy in "their houses, papers and effects"—even assuming that all or some of these existed, the concept is merely ironic.

The legal depth of the degradation which poverty entailed during our early years as a nation can be seen clearly in the language and result of an early United States Supreme Court case, *City of New York v. Miln*, decided in 1837.[28]

New York had passed legislation excluding poor persons from entry into the state. The issue was whether such an approach to the poor was within New York's police power and constitutional. The Supreme Court held that it was, making reference, in its opinion, to "the moral pestilence of paupers,"[29] and reasoning that it was as constitutional to take precau-

---

[26] Articles of Confederation 1777, art. IV. See Bingham's 1859 speech in Congress (in opposition to the admission of Oregon into the Union because of its constitutional provision that "no free Negro or mulatto, not residing in this State at the time of the adoption of this constitution, shall ever come, reside or be, within this State, or hold any real estate, or make any contract, or maintain any suit therein . . . ."): "I . . . refer gentlemen to the Journal of the Continental Congress, volume 2, page 606. . . . [I]n that Congress, on the 25th of June, 1778, the Articles of Confederation being under consideration, it was moved by delegates of South Carolina to amend the fourth article, by inserting after the word 'free' and before the word 'inhabitants,' the word 'white,' so that 'the privileges and immunities of the citizens in the several States should be limited exclusively to white inhabitants.' The vote on this amendment was taken by States, and stood two States for, and eight against, and one equally divided. This action of the Congress of 1778 was a clear and direct disavowal that *all free inhabitants, white and black, except 'paupers, vagabonds, and fugitives from justice'* (which were expressly excepted), 'were entitled to all the privileges and immunities of free citizens in the several States.'" Address by John A. Bingham, 1859, in TENBROEK, EQUAL UNDER THE LAW 320, 334, 336-37 (1965). (Emphasis added.)

[27] See note 78 *infra*.

[28] 36 U.S. (11 Pet.) 102 (1837).

[29] *Id.* at 142.

tions against the dangers of poverty by excluding the poor as it was to take similar police measures against "convicts" or "infectious articles."[30] In the highest court in the land, poverty was thus seen to be a species of immorality; like crime or pestilence, it was within a state's police power; and poor persons were thereby placed on a par with convicted criminals and contaminated commodities.

Similar language to that employed in *Miln* continued to be "casually repeated in numerous later cases up to the turn of the century."[31] Indeed, it was not until 1941, when the issue presented in *Miln* was again brought to the Supreme Court in *Edwards v. California*,[32] that the high court finally repudiated the equation of poverty with immorality. It had taken more than one hundred years for poverty stricken persons to progress, in the eyes of the law, from the dignity of treatment accorded to contaminated commodities to that of uncontaminated ones. Yet the decision marked a watershed in the development of our intellectual and legal attitudes toward poverty.

B. The Turning Point

The *Edwards* case, like *Miln*, arose over the issue whether California could constitutionally exclude the victims of the great depression from seeking new horizons in the "golden state." En route to its decision, the Court said that whatever may have been the view in 1837, "we do not think that it will now be seriously contended that because a person is without employment and without funds he constitutes a 'moral pestilence.' Poverty and immorality are not synonymous."[33] To be sure, this was important language; it was indeed time to recognize that the mere condition of being without funds was neither a function of personal choice, necessarily, nor a mark of moral fault. But, unfortunately, its actual holding was drastically limited. The Court reasoned that interstate transportation of persons was "commerce"; that the exclusion of poor persons was not an exercise of a state's police power but a mere economic regulation; and since the contemplated exclusion burdened interstate commerce, the regulation of which was constitutionally reserved exclusively for Congress, California's law violated the commerce clause. Though doubtless a step in the right direction—the poor had at least been elevated to a level with noninfectious articles of commerce—the *Edwards* decision shed little light on the question of the constitutional rights of the poor *as persons* beyond

---

30 *Ibid.*

31 Edwards v. California, 314 U.S. 160, 176 (1941).

32 *Ibid.*

33 *Id.* at 177.

suggesting that they were not to be regarded as immoral merely because of their poverty.

Justice Jackson alone rose to the occasion and, in a separate concurring opinion, undertook to set forth a general, theoretical consideration of the relationship between poverty and the Constitution. In pertinent part he said:

> Does "indigence" . . . constitute a basis for restricting the freedom of a citizen, as crime or contagion warrants its restriction? We should say now, and in no uncertain terms, that a man's mere property status, without more, cannot be used by a state to test, qualify, or limit his rights as a citizen of the United States. "Indigence" in itself is neither a source of rights nor a basis for denying them. The mere state of being without funds is a neutral fact—constitutionally an irrelevance, like race, creed, or color.[34]

Here was a new note! For the first time language in a Supreme Court decision recognized that there could be a contradiction between the fact of poverty and the constitutional guarantees of freedom. In insisting that the mere state of being without funds must be a constitutional irrelevance, Justice Jackson opened up the entire question of how the stubborn, brutal, and invidious fact of poverty was to be rendered constitutionally "neutral." What was momentous in Justice Jackson's opinion was the understanding that no more legitimately than race or creed could poverty be suffered to diminish constitutional freedoms. To the extent that poverty did have that effect, it was itself unconstitutional! Freedom to have constitutional freedom thus implied freedom from poverty.

C. The New Approach

Before the Court was again confronted with the issue of the conflict between poverty and the Constitution, another fifteen years were to pass. Then *Griffin v. Illinois*,[35] in 1956, presented the question whether justice in the form of equal protection and due process of law required a state to provide a trial transcript at its own expense to an indigent convict who could not otherwise effectively take advantage of the right to appeal which Illinois made generally available to all who could afford it. The Court split on the question. Five justices thought that the guarantee of equal protection required Illinois to provide equal access to its courts of criminal appeal even if that meant paying for transcripts so the poor could have them. Four Justices, dissenting, questioned whether any state was constitutionally compelled to make persons "economically equal before its bar of justice."[36] Taking up the challenge, Justice Frankfurter, in a con-

---

34 *Id.* at 184-85.
35 351 U.S. 12 (1956).
36 *Id.* at 28.

curring opinion, asked rhetorically whether a state could constitutionally limit appeals from criminal convictions to those persons who could afford to pay a fee of five-hundred dollars.[37] Justice Harlan countered by asking whether states were violating the Constitution in requiring tuition fees for admission to state colleges, though many who might otherwise choose to attend were thus excluded.[38]

Here was the Supreme Court seriously and forthrightly wrestling with the challenge which Anatol France had laid down years before when he questioned the value of a legal guarantee of equality in the face of economic facts which made realization of the guarantee by the poor impossible. The members of the Supreme Court were apparently agreed that where fundamental rights are concerned, the Constitution requires equality of access to them even if that means that the state must bear the cost. The justices divided over the question whether the right to appeal was a fundamental right or a mere luxury.

The stage was thus set for the question: Assuming that a person's poverty does stand in the way of a fundamental right; that poverty and only poverty blocks access to an aspect of justice which all agree is "implicit in the concept of ordered liberty"[39]—under such circumstances, is a state constitutionally required to neutralize the fact of poverty, to "equalize" the poor man by providing the money or other necessities needed to realize the right?

Seven years later, in the landmark case of *Gideon v. Wainwright*,[40] the Court provided the answer by unanimously holding that at least as to state prosecutions involving the possibility of a substantial prison sentence, due process of law requires that defendants have access to representation by counsel regardless of their ability to pay the fee. The Court's basic assumption was that the right to counsel in such circumstances is a fundamental right. The ability to hire the services of an outstanding attorney would, to be sure, still turn on the condition of a man's purse, as would access to other "luxuries." But, as to the right to be represented by a lawyer who can do an adequate job, it is the Constitution, not one's purse, which guarantees that.

In these few cases, legal attitudes toward the poor may be said to have taken a new direction pointing to a narrowing of the gap between the principle that fundamental rights belong equally to all and the persistent fact of second class citizenship for the poor.[41] Though this new under-

---

[37] *Id.* at 22.

[38] *Id.* at 34-36 (dissenting opinion).

[39] *Cf.* Palko v. Connecticut, 302 U.S. 319 (1937).

[40] 372 U.S. 335 (1963).

[41] See WALD, LAW AND POVERTY 1965, at 4 n.9 (1965): "There is, of course, as yet no constitutional right to counsel in civil proceedings . . . . Some have questioned the validity of the

standing of the guarantee of equality and due process has thus far been applied only to the aspect of the conflict between poverty and constitutional rights bearing upon the process of criminal law, it is clear that the logic of these decisions extends to other areas. In the field of fundamental constitutional rights, as in the field of full employment, it appears that we are coming to understand that reliance is no longer to be placed in *laissez faire*. If the automatic forces of the market will not do the job, men must. And therefore the task now is to accelerate the process whereby the gap between principle and practice can be eliminated. It is time to move from dedication in principle to realization in practice of the Constitution's great guarantees of first class citizenship for all.

Some speculation may be justified as to the extent to which the logic of *Griffin* and *Gideon* will require economic support from the government to be furnished to persons outside the area of criminal law. The most fundamental needs are clearly for food, shelter, and clothing. To what extent are they merely luxuries and to what extent are they not only biological and social but also *constitutional* necessities?

It would be perverse to say that one has a fundamental right to be assisted by a lawyer when charged with crime, but that he has no right to such food or medicine as might be required to keep him reasonably healthy and attentive during the process of his trial. If the defendant is a diabetic who requires insulin in order to stay out of a state of shock it would seem that the constitutional right to a fair trial would require him to be supplied with insulin in the same way that it would entitle him to be furnished with counsel. But if a person charged with crime has a right to such assistance, on what principle is one innocent of such a charge to be denied equal access to assistance? Is a person's right to meaningful participation in the processes of citizenship less fundamental than one's right to defend himself when accused of crime? What constitutional guarantees other than those which are bound up with the criminal law are denied to persons because of their poverty? Does the fourth amendment's guarantee of the right to be secure in one's person, papers, house, and effects presuppose housing for the people of America? If it does, then clearly the condition of being unable to pay rent can deprive one of this aspect of the right to privacy as effectively as the inability to pay counsel fees could, prior to *Gideon*, deprive one of the right to counsel. Does not the right to privacy therefore imply that poverty can not constitutionally be allowed to stand in the way of minimally adequate housing? If poverty

---

distinction . . . ." Former Attorney General Kennedy, for example, in his Address on Law Day at the University of Chicago Law School, May 1, 1964 said: "We have secured the acquittal of an indigent person—but only to abandon him to eviction notices, wage attachments, repossession of goods and termination of welfare benefits." *Ibid.*

is to be a constitutionally neutral fact, it must not deprive persons of the guarantees of the fourth amendment any more than of the other fundamental guarantees. Moreover, if the answer here is in the affirmative and the state is under a constitutional obligation to provide persons with housing, are there not some minimal requirements which must be adhered to so that the right is meaningful? For example, if the state must provide a transcript, obviously it need not be bound in leather, but it must be reasonably accurate and legible; if the state must provide a lawyer, obviously he need not be the attorney general, but he must be reasonably competent; if the state must provide housing for those who would otherwise be without shelter, it obviously need not be the governor's mansion, but it must be minimally consistent with basic standards of health and decency. Clearly neither the poorhouse nor the jailhouse will constitute housing which is meaningfully relevant to the constitutional right to privacy. If rat infested, dilapidated, oppressive slum dwellings can produce disease, depression, and other mental disorders and render privacy even in the sense of access to reasonable seclusion meaningless,[42] such dwellings do not constitute housing in the sense required in order for the right to privacy not to be a mockery of constitutional protection.

To be sure, considerations such as these point in the direction of deep changes in the interpretation of our constitutional law. But this is no more than what the Constitution itself requires. Indeed, as the late Justice Frankfurter once said, "it is the very nature of a free society to advance in its standards of what is reasonable and right. Representing as it does a living principle, due process is not confined within a permanent catalogue of what may at a given time be deemed the limits or the essentials of fundamental rights."[43] Moreover, the economic shift from a *laissez faire* to a welfare state system requires appropriate changes in legal conceptions in order that the law may remain viable. However questionable the old assumption that there is no state action in or responsibility for the ordinary processes of economic life may have been prior to the New Deal, there is today no doubt that government policy is highly relevant to, if it does not wholly determine, the degree of the realization or frustration of virtually every basic human need. From stagnation to accelerated growth

---

[42] See Paulsen, The Legal Needs of the Poor and Family Law 18, 20 (1964): "A small unattractive apartment in the heart of New York City on a hot summer's day can produce mental troubles almost by itself."

"Positive motivation withers in the midst of rats, refuse strewn alleys, peeling plaster, broken windows, cold radiators, and leaky ceilings. Nearly 1,000 adults and children live in one slum block of the District of Columbia." Wald, *op. cit. supra*, note 41, at 13. Another stimulus to "positive motivation": "Negroes are apt to pay up to 30 percent more rent for the same facilities as white tenants." *Ibid*, citing May, The Wasted Americans 131 (1964).

[43] Wolf v. Colorado, 338 U.S. 25, 27 (1949).

rates, unemployment to full employment, miserably inadequate to minimally decent housing, polluted air and water to fresh air and clean
streams and bays—in almost every way that men measure welfare, the
Great Society not only assumes but proclaims that the guiding hand is
neither invisible nor anonymous but the government's.

Since it is clear that the level of employment, or the character of education, or the nature of housing is a reflection of policy; since we know,
for example, that budgeting twelve billion dollars will bridge the so-called
"poverty gap";[44] that, in short, there is no greater inevitability to growing

[44] Depending on the figures one uses, either one-fifth or two-fifths of the American
people are poverty-stricken. According to the President's council of economic advisers, the
poverty line for an urban family of four is about $3,000 in annual income. This is a pretty
low floor as can be seen from the fact that such a budget will allow a daily expenditure of
seventy cents per person for food and a dollar and forty cents for all other needs including
rent, clothes, medical care, etc. See Miller, *Who Are The Poor*, 200 THE NATION 609 (1965).
Still, according to the 1960 census, the families constituting the lowest fifth of the income
hierarchy received less than $2,798 annually. According to the Heller Committee For Research
in Social Economics of the University of California, a "modest but decent" annual income for
such a family would be $5,500 to $6,500 depending on the city of residence. According to the
1960 census figures again, the families constituting the second lowest fifth of the income
hierarchy had incomes between $2,798 and $4,812. Taking the poverty line at the official
$3,000 figure thus leaves a fifth of the American people in limbo between poverty and de-
cency, and classifies about 34.5 million persons as poverty-stricken, subsisting at incomes
below this minimum poverty line. In 1963 these persons (half of whom are children) received an aggregate income that was about $12 billion *below* their estimated minimum
requirements. This is the so called "poverty-gap."

Given the fact that the government has not appropriated even a twelfth of this sum for
the annual budget of the war on poverty, it must unfortunately be concluded that so far, at
least, the war is more talk than fight. The need is to prevent the "war" from degenerating
into mere propaganda: We must do what we can to see to it that the words are matched
with deeds. That will almost certainly depend on the amount of attention the poor themselves are able to focus upon their needs. For it seems pretty clear that, as Alan Harrington
remarked recently, the war on poverty has been a reaction to the pressures generated by the
civil rights revolution, and would not otherwise have occurred.

Who are "the poor"? About two million families, a fourth of the poor living below the
poverty line, are headed by persons who work full time. "This figure dramatizes the fact that
low wages are still a major cause of poverty in the United States." Miller, *supra* at 610.
Another million and a half family heads work at full time jobs but are not employed an
entire year because of illness or layoffs. About two million families, another quarter of the
poor, are headed by women. Miller estimates that about $5 billion would bring all families
headed by women up to the minimum poverty line requirements. Right now however, though
$260 per month is the minimum necessary standard for a family of four headed by a woman,
only three states set their minimum budgets at or above this level. In several states the
median AFDC standard for such a family was $150 and for the country as a whole it is
$203. Even so, only "nineteen states actually make payments sufficient to bring all eligible
AFDC families up to their own excessively modest minimums. The others set dollar maximums
on the payments to any one family, regardless of size or needs, or, for fiscal reasons pay only
a percentage of the sum that elaborate investigation has shown to be needed." See Burns, *The
Poor Need Money*, 200 THE NATION 613-14 (1965).

Though the nonwhite population is about 11.8% of the total, about 25% of the poor are
nonwhite. The meaning of these figures takes on further significance when it is realized that

up absurd in Harlem or Watts than there was in Autherine Lucy or James Meredith being denied college educations, it follows that the government is constitutionally responsible in these areas in a way which the law must recognize upon pain of losing contact with reality. When former Attorney General Kennedy declared that twenty per cent of our population is "serving a life sentence of poverty"[45] his words accurately implied that a conscious choice, a negligent or deliberate policy condemns these millions. But by what constitutional authority may they be so "convicted"? If a legislative refusal to appropriate twelve billion dollars is the cause of their condemnation, are they not being punished unconstitutionally? Have they not been deprived of a judicial trial? Have they not been subjected to what is in effect a bill of attainder? Have they not been sentenced to cruel and unusual punishment? Are they not deprived of equal protection and due process of law?

Attorney General Katzenbach has noted the inequality between the poor and the comfortable in relation to the law. "To us," he said, "laws and regulations are protections and guides, established for our benefit, and for us to use. But to the poor, they are a hostile maze, established as harrassment, at all costs to be avoided."[46] Former Attorney General Kennedy went further. "The poor man," he said, "looks upon the law as an enemy, not as a friend. For him the law is always taking something away."[47] The law, as it were, is "separate" but hardly equal. Attorney General Katzenbach has added: "Small wonder then that the poor man

---

in 1940 the unemployment rates were 13% and 14.5% for whites and nonwhites respectively. By 1962 the corresponding figures were 4.9% for whites and 11% for nonwhites. Though Negro unemployment was only 12% above white in 1940, it was 125% greater in 1962. This reflected the fact that as unemployment increased after the war, it tended to concentrate among the unskilled and semi-skilled for various reasons, mainly the impact of the new technologies. In any event, the "race-gap" had grown approximately tenfold! Another aspect of this process appears in the fact that the gap between the earnings of Negro and white workers has grown steadily since the end of World War II. S. Doc. No. 86, 88th Cong., 2d Sess., 38 n.2 (1964); SELECT SUBCOMM. ON POVERTY OF THE COMM. ON LABOR AND PUBLIC WELFARE, THE WAR ON POVERTY, A COMPILATION OF MATERIALS RELEVANT TO S. 2642, at 38 n.2. In the light of such trends it should surprise no one that 44% of all recipients of Aid to Needy Children are Negro, more than 80% in ten northern cities. MAY, THE WASTED AMERICANS 23 (1964).

It is therefore to be expected that the drive for equality which has so rearranged the constitutional topography of the United States; this revolution in constitutional theory and law which has even driven the courts into reapportionment of political districts; this *civil rights revolution* is also going to compel us to come to grips with the relation between poverty and the constitution.

[45] Quoted in address by Attorney General Katzenbach in *Justice, Justice, Shall Ye Pursue*, to the Conference on Extension of Legal Service to the Poor, Washington, D.C., Nov. 12, 1964, p. 6.

[46] Quoted in WALD, *op. cit supra* note 40, at 6 n.14.

[47] *Id.* at n.13.

does not respect the law. He has little reason to believe it is his guardian; he has every reason to believe it is an instrument of the Other Society, of the well-off, the well-educated, the well-dressed, and the well-connected. The poor man is cut off from this society—and from the protection of its laws. We make of him a functional outlaw."[48]

But if as the Supreme Court said in the school desegregation cases, "separate" is "inherently unequal" even though "similar," what shall we say of it when it is hostilely dissimilar? If inequality generates in Negro students sent to segregated schools "a feeling of inferiority as to their status in the community that may affect their hearts and minds in a way unlikely ever to be undone,"[49] what shall we say of a system of law which strikes fear into the hearts and minds of the poor, which appears to them as a "hostile maze," "an enemy," and "at all costs to be avoided"?[50]

Such wrongs require remedies. This is not, of course, to suggest that immediate litigation of these questions is necessarily either possible or desirable as a strategic matter. But that is not the point here. Historically, the appeal to constitutional rights has served the needs of the poor and oppressed as a rallying cry, an inspiration, an ideal even though the courts denied that there were such rights as were appealed to. Nevertheless, the energies which were thus kindled brought ultimate success to the struggle for constitutional change and progress. From the abolitionists and suffragettes to the NAACP, CORE, SNCC, and The Welfare Rights Organization, the cry for justice, the demand for freedom, equality, and dignity has invoked, and derived power and sustenance from, the notion of constitutional entitlement. If there is to be a war against poverty, let us help to make it as effective as possible. It is clear that the poor will themselves have to bear the major brunt of the struggle, but we of the legal profession can help. As Attorney General Katzenbach has said, "One of the threshold problems in this new area is simply to make rights known. . . . For a poor person to hold rights in theory satisfies only the theory. We have to begin asserting those rights—and help the poor assert those rights. Unknown, unasserted rights are no rights at all."[51] We can show how the logic and the history, the rhetoric, and even some precedents regarding freedom, equality, and justice are with the poor whether or not courts are yet prepared to vindicate their rights. As we work together in these ways, we shall hasten the process of vindication. But, if this is not done, the law and the Constitution can not but seem at best to be irrelevant to and at

---

[48] Address by Attorney General Katzenbach to the National Conference on Law and Poverty, June 1965.

[49] Brown v. Board of Educ., 347 U.S. 483, 494 (1953).

[50] WALD, op. cit. supra note 41, at 6 n.14.

[51] Katzenbach, supra note 45, at 10-11.

worst a mockery of the deepest needs and hopes of millions of Americans. In a profound sense, the war against poverty is a war in defense of the constitution.

III

THE MEANS TEST, CHARITY, AND UNCONSTITUTIONAL CONDITIONS

Charity implies discretion. It presupposes the power to withhold as well as grant. When the means of existence may be manipulated, withheld, granted, those who have power over the means, also have power over the persons dependent upon those means. But, to speak of some having the power to withhold or grant the means of other's existence, is to speak of slavery. Nor is slavery inconsistent with charity. History informs us that benevolence has been found in all forms of despotic institutions. For charity depends upon power; indeed, it presupposes the existence of a great inequality of power as between the giver and the taker of charity. Charity in this sense therefore presupposes despotism. And while despots may be cruel or benevolent, it is their power to make the choice which earns them that title. Given despotic conditions, charity may certainly be ameliorative. But charity does not square with freedom. Historically, when paupers were regarded as criminals, or at least as immoral, it was taken for granted that they had either forfeited or failed to earn the rights of respectable citizens. Unlike the latter, they were not only not entitled to privacy, they were lucky to avoid imprisonment. When provided with charity in the form of shelter, they discovered that a house is not a home if it is a house of correction, an almshouse, or a poorhouse.

In any event, one who depends upon charity is one who depends upon the goodwill of a master. One who depends upon the goodwill of a master may be a slave, but he cannot be a free man; dependence is incompatible with independence; being forced to please another, one is precluded from pleasing himself. All this defines a condition which is the very opposite of that which the right to privacy is intended to protect. The principle of charity is at war with the principle of privacy, just as the principle of slavery was at war with the principle of equality, or freedom, or democracy.[52]

---

[52] An exchange of correspondence between a slaveholder and her fugitive slave, published in the Liberator, April 27, 1860, is illustrative. The slaveholder wrote: "I write you these lines to let you know the situation we are in,—partly in consequence of your running away and stealing Old Rock, our fine mare. Though we got the mare back, she never was worth much after you took her;—and, as I now stand in need of some funds I have determined to sell you and I have had an offer for you but did not see fit to take it. If you will send me one thousand dollars, and pay for the old mare, I will give up all claim I have to you. . . . If you do not comply with my request, I will sell you to someone else, and you may rest assured that the time is not far distant when things will be changed with you. . . . You know that we reared you as we reared our own children; that you was [sic]

The abolitionists believed and argued that slavery violated the fundamental basis upon which governments are instituted, the protection of the natural rights of men. Slavery was in their view, therefore, in violation of the political philosophy which underlay the establishment of our government, the basic and self-evident truth that all men are created equal and are endowed with inalienable rights of life, liberty, and the pursuit of happiness. Since on this view, the Constitution was an instrument which was created in the light of and to protect these values, slavery, which was at war with them was also in conflict with the constitution even prior to the Civil War amendments.[53]

The abolitionists did not, however, campaign against poverty or the treatment of the poor. The propagandists of the slaveowners tried to respond to antislavery arguments in part by arguing that the slave was better off than the wage worker; that the conditions of his existence frequently reduced him to a level of poverty rendering his circumstances at best similar but generally inferior to those of the chattel slave. But the propaganda was not very effective. The conditions of poverty in which the wage worker might find himself were impersonal. They were not permanent. They were not a function of any individual's or group's policy; indeed the assumption was that no individual or group of individuals had any control over these matters. Moreover, the existence of the frontier and the dynamic and open character of the society legally and economically provided a substantive basis for individual hope, freedom, dignity, even when down and out.

In today's America, practically all of these conditions are, if not reversed, radically changed, and poverty increasingly takes on the aspects of slavery. Today it is not the impersonal and inscrutable forces of the market which determine the character of the lives of the poor and their

---

never abused, and that shortly before you ran away, when your master asked if you would like to be sold, you said you would not leave him to go with anybody." The fugitive slave replied: "You say you have offers to buy me, and that you shall sell me if I do not send you $1,000, and in the same sentence, you say, 'You know we raised you as we did our own children.' Woman, did you raise *your own children* for the market? Did you raise them for the whipping post? Did you raise them to be driven off, bound to a coffle in chains? Where are my poor bleeding brothers and sisters? Can you tell?. . . . But you say I am a thief because I took the old mare along with me. Have you got to learn that I had a better right to the old mare, as you call her, than Manesseth Logue had to me? Is it a greater sin for me to steal his horse, than it was for him to rob my mother's cradle, and steal me? If he and you infer that I forfeit all my rights to you, shall not I infer that you forfeit all your rights to me? Have you got to learn that human rights are mutual and reciprocal, and if you take my liberty and life, you forfeit your own liberty and life? Before God and high heaven, is there a law for one man which is not a law for every other man?" Quoted in APTHEKER, A DOCUMENTARY HISTORY OF THE NEGRO PEOPLE IN THE UNITED STATES 449-51 (1951).

[53] See tenBroek, *supra* note 22.

destiny; it is not a matter of the invisible hand arranging their fate; but rather the legislative and bureaucratic hand of state. Policy, law, regulations, administrators, social workers, probation officers—these are the responsible and manipulative personal forces which shape the lives of millions; not the invisible hand of fate, but the accountable power of government.

But if that power is accountable, to whom is it accountable? The unfortunate fact is that this power, which theoretically is accountable to all citizens, is not accountable to the poor, but it is rather the other way around. Because the welfare program is so largely constructed on the principle of charity as embodied in the means test approach, those who dispense the means of existence virtually maintain the recipients of welfare in a condition of bondage. Incurring the ill will of such persons can result in deprivation of desperately needed funds, being forced to change one's deepest habits,[54] or even losing one's children or going to jail. Even if welfare grants were adequate to the task of allowing for the acquisition of the physical prerequisites of privacy, the conditions under which they are dispensed would destroy the possibility of achieving it.

Free men are those who have and use the power to manage their affairs in accordance with their own judgment; they determine for themselves whether their needs are being met. That must be the direction in which power is accountable in a free society. But the basis upon which welfare benefits are distributed is directly contrary to these assumptions: Need is judged not by the recipient of the grant, but by its dispenser; moreover, the grant varies with the dispenser's judgment of the existence, size, and character of the need and also the character of the recipient. The means test or charity principle upon which welfare assistance is based, thus violates and is utterly incompatible with the right to privacy because the latter is centrally concerned with the freedom to be an individual, a functioning member of a self-governing community, while the means test renders impossible "the direction of one's affairs, the whole basic principle of self-management."[55] Twelve years ago, tenBroek and Wilson in a seminal article[56] masterfully analyzed the contradiction between these principles:

---

[54] "Appellant also argues that he has a right to live as he pleases . . . . One would admire his independence if he were not so dependent . . . . One is impressed with appellant's argument that he enjoys the life he leads in his humble 'home' as he calls it . . . .

"It is true, as appellant argues, that the hardy pioneers of our country slept in beds not better than the one he has chosen, . . . but unlike the appellant, . . . they did not call upon the public to support them . . . ." Wilkie v. O'Connor, 261 App. Div. 373, 375, 25 N.Y.S.2d 617, 619 (1941).

[55] tenBroek & Wilson, *Public Assistance and Social Insurance—A Normative Evaluation*, 1 U.C.L.A.L. REV. 237, 264 (1954).

[56] *Ibid.*

Under it [the means test], the individual recipient soon loses control of his daily activities and the whole course and direction of his life. The capacity for self-direction presently atrophies and drops away. It is the welfare agency rather than the individual which decides what wants shall be taken into account. It is the welfare agency which decides what needs shall be budgeted. It is the welfare agency which decides how much shall be allocated to meet each of them. The smallness, character and scrutiny of the budget result in a welfare agency domination of a supposedly free consumption choce and a corresponding frustration of the principle of cash payments. It is the welfare agency, moreover, which decides what resources are to be treated as available for the individual's support and how he is to utilize them for that purpose. The agency tells him when, how and in what circumstances he can dispose of his property, what returns he must get and the manner of its payment. In these circumstances, it is an idle formalism to say, as many state statutes and rules do say, that the payment is an over-all amount no part of which is required to be spent for any given purpose or that there shall be no dictation as to where and how a recipient shall live. The formal sanctions are there and are compelling. If the recipient does not live up to the conditions and do so with alacrity, he may be removed from the rolls or have his budget reduced. The alternatives are thus obedience or starvation. The informal sanction—consisting of the social worker's participation in the recipient's affairs—are also there and are no less continuing and impressive than the formal. With each new item budgeted or eliminated, with each new resource tracked down and evaluated, the social worker's influence increases. This is an inevitable concomitant of the means test. It results from the nature and extent of the system. It is bred and nourished by the provisions of the statutes and the rules issued under them. It is in the flexible joints of the cumbersome machinery. It is in the inescapable confinements of the budget. It is in the idleness, defeatism and waning spirit of the recipient. Whatever the social worker's wishes and intentions, her hand becomes the agency of direction in his affairs. . . .

. . . [D]ignity is jeopardized by the initial investigation, by the searching inquiry into every intimate detail of need, living habits, family relations, by the setting up of a detailed budget of expenditures subject to repeated examination and review, by the continuously implied and often explicit threat that if behaviour is uncooperative or unapproved, aid will be reduced or stopped . . . and, finally by the constant tendency of the whole system to push living standards down below a minimun of decency and health.

. . . [M]eans test aid is fundamentally antithetical to the idea of equality. A system which makes so much depend upon a minute examination of every aspect of the individual's situation necessarily involves personalized judgments by officials and invites arbitrary and whimsical exercises of power, prevents the enforcement of a uniform rule . . . renders it impossible for the recipient himself to determine to what he is entitled . . . for complying with the purpose of providing a minimum standard of living, disability and absence of income, or age and absence of income [the latter can easily be determined from income tax returns] are the factors of relevance in determining eligibility. Equality requires that all who possess them should be treated alike. In this regard, means test aid stands in striking contrast not only to the requirements of equality but also to the manner in which assistance is granted to other groups: to youth by public education; to farmers by parity payments and other assistance; to industrialists and others by tariffs; to labor by minumum wages. In none of these cases is aid granted by an individual means test or by an invasion of rights of self-management in personal affairs. Assistance is upon a group basis, with need determined or presumed from characteristics of the group or situation in which they find themselves and with allocations of aid upon a fixed grant formula. . . .

. . . Since means test aid requires that all income and resources of the recipient be applied to meet his current needs, and since the public assistance grant is reduced by the amount of any such available income or resources, the usual financial motive for effort and endeavor is removed.[57]

It is sometimes said, by persons of good will, that the "means test" is simply a name for government's efforts to prevent cheating; that it is a necessary and common device, encountered, for example, in the income tax; and that it does not discriminate against the poor. The point which such criticism misses is that a test which considers means is not necessarily a means test. Surely, the income tax considers "means." But it is not a means test. A means test concerns itself with the question whether an individual or a family has sufficient resources (including everything from labor power, to a change in consumer values and tastes, to savings) to justify denial or diminution of assistance to help secure the bare minima of existence. Such a question always and necessarily involves the substitution of the welfare agent's judgment and information for that of the recipient's. The agent in a real sense thus becomes the recipient, taking over his most intimate and basic functions, pre-empting his freedom, dignity, and humanity and destroying his privacy. This is not the case in any sense in the other situations where "means" are considered, as in the income tax. First, the income tax does not even attach unless some minimal income, exempt from taxation, is exceeded. As to the excess, the way it is handled is strictly the taxpayer's business. Moreover, in addition to being independent in the ways he chooses to use his income, he is also independent of the threat of having his necessaries cut off if he does not please some agent who thinks he knows better than the taxpayer how his income and resources should be deployed. Indeed, the tax agents may not search financial records without a court order if the taxpayer chooses to

[57] *Id.* at 264-66.

resist scrutiny.[58] Not only is such resistance not a matter of losing the bare necessities of existence, but once a court order issues, permitting such searches, they are strictly and narrowly limited to financial records; they have no bearing upon such questions as how a mother is to bring up her children; whether she should work or stay home; how much rent is within reason; what sort of neighborhood she may live in; whether she may move; what resources her relatives possess; and whether she is having an affair.

These are the reasons why the means test approach of our current welfare practices and the laws and regulations which require and sanction them are incompatible with the right to privacy and other fundamental constitutional guarantees.[59] The means test should therefore be stricken from our welfare programs as an unconstitutional condition. Striking the means test would at the same time eliminate other unconstitutional practices such as midnight raids, relatives responsibility requirements, and residence requirements. But the charity principle still will linger in the inadequacy of the grants themselves, and this will require a different constitutional attack.

Unconstitutional conditions may not be attached to rights, privileges, or gratuities. In the recent case of *Torcaso v. Watkins*,[60] the Supreme Court said that this point was "settled by our holding in Wieman v. Updegraff . . . . We there pointed out that whether or not 'an abstract right to public employment exists,' Congress could not pass a law providing 'that no federal employee shall attend Mass or take any active part in missionary work.' " In *Sherbert v. Verner*,[61] the Supreme Court further

---

[58] *Cf.* United States v. Powell, 379 U.S. 48 (1964).

[59] In Department of Mental Hygiene v. Kirchner, 60 Cal. 2d 716, 388 P.2d 720, 36 Cal. Rptr. 488 (1964), the responsibility of relatives provisions were striken out of the California law dealing with the mentally irresponsible. The California Supreme Court held that public responsibility for the mentally ill requires the costs of that responsibility to be borne by the public and that "a statute obviously violates the equal protection clause if it selects one particular class of persons for a species of taxation . . . . [for the cost of programs properly benefiting the public] cannot be arbitrarily charged to one class in the society." *Id.* at 722, 720, 388 P.2d at 724, 722, 36 Cal. Rptr. at 492, 490. It can be argued, also, that the means test as a whole, which Professor tenBroek has shown to be largely motivated by cost-cutting considerations and thus to constitute a species of regressive and special taxation, violates the guarantee of equality. Certainly the provision of assistance to the aged and the families with needy children for example is as valid a public function as the hospitalization of the mentally irresponsible. And certainly it is as valid a public function as the provision of public schools, or assistance to farmers. Yet the latter, though similarly situated with reference to public support and benefit, are not treated the way welfare recipients are, either with respect to the financial or the privacy aspects of the means test. The classification of welfare recipients is therefore arbitrary and invidiously discriminatory and violative of the guarantee of equal protection.

[60] 367 U.S. 488, 496 (1961).

[61] 374 U.S. 398, 404-05 (1963).

pointed out that "it is too late in the day to doubt that the liberties of religion and expression may be infringed by the denial or placing of conditions upon a benefit or privilege . . . . In *Speiser v. Randall* . . . we emphasized that conditions upon public benefits cannot be sustained if they so operate, whatever their purpose, as to inhibit or deter the exercise of First Amendment freedoms."

Where fundamental constitutional rights are involved, such as the right to privacy, "conditions upon public benefits cannot be sustained if they so operate, whatever their purpose, as to inhibit or deter [their] . . . exercise . . . ."[62]

There can be no question but that the conditions labeled the "means test" under which welfare benefits are distributed "inhibit or deter" the exercise of the right to privacy. It is clear that these conditions not only inhibit and deter but violate this fundamental right. The much publicized midnight raids in the course of which teams of fraud investigators ransack the homes of welfare recipients looking for "men in the home" are clearly unconstitutional violations of the fourth amendment, as Reich has shown.[63] Yet such raids are only the most spectacularly unconstitutional aspects of the means test approach. A simple declaration of the unconstitutionality of the means test principle would render the entire machinery of man-hunting, the complete cop-kit of fraud investigators, bedroom snoopers, child disturbers utterly irrelevant to the welfare process, as indeed they are now except for their deleterious effects upon any of the legitimate or constructive purposes of welfare. Doubtless test cases now pending will result in a judicial declaration of the unconstitutionality of midnight raids.[64] The danger inherent in this situation is that persons concerned with the protection of privacy will feel that the problem will have been solved since the most visible manifestation of the abuse of the right will have been stopped. But the subsurface part of the iceberg will not have been disturbed by such a victory and the danger is that in the legitimate celebration of such a genuinely significant step forward in the vindication of the fundamental rights of Americans and of the principle that the condition of a man's purse should not condition his fundamental rights, the unfinished task will be forgotten.

It is important therefore to emphasize that the means test is unconstitutional as a violation of or at the least a deterrence to or inhibition upon

---

[62] *Id.* at 405.

[63] Reich, *Midnight Welfare Searches and the Social Security Act*, 72 Yale L.J. 1347 (1963).

[64] Parrish v. Civil Service Comm'n, 1 Civil no. 22, 556, 1st Dist. Cal., *appeal filed* Jan. 7, 1965. Benny Parrish, a social worker, was fired for insubordination when he refused on legal and constitutional grounds to participate in a mass "bed check" operation conducted by the Alameda County Welfare Department in January 1963.

the exercise of the right to privacy. The only justification which can be brought forward in support of the means test approach is that by using it the state can shave the costs of the program. What is balanced against the fundamental right to privacy, therefore, is the state's interest in economy. Long ago in the case of *Schneider v. Irvington*,[65] Justice Roberts pointed out that fundamental civil liberties were not to be endangered on grounds of economy. Doubtless the requirements of the fourth amendment add to the costs of operating government; but no court would entertain the suggestion that the use of warrants be curtailed because it would be cheaper to dispense with the use of judges. The costs of protecting fundamental rights are real enough and they must be borne. It is doubtful that an argument could be persuasively constructed to suggest that a justification for the means test is the state's right to "rehabilitate" welfare recipients. If the poor are not by the fact of their poverty rendered immoral, their poverty can hardly serve as a justification for discriminating between them and the rest of the population in moral terms. Rehabilitation, if it is to be meaningful, can not be properly approached punitively. The means test is an outgrowth of outworn and unconstitutional assumptions such as the assumption that poor persons are morally responsible for their plight and that their bad character needs careful scrutiny in order to prevent cheating.

In any event, the state must bear the burden of proof if it wishes to save a practice which violates, inhibits, or deters fundamental rights. This is a particularly heavy burden: "[W]here there is a significant encroachment upon personal liberty, the State may prevail only upon showing a subordinating interest which is compelling."[66] Such a practice or law must be shown to be "necessary, and not merely rationally related, to the accomplishment of a permissible state policy."[67] This latter requirement renders it virtually impossible for the means test to withstand a constitutional assault in the name of the right to privacy because there is no necessary connection of the sort required. The test for the presence of a necessary connection rather than a rational relation is the test as to whether the state can prove that no alternative methods are available to it whereby it can serve its legitimate purposes without violating, inhibiting, or deterring fundamental rights.[68] Does the state desire to rehabilitate persons? The alternative of making teachers and schools and employment of an attractive character available to the recipients can certainly not be shown to be unavailable. What evidence can the state offer that such alternatives are

[65] 308 U.S. 147 (1939).
[66] Bates v. City of Little Rock, 361 U.S. 516, 524 (1960).
[67] McLaughlin v. Florida, 379 U.S. 184, 196 (1964).
[68] Sherbert v. Verner, 374 U.S. 398 (1963).

not viable? "Mere legislative preferences or beliefs may well support regulation directed at other personal activities, but be insufficient to justify such as diminishes the exercise of rights so vital to the maintenance of democratic institutions."[69] Finally, "precision of regulation must be the touchstone in an area so closely touching our most precious freedoms."[70] Even "though the governmental purpose be legitimate and substantial, that purpose cannot be pursued by means that broadly stifle fundamental personal liberties when the end can be more narrowly achieved. The breadth of legislative abridgment must be viewed in the light of less drastic means for achieving the same basic purpose."[71] The essence of the means test inheres in the amount of discretion vested in official persons to make determinations about the lives of others. As we have seen, this is as broad a power as the right which the recipient would have, under normal circumstances, to determine his own needs, likes, and desires. This hardly comports with the "precision" required of regulation in areas so "closely touching our most precious freedoms."[72] This is not precision but annihilation. The breadth of this power may also be appreciated by viewing it from a slightly different angle of vision. As a condition of receiving assistance, mothers of needy children must "cooperate" with the district attorney's office,[73] generally for purposes of locating absent fathers. As a result, many county law enforcement officers use lie detectors on AFDC mothers and fathers.[74] An opinion of the California legislative counsel states that "the use of such a device . . . suggests a refusal on the part of the county to accept an applicant's statements as truthful and certainly does not demonstrate respect for the integrity and self esteem of the applicant."[75] Disrespect for the right of privacy inevitably issues in a reversal of the presumption of innocence and the tendency to supervise totally, to maintain total surveillance, and thus progressively to undermine the right to the point of extinction.[76]

---

[69] Schneider v. Irvington, 308 U.S. 147 (1939).

[70] NAACP v. Button, 371 U.S. 415, 438 (1963).

[71] Shelton v. Tucker, 364 U.S. 479, 488 (1960).

[72] NAACP v. Button, 371 U.S. 415, 438 (1963).

[73] See, e.g., CAL. WELFARE & INST'NS CODE § 11477.

[74] See tenBroek, California's Dual System of Family Law: Its Origin, Development, and Present Status, 17 STAN. L. REV. 614, 666 (1965).

[75] Opinion of the California Legislative Counsel No. 4247 (July 15, 1960), quoted in tenBroek, supra note 53.

[76] Compare the recent statement of Gunnar Myrdal at a national conference on poverty held at the University of California, Berkeley, February 26-28, 1965: "The social security system, including the provision of health facilities for all who need it, has to be reformed in a radical fashion. Incidentally, I believe somebody should look into the history of social security in America and how it is continually imprisoned in out-dated conceptions. I think it is too closely related to that old man Bismarck and our old friend Lloyd George, who were pioneers in this field, but who characterized the social problem as eine Arbeiterfrage.

The means test, it must be concluded, is an unconstitutional condition parasitically fastened upon and destructive of the privacy of millions of Americans.

IV

THE UNCONSTITUTIONALITY OF INADEQUATE WELFARE GRANTS

The right to counsel is guaranteed by and is an obligation of government. The obligation can be discharged in two ways, either through the "private" arrangements which usually suffice to make it possible for those who desire counsel to employ a lawyer, or through "public" provision of the services of lawyers for those who cannot privately arrange for them.

In the same way, the right to privacy is an obligation of government. Though private arrangements generally have sufficed with regard to securing this right for very many, it is understood that where private arrangements prove inadequate, government provision must fill the gap.

As we have seen, unconstitutional conditions, such as requiring those for whom counsel is to be provided to adhere to a particular religion, may not be attached to the provision of any governmental service whether it is the provision of an obligation or a gratuity. That would merely be to attempt to do indirectly what could not be done directly.

The direct governmental obligation to provide counsel to those who cannot privately engage a lawyer is capable of being subverted in many ways: one, of course, is the method of requiring the forfeiture of another constitutional right as the price of providing this one—as in the example of the forfeiture of religious freedom; another, is simply the insufficiency of the very right ostensibly being furnished—as, for example, would be the case if the lawyer provided to an indigent defendant were inadequately trained to do the job.[77] And, of course, the same result would obtain if the government flatly declined to furnish a lawyer at all.

In the same way, the governmental obligation to protect the right to privacy can be variously subverted and undermined. Certainly, no one would deny that the government could not constitutionally require adherence to a particular religion as a condition of furnishing food or shelter to the destitute. Neither would anyone contend that the government could constitutionally require all shelters furnished to the indigent to be bugged and equipped with hidden cameras for the purpose of providing the welfare authorities with the opportunity for total surveillance. By the

---

I am proud that in my own country, Sweden, when we inaugurated an old-age pension reform in 1911, the labor party was eager to stress that we did not want to have the benefits subject to any condition except residence in the country. We wanted to give security to all as a right of citizenship. . . . This, of course, also simplifies the whole administration." Quoted in GORDON, POVERTY IN AMERICA 437 (1965).

[77] See, e.g., Brubaker v. Dickson, 310 F.2d 30 (9th Cir. 1962).

same token, the provision of food or shelter inadequate to the purpose of maintaining the minimal standards for political and social existence, given the ability to make adequate provision, would undermine the right to privacy.

A. Beyond Unconstitutional Conditions

The doctrine of unconstitutonal conditions is vital to the task of maintaining the integrity of the Constitution and the principles which it must serve. It serves to shore up constitutional rights against the erosion which can attend government action. But it does not help in the case of govermnental inaction, the case where the government refuses to do anything.

This poses a practical problem, particularly in the welfare field, in the following way. As a practical matter, it is clear that we as a nation will not allow anyone to starve or be deprived of shelter. But even if no one will be allowed to starve, or live in the street like a stray cat, the "other America" is still a reality, and the people in the other America, though they may be hidden from view, do not necessarily enjoy privacy. As a matter of fact, we know that they do not participate in the enjoyment or use of their fundamental rights and that the reason is simply that they are not meaningfully available to them.

Here it should be remembered that the paupers of seventeenth-century England were not allowed to starve either, or to live in the streets. But that did not mean that they were given the minimal means of privacy or dignified existence. In the same way, the mere fact that we will make provision for the poor, and that in the process we will refrain from committing outrages upon them such as sending them to jail, or requiring them to wear big P's for "pauper" emblazoned on their clothes (as used to be required in the state of Pennsylvania);[78] or raiding their homes at night, or forcing them to adopt or relinquish any religious or political beliefs (though we have attempted the latter in the form of loyalty oaths as a condition of housing[79] and are attempting it even now in other connec-

---

[78] "The need for or the actual receipt of assistance created . . . a veritable *'pauper statis.'* Thus the pauper was required to wear a badge with the letter P, a practice which was first given statutory sanction by the Pennsylvania Poor Law Amendment Act of 1718, 3 Pa. Stat. at L. 1712-1724, 221 (1896); he was required to be farmed out to the bidder at public auction, see, *e.g.*, Indiana Poor Law of 1807 . . . ; he could be thrown into the poor-house against his will, see, *e.g.*, Harrison v. Gilbert, 71 Conn. 724, 43 Atl. 190 (1899) (denying a writ of habeas corpus); he could and apparently still can, without violation of the constitutional guarantees, be forcibly removed to his place of settlement; Lovell v. Seeback, 45 Minn. 465, 48 N.W. 23 (1891); he lost the right to vote and still does under the constitution of Massachusetts, Mass. Const. Art. of Amendments III, and Texas, Tex. Const. Art. VI, Sec. 1." RIESENFELD & MAXWELL, MODERN SOCIAL LEGISLATION 709 (1950).

[79] The courts of three states rejected the notion of conditioning public housing on loyalty tests. Housing Authority v. Cordova, 130 Cal. App. 2d 883, 279 P.2d 215 (Super.

tions[80])—all this does not mean that we shall be furnishing the essentials of the right to privacy or other fundamental rights.

If we are to provide those essentials necessary to the meaningful exercise of the right to privacy, we shall have to establish minimal criteria of privacy in order to meet the practical problem posed not by the refusal to furnish any assistance at all, and not by the imposition of outrageous unconstitutional conditions of high visibility such as mass midnight raids, nor even by the more subtle though not less virulent unconstitutional invasion of privacy which the means tests approach involves, but by the meagreness of the grant, the insufficiency of the funds, and the inadequacy of the housing provided.

The establishment of such criteria is not an insuperably difficult task; the President's Council of Economic Advisers, the Heller Committee, and others are constantly working on such questions.

The difficult task is making it clear and winning acceptance for the proposition that decent minimal standards are constitutionally required because the freedom of the individual is as much threatened by the failure to meet them as it is when the criminal courts fail to provide counsel and other minimal prerequisites of due process. And it must be made clear that poverty is not a constitutionally acceptable reason for deprivation of freedom in either case. Freedom of this sort is not for sale.

Yet, as we have noted, a root problem which must be dealt with is the persistence of the habit of thought that views access to the basic necessities of life by those who lack them not as a matter of right, of entitlement, but as a matter of charity. On this approach, it is not a matter of constitutional concern if the basic necessities are not available to all even if the power to make them available is unquestioned. The provision of some or all of such necessaries is seen as a matter of legislative discretion, and the implication, therefore, is that if the legislature should choose *not* to provide any welfare benefits it would be as constitutionally free as if it chose *to* provide them.

In order to appreciate the depth to which this gnarled root reaches in the psychology of the nation, it may be useful to recall that it was only yesterday, figuratively speaking, that the Supreme Court held that the Constitution even *permitted* legislative protection of the poor and dependent against the ravages of unrestrained economic power.

Not until 1936, for example, did the Supreme Court agree that the rights of employers could constitutionally be limited by legislatures

---

Ct. 1955); Chicago Housing Authority v. Blackman, 4 Ill. 2d 319, 122 N.E.2d 522 (1954); Lawson v. Housing Authority, 270 Wis. 269, 70 N.W.2d 605 (1955).

[80] The Economic Opportunity Act, 78 Stat. 533 (1964), 42 U.S.C. § 2966 (1964), as amended, 42 U.S.C. § 2966 (Supp. I, 1965), includes a loyalty oath requirement.

desirous of protecting the worker even if only to provide for minimum wages. In the midst of the most cataclysmic economic crisis the nation had ever known, only the barest majority of the Court could be mustered to agree that there was no equality of power between sweat shop employers and workers who were defenseless against a denial of a minimally decent wage, and that minimum wage legislation was therefore not a violation of freedom of contract and a denial of due process. "What these workers lose in wages," the Chief Justice angrily remarked, "the taxpayers are called upon to pay. The bare cost of living must be met . . . . The community is not bound to provide what is in effect a subsidy for unconscionable employers."[81] Indeed, the validity of the Social Security Act was attacked in the Supreme Court the following year, partly on the ground that the law was class legislation and not in the interest of the general welfare. This time, Justice Cardozo, again for the narrowest majority, found it necessary to point out some facts of life which one would have thought were so immense and insistent as not to be avoidable:

> During the years 1929 to 1936, when the country was passing through a cyclical depression, the number of the unemployed mounted to unprecedented heights. Often the average was more than ten million; at times a peak was attained of 16 million or more. Disaster to the breadwinner meant disaster to dependents. Accordingly the roll of the unemployed, itself formidable enough, was only a partial role of the destitute or needy. The fact developed quickly that the states were unable to give the requisite relief. The problem had become national in area and dimension. There was need of help from the nation if the people were not to starve.[82]

But even in the face of such unprecedented catastrophe men pressed the argument that the nation could not constitutionally provide unemployment insurance. To this Justice Cardozo impatiently responded: "It is too late today for the argument to be heard with tolerance that in a crisis so extreme the use of the moneys of the nation to relieve the unemployed and their dependents is a use for any purpose narrower than the promotion of the general welfare."[83]

Thus, reluctantly, under the most relentless and implacable pressure, was the constitutionality of the state's *discretion* to enact welfare measures finally acceded to by the Supreme Court. Some of the welfare measures seemed to have the character of insurance or property rights; others were more like simple charity. Some commentators have urged, in their desire to protect the poor person's access to benefits, that they should all be viewed as property rights. That would, of course, be an improve-

---

81 West Coast Hotel v. Parrish, 300 U.S. 379, 399 (1936).
82 Steward Machine Co. v. Davis, 301 U.S. 548, 586 (1937).
83 *Id.* at 586-87.

ment. But legislative discretion to confer benefits is also of course discretion to terminate them. Even if they are viewed not as gratuitous privileges, but as property rights bestowed by statute, future welfare benefits may be rescinded with the statute that bestows them. To be sure, the procedural protection available in the latter case is somewhat more substantial than in the former, while the benefits are provided; but one must question the assumption that equates the protections against deprivation of property with those against deprivations of fundamental human rights.

Fundamental human rights, it must be understood, are not mere property rights—though, to be sure, economic support is a partial condition of their existence. Yet, we commonly view access to the bare necessities of existence not as a matter of constitutional entitlement, even on the level of property rights. It is merely a matter of discretion, largesse, or charity.

B. Property Rights versus Human Rights

If the right to privacy is a fundamental human right, it is not a lesser right than the right to counsel. Gideon was not provided with a lawyer because there were "good-hearted people" willing to "help" him. He did not say, "Please, out of the depths of your generosity may I have the privilege of the assistance of counsel?" His position before the state was not that of a suppliant; it was that of a sovereign, a citizen. He said, "I cannot be tried unless counsel is provided because the Constitution forbids it." He did not acquire that right or lose it with any personal acquisition or loss of funds. Though there is an economically measurable cost attached to the right Gideon claimed, that right is not for sale. It costs money to have judges, but it does not follow that judgments can be purchased. Gideon's right stemmed from his status as a human being in a society where sovereignty is in the people; it had nothing to do with the status of his purse; it had everything to do with the constitutional scheme of our society. That scheme locates the fundamental rights in the people—not the rich or the employed, but the people. Those rights do not depend upon the good will of anyone, of any class, or of any government. The only power which government possesses with regard to them is the power to protect them. Indeed, in that regard, government not only is empowered to do so, it is under the most basic obligation to do so, for that is why governments, according to the political philosophy underlying our Constitution and expressed in the Declaration of Independence, are instituted. These reasons have nothing to do with mere property rights. It is not true that civil liberty depends on property rights.[84] If it were, we should have to explain why the Constitution protects property only to the extent that

---

[84] But see Reich, The New Property, 73 YALE L.J. 733, 771 (1964): "Indeed, in the final analysis the Bill of Rights depends upon the existence of private property."

a rational basis for dealing with it is required of a legislature, thus satisfying due process,[85] whereas the Constitution protects fundamental human rights far more stringently. [86] The answer, surely, must be close to the fact that the forms in which property is held could alter drastically without threatening our constitutional structure, but the constitutional structure itself obviously could not be so dealt with. As Justice Holmes once put it, the Constitution did not enact Mr. Herbert Spencer's social statics or any other specific economic doctrine.[87] The essence of the Constitution is the political doctrine which it embodies. Free speech, privacy, freedom from self-incrimination—these are simply not to be experimented with (as property, however, may be) on rational grounds without first amending the Constitution. And legislatures do not possess that authority. The fact that men must eat if they are to have the strength to speak is therefore an important clue as to the distinction between "property" and "fundamental rights." That which is essential to the exercise of fundamental rights must be treated as part of them. That which is not essential to their exercise must not be treated as if it were. A minimum income therefore cannot rightly be viewed as "property" and property should not be confused with civil liberty.

Thus, in the realm of fundamental rights—at least in the area of the fundamental right to counsel—it is clear that the notion of charity is out of place; that the notion of such rights as a function of or dependent upon property or economic power is alien; that the philosophy expressed in the phrase "who pays the piper calls the tune" is excluded. Moreover, it is also clear that refusal to provide counsel to indigent defendants could not be justified in any of the ways that courts justify the cancellation or revocation of a property right. A "rational basis" would not justify such a legislative decision. If it could be justified at all, it would be possible to do so only on grounds of grave national emergency rendering the government incapable of maintaining the courts.[88] It is, however, difficult to believe that even such circumstances could justify such discrimination against the poor any more than it would justify such discrimination against a particular racial or religious group.

[85] Cf. Ex Parte Milligan, 71 U.S. (4 Wall.) 2 (1886).

[86] "[T]he existence of facts supporting the legislative judgment is to be presumed, for regulatory legislation affecting ordinary commercial transactions is not to be pronounced unconstitutional unless in the light of the facts made known or generally assumed it is of such a character as to preclude the assumption that it rests upon some rational basis within the knowledge and experience of the legislators." United States v. Carolene Prods. Co., 304 U.S. 144, 152 (1939).

[87] See Lochner v. New York, 198 U.S. 45, 75 (1905) (dissenting opinion).

[88] "[O]nly the gravest abuses, endangering paramount interests, give occasion for permissible limitation." Thomas v. Collins, 323 U.S. 516, 530 (1945).

The fact, however, is that we treat those of our citizens for whom the costs of necessaries must be met out of public rather than private funds as though they are second-class citizens. But if fundamental constitutional rights are not for sale where is the authority for issuing second-class rights to be found? The answer is that there is no such authority; that the reason for the practice is to be found in incorrect, outmoded, and muddled attitudes that do not square with constitutional assumptions. Constitutionally, people must be provided with the essentials for behaving as sovereign citizens. If that means a minimum income for all who need it, minimum education, housing—so be it.[89]

Of course there will be those who will throw up the straw man of "socialism" or "paternalism"; but such arguments are specious. Constitutionally, they are irrelevant; politically, they are misconceived. Even Friedrich Hayek, certainly no advocate of "socialism," has argued that "there is no reason why in a society which has reached the general level of wealth which ours has attained, . . . security [the certainty of a given minimum of sustenance for all] should not be guaranteed to all without endangering general freedom."[90] Moreover, it is not a question of "endangering" freedom; rather, it is a question of realizing it. Furnishing counsel to an indigent defendant is not a danger to freedom; it is a protection and a condition of it. Providing all persons with the minimal prerequisites of privacy is a guarantee and a condition of and not a threat to freedom.

On the contrary, the threat to freedom comes rather from those who consider the recipients of welfare to be less than full citizens and persons, even if not quite criminals, and therefore fair game for treatment they would consider unconstitutional if applied to persons of means. For it is

---

[89] The California Supreme Court in Manjares v. Newton, 64 AC 378, 411 P.2d 901, 49 Cal. Rptr. 805 (1966), held that there was an affirmative duty to provide transportation to students.

[90] HAYEK, THE ROAD TO SERFDOM 120 (1944); cf. Milton Friedman's suggestion of the "Negative Income Tax," which would bring all incomes up to some socially acceptable minimum. Robert Heilbroner has recently commented on such suggestions, "Indeed, I think such a plan is the most effective next step we can take in alleviating the misery of many impoverished persons, and I am happy to note its inclusion in the recent report of the President's Commission on Automation . . . . But alleviating poverty is one thing, and shoring up all incomes close to the line of present earnings is another. A world in which labor (including middle-class labor) no longer felt the lash of necessity would no doubt be a better world, but it would not be a world that the market system could control." Heilbroner, *The Controversy over Automation*, The New York Review, March 17, 1966, pp. 12, 15. Compare Article 25 (1) of the Universal Declaration of Human Rights: "Everyone has the right to a standard of living adequate for the health and well-being of himself and of his family, including food, clothing, housing and medical care and necessary social services, and the right to security in the event of unemployment, sickness, disability, widowhood, old age or other lack of livelihood in circumstances beyond his control."

such attitudes, the attitude which confuses property with human rights, which considers wealth not merely a mark of fortune but of moral and political superiority, which envisions the provision of necessaries as charity, which sees poverty as a function of personal fault, which seeks to coerce conformity under the banner of "rehabilitation"—attitudes which in short are self-righteously or even negligently consistent with the willingness to intrude upon and manage the lives of others, these are the real threat to freedom. It is the right to *invade* privacy which such attitudes nurture, and the very greatest danger to freedom is that we shall become insensitive to the outrage in proportion to its increasing practice.

Privacy is the protection of the person against authority; it is the guarantee that the individual and not the state shall remain primary; that the state shall serve the needs of the individual, not that the individual shall be a servant of the state. It is therefore the protection of the authority of the person. Respect for privacy, respect for individual integrity, requires that one respect oneself. The government agent or private person who taps wires, who plants bugs, who snoops upon the intimacy of others cannot have any respect for his own privacy, for as a matter of principle he could have no objection to others doing to him what he himself practices. He thereby demonstrates disrespect for the rights of others as well as himself. How can we avoid the conclusion that he is the most dangerous threat to constitutional freedoms? For who will defend the Constitution if its guarantees are only to be found in its parchment? The only ultimate protection of constitutional freedom is in its practice. The alarming presence and increase of attitudes and practices violative of privacy in America is what endangers freedom. This is the source of "Big Brother's" power.

The protection of the right to privacy is therefore not merely a protection of the private rights of individuals, but it is also a protection of a most fundamental aspect of the public interest. It is a protection of freedom itself. That is why no infringement of so fundamental a right can be justified on any grounds which might suffice to justify invasions of lesser rights such as property rights. Property rights may be regulated and abridged *in* the public interest. Privacy, like freedom of speech, is itself an aspect *of* the public interest.

Civil liberty is indivisible; there cannot be one law for the poor and another for the rich; there cannot be one freedom for the whites and another for the blacks; there cannot be one standard of privacy for the righteous, or the loyal, or the good, and another for the wicked, the disloyal, and the bad. Civil liberty is not for sale and it is not a matter of charity. No man and no government has the discretion to divide it, dole it, or withdraw it. That is the meaning of equality: not that all must be identical, but that all are entitled to live under and enjoy the genuine protection of equal laws; not that all shall have the same happiness, but that all shall have the same right to pursue it, each in his own way, and not as someone else determines. "Each in his own way" and "not as someone else determines" implies, of course, that none shall through his pursuit interfere with the capacity of others to conduct theirs. That is the meaning of the indivisibility of liberty. That is the content of the guarantee of privacy. Poverty degrades people, divides liberty, and undermines privacy. That is why poverty must be rendered a "neutral" fact. That is why poverty must be defeated.

Unconstitutional Conditions: Welfare Benefits with Strings Attached

Robert M. O'Neil*

MAY A STATE COMPEL a foreign corporation, in order to transact business within the state, to forego removal of lawsuits to the federal courts?[1] May the same state require recipients of welfare benefits to agree not to join certain political organizations while they receive benefits? Surprisingly, constitutional law has tended to view these two questions as almost equivalent. Both, it has been said, raise problems of unconstitutional conditions.

The vital differences between these two cases should be rather obvious. Both the corporation and the welfare-seeker face, to be sure, a superficially similar choice: whether to accept the benefit encumbered by the condition, or forego the benefit because of reluctance to submit to the condition. But that theoretical if beguiling similarity obscures critical differences which warrant different legal analysis. The choice facing the corporate management calls for an essentially practical, economic decision— is it worth relinquishing the opportunity to remove cases to the federal courts in order to carry on local business? If the price is excessive, many other markets beckon. Even if the state which imposes the offensive condition happens to be the site of the principal or most logical market, the corporation may avoid the condition by incorporating there. Thus the decision whether to accept or reject the condition in order to obtain the benefit is an unemotional, objective one.[2]

---

* A.B., 1956, A.M., 1957, LL.B., 1961, Harvard University; Acting Associate Professor of Law, University of California (Berkeley).

[1] The case on which the question is based is Doyle v. Continental Ins. Co., 94 U.S. 535 (1877). The Court's holding that such a condition could constitutionally be imposed was overruled in Terral v. Burke Constr. Co., 257 U.S. 529 (1922). See generally Willcox, *Invasions of the First Amendment Through Conditioned Public Spending*, 41 CORNELL L.Q. 12, 22-23 (1955).

[2] This is not to say, of course, that the corporate decision may not be a difficult and even painful one for those charged with making it. In a time of greater solicitude for the foreign corporation than the present, the Supreme Court held that California could not constitutionally compel a contract carrier seeking to do business within the state to assume the burdens of a common carrier as a condition of the "privilege" of using the state's highways. Mr. Justice Sutherland spoke feelingly of the dilemma facing the corporation confronted with such an unpalatable option: "In reality, the carrier is given no choice, except a choice between the rock and the whirlpool,—an option to forego a privilege which may be vital to his livelihood or submit to a requirement which may constitute an intolerable burden." Frost & Frost Trucking Co. v. Railroad Comm'n, 271 U.S. 583, 593 (1926). For the Court's lack of corresponding solicitude for the dilemma of individuals seeking conditioned benefits, see, e.g., Hamilton v. Regents of the Univ. of Calif., 293 U.S. 245 (1934).

The dilemma of the indigent welfare-seeker contrasts sharply. In the first place, the very fact of asking for public assistance imposes an unavoidable stigma. Second, the consequence of refusing the benefit is quite different: An indigent person's ability to survive without public assistance is hardly comparable to the ambitious corporation's quest for new markets.[3] Third, the effects of compliance with the condition are usually quite different: A compelled loyalty oath, for example, may subtly coerce avoidance not only of "disloyal" groups but of all controversial political affiliation,[4] while the inability to remove corporate suits to the federal courts seems unlikely to carry profound collateral consequences.

Thus the cases of the welfare-seeker and the interstate business seem so fundamentally different that constitutional scholars and courts should long ago have stopped trying to fit them to the same mold. This article will suggest some principles of constitutional analysis more germane to the problems of welfare benefits than those that have been developed in the corporate context. A fresh look of this sort is already overdue. The need for a thorough reexamination is heightened by the expansion of government welfare and other benefit programs. The conditioning of benefits, indeed, is one of the pressing constitutional problems confronting lawyers in the welfare state.

I

TYPES OF CONDITIONED BENEFITS

The initial task is to identify the various forms of benefits which have been conditioned by government programs of spending. This is a necessary first step before considering the more important matters of types of conditions and reasons for imposing them.

Before classifying benefits, however, we must inquire whether there are any opportunities afforded by government to its citizens which are constitutionally exempt from encumbrances. Freedom of speech, for example, is clearly a "right" of the highest priority. One may not be compelled to pay for the opportunity to speak,[5] nor required to submit to previous censorship.[6] But a speaker may be compelled to register with local authorities or obtain a minimal permit before he speaks, so long as no infringement of his message is involved.[7] The other government

---

[3] See generally, for a sympathetic view of the problems confronting the welfare-seeker, Reich, *Individual Rights and Social Welfare: the Emerging Legal Issues*, 74 YALE L.J. 1245-46 (1965).

[4] See note 30 *infra* and accompanying text.

[5] Murdock v. Pennsylvania, 319 U.S. 105 (1943).

[6] Cantwell v. Connecticut, 310 U.S. 296 (1940).

[7] *Compare* Poulos v. New Hampshire, 345 U.S. 395 (1953), *with* Thomas v. Collins, 323 U.S. 516 (1945).

benefit which seems most clearly a "right" is the franchise. It might be thought that voting is so essential to a democracy that no conditions could be imposed upon the franchise. Recently, however, it has taken a constitutional amendment[8] and a major Supreme Court decision to abolish the last vestiges of the poll tax.[9] Even the most recent federal legislation protecting the franchise seems to assume the validity of some conditions and qualifications upon its exercise.[10] Thus it appears that few if any forms of government benefit are so essential or of such a high order that they cannot constitutionally be conditioned in any way.

The most inviting distinction in the field of government benefits is the one that has been drawn between "rights" and "privileges." Those who start with this distinction then conclude that a "privilege," being a mere government gratuity, can be conditioned without limit because it could be withdrawn without notice or formal proceeding.[11] "Rights," on the other hand, have to be treated circumspectly because they are in some sense "vested," and cannot be summarily withdrawn or arbitrarily denied. The distinction is circular as well as illusory. Recent scholarship has shown how flimsy it is, and has urged that it should be abandoned,[12] although there are courts which cling to the security it affords in analyzing government benefits.[13]

To break out of the right-privilege circle, it would be more useful to

---

8 U.S. CONST. amend. XXIV.

9 Harper v. Virginia State Board of Elections, 86 S. Ct. 1079 (1966).

10 Only certain types of literacy tests are prohibited by the Civil Rights Act of 1964, 78 Stat. 241, 42 U.S.C. § 1971(a)(2)(C) (1964), or suspended by the Voting Rights Act of 1965, 79 Stat. 437, 42 U.S.C. §§ 1973-73p (Supp. I, 1965). Where such tests are administered in writing and are not used for racially discriminatory purposes, they may still be permitted.

11 The most durable statement of the "privilege" concept, if not the soundest, was Justice Holmes' epigram in the case involving a municipal ban on the political activities of city employees: "The petitioner may have a constitutional right to talk politics, but he has no constitutional right to be a policeman." McAuliffe v. Mayor & Board of Aldermen, 155 Mass. 216, 220, 29 N.E. 517 (1892). In a similar vein is Professor Hale's classic statement: "[The] doctrine of unconstitutional conditions . . . is difficult to support logically. If I have no ground for complaint at being denied a privilege absolutely, it is difficult to see how I acquire such a ground merely because the state, instead of denying me a privilege outright, offers me an alternative, however harsh." Hale, *Unconstitutional Conditions and Constitutional Rights*, 35 COLUM. L. REV. 321-22 (1935).

12 See, e.g., French, *Comment: Unconstitutional Conditions: An Analysis*, 50 GEO. L.J. 234, 236-39 (1961).

13 Probably the last clear adherence to the "privilege" concept in Supreme Court jurisprudence was Adler v. Board of Educ., 342 U.S. 485, 492 (1952). Although the Court has never squarely repudiated the doctrine, recent decisions have conveniently avoided consideration of the right-privilege distinction. *E.g.*, Sherbert v. Verner, 374 U.S. 398 (1963). But lower courts occasionally take solace in the distinction. See, e.g., Thompson v. Gleason, 317 F.2d 901, 906 (D.C. Cir. 1962). For a summary of the development, see Linde, *Justice Douglas on Freedom in the Welfare State: Constitutional Rights in the Public Sector*, 39 WASH. L. REV. 4, 31-32 (1964).

speak of a single category of "benefits." This category runs the gamut from the most securely protected activities sanctioned or underwritten by government (such as the practice of the basic professions under government license), to the most ephemeral government gratuities (bonus payment or rewards for valor, for example). Thus no distinction need be drawn at any arbitrary point between "rights" and "privileges"; it need only be recognized that in terms of the interests both of the donor and of the recipient, some forms of government benefits are more valuable than others, and should be more fully safeguarded.[14] But the withdrawal or conditioning of all types of benefits should be analyzed according to the same constitutional principles.

A complete catalogue of the kinds of government benefits now provided in the United States would serve no useful purpose; an illustrative survey should suffice here. Public employment is usually seen as a distinct category—partly because employment is a very important kind of opportunity to the recipient, and partly because there are more cases dealing with the conditioning of employment than any other benefit.[15] But employment is not really different in kind from other benefits, and the creation of a discrete category may therefore obscure the assimilation which is urged here.

Public education is another class of benefits sometimes singled out for special treatment. Elementary and secondary education has always been among the most vital opportunities afforded by government, and the courts have been careful to protect the rights of students and parents.[16] Also recent changes in the character of public higher education, from bare luxury to near necessity, have obviously altered its position on the hierarchy of benefits,[17] and may have rendered obsolete most of the old cases about conditioning the privilege of attending a state university.[18]

---

[14] This appears to have been the United States Supreme Court's disposition in recent cases. For example, in the process of deciding that a political deportee forfeited all claims to social security, the Court nevertheless recognized that his claim to benefits "is of sufficient substance to fall within the protection from arbitrary governmental action afforded by the Due Process Clause." Flemming v. Nestor, 363 U.S. 603, 611 (1960). The need to draw such a distinction has been similarly avoided in other recent decisions involving the withdrawal or conditioning of government benefits, e.g., Schware v. Board of Bar Examiners, 353 U.S. 232, 239 n.5 (1957); Wieman v. Updegraff, 344 U.S. 183, 192 (1952).

[15] For an extended discussion of the special problems of conditioned access to public employment, see Linde, *supra* note 13, at 31-46.

[16] See, e.g., Comment, 37 U. Colo. L. Rev. 492 (1965); note 57 *infra*.

[17] See Van Alstyne, *Student Academic Freedom and the Rule-Making Powers of Public Universities: Some Constitutional Considerations*, 2 Law in Transition Q. 1, 6-8 (1965).

[18] *Compare*, e.g., Hamilton v. University of Calif. Board of Regents, 293 U.S. 245 (1934); North v. Board of Trustees, 137 Ill. 296, 27 N.E. 54 (1891), *with* the more recent pronouncements in, e.g., Dixon v. Alabama State Board of Educ., 294 F.2d 150 (5th Cir. 1961); Connelly v. University of Vt., 244 F. Supp. 156 (D. Vt. 1965); Knight v. Board of Educ.,

Many government benefits come in the form of licenses or permits. Running the gamut from admission to the basic professions to weekend fishing licenses, benefits of this sort are among the most important that government can offer to the citizen. Nowhere has the classic right-privilege distinction proved more pernicious. Yet nowhere is it more apparent that some types of conditions are not only legitimate but essential. For example, few would question the wisdom of ascertaining a doctor's or lawyer's professional skills before turning him loose upon a trusting public. Having said that does not, however, always determine where to draw the line between legitimate tests of professional qualification and illegitimate tests of unrelated personal characteristics. Mr. Justice Douglas has argued that "nothing in a man's political beliefs disables him from setting broken bones or removing ruptured appendixes safely and efficiently";[19] but the cases that now trouble the courts tend to be subtler than the one about which Douglas was speaking.

It would be easy, but misleading, to overlook the category of government benefits comprised of opportunities to use various public facilities. While we tend to take for granted access to public parks and playgrounds, there has been much controversy over such less obvious benefits as the use of the mails[20] and of high school auditoriums for public meetings.[21] When one considers the whole range of public facilities that have been made available to the citizen, and to citizen groups, for essentially nongovernmental activities, the significance of this class of government benefits becomes apparent.

Finally, there are the myriad governmental benefits that have characterized the development of the welfare state. Most of these benefits are designed to remedy or offset the effects of unequal distribution of resources in the private sector or to cushion the impact of illness or other misfortunes—unemployment compensation, workmen's compensation,

---

200 F. Supp. 174 (M.D. Tenn. 1961); Manjares v. Newton, 64 A.C. 378, 411 P.2d 901, 49 Cal. Rptr. 805 (1966).

[19] Barsky v. Board of Regents, 347 U.S. 442, 474 (1954) (Douglas, J., dissenting). The questions of relevance of qualifications and conditions to the purposes of the benefit program, and of the relationship between the condition and the alleged purpose, will be considered more fully in the text accompanying notes 97-102 infra.

[20] Compare Milwaukee Social Democratic Publishing Co. v. Burleson, 255 U.S. 407 (1921), with Lamont v. Postmaster General, 381 U.S. 301 (1965); Hannegan v. Esquire, Inc., 327 U.S. 146 (1946); United States v. 18 Packages of Magazines, 238 F. Supp. 846 (N.D. Cal. 1964).

[21] See, e.g., Bynum v. Schiro, 219 F. Supp. 204 (E.D. La. 1963); American Civil Liberties Union v. Board of Educ., 59 Cal. 2d 203, 379 P.2d 4, 28 Cal. Rptr. 700 (1963); American Civil Liberties Union v. Board of Educ., 55 Cal. 2d 167, 359 P.2d 45, 10 Cal. Rptr. 647 (1961); Danskin v. San Diego Unified School Dist., 28 Cal. 2d 536, 171 P.2d 885 (1946); Blease, The Civic Center Act and the Freedom of Speech, 2 CALIF. COMM'N ON LAW & SOCIAL ACTION L. COMMENTARY 43 (1964).

medical care payments, social security, college scholarships, rent subsidies, and the like, to mention but a few of the commoner forms of welfare payments. It is the conditioning of such benefits that poses the most serious constitutional problems today, for several reasons: first, because the "privilege" dogma has clung most assiduously to welfare benefits; second, because those affected by such conditions are less able to resist or to litigate the questions than those affected by conditions on other forms of benefits; and third, because conditions imposed on welfare benefits are likely to be most remote from the purposes or aims of the benefit program itself. It is these factors which serve to focus the principal attention of the present article upon conditioning of welfare benefits, though in so doing we must not slight problems of conditioned benefits of the other varieties previously discussed.

Before moving on, something should be said about the inherent limitations of any classification of benefits such as we have just set forth. The distinctions drawn in this section are of descriptive significance only. This brief survey has reflected none of the analytical distinctions that would be essential to the making of constitutional judgments about the legitimacy of conditions. There has been, for example, no attempt here to rank benefits in order of their value or importance either to the recipient or to the benefactor. Some attention will be given to such distinctions in a later section where functional differences figure more prominently. Here the object has been only to present a gross descriptive survey for its reference value.

II

TYPES OF CONDITIONS

It seems appropriate at the outset to survey the various types of conditions much as we have just surveyed the benefits.[22] It should be stressed again that some conditions are not only legitimate but essential to any orderly system of government regulation. Medical licenses could hardly be issued, for example, without some demonstration of professional training and skill. And the appropriation of federal and state funds must constitutionally be accompanied by a stipulation, express or implied, that they not be spent for racially discriminatory purposes.[23] Conditions, then, may

---

[22] No attempt will be made to illustrate all the types of conditions described in this section. Indeed, some of them may be hypothetical, although unintentionally. For a survey of some of the most onerous forms of conditions still found in welfare legislation, see Reich, *supra* note 3, at 1246-51.

[23] See, *e.g.*, Smith v. Holiday Inns of America, Inc., 336 F.2d 630 (6th Cir. 1964); Simkins v. Moses H. Cone Memorial Hosp., 323 F.2d 959 (4th Cir. 1963). Today the constitutional obligation has been strongly reinforced by the statutory obligation of Title VI of the Civil Rights Act of 1964, 78 Stat. 252 (1964), 42 U.S.C. §§ 2000d-2000d-4 (1964).

be benign and beneficial as well as malevolent and devious. The survey which we are about to undertake must, therefore, view the conditioning process with an objective and impartial eye.

There are many government benefit programs which are "conditioned" only to the extent that limits of monetary amount or duration are imposed upon the eligibility of a particular individual. Unemployment compensation may run out after twenty-six weeks, for example, or medical expenses may be reimbursable only up to 5,000 dollars. (Sometimes, of course, the beneficiary has a choice regarding the condition: he may purchase a hunting license for the entire season at twenty-five dollars, or a weekend permit for ten dollars.) Such conditions as these are unlikely to be used for ulterior purposes, even where the dispensing government seems unduly parsimonious. Nor do such limitations often deter constitutionally protected conduct.

More troublesome are various conditions imposed in the nature of *qualifications*. If professional skill is the requisite qualification for a license, questions may arise with respect to the manner of ascertaining the skill. Many benefits are restricted in terms of the qualification of residence or citizenship—state jobs may, for example, be open only to residents of the state, or relief rolls may be closed to persons who have newly migrated to the city or the county.[24] These qualifications, although sometimes harsh, and arguably unconstitutional, should be clearly distinguished from other qualifications, such as race or ancestry, which rest upon a closed, fixed class or involuntary status. Most people can *become* citizens or residents; a Negro cannot *become* Caucasian, and a person who was born in another land cannot acquire native grandparents. Yet the courts have occasionally sustained even qualifications based upon an involuntary status or closed class.[25]

Two qualifications which have been particularly troublesome with regard to welfare benefits are indigency and residence. It is not unreasonable for a community to decide that preference should be given in the disbursement of a limited welfare fund to those who are really needy, and

[24] For a thorough discussion of the nature, effect, and constitutionality of various residence qualifications upon welfare benefits, see Harvith, *The Constitutionality of Residence Tests for General and Categorical Assistance Programs*, this symposium.

[25] The classic example is Goesaert v. Cleary, 335 U.S. 464 (1948), sustaining a Michigan statute restricting employment as a barmaid to those women who were the wives or daughters of male owners of licensed taverns or other liquor establishments. Although the Court conceded that "Michigan cannot play favorites among women without rhyme or reason," *id.* at 466, its majority concluded that a plausible basis for the classification had been shown, even though entry into that class was really not subject to the applicant's volition. *Id.* at 466-67. *But cf.* Morey v. Doud, 354 U.S. 457 (1957), a later and somewhat different treatment of the problem of the closed or involuntary class.

to those who have been members of the community for a substantial length of time. But determination of indigency may involve the use of a means test, the constitutionality of which has recently been drawn in question.[26] And the residence qualification, particularly where designed to exclude needy newcomers from the community altogether, may conflict with the United States Supreme Court's view of how far a state may go in insulating its treasury from the claims of indigent migrants.[27]

Certain benefit programs require an applicant to supply information in connection with his application. Undoubtedly the government which gives away money has a valid interest in knowing the correct name and home address of everyone to whom it makes payments. But what of information about the applicant's marital status, or the nature of his employment, which may be pertinent to some programs, but not to others? Requests for information about an indigent applicant's income and assets, while innocent enough to the middle-class eye, may have deterred thousands of elderly poor persons from seeking medical attention they obviously needed.[28]

Most troublesome have been requests for information about political affiliations. Even an open-ended question about past membership in political groups may discourage the benefit-seeker and deter future applicants from questionable affiliations. Inquiries about present political associations may force applicants to the choice of declining the benefit or disaffiliating with organizations which are thought suspect. Even these few illustrations suggest, therefore, that inquiries ostensibly seeking only particular, specific information may have collateral consequences far beyond the process of supplying the requested information.[29]

---

[26] For a trenchant discussion of the constitutional questions raised by the means test and other similar exactions, see Bendich, *Privacy, Poverty and the Constitution*, this symposium.

[27] See Edwards v. California, 314 U.S. 160 (1941); Meyers, *Federal Privileges and Immunities: Application to Ingress and Egress*, 29 CORNELL L.Q. 489 (1944); Roback, *Legal Barriers to Interstate Migration*, 28 CORNELL L.Q. 286, 483 (1943); Note, *Depression Migrants and the States*, 53 HARV. L. REV. 1031 (1940).

[28] For a discussion of some of the effects of the means test, see tenBroek & Wilson, *Public Assistance and Social Insurance—A Normative Evaluation*, 1 U.C.L.A.L. REV. 237, 264-67 (1954).

[29] The most important case invalidating such a merely informational request made of a public beneficiary is Shelton v. Tucker, 364 U.S. 479 (1960). The Supreme Court there struck down as violative of the freedom of association an Arkansas statute requiring every public school or college teacher to file annually an affidavit listing every organization to which he had belonged or regularly contributed within the preceding five years. The Court stressed the danger, or at least the fear, that disclosure of unpopular or "disapproved" affiliations might jeopardize the teacher's nontenure position; the probable deterrence of such a requirement to free political association and affiliation; and the sweeping, unqualified scope of the statute's demand. *Cf.* Lamont v. Postmaster General, 381 U.S. 301 (1965).

Some inquiries go beyond specific information, moreover, and call upon the applicant to make a subjective judgment about his affiliations. Illustrative is the demand for a declaration that the applicant belongs to no "subversive organizations" or to any group which advocates the violent overthrow of the government. Even when a requirement of "knowing" membership is added, the judgment may be a treacherous one for the layman to make. Thus the broader the question and the less precise the information sought, the more likely is the question to have collateral deterrent effects upon the political activity of the applicant.[30]

Similar though perhaps more acute problems of judgment are raised by demands for an applicant's declaration about or renunciation of certain future political activity. The typical loyalty oath is a prime example, and will be considered more fully below. Another illustration is the ban imposed on public employees' partisan political activity by the federal Hatch Act[31] and similar state legislation.[32] Such a ban may be imposed either in the form of an explicit declaration, or by a renunciation implicit in the mere acceptance of any government employment in the covered class. There are various other forms of the "I shall not . . . so long as I receive the benefit" condition, but these two illustrations will suffice for the moment.

Some benefit programs seek an affirmative undertaking on the part of the beneficiary. A student who has part of his higher education financed by the R.O.T.C., or all of it subsidized through attendance at a service academy, thereby obligates himself to serve in the armed forces for a certain period after graduation. A recipient of National Defense Education Act assistance may turn the loan into a grant—and thus receive an additional benefit of value—by becoming a school teacher for a certain period after college.[33] These conditions are innocent enough. But consider the more difficult case of the recipient of aid for dependent children who must agree to prosecute the errant father of her children for nonsupport if and when he can be located. In all these cases, the condition is pertinent

---

30 See, e.g., Baggett v. Bullitt, 377 U.S. 360, 371-73 (1964); Cramp v. Board of Pub. Instruction, 368 U.S. 278, 287 (1961); Wieman v. Updegraff, 344 U.S. 183, 190 (1952); Danskin v. San Diego Unified School Dist., 28 Cal. 2d 536, 548-50, 171 P.2d 885, 893 (1946); Collings, *Unconstitutional Uncertainty—An Appraisal*, 40 CORNELL L.Q. 195, 219-20 (1955); cf. Pollitt, *Statutory Comment, Campus Censorship: Statute Barring Speakers From State Educational Institutions*, 42 N.C.L. REV. 179, 186-96 (1963).

31 See note 56 *infra* and accompanying text.

32 For a discussion of local and state legislation similar to the Hatch Act, see material cited in note 57 *infra*.

33 National Defense Education Act § 205(b)(3), 72 Stat. 1584 (1958), 20 U.S.C. § 425(b)(3) (1964), provides for the cancellation of up to one half of the entire loan for service as a full-time teacher in a public or other nonprofit secondary or elementary school, at the rate of ten per cent per complete academic year of such service.

to the program of which the benefit is a part. But the acceptance of the condition may nevertheless exact of the beneficiary a heavy price, and one that may not be fully appreciated at the time the application is made.

Finally, there are conditions which demand no affirmative act of the applicant at the start, but which erode his future protection by relinquishing to the government certain rights which could not have been withdrawn directly. For example, a welfare recipient may have to consent to certain kinds of searches that would otherwise violate his constitutional right of privacy.[34] Of course, some legal protections simply cannot be bargained away, and public policy will invalidate a state's attempt to exact such a waiver. In the meantime, however, the *in terrorem* effect of mere acceptance of such a condition cannot be overlooked—particularly in the case of the indigent and uncounselled welfare recipient.

One other distinction should be noted among conditions that may encumber government benefits. Some conditions are explicit and obvious to the applicant, even if their significance is not always fully apparent. This is the case where one must sign a loyalty oath before starting work, or must disclose certain information before his application is processed. Other conditions, however, may be more subtly imposed or accepted by acquiescence. The recipient of a radio or television license, for example, does not in terms agree to comply with the "fairness" doctrine, not to censor political broadcasts, and the like, but he is as much on notice of the policies of the FCC and the provisions of the Communications Act as though he had taken such an oath. That is no great hardship for the well-counselled businessman. But it may be unreasonable to expect the indigent welfare recipient to anticipate the forfeiture of his benefits for doing or failing to do certain things which are enumerated only in administrative rulings or regulations, or buried in the pages of a compendious code. Thus, as we shall consider more fully below, the form in which a condition is imposed may often be as significant as its substance.[35]

---

34 There is considerable doubt whether such an essentially involuntary "consent" will be valid. For a discussion of the difficult constitutional questions, see Reich, *Midnight Welfare Searches and the Social Security Act*, 72 YALE L.J. 1347, 1348-50 (1963).

35 No survey of the types of conditions attached to government benefits within the United States would be complete without some reference to the various conditions attached to our foreign aid and international development programs. Some conditions are, of course, obvious in their relationship to the purposes of the program to which they are attached—*i.e.*, military assistance is available only for military expenditures, for the purposes of peace and stability; development loans and grants are available only for specified purposes, and so on. More controversial are the other forms of conditions designed to achieve purposes less immediately related to the aims of the aid or development program itself. There are, for example, conditions designed to make aid administrators act more wisely in accomplishing aid purposes than the Congress believes they will act without restrictions—*e.g.*, the provision of 75 Stat. 442 (1961), as amended, 22 U.S.C. § 2361(a)(1) (1964), that funds should not

III

THE RATIONALE OF CONDITIONS: WHY GOVERNMENTS IMPOSE
RESTRICTIONS ON BENEFITS

Conditions or qualifications on benefits may serve a broad range of governmental interests and purposes. The stated purpose, if any, for imposing a condition may of course not be the real purpose; both silence and dissimulation may make it difficult to determine the real purpose or motive behind a particular condition.[36] But a survey of the various conditioned benefit programs suggests certain common objectives. Among such general purposes would undoubtedly appear the following:

---

be obligated for projects requiring substantive technical and financial planning until such planning is done and a reasonably firm estimate of the cost to the United States is developed; and the provisions of 75 Stat. 426 (1961), as amended, 22 U.S.C. § 2161(e) (1964), and 76 Stat. 257 (1962), as amended, 22 U.S.C. § 2211(e) (1964), which require application by the country and some planning evaluation before funds are reserved for assistance.

Other conditions attached to American aid funds are designed to achieve a variety of domestic policy objectives: 75 Stat. 439 (1961), 22 U.S.C. § 2354(a) (1964), generally limits procurement with appropriated funds to the United States; 75 Stat. 439 (1961), 22 U.S.C. § 2354(d) (1964), precludes discrimination against the United States marine insurance industry in A.I.D. financed transactions; and 75 Stat. 444 (1961), as amended, 22 U.S.C. § 2370(d) (1964), prohibits assistance to productive enterprises which are competitive with U.S. enterprises.

Other conditions are designed to prevent aid from going to countries which are politically unacceptable to the United States or which are acting so as to jeopardize United States private investors or other interests. For example, 75 Stat. 444 (1961), as amended, 22 U.S.C. § 2370 (Supp. I, 1965), is largely concerned with prohibiting aid to various Communist bloc or Communist-dominated countries (except for very limited Presidential waiver provisions contained in 75 Stat. 444 (1961), as amended, 22 U.S.C. § 2370(f) (1964), which in a sense place "conditions upon the condition"). 75 Stat. 436 (1961), as amended, 22 U.S.C. § 2314 (1964), seeks to limit military assistance to free-world allies; and the Battle Act (Mutual Defense Assistance Control Act of 1951), 65 Stat. 645 (1951), as amended, 22 U.S.C. § 1611b(b) (1964), requires the termination of assistance to countries that knowingly permit shipment to Communist bloc nations of certain categories of strategic materials.

36 The discernment of legislative purpose or intent is always a treacherous business. For a profound analysis of many of the problems, see Wofford, *The Blinding Light: The Uses of History in Constitutional Interpretation*, 31 U. CHI. L. REV. 502 (1964). The attempt is not futile, however. For some cases in which the United States Supreme Court has considered and determined *the* (or *a*) legislative purpose, see, *e.g.*, McLaughlin v. Florida, 379 U.S. 184, 193 (1964); Griffin v. County School Board, 377 U.S. 218, 231-32 (1964); Kennedy v. Mendoza-Martinez, 372 U.S. 144, 170-84 (1963); United States v. Butler, 297 U.S. 1, 68-78 (1936). While *Butler's* reliance, 297 U.S. at 90, for inquiry into legislative motive upon the now discredited principle of the Child Labor Tax Case, 259 U.S. 20 (1922), may have been undermined by United States v. Darby, 312 U.S. 100, 114-15 (1941), the deference which *Darby* accords to the legislative judgment, regardless of motive or purpose, applies particularly to Commerce Clause cases. *Darby* does not necessarily preclude inquiry into legislative purpose to determine validity of statutes affecting racial or religious equality, or freedoms of expression and association. Indeed, any doubts about *Darby's* encroachment upon that judicial domain should have been resolved by *Mendoza-Martinez*, in which judicial determination of legislative motive was the principal basis for invalidating the statute.

1. Gather Relevant Information

Some conditions or qualifications only seek general information necessary in the administration of the program. Where such information cannot affect the status or eligibility of the individual recipient, its gathering is unlikely to deter acceptance of benefits. But where the information does remain in the individual recipient's file, or where the very act of giving the information offends or embarrasses the applicant, it may be difficult to serve even this relatively innocuous purpose without to some degree deterring acceptance of benefits.

2. Ensure that Benefits Are Restricted to Eligible Applicants

Many conditions and qualifications seek to ascertain that the benefits go only to those who need them or are qualified to enjoy them. It seems reasonable enough to determine that a scholarship applicant is really a student, that a social security claimant has reached the retirement age, and that a doctor is medically trained and skilled before he can begin to practice. The legitimacy of other conditions and qualifications designed to narrow the channels of distribution of official largesse depends, of course, upon the validity of the criteria of eligibility. Even with qualifications which are obviously legitimate, there may be some question whether the *amount* or *type* of information sought is really necessary to determine eligibility, but such questions do not concern us at this stage.

3. Reduce the Cost of the Program

Some conditions and qualifications which appear only to determine eligibility may in fact be designed for the ulterior though closely related purpose of economy. Although evidence is very difficult to gather, there are occasional impressions from legislative history and extra-legislative statements that the real motive for imposing conditions may be to deter or exclude persons who are in fact eligible, and thus reduce the cost of the program. Indeed, the imposition of conditions may constitute one of the subtlest and most effective ways of doing precisely this.

4. Promote a Strong Governmental Interest

Apart from the immediately related interests in economy and in restricting benefits to those for whom they were intended, conditioned benefit programs may seek to achieve a host of other governmental objectives. It would be pointless to catalogue those interests here. It will be sufficient for the moment to suggest two general distinctions: First, between purposes directly relevant to the benefit program itself and those which are independent or unrelated; and second, between those governmental interests which would support direct regulation of the behavior covered by the condition, and those which would not. As will be suggested below, relevance and the availability of direct regulatory power both bear upon the validity of conditions, though neither should be dispositive.

5. Promote Loyalty or Deter Disloyalty

The hardest constitutional questions about conditioned government benefits have involved loyalty oaths and disloyalty bars. Two points should be made here: First, loyalty to the dispensing government is undoubtedly more relevant to certain benefits—for example, security clearances for work in top secret defense programs[37]—than to others such as residence in public housing projects and receipt of tax exemptions.[38] The difference between the underlying government interests in these two examples is the difference between protection of highly sensitive programs which could be jeopardized by disloyal persons, and the use of random methods to promote "loyalty" regardless of the nature of the program.

The other point is that the significance of loyalty conditions may depend a great deal upon the *form* in which they are imposed. Persons of impeccable loyalty and integrity may be deterred from signing sweeping loyalty oaths; indeed, they are probably more likely to refuse the benefit by renouncing the condition than the disloyal persons at whom the condition is ostensibly directed. On the other hand, persons of conscience and scruple are probably less likely to refuse benefits available only to the loyal when they are told that they would forfeit the benefits only if their

---

[37] It is relatively easy, for example, to perceive the interest behind the provisions for security clearance of contractors and licensees working with restricted data from Atomic Energy Commission files, 68 Stat. 942 (1954), as amended, 42 U.S.C. § 2165 (1964). Less obvious is the federal interest in requiring security clearances of all participants in the Peace Corps, 75 Stat. 624 (1961), 22 U.S.C. § 2519 (1964). Considerably less apparent is California's interest in requiring a loyalty oath of persons occasionally employed as models for art classes at a junior college—but models, like other employees of the college, are covered by the general loyalty oath requirements, CAL. GOV'T CODE § 18150. See San Francisco Chronicle, March 25, 1966, p. 1, col. 4-5, p. 7, col. 1-2.

[38] See the pointed comment of the General Counsel of the Department of Health, Education and Welfare: "Perhaps the chief motive for the imposition of such conditions [loyalty oaths and qualifications] is a feeling that the government ought not to be required to help those who would overthrow it. But while ingratitude to a generous government may well be a sin, the fact remains that the first amendment protects ingrates as well as the grateful and, as the Jehovah's Witness cases abundantly testify, the cantankerous as well as the meek." Willcox, *Invasions of the First Amendment Through Conditioned Public Spending*, 41 CORNELL L.Q. 12, 48 (1955). For a survey of some of the curious forms of loyalty requirements adopted in the 1950's, and some observations about their relevance to governmental interests, see *id.* at 48-52 & nn. 146-51; note 111 *infra*.

disloyalty were proved in court.[39] This is a point to which we shall return later.

6. Ambiguous or Multiple Purposes

Some cases disclose no declared purpose for the conditioning of government benefits. In other cases the conditions may serve multiple and not always harmonious purposes. It has been said, for example, that the Job Corps administered by the Office of Economic Opportunity systematically refuses to accept applicants with criminal records.[40] Perhaps the administrators simply feel that former delinquents are bad risks and might disrupt the training camps. Or perhaps they believe that federal funds ought to be used first to train those whose untarnished records show them to be deserving citizens. Or perhaps there is some element of deterrence at work, assuming that if a criminal record will disqualify one for the Job Corps, and if the Job Corps is considered desirable, some delinquency might thus be prevented. Any or all of these purposes might explain the disqualification in question. Or perhaps, out of unfamiliarity with the practical administration of the Job Corps, we have missed the real purpose of the delinquent-disqualification rule which differs from any of the foregoing. Suffice it to say that discernment of the real legislative motives is not always easy.

IV

EVOLUTION OF THE LAW OF UNCONSTITUTIONAL CONDITIONS[41]

The unconstitutional conditions doctrine originated with the case of the foreign corporation seeking permission to do local business. The

[39] See Justice (as he then was) Traynor's comment: "There are some who refuse to make the required declaration, not because they advocate overthrow of the government, but because they conscientiously believe that the state has no right to inquire into matters so intimately touching political belief. Rightly or wrongly they fear that such an inquiry is the first step in censorship of unpopular ideas." First Unitarian Church v. County of Los Angeles, 48 Cal. 2d 419, 447, 311 P.2d 508, 525 (1957) (dissenting opinion), rev'd, 357 U.S. 545 (1958).

The *New York Times* has recently observed editorially, apropos the loyalty oath required of certain applicants for Medicare under the 1965 legislation: "Furthermore . . . [loyalty oaths] are useless; for what genuine subversive would hesitate to swear loyalty if to do so served his purpose? Only the conscientious are likely to be the victims. A by-product in the McCarthy heyday of loyalty oaths was that many thinking people in such fields as teaching and the sciences simply bowed out rather than subject themselves to this humiliation." N.Y. Times, Jan. 17, 1966, p. 46, col. 2.

[40] Reich, *Individual Rights and Social Welfare: The Emerging Legal Issues*, 74 YALE L.J. 1245, 1251 (1965).

[41] Probably the most thorough history of the development of the doctrine of unconstitutional conditions is in Willcox, *supra* note 38, at 22-44. See also, for general discussions, HENDERSON, THE POSITION OF FOREIGN CORPORATIONS IN AMERICAN CONSTITUTIONAL LAW 132-47 (1918); Hale, *Unconstitutional Conditions and Constitutional Rights*, 35 COLUM. L. REV. 321 (1935); Merrill, *Unconstitutional Conditions*, 77 U. PA. L. REV. 879 (1929); Note, *Unconstitutional Conditions*, 73 HARV. L. REV. 1595 (1960).

claimed basis of authority to impose conditions upon the entry of such a corporation was the nondomiciliary state's absolute power to exclude all corporations from the local market. In 1877 the Supreme Court held that Wisconsin could oust a foreign corporation for having removed a case to the federal court in violation of a condition of entry because the corporation "has no constitutional right to do business in that State; that State has authority at any time to declare that it shall not transact business there."[42] There were dissents, even in the beginning. In the case just cited, for example, Justice Bradley challenged the majority's assumption that "the greater always includes the less" and termed "unsound" the conclusion that "if the State may exclude the . . . [corporation] without any cause, it may exclude them for a bad cause . . . ."[43]

The critical turning point came in 1926, when the Court held that California could not require a foreign trucking corporation to accept the status of a common carrier in order to do business in the state as a contract carrier.[44] Although declining to repudiate the old view completely, the Court declared simply that "the power of the State in that respect is not unlimited; and one of the limitations is that it may not impose conditions which require the relinquishment of constitutional rights."[45]

Until quite recently, the foreign corporation cases have set the pattern. They have generally determined what conditions are reasonable under the constitutional standard. But there have not been many such cases of late—whether because the states have become more subtle in their regulation of entry by foreign corporations, or because the courts have been less anxious to protect such corporations from state regulation.[46]

The center of the unconstitutional conditions stage has now been taken over by the newer problems with which we are concerned in this article—government employment, education, licensing, and welfare benefits. Despite the significant differences between these activities and government regulation of foreign corporations, substantially the same principles have usually been invoked. The results of this curious assimilation have been, as we shall see, far from satisfactory.

The confusion about applying the unconstitutional conditions doctrine outside the foreign corporations area is well illustrated by the quandary of Mr. Justice Holmes. It was Holmes who once insisted, in defense of a city's ban on political activities by certain of its employees, that a police

---

[42] Doyle v. Continental Ins. Co., 94 U.S. 535, 542 (1877).

[43] *Id.* at 543-44 (dissenting opinion).

[44] Frost & Frost Trucking Co. v. Railroad Comm'n, 271 U.S. 583 (1926). *But cf.* Stephenson v. Binford, 287 U.S. 251 (1932), for assurance that *Frost* did not represent total repudiation of the old doctrine.

[45] Frost & Frost Trucking Co. v. Railroad Comm'n, *supra* note 44, at 593-94 (1926).

[46] For a discussion of the continuing vitality of the foreign corporation-conditioned entry cases, see Note, *Unconstitutional Conditions*, 73 HARV. L. REV. 1595. 1605-09 (1960).

officer "may have a constitutional right to talk politics, but he has no constitutional right to be a policeman."[47] It was Holmes, too, who (as a state judge) saw no great constitutional difference between a city's absolute refusal to open its parks for speeches and rallies, and its conditioning of such use upon a permit granted by the mayor in his unfettered discretion.[48]

It was also Justice Holmes, however, who balked when a majority of the Court deemed the fourth-class mailing privilege a gratuity which the Post Office Department might grant or deny arbitrarily. "The United States may give up the Post Office when it sees fit," warned Holmes, "but while it carries it on the use of the mails is almost as much a part of free speech as the right to use our tongues . . . ."[49] Here is the essence of the modern notion of unconstitutional conditions. It was particularized, though, in Justice Brandeis' dissent in the same case. "Congress may not through its postal police power," declared Brandeis, "put limitations upon the freedom of the press which if directly attempted would be unconstitutional."[50]

When a similar question of the use of low cost mailing privileges came before the Court two decades later, the majority was ready to accept the Holmes-Brandeis view:

> [G]rave constitutional questions are immediately raised once it is said that the use of the mails is a privilege which may be extended or withheld on any grounds whatever. . . . Under that view the second-class rate could be granted on condition that certain economic or political ideas not be disseminated. The provisions of . . . [the statute] would have to be far more explicit for us to assume that Congress made such a radical departure from our traditions and undertook to clothe the Postmaster General with the power to supervise the tastes of the reading public of the country.[51]

Given such statements, one might suppose that the unconstitutional conditions doctrine today consistently protects the recipient of government benefits. That is still far from the case, however, as a quick review of recent Supreme Court decisions will indicate. In the field of public employment, for example, the Court first held that states may demand loyalty oaths as a condition of obtaining and holding a government job.[52]

---

[47] McAuliffe v. Mayor & Board of Aldermen, 155 Mass. 216, 220, 29 N.E. 517 (1892).

[48] Commonwealth v. Davis, 162 Mass. 510, 39 N.E. 113 (1895). The Supreme Court affirmed the conviction in Davis v. Massachuetts, 167 U.S. 43 (1897), finding nothing unconstitutional in the conditional exercise or the discretionary delegation of the city's power to deny all use of its parks for public expression.

[49] Milwaukee Social Democratic Publishing Co. v. Burleson, 255 U.S. 407, 437 (1921) (dissenting opinion).

[50] *Id.* at 430-31.

[51] Hannegan v. Esquire, Inc., 327 U.S. 146, 156-57 (1946).

[52] Garner v. Board of Pub. Works, 341 U.S. 716 (1951).

But subsequent cases have invalidated various types of loyalty oaths as excessively broad or uncertain,[53] or for failure to deal only with *knowing* membership in the proscribed organizations.[54] The federal Hatch Act,[55] which drastically curtails the political activities of civil servants, has been upheld;[56] but similar county charter provisions have been struck down by at least one state supreme court on federal constitutional grounds.[57]

The United States Supreme Court permitted the termination of social security benefits because the beneficiary was deported on grounds of political activity that would have caused no forfeiture either at the time the activity occurred or at the time the beneficiary was first covered by social security.[58] Yet, a few years later, the Court held that a state might not constitutionally deny unemployment compensation to a Seventh-Day Adventist who was declared unavailable for suitable work only because her religion prevented her from accepting Saturday employment.[59] In the field of public education, the Court has never overruled its 1934 decision permitting the University of California to condition admission on willingness of students to take at least two years of R.O.T.C. training[60]—although the rationale of that decision is difficult to square with more recent pronouncements on public education.[61]

Finally there is the bizarre series of cases dealing with admission to

---

[53] Baggett v. Bullitt, 377 U.S. 360 (1964); Cramp v. Board of Pub. Instruction, 368 U.S. 278 (1961).

[54] Wieman v. Updegraff, 344 U.S. 183, 190 (1952). *Cf.* Elfbrandt v. Russell, 86 S. Ct. 1238 (1966).

[55] 53 Stat. 1148 (1939), as amended, 5 U.S.C. § 118i (1964): "No officer or employee in the executive branch of the Federal Government, or any agency or department thereof, shall take any active part in political management or in political campaigns."

[56] United Pub. Workers v. Mitchell, 330 U.S. 75 (1947).

[57] Fort v. Civil Serv. Comm'n, 61 Cal. 2d 331, 38 Cal. Rptr. 625, 392 P.2d 385 (1964); Kinnear v. City & County of San Francisco, 61 Cal. 2d 341, 38 Cal. Rptr. 631, 392 P.2d 391 (1964).

[58] Flemming v. Nestor, 363 U.S. 603 (1960).

[59] Sherbert v. Verner, 374 U.S. 398 (1963).

[60] Hamilton v. Regents of the Univ. of Calif., 293 U.S. 245 (1934). On the logical difficulty of reconciling *Hamilton* with later cases such as *Sherbert*, see Linde, *Justice Douglas on Liberty in the Welfare State: Constitutional Rights in the Public Sector*, 40 WASH. L. REV. 10, 19-22 (1965).

[61] See, *e.g.*, Griffin v. County School Board, 377 U.S. 218 (1964); School Dist. of Abington Township v. Schempp, 374 U.S. 203 (1963). Although these cases deal with elementary and secondary education rather than the higher education with which *Hamilton* was concerned, other cases indicate the changing attitudes of the Court with respect to higher education. See, *e.g.*, McLaurin v. Oklahoma State Regents, 339 U.S. 637 (1950); Sweatt v. Painter, 339 U.S. 629 (1950); Sipuel v. Board of Regents, 332 U.S. 631 (1948), *reversing*, 119 Okla. 36, 180 P.2d 135 (1947); Dixon v. Alabama State Board of Educ., 294 F.2d 150 (5th Cir.), *cert. denied*, 368 U.S. 930 (1961); Knight v. State Board of Educ., 200 F. Supp. 174 (M.D. Tenn. 1961); Van Alstyne, *Student Academic Freedom and the Rulemaking Powers of Public Universities: Some Constitutional Considerations*, 2 LAW IN TRANSITION Q. 1, 6-8 (1965).

the bar. At the close of World War II the Court sustained Illinois' power to refuse admission to an applicant solely because he would not promise to bear arms in support of the state.[62] Twelve years later the Court held that a state bar could not reject an otherwise qualified applicant simply on suspicion he had been a Communist—at least not on grounds of "bad moral character."[63] At that time the Court declined to classify bar admission as a "right" or a "privilege," but indicated only that it was an opportunity of sufficient importance to the individual that it could not be arbitrarily withheld.[64] Yet within a few years the Court seemingly abandoned that view by allowing a state to reject a bar applicant who refused to answer questions about his alleged past Communist affiliations.[65]

The course of these decisions is far from consistent, and makes it hazardous to predict future developments. This background suggests that if the case law governing conditioned benefits in public employment, education, and licensing is now uncritically transferred to the burgeoning field of conditioned public welfare benefits, the results could be most unfortunate. Before such a transfer is made, therefore, it seems essential to formulate more rational, more discriminating, and more appropriate principles for judging the constitutionality of conditioned benefits.

V

A SUGGESTED FRAMEWORK FOR TESTING CONDITIONED BENEFITS

Two legal premises underlay the old view that government could impose virtually any condition it wished upon the offer or grant of a benefit. The first premise was that government is not constitutionally compelled to extend any benefits.[66] The second premise was that given the power of total exclusion or flat denial, the government could exercise the "lesser" power of making the benefit available only on certain condi-

---

[62] *In re* Summers, 325 U.S. 561 (1945).

[63] Schware v. Board of Bar Examiners, 353 U.S. 232 (1957); Konigsberg v. State Bar, 353 U.S. 252 (1957).

[64] Schware v. Board of Bar Examiners, *supra* note 63, at 239 n.5.

[65] Konigsberg v. State Bar, 366 U.S. 36 (1961). The Court stressed that the applicant was disqualified by his failure to respond candidly to the questions, and not any inference about his past political affiliations. *Cf.* Slochower v. Board of Higher Educ., 350 U.S. 551 (1956), which led to his rejection. *But cf.*, for a still later, and somewhat different view of the constitutional status of admission to the bar, Willner v. Committee on Character and Fitness, 373 U.S. 96, 102 (1963).

[66] This premise would not apply, of course, to any benefits deemed "rights" rather than "privileges." But in the early days few, if any, government benefits were held to be "rights" that could not constitutionally be withdrawn or denied. Even the franchise, which was not extended to all citizens, and upon which qualifications were widely imposed, was presumably a "privilege" rather than a "right." If the franchise could be denied or withdrawn, then *a fortiori* government was not obligated to extend to all citizens, without qualifications, such other benefits as employment, education, and welfare payments.

tions.[67] It mattered not, therefore, whether the dispensing government could constitutionally have achieved the same objective by direct regulation, for the beneficiary always had the theoretical option of avoiding the indirect regulation by refusing the benefit.

The first of these premises has been trenchantly criticized by Professor Charles Reich in his recent articles.[68] His theory of "entitlement" suggests that even welfare benefits are no longer gratuities but have assumed at least some of the characteristics of "rights." If that argument prevails, it may be unnecessary even to consider the second premise or the question whether government may achieve indirectly what it cannot accomplish directly.

But there is some doubt how the Reich theory of "entitlement" will fare in the courts.[69] Thus it is still worth tackling the second premise, that given the "greater" power of exclusion, government can exercise the "lesser" power of conditioning admission. Half a century ago Professor Thomas Reed Powell argued forcefully that there is no principle of *logic* which comprehends the power to impose any conditions whatever within the power to exclude or refuse benefits unconditionally.[70] Yet the fallacy persisted, perhaps because exposure of bad logic is not always an antidote for *stare decisis*.[71]

There are other flaws, moreover, in the logic of this second premise. To say that because government can exclude an applicant or deny a benefit summarily, and without giving reasons, it can grant or admit on any

[67] See Davis v. Massachusetts, 167 U.S. 43, 48 (1897): "The right to absolutely exclude all right to use, necessarily includes the authority to determine under what circumstances such use may be availed of, as the greater power contains the lesser." See notes 11, 48 *supra*.

[68] Reich, *The New Property*, 73 YALE L.J. 733 (1964); Reich, *Individual Rights and Social Welfare: The Emerging Legal Issues*, 74 YALE L.J. 1245 (1965). See also the thoughtful criticism of the Reich theories by Professor Joel Handler. Handler, *Controlling Official Behavior in Welfare Administration*, this symposium.

[69] It should be apparent that the Reich theory tends to accept the right-privilege distinction, by turning that distinction to the advantage of welfare recipients and applicants. Professor Bendich seems to view the problem in a similar light, for he also argues that certain benefits have become "rights" and cannot be treated as gratuities any longer. See Bendich, *supra* note 24. For reasons discussed earlier in this article, however, it may be sounder to reject altogether the right-privilege distinction, or—as the courts have tended increasingly to do—simply to disregard it on the theory that the claim involved, whether one of right or privilege, is entitled to major constitutional safeguards. See, *e.g.*, Schware v. Board of Bar Examiners, 353 U.S. 232, 239 & n.5 (1957); Slochower v. Board of Higher Educ., 350 U.S. 551, 555-56 (1956); Wieman v. Updegraff, 344 U.S. 183, 192 (1952).

[70] Powell, *The Right To Work for the State*, 16 COLUM. L. REV. 99, 110-12 (1916). For a more modern indictment of the "privilege" notion, see French, *Comment: Unconstitutional Conditions: An Analysis*, 50 GEO. L.J. 234, 239-42 (1961).

[71] See, *e.g.*, Adler v. Board of Educ., 342 U.S. 485, 492 (1952); American Communications Ass'n v. Douds, 339 U.S. 382, 408 (1950); Thompson v. Gleason, 317 F.2d 901, 906 (D.C. Cir. 1962); *cf.* Flemming v. Nestor, 363 U.S. 603, 608-10 (1960).

condition, is analogous to the argument that the government may use its undoubted power to instantly execute a convicted killer as the basis for killing him by slow torture. Obviously the doctrine of cruel and unusual punishment intercedes, recognizing that the greater power does not always include the lesser.[72] Or, to take another analogy, the undoubted power of a businessman to close down altogether in order to prevent labor unionization does not give him the "lesser" power to close down part of his business for that purpose, or to transfer struck work to another plant, or to take various other seemingly less drastic antiunion measures.[73]

The arguments against the greater-includes-the-lesser theory in the conditioned benefits field are also quite strong. Most important is the psychological impact of merely offering a conditioned benefit. The unexplained denial of a benefit will probably not deter any conduct other than the enjoyment of the benefit itself. But where conditions are imposed or reasons are given, the natural human response is to be influenced by the condit'   qualification itself, unless of course the benefit is either worthless or readily available elsewhere without conditions. Thus the very fact of attaching the conditions to government benefits probably influences human conduct *more* extensively than the flat denial or withdrawal of the benefit, not less. Regardless of whether one is a "greater" government power than the other, it should be apparent that these are very different forms of regulation with quite distinct effects upon prospective beneficiaries.

Thus the "greater" power to withhold the benefit does not logically subsume the "lesser" power to grant it conditionally. But this does not, of course, mean that all conditions are constitutionally bad. Indeed, many conditions are legitimate, and some (such as the condition that federal grants to the states not be spent for racially discriminatory programs[74]) may even be constitutionally required.[75] The problem for the constitutional scholar is to differentiate the valid from the invalid conditions. This task requires a more discriminating and more uniform set of tools than are now available. We shall consider various questions that might be used to appraise the validity of a particular condition. Undoubtedly no one condition would respond to analysis under all these criteria; only those that are appropriate need be invoked in each instance. The final resolution

---

[72] See Trop v. Dulles, 356 U.S. 86 (1958), in which the Court found that the denaturalization of a person for being a wartime deserter was a cruel and unusual punishment even though he could have been summarily executed for the desertion. *Cf.* Robinson v. California, 370 U.S. 660 (1962); Louisiana *ex rel.* Francis v. Resweber, 329 U.S. 459 (1947).

[73] Textile Workers Union v. Darlington Mfg. Co., 380 U.S. 263 (1965).

[74] Title VI, Civil Rights Act of 1964, 78 Stat. 252 (1964), 42 U.S.C. §§ 2000d-2000d-4 (1964).

[75] See Bolling v. Sharpe, 347 U.S. 497 (1954).

of the condition's constitutionality might then depend upon a balancing of the results.

A. Could the Object of the Condition Be Achieved Directly?

It is sometimes said that a conditioned benefit may not be used to bring about a result that the government is powerless to achieve through direct regulation.[76] In at least two situations this proposition seems sound. First is the case in which government discriminates among beneficiaries along lines that would clearly violate the fourteenth amendment's equal protection clause if the discrimination resulted from direct regulation.[77] Government may no more discriminate against Negroes, or Catholics, or Mexicans, as such, through conditioned benefits than it may directly impose disabilities upon such groups.[78]

The second case in which the absence of direct power may well be conclusive is the indirect attempt to force the surrender of a right clearly protected by the first amendment.[79] There is little doubt, for example, that a government could not offer employment on condition that its employees agree not to attend church while so employed. Nor could a state university compel its students to give up all writing or publishing while they remained on the campus. Beyond these obvious cases, though, the significance of a lack of direct power is much less clear. The federal Hatch Act, for example, denies to federal civil servants certain important political activities which surely could not be closed to any group of persons employed in the private sector.[80] Yet the Hatch Act has been held constitutional,[81] suggesting that even where the infringements of first amendment rights may be substantial, the absence of governmental power to achieve the same end through direct means is not always dispositive.[82]

---

[76] See, e.g., Buckley v. Meng, 35 Misc. 2d 467, 475, 230 N.Y.S.2d 924, 934 (Sup. Ct. 1962); cf. Lawson v. Housing Authority, 270 Wis. 269, 275, 70 N.W.2d 605, 608 (1955). More discriminating is the Supreme Court's recognition that "under some circumstances, indirect 'discouragements' undoubtedly have the same coercive effect upon the exercise of First Amendment rights as imprisonment, fines, injunctions or taxes." American Communications Ass'n v. Douds, 339 U.S. 382, 402 (1950).

[77] See Missouri ex rel. Gaines v. Canada, 305 U.S. 337 (1938); Garner v. Board of Pub. Works, 341 U.S. 716, 725 (1951) (opinion of Frankfurter, J.); Bynum v. Schiro, 219 F. Supp. 204 (E.D. La. 1963).

[78] See Linde, supra note 60, at 12.

[79] See, e.g., Thomas v. Collins, 323 U.S. 516, 540 (1945); Danskin v. San Diego Unified School Dist., 28 Cal. 2d 536, 547-48, 171 P.2d 885, 892-93 (1946).

[80] See United Pub. Workers v. Mitchell, 330 U.S. 75, 110-11 (1947) (Black, J., dissenting); cf. Fort v. Civil Serv. Comm'n, 61 Cal. 2d 331, 338, 392 P.2d 385, 389, 38 Cal. Rptr. 625, 629 (1964).

[81] United Pub. Workers v. Mitchell, supra note 80.

[82] See also French, supra note 70, at 242-43, for comments about the logical inadequacy of the notion that absence of direct power precludes the use of indirect means.

Perhaps the Hatch Act cases should be read more narrowly, however, because of the Court's deference to the government's interest in the integrity of the civil service.

Other cases further undermine the proposition that "government may not do indirectly what it can't do directly." It is highly doubtful, for example, whether the federal government could constitutionally conscript prospective teachers for compulsory classroom service after college graduation. Yet those doubts do not necessarily invalidate the provision of the NDEA loan program which seeks to induce students to sign up for one to five year teaching stints as a condition of partial forgiveness of the debt they incur to finance their higher education.[83] These examples demonstrate that the absence of direct power does not always preclude the use of indirect methods.

Indirect inducements are, however, suspect in such cases, and a finding that direct power is lacking should militate against the validity of the condition for several reasons. First, there is the probable difference in procedural safeguards and in the susceptibility of the restriction to judicial challenge. The contrast may be illustrated by recent congressional efforts to bar Communists from leadership positions in the labor movement. In the Taft-Hartley Act, indirect means were employed: Section 9(h) made it a condition of resort to the NLRB that the union declare it had no Communists among its officialdom.[84] In an early test, the Supreme Court sustained that condition against a barrage of constitutional attacks.[85] A decade later, in the Landrum-Griffin Act, the Congress substituted criminal penalty for condition by providing for the prosecution of Communist labor leaders.[86] In its first Supreme Court test, this direct method was held invalid as a bill of attainder.[87] Of course there were other differences between the two cases, but the juxtaposition suggests an important principle: The denial or withdrawal of a conditioned benefit is seldom surrounded with the procedural safeguards that are essential to a criminal prosecution. For this reason, the direct means is constitutionally preferable to the indirect, even where both are permissible.

---

83 National Defense Education Act § 205(b)(3), 72 Stat. 1584 (1958), as amended, 20 U.S.C. § 425(b)(3) (1964); see note 34 *supra*.

84 Labor Management Relations Act § 9(h), 61 Stat. 143 (1947).

85 American Communications Ass'n v. Douds, 339 U.S. 382 (1950). Significantly, the Court did suggest more than once during the opinion that "the loss of a particular position is not the loss of life or liberty." *Id.* at 409; *cf. id.* at 402.

86 Labor-Management Reporting and Disclosure Act (Landrum-Griffin Act) § 504, 73 Stat. 536 (1959), 29 U.S.C. § 504 (1964).

87 United States v. Brown, 381 U.S. 437 (1965). Although the Supreme Court struck down the statute as a bill of attainder, the court of appeals had reached the same result under the first and fifth Amendments, Brown v. United States, 334 F.2d 488 (9th Cir. 1964), *aff'd*, 381 U.S. 437 (1965).

A second consideration is the relative availability of judicial review. One need only recall the difficulty of the New York teachers in getting a constitutional test of the Feinberg law,[88] or of federal employees in challenging the Hatch Act's political prohibitions on the merits.[89] It has been widely assumed that many conditions—the loyalty oath under the Medicare program,[90] and the since repealed affidavit required of NDEA loan recipients,[91] for example—are simply beyond judicial challenge according to present principles of standing and justiciability.[92] The fault may lie with the rules of standing, of course, rather than in the use of indirect methods to promote questionable government interests.[93] But until these barriers to constitutional litigation are relaxed, they afford an additional ground for preferring the direct to the indirect route.

This discussion suggests that the question "could it be done directly?"

---

[88] Adler v. Board of Educ., 342 U.S. 485 (1952).

[89] United Pub. Workers v. Mitchell, 330 U.S. 75, 86-91 (1947).

[90] The Medicare program was established by Subchapter XVIII of the Social Security Act, added by 79 Stat. 291 (1965), 42 U.S.C.A. § 1395 (Supp. 1965). The oath required of applicants for Medicare who have never been covered by Social Security is not part of the statute, but rather an administrative addition to the application form. The oath requires the affected applicant to certify that he is not now, and has not been for the previous twelve months, "a member of any organization which is required to register under the Internal Security Act of 1950, as amended, as a Communist-action organization, a Communist-front organization, or a Communist-infiltrated organization." There have been recent efforts in Congress to obtain the abolition of the oath, strongly supported by the American Civil Liberties Union and other interested groups. See N.Y. Times, Jan. 11, 1966, p. 6, cols. 3 & 4; Jan. 4, 1966, p. 8, cols. 3 & 4. Eventually the Commissioner of the Social Security Administration, which originally deemed the oath to be required by the statute, also sought its abolition by Congress. N.Y. Times, Feb. 10, 1966, p. 50, col. 8.

[91] The oath was originally required of all applicants for National Defense Education Act loans by section 1001(f) of the National Defense Education Act of 1958, 72 Stat. 1602 (1958). It was repealed in 1962, 76 Stat. 1069 (1962). In its place was substituted a simple oath of allegiance requirement, together with a provision compelling applicants to submit lists of all major criminal convictions.

Also of recent interest in this regard is the repeal by Congress of the short-lived requirement that Poverty Program workers disavow membership in and support of "any organization that believes in or teaches, the overthrow of the United States Government by force or violence or by any illegal or unconstitutional means." Economic Opportunity Act of 1964, § 616, 78 Stat. 533, repealed by 79 Stat. 979 (1965).

[92] For recent examples of legislation which purports in terms to preclude judicial review of determinations in public welfare programs, see, e.g., 79 Stat. 59 (1961), 42 U.S.C. § 2514(c) (1964); 76 Stat. 26 (1962), 42 U.S.C. § 2583(g) (1964). Not all statutes which purport to make decisions "final" or "unreviewable" are accorded the desired deference by courts asked to review their application. E.g., United States v. California Eastern Line, 348 U.S. 351 (1955); see 4 DAVIS, ADMINISTRATIVE LAW ch. 28 (1958). For some of the practical difficulties involved in obtaining judicial review of decisions denying or withdrawing welfare benefits, see generally Mandelker, *Judicial Review in General Assistance*, 6 J. PUB. L. 100 (1957); note 123 *infra*.

[93] *Cf.* Jaffe, *Standing to Secure Judicial Review: Public Actions*, 74 HARV. L. REV. 1265 (1961).

is still pertinent, even though a negative answer is not dispositive. The use of indirect means to circumvent the absence of direct regulatory power is inherently suspect on several grounds. At the very least, the effect of the condition should be scrutinized more critically where direct power is lacking. Moreover, it might be appropriate to require in such a case that the denial or withdrawal of the benefit be made judicially reviewable through prescribed channels[94] (to the extent permitted by constitutional limitations on court jurisdiction), and that procedural safeguards of a judicial character accompany any administrative proceeding for such denial or withdrawal.[95] More will be said below about procedure and judicial review.[96]

B. How Relevant is the Condition to the Benefit?

Relevance is another deceptively simple criterion the utility of which is exaggerated; not every condition is necessarily invalid because it is not directly relevant to the purposes of the program. Whether the less relevant condition may be sustained despite its attenuation depends upon other factors including the strength of the underlying government interest and the effect of the condition upon the recipient.

Nonetheless, relevance should be an important factor in the balance. A loyalty oath, for example, should be tolerated more readily when it restricts the employment of persons for top secret defense jobs than when it restricts admission to a public housing project.[97] And, as has often been

---

[94] Cf. the judicial review provision of the Elementary and Secondary Education Act of 1965, Title II, § 211, 79 Stat. 33, 20 U.S.C. § 241k (Supp. I, 1965). In a much earlier proposed statute for federal aid to education, which passed the House but not the Senate, private taxpayers were authorized to bring suit to prevent improper expenditure or to enforce compliance with the statute. H.R. 4643, § 5, 81st Cong., 1st Sess. (1949).

[95] Cf. the development of quasi-judicial procedures for the suspension or expulsion of college students who could once be dismissed by the most summary or perfunctory of hearing procedures. See, for examples of the newer approach, University of Oregon Student Conduct Program, Pt. I, § A(4) (1964); University of California Policies Relating to Students and Student Organizations, Use of University Facilities, and Non-Discrimination, Section II, Pt. E, July 1, 1965.

[96] See notes 118-24 infra and accompanying text.

[97] See Willcox, Invasions of the First Amendment Through Conditioned Public Spending, 41 CORNELL L.Q. 12, 49-50 (1955): "Though we can hardly expect the courts to reject loyalty tests as irrelevant to even non-sensitive public employment, their relevance to non-sensitive private employment or occupations financed by the government stands in a quite different posture. Unless in particular situations some reason for such tests can be shown other than the mere fact that the government is footing the bill, it is submitted that the tests, if imposed by government, are unconstitutional conditions in violation of the first amendment." If the test of relevance is uniformly applied, it would be hard to imagine a benefit to which loyalty is less relevant than that of burial in a national cemetery. Yet the Attorney General of the United States recently denied that honor to the remains of one Robert G. Thompson, a decorated World War II veteran who would have been

suggested, a test of professional competence may be proper as a condition of admission to legal or medical practice, while a test of political beliefs should be rejected because it is irrelevant.[98]

One might approach the issue of relevance by asking two further questions about a conditioned benefit: (1) How strong is the government's interest in the benefit program? (2) How strong is the government's interest in the activity to which the condition applies? These two questions cannot, however, really be separated. A government undoubtedly has a stronger interest in deterring professional incompetence in the practice of licensed professions than in deterring immorality among residents of housing projects. It makes little sense, however, to say abstractly that the government's interest in the licensing of the professions is stronger than its stake in providing low cost shelter for needy citizens; or that ensuring competence is more vital to the functions of government than promoting morality. These statements become meaningful only when a *particular condition* is judged in relation to a *particular benefit;* neither the importance of the benefit program nor that of the condition can be evaluated in isolation. It is the criterion of relevance which juxtaposes them in such a way as to facilitate meaningful comparison.

Suppose, however, that the condition is not directly relevant to the program of which the encumbered benefit is a part. Then an alternative question should be asked: Is the condition relevant to some *other* valid governmental purpose? If it is, the lack of relevance to the program involving the particular benefit may be less serious. To illustrate: When government funds are allocated to assist communities in ending racial

---

eligible for burial in the Arlington National Cemetery but for the fact of his conviction as a leading Communist conspirator. He had also been sentenced for jumping bail, but the disqualification for interment was based on his allegedly subversive background. N.Y. Times, Jan. 28, 1966, p. 1, col. 2, p. 11, col. 1-2. Although it is difficult to determine the relevance of this qualification to the federal interest in maintaining the cemetery as a national shrine, at least one observer finds such a relationship. See the recent comment of Representative Charles E. Bennett of Florida: "If this can be justified, we can justify burying there Benedict Arnold, Aaron Burr and a host of others who at one time in their lives contributed something to America, but turned their back on the country that had helped them to secure all the good things they had attained." Los Angeles Times, Jan. 25, 1966, Pt. I, p. 6, col. 2. Similar questions of relevance to the purpose of the benefit program may be raised about the declaration of loyalty required of certain applicants for Medicare benefits. See note 84 *supra.* The disclaimer has been attacked on various grounds in the press, *e.g.,* N.Y. Times, Jan. 17, 1966, p. 46, col. 2, and by the American Civil Liberties Union, N.Y. Times, Jan. 4, 1966, p. 8, col. 3-4. Bills to eliminate it have been introduced both in the House, 112 CONG. REC. 6-8 (daily ed. Jan. 10, 1966), and in the Senate, 112 CONG. REC. 344 (daily ed. Jan. 17, 1966). Finally, even the Social Security Administration of the Department of Health Education and Welfare asked Congress to remove any implication of such a requirement. N.Y. Times, Feb. 10, 1966, p. 50, col. 8; see note 90 *supra.*

[98] See, *e.g.,* Barsky v. Board of Regents, 347 U.S. 442, 474 (1954) (Douglas, J., dissenting).

segregation in the public schools, the condition that such funds not be used for discriminatory purposes is obviously relevant to the whole program.[99] But when federal funds are appropriated for school construction, or hospital construction, or any of a number of other legitimate federal objectives, the condition of racial nondiscrimination is only remotely relevant to the purpose of the benefit program.[100] Yet that lack of relevance is not disabling so long as some valid governmental purpose—here the elimination of racial barriers—is furthered by imposing the condition.

Once the relevance of the condition to some legitimate government end is established, a further question should be asked: Is there a rational relationship between the condition and the end sought by the government program of which the benefit is a part? Rationality is not something that courts can easily determine. Yet there are a number of cases in the equal protection field deciding whether a particular classification bears a rational relationship to a governmental interest.[101] Perhaps the same canons of rationality can be applied here; courts have occasionally invalidated conditions which were irrationally related to the asserted purpose.[102] Such decisions are necessarily imprecise, however, and the principle of rationality is unlikely to catch any but the most arbitrary condition. A sounder approach to the rationality of the link between condition and governmental interest may be suggested by the question we next consider—whether there is a better way of doing what the condition seeks to do.

---

99 Section 405 of the 1964 Civil Rights Act, 78 Stat. 247, 42 U.S.C. § 2000c-4 (1964), does not expressly condition grants of aid for desegregation upon the assurance that they not be used for discriminatory purposes, but that condition is implicit—apart from the general nondiscrimination guarantee of Title VI of the Act. See note 23 *supra*.

100 Since enactment of the 1964 Civil Rights Act, extensive use has been made of federal funds to encourage public school desegregation in the South, Wall St. Journal (S.F. ed.), Jan. 24, 1966, p. 1, col. 4, p. 13, col. 1-3, and to reduce racial barriers in hospitals, Wall St. Journal, Feb. 2, 1966, p. 12, col. 4; N.Y. Times (city ed.), March 9, 1966, p. 26, col. 1-2. A recent report of the United States Civil Rights Commission views with satisfaction the use of federal funds in various programs to speed desegregation. U.S. COMM'N ON CIVIL RIGHTS, TITLE VI . . . ONE YEAR AFTER (1966). See also THE POTOMAC INSTITUTE, INC., THE FEDERAL DOLLAR AND NONDISCRIMINATION (1965).

101 E.g., McLaughlin v. Florida, 379 U.S. 184 (1964); Morey v. Doud, 354 U.S. 457 (1957).

102 E.g., Konigsberg v. State Bar, 353 U.S. 252, 273-74 (1957); Slochower v. Board of Higher Educ., 350 U.S. 551, 558 (1956); Fort v. Civil Serv. Comm'n, 61 Cal. 2d 331, 337-38, 392 P.2d 385, 389, 38 Cal. Rptr. 625, 629 (1964); Syrek v. California Unemployment Ins. Appeals Bd., 54 Cal. 2d 519, 529-30, 354 P.2d 625, 631, 7 Cal. Rptr. 97, 103 (1960); Housing Authority v. Cordova, 130 Cal. App. 2d 883, 279 P.2d 215 (1955); Chicago Housing Authority v. Blackman, 4 Ill. 2d 319, 326, 122 N.E.2d 522, 526 (1954); Lawson v. Housing Authority, 270 Wis. 269, 287-88, 70 N.W.2d 605, 615 (1955). The courts in the three cases last cited invalidated as irrational state and federal attempts to deny certain "subversive persons" access to governmentally assisted housing. For a discussion of the application of the rationality test to these cases, see Note, 53 COLUM. L. REV. 1166 (1953).

C. What Alternative Means, if Any, Would Achieve the Same End?

It is now time to consider the potential contribution of the principle of the "less onerous alternative."[103] Where a condition may deter constitutionally protected expression or political activity, courts increasingly hold that government may not employ restrictions more drastic than are absolutely necessary.[104] Thus, to return to the case of the ban on political activity by civil servants, if the real evil is partisan pressures brought by superiors upon their subordinates, the government interest might be adequately served by direct criminal sanctions against such improper pressures.[105] Partly on this ground, the California Supreme Court recently invalidated such a condition on public employment, finding no proof of the inadequacy of more precise and direct criminal proscriptions.[106]

The doctrine of the less burdensome alternative is most applicable, of course, to conditions that threaten freedom of expression. But even where less basic constitutional liberties are in jeopardy, proof of the sufficiency of less onerous forms of regulation should be persuasive. In the field of conditioned benefits—particularly where there is doubt about government's power to act directly—perhaps the government should bear the burden of proving that no less onerous means can be found.

It might be that some other form of condition, rather than direct regulation, would be less burdensome and thus preferable. For example, a California city or county may still be able to impose narrow restrictions on the partisan political activities of its civil servants if it can show that the condition is no broader than the regulable evil.[107] Thus the judgment that one form of condition is unduly burdensome does not necessarily force government to choose between resort to direct regulation and terminating the program, but may simply require that the condition be rewritten in narrow terms more appropriate to the governmental interest.

---

[103] See Dean Milk Co. v. City of Madison, 340 U.S. 349, 354-56 (1951); Schneider v. State, 308 U.S. 147, 164 (1939). On the obligation to employ the least onerous alternative where freedoms of expression and association are directly affected, see generally Wormuth & Mirkin, *The Doctrine of the Reasonable Alternative*, 9 UTAH L. REV. 254, 267-93 (1964).

[104] *E.g.*, Sherbert v. Verner, 374 U.S. 398, 407 (1963); Shelton v. Tucker, 364 U.S. 479, 487-88 (1960).

[105] See United Pub. Workers v. Mitchell, 330 U.S. 75, 113-14 (1947) (Black, J., dissenting); Linde, *supra* note 60, at 33, 37.

[106] Fort v. Civil Serv. Comm'n, 61 Cal. 2d 331, 338, 392 P.2d 385, 389, 38 Cal. Rptr. 625, 629 (1964); Kinnear v. City & County of San Francisco, 61 Cal. 2d 341, 392 P.2d 391, 38 Cal. Rptr. 631 (1964).

[107] In *Fort, supra* note 106, the California Supreme Court suggested the possibility of such narrower legislation: "A strong case, we think, can also be made for the view that permitting a public employee to run or campaign against his own superior has so disruptive an effect on the public service as to warrant restriction. It is, of course, possible to draw a restrictive provision narrowly in order to deal specifically with such abuses." *Id.* at 338, 392 P.2d at 389, 38 Cal. Rptr. at 629.

In any case, the theoretical availability of less onerous forms of regulation offers a useful criterion for judging any condition on a government benefit.

D. How Important is the Benefit to the Individual Recipient?

At the risk of rousing the ghost of the right-privilege distinction, we should consider the relative importance to the recipient of the encumbered benefit. Obviously the individual has a greater interest, and should receive more protection, in the enjoyment of a license to practice his profession than in a Christmas bonus. Whether one is a "right" and the other a "privilege" need not be considered, so long as the various forms of government benefits be roughly located on the spectrum of importance.

This question may be misleading and mischievous, however, unless one looks closely at the particular interest of the particular beneficiary. For example, twenty years ago social security might have been regarded as a mere gratuity (if one can overlook the substantial investment which the individual claimant has made during his years of employment). Recently, however, patterns of saving and insurance have probably changed in reliance upon the very existence of government assistance to cover emergencies and contingencies that once had to be met from private sources. The same shift will presumably occur with regard to the medical care of the elderly, as the first phase of Medicare goes into effect. Thus any court now called upon to weigh the importance of social security or unemployment compensation benefits should take account of the changes which reliance upon the very existence of such funds have brought about on the beneficiary's part. In addition, there may be less direct, but equally important, reliance on the part of persons obligated to support the beneficiary, which should not be lightly upset.

E. Are Equivalent Benefits Available in the Private Sector?

The importance of the benefit to the recipient is undoubtedly affected by the availability of similar opportunities from nongovernment sources. One who declines to take the loyalty oath required of faculty members at a state university can, for example, always teach at a private college.[108] But this is much less true for teachers in elementary and secondary schools, where the private share of total employment is very much smaller —even if one includes the church-affiliated schools, which are not a meaningful equivalent for all teachers. There are coming to be "public"

---

108 Keyishian v. Board of Regents, 345 F.2d 236, 239 (2d Cir. 1965). *But cf.* Adler v. Board of Educ., 342 U.S. 485, 492 (1952), in which the Supreme Court suggested that New York public school teachers who objected to the required loyalty oath "may work for the school system upon the reasonable terms laid down by the proper authorities of New York. If they do not choose to work on such terms, they are at liberty to retain their beliefs and associations and go elsewhere."

or "governmental" branches of professions and occupations that were once confined almost wholly to the private sector. It is no answer to a public health doctor, for example, to say that the door of private practice is open when the door of state employment is closed by an unacceptable condition.[109] Certain kinds of public health work are carried on *only* by the government, even though most physicians still work in the private sector of our society. As the public sector share of total employment grows, moreover, the availability of private-sector alternatives will diminish for many occupations.

The availability of nongovernmental equivalents is most relevant to a study of burgeoning welfare benefits. For some senior citizens, private medical insurance has always been readily accessible. But for others— particularly those for whom Medicare now offers the greatest hope—the cost of premiums has always placed private insurance beyond reach. The same is true of other forms of insurance, and of private savings. Thus the mere existence of private-sector programs, and even their widespread use, does not always mean that most people enjoy meaningful alternatives to government benefits. Ironically, such alternatives are least viable for those who are most in need of the benefits offered by the public sector. The intensity of the dilemma facing the applicant or beneficiary undoubtedly depends very much upon the availability of private-sector alternatives. The condition should be judged somewhat more critically when such alternatives are unavailable, even though this factor by itself is unlikely to be dispositive.

F. How Does the Condition Influence the Beneficiary's Judgment?

The psychological effect of the condition upon the beneficiary points up most vividly the difference between the typical foreign-corporation

---

[109] For more sympathetic consideration of the dilemma facing the beneficiary or applicant who objects to conditions that may deter freedom of expression or conscience, see Sherbert v. Verner, 374 U.S. 398 (1963); Fort v. Civil Serv. Comm'n, 61 Cal. 2d 331, 392 P.2d 385, 38 Cal. Rptr. 625 (1964); Syrek v. California Unemployment Ins. Appeals Board, 54 Cal. 2d 519, 354 P.2d 625, 7 Cal. Rptr. 97 (1960). The *Syrek* case is particularly illustrative. Syrek, an applicant for unemployment insurance, had declined the first job offered to him, a civil service position, on the ground that he conscientiously opposed taking the loyalty oath which would accompany that position. There was no equivalent employment available to Syrek in the private sector. Thus the court held that he was entitled to unemployment benefits, having declined to accept suitable employment for "good cause." The court not only found a lack of rational relation between the oath requirement and the unemployment insurance program, but further concluded that by forcing unemployed persons to become reluctant signatories, the interaction of the two legislative programs actually worked at cross purposes. The court perceived the dilemma of the conscientious applicant: "The pressure put on an unemployed person to take the oath or go without benefits, perhaps when he is in desperate circumstances, may lead to the taking of the oath with reservations, or with actual falsehood." *Id.* at 530, 354 P.2d at 631, 7 Cal. Rptr. at 103.

case and the case of the welfare-seeker. However onerous the cost, the corporation need only sacrifice economic interests in order to receive the benefit. Certain conditions imposed upon government employees and welfare recipients, however, exact a far different price: The requirement of a loyalty oath, or an enumeration of political affiliations, or a declaration of belief in God, directly affects liberties of conscience and expression which enjoy top constitutional priority.[110] This difference should bear heavily upon the validity of the condition.

In making that assessment, moreover, the courts should take greater account than heretofore of the potential contribution of psychology. We should not assume that the individual resolves his dilemma in the same manner as the corporate officers, or even that the individual's decision is wholly rational. Analysis of the psychological impact of the condition upon an applicant might consider two levels of response: First, reaction to the very presence of any condition; and second, the impact of the particular condition.

The very fact that an offer of aid has strings attached to it is undoubtedly significant. The welfare seeker is in line precisely because he is poor and presumably without other means of support; he cannot be expected to view the offer of welfare, with or without conditions, in complete equanimity. It is surely naïve to suppose that he approaches the possible loss or forfeiture of a benefit in the same frame of mind as do the corporate managers. We need to know a great deal more than lawyers presently do about the psychological effects of being told that because one is poor, or unemployed, or simply wants to work for the government, he must restrict his activities in ways that government does not ask self-sufficient people to do. It probably makes little difference to him whether or not government *could* constitutionally impose similar restrictions on non-beneficiaries. It is enough for him that other people are not in fact so encumbered.

At the second level, law and psychology surely need to collaborate more closely to understand how a beneficiary decides whether or not to accept a particular condition. Courts have tended to assume that a welfare applicant is capable of making a reasoned choice whether the price attached to the benefit he seeks is worth paying. Is it not equally plausible, however, that even the well qualified applicant may sometimes decline the aid, even if the price seems rather low, simply because the nature of

---

[110] Lamont v. Postmaster General, 381 U.S. 301, 307 (1965); Baggett v. Bullitt, 377 U.S. 360, 372-73 (1964); Cramp v. Board of Pub. Instruction, 368 U.S. 278, 287 (1961); Torcaso v. Watkins, 367 U.S. 488 (1961); Speiser v. Randall, 357 U.S. 513, 526 (1958); Kovach v. Maddux, 238 F. Supp. 835, 843-45 (M.D. Tenn. 1965); Danskin v. San Diego Unified School Dist., 28 Cal. 2d 536, 547-48, 171 P.2d 885, 892-93 (1946); *cf.* School Dist. of Abington Township v. Schempp, 374 U.S. 203, 288-94 (1963) (Brennan, J., concurring).

the condition offends him?[111] Is this not especially likely to be his response where the condition is directed at matters of conscience or expression, which are particularly sensitive and private interests? The law in its present state of knowledge can do no more than raise such questions. Only with the aid of psychology can it begin to answer them. But answers must surely be found before intelligent judgments are made about the overall effect and validity of conditioned welfare benefits.

G. In What Form Is the Condition Imposed?

Any judgment about the validity of conditioned benefits should consider the form and clarity of the condition. Some conditions are fully explained to the applicant at the time the benefit is offered, and the consequences of a breach are made quite clear. Other conditions, however, remain largely obscure, and the withdrawal of the benefit may catch the beneficiary by surprise. Especially suspect should be conditions which are imposed after the benefit has been sought or granted. Consider, for example, the case of the political deportee's forfeiture of social security benefits which the Supreme Court recently upheld.[112] The beneficiary, a Bulgarian, had entered the United States more than twenty years before enactment of the Social Security legislation. He became a Communist during the 1930's, when party membership was neither illegal nor a ground for deportation. For two decades he and his employer had made regular contributions to the social security program. Shortly before his retirement, Congress decreed that any person deported from the country because of past Communist party membership (which had since been made a ground for deportation) would forfeit all social security benefits. After the man had been deported under this law his wife (who was not deported) tried unsuccessfully to obtain social security on his account. The courts agreed with the Administrator that the denial of benefits was constitutional.

This was a case in which the potential beneficiary was taken by surprise in two major respects: At the time he began contributing to the social security program, and thus made his first "application" for benefits, there was no warning that his political activities might eventually jeopardize his claim.[113] Second, at the time he became a Communist he had no reason to fear forfeiture of his benefits. Perhaps he could not in fact have withdrawn from the social security program even if he knew of all the

---

[111] See First Unitarian Church v. County of Los Angeles, 48 Cal. 2d 419, 446-47, 311 P.2d 508, 525 (1957) (Traynor, J., dissenting), rev'd, 357 U.S. 545 (1958); 112 CONG. REC. 6 (daily ed. Jan. 10, 1966) (remarks of Representative Ryan); N.Y. Times, Jan. 17, 1966, p. 46, col. 2; note 39 supra.

[112] Flemming v. Nestor, 363 U.S. 603 (1960).

[113] Id. at 621-22 (Black, J., dissenting).

consequences; but so long as uncovered occupations were theoretically available to him, as they were during the entire period in question, even that argument is untenable.

In addition to the adequacy and timing of notice of the consequences, the specificity of the language in which the condition is stated also seems relevant. This factor has been invoked by recent Supreme Court decisions invalidating state loyalty oaths because of sweeping and uncertain provisions.[114] A state may still require a loyalty oath of public employees, but "the measures which purport to define disloyalty must allow public servants to know what is and what is not disloyal."[115] Whether courts will now demand the degree of specificity that would be required if the same governmental interests were effectuated through direct criminal sanctions remains for speculation. Since indirect restrictions may actually work greater mischief than direct restraints, no less strict a standard should be applied to the language of an oath than that of a criminal law.

Finally, adequate notice requires not only an understanding that *something* will happen if the condition is breached, but a full appreciation of the actual consequences. Thus, one who lists his political affiliations in applying for government employment may be willing to risk not getting the job if one of his organizations is unlawful, or risk losing the job if it is later proved he has falsified his record. But he may not be willing to take the chance that the list will be circulated around the state government, or turned over to a legislative investigating committee, for whatever reprisals may follow such wider dissemination. Similarly, under the recently invalidated postal law[116] one who requested delivery of Communist publications might have been willing to apprise the local post office of his interest in such materials. But he may have been quite unwilling to have his private employer know that he asked to receive Communist propaganda. If any such circulation of the request card had been contemplated, the power of government to impose the condition at all would be rendered much more suspect by the hidden collateral consequences of compliance.[117]

H. What Procedures Are Provided for Determining a Breach of the Condition?

When government moves against the individual by direct regulation, it cannot deprive him of his property or liberty without fair and formal

---

[114] Baggett v. Bullitt, 377 U.S. 360 (1964); Cramp v. Board of Pub. Instruction, 368 U.S. 278 (1961); Wieman v. Updegraff, 344 U.S. 183 (1952).

[115] Baggett v. Bullitt, *supra* note 114, at 380; see Morris, *The University of Washington Loyalty Oath Case*, 50 A.A.U.P. BULL. 221 (1964).

[116] Section 305(a) of the Postal Service and Federal Employees Salary Act of 1962, 76 Stat. 840, 39 U.S.C. § 4008(a) (1964), held unconstitutional in Lamont v. Postmaster General, 381 U.S. 301 (1965).

[117] Lamont v. Postmaster General, 381 U.S. 301, 307 (1965); *cf.* Shelton v. Tucker, 364 U.S. 479, 486-87 (1960).

proceedings. One example will vividly illustrate the distinction. If a state university student steals a book from the campus library, he has probably both violated the general criminal law and subjected himself to campus discipline. If the offense is serious enough, he may even risk loss of the "privilege" of student status. On the one hand, he cannot be jailed or fined (the direct form of regulation) without a criminal trial before an impartial judge (and perhaps a jury), the right to be represented by counsel, the privilege against self-incrimination, the right to confront his accusers, and the right of appeal. Yet for the same act, indirect regulation—even leading to the suspension or expulsion of the student, probably far more drastic in his view than the direct sanctions of the criminal law —might be decreed following only a perfunctory administrative hearing on the campus, or possibly even without a hearing.[118] And the standard justifying the impairment or withdrawal of student status might be nothing more precise than "conduct unbecoming a student" or "behavior inimical to the university"—standards which surely would never stand up in a criminal proceeding.

This contrast suggests that the procedures provided for withdrawal of the benefit are important in determining the validity of the withdrawal. Although indirect forms of regulation are seldom accompanied by the safeguards of direct criminal regulation, the protections available to the government beneficiary vary considerably. To return to the case of the state university student, for example, courts and educational administrators alike are requiring ever stricter procedures before expulsion or suspension can be decreed.[119] Perhaps a university which guarantees every student a trial-type hearing for disciplinary proceedings should be permitted to impose more onerous conditions upon attendance than the college which retains the right to eject students summarily. Of course in practice the institution which is most equitable in its disciplinary procedures is also likely to be most enlightened in its substantive regulation of student conduct. The important point is that the sufficiency of procedures should be weighed in the balance in determining the validity of the condition.[120]

---

[118] See Van Alstyne, *supra* note 61, at 2-6.

[119] See Dixon v. Alabama State Board of Educ., 294 F.2d 150 (5th Cir.), *cert. denied*, 368 U.S. 930 (1961); Connelly v. University of Vt., 244 F. Supp. 156 (D. Vt. 1965); Knight v. State Bd. of Educ., 200 F. Supp. 174 (M.D. Tenn. 1961); Johnson, *The Constitutional Rights of College Students*, 42 TEXAS L. REV. 344 (1964); Seavey, *Dismissal of Students: "Due Process,"* 70 HARV. L. REV. 1406 (1957); Van Alstyne, *Procedural Due Process and State University Students*, 10 U.C.L.A.L. REV. 368 (1963); Note, *Private Government on the Campus—Judicial Review of University Expulsions*, 72 YALE L.J. 1362 (1963); note 88 *supra*.

[120] For recent suggestions that the adequacy of procedures, and particularly the availability of a hearing, should have some bearing on the validity of conditions encumbering government benefits, see Willner v. Committee on Character and Fitness, 373 U.S. 96 (1963);

Another relevant aspect of procedure is the allocation of the burden of proof. The United States Supreme Court struck down California's qualified property tax exemption for veterans on the rather narrow ground that the eligibility provision required the applicant to demonstrate his loyalty.[121] The placement of the burden of proof, the Court held, was likely to deter a taxpayer's speech and political activity: "The man who knows that he must bring forth proof and persuade another of the lawfulness of his conduct necessarily must steer wider of the unlawful zone than if the State must bear these burdens."[122] The Court did not preclude California from denying tax exemptions to disloyal veterans. The state might even require veterans to file loyalty oaths as the condition of claiming the exemption—so long as the state bore the burden of proof in any contest over the validity of the declaration. The decision turned, then, on the quite narrow but important ground of burden of proof. Even where the information in issue is less sensitive than that concerning political affiliations—determination of indigency, for example—the allocation of the burden of proof may constitute a major protection to the beneficiary in case of a dispute over his qualifications.

Finally, some attention should be given to the availability of judicial review. We have observed that direct regulation is preferable to conditioning of benefits because the former can usually be challenged directly in court on its merits. But the immunity of conditioned benefits to constitutional attack is not endemic. There have been recent legislative attempts to arrange test cases and thereby circumvent the historic barriers.[123] But many welfare benefit programs remain virtually immune from constitutional attack. In some programs, indeed, unreviewability is virtually ensured by explicit declarations in the statute to the effect that the administrative decision is "final." Other programs are effectively unreview-

Cafeteria & Restaurant Workers Local 473 v. McElroy, 367 U.S. 886 (1961); Flemming v. Nestor, 363 U.S. 603, 636, 640 (1960) (Brennan, J., dissenting); Greene v. McElroy, 360 U.S. 474, 492, 496-97 (1959); Garrott v. United States, 340 F.2d 615 (Ct. Cl. 1965); Rudder v. United States, 226 F.2d 51, 53 (D.C. Cir. 1955); Heckler v. Shepard, 243 F. Supp. 841 (D. Idaho 1965); Reich, *Individual Rights and Social Welfare: The Emerging Legal Issues*, 74 YALE L.J. 1245, 1252-53 (1965).

[121] Speiser v. Randall, 357 U.S. 513 (1958).

[122] *Id.* at 526. Recently the Court has extended the *Speiser* rationale to the motion picture censorship context. Freedman v. Maryland, 380 U.S. 51, 58 (1965), requires that "the burden of proving that the film is unprotected expression must rest on the censor."

[123] *Compare* the rather generous judicial review provisions accompanying recent federal programs of aid for education, *e.g.*, 72 Stat. 554 (1958), 20 U.S.C. § 641 (1964); 79 Stat. 33, 20 U.S.C. § 241k (Supp. I, 1965); H.R. 4643, § 5, 81st Cong., 1st Sess. (1949), *with* some recent and rather restrictive provisions in federal welfare programs, *e.g.*, the "finality" provision for certain occupational training grants, 75 Stat. 59 (1961), 42 U.S.C. § 2514(c) (1964), and similar provisions regarding training allowances, 76 Stat. 26 (1962), 42 U.S.C. § 2583(g) (1964). See notes 92 and 94 *supra.*

able because no person has the requisite standing to protest the denial or withdrawal of the benefit, at least in the federal courts.[124] Both the availability and the scope of judicial review of administrative decisions concerning government benefits should probably play a greater role than they have heretofore.

CONCLUSION

The application of these criteria will undoubtedly make more difficult many cases which now appear relatively easy. Such criteria would, for example, preclude the ready judgment that a condition is permissible because the benefit to which it is attached is a mere "privilege." These criteria would also postpone the judgment that a condition is necessarily invalid because it lacks either relevance to the benefit program, or a foundation in direct regulatory power. Suspended judgment and critical examination of all the factors are essential in these cases, however, unless we are ready to treat the welfare recipient like the foreign corporation for purposes of conditioned benefits. At some time, the courts may adopt the "entitlement" theory of welfare benefits, thus rendering less necessary the kind of analysis to which this article is directed. But until that time comes, it is probably better to escape slowly from the shackles of the old corporation and "privilege" cases than to try to make the sudden and dramatic break which "entitlement" requires. The process of emancipation must be guided through discriminating, and legally familiar, channels. The criteria suggested here are designed to ease that transition.

Even if the courts do determine that welfare benefits partake of some of the qualities of "property," the criteria outlined here may still be useful. For the property concept is not monolithic or unidimensional; government permissibly conditions more traditional proprietary interests to an extent determined by, among other factors, the strength of its interest in the particular restriction, the relevance of that restriction to some permissible governmental objective or program, and the character of the owner's interest in the unfettered use of the property. These criteria suggest obvious and strong parallels by which to evaluate the constitutionality of conditions upon government benefits, whether or not the beneficiary's interest is viewed as proprietary.

One matter remains, and will have to wait for another day. The criteria suggested here are obviously not self-applying. There is no inherent order of priority or preference among them, no natural weight to be given in the balancing process. The development of general formulae to structure the balancing process will have to await further study of the particular criteria—for example, the psychological impact of certain types

---

[124] See United Pub. Workers v. Mitchell, 330 U.S. 75, 86-91 (1947); note 92 *supra*.

of conditions—and extensive field research on the nature, purpose, and use of conditions of many kinds. For the moment, about all that can safely be said is that balancing of the criteria is (1) necessary, (2) difficult, and (3) inhospitable to generalization. But even without general formulae, the balancing process should be roughly workable; there has already been some limited use of an *ad hoc* balancing approach to conditions. Whatever else may be said of the criteria-balancing approach to conditioned welfare and other government benefits, it is at least more flexible than what we now have.

Controlling Official Behavior in Welfare Administration†

Joel F. Handler*

L AWYERS HAVE ALWAYS BEEN CONCERNED with controlling the actions of government. What is new today is that attention has shifted to welfare administration. The shift, of course, reflects the larger national interest in civil rights and poverty. The legal profession's reaction to the national interest has been an increasing awareness and apparent (if somewhat halting) willingness to do something about providing legal services for the underprivileged, the Negro, and the dependent poor. Within these broader shifts in attitudes, it is natural that lawyers would begin to concern themselves with the problems raised by government activity in the welfare field. Public welfare has been around a long time; attention is now being directed at it as part of the broad national movement for civil justice.

To a very considerable extent, lawyers cast the problem in traditional terms: How can the socially approved interests of the individual be protected in the government welfare programs? The concern of lawyers in the welfare field is timely. Existing welfare programs, which were aimed primarily at assistance or income maintenance, are being extended. But more important, government welfare programs are taking on new goals and purposes. The dependent poor are not only to be helped financially, but the new programs are designed to strengthen family life and to move the dependent poor toward self-support and independence, to improve their life-chances by "breaking the cycle of poverty." The War On Poverty is the most popular example. The Social Security Act,[1] particularly in its recent amendments concerning aid to families with children, bristles with the new approach. The Aid to Dependent Children program (ADC) has been changed to "aid and services to needy families with children" (AFDC).[2] The purposes have been restated "to help such

---

† This article grew out of two related efforts: (1) the Russell Sage Law and Sociology Program at the University of Wisconsin, and, more particularly, the Administrative Law Seminar which was given for graduate students in that program; and (2) a study of the administration of the AFDC program in Wisconsin now getting under way under the direction of Professor Anthony F. Costonis, Department of Sociology, Wisconsin University, and myself.

* A.B., 1954, Princeton University; LL.B., 1957, Harvard University. Associate Professor of Law, University of Wisconsin.

[1] 49 Stat. 620 (1935), as amended, 42 U.S.C. §§ 301-1394 (1964), as amended, 42 U.S.C. §§ 302-1396d (Supp. I, 1965).

[2] 76 Stat. 185 (1962), as amended, 42 U.S.C. §§ 601-09 (1964), as amended, 42 U.S.C. §§ 602, 603, 606 (Supp. I, 1965).

parents or relatives to attain or retain capability for maximum self-support and personal independence consistent with the maintenance of continuing parental care and protection . . . ."[3] The amendments call for increased services such as accelerated programs in education, vocational rehabilitation, counselling, mental health, and community organization work.[4] The War On Poverty and the changes in the Social Security Act offer new hope for the dependent poor to escape many of the problems that they have known. But the new programs also pose new threats to the interests and freedom of the welfare clients; they may further weaken or debilitate family life and result in further loss of personal dignity.[5]

It is to the danger or threats to the freedom and dignity of the individual that the recent literature of the lawyers has turned. A good way to discuss the issues is to examine the work of Professor Charles Reich. His three articles—*Midnight Welfare Searches and the Social Security Act*,[6] *The New Property*,[7] and *Individual Rights and Social Welfare: The Emerging Legal Issues*[8]—have received a great deal of attention. They purport to define some of the more important issues, and suggest how we should solve them. Much new legal research adopts Reich's analysis and approach.[9]

Reich catalogues certain "ills" of present-day welfare administration. Welfare officials have attempted to impose moral codes on welfare recipients. Privacy has been unnecessarily invaded under the guise of eligibility and need investigations. Welfare laws sometimes impose financial responsibility on relatives of welfare recipients that are much broader than duties imposed on relatives of nonwelfare persons. The residence of welfare recipients is usually restricted; in some states, there are "removal" laws. Several states require work or vocational retraining as a

---

[3] 70 Stat. 848 (1956), as amended, 42 U.S.C. § 601 (1964).

[4] See 76 Stat. 173 (1962), 42 U.S.C. §§ 603(a)(3), (c)(1) (1964) (the states are offered a seventy-five per cent grant-in-aid to develop these new programs); BUREAU OF FAMILY SERVICE, U.S. DEP'T OF HEALTH, EDUC. & WELFARE, HANDBOOK OF PUBLIC ASSISTANCE ADMINISTRATION, PART IV §§ 4050-53.5 (Rev. Nov. 30, 1962).

[5] Some of the far-reaching implications of the new welfare programs are discussed in Handler & Rosenheim, *Privacy in Welfare: Public Assistance and Juvenile Justice*, 31 LAW & CONTEMP. PROB. (1966) (to be published).

[6] 72 YALE L.J. 1347 (1963).

[7] 73 YALE L.J. 733 (1964).

[8] 74 YALE L.J. 1245 (1965).

[9] See, *e.g.*, the statement of purposes of the newly established Project on Social Welfare Law at the New York University School of Law, 1 Welfare Law Bull., Dec. 1965, p. 1 (quoted in text accompanying note 64 *infra*), and Columbia University School of Social Work: Center on Social Welfare Policy and Law, Memorandum on the "social welfare law testing" function of the Center 1. This memorandum has been reprinted in *Practical Lawyer*, April 1966.

condition of receiving aid. Public housing authorities may deny admission or terminate leases of people who have police records or whom the authorities think keep undesirable company or engage in immoral conduct. Often welfare recipients are required to take loyalty oaths not required of the general public. Under the means test, welfare officials have great powers over the family budget; independence is restricted by official supervision.[10]

The "ills" that Reich (as well as others) are concerned with fall into two broad categories. On the one hand, the day-to-day administration has resulted in many instances of plainly lawless administrative behavior; that is, administrative officials are acting contrary to the Constitution and/or statutory terms, and clients are being deprived of rights embodied in constitutional and statutory law. On the other hand, there is concern over unwarranted interferences in the interests of welfare clients that are not clearly defined legal rights. These would include various aspects of privacy, moral behavior, and the manipulation of welfare clients in such matters as employment, retraining, counselling, mental health, and other rehabilitative services. In this latter category, there is a feeling that welfare clients are being made to adopt behavior not required of other people by the state, or that welfare clients are made to forego activities and enjoyments that other people are allowed to enjoy.

The ills come about in two ways. First, there is bad substantive legislation. Welfare statutes often contain provisions which impose unnecessary hardships on the recipients. These would include residence requirements, responsibility provisions, loyalty oaths (included in the Economic Opportunity Act),[11] and the notice to law enforcement provision in the ADC program. Second, there are broad delegations of authority to welfare agencies which allow them to define critical substantive matters. Generally, the federal welfare statutes allow the states to determine the criteria of need, levels of income and resources, and the minimum level of living for the recipients.[12] When eligibility criteria are set forth in the legislation (federal and state), the criteria often conflict, or are vague, and the agencies have choice over which criteria to choose in any given situation. Or, the statutes are silent as to critical substantive areas, giving the agencies an even freer hand. In the day-to-day administration, the power granted through delegations of authority is increased by the agency practice of deciding issues on a case-by-case basis rather than promulgating and publishing rules in advance, the discretionary powers of enforcement,

---

[10] Reich, *supra* note 8, at 1247-51.

[11] 79 Stat. 973, 42 U.S.C. § 2714(d) (Supp. I, 1965).

[12] See Burns, Social Security and Public Policy 228-31 (1956).

the power to delay, investigate, and harass, and the fact that people dependent on welfare are over-anxious to please officials rather than run the risk of punishment.

The remedies or solutions that Reich proposes have a ring familiar to lawyers. In welfare the government should not be allowed to impose any conditions that would be unconstitutional if imposed on persons not on welfare; government can't "buy up" constitutional rights. The substantive provisions of welfare statutes must be stripped of all that is not relevant to the purposes of the programs, such as loyalty requirements for tenants in government housing. In addition, "to the extent possible, delegated power to make rules ought to be confined within ascertainable limits, and regulating agencies should not be assigned the task of enforcing conflicting policies. Also agencies should be enjoined to use their powers only for the purposes for which they were designed."[13] But because it is so difficult to define in statutes what is relevant and to confine administrative discretion, Reich puts heavy emphasis on "basic" procedural safeguards. "In the case of a decision removing a family from public housing, or a decision denying aid to families with dependent children, generally the matter is finally determined at some level within the appropriate agency, after investigation by the agency, and with comparatively informal procedures, if any, available to the persons affected."[14] He calls for "full adjudicatory procedures."[15] Reich is not very specific about what he means by this ("procedures can develop gradually and pragmatically")[16] but appears to favor quite strongly the following: advance notification and publication of regulations that will govern future agency decisions; notice of proposed action, including a "full statement of the basis for it"; a trial-type hearing with the right to be represented by counsel; a separation of functions of investigator and judge; a decision based on competent evidence in the record; reasons in support of the decision; and "some form of review" (perhaps "within the agency, and, ultimately, in the courts").[17] Finally, Reich develops his idea of "entitlement." His conclusion is that the poor are entitled to welfare as a matter of "right" and not of "privilege." "The idea of entitlement is simply that when individuals have insufficient resources to live under conditions of health and decency, society has obligations to provide support, and the individual is entitled to that support as of right." At the risk of oversimplification, the objective

---

[13] Reich, *supra* note 7, at 782-83.
[14] Reich, *supra* note 8, at 1252.
[15] *Id.* at 1253.
[16] *Ibid.*
[17] *Ibid.*

of this position is to promote individual security by rejecting the case law justifying government interference on the ground that what the individual is claiming is a "mere gratuity" rather than a "right."[18]

Reich's strategy is quite clear. What he wants to do, in essence, is elevate the position of the welfare recipient to a position similar to that of a person whose business interests are regulated by government. In business regulation, government agencies are dealing with a "right"— property. Constitutional limits, more or less, are applicable. Through the years statutory and judicially-imposed procedural safeguards have developed. Reich introduces his argument for procedural safeguards in the welfare field by talking about and listing specifically the types of procedural safeguards developed in business regulation. (These were basically the "full adjudicatory" procedures discussed above.)

> These procedures, however cumbersome they may seem, have come to represent a fundamental standard of fairness in administrative process. They may be exaggerated and misused until they produce inordinate delay and expense, but they represent effective checks on the characteristic evils of proceedings in any large public or private organization: closed doors, Kafka-like uncertainty, difficulty in locating responsibility, and rigid adherence to a particular point of view. They are fundamental safeguards for those who must deal with government.[19]

What Reich is doing then, is giving welfare recipients legally protectible rights (similar to "standing"), procedural safeguards with which to assert those rights, and, he adds, the ability to protect the rights through representation by counsel. Welfare clients would then be in a position similar to regulated industries, and in "business regulation . . . lawyers have made paper procedures a practical reality."[20]

In analyzing this very appealing approach, I will first examine the assumptions underlying Reich's view as to what the process of business regulation is like. We will see how much lawyers have in fact made a "practical reality" out of "paper procedures." More important, an examination of the administrative process in business regulation will shed light on some basic institutional and structural problems which apply to welfare administration. Second, I will discuss some of the particular problems of judicializing welfare administration. The main example will be the AFDC program. Third, I will suggest different avenues if we are to accomplish Reich's, as well as our, goal of civil justice.

---

18 *Id.* at 1256.
19 *Id.* at 1253.
20 *Id.* at 1252.

I

THE ANALOGY TO ADMINISTRATIVE REGULATION OF BUSINESS INTERESTS

The procedural safeguards in the administration of business interests, which Reich has in mind, arise in many types of situations. Typically, they come into operation when a person or business is claiming that an agency is acting contrary to law. The person may claim, for example, that the agency is taxing him illegally, or is wrongly applying a health regulation to his restaurant. The person may also be complaining about the failure of an agency to give him permission to do something, such as denying an application for a zoning variance. In situations like these (and if the matter cannot be settled), the claimant, with counsel, presents his claim to the agency which then conducts a trial-type hearing. The agency (or a hearing officer) acts like a judge. Although agencies are generally not bound by formal rules of evidence, the decision usually must be based on evidence in the record and the type of evidence cannot stray too far afield from that typically presented in court. If the claimant is still unhappy with the agency decision, he can seek judicial review. Again there are variations, but we will assume that the review will be appellate court review rather than a trial de novo. The appellate court is asked to "review" the administration action, to see whether the administrative behavior was authorized by law. The claim can be that there was no authority for the agency to act at all in this situation (for example, no statutory jurisdiction), or that the agency misapplied the statute, or that there was insufficient evidence to support the decision, or that there was bias, and so forth.

If the court thinks that the claimant is correct, the remedy may be to nullify the administrative decision and thus to allow the claimant to use his property as he intended free from official interference. Such would be the case, for example, if the court decided that the particular health regulation did not apply to the claimant's business. On the other hand, if the court decides that there was insufficient evidence to support the agency decision, the court may send the case back to the agency for a "new trial." This may also happen even if the court thinks that the agency has misconstrued the statute. The court may still think that the basic substantive decision should be made by the agency rather than the court. But the court will insist that the administrative decision be legal.

In these examples, we note that there is no question about the protectibility of the claimant's interest; he is seeking to prevent interference with land or money or other types of property in which he has "rights." In addition, there is generally no question about knowledge or resources on the part of the claimant. He knows what he wants to do with his property;

the agency has told him what he can or cannot do with the property; he has legal counsel of his own choosing to advise him. Reich's solutions would place the welfare recipient in a similar position—he would have rights, he would have procedural safeguards, and he would be given counsel.

The fact of the matter is that even in the administration of business regulation, very little of the type of control of administrative behavior that Reich talks about exists. It is now commonplace to reiterate that the informal procedures are truly "the lifeblood of the administrative process."[21] Davis estimates that "perhaps eighty or ninety per cent of the impact of the administrative process involves discretionary action in absence of safeguards of hearing procedures."[22] These are cases which are disposed of without a trial-type hearing or a record upon which the decision is based. Sometimes the informal adjudication consists of "settlement cases"—the party is entitled to a formal hearing if he wants one, but the case is settled prior to the hearing. In others, sometimes called the "pure administrative process," no formal hearings are provided prior to the formal decision (for example, inspection or tests of physical properties).[23] I cannot here describe in any detail the characteristics and range of problems encompassed by the informal administrative process. I will point out instead some highlights and examples of some aspects that have particular relevance to the problems raised by welfare administration and the program of "rights" that Reich calls for.

A great deal of informal adjudication is present when agencies have the power to enforce statutes. These agencies are able to negotiate settlements and regulate behavior without using formal procedures and without judicial review. In nonadministrative law contexts, the regulatory practices of the police and the administrators of juvenile justice are familiar examples. These officials "settle" cases and impose sanctions without any resort to courts or other formal procedures.[24] This is also true of many administrative agencies. One prominent example is the Federal Trade Commission. The statute provides for hearings, findings of fact, and orders to cease and desist.[25] The vast majority of the results obtained by the FTC are through stipulation and consent orders rather than cease and desist orders. Many deceptive practices are disposed of through administrative treatment upon assurance that the party will discontinue the

---

[21] Att'y General's Comm. on Administrative Procedure, *Report*, S. Doc. No. 8, 77th Cong., 1st Sess. 35 (1941).

[22] DAVIS, ADMINISTRATIVE LAW—CASES, TEXT, PROBLEMS 70 (1965).

[23] On the "pure administrative process," see GELLHORN & BYSE, ADMINISTRATIVE LAW 657-65 (4th ed. 1960).

[24] See generally Note, 79 HARV. L. REV. 775 (1966).

[25] 38 Stat. 719 (1914), as amended, 15 U.S.C. § 45 (1964).

practice. It is claimed that "if the Federal Trade Commission were compelled to discontinue its stipulation and consent order procedures, it would have to forego a major part of its activity."[26] It is also said that "the fact that stipulation and consent orders are based on consent does not mean that parties are necessarily protected against exercise of arbitrary power."[27] There is little difference between the "quasi-judicial" independent Commission and the wholly nonjudicial Antitrust Division of the Justice Department in the matter of informal adjudication. In recent years, between eighty-five and ninety per cent of the antitrust decrees were obtained under consent procedures.[28] The FTC, with its judicialized structure and procedural rights and safeguards, operates to a large extent as strictly a prosecuting agency.

The regulation of banking is another prominent example.

> The striking fact is that the banking agencies use methods of informal supervision, almost always without formal adjudication, even for the determination of controversies. . . . A single example will suggest the spirit of the regulatory system. The Board of Governors of the Federal Reserve System has authority, after hearing, to suspend any member bank for "undue use" of its credit for speculative purposes inconsistent with sound credit conditions. . . . What happens is that the Board enforces the statute through methods of bank examiners, who call to the bank's attention the items which require correction. A bank which is inclined to disagree does not typically stand on its supposed rights and defy the Board to start a formal proceeding; suspension is too drastic a remedy for the bank to risk. The bank deals informally with the Board's representatives until some mutually satisfactory solution is worked out. Adjudication gives way almost entirely to supervision. . . . The sanction is not the power of suspension but the power of instituting proceedings.[29]

A third example involves the Securities and Exchange Commission's power over registration and acceleration. Because the mere announcement that a stop-order proceeding is so harmful, the decisive administrative determination, as far as the registrant is concerned, is the letter of comment from the SEC staff suggesting changes in the registration statement. "The registrant may be inclined to disagree with the staff's policies and may even think that the staff is arbitrary or unreasonable. But even if the registrant could convince a reviewing court that this is so, the registrant is in practical effect at the mercy of the Commission."[30] The statute provides that the effective date of a registration statement is twenty days after

---

26 Massel, *The Regulatory Process*, 26 LAW & CONTEMP. PROB. 181, 187 (1961).

27 DAVIS, *op. cit. supra* note 22, at 75.

28 Massel, *supra* note 26, at 192.

29 DAVIS, *op. cit. supra* note 22, at 76.

30 *Id.* at 73.

filing.[31] Registrants, however, usually want the date accelerated, and the Commission has discretionary power to grant the request.[32]

> Business reasons usually make acceleration . . . so compelling that the registrant is willing to yield to onerous conditions. The SEC uses its discretionary power . . . to bargain for what it thinks the public interest may require; indeed, it sometimes requires substantive action having nothing to do with full disclosure. . . . The manner in which the SEC uses the acceleration power has long been highly controversial, but no registrant has been able to challenge it in a reviewing court.[33]

The SEC example, as well as the others, raises another aspect of the informal administrative process—regulation by fear of prosecution or publicity. The main weapon in the arsenal of the SEC, in the above example, is the potentially disastrous effects of publicity and delay. There are numerous examples in the literature of regulation by threats of adverse publicity. The Food and Drug Administration decided to stop salad oil and margarine makers from making claims about cholesterol and heart disease. According to H. Thomas Austern:

> The FDA did not reach that conclusion by taking evidence or by offering any facts or opinions for expert discussion and criticism at a public hearing. It did not issue any formal regulation. It held no hearings. It made no formal findings. Instead, it published what it called a "Statement of Policy." It simply announced that it would hereafter consider as false and misleading any label claim that the use of a non-animal fat had any relation to heart disease. In the accompanying Press Release, which was hardly a legal document, it went even further. It announced that any label reference to "cholesterol" would also be illegal, because it might falsely imply some relation to heart disease. . . .
> Whether the FDA was right or wrong, the fact is that every margarine manufacturer has acquiesced.[34]

After discussing other FDA examples of this type of regulation (including the cranberries), Austern concludes:

> That is why no experienced Food and Drug lawyer resorts to court save in extremis—why here the conventional talk about the "administrative process" and "court review" is largely academic, why seizures usually go uncontested, why what I shall call "jawbone enforcement" is the real area of administrative activity, why reported decisions and formal regulations bear as little relation to what really goes on as the

---

[31] 48 Stat. 79 (1933), as amended, 15 U.S.C. § 77h (1964).

[32] *Ibid.*

[33] Davis, *op. cit. supra* note 22, at 73-74.

[34] Address by H. Thomas Austern, *Sanctions in Silhouette*, Second Annual Charles Wesley Dunn Food and Drug Law Lecture, delivered at the Harvard Law School, March 22, 1960, reprinted in Gellhorn & Byse, *op. cit. supra* note 23, at 671-72.

visible top of an iceberg to the whole, and why the question of enforcement of administrative views by Madison Avenue techniques of publicity demands such close scrutiny in this field.[35]

Reich, in drawing upon the analogy of the administration of business regulation to support his arguments for "judicializing" welfare administration, seems to give the impression that administrative decisions are generally carried out with all the procedural safeguards: advance publication of rules, notice, formal trial-type hearings, competent and relevant evidence, decisions based on the record. His description leaves out the most significant area: informal administration, where none of these procedural safeguards are used. He is quite wrong in asserting that lawyers have made a "practical reality" of the judicial-type procedures. The existing evidence points in the opposite direction. According to persons intimate with the administrative process, it seems rare indeed when judicial-type procedures are used to attempt to control administrative behavior.

It might be argued that the fact that judicial-type procedures are not used or are circumvented in business regulation does not detract from their value; it only means that reform is needed with business regulation as well as welfare administration. The fact is, however, that arguments over procedures in administration have been raging for years, and many able and serious students of the administrative process argue for *less*, not more, judicial-type procedure. It is claimed, for example, that many regulatory agencies simply could not administer their programs if all decisions on cases and policies had to go through formalized hearing procedures.[36] The same is true with regard to enforcement agencies. In many situations the parties may be better off if minor infractions can be settled informally.[37] Several critics take issue with the popular notion (usually put forward by lawyers) that adjudication can be considered separate from policy formulation. They argue that many administrative policies have to be formulated on a case-by-case approach, with observation of a gradual development, rather than the promulgation of rules in advance.[38] Marver Bernstein suggests, as a hypothesis, that the "continuing judicialization of administrative regulation . . . has encouraged the growth of nonad-

---

[35] *Id.* at 673.

[36] Massel, *supra* note 26, at 187.

[37] *Ibid.*

[38] Mark Massel, of the Brookings Institution, for example, states that "The criticisms of policy-making seem to be founded on the assumption that the agencies refuse to issue rules because of timidity, inability, and ineffectiveness. There seems to be no room allowed for the possibility that there exist reasonable grounds for the agency practice or institutional pressures against such a practice." *Id.* at 189. See generally Shapiro, *The Choice of Rulemaking or Adjudication in the Development of Administrative Policy*, 78 HARV. L. REV. 921 (1965).

versary methods to dispose of regulatory business and may have stimulated wider recourse to ex parte contacts and communications."[39] That is to say, more stringent "due process" requirements may result in more nonformal regulations or less regulations altogether; more rigid and formal hearing requirements may result in increased pressures for informal settlements. Running through many of the arguments of informed critics like Massel, Bernstein, Gellhorn, Byse, as well as many others, is the view that lawyers have wrongly looked at administrative agencies through judicial-colored glasses and have evaluated the administrative process in terms of how well administrative procedures match up to court procedures. This approach concentrates on the independent regulatory agencies and ignores the vast amount of regulation carried on by executive departments; it fails to recognize that the agencies were set up, in part, because the courts and legislatures could not handle the programs that the agencies are charged with; it misses the very important regulatory activity that goes on without judicial-type procedures and the value of the informal process; and it has resulted in sometimes harmful and sometimes futile attempts to engraft on agencies procedural requirements unsuited for the conduct of their business.[40]

But, it may be argued that even though "rights" embodied in judicial-

---

[39] Bernstein, *The Regulatory Process: A Framework for Analysis*, 26 LAW & CONTEMP. PROB. 329, 345 (1961).

[40] Gellhorn and Byse, in commenting on informal adjudication, say:

"Procedural forms are not fetishes. They are means to ends. The ends are correct determinations of disputable questions, with safeguards against abusive exercises of governmental authority.

"In some circumstances it has been concluded, and rightly so, that a record of past happenings can be reconstructed with greatest fidelity by requiring narrations concerning them to be made with full solemnity—under oath, in a public forum, and subject to that process of refinement and qualification known as cross-examination. . . .

"In other circumstances . . . a different method seems warranted. An investigatory technique supplants the judicialized hearing. It is the technique which, after all, is employed almost exclusively—except by government—to develop the facts on which the gravest judgments turn. To suggest that it is no longer an apt tool merely because it is in official hands, would be an absurdity. The groupings of cases mentioned in these pages . . . suffice to refute . . . the contention that administration is necessarily defective to the extent that it tolerates basic departures from the procedure of courts. . . .

"The extension of unconventional processes presupposes a subordinate personnel equipped to use them fairly and an administrative hierarchy fired with a sense of responsibility for scrupulously just results. There is no reason to suppose that public administration through official agencies is incapable of developing professional traditions and standards comparable with those developed by public administration through the courts.

"It is here that the experience of life offers lessons: the formalized hearing is a method of getting at the truth and of assuring justice; but it is only one of many methods. No particular means is invariably synonymous with the fair result. No one device can properly assert a monopoly over the procedural virtues, and thus debar efforts to build new, perhaps more direct roads to justice." GELLHORN & BYSE, *op. cit. supra* note 23, at 664-65.

type procedures are not used very often, it is still important that they exist; it is still within the power of private citizens and companies to check illegal and unwarranted official behavior if the need should arise. This argument may or may not be true. First, as some of the above examples show (and these are not atypical cases), in many instances people and businesses are not *able* to use the judicial-type procedures. The costs or the risks involved are too high—even in situations where they feel that government action is unwarranted. Later I will discuss why this happens.

Second, the argument is dangerous and, if implemented, can be productive of much harm. By ignoring the realities of administration, and particularly the informal process, it leads one into thinking that the important problems of controlling official behavior will be solved by enacting a program of rights. The informal process exists. It cannot be legislated away. In many situations, there is persuasive evidence that the informal process works fairly and fulfills legislative goals.[41] No doubt there are many instances where this is not true.[42] But the informal process is intimately connected with the formal process. Enacting a formal program of rights and judicializing the administrative procedure may make the informal process more fair. On the other hand, changing the formal process may destroy much of the value of the informal process; in other instances, it may lead to even more lawless administrative behavior.[43] Reich pays little or no attention to the problem of implementing his program or to whether the harm caused by an effective use of these rights (if that is ever possible) outweighs the good. It is premature to defend his position on the ground that "it is good as far as it goes" because of his failure to calculate the costs of judicializing administrative procedures. The easy assumption that because agencies decide individual cases they are therefore like courts and should act like courts ignores the very different institutional and structural characteristics of administrative agencies. These points will be discussed in detail in the following section which deals specifically with welfare administration.

The discussion about the inappropriateness of the analogy to the

---

[41] For an excellent and exhaustive analysis of the intimate relationship between the formal and informal process in the administration of the automobile dealers statutes, see Macauley, *Changing A Continuing Relationship Between A Large Corporation and Those Who Deal With It: Automobile Manufacturers, Their Dealers, and The Legal System* (pts. 1, 2), 1965 WIS. L. REV. 483, 740. Professor Macaulay presents a persuasive case that the informal process in Wisconsin better serves the competing interests than the formal legal system.

[42] See Levy, *Protecting the Mentally Retarded: An Empirical Survey and Evaluation of the Establishment of State Guardianship in Minnesota*, 49 MINN. L. REV. 821 (1965).

[43] See LaFAVE, ARREST: THE DECISION TO TAKE A SUSPECT INTO CUSTODY (1965); LaFave & Remington, *Controlling the Police: The Judge's Role in Making and Reviewing Law Enforcement Decisions*, 63 MICH. L. REV. 987 (1965).

administration of economic regulation would not be complete without mentioning that all-important guardian and protector of individual rights, the reviewing court. Whatever the injustice committed at the administrative level, the opportunity to go to court means that ultimately the rights of the individual will be secure against lawless administrative behavior. Of course, there have been instances where appellate courts have checked lawless administrative behavior; and it might be demonstrated that the availability of judicial review does have some impact on some administrative agencies. But, in the main, it seems doubtful to rely on reviewing courts to accomplish significant changes in administrative behavior. First, much of the informal administrative process is not susceptible to judicial review.[44] Second, at least in federal administrative law, the impact of the reviewing courts has been characterized as sporadic, clumsy, and largely ineffective.[45] The courts have been concerned almost exclusively with matters of procedure; what the agencies *do* to people and their property is largely beyond judicial scrutiny, as long as procedural steps are properly taken or adequate "findings" are made. Judicially developed doctrines of limited scope of review of questions of fact and of law, expertise, and primary jurisdiction all have served to hasten the flight of courts from supervising the substance of administrative programs and from serious attempts to control official behavior. Howard Westwood says:

> In the case of the federal agencies, it is my observation that the appellate court decisions—especially those of the Supreme Court—do not greatly affect the day-to-day problems that arise in the practice before the agencies. . . . This conclusion would be difficult to prove and, based as it is upon personal experience, it may well be faulty. Yet, as I look upon a considerable experience I find little significant impact of the advance sheets upon what actually goes on from one day to the next in agency practice.[46]

Agencies, reports Westwood, usually do not pay very much attention to court decisions involving different agencies.

> And even the agency directly involved in an appellate case often is not drastically affected thereby. A little adjustment of procedure, another form of words in "findings," a slightly different evidentiary presumption—and life goes on rather as before in many, many cases; or, indeed, the appellate decision may have no effect at all save in the specific case immediately involved. The point of the matter is that the agency's own decisions (and sometimes the decisions of sister agencies on related problems) are usually more important as precedents than

---

[44] See Davis, *op. cit. supra* note 22, at 72.

[45] See, *e.g.*, Att'y General's Comm. on Administrative Procedure, *Report*, S. Doc. No. 8, 77th Cong., 1st Sess. 76-77 (1941); Westwood, *The Davis Treatise: Meaning to the Practitioner*, 43 Minn. L. Rev. 607, 608 (1959).

[46] Westwood, *supra* note 45, at 608.

the rulings of the appellate courts. Important, too, is a "feel" for the way the agency and its staff will react to a situation, a "feel" not to be disclosed in any precedents at all.[47]

Frank Newman points out that reviewing courts can only deal effectively with "judicial review law," "but law relating to agency powers and procedures is quite different, for judges inevitably can deal only with tiny pieces of it."[48] The "right" to judicial review, as a method of controlling administrative behavior, may be largely one of paper only. Judicial review is simply not applicable to many administrative decisions; and when it is available, the court may decline to make the substantive decision anyway.

II

APPLYING JUDICIAL TECHNIQUES TO THE ADMINISTRATION OF WELFARE

The importance of the discussion in the preceding section does not lie solely in exposing some of the futility and difficulties in the attempt to judicialize the administration of business regulation. It sheds light on some of the basic aspects of administrative processes; the lessons learned in the administration of business regulation should help in avoiding the pitfalls of attempting to control official behavior in welfare administration by imposing similar techniques.

I will use as my example the AFDC program, which is a grant-in-aid program administered under the Social Security Act. The Act sets forth relatively few mandatory requirements on the states as conditions for participation (for example, a state can have a residence requirement but it cannot be for longer than one year);[49] most of the federal statutory provisions are permissive (for example, a state *may* extend the program where need is caused by the unemployment of a parent).[50] As stated earlier, the federal statute generally leaves to the states the determination of the criteria of need, the levels of income and other sources that will be included in the budget, and the levels of income to be paid to the families (subject to a federally imposed maximum). In Wisconsin, as well as many other states, the state agency (Wisconsin State Department of Public Welfare, Division of Public Assistance) supervises the program, but the actual administration is carried on by county welfare agencies. The Wisconsin Division of Public Assistance assists the counties in the development of their programs, supervises their activities, and advises the local agencies of federal and state requirements. At both the federal and state

---

[47] *Id.* at 609.

[48] Newman, *The Literature of Administrative Law and the New Davis Treatise,* 43 MINN. L. REV. 637, 644 (1959).

[49] 49 Stat. 627 (1935), as amended, 42 U.S.C. § 602(b) (1964).

[50] 75 Stat. 75 (1961), as amended, 42 U.S.C. § 607 (1964).

levels there has been a conscious attempt to provide flexibility and a large measure of autonomy and discretion at the county level.

One of the discretionary decisions that is made at the county level is whether the AFDC mother should work. When the program was first enacted, the policy was to provide financial assistance so that the mother would not have to leave the home in order to work. Attitudes have changed, and it is now recognized that in certain situations if the mother has a job it may be beneficial to both the mother and the children (assuming adequate day care). Whether the mother should work or not is a decision that must be made on the basis of each family's needs. One of the dangers, of course, is that mothers will be "encouraged" to work in order to save public money, since her earnings will be included in the family budget. The Wisconsin regulations go to great length in suggesting criteria to be used by the county caseworkers in making this decision.[51] The caseworkers are specifically told that the mother should work only if her working will contribute to the strengthening of family life and promote other rehabilitative goals; the decision must not be made in order to save public money.

Assume that in a particular case, a caseworker decides that the mother should work. Assume further that this decision was made to save public money and that it was not in the "best interests" of the family. The mother, for example, is genuinely reluctant to leave her children in the hands of the available day-care help. To a very great extent, the mother already has the "rights" that Reich calls for. In distinguishing the Social Security Act from other welfare programs, he says that "the framers of the Act had a clear concept concerning the 'right' to public assistance, and provided devices to protect these rights. Thus, in the program for aid to families with needy children, the Act requires that states afford an opportunity for a fair hearing to any individual whose claim is denied or not acted upon with reasonable promptness . . . ."[52] Wisconsin faithfully implements the purpose of the Social Security Act to provide procedural regularity and fairness. There is advance publication of the rule governing the situation; indeed, the fullness and clarity of the Wisconsin regulation is probably unusual. The state statute provides for a prompt, fair hearing not only when a claim is denied but also when an individual is dissatisfied with the amount of the grant.[53] The regulations set forth detailed procedures which display a careful balance between fairness and informality.[54]

[51] Div. of Public Assistance, Wis. State Dep't of Public Welfare, Regs. § III, ch. III, (Need Determination) 47.

[52] Reich, *supra* note 8, at 1246, referring to the amended 42 U.S.C. § 602 (1964).

[53] Wis Stat. § 49.50(8) (Supp. 1961).

[54] Div. of Public Assistance, Wis. State Dep't of Public Welfare, Regs. § I, ch. III, Rule No. PW-PA 20.18, as amended (1951).

The appeal is heard by a special representative of the state Division of Public Assistance, and not by the county welfare department.[55] Yet, it is easy to see how Reich's program of rights will be of little use to the mother in this type of situation.

One of the critical facts to realize is that at the point where the case-worker tells the mother that she must take a job, the mother is still in the program. She and her family are currently receiving assistance and she will probably not be able to support her family with her earnings; besides, she does not want to leave her children. She knows that tomorrow and the next day the same caseworker will be making other decisions that affect vitally her level of living and style of life. She may want extra money to give herself or her children special vocational training; she may want a referral for herself or one of her children for mental health services or counseling; she may want the earnings of her children set aside for future higher education; or she may want to move to a better apartment in a better neighborhood. There are literally countless decisions that the case-worker may be called upon to make that can help this family: Boy Scout fees, a graduation dress or money for the graduation dance, money for a band instrument, money for tools to learn a trade, and so on.[56] These can be matters of great importance to any of us; and they are decided by the county caseworker.

In short, in calculating whether to fight the decision about working, the mother has to weigh the costs to her on-going relationship with the local agency; what will happen to her tomorrow if she disagrees with the case-worker this time and "goes over his head"? She is now beginning to think that in the "long run" it would be "better" for her family if she agreed with the caseworker and went to work. Reich is absolutely right in stating that caseworkers in these situations have great power over their clients. What he fails to realize is that this power largely nullifies a program of rights. This is one of the lessons that we learn from the administration of business regulation; why there is so much informal administrative adjudi-cation. The bankers will have to deal with the federal examiners next month; securities dealers and traders and manufacturers of food and drugs are under constant supervision by government officials; the same is true in commercial broadcasting and transportation. In these fields, as

---

[55] *Ibid.*

[56] The Wisconsin regulations explicitly recognize the importance of these items. For example, "additional special needs [for children] . . . may be the following: lunches, transportation, costs of special courses of training, participation in school band or orchestra, athletic activities or in community activities (such as Scouts, 4-H); union dues, health insurance (if not deducted by employer); regular payments on equipment such as bicycle, lawn mower, special clothing, or tools and equipment of employment." Div. of Public Assistance, Wis. State Dep't of Public Welfare, Regs. § III, ch. III-51 (Revised 1965).

well as others, the complaints about the unchecked discretionary powers of officials and the lack of procedural safeguards and judicial control are loud. The reason is not because procedural rights and judicial review are not provided for; they are. It is because the relationships between the regulators and the regulated interests are such that the latter are effectively discouraged from exercising those rights.

It is curious, then, that where knowledgeable and powerful economic interests forego procedural rights and succumb to lawless official behavior, one would argue that a program of rights would control officials in the welfare field. Again, there is solid evidence to the contrary. In the administration of juvenile justice, quite often the "clients" have at least some of the rights; indeed, a juvenile cannot be declared a delinquent, or neglected, or dependent without a formal court proceeding. Yet it is found that the effective decisions are made by the police and probation officers, not the judges. In many instances, the juveniles, rightly or wrongly, think that it is to their advantage to play ball rather than to fight. One of the reasons is that they know that even if they win today, the officer will have another chance tomorrow. Reformers here also call for a program of rights. I have argued elsewhere that before rights can be made effective in this field, there has to be knowledge, ability or resources, *and clear, practical advantages for using these rights*.[57] All of these conditions present formidable hurdles in the area of juvenile justice. The same would seem to be true in the welfare field. The dependent poor, we are told, are bewildered, confused, and have a deep sense of helplessness; many suffer from mental illness. Legislation, regulations at the state level, and appellate court opinions would seem to have little impact on these people in their face-to-face encounters with county welfare officials.[58]

Of course, there are situations where the victims of government will use their rights, where they will fight. Again, these cases are instructive; they indicate the significance of the on-going relationship. Formal administrative hearings and court cases are long and hard fought in the allocation

---

[57] Handler, *The Juvenile Court and the Adversary System: Problems of Function and Form*, 1965 WIS. L. REV. 7. See also Sparer, *The Role of the Welfare Client's Lawyer*, 12 U.C.L.A.L. REV. 361, 378 (1965): "The public welfare worker, however, presents a different situation. Generally, he initially makes the ruling which necessitates the client going to the lawyer. This presents the attorney with a double danger. On the one hand, he needs to remember that he cannot afford, for his client's sake, to make an enemy of the public social worker. Although antagonism to the worker's decision will often result, the lawyer's function should not be to undermine the welfare worker and inspire needless hostility. The welfare worker, after all, remains with the client if the lawyer wins the latter's case. There are ways other than the flat denial of eligibility to make a welfare recipient's life intolerable. Indeed, these may be beyond the redress of the legal process."

[58] These exact points are made by Levy, *supra* note 42, where there is also a full program of rights.

of TV channels, or airline routes, or franchises, or when licenses are revoked. But these are in the nature of "either-or" situations. The airline gets the route or it does not; the company or individual can stay in business or it can't. Similarly, if we look at the cases where Reich and others call for judicial-type rights and judicial control, we find also that they tend to be extreme "either-or" situations. Reich's cases, in welfare, generally deal with situations where clients are denied entrance to the program or are thrown out. In the midnight raid situation, state statutes and regulations deny AFDC aid if there is a man living in the house; the theory is that a man using the "privileges" of marriage ought to bear the responsibilities as well. Enforcement officials conduct raids on the homes of clients, late at night and without a warrant, to find evidence of the man. If such evidence is found, the client is thrown out of the program. Other cases deal with the improper or illegal use of eligibility requirements to prevent clients from entering the program. I would not minimize the importance of protecting people from this type of lawless official behavior; these issues are poignantly critical for the people involved. But they are cases where people have been cut off from the program or denied entrance; if they want in, they have no recourse but to fight and to appeal ultimately to agencies outside of the administrative bureaucracy, that is, the courts. For these people, future risks in the on-going administrative relationship are of considerably less relative importance than they are to the mother who has been told that she must work. These people are now interested in survival, not higher education. Reich, then, is talking primarily about the extreme cases. His discussion and solutions do not touch the mass of people in welfare administration, the people who have to deal day to day with officials and who are subject to the more elusive forms of administrative manipulation and interference.

In addition, even if we assume that the mother who has been told that she must work is resourceful and has the courage to challenge the caseworker's decision, and is willing to risk subsequent administrative disapproval, we may ask what her chances are of winning? Under the Wisconsin statutes, the AFDC mother has no absolute right not to work; the statute provides, instead, that the county "may require the mother to do such remunerative work as in its judgment she can do without detriment to her health or the neglect of her children or her home . . . ."[59] The mother's "right," then, depends on the existence of certain underlying facts and the evaluation of those facts; she is not required to work if working, in her particular family situation, will defeat the objectives of the program. This conditional aspect, of course, is true for most rights: A family is eligible

---

[59] WIS. STAT. § 49.19(6) (1957).

under the Social Security Act if it is needy; a person is entitled to receive benefits if he is "under a disability";[60] an applicant for an occupational license (or a driver's license) has to be competent, and so forth. Reich correctly points out that the "rights" of the mother (and in the other examples) are largely procedural: She is entitled to a fair hearing as to whether under the particular facts and under the regulations properly construed she should be required to work.

This dependence of "rights" on underlying and often complicated facts seriously qualifies the right of appeal. The caseworker, we may be sure, is familiar with the state regulations and will tailor his reasons to fit them. In his "professional" judgment, it would be good for both the mother and the children if the mother took the job; the latest medical reports say that she is physically and mentally able to work; this is a job suited to her abilities; she will be better integrated into the community if she is a working mother; the day-care help is very competent (in fact, the center or the person is "certified" by the state or the county). And, of course, there will be no hint that the purpose of the mother working is to save the public money. If this case gets to an appellate court, what will the court review? Will the court substitute its judgment on the substantive question for that of the professional worker in the field? Should the court? From the experience in judicial review of administration of business regulation, the reviewing court will probably examine the procedural steps taken, find "substantial evidence in the record" to support the agency's determination, and affirm the decision. I would guess that the most the mother could hope for, unless the administrative decision was outrageous and stupid, and she had very strong evidence, is that the reviewing court would reverse and remand the case to the agency for further findings. The court, in effect, would ask the agency to reconsider its decision. This generally is what happens when regulated business interests "win" in the reviewing courts.

A program of rights builds on the courtroom experience of lawyers and is subject to the limitations of that system of legal control. Control of government through court processes requires activity by the individual. If the person does not object to the official decision, the control does not come into play. I have already touched on the difficulties of getting individuals to act: In business regulation, the power of officials influences others to submit to informal regulation; in welfare administration, this power exists, and in addition, there are severe limitations concerning the personalities and resources of the dependent poor.

But there is another basic limitation to this adversary-oriented system of control. It is essentially negatively oriented; its emphasis is on blocking

---

[60] 70 Stat. 815 (1956), as amended, 42 U.S.C. § 423 (1964), as amended, 42 U.S.C. § 423 (Supp. I, 1965).

or preventing government activity. It has at its base a philosophical position about the function of property, the proper relationship between the state and the individual, and the role of law and legal institutions in preserving or maintaining that relationship. It is predicated on assumptions that if government is checked or prevented from making unwarranted intrusions, then the individual, free from lawless behavior, will behave in socially useful ways. Reich's *New Property*[61] is laden with this belief. The purpose of property, he says, is to create a boundary between the individual and the state; within that zone the individual will have dignity, the capacity to defy the majority, to act, if he wants, with whim and caprice; it will create "precincts sacred to the spirit of individual man."[62] This is an old view in America. Reich himself says that the "Bill of Rights depends upon the existence of private property. Political rights presuppose that individuals and private groups have the will and means to act independently."[63] This view limits the use of law and legal institutions to the establishment of clear rights in individuals and the defense of those rights against government (and others). Reich himself concludes:

> We need a radically new approach to the field of social welfare. Today the nation's poor stand as far from the enjoyment of basic rights as did the Negro at the beginning of the Civil Rights movement. As in the case of the Negro, the avenue of reform must be through law. In a society that is highly organized, institutional and bureaucratic, law is the essential means by which individuals are protected; law alone can ensure the fairness and lack of oppression that is essential to individual independence. . . .
>
> We need organized legal research to examine statutes, regulations, manuals and practices to determine where changes are needed. We need institutions capable of financing both legal research and test cases to determine the extent of rights in given areas. And we need lawyers to represent individual clients who cannot pay for help or secure that help from any existing organizations; *it is only through individual cases that the law comes into being and keeps on growing.*[64]

The newly established Project of Social Welfare adopts this same view of the role of law. In its statement of purposes, it says:

> The Project will focus on the substantive and procedural rights of persons entitled to public benefits, such as rights to unemployment insurance, workmen's compensation, social security insurance, public assistance, public housing, child welfare services, and education or training programs. The Project will seek ways to clarify the legal rights and protections connected with these benefits, all of which are based

---

[61] Reich, *The New Property*, 73 YALE L.J. 733 (1964).

[62] *Id.* at 778.

[63] *Id.* at 771.

[64] Reich, *Individual Rights and Social Welfare: The Emerging Legal Issues*, 74 YALE L.J. 1245, 1256-57 (1965). (Emphasis added.)

on varying factors of entitlement. It will consider possible infringement of constitutional, statutory, and other rights in the administration of social welfare programs, such as arbitrary or unreasonable eligibility requirements, inequitable distribution of benefits, use of "midnight" and other unreasonable searches, release of privileged information, and restrictions on freedom of movement. The Project will also devote attention to legal protection of the public at points of special vulnerability, including consumer protection, commitment of the mentally ill and retarded, and landlord-tenant relationships.[65]

This is not the place to say whether Reich's and the Project's view of the proper relationship of the state and the individual is correct or not. But it is important to recognize quite clearly that this view is not entirely the view of the recent amendments to the Social Security Act and the Economic Opportunity Act. These programs want to assist people, to give them income, but they also want to do more. They want the states, the counties, and the local government units to rehabilitate families and individuals as well as provide income maintenance. They want new programs that will move the dependent poor into middle-class America. The authors of these programs do not view the problem in the same way that Reich does. Social objectives will not necessarily be accomplished by giving people property and offering them services to use as they see fit. The purpose is not to restrain government from interfering with the behavior of people, which, if let alone, will produce individualism, dignity, and spirit. The purpose, at least in part, is to encourage government to interfere to change the dependent poor into the type of person which Reich implies now exists.

It is perfectly clear that the traditional adversary techniques of controlling administrative behavior are not capable of accomplishing some of the important goals of the new programs. Prospective recipients will not be able to get a reviewing court to require a state or county agency or local government unit to take advantage of a federal grant-in-aid to institute or expand mental health services, counseling, vocational rehabilitation, or other community projects. Davis calls this the discretion to do nothing.[66] Welfare officials have the power to thwart the new legislative programs by simply doing nothing. This form of official behavior is beyond the traditional judicial-type techniques of control.

Whether or not the country was wise in adopting the new rehabilitative programs is not the subject of this article. I have mentioned briefly, in the introductory remarks, the dangers that these programs pose for the individual. They also offer, it is argued, great promise—a real chance to im-

---

[65] Welfare Law Bull., Dec. 1965, p. 1. See also Columbia University School of Social Work: Center on Social Welfare Policy and Law, Memorandum on the "social welfare law testing" function of the Center 1.

[66] DAVIS, *op. cit. supra* note 22, at 71.

prove the life-chances and style of life of the dependent poor. At any rate, the elected representatives of the people apparently think that in the long run the new programs will do more for the dependent poor than the older assistance programs. Reich's program of rights does not touch this problem of controlling welfare officials, the problem of implementing national and state legislative goals. And this may be the most important issue of all.

In summary, the "radical approach" to the problem of controlling official behavior in welfare administration is not really radical at all. It relies on the traditional adversary methods of establishing rights and providing judicialized procedures to protect those rights against government. It may be that statutory rights, judicial-type controls, and judicial review will help in eliminating certain obnoxious features of welfare programs and provide redress for the outrageous cases. But how much help and whether there will be a net gain are the crucial questions. The experience of the administration of business regulation and the peculiar problems of welfare administration cast doubt on the benefits to be gained from a program of rights. Its lack of utility in helping to fulfill the broader legislative goals—the rehabilitative or people-changing aspects of welfare programs—is manifest. But what is really unknown are the costs of these reforms—the impact on the informal process, the unintended consequences of formal procedural requirements, lawyers, judicial decisions. There is persuasive evidence that current judicial supervision of the police in some areas of administration has resulted in *more*, not less, lawless behavior.[67] We may be fairly certain that welfare officials disposed to use the midnight raid and similar tactics will not change their ways merely because a supreme court tells them to stop. The civil rights movement is beginning to rely more on administration than litigation in court. This is not to argue that rights, lawyers, courts, and due process should not be used. It is only to point out that we are dealing with administrative systems. We must consider the whole operation of the systems and the relationship of the reforms to the rest of the systems.

III

CONTROLLING OFFICIAL BEHAVIOR THROUGH LEGISLATIVE AND ADMINISTRATIVE TECHNIQUES

We need a change in focus. We ought to examine the possibilities of statutory and administrative methods of control. Line officials in welfare

---

[67] See authorities cited in note 43 *supra*. In the running dispute over whether probation reports should be disclosed to defense counsel, it is suggested that if disclosure is required, the caseworkers will write their reports "differently." See, *e.g.*, Dembitz, *Ferment and Experiment in New York: Juvenile Cases in New Family Court*, 48 CORNELL L.Q. 499, 517 (1963); Paulsen, *The New York Family Court Act*, 12 BUFFALO L. REV. 420, 435 (1963).

operate in a maelstrom of conflicting pressures: the persistent drive to cut costs, local hostilities towards welfare recipients, moralistic demagoguery, prejudice, overwork, lack of adequate compensation, lack of proper professional training, poor relationships with federal, state, and local agencies.[68] Most of the distress over welfare is probably not caused by the people who administer welfare, but by those who never were sympathetic with welfare. Legislative standards of eligibility and need determination make welfare officials fraud investigators and keepers of public morality.[69] The traditional adversary method of controlling official behavior attempts to block or change activity once undertaken. An approach that looks to statutory and administrative methods of control focuses on the nature of the causes and conditions of official behavior and then seeks ways of changing the causes and conditions. We need information on the types of activities that officials engage in and why, and the types of legislative changes officials react to and why. Administrative programs can be recast to make them more susceptible to fulfillment, personnel practices might be changed, and new methods of rewards and punishments can be built into the administrative system to strengthen the hand of the line officials. The task is to make sure that the legislative program is carried out by the line officials; this involves not only correcting lawlessness in the traditional sense of the mishandling of individual cases, but also in the broader sense of fulfilling legislative goals.

The difficulties of implementing the AFDC program are illustrative of many of the problems facing most of our comprehensive social welfare programs. In the first instance, the three-tiered bureaucratic structure of federal leadership and financial support, but state and local implementation, presents special problems of coordination and control. The Social Security Act provides the basic framework for the administration, organization, and implementation of the AFDC program.[70] At the federal level, the Department of Health, Education, and Welfare, and more specifically, the Bureau of Family Services, has the responsibility for the administration of the program. The Bureau, through control and review devices, interprets and explains the federal position. In addition, the Bureau, through its regional representatives, assists the states in the design of their programs. On the state level, the Act provides that a single state agency must be responsible for the administration of the program. The state

---

[68] See Sparer, *supra* note 57, at 375.

[69] Compare Rosenheim, *Vagrancy Concepts in Welfare Law*, this symposium; Handler & Rosenheim, *Privacy in Welfare: Public Assistance and Juvenile Justice*, 31 LAW & CONTEMP. PROB. (1966) (to be published).

[70] See Wedemeyer & Moore, *The American Welfare System*, this symposium, for a description of the statutory framework of the welfare system under the Social Security Act.

agency may administer the program itself or it may supervise a program administered by the counties or other political subdivisions. Wisconsin, as stated earlier, has elected to choose the latter organizational structure.

At both the federal and state levels, there has been a conscious attempt to provide flexibility to lower governmental units. Within the sphere of local autonomy, the role of the county welfare director is particularly important. He establishes both the formal and informal policy concerning the following areas: the design of the program, the mobilization of staff, the supportive community resources, and the encouragement of families to take advantage of the available services. The staff of the agency is under the supervision of the welfare director; his style of leadership, both in philosophy and in administration, will largely determine the content of the program.

This is the three-tiered bureaucratic structure so familiar in many welfare programs. What are the techniques of coordination and control that are employed to ensure that legislative standards are being carried out? The states are not required to enter the program (although all of them have). The basic incentive is the financial support provided by the federal government in the form of grants-in-aid. The federal government uses a number of techniques by which it attempts to ensure that the monies are being spent for the purposes intended. Sometimes it requires the states to enact specific statutory requirements as a condition of participation. These requirements may leave no room for state statutory deviation and confer only narrow administrative discretion. On the other hand, the federal government may prescribe certain minimum or maximum requirements as a condition of participation; the state statutes can deviate above or below the line, as the case may be, and there can be broad administrative discretion.[71] The federal government can make available additional or supplementary programs which the state is not required to adopt as a condition of participation in AFDC. Again, the additional programs can have fixed, narrow requirements or broadly defined requirements. Finally, the federal government may not take a position at all on certain issues.

All of these alternatives have been exercised in the relationship be-

---

[71] The terms "broad" and "narrow" administrative discretion are admittedly crude, if not awkward. In a study of a bureaucracy, such as found in the AFDC program, a critical issue is the types and kinds of policy-making decisions delegated and exercised at the several hierarchical levels. Every administrative decision requires a policy decision in the sense of supplementary interpretation. The delegation of administration to the Department of Health, Education, and Welfare, the states, and the local units carries with it the delegation of differences in the range of power. Sometimes the delegation is very narrow (for example, the age requirements of the AFDC children); sometimes, very broad (for example, providing counseling services). For the purposes of this paper, we are only distinguishing between two polar types—narrow and broad. Further research and analysis will require more refined categories.

tween the federal and state governments. Important substantive decisions have been delegated to the states and from the states to the counties. Little attention has been paid to the nature and consequences of the delegations to the states: why choices were made between mandatory and permissive requirements and the consequences of these choices; why the states and counties make the substantive decisions that they do and the intended and unintended consequences of these decisions. The Social Security Act was amended recently to allow AFDC payments to be made where need was caused by the unemployment of the parent.[72] The purpose of the amendment was to mitigate the harshness of the existing program which required the breadwinning parent to be absent from the home; instances were reported where fathers were forced to leave a stable family situation so that the family could be eligible for benefits. The new federal program (AFDC-U) was permissive for the states; they could take advantage of an additional grant-in-aid if they wanted, but it was not a condition of continued participation in the existing program. One would have expected Wisconsin, with its long tradition of liberalism in welfare, to have speedily amended state legislation to take advantage of the new program. Yet, on two occasions proposed amendments failed to pass the legislature. Part of the reason was budgetary. But, in addition, many of the county welfare directors and caseworkers opposed the legislation. The reason was that the new program, if adopted, would have imposed vastly different tasks on those line officials. They felt that under the new program, they would be forced to devote much of their energy and time to finding jobs for AFDC parents. They would be diverted from what they considered to be their main tasks: that of rehabilitating and strengthening family life.

It would be a mistake, I think, to assume that the opposition of the Wisconsin line officials was merely another manifestation of bureaucratic resistance to change. Under certain conditions, public officials not only welcome change, but even initiate change on their own.[73] It would also be a mistake to think that these officials were opposed to giving assistance to needy families where the husband was not absent. The reaction of the Wisconsin line officials shows the importance of learning why officials react as they do. The amendment to the Social Security Act was designed to ameliorate what was thought to be a harsh result under the existing program. One would guess, however, that if Wisconsin had adopted the AFDC-U program, without other significant changes, grants would have been given to these families but little serious effort would have been made by the county caseworkers to find jobs for unemployed fathers. Of course, it could still be argued that the results would have been good

---

[72] 75 Stat. 75 (1961), as amended, 42 U.S.C. § 607 (1964).
[73] BLAU, THE DYNAMICS OF BUREAUCRACY, ch. 13 (rev. ed. 1964).

—the families would have been getting needed assistance; but an important aspect of the federal statutory policy (whether wise or not) would not have been carried out by the line officials. This type of official lawlessness is not susceptible to control by a program of rights. With better information as to attitudes, perhaps the legislation could have been recast to insure more sympathetic and cooperative responses by the caseworkers.

Another example of a federally-initiated change is the requirement of notice to law enforcement officials if need is caused by the desertion of a father (the NOLEO amendment).[74] The amendment was an effort by Congress to stimulate the enforcement of the responsibilities of husbands to support their families. As distinguished from AFDC-U, the states were required to adopt NOLEO. NOLEO has resulted in a great variety of administration on the state and local level. Several states have gone beyond the mere notice to law enforcement officials required by federal law and insist that mothers cooperate actively with law enforcement officials.[75] There is some evidence that the operation of such policies has destroyed reconciliation possibilities in some families; in others, mothers have refused to cooperate, thus defeating the policy of supplying aid to needy children.[76] Perhaps more seriously, the involvement of local law enforcement officials and the local courts by the NOLEO amendment has increased the chances of repressive and brutal treatment of welfare clients. One of the results of the amendment was to shift the decision to use criminal processes from the welfare agency to the law enforcement officials. This might result in lower welfare costs, but it also might have exacerbated problems of controlling or preventing local indiscriminate and predatory attacks on welfare recipients.[77]

Similar problems of coordination and control apply in the flexible arrangements between the state and the local government units. In Wisconsin, the State Division of Public Assistance attempts to maintain a certain state-wide consistency. A review of state regulations and interviews with state officials indicate that state control and state uniformity are greatest for the assistance components of the program. State regulations go into very great detail in this area, even to the point of providing specific dollar allowances for necessities. Any deviations from these regulations must be in writing and are scrutinized very carefully by the

---

[74] 64 Stat. 550 (1951), as amended, 42 U.S.C. § 602(a)(10) (Supp. I, 1965).

[75] For a discussion of federal objectives in enacting, and federal policies in implementing the NOLEO amendment, with an analysis of the states' reactions thereto, see McKEANY, THE ABSENT FATHER AND PUBLIC POLICY IN THE PROGRAM OF AID TO DEPENDENT CHILDREN 48-68 (1960).

[76] *Id.* at 64-67.

[77] tenBroek, *California's Dual System of Family Law: Its Origin, Development, and Present Status*, 17 STAN. L. REV. 614, 659-66 (1965).

state district supervisors. On the other hand, state regulations may be very ambiguously stated, indicating standards for the county agency to achieve rather than rules to be followed. Invariably, these are usually in the area governing the service components of the program. For example, the Division strongly encourages the local agencies to motivate AFDC children to continue their education and training. The state provides monies for this purpose but the local agency decides whether or not to follow this lead.[78]

One of the principal reasons why it is so difficult to control official behavior in the service aspects of the program is that decisions in this area are not readily quantifiable. It is relatively easy for supervisory state and federal officials to check numbers of people on welfare and the dollar amounts spent for necessities. It is far more difficult to check the caseworker decisions denying a family request for extra needs and services. The decision about requiring a mother to work, discussed above, illustrates the difficulties of supervising the exercise of broad administrative discretion based on an assessment of individual family situations. The difficulties of intelligent quantification limit the use of one of the principal tools of supervision—statistical reporting. For many types of administrative decisions, statistical reporting works well. It allows supervisors to tell at a glance the output of subordinates. The subordinates themselves can evaluate their own performances. It avoids what is often a more imprecise qualitative evaluation. It lessens the unpleasantness of personal criticisms; instead of the supervisor telling the subordinate his

---

[78] The above examples, dealing with the problems of implementing legislative goals at the lower levels of the bureaucracy, illustrate the importance of the attitudes or predispositions of line officials in the administration of the program. Alan Keith-Lucas emphasized this condition of administration in his study of ADC in two states. State A, in general, emphasized financial eligibility more than State B. For example, under the NOLEO amendment, State B only required the notice. State A, however, went further; it required, as a condition of eligibility, that a deserted wife file a nonsupport charge against her husband, and that an unmarried mother file a charge against the putative father. State A, as another example, required an incapacitated father to accept rehabilitation, including surgery, as a condition of eligibility. State B was more flexible. State A treated the employment of a mother as a condition of eligibility, but State B treated this as only a factor "to be considered in establishing need." Keith-Lucas examined the decisions of two caseworkers in County A of State A and two caseworkers in County B of State B concerning the employability of mothers. He found that the workers in each of the counties had different results (that is, the proportion of mothers actually working) and, that despite the differences in the state policies, the overall results between the two counties were the same. Each county had one caseworker with a high proportion of mothers working and one with a low proportion of mothers working. It was his conclusion that "the worker's predilections play a major part" in enforcing the state policies concerning the employment of the mothers; it was their attitudes toward work—its social and rehabilitative, as well as economic, value—which probably accounted for (a) the differences within the same county agency and (b) the overall similarity between the two states. KEITH-LUCAS, DECISIONS ABOUT PEOPLE IN NEED 218-21 (1957).

impression of the subordinate's work, he can show the subordinate his record as compared to the records of his co-workers. Statistical reporting also facilitates changing the production goals of line officials. In the public employment agency that Peter Blau studied, a new supervisor changed the reporting from the number of clients interviewed to measures of job placement. Under the previous regime, workers became more interested in just interviewing clients rather than making serious efforts to find jobs for them. Workers modified their behavior under the new system.[79]

Statistical reporting also has important limitations. Blau's example of the employment agency illustrates one of the limitations; it can result in what the sociologists call the "displacement of goals." If the performance of workers is based on the statistical reports, then making a good report can become the goal of the workers which may conflict with the goal of the administrative program. In the employment agency, the goal was finding jobs for people, and not just interviewing a great number of people. Anthony Costonis, in his work on a large Veterans' Administration Hospital, examined the performance of four units dealing with mental health patients.[80] One of the units was "treatment oriented"; it kept patients longer than the other units and it frequently readmitted previous patients for further treatment. Another unit was "rules oriented"; it discharged patients earlier than the other units and there were few re-admissions. The statistical reporting method of supervising performance in this large bureaucracy favored the "rules oriented" unit; it "treated" more patients per unit of time and was able to terminate care for more patients. Output was measured by the number of patients who "completed" treatment. If the quality of mental health services was better in the "treatment oriented" unit, then the method of evaluating performance resulted in a displacement of goals by the "rules oriented" unit. Costonis suggests that the exigencies of administrative control in the large bureaucracy impelled this result, even though its questionableness was recognized. It was felt by the evaluators at the top that there was simply no other adequate administratively feasible method of supervising performance than the number of patients who "completed" treatment. Better methods of control, to avoid this displacement of goals, had to await technological improvement.

Statistical reporting, as a method of controlling line officials, presents similar issues for welfare administration. A caseworker decision discouraging a client's request for extra money or services will often not show up in the report to the top; an affirmative decision will, and may have to be

---

[79] BLAU, *op. cit. supra* note 73, at 12.

[80] Costonis, A Study of Decentralization in a Mental Hospital, 1966 (unpublished thesis in the University of Chicago, Dep't of Sociology).

justified. The use of statistical reporting as the principal supervisory tool may dampen the willingness of line officials to implement rehabilitative programs. But the reverse may also be true; using statistical reporting in the rehabilitative areas may stimulate line officials to overact which may result in harmful consequences. A well-meaning supervisory emphasis on the *numbers* of AFDC people working or receiving mental health services, extended budget counselling, or vocational rehabilitation might result in the type of coercion or manipulation we seek to avoid. The point is obvious. In some instances, this standard method of administrative control is a relatively inexpensive and efficient way to stimulate proper official behavior. In other areas, lack of technology and the failure to refine criteria prevent the use of this technique which, if unthinkingly applied, can change administrative behavior in unintended and harmful ways.

These are some of the constraints and opportunities provided by the welfare bureaucracy that affect the operation of the program. But there are other factors which will affect the content of the program on the local level. In a service-oriented welfare program, no single agency by itself can accomplish all of the rehabilitative objectives. Cooperation and support must be obtained from other agencies within the community. Some communities develop elaborate mechanisms for increasing inter-agency efficiency in the handling of welfare problems. These include community-wide welfare services, social service exchanges, and handbooks on welfare agencies. In these endeavors, some communities are more successful than others, and in other communities, local agencies, which may be public or private, may be reluctant to commit their resources to AFDC families. These are contingencies over which the county agency has little control. Yet, they clearly can have an impact on the type of services which the agency will be able to provide its clients.

Another factor which can affect the content of the program is the community's generalized commitment to social welfare. While most American communities support traditional services, such as education, there is a great deal of variety in the support they provide for the more comprehensive service programs. This has been especially true for the programs oriented toward the dependent poor. The stance that the community adopts, particularly as it is reflected in the local leadership, will affect the county agency; county boards are elected, and they select the welfare directors. Blau and Scott argue that studies of other administrative programs indicate that if the environment is hostile, the officials will gradually retreat from the original goals of the program to more modest goals.[81]

---

[81] BLAU & SCOTT, FORMAL ORGANIZATIONS 231 (1962).

In many areas, welfare administration, or at least AFDC and similar relief programs, operate in such environments.

Of crucial importance to the AFDC program is the community's resource base. This includes the health, recreation, and education facilities required to help families obtain self-sufficiency, better family functioning, and social integration within the community. In addition, it includes the local economic structure and level of prosperity. Communities vary in the extent to which such facilities and resources exist. In any one community, these factors—social, political, and economic—very likely converge to form a pattern to which the local agency must adapt itself and its programs. There is probably a very close relationship between the posture that the agency adopts and the context within which the agency is operating. It is important to determine the precise nature of this relationship since these factors are some of the essential preconditions which will determine the extent to which the objectives of the program will be achieved. Statutory changes like the NOLEO amendment may serve to increase the vulnerability of welfare administration to community or environmental control. A similar effect may be produced by the basic grants-in-aid or matching costs approach itself. tenBroek argues that a major cause of the harshness and restrictiveness of welfare programs is a deeply felt need to save public money.[82] This manifests itself in resentful attitudes towards welfare recipients. Local prosecutors campaign on getting cheaters off the welfare rolls. We remember the Newburgh episode. It may be, then, that the grants-in-aid approach needs rethinking. The theory behind requiring the states to match funds is that this will result in the states supervising more carefully the costs of the program. The same theory is apparently behind the practice of federally-imposed maximum benefits.[83] We don't know whether these theories have any foundation in fact. Many states do not grant the maximum benefits and many do not take advantage of several programs at all. Why states go into programs, why they stay out, and why they impose dollar limits lower than the maximum is unknown. In the meantime, the matching system may be having a devastating effect on the goals of the Social Security Act. By "costing" the states to participate, the system may be fanning local hostile attitudes towards welfare.

The final contingency or condition of the administration of the program may be the most important—the families. The AFDC families, as a group, have been defined by the legal system as being in need of assistance. This means that the families have two distinct statuses: one legal and the other social. The legal status (as participants in AFDC) involves

---

[82] tenBroek, *supra* note 77, at 676-77.
[83] BURNS, SOCIAL SECURITY AND PUBLIC POLICY 240-43 (1956).

problems of rights, obligations, and other relationships between the families and the government bureaucracy. The social status involves the position of the families in the wider society. With respect to social status, AFDC families are drawn primarily from the lower class. In the first instance, their problems stem from this fact. Lower class problems can be economic-material (that is, related to the level of living) or they can be behavioral-attitudinal (that is, related to style of life). Thus, AFDC families are often "multiproblem" families. At the same time, this distinction calls attention to the fact that all AFDC families do not face the same types of problems. In one family, the most pressing problem may be one of inadequate childcare; in another, inadequate housing; in a third family, it could be both. The only problem that is common to all AFDC families is economic instability, since eligibility requirements are based on level of living criteria.

Prior to the amendments to the Social Security Act,[84] the ADC program was directed to the level of living problems. Most of the aid was in the form of financial assistance, with little provision for service. Moreover, the approach was typically in the form of "working with the cases at the level they are." As a consequence, little was done to improve the life-chances of the AFDC families or to move them towards self-support and independence. With the emphasis now on service and family rehabilitation, the approach is oriented not only to problems of level of living but also to problems associated with style of life. In this respect, the new approach to the program is to develop a more comprehensive attack upon the various problems which these families face. In the broader sociological perspective, the new program is an instrument of social mobility for the families. The underlying expectation appears to be that the program can move the members of AFDC families into middle-class positions as a result of successful rehabilitation.

The substantive impact of the program is inextricably tied to the impact of the program which results from the legal status of the AFDC families. As stated earlier, once programs move away from merely supplying assistance money to comprehensive services, the families face the prospect of greater control over their lives by the administrators of the program. The services aspects offer the most promise, but also the greatest threats to the freedom of the individual and the dignity of the family.

These are the factors which bear on how a comprehensive welfare program affects welfare recipients: legislation and regulations, the relationship of officials to each other within the bureaucratic structure, the relationship between the various structures, the impact of the environ-

---

[84] Social Security Amendments of 1956, ch. 836, §§ 312(c), 342, 70 Stat. 849, 852, as amended, 42 U.S.C. § 603(a) (Supp. I, 1965).

ment, and the welfare recipients themselves. The various factors or conditions are related through formal and informal processes—styles of leadership, attitudes, customs, as well as statutes, rules, procedures. A comprehensive welfare program is a complex system. Controlling the behavior of line officials in this complex system has a double aspect. Lawyers tend to focus on restraining officials, preventing them from doing wrong by attacking through the adversary system. I have argued here that this approach may have only marginal utility, particularly since we do not understand the total administrative system. The costs might outweigh the gains. We should be concerned about strengthening the administrative system, creating conditions under which officials will be more likely to fulfill legislative goals. This will prevent official lawlessness, as lawyers conceive of the problem, but it will also prevent lawlessness in the broader legislative sense. Some of the conditions of welfare administration are either not susceptible to change or can be changed only very slowly; these would usually involve conditions arising out of the community context. But job security, social cohesiveness among officials, new devices of control and stimulation, and other aspects of working conditions can affect the willingness of officials to innovate, to accept responsibility and changes from the top, and to further the goals of the program.[85] Working conditions can aid professionals in their willingness to act in the desired way. Legislation and administrative regulation and supervision can do much to create a more favorable climate for officials, which, in turn, can affect materially the service given to clients.

[85] See Blau, *The Dynamics of Bureaucracy*, in COMPLEX ORGANIZATIONS 343-55 (Etzioni ed. 1964).

Vagrancy Concepts in Welfare Law[†]

*Margaret K. Rosenheim**

I**N A RECENT SERIES OF ARTICLES** exhaustively discussing "California's Dual System of Family Law,"[1] Professor Jacobus tenBroek states a persuasive case for concluding that vagrancy concepts infuse the welfare system, and thus the family law of the poor—so much of which appears in welfare statutes. It is his contention that vagrancy concepts are maintaining a firm hold on life within the welfare system, even though their tenure in criminal law appears to be in jeopardy. He concludes that "the relationship of the poor law and other public aid provisions to the vagrancy statutes is as intimate today as it was in the time of the Tudors."[2]

In this paper I attempt to support my basic agreement with tenBroek's thesis. This requires a look at vagrancy as a criminal offense and at the development of welfare laws which aim to accomplish the same ends. The discussion suggests policy issues which permeate the historical development of the vagrancy idea and pose hard choices to present-day legislators, administrators, and other policymakers.

I

PRELIMINARY OBSERVATIONS

The very term **vagrancy** has an old-fashioned ring to it these days. Like the vagabond or beggar, the vagrant has disappeared from public view. But if his press releases are rare and generally unfavorable it cannot be said that he plays no role in modern criminal and welfare law systems; it is rather that he plays bit parts of which the general public is unaware and the professions dealing with him are quietly ashamed.[3]

[†] The fugitive character of many materials relied on in this article attests to my extraordinary dependence on a number of administrators and critics of social welfare. I gratefully acknowledge help from Miss Elizabeth Wickenden of the National Social Welfare Assembly, Miss Mary Claire Johnson and Mrs. Janet Kahlert of the Illinois Department of Public Aid, and staff members too numerous to identify in the U.S. Department of Health, Education, and Welfare, the U.S. Department of Labor, and the Office of Economic Opportunity. Public aid staff in several states also generously supplied me with information as did many colleagues, and I am greatly indebted to Barry Roberts for research assistance. Errors of fact or interpretation remain, however, solely my responsibility.

* J.D., University of Chicago. Professor, School of Social Service Administration, University of Chicago.

[1] tenBroek, *California's Dual System of Family Law: Its Origin, Development, and Present Status* (pts. 1, 2), 16 STAN. L. REV. 257, 900 (1964); (pt. 3), 17 STAN. L. REV. 614 (1965) [hereinafter cited as tenBroek with appropriate volume and page].

[2] tenBroek, 17 STAN. L. REV. 675.

[3] Among the more outspoken critics of the crime of vagrancy should be numbered

Who is the vagrant? It is difficult to answer this basic inquiry and to discuss intelligibly the problems associated with vagrancy because of the amorphousness of the concept. Vagrancy has covered a variety of acts and statuses in the course of its history in England and the United States. Furthermore, the use to which vagrancy concepts have been put, in criminal law or in association with poor relief of either ancient or modern type, has shifted according to the compelling economic and social requirements of the times.

A. The Crime of Vagrancy

1. England

Discussions of vagrancy typically hark back to Sir James Fitzjames Stephen's identification of three stages—vagrancy as the criminal aspect of the poor law, as a crime of status, and as a crime of conduct.[4] An intertwining of criminal and welfare law approaches is discernible throughout six hundred years of history, the interaction varying according to Parliament's response to the changing economic and social problems of the times.

The first stage runs from 1349 to 1547. Starting with the Statutes of Laborers[5] and proceeding into the fifteenth century the vagrant emerges

---

Douglas, *Vagrancy and Arrest on Suspicion*, 70 YALE L.J. 1 (1960); Foote, *Vagrancy-Type Law and Its Administration*, 104 U. PA. L. REV. 603 (1956); Lacey, *Vagrancy and Other Crimes of Personal Condition*, 66 HARV. L. REV. 1203 (1953); Sherry, *Vagrants, Rogues and Vagabonds—Old Concepts in Need of Revision*, 48 CALIF. L. REV. 557 (1960); Note, 37 N.Y.U.L. REV. 102 (1962). Their comments range over the ineffectiveness of vagrancy prosecutions to achieve crime prevention, substantive questions of constitutionality and statutory interpretation, and the differential enforcement of vagrancy laws. To these may be added the point that some aspects of vagrancy enforcement may overburden the criminal justice system "with functions it cannot effectively perform [thereby diverting] . . . energies and resources from those vital functions of public order that the criminal law, and only the criminal law, can perform." Allen, *The Borderland of the Criminal Law: Problems of "Socializing" Criminal Justice*, 32 SOCIAL SERVICE REV. 107, 110 (1958), reprinted in ALLEN, THE BORDERLAND OF CRIMINAL JUSTICE 7 (1964). Critics of the welfare system's treatment of the vagrant are cited in later sections of this article.

[4] See 3 STEPHEN, HISTORY OF THE CRIMINAL LAW OF ENGLAND 266-75 (1883).

[5] 23 Edw. 3, c. 1-8 (1349); 25 Edw. 3, c. 1-7 (1350). The first statute is usually considered to mark the starting point of the modern relief system. Its objectives were maintenance of wages at the level prevailing prior to the Black Death, enforcement of the customary terms of services in the face of marked tendencies to migrate for employment, and prohibition of almsgiving to be able-bodied. The Statute directed that:

> every man and woman . . . of what condition he be, free or bond, able in body, and within the age of threescore years, not living in merchandize, nor exercising any craft, nor having of his own whereof he may live, nor proper land, about whose tillage he may himself occupy, and not serving any other . . . shall be bounden to serve him which so shall him require. And take only the wages, livery, meed, or salary, which were accustomed to be given in the places where he oweth to serve . . . . Statute of Laborers, 1349, 23 Edw. 3, c. 1.

as a stranger and wanderer who threatened the demise of a crumbling feudal society.[6] Regulation of wages and prices and prohibition of wandering were the measures adopted to prevent the exploitation of a short labor supply, greatly depleted by the Black Plague, and to maintain the *status quo* in which roles and responsibilities were clearly defined. Laborers were curbed under penalty of law from departing from their customary places of employment without letters proclaiming the legitimacy of their travels. Employers, too, for a time, were penalized for paying wages above scale.[7] Vagrancy control had a clear economic objective.

Even in this early stage, however, other factors emerged to shape the legislation. Crime prevention, for one, was soon identified as a reason for prohibiting wandering and begging.[8] The unattached stranger lacking visible means of support was seen as a predator, a threat to public safety. Repressive measures directed at him increased in number and severity throughout most of this period.[9] Begging was early restricted

Penalties were exacted of both giver and taker for failure to comply with the terms of the law. The second Statute of Laborers sought to promote compliance by detailed prescription of wages and other terms of service.

[6] Successive enactments throughout the latter half of the fourteenth and the fifteenth centuries attest to the insufficiency of the Statutes of Laborers to attain their stated goals. Chief among the acts of Parliament are: 12 Rich. 2, c. 7 (1388), distinguishing the impotent from the able-bodied poor with implied permission for the former to beg; 2 Hen. 5, c. 4 (1414), conferring summary powers on the justice of the peace with respect to violations of laws controlling labor; and 11 Hen. 7, c. 2 (1494), permitting confinement in the stocks to be substituted for jail. General discussions of the legislation are available in DE SCHWEINITZ, ENGLAND'S ROAD TO SOCIAL SECURITY 1-13 (1943); 1 NICHOLLS, HISTORY OF THE ENGLISH POOR LAW 1-106 (1854) [hereinafter cited as NICHOLLS]; and 3 STEPHEN, *op. cit. supra* note 4, at 266-69.

[7] Statute of Laborers, 1349, 23 Edw. 3, c. 3: "that no man pay, or promise to pay, any servant any more wages, liveries, meed, or salary, than was wont . . . . Nor that in any other manner shall demand or receive the same, upon pain of doubling of that, that so shall be paid, promised, required, or received, to him which thereof shall feel himself grieved, pursuing for the same." Penalties on employers were removed by 4 Hen. 5, c. 4 (1416). See 1 NICHOLLS 72-73.

[8] Nicholls, Poor Law Commissioner turned historian, sees repression of vagabondage and vagrancy as the primary purpose of the early laws: "Many of those who had struggled for and asserted their own freedom, resorted to begging and vagabondism, and not infrequently to violence, whenever employment, or the means of honest livelihood, was not readily obtainable, and sometimes, perhaps, when it was. The idle and evil-disposed were of course the first to do this, and the unsettled character of the period fostered and gave licence to the vocation of a beggar, which, moreover, received direct encouragement from the almsgiving inculcated by churchmen, and practised by the religious communities." 1 NICHOLLS 31-32.

[9] Nicholls notes that the alternation between severe and more lenient measures of vagrancy control, evident in later eras, was discernible in the fifteenth and sixteenth centuries. *Id.* at 98-99, 104-05, 119, 134-35, 185-88, 200-01. 22 Hen. 8, c. 12 (1530), marks the beginning of reliance on mutilation for "undesirables," such as charlatans. See 3 STEPHEN,

to the "impotent poor,"[10] thus confirming national reliance on begging as a poor relief measure while closing this avenue of recourse to either the laborer whose search for employment failed or the able-bodied person bent on a life of indolence or crime. By the dawn of the great Tudor period crime prevention had become a primary object of vagrancy laws.

Second, the emergence of a secular poor relief system had consequences for vagrancy. The break-away of the able-bodied from serfdom inevitably produced failures and brought with it the recognition of poverty and want as appropriate subjects of national policy.[11] One indispensable ingredient of an effective assault on extreme poverty and suffering was organized public relief. Whether relief was dispensed under the auspices of the medieval church or under secular administration, as occurred during the Tudor reign in England, an effective relief scheme had to comprehend the entire jurisdiction, distinguish at least to some degree among the types of poverty and the measures appropriate to relieve each type, and contain an element of compulsion so far as donation was concerned. All these elements were present in canon law.[12] They later appeared as secular commands in the sixteenth-century statutes which led up to the famous Elizabethan Poor Law in 1601.[13]

---

op. cit. supra note 4, at 271. Enslavement, banishment, and impressment came later. Id. at 271-73.

[10] The distinction between able-bodied and impotent poor was first introduced in 12 Rich. 2, c. 3 (1388), whereby a person able to serve is commanded to remain and labor "in the hundred, rape or wapentake where he is dwelling" and "beggars impotent to serve" are directed to remain where resident or born. This statute provided no relief for the impotent (probably because church law already provided a poor relief system; see TIERNEY, MEDIEVAL POOR LAW 129 (1959)) but the prohibition against begging was limited to the able-bodied. This statute also contained the germ of the law of settlement, it should be noted. Ibid. Direct relief of the impotent poor is first statutorily prescribed in 27 Hen. 8, c. 25 (1535).

[11] 1 NICHOLLS 68.

[12] The presence of these elements has often been overlooked with the result that poor relief legislation is commonly dated from the sixteenth century. Tierney argues that "the occasional fragments of secular legislation that one comes upon in the medieval period, insofar as they related to the relief of poverty and not to the suppression of vagrancy, were almost invariably mere reenactments of principles drawn from the canonistic works which contained the main body of medieval law in the field. . . . Medieval canon law is no obscure eddy, outside the main stream of poor law history, but an important and neglected stretch of the main stream itself." TIERNEY, op. cit. supra note 10, at 5-6. Authorities differ on the extent to which canon law was effectively implemented. Whereas Jordan characterizes the "medieval system of alms" as "at once casual and ineffective in its incidence," JORDAN, PHILANTHROPY IN ENGLAND 1480-1660, at 17 (1959), Tierney states that an archdiaconal visit in 1520 found the provision of parochial poor relief "tolerably satisfactory" in 158 of 193 parishes, TIERNEY, op. cit. supra note 10, at 128. In the latter's view the system's greatest shortcoming was the failure "to develop a constructive approach to the problem of the able-bodied unemployed . . . ." Id. at 132.

[13] 43 Eliz. 1, c. 2 (1601). A succinct and penetrating analysis of Tudor poor law development in relation to vagrancy control and the system of labor exchange is available in

With the introduction of poor relief based on taxation and secular administration the interconnections between control of vagrancy and the function of public aid were temporarily loosened. As the poor relief system extended its scope and powers it commanded techniques for dealing with the able-bodied poor.[14] Certain types of vagrants were dealt with by the welfare system, leaving others to the criminal law.

Thus 1547 is considered to mark the beginning of the second stage in vagrancy history;[15] vagrancy became a crime of status to be employed as a weapon against beggary—at times a national disgrace[16]—and other

---

tenBroek, 16 STAN. L. REV. 258-79. See LEONARD, THE EARLY HISTORY OF ENGLISH POOR RELIEF (1900), for an account of legislation and administration from 1500 to the 1680's. A convenient summary of Tudor legislation is available in DE SCHWEINITZ, op. cit. supra note 6, at 20-29. 1 NICHOLLS 1-210, discusses all enactments from Athelstan to James I. A standard reference is WEBB & WEBB, ENGLISH LOCAL GOVERNMENT: ENGLISH POOR LAW HISTORY, PART I: THE OLD POOR LAW (1927). The major statutes are 27 Hen. 8, c. 25 (1535), ordering alms to be collected for relief of the impotent and for putting to work the able-bodied poor; 14 Eliz. 1, c. 15 (1572), introducing taxation; 18 Eliz. 1, c. 3 (1576), defining purposes of work relief and inaugurating the principle of relatives' responsibility in the bastardy provisions; and 39 Eliz. 1, c. 3 & 4 (1597), establishing overseers of the poor, authorizing erection of houses of correction, extending relatives' responsibility, and strengthening administrative machinery.

[14] By the time of the codification in 1601, 43 Eliz. 1, c. 2, the poor law made available tax funds for the impotent and charged the overseers of the poor with apprenticing or punishing, or purchasing work stuffs ("a convenient stock of flax, hemp, wool, thread, iron and other necessary ware and stuff") for employment of the able-bodied as their ages, conditions, and attitudes might require. See 14 Eliz. 1, c. 5 (1572); 18 Eliz. 1, c. 3 (1576); 39 Eliz. 1, c. 1-5 (1597); WEBB, op. cit. supra note 13, at 54-59. Accounts of the developing national policy toward poverty and unemployment in the sixteenth century are also available in JORDAN, op. cit. supra note 12, at 77-101, and tenBroek, 16 STAN. L. REV. 258-91. Prior to 39 Eliz. 1, c. 3 (1597), explicitly directing the overseers to provide work for the able-bodied unemployed, the choices open to such persons were narrow. Jordan notes a proposed statute for a public works program drafted in 1531, JORDAN, op. cit. supra note 12, at 84, but it appears that institutionalized publicly-financed work programs (as distinct from compulsory labor in the House of Correction) were a late seventeenth-century innovation in England. See DE SCHWEINITZ, op. cit. supra note 6, at 47; LEONARD, op. cit. supra note 13, at 221-36. However deficient the administration of work provisions the notable fact is that relief was no longer denied to the able-bodied, whereas today public assistance may be unavailable to the able-bodied or available in less adequate measure than is the case for groups of unemployables receiving public support. See text accompanying notes 37-38 infra.

[15] 1 Edw. 6, c. 3 (1547). Penalties provided included branding, slavery, and death.

[16] Jordan paints a vivid picture of the social dislocations of the late fifteenth and early sixteenth centuries which gave rise to the stream of legislation. JORDAN, op. cit. supra note 12, at 59-65, 67-76, 78-86. And see LEONARD, op. cit. supra note 13, at 11-21, detailing causes of reform of the poor relief system in England and on the Continent. As Leonard notes, the countries of Western Europe were equally infested by a "plague of vagrants" whose vagaries troubled a number of contemporary writers. Id. at 13. Thus it was written in 1494:

> Bold begging charms full many a fool,
> For begging has become the rule

conduct regarded as threatening or reprehensible. Now that poor relief was an accepted public responsibility buttressed by taxation and formal assignment of duties of administration, the vagrant no longer was identified primarily as a wanderer in search of employment. He became instead an object of control because of his roguery, his threat to public security, his flaunting of prevailing moral values. By an act of 1744, consolidating and extending prior enactments, the crime of vagrancy encompassed idle wanderers, beggars, persons pretending to be seafarers, persons "wandering in the habit or form of Egyptians," and persons running away from their wives and children. It grouped the offenders into three classes, the disorderly, rogues and vagabonds, and incorrigible rogues, and assigned a specific punishment to each.[17] Status and conduct were intermingled in the vagrancy definition, the apparent object being to control persons thought likely to commit crimes as well as persons whose behavior was offensive to prevailing moral values.

In the third stage, dated from 1824, vagrancy concepts deriving from

---

And ranks among our best professions:

. . .

To beg some men will always choose,
Though they could work if but they would,
They're young and strong, their health is good,
Save that their back they'll not incline,
These sluggards have a corpse's spine.

2 BRANT, SHIP OF FOOLS 208-09 (Zeydel transl. 1944). Adaptations of Brant, published in 1509, did full justice to his disapproval of begging. See, e.g., 1 BRANT, SHIP OF FOOLS 301-06 (Barclay transl. 1874). A century later, a distinguished foreign visitor expressed relief and satisfaction at the reduction of begging in England and gave a plausible explanation of the cause: "It is a pleasure to go about [at the Royal Exchange] for one is not molested or accosted by beggars, who are elsewhere so frequently met with in places of this kind. For in all England they do not suffer any beggars except they be few in number and outside the gates. Every parish cares for its poor. Strangers are brought to the hospital, but those that belong to the Kingdom or have come from distant places are sent from one parish to another, their wants being cared for, till at last they reach their home." *Diary of the Duke of Stettin's Journey* (1602), quoted in 2 TREVELYAN, HISTORY OF ENGLAND 124 (3d ed. 1945).

[17] 17 Geo. 2, c. 5 (1744); see 3 STEPHEN, *op. cit. supra* note 4, at 272-73. Nicholls observes that "vagrancy, mendicancy, and pauperism are so mixed up together, that it is not surprising the earlier statutes should have applied to them indifferently, and that it was not until a late period, and after a special provision had been made for the relief of the destitute poor, that vagrants were dealt with as a separate class . . . ." 2 NICHOLLS 208. The arrival of gypsies in England may have hastened the identification of a crime-preventive function of vagrancy. Gypsies were first included among the idle persons listed in a vagrancy statute in 1530, 22 Hen. 8, c. 12, the same year in which a law prohibiting their entry into the kingdom was enacted, 22 Hen. 8, c. 10. I am indebted to Professor David Matza of the University of California, Berkeley, for calling to my attention the possibility that fear of gypsies was a significant reason for expanding vagrancy concepts in the sixteenth, seventeenth, and eighteenth centuries. *Cf.* Chambliss, *A Sociological Analysis of the Law of Vagrancy,* 12 SOCIAL PROBLEMS 67 (1964).

status were pruned from the criminal law of England.[18] The final excision occurred in 1937 in *Ledwith v. Roberts*, which made reasonable cause to suspect proscribed acts had been committed a requirement for vagrancy arrest.[19]

2. The United States

Here, as tenBroek states, the stages in vagrancy development of the poor law penal aspect, crime of status, and crime of conduct "have not been successive but simultaneous."[20] There are two major sources of vagrancy concepts in current law, the criminal law and the welfare law. The intermingling of crimes of status and of conduct is readily apparent in criminal statutes on vagrancy. In a number of states the vagrancy definition includes not only a person committing such acts as begging, prostitution, disorderly conduct, and desertion but also a person with the status of idleness, dissolute misspending of time, habitual drunkenness, association with thieves or prostitutes, and the like.[21] No longer a keystone of labor legislation, vagrancy occupies a subsidiary role in criminal law, joining the lists of petty crimes. But in numbers affected it remains significant,[22] and it provides avenues for officialdom to protect society against "moral pestilence" and to serve such diverse humane ends as giving shelter to the aged or drying out alcoholics when alternative remedies are not readily available.[23]

Criticism by legal theorists has been almost uniformly directed to clarifying the several purposes served by such laws.[24] Questions have been raised both as to the theory and implementation of the laws. They are attacked as unconstitutional on the grounds of vagueness, unreasonableness of classification, and discriminatory enforcement; they are said to be inadequate to meet the goal of crime prevention—often an express justification for their existence.

One can hazard the guess that the days of the "old-style" crime of vagrancy are numbered.[25] Some modern criminal codes omit vagrancy

---

[18] 5 Geo. 4, c. 83 (1824). Although concepts reminiscent of status are embodied in this act, the emphasis is placed on conduct. See 3 Stephen, *op. cit. supra* note 4, at 273.

[19] Ledwith v. Roberts, [1937] 1 K.B. 232, 275-77 (C.A. 1936).

[20] tenBroek, 17 Stan. L. Rev. 671-72.

[21] Note, 37 N.Y.U.L. Rev. 102, 108-14 (1962).

[22] *Id.* at 102 n.3, citing FBI, Uniform Crime Reports 101 (1959).

[23] Foote, *supra* note 3, at 631-37; Lacey, *supra* note 3, at 1217-19.

[24] See authorities cited at note 3 *supra. But see* Perkins, *The Vagrancy Concept*, 9 Hastings L.J. 237 (1958).

[25] A writ of certiorari was granted by the Supreme Court to a party challenging the District of Columbia vagrancy ordinance as void for vagueness, Hicks v. District of Columbia, 379 U.S. 998 (1965), but was subsequently dismissed as improvidently granted, 86 Sup. Ct. 798 (1966).

as a distinct offense, seeking to achieve control of that behavior which is widely deplored and deemed harmful to society by more direct means. Thus the Illinois criminal code discards vagrancy but retains the crimes of gambling, prostitution, keeping of disorderly houses, disorderly conduct, and pimping.[26] Similarly, the Model Penal Code, in section 250.2 (Disorderly Conduct) subsumes certain vagrancy-type offenses regarded as socially dangerous.[27] Conduct harmful simply to the actor is omitted. We may expect this trend to continue.

But before congratulating ourselves on the abolition of a crime widely condemned as outdated and inevitably presenting opportunities for grossly discriminatory enforcement, we must ask if any unfinished business remains. Is it true, as tenBroek claims, that "this class of offenders, for such they are still regarded, has simply moved along with penal sanctions to the welfare program"?[28] And if the claim can be supported, does the incorporation of vagrancy concepts in welfare law raise issues comparable to those identified with the crime of vagrancy?

B. Modern Welfare Programs

The suggestion that the spirit of vagrancy offenses lingers on in the modern welfare system may come as a surprise to many. On the face of it this system is established to achieve goals which are remote from the policies that historically have governed vagrancy. Vagrancy-type offenses reach certain kinds of personal conduct. We are not accustomed to thinking of the availability of public support and services as predicated on the proof of worthiness or the absence of immoral or imprudent conduct. Nor would we usually characterize the welfare system as seeking to curtail labor mobility, as did the vagrancy law in an early period. Population mobility is, indeed, an accustomed and valued feature of American society, notwithstanding the problems attendant on attaining it to a high degree. One considerable virtue of Old-Age, Survivors, and Disability Insurance, in fact, is that it affords coverage anywhere in the United States regardless of the number of changes of employment a worker may experience.

It is perhaps precisely the widespread knowledge and acceptance of OASDI which impedes recognition of the policies and problems associated with other programs that are also part of the welfare system. The importance of OASDI and Medicare deflects popular attention from other component parts. Elsewhere in this Symposium the components of the

---

26 Ill. Laws 1961, at 2044, repealing ILL. REV. STAT. ch. 38, § 270 (1957); ILL. REV. STAT. ch. 38, §§ 28-1, 11-14, 11-17, 26-1, 11-19 (1965).

27 MODEL PENAL CODE § 250.2 (Proposed Official Draft 1962).

28 tenBroek, 17 STAN. L. REV. 675.

entire welfare system are described and the major trends, shortcomings, and conflicts identified.[29] Here it is appropriate to stress only the welfare programs which incorporate vagrancy concepts—those programs which make provision for support of the able-bodied and their dependents. Thus this article focuses on public assistance,[30] with specific reference to general assistance and Aid to Families with Dependent Children (AFDC), and to a far lesser degree on unemployment insurance.

The selection of these categories follows naturally from the thesis that the accommodation of the needs of able-bodied persons in a system of social provision puts that system to its severest test.[31] To the extent that the spirit of vagrancy hovers over the welfare system at all, its corporeal manifestations occur in those programs which provide financial relief to people in an age group which contains the bulk of the producers in our economy. This same age group harbors those whose immoral or otherwise aberrant behavior is perceived as the greatest threat to society, in part because of the realization that the behavior may interpose obstacles to fulfilling an expected economic role. Thus an unmarried mother receiving AFDC may, by her sexual conduct, be burdened with additional illegitimate children who interfere with her assumption of an economically productive role, a role increasingly borne by women in modern society. Likewise, the apathy or lack of job skills of a male aged forty which result in unemployment is of greater consequence than the same limita-

---

[29] Wedemeyer & Moore, *The American Welfare System,* this symposium.

[30] Modern critiques of welfare laws demonstrate thorough awareness of the punitive character of many of these laws. Students of social welfare have never lost sight of poor law's dominant influence upon general assistance. The broad recognition of poor law influences in federally-aided public assistance, however, is probably of fairly recent origin, for these programs, established in 1935, with their emphasis on rights, hearings, unrestricted money payments, *etc.,* bore little superficial resemblance to old-style poor relief. See U.S. BUREAU OF PUBLIC ASSISTANCE, SOCIAL SECURITY BD., MONEY PAYMENTS TO RECIPIENTS OF OLD-AGE ASSISTANCE, AID TO DEPENDENT CHILDREN, AND AID TO THE BLIND (Bureau Circular No. 17, 1944); Ball, *Social Insurance and the Right to Assistance,* 21 SOCIAL SERVICE REV. 331 (1947). *But see* Note, *Abolish the Means Test for Old Age Assistance,* 17 SOCIAL SERVICE REV. 213 (1943); *cf.* Smith, *Elements of the Judicial in Security Programs,* 17 SOCIAL SERVICE REV. 424 (1943). The changing view of public assistance is no doubt attributable to innumerable factors, including growing knowledge of administrative abuses and inconsistencies, professional criticism of individualized, therapeutically-directed techniques for relief of economic need, and increasing support for impersonal generalized methods of income maintenance. See generally KEITH-LUCAS, DECISIONS ABOUT PEOPLE IN NEED (1957); Bentrup, *The Profession and the Means Test,* Social Work, April 1964, p. 10; Kahn, *Social Services in Relation to Income Security,* 39 SOCIAL SERVICE REV. 381 (1965); Mencher, *Perspectives on Recent Welfare Legislation, Fore and Aft,* Social Work, July 1963, p. 59; Reich, *The New Property,* 73 YALE L.J. 733 (1964); Reich, *Individual Rights and Social Welfare: The Emerging Social Issues,* 74 YALE L.J. 1245 (1965); Schwartz, *A Way to End the Means Test,* Social Work, July 1964, p. 3.

[31] For an illuminating discussion of income maintenance policies respecting the able-bodied, see BURNS, SOCIAL SECURITY AND PUBLIC POLICY 56-79 (1956).

tions in one of seventy. Thus the vagrancy concepts discernible in modern welfare programs are primarily those with an economic flavor—idleness and wandering without visible means of support, desertion of family whose members become public charges, illicit intercourse which results in additional children. The criminal types of vagrancy, by comparison, have little carryover into welfare practice.

What, then, are provisions for the able-bodied—or persons who are so regarded by the public? They may be classified as public assistance for the unemployed adult male and his dependents and for mothers of dependent children. A social insurance program for the unemployed may be added to the list. Note should also be taken of the increasing availability of job training programs and other services which, in addition to protective features, afford an avenue of income support.

The genesis of these modern programs, for all practical purposes, is the poor law and earlier religious institutions on which it built. As we have seen, the able-bodied idler or wanderer was an unwelcome challenge even then. The medieval observer scarcely knew what to make of the vagrant. Both canonists and secular lawmakers seem to have ignored the important distinction between various kinds of able-bodied persons and were content with an elementary, though admittedly significant, differentiation between able-bodied and impotent.[32] Nonetheless, the Elizabethan Poor Law, while lacking a sophisticated classification of the stalwart, had at least the considerable merit of affording a total and flexible nationwide system of relief. In the accretions of sixteenth-century legislation parish officials gained a rich variety of measures which permitted them to deal with the varying problems of the able-bodied.[33] Thus distinctions absent in theory could, if desired, be drawn in practice.

Unfortunately, by this test, our present welfare system must be graded as deficient. In a line of direct descent from their English forebears, the able-bodied still wear the mantle (or the rags) of the sturdy beggar, and in some respects public provision for their relief is less adequate than four hundred years ago. This judgment is supported by examination of current programs.

The legacy of the poor law approach is most apparent in the public assistances, for these programs, like their ancestor, are based on proof of need. One class of public assistance programs, and the most important as measured by numbers and expenditures, is the categorical assistances. These programs are based on grants-in-aid established in the Social

---

[32] Tierney comments on the failure of the canonists to undertake a badly-needed "scholastic critique of employability in able-bodied vagrants"—to distinguish those who were idle, unable to find work, looking for better work, or intermittently employed. TIERNEY, *op. cit. supra* note 10, at 119; see *id.* at 119-20, 128-32.

[33] See note 14 *supra*.

Security Act[34] and presently include the aged, blind, disabled, families with dependent children, and medical assistance titles.[35] With the exception of the medical programs, categorical assistance is geared to the unemployable. By their nature these categories rest on federal-state legislation and combinations of financing from federal, state, and sometimes local governments.[36] The other type of assistance program is general assistance, the most "residual" of all residual programs but nevertheless not comprehensive in every state of the needy left out of the other programs.[37] The latter aspect deserves emphasis. Since able-bodied men typically are omitted from coverage under the categorical assistances,

---

[34] 49 Stat. 620 (1935), as amended, 42 U.S.C. §§ 301-1394 (1964), as amended, 42 U.S.C. §§ 302-1396d (Supp. I, 1965).

[35] Social Security Act, Subchapter I, Grants to States for Old-Age Assistance and Medical Assistance for the Aged [hereinafter cited as OAA and MAA], 49 Stat. 620 (1935), as amended, 42 U.S.C. §§ 301-06 (1964), as amended, 42 U.S.C. §§ 302-06 (Supp. I, 1965); Subchapter IV, Grants to States for Aid and Services to Needy Families with Children [hereinafter cited as AFDC], 49 Stat. 627 (1935), as amended, 42 U.S.C. §§ 601-09 (1964), as amended, 42 U.S.C. §§ 602-06 (Supp. I, 1965); Subchapter X, Grants to States for Aid to the Blind [hereinafter cited as AB], 49 Stat. 645 (1935), as amended, 42 U.S.C. §§ 1201-06 (1964), as amended, 42 U.S.C. §§ 1202-06 (Supp. I, 1965); Subchapter XIV, Grants to States for Aid to the Permanently and Totally Disabled [hereinafter cited as APTD], 64 Stat. 555 (1950), as amended, 42 U.S.C. §§ 1351-55 (1964), as amended, 42 U.S.C. §§ 1352-55 (Supp. I, 1965); Subchapter XVI, Grants to States for Aid to the Aged, Blind, or Disabled, or for such Aid and Medical Assistance for the Aged [hereinafter cited as combined category], 76 Stat. 197 (1962), as amended, 42 U.S.C. §§ 1381-85 (1964), as amended, 42 U.S.C. §§ 1382-85 (Supp. I, 1965); and Subchapter XIX, Grants to States for Medical Assistance Programs [hereinafter cited AMI], 79 Stat. 291, 42 U.S.C. §§ 1396-96d (Supp. I, 1965). As of August 1965, the public assistance caseloads were: OAA, 2,144,534 recipients; MAA, 264,687; AB, 95,135; APTD, 563,113; AFDC, 4,388,240 (in over one million families). Persons on general assistance (GA) totalled 662,000. See Welfare in Review, Dec. 1965, p. 26, Table I.

[36] The percentage of federal funds expended on public assistance grants, services, training, and administration ranges from a low of 40% (Nevada) to a high of 78.6% (Mississippi) for the categories. A breakdown by categories reveals that the highest proportion of federal funds is expended in OAA (64.3%) and the lowest in AB (48.3%). Bureau of Family Services, U.S. Dep't of Health, Educ. & Welfare, Source of Funds Expended fiscal year ended June 30, 1964, Dec. 1964. The national average for assistance alone under the categorical programs is 56 per cent federal funds. For a listing of the assigned "federal" percentage and "federal medical" percentage for which each state was eligible as of 1964, see BUREAU OF FAMILY SERVICES, U.S. DEP'T OF HEALTH, EDUC. & WELFARE, CHARACTERISTICS OF STATE PUBLIC ASSISTANCE PLANS: GENERAL PROVISIONS—ELIGIBILITY, ASSISTANCE, ADMINISTRATION 116 (Public Assistance Rep. No. 50, 1964) [hereinafter cited CHARACTERISTICS OF STATE PLANS]. The federal percentage (that is, the basis for calculating reimbursement of money payments) ranged from 50% to 65%, with 19 of the 51 jurisdictions affected by the formula receiving 50% matching and 16 receiving 65%. The remaining 16 jurisdictions fell in between. A somewhat similar distribution applies to the states with respect to the federal medical percentage, a reimbursement formula running from 50% to 80% (50-83% following 1965 amendments, 79 Stat. 351, 42 U.S.C. 1396d(b) (Supp. I, 1965)) matching on *vendor* medical payments (19 states receiving 50%, 11 states 70-80% matching).

[37] See generally BUREAU OF PUBLIC ASSISTANCE, U.S. DEP'T OF HEALTH, EDUC. & WELFARE, CHARACTERISTICS OF GENERAL ASSISTANCE IN THE UNITED STATES (Public Assistance Rep. No. 39, 1959) [hereinafter cited as CHARACTERISTICS OF GA].

their needs must be met under general assistance, if at all. We know, however, that the unemployed or underemployed are ineligible for income maintenance in a number of jurisdictions.[38] Hence, certain needy persons do not, under the present system, have access to public support.

The able-bodied needy have another avenue of recourse in the face of adversity: unemployment insurance, a federally authorized,[39] state-administered social insurance program. Instituted during the Depression as a counter-cyclical measure, it was never intended to cope with long-term unemployment. Thus for the idle and wandering vagrant it may be a wholly inadequate measure; not only is the duration of benefits limited but existing conditions of entitlement may also prove impossible for him to fulfill.[40]

The third, and much newer, method of social provision for the able-bodied is the product of public concern over technological changes affecting employment and social factors affecting motivation to work. Emerging are programs of job training, basic literacy training, and employment "etiquette," all reflecting both economic and rehabilitative goals.[41] With the vagrant in mind, we may conclude that these programs have particular relevance to the long-identified social problems reflected in vagrancy concepts. The idle person may well be one who cannot find work; on the other hand, he may lack incentive to seek employment or the personal capacity to retain it. In any case, he is an appropriate object of public concern. The types of social control and aid best calculated to resolve or minimize his difficulties are, however, subject to debate.

---

[38] E.g., Ariz. Rev. Stat. § 46-233 (Supp. 1965):

A. No person shall be entitled to general assistance who does not meet and maintain the following requirements:

· · · ·

4. Is not employable according to the findings of the state department.
Part B of the statute does allow for emergencies, however.

[39] 49 Stat. 626 (1935), as amended, 42 U.S.C. §§ 501-03 (1964).

[40] He must work in a covered type of employment for a firm of specified size and/or a firm with certain size payroll; be able to, available for, and in most states actively seeking work; and be free of disqualifications, such as discharge for misconduct or voluntary quit. See generally Bureau of Employment Security, U.S. Dep't of Labor, Comparison of State Unemployment Insurance Laws (BES No. U-141, 1966).

[41] The Economic Opportunity Act of 1964 provides for work-training programs for unemployed young men and women, 78 Stat. 512, 42 U.S.C. § 2731 (1964), for part-time employment among students in institutions of higher education, particularly those students from low-income families, 79 Stat. 1249, 42 U.S.C. § 2751 (Supp. I, 1965), and for community action programs, where the emphasis is to assist communities where unemployment and underemployment have given rise to poverty and related ills, 78 Stat. 518, 42 U.S.C. § 2785(c) (1964). Under the Manpower Development and Training Act of 1962, training programs are to be devised for both the unemployed and underemployed, 79 Stat. 75, 76, 42 U.S.C. §§ 2572a, 2572c (Supp. I, 1965), with priority going to the unemployed, 76 Stat. 26, 42 U.S.C. § 2582(c) (1964). Thus these newer programs are not in all instances restricted to the indigent or to the unemployed.

It is within the context of social provision for the able-bodied poor that the carryover of vagrancy concepts should be examined. What is the function of vagrancy concepts in this setting? How appropriate are these ideas to the fulfillment of the various aims of the welfare system? Finally, are there alternative concepts available to guide the future growth of social policy?

II.

VAGRANCY CONCEPTS AND WELFARE LAW

To consider these questions fruitfully it is useful to look in some detail at selected welfare programs. In order to highlight the conflicting social values involved I examine the requirements of the programs according to sex and age. This may result in a certain overlapping in the treatment of programs but should ease the identification of issues which stem from the application of vagrancy concepts to different groups of needy persons.

A. Welfare Law and the Male Vagrant

The key element of vagrancy so far as men are concerned is quite plainly the idea of idleness and absence of visible support. Isolating this element amidst a plethora of other statuses and types of conduct comprehended in vagrancy laws, however, does not move us far forward. Immediately such questions arise as: Why idle—voluntarily or otherwise? Where idle—in one fixed spot or wherever one's wanderings may lead?

1. The Wanderer or Transient

If the purpose of early vagrancy legislation was labor *immobility* and concomitant wage-fixing, the purpose of these laws at a later date was protection of the community against strangers—for fear of their predatory habits, their apparent differences in modes of conduct, and the possibility of their becoming public charges. Similar concerns appear to affect the welfare system's indifference to the transient of today. Failure to provide income for modern "wanderers" is most apparent in the prerequisites of durational residence which characterize state public assistance laws.[42] These requirements are permitted under the federally-aided categories despite the premium placed in our twentieth-century economy on labor mobility. Grant-in-aid programs, with two notable exceptions, permit imposition of durational requirements. States, in turn, avail themselves

---

[42] CHARACTERISTICS OF STATE PLANS *passim;* CHARACTERISTICS OF GA *passim;* Mandelker, *The Settlement Requirement in General Assistance* (pt. 1), 1955 WASH. U.L.Q. 355, (pt. 2), 1956 WASH. U.L.Q. 21.

of the option.[43] In general assistance, furthermore, the exclusively state-controlled standards have produced even higher residence periods than are common in the federal-state categories.[44]

Insistence on durational periods of residence makes itself felt among the needy not only by persons legitimately characterized as "transient" but by those who by any other test would be regarded as firmly settled in a community.[45] How can we, under contemporary living conditions, look on a resident of three years as transient? In seventeenth-century America obstacles to travel and establishment of a means of livelihood may have justified so regarding the newcomer. Fear of the possibility of his dependency operated to exclude him from entry into communities unless guarantees of "keeping the parish free" could be extended.[46] No such promises are exacted or tolerable at present. Yet the tension between welcoming the stranger and resisting responsibility for his dependency persists, with painful results in some cases.

The wanderer, as a result, is often not an object of organized public charity, for lack of ability to meet a crucial test of entitlement—residence.

---

[43] With but two exceptions the categorical aid laws permit state restrictions of eligibility based on length of residence. See 42 U.S.C. §§ 302(b)(2)(A), 1202(b)(1), 1352(b)(1), 1382(b)(1)(A) (1964) (OAA, AB, APTD, combined; not to exclude one who has resided therein for five out of the last nine years); see also 42 U.S.C. § 602(b) (AFDC, one year per child or parent). The two exceptions are, significantly, medical vendor payment programs. See 42 U.S.C. §§ 302(b)(2)(B) (1964), 1396a(b)(3) (Supp. I, 1965) (MAA and AMI) ("state plan shall not contain any residence requirement which excludes any individual who resides in the State."); cf. BUREAU OF FAMILY SERVICES, U.S. DEP'T OF HEALTH, EDUC. & WELFARE, HANDBOOK OF PUBLIC ASSISTANCE, pt. IV, § 3620: "Every individual should be held to live or reside somewhere; that is, he should not be adjudged to be without a residence."

[44] See CHARACTERISTICS OF GA passim. A settlement requirement, as well as a durational period of state residence, is common. In some states, localities are authorized to set their own settlement standards. Acquisition of settlement may require proof of a period of residence within a county without receipt of public or private assistance. See Mandelker (pt. 2), supra note 42, at 25-33. Compare 13 & 14 Car. 2, c. 12 (1662) (prohibiting acquisition of settlement by any person within forty days of his arrival if resident in a dwelling whose rental value was less than ten pounds a year). Marshall states that those affected by this law included "not only the old, the infirm, the helpless, and the infants, but also all those agricultural labourers who worked for, and were dependent on, their wages; it affected the great class of manual workers of every kind; it affected most of the smaller manufacturers, such as the spinners, the weavers, the dyers, and the shearers; it affected, too, the large class of small craftsmen . . . . In short, [it] . . . included the greater part of the lower working class under the designation of 'The Poor.'" MARSHALL, THE ENGLISH POOR IN THE EIGHTEENTH CENTURY 2 (1926).

[45] A brief account of mobile groups in the population and services presently available to them is contained in Migrants, Transients, and Nonresidents, 15 ENCYCLOPEDIA OF SOCIAL WORK 512-18 (1956). The impact of residence restrictions is detailed in Simons, Services to Uprooted and Unsettled Families, in NATIONAL CONFERENCE ON SOCIAL WELFARE, THE SOCIAL WELFARE FORUM, 1962, at 169 (1962).

[46] See 1 ABBOTT, PUBLIC ASSISTANCE 150-55 (1940).

That he does not starve more often than he does is a tribute to private philanthropy and the "hardship" clauses in many general assistance statutes. Yet this solution smacks of *ad hoc* and unpredictable resolutions to a common enough plight. It is not a thoughtful attempt to deal with an eminently predictable social problem—the existence among newcomers of a few sure to become dependent upon others to save themselves from destitution. What measures should be taken to wholly eliminate this group's problems is the subject of another inquiry.[47] It is sufficient to say that suggestions abound.

---

[47] How to define the problems which require social action is also beyond the scope of the present inquiry but it should be noted that the "rootless" are as heterogeneous a group as the poor, or those labeled vagrants, for that matter. Some transiency is attributable to the type of employment which the individual pursues, for example, migratory agricultural labor. Customarily this transient is accompanied by his entire family, for their earnings significantly inflate what he brings in and are indispensable to reaching even a subsistence standard of living.

Another type of person that residence requirements may hurt is the worker who moves, frequently with a family, to seek permanent employment in another locality. Whether previously employed or not, his mobility is generated by a desire for self-betterment. It is the better-educated, more skilled, and younger members of the labor force who tend to move, and to areas of low unemployment. See U.S. DEP'T OF LABOR, MANPOWER REPORT OF THE PRESIDENT AND A REPORT ON MANPOWER REQUIREMENTS, RESOURCES, UTILIZATION, AND TRAINING 145-48, 271-76 (1965) [hereinafter cited as MANPOWER REPORT]. This profile of worker mobility runs counter to the belief that people move to receive public assistance.

Yet another type of "transient" is the solitary drifter. He may move from one locality to another, taking employment from time to time, and he is often caught up in the law enforcement net as a vagrant. See generally Foote, *supra* note 3. By definition he is a faceless member of society and his numbers can only be approximated from the contacts with private and public charities and a count of police blotters. This man is not uncommonly confused with the residents of Skid Row, yet it is false to conclude that the inhabitants of such metropolitan areas are transients in any legally important sense. With respect to entitlement for assistance, for example, the significant facts are residence and/or settlement in geographically defined areas. The Skid Row resident is often a longtime inhabitant of that area who, if transient at all, moves within the area without jeopardizing residence or settlement. See, *e.g.*, *Migration and Mobility*, in TENANTS RELOCATION BUREAU, CITY OF CHICAGO, THE HOMELESS MAN ON SKID ROW 38-39, 100-01, Table X (1961) (56% of the men were residents on Skid Row for one year or more, 29% for five years or more; about 70% were in Chicago continuously for twelve months prior to the time of interview).

By contrast, note that the study of migration of workers reveals that one out of fifteen persons moves from one county to another each year and about half the migrating group (or one out of thirty persons) move to another state. MANPOWER REPORT 147, 271. The unemployed, many of whom are presumably poor, form a substantial proportion of the workers who migrate (10% of the employed and 37% of the unemployed migrants gave as their reason for migrating "to look for work." See MANPOWER REPORT 271, Table J-2.) Furthermore, the unemployment rates among migrants exceed the rates for nonmigrants. *Id.* at 150, Table 25. Nonetheless, unemployed workers who migrate tend to have lower rates of unemployment than do the unemployed who stay put, *id.* at 149, Chart 28, a fact which becomes readily understandable if we look at the more desirable characteristics (age, race, occupation, education) of migrants as compared to nonmigrants,

But the point stressed here is that public assistance laws make no substantial effort to resolve the economic problems of transients and persons with short periods of residence. The one substantial exception to this indictment of American efforts occurred in the 1930's when, under the first Roosevelt administration, measures of relief for the unsettled were introduced.[48] From 1933 to 1935, the Federal Emergency Relief Administration aided the needy without regard to residence or settlement through its Transients Bureau, a federally administered and funded operation, and through state programs to which federal funds contributed a high though variable proportion of total expenditures.[49]

The experiment ground to a halt with passage of the Social Security Act. Creating a pattern of categorical assistances for presumed unemployables, the act established maximal periods of residence that state plans could adopt to receive federal matching.[50] The pattern remains unaltered to date with the exception of the recently added medical care programs.[51] Thus the newcomer is precluded from assistance absent a showing of the one or three or five years that happens to be demanded, however well integrated into community life he has become. Federal policy, by which the poorer states now receive up to eighty per cent federal matching under the categories, has tolerated durational periods where leverage for improvement exists. Not surprising, then, is the application of stiffer conditions in the wholly state and state-local program of general assistance. The vagrant-"wanderer" continues to pay a price for his mobility.

and, further, consider that areas of migration loss tend to be economically deprived according to several criteria. *Id.* at 151-54. Because, however, "migration is by no means a fully effective mechanism for bringing workers to jobs," *id.* at 158, the *Manpower Report* recommends a variety of measures to assure smoother matching of workers to jobs, *id.* at 158-75. Voices in other quarters have recommended improvements in existing programs to support the migrant and his family while the search for employment goes on. See, *e.g.*, Simons, *Social Services for the Mobile Poor in Urban Areas*, in NATIONAL CONFERENCE ON SOCIAL WELFARE, SOCIAL WORK PRACTICE 162 (1965).

[48] A beginning at federally-funded relief had been made in the Hoover Administration by authorizing the Reconstruction Finance Corporation to lend funds to the states for relief and work relief. Emergency Relief and Construction Act of 1932, ch. 520, § 1, 47 Stat. 709. Payment on these loans was waived in 1934, Act of June 18, 1934, ch. 586, § 14, 48 Stat. 996. See generally *The Long History of the Movement Toward Federal Aid for Social Welfare*, in 1 ABBOTT, PUBLIC ASSISTANCE 645-90 (1940).

[49] Federal Emergency Relief Act of 1933, ch. 30, 48 Stat. 55. The principal feature of FERA was the creation, in § 3, of a Federal Emergency Relief Administration, all the powers of which were to be exercised by a Federal Emergency Relief Administrator. Section 4 provided grants to the states for relief of need of persons and their dependents, whether resident, transient, or homeless. The problems of transients and nonresidents up to the mid-30's are illustrated in 1 ABBOTT, *op. cit. supra* note 48, at 176-79, 283-345. See also BROWN, PUBLIC RELIEF: 1929-1939, at 259-63 (1940).

[50] *E.g.*, 49 Stat. 627, as amended, 42 U.S.C. § 602(b) (1964).

[51] 76 Stat. 200 (1962), 42 U.S.C. § 1382(b)(2)(B) (1964); 79 Stat. 348, 42 U.S.C. § 1396a(b) (Supp. I, 1965).

2. *"Idle and Without Visible Means of Support"*

(a) *Introductory Comments.*—Who shall be considered idle? In England the footloose laborer, described above, was often labeled idle whether or not he sought employment. At present it seems unlikely that a man actively looking for work would be treated as vagrant but occasionally examples are furnished that suggest otherwise.[52] Furthermore, the person who works intermittently in order to support extended periods of idleness at a subsistence level may be outwardly indistinguishable from one who is chronically idle.

For the criminal law the central question is whether idleness itself should be circumscribed.[53] For welfare law, particularly public assistance and unemployment insurance, the issue is different: It is whether, given the existence of income need, idle persons receiving grants or benefits may be asked to conform to standards of conduct related to work and self-improvement. As might be expected, income maintenance programs reflect important distinctions on this point arising out of popular views as to the employability of the various groups for whom income support is provided. A more lenient attitude is held, quite understandably, toward persons who are involuntarily rather than voluntarily idle.

Now the initial observation to be made is banal but important: that in practice, identification of the involuntarily idle presents far greater difficulties than a theoretical formulation might lead one to suspect. This is so, in part, because there exist on any day of the year unfilled jobs, some of which are available in theory to those currently out of work.

From the welfare perspective the direction of modern laws is toward identifying circumstances under which certain persons shall be deemed unemployable so far as entitlement to benefits is concerned. Examples of this approach exist in social welfare programs which establish tests of unemployability or of genuine retirement from the labor market. Thus a finding of disability deemed to be permanent, hence to preclude employment, is necessary under the federally-aided assistance program, Aid to the Permanently and Totally Disabled (APTD).[54] Another example, this from social insurance, is the requirement of registration at an employment service office as a prerequisite to receipt of unemployment

---

[52] See Foote, *supra* note 3, at 620.

[53] On the legality of proscribing sheer idleness, see discussion in Lacey, *supra* note 3, at 1220. Perkins, *supra* note 24, at 238, claims that "the concept of idleness *per se* as a crime had disappeared before it had an opportunity to be molded into the common law"; in his view it is idleness in combination with wandering, looseness, disorderly conduct, or absence of visible support that gives rise to punishable vagrancy. *Id.* at 239-44.

[54] 64 Stat. 555 (1950), as amended, 42 U.S.C. §§ 1351-55 (1964), as amended, 42 U.S.C. §§ 1352-55 (Supp. I, 1965).

compensation. It is coupled with a requirement to accept employment under specified conditions and, in many states, to actively seek work.[55]

By contrast, for receipt of Old-Age Insurance, retirement from the labor market rather than individually-determined unemployability is a test of entitlement.[56] The presumptive unemployability of persons over sixty-five, reinforced by the retirement test, affords a method of balancing the desires to provide income as a matter of right to the aged and at the same time to limit the financial drain on the system by reducing benefits to those whose current earnings demonstrate a substantial degree of participation in the labor market. Note, however, that neither proof of unemployability nor proof of need are required for receipt of Old-Age benefits; the test is measured by dollars of previously earned income.

What of the able-bodied unemployed, neither covered by insurance nor presumed unemployable? Only public assistance affords such persons the possibility of income maintenance and only under certain circumstances. Here the hand of poor law history is felt with the result, in tenBroek's words, that "idleness [which] in the rich has always been envied . . . in the poor . . . is as socially reprehensible as ever."[57]

While critical attitudes toward the idle poor have long characterized poor relief, they became an especially important determinant of policy

---

[55] See COMPARISON OF STATE UNEMPLOYMENT INSURANCE LAWS, *op. cit. supra* note 40, at 47-87. See generally ALTMAN, AVAILABILITY FOR WORK (1950); BURNS, *op. cit. supra* note 31, at 70-79. The similarities between the available-for-work test of unemployment compensation and compulsory work relief administered by poor law (now public assistance) officials are discussed in Mandelker, *Refusals to Work and Union Objectives in the Administration of Taft-Hartley and Unemployment Compensation*, 44 CORNELL L.Q. 477 (1959). Mandelker further notes that "no judicial interpretation of these [general assistance work-requirement] statutes has been found, but the available evidence indicates that the work refusal requirement in poor relief is administered in terms of minimizing the relief load, without much consideration of individual preferences. This is so in spite of a study during the depression of the 1930's, indicating that only about 3% of the reported refusals of relief applicants to accept jobs were unjustified. The explanation lies in the nature of the program. Poor relief grants aim at the guarantee of aid at a subsistence level; higher standards cannot be expected in the administration of the work refusal requirement." *Id.* at 482; see note 85 *infra* and accompanying text.

[56] 49 Stat. 623 (1935), as amended, 42 U.S.C. § 403 (f) (1964), as amended, 42 U.S.C. § 403 (f) (Supp. I, 1965). Effective as of taxable years after December 31, 1965, retired beneficiaries may earn up to 150 dollars a month or 1800 dollars a year without loss of benefit. If earnings exceed 1800 dollars, 1 dollar in benefits will be withheld for each 2 dollars in earnings up to 3,000 dollars and for each 1 dollar of earnings thereafter. The retirement test is inapplicable to individuals who have reached age seventy-two. See generally COHEN, RETIREMENT POLICIES UNDER SOCIAL SECURITY (1957); Myers, *Earnings Test under Old-Age, Survivors, and Disability Insurance*, Social Security Bull., May 1964, p. 3.

[57] tenBroek, 17 STAN. L. REV. 675.

in 1834 with enactment of the new Poor Law[58] hard on the heels of the Speenhamland fiasco.[59] Previous experimentation with workhouses and public works culminated in the adoption of the principle of less eligibility as the guideline to the level of public support, with the imposition of the workhouse test as the administrative technique for implementing it. Thereafter, the standard of living on relief was to be lower than that of the lowest paid labourer and available only in the form of indoor (workhouse) relief.[60]

Iniquities of this system have been regaled at length, no more powerfully perhaps than by Dickens.[61] Intended to be hygienic and corrective, the workhouses degenerated into places of sickness, corruption, and the

---

[58] 4 & 5 Will. 4, c. 76 (1834). For evaluations of the new Poor Law of 1834, see generally DE SCHWEINITZ, ENGLAND'S ROAD TO SOCIAL SECURITY 128-39 (1943); WEBB, op. cit. supra note 13, at 56-102.

[59] The justices of the peace, meeting in Speenhamland in 1795, set a scale to relieve indigent families and supplement laborers' earnings which fell beneath the scale. By the time the Royal Commission on the Poor Laws was appointed in 1832, there was widespread opposition in England to this method of income maintenance on the ground that it pauperized the laboring class. See generally DE SCHWEINITZ, op. cit. supra note 58, at 69-78 (1943); POLANYI, THE GREAT TRANSFORMATION 77-85 (Beacon Paperback ed. 1957).

[60] Chadwick's biographer, Finer, credits him with major responsibility for the principles underlying the new Poor Law and demonstrates Chadwick's debt to Bentham who introduced the principles of lenity, economy, and less-eligibility into discussion of penal reform. See FINER, LIFE AND TIMES OF SIR EDWIN CHADWICK 39-49, 69-95 (1952).

Lenity laid down the rule that health be protected, which Chadwick interpreted to require proper ventilation, hygienic standards, and hospital care. Economy called for strict disciplinary measures in enforcing work, contracting from the public for supplies, and dull, unpalatable, but unlimited food. Less-eligibility is worth parallel quotation:

BENTHAM	THE POOR LAW REPORT
The ordinary condition of a convict Saving the regard due to life, health, and bodily ease ought not Be made more eligible than that of	His [the pauper's] situation on the whole shall not be made really or apparently so eligible as the
The Poorest class of subjects living in a state of innocence and liberty.	situation of the independent labourer of the lowest class.

Id. at 75, quoting BENTHAM, PANAPTICON 122-23 (Works, Bowering ed. vol. iv) and HIS MAJESTY'S COMMISSIONERS FOR INQUIRING INTO THE ADMINISTRATION AND PRACTICAL OPERATION OF THE POOR LAWS, REPORT 228 (1834).

[61] Aside from the well-known indictment in *Oliver Twist* (1838), Dickens elsewhere castigated the operators of workhouses, Poor Law officials generally, and private benefactors whose zealous espousal of foreign causes blinded them to evils close at hand. See, *e.g.*, OUR MUTUAL FRIEND (1865), and BLEAK HOUSE (1835). It seems likely that he was as accurate in describing the weaknesses of the contemporary welfare system as in his strictures against the legal system. No less an authority than Sir William Holdsworth vouches for Dicken's perceptiveness and factual precision in the latter respect. HOLDSWORTH, DICKENS AS A LEGAL HISTORIAN (1929).

indiscriminate herding together of the ill, aged, insane, criminal, and youthful types. More important from my standpoint in this inquiry, poor relief administration in the nineteenth century revealed an over-emphasis on the able-bodied with consequent distortion of methods applied to other dependent classes.[62] Moreover, policy toward the able-bodied failed to discriminate as to the circumstances preventing employment or giving rise to need. The simple assumption was that the able-bodied were voluntarily idle and policy must provide an effective deterrent to their reliance on public support. The 1834 deterrent was the workhouse. What is its modern counterpart?

(b) Conditions Relating to Employment in Current Income Mainte-nance Programs.—The intertwining of idleness as a vagrancy offense and of poor relief measures applied to the idle—that is, the unemployed—is visible in English and American history. It remains to discover whether the punitive overtones of vagrancy and the new poor law resound in the modern welfare system. At the outset, let it be said that the language of repression and of penal goals has been discarded for newer concepts phrased in terms of work incentive and training or job skill upgrading. We turn to specific programs to interpret the new vocabulary.

(i) General Assistance.—In the first place, the able-bodied male, even if fulfilling residence or settlement requirements, is not, in many states, entitled to any income maintenance whatsoever.[63] Furthermore, a distinction must be drawn between states which permit aid for the totally unemployed and those which also extend it to the underemployed. Within some states making general assistance available to unemployed men, particular localities have the power to determine whether aid will be extended. Beyond this, it is difficult to generalize. Being subject to no federal control, general assistance programs vary greatly, and competent reports on their administration appear sporadically and are based in

---

[62] The Webbs estimate that in 1833 able-bodied men on relief totalled about 100,000 out of a grand total of 700,000 in workhouses or receiving outdoor relief. WEBB & WEBB, ENGLISH LOCAL GOVERNMENT: ENGLISH POOR LAW HISTORY, PART II: THE LAST HUN-DRED YEARS 88 n.1 (1929). On the absence of statistics on pauperism to support the con-clusions and recommendations of the Royal Commission of 1832-34, see id. at 82-90.

In 1966, if all general assistance families are counted as having one able-bodied unemployed adult, and if all AFDC families are (quite unreasonably, of course) treated likewise, the estimate is approximately 1,300,000 able-bodied dependent poor. If, in addition, all recipients of unemployment insurance are added, the total increases to slightly under 2,300,000. Social Security Bull., Jan. 1966, pp. 54, 55. At its largest, however, this sum is a minor proportion of the "unemployable" indigent and presumed-to-be needy groups aided through assistance (6.5 million, excluding AFDC and general assistance heads, counted above as "able-bodied") and social insurance (25.5 million, excluding beneficiaries of railroad retirement, federal civil service, temporary disability, and all types of un-employment insurance). Id. at 46, 55.

[63] See note 38 supra.

large part on estimates. The isolated bits of testimony available form a picture of discretionary administration of income provision under which conditions of the grant are markedly less favorable than those under the categorical programs.[64] It seems reasonable to assume, then, that the idle person receiving general assistance has frequently been subjected to experiences similar to those awaiting the committed vagrant —so many days at hard labor, albeit undertaken outside of jail and by one who is able to go home at night.[65]

(ii) *AFDC-UP.*—Eighteen states offer a better solution through AFDC-UP, the addition to AFDC which permits federal matching of grants to needy families containing an unemployed parent.[66] Heretofore the policy underlying all the federal categories limited grants to persons deemed unemployable. Under AFDC, "dependent child," as earlier defined, meant children whose need for financial aid arose out of illegitimacy, or the death, desertion, disability, or continued absence from the home of parent or parents, and who were receiving care from one of several enumerated categories of relatives.[67] In 1961 the program was enlarged to allow states to include children in families with unemployed parents in the home.[68] In 1962 the unemployed parent himself was added, further increasing the amount the federal government would match.[69]

At the same time that presence of the unemployed parent was removed as a bar to receipt of AFDC, Congress imposed conditions designed to stimulate the employment or enhance the employability of that parent—

---

[64] See, *e.g.*, Breul, Survey of the Administration of General Assistance in Bloom Township, Illinois, Dec. 1963.

[65] The well-publicized case of People v. LaFountain, 21 App. Div. 2d 719, 249 N.Y.S. 2d 744 (1964), is instructive on this point. See generally Mandell, *The Crime of Poverty*, Social Work, Jan. 1966, p. 11; *cf.*, MASS. ANN. LAWS ch. 117, § 20 (1958) ("The board of public welfare . . . may and in cases of tramps and vagrants shall require any person applying for and receiving food or lodging to perform, if physically able, a reasonable amount of labor in return therefor, and may detain him for no more than twenty hours . . . until the labor . . . has been performed."). (Repealed, Mass. Acts 1965, ch. 523, § 4.)

[66] At the time of preparation of this article the states were: California, Connecticut, Delaware, Hawaii, Illinois, Kansas, Maryland, Massachusetts, Michigan, New York, Ohio, Oklahoma, Oregon, Pennsylvania, Rhode Island, Utah, Washington, West Virginia. Welfare in Review, Dec. 1965, p. 39.

[67] 49 Stat. 629 (1935), as amended, 42 U.S.C. § 606(a) (Supp. I, 1965). Relatives specified include parents, grandparents, siblings, stepparents, step-siblings, uncles, aunts, first cousins, and nephews and nieces. This listing of relatives is subtantially as enacted in 1935. Note, however, that the prototype for AFDC, Mother's Pension laws, tended to be more restrictive in describing the eligible caretaker class and the conditions of parental deprivation giving rise to eligibility in the first instance. See U.S. SOCIAL SECURITY BD., SOCIAL SECURITY IN AMERICA 233-37 (1937).

[68] 75 Stat. 75 (1961), as amended, 42 U.S.C. § 607 (1964).

[69] 76 Stat. 190 (1962), 42 U.S.C. § 606(b)(1) (1964). See generally Cohen & Ball, *The Public Welfare Amendments of 1962*, 20 PUBLIC WELFARE 191 (1962).

that is, to eliminate his idleness and lack of means of support. Thus every state seeking to avail itself of AFDC-UP must include, in its state plan, provisions assuring the welfare department's cooperation with public employment offices in finding employment for the parent, termination of aid to families "if, and for as long as, the unemployed parent refuses without good cause to accept employment," and use of existing vocational educational facilities for retraining programs. Receipt of aid is contingent upon parental participation in retraining when the caseworker recommends it.[70]

The public policy seems clear enough: Congress, upon making unemployment ground for receipt of aid under the AFDC program, concluded that the states should step up efforts to reduce unemployment.[71] This policy manifests the public preference for employment over relief, not only for its effect on relief expenditures, but equally for the personal satisfactions gained by formerly-dependent individuals.

Section 407 of the AFDC title[72] seeks to accomplish this result. States which fail to meet employment and training provisions receive no federal matching. Note that these new provisions relate entirely to the conditions to be imposed, under the state plan, upon the parent; it is his uncooperativeness, in the absence of "good cause," which triggers termination of the grant to himself, to any other eligible relative, and to the child or children who are receiving aid.

A later provision tackles the problem of parental unemployment from a different aspect. Section 409, enacted in 1962 as one of the so-called "service amendments,"[73] makes possible federal matching of "payments for work performed . . . for the State agency or any other public agency under a program . . . administered by or under the supervision of such State Agency . . . ." The concept is broadly conceived. It comprehends

---

[70] These requirements are stated as additional state plan requirements. 75 Stat. 75 (1961), as amended, 42 U.S.C. § 607 (1964). For federal matching the states must show that the specified provisions have been met. Note, however, that no federal funds were made available at this time (1961) to support the states in the development of work referral or retraining services. See text accompanying notes 72, 73 *infra*.

[71] *Cf.* the statement accompanying the 1962 amendments, 76 Stat. 186 (1962), as amended, 42 U.S.C. § 609(a) (1964), in the Senate Report: "The committee recognizes that some provision must be made to deal with the problem of providing useful work for the unemployment parent. . . . The committee believes that states should be permitted, if they wish, to have community work and training programs for employable people, and provides for such a program as a part of the aid to dependent children program. Under the provisions of the bill, states that wish to have such programs could do so if they fulfill certain safeguarding provisions. If a state plan is approved, assistance could be denied if the individual refuses without good cause to take the work offered." S. REP. No. 1589, 87th Cong., 2d Sess. 11 (1962).

[72] 75 Stat. 75 (1961), as amended, 42 U.S.C. § 607 (1964).

[73] 76 Stat. 186 (1962), as amended, 42 U.S.C. § 609(a) (1964).

"community work and training programs of a constructive nature" for the avowed purpose of encouraging "the conservation of work skills and the development of new skills for individuals who have attained the age of 18 and are receiving" AFDC.[74]

Despite the use of new language, with the emphasis on "conservation" or "development" of work skills, there is a suspicion that Congress feared the possibility of confusion with old-fashioned work relief.[75] A desire to head off abuses previously associated with work relief may be read into the insertion of state plan requirements of a protective nature. Section 409(a) adumbrates a host of conditions related to the recipient's personal and career protection. Health and safety standards must be observed; rates of pay for work performed in community work and training must be those prevailing in the community; work must be useful and displace no regular workers. Further, state plans must provide for mandatory budgeting of work expenses, affording opportunities to seek employment and any other training available, coverage under workmen's compensation, and recognition of "good cause" as a ground for refusal to perform work requested. An additional safeguard, especially pertinent to mothers, is the insistence on "appropriate arrangements for the care and protection of the child during the absence from the home of any such relative performing work under such program in order to assure that such absence and work will not be inimical to the welfare of the child."[76]

By these amendments, conditions relative to work relief, acceptance of employment, and assignment to training projects have been inserted into a federal program of public assistance for the first time since the 1940's. In conception they resemble earlier methods of conditional support to able-bodied paupers, notwithstanding obvious efforts to install a "new look" into efforts to deter malingerers and the apathetic from ready reliance on a public source of income. But can anything be said against such a commendable purpose? And what do the burgeoning programs of work relief and training have to do with the concept of vagrancy?

The answers to these questions appear to turn on what the essential purposes of the new requirements are. To the extent that repressive

---

[74] *Ibid.* While the community work and training programs are not limited to states which adopt AFDC-UP, in fact the ten states presently administering such programs are within the group of eighteen jurisdictions which have AFDC-UP. See Welfare in Review, Feb. 1966, p. 29.

[75] See S. REP. No. 1589, *op. cit. supra* note 71, at 11: "The bill contains several safeguards that will assure that the projects will be useful and also that the individual worker will be protected against possible abuse or exploitation."

[76] 76 Stat. 187 (1962), 42 U.S.C. § 609(a)(4) (1964).

policies motivate their enactment and administration, they may fairly be compared to work relief, or what is more accurately called work-for-relief.[77] In this sense they closely resemble the vagrancy offense in that their objective is the punishment of idleness, in this instance through presenting a choice between privation or work or training, no matter how uncongenial. Ascertaining legislative intent and accurately characterizing administrative practice are far from simple tasks. It is probable, for one thing, that legislators and administrators alike are motivated not only by deterrent policies[78] but equally by policies conceived as genuinely therapeutic.[79] In the last analysis, we can best interpret the goals of community work and training in the light of past experience with such undertakings and the present available alternatives.

The overall aim of the public policy under consideration is employment. For marginal members of the labor force attainment of this goal is thought to require indoctrination in work habits, training geared to

[77] A summary and evaluation of work relief in the United States is contained in FEDER, UNEMPLOYMENT RELIEF IN PERIODS OF DEPRESSION 352-53 (1936). See also BUREAU OF FAMILY SERVICES, U.S. DEP'T OF HEALTH, EDUC. & WELFARE, WORK RELIEF: A CURRENT LOOK (Public Assistance Rep. No. 52, 1962); COLCORD, KOPLOVITZ & KURTZ, EMERGENCY WORK RELIEF (1932); HOWARD, THE WPA AND FEDERAL RELIEF POLICY (1943); MACMAHON, MILLETT & OGDEN, THE ADMINISTRATION OF FEDERAL WORK RELIEF (1941). See generally FEDER, op. cit. supra, at 31-34, 67-70, 123-25, 168-85, 214-17, 278-76. The principal objections to work relief have centered on its use as a work test, regarded as wholly unsuitable in severe depressions, the inappropriateness of work provided in terms of physical demand and needs of the economy, competition with industry, and its high cost relative to direct relief. Critics have also questioned the wisdom of limiting wages received as work relief to the amount of budgeted need to which the recipient is entitled and some have urged that earnings from work relief exceed direct relief (yet be low enough so as not to reduce the incentive to seek employment in the private sector). E.g., BENNETT, UNEMPLOYMENT AND RELIEF 176-79 (1955). A necessary distinction between work relief and public works is usually noted; the equally useful distinction is less often drawn between work relief (work of tangible value to the community designed to maintain morale and skills of employables; Works Progress Administration programs furnish an example) and work-for-relief (work for purposes of establishing eligibility; a work test; further distinguishable from work relief by limiting work to that needed to amount of relief grant in contrast to WPA policy of paying flat weekly wages). Id. at 123. The current community work and training programs may be said to combine these different objectives.

[78] However distant the evils of Speenhamland, see POLANYI, THE GREAT TRANSFORMATION 77-85 (Beacon Paperback ed. 1957), may seem to be, twentieth-century commentators also have feared the pauperizing effects of indefinite welfare support. See Lampman, Approaches to the Reduction of Poverty, reprinted in POVERTY IN AMERICA 418 (Ferman, Kornbluh & Haber eds. 1965); Editorial, N.Y. Times, Feb. 4, 1966, p. 30, col. 1. Compare Schwartz, A Way to End the Means Test, Social Work, July 1964, p. 3, at 8-10. See generally HOPKINS, SPENDING TO SAVE 108-25, 160-78 (1936).

[79] Martz & Huyck, From Work Relief to Rehabilitation Through Work and Training, in U.S. DEP'T OF HEALTH, EDUC. & WELFARE, NEW DIRECTIONS ON HEALTH, EDUCATION, AND WELFARE 250, 254-57 (1963); Truelson, One-by-One Approach to People's Problems, 23 PUBLIC WELFARE 116 (1965). See also S. REP. No. 1589, op. cit. supra note 71, at 11.

specific jobs and, sometimes, social services designed to heighten the motivation to move into the mainstream of economic and social life.[80] The underlying assumptions, of course, are that jobs will be widely available and that in a society based on a work ethic the good of all, and especially of the dependent poor themselves, will be furthered by diminishing the ranks of the unemployed.

Community work and training programs appear to move in the direction of increasing employment opportunity. Yet certain inconsistencies in supporting policies can be identified. Some are inherent in the statutory scheme. For instance, work must be useful and paid for at prevailing rates.[81] Its availability, however, hinges on its not being performed under existing labor market conditions. Thus one recommended form of work, euphemistically entitled training, is clearing brush on secondary roads.[82] This, it is submitted, may be socially useful, but its immediate value to the recipient whose job opportunities today lie largely in industry or service occupations can be seriously challenged.

---

[80] Levine, *Seeking Out Employment Opportunities*, Employment Service Rev., Dec. 1965, p. 1.

[81] 76 Stat. 186 (1962), 42 U.S.C. §§ 609(a)(1)(B), (C) (1964).

[82] See *Guidelines for Programming*, in BUREAU OF FAMILY SERVICES, U.S. DEP'T OF HEALTH, EDUC. & WELFARE, HANDBOOK OF PUBLIC ASSISTANCE ADMINISTRATION, SUPPLEMENT B, § B-2130.9 (in reference to Title V of the Economic Opportunity Act, 78 Stat. 527, 42 U.S.C. §§ 2921-23 (1964), as amended, 42 U.S.C. §§ 2922, 2923 (Supp. I, 1965)): "With the Administration's strong interest in beautification, welfare agencies are encouraged to include work experience units in this area in their Title V projects. Roadside beautification, including removal or fencing off of junk car 'graveyards,' would be particularly appropriate along secondary roads because of their proximity to the homes of Title V participants. State and local highway departments would be sponsors for such projects. In addition, beautification work may be done for park or recreation departments, schools, forestry agencies, etc. Through constructive work experience in beautification, participants may learn, along with good work habits, skills in grading land, planting trees, lawns and shrubbery; and conservation work and some construction (roadside rest stops, camp sites). This work experience must adhere to the requirements governing Title V projects . . . ."

A study of work relief conducted by the Bureau of Family Services in 1961 revealed that the majority of work projects then in operation were of a maintenance or custodial character: "These conclusions about work relief by the Bureau of Family Services are based on observations of the program as currently conducted. Some of them confirm what was learned by public welfare people in the 1930's and recorded in their experiences.

1. Properly administered work relief projects can help recipients become better able to compete for jobs in the regular labor market. But according to the inquiry, few projects are doing so. The Bureau believes that this is because many welfare agencies were not equipped to classify recipients according to their work capacities and did not offer enough different kinds of work. . . .

4. The problem that earlier work relief administrators faced in selecting projects still exists: Projects that are useful to the community are more likely to interfere with regular employment, and hence are difficult to justify as work relief."

WORK RELIEF, *op. cit. supra* note 77, at 15.

In addition, if either work or training have real value to the recipient, why is he not rewarded beyond the amount of his grant?[83] Why does his participation in work or training cease when the grant has been earned, unless of course he chooses to "volunteer"? Further, we may ask, is the type of training, for training receives the emphasis rather than work in a number of states, soundly geared to the employment market?[84] Is a welfare administration equipped to operate programs of training which will coincide with labor market demands?

Another source of difficulty is the opportunity for discretionary administrative practices under the work and training programs. So long as the recipient's participation is prerequisite to receipt of assistance, his fate lies in the hands of the staff. It is the caseworker who decides on referral for work or training, and the caseworker or a farther-removed staff member who determines whether refusal to participate is based on "good cause."[85]

In all fairness, two observations should be made. One is that work and training for the recipient of assistance, though theoretically available in other departments of government, is in fact often unavailable outside the

---

[83] "In most of the agencies visited, work relief recipients worked about two weeks out of the month." *Id.* at 11. See also MORELAND COMM'N, REPORT ON PUBLIC WELFARE IN THE STATE OF NEW YORK 61-62 (1963).

[84] Training receives verbal emphasis today as compared to 1961 and under the new title V training projects funded by OEO training programs are rapidly expanding. Questions respecting the suitability of the training programs for individual recipients and the considerable discretionary authority vested in the caseworker have been raised, notwithstanding the general concurrence in training goals as appropriate replacement of working-out-relief assignments. See address by Arnold Weber, Professor, Graduate School of Business, University of Chicago, *The Role and Limits of National Manpower Policies*, Eighteenth Annual Meeting of the Industrial Relations Research Association, Dec. 1965; GREENLEIGH ASSOCIATES, PUBLIC WELFARE: POVERTY, PREVENTION OR PERPETUATION, A STUDY OF THE STATE DEPARTMENT OF PUBLIC ASSISTANCE OF THE STATE OF WASHINGTON 40 (1964) (reporting on small portions of recipients in job training and rehabilitation programs).

[85] See, *e.g.*, GREENLEIGH ASSOCIATES, REPORT TO MORELAND COMMISSION ON WELFARE 51-55 (1962). It seems reasonable to predict that both caseworker and administrator initiating a particular training referral or training project will regard it as suitable. For an historical footnote, see Serota, *The Myth of Work Refusals*, in AMERICAN ASS'N SOCIAL WORKERS, THIS BUSINESS OF RELIEF 33 (1936). Consider refusal to perform "work" (to participate in work experience and training project activities) for good cause. title V projects for AFDC recipients, see text accompanying notes 87-96 *infra*, must allow the good cause ground, 42 U.S.C. § 609(a)(1)(G) (1964), the objective being protection of recipients from unjustified termination of their grants. Criteria for judging the reasonableness of refusals inevitably elicit discretionary administration of such items as "obviously unsuitable work experience or training assignment," assignment to a job "that, combined with heavy home burdens, would make excessive demands," lack of child care, or "special needs of children." BUREAU OF FAMILY SERVICES, *op. cit. supra* note 82, at § B-2463. Consider also: "[R]efusal to accept assignment, to continue on a project, or to transfer to another assignment in the project, may indicate the need for counseling, medical care, psychiatric help or special social services." *Ibid.*

welfare department, thus forcing it into this business.[86] Second, the problems alluded to above are not unique to public assistance. On the contrary, they have plagued administration of unemployment insurance, and because of many of the same underlying attitudes; unemployment must be a person's own fault, and only repressive measures will keep him from a life of dependency.

Nonetheless, the problems of administering work and training requirements, in my opinion, are most acute in AFDC and general assistance, the programs which attract the most inarticulate and socially-defective clientele by virtue of their residual nature. Within these two programs, evidence indicates that, at least to some extent, the attitudes which shape the implementation of the requirements arise from the same punitive instincts which have maintained the crime of vagrancy.

(c) *Demonstration Projects under EOA.*—Closely related to the community work and training provisions of AFDC are the demonstration projects instituted in 1962 under section 1115 of the Social Security Act[87] and further extended by title V of the Economic Opportunity Act of 1964.[88] The purpose of this set of provisions is twofold: to enable states to experiment with new types of programs as demonstrations, thereby avoiding the customary federal requirement of state-wi availability of service; and to encourage projects designed to enhance employability or capacity for self-support. Whereas community work and training under AFDC is restricted to that class of recipients, the title V projects are open to recipients under any of the categories and to persons likely to become recipients. As of November 11, 1965, 46,500 persons were enrolled in a total of 139 projects distributed over forty-two states and involving a wide range of training.[89]

What proportion of the caseload of presumably able-bodied recipients of assistance is represented in the trainee caseload? The question cannot be answered. Only a poor estimate can be hazarded on the basis of inferences drawn from data on AFDC-UP. From November 1965 statistics on assistance programs, we find that 17,653 adult recipients were enrolled in community work and training under AFDC.[90] As of this date 5,600

---

[86] "The poor have been relatively neglected by the public employment services of Detroit and by other services which exist to counsel, train, and place in jobs the able-bodied or the disabled." GREENLEIGH ASSOCIATES, STUDY OF SERVICES TO DEAL WITH POVERTY IN DETROIT, MICHIGAN 21-22 (1965). See also *id.* at 21-24, 62-76.

[87] 76 Stat. 192 (1962), as amended, 42 U.S.C. § 1315 (Supp. I, 1965).

[88] 78 Stat. 527, 42 U.S.C. §§ 2921-23 (1964), as amended, 42 U.S.C. §§ 2922, 2923 (Supp. I, 1965).

[89] Office of Special Services, U. S. Bureau of Family Services, Work Experience and Training Report to the Office of Economic Opportunity, Nov. 25, 1965.

[90] BUREAU OF FAMILY SERVICES, U.S. DEP'T OF HEALTH, EDUC. & WELFARE, ADVANCE RELEASE OF STATISTICS ON PUBLIC ASSISTANCE, Table 9 (Nov. 1965).

enrollees in the title V projects were AFDC adults drawn from community work and training programs.[91] To state the facts negatively, 40,900 of the 46,500 total on title V projects were not drawn from community work and training programs. The data should not be interpreted, however, to signify that AFDC adults are not being trained in the title V projects. On the contrary it is more plausible to hypothesize that most trainees are drawn from AFDC, the program with the highest potential of employables, with a sizable enrollment in states which do not have AFDC-UP and hence no community work and training program.[92]

Two curious anomalies underlie any effort to advance a consistent interpretation of the purpose of title V projects. One is the fact that compulsion exists for AFDC recipients;[93] not so for recipients in other categories to whom enrollment in title V projects is offered. The other derives from the facts on enrollment; at this point a substantial proportion of trainees are females. One might expect a genuine employment opportunity program to reach out for all unemployed males in an effort to restore them to the status of primary earner in the family.[94] It is a

[91] Note 89 supra.

[92] Cf. BUREAU OF FAMILY SERVICES, op. cit. supra note 82, § B-2123; Truelson, Helping Needy People Get Jobs and Hold Them, Welfare in Review, Nov. 1965, p. 14; see note 74 supra.

[93] By incorporation, see 42 U.S.C. § 2922 (Supp. I, 1965), referring to 42 U.S.C. § 1315 (Supp. I, 1965) (demonstration projects), referring to title IV, AFDC.

[94] See Truelson, supra note 92, at 15. Forty-four per cent of the title V trainees nationwide are female. Ibid. Original plans for a title V project in Wayne County, Michigan called for training of 1700 AFDC-UP males, to be followed by training for about 1000 AFDC-UP mothers with children over fourteen. "The favorable employment market has resulted in a reduction . . . in caseload . . . reflected in the preponderance of ADC mothers in the projects even though priority is given to unemployed fathers as the law suggests . . . .

TITLE V PARTICIPANTS

	Oct. 31, 1965 Men	Women	Total
White	306	245	551
Non-White	735	1318	2053
Total	1041	1563	2604

Of the men, 714 were receiving work experience and training, 158 training only. For women the situation was reversed." Mich. Dep't Social Services, Work Experience Program, Nov. 65.

This seems to be in accord with stated federal policy. "The estimated participation in the title V program is 2,110,000 persons. This number includes 1,750,000 part-time employed and unemployed heads of families and 220,000 AFDC mothers of the over 1 million AFDC families. Our immediate target is 350,000 needy, hardcore, unemployed persons including the 220,000 AFDC mothers I mentioned" Address by Andrew R. N. Truelson,

status which, we have been told, critically affects the movement of Negro families out of poverty and into the relative affluence and stability of the middle class.[95] A counterargument points to the rapid turnover of AFDC-UP families receiving aid because of parental unemployment. Such a high turnover, it is suggested, precludes extended training efforts directed at male recipients. To this two responses may be offered: Comparisons of numbers of assistance recipients with numbers currently reported in training belies the assertion that no men exist to be trained. Furthermore, a dwindling number of primary breadwinners for the

---

The Work Experience Program under Title V of the Economic Opportunity Act 5, American Public Welfare Ass'n, National Biennial Round Table Conference, Dec. 3, 1965. Similarly, in the community work and training programs supported under AFDC, the majority of trainees are apparently women. In some states the relatively high proportion of women in training programs is a consequence of a tight employment market for men and a rapid turnover of AFDC-UP cases. In West Virginia, where all 8610 families receiving AFDC-UP are listed as having an adult participant in a community work and training program, it is probable that the average length of an AFDC-UP case is considerably longer than other AFDC-UP states and/or the emphasis in administration is on work, not training. Welfare in Review, Dec. 1965, p. 39.

[95] With respect to Negro males, the point has repeatedly been stressed that access to rewarding employment is essential not only to self-esteem but to family stability. See generally THE NEGRO AMERICAN (Daedalus, pt. 1, Fall 1965; pt. 2, Winter 1966). The point would seem equally applicable to unemployed white males. Whereas Department of Labor statistics routinely classify MDTA trainees by both sex and race, data on the welfare-sponsored training programs so far published give only sex and types of training provided by project (not by trainees enrolled). Analysis and evaluation of the Title V and AFDC-UP training programs demand cross-classification by sex, race, and type of training provided to individual enrollees (the last-named will soon be available; personal communication to the author from Andrew R. N. Truelson, Ass't Director, Special Services, Welfare Administration, dated Jan. 21, 1966). It would also be useful to have a breakdown by category of enrollees who are public assistance recipients. At this writing Title V project approval is restricted to projects serving categorical assistance recipients or "categorically related" persons (for example, parents of youngsters up to age twenty-one) notwithstanding legislative authorization to serve "other needy persons." See WELFARE ADMINISTRATION, U.S. DEP'T OF HEALTH, EDUC. & WELFARE, HANDBOOK TRANSMITTAL NO. 73 (Dec. 21, 1965).

To be sure, restricting enrollment in training programs to men might set off a hue and cry about discrimination against women. *Cf.* Civil Rights Act of 1964, §§ 703(a)-(e), 42 U.S.C. §§ 2000e-2(a)-(e) 1964. But it is not necessary to bar women from training programs altogether in order to give priority in design and implementation of such programs to males of relatively young age who have recently assumed or may be expected to assume family responsibilities. As long as men fill the role of primary breadwinner in American society, aiding the disadvantaged among them to fill this role more successfully would appear to be sound national policy. In addition, it should be noted that the training programs for women may be perpetuating a well-recognized type of discrimination against women: training them for jobs which are low-paid and offer irregular employment and few fringe benefits. If, as is argued, these are jobs that men often will not take and women should not have to take, what do we make of welfare-sponsored policies which direct women to enroll in training programs leading to these jobs? See generally Peterson, *Working Women*, in THE WOMAN IN AMERICA 671, 681-87 (Daedalus, Spring 1964).

training programs should perhaps force a reevaluation of the whole effort. Further attention to this issue is given in a later section.[96]

(*d*) *Other Training Programs.*—Welfare programs are neither the exclusive nor the primary setting for training efforts at the present. There are now several work and training programs outside the income maintenance programs. Some reflect new approaches generated by apprehensions that automation has produced new labor market problems or the conviction that a new set of manpower policies is needed in the United States.[97] Other programs are extensions or modifications of earlier public efforts; an example is the Youth Conservation Corps within the Job Corps program of the Economic Opportunity Act of 1964.[98] Its lineage is traceable back to the depression program of the Civilian Conservation Corps.[99]

All of these programs secure enrollees voluntarily. Indeed, voluntary enrollment is essential since full coverage of target populations is neither intended nor feasible in the immediate future. The underlying goal is to provide training and education for able-bodied persons who are seen as particularly vulnerable to the risks of unemployment or intermittent, unrewarding employment.[100] The hope is that the variety in types of programs and in enrollment techniques will attract members of these identified groups and produce the results desired. By December 1964, 340,000 trainees had been approved for training projects under the Manpower Development and Training Act whereas in the Neighborhood Youth Corps under the Economic Opportunity Act 308,000 training spaces had been allotted.[101] By comparison, the numbers being trained under public assistance auspices look small.[102]

The social ills to be remedied by these particular programs are

---

[96] See text commencing with footnote 119 *infra*.

[97] *E.g.*, the Manpower Development and Training Act of 1962, 76 Stat. 23, as amended, 42 U.S.C. §§ 2571-2620 (1964), as amended, 42 U.S.C. §§ 2571-2620 (Supp. I, 1965), and the Area Redevelopment Act, 75 Stat. 47 (1961), as amended, 42 U.S.C. §§ 2501-25 (1964), as amended, 42 U.S.C. §§ 2513, 2514 (repealed), 2525 (Supp. I, 1965).

[98] Economic Opportunity Act of 1964, 78 Stat. 511, 42 U.S.C. § 2720 (Supp. I, 1965): "Within the Job Corps there is authorized a Youth Conservation Corps in which at any one time no less than 40 per centum of the male enrollees under this part shall be assigned to camps where their work activity is directed primarily toward conserving, developing, and managing the public natural resources of the Nation, and developing, managing, and protecting public recreational areas."

[99] Civilian Conservation Corps Reforestation Relief Act, ch. 17, 48 Stat. 22 (1933).

[100] These programs, in effect, permit rendering compensatory treatment to unemployed Negro youth and adults without so labelling the efforts. See TRANSCRIPT, CONFERENCE ON THE NEGRO AMERICAN 288-99 (Daedalus, Winter 1966).

[101] U.S. BUREAU OF THE BUDGET, THE BUDGET OF THE UNITED STATES GOVERNMENT FOR FISCAL YEAR ENDING 1967, App. 125 (1966).

[102] See text accompanying notes 89-91 *supra*.

essentially the same that AFDC seeks to eradicate through its work and training. But the approaches differ markedly. One has open enrollment, the other required participation. One heavily relies on "indigenous" leaders to hurdle the barriers of communication and make participation seem more meaningful and less formidable; the other is dominated (or so it has been claimed) by middle-class persons whose language and values set barriers between themselves and the client group.[103]

(e) *Conclusion.*—A review of various work and training programs designed for assistance recipents identifies features more readily explained as reflections of dislike of idleness than of the unique requirements of the population in the recipient status. The effectiveness of these various attacks on unemployment has yet to be measured in any systematic way. In light of the value placed on freedom of choice and dignity in our society, however, elements of compulsion in any welfare program ought to rest on a carefully justified necessity. To be required to do what is good for oneself is a far different approach to human ills than the assurance of aid to self-betterment. In general, our tendency has been to endorse the latter approach and to insist on closely reasoned explanations to support the former. The vagrancy concept, we may conclude, lies in the background of these compulsory programs.

3. The Deserting Father: Is He a Welfare Vagrant?

A common element of the vagrancy offense is desertion of a family with the consequence of their becoming public charges.[104] It should be noted that desertion and nonsupport laws have always been applicable to parents, mainly fathers, who shirk their duties. Further, relatives' responsibility provisions have been available since 1597[105] and have ap-

---

[103] Among useful items in a rapidly expanding literature on problems engendered by the middle-class bias of social workers and on indigenous leadership potential are: HUNTER, THE SLUMS: CHALLENGE AND RESPONSE 265-68 (1964); SILBERMAN, CRISIS IN BLACK AND WHITE 308-55 (1964); Brager, *Organizing the Unaffiliated in a Low-Income Area,* in SOCIAL WELFARE INSTITUTIONS 644 (Zald ed. 1965); Cloward & Epstein, *Private Social Welfare's Disengagement From the Poor,* in *id.* at 623; Cohen, *Social Work and the Culture of Poverty,* in MENTAL HEALTH OF THE POOR 128 (Riesman, Cohen & Pearl eds. 1964).

[104] First introduced as a vagrancy concept in 1744, 17 Geo. 2, c. 5, it applied to one who deserted his family if they became a charge on the parish. See Rex v. Hall, 3 Burr. 1636, 97 Eng. Rep. 1022 (K.B. 1765); Perkins, *The Vagrancy Concept,* 9 HASTINGS L.J. 237, 246-47 (1958). Lacey identifies ten states as including in the definition of vagrant one who fails to support his family, without the further requirement of showing that the family is a public charge. Lacey, *Vagrancy and Other Crimes of Personal Condition,* 66 HARV. L. REV. 1203, 1209 (1953). A common fate for him who refuses work relief or job offers appears to be a threat of referral for prosecution for nonsupport. See Mandell, *The Crime of Poverty,* Social Work, Jan. 1966, p. 11, at 12; Reich, *Individual Rights and Social Welfare: The Emerging Social Issues,* 74 YALE L.J. 1245, 1249 (1965).

[105] 39 Eliz. 1, c. 3 (1597).

plied to a wider circle of relatives than do the nonsupport provisions. Welfare statutes derived from the poor law have quite universally retained some form of relatives' responsibility, raising the most perplexing problems of policy.[106] Until the 1952 amendment of the AFDC title for Notification of Law Enforcement Officers (NOLEO),[107] the problems centered on discretionary application of responsibility provisions by public assistance workers. NOLEO brought additional elements of discretion and repression which reflect vagrancy concepts.

NOLEO is the product of public concern over mounting proportions of AFDC families whose eligibility arises from a parent's desertion. It requires notification to law enforcement officers of the furnishing of aid to families where a parent has abandoned or deserted; this duty has been reinforced in some states by requiring the child's custodian to file charges for child support.[108] The net effect of NOLEO is to limit assistance agency discretion in determining what support action is reasonable in each case, particularly in states with a mandatory filing requirement.

NOLEO, then, highlights a conflict in values which has long persisted.[109] On the one hand, the public can be said to deserve protection from the burden of supporting families when the parents are able to. While parental support is usually forthcoming voluntarily, and increased amounts often follow from assistance agency interpretation of parental duties,[110] inevitably cases appropriate for legal action will arise, even though their numbers be small. Recourse to legal action may buttress the sense of moral obligation and thus be important as a deterrent.

Opposing arguments stress the punitive consequences of federal-state reporting and state filing provisions. Insistence on pursuit of remedies may hamper efforts to restore the family unit and force the child's custodian, typically his mother, to the hard choice of ineligibility for assistance or irreversibly widening the gap between parents. Bearing the brunt of the choice is the child, the primary object of public protection under AFDC. Further, it is urged, the rewards of implementing support laws are small. Collections are insignificant. The referral to law enforce-

---

[106] SCHORR, FILIAL RESPONSIBILITY IN THE MODERN AMERICAN FAMILY (Dep't of Health, Educ. & Welfare 1960); Lewis & Levy, *Family Law and Welfare Policies—The Case for "Dual Systems,"* this symposium; Mandelker, *Family Responsibility Under the American Poor Laws,* 54 MICH. L. REV. 497, 607 (1956); Rheinstein, *Motivation of Intergenerational Behavior by Norms of Law,* in SOCIAL STRUCTURE AND THE FAMILY 241-55 (Shanas & Streib eds. 1965).

[107] 64 Stat. 550 (1950), as amended, 42 U.S.C. § 602(a)(10) (Supp. I, 1965). Federal law requires only notification; it does not require that action to locate the absent parent be taken by state agency or applicant.

[108] *E.g.,* ILL. REV. STAT. ch. 23, § 601.1 (1965); see Belknap, *An Analysis and Criticism of the Program of Aid to Dependent Children,* 6 J. PUB. L. 25, 42 (1957).

[109] Taylor, *Support from Absent Parents in ADC,* 14 PUBLIC WELFARE 114 (1956).

[110] Belknap, *supra* note 108, at 44.

ment officers is a formal gesture in many places because of the workload otherwise borne by prosecutors' offices, the difficulties of proof and tracing the absent parent, and the lack of enthusiasm for vigorous enforcement.[111]

In short, as in the case of work requirements, the policies underlying the requirements of NOLEO are easier to defend than the inconsistencies in administration. AFDC and general assistance, furthermore, in their continued reliance on relatives' responsibility, contrast to other welfare programs with similar avowed purposes of income support. Thus the social insurances make benefits contingent on membership in a class without regard to other family resources. Moreover, experience suggests that application of relatives' responsibility provisions often occurs in families which have a tenuous hold on security, and the deduction of support from the relatives' income depresses their own living standards.[112]

In the case of AFDC, however, parents of minor children, under domestic relations law as well as welfare laws, have a duty to support which no authorities have yet suggested be removed. The essential problem in AFDC is one of practice rather than principle. The accommodation of conflicting values believed to affect family unity is difficult to achieve. And as Professors Lewis and Levy suggest, the abolition of support features under public assistance would result in unequal treatment of families where support is rendered voluntarily and thus calculated in the determination of total need.[113]

The inequities arise from two factors: grossly varying methods of implementing support laws, signifying that a high degree of discretion is often exercised by caseworkers as well as prosecutors; and the reinforcement of support duties by required recourse to law enforcement, a measure not imposed on self-supporting families nor on families who derive income from other governmental forms of income maintenance. We should also note that OASDI records are available to trace the location of the deserting parents, an exception to the general rule of confidentiality which prohibits access by outside agencies or persons.[114]

Resolution of the basic conflicts in policy seems unlikely unless all income maintenance programs take a measure of economic need in family units as a determinant of benefits.[115] The contributory feature of

---

[111] See *id.* at 42-45. See also BURNS, SOCIAL SECURITY AND PUBLIC POLICY 80-93 (1956).

[112] Rheinstein, *supra* note 106, at 249-55; Rosenheim, *Social Welfare and Its Implications for Family Living*, in SOCIAL STRUCTURE AND THE FAMILY 237 & nn.65-66 (Shanas & Streib eds. 1965).

[113] See discussion of "substitute parent" policies in Lewis & Levy, *supra* note 106, at 761-80.

[114] 53 Stat. 1398 (1939), as amended, 42 U.S.C. § 1306 (1964), as amended, 42 U.S.C. § 1306 (Supp. I, 1965).

[115] BURNS, *op. cit. supra* note 111, at 92.

OASDI renders it improbable that a program of demonstrated need will soon supplant benefits accumulated over time under a program which merely presumes the likelihood of need. At the same time, the general approval of parental support of minor children indicates that the public assistance programs' consideration of parental resources will continue. The infusion of the vagrancy concept is related to implementation—to the required use of law enforcement methods in cases of poor families with deserting parents and to the discretionary standards employed by those charged with administration and enforcement. It is to this level of reform that immediate efforts must be bent.

B. The Female Vagrant in Welfare Law

The recognition of appropriate policy differences in welfare law based on sex is a matter of recent origin. An historical review of the vagrancy aspect of the poor laws, for example, makes clear that women, men, and what we today consider children were equally included within its scope.[116] These measures were directed impartially to all though their enforcement may have differed. Indeed, the repeated expressions of concern about public safety which preface vagrancy laws[117] suggest that the idle male, with his assumed predilection for criminal conduct, was the principal target.

Whatever the historical truth of the matter, in our own time idleness and the lack of visible means of support among women have been singled out for disapprobation in relatively few and specific instances. From the standpoint of vagrancy offense the "idle" woman summons up the image of a prostitute, drug peddler, or other malfeasant. From the

---

[116] See 1 NICHOLLS *passim*. The Statute of Labourers applied to every man and woman "within the age of threescore years." 23 Edw. 3, c. 3 (1349). In 1535, authority was first given for the compulsory apprenticing of vagrant children between the ages of five and fourteen. 27 Hen. 8, c. 25 (1535). Being the child of a vagrant likewise subjected one to compulsory apprenticeship (till age twenty-four for sons, age twenty for daughters, with slavery and punishment for those who rebelled). 1 Edw. 6, c. 3 (1547). Jordan states that the vagrant class contained "a breed of men, their women and their children, [who] had insulated themselves from a society of which they were no more than a festering part." JORDAN, PHILANTHROPY IN ENGLAND 1480-1660, at 79 (1959). In subsequent discussion, however, his references to vagrants are to men. *Id.* at 79-98.

[117] See, *e.g.*, the plaintive preamble to 22 Hen. 8, c. 12 (1530): "In all places throughout this realm, vagabonds and beggars have of long time increased, and daily do increase in great and excessive numbers, by the occasion of idleness, mother and root of all vices, whereby hath insurged and sprung, and daily insurgeth and springeth, continual thefts, murders, and other heinous offences and great enormities, to the high displeasure of God, the unquietation and damage of the King's people, and to the marvellous disturbance of the common weal." See also LEONARD, THE EARLY HISTORY OF ENGLISH POOR RELIEF *passim* (1900); 3 STEPHEN, HISTORY OF THE CRIMINAL LAW OF ENGLAND 391-96 (1883); WEBB & WEBB, ENGLISH LOCAL GOVERNMENT: ENGLISH POOR LAW HISTORY, PART I: THE OLD POOR LAW 1-59 (1927).

point-of-view of welfare, the malingerers and employable women are the prime targets; it is the administrator's duty to keep them off the welfare rolls.

But how do we identify the "voluntarily" idle among women? What welfare policies are suited to prevailing attitudes toward working women? If women are generally regarded either as out of the labor force or as *secondary* workers,[118] should it be public policy to insist they be *primary* workers in the case of the poor?

1. Working Mothers and AFDC

Consider the confusion of policies surrounding Aid to Families with Dependent Children. It has repeatedly been said that AFDC was established for a needy group which like the other original public assistance categories was outside the labor market. The forerunners of AFDC, we are told, were predicated on the desire to foster the mother's invaluable presence in the home as child caretaker,[119] and possibly were stimulated in the early depression years by labor's wish to limit the ranks of those seeking employment principally to males.[120] These Mother's Pension laws were enacted to afford financial aid outside of the almshouse or poor farm for dependent children.[121]

It is not clear, however, whether AFDC, or its precursors, was designed to wholly eliminate maternal employment or to offer an alternative to the prevailing mode of child care for dependent children, namely institutionalization.[122] We may mislead ourselves by speaking of the history of AFDC as though the original impetus was to provide a

---

[118] *But cf.* Civil Rights Act of 1964, §§ 703(a)-(e), 42 U.S.C. §§ 2000e-2(a)-(e) (1964); note 95 *supra*.

[119] The classic formulation of the case in favor of outdoor relief for mothers and children is found in the initial resolution of the CONFERENCE ON THE CARE OF DEPENDENT CHILDREN, PROCEEDINGS 9-10 (1909). See also U.S. SOCIAL SECURITY BD., SOCIAL SECURITY IN AMERICA 233-34 (1937).

[120] In many states during the depression mothers were classed as unemployables. Bookman, *A Community Program for Reducing Unemployment and Relief*, 11 SOCIAL SERVICE REV. 367 (1937). This author argues against such a designation for mothers or other groups (that is, those between fifty and sixty-five, the physically handicapped) because of its stigmatizing effect and its deterring the rehabilitative programs which he espouses. *Id.* at 365-67.

[121] See New York State Comm. on Relief for Widowed Mothers, *Report*, extracted in 2 ABBOTT, THE CHILD AND THE STATE 251-53 (1938).

[122] Proponents of Mother's Pension laws stressed the greater expense of the alternative, institutionalization. *Id.* at 252-55. The Commission on the Support of Dependent Minor Children of Widowed Mothers of Massachusetts recommended that aid be limited to young children in a good family, believing that "the widow without children or with children grown up is in a situation that she can generally manage." *Id.* at 250. Note that under AFDC, with its more liberal coverage, the number of one-child families supported was larger than under Mother's Pension programs. LUNDBERG, UNTO THE LEAST OF THESE 178 (1947).

choice between employment and nonemployment. It might better be characterized as offering mothers an alternative to institutionalization of their children or to starvation where employment was not a live possibility or brought insufficient income for the entire family. The latter possibility is supported by our knowledge that working women do not represent a new phenomenon, though undeniably our attitudes toward the acceptable reasons for women seeking employment have broadened. Lower-class women generally have been expected to work when the possibility was open to them.[123]

Income maintenance policies respecting dependent children will depend on the issues we frame. Possible alternative policy questions are: Should women be supported to care for their children at home and be prohibited from working; should they work and place the children under the care of others; or should they be encouraged to pursue dual careers?

If the history of Mother's Pensions is murky as to permissible answers, current policy is also opaque. The various purposes set forth in the first clause of the AFDC title read:

> For the purpose of encouraging the care of dependent children in their own homes or in the homes of relatives by enabling each State to furnish financial assistance and rehabilitation and other services, as far as practicable under the conditions in such State, to needy dependent children and the parents or relatives with whom they are living to help maintain and strengthen family life and to help such parents or relatives to attain capability for the maximum self-support and personal independence consistent with the maintenance of continuing parental care and protection, there is hereby authorized to be appropriated for each fiscal year a sum sufficient to carry out the purpose of this title.[124]

The legislative history of this section is instructive. Originally the statement of purpose read: "for the purposes of enabling each State to furnish financial assistance . . . to needy dependent children . . . ."[125] The straightforward aim of the federal title was to expand relief measures already on the books of many states.[126] And so it remained until 1956 when concern for what seemed to be a growing number of

---

[123] Peterson, *supra* note 95, at 671-73; see also Rossi, *Equality Between the Sexes*, in THE WOMAN IN AMERICA 615 (Daedalus, Spring 1964) (*"for the first time in the history of any known society, motherhood has become a full-time occupation for adult women"*: italics in original). Compare BUREAU OF FAMILY SERVICES, U.S. DEP'T OF HEALTH, EDUC. & WELFARE, HANDBOOK OF PUBLIC ASSISTANCE ADMINISTRATION, pt. IV, § 3401.1, expressing very measured approval of mothers' working.

[124] 49 Stat. 627 (1935), as amended, 42 U.S.C. § 601 (1964).

[125] Social Security Act of 1935, ch. 531, § 401, 49 Stat. 627.

[126] U.S. SOCIAL SECURITY BD., SOCIAL SECURITY IN AMERICA 233-49 (1937). Congress displayed little interest in this title. WITTE, THE DEVELOPMENT OF THE SOCIAL SECURITY ACT 164 (1962).

hard core families on AFDC led Congress to encourage extension of services as well as financial aid.[127] This had long been the goal of social work.[128] While a number of states had already made notable efforts to extend services, as distinct from cash payments, to selected public assistance cases, the belief was that services would be broadened if explicitly spelled out in the federal act as a desirable function. Thus came into being the additional phrases: "encouraging the care of dependent children in their own homes" by giving financial aid "and other services"—services not only to the children but also to "the parents or relatives with whom they are living."[129]

The expanded concept had an immediate practical effect. Federal matching in administrative costs (in 1956, as before, at the rate of fifty per cent without ceiling) covered social and other specialized services as well as the costs of administering disbursement of money payments and of medical care.[130] An added incentive to the states was provided by the 1962 amendments—an increase in federal matching for specialized services from fifty to seventy-five per cent.[131]

Parallel changes are reflected in state law. In its general provisions the Illinois Public Assistance Code declares: "The principal aim in promoting assistance and services shall be to aid those persons who can be so helped, to become self-supporting or attain self-care." Service is to encourage recipients in "developing their self-reliance and realizing their capacities for self-care, self-support, and responsible citizenship." Further, "all public assistance policies shall be formulated and administered with the purpose of strengthening the family unit."[132] In the AFDC article the goals of service for this category are enumerated:

"Services" means guidance and counseling provided directly by the staff of the county departments and the STATE DEPARTMENT, or

---

127 Schottland, *The Social Security Amendments of 1956*, Social Security Bull., Sept. 1956, pp. 10-11. Background on the amendments is contained in Cohen & Fauri, *The Social Security Amendments of 1956*, 14 PUBLIC WELFARE 183, 193-96 (1956).

128 Belknap, *supra* note 108, at 33-34.

129 70 Stat. 848 (1956), as amended, 42 U.S.C. § 601 (1964).

130 Schottland, *supra* note 127, at 11.

131 Increased federal participation provides a lever to implement the "new look" provided by the 1962 amendments, 76 Stat. 175, 42 U.S.C. § 603(a)(3) (1964). See Editorial, 20 PUBLIC WELFARE 89, 90 (1962). The underlying rationale of the 1962 amendments, and the earlier ones in 1956, 70 Stat. 848, as amended, 42 U.S.C. § 601 (1964), is that the poor have many "needs," of which only one is financial; counseling and other services are necessary to hasten their elevation into the ranks of the middle class. See generally Cohen & Ball, *The Public Welfare Amendments of 1962*, 20 PUBLIC WELFARE 191 (1962); Schorr, *The Trend to Rx*, Social Work, Jan. 1962, p. 59; tenBroek, *The 1956 Amendments to the Social Security Act*, 6 J. PUB. L. 123 (1957). *But cf.* Mencher, *Perspectives on Recent Welfare Legislation, Fore and Aft*, Social Work, July 1963, p. 59; Wilson, *Public Welfare and the New Frontier*, 36 SOCIAL SERVICE REV. 253 (1962).

132 ILL. REV. STAT. ch. 23, § 101 (1965).

through co-operating governmental and private agencies, to assist children and their parents or other adults who provide them with care and supervision in preventing or overcoming financial dependency or social maladjustment; in maintaining and strengthening family life; in increasing the capacities of the parents or other adults for attaining, or maintaining, a decent and healthful standard of living for themselves and the children; and in encouraging and aiding the parents or other adults in providing the children with maximum opportunities for realizing their full potentialities for development.[133]

If we look further into the AFDC portion of the Public Assistance Code we find that establishing eligibility requires, *inter alia*, "that the parent or parents have met, where applicable, the requirements for employment, or training or retraining for employment, for participation in educational programs designed to enhance opportunities for employment, and for participation in training and service projects."[134] The ground rules are spelled out in later sections. Significantly, services for purposes other than achieving self-support are not further referred to in the AFDC article.

The tough questions, however, arise in administration. Who qualifies for aid under a program designed to fulfill multiple objectives, at times mutually incompatible? And who determines who will qualify? The answers vary from state to state but some points are plain. First, administrative regulations and manuals provide pertinent sources of information designed to guide the caseworker initially and then his superior in review in determining applicability of the different program objectives. Second, we can be quite sure that no amount of "manualizing" will decide all those cases in which self-support and a mother's presence at home are twin aims of public policy. Reasonable doubt will sometimes arise as to the priority of one policy as against another, even though statute and administrative interpretation attempt to offer guidance.[135]

---

133 ILL. REV. STAT. ch. 23, § 601 (1965).

134 ILL. REV. STAT. ch. 23, § 603 (1965).

135 Consider the explicit reference in the Illinois Public Assistance Code, ILL. REV. STAT. ch. 23, § 605.3 (1965). On employment of mothers, rules and manuals reflect efforts to protect competing interests sensibly. For example, "If a parent who is requesting or receiving assistance for his or her children, or other adult whose needs are included in the assistance budget, refuses to accept available employment for which he or she is qualified, eligibility on the basis of need cannot be established provided that a suitable plan for the children can be arranged during the absence of the parent or other adult, taking into consideration the age, health, and welfare of the children. In no case shall this rule require consideration of potential employment of a mother or person acting in place of the mother when the youngest child in the eligible group is less than two years of age." MICH. SOCIAL WELFARE COMM., rule 26a, § I. Consider MICH. DEP'T SOCIAL SERVICES, MANUAL § 320-20A: "The primary responsibility and the most important job of any mother is to provide adequate care for her children. Under certain circumstances a mother may be able to provide such care and at the same time work outside the home to support the family. The purpose of this rule is to insure that the ADC program is administered in

Factors such as past employment experience, work skills, age of children, state of local labor market, and child care resources are among the usual criteria presented for the caseworker's use. The worker's inclinations, informal orders from superiors, guides from agency directors, and public criticism of the program also apparently play a role, perhaps more important than the articulated criteria.[136]

Consider, for example, the admonitions and directives to staff contained in the following statements of one state department director:

> We need to stress again the vast responsibility which lies ahead in the orderly movement of ADC mothers into employment or on the path to employment, through education and training programs.
>
> These 45,000 women who are the heads of their families have a dual role—that of homemaker and that of breadwinner. This idea is accepted without a question as a national pattern. There is no valid reason why it should be otherwise. . . .
>
> More than 4,000 ADC grantees in the state have finished high school. Their potential is good and they, too, should have a high priority in

such a way as to restore families, whenever possible, to a condition of financial and social independence, recognizing that the majority of families seeking aid are anxious to become self-supporting. The rule applies to any adult in the assistance group except the mother (or person acting in the place of the mother) of the child under two years of age. In applying this rule an adult is defined as any person who has attained 18 years of age."

And see competing objectives set forth in another state manual with respect to the mother's employment: "(1) The need for the mother's services at home depends upon the number, age and special needs of the children; incapacity of the father; the mother's acceptance of homemaking responsibility; and the availability of a mother-substitute to assure the adequate care of the children at home; (2) Her potential for employment depends upon her training and capacity for employment, the economic feasibility, the job availability and her physical and emotional ability to assume the dual responsibility of mother and breadwinner." Columbia University School of Social Work: Center on Social Welfare Policy and Law, Memorandum on the "social welfare law testing" Function of the Center 15. The Memorandum comments on this regulation: "The regulation may give an initial impression of reasonable guidelines. It does not take much imagination, however, to visualize the kind of opposite results easily reached in the same kinds of cases. Such breadth to discretionary situations translates itself in practice to arbitrary decision-making. There is a need, of course, to avoid rigid rules; and perhaps, in this area, satisfactory guides could not be worked out without incorporating a provision that the ultimate decision as to whether the welfare of her children is better served by staying at home or going to work must be made by the mother."

See also findings and conclusions reported in Cal. Dep't of Social Welfare, Parental Behavior in ANC Families 28, July 16, 1960: "The number of ANC families reported to be having problems in meeting certain program requirements [i.e., reporting changes in income, planning for employment, and participating in rehabilitation plans] suggest the need for further study to determine if these requirements are realistic, unless additional services are available . . . ." See also Cal. Dep't of Social Welfare, Study of Discontinuance for Lack of Cooperation in the Aid to Needy Children Program, July, 1960, reporting on improper discontinuance of aid in cases where parent refused employment.

136 See policies and practices criticized in D.C. CHAPTER, NATIONAL ASS'N SOCIAL WORKERS, THE PUBLIC WELFARE CRISIS IN THE NATION'S CAPITAL 33-35 (undated); Memorandum on Social Welfare Testing, op. cit. supra note 135, at 15.

our endeavor to require recipients to utilize their capacities fully to attain self-dependence.

Looking further, we see that 13,500 ADC grantees have some high school education, and more than 5,000 have finished the eighth grade. This group of recipients, totaling over 18,500, have demonstrated in their limited academic progress some capacity for achievement. They appear to have average to good potential for either immediate employment, or placement in vocational training classes to learn marketable skills.

The more than 11,000 who have some elementary schooling and the 500 to 600 who have no schooling defy any ready generalization, and the task of elevating many of them to wage earner status may be a lengthy process. For that reason, they should be started toward that goal as quickly as possible.

We will provide you with county-by-county information concerning these 45,000 women, and focus attention on the progress that is being made to accomplish the goals we have set for them. Moving them toward self-support is the first order of business in every county of the state.

The care of the children in the family is a problem to be recognized and solved. Again, let us consider the situation in the light of all working mothers who are faced with the responsibility for planning the care of their children while they are away from home on the job. Some place the children in the care of relatives; some locate a dependable woman to stay in the home with the children or to care for them in her own home; others leave them in nurseries or day-care arrangements. . . .

I have mentioned that we will inaugurate education and training programs to reach recipients wherever they live. This is entirely feasible because if public transportation is lacking, other transportation plans can be made. Here again, the situation of public aid recipients is no different from others who must commute to schools and training programs, or to jobs in other communities. We expect aid recipients to do the same.

If jobs cannot be found in their community of residence but are available elsewhere, we will expect them to move—voluntarily or involuntarily. . . . Mobility has always been a characteristic of our national culture. We can understand that inclination for people to stay in familiar surroundings, but we cannot condone the continuation of assistance funds to individuals or families in a favored location, when they can become self-supporting by moving to a location where opportunities are better.[137]

The statement underscores the importance of discretion in planning for each AFDC mother. At the same time it reflects a welfare director's

---

137 Swank, Programs, Trends, Goals, Public Aid in Illinois 15-16, Oct. 1965.

determination to hasten acquisition of dual careers by recipient mothers. Both the policy and the practice give rise to serious problems. So long as dual careers are seen as appropriate goals for AFDC mothers, discretion must be lodged in assistance staff in order to avoid the result the program was designed to obviate—automatic insistence on working regardless of personal circumstances. The development of less discretionary standards for determining suitability of employment would appear, by the nature of the relevant criteria, to be exceedingly difficult.[138] Internal administrative checks and test cases may be useful to curb extreme abuse but unsuited to promoting equality of treatment. So long as a decision hangs on evaluating child care arrangements, for example, the assistance staff must necessarily weigh the child's age, his particular behavior problems, and the quality of adult supervision. The mixture of relevant criteria is complex without even introducing the possibility that other factors may influence the final decision. Furthermore, the enthusiasm of many middle-class women for employment may produce in the staff, itself usually drawn from the middle class, an unrealistic view of the stresses of employment on families headed by one, presumably lower-class, parent.[139]

Thus we face squarely the question of policy. Is it socially desirable that AFDC mothers be required to work or to seek self-betterment by the agency which provides them with income? Why has the question taken on new significance so recently? Here recourse to vagrancy concepts may be instructive. The current stance of the AFDC program is to encourage self-support—and to penalize disinclination to achieve it. This approach contrasts with earlier pronouncements. It may be said that the change stems from today's widespread job opportunities as well as more hospitable attitudes toward women in employment. But in the face of social and economic changes we might well ask why there are unemployed women. Can we not safely assume that relief is an undesired status so far as the recipients as well as the general public are concerned?[140] The reasonable conclusion appears to be that most women on AFDC are unemployed because they are unable to solve child care problems or to find employment. In the latter instance, employment may be foreclosed by the mother's low level of literacy or other personal problems. Society agrees that some publicly mounted attack on these problems is overdue. Granting the existing consensus to promote employment opportunities for the dependent poor, it remains to consider the propriety

---

138 See warnings in Mapes, *The Mother's Employment—Whose Decision in ADC?*, 8 PUBLIC WELFARE 75 (1950).

139 See Belknap, *supra* note 108, at 40.

140 See Briar, *Welfare From Below: Recipients' Views of the Public Welfare System*, this symposium.

of hinging receipt of income upon participation in a plan of living which someone else has concocted. The fact that the good of the individual as well as the social good is the lodestar of this policy does not dispose of the evils of compulsion.

The introduction of compulsion, in fact, strengthens a comparison of these new elements of required "services" to old vagrancy concepts, the more so today when alternative methods of hastening entry into employment can be used. The presence of compulsion leads to the possibility of punitive results, for the choice is between forced training or employment and discontinuance of support. Only "good cause," a concept of uncertain meaning to caseworkers and ill-interpreted to clients, can rescue mothers regarded by their workers as employable. One way to resolve it is to insist "that the ultimate decision as to whether the welfare of her children is better served by staying at home or going to work must be made by the mother."[141]

To conclude, I would argue that the requirement of participation in work and training, now discretionarily applied to mothers in AFDC families, reflects the old vagrancy concept proscribing idleness without visible means of support. Moreover, in a society which has invented other means to cope with persistent unemployment among the disadvantaged, predicating receipt of relief upon fulfilling this requirement is especially harsh. Rising taxes and fearful recognition of the signs of alienation of nonwhite persons from middle-class values may underlie the emphasis on accelerating self-support. The promotion of self-support among female heads of household should, however, be considered on its own terms and in connection with more general problems of unemployment among the nonwhite. Incorporation of self-support requirements in AFDC obscures consideration of more basic issues at the same time that it reflects the disapprobation of certain groups and statuses which has so long characterized vagrancy.

2. Morality and AFDC

Similar conclusions may be drawn about requirements respecting personal conduct which permeate AFDC law and administration. The vagrant as a prostitute or person of dissolute character is a notion reflected in the rules relating to the AFDC mother who invites a man into her house, fails to keep a suitable home, or resorts to park or country lane for purposes of extramarital relations.[142] Comments herein will be limited to the suitable home requirement because of its pervasive influence on AFDC.

---

141 Memorandum on Social Welfare Testing, *op. cit. supra* note 135, at 15.
142 See tenBroek, 17 STAN. L. REV. 674.

Suitability of the home, broadly speaking, comprehends a range of conduct and environmental circumstances; in practice, however, the term is a euphemism for standards of sexual conduct of the mother.[143] It should be clearly understood that each state sets its own standard of conduct for the relative with whom the AFDC child resides. Its statutes and administrative regulations must be consulted.

Suitability requirements are a long-standing feature of AFDC laws and the Mother's Pension antecedents.[144] One state commission investigating the merits of a Mother's Pension law, for example, clearly indicated its intent to limit aid to families headed by worthy mothers:

> The commission rejects the principle of payment by way of indemnity for loss [such as the death of husband]. It proposes the principle of payment by way of subsidy for the rearing of children. The terms "pension," "indemnity" and "compensation" are irrelevant, *but the term "subsidy" implies that a condition exists which, aided, will result in positive good for the State. Subsidy makes it feasible that children should stay with their worthy mothers* in the most normal relation still possible when the father has been removed by death. It is intended not primarily for those with least adequate incomes under the present system of aid, but for the fit and worthy poor. What a good mother can do for her own children no other woman can do, and no different device can do . . . .
>
> The commission believes that no aid can be given, except under the poor-law and by private societies, to widows unfit to spend money for the improvements of their families. Aid may have to be given them hesitatingly, without assurance, and under abundant supervision. When even then family life is not really maintained, separation of the children may be resorted to as being genuinely in their interests. Whether it is then best that they be boarded out or placed in institutions must depend on a variety of circumstances.[145]

The fitness test could often be met, for in the period prior to survivors' benefits under OASDI, widows with dependent children formed a large, appealing group among the persons aided by AFDC.[146] While widowhood is no guarantee of worthiness, the problems of widows

---

[143] Suitable home policies almost invariably are applied to homes in which one or more children are illegitimate. Familiar crime-preventive concepts, such as proscription of association with known thieves and prostitutes, could be said to influence determinations of the suitability of home, a required finding in some state AFDC programs. I have never heard of cases where it has been attempted, however, and Bell's study of suitability indicates that the standard is the promiscuity of the mother and/or births of illegitimate children. See BELL, AID TO DEPENDENT CHILDREN 179 (1965). Compare the varied meanings of the "man in the house" rule, listed in Memorandum on Social Welfare Testing, *op. cit. supra* note 135, at 25.

[144] BELL, *op. cit. supra* note 143, at 3-19.

[145] Mass. Comm'n Rep. in 2 ABBOTT, *op. cit. supra* note 121, at 250. (Emphasis added.)

[146] Perkins, *AFDC in Review* 1936-1962, Welfare in Review, Nov. 1963, p. 1, at 7.

raising young children command more sympathetic attention from the public than the problems of women whose child-care burdens stem from the derelictions of their husbands or their own imprudent sexual behavior. Needless to say, the AFDC program presently draws the problem families most vulnerable to public attack.[147]

By the early 1950's, social workers, minority group leaders, and others were expressing vigorous dissatisfaction with the use of suitability provisions.[148] Concurrent with widely publicized attacks on AFDC, state administrations were said to be employing suitability criteria discriminatorily, based on characteristics of the mothers, and arbitrarily, considering the program's avowed goal of support for needy children. On the latter point evidence was adduced that children found living in unsuitable homes were ineligible for AFDC grants—thus deprived of financial aid—but were nonetheless permitted to remain in these allegedly harmful surroundings. The unfairness of the suitability criterion as applied was urged upon the states to little avail. Finally, a strategy emerged to exploit the conformity requirements of the federal act, with Louisiana as the test state and numerous interested organizations urging abolition of the suitability standard.[149] On January 16, 1961, after a review of the history of approved state plans with suitable home features, the Social Security Commissioner concluded a finding of nonconformity could not be supported. The following day, however, the Secretary of the Department of Health, Education, and Welfare moved to modify the suitable home standard under what is known as the "Flemming ruling."[150] Congress followed suit, and as a consequence, states are required to formulate plans of child care for any children living in an "unsuitable" home.[151] To enable the states to bear the financial burden of foster care, Congress extended payment of AFDC grants to include foster homes and institutions.[152] Participation in these new variants of AFDC rests on the state's enactment of parallel legislation and now includes twenty-three states.[153]

Many state laws are silent on home conditions. Those which take account of them use varying formulae for suitability determination. In New York State, for example, the agency must find that "the parent or other relative is a fit person to bring up such child or minor so that his

147 *Ibid.* See also Mugge, *Aid to Families with Dependent Children: Initial Findings,* Social Security Bull., March 1963, p. 3.
148 BELL, *op. cit. supra* note 143, at 137-51.
149 *Ibid.*
150 *Ibid.*
151 75 Stat. 77 (1961), as amended, 42 U.S.C. § 604(b) (1964). See also 76 Stat. 185 (1962), 42 U.S.C. § 602(a)(13) (1964).
152 75 Stat. 76 (1961), as amended, 42 U.S.C. § 608 (1964).
153 CHARACTERISTICS OF STATE PLANS *passim.*

physical, mental and moral well-being will be safeguarded,"[154] and further that "the religious faith of the child or minor shall be preserved or protected."[155] Michigan retains a suitable home requirement but now meets previous objections raised by Washington by assuring general assistance for the child so cut off from AFDC funds.[156] The net effect of this strategy, it has been claimed, is to produce two standards of support to children in their own homes—one, general assistance, the other, the "elite" program of AFDC.[157]

Thus the AFDC mother is an object of public disapproval. The desirability of supporting her at home is once again open to question, and her conduct, while in the home and caring for her children, is subject to far greater scrutiny and control than nonrecipients experience. She is the object of "services," for her compulsory,[158] and of special investigation.[159]

---

[154] N.Y. Soc. Welfare Law § 349(A)(2).

[155] N.Y. Soc. Welfare Law § 349(C).

[156] See Bell, op. cit. supra note 143, at 150. This is required by 42 U.S.C. § 604(b).

[157] Bell, op. cit. supra note 143, at 111-23.

[158] See Ill. Public Aid Comm'n [now Dep't Public Aid], Manual Release No. 63.8 (May 15, 1963):

The Illinois Public Aid Commission has always encouraged and expected county departments to offer social services, in addition to financial assistance, to those applicants and recipients who are in need of such services. Provision of stipulated services, as needed and on an individualized basis, is *mandatory* for *all ADC and ADC-U cases* and for designated OAA, BA, and DA cases, effective May 1, 1963. Other services may be provided, as needed, when resources for provision of the services are available and staff time permits. (Emphasis added.)

For a discussion of issues arising from the new "service" orientation of public assistance, see Handler & Rosenheim, *Privacy in Welfare: Public Assistance and Juvenile Justice*, 31 Law & Contemp. Prob. (to be published 1966).

[159] See, *e.g.*, provisions in the *Louisiana Manual of Public Assistance* which relate to establishing crucial facts of eligibility:

[W]hen the parent applying for or receiving ADC is maintaining or has maintained a nonlegal marital union as defined above, deprivation of parental support must be established in accordance with 2-740 B. in relation to this parent and this parent's latest nonlegal spouse. (§ 2-742.1)

. . . .

It is recognized that the client has a right to participate in social activities, including dating. The fact that a mother has dates with a man does not in itself establish that a nonlegal marital union exists. However, the worker shall be alert to and follow up on clues which indicate that the relationship is more than that of dating or courtship.

It is necessary to take into consideration the mother's past pattern of living in evaluating the situation, as well as whether both she and the man are free to marry.

If the mother is not known to have given birth to a child out of wedlock and does not have a past history of nonlegal marital unions; if both she and the man in question are legally free to marry; and if they are together during conventional, or acceptable, hours for dating; the department would not presume that a nonlegal marital union exists.

She is, in short, a minor criminal—a vagrant, an adulteress, a fornicator—in a nation where criminal laws condemning this kind of conduct have died either through disuse or repeal. The sanctions differ—she suffers *no* assistance or more restricted assistance instead of imprisonment—yet she is penalized for conduct which in the rest of us is widely regarded to be none of the public's business.

C. Idle Children as "Welfare Vagrants"

The school dropout of modern days comes perilously close to the classical vagrant of history.[160] As commonly described the dropout is male, feckless, and delinquency-prone. From a welfare perspective he represents the tough case which puts to test our public policies respecting support of economically-deprived young people. Should support provided through a welfare system be conditioned solely on age? Or should it, as in the instance of the men and women discussed above, sometimes be made contingent on qualifications of self-betterment or productive ability?

The bulk of children who derive support from public income maintenance are entitled on the bases of age and relationship. Thus under OASDI, to take the largest program, benefits are payable to children who are unmarried (with certain exceptions) and under eighteen (or

---

On the other hand, if either is not free to marry or if the client and the man stay away from home overnight, or he stays in the home to very late hours or overnight, or is in and out of the home at his will at all hours, *this is not dating and a nonlegal marital union shall be presumed to exist.*

When there is indication that the relationship may be more than that of normal courtship this should be discussed with the client, who should be asked for a true and full account concerning the length of time she has been seeing the man in question, where she usually sees him, the frequency of their dates and where they go. (§ 2-742.2-J) (Emphasis added.)

Special investigation units commonly exist in the large cities with high AFDC rolls, though some state systems also use them. See, *e.g.*, LA. REV. STAT. ANN. § 46:102(4) (Supp. 1965). The legal questions arising from the practices of these units have been noted. See Reich, *Individual Rights and Social Welfare: The Emerging Social Issues*, 74 YALE L.J. 1245, 1248 (1964); Memorandum on Social Welfare Testing, *op. cit. supra* note 135, at 5-6. See generally Handler & Rosenheim, *supra* note 158. Federal policy now requires the states to use investigatory techniques that meet standards of individual dignity and legality. See HANDBOOK OF PUBLIC ASSISTANCE ADMINISTRATION, pt. IV, *op. cit. supra* note 123, at §§2220(1), 2230(1) (effective July 1, 1967, HANDBOOK TRANSMITTAL No. 77).

160 At exactly what age children were considered employable and therefore subject to vagrancy laws if found wandering and idle is somewhat difficult to say. Information is sparse concerning the circumstances of agricultural labor of children, and for the early period under discussion here (fourteenth to sixteenth centuries) the vagrancy problem was associated with supposedly unjustifiable departures from service in husbandry. See 12 Rich. 2, c. 5 (1389) (forbidding apprenticeships to boys and girls who had worked up to the age of twelve in agriculture). In trade, children of very young age were employed prior to the factory system but the organized trades dependent on apprenticeship appear to have favored twelve or fourteen as minimum ages of entry. DUNLOP & DENMAN, ENGLISH APPRENTICESHIP AND CHILD LABOUR 98 (1912).

under twenty-two if attending school) and can show a dependency on an insured individual.[161] By comparison, AFDC looks to both need and age and permits the states to set more refined qualifications of eligibility.

As originally passed in 1935, the AFDC title identified dependent children as needy youngsters up to age sixteen.[162] The chosen age coincided with the generally accepted age limit in the states' Mother's Pension and compulsory education laws.[163] Generally, children under sixteen were eligible for ADC without further qualification. A few states, however, additionally required that the child be regularly attending school,[164] and Congress adopted this formula when, in 1939, it raised the age of eligibility to eighteen with respect to children in school.[165] In 1956 the act was amended to eliminate the school attendance requirement, thereby permitting federal matching under state laws which declared children up to eighteen to be eligible.[166] In 1964 and 1965 Congress once more returned to the age factor. It first permitted inclusion in the grant of children between eighteen and twenty-one who are "regularly attending a high school in pursuance of a course of study leading to a high school diploma or its equivalent, or regularly attending a course of vocational or technical training designed to fit him for gainful employment."[167] By the amendments of 1965 the requirements were clarified and now extend simply to students in the named age group "regularly attending a school, college, or university."[168]

Federal and state policies increasingly favor support of youth over compulsory school age who are pursuing their education. This reflects the premium on educational attainment in the modern labor market. Extension of the age of dependency is one method to encourage a youthful recipient, whose employment risks may already be substantial, to complete a course of study which may assure him of a lifetime of productivity. The calculus of assistance reinforces this point; if the average cost of maintaining an eighteen-year-old in school until he reaches twenty-one is, let us say, 912.60 dollars, it is still a small price to pay in order to avoid incurring public aid expenditures for this individual (and his future dependents) over an extended period of time. The cost of main-

---

161 53 Stat. 1364 (1939), as amended, 42 U.S.C. § 402(d), as amended, 42 U.S.C. § 402(d) (Supp. I, 1965).

162 Social Security Act of 1935, ch. 531, § 406, 49 Stat. 629.

163 U.S. SOCIAL SECURITY BD., SOCIAL SECURITY IN AMERICA 235-36 (1937).

164 Belknap, *An Analysis and Criticism of the Program of Aid to Dependent Children,* 6 J. PUB. L. 25, 35 (1957).

165 Social Security Act Amendments of 1939, ch. 666, § 403, 53 Stat. 1380.

166 Social Security Act Amendments of 1956, ch. 836, § 322, 70 Stat. 850.

167 Social Security Act Amendments of 1964, § 2, 78 Stat. 1042.

168 79 Stat. 422, 42 U.S.C. § 606(a)(2) (Supp. I, 1965).

taining one student for three years is less than the cost of a family of four for eight months.[169]

So much, then, for the arguments in favor of including in a public assistance program youth who are still in school. What of the boys or girls who are over the school-leaving age, out of school, and not seeking employment? (In this inquiry I put aside the question of whether they can find employment if they look.) Should they be included in an AFDC grant? Should they be required to fulfill additional conditions to qualify?

As far as federal law is concerned, an idle child between school-leaving age and age eighteen is not barred from AFDC by reason of idleness, and the majority of states also establish age—and age only—as the eligibility factor.[170] There are still, however, a substantial number of states which, even with respect to children under eighteen, require attendance at school as a condition of participation in the grant. As reported in 1964 by the Bureau of Family Services, twenty-one states require school attendance for all children or for those over sixteen but under eighteen.[171] One state, Texas, excludes all children over age sixteen regardless of educational status.[172]

Welfare policy respecting "productive activity" for youth, especially those in the school dropout class, appears to rest on the conviction that idleness breeds mischief. Beyond this general statement, however, agreement is less apparent. Many commentators emphasize productive activity, whether in training programs or in school, not so much as a means to prevent idleness per se but as a means to enhance personal ability to participate in and thereby strengthen a democratic society.[173] If one views school dropout rates, however, more as an indicator of *school* failure than the failure of youth, one can evaluate state policies making inclusion in AFDC contingent on a youth's educational status as doubling the injustice to school dropouts.

---

169 This calculation is based on personal allowance figures currently used in computing grants in Illinois; in both examples it excludes rent since rent is budgeted (within a maximum) as paid. The child's allowance is 30.80 dollars a month, with an additional 15 cents for lunch. Maintenance until age twenty-one will cost 912.60 dollars for three nine-month school years. A family of four with two parents (30.80 dollars each month), one child between thirteen to seventeen years (36.25 dollars) and one child between six to twelve years (27.30 dollars) will require 125.65 dollars a month for personal allowances. The sum for eight months is 1005.20 dollars. Ill. Dep't Public Aid, Monthly Budget Chart (8-7-64).

170 CHARACTERISTICS OF STATE PLANS *passim.*

171 Arizona, Arkansas, California, Colorado, District of Columbia, Georgia, Idaho, Indiana, Iowa, Kentucky, Louisiana, Mississippi, Missouri, Nebraska, Nevada, New Hampshire, New Mexico, Oklahoma, Tennessee, Vermont, Virginia. CHARACTERISTICS OF STATE PLANS *passim.*

172 *Id.* at 98.

173 *E.g.,* CONANT SLUMS AND SUBURBS (1961).

Suppose we agreed, in contrast to the present piecemeal approach, that needy minors ought to be universally eligible for public financial support. There would still remain the question of whether special conditions should be attached to receipt of assistance. Should youth, equally with the able-bodied male and female adults already discussed, be required to seek employment, to participate in training, or to accept employment or work relief offered them? What is the preferred attack on idleness in youth?

Initially we should note that public assistance adopts a case-oriented approach which markedly contrasts with the broad-scale "up-grading" approaches to education and training recently adopted under well-publicized federal legislation. Notable examples are the Manpower Development and Training Act, and titles I and II of the Economic Opportunity Act.[174]

Underlying both MDTA and EOA strategies is the conviction that most people, younger and older, including those considered alienated from society, will respond favorably to offers for training which in turn promises employment. Both sets of programs are premised on reaching target populations through voluntary enrollment, reinforced, to be sure, by publicity and persuasion. Such criticism as the new programs have received has been focused on inadequate planning or imperfect execution; the principle of voluntary enrollment has withstood the test of operation.

The public assistance approach to able-bodied youth, on the other hand, reflects the characteristic case-oriented approach of other assistance programs, a stigmatization of the able-bodied dependent poor. States that condition aid on school attendance approve support only when it is used to maintain those engaged in socially approved activity. The few anomalous cases requiring work and training referrals for youth between sixteen and eighteen in order to qualify them for an AFDC grant illustrate an informal policy in the same vein.[175]

Treatment of the earnings of an AFDC child provides another dramatic illustration of the policies which pervade all the public assistances. Let me restate the central principle of these programs—relief of need. Need is determined by measuring income and resources available to the

---

[174] See note 41 *supra* and accompanying text.

[175] Consider, however: "Employable youths 16 through 18 years of age, who are not in full time school attendance, are to be referred to Welfare Rehabilitation Service [for training, employment referral, or assignment to work relief] as soon as assistance is authorized. . . . Youths 16 through 18 years of age are given special services by Welfare Rehabilitation Service, *but elegibility of the family is not dependent on their cooperation.*" (Emphasis added.) Cook County Dep't of Public Aid, CCPA Bull. No. 65.1, March 1, 1965. Notwithstanding the voluntary aspect of the referral, instances of holding up the assistance grant for noncooperation of the youth have been reported to the author.

recipient and members of his family against a predetermined subsistence budget for the usual items of consumption, possibly expanded under special circumstances. Thus it is argued that to assure equality of treatment of recipients within a state demands that a child's earnings must be deducted from the grant so that similar-sized family units have equal levels of income. If, however, equality of treatment among the recipient class is urged as the value which demands these results, the equality principle here advanced works a discrimination between recipients and non-recipients who pay taxes on their more substantial incomes: The earnings of the latter are never taxed at a one hundred per cent rate. The equality, then, is confined to the very poor on assistance, and the sentiments favoring it are explicable primarily in terms of limited state appropriations which offer the recipient group a very low level of living. Each dollar appropriated must be stretched if the level is to rise or be maintained. Thus each dollar earned in a recipient family is a dollar of gain for the group as a whole.

Furthermore, even if the equality principle can be defended in its own terms it runs contrary to another value vigorously promoted—monetary incentive as a device for stimulating work. This is the value which attracts enrollees into the newer training programs and which has supported such modifications of assistance policy as have occurred. The modifications have been introduced unsystematically, however, with strikingly disparate results.

Thus, to take the AFDC child, note the different earnings treatments available to or imposed on the states at present. A youth who seeks employment and finds it on his own is a "resource" to his family. His income must be included in the calculation of need unless state law permits disregarding it according to the permissible methods of current federal law. The federal act now allows states to disregard as much as fifty dollars a month per child, to set aside without restriction "earned or other income" for his future identifiable needs, and, besides, to disregard an additional five dollars.[176] But note, this newest version of the federal act merely sets the permissible limits of state policy. It does not direct state treatment as do the programs of Aid to the Blind or relevant titles of the Economic Opportunity Act. A child enrolled in a Neighborhood Youth Corps program under EOA is entitled to his earnings in full as to the first eighty-five dollars and to half the excess.[177] Thus within the same family, earnings of two or more children may be treated differently according to their source.

---

[176] 53 Stat. 1379 (1939), as amended, 42 U.S.C. § 602(a)(7) (Supp. I, 1965). Note that the fifty dollar and future-identifiable-needs "disregards" apply only to the child. The adult caretaker is not directly benefitted by this policy.

[177] 78 Stat. 534, 42 U.S.C. § 2981 (1964).

Perhaps the reasonable conclusion to draw is that EOA, establishing a national program, could more readily adopt a liberal policy toward earnings and that the restrictive treatment in public assistance will, by startling contrast, produce its own continuing modification. The area of state decision-making remains substantial, however, and federal legislation of a permissive nature may not be decisive in state legislatures where the size of assistance appropriations is uppermost in the mind. It seems quite possible indeed that differential treatment of earnings will persist. If this forecast proves accurate, the popular attitudes toward able-bodied recipients may be blamed. For the child in his teens no longer looks helpless, appealing, or dependent; he more closely resembles, in popular opinion, the idle, threatening wastrel that his publicly-supported parents are supposed to be, and he is treated accordingly.

III

ELIMINATION OF VAGRANCY CONCEPTS FROM WELFARE LAW:
UNFINISHED BUSINESS

I have tried to demonstrate that certain vagrancy concepts significantly infuse the letter and spirit of welfare programs in the United States today. One may ask, however, "What of it"? Is it inappropriate under the welfare system to accomplish ends which are regarded by many legal theorists as improper subjects of criminal law? Obviously the fact that some have concluded it advisable to eliminate, as an end of the criminal law, the control of conduct not socially harmful does not dispose of the question. For one thing, there are dissenting voices to the proposition as advanced in the context of criminal jurisprudence. More compelling is the point that the goals of welfare law are and should be different from the aims of criminal justice.

Thus we must consider the desired aims of a welfare system in order to evaluate methods demonstrably infused with vagrancy concepts. To say that a welfare system should relieve want and provide services to enhance the competence of individuals in their social and personal functioning is a global way of expressing these aims. It fails to establish, however, the validity of conditions or priorities which are necessary guidelines to fulfillment of the aims. I assume that attainment of universal services is some time ahead, if for no other reason than that our desires exceed our resources.[178] Income maintenance for all, on the other hand, is immediately attainable if we will it.[179] Thus with respect to financial

---

[178] With respect to the acute shortage of manpower to provide services, see generally U.S. DEP'T OF HEALTH, EDUC. & WELFARE, TASK FORCE REPORT, CLOSING THE GAP IN SOCIAL WORK MANPOWER (Nov. 1965).

[179] See Schwartz, A Way to End the Means Test, Social Work, July 1964, p. 3; cf. FRIEDMAN, CAPITALISM AND FREEDOM 161-76 (1962).

support for the needy, its theoretical availability sharpens the issues: Should it be offered with no strings attached? Here we are forced to balance the costs of social policies in consideration ignorance of the probable outcomes. Yet, as the task is undertaken, one consoling point appears. We can at least advance well-informed guesses about the costs of prevailing methods, even if estimates of future results project us into terra incognita. From this point of view an evaluation of vagrancy concepts in the welfare system may be offered.

In his guise as wanderer, the "welfare-vagrant"[180] is no more effectively inhibited from moving by existing welfare laws than by the poor law and vagrancy statutes of old. He is asked to assume consequences, however, which the less mobile among us do not risk, and this result attends in an age when mobility of the able-bodied is a necessary element of modern manpower and labor market policy. Laws which elevate the importance of residence, therefore, mirror popular concern about increased financial burdens. Allocation of these burdens, nevertheless, is neither significantly affected nor, I may add, sensibly dealt with by welfare laws which place a premium on residence. Economic opportunity and salubrious climate may well have far more bearing on mobility. The paradox is that laws designed to curb the mobility of undesirables fail in their objective and catch up in their net of residence requirements many whose characteristics place them among the desirable or worthy group of needy persons.

In the guise of idle persons lacking visible means of support, the "welfare-vagrants" of today are treated as though work were an occupation which they shun. Yet all attempts to study this assertion belie its accuracy as a generalization. The fluctuations of assistance caseloads made up of the able-bodied bear the closest parallel to fluctuations of the labor market.[181] Undoubtedly the general conclusion drawn from this fact—that motivation to work coupled with the low levels of living afforded on income maintenance generates the observable turnover in relief rolls—is riddled with individual exceptions. Furthermore, past documentation of a parallel between high unemployment and high caseloads for public assistance is no sure predictor that such fluctuations will cease if levels of assistance are raised to approach more closely the wages

---

180 That is, the able-bodied unemployed; residence laws may have different effects on some public assistance recipients contemplating a move. Studies of assistance caseloads repeatedly demonstrate, however, that most recipients are not newcomers to the jurisdiction.

181 Lynch, *Effect of Seasonal Variations in Employment Opportunities on Unemployed—Parent Segment of Aid to Families with Dependent Children*, Welfare in Review, May 1964, p. 10, at 10-14; Perkins, *AFDC in Review 1936-1962*, Welfare in Review, Nov. 1963, p. 1, at 9-11.

offered in low-paid employment.[182] The significance of these observations for welfare policy, I would argue, is twofold: the necessity of giving special attention to the "hard-core" cases of unemployed persons, and of continued concern for the relationship between prevailing wages and salaries and the level and mechanisms of public income maintenance.

One can hardly escape the conclusion that attitudes toward income maintenance programs for the able-bodied have markedly changed since the modern programs were inaugurated in 1935. This shift in attitudes has left its mark on both law and practice. Nor should the result surprise us. Welfare in 1930's was seen as a boom for some of the middle as well as the lower class. It was evident to all that suffering was not the exclusive product of individual fault. Blame then attached to the malfunctioning of a world economy. With universal recognition of the economic causes of poverty, social policy in the 1930's aimed at providing monetary support in as dignified a manner as possible. The stress was on the aged and on the unemployed; other categories were eased in.[183] In all instances the notion of "right" was emphasized and the payment of grants in cash coupled with state plan requirements in categorical assistance and unemployment insurance symbolized a national commitment to preserve a large area of freedom of choice and dignity for recipients who were pawns of fate.

Thirty years later the recipient-beneficiary population among the able-bodied has a new look. Just as Professor Friedman describes the change in the tenant population in public housing,[184] so too in the welfare system the persons in receipt of funds from AFDC or unemployment insurance are those not benefiting from an improved economy. One popular explanation is related to fault; these people are, it is said, unwilling to work or unable to find employment because of their personal deficiencies. This attitude is expressed in law, as well as in practice. The vagrancy concepts, traced above, include welfare provisions which are creatures of legislation or administrative emphasis occurring since 1950.[185] Protective payments, work and training programs, the NOLEO amendment—all of these are relatively new and reflect sentiments which are repressive, on the one

---

182 *Cf.* Burns, *Social Security in Evolution*, 39 Social Service Rev. 129, 140 (1965).

183 See authorities cited in note 126 *supra*. The clear intention of the framers of the Social Security Act was to establish social insurance as the first line of defense against want, relegating public assistance to a minor and residual role. See tenBroek & Wilson, *Public Assistance and Social Insurance*, 1 U.C.L.A.L. Rev. 237, 238 (1954).

184 Friedman, *Public Housing and the Poor: An Overview*, this symposium.

185 See generally Wickenden, Poverty and the Law: The Constitutional Rights of Assistance Recipients, Feb. 25, 1963; Wickenden, *The Indigent and Welfare Administration*, in Proceedings of the Conference on The Extension of Legal Services to the Poor 41 (U.S. Dep't of Health, Educ. & Welfare 1964).

hand, or reformatory, on the other. The danger that the two may merge is well worth noting.

Certain provisions have, of course, been with the programs all along. Suitable home requirements, for one, are old, but what is new is the nature of the population to whom they potentially apply. For such requirements were less threat to the "deserving" poor in 1935; its membership could fulfill the condition. Now, possessing a matured OASDI program, we find that the group remaining on AFDC is, by and large, one ineligible for OASDI. And to considerable degree these "social insurance-ineligibles" are composed of persons whose conduct we disapprove of—the long-term unemployed, the family with an absent parent, the family of the unwed mother. The facts give rise to stereotypes, and these stereotypes generate the pressure for legislative change. Thus we move away from programs offering money payment and emphasizing right toward programs which attach more strings to receipt and expenditure of funds and which proclaim service as an important means toward attainment of self-support. The social pressures for conformity, protection, and economy are manifest in our welfare laws. Undergirding vagrancy throughout its tangled history they now re-emerge in the welfare system.

So far in this article I have argued that the transfusion of vagrancy concepts into welfare programs has for the most part failed to meet the avowed aims of public policy and has had inhuman consequences for individual clients. But a word should be added on the impact of these concepts on the bureaucracy which administers the programs. If the policy adopted toward treatment of the able-bodied is characterized by suspicion and denial, it stands to reason that it takes a toll from those executing the letter and the spirit of the law at the same time that it encourages slyness and chicanery by persons on the receiving end. Harsh measures carry within them the seeds of corruption. At least within the public assistance programs, workers sooner or later become committed to unbending application of the rules[186] or to most strenuous efforts to avoid intolerably severe consequences. Neither extreme promotes a reasonable consistency in administration nor creates an atmosphere in which legislative and administrative change is freely sought whenever conditions call for it. The caseworkers in many public assistance programs are neither masters of their own small barks nor even confident of safe

---

[186] Bentrup, *The Profession and the Means Test*, Social Work, April 1964, p. 10, at 15: "Workers not infrequently share with amusement their exploits in 'tripping up' one or another client. Nor does this effect stop with the worker; it has its subtly pervasive influence on the whole administrative structure." See also Blau, *Orientation toward Clients in a Public Agency*, 5 ADMINISTRATIVE SCIENCE Q. 341 (1960), reprinted in SOCIAL WELFARE INSTITUTIONS 654 (Zald ed. 1965).

passage. Their voyages are subject to the tides of public opinion, the endless waves of manual dicta, and the limits of their own endurance.

In the nature of its difficulties and its triumphs a welfare system is like many other large-scale social systems.[187] It promotes standardization at a scale once unheard of. It offers opportunities for aid unknown to earlier times. It also contains unwieldy bureaucratic structures. It has self-perpetuating tendencies and comes to regard its formal functions as limited by those traditionally assigned. Like other social systems, welfare can ill afford to tolerate a single-purpose focus. Instruction as well as income maintenance, counselling as well as clothing, can properly be demanded of this social protection complex. To insist on a restrictive vision of the functions of welfare is to encourage the growth of informal mechanisms and tiers of formal exceptions. In this development would lie the dangers inherent in confusion of purpose and absence of priorities to guide the expenditures of money and talent. Yet multiple purposes must be clearly spelled out and their interrelations articulated.

The vagrancy remnant in the welfare system is at once a symptom of its singlemindedness and a test of its creativity. The criminal and welfare law provisions directed at this shadowy, ill-defined person stigmatize him as an outcast from the mainstream of public life. To alter the impact of either system it is first necessary to recognize the consequences it produces. For the crime of vagrancy this task has been performed, and I have tried to trace the same process of rejection in another area. Yet I cannot conclude without remarking that abolishing the vagrancy remnant in the systems, even though it is limited, poses most difficult problems.[188] Not all those labelled vagrants are, or have been, poor; neither are all the poor uniformly stigmatized.[189] Counterfeiters and gypsies and disorderly persons have been vagrants—though not necessarily poor. The aged and disabled who are poor, furthermore, do not seem to bear or feel the full force of the public's scorn. It is the able-bodied unemployed—characterized as apathetic or rebellious, wanton and irresponsible—who form the target of concern. The persistence of public indignation is perhaps our best indicator of the odds against complete success in replacing untutored emotion with balanced appraisal of policy.

Two commonly encountered solutions to the ills which plague the income maintenances, and most especially public assistance, are the sub-

---

[187] See generally BLAU, BUREAUCRACY IN MODERN SOCIETY (1956); BLAU, THE DYNAMICS OF BUREAUCRACY (1955).

[188] Cf. Sherry, Vagrants, Rogues and Vagabonds—Old Concepts in Need of Revision, 48 CALIF. L. REV. 557, 566 (1960).

[189] For an enlightening discussion of the stigmatization of the poor, which came to my attention after completing this article, see Matza, Poverty and Disrepute, in CONTEMPORARY SOCIAL PROBLEMS 619 (2d ed. Merton & Nisbet 1966).

stitution of more objective principles to guide income distribution to the needy and the separation of service function from financial aid.[190] Perhaps the merits of these strategies are great; I personally endorse them. But their consequence for eliminating the attitudes and aberrational policies discussed here is problematical. Regardless of the form of payment, programs within the welfare system today reflect differences which can only indicate a general recognition that the various eligible populations differ—at least as publicly viewed. The low levels of grants to AFDC, the persistent lag in bringing unemployment benefits to closer approximation of wage scales, the differential application of services to categories within the public assistances—these are among the signs suggestive of popular distinctions between the employable and the other dependent poor. And past experience indicates that a change in name, a change in form, will not alone suffice to change the content or the modes of public aid. Thus the "welfare-vagrants," whether men or women, young or old, must be faced for what they are—problems to a society which has demonstrated little skill in their solution and little maturity in recognizing its failures. These people squarely pose a test of what the public will freely grant, what it will withhold, and why. In these terms they become appropriate subjects of public debate so that conflicting values are identified, periodically resolved, and once again appraised and re-examined.[191]

For now, the saving grace so far as mitigating the repressive effect of vagrancy concepts on the welfare system may well be the rise of competing programs within the system whose goals are not yet firmly and irrevocably established. As these programs are accepted new ways of handling "problem people" such as the vagrant are introduced. By means of developments *outside* the traditional structure of welfare, there are available various lines of attack on opportunity provision, on work training, on stimulating people to participate in the "Great Society." Such measures, and techniques yet to receive legislative benediction, present new ways of rehabilitating and reaching the unfortunate people in our land who are lacking in employment, education, parental capabilities, or self-esteem. They also offer leverage to hasten rejection of outmoded concepts. In the last analysis, however, whether the legacy of personal fault or the lure of building multi-purpose systems for a complicated world will shape the future is for the public to say.

---

190 See Kahn, *Social Services in Relation to Income Security*, 39 SOCIAL SERVICE REV. 381 (1965); *cf.* Hoshino, *Can the Means Test Be Simplified*, Social Work, July 1965, p. 98. See also Mencher, *Perspectives on Recent Welfare Legislation, Fore and Aft*, Social Work, July 1963, p. 59; Schwartz, *A Way to End the Means Test*, Social Work, July 1964, p. 3.

191 Wickenden, *Welfare Services*, in IN AID OF THE UNEMPLOYED 252, 270-71 (Becker ed. 1965).

The Constitutionality of Residence Tests for General and Categorical Assistance Programs†

Bernard Evans Harvith*

IN THE UNITED STATES, constitutional rights are being infringed by residence tests for eligibility for state and federal welfare assistance. "Residence test" here, and throughout this paper, refers to *a period of residence* in a state necessary to qualify a person for welfare payments. These tests are derived historically from the concept of settlement, the idea that each individual belonged to a certain place which had the obligation of supporting him in time of need.[1] This concept is traceable to the English poor laws.[2] While this article does not deal specifically with other derivatives of the settlement tradition, such as removal[3] and "warning-out,"[4] much of the analysis is applicable to these provisions.

Also, this article does not analyze extensively the validity of a requirement of residence, with no minimum period being required. The fourteenth amendment makes residence the determining factor for state citizenship[5] and some of the arguments made here may founder in the face of the reasonableness of a distinction between citizens and noncitizens of a state.

First, this article will examine the constitutionality of residence tests for general or public assistance,[6] a form of welfare program entirely fi-

---

* A.B., 1960, University of Rochester; LL.B., 1963, Harvard University; LL.M., 1964, New York University. Visiting Assistant Professor of Law and Legal Director, Project on Social Welfare Law, New York University School of Law.

† This paper was prepared as part of the author's work for the Project on Social Welfare Law. The views expressed are the responsibility of the author.

The author is indebted to Professor Charles Ares, New York University School of Law and Professor Arvo Van Alstyne, University of California at Los Angeles, for their comments upon the conference draft of this paper.

1 See Mandelker, *The Settlement Requirement in General Assistance*, 1955 WASH. U.L.Q. 355-56.

2 See *id.* at 355, 356-57.

3 See generally Mandelker, *Exclusion and Removal Legislation*, 1956 WIS. L. REV. 57.

4 See Mandelker, *The Settlement Requirement in General Assistance*, 1956 WASH. U.L.Q. 21-22.

5 U.S. CONST. amend. XIV, § 1.

6 The constitutionality of residence tests for general assistance is discussed in TENBROEK, THE CONSTITUTION AND THE RIGHT OF FREE MOVEMENT (1955) [hereinafter cited as TENBROEK]; LoGatto, *Residence Laws—A Step Forward or Backward?*, 7 CATHOLIC LAW. 101 (1961) [hereinafter cited as LoGatto]; Feinberg, Settlement Laws: A Constitutional Assault (unpublished paper prepared in 1964 by student at New York University School of

nanced by state and local units and defined by state legislation. According to a compilation published in 1961,[7] residence tests for general assistance range from five years[8] to no required period.[9] States frequently require one[10] or three[11] years of residence. Some require that the residence be in the county,[12] and others require a shorter period in the county or township in addition to the longer period in the state.[13] One variant is to require a shorter period for those who were self-supporting when they became residents.[14] Other states have emergency provisions making assistance available in certain cases to those who do not meet the residence test.[15] The constitutional validity of residence tests for general or public assistance will be considered in the face of challenges based upon: (1) a freedom of interstate movement which may be protected against state action by the commerce clause,[16] the privileges and immunities clause of the fourteenth amendment, or the privileges and immunities clause of article IV, or (2) the equal protection clause of the fourteenth amendment.

Second, this article will discuss the validity of residence tests for categorical assistance programs, which are defined in the Social Security Act and involve federal financial participation in state plans meeting specified federal standards. Categorical assistance programs[17] include: (1)

Law) [hereinafter cited as Feinberg]; Hohlt, Residence Requirements: Are They Unconstitutional? (unpublished paper prepared in 1965 by student at Columbia Law School) [hereinafter cited as Hohlt]; Nathanson, Residence Requirements in Public Welfare Law (unpublished paper prepared in 1965 by student at Columbia Law School) [hereinafter cited as Nathanson]; Pierson, The Constitutionality of District of Columbia Residence Requirements for Public Assistance (undated mimeographed memorandum) [hereinafter cited as Pierson]; Note, 12 Wyo. L.J. 50 (1957). See also, on freedom of movement generally, CHAFEE, THREE HUMAN RIGHTS IN THE CONSTITUTION OF 1787, at 162-213, 221-23 (1956).

7 NATIONAL TRAVELERS AID ASS'N, ONE MANNER OF LAW—A HANDBOOK ON RESIDENCE REQUIREMENTS IN PUBLIC ASSISTANCE 8-13 (1961).

8 E.g., N.H. REV. STAT. ANN. § 164:1 (1964 Replacement ed.).

9 E.g., HAWAII REV. LAWS § 108-15 (Supp. 1963); N.Y. Soc. WELFARE LAW §§ 117, 131, 132, 138, 139, 157, 158.

10 E.g., ALASKA COMP. LAWS ANN. § 47.25.300 (1962).

11 E.g., CAL. WELFARE & INST'NS CODE § 2555.

12 E.g., IOWA CODE § 252.16 (Supp. 1965).

13 E.g., IND. ANN. STAT. § 52-147 (1964).

14 VA. CODE ANN. § 63-330 (1950).

15 E.g., ORE. REV. STAT. § 411.720 (Supp. 1963).

16 U.S. CONST. art. I, § 8, cl. 3.

17 The Social Security Act, 49 Stat. 620 (1935), as amended, 42 U.S.C. §§ 301-1394 (1964), as amended, 42 U.S.C. §§ 301-1396d (Supp. I, 1965), is the focus of much of the discussion in this article. For discussion of the structure and administrative operation of the Social Security System, see Wedemeyer, *The American Welfare System*, this symposium.

Old Age Assistance,[18] (2) Aid to the Blind,[19] (3) Aid to the Disabled,[20] (4) Medical Assistance for the Aged,[21] (5) programs combining any of the foregoing,[22] (6) Aid to Needy Families with Children,[23] and (7) Medical Assistance under Title XIX.[24] State plans qualify for federal financial participation if, in regard to the first three of these programs (or any or all of them in a combined program), any residence test imposed does not exceed five of the nine years immediately preceding application, and continuous residence during the last year.[25] A qualifying Aid to Needy Families with Children state program may impose only a residence requirement not exceeding one year, or in the case of a child under age one, not exceeding one year of residence, before the child's birth, by the parent or other relative with whom the child is living.[26] Medical Assistance for the Aged and Title XIX Medical Assistance Plans qualify only if open to all residents of the state,[27] so these programs are removed from consideration in this article.

According to a compilation published in 1961, state programs for the types of categorical assistance allowing residence tests range from having the maximum tests allowable to having no residence tests.[28] This article will examine the constitutionality of residence tests for categorical assistance in light of (1) a freedom of interstate movement protected against federal government interference, and (2) the equal protection of the law safeguarded by the due process provision of the fifth amendment.

---

[18] Social Security Act, Title I, 49 Stat. 620 (1935), as amended, 42 U.S.C. §§ 301-06 (1964), as amended, 42 U.S.C. §§ 302-06 (Supp. I, 1965).

[19] Social Security Act, Title X, 49 Stat. 645 (1935), as amended, 42 U.S.C. §§ 1201-06 (1964), as amended, 42 U.S.C. §§ 1202-06 (Supp. I, 1965).

[20] Social Security Act, Title XIV, 64 Stat. 555 (1950), as amended, 42 U.S.C. §§ 1351-55 (1964), as amended, 42 U.S.C. §§ 1352-55 (Supp. I, 1965).

[21] Social Security Act, Title I, 49 Stat. 620 (1935), as amended, 42 U.S.C. §§ 301-06 (1964), as amended, 42 U.S.C. §§ 302-06 (Supp. I, 1965).

[22] Social Security Act, Title XVI, 76 Stat. 197 (1962), 42 U.S.C. §§ 1381-85 (1964), as amended, 42 U.S.C. §§ 1382-85 (Supp. I. 1965).

[23] Social Security Act, Title IV, 49 Stat. 627 (1935), as amended, 42 U.S.C. §§ 601-09 (1964), as amended, 42 U.S.C. §§ 602-06 (Supp. I, 1965).

[24] Social Security Act, Title XIX, 79 Stat. 343, 42 U.S.C. §§ 1396-96d (Supp. I, 1965), providing for qualifying state plans for Medical Assistance to the aged, blind, disabled, and families with dependent children.

[25] 49 Stat. 620 (1935), as amended, 42 U.S.C. § 302(b)(2) (1964); 49 Stat. 645 (1935), as amended, 42 U.S.C. § 1202(b)(1) (1964); 64 Stat. 555 (1950), as amended, 42 U.S.C. § 1352(b)(1) (1964); 76 Stat. 198 (1962), as amended, 42 U.S.C. § 1382(b)(2) (1964).

[26] 49 Stat. 627 (1935), as amended, 42 U.S.C. § 602(b)(2) (1964).

[27] 49 Stat. 620 (1935), as amended, 42 U.S.C. § 302(b)(2) (1964); 76 Stat. 198 (1962), as amended, 42 U.S.C. § 1382(b)(2) (1964) (Medical Assistance to the Aged in combined program under Title XVI); 79 Stat. 349, 42 U.S.C. § 1396a(b)(3) (Supp. I, 1965).

[28] NATIONAL TRAVELERS AID ASS'N, ONE MANNER OF LAW—A HANDBOOK ON RESIDENCE REQUIREMENTS IN PUBLIC ASSISTANCE 8-13 (1961).

I

THE CONSTITUTIONALITY OF RESIDENCE TESTS FOR GENERAL ASSISTANCE PROGRAMS

A variety of federal constitutional provisions may be cited in support of an attack on the validity of residence tests for state general assistance programs. However, it is important not to lose sight of the forest as we investigate particular hoary oaks and tiny seedlings of legal doctrine. Fortunately, the grounds for attack can be grouped in two general categories: (1) an infringement of a constitutionally protected freedom of movement, and (2) a denial of equal treatment of newcomers as compared to settled residents of the state. Before analyzing these categories, it will be useful to examine the very limited case law directly in point, to dispose of a spurious argument, and to distinguish one case.

A. Cases Directly in Point

1. The One Direct Authority

In *People ex rel. Heydenreich v. Lyons*,[29] in 1940, the Supreme Court of Illinois upheld a state statute requiring applicants for assistance to have resided in the city or other pertinent local governmental unit for the three years immediately preceding the date of application. The court pointed out that since a state has no constitutionally imposed or common law duty to provide assistance,[30] "a large degree of discretion rests upon the State when it elects to furnish relief."[31] In analyzing a claim that the test denied equal protection, the court stated: "The Fourteenth Amendment . . . . merely requires that the classification shall be based on a real and substantial difference having a rational relation to the subject of the particular legislation."[32] The court found that the legislative purpose underlying the residence test was to guard against the costs of providing assistance payments to an "influx of unfortunate transients"; that is, to reduce the financial burden of assistance and to prevent any need for "reducing the aid to which permanent residents of Illinois should justly have first claim."[33] Therefore, the residence test was held to be a reasonable classification, made pursuant to a valid state purpose. This holding was facilitated by the fact that the court construed the residence test so as to remove the discriminatory aspects being alleged by the parties. The relators, in general, seem to have met even a strict interpretation of the residence test except for short periods when they were absent

---

29 374 Ill. 557, 30 N.E.2d 46 (1940).
30 *Id.* at 564-66, 30 N.E.2d at 50-51.
31 *Id.* at 565, 30 N.E.2d at 51.
32 *Id.* at 564, 30 N.E.2d at 51.
33 *Id.* at 566, 30 N.E.2d at 51.

from their usual residence to seek and pursue work, when employment was not available near their usual residence.[34] The court's interpretation of the purpose of the legislature made residence largely a matter of intention.[35] "To construe the statute so as to preclude a temporary departure from the particular governmental unit by persons who have long resided there would impute a harsh and unconscionable intent to the legislature."[36] Therefore, the court concluded, "A 'residence' or 'settlement' for poor relief purposes once acquired is not necessarily lost or defeated by a voluntary absence for the purpose of obtaining work."[37]

The court did not have to face the equal protection question squarely. Moreover, the landmark decision dealing with freedom to travel interstate, *Edwards v. California*,[38] was not decided until a year later. Also, *Heydenreich* is only a state court opinion. All of these factors serve to reduce the value of this case as authority.

2. The Chirillo Dissent

In re Chirillo,[39] a 1940 decision by the Court of Appeals of New York, found four justices dismissing a direct appeal challenging the constitutionality of a removal statute, since other issues were also involved.[40] Three dissenting justices[41] would have reached the constitutional issues and upheld the statute against arguments based on the due process, equal protection, and privileges and immunities clauses of the fourteenth amendment, the privileges and immunities clause of article IV, and the commerce clause.

The dissent argued that New York, before adoption of the Constitution, "possessed the powers of a sovereign nation, which included the power to refuse admittance to, or to deport, a person coming from without its borders, whether or not that person crossed the state line with the intention of seeking permanent residence . . . ."[42] The state retains this power, except as limited by the United States Constitution. Due process requires only that regulations promote "the public welfare through having a real and substantial relation to that end, and shall not be unreasonable, arbitrary or capricious."[43] That the New York statute meets this

---

[34] *Id.* at 561, 567, 30 N.E.2d at 49, 52.

[35] *Id.* at 565-66, 30 N.E.2d at 51.

[36] *Id.* at 566, 30 N.E.2d at 51.

[37] *Id.* at 566, 30 N.E.2d at 52.

[38] 314 U.S. 160 (1941).

[39] 283 N.Y. 417, 28 N.E.2d 895 (1940).

[40] *Id.* at 418-21, 28 N.E.2d at 895-96; *id.* at 421-24, 28 N.E.2d at 896-98 (concurring opinion of Lehman, C.J., for three of four majority justices).

[41] *Id.* at 424-39, 28 N.E.2d at 898-905.

[42] *Id.* at 431, 28 N.E.2d at 901.

[43] *Ibid.*

test is shown by: (1) the long history of removal legislation at common law, (2) the safeguards incorporated in the statute, and (3) the size and growth of the state's welfare burdens and its grants per person which exceed those of other states.[44]

The dissenters argued that the commerce clause does not, "in the absence of congressional pre-emptions," bar exercises of the police power "within reasonable restrictions, even though there may be interference with interstate commerce."[45] The removal statute does not prevent any person from entering the state; removal is possible only after an application for welfare assistance. The privileges and immunities clause of article IV prevents a state from discriminating against another state's citizens.

> To hold that this clause protects the right of a citizen to be sup-
> ported at public expense in any community to which he may journey,
> it is necessary to find that there is inherent in State citizenship a con-
> stitutional right to be supported at public expense free from any limi-
> tations whatsoever. . . . No such right exists. "Neither aliens nor
> citizens of other states are invested by the Constitution with any in-
> terest in the common property of the people of this state."[46]

There is no discrimination based on state citizenship, the dissent continued, since New York citizens applying for assistance may also be removed to their place of settlement if it is in another county.[47] The same
argument disposes of any claim that the equal protection clause is violated. The removal statute treats similarly all persons similarly located;
that is, those applying for assistance.[48] The privileges and immunities
clause of the fourteenth amendment is inapplicable, since the privileges
and immunities of United States citizens are only those resulting "from
other provisions of the Constitution and from the laws of Congress."[49]
No federal statute applies and no other provision of the Constitution is
violated.

B. An Improper Argument: The Absence of a Duty to Enact Assistance Programs Allows a State to Condition Such Programs as It Wishes

It is now necessary to dispose of the contention that, since neither
the common law nor the state or federal constitutions impose a duty on
a state to provide welfare assistance, the state can condition a grant of

---

44 *Id.* at 432-34, 28 N.E.2d at 901-02.
45 *Id.* at 435, 28 N.E.2d at 903.
46 *Id.* at 436, 28 N.E.2d at 903.
47 *Id.* at 436-37, 28 N.E.2d at 903-04.
48 *Id.* at 437, 28 N.E.2d at 904.
49 *Id.* at 438, 28 N.E.2d at 904.

such assistance as it wishes, even in derogation of constitutional rights.[50] If this contention is correct, the remainder of this article is a futile exercise.

The *Chirillo* dissent argued that removal, being possible only after an application for assistance, could not infringe any freedom to enter the state.[51] The application for assistance would waive any constitutional right to free interstate movement, including the right to remain. An assistance applicant "is bound to accept the relief *cum onere,* or with the limitation of the reasonable provisions of the Public Welfare Law."[52] It is unclear whether the dissenters were describing the conditions as "reasonable" or saying they were required to be so.

In *Heydenreich,* a power to condition assistance was recognized. The Illinois court stated that "since there is no legal obligation upon the State, . . . in the absence of legislative action, to support its poor, it follows, necessarily, that a large degree of discretion rests upon the State when it elects to furnish relief."[53] This discretion was considered broad enough to include residence tests.

The invalidity of this contention seems evident from the 1963 decision of the United States Supreme Court in *Sherbert v. Verner,*[54] which held unconstitutional the application of a state unemployment compensation statute to deny benefits to a Seventh Day Adventist who could not find work because her religion prevented her from laboring on Saturday. The Court rejected an argument that since the compensation benefits were a privilege and not a right, the state could condition them even if a constitutional right is infringed thereby.[55]

Admittedly *Sherbert,* like *Speiser v. Randall,*[56] the major authority cited in support of the Court's holding,[57] involved a condition operating "to inhibit or deter the exercise of First Amendment freedoms."[58] It is well settled that such freedoms occupy a preferred position in the galaxy

---

[50] See, *e.g.*, People *ex rel.* Heydenreich v. Lyons, 374 Ill. 557, 30 N.E.2d 46 (1940). *Contra,* Reich, *Individual Rights and Social Welfare: The Emerging Legal Issues,* 74 YALE L.J. 1245, 1255-56 (1965). For a more complete analysis than that which follows, see O'Neil, *Unconstitutional Conditions: Welfare Benefits With Strings Attached,* this symposium. See also Linde, *Constitutional Rights in the Public Sector: Justice Douglas on Liberty in the Welfare State,* 40 WASH. L. REV. 10-34 (1965).

[51] 283 N.Y. at 435, 28 N.E.2d at 903.

[52] *Id.* at 436, 28 N.E.2d at 903.

[53] 374 Ill. at 565, 30 N.E.2d at 51.

[54] 374 U.S. 398 (1963) (7-2 decision, with Justices Douglas and Stewart each concurring separately, and Justices Harlan and White dissenting). See Feinberg 32-33; Note, *Unconstitutional Conditions,* 73 HARV. L. REV. 1595 (1960).

[55] 374 U.S. at 404-06.

[56] 357 U.S. 513 (1958).

[57] 374 U.S. at 405.

[58] *Ibid.*

of constitutional rights.[59] However, since freedom of interstate movement has been analogized, in importance, to such freedoms,[60] *Sherbert* is highly relevant to a consideration of the validity of residence tests for public assistance.

Sherbert conceivably could be distinguished on the ground that unemployment compensation is an insurance program, different in kind from assistance. However, the Court gave no indication that such a distinction would be significant. The underlying policy of the decision, opposition to allowing a state to either buy up constitutional rights or treat similarly situated persons differently, would seem equally applicable to the assistance situation.

The extent of the Court's protection of constitutional freedoms is indicated by its express statement that conditions, "whatever their purpose," were invalid if they merely inhibited or deterred the exercise of first amendment freedoms.[61] The Court did admit that there might be "some compelling state interest" which could justify such infringement, but "in this highly sensitive constitutional area, 'only the gravest abuses, endangering paramount interests, give occasion for permissible limitation,' . . . . No such abuse or danger has been advanced in the present case."[62] While the majority stated that the only "danger" argued to them was that of fraudulent claims leading to dilution of the state's unemployment compensation fund, the dissent[63] stressed the state's interest in accumulating funds, when employment was available, to tide workers over jobless periods.[64] Therefore, the holding in *Sherbert* would seem to blunt an argument that residence tests are justified to protect the state's treasury. The economic threat in *Sherbert* arguably was less than that caused by in-migrating indigents. But the holding in *Edwards v. California*[65] would seem to destroy any attempt to stress the extent of an economic threat posed by such migrants. There, the Court acknowledged California's economic plight, resulting from heavy in-migration of poor refugees from the Dust Bowl. The majority held that aiding indigents to enter the state could not be barred for that reason, because of the commerce clause. The concurring justices reached a similar result, but applied the privileges and immunities clause of the fourteenth amendment.[66]

---

[59] *E.g.*, Kovacs v. Cooper, 336 U.S. 77, 89-97 (1949) (concurring opinion of Frankfurter, J.) and cases cited therein; FREUND, THE SUPREME COURT OF THE UNITED STATES 32-33, 74-87 (Meridian ed. 1961).

[60] Aptheker v. United States, 378 U.S. 500, 517 (1964).

[61] 374 U.S. at 405.

[62] *Id.* at 406-07.

[63] *Id.* at 418.

[64] *Id.* at 418-19.

[65] 314 U.S. 160 (1941).

[66] *Id.* at 177, 181.

Perhaps the only state purposes which can justify conditions infringing basic constitutional rights are efforts to meet other fundamental human needs, such as a uniform day of rest, used in *Sherbert*[67] to explain a Sunday law case.[68]

C. A Distinguishable Case—Flemming v. Nestor

Flemming v. Nestor,[69] while distinguishable from the situations of residence tests for general and categorical assistance, might be thought to contradict some of the analysis in this article. In *Flemming*, a five-to-four decision of the Supreme Court in 1960, five Justices, speaking through Justice Harlan, upheld a provision of the Social Security Act[70] terminating old-age benefits for aliens deported from the United States for having been members of the Communist Party. While this case dealt with a federal statute, the majority's reasoning might be thought to support the proposition that state or federal legislatures may restrict eligibility for public benefit programs as long as any arguably valid legislative purpose may be conjured up by the Court, regardless of either the actual intent of the legislators or the effect of the restrictions. Presumably, such an analysis of *Flemming* would explain *Sherbert* as an exception confined to situations where the restriction infringes freedom of religion. Moreover, *Flemming* dealt with benefits which are easier to call vested rights than are those provided under assistance programs.

The majority rejected contentions that the statute violated the due process clause of the fifth amendment, the bans in article I, section 9 on bills of attainder and ex post facto laws, and the sixth amendment forbidding imposition of criminal punishment without a jury trial. They argued that the employee acquires no vested property rights from his payment of Social Security taxes, and that no punishment was involved, since the statute was aimed at "the activity or status from which the individual is barred," rather than "the person or class of persons disqualified."[71]

In *Flemming* the majority applied very strong presumptions of constitutionality: (1) After stating that "the Due Process Clause can be thought to interpose a bar only if the statute manifests a patently arbitrary classification, utterly lacking in rational justification,"[72] Justice Harlan inquired if there was a valid purpose which Congress might have been implementing. Having found such a motivation—the desire to

---

[67] 374 U.S. at 408.

[68] Braunfield v. Brown, 366 U.S. 599 (1961).

[69] 363 U.S. 603 (1960).

[70] Social Security Act § 202(n), 49 Stat. 623 (1935), as amended, 42 U.S.C. § 402(n) (1964).

[71] 363 U.S. at 614.

[72] *Id.* at 611.

have Social Security payments spent in the United States to bolster national production, he argued that it was "constitutionally irrelevant whether this reasoning in fact underlay the legislative decision."[73] Therefore, the statutory classification was not arbitrary or irrational. (2) In considering the allegations that the statute imposes punishment and is a bill of attainder, ex post facto law, or violation of the sixth amendment, Harlan stated:

> [O]nly the clearest proof could suffice to establish the unconstitutionality of a statute on such a ground. Judicial inquiries into Congressional motives are at best a hazardous matter and when that inquiry seeks to go behind objective manifestations it becomes a dubious affair indeed. Moreover, the presumption of constitutionality with which this enactment, like any other, comes to us forbids us lightly to choose that reading of the statute's setting which will invalidate it over that which will save it.[74]

The precedential value of *Flemming* for cases dealing with residence tests for assistance is weak for the following reasons:

(1) The statute in *Flemming*, unlike that in *Sherbert*, and unlike a residence test affecting freedom of movement, does not treat a person differently because he chose to exercise a preferred constitutional right. The Court had previously held that the conduct underlying the termination of old-age benefits was sufficient to justify deportation of an alien.[75] Freedom of movement has been analogized to first amendment rights.[76]

(2) Harlan's presumptions and conjuring up of a possible, valid legislative purpose are inconsistent with the Court's approach in *Sherbert* in 1963; in other first amendment cases, and especially those dealing with freedom of speech, to which freedom of movement has been analogized;[77] in the 1963 decision in *Kennedy v. Mendoza-Martinez*,[78] which, like *Flemming*, found the Court inquiring if the purpose of Congress was punishment; in *Griffin v. County School Board of Prince Edward County*[79] in 1964; and in *Aptheker v. Secretary of State*,[80] also in 1964.

In *Sherbert*, the Court held that only a "compelling state interest" could justify infringing "appellant's First Amendment right. It is basic

---

[73] *Id.* at 612.

[74] *Id.* at 617.

[75] Galvan v. Press, 347 U.S. 522 (1954).

[76] Aptheker v. Secretary of State, 378 U.S. 500, 516-17 (1964) (majority opinion by Goldberg, J.); *id.* at 519, 520 (concurring opinion of Douglas, J.).

[77] See note 76 *supra*.

[78] 372 U.S. 144 (1963). The author is indebted to Acting Associate Professor Robert M. O'Neil, of the University of California School of Law, Berkeley, for suggesting the relevance of this case to a discussion of the continued viability of the Court's attitude in *Flemming*.

[79] 377 U.S. 218 (1964).

[80] 378 U.S. 500 (1964).

that no showing merely of a rational relationship to some colorable state interest would suffice; in this highly sensitive constitutional area, 'only the gravest abuses, endangering paramount interests, give occasion for permissible limitation.' "[81] The Court stated that if it were to consider the justifications argued by the state, but not raised below, and "even if the possibility of spurious claims did threaten to dilute the fund and disrupt the scheduling of work, it would plainly be incumbent upon the appellees to demonstrate that no alternative forms of regulation would combat such abuses without infringing First Amendment rights."[82]

The preferred position of first amendment freedoms, especially those of speech and press, has even led Justice Frankfurter to worry about an implication "that any law touching communication is infected with presumptive invalidity."[83] In any event, clearly no presumption of validity of the type indulged in by Harlan in *Flemming* would be applied to statutes challenged as infringing free speech.[84]

In *Kennedy v. Mendoza-Martinez*, Justice Goldberg's majority opinion investigates in detail and with care the legislative history of a federal statute and its antecedents, to determine if the purpose of Congress was to punish.[85] Here is a search for the actual intent, rather than a possible intent which may have been chimerical, as in Harlan's opinion in *Flemming*. *Mendoza-Martinez* is especially significant since it was not a case involving first amendment freedoms.

In the *Prince Edward County* school case, the Court showed itself very willing to look through a discriminatory statute to ascertain if racial discrimination was the motivating purpose.[86] It is certainly not illogical to assume that the justices will be as inquiring when the underlying aim might be to discriminate against the newcomer or to deter and penalize freedom of movement.

In *Aptheker*,[87] the Court held applicable to congressional legislation affecting freedom of movement, the rule applied in first amendment cases[88] that the Court will examine the validity of a statute on its face and may "take into account possible applications of the statute in other factual contexts besides that at bar."[89] The attitude here is almost

---

[81] 374 U.S. at 406.

[82] *Id.* at 407.

[83] Kovacs v. Cooper, 336 U.S. 89, 90 (1949) (concurring opinion of Frankfurter, J.).

[84] See McKay, *The Preference for Freedom*, 34 N.Y.U.L. Rev. 1182 (1959).

[85] 372 U.S. at 169-84.

[86] 377 U.S. at 231, where Justice Black based his determination as to purpose on his lengthy analysis of the record in the case.

[87] 378 U.S. at 516-17.

[88] *E.g.*, Winters v. New York, 333 U.S. 507, 518-20 (1948); Thornhill v. Alabama, 310 U.S. 88, 97-98 (1940).

[89] 378 U.S. at 516, quoting NAACP v. Button, 371 U.S. 415, 432 (1963).

opposite that of Harlan in *Flemming;* according to *Aptheker,* the imagining will be of situations where the statute may apply unconstitutionally.

(3) The presumptions in *Flemming* will not apply where there is a clear manifestation of legislative intent, and such information does exist in regard to residence tests for assistance.[90]

(4) The actual purpose behind assistance residence tests, saving public funds by deterring the poor from migrating into the state and delaying the time when newcomers become eligible, is not a valid purpose, as will be argued in this article. The threat to the public purse argument was rejected by the Court in *Edwards v. California*[91] in 1941. The Court stated in *Sherbert*[92] that *Flemming* was distinguishable because of "the compelling federal interests" which underlay congressional enactment of the statute there challenged. In light of this statement and of the strong dissents in *Flemming,*[93] it would seem that very compelling governmental purposes indeed will be needed, in the future, to support conditioning of public benefits in a way that affects important constitutional rights.

(5) Even if the Court were to search for a valid purpose which a legislature might have had when passing assistance residence tests, no such purpose will be found, or at least no valid purpose will be found which could not be served by a much less restrictive statute, as this article will demonstrate, principally because of *Edwards* and the fourteenth amendment, which provides that all residents of a state, including newcomers, are citizens thereof.[94]

(6) *Flemming* did not deal with the rights of a member of the body politic, a person who was presently a United States and state citizen, or a resident of a state and of the United States. While not expressly so stating, the majority opinion smacks of the tang of earlier cases concerning the discretion of Congress in regard to deporting aliens.[95] This distinction is especially important in regard to an attack of residence tests as denying equal protection. The fact of deportation on specific grounds may be a valid basis for discriminating against a person, but it is difficult to make the same argument in regard to the fact of interstate movement, since the fourteenth amendment makes all residents of a state, including newcomers, citizens thereof.

---

[90] See note 147 *infra.*

[91] 314 U.S. 160 (1941).

[92] 374 U.S. 398, 409 n.9 (1963).

[93] 363 U.S. at 621 (Black, J.), 628 (Douglas, J.), 634 (Brennan, J., Warren, C.J., and Douglas, J.).

[94] U.S. Const. amend. XIV. § 1, cl. 1.

[95] *E.g.,* 363 U.S. at 616. An example of the earlier cases is Galvan v. Press, 347 U.S. 522, 530-32 (1954).

(7) In *Flemming*, four justices, a majority of those still sitting,[96] would have held the statute unconstitutional. Justice Black[97] argued it was a taking of property without just compensation, a violation of the due process clause of the fifth amendment, a bill of attainder, and an ex post facto law. Justice Douglas[98] contended it was a bill of attainder, and he joined Justice Brennan and Chief Justice Warren[99] in finding an ex post facto law and an imposition of a criminal punishment without a jury trial, in violation of the sixth amendment.

(8) While Nestor had a strong argument unavailable to the assistance applicant, deprivation of an accrued property right arising from payment of Social Security taxes, the *Flemming* majority rejected that view,[100] although Black[101] and Douglas[102] would have held the statute invalid on grounds requiring the finding of such a right. Furthermore, the invalidity of assistance residence tests as (1) interfering with freedom of movement, and (2) denying equal protection, is not dependent upon the existence of a property right to assistance payments.

D. Infringement of Freedom of Interstate Movement

Invalidation of a residence test as an infringement of a freedom of interstate movement protected by the federal constitution requires two analytical steps: (1) determining the existence and constitutional basis of such a freedom, and (2) finding that the residence test is an improper infringement of that right. It seems logical to begin by establishing what is a vital portion of the second finding: that residence tests for general assistance do affect interstate movement. The same argument will, of course, apply to the impact of residence tests for categorical assistance.

Residence tests for general assistance *prevent* the interstate migration of persons unable to exist without public assistance in their new home for the period of residence required, if the potential migrant recognizes his situation and reacts sensibly. Residence tests also *penalize* those who do migrate for the fact of having moved interstate. Also, a clear distinction should be made between those persons whose only reason for migrating is to obtain higher assistance payments, and those persons who will be deterred from migrating if residence requirements in

---

96 Of the five-man majority, Justices Harlan, Clark and Stewart remain; Justices Frankfurter and Whittaker are no longer sitting.

97 363 U.S. at 621-28. Although not listed as concurring in the dissents written by Douglas and Brennan, Black stated that he agreed with the views expressed therein. *Id.* at 621.

98 *Id.* at 628-34.

99 *Id.* at 634-40.

100 *Id.* at 609-11. This conclusion of the majority is criticized in Reich, *The New Property*, 73 YALE L.J. 733, 769-71 (1964).

101 363 U.S. at 623-25, 627.

102 *Id.* at 631-32.

the new state would prevent them from receiving, for even a short period of time, their present level of assistance. The latter are not motivated by any desire to get higher payments, but must be included in an enumeration of persons prevented from migrating by residence tests.

Clearly, residence tests affect interstate movement. Therefore it is necessary to consider whether there is a freedom of interstate movement and if the effect of residence tests thereon is unconstitutional.

1. The Commerce Clause

The commerce clause of the federal constitution[103] has been discussed by several writers[104] as a ground for invalidating residence tests and other state legislation impeding a freedom of interstate movement of persons. This freedom amounts to a right not to have interstate movement of persons controlled by the states, absent an overriding state interest.

An argument built upon the commerce clause has two main components: (1) interstate movement of persons is commerce, and (2) such commerce may be regulated only by Congress, with limited exceptions inapplicable to the assistance residence test situation. State regulation of the movement of persons, when necessary on grounds of health,[105] is such an exception.

(a) The Edwards Case.—The case from which any analysis of assistance residence tests and freedom of movement must start, is Edwards v. California.[106] The nine justices of the United States Supreme Court agreed in the result, holding unconstitutional a state statute making it a misdemeanor knowingly to bring a nonresident indigent into the state. A majority of five, in an opinion by Justice Byrnes, based their conclusion on the commerce clause.[107] They held that "the transportation of indigent persons from State to State clearly falls within . . . [the class of subjects related to interstate commerce which can only be regulated by Congress]."[108] Four justices (Justices Black and Murphy concurring in an opinion by Justice Douglas,[109] and Justice Jackson concurring separately)[110] thought the state statute invalid because it infringed a freedom of interstate movement which is a privilege or

---

103 U.S. CONST. art. I, § 8, cl. 3.

104 E.g., Pierson III-A-3-9; Hohlt 10-11; TENBROEK 7-11; Feinberg 41-44.

105 An extreme example of application of this exception is Compagnie Francaise de Navigation a Vapeur v. Louisiana State Bd. of Health, 186 U.S. 380 (1902). See TENBROEK 9.

106 314 U.S. 160 (1941).

107 U.S. CONST. art. I, § 8, cl. 3.

108 314 U.S. at 176.

109 Id. at 177.

110 Id. at 181.

immunity of a United States citizen guaranteed against state abridgement by the fourteenth amendment.[111]

The majority expressed no view contrary to the conclusion that freedom of movement is such a privilege or immunity, finding it unnecessary to reach that question.[112] Also, Douglas' concurring opinion begins: "I express no view on whether or not the statute here in question runs afoul of Art. I, § 8 . . . ."[113] Therefore, three concurring justices did not contradict the majority's view of the commerce clause. Only Justice Jackson disputed a ground for decision relied upon by another justice in this case. He thought the commerce clause inapplicable to "migrations of a human being."[114] It is fair to summarize *Edwards* as representing a vote of 5-1 for finding a violation of the commerce clause and of 4-0 for finding a violation of the privileges and immunities guarantee of the fourteenth amendment.

The majority clearly repudiated Jackson's argument for rejecting the Court's reliance on the commerce clause: "[I]t is settled beyond question that the transportation of persons is 'commerce,' within the meaning of that provision [the commerce clause]."[115] This conclusion was supported by citation of proper authorities.[116]

The established construction of the commerce clause was stated by Chief Justice Stone in *Southern Pac. Co. v. Arizona:*[117]

> Ever since . . . *Cooley v. Board of Wardens*,[118] . . . it has been recognized that, in the absence of conflicting legislation by Congress, there is a residuum of power in the state to make laws governing matters of local concern which nevertheless in some measure affect interstate commerce or even, to some extent, regulate it . . . .
> But ever since *Gibbons v. Ogden*,[119] . . . the states have not been deemed to have authority to impede substantially the free flow of com-

---

[111] U.S. Const. amend. XIV, § 1.

[112] Justice Byrnes, after deciding the case under the commerce clause, stated: "In the view we have taken it is unnecessary to decide whether the Section is repugnant to other provisions of the Constitution." 314 U.S. at 177. That one of these other provisions was the privileges and immunities clause of the fourteenth amendment is shown by an examination of the summaries of the arguments of appellant, *id.* at 163; of the amicus curiae, *id.* at 164; and of appellee, *id.* at 170.

[113] *Id.* at 177.

[114] *Id.* at 182.

[115] *Id.* at 172.

[116] *Id.* at 172 n.1, citing Gloucester Ferry Co. v. Pennsylvania, 114 U.S. 196, 203 (1885); Leisy v. Hardin, 135 U.S. 100, 112 (1890); Covington Bridge Co. v. Kentucky, 154 U.S. 204, 218 (1894); Hoke v. United States, 227 U.S. 308, 320 (1913); Caminetti v. United States, 242 U.S. 470, 491 (1917); United States v. Hill, 248 U.S. 420, 423 (1919); Mitchell v. United States, 313 U.S. 80 (1941).

[117] 325 U.S. 761, 766-67 (1945).

[118] 53 U.S. (12 How.) 299 (1851).

[119] 22 U.S. (9 Wheat.) 1 (1824).

merce from state to state, or to regulate those phases of the national commerce which, because of the need of national uniformity, demand that their regulation, if any, be prescribed by a single authority.

As Professor Allison Dunham has remarked, "all modern cases say something similar to Chief Justice Stone's statement."[120] Stone, discussing those phases of national commerce where uniformity requires exclusive congressional power, cited *Edwards*.[121] Therefore, there seems to be no doubt that interstate movement of persons is a form of commerce which, generally, the states may not regulate.

In view of the "health" exception to the ban on state regulation of interstate movement, it is significant that, in *Edwards*, the Court rejected a view of the poor as a "moral pestilence."[122]

More important is the dictum of the majority: "The nature and extent of [a state's] . . . obligation to afford relief to newcomers is not here involved. We do, however, suggest that the theory of the Elizabethan poor laws no longer fits the facts."[123]

(b) *Crandall and Williams—Interference With Egress.—Crandall v. Nevada*[124] was decided much earlier than *Edwards* and before the passage of the fourteenth amendment. The Court invalidated a state tax upon all persons leaving the state by commercial vehicle. The decision was based upon the needs of the country and the concomitant rights of its citizens that the latter be unhampered in approaching the seats of government, the courts, public offices, and seaports.[125] Justice Stone, dissenting in *Colgate v. Harvey*[126] in 1935, in an opinion joined by

---

[120] Dunham, *Congress, the States and Commerce*, 8 J. Pub. L. 47, 49 (1959). "For other expressions of this doctrine, see California v. Zook, 336 U.S. 725, 728 (1949); Cities Service Co. v. Peerless Co., 340 U.S. 179, 186 (1950)." *Id.* at 49 n.17.

[121] 325 U.S. at 768.

[122] 314 U.S. at 177. Paupers, vagabonds, and convicts were referred to as a "moral pestilence" in City of New York v. Miln, 36 U.S. (11 Pet.) 102, 142 (1837), discussed in Subsection II, *D, 1 infra*. The view expressed in *Edwards* is consistent with Robinson v. California, 370 U.S. 660 (1962), where the Court invalidated a criminal law penalizing the status of being a narcotics addict and applying to a person "whether or not he has ever used or possessed any narcotics within the State, and whether or not he has been guilty of any antisocial behavior there." *Id.* at 666. While this decision was based on the prohibition in the eighth amendment against cruel and unusual punishment (here applied to the states through the fourteenth amendment), the underlying policy would also appear to run counter to any attempt to exclude the poor as a group.

[123] 314 U.S. at 174.

[124] 73 U.S. (6 Wall.) 35 (1867). One amazing aspect of this case is that Crandall, who had sought a writ of error, was not represented at the oral argument and no brief was filed on his behalf. Justice Miller noted this situation at the beginning of his opinion. *Id.* at 39. The reasons underlying the Court's decision must have been strong to have overcome the failure of Crandall to present any argument to the Court.

[125] *Id.* at 43-44.

[126] 296 U.S. 404, 436 (1935) (dissenting opinion). The opinion from which Mr. Justice Stone dissented was subsequently overruled. Madden v. Kentucky, 309 U.S. 83 (1940).

Justices Brandeis and Cardozo, discussed *Crandall* and stated: "No one could doubt that if the decision had been made at any time after *Railroad Co. v. Maryland*,[127] . . . and until the present moment, it would have been rested on the commerce clause."[128]

In *Crandall*, the Court considered the commerce clause argument and found it unconvincing:

> It may be that under the power to regulate commerce among the States, Congress has authority to pass laws, the operation of which would be inconsistent with the tax imposed by the State of Nevada, but we know of no such statute now in existence. Inasmuch, therefore, as the tax does not itself institute any regulation of commerce of a national character, or which has a uniform operation over the whole country, it is not easy to maintain . . . that it violates the clause of the Federal Constitution which we have had under review.[129]

Justice Miller then stated that the Court did not "concede" that the case had to be decided under the commerce clause.[130] Moreover, as will be discussed later, Justices Douglas, Black and Murphy, concurring in *Edwards*,[131] explicitly disagreed with Stone[132] and interpreted *Crandall* as holding that "the right to move freely from State to State was a right of *national* citizenship," a right which upon the subsequent passage of the fourteenth amendment was protected by its privileges and immunities clause against state action.[133]

Williams v. Fears,[134] in 1900, found the Supreme Court again dealing with a state tax affecting egress. In upholding a Georgia statute taxing "emigrant agents," who hired persons in Georgia to work outside the

---

[127] 88 U.S. (21 Wall.) 456 (1874).

[128] 296 U.S. at 444. Justice Stone's statement is quoted with approval in Anderson v. Mullaney, 191 F.2d 123, 127 (9th Cir. 1951), *aff'd on other grounds*, 342 U.S. 415 (1952).

[129] 73 U.S. (6 Wall.) at 43.

[130] *Ibid.* Justice Miller also refused to "concede" that the case must be decided under article I, section 10, clause 2 of the Constitution: "No State shall, without the Consent of the Congress, lay any Imposts or Duties on Imports or Exports, except what may be absolutely necessary for executing it's inspection laws . . . ." *Ibid.* This provision and the commerce clause were assumed by the Supreme Court of Nevada and by counsel for Nevada to be the sole bases of decision. *Id.* at 40-41. See 2 WARREN, THE SUPREME COURT IN UNITED STATES HISTORY 415 (Rev. ed. 1926).

[131] 314 U.S. at 177.

[132] *Id.* at 179.

[133] *Ibid.*

[134] 179 U.S. 270 (1900). See Feinberg 29, quoting Joseph v. Randolph, 71 Ala. 499, 508 (1882), to the effect that the tax in *Williams* restrained "personal mobility, its 'obvious purpose . . . [being] to seriously clog and impair the laborer's right of free emigration.'" This view is supported by Georgia's failure to tax the hiring of workers to labor within the State, a discrimination challenged on equal protection grounds in *Williams*, with the Court doing an extremely poor job of explaining its rejection of this contention. 179 U.S. at 275-76. The Court did note that many other occupations were taxed, *id.* at 275, but failed to see that some of these taxes, at least, were prohibitive. See *ibid.*

state, the Court rejected a commerce clause argument on the ground that the agents' activities were not sufficiently related to commerce. This case is not troublesome for the present analysis because this limited view of commerce is not tenable after *Wickard v. Filburn*.[135] Indeed, *Williams* viewed in this light, supports protection of freedom of movement since the Court stated: "Undoubtedly the right of locomotion, the right to remove from one place to another according to inclination, is an attribute of personal liberty, and the right, ordinarily, of free transit from or through the territory of any State is a right secured by the Fourteenth Amendment and by other provisions of the Constitution."[136]

(c) *Miln, Henderson and The Passenger Cases*.—The opinions of the United States Supreme Court in *City of New York v. Miln*,[137] *The Passenger Cases*,[138] and *Henderson v. Mayor of New York*,[139] between 1837 and 1875, show the development of the concept of the commerce clause as a bar to state action regulating in-migration,[140] and, therefore, are precursors of *Edwards*.

In *Miln*, the majority upheld a New York statute requiring masters of vessels to report to the Mayor of New York City the name, birth place, last legal settlement, occupation, and age of all passengers disembarking there from any foreign country or other state of the United States. The Court held that the statute was a regulation under the police power and not of commerce. Justice Story, dissenting,[141] disagreed, noting that the late Chief Justice Marshall had taken the same position on an earlier hearing of the case.[142]

In *The Passenger Cases*, while the Court split 5-4 and required eight opinions, it does seem clear that the majority held that state taxes on

---

135 317 U.S. 111 (1942).

136 179 U.S. at 274.

137 36 U.S. (11 Pet.) 102 (1837).

138 48 U.S. (7 How.) 282 (1849).

139 92 U.S. 259 (1875).

140 See TENBROEK 7-8; Feinberg 19-20, 22-23.

141 36 U.S. (11 Pet.) at 153.

142 *Id.* at 160. As is noted in LOCKHART, KAMISAR & CHOPER, CONSTITUTIONAL LAW 298 (1964), "Story's reference is to an earlier argument of the same case in 1834, when two justices who would have concurred with Marshall and Story were absent. Rather than to let a minority of the Court uphold the New York Act by a 3 to 2 vote, Chief Justice Marshall announced for the Court the previously unknown 'practice . . . not (except in cases of absolute necessity) to deliver any judgment in cases where constitutional questions are involved, unless four justices concur in opinion, thus making the decision that of a majority of the whole court.' [33 U.S. (8 Pet.) 118, 121 (1834)] The Court ordered reargument. . . . At the reargument only Story remained of the 4 who would have voted against the New York Act in 1834."

passengers arriving from foreign ports were invalid under the commerce clause.[143]

The law was clarified further in *Henderson v. New York*, where a unanimous Court held unconstitutional, on commerce clause grounds, a New York statute requiring the owner or consignee of a vessel to supply a three hundred dollar bond for each alien passenger landed, to indemnify the state for any relief needed by the passenger, or, in lieu of the bond, the owner or consignee to pay $1.50 for each such passenger. Failure to supply the bond or pay $1.50 made the carrier liable for a 500 dollar fine which was a lien on the ship.[144]

While these cases dealt mainly with foreign commerce, perhaps their greatest significance for present purposes is the dictum of Chief Justice Taney, dissenting in *The Passenger Cases*,[145] quoted by the Court in *Crandall*:

> Living as we do under a common government, charged with the great concerns of the whole Union, every citizen of the United States . . . is entitled to free access, not only to the principal departments established at Washington, but also to its judicial tribunals and public offices in every State. . . . We are all citizens of the United States, and as members of the same community must have the right to pass and repass through every part of it without interruption as freely as in our own States.[146]

(d) Can Edwards and Crandall Be Distinguished?—It may be objected that the assistance residence test case differs from *Edwards*, which involved a criminal penalty for helping certain persons move interstate, and *Crandall*, which taxed interstate travel. Residence tests for welfare assistance are not intended—at least primarily—as a regulation of commerce or of personal travel. The main purpose is protection of the

---

[143] See Henderson v. Mayor of New York, 92 U.S. at 266-67, so interpreting *The Passenger Cases*. For the details of the statutes invalidated, see 48 U.S. (7 How.) at 283-86. See generally 2 WARREN, THE SUPREME COURT IN UNITED STATES HISTORY 168-82 (Rev. ed. 1926).

[144] 92 U.S. at 261. In a companion case, Chy Lung v. Freeman, 92 U.S. 275 (1875), the Court invalidated, as infringing congressional control of foreign commerce, a California statute requiring ship captains to post bonds before certain classes of alien passengers may be landed, those classes including paupers and lewd women. The plaintiff was alleged to be in the latter cateory. As an alternative to posting bond, the captain could pay whatever sum of money the state's Commissioner of Immigration "may in each case think proper to exact." *Id.* at 278. The Court found that this statute amounted to legalizing extortion. *Ibid.* Since it went far beyond any enactment necessary and proper to protect the state from paupers and convicted criminals, the Court was "not called upon" to determine the constitutionality of legislation so suited for that purpose. *Id.* at 280. This case is discussed in tenBROEK 8.

[145] 48 U.S. (7 How.) at 491-92, quoted in Feinberg 19.

[146] 73 U.S. (6 Wall.) at 48-49.

state treasury.[147] Because this was the motivation for the statute invalidated in *Edwards*, this "purpose" will not distinguish that case. Furthermore, the "protecting the public purse" argument is usually phrased as protecting it against newcomers,[148] thereby indicating a clear "purpose" to discriminate against them.

Any argument that residence tests might be intended to bar newcomers from assistance until (1) they have been in a state long enough to contribute to its economy and hence the tax base from which the state funds such assistance, or (2) they have exhausted the possibilities of aid from private charity, ignores the fact that time spent in a state and therefore residence tests are unrelated to either goal.

The only arguably valid purposes that a state might claim for residence tests are (1) to prevent an influx of the poor whose sole or primary motive in migrating was to obtain higher assistance benefits than those for which they were eligible in their former home state, and (2) to furnish a means of determining bona fide residence. As will be explained later, means less restrictive of freedom of movement and less discriminatory against newcomers exist for dealing with these objectives.[149] Therefore, they should not be held to be capable of supporting the validity of residence tests.

An attempt to distinguish *Edwards* as involving a criminal statute should fail for two reasons: (1) the effect on commerce of a fine or short jail term for a person knowingly assisting an indigent to enter a state would seem to be no greater than the effect on movement of residence tests denying poor newcomers the necessities of life; and (2) the *Edwards* holding has been applied to invalidate civil statutes. A recent decision by the widely respected Judge Justine Polier of the New York Family Court, *In re Higgins*,[150] held that under the rationale of either the majority or concurring opinions in *Edwards*, certain demands made by Michigan in connection with placement of a child there were unconstitutional.[151]

---

[147] *E.g.*, N.Y. Times, April 30, 1965, p. 1, col. 3 (reporting recommendations of New York State Committee on Welfare Costs); N.Y. Herald Tribune, Sept. 28, 1965, p. 11, col. 1 (report that local official will ask county board to request passage of residence test); see, *e.g.*, LoGatto 105-06.

[148] See note 147 *supra*.

[149] See *infra* subsection I, E, 5.

[150] 46 Misc. 2d 233, 259 N.Y.S.2d 874 (Family Ct. 1965), also reported in the New York Law Journal, May 20, 1965, p. 17, col. 5, as *Matter of Anonymous* (The Little Ivy case).

[151] The child had been adjudged neglected by the New York Family Court, which discharged her into the custody of a maternal aunt living in Michigan. The Michigan Department of Social Welfare, as a condition for approving the placement, asked the New York court to sign an interstate agreement or a statement of the court retaining legal liability for the child. In other words, Michigan wanted New York to agree to reimburse Michigan for any future welfare expenditures for this child, who was not now receiving welfare. Judge

In *Anderson v. Mullaney*,[152] discussed in the next subsection of this article, the Ninth Circuit, in invalidating a license fee discriminating against nonresident commercial fishermen, treated the statute under attack as civil, although there seem to have been criminal penalties for fishing without the required license.[153]

Next it may be argued that residence tests do not purport to bar interstate travel; they merely impede it. But for persons unable to live without public assistance for the required period, a residence test does bar interstate movement. If this is merely impeding travel, the tax in *Crandall* merely impeded travel for persons unable to pay it. Furthermore, Justices Douglas and Goldberg, concurring in *Bell v. Maryland*,[154] indicated that state action is unconstitutional even if it merely hinders interstate movement. Douglas, with the concurrence of Goldberg, viewed a state trespass conviction for refusal to obey a racially motivated request to leave a public accommodation, as invalid state action infringing the right to travel.[155]

> Is the right of a person to eat less basic than his right to travel, which we protected in *Edwards v. California* . . . ? Does not a right to travel in modern times shrink in value materially when there is no accompanying right to eat in public places?
>
> The right of any person to travel *interstate* irrespective of race, creed, or color is protected by the Constitution. *Edwards v. California, supra.* Certainly his right to eat at public restaurants is as important in

---

Polier's decision invalidated the Michigan statute (MICH. COMP. LAWS § 400.14(d) (1948)) which required such a guaranty before the Welfare Department could approve placement in Michigan of an out-of-state child. The decision also seems to imply the unconstitutionality of the New York statute, N.Y. SOC. WELFARE LAW § 374-a (1960) (enacting the Interstate Compact on the Placement of Children), and administrative practice, see 46 Misc. 2d at 234, 259 N.Y.S.2d at 875, under which a child will not be sent to another state unless the latter consents, at least where refusal of consent is predicated on the child's poverty or that of the person with whom placement is proposed. *In re Higgins* is highly relevant to an analysis of residence tests since it applied the *Edwards* result to invalidate civil law requirements, whereas *Edwards* voided a criminal statute. Moreover, the statement by Judge Polier, that efforts to require the sending state to retain liability for future welfare needed by a child seriously delay and often prevent the best placement, *id.* at 240, 259 N.Y.S.2d at 881, indicates strong policy reasons for rejecting the concept of settlement and residence tests as inappropriate for our mobile society, at least in regard to child placement. It is submitted that the effects of residence tests for assistance, discussed in the present article, similarly indicate that such tests are anachronisms.

[152] 191 F.2d 123 (9th Cir. 1951).

[153] ALASKA COMP. LAWS ANN. § 16.05.720 (1962).

[154] 378 U.S. 226, 242, 286 (1964); see Feinberg 24-25. The concurring opinion of Douglas, with Goldberg concurring in parts II-V thereof, begins at 378 U.S. at 242. The concurring opinion of Goldberg, with Douglas concurring in parts II-V thereof, begins in *id.* at 286. The opinion of the Court never reached the constitutional issues. Goldberg and Douglas would have done so, as would the three dissenting justices. *Id.* at 318. Only Goldberg and Douglas used a right-to-travel analysis.

[155] *Id.* at 247, 250-51, 255.

the modern setting as the right of mobility. In these times that right is, indeed, practically indispensable to travel either interstate or intra-state.[156]

Justice Goldberg, with the concurrence of Justice Douglas, in discussing the congressional history of the fourteenth amendment and related legislation, stated: "The recurrent references to the right 'to go and come at pleasure' as being 'among the natural rights of free men' reflect the common understanding that the concepts of liberty and citizenship embraced the right to freedom of movement, the effective right to travel freely."[157] *Edwards v. California* is also authority for the invalidity of state legislation which merely hinders the right to travel. The offense there was knowingly bringing a nonresident into the state.[158] By making such conduct a crime, California in effect prevented others from knowingly assisting nonresident indigents to cross the state line.

An attempt to distinguish *Crandall* and *Edwards* with a necessity argument will also fail, because it is very unlikely that any state today could claim a greater threat to its welfare budget than that faced by California when it enacted the statute voided in *Edwards*.

A similar fate awaits any argument based upon the long history of residence tests and of the underlying concept of settlement.[159] The legislation before the Court in *Edwards* could also claim the support of hoary antecedents and of the settlement concepts.[160] The view of the poor as a "moral pestilence," the basis for much of the prior authority which might be cited in contending for the validity of residence tests, was expressly rejected by the Court in *Edwards*.[161] Finally, constitutional doctrine must grow to meet the requirements of a changing society and evolving concepts of human dignity and the needs which must be met to maintain it. The United States becomes more one nation every year, with greater mobility of population.[162] It seems fair to say that an

---

[156] *Id.* at 255.

[157] *Id.* at 293 n.10, citing CONG. GLOBE, 39TH CONG., 1ST SESS., at 322, 41-43, 111, 475. Justice Black, writing on behalf of the three dissenters, disagrees with Goldberg's reading of some of his authority regarding the right of the colored man "to go where he pleases." *Id.* at 337 n.25.

[158] 314 U.S. at 171.

[159] See Mandelker, *The Settlement Requirement in General Assistance*; 1955 WASH. U.L.Q. 355-58.

[160] See 314 U.S. at 174; Mandelker, *Exclusion and Removal Legislation*; 1956 WIS. L. REV. 57, 59-60.

[161] 314 U.S. at 177.

[162] See, *e.g.*, Legislation Note, *Voting Rights—Residence Requirements for Voting in Presidential Elections*, 18 VAND. L. REV. 337 (1964): "In the 1960 presidential election, between five and eight million American citizens, otherwise qualified to vote, were disenfranchised by virtue of their having changed places of residence during the year preceding the election," citing Scammon, *The Electoral Process*, 27 LAW & CONTEMP. PROB. 299, 304

increasing awareness of human needs and of the obligation of government to meet them has developed and includes, in the minds of many Americans, a feeling that the poor should not be deterred from interstate migration. Indeed, the needs of the economy for a fluid supply of manpower will be best met if free interstate movement is available to those with little or no funds.

A more sophisticated argument would be that *Edwards* represents (1) a severe, direct burden on freedom of movement, and (2) a strong necessity for the legislation, and *Crandall* combined (1) a minor, indirect burden on this freedom, and (2) no necessity for the tax statute. The residence test situation combines the aspects of each case most favorable to upholding the legislation—a minor, indirect burden on commerce and a strong necessity—and does not involve the unfavorable aspects which outbalanced these factors in *Edwards* and *Crandall*.

An answer to this argument may be made as follows: (1) Residence tests impose a severe burden on interstate movement, if severity is judged from the standpoint of the relevant citizens, those without the financial ability to support themselves in a state for the period of residence required for welfare assistance. (2) If severity is judged by the number of people prevented from migrating, the extent of the benefit to the state (the necessity for the test) will vary directly with the burden on commerce. The reduction in welfare costs will be commensurate, to a large extent, with the number of people deterred from entering. Admittedly, there will be a saving in regard to each newcomer, but the brevity of the residence period indicates that this saving will not be great. The substantial economies arise when potential long-term welfare recipients are unable to enter. (3) *Edwards* lends no support to the contention that its holding was based upon a balancing of burden on commerce against necessity for the statute. The Court made it clear that a desire to exclude paupers was not a constitutionally cognizable justification for any state legislation.[163] Similarly, the Court in *Crandall* did not stress the lack of any compelling reason for the state tax statute.

Also, it does not seem proper to distinguish *Edwards* and *Crandall* as involving a more direct interference with interstate movement than that imposed by assistance residence tests. The statute invalidated in *Edwards* penalized the person who knowingly assisted the nonresident indigent to enter California. The tax in *Crandall* struck directly at the pocketbook of the migrant, but so do the residence tests. Moreover, losing eligibility

---

(1962). See also Schmidhauser, *Residency Requirements for Voting and the Tensions of a Mobile Society*, 61 MICH. L. REV. 823, 824-30 (1963).

[163] 314 U.S. at 176-77.

for assistance probably is, to an indigent, a worse penalty than a threat of fine or imprisonment.

(e) *Two Recent Federal Cases.*—Two cases arising in Alaska lend strong support to a commerce clause analysis: One of them, through its alternative holding based upon the privileges and immunities clause of article IV, also aids that line of attack upon residence tests. In *Anderson v. Mullaney,*[164] the Ninth Circuit, with one judge dissenting on other grounds,[165] held that the portion of a license fee[166] for nonresident fishermen which exceeded the fee for resident fishermen was an unconstitutional burden on interstate commerce in commercial fishermen and void. This case was affirmed on other grounds by the United States Supreme Court.[167] The Ninth Circuit noted the existence of an argument under the privileges and immunities clause of article IV,[168] but found it unnecessary to reach that question.[169] In *Brown v. Anderson,*[170] a federal district court judge, in alternative holdings relying upon the commerce clause and article IV protection of privileges and immunities, held unconstitutional an Alaska statute[171] authorizing the closing of certain fishing areas to nonresident fishermen while allowing residents to fish there.

Anderson v. Mullaney indicates the great strength of the commerce clause's guarantee of freedom of interstate movement, since the tax charged nonresidents was only fifty dollars, a mere forty-five dollars more than the five dollar tax on residents.[172] Such a differential would seem to be much less of a hindrance to interstate travel than are the residence tests for welfare assistance programs. Alaska was a territory in 1951, but the Ninth Circuit held that the same rules applied to commerce from and to a territory as governed interstate commerce.[173]

---

164 191 F.2d 123 (9th Cir. 1951), *aff'd on other grounds,* 342 U.S. 415 (1952).

165 *Id.* at 134. Part (B) of the dissenting opinion of Chief Judge Denman may be read as rebutting part of the majority's commerce clause argument. In Part (B), he argues that plaintiffs failed to carry their burden of proving that the license fee for nonresidence is arbitrary or excessive.

166 Alaska Sess. Laws 1949, ch. 66.

167 *Sub nom.* Mullaney v. Anderson, 342 U.S. 415 (1952).

168 191 F.2d at 126.

169 *Id.* at 133.

170 202 F. Supp. 96 (D. Alaska 1962).

171 Alaska Sess. Laws 1961, ch. 62. This provision has been deleted from the Alaska statutes.

172 191 F.2d at 125.

173 *Id.* at 127. The Ninth Circuit cited as authority its prior decision in Inter-Island Steam Nav. Co. v. Territory of Hawaii, 96 F.2d 412, 416, 417 (9th Cir.), *aff'd on other grounds,* 305 U.S. 306 (1938), and the following cases in which the Ninth Circuit said the cited proposition "has been assumed to be true": McLean & Co. v. Denver & Rio Grande R.R. Co., 203 U.S. 38, 49 (1906); Hanley v. Kansas City Southern Ry. Co., 187 U.S. 617, 620 (1903); Inter-Island Steam Nav. Co. v. Territory of Hawaii, 305 U.S. 306, 313 (1938)

Brown is especially pertinent to an examination of residence tests for assistance, since the argument was made and rejected there that the state statute condemned was necessary to protect the citizens of Alaska against the costs of caring for the indigent.[174] Discussion of this holding will be deferred,[175] since the main thrust of the opinion was directed to the privileges and immunities issue.

(*f*) *The Power of Congress.*—A commerce clause analysis is vulnerable: if the unconstitutionality of residence tests is based upon the exclusive power of Congress to regulate such commerce, Congress could override this objection with an enabling statute. The widespread use of residence tests in many states,[176] and the recurrent requests to enact them in others,[177] indicate that considerable pressure would be put on Congress to undercut any Supreme Court decision invalidating residence tests under the commerce clause.

That Congress is not necessarily opposed to residence tests for assistance programs may be indicated by the conditions set by the Social Security Act for state categorical assistance plans qualifying for federal financial participation. Congress expressly states that plans which meet the other criteria qualify if their residence requirements are within the parameters set forth.

(*g*) *Has Congress Acted?*—Even if it be concluded that, in the absence of contrary congressional intent, the states may not impose residence requirements affecting interstate movement of persons, the congressional approval of limited tests for categorical assistance may be interpreted as an implicit indication that Congress is not opposed to residence tests for other state public benefit programs, and especially not for general assistance programs, which aid needy persons who do not qualify for federally-aided assistance and federal insurance programs. A strong argument can be made that (1) it would be anomalous for Congress to have a different policy for different assistance programs, (2) it would be especially anomalous for Congress to give the states less freedom in setting standards for programs entirely state-funded than for those partially federally-financed, and (3) any such distinctions of policy would run afoul of the equal protection guarantee implicit in fifth amendment due process.[178] A subsidiary question which would arise if

---

174 202 F. Supp. at 101-02.

175 See *infra* subsection II, *D, 3, a.*

176 See National Travelers Aid Ass'n, One Manner of Law—A Handbook on Residence Requirements in Public Assistance 8-13 (1961).

177 See, *e.g.*, N.Y. Times, April 30, 1965, p. 1, col. 3 (a report of the recommendations of the New York State Committee on Welfare Costs); N.Y. Herald Tribune, Sept. 28, 1965, p. 11, col. 1 (Supervisor of Riverhead, L.I., will ask county board to request passage of residence test).

178 See *infra* subsection III, *B.*

this analysis is accepted, is whether or not the implicit congressional approval extends only to public assistance residence tests which are within the limits set in the Social Security Act for categorical assistance.

However, the foregoing analysis would attribute to Congress an intent far exceeding that which was present in the legislators' minds when they approved limited residence tests for categorical assistance.[179] Freedom of interstate movement is an aspect of commerce involving such important human rights that Congress should be required to legislate explicitly in regard to residence tests for assistance, in order to regulate that commerce.

Nevertheless, the possibility of a contrary decision, and the power of Congress to act expressly, makes the commerce clause something less than an ideal road to the abolition of residence tests for public assistance. (h) *The Rights of Nonresidents.*—The constitutional guarantee of freedom of movement, under the commerce clause or otherwise, may require a state to extend its assistance programs to nonresidents. Persons presently receiving assistance in their home state will be deterred from traveling to and through other states if they may thereby risk termination of assistance from their old home state, without qualifying for assistance in states they visit. Even if inconsistent determinations as to residence are avoided, travel is discouraged unless the traveler can be assured of assistance in the state where he needs it.

The situation of the migratory worker[180] is probably the most striking example of the effect on freedom of movement of residence tests for assistance. Mobility of the labor force, including seasonal workers, promotes the efficiency of economic enterprises and therefore the growth of the gross national product.[181] In situations like that of the migratory farm worker, who may not intend to become a citizen of any state he enters while following the harvests, residence tests for welfare diminish his freedom to move in search of this work. In the event of family tragedy, inability to find the work anticipated, or some other difficulty, he and his family will not be eligible for welfare benefits. The worker's willingness to take these risks will be reduced. However, this view must

---

[179] Indeed, when the Social Security Act was passed in 1935, *Edwards* had not been decided, and in all probability the members of Congress allowed residence tests largely because they were a traditional part of assistance programs. It may well be that the traditional trappings were useful to coat the bitter pill of assistance which was partially federally financed, a deviation from prior practice.

[180] See *e.g.*, WRIGHT, THEY HARVEST DESPAIR (1965); The Comm. of Labor and Social Security Legislation, The Ass'n of the Bar of the City of New York, *Migratory Labor*, Reports of Committees of The Association of the Bar Concerned with Federal Legislation, June, 1965, p. 108; Feinberg 40; Givens, *Legal Disadvantages of Migratory Workers*, 16 LAB. L.J. 584 (1965).

[181] See Nathanson 17-18.

contend with the apparent reasonableness of discriminations based on state citizenship, in regard to state programs. The more humane policy of requiring assistance to be offered on an equal basis to nonresidents will also raise worries about welfare recipients who winter in Florida and summer on Cape Cod. Arguably, an adequate answer is the low rate of assistance payments, making such a life unattractive.

It seems fair to conclude that the unconstitutionality of a requirement of residence is less clear than that of a required period of residence. In light of the equal protection guarantee, which extends to all persons subject to a state's jurisdiction, and the importance of freedom of movement, the better result is to hold invalid the restriction of assistance to residents.

(*i*) *Possible Difficulties with an "Interference with Freedom of Movement" Analysis.*—Before two other constitutional provisions that may protect freedom of interstate movement are examined, it may be best to consider—in this subsection and in the one that follows—certain objections to a freedom of movement analysis that may be troubling the reader, although these arguments are applicable whether that freedom is regarded as protected under the commerce clause or some other constitutional provision.

One possible argument in opposition to an interference with freedom of movement analysis is as follows: If a state is to be forbidden to enact welfare legislation restricting or discouraging interstate freedom of movement, the logic of such a rule would also require a state to provide benefits equivalent in buying power, and so conditioned as to be comparable, to those available in other states. Each state will be forced to match, in buying power, the benefits available in the most generous state. Otherwise, potential migrants from that state might be deterred. But such an approach contravenes the well-settled rule that no state is constitutionally required to have welfare programs.[182] Rights which may accrue under established programs are far different from notions of a general right to the creation of welfare programs. There will be the greatest hindrance to free movement when no welfare program exists in a state while other states have such programs. These anomalies suggest that the constitutionality of assistance programs should not be evaluated in terms of interference with interstate freedom of movement.

This argument overlooks the need to weigh all of the following factors in evaluating the constitutionality of residence tests and of a state's failure to have certain welfare programs: (i) the effect on freedom of interstate movement; (ii) the purpose behind the state legislation or

---

[182] *E.g.*, People *ex rel.* Heydenreich v. Lyons, 374 Ill. 557, 565, 30 N.E.2d 46, 51 (1940).

lack thereof; (iii) the state's interest in pursuing its policy; (iv) the proximate cause of the effect on migration; and (v) the distinction between state action and inaction.

(i) *Effect.*—While a state's failure to have a particular welfare program may be a greater deterrent to in-migration than a residence test for that program, especially if the required residence period is relatively short, the impact of a state's policy against having a program is not confined to newcomers. Therefore, that policy avoids the discriminatory aspect which permeates residence tests. Discrimination against newcomers not only is an effect which may be indicative of the state's purpose, but also provides a way to delineate the areas where the courts may apply constitutional protection for freedom of movement, without logically having to undertake supervision of all aspects of state policy-making influencing in-migration. If the courts will invalidate the failure of a state to have certain welfare programs, the same analysis would require them to also hold unconstitutional state minimum wage, education, taxation, and all other policies which may influence the decision of persons to move to that state. Therefore, discrimination against the newcomer should be viewed as the crucial effect under the commerce clause analysis, as well as in regard to other grounds for invalidating assistance residence tests.[183]

(ii) *Purpose.*—A state may choose not to create welfare programs for reasons totally unrelated to any intent to deter or penalize ingress of persons from other states. Similarly, a state may decide not to match the benefits or liberal conditions of other states' welfare benefits. On the other hand, an intent to discriminate against newcomers, although phrased more politely, is frequently expressed as the reason for enactment of assistance residence tests.[184] And even in the absence of an express statement of intent, it is difficult to envision any nondiscriminatory state interest served by such tests or any arguably valid discriminatory state interest so served which could not be satisfied by a statute less restrictive of individual rights.[185]

(iii) *State's Interest.*—A state's interest in being allowed to choose not to have a particular assistance program is greater than its interest in having a residence test for that program upheld, because the expenditures avoided by the former policy are much larger.

(iv) *Proximate Cause.*—A strong argument may be made, as will be shown shortly,[186] that the residence test of the actual or potential new

---

183 See *infra* subsections I, *D*, *2*; I, *D*, *3*; I, *E*; II, *B*.
184 See note 147 *supra.*
185 See *infra* subsection I, *E*, *5*.
186 See *infra* subsection I, *D*, *1*, *i*, *v*.

state of abode, rather than the existence of an assistance program in the state from which the migrant will move (and the refusal of that state to continue assistance after he leaves), is the cause of any infringement of freedom of movement. Causation is less clear when the lack of an assistance program in the new home state is compared with the existence of such a program in the former home state. The policy of one state against having an assistance program would not deter movement if the former home state did not have a program. Also, the decision not to have a program, like the decision to enact one, is unlikely to have been motivated by a desire to deter or penalize migration.

(v) *State Action and Inaction.*—When a state acts affirmatively, it may be easier to attribute a purpose, than when the state does not act. There are many explanations for state inaction that are unrelated to an intent to interfere with interstate movement. It would be extremely difficult for a court to ascertain these reasons, and an attempt to do so would lead judges into examinations of the bases for all sorts of programs or the lack thereof. It seems fair to say that when a state acts affirmatively, it gives more consideration to effects and purposes than when a state does not act—and that therefore a higher standard should be applied to action than to inaction in weighing various other factors to ascertain constitutionality.

Consideration of the five factors just discussed indicates that there would be nothing illogical in holding assistance residence tests unconstitutional although at present the law is well-settled that a state is not required to have welfare programs. A similar argument will dispose of the corollary contention that it would be anomalous to invalidate residence tests but not require a state with an assistance program to match in benefits the buying power of assistance benefits available in the state from which a migrant moves.

Another possible objection to a freedom of movement analysis is that the existence of an assistance program in the potential migrant's present state of residence, and the refusal of that state to continue assistance after the migrant moves to another state, is as much the cause of inhibiting interstate movement as is the residence test in the contemplated new state of residence.

However, the old home state (1) did not enact an assistance program with the purpose of deterring interstate movement, and (2) is treating all of its citizens alike, since state citizenship is governed by residence, under the fourteenth amendment. The state with the residence test (1) probably enacted it with a purpose of deterring interstate movement, and (2) is treating certain state citizens unequally. Therefore, the residence test, rather than the old home state's assistance program, must

be the legislation evaluated in terms of infringing freedom of movement.
(j) Must a State Encourage and Reward Interstate Movement?— If it
is agreed that a state may not penalize interstate movement, does it
follow that such movement must be encouraged and rewarded? Where a
state's assistance benefits are greater in purchasing power than those
available in the state from which a potential migrant considers moving,
he may be encouraged to move. May his new state of residence reduce
the benefits for which he is eligible to the equivalent of those available in
his former state? Under a freedom of movement analysis, the answer
would seem to be in the affirmative. However, as will be discussed in
subsection I, E of this article, providing lower assistance payments to
some newcomers would seem to contravene the state citizenship and
equal protection clauses of the fourteenth amendment.

2. The Privileges and Immunities Clause of the Fourteenth Amendment

The fourteenth amendment reads, in relevant part: "No State shall
make or enforce any. law which shall abridge the privileges or immunities
of citizens of the United States . . . ."

(a) The Concurring Opinions in Edwards.—The leading authority supporting the protection of a freedom of interstate movement under the
privileges and immunities clause of the fourteenth amendment is the
concurring opinion of Justice Douglas in *Edwards v. California.*[187] He
declared: "The right to move freely from State to State is an incident of
national citizenship protected by the privileges and immunities clause of
the Fourteenth Amendment against state interference."[188] Douglas, joined
by Black and Murphy, argued that *Crandall v. Nevada*[189] held that "the
right to move freely from State to State was a right of *national* citizenship."[190] This right was then protected against state interference by the
privileges and immunities clause when the fourteenth amendment was
adopted, under the doctrine laid down in the *Slaughter-House Cases.*[191]
There the Court gave as its first example of a right protected under that
clause—that is, of those privileges and immunities "which owe their
existence to the Federal government, its National character, its Constitution, or its laws"[192]—the right to come to the seat of government and
the seaports, and cited *Crandall* as authority.[193]

---

[187] 314 U.S. 160, 177 (1941).

[188] *Id.* at 178.

[189] 73 U.S. (6 Wall.) 35 (1867).

[190] 314 U.S. at 179.

[191] 83 U.S. (16 Wall.) 36 (1873). Douglas's argument appears in 314 U.S. at 179.

[192] *Id.* at 79 (cited in Feinberg 20); see Hague v. C.I.O., 307 U.S. 496, 520-21 n.1, 526
(1939) (concurring opinion of Stone, J.).

[193] 83 U.S. (16 Wall.) at 79.

Since Douglas' argument hinges upon his reading of *Crandall*, a not unambiguous opinion, it might be thought fairly weak authority. However, there seems no doubt that even without *Crandall*, Douglas would regard freedom of interstate movement as a privilege and immunity of national citizenship.

Justice Douglas found further support for his interpretation of the privileges and immunities clause of the fourteenth amendment in *Corfield v. Coryell*,[194] a case construing the privileges and immunities clause of article IV and decided on circuit by Justice Washington in 1823. While his view of that clause as protecting "natural rights" has been rejected,[195] Justice Washington's words are important as an early recognition of freedom of interstate movement:

> The inquiry is, what are the privileges and immunities of citizens in the several states? We feel no hesitation in confining these expressions to those privileges and immunities which are, in their nature, fundamental; which belong, of right, to the citizens of all free governments; and which have, at all times, been enjoyed by the citizens of the several states which compose this Union, from the time of their becoming free, independent, and sovereign. . . . The right of a citizen of one state to pass through, or to reside in any other state, for purposes of trade, agriculture, professional pursuits, or otherwise; . . . may be mentioned as [one] . . . of the particular privileges and immunities of citizens, which [is] . . . clearly embraced by the general description of privileges deemed to be fundamental . . . .[196]

If Douglas' view of the privileges and immunities clause is accepted, his words seem particularly pertinent to a consideration of the validity of residence requirements for welfare assistance in light of the effect of such tests on interstate movement:

> If a state tax on that movement, as in the *Crandall* case, is invalid, *a fortiori* a state statute which obstructs or in substance prevents that movement must fall. That result necessarily follows unless perchance a State can curtail the right of free movement of those who are poor or destitute. But to allow such an exception to be engrafted on the rights of *national* citizenship would be to contravene every conception of national unity. It would also introduce a caste system utterly incompatible with the spirit of our system of government. It would permit those who were stigmatized by a State as indigents, paupers, or vagabonds to be relegated to an inferior class of citizenship. It would prevent a citizen because he was poor from seeking new horizons in other States. It might thus withhold from large segments of our people that mobility which is basic to any guarantee of freedom of opportunity. The result

---

[194] 6 Fed. Cas. 546 (No. 3230) (C.C.E.D. Pa. 1823).
[195] See note 233 *infra* and accompanying text.
[196] 6 Fed. Cas. at 551-52.

would be a substantial dilution of the rights of *national* citizenship, a serious impairment of the principles of equality.[197]

Justice Douglas' argument is strongly supported by dictum in *Twining v. New Jersey*[198] in 1908, in an opinion for eight justices including Justice Holmes. The Court stated that the privileges and immunities of United States citizens, protected by the fourteenth amendment, "are only such as arise out of the nature and essential character of the National Government, or are specifically granted or secured to all citizens or persons by the Constitution of the United States" and "among the rights and privileges of National citizenship recognized by this court are the right to pass freely from State to State, *Crandall v. Nevada* . . . ."[199]

This authority is undercut by language, again of eight justices, in *United States v. Wheeler.*[200] In this case involving private action to deport United States citizens from a state, the Court found

> that the case of *Crandall v. Nevada,* . . . is inapplicable, not only because it involved the validity of state action, but because the state statute considered in that case was held to directly burden the performance by the United States of its governmental functions and also to limit rights of the citizens growing out of such functions; and hence it also follows that the observation made in *Twining v. New Jersey* . . . to the effect that it had been held in the *Crandall Case* that the privilege of passing from State to State is an attribute of national citizenship, may here be put out of view as inapposite.
>
> With the object of confining our decision to the case before us, we say that nothing we have stated must be considered as implying a want of power in the United States to restrain acts which, although involving ingress or egress into or from a State, have for their direct and necessary effect an interference with the performance of duties which it is incumbent upon the United States to discharge, as illustrated in the *Crandall Case, supra.*[201]

However, Douglas, in *Edwards*,[202] argued that in *Wheeler* the Court was in error in its analysis of *Crandall*. He acknowledges that Justice Miller "emphasized that the Nevada statute would obstruct the right of a citizen to travel to the seat of his national government or its offices throughout the country."[203] Douglas then states:

> But there is not a shred of evidence in the record of the *Crandall* case

---

197 314 U.S. at 181.

198 211 U.S. 78 (1908).

199 *Id.* at 97. The dissenting opinion of Justice Harlan, *id.* at 114, expressly declined to list the privileges and immunities protected by the fourteenth amendment. *Id.* at 123.

200 254 U.S. 281 (1920) (8-1 decision, Justice Clarke dissenting without opinion).

201 *Id.* at 299-300.

202 314 U.S. at 178-79.

203 *Id.* at 178.

that the persons there involved were en route on any such mission . . . .
The point which Mr. Justice Miller made was merely in illustration of
the damage and havoc which would ensue if the States had the power
to prevent the free movement of citizens from one State to another.
This is emphasized by his quotation from Chief Justice Taney's dissenting opinion in the *Passenger Cases* . . .: "We are all citizens
of the United States; and, as members of the same community, must
have the right to pass and repass through every part of it without inter-
ruption, as freely as in our own States."[204]

Therefore, Douglas concludes that the *Wheeler* opinion erred in
limiting *Crandall* "to a holding that the statute in question directly
burdened 'the performance by the United States of its governmental
functions' and limited the 'rights of the citizens growing out of such
functions.' "[205]

Douglas could also have supported his reading of *Crandall* by noting
that Justice Miller's reasons for his holding extended beyond (1) the
right of the government to call citizens to the capital city, to secondary
centers of government, to ports of entry, and to land offices, revenue
offices, and subtreasuries, and (2) the right of the citizen to access to
all these governmental locations.[206] Justice Miller also stated that a
United States citizen "has a right to free access to its sea-ports, through
which all the operations of foreign trade and commerce are conducted."[207] Moreover, the quotation from Chief Justice Taney includes
the following language: " 'And a tax imposed by a State, for entering
its territories or harbors, is inconsistent with the rights which belong to
citizens of other States as members of the Union, and with the objects
which that Union was intended to attain.' "[208] It would seem that *Crandall* reflects the view that one of the objects of the Union was to protect
freedom of interstate movement.

Justice Jackson's concurring opinion in *Edwards*[209] stressed the
relationship between the clauses of the fourteenth amendment which (1)
define United States citizenship, and (2) forbid any state to abridge the
privileges or immunities of United States citizens. He would have held

> that it is a privilege of citizenship of the United States, protected
> from state abridgment, to enter any state of the Union . . . for gaining
> resultant citizenship thereof. . . .
> . . . State citizenship is ephemeral. It results only from residence

---

204 *Id.* at 178-79.

205 *Id.* at 179.

206 73 U.S. (6 Wall.) 35, 43-44 (1867).

207 *Id.* at 44.

208 *Id.* at 49, quoting The Passenger Cases, 48 U.S. (7 How.) 283, 492 (1849) (dissenting opinion).

209 314 U.S. at 181.

and is gained or lost therewith. That choice of residence was subject to local approval is contrary to the inescapable implications of the westward movement of our civilization.[210]

Jackson noted that freedom of interstate movement is not unlimited, but that "indigence" is not a valid reason for restricting such movement.[211] "[A] man's mere property status, without more, cannot be used by a state to test, qualify, or limit his rights as a citizen of the United States. 'Indigence' in itself is neither a source of rights nor a basis for denying them. The mere state of being without funds is a neutral fact—constitutionally an irrelevance, like race, creed, or color."[212]

(b) *Kent, Aptheker, Zemel and Guest.*—The importance of the constitutional right to free movement interstate has been reiterated by the Supreme Court in three cases dealing with freedom of international travel: *Kent v. Dulles*,[213] *Aptheker v. Secretary of State*,[214] and *Zemel v. Rusk*.[215] While these statements are not explicit as to the constitutional basis for freedom of interstate movement, the citation of *Edwards* in these cases[216] indicates the Court would base its protection against state action either on the commerce clause or the privileges and immunities clause of the fourteenth amendment. These cases will be discussed at length in the portion of this article dealing with residence tests for categorical assistance.[217]

The Supreme Court, on March 28, 1966, in some of the opinions in *United States v. Guest*,[218] again noted the importance of the constitution-

---

[210] *Id.* at 183.

[211] *Id.* at 184-85.

[212] *Ibid.*

[213] 357 U.S. 116, 125-27 (1958).

[214] 378 U.S. 500, 505-06 (1964).

[215] 381 U.S. 1, 14-16 (majority opinion), 23-24 (dissenting opinion of Douglas and Goldberg, JJ.) (1965).

[216] 357 U.S. at 126; 381 U.S. at 15. In *Aptheker*, Douglas concurred, cited *Edwards*, and repeated his view in that case that freedom of movement interstate should be based on the privileges and immunities clause of the fourteenth amendment. 378 U.S. at 519.

[217] See *infra* subsection III, *A*.

[218] 86 Sup. Ct. 1170 (1966). The right to travel is discussed in *id.* at 1177-79 (opinion of the Court by Stewart, J.); (opinion of Harlan, J., concurring in part and dissenting in part); 1183 n.3 (opinion of Justice Brennan, J., Warren, C.J., and Douglas, J., concurring in part and dissenting in part). The latter opinion does not cite any constitutional provision as the basis for the right to travel. Justice Stewart mentions various cases and bases discussed in the present article, *id.* at 1178, finds it unnecessary to determine the basis or bases, *id.* at 1179, and says there is no doubt that the nine justices "all have agreed that the right exists." *Ibid.* Justice Harlan notes several bases for the right, *id.* at 1181-85, including the due process clauses of the fifth and fourteenth amendments, which were recommended, although without much supporting analysis, by Professor Chafee, in THREE HUMAN RIGHTS IN THE CONSTITUTION OF 1787, at 192-93 (1956). The present article does not discuss the due process clause of the fourteenth amendment as a basis for protecting freedom of travel, since the relevant problem—at least in regard to residence tests—seems to be improper classification, and therefore is best analyzed under the equal protection clause. See generally Tussman & tenBroek.

ally-protected right to travel. The high priority given this right, and its wide-ranging impact was stressed earlier in the dissenting opinions of Justices Black and Douglas in *New York v. O'Neill*[219] and *Williams v. North Carolina*.[220]

The Equal Protection of the Laws, 37 CALIF. L. REV. 341 (1949). For the same reason, the present article discusses the equal protection guarantee incorporated in the due process clause of the fifth amendment, rather than the due process aspect thereof.

[219] 359 U.S. 1 (1959); see Feinberg 19, 26-28. In this case, seven justices, in an opinion by Justice Frankfurter, held that the Uniform Law to Secure the Attendance of Witnesses from Within or Without a State in Criminal Proceedings, FLA. STAT., §§ 942.01-.06 (1963), under which a witness in a state could be ordered by a court therein to go or be sent in custody to another state to testify in a criminal proceeding, did not violate the privileges and immunities clause of the fourteenth amendment. Frankfurter argued that even if under that clause "broad scope" were given to the right of "ingress and egress" across state lines, (1) the Uniform Act limits the right no more than does the admitted power of the ordering state to hold the witness for appearance in its own criminal proceedings, 359 U.S. at 7; (2) "the obligation to give testimony" is a restriction on the claimed right, *ibid.*; (3) "at most" there is only "a temporary interference with voluntary travel," *ibid.*; and (4) the policy behind the right is consistent with the aims of the Uniform Act: "The privilege of ingress and egress among the States . . . was to prevent the walling off of States, what has been called the Balkanization of the Nation. The requirement which respondent resists conduces . . . toward a free-willed collaboration of independent states." *Id.* at 7-8.

Douglas and Black, in dissent, *id.* at 12, would have held that freedom of interstate movement, whether based on the fourteenth amendment privileges and immunities clause, on the commerce clause, or on a basic liberty inherent in national citizenship, is limited by the extradition clause of the Constitution, art. IV, § 2, applicable to fugitives. They argued that the states have no authority to expand the extradition power. The Uniform Act allows "a State to pick a citizen up and forcibly remove him from its boundaries where there is no basis for extradition." 359 U.S. at 15. "To say that there is no interference here because O'Neill will be free to return to Florida later is to trifle with a basic human right." *Id.* at 16. But Douglas did state: "This right of freedom of movement even of the innocent may not be absolute. Perhaps a State could stop a migrant at its borders for health inspection. There may be other narrow and limited qualifications to this right of free ingress and egress which a State may impose." *Id.* at 15.

[220] 325 U.S. 226 (1945). In this second Supreme Court case involving the same prosecution, the majority had upheld a North Carolina conviction for bigamous cohabitation, against a man and woman who, domiciled in that state, had gone to Nevada and obtained divorces from their respective spouses, married each other, and returned to North Carolina. The majority held that domicile in a state is required for jurisdiction to grant a divorce decree and that the Nevada decree was subject to collateral attack on the ground that the parties were never domiciled in Nevada, even though the record of the Nevada proceedings purported to show jurisdiction. Black and Douglas, in dissent, *id.* at 261, argued that one consequence of the majority's holding "is to subject people to criminal prosecutions for adultery and bigamy merely because they exercise their constitutional right to pass from a state in which they were validly married into another state which refuses to recognize their marriage. Such a consequence runs counter to the basic guarantees of our federal union. *Edwards v. California.* . . . It is true that persons validly married under the laws of one state have been convicted of crime for living together in other states. But those state convictions were not approved by this Court." *Id.* at 265. Black's citation of *Edwards* is to the majority opinion based upon the commerce clause, despite the fact that Black joined Douglas in arguing in *Edwards* for basing freedom of movement upon the privileges and immunities clause of the fourteenth amendment. Undoubtedly Black's view is that under either of the analyses in *Edwards*, such a freedom of movement exists.

(c) *Freedom of Interstate Movement and a Civil Rights March.*— The importance of the right to move freely interstate is underscored by a recent Alabama per curiam opinion holding the interest of the state, acting under its police power, in punishing "conduct calculated to provoke a breach of the peace,"[221] insufficient to overcome this constitutionally protected right.[222] Especially important is the context in which this case, *Hanson v. State*, was decided by the Court of Appeals of Alabama: a march into Alabama in protest against the murder of a civil rights pilgrim,[223] a march which the state alleged tended "to create racial tensions at a time when said racial tension was already high and the general public apprehensive of racial violence in this State."[224] The governor of Alabama had requested that the march not be held.[225]

The Alabama court clearly based its decision on freedom of movement, probably relying upon the privileges and immunities clause of the fourteenth amendment. However, the commerce clause might have been regarded as the source of the constitutional guarantee.[226]

---

[221] ALA. CODE ANN. tit. 14 § 119(1) (Supp. 1963) makes disturbing the peace "by . . . conduct calculated to provoke a breach of the peace" a misdemeanor.

[222] Hanson v. State, 42 Ala. App. 409, 166 So. 2d 886 (1964). This decision does not seem to have been appealed.

[223] See Zellner v. Lingo, 218 F. Supp. 513, 514 (M.D. Ala. 1963), aff'd *per curiam*, 334 F.2d 620 (5th Cir. 1964).

[224] 42 Ala. App. at 410, 166 So. 2d at 886.

[225] *Ibid.*

[226] The Court of Appeals of Alabama did not feel it was necessary to write a full opinion. The per curiam opinion merely set forth the complaint and held it failed to state an offense, citing the following five cases: Edwards v. California, 314 U.S. 160 (1941); Zellner v. Lingo, 218 F. Supp. 513 (M.D. Ala. 1963) [aff'd *per curiam*, 334 F.2d 620 (5th Cir. 1964)]; Opinion of the Justices, 275 Ala. 547, 156 So. 2d 639 (1963); *Ex parte* Lavinder, 88 W. Va. 713, 108 S.E. 428 (1921); Constantin v. Smith, 57 F.2d 227 (E.D. Tex.) [aff'd *sub nom.* Sterling v. Constantin, 287 U.S. 378 (1932)].

In *Zellner*, a federal district court judge, applying the doctrine that equity will not enjoin a criminal prosecution, refused to enjoin the prosecution of the appellants in *Hanson*. However, he probably influenced the decision of the Alabama Court of Appeals since he quoted at length from the concurring opinion of Mr. Justice Douglas in *Edwards*, 218 F. Supp. at 515, and expressly disclaimed any approval of the state's prosecution of defendants. *Id.* at 518.

Since the federal court quoted Douglas's language relying upon the privileges and immunities clause of the fourteenth amendment, but purported to be quoting the opinion of the majority, see 218 F. Supp. at 515 (where the quotation from Justice Douglas is given as what "the Supreme Court of the United States in Edwards v. California, . . . stated . . . ."), and since the Alabama court merely cited *Edwards*, with no indication of reliance upon a concurrence, 42 Ala. App. at 410, 166 So. 2d at 887, there may be doubt as to the basis for *Hanson*. Probably it is grounded upon the privileges and immunities clause, because the Alabama court also relied upon *Zellner*.

The *Opinion of the Justices* was cited in *Hanson* apparently for its holding that the governor is authorized by the state constitution "to employ such forces as are available to him," including military forces, "to keep the peace . . . ." 275 Ala. 547, 549, 156 So. 2d 639, 641 (1963).

In *Ex parte Lavinder* the Supreme Court of Appeals of West Virginia held invalid the

(d) Residence Tests for General Assistance Infringe the Freedom of Interstate Movement Protected By the Privileges and Immunities Clause of the Fourteenth Amendment.—With the exception of the question discussed in the next subsection, the analysis of the way residence tests for general assistance infringe a freedom of movement protected by the privileges and immunities clause of the fourteenth amendment parallels the argument made earlier[227] concerning the violation of such a freedom protected by the commerce clause. The different constitutional provisions safeguarding the right do not change its parameters, in this instance. The same attempts may be made to distinguish *Edwards*, and the same answers may be made.[228]

(e) Effect of the Allowance of Residence Tests for Categorical Assistance.—Does congressional approval of limited residence tests for categorical assistance programs vitiate an argument against such state-imposed tests made under the privileges and immunities clause of the fourteenth amendment? The obvious answer might seem to be that Congress has no power to exempt states from the requirements of the fourteenth amendment. But the problem is not that simple. Adequate analysis hinges upon whether or not there is a relationship between the commerce power and the privilege or immunity being considered. If the right to travel interstate, protected by the privileges and immunities clause of the fourteenth amendment, is only a right to travel unhindered by states

---

governor's declaration of martial law in a certain county. The court held that martial law was proper under the federal constitution only where an actual state of war existed, and that such a situation could exist only with the presence of military troops in the field. 88 W. Va. at 720, 108 S.E. at 431. In this case, martial law was being enforced by civilian officials. Probably this opinion was cited in *Hanson* for the proposition that the governor of a state may not, by executive order, curtail the rights of citizens under the federal constitution and regular civil laws, in the absence of an actual state of war. *Constantin v. Smith* is in accord, stressing that *Lavinder* and many other cases dealing with martial law stand for the doctrines that the courts may inquire into the state of facts alleged to justify martial law, 57 F.2d at 236, and that in the absence of the necessity for such law, constitutional guarantees may not be suspended, *id.* at 240. The basis for this decision is somewhat confused; the court seems to rely upon (1) the Texas Constitution and (2) the due process clause of the federal constitution. *Id.* at 237. Similarly, the *Lavinder* holding seems grounded upon an interpretation of the federal and state constitutions and state statutes, with the basic federal constitutional provision which required interpretation apparently being the war power. 88 W. Va. at 717-21, 108 S.E. at 430-31.

Despite the cryptic citation of authority, there seems to be no doubt that *Hanson* stands for the proposition that in the absence of a state of war, basic constitutional guarantees and rights under civil law may not be suspended, and that there is a constitutional right of interstate travel which is so protected. The only uncertainty about the holding is whether it relies upon the privileges and immunities clause of the fourteenth amendment or the commerce clause. The citation of *Edwards* and *Zellner* shows that the court saw one of these clauses, probably the former, as guaranteeing such a right to travel interstate.

[227] *Supra* subsection I, *D, 1*.

[228] *Supra* subsection I, *D, 1, d*.

but within the limits set by Congress acting under the commerce clause, this freedom may be abridged by a state acting pursuant to a congressional mandate which is a proper delegation of legislative power. Here, the limits set for permissible residence tests are so narrow that an argument of improper delegation is almost certain to fail. However, the better reading of the concurrences in *Edwards* does not tie the privilege to the commerce clause, and, as will be argued later, freedom of interstate movement is also protected against federal action.[229]

3. The Privileges and Immunities Clause of Article IV

Article IV, section 2, clause 1 of the Constitution states: "The citizens of each State shall be entitled to all privileges and immunities of citizens in the several States." This language bars discrimination by a state against a citizen of another state in favor of its own citizens;[230] it does not affect a state's regulation of its own citizenry.[231] An older view that the clause recognized certain "natural rights" and protected citizens against another state's infringement of them, promulgated by Justice Washington in *Corfield v. Coryell*,[232] has been rejected.[233]

(a) *Toomer v. Witsell.*—Not all discriminations against citizens of other states are barred. The Court stated in 1948 in *Toomer v. Witsell*:[234]

> [T]he privileges and immunities clause [of Article IV] is not an absolute. It does bar discrimination against citizens of other States where there is no substantial reason for the discrimination beyond the mere fact that they are citizens of other States. But it does not preclude disparity of treatment in the many situations where there are perfectly valid independent reasons for it. Thus the inquiry in each case must be concerned with whether such reasons do exist and whether the degree of discrimination bears a close relation to them. The inquiry must also, of course, be conducted with due regard for the principle that the States should have considerable leeway in analyzing local evils and in prescribing appropriate cures.

The Court further declared that "the purpose" of the clause was "to outlaw classifications based on the fact of non-citizenship unless there is something to indicate that non-citizens constitute a peculiar source of the

---

[229] See *infra* subsection II, A.

[230] Slaughter-House Cases, 83 U.S. (16 Wall.) 36, 77 (1873); New York v. O'Neill, 359 U.S. 1, 6 (1959); Hague v. C.I.O., 307 U.S. 496, 511 (1939) (opinion of Roberts and Black, JJ.; there was no majority opinion).

[231] Slaughter-House Cases, *supra* note 230, at 77.

[232] 6 Fed. Cas. 546 (No. 3230) (C.C.E.D. Pa. 1823).

[233] Hague v. C.I.O., 307 U.S. 496, 511 (1939) (opinion of Roberts, J., with whom Black, J., concurred); *id.* at 520 n.1 (concurring opinion of Stone, J.).

[234] 334 U.S. 385, 396 (1948).

evil at which the statute is aimed."[235] This language may indicate that the state has the burden of proving a sufficient justification for a classification based on noncitizenship. Placing the burden on the state seems consistent with the aim of the privileges and immunities clause, "to help fuse into one Nation a collection of independent, sovereign States."[236] A state should have the burden of justifying legislation infringing such a vital constitutional policy.

In *Toomer* the Court found no evidence that noncitizen fishermen used different fishing methods or different size boats or required more costly enforcement of fishing regulations.[237] Therefore South Carolina's discriminatory regulation of commercial shrimp fishing violated the privileges and immunities clause of article IV. Even if proven, increased burdens imposed by nonresidents "would not necessarily support a remedy so drastic as to be a near equivalent of total exclusion."[238]

When these yardsticks are applied to assistance residence tests, a determination of constitutionality requires a showing that newcomers "constitute a peculiar source" of the high welfare bill, the general evil the tests are enacted to alleviate.[239] The Court in *Toomer* discussed the "peculiar source" in terms of whether or not each noncitizen boat produced an impact differing in kind or degree. No examination was made of the percentage of the evil which was due to nonresidents. It is submitted that a "peculiar source" exists only where the impact of each unit is different from the impact of each citizen unit. If the *Toomer* test is satisfied by a showing that nonresidents produced a substantial percentage of the evil, in some states the factual situation may support a finding that welfare residence tests do not violate article IV's privileges and immunities clause. The apparently inconclusive results of existing studies will be discussed later.[240]

Toomer would seem to overrule, implicitly, *McCready v. Virginia*,[241] which held that the privileges and immunities clause is not violated by exclusion of other states' citizens from planting oysters in a state's tidelands, because they are part of the common property of the state's

---

[235] *Id.* at 398.

[236] *Id.* at 395.

[237] *Id.* at 398.

[238] *Ibid.*

[239] See materials cited note 147 *supra*. If it is argued that the purpose of assistance residence tests is to prevent an influx of the indigent, the answer is that Edwards v. California, 314 U.S. 160 (1941), invalidates that purpose. If it is argued that the tests are intended to prevent an influx of the indigent persons motivated solely or primarily by a desire to obtain higher assistance benefits than those available in their former state, the residence test is invalid as too broadly drawn. See *infra* subsection I, *E*.

[240] See *infra* subsection I, *E*.

[241] 94 U.S. 391 (1876).

citizenry. While the Court in *Toomer* carefully distinguished *Mc-Cready*,[242] the reasoning of the *Toomer* opinion, especially the "peculiar source" test, undermines *McCready* and cases following it.[243]

The death knell of the common property doctrine was sounded in *Toomer:*

> The whole ownership theory, in fact, is now generally regarded as but a fiction expressive in legal shorthand of the importance to its people that a State have power to preserve and regulate the exploitation of an important resource. And there is no necessary conflict between that vital policy consideration and the constitutional command that the State exercise that power, like its other powers, so as not to discriminate without reason against citizens of other States.[244]

The decline of *McCready* is further illustrated by *Anderson v. Mullaney*[245] and *Brown v. Anderson*,[246] two recent federal cases already discussed,[247] which invalidated on commerce clause grounds—and in the latter, alternatively, under article IV's privileges and immunities clause—license fees and fishing regulations discriminating against nonresidents. On the privileges and immunities issue *Brown* followed *Toomer*,[248] which the judge states "put at rest" the common ownership theory of *Mc-Cready*.[249] More important was *Brown's* rejection of the contention that the statute was "a reasonable regulation" because "it provides a means to prevent or alleviate the possible destitution of the residents of the State of Alaska," who "could become a burden upon the citizens of Alaska and not on non-residents."[250] The judge stated: "There is no exception in the privileges and immunities clause providing for differentiation on the basis of the general welfare of citizens of any State. . . . We cannot agree with defendants that there is any authority to avoid the effect of the privileges and immunities clause solely under the guise of avoiding economic losses to residents."[251] This language, although

---

[242] 334 U.S. at 401.

[243] *E.g.*, Patsone v. Pennsylvania, 232 U.S. 138 (1914). In this case, Justice Holmes writing for the Court used the "peculiar source" terminology, *id.* at 144, but was much less willing than the Court in *Toomer* to examine the factual basis for concluding that a certain group could be so described. *Id.* at 144-45.

[244] 334 U.S. at 402.

[245] 191 F.2d 123 (9th Cir. 1951) (one judge dissented on other grounds), *aff'd on other grounds sub nom.* Mullaney v. Anderson, 342 U.S. 415 (1952).

[246] 202 F. Supp. 96 (D. Alaska 1962).

[247] See *supra* subsection II, *D, 1, e*.

[248] 202 F. Supp. at 101-02. Earlier in the opinion, the judge quotes the privileges and immunities clauses of both article IV and the fourteenth amendment, *id.* at 100, and thereafter does not identify which clause he is applying. But his reliance on *Toomer* makes it clear that he means the article IV clause.

[249] *Id.* at 102.

[250] *Id.* at 101-02.

[251] *Id.* at 102.

applied to a different constitutional provision, is similar to that in *Edwards* and appears directly relevant to the assistance resident test situation.

(*b*) *Residence Tests for Voting—A Valid Analogy?*—Dictum by the Supreme Court in *Blake v. McClung*,[252] in 1898, supports the validity of residence tests for voting and office-holding in the face of an attack under the privileges and immunities clause of article IV. The first Justice Harlan stated that a citizen of one state is not entitled, by that clause, "to enjoy in another State *every* privilege that may be given in the latter to its own citizens. There are privileges that may be accorded by a State to its own people in which citizens of other States may not participate except in conformity to such reasonable regulations as may be established by the State."[253] One of the examples of a permissible requirement that he then noted was a state-imposed period of residence test for voting and office-holding.[254]

Since these situations are easily distinguishable from the welfare test, in regard to both the state's interest necessitating the test and the impact of the test on the migrant, this dictum does not raise any serious barrier to the conclusion that welfare residence tests violate article IV's privileges and immunities clause. The voting analogy will be discussed later in this article,[255] since the more recent cases deal with the equal protection clause.

(*c*) *Are Paupers Protected by the Clause?*—The provision in the Articles of Confederation[256] parallel to the privileges and immunities clause of article IV of the Constitution expressly excluded from its shelter "paupers, vagabonds, and fugitives." This exception was not included in the constitutional provision.

Confusion may arise from the Supreme Court's statement in *United States v. Wheeler*[257] that "the text of Article IV, sec. 2 of the Constitution, makes manifest that it was drawn with reference to the corresponding clause of the Articles of Confederation and was *intended to perpetuate its limitations.*" It seems unlikely that the Court was referring to the exception of paupers and others. The quoted language appears in a discussion which (1) twice refers to the "limitation" in the Articles'

---

[252] 172 U.S. 239, 256 (1898) (7-2 decision). Subsection I, *E*, 7 *infra* discusses recent cases which seem to indicate that the equal protection clause of the fourteenth amendment is not violated by short residence tests for voting.

[253] 172 U.S. at 256.

[254] *Ibid.*

[255] See *infra* subsection I, *E*, 7.

[256] Articles of Confederation, art. IV, § 2; see TENBROEK 12.

[257] 254 U.S. 281, 294 (1920). (Emphasis added.)

provision which inhibited the states from discriminating,[258] and (2) logically can be read with the limitations perpetuated meaning this restraint on discrimination.[259] Also, that case involved no question requiring the Court to consider the inclusion of "paupers, vagabonds, and fugitives." There is little chance that the Founding Fathers absent-mindedly omitted the exception. The following section of article IV,[260] like that in the Articles of Confederation,[261] deals with extradition of fugitives.

Regardless of the Court's meaning and of the intent of the Fathers, construction of the Constitution changes with the needs and views of our society,[262] and since *Edwards v. California*[263] rejected a view of the poor as "a moral pestilence,"[264] there can be little doubt that the privileges and immunities clause of article IV should be read as extending its protections to the poor.

(*d*) *Is Discrimination Against New Citizens of a State Barred?*—It may also be contended that the privileges and immunities clause of article IV has no bearing on the validity of residence tests, since it protects only citizens of other states, and newcomers attacking assistance residence requirements are citizens of the state where they now reside. The citizenship part of this argument is supported by the fourteenth amendment, which states, in relevant part: "All persons born or naturalized in the United States, and subject to the jurisdiction thereof, are citizens . . . of the State wherein they reside." It should be noted that this provision imposes, for acquisition of state citizenship, a requirement of residence, but no requirement of any minimum period of residence.

Residence tests for welfare programs violate the privileges and immunities clause of article IV precisely because they impair the privilege of free interstate movement, since a potential migrant will face discriminatory treatment after he becomes a resident and therefore a citizen of the state he wishes to enter. In *Blake v. McClung*,[265] Justice Harlan stated, "The Constitution forbids only such legislation affecting citizens of the respective States as will substantially or practically put a citizen of one State in a condition of alienage when he is within *or when he removes to another State*."[266] Therefore, the clause bars certain discrimination against the new citizen who recently was a citizen of another state.

---

258 *Ibid.*

259 See *id.* at 294-95.

260 U.S. CONST., art. IV, § 2, cl. 2.

261 Articles of Confederation, art. IV, § 2.

262 *E.g.*, JACKSON, THE STRUGGLE FOR JUDICIAL SUPREMACY 174 (1941).

263 314 U.S. 160 (1941).

264 *Id.* at 177.

265 172 U.S. 239 (1898).

266 *Id.* at 256. (Emphasis added.)

It may be that welfare assistance is so vital to life that its denial places an otherwise eligible newcomer in a position of "alienage" and therefore is impermissible, even where the newcomer remains a resident and citizen of another state. The reasons of economic policy supporting such a conclusion have already been examined in connection with the possibility of protecting, under the commerce clause, a nonresident's right to assistance.[267]

In regard to newly arrived residents, the argument for the inapplicability of the privileges and immunities protection of article IV is at the same time an argument for finding that residence tests violate the equal protection clause of the fourteenth amendment. While the latter provision speaks in terms of persons subject to the state's jurisdiction, a discrimination seems especially repugnant to the letter and spirit of the clause when it is against citizens of the state. If a state may remove itself from castigation under article IV, on the grounds that the persons discriminated against are citizens of that state, the state cannot be heard to say the complainants are not citizens for purposes of the equal protection clause. In other words, the class of persons not protected by the article IV clause is a class which is protected under the equal protection clause.

(e) Conclusion.—A conclusion that article IV's privileges and immunities clause may be a successful means of attacking welfare residence tests must be tempered by recognition that (1) facts may exist meeting the "peculiar source" test, at least under a percentage interpretation, and (2) the analysis of discrimination against the new citizen as discrimination against another state's citizens considering becoming such, may not be accepted by the courts.

E. Denial of Equal Protection of the Laws

The equal protection clause of the fourteenth amendment forbids any state to "deny to any person within its jurisdiction the equal protection of the laws." The Court has made it clear that "the guaranty of 'equal protection of the laws is a pledge of the protection of equal laws.' "[268] When a state law treats classes of persons differently, it is valid only if the classifications made are reasonable in light of the statute's purpose.[269]

---

267 See *supra* subsection I, D, 1, h.

268 Skinner v. Oklahoma, 316 U.S. 535, 541 (1942), quoting Yick Wo v. Hopkins, 118 U.S. 356, 369 (1886).

269 *E.g.*, Carrington v. Rash, 380 U.S. 89, 93 (1965); Allied Stores of Ohio v. Bowers, 358 U.S. 522, 527-28 (1959), and cases cited therein; Watson v. Maryland, 218 U.S. 173, 179 (1910); Bachtel v. Wilson, 204 U.S. 36, 41 (1907); see Tussman & tenBroek, *The Equal Protection of the Laws*, 37 CALIF. L. REV. 341, 344-53 (1949).

1. Discrimination Between State Citizens

While the equal protection guarantee is not restricted to citizens, it should be more difficult to sustain the reasonableness of discriminations between citizens of a state than it is to uphold diverse treatment of citizens and noncitizens. The applicant for assistance, if a resident of the state, is a citizen thereof. The fourteenth amendment so declares and does not require, for state citizenship, any period of residence in the state. Residence tests, then, must pass the test of being reasonable classifications among the citizens of the same state. The question becomes whether or not it is reasonable to discriminate, in this context, against state citizens who are newcomers.

2. A Test for the Reasonableness of a Classification

The reasonableness of a classification may be tested, under the equal protection clause, by comparing (1) the necessity for the discrimination (that is, the importance to the state of having this diverse treatment) with (2) relevant differences in the situations of those treated unequally, and (3) the impact of the discrimination upon individual rights and other human values. The Supreme Court made it clear in *Oyama v. California*[270] that disparate treatment may not be justified "because of some remote administrative benefit to the State."[271] In other words, the rights of a class of persons may not be unduly infringed when a less restrictive statute—albeit requiring greater administrative effort—could satisfy the same needs of the state. The continued and increasing vitality of this rule is shown by the reliance on it in *Carrington v. Rash*,[272] from which the language just quoted is taken. There the Court held that the equal protection clause was violated by a Texas constitutional provision which "prohibits 'any member of the Armed Forces of the United States' who moves his home to Texas during the course of his military duty from ever voting in any election in that State 'so long as he or she is a member of the Armed Forces.' "[273] The fundamental defect of this provision was barring military personnel from becoming Texas residents for voting purposes regardless of their intentions. The citation of *Oyama* supported the Court's rejection of an argument that the Texas rule was necessary to avoid the onerous administrative tasks involved in

---

[270] 332 U.S. 633, 646-47 (1948).

[271] Carrington v. Rash, 380 U.S. 89, 96 (1965) (7-1 decision) citing *Oyama; accord,* Harman v. Forssenius, 380 U.S. 528, 542-43 (1965) (8-1 decision, Harlan, J., agreeing only in part with the majority).

[272] *Supra* note 271.

[273] 380 U.S. at 89, paraphrasing and quoting in part Tex. Const., art. VI, § 2.

determining which military personnel stationed in the state had a bona fide intention to become residents.[274]

It is appropriate at this point to consider whether or not the classifications invalidated in *Oyama* and *Carrington* should be distinguished from residence tests as involving a different defect regarding inclusiveness. This requires comparing the group covered by the statute with the class of persons connected with the mischief at which the statute is aimed.[275] Several arguments indicate that *Oyama* and *Carrington* should not be so distinguished:

(1) The opinions of the Court in those cases do not indicate preoccupation with overinclusiveness or underinclusiveness. As the Court said in *Carrington*, the question was " 'whether the classifications drawn in a statute are reasonable in light of its purpose . . . .' "[276]

(2) The classifications in *Carrington* and in the residence test situation each can be viewed as either overinclusive or underinclusive. In *Carrington*, the Court stressed the fact that Texas had singled out servicemen, and had not applied the same rule to other groups whose bona fide residence might be in doubt.[277] This would indicate underinclusiveness, but the Court also noted that Texas had been able to distinguish among servicemen, in regard to bona fide residence, for legal purposes other than voting, and this would indicate overinclusiveness. Similarly, in the residence test situation, the class treated differently is too broad if the legislature is worried about good faith residence, and the class is too narrowly drawn if the purpose of the solons is merely to reduce the number of persons eligible for welfare assistance, or to eliminate those persons whose past contributions to the state's economy do not equal all or some specific portion of the assistance sought, or to make eligible for public assistance only those persons for whom aid from private charities is unavailable. In *Oyama*, the crucial issue was the basis of the classification (national origin) rather than its inclusiveness.

(3) The overriding factor is that in regard to denial of eligibility for assistance, an overinclusive classification is worse than an underinclusive one. The former will result in human suffering and, in some cases, a threat to life itself, while the latter causes, at most, waste of public funds. While such waste may result in higher taxes and some discomfort for persons, in all likelihood increased tax burdens will be borne by families other than those on the margin of subsistence. Whether the situation is viewed

---

[274] *Id.* at 96. Worry about large administrative expenditure was stressed by Justice Harlan dissenting. *Id.* at 99-100.

[275] Tussman & tenBroek, *supra* note 269, at 345-48.

[276] 380 U.S. at 93, quoting McLaughlin v. Florida, 379 U.S. 184, 191 (1964).

[277] 380 U.S. at 95-96.

as involving overinclusiveness or underinclusiveness, the Court should apply a stricter test to classifications involving life itself, than to those in cases like *Oyama* and *Carrington*, involving land ownership and voting.[278]

(4) The Court rejected in *Oyama* and *Carrington*—both arguably cases of overinclusive classifications, and the latter clearly having an underinclusive aspect—the administrative convenience justification which, in what is probably the leading article on equal protection, is posited as applying in some underinclusive classification situations.[279]

It is submitted that the overinclusive-underinclusive distinction is not helpful in regard to assistance residence tests. Analysis should depend upon the need for and purpose of the classification, relevant differences in the situations of those treated differently, and the impact of the discrimination upon individual rights and other human values, most especially, life itself.

3. Oyama v. California

The decision of the Supreme Court in *Oyama v. California*[280] is relevant to the question of the compatibility of assistance residence tests with the equal protection clause of the fourteenth amendment. The majority held violative of that clause and of the privileges of United States citizens, a California statute which, in effect, imposed different presumptions regarding property ownership upon the class of minor citizens whose parents were aliens incapable of naturalization. "The cumulative effect . . . was clearly to discriminate against Fred Oyama. He was saddled with an onerous burden of proof which need not be borne by California children generally."[281] "Thus, as between the citizen children of a Chinese or English father and the citizen children of a Japanese father, there is discrimination . . . ."[282] The privilege of citizens violated was that of owning land.[283] While the majority also gave this second ground for their holding, they depended primarily upon the equal protection clause.[284] That guarantee was also relied upon by the

---

[278] The distinction is even more obvious between the assistance situation and cases involving economic regulation, such as Railway Express Agency v. New York, 336 U.S. 106 (1949), where the Court upheld a statute barring advertising on trucks except for advertisements of goods sold by the truck's owner.

[279] Tussman & tenBroek, *supra* note 269, at 349.

[280] 332 U.S. 633 (1948).

[281] *Id.* at 644

[282] *Id.* at 645

[283] *Id.* at 640, 646-47

[284] Most of the majority's analysis is devoted to this issue, *id.* at 640-47. The right to own land seems to have been relevant only to undercutting any justification for the unequal treatment. *Id.* at 64

four concurring justices, being the only provision cited by Murphy and Rutledge,[285] and a major basis for the opinion of Black and Douglas.[286] Reed and Burton,[287] and Jackson in a separate opinion,[288] dissented on the ground that it is anomalous to find the presumptions unconstitutional, while assuming the validity of the underlying provisions of the California Alien Land Law forbidding aliens to own land if they were ineligible for American citizenship. The thrust of the presumptions was aimed at such alien parents to prevent them from evading the law by holding property in the names of citizen children.[289]

In *Oyama*, the invalid discrimination was based upon the parent's status as an alien of particular descent, that is, upon the status of a person who, although a resident, was not and could not become a citizen of the state. The fourteenth amendment requires United States citizenship as a prerequisite for state citizenship; at the time *Oyama* was decided, Japanese nationals were not eligible for naturalization.[290] Residence tests for assistance posit a difference in treatment upon what may well be an even more invalid basis: the status of one who recently became a resident *and* state citizen.

Oyama may be distinguished because the discrimination is vested upon the child because of the parent's status. But while the Court expressly found no need to decide if the statutory presumptions denied equal protection to the parent,[291] or if the ban on alien landholding was similarly invalid,[292] affirmative answers seem indicated by the rationale of the decision, by the language of the fourteenth amendment requiring states to give equal protection of the laws to all persons subject to their jurisdiction and not just to citizens, and by the fact that four concurring and three dissenting justices would have faced these questions.

Oyama does contain an indication that the majority holding should

---

285 *Id*. at 65

286 *Id*. at 647. Black and Douglas, the only deciding Justices now on the Court, would have decided the case "on the broader grounds that the basic provisions of the California Alien Land Law [forbidding aliens to own land] violate the equal protection clause of the Fourteenth Amendment and conflict with federal laws and treaties governing the immigration of aliens and their rights after arrival in this country," *ibid*, and would have overruled previous decisions of the Court to the contrary, *id*. at 649. (The prior decisions referred to were Terrace v. Thompson, 263 U.S. 197 (1923); Porterfield v. Webb, 263 U.S. 225 (1923); Webb v. O'Brien, 263 U.S. 313 (1923); Frick v. Webb, 263 U.S. 326 (1923), all cited in 332 U.S. at 649 n.3.). Justices Murphy and Rutledge would have reached the same result, but relied only on the equal protection clause. 332 U.S. at 650.

287 *Id*. at 674.

288 *Id*. at 684.

289 *Id*. at 646.

290 *Id*. at 635 n.3.

291 *Id*. at 647.

292 *Id*. at 646.

have been, or at least could have been, based on the unequal treatment of the parent. California argued, in response to a charge of racial discrimination against the child, that its statute applied to any recipient of a gift from the father, Kajiro Oyama.[293] The majority opinion responded that the statute made the racial descent of the father determinative,[294] thereby showing that these justices were focussing on the parent's status.

This portion of the opinion[295] and express statements by two of the concurring justices[296] provide a basis for distinguishing *Oyama* as merely another case invalidating racial discrimination. But language earlier in the majority opinion seems to indicate that considerable weight was put upon a factor more akin to that present in assistance residence test cases; the Court stated that the pertinent constitutional deficiency was discrimination against the child "based solely on his parents' country of origin."[297] Similarly, the residence test penalizes those who enter from another state of the United States.

It might be argued that landholding is a right, whereas receipt of welfare assistance is a privilege, or a right in regard to which different standards of equal protection should apply. However, the *Oyama* holding can be read broadly as being based upon a state's duty to treat equally similarly situated residents of the state, regardless of their origins. If unequal treatment may not be based upon Japanese nationality, how can it be based on recent citizenship of another state of the United States, unless the time factor is to be determinative? But since a federal statute[298] granting citizens the right to own land was held in *Oyama* to undermine a justification based upon the father's status as an alien,[299] the right of free interstate movement—a constitutionally protected,[300] and therefore higher class of, right—should serve to destroy any rationale bottomed on recent interstate migration. Moreover, in defining state citizenship the fourteenth amendment makes no distinction between newcomers and long-term residents.

4. *Arguably Valid State Purposes Served by Residence Tests for Public Assistance*

The major constitutionally permissible state objective arguably served by a residence test for welfare assistance is avoiding having indi-

---

293 *Id.* at 644.
294 *Id.* at 645–46.
295 *Ibid.*
296 *Id.* at 650.
297 *Id.* at 640.
298 REV. STAT. § 1978 (1875), 42 U.S.C. § 1982 (1964).
299 332 U.S. at 646.
300 U.S. CONST. art. VI, § 2.

gents enter the state for the sole or primary purpose of receiving welfare. While the Court did not reach the equal protection argument in *Edwards v. California*,[301] the thesis underlying the majority and concurring opinions bars a state from seeking to protect the public purse by excluding, or hindering the entry of, all nonresident indigents, including those who have a reason for entering other than a desire to collect welfare. In *Edwards* the Court rejected California's very real argument that the influx of "Okies" and other fugitives from the impact of the Depression and Dust Bowl imposed severe costs on the state.[302] It might be thought that residence tests present a better case for constitutionality than did the statute in *Edwards*, since they do not bar interstate movement, but only deny assistance payments for a period after arrival. Two answers exist: (1) residence tests do bar interstate movement for some persons who are unable to exist in a new state for the required period without public assistance, and (2) the rationale of *Edwards* extends to state statutes which penalize, as well as those which bar, interstate movement. The statute in *Edwards* merely hindered such movement by nonresident indigents, by making it a misdemeanor to knowingly assist one to enter the state.

The next question is whether or not a legislature could reasonably find that there is any danger to the public purse from in-migrants motivated primarily by a desire to receive welfare, or even any danger from all indigents moving to the state, if *Edwards* were not felt to bar the state from protecting its coffers against every such migrant. It is submitted that a careful, impartial analysis must answer that the existing studies, while not conclusive, seem to indicate that in either case the threat to the public purse is not as great as advocates of residence tests often contend. The existence of a substantial threat, again in either case, seems to vary, depending on the situation in each state.

Some commentators[303] have concluded that existing studies indicate that residence tests for assistance are not necessary to serve the purpose usually given as the justification for them: to protect the public purse against costs imposed by a large in-migration of indigents seeking or needing welfare benefits.[304] However, certain studies which might be thought to support this view actually are inconclusive. For example, Rhode Island's

---

[301] 314 U.S. 160 (1941); *compare id.* at 177 (the majority saying they do not have to reach other constitutional questions) and the grounds for decision given in the concurring opinions, *id.* at 177-81 and 181-86, *with* the equal protection arguments made, 86 L. Ed. 120, 122.

[302] 314 U.S. at 173.

[303] *E.g.,* Leet, *Rhode Island Abolishes Settlement*, 18 Soc. Serv. Rev. 281, 283-84 (1944); Falk, *Social Action on Settlement Laws*, 18 Soc. Serv. Rev. 288, 294 (1944); see LoGatto 106-07.

[304] See *supra* note 147.

experience, during World War II, with abolishing all settlement and residence tests and finding that welfare costs declined despite the fact that Rhode Island paid higher welfare benefits than surrounding states,[305] neither proves nor disproves the efficacy of the tests. The period 1942-44 was a time of very high and rising employment resulting from the demands of war production combined with the presence of about fifteen million men in the armed services.[306]

Even if a state abolished residence tests and found that its welfare costs increased, this would not prove that people came to the state to get higher assistance. The increase might be attributable to persons previously deterred from moving to the state by unwillingness to lose welfare benefits for which they were presently eligible in another state. Such persons would move once the new state allowed them to obtain the same level of benefits.

Any statement that a State Welfare Department was "unable to locate a single individual who has moved into the state in order to secure assistance"[307] cannot be accepted without serious doubts about the manner in which the Department sought to locate such persons. It would be naive to believe that indigents are so honest or so untutored in the answers expected by welfare agencies as to admit any such purpose, even if it were the major reason for their migration.

Doubts arise also about the interpretation which should be given to reports[308] from New York, which has no residence test. These reports show that a small percentage—3.5% in 1946; about 1.5% in 1955-58—of those receiving welfare in New York State had been residents for less than one year. Fair analysis must consider the effect on welfare costs, not only of each year's newcomers, but also of newcomers in the past who might have been deterred from coming to New York if the state had had a period of residence test.[309] Father LoGatto has written:

> The New York State Department of Social Welfare reported that in 1955 non-residents made up only 1.8% of the case load. According to

---

[305] Reported in Leet, *supra* note 303, at 283-84; see also Falk, *supra* note 303, at 294.

[306] See, *e.g.*, MORISON & COMMAGER, 2 THE GROWTH OF THE AMERICAN REPUBLIC 686-87 (4th ed. revised 1956). Fleet's article, *supra* note 305 recognizes the effect of war production in creating jobs and reducing welfare costs, *id.* at 283-84, and notes that in Rhode Island in the year after elimination of the settlement and residence requirements for public assistance, the percentage reduction in the public assistance rolls was "just a little bit more than the drop for the entire nation." *Id.* at 283.

[307] Leet, *supra* 303, at 283.

[308] NEW YORK STATE DEP'T OF WELFARE, THE MOVEMENT OF POPULATION AND PUBLIC WELFARE IN NEW YORK STATE 13 (1958); N.Y. Times, Feb. 16, 1961, p. 21, col. 5, cited in LoGatto 107 n.38; New York State Ass'n of Councils and Chests, "Residence" as a Requirement for Public Assistance, Memorandum No. 1, Dec. 1956, cited in LoGatto 107 nn. 37, 39-40.

[309] See LoGatto 107.

testimony presented last year [1961], only 1.5% had not lived in the state for a period of one year.

As for duration of dependency, and this is an important consideration since an annual increase of even 1.5% per year could reach a staggering proportion in time, it was found in New York City that the average duration of assistance to non-residents was six months for state charges and ten months as to local charges or a total of sixteen months. It must be borne in mind here that this average included such cases as aid to dependent children, aid to the blind, and old age assistance which generally are long term cases. In upper New York State, a study revealed an average length of care of fourteen months. To round out the picture, the same study shows about 18% of the 1.8% of needy non-residents require help over a long period of time.[310]

An example will illustrate how the increases might accumulate. If 18% of 1.8% per year, or .324%, is multiplied by a period of ten years, the result is a 3.24% increase in welfare costs, assuming that cost per needy nonresident is the same as cost per needy resident. To this must be added the 1.8% entering each year and requiring an average of more than one year of assistance, for a total increase exceeding 5% in an eleven year period. A portion of those entering, who would be deterred by a residence test, will have children who will also require welfare assistance, but who will be counted statistically as residents if born of resident parents. According to a 1962 report by Greenleigh Associates, in New York, of families receiving Home Relief, Aid to Dependent Children, or Aid to the Disabled, in about twenty-five per cent of the cases the head of the household had parents who had been welfare recipients.[311] This report also indicates, in a backhanded way, that newcomers do place a noticeable burden on New York's welfare programs: "The public assistance recipients are not newcomers to New York State. Many are natives and at least eighty per cent have lived in the state more than five years."[312] Moreover, in New York many eligible for assistance do not receive it.[313] It is realistic to assume that newcomers are in this category in numbers disproportionate to the percentage of newcomers on welfare rolls or among the poor generally. It is the recent migrant who is most likely to be

---

[310] *Ibid.*, citing New York State Ass'n of Councils and Chests, *supra* note 308.

[311] GREENLEIGH ASSOCIATES, REPORT TO THE MORELAND COMMISSION ON WELFARE OF FINDINGS OF THE STUDY OF THE PUBLIC ASSISTANCE PROGRAM AND OPERATIONS OF THE STATE OF NEW YORK 9 (Nov. 1962).

[312] *Id.* at 17.

[313] See Sparer, *The Role of the Welfare Client's Lawyer*, 12 U.C.L.A.L. REV. 361, 371 (1965). The figures cited therein deal with persons living in poverty who do not receive assistance. However, it is very difficult to believe that all of those persons are not eligible. In Westchester County "more than five times as many people are living in abject poverty as are receiving aid from the Westchester County Department of Public Welfare," according to a statement by the president of the Westchester Council of Social Agencies appearing in the N.Y. Times, Oct. 23, 1964, p. 37, col. 6, and quoted in 12 U.C.L.A.L. REV. at 371.

unaware of the techniques and demands of living in a new environment—especially if it is urban—including the welfare assistance eligibility requirements and application procedures of a particular city, county, or state.[314] The migrant poor in many cases lack the educational prerequisites to being able to learn quickly about these aspects of their new environment.[315] And migrants, more than other indigents, lack even rudimentary political and organizational contacts which could help them apply for welfare.

Because the rationale in *Edwards* invalidates the objective of merely guarding the state treasury against the needs of migrant indigents, the analysis (or the numbers game) has one more step: ascertaining the impact on welfare costs of those who come to a state solely to obtain welfare. On this subject, there is little information. However, it is fallacious to argue that if there are few persons of this type who would be deterred by residence tests, this demonstrates that such tests do not have substantial impact on interstate freedom of movement. There may be many who desire to move to another state for reasons unrelated to obtaining higher welfare payments, but who will be deterred from migrating by residence tests making them ineligible to receive in the new state the same level of assistance they are receiving in their present state. For them, losing present benefits rather than obtaining higher ones is the critical issue. Furthermore, impact on freedom of movement under a constitutional system devoted to individual rights should be measured in terms of impact on such freedom for each person whose situation is considered.

A fair conclusion seems to be that, in at least some states, it is not unreasonable for the legislature to conclude that a useful saving in welfare costs may be obtained by residence tests discouraging those who would enter the state solely because of its welfare programs. In New York, for example, a one per cent saving in welfare costs would amount to several million dollars.[316] Perhaps future studies will demonstrate that a very small percentage of those in-migrants who would be deterred by a residence test come solely to obtain welfare.[317]

---

314 *E.g.*, Seligman, *The Enduring Slums*, in THE EDITORS OF FORTUNE, THE EXPLODING METROPOLIS 95 (Doubleday Anchor ed. 1958).

315 *Ibid.* Governor Rockefeller has declared that the federal government should give New York City special aid to help alleviate the "educational and cultural lag among rural migrants" from Puerto Rico and the South. N.Y. Times, Nov. 20, 1965, p. 23, col. 6.

316 In 1962 a one per cent saving in New York would have been four million dollars. See GREENLEIGH ASSOCIATES, *op. cit. supra* note 311, at *i*.

317 It is "the firm conviction of social workers and the New York City Commissioner of Welfare, among others, that people simply do not migrate for the purpose of receiving welfare aid." Sparer, *supra* note 313, at 376, citing Statement on the Proposal to Enact a Residence Law for Public Assistance, James R. Simpson (*sic*, for Dumpson), Commissioner of Welfare, New York City, 1959.

Another arguably valid reason for requiring a minimum period of residence is to determine if the newcomer has a bona fide intent to reside in the state, and thereby to become a state citizen.

5. The Arguably Valid Purposes Served by Residence Tests Can Be Met by a Statute Less Restrictive of Individual Rights

The arguably valid purpose of preventing people from moving to a state with the primary aim of receiving higher assistance payments can be dealt with by a statute much less restrictive of individual rights and much less discriminatory than residence tests. Such a statute would bar from welfare assistance, permanently or for the period of residence now required, any person whose sole or primary purpose in entering the state was the receipt of assistance. A series of rebuttable presumptions regarding intention might be established or a list of factors to be considered in that regard might be provided. An example of such a statute, although it is possible to quarrel with the fairness of some of its details and its administration,[318] is the New York Welfare Abuses Law,[319] set

---

The three-member majority of the five-man New York State Committee on Welfare Costs (a group appointed by Governor Rockefeller), recommended adoption of a one-year residence test, but "said it was aware that 'not too many people come to New York State simply to get the benefits of public assistance.'" N.Y. Times, April 30, 1965, p. 1, col. 3, p. 24, col. 1.

[318] See Sparer, *supra* note 313, at 375-77.

[319] N.Y. Soc. Welfare Law § 139-a:
Special Provisions to avoid abuse of assistance and care.

1. Where a public welfare official has reason to believe that an applicant for home relief or aid to dependent children came into the state for the purpose of receiving such public assistance or care, he shall conduct an investigation according to the provisions of subdivisions two and three of this section to determine whether such applicant is undeserving of and ineligible for assistance in accordance with subdivision four of this section.

2. In the course of the investigation by the public welfare official to ascertain the facts supporting the application and to obtain such information as may be required by the regulations of the department, he shall direct his inquiry towards ascertaining whether or not the applicant came into the state for the purpose of receiving public assistance or care and in making such inquiry the public welfare official shall expressly consider whether proof has been submitted as to one or more of the following:

a. That the applicant is gainfully employed at the time of the application, or

b. That the applicant has been gainfully employed since his arrival in the state for a period of at least one month during his first year of residence in the state, or

c. That the applicant had reasonable assurance of gainful employment before his arrival in the state, or

d. That the applicant had reliable assurance of adequate private aid, maintenance or support or resources from relatives, friends or other sources in this state for himself and for any person dependent upon him for maintenance or support who preceded, followed or accompanied the applicant to this state, or

e. That the applicant for the first six months after his entry into the state made no application for public assistance or care, or

out in full in the footnote. While fair administration of such a statute involves administrative difficulties, they do not seem to exceed those the

---

f. That in the case of an applicant who has entered the state within six months of the date of his application, such applicant entered the state for some purpose other than to receive public assistance or care.

3. In addition, where the applicant is a person who, by reason of age, physical and mental condition, is capable of working and who is or should be available for employment, he shall submit with his application a certificate from the appropriate local employment office of the state department of labor issued within a two week period from the date of his application stating that such employment office has no order for an opening in part-time, full-time, temporary or permanent work of any kind to which the applicant could properly be referred by such office, taking into consideration only his physical and mental capacity without reference to his customary occupation or acquired skill. Such a certificate, however, shall not be required of persons who cannot register with such employment office because of age, health or other disability or are otherwise not available for employment.

4. If as a result of such an investigation and upon the proof submitted by the applicant, by affidavit or otherwise, the public welfare official determines that such applicant came into the state for the purpose of receiving public assistance or care and accordingly is undeserving of and ineligible for assistance, the application shall be disapproved. It shall be evidence that a person is not undeserving of and ineligible for assistance if the investigation revealed an affirmative answer to either paragraphs, a, b, c, d, e, or f of subdivision two of this section. If in the case of a person who falls within the purview of paragraph f of subdivision two of this section, the applicant fails to submit proof to the public welfare official that he entered the state for some purpose other than to receive public assistance or care, he shall be presumed to have come into the state for the purpose of receiving public assistance or care and accordingly to be undeserving of and ineligible for assistance. A person shall not be determined to be undeserving of and ineligible for assistance if a certificate as required by subdivision three of this section has been submitted. If either home relief or aid to dependent children is granted on the basis of such a certificate, such assistance or care shall be terminated to any person who, by reason of age, physical and mental condition, remains capable of working and who is or should be available for employment and who remains eligible for registration with the employment office if such person:

a. wilfully fails to obtain and file with the public welfare district at least once in every two-week period a new certificate of the type required to be filed in accordance with subdivision three of this section, or

b. wilfully fails to report for an interview at an employment office with respect to employment when requested to do so by such office, or

c. wilfully fails to report to such office the result of a referral to employment, or

d. wilfully fails to report for employment, or

e. refuses to accept employment for any reason other than his physical or mental condition.

Such wilful failures or refusals as above listed shall be reported immediately to the public welfare district by such local employment office.

5. Notwithstanding any inconsistent provision of this section, an applicant in immediate need of public assistance or care for himself or for any person dependent upon him shall be granted such assistance or care on a temporary emergency basis.

6. If the public welfare official determines that the applicant is undeserving of and ineligible for assistance hereunder, he shall notify the applicant of his decision in writing.

Supreme Court, in effect, imposed on Texas in *Carrington*,[320] if Texas wishes to contest the residence of servicemen stationed there. However, it should be noted that in *Carrington* the Court placed considerable emphasis upon the fact that Texas did ascertain bona fide residence for other classes of voters and for other purposes.[321] It may be objected that states lack the experience necessary to demonstrate that it is possible to identify those entering solely to obtain welfare. In reply it may be said: (1) It is unclear to what extent, if any, the decision in *Carrington* depended upon the existence of these facts; (2) in any event, state experience in ascertaining bona fide residence is analogous; and (3) nothing in the New York experience has indicated that the task is impossible—the Welfare Abuses Law illustrates a list of factors which may be consulted. It is submitted that these contentions overcome the objection.

An even less restrictive statute, which would deal effectively with persons coming to a state solely or primarily to get higher welfare benefits than those available in their former home state, would allow newcomers shown to have such an intent, to collect only such welfare assistance as would equal that for which they were eligible in their prior state of residence. The restriction of assistance payments could be imposed permanently or only for a limited time after the arrival of the newcomer with the requisite intent.

Similarly, the rule of *Oyama* and of *Carrington* disposes of the argument that residence tests are necessary to show a bona fide intent to become a resident and state citizen. Other factors may be looked to in this regard, including those used in examining the reasons for a person's entering the state. Moreover, requiring a period of residence as a means of ascertaining a bona fide intent to reside seems incompatible with the fourteenth amendment's definition of state citizenship, which encompasses all residents, including those who have just arrived.

The existence of more restrained methods of handling the only arguably valid purposes of residence tests for assistance renders those tests

---

7. If an application is not acted upon by the public welfare official within thirty days after the filing of the application or if the applicant is determined by the public welfare official to be undeserving of and ineligible for assistance, the applicant may appeal to the department, which upon receipt of the appeal shall review the case, shall give the applicant making the appeal an opportunity for a fair hearing thereon and within thirty days render its decision. The department may also, on its own motion, review any such decision made, or any case in which a decision has not been made by the public welfare official within the time specified. All decisions of the department shall be binding upon the public welfare districts involved and shall be complied with by the public welfare officials thereof.

320 See Carrington v. Rash, 380 U.S. 89, 96 (1965).

321 *Id.* at 95-96.

violative of equal protection under the tests laid down in *Oyama* and *Carrington*.

Fairness would seem to require that statutes like those suggested should place the burden of proof on the state to show that obtaining welfare was the sole reason for entering the state. So structured and administered in good faith, such a statute should avoid the harmful aspects of residence tests while still safeguarding the public purse insofar as is constitutionally permissible.

Worries that such a statute might be unfairly administered so as to discriminate against newcomers raise a legislative rather than a constitutional question. The courts must assume bona fide application of statutes until the contrary is shown. Then, it can be enjoined. Also the defect of improper administration is inherent in residence tests themselves.

6. Are the Arguably Valid Purposes Really Valid?

It is by no means clear that a state may deny assistance to, or reduce the level of assistance for, newcomers whose sole or primary reason for migrating was to obtain higher welfare benefits. The rationales of *Edwards* and of the state citizenship and equal protection provisions of the fourteenth amendment seem to require that a state treat all of its citizens equally, regardless of length of residence or intent in entering the state. Furthermore, denial of assistance would contravene the freedom of movement analysis made earlier, concluding that a state providing higher assistance benefits than the newcomer's former home state is required to provide at least the equivalent of the benefits for which he was eligible there.

It might be argued that when a newcomer arrives, having moved solely to obtain higher assistance payments, his "bad purpose" eliminates any need to worry about equal protection and freedom of movement in regard to him. On the other hand, the newcomer desiring higher benefits only has the purpose of becoming a citizen of a state with more humane social welfare policies. This motive seems little different from that of persons who are attracted to a state because it has better public universities, provides more aid per grade school pupil, has finer public recreation facilities, or furnishes superior services in any other area of public programs. Certainly the alleged "bad purpose" is not so evil that it should result in penalizing interstate movement and denying equal protection. Nor would the fourteenth amendment's state citizenship provision seem to allow examination of the newcomer's purpose in becoming a resident.

To this argument it might be replied that the state certainly can seek to ascertain if the newcomer is a bona fide resident, and that persons migrating solely to obtain higher assistance payments do not have an intention to remain indefinitely, the requisite intention for becoming residents. They will leave if such payments are reduced or another state provides a more generous program. But the same may be true of persons attracted to a state by any other state program. Additionally, it can be argued that a state may not make eligibility for assistance depend on residence, since the guarantee of the equal protection clause is not limited to state citizens, but extends to all persons subject to the state's jurisdiction.

It is uncertain whether a state may refuse to extend assistance eligibility to nonresidents and to those who became residents with the purpose of obtaining higher welfare payments. It is submitted that the rule more consistent with the nature of the Federal Union, the language of *Edwards*, freedom of movement, and equal protection, is that a state may not so limit assistance. In any event, the arguably valid state purposes underlying such limitations may be pursued by measures less restrictive than residence tests, which therefore clearly are invalid.

Moreover, aside from constitutional requirements, the realities of welfare administration probably make it desirable for a state not to confine assistance to those becoming residents with a purpose other than that of obtaining higher assistance benefits. Investigating residence and motives for becoming residents will require the expenditure of time and money which might be better spent in providing services to the needy. When state administrators are applying state standards and are under pressure to conserve state resources, even the best system of presumptions designed to protect newcomers may be insufficient to prevent frequent, unwarranted findings of a sole or primary intent to obtain higher welfare benefits or of a lack of a bona fide intent to become a resident.[322]

7. The Voting Cases

One-year residence tests for voting have been held valid in the face of attacks under the equal protection clause. *Drueding v. Devlin*,[323] decided by a three-judge federal district court in 1964, rejected an attack upon state-imposed residence requirements for voting for President and Vice-President. Maryland required one year of residence in the state and six months in the county.[324] The court found that these tests did not violate the equal protection clause of the fourteenth amendment. The judges noted (1) that many states have a one-year residence requirement and that Congress imposed such a test in implementing the twenty-

---

[322] Sparer, *supra* note 313, at 375-77.

[323] 234 F. Supp. 721 (D. Md. 1964), *aff'd per curiam*, 380 U.S. 125 (1965), discussed in Feinberg 14-16.

[324] MD. CONST. art. I, § 1.

third amendment, allowing District of Columbia voters to participate in Presidential elections;[325] (2) that steps were being taken in Maryland to reduce the residence period required to vote in such elections,[326] and (3) that the Court of Appeals of Maryland stated the purposes of the residence tests were (a) to identify the voter and protect against fraud, and (b) "to insure that the voter will 'become in fact a member of the community, and as such have a common interest in all matters pertaining to its government.' "[327] The district court holding was affirmed in a per curiam opinion by the Supreme Court.[328] The strength of this affirmance as precedent may be weakened by the fact that it was rendered at a time when it was evident that voting rights legislation would be considered by Congress,[329] and when steps were being taken in Maryland to reduce the residence period. The Court may have felt the time inappropriate for careful consideration of the equal protection challenge to these residence tests for voting. Also, a reversal of the three-judge court would have impliedly overruled *Pope v. Williams*,[330] upon which it had relied.[331] In *Pope*, a 1904 case, the Supreme Court upheld a one-year residence test for voting in state elections, against challenges based upon the equal protection clause, freedom of movement, and the definition of state citizenship in the fourteenth amendment.[332] Actually, the requirement in *Pope* was even more restrictive: New residents entering the state after a given date had to record their intention of becoming residents and were not allowed to vote until one year after the date of so recording.[333] But the *Pope* holding was based on views of the right to vote in state elections in all probability not acceptable today: "A state, so far as the Federal Constitution is concerned, might provide by its own constitution and laws that none but native-born citizens should be permitted to vote . . . ."[334] Oddly enough, the Court made this statement

---

[325] 234 F. Supp. at 725, giving no citation but apparently referring to D.C. Code § 1-1102(2) (Supp. V, 1966).

[326] 234 F. Supp. at 725: "As a result of this case the Attorney General of Maryland has recommended to the Legislative Council that the provisions in question be amended to shorten the length of residence requirements for voting for presidential electors."

[327] *Id.* at 724, quoting Shaeffer v. Gilbert, 73 Md. 66, 70, 20 Atl. 434, 435 (1890).

[328] Drueding v. Devlin, 380 U.S. 125 (1965).

[329] The Supreme Court affirmed per curiam on March 1, 1965. On March 15, 1965, President Johnson addressed a joint session of Congress and called for voting rights legislation. He transmitted the proposed bill to Congress on March 17, 1965. Christopher, *The Constitutionality of the Voting Rights Act of 1965*, 18 Stan. L. Rev. 1, 36 (1965). However, prior to March 15, 1965, it was clear that there would be voting rights legislation considered in that session of Congress. See *id.* at 8.

[330] 193 U.S. 621 (1904), discussed in Feinberg 14-15.

[331] 234 F. Supp. at 724.

[332] 193 U.S. at 624-25.

[333] *Id.* at 622 n.1.

[334] *Id.* at 633.

after recognizing that states could not make discriminations between individuals which violated the Constitution.[335]

However, the argument that the Court, in the next case, might invalidate period of residence requirements for voting is badly weakened by dictum in a 1965 opinion joined by seven justices, in *Carrington v. Rash*: "Texas has unquestioned power to impose reasonable residence restrictions on the availability of the ballot. *Pope v. Williams*, 193 U.S. 621."[336] The present analysis must accept the likelihood that the Court will uphold short residence period requirements for voting. Then, it is important to ascertain if there are significant reasons for treating residence tests for assistance differently. In any event, it should be noted that *Pope* and *Drueding* involved relatively short residence tests, and therefore are distinguishable when longer periods are required, for voting or welfare.

The major reasons for residence tests for voting seem to be (1) to protect against fraud, and especially against an influx of alleged "residents" immediately before a close election; and (2) to ensure that voters will have had time to become aware of community problems, the qualifications of candidates, and the respective positions of political groups. The requirement that voters have cast in their lot with the community is an amalgam of both of these objectives.[337]

The major reason for residence tests for assistance programs is financial—protection of the public purse by reducing welfare costs by discouraging in-migration by the indigent, and by eliminating, for each newcomer, a period of time during which he can collect assistance.

Therefore, the rationales for residence tests for voting and assistance differ, being protection of the integrity and intelligence of the voting process as opposed to protection of the public purse and the taxpayers. The effects of such tests also differ. Residence tests for voting are unlikely to deter in-migration and freedom of interstate movement, and do not involve risk to life. Residence requirements for assistance are likely to deter interstate movement by indigents, and may cause great suffering and even loss of life. Moreover, the voting requirement affects only adults, while the assistance test may penalize children who suffer because their parent or parents changed residences, a factor over which the children have no control.

---

[335] *Id.* at 632. Since the fourteenth amendment makes all native-born and all naturalized citizens of the United States also citizens of the state in which they reside, it would obviously seem to follow that the equal protection clause would be violated by the voting discrimination suggested in the quotation appearing in the text.

[336] 380 U.S. 89, 91 (1965).

[337] Schmidhauser, *Residency Requirements for Voting and the Tensions of a Mobile Society*, 61 MICH. L. REV. 823, 828 (1963); Legislation Note, *Voting Rights—Residence Requirements for Voting in Presidential Elections*, 18 VAND. L. REV. 337 (1964).

Balancing rationales against effects—and it would seem that there is a much greater need to protect the integrity of the electoral process than to avoid the expenditure of extra welfare dollars—leaves no doubt that it is much easier to uphold residence tests in the voting context than in the welfare area.

8. The State's Common Property Argument

It may be contended that the public funds of a state are the common property of its citizens, and by analogy to McCready v. Virginia,[338] outsiders may be barred from participating in welfare programs paid for out of this common property. In McCready, the Supreme Court held that a state holds its tidelands as the common property of its people and can prohibit other states' citizens from planting oysters thereon.

Even assuming that McCready is still good law, a dubious proposition in light of Toomer v. Witsell[339] and other cases already discussed,[340] the common property argument must fall because a residence test for welfare assistance discriminates, not against another state's citizens, but against new citizens of the state imposing the test. Any attempt to argue that the period of residence would ensure that assistance recipients would have participated in providing the public revenue upon which they are drawing must be rejected. There is no relationship between living in a state for a period of time and paying taxes sufficient to cover the cost of subsequent welfare aid. Some newcomers might pay huge taxes in a short time, and subsequently require little or no assistance. Others might reside for the required period without paying any taxes, and then receive welfare payments for the rest of their lives.

Also, the McCready type of situation is distinguishable from that involving residence tests for welfare, which may be essential to maintenance of life itself.

The common property argument, like the other attempted justifications previously considered, is insufficient to overcome the fourteenth amendment's definition of state citizenship and guarantee of equal protection of the laws.

F. Conclusion Regarding Residence Tests for General Assistance

Residence tests for general assistance should be held unconstitutional under either a freedom of movement or an equal protection analysis. Since several grounds exist for finding that there is a constitutionally

---

[338] 94 U.S. 391 (1876). See also Patsone v. Pennsylvania, 232 U.S. 138 (1914) (Holmes, J.); Geer v. Connecticut, 161 U.S. 519, 529 (1896).

[339] 334 U.S. 385 (1948).

[340] See supra subsection I, D, 3, a, for the discussion of Toomer, and subsections I, D, 1, e, I, D, 3, a for discussion of other cases undermining McCready.

protected freedom of interstate movement, the Court may eventually rely, not upon any discrete constitutional clause, but upon a general right to travel with roots in several provisions. An analogous development has been that of the right of privacy, or at least of marital privacy, as was evidenced by *Griswold v. Connecticut*.[341]

If neither the infringement of freedom to move interstate nor denial of equal protection is held to be sufficient to invalidate residence tests for general assistance, the cumulative impact of such tests on these two vital constitutional safeguards should provide an adequate basis for such a holding.

II

THE CONSTITUTIONALITY OF RESIDENCE TESTS FOR CATEGORICAL ASSISTANCE PROGRAMS

For categorical assistance programs under the Social Security Act, Congress allows limited residence requirements in state plans qualifying for federal financial participation. In regard to Old-Age Assistance,[342] Aid to the Blind,[343] Aid to the Permanently and Totally Disabled,[344] and programs combining them,[345] the Secretary of Health, Education and Welfare "shall not approve" any state plan with a residence requirement excluding "any resident of the State who has resided therein five years during the nine years immediately preceding the application for [the aid] . . . and has resided therein continuously for one year immediately preceding the application." For Aid to Needy Families with Children,[346] a state may not deny

> aid with respect to any child residing in the State (1) who has resided in the State for one year immediately preceding the application for such aid, or (2) who was born within one year immediately preceding the application, if the parent or other relative with whom the child is living has resided in the State for one year immediately preceding the birth.

These federal standards define the permissible maximum exclusions. A state may have less restrictive residence tests and still qualify for federal financial participation.

Qualifying state plans for Medical Assistance to the Aged, under Title I of the Social Security Act[347] or under Title XVI[348] (where it may

---

[341] 381 U.S. 479 (1965).

[342] 49 Stat. 620 (1935), as amended, 42 U.S.C. § 302(b)(2) (1964).

[343] 49 Stat. 645 (1935), as amended, 42 U.S.C. § 1202(b)(1) (1964).

[344] 64 Stat. 555 (1950), as amended, 42 U.S.C. § 1352(b)(1) (1964).

[345] 76 Stat. 198 (1962), as amended, 42 U.S.C. § 1382(b)(2) (1964).

[346] 49 Stat. 627 (1935), as amended, 42 U.S.C. § 602(b)(2) (1964).

[347] 49 Stat. 620 (1935), as amended, 42 U.S.C. § 302(b)(2) (1964).

[348] 76 Stat. 198 (1962), as amended, 42 U.S.C. § 1382(b)(2) (1964).

be combined with other categorical assistance programs), and qualifying plans for Medical Assistance under Title XIX,[349] must not incorporate any residence test other than a requirement of residence in the state.

This allowing of residence tests by Congress would seem to be unconstitutional only if the tests violate (1) a freedom of interstate movement protected against congressional action, or (2) an equal protection of the federal laws guarantee read into the due process clause of the fifth amendment. These residence requirements also may be invalid as products of an unconstitutional delegation of legislative power to the states by Congress. This argument seems to be merely another way of stating the federal equal protection contention. Moreover, state statutes meeting federal requirements can be held invalid as violating a freedom of interstate movement or as infringing the equal protection clause of the fourteenth amendment, according to the arguments already given in regard to state public assistance programs, with the exception of the commerce clause analysis. Congress cannot empower a state to violate the Constitution, but it can, under the commerce power, authorize state action which would otherwise violate the commerce clause. Of course, such authorization is effective only if the relevant federal statute is constitutional.

A. Infringement of a Freedom of Interstate Movement Protected Against Federal Action

Residence tests for categorical assistance infringe a freedom of movement within the United States which is protected against federal action by the due process clause of the fifth amendment—unless there is a sufficient justification for this interference with personal liberty.

The existence of such a freedom of interstate movement was recognized by a federal district court in 1943, in *Ebel v. Drum*.[350] In that case, the court invalidated an order excluding an alleged pro-Nazi from "military areas comprising a large portion of the United States,"[351] but stated that an exclusion order supported by military necessity would be valid,[352] where the degree of restriction was reasonably related to the degree of danger.[353] Judge Ford stated:

> Congress . . . with its knowledge of the limitations of governmental war power . . . did not—nor could it constitutionally—authorize the imposition of such drastic restrictions as are here involved upon the right guaranteed our citizens under the Fifth Amendment to be free

---

[349] 79 Stat. 349, 42 U.S.C. § 1396a(b)(3) (Supp. I, 1965).
[350] 52 F. Supp. 189 (D. Mass. 1943); see Feinberg 24 n.100.
[351] 52 F. Supp. at 190.
[352] *Id.* at 195.
[353] *Id.* at 196.

from physical restraint in moving freely from state to state . . . unless the exercise of the war power was reasonable and necessary at the time and place of its application.[354]

The judge then held that the evidence did not warrant a finding that "a real and present danger to our military resources" existed to support the exclusion order.[355]

The Supreme Court at least hinted at a freedom of movement—or more precisely a right to remain, an element of such a freedom—in *Korematsu v. United States*,[356] where the Court in an opinion by Justice Black declared that "nothing short of apprehension by the proper military authorities of the gravest imminent danger to the public safety can constitutionally justify" exclusion from the area in which one's home is located.[357] Justice Murphy's dissent[358] was more explicit. Finding that the exclusion order violated the equal protection clause, he stated: "It further deprives these individuals of their constitutional rights to live and work where they will, to establish a home where they choose and to move about freely."[359]

Since *Kent v. Dulles*,[360] in 1958, there can be no doubt that a majority of the Supreme Court has recognized the existence of a freedom of interstate movement protected under the due process clause of the fifth amendment. The holding in *Kent* was an interpretation of congressional intent regarding the Secretary of State's discretion in issuing passports. However, the opinion of Justice Douglas, for a majority of five, clearly recognized a freedom of movement operative in regard to travel within the United States as well as travel to foreign countries:

> The right to travel is a part of the "liberty" of which the citizen cannot be deprived without due process of law under the Fifth Amendment. . . . Freedom of movement across frontiers in either direction, and inside frontiers as well, was a part of our heritage. Travel abroad, like travel within the country, may be necessary for a livelihood. It may be as close to the heart of the individual as the choice of what he eats, or wears, or reads. Freedom of movement is basic in our scheme of values.[361]

The quotation of this passage with approval in Justice Goldberg's opinion

---

354 *Ibid.*

355 *Ibid.*

356 323 U.S. 214 (1944).

357 *Id.* at 218.

358 *Id.* at 233. Justice Murphy again referred to freedom of interstate movement in his concurring opinion in *Ex parte* Endo, 323 U.S. 283, 308 (1944).

359 *Id.* at 235.

360 357 U.S. 116, 125-27 (1958) (5-4 decision); see Feinberg 23-24.

361 357 U.S. at 125-26, quoted in Feinberg 23-24.

for the Court in *Aptheker v. Secretary of State*[362] in 1964 shows the continued viability of this freedom of movement, although *Aptheker* was another case dealing with travel abroad.

Aptheker held violative of the fifth amendment a federal statute which in effect "prohibits travel anywhere in the world outside the Western Hemisphere by members of any 'Communist organization,' "[363] since the statutory infringements of the right to travel exceeded those necessitated by the national security. The Court stressed that less restrictive tools were available to Congress,[364] but clearly recognized the power of Congress to inhibit freedom of movement when necessary to national security.[365]

As recently as May 3, 1965, the Supreme Court, in *Zemel v. Rusk*,[366] reaffirmed its view that freedom of interstate and international movement is part of the liberty protected by the fifth amendment against being taken without due process.[367]

> However, the fact that a liberty cannot be inhibited without due process of law does not mean that it can under no circumstances be inhibited.
> The requirements of due process are a function not only of the extent of the governmental restriction imposed, but also of the extent of the necessity for the restriction.[368]

Justice Warren, for the majority, found grave necessities justifying restriction of travel to Cuba: (1) hindering the spreading of subversion from "the only area in the Western Hemisphere controlled by a Communist government";[369] and (2) avoiding involvement by the United States in dangerous international incidents that might arise from improper imprisonment of United States citizens in Cuba and the statutory duty[370] of the President to " 'use such means, not amounting to acts of war, as he may think necessary and proper' to secure" their release.[371] Warren then acknowledged circumstances in which freedom of inter-

---

362 378 U.S. 500, 505-06 (1964) (6-3 decision, with Black and Douglas, JJ., each concurring in a separate opinion). Justice Goldberg omitted one small portion of the language quoted in the text. Justice Black would hold the entire act, of which the statute here is a part, invalid on several grounds. 378 U.S. at 518-19. Justice Douglas's separate opinion underscored the importance of freedom of movement. *Aptheker* is discussed in Feinberg 24.

363 378 U.S. at 507.

364 *Id.* at 512-14.

365 *Id.* at 509.

366 381 U.S. 1 (1965).

367 *Id.* at 14-15.

368 *Id.* at 14.

369 *Ibid.*

370 REV. STAT. § 2001 (1875), 22 U.S.C. § 1732 (1964).

371 381 U.S. at 15.

state movement could be infringed without violating due process: "[T]hat freedom does not mean that areas ravaged by flood, fire or pestilence cannot be quarantined when it can be demonstrated that unlimited travel to the area would directly and materially interfere with the safety and welfare of the area or the Nation as a whole."[372] The stringency of the necessity required is shown by the next two sentences. "So it is with international travel. That the restriction which is challenged in this case is supported by the weightiest considerations of national security is perhaps best pointed up by recalling that the Cuban missile crisis of October 1962 preceded the filing of appellant's complaint by less than two months."[373]

Residence tests for categorical assistance hinder and penalize interstate migration, thereby infringing freedom of interstate movement, in the same way that residence tests for general assistance do.[374] Since freedom of interstate movement may be abridged by Congress for sufficiently compelling reasons, it is imperative to consider what congressional purposes could underlie the permissive residence test provisions for categorical assistance. Perhaps Congress wished to allow a state to deter needy persons from migrating there in order to receive categorical assistance benefits.[375] This purpose should not include a desire to bar the uprooted from categorical assistance; instead it should be limited to protection of the state's treasury. In a federal nation, programs largely federally financed should not be designed to exclude recent interstate migrants. As will be discussed shortly, such a discrimination is unreasonable and therefore violative of the equal protection guarantee inherent in the due process clause of the fifth amendment.[376] Since the purpose should be only to protect state treasuries, Congress could use a means less restrictive of freedom of movement—federal payment of the entire costs of categorical assistance for newcomers. Therefore, the categorical assistance residence test provisions suffer from the same deficiency as the statute in *Aptheker*: an inhibition of freedom of movement which exceeds that necessitated by permissible congressional objectives.

Moreover, the desire to protect state funds against an influx of the indigent would also seem to be an improper basis for limiting freedom of interstate movement, in light of the majority opinion in *Edwards v. California*.[377] Since health quarantines may be a justification for infringing

---

[372] *Id.* at 15-16.
[373] *Id.* at 16.
[374] See *supra* subsection I, *D*.
[375] *But see supra* note 179.
[376] See *infra* subsection II, *B*.
[377] 314 U.S. 160, 173 (1941).

freedom of movement, it is important to note that in *Edwards* the Court rejected the view of the poor as a "moral pestilence."[378]

Any argument that Congress may have intended its allowance of residence tests to bar newcomers from categorical assistance until (1) they have been in a state long enough to contribute to its economy and hence to the tax base from which the state's share of such assistance is drawn, or (2) they have exhausted the possibilities of aid from private charity, ignores the fact that residence tests are unrelated to either goal. If Congress intended to discourage interstate movement, its purpose was invalid.

The importance of freedom of movement in the hierarchy of constitutionally protected rights is shown by Justice Goldberg's citation, in *Aptheker*,[379] of first amendment cases[380] to support the Court's examination of the statute on its face, "since freedom of travel is a constitutional liberty closely related to rights of free speech and association."[381] Concurring in *Aptheker*, Justice Douglas wrote:

> We noted in *Kent v. Dulles* . . . that "freedom of movement," both internally and abroad, is "deeply engrained" in our history. I would not suppose that a Communist, any more than an indigent, could be barred from traveling interstate. . . . If, as I think, the right to move freely from State to State is a privilege and immunity of national citizenship (see *Edwards v. California*, 314 U.S. 160, 178), none can be barred from exercising it, though anyone who uses it as an occasion to commit a crime can of course be punished. But the right remains sacrosanct, only illegal conduct being punishable.[382]

Douglas then details the importance of freedom of movement and severely restricts the power to interfere with it:

> Freedom of movement, at home and abroad, is important for job and business opportunities—for cultural, political, and social activities—for all the commingling which gregarious man enjoys. . . .
>
> Freedom of movement is kin to the right of assembly and to the right of association. . . .
>
> War may be the occasion for serious curtailment of liberty. Absent war, I see no way to keep a citizen from traveling within or without the country, unless there is power to detain him. . . . This freedom of movement is the very essence of our free society, setting us apart.[383]

---

[378] *Id.* at 177.

[379] 378 U.S. at 516-17. Justice Douglas, concurring, agreed that freedom of movement was closely related to first amendment rights. *Id.* at 520. The dissenting opinion of Justice Clark attacked this use of first amendment cases. *Id.* at 523.

[380] NAACP v. Button, 371 U.S. 415 (1963); Thornhill v. Alabama, 310 U.S. 88 (1940).

[381] 378 U.S. at 517.

[382] *Id.* at 519.

[383] *Id.* at 519-20.

It is submitted that there is no reason of sufficient importance to justify congressional sanction of residence tests for categorical assistance. Such tests are an unconstitutional infringement of interstate freedom of movement.

B. Denial of the Equal Protection Guarantee Incorporated in the Due Process Clause of the Fifth Amendment

1. The Scope of the Guarantee

Since *Bolling v. Sharpe*,[384] there has been no doubt that the due process clause of the fifth amendment includes an equal protection guarantee applicable to federal action. While *Bolling* involved racially segregated schools, the Court has held that this equal protection requirement also bars an unreasonable classification not based on race. In *Schneider v. Rusk*,[385] the majority invalidated a portion of the Immigration and Nationality Act of 1952 which removed the citizenship of a naturalized citizen "having a continuous residence for three years in the territory of a foreign state of which he was formerly a national or in which the place of his birth is situated,"[386] unless he resided there while employed by the United States.

> This statute proceeds on the impermissible assumption that naturalized citizens as a class are less reliable and bear less allegiance to this country than do the native born. This is an assumption that is impossible for us to make. Moreover, while the Fifth Amendment contains no equal protection clause, it does forbid discrimination that is "so unjustifiable as to be violative of due process." *Bolling v. Sharpe*, 347 U.S. 497, 499.[387]

The dissenting opinion[388] of Justice Clark, joined by Justices Harlan and White, did not contest the majority's reading into the due process clause of the fifth amendment an equal protection guarantee against unjustifiable discrimination. The dissenters merely contended that the classification in this case satisfied the test of being "reasonably devised to meet a demonstrated need."[389]

A view of fifth amendment equal protection, broader than a bar on

---

[384] 347 U.S. 497 (1954); *accord*, Colorado Anti-Discrimination Comm'n v. Continental Air Lines, 372 U.S. 714, 721 (1963) (dictum) (a federal statute requiring that job applicants be turned away because of race would violate the due process clause of the fifth amendment).

[385] 377 U.S. 163 (1964) (5-3 decision); see Naden, Equal Protection and Federal Incorporation of State Standards in Federal Legislation: A Tough Proposition 4-5, 1965 (unpublished paper prepared for the Welfare Law Seminar taught at New York University School of Law, Fall 1965).

[386] 66 Stat. 269 (1952), 8 U.S.C. § 1484 (1964).

[387] 377 U.S. at 168.

[388] *Id.* at 169.

[389] *Id.* at 176-77.

racial discrimination, is also evident from two other dissents. The dissenting opinion of Black, Warren, and Douglas in *Pennsylvania R.R. v. Day*,[390] argued that the Railway Labor Act,[391] as construed to allow the railroad, but not the employees, an adjudication of wage claims before a judge and jury, after an initial determination at an administrative hearing, "denies employees equal protection of the law in violation of the Due Process Clause of the Fifth Amendment."[392] Furthermore, Black indicated in his dissent in *Griswold v. Connecticut*,[393] that

> *Bolling v. Sharpe* . . . merely recognized what had been the understanding from the beginning of the country, an understanding shared by many of the draftsmen of the Fourteenth Amendment, that the whole Bill of Rights, including the Due Process Clause of the Fifth Amendment, was a guarantee that all persons would receive equal treatment under the law.[394]

It is apparent that the Court does not regard the equal protection aspect of fifth amendment due process as limited to barring racial discrimination. This conclusion is buttressed by the diverse instances in which lower federal courts have cited *Bolling* in considering whether or not federal action denied the equal protection guaranteed by the fifth amendment.[395]

---

[390] 360 U.S. 548, 554 (1959).

[391] 44 Stat. 577 (1926), as amended, 45 U.S.C. § 151-63 (1964).

[392] 360 U.S. at 554.

[393] 381 U.S. 479, 507 (1965).

[394] *Id.* at 517 n.10. However, Justice Black's view of *Bolling* may have been tempered by the context in which it was expressed; he was attempting to refute a citation of that case as supporting what Black read as an argument "that judges have power to use a natural law due process formula to strike down all state laws which they think are unwise, dangerous, or irrational." *Ibid.*

[395] These situations, other than racial discrimination, include the following: (1) a special Selective Service category for doctors, Bertelson v. Cooney, 213 F.2d 275 (5th Cir. 1954) (upheld as reasonable); (2) construction of a statute resulting in "differentiation tax-wise between partnerships organized in states adhering to the common law, non-entity, view and partnerships organized in states following the civil law, entity view," Stagg, Mather & Hough v. Descartes, 244 F.2d 578, 582 (1st Cir. 1957) (this construction rejected); (3) discrimination regarding National Labor Relations Board action between cases involving chain restaurants and those of hotel chain restaurants similarly involved with interstate commerce, NLRB v. Gene Compton's Corp., 262 F.2d 653 (9th Cir. 1959) (no evidence of such discrimination found); (4) "exempting industrial gas [gas sold by a pipeline company to a distributing company for resale for industrial purposes only] from the Federal Power Commission's power to suspend rates and . . . from the discretionary power of the Commission to require security from the supplier to make reparations in cases where new rates are set aside by the Commission as unreasonable after the period of suspension has expired," where these exemptions did not apply to nonindustrial gas, Pacific Natural Gas Co. v. FPC, 276 F.2d 350, 353-54 (9th Cir. 1960) (upheld as reasonable); (5) electoral apportionment favoring one regional class of a territory's voters over another, Dyer v. Kazuhisa Abe, 138 F. Supp. 220, 227 (D. Hawaii 1956) (held: violation of fifth amendment due process; alternative holding: denial of equal protection, which was guaranteed by the Organic Act of Hawaii,

Of special interest to the present inquiry are cases in which federal courts have discussed discriminations involving indigents. In *Henderson v. United States*,[396] a federal district court held that where no funds were available to pay for a free transcript, although a federal statute[397] provided for furnishing one, for an indigent appealing a federal criminal conviction, the judgment and sentence must be vacated. Citing *Bolling*, the judge stated, "While the states are prohibited by the Equal Protection Clause of the Fourteenth Amendment from effectively discriminating against indigent petitioners in collateral proceedings, the same prohibition is imposed in federal proceedings by the Due Process Clause of the Fifth Amendment."[398]

In *Hyser v. Reed*,[399] two judges of the District of Columbia Circuit, concurring in part and dissenting in part, construed a statute[400] to avoid the fifth amendment due process problems entailed by a reading not allowing the appointment of counsel to represent indigent parolees at parole revocation hearings.

> The Supreme Court has repeatedly held that in criminal trials, discrimination "on account of poverty" is as unjustifiable as discrimination "on account of religion, race, or color," because it "bears no rational relationship to a defendant's guilt or innocence." . . . Poverty bears no more relationship to the question of parole violation than to the question of guilt. Therefore congressional discrimination against parolees who cannot afford counsel would raise serious problems of due process of law. To avoid such problems we should construe the statute to provide for the appointment of counsel for such parolees.[401]

In *Fulwood v. Clemmer*,[402] another concurrence in the District of

---

31 Stat. 141, as amended); (6) different treatment, under a nonretroactive statute, regarding inheritance of illegitimate children resulting from adultery who were born before a certain date, Marquez v. Aviles, 252 F.2d 715 (1st Cir. 1958) (held: not unreasonable to enact statute which was not retroactive); and (7) different treatment regarding punishment and control "of persons over and those under twenty-two years of age" convicted of a misdemeanor, Cunningham v. United States, 256 F.2d 467, 472 (5th Cir. 1958) (upheld different treatment of youthful offenders as reasonable).

396 231 F. Supp. 177 (N.D. Cal. 1964); see Naden, *op. cit. supra* note 385, at 5-6.

397 28 U.S.C. § 753(f) (1964).

398 231 F. Supp. at 178.

399 318 F.2d 225 (D.C. Cir. 1963).

400 18 U.S.C. § 4207 (1964).

401 318 F.2d at 255 (Bazelon, C.J., and Edgerton, J., concurring in part and dissenting in part). The majority, Judge Washington concurring, and Judges Fahy and Wright concurring in part and dissenting in part, did not believe appointment of counsel was necessary, but regarded the question as solely one of procedural due process. *Id.* at 238-39, 247-48, 260, 262. Judge Wright also declared in a separate opinion that he "would have a probation officer appointed to assist in [the parolee's] . . . defense if he denies the charges and is not represented by counsel." *Id.* at 262.

402 295 F.2d 171 (D.C. Cir. 1961).

Columbia Circuit stated in dictum that, because of the equal protection requirement incorporated in fifth amendment due process, "it may follow that a federal court's refusal to file the non-frivolous petition of an indigent in circumstances in which a non-indigent might file would deny a constitutional right."[403]

2. Denial of Equal Protection by Residence Tests for Welfare Assistance

There are two reasons why federally sanctioned residence tests for welfare assistance may violate the equal protection of the laws guaranteed by the due process clause of the fifth amendment: (1) They are an unreasonable classification between new residents and other citizens of a state, and, generally, between recent migrants and more settled persons throughout the country, and (2) they discriminate unreasonably among new residents of different states.

(a) *An Unreasonable Classification Between New Residents and Other Citizens of a State.*—Supporting the first proposition is the argument already stated in regard to state-imposed residence tests and the equal protection clause of the fourteenth amendment.

Possibly a classification must be more unreasonable to violate the equal protection guarantee of the fifth amendment due process clause than that of the fourteenth amendment. In *Bolling*, the Court stated:

> The Fifth Amendment . . . does not contain an equal protection clause as does the Fourteenth Amendment . . . . But the concepts of equal protection and due process, both stemming from our American ideal of fairness, are not mutually exclusive. The "equal protection of the laws" is a more explicit safeguard of prohibited unfairness than "due process of law," and, therefore, we do not imply that the two are always interchangeable phrases. But, as this Court has recognized, discrimination may be so unjustifiable as to be violative of due process.[404]

But the Court continued:

> Although the Court has not assumed to define "liberty" with any great precision, that term is not confined to mere freedom from bodily restraint. Liberty under law extends to the full range of conduct which the individual is free to pursue, and it cannot be restricted except for a proper governmental objective. Segregation in public education is not reasonably related to any proper governmental objective, and thus it imposes on Negro children of the District of Columbia a burden that constitutes an arbitrary deprivation of their liberty in violation of the Due Process Clause.[405]

---

403 *Id.* at 174 (Edgerton, J.).
404 347 U.S. at 499.
405 *Id.* at 499-500.

In short, the fifth amendment bars classifications "not reasonably related to any proper governmental objective." This test seems to be a twin of that employed under the equal protection clause of the fourteenth amendment.[406]

Therefore, the better view of the due process clause of the fifth amendment is that its equal protection facet, applying to the federal government, is identical with that of the fourteenth amendment, applying to the states. As the Court said in *Bolling*, speaking of the fourteenth amendment's prohibition against "maintaining racially segregated public schools, it would be unthinkable that the same Constitution would impose a lesser duty on the Federal Government,"[407] in regard to equal protection of the laws.

(b) *An Unreasonable Discrimination Among New Residents of Different States.*—Arguably, assistance residence tests discriminate unreasonably among new residents of different states because it is unreasonable for Congress to allow states to have varying residence tests for eligibility under a program involving a substantial federal financial participation. It is hard to see how such permissiveness can be reasonably related to any proper objective of the federal government.

The objective of protecting states, or allowing states to protect themselves, against a heavy influx of indigents is improper under the rationale of *Edwards v. California*.[408] The most valid congressional motivations would be (1) a desire to allow states freedom to choose their own residence tests, (2) an unwillingness to require a state to pay its portion of the cost of assistance to a newcomer until he has lived there long enough to show a bona fide intention to become a resident, and (3) an unwillingness to require a state to pay its portion of the cost of assistance to a newcomer who migrated solely or primarily in order to obtain higher categorical assistance payments than those for which he was eligible in his former state. The first aim, while it can be supported by references to the federal nature of the Union and to the traditionally state-level and county-level character of settlement concepts,[409] founders in the face of the unconstitutional nature of state-imposed residence tests and the increasingly national character of the country, with its growing, mobile population. The second motivation, similarly, is invalid because it contradicts the definition of state citizenship in the fourteenth amendment. The third objective could be achieved, without affecting freedom of move-

---

406 See *supra* subsection I, *E*.

407 347 U.S. at 500.

408 314 U.S. 160 (1941).

409 Mandelker, *The Settlement Requirement in General Assistance*, 1955 WASH. U.L.Q. 355, 366-68.

ment or denying equal protection, by requiring that the benefits available under categorical assistance programs in all states be equivalent in purchasing power, or by having the federal government pay the entire increment in benefits, or even the entire benefits, of persons shown to have migrated with such a motive. Residence tests are much too broad, in terms of the classes they affect, just to achieve the second and third objectives.

Supporters of the limited state options for residence tests in categorical assistance programs may rely upon Supreme Court decisions, under the equal protection clause of the fourteenth amendment, upholding state legislation applying different rules in different parts of the state.

In *Salsburg v. Maryland*,[410] the Court held that the equal protection clause was not violated by a state statute permitting the admission, in one county, of evidence obtained by unlawful search and seizure, although the statute barred evidence so obtained, in similar gambling prosecutions in other counties. While the precise holding was rendered moot by *Mapp v. Ohio*,[411] language in *Salsburg* seems to support the validity of discrimination between people living in different territories of the state. The Court stated:

> There seems to be no doubt that Maryland could validly grant home rule to each of its 23 counties and to the City of Baltimore to determine this rule of evidence by local option. It is equally clear, although less usual, that a state legislature may itself determine such an issue for each of its local subdivisions, having in mind the needs and desires of each. Territorial uniformity is not a constitutional requisite.[412]

The Court held that "the Equal Protection Clause relates to equality between persons as such rather than between areas."[413]

However, *Salsburg* and the cases upon which it relies are all distinguishable as involving procedural matters.[414] And in *Salsburg*, the Court

---

410 346 U.S. 545 (1954) (7-1 decision; Douglas, J., dissented on the grounds which would command a majority in Mapp v. Ohio, 367 U.S. 643 (1961)).

411 367 U.S. 643 (1961).

412 346 U.S. at 552.

413 *Id.* at 551, where the Court said this proposition was established in Missouri v. Lewis, 101 U.S. 22 (1879), which stated that (1) equal protection "means that no person or class of persons shall be denied the same protection of the laws which is enjoyed by other persons or other classes in the same place and under like circumstances," *id.* at 31, and (2) "there is nothing in the Constitution to prevent any State from adopting any system of laws or judicature it sees fit for all or any part of its territory," *ibid.*

414 As already noted in the text, *Salsburg* involved the admission of evidence. Ocampo v. United States, 234 U.S. 91 (1914), challenged a denial of a right to a preliminary examination in criminal cases to inhabitants of part of the Philippine Islands, *id.* at 98, and relied mainly upon Missouri v. Lewis, *supra* note 413, as authority. *Id.* at 98-99. Missouri v. Lewis, also relied upon in *Salsburg*, see *supra* note 413, upheld a statute requiring that appeals from part of the state go to a separate appellate court rather than to the state's supreme court.

spoke of "the liberal legislative license allowed a state in prescribing rules of practice"[415] and recognized that "a state has especially wide discretion in prescribing practice relating to its police power, as is the case here."[416]

Of more assistance to advocates of territorial diversity in regard to substantive law is *McGowan v. Maryland*,[417] decided by the Court in 1961. The majority held valid under the equal protection clause Maryland's Sunday Laws, although they permitted certain retailers in one county to sell specified merchandise on Sunday while forbidding retailers in other Maryland counties to do so.[418] The justices stated:

> [W]e have held that the Equal Protection Clause relates to equality between persons as such, rather than between areas and that territorial uniformity is not a constitutional prerequisite. With particular reference to the State of Maryland, we have noted that the prescription of different substantive offenses in different counties is generally a matter for legislative discretion. We find no invidious discrimination here. See *Salsburg v. Maryland, supra.*[419]

While the Court's reliance upon *Salsburg* may be criticized,[420] *McGowan* stands as Supreme Court authority supporting territorial discrimination within a state in regard to substantive law. Therefore, it is necessary to see if that case is distinguishable in significant respects from

---

101 U.S. at 29-32. Appeals from the separate appellate court to the state supreme court were allowed only in certain cases. *Id.* at 29. The other cases *Ocampo* cited as authority, 234 U.S. at 99, are also distinguishable as procedural cases: Hayes v. Missouri, 120 U.S. 68, 72 (1887) (criminal case; different number of peremptory challenges to jurors in capital cases in cities having a population over 100,000); Chappell Chem. Co. v. Sulphur Mines Co. (No. 3), 172 U.S. 474 (1899) (civil case; trial by jury abridged in part of state); Mallett v. North Carolina, 181 U.S. 589, 598 (1901) (criminal case; state allowed an appeal from Superior Court for the Eastern District of the state and not from such court for Western District).

415 346 U.S. at 550.

416 *Ibid.*

417 366 U.S. 420 (1961).

418 *Id.* at 427.

419 *Ibid.*

420 The second sentence of the quotation is an unfair use of *Salsburg,* bacause therein at the pages referred to, 346 U.S. at 552-53 (see 366 U.S. at 426, the *"supra"* referred to in the quotation), the text notes that Maryland has prescribed "different substantive offenses in different counties," 346 U.S. at 552, and then states that such "variations" are "a matter for legislative discretion, not judicial supervision, except where there is a clear conflict with constitutional limitations," *id.* at 552-53. Besides this circular statement, the only basis for *McGowan's* citation is a footnote which lists some statutes discriminating territorially, but the list follows this statement, "without appraising their validity, but as illustrating Maryland practice, we find Flack's Md. Ann. Code, 1951, full of such examples." *Id.* at 552 n.8. Therefore, the main prop for the words of the *McGowan* majority about territorial discrimination in substantive law is flimsy. The same defect appears in the separate opinion of Frankfurter and Harlan, 366 U.S. 459, which relies on *Salsburg* and *Missouri v. Lewis* as authority for its conclusion "that the provision of different Sunday regulations for different regions of a State is not *ipso facto* arbitrary," *id.* at 537.

the categorical assistance situation. The latter, unlike *McGowan*, involves: (1) a program which in many cases will be vital to life itself, or at least to a life with the basic necessities available; (2) a benefit granted by government rather than a police power regulation; and (3) differentiation by the federal government between people in different states, rather than by a state between people in its different parts. If the equal protection guarantees under the fifth and fourteenth amendments have similar metes and bounds, the third distinction is not important. The benefit-granting nature of assistance is significant; when the federal government uses general tax revenues to meet a national problem involving need on the part of many citizens, the needy in all states should be treated alike. Certainly the federal participation would be a sufficient ground to justify congressional action banning residence tests for categorical assistance. Similarly, it is an adequate basis for the courts to compel the same result. The vital-to-life argument is still more compelling. A suit challenging residence tests for categorical assistance would be an apt place for the court to quote the following language from the majority opinion of the Fourth Circuit in *Simkins v. Moses H. Cone Memorial Hospital:*[421]

> We deal here with the appropriation of millions of dollars of public monies pursuant to comprehensive governmental plans. But we emphasize that this is not merely a controversy over a sum of money. Viewed from the plaintiffs' standpoint it is an effort by a group of citizens to escape the consequences of discrimination in a concern touching health and life itself.

The comprehensive plan plus the vital need for the assistance should require uniformity of treatment.

Moreover, reliance upon the Court's language in *McGowan* should be tempered by a realization that the fact situation before the justices was one where "local option" made a lot of sense. For example, manufacturing towns may well have different needs, regarding a weekly day of rest, than resort areas. No similarly strong justification for diversity between states exists in regard to the life-sustaining, largely federally-funded categorical assistance programs.

But even if *McGowan* leads to a refusal to find a violation of fifth amendment due process because of diverse treatment of newcomers residing in different states, the due process clause of that amendment is still violated because Congress sanctions discrimination by the states against newcomers, as has already been argued.

C. Conclusion Regarding Residence Tests for Categorical Assistance

The conclusion seems unmistakable that residence tests for categorical assistance violate the Constitution in several ways: (1) they infringe a

---

[421] 323 F.2d 959, 967 (4th Cir. 1963) (3-2 decision), *cert. denied*, 376 U.S. 938 (1964).

freedom of movement constitutionally protected against federal action; (2) they contravene the equal protection guarantee incorporated in the due process clause of the fifth amendment; and (3) in exercising the option provided by Congress, the states infringe (a) a freedom of movement constitutionally protected against state action and (b) the equal protection clause of the fourteenth amendment, in the same manner as when states impose residence tests for general assistance. Moreover, even if none of these arguments alone is sufficient to establish the invalidity of residence tests for categorical assistance, their cumulative impact on several constitutional protections makes clear the unconstitutionality of those tests.

While the command of the Constitution seems clear, perhaps the most politic way to dispose of residence tests for categorical assistance would be for Congress to forbid them but provide for federal payment of all costs of such assistance to persons who have not resided in the state for one year.[422] Indeed, the reasoning of *Edwards*, that the states are all part of a federal union and "must sink or swim together,"[423] would indicate that the ultimate solution for the problems purported to be dealt with by residence tests should be federal legislation either (1) making all assistance programs federal programs totally funded from the national revenue, or (2) shifting the present tax structure to increase the tax revenue of the states. Under the present arrangement, acceptance of the conclusions reached in this paper regarding freedom of movement and equal protection, may impose severe burdens upon certain states. However, the tax structure is not decisive in examining constitutional guarantees, and *Edwards* rejected the economic contentions that would be made in arguing that residence tests for general and categorical assistance are constitutional. Hopefully, the federal union rationale which has been accepted by the Supreme Court will also find favor with Congress, and fair provisions will be made to alleviate unusual burdens borne by those states which attract large numbers of new residents.

---

[422] See Nathanson 22-27 (including a discussion of legislation which has been introduced into Congress at various times); Hohlt 12-13; Mandelker, *The Settlement Requirement in Public Assistance*, 1956 WASH. U.L.Q. 21, 49-50.

[423] Edwards v. California, 314 U.S. 160, 170 (1941), quoting Justice Cardozo in Baldwin v. Seelig, 294 U.S. 511, 523 (1935).

Public Housing and the Poor: An Overview†

Lawrence M. Friedman*

PUBLIC HOUSING became a reality in the United States only in the days of the New Deal. There were some gingerly steps toward public housing during the First World War, and a few more in the states in the Twenties, but a serious, living program had to wait for the days of the great depression.[1] The major piece of federal legislation on housing was the Wagner-Steagall Act of 1937[2] which, despite a gloss of amendments, remains on the statute books today, hardly altered in its basic design. On September 1, 1937, President Roosevelt signed the bill[3] which was to begin a "new era in the economic and social life of America."[4] Hopes ran high in the early years of the program. The wall of resistance to federally supported housing had been breached. A "real start" would be made "at last" toward "wiping out . . . city slums."[5] The states passed enabling legislation, local housing authorities were formed, and the flow of cash into public housing began in earnest. "In city after city," wrote Nathan Straus in 1939, "the sound of the wrecker's hammer is heard, sites are being cleared, the excavators are at work, and the superstructures are going up . . . . [By] next summer . . . five thousand families will be moving from the slums into new and decent homes."[6] In the years since then, public housing has become a familiar aspect of the urban landscape. By the end of 1965 every state had some public housing units in planning or operation,[7] and

---

† Some of the material on which this paper is based was gathered in the course of interviews. Some individuals who were interviewed would prefer not to be quoted directly. Some of the information supplied must be treated as confidential. Consequently, supporting authorities for some statements have been omitted.

* B.A., 1948, J.D., 1951, LL.M., 1953, University of Chicago. Professor of Law, University of Wisconsin Law School.

[1] On the forerunners of the Wagner-Steagall Act, see FISHER, TWENTY YEARS OF PUBLIC HOUSING (1959); a good short account is Riesenfeld & Eastlund, *Public Aid to Housing and Land Redevelopment*, 34 MINN. L. REV. 610 (1950). On the Wagner-Steagall Act itself, see McDONNELL, THE WAGNER HOUSING ACT: A CASE STUDY OF THE LEGISLATIVE PROCESS (1957).

[2] 50 Stat. 888 (1937), as amended, 42 U.S.C. §§ 1401-30 (1964), as amended, 42 U.S.C. §§ 1402-21b (Supp. I, 1965).

[3] N.Y. Times, Sept. 3, 1937, p. 1, col. 3.

[4] Letter from Franklin D. Roosevelt to Nathan Straus, Administrator of the United States Housing Authority, March 17, 1938, quoted in STRAUS & WEGG, HOUSING COMES OF AGE 189 (1938).

[5] N.Y. Times, Sept. 3, 1937, p. 16, col. 3.

[6] Straus, *Housing—A National Achievement*, Atlantic Monthly, Feb. 1939, pp. 204, 210.

[7] As of the end of 1963, Utah, Wyoming, and Iowa had no units of public housing. HOUSING AND HOME FINANCE AGENCY, ANNUAL REPORT 306 n.1 (1963). Iowa since has passed enabling legislation. IOWA CODE ANN. § 403A (Supp. 1964). At the end of 1964, every state had one or more local public housing authorities, except Oklahoma and this state had two

more than 2,100,000 people lived in low-rent public housing.[8] In New York City more than half a million people lived in public housing units built with the aid of federal, state, or city money.[9] The overwhelming majority of these units were products of the federal program. New York City had more public housing than any other city; but every major city and a host of minor ones ran more or less substantial programs of their own.[10] As of October 1964, 26,175 people lived in public housing in Detroit, Michigan; Duluth, Minnesota, at the end of 1964, operated three hundred units divided into three separate projects.[11] Whatever else these figures signified, they meant that vast tracts of slum wasteland had been cleared and that millions of people over the last thirty years had been rehoused in units which met at least minimum sanitary and spatial standards.

But to judge by some newspaper and magazine accounts—and even by the words of housing experts—the public housing program had betrayed its fond expectations. In 1937 Catherine Bauer, a highly respected expert on housing, praised the Wagner-Steagall Act as "progressive legislation"—a hopeful first step toward the goal of good housing for all.[12] Twenty years later, in 1957, Miss Bauer returned to the subject in an article in *Architectural Forum*. The title was significant: "The Dreary Deadlock of Public Housing."[13] She found little to praise in the program as it had evolved. Rather, she saw rigidity and paternalism in management, crudity and segregation in project design, and a deplorable fragmentation of over-all housing policy. In the following issue of the magazine, eleven housing experts commented on her article and made suggestions for change.[14] Not one of the eleven disagreed with her general thesis: that the public housing movement was stagnant; that politically the program was at a standstill; that existing projects were badly conceived and perhaps did more harm than good; and that the whole program

---

projects federally owned and operated. HOUSING AND HOME FINANCE AGENCY, ANNUAL REPORT 235, 239, Tables IV-1, IV-3 (1964).

[8] *Id.* at 235.

[9] New York City Housing Authority, Project Statistics 26, Dec. 31, 1964.

[10] Every city of more than one million population ran a public housing authority aided housing program, and 89% (42 out of 47) of the cities of more than a quarter million and less than a million. Sixty-three per cent of the cities with more than fifty thousand and less than two hundred fifty thousand had programs. HOUSING AND HOME FINANCE AGENCY, ANNUAL REPORT 240 (1964).

[11] Information supplied by the respective housing authorities.

[12] *Now, at Last: Housing*, New Republic, Sept. 8, 1937, pp. 119, 121.

[13] Bauer, *The Dreary Deadlock of Public Housing*, Architectural Forum, May 1957, p. 140.

[14] *The Dreary Deadlock of Public Housing—How to Break It*, Architectural Forum, June 1957, p. 139.

needed radical reformation. This was the twentieth anniversary of the Wagner-Steagall Act.

It was a bad time for the image of public housing. Harrison Salisbury, Russian correspondent for the *New York Times*, came home to write his reactions to the domestic scene. What he saw in New York's housing projects profoundly shocked him—for example, the "stench of stale urine that pervades the elevators" in Fort Greene Houses, Brooklyn.[15] He had other things to report about the "new ghettos," as he called them. They were "human cesspools worse than those of yesterday."[16] Fort Greene and similar projects were "monsters, devouring their residents, polluting the areas about them, spewing out a social excrescence which infects the whole of our society."[17] The slums themselves had rarely felt such a tongue-lashing.

Salisbury's conclusions were published in book form and widely read. They were by no means the last such attack on public housing. Readers of the *Chicago Daily News*, in April 1965, were invited to share a sense of wrath and dismay toward public housing. A sensational series of articles excoriated the Robert R. Taylor homes, Chicago's "$70 Million Ghetto." Taylor was the "world's biggest and most jam-packed housing development," an "all-Negro city within a city," a "civic monument to misery, bungling and a hellish way of life," a " 'death trap,' a concentration camp." Its tenants—who sometimes called their home "the Congo Hilton" —lived in misery, "grappling with violence and vandalism, fear and suspicion, teen-age terror and adult chaos, rage, resentment, official regimenting."[18] In the same year, a tenant of the Syracuse Housing Authority described her home as "nothing but a prison camp." In Syracuse, under the impetus of the war against poverty, the Negro poor organized to do battle with those they identified as their oppressors. Prominent among these oppressors were officials of the local housing authority. To judge by the outcry, public housing in Syracuse was also worse than the slums.[19]

Public housing does not totally lack defenders, but they have spoken softly of late. It is hard to think of any prominent housing figure outside of government who defends the program as it is. Politically, the program has little appeal. Appropriations for additional units have been grudgingly voted in Congress; time and time again requests have been scaled down. What is perhaps more significant, authorizations have often gone begging

---

[15] SALISBURY, THE SHOOK-UP GENERATION 74 (1958).

[16] *Id.* at 75.

[17] *Id.* at 77.

[18] Chicago Daily News, April 10, 1965, p. 1, col. 1.

[19] The tenant quotes are from The Tenants Report, Public Housing: Syracuse Style, This Is the Way It Is, 1965. Materials on the Syracuse movement were supplied to me by Professor Warren C. Haggstrom of Syracuse University.

because local government agencies have not been interested in applying for federal grants—authorized units have "washed away."[20] This is perhaps the darkest symptom of all: A program must be genuinely unpopular if free federal money is spurned. The unpopularity of public housing need not be left to oblique inference. In scores of cities and small towns, public housing has been put to the test by the voters. Where it is legally possible, opponents have demanded referenda on the question. In a distressing number of cases, bond issues to finance the program have failed or public housing has been voted out of town.[21]

Where does the trouble lie? Is it in the conception, the shape of the public housing program? Is it in its mode of administration? Perhaps the problems lie in both. The indictment is clear: Public housing, ostensibly designed to clear the slums and to alleviate the sufferings of the poor, has failed to do either. We turn now to the facts.

I

THE PUBLIC HOUSING PROGRAM: CONCEPTION AND DESIGN

The public housing law is one of a vaguely defined group of statutes called "social" or "welfare" legislation.

It would be a mistake to suppose (if anyone did) that the Wagner-Steagall Act[22] arose solely out of a gradual persuasion of decent-minded people that the slums were odious, crowded, and evil, and that the federal government had a duty to relieve the sufferings of the poor. The social and economic conditions in the slums provided the opportunity, the background, and much of the emotive power of the law. Yet reformers had long dreamed in vain of public housing. And the slums were surely no worse than they had been in the nineteenth century, though possibly they were larger.

In 1937 the country was suffering from a deep and dangerous depression. Fully one-quarter of the work force was unemployed during the worst days of the depression. In the spring of 1933, thirteen to fifteen million were unemployed.[23] Millions of families were barely making a living. The number of "poor people" in the country had been vastly increased; indeed, many of the "poor people" were formerly members of the middle class, who had enjoyed prosperity in the twenties. They retained their middle-class culture and their outlook, their articulateness, their

---

[20] Seligman, *The Enduring Slums*, in THE EXPLODING METROPOLIS 92, 105 (1958).

[21] *E.g.*, in elections in April and June 1961, Rapid City, South Dakota, and Marin County, California, turned down low-rent proposals. 18 J. OF HOUSING 289 (1961).

[22] 50 Stat. 888 (1937), as amended, 42 U.S.C. §§ 1401-30 (1964), as amended, 42 U.S.C. §§ 1402-21b (Supp. I, 1965).

[23] BROWN, PUBLIC RELIEF 1929-1939, at 65 (1940).

habit of expressing their desires at the polls. There were, therefore, millions of candidates for public housing who did not belong (as later was true) to the class of the "problem poor"; rather they were members of what we might call the submerged middle class. The attractiveness of public housing was enormously enhanced because the potential clientele was itself enormous, composed of millions of relatively articulate citizens, angry and dispirited at their unjust descent into poverty. Public housing was not supported by the dregs of society; a discontented army of men and women of high demands and high expectations stood ready to insist on decent housing from government or at least stood ready to approve and defend it. The political climate was receptive to federal planning and federal housing—not so much as a matter of radical ideology, but out of a demand for positive programs to eliminate the "undeserved" privations of the unaccustomed poor.

Moreover, business was stagnant in the thirties. Programs of social welfare and relief were tested by their ability to create new jobs and prime the business pump as much as by their inherent welfare virtues. Public works programs were exceedingly popular for this reason.[24] A vast federal program of house building naturally received the enthusiastic support of manufacturers of building supplies and workers in the building trades. The normal opposition to "socialized" housing made its appearance in debate,[25] but it was weak and somewhat muted. Nonetheless, business support for the act was conditioned upon the act being so structured as to avoid any actual government competition with business. Homes would be built only for those who could not possibly afford to buy them on their own. A clear wall must separate the public and the private sector. This too was only partly ideological. Government, it was felt, should not cut into the markets of private industry; it must stimulate fresh demand and make fresh jobs—otherwise the effect of the program on the economy would be wasted.

During the depression, the volume of private housing construction was very low. In 1925, 900,000 housing units were constructed; in 1934, only 60,000.[26] Yet in one sense no housing shortage developed. During much of the depression, plenty of apartments stood vacant.[27] People who were poor doubled up with relatives, lived in "Hoovervilles" and shanties, returned to rural areas, and in general failed to consume the housing supply. Rents were extremely low. The high vacancy rate posed a potential danger for

---

24 MITCHELL, DEPRESSION DECADE 314-38 (1947).

25 E.g., 81 CONG. REC. 8079 (1937) (remarks of Senator Walsh).

26 BROOKINGS INSTITUTION, THE RECOVERY PROBLEM IN THE UNITED STATES 183-84 (1936).

27 Id. at 184-85.

the program. If public construction increased the housing supply during a period in which many dwellings stood vacant, rents would decrease still more and vacancies would increase. In a decade willing to kill baby pigs and impose acreage controls on farmers, one could hardly expect to see government flooding the housing market with new units. And in fact, the Wagner-Steagall Act was careful to avoid the problem of over-supply. No units were to be built without destroying "dwellings . . . substantially equal in number to the number of newly constructed dwellings provided by the project."[28] This provision—the so-called "equivalent elimination" provision[29]—killed two birds with one stone. It neutralized potential opposition from landlords and the housing industry by removing the danger of over-supply; at the same time, by making slum clearance a part of the law, it appealed to those whose desire for public housing stemmed from their loathing of the slums and slum conditions. The Wagner-Steagall Act was thus shaped by the force of concrete social conditions; what emerged was a program geared to the needs of the submerged middle class, tied to slum clearance, and purged of any element of possible competition with business.[30]

Constitutional difficulties played a part in determining one of the most notable features of the program—its decentralization. From 1933 on, the Public Works Administration had run its own public housing program.[31] In 1935 a federal district court case held that the federal government had no power under the constitution to clear land and build public housing. It was not proper, said the court, for the federal government "to construct buildings in a state for the purpose of selling or leasing them to private citizens for occupancy as homes."[32] The federal government never appealed this decision. In 1935 the government's prospect of sympathetic treatment by the United States Supreme Court seemed bleak; attempting to overturn the adverse housing decision might risk the whole program of public works. On the other hand, no important legal barriers stood in the

---

28 50 Stat. 891 (1937), as amended, 42 U.S.C. § 1410(a) (1964), as amended, 42 U.S.C. § 1410(a) (Supp. I, 1965).

29 Robinson & Altman, *Equivalent Elimination Agreements in Public Housing Projects*, 22 B.U.L. REV. 375, 376 (1942).

30 The 1949 act, to make the point crystal clear, provided that no annual contribution contract be entered into unless the local agency demonstrates "that a gap of at least 20 per centum . . . has been left between the upper rental limits for admission to the proposed low-rent housing and the lowest rents at which private enterprise unaided by public subsidy is providing . . . decent . . . housing." 63 Stat. 422 (1949), as amended, 42 U.S.C. § 1415 (7)(b)(ii) (1964).

31 FISHER, TWENTY YEARS OF PUBLIC HOUSING 82-89 (1959).

32 United States v. Certain Lands, 9 F. Supp. 137, 141 (W.D. Ky.), *aff'd*, 78 F.2d 684 (6th Cir.), *dismissed*, 294 U.S. 735 (1935), 297 U.S. 726 (1936). See also United States v. Certain Lands, 12 F. Supp. 345 (E.D. Mich. 1935).

way of a decentralized program. Washington could supply money and a certain amount of benign control; title to property and the motive force in condemnation could remain vested in local public agencies. A key New York state decision strengthened this view, distinguishing the federal cases as inapplicable to state power.[33] Moreover, decentralization was politically attractive to those who dreaded further expansion of the "federal octopus."

Financial considerations had an important impact on the design of the housing law. If the federal government had made outright grants to local authorities to build houses, immense amounts of money would have been immediately required. Under the act, however, local authorities were invited to borrow money through bond issues; with the proceeds, they were to acquire sites, clear them, and put up houses. The federal government would enter into "contracts" with local housing authorities, under which the federal government would agree to make annual contributions for a long period of time. The federal government would pay (in essence) enough money for the interest on the bonds and the amortization of the principal. Operating expenses for the housing projects would come out of current rents. In this way, federal contributions would be kept relatively small; housing could be built on the installment plan, and paid for over a period of fifty or sixty years.[34]

Note, too, that the tenants were only partially subsidized. They were not given "free" housing. Each tenant had to pay his rent. Project rents had to be sufficient to pay operating costs—maintenance, administration, and payments in lieu of taxes to local government for fire and police protection and other municipal services.[35] Though the federal act was discreetly silent on the subject, the rent requirement meant that the unemployed and the paupers were not welcome in public housing. They could not pay the rent, any more than in private housing. There are "some people," said Senator Wagner, "who we cannot possibly reach; I mean those who have no means to pay the rent. . . . [O]bviously this bill cannot provide housing for those who cannot pay the rent minus the subsidy allowed."[36] The projects were for poor but honest workers—the members of the submerged middle class, biding their time until the day when they regained their rightful income level. The tenants were not to receive any "charity." The difference between a dole and a subsidy is psychologically powerful, whether or not the distinction is good economics. The working

---

[33] New York Housing Authority v. Muller, 270 N.Y. 333, 1 N.E.2d 152 (1936).

[34] 50 Stat. 892 (1937), as amended, 42 U.S.C. §§ 1410(b), (c) (1964), as amended, 42 U.S.C. § 1410(c) (Supp. I, 1965).

[35] The so-called "in-lieu" payments. See 63 Stat. 428 (1949), as amended, 42 U.S.C. § 1410(h) (1964), as amended, 42 U.S.C. § 1410(h) (Supp. I, 1965).

[36] 81 CONG. REC. 8099 (Aug. 3, 1937).

class residents of public housing were not to receive a gift from the government, but their rightful due as citizens. Public housing, arguably, was no more "charitable" than the free land of the homestead act of 1862 —an earlier form of middle-class subsidy. Decent, sanitary apartments were a stepping-stone to a fee simple cottage—the American dream. Perhaps a radical fringe of housing reformers looked on public housing as something more fundamentally "public"; but the core of support lay in an old and conservative tradition.

If this general analysis is correct, what would happen to public housing if a rising standard of living released the submerged middle class from dependence on government shelter? Public housing would be inherited by the permanent poor. The empty rooms would pass to those who had at first been disdained—the unemployed, "problem" families, those from broken homes. The program could adapt only with difficulty to its new conditions, because it had been originally designed for a different clientele. To suit the programs to the needs of the new tenant would require fresh legislation; and yet change would be difficult to enact and to implement precisely because the new clientele would be so poor, so powerless, so inarticulate. The political attractiveness of public housing would diminish. Maladaptations to reality in the program would disenchant housing reformers; they would declare the program a failure and abandon it to search out fresh cures for bad housing and slums.

All this is precisely what has happened, as a brief sketch of the history of public housing since 1937 will illustrate. The first public housing projects were, in general, low-rise rowhouses; they blended in fairly well with their surroundings. Some of them, outside the major cities, were "suburban" in location and design. The residents were members of the submerged middle class, and the projects were literally stepping-stones to middle-class life and a home of one's own. We may take as an archetype of the stepping-stone project Middletown Gardens, in Delaware County, Indiana—a "112-unit low-rent housing community built on an 80-acre outlying tract: 15 acres in houses, 33 in gardens, 7 a recreation grove, 4 a ball field, 21 untouched timber."[37] Here, according to a report in 1944, one-quarter of the families were able to save enough money to buy their own homes.[38] Of course, rising incomes helped. But only the submerged middle class partook of the benefits of rising incomes.

The outbreak of war interrupted the progress of public housing. Housing construction had to be suspended during the emergency, except where it served some wartime purpose. As early as June 1940, when the

---

[37] 1 J. of Housing 47 (1944).
[38] 2 J. of Housing 9 (1945).

war was still a distant thunder, Congress passed a defense housing act,[39] which provided for construction of units for workers. Under this act, contracts with local housing authorities could be revised and low-income units diverted to defense housing. The Wagner-Steagall Act was then only three years old. Moreover, when victory was in sight, the emphasis in construction changed from defense to veterans' housing. Construction of veterans' housing began in earnest at the end of the war.[40] During the war, conditions underlying the housing market were fundamentally altered. No longer was there a housing surplus, together with a surplus of the honorable poor. Private building completely halted during the war; defense factories soaked up all the employables and put high wages in peoples' pockets. The result was a stupendous housing shortage—the supply of housing remained constant while the demand multiplied inordinately. This demand would have driven rents to fabulous levels, except for stringent national controls on rents and evictions.

The end of the war was traumatic in one regard: It threatened to bring to a close a period of prosperity—prosperity which was doubly welcome because of the long depression it replaced. No one wanted war, but no one wanted poverty either. Clearly, a high level of construction was one guarantee against depression; and government had to be prepared to give subsidies, prime pumps, and do whatever was politically necessary to keep construction healthy and high. The beneficiaries of the new housing programs were the veterans and the middle class generally. Prosperity meant an end of concentrated political demand for minimum housing built in the city for the submerged middle class. The major need now was for veterans' houses, individually owned and detached from those of their neighbors. This was the only new program appealing both to homeowners and builders. To keep land costs down, any such mass development had to be outside of town. Thus began the suburban housing boom, financed by vast infusions of public money. The money was paid, however, in the form of subsidy, aid to private enterprise, mortgage insurance, and tax breaks. It was never "charity." Moreover, a little public money went a very long way. Meanwhile, old-style public housing languished.

---

[39] 54 Stat. 681 (1940), as amended, 42 U.S.C. §§ 1501-05 (1964). Later in the same year the Lanham Act was passed making further provisions for defense housing. 54 Stat. 681 (1940), as amended, 42 U.S.C. §§ 1521-23, 1541-50 (1964).

[40] An Act of June 23, 1945, amended the Lanham Act to authorize the Housing Administrator to use his powers to "provide housing for distressed families of servicemen and for veterans and their families." 59 Stat. 260 (1945), as amended, 42 U.S.C. §§ 1571-73 (1964). A Joint Resolution of December 31, 1945, appropriated $160,000,000 to be used for these purposes. 59 Stat. 674 (1945), as amended, 42 U.S.C. § 1572 (1964). In 1946 a "Veterans' Emergency Housing Act" was passed. Act of May 22, 1946, ch. 268, 60 Stat. 207. See also Robinson & Robinson, *State Spending for Veterans' Housing*, 1949 Wis. L. Rev. 10 (1949).

Worse than that: Public housing was now boxed in, in the core of the cities. Outlying sites, on the fringes of the metropolitan areas, where land was raw and cheap, were no longer available; this land was *de facto* reserved for veterans' subdivisions. Public housing was losing its best sites —and its best clientele. The submerged middle class moved out as fast as it reasonably could. Indeed, those who would have liked to stay were not given the option; they were simply thrown out. After the war, comfortable tenants who enjoyed their subsidized homes frequently wanted to continue where they were. But the most they could achieve was a measure of delay. Their struggle against eviction from public housing had to be abandoned.[41] Pressure built up to force people to give up subsidized apartments and buy subsidized homes instead. The economy (it was thought) depended on the health of the suburban building boom; the nation could not afford to let people with good incomes go on living with New Deal subsidies. The sharp, bitter struggle over evictions was not a struggle of rich against poor. It was a struggle between middle-class veterans and defense workers, on the one hand, and business interests on the other. The scale tipped in favor of business presumably because of the strong general interest in a healthy level of construction. The dispossessed veterans were (in part) paid off by subsidized mortgages and a whole host of government programs which eased the journey to the suburbs.[42] Public housing, meanwhile, was relegated to the permanent poor in the city, and to the new urban immigrants. In the big cities, these were chiefly Negroes from the South.[43] The compromise of the late 1940's and early 1950's meant reinforcement of the notion that public housing was exclusively for those who were certainly, indisputably, and irreversibly poor.[44]

But this development meant that the political strength of public housing had eroded and would continue to erode. The new tenants were precisely those who had the least power in our society, the least potent voice in the councils of city hall. The middle-class masses, moreover, were spending their sweat and treasure in a wild flight from the slums and their residents. Now that they had attained the status of suburban property owners, they had no intention of giving up their property values and their hard-won status by allowing their former neighbors (and even less de-

---

[41] See *FPHA Opens Drive for Removal of High-Income Families*, 4 J. OF HOUSING 143 (1947); 7 J. OF HOUSING 27 (1950).

[42] See generally BEYER, HOUSING: A FACTUAL ANALYSIS 126-28, 237-46 (1958).

[43] On the postwar movement of Negroes, see generally TAEUBER & TAEUBER, NEGROES IN CITIES (1965).

[44] It was in 1949 that federal law first insisted that public housing agencies not "discriminate against families . . . [whose] incomes are derived in whole or in part from public assistance . . . ." 63 Stat. 422 (1949), as amended, 42 U.S.C. § 1415 (1964), as amended, 42 U.S.C. § 1415 (Supp. I, 1965).

sirable people) to move in. The slums were not to follow them into the suburbs. Race and income prejudice was by no means confined to the suburbs. It flourished in the city, too, particularly in the little enclaves of frame houses that formed ethnically homogeneous, proud, and self-contained neighborhoods. These sub-cities would also resist public housing in their midst. Public housing no longer meant homes for less fortunate friends and neighbors, but rather, intrusions of "foreigners," the problem poor and those least welcome "forbidden neighbors," the lower class Negro. Public housing not only lost its political appeal but what was left of the program was confined to the core of the city. Public housing remained tied to slum clearance and rebuilding out of necessity. The suburbs and the middle-class areas of the city had shut their doors. Vacant land could not be used for sites unless the land happened to lie in skid row or a Negro neighborhood.[45]

Land in the core of the city was far more expensive than the raw land of the suburbs. City land had to be bought, cleared of commercial and residential properties, and then redeveloped. Labor and material costs were high and kept rising. So did the buildings. The cost squeeze meant the end of low-rise, "home-style" housing projects. The buildings turned into towers—six-story, ten-story, then nineteen, twenty or more in New York and Chicago.[46] Costs and the enmity of the outside world squeezed the buildings into the heart of the slums. The ratio of Negroes to whites increased radically.[47] The whites streamed out. By the early 1950's, project managers had to learn to cope with "problem" families. The texture of life in the projects changed for the worse; since more delinquent families lived in them, they were the locus for more and more delinquency. The attention of the public was now directed to public housing not as a hopeful program of reform but as the site of public folly and private decay—vandalism, crime, and unrest. The sordid facts of life in public housing merely reinforced the passionate resistance of the rest of the city to public housing projects. Who wanted such places in their neighborhood? It was a vicious circle. And when the intellectual community looked out of its own windows and saw the projects in the distance—drab, ugly blocks of cement standing like soldiers—when they observed that public housing built ghettos for Negroes and the despondent classes, they, too, called for

---

[45] See the now classic study of Chicago's site location problems, MEYERSON & BANFIELD, POLITICS, PLANNING AND THE PUBLIC INTEREST (1955).

[46] For a description of the beginnings of this process, see Riley, *Cost Reductions Pioneered in New York Public Housing*, 5 J. OF HOUSING 105, 106 (1948).

[47] By the end of June 1963, almost 96% of the occupants of public housing in Washington were Negro. WEAVER, THE URBAN COMPLEX 251 (1964). Since 1955 Negroes have been in the majority in St. Louis' public housing. Information supplied by the St. Louis Housing Authority.

a halt. Right and left wings, oddly enough, agreed that the program had outlived its utility; both called for a curtailment of fresh building.[48] Some have even urged the abandonment of existing projects, and Charles Abrams has called it a fiction that "public housing must be owned by the city forever,"[49] a fiction which, if lived by, would result in public housing becoming the "concentrated retreats" of the "saddest and bitterest assemblage of mortals ever permitted a foothold on earth."[50]

Ironically, the same forces that have crippled public housing have made possible the one bright exception to the "dreary deadlock": housing for the elderly. In many cities today the *only* public housing being built is housing for the elderly. The Wagner-Steagall Act of 1937 said nothing about old people; but in the last decade, the law has increasingly favored the elderly. The trend began modestly enough in 1956, when, for the first time, public housing was opened up to unmarried people (not members of a "family") who were sixty-five years of age or more.[51] In the 1960's much more positive inducements have been offered. The 1961 act offered a subsidy of up to 120 dollars per unit occupied by "senior citizens," where such assistance was necessary to operate these units in the black.[52] In this regard, federal law has merely mirrored local opinion. Milwaukee, for example—a city notoriously hostile to public housing—has eagerly embraced housing for the elderly.[53] In Chicago, 5,661 units were under construction as of June 30, 1964; 4,345 of these were reserved for the elderly.[54] And Marin County, California, three years after defeating a public housing proposal, voted overwhelmingly to support a proposed 200-unit development for the elderly.[55] In 1964, 52.6 per cent of the new units placed under contract "were to be designed specifically for the elderly."[56]

---

[48] It is no surprise that a conservative like Milton Friedman would favor a cash subsidy to poor people over the erection of public housing. FRIEDMAN, CAPITALISM AND FREEDOM 178 (1962). This proposal has points in common with the proposals for rent certificates or subsidies which are now so much in favor with housing "liberals," and specifically in that the plans contemplate abandonment of the program of building high-rise "projects." For a discussion of income subsidies, see WENDT, HOUSING POLICY—THE SEARCH FOR SOLUTIONS 217-25 (1963); *The Dreary Deadlock of Public Housing—How to Break It*, Architectural Forum, June 1957, p. 139.

[49] ABRAMS, THE CITY IS THE FRONTIER 37 (1965).

[50] *Id.* at 38.

[51] 70 Stat. 1104 (1956), as amended, 42 U.S.C. § 1402(2) (1964), as amended, 42 U.S.C. § 1402(2) (Supp. I, 1965).

[52] See generally Spector, *Housing for Senior Citizens*, 11 N.Y.L.F. 30 (1965).

[53] See MILWAUKEE HOUSING AUTHORITY, HOUSING ACCOMMODATIONS OF ELDERLY PERSONS IN THE CITY OF MILWAUKEE (1958).

[54] Chicago Housing Authority, Fact Sheets, Table 3, June 30, 1964.

[55] 21 J. OF HOUSING 513 (1964).

[56] HOUSING AND HOME FINANCE AGENCY, ANNUAL REPORT 235 (1964).

It is easy to see why housing for the elderly is succeeding where public housing in general has failed. Housing for the elderly taps the only remaining reservoir of poor people who are also white, orderly, and middle-class in behavior. Neighborhoods which will not tolerate a ten-story tower packed with Negro mothers on AFDC might tolerate a tower of sweet but impoverished old folks. Old people are never vandals; they do not whore and carouse. Many of them are honest working-class people caught in a trap set by low retirement incomes, small pensions, inadequate savings, and high medical bills. Furthermore, housing for the elderly helps solve a problem all too common for middle-class people—what to do with aged, dependent parents. Subsidized housing for the grandparents is a solution to many people's troubles. Moreover, the old people are more likely than the problem poor to be grateful, docile, and unseen.[57]

II

ADMINISTRATION OF PUBLIC HOUSING

In the preceding section of this paper, we have sketched the history of public housing and advanced the thesis that the program was designed originally for the submerged middle class. That class no longer needs or wants public housing, except in the special cases of the elderly and the handicapped. Public housing has been inherited by the dependent poor and by the low-income urban Negro, and as a result, the program has become less popular politically. This unpopularity in turn has adversely affected the design of the program. We shall now briefly look at some aspects of the administration of public housing, as it has been affected by the change in clientele, and as it affects the welfare of the post-war tenants.[58]

When public housing was conceived of as subsidized shelter for members of the submerged middle class, it did not call for modes of administration different from those which any ordinary landlord would be called upon to use. Housing was run on a business-like basis. Tenants were expected to pay their rent, and pay it promptly. The pages of the *Journal of Housing* are full of accounts of successful managers who achieved one hundred per cent rental payments—sometimes through the use of tough methods. In Buffalo, it was reported in 1945 that managers "competed"

---

[57] Similarly, special favors have been accorded in recent years to public housing for the handicapped. See, *e.g.*, 73 Stat. 667 (1959), as amended, 12 U.S.C. § 1701(q) (1964), as amended, 12 U.S.C. § 1701(q) (Supp. I, 1965).

[58] Good general assessments can be found in SCHORR, SLUMS AND SOCIAL INSECURITY 85-93 (1964); Mulvihill, *Problems in the Management of Public Housing*, 35 TEMP. L.Q. 163 (1962).

for one hundred per cent rent collections; some managers "attach the three-day [eviction] notice to the tenant's door, for public view."[59]

In the early 1950's, housing officials began giving voice to uneasiness at the change in character of their tenants. Managers and housing officials worried out loud about the large number of "problem families" moving into their buildings.[60] Mrs. Bette Jenkins of Detroit, writing in the *Journal of Housing* in 1951, thought that projects had a duty to accept problem families; but even she wondered whether there was "some danger that public housing might become labeled as a catchall for all the people who do not tend to make satisfactory personal judgments."[61] Some less tender-hearted officials began to strengthen discipline. In 1956, for example, the New York City Housing Authority announced a "get tough" policy to get rid of families that could not control delinquent children.[62] Other projects tried injecting massive doses of paternalism, in an effort to cure rather than to kill. Public housing, in the opinion of most housing officials, had to "accept family rehabilitation responsibility."[63] In Newark, Detroit, and Nashville, management tried to use social workers, tenant relations experts, or other devices to help "problem families" adjust.[64] Problem families have remained a problem. The change in the clientele of public housing has continued until the present time, except insofar as housing for the elderly alters the picture. In many cities, it is not unusual if more than a third of the tenants derive all their income from welfare checks; and in individual projects the percentage may run higher.[65] Naturally, under these circumstances public housing becomes more "institutional." Public housing is more than shelter; it also provides a place for golden-age clubs and well-baby clinics.[66] In Chicago, housing projects have their own public

---

[59] 2 J. OF HOUSING 79 (1945). See also 3 J. OF HOUSING 154 (1946) (Philadelphia); 4 J. OF HOUSING 49, 50 (1947) ("hard-boiled" tactics in Wilmington, North Carolina and in New Orleans).

[60] See, *e.g., How Much "Selection" Should There Be in Public Housing Tenant Selection? Four Answers*, 8 J. OF HOUSING 91 (1951); Aronov, *The Problem Family*, 11 J. OF HOUSING 425 (1954).

[61] Jenkins, *"Problem Families"—New Answer to Their Housing Eligibility Status*, 8 J. OF HOUSING 283 (1951).

[62] N.Y. Times, Jan. 31, 1956, p. 23, col. 5.

[63] Filker, *Public Housing Management Must Accept Family Rehabilitation Responsibility*, 13 J. OF HOUSING 168 (1956).

[64] 14 J. OF HOUSING 131 (1957) (Detroit); 15 J. OF HOUSING 13 (1958) (Newark); 12 J. OF HOUSING 188 (1955) (Nashville).

[65] In Chicago in 1964, 2,067 out of 4,345 families in the Taylor homes and 1,965 out of 3,597 Aid for Families of Dependent Children in the Cabrini-Green project received some form of government assistance. 1,736 families in Taylor were on AFDC. Chicago Housing Authority, Fact Sheets, Table 9, 1964.

[66] See, *e.g.,* Welcome to Your Home 17-18 (undated), a pamphlet of The Baltimore Urban Renewal and Housing Agency, listing "the Men's Club, the Women's Sewing Club,

assistance offices, located right on the premises, with the case load drawn exclusively from the project. Many large projects have enough young children to fill their own elementary school, which may also be located right on the grounds. Housing managers and their staff workers can easily communicate with teachers and social workers; public housing can be more highly "administered" and more paternal and institutional. The size and design of the projects, as well as the homogeneity of the tenants, encourages this response to conditions.

What has become of the administration of public housing as the type of resident has changed? What kind of rules are made and enforced? What kind of programs are carried out? In order to answer these questions, tenant selection will be briefly discussed followed by a slightly more detailed account of tenure and eviction. Consideration of these points will suggest some propositions about public housing administration that may have wider implications.

A. Tenant Selection

Tenant eligibility is determined by statute and local rule. Federal law makes relatively few demands on administration, insisting only that only poor persons be allowed in public housing. The Wagner-Steagall Act[67] limited tenancy to "families of low income" who could not "afford to pay enough to cause private enterprise in their locality . . . to build an adequate supply of decent, safe, and sanitary dwellings for their use." Income limits were part of the federal law—the Act was restricted to families "whose net income at the time of admission does not exceed five times the rental."[68] Between 1949 and 1961, the federal statute specifically stated that public housing agencies were not to "discriminate against families, otherwise eligible for admission to [public] housing, because their incomes are derived in whole or in part from public assistance."[69] Federal law also asks local agencies to adopt admission policies which "give full consideration" to their "responsibility for the rehousing of displaced families,—to the applicant's status as a serviceman or veteran," his age, disability, housing

---

the Golden Age Club, the Mothers' Club . . . classes in Home Nursing, Nutrition, or First Aid . . . Boy Scouts, Girl Scouts, Y-Teens . . . a recreation program . . . Well Baby Clinics . . . ."

[67] 50 Stat. 888 (1937), as amended, 42 U.S.C. § 1402(2) (1964), as amended, 42 U.S.C. § 1402(2) (Supp. I, 1965).

[68] 50 Stat. 888 (1937), as amended, 42 U.S.C. § 1402 (1964), as amended, 42 U.S.C. § 1402 (Supp. I, 1965). For families with three or more minor dependents, the ratio was six to one. In 1958 specific income-rent ratios were dropped from the statute, leaving the matter to the discretion of local authorities and state statutes; the federal statute still required that families be "of low income," however. 73 Stat. 680 (1959), as amended, 42 U.S.C. § 1402 (1964), as amended, 42 U.S.C. § 1402 (Supp. I, 1965).

[69] Act of July 15, 1949, § 301, 63 Stat. 422.

conditions, and urgency of housing need.[70] Other than this, federal law is silent on eligibility for public housing; and indeed, the statute offers little guidance as to the administration of projects or the termination of tenancy.[71] In the 1950's, during the palmy days of McCarthyism, the so-called "Gwinn amendment" briefly made nonmembership in subversive organizations a condition of tenancy.[72] The Gwinn amendment reminds us of the *possibility* that onerous conditions for eligibility can be written into federal law. On the other hand, the life of the Gwinn amendment was short and the reaction of courts quite hostile.[73] The experiment has not been repeated.

State laws are not much more explicit than federal law. The states have followed the federal lead in prescribing income limits. More than thirty states have the five-to-one ratio or some variant;[74] a few have a different ratio, or a flexible maximum coupled with a general requirement of poverty; a few simply delegate authority to local projects to fix rent scales.[75] Some states specifically provide for the problem of the over-income tenant; in New Jersey, for example, he may continue to occupy his quarters until his income is more than twenty-five per cent over the maximum for entry.[76] A few states add a detail here or there—by spelling out their preference for veterans, for example.[77] But in the main, tenant selection is controlled by the housing authorities themselves. Some of them have their own preference lists—giving special place or exemption from some prerequisite to veterans, to persons in desperate need of housing, or even to students.[78]

The selection process has not been carefully studied. If there were abuses, no one in government seemed to have heard of them. Within categories of preference, selection is made on a first-come-first-served basis, although screening out of "undesirables" is often practiced with the aid of social workers. If responsible officials discriminated among applicants there would be no machinery for correcting these abuses. We may be fairly

---

[70] 50 Stat. 891 (1937), as amended, 42 U.S.C. § 1410(g)(2) (1964), as amended, 42 U.S.C. § 1410(g)(2) (Supp. I, 1965).

[71] See 50 Stat. 891 (1937), as amended, 42 U.S.C. § 1410(g)(3) (1964), as amended, 42 U.S.C. § 1410(g)(3) (Supp. I, 1965).

[72] Act of July 31, 1953, § 101, 67 Stat. 307.

[73] See, *e.g.*, Lawson v. Housing Authority, 270 Wis. 269, 70 N.W.2d 605 (1955).

[74] *E.g.*, NEB. REV. STAT. 14-1422 (1962).

[75] N.Y. PUB. HOUSING § 156 (six-to-one ratio); LA. REV. STATS. § 40:478 (1960) (no specific ratio, but a general requirement of "low income" and a list of factors to be considered); MONT. REV. CODES ANN. § 35-103(18) (1961) ("low income" to be determined by local authority).

[76] N.J. STATS. ANN. § 55:14H-20 (1964).

[77] *E.g.*, NEV. REV. STAT. § 315-510.

[78] San Francisco waives a one-year residency requirement for students. San Francisco Housing Authority, Low-Rent Housing—Policy, Part I, sec. I, p. 3 (rev. Feb. 1964).

confident that "discrimination" in the usual sense does not occur. One cannot think of any reasons offhand why officials should play favorites. Applicants are too poor to offer much of a bribe. A class difference separates officials from applicants; a project manager is highly unlikely to have a cousin or sister-in-law anxious to be moved from the bottom to the top of the waiting list. This, indeed, is a general characteristic of welfare administration, as opposed to, for example, the enforcement of housing codes or the administration of regulatory programs that affect businessmen. The selection process is therefore likely to be fair, in the sense of conforming to general rules, and will remain fair in this sense even though applicants have no "rights" and no meaningful review. But though fair, selection may be blind, rule-bound, and unwilling to temper principle to the dictates of common sense. Recently complaints that filtered through legal aid services and agencies of the War on Poverty have brought some examples to light. One housing authority, for example, tried to evict two Puerto Rican brothers, seventeen and eighteen years old, after their mother died and left them orphaned, on the grounds that the authority could not enter into a lease with minors.[79] The Housing Authority of New Bern, North Carolina, adopted a rule which called for the eviction of any tenant to whom "additional illegitimate children" were born during tenancy.[80] Perhaps many additional injustices are hidden in the criteria of selection or in the manner in which screeners work and perceive their work. These injustices, however, are not easily cured. What reform calls for here is not enforcement of rules, but changes in rules. And that in turn requires political pressures upon management—a theme to which we shall return.

Race discrimination was not unknown in the early days of public housing; indeed, the Public Housing Authority deliberately encouraged segregation in some cities.[81] Race discrimination has been abandoned as policy by the PHA; race is no longer officially a criterion for eligibility[82]

---

[79] I am indebted to Edward V. Sparer, Legal Director, Center on Social Welfare Policy and Law, of Columbia University School of Social Work, for this example, drawn from a paper, *The Poor Man's Lawyer and Governmental Agencies*, delivered by Mr. Sparer to the National Conference on Law and Poverty, sponsored by the Department of Justice and the Office of Economic Opportunity, June 24, 1965, at Washington, D.C.

[80] The legality of this rule is currently being tested. I am indebted to Mr. Sparer for this example, too.

[81] *E.g.*, in San Diego, see DAVIS & MCENTIRE, RESIDENCE AND RACE 320 (1960). In fairness to PHA, it ought to be pointed out that public housing accommodations were generally available to Negroes "in accordance with need . . . in striking contrast to the discriminatory distribution of local, state and Federal funds," and that it was white prejudice that defeated many attempts by housing officials to break out of the ghetto. WEAVER, THE NEGRO GHETTO 179 (1948).

[82] For the PHA regulation, promulgated during the Kennedy administration, see 24 C.F.R. § 1500.6 (1963).

or assignment to a project. Many Southern projects are still totally segregated. For example, there are seven projects in Anniston, Alabama—three all-white and four all-Negro.[83] And there is a great deal of *de facto* segregation in public housing in the North. It is as distasteful to Negroes as *de facto* school segregation. The remedies are if anything more elusive. In many cities, a majority of public tenants are Negroes. This is true in Chicago, for example. Chicago has virtually no all-white housing projects; but it has many all-Negro projects; and in some projects the percentage of white tenants is far greater than the percentage of whites in public housing in general.[84] Spreading the few white tenants equally throughout the city would simply drive many of them out of public housing, without benefiting the Negro particularly. Yet the present pattern *is* one of *de facto* segregation. Public housing is, by and large, located in Negro areas and is inhabited by Negroes. Projects are so large in the major urban areas that a project would be impossible for a white, middle-class community to digest, if some giant hand picked it up and transported it to the urban fringe. We have seen how political and social forces have transformed public housing into Negro ghetto housing. *De facto* segregation illustrates quite the opposite point from tenant selection. Here, the granting of formal rights to Negroes to demand desegregated projects would be meaningless in many cities, not because no real abuses exist, but because the problem is so basic that only a radical solution can remedy the matter; rights are not enough.

B. Tenure and Eviction

Once a family has moved into public housing, it becomes subject to rules regarding tenure and eviction. As is true of eligibility and selection, these rules are largely local. Since federal law, state statutes, and local rules all agree that only the poor may live in public housing, a tenant is liable to lose his right to stay if his income exceeds the maximum set for the particular project.[85] In addition, however, his tenure is jeopardized if he misbehaves or breaches the terms of his lease. Misconduct may bring down upon him a variety of sanctions—fines, withholding of privileges, eviction. Eviction is the ultimate and major sanction of the authority, and the only one susceptible currently to any measurement. We shall, therefore, confine our discussion to the legal position of the tenant with regard to eviction.

---

[83] Home and Housing Finance Agency, Low Rent Project Directory, June 30, 1965, p. 38.

[84] In Chicago in 1964, whites were a tiny minority of the families in public housing (2,472 out of 29,386) ; yet in one project of 139 families, there were no Negroes at all. Figures taken from Chicago Housing Authority, Racial Occupancy as of June 30, 1964, Table 12 (undated mimeo).

[85] In practice, there is considerable administrative leeway.

The tenant has virtually no protection against eviction. His lease is rigged against him, and his tenancy is on a month-to-month basis. Leases for a year, or two years, which are common for tenants in private buildings, are unknown in public housing. Nothing in any state statute requires a short-term lease explicitly; yet there is probably no housing authority in the country which regularly grants more than a month-to-month lease to its tenants.[86] On thirty days' notice then, any public housing tenant in the country can lose his rights to his home.

Does a housing authority need a *reason* for eviction, or may it avail itself of the privilege of the short-term lease? This question has been more frequently litigated than any other issue of landlord-tenant rights in public housing, although there are few reported cases. Project managers are apt to be aware of the reported or unreported test case in their community, and what it decided. This is true in Milwaukee and Chicago.[87] In general, housing authorities have insisted that they do not need to assign any reasons for termination; they insist that they may evict at the end of the month's term by complying with the general landlord-tenant statutes— like any other landlord whose tenants hold under a month-to-month lease. The courts have usually agreed with the landlords.[88] One fairly recent New York case held the housing authority to a somewhat higher standard and was willing to hold that an eviction was not "reasonable."[89] But this holding is quite exceptional. Other cases—including several in New York[90] —have upheld the authority's view of the law. It does not much matter whether the authority's right to evict is absolute, or whether it must at least comply with its own regular procedures. In either event, the tenure of residents in public housing is as precarious as that of any slum-dweller —perhaps more so.

Evictions are probably not common in any housing project,[91] even if

---

[86] An examination of leases from more than thirty housing authorities, in big cities and little ones, and from every part of the country, confirms this.

[87] In Chicago, the case is Chicago Housing Authority v. Ivory, 341 Ill. App. 282, 93 N.E.2d 386 (1950); see 7 J. OF HOUSING 432 (1950). For reports of other cases, see 6 J. OF HOUSING 150 (1949); 11 J. OF HOUSING 278 (1954); 21 J. OF HOUSING 384 (1961).

[88] *E.g.*, Walton v. City of Phoenix, 69 Ariz. 26, 208 P.2d 309 (1949).

[89] Sanders v. Cruise, 10 Misc. 2d 533, 173 N.Y.S.2d 871 (Sup. Ct. 1958).

[90] *E.g.*, Smalls v. White Plains Housing Authority, 34 Misc. 2d 949, 230 N.Y.S.2d 106 (Sup. Ct. 1962).

[91] In Minneapolis, with 2,462 dwelling units, forty-eight families were asked to leave in the fiscal year ending September 30, 1964. Twelve of these were "community problems" (misconduct). Letter from V. E. Dale, Director of Management, Housing and Redevelopment Authority, Minneapolis, Aug. 12, 1965. Public housing in Minneapolis is predominantly white and more than one half of the units are for the elderly. But in the same period St. Louis (largely Negro, nonelderly) had only eighty-one involuntary move-outs of "undesirable tenants," out of a low-rent population of more than 25,000. St. Louis Housing Authority, Move-Out Study (undated mimeo).

we consider tenants as "evicted" if they are asked to leave and they comply without court order. The threat of eviction, however, may be a meaningful and potent sanction even if it rarely has to be carried out.[92] The reported cases suggest that some authorities are anxious to rid themselves of troublemakers. In one case, the tenant's children were a nuisance.[93] In another, a member of the family was alleged to be a dope addict.[94] In another, the head of the family was in jail.[95] There is a continued search for the submerged middle class, that lost legion whose ghost still haunts the program. And, to be sure, the safety and happiness of all may depend upon getting rid of the few. No one denies that management needs the right to protect the other tenants and the property by eliminating people who destroy the walls or the peace of their neighbors. But even the fragmentary evidence of the cases raises disquieting doubts whether management has restricted itself to clear-cut cases of gross misconduct.

There are similar doubts in regard to rule-making powers. Authorities may evict without reason; in addition, and in consequence, they have very broad powers to impose rules and regulations upon the tenants—provided only that the rules are not illegal or so scandalous as to arouse rebellion. Again, many rules and regulations are perfectly salutary and indeed necessary. But others are debatable. It would be a rare housing project, for example, which permitted dogs in high-rise buildings. Half a million people in New York City must choose between subsidy and pets. Bills are regularly introduced into the legislature to let tenants have their cats and dogs, but the housing authority has beaten back every attempt.[96] The New Orleans housing authority allowed seeing-eye dogs for blind tenants only after considerable hullabaloo.[97] Normally, management can be quite stiff-necked toward its constituency, and its view of "the good of the project" is unassailable.

---

[92] The San Francisco Housing Authority "has never had to evict for over-income or misconduct. Many thirty-day lease cancellation notices have been served for the two latter reasons, however. The families moved prior to the necessity of taking final action." Letter from Fred S. Threefoot, Manager, Rental Office, San Francisco Housing Authority, Aug. 19, 1965.

[93] Smalls v. White Plains Housing Authority, 34 Misc. 2d 949, 230 N.Y.S.2d 106 (Sup. Ct. 1962).

[94] Sanders v. Cruise, 10 Misc. 2d 533, 173 N.Y.S.2d 871 (Sup. Ct. 1958).

[95] New York City Housing Authority v. Watson, 27 Misc. 2d 618, 207 N.Y.S.2d 920 (Sup. Ct. 1960).

[96] N.Y. Times, March 25, 1964, p. 35, col. 4; see *"Man's Best Friend" Is Cause for Eviction*, 6 J. OF HOUSING 150 (1949), reporting an eviction in Stockton, California, in 1948, for ownership of a dog. In most cities, the lease or tenants' handbook specifically forbids pets. Goldfish and canaries are sometimes expressly exempted (*e.g.*, in Bayonne, New Jersey). The housing authority of Kansas City, Kansas, feels called upon specifically to outlaw chickens and ducks as well as the usual dogs and cats.

[97] I am indebted to Professor Jacobus tenBroek for this information.

C. *Control of Management Behavior*

Since management is formally free to do more or less as it wishes, what limits can be placed upon its power? Judicial review is a natural answer for a lawyer. Judicial review—indeed, administrative review—of the rule-making and rule-enforcing power of the housing authorities is virtually nonexistent. Yet one must hesitate to ask for more. There is no reason to believe that judicial review would amount to more than an insistence on elementary (and empty) form. Since the authorities have secured for themselves formal freedom to evict without reasons, there is no *formal* impediment to governance by informal rules. Nothing requires the authorities in most cities to promulgate definite regulations which the tenants must follow. Of course, most authorities do publish either formal rules or handbooks and guides which embody rules and regulations. Rules also appear in the leases, though in that form it is doubtful if they are read. The problem is not secret rules, since management is not insane: It wants its rules to be known and to be followed. The problem is what the rules say and who decides them. It is hard to believe that the courts are either willing or able to run the housing authorities. They might require the authority to comply with certain rule-making procedures, but they are not likely to care what the rules say.[98]

Nor are judges likely to be more enlightened than the average man on problems of the poor. In an eviction case, the Supreme Court of Westchester County, New York, reminded petitioner that "the [Housing] Authority is composed of public-spirited citizens serving without compensation," who acted in ways thought "necessary for the administration of the project and the welfare of all of the tenants," and thus not lightly to be altered.[99] There is an implication that the petitioning tenant was both presumptuous and ungrateful. Such an attitude holds little promise of gain for dissatisfied tenants.

How much can we expect from the tenants themselves? Tenants are "organized" in many projects, but for welfare or social purposes, not to run anything which management considers important. Activist tenant organizations may have existed and flourished to a greater degree in some of the early projects. In those days, the projects were crowded with members of the submerged middle class; and among these were people who were politically active and anxious to form tenant organizations. Indeed, Harrison Salisbury claims that bureaucratic management helped stamp out tenant organizations, because left-wing activists among the tenants

---

[98] See Handler, *Controlling Official Behavior in Welfare Administration*, this Symposium.
[99] Smalls v. White Plains Housing Authority, 34 Misc. 2d 949, 951, 230 N.Y.S.2d 106, 109 (Sup. Ct. 1962).

proved to be too much of an annoyance.[100] The passage of the Gwinn amendment suggests that there might be some substance to this charge. But in any event, the change in clientele of public housing, from the submerged middle class to the dependent poor, would in itself explain a decrease in group participation among tenants. The normal state of mind in public housing may be one of apathetic detachment.[101] And the officially approved state of mind for the dependent poor is a combination of shuffling servility and childish zest for arts and crafts.

Quite another sort of tenant organization has arisen recently. The Syracuse tenant organization can be taken as symptomatic of a latter-day unrest. This organization bitterly objects to certain of the rules imposed upon tenants by management. For example, they complain that management assesses unfair fines and penalties. Tenants have claimed that they must pay for broken windows, whether they themselves caused the breakage or not. And alongside their specific complaints goes a more general one: that they have no power or voice in the management. They demand "a voice and a vote."[102]

Is there sufficient evidence to judge whether the unrest at Syracuse arises because the housing administrators there are unusually harsh, or obtuse, or simply that the tenants are uncommonly restless? When residents of Chicago's Taylor homes call their project worse than the slums and use the nickname "Congo Hilton," are we hearing the voice of most tenants, a few tenants, or all tenants? Are we hearing a protest against a particular style of management, against management in general, or against conditions in society in general? Our lack of knowledge is itself an important point. The tremendous leeway of management has the legal and social result of plunging management practices into the deepest obscurity. This lessens the extent to which the outside community can exert its influence. And the outside community has not been interested. As far as the public has been concerned, public housing projects (like mental hospitals and prisons) are warehouses where the poor can be stored and ignored. The literature on the management of public housing is nonexistent—a literature of silence. Managers write hints to each other in the trade journals; Washington advises and consents from above. An outside appraisal has been almost totally absent. The·tremendous polemic literature over public housing has to do with the way projects look—the

---

[100] SALISBURY, THE SHOOK-UP GENERATION 81 (1958).

[101] But at least one observer has analyzed a wide variety of "types" among slum and public housing dwellers. Salzman, *Redevelopment Effectiveness Contingent on Understanding Slum Occupants*, 13 J. OF HOUSING 289 (1956).

[102] The Tenants' Report, *supra* note 19. For one study of attitudes of tenants, see Hollingshead & Regler, *Attitudes Toward Slums and Public Housing in Puerto Rico*, in THE URBAN CONDITION 229-45 (Duhl ed. 1963).

aesthetics of the projects, which means nothing or almost nothing to the residents[103]—and with the misbehavior of the tenants, not with misbehavior toward them. The recent polemic literature tends to conclude, as one writer neatly put it, that the tenants are the "same bunch of bastards"[104] they were before they moved in. It follows somehow that public housing is a failure and ought to be replaced. That the projects are misguided or mismanaged in operation rather than in conception is a possibility rarely considered. That meaningful reforms may be possible within present projects must at least be weighed as a chance before being rejected. Can society, or the tenants, control and improve public housing—as it is, not as it might be?

D. Management Styles

It is common to confuse the possibility of abuse with actual abuse. Custom, sentiment, and social forces are potent curbs on behavior even when no formal rule binds. We must be hesitant, therefore, in ascribing evils to all public housing management, even though there are few formal limits on management behavior. For one thing, there is no one style of management. The projects themselves are too different for one style of management. There are two polar types of project. One is the institutional, high-rise ghetto, largely inhabited by poor Negroes in the big city and characterized by a high number of "problem" families. Then there are communities of the submerged middle class—projects for the elderly, and low-rise, low-key projects in smaller communities or on the fringes of metropolitan areas (many of them built in the early days of public housing). Clearly, the two types call for—and must get—different styles of management.

Project managers have considerable administrative discretion. Projects are relatively autonomous administrative units. This too makes for a great deal of variation in governing public housing. A Chicago manager reports that he does not follow the policy of expelling over-income tenants. He "goes along" with his high-paid tenants for a year or even two. These are "good" tenants and he does not want to lose them. If he waits long enough,

---

[103] This point is hardly susceptible of proof, and many learned men swear to the contrary, for example, Lewis Mumford, who is sure that esthetic degradation in the modern city has vast, evil consequences: "[N]ever before in recorded history" have people "lived in such a savagely deteriorated environment, ugly in form, debased in content." It is hard to deny the indictment, which he adroitly subjoins to a catalog of the undoubted harm to health which arises out of slums. Yet many people live lives of agony in slum buildings which were once gorgeous mansions, and the rich too live often in vulgar, ugly—but comfortable—buildings. Is the poor child who grows up in Florence or Venice ahead of the child of "Coketown"? MUMFORD, THE CITY IN HISTORY 466-74 (1961).

[104] Seligman, *The Enduring Slums*, in THE EXPLODING METROPOLIS 92, 106 (1958).

the income limit at the project may be raised; or the tenant may lose his job. In any event, this manager evicts as few over-income tenants as he possibly can. The same manager regards "quarter parties" (parties at which admission is charged, usually a quarter, and drinks and sandwiches sold at a quarter apiece) as grounds for summary expulsion. Some managers in Milwaukee, on the other hand, have never heard of this practice; but they take a more stringent view of over-income tenants. Intensive study would no doubt reveal further variations. Administration variation can be enormous, even when separate administrators are governed by the same formal rules; and variation can be small even though no formal rules bind administrators. The same is true of the management of public housing. As if through some giant conspiracy, all public housing projects force their tenants to sign a month-to-month lease. The universal use of a month-to-month lease is an example of a consistency of practice which is not required by formal law. Practice in regard to over-income tenants shows variations in administration, on the other hand, though formal law seems to require uniformity. Attitudes of management toward misconduct and eviction show still another pattern. Here it is the *absence* of formal rule that permits management practices to vary.

Variations in management style are probably related to the type of project. The conscientious manager of a Negro ghetto is naturally eager to keep well-behaved tenants who set a good example; he is loathe to evict them if their income goes up. The manager of a "middle-class" project has no need for good examples; his role is to provide subsidized shelter for people who are temporarily earning less than they could and should; or for the elderly whose income does not fluctuate. Variations of this sort between types of project are understandable, and, to a large degree, justified. There may be other variations which are less justified but which remain locked away from prying eyes.

One source of difficulty is that the goals of public housing have never been agreed upon, even by those who strongly support the program—even perhaps within the minds of many housing officials or project managers. Is it the duty of public housing to provide a subsidized, sheltered home for the respectable, unfortunate poor? This is probably the predominant goal of housing for the elderly. Is it the duty of public housing to provide minimum facilities for the poor—to protect them from fire and rat bites, and incidentally, to protect the city from the spread of fire and infection? Or is it the duty of public housing to rehabilitate the dependent poor, by providing them with a total new environment and a massive infusion of social services?

These three goals are to a degree incompatible. They certainly cannot coexist in one project; they imply different rules, strategies, and modes of management. Housing for the submerged middle class can be and perhaps should be run in the same way that a major private landlord runs his apartment house. On the other hand, these projects are *not* private; they are run by government employees, and they are not subject to the discipline of a competitive market. There is no reason why "middle-class" public housing, including housing for the elderly, should not give its tenants a full battery of legal rights, long-term leases if anybody wants them, a strong tenant voice in project affairs not as a matter of administrative grace, but of right, and tenure from eviction except for cause established by reasonable rules concurred in by tenants. We might even insist that internal procedures be judicialized to a degree. It is hard to think of any legitimate prerogative or duty of administration which would be harmed by adding some procedural and substantive restraints. On the other hand, it is precisely in these projects that abuse of discretion is least likely to occur and is least likely to endanger the prerogatives of tenants.

Projects inhabited by the dependent poor present much more difficult questions. The present state of affairs is certainly not ideal. The month-to-month lease is unnecessary and ought to be eliminated. Its value lies in the broad discretion it affords to housing administrators. Administrative discretion may be a good thing under many circumstances, but only if flexibility serves some real function; there is no reason to insulate managers completely from responsibility and embarrassment through the device of a short-term lease. And no device should be neglected that might increase the stake of the poor in their homes, their communities, and in their circle of neighbors.

Do we conceive of housing projects for the dependent poor as custodial? Or do we think of them as providing an environment within which society can attempt to rework wasted lives and untie the knots of decadence? These competing goals may imply competing rules of government. A custodial project may be as hard and orderly as a prison; but it might also be run on easy-going permissive terms. To create a total environment, however, a certain amount of discipline is essential—discipline to prevent tenants from living in terror, discipline to create a climate of order which is a prerequisite for rehabilitation. Those who wish to reform public housing—particularly those who complain that the projects are ugly, grim enclaves, shut off from the community—frequently suggest scattering pocket-size projects about town, and even insinuating a subsidized tenant or two into private housing.[105] One can readily agree that

---

[105] This is the theory that underlies one form of "rent subsidy," which has long been a favorite of authorities on housing. *E.g.*, BROWN, PUBLIC HOUSING IN ACTION: THE RECORD OF PITTSBURGH 88 (1959). The 1965 housing law authorized a limited program of rent subsidies and also a program of leasing space in private housing by local public authorities. 79 Stat. 451,

in the long run, the solution to the social ills of the Negro ghetto must include breaking down the walls that separate the poor Negro from his white neighbors. But in the short run, and within slum communities, a sheltered enclave is a vital prerequisite for the offering of massive social services to public housing tenants. Teachers and social workers should be able to walk unafraid on the grounds at least by daylight. There should be space for playgrounds and meeting rooms. If existing communities are destroyed by private building or by civic projects, public housing can at least provide a stable locale where the community could possibly be rebuilt. The isolation of the projects may be, in absolute terms, an evil; but the most radical causative factors producing that isolation arise out of political forces which condemn public housing to internal exile and high-rise life. These forces, at least in the short run, are not likely to be overcome.

These remarks must not be taken as an endorsement of the present system of building high-rise, segregated housing in the core of a city for those who cannot afford better housing. Practically everyone agrees that "vest-pocket" projects, mixed-income projects, and the insinuation of the poor into middle-class neighborhoods through rent subsidies and similar programs is far better than the present system. I would entirely agree. Others insist that tenants whose incomes rise should be allowed to buy their apartments or at least stay on and exert their good influence on their neighbors. But the danger of all these programs is that they are likely to benefit only the members of the submerged middle class. Who will be selected to live in the middle-income building? No doubt a tenant who can "pass" for middle class. Once again, we may be propounding solutions which subsidize and encourage all but the rock-bottom poor. A Utopian vision of the future should not be used to harm the helpless of today.

Since the huge, evil barracks are likely to be with us for many years, how shall we govern them? Once it is agreed that a certain amount of discipline, rules, order, and police is necessary in public housing for the poor, we can address ourselves to the difficult task of finding a level of discipline as consistent as possible with administrative requirements, the rehabilitative goal, and the wishes and needs of the tenants. Undoubtedly, we could do with less "management" and less rules. It would be good to see more debate on issues of policy—and on smaller questions, too. Is there really no way to let tenants have pets? It is so easy to forbid pets— a stroke of the pen will do it. It is not quite so easy to calculate the costs

12 U.S.C. § 1701(s) (Supp. I, 1965). The rent subsidy program was concerned mainly with encouraging new business construction; it was not funded in 1965 and attempts to appropriate a paltry amount for the program were barely succeeding as of early May 1966 despite the most strenuous Administration efforts.

and the benefits of cats and dogs and to try to devise some method of letting tenants have their pets without harming the project. It is probably correct to assume that hard-core slum projects cannot govern themselves as smoothly and easily as "middle-class" projects. But surely the answer is not to deny any rights—formal or informal—to tenants. Internal procedures should, perhaps, be formalized, if only to enhance the self-respect and dignity of some of the tenants. In general, ways should be sought to make tenants feel more of a stake in a place which, after all, and despite its defects, is their home and which is in theory run for *their* benefit, not the benefit of the government. Equally important, perhaps, is a need for outside, independent controls over management—not legal controls, necessarily, but the kind of disciplined control which public opinion imposes on issues and institutions which arouse articulate members of the middle class to nag at their public servants. If the poor cannot nag by themselves, somebody must do it for them—lawyers, perhaps; latter-day reformers of the Jane Addams stamp; professors, if they can be induced to interest themselves; politicians of the opposition party.

The militancy of the poor is a new factor in the situation. It is an easy, and safe, prediction that attacks on the mode of management of public housing will increase as time goes on. The rumblings out of Syracuse and elsewhere are ominous and revealing. Yet in another sense these rumblings are a sign of great hope. The militancy of the poor—particularly the Negro poor—has a tremendous potential for bringing about social reform. In one sense, it is almost the only hope for administrative overhaul; the other champions of the tenants are fickle and sporadic. In the long run, the ills of public housing are not going to be cured by administrative reform or by giving tenants "rights" which they cannot use or are untrained to use. In the long run the only solution is to break down the ghetto walls and win acceptance for the Negro poor in the general society. This means, then, that the solution must be political. But when the tenants organize and make demands, and assault the prerogatives of management, they are seeking a political solution; and thus, paradoxically, the achievement of useless rights may turn out to be useful, since what will have happened will have been a shift in the balance of power. And power is the matter at stake, not formality.[106]

Not that there are no dangers in militancy. Angry cliques of tenants, though we may (and *must*) trust them to measure their own self-interest,

---

[106] When a tenant organization sues to have a rule or practice of an authority declared "unconstitutional," this may be as much an attempt at a political solution as trying to get a law passed would be. The act of vindicating rights is often the act of creating rights. Appeal to the courts is an appeal to another power-granting or power-ratifying authority in our society. Though new rights created through legal action may have (in some theoretical sense) "always existed," for practical purposes they were unborn, not dormant.

cannot be expected to diagnose the ills of the system perfectly, since no one else can. And so we are likely to hear complaints against managers that are unjustified, or reflect unavoidable conditions, or which are simply unreasonable. But if we are willing to let people govern themselves, we must be willing to let them commit the unreasonable in their lives. Still, the Negro poor are a minority. For any minority, life in a democracy is a process of striking workable bargains with the majority; and the majority is white. The whites must feel that the costs of resistance to Negro pressures are not worth the annoyance of civil disorder; that segregation bears too high a price, that the comfortable old order of rule and of despotism (benevolent and otherwise) is no longer feasible. The militancy of the poor demonstrates to the others how high the price really is; but militancy is most effective when it appears to be strong but self-controlled, principled but ready to bargain. Otherwise, opposition sees no alternative to continued resistance. In the case of public housing, it is neither honest nor desirable to clamp down the lid on rebellious tenants (even when action is taken "for their own good"); the likely result is simply more angry frustration—even if we were sure (which we are not) that we knew what is good for other men.

In any dispute between tenants and managers, the outside public will control, if it wishes. The general community is woefully ignorant of public housing; it ought to know more. It must realize that many of the ills of public housing are caused by conditions insisted upon by the very people who criticize the outcome. Moreover, doubts ought to be resolved on the side of the tenants: This the community must understand. Public housing is meaningless or hypocritical if it is not an effective vehicle to make better the life of the poor. That is the object, or ought to be; management is only an instrument. Bureaucratic convenience and paternalism are not the point of public housing; they are perversions. Much of the fault for present ills can be found in the long shadow of history, as this paper has attempted to show. But the program is not incurable. What is needed, quite simply, is more subtle flexibility, in fitting the means to the ends.

Protecting the Interests of the Indigent Tenant: Two Approaches

Carl Schier*

THE PERSON WITH INADEQUATE MEANS, seeking a suitable family dwelling in the city, is often a hapless figure. Space can be had only on a short-term basis, and most available housing is run-down, dirty, and without adequate services.[1] Furthermore, if the community is progressive and in the throes of redevelopment, one never knows when the neighborhood will be slated for wholesale destruction.[2] Hence, many poor families are little better than transients within the metropolis, resettling periodically in one blighted area or another.[3]

For some, public housing fills the need for shelter. It is secure from condemnation by the local planning authority and adequate in the sense that it is warm and dry and provides more creature comforts than private fare.[4] It is also scarce.[5] A great need exists for additional units, and many of the yearly contracts must be placed in an eligible "pool" until units are vacated.[6] But even though the demand is high, the poor do not like

---

* B.A., 1959, Lehigh University; LL.B., 1963, University of Michigan. Assistant Director for Research, Urban Law Program, University of Detroit School of Law. For a discussion of the Urban Law Program at the University of Detroit, see Miller & Daggitt, *The Urban Law Program of the University of Detroit School of Law*, this symposium.

[1] In 1960, 12.4% of all of Detroit's housing, or 63,635 units, were either deteriorating or dilapidated. 2 U.S. BUREAU OF THE CENSUS, DEP'T OF COMMERCE, CENSUS OF HOUSING: 1960, pt. 3, at 57-59 (1963). For a general description of the manner in which the poor are housed, see AGEE & EVANS, LET US NOW PRAISE FAMOUS MEN (1960); MAY, THE WASTED AMERICANS 123-30 (1964).

[2] In Detroit's Gratiot project, for example, 129 acres were cleared, during a ten-year period, to bare earth, requiring relocation of 1,958 families and 989 single persons, who had been living in 1,550 dwelling units. DETROIT HOUSING COMM'N, GRATIOT REDEVELOPMENT PROJECT, FINAL REPORT 6 (1964). See generally ANDERSON, THE FEDERAL BULLDOZER 52-70 (1964).

[3] 5,530 families and single persons were uprooted in Detroit's ten redevelopment projects. DETROIT HOUSING COMM'N, QUARTERLY REPORT, FOURTH QUARTER 15 (1964). There is no way of knowing how many families moved from the seven projects that were formerly residential in character, only to find they had relocated in a proposed redevelopment area, but interviews indicate many families moved twice, and others expect to move again.

[4] The Detroit Housing Commission leaflet advertises: "All dwellings have range and refrigerator—All units have private bath and ample closet space in addition to living room, kitchen, bedrooms and parking facilities." Detroit Housing Comm'n, Modern Housing with Reasonable Rent, 1963.

[5] For example, the 1960 census report showed Detroit with 78,437 units that needed or would soon need replacing or repair, 2 U.S. BUREAU OF THE CENSUS, *op. cit. supra* note 1. Available public housing now totals 8,113 units, and no new units have been built since 1960. DETROIT HOUSING COMM'N, *op. cit. supra* note 3, at 12.

[6] In Detroit, as of December 31, 1965, 790 families waited in the eligible pool. DETROIT HOUSING COMM'N, *op. cit. supra* note 3, at 14.

projects. Living in one adds to the burden of being poor because it strips away disguise and pretense and identifies poverty by address.[7] Raising families there is difficult, high-rise buildings provide no place to play, and the stark, sterile surroundings are more confinement than home to the children.[8] Such places have become, in many instances, dormitories housing refugees from the war against poverty.

For these reasons, one may assume that large numbers of poor families will be relying on private accommodations for the foreseeable future.

Since the cost of outright ownership is prohibitive, and since the market could not supply a sufficient number of single family dwellings in the event the means to purchase magically appeared at hand, the poor will rent, and the party to whom they must look to meet their housing needs will be the private landlord.

It would seem that adequate housing for the indigent tenant would depend on the fulfillment of the following conditions: (1) adequate space at reasonable cost; (2) a term of sufficiently long duration to ensure a degree of permanency; (3) maintenance of the leased premises and common areas in a habitable state, or at least a condition that meets housing code requirements, at the time of letting and throughout the term; (4) provision of basic services, such as heat, light, and water; and (5) an assurance of privacy. The urgent question is whether the law provides a means to meet these conditions.

Public law provides a limited resource for the attorney seeking relief for his clients. Where the perplexing question is how to find adequate space at a price the tenant can afford, the long term remedy will lie only in the public law sector. Housing is in short supply, and the demand is high. In addition, the market is distorted by considerations of race and poverty, hence the asking price reflects considerations which have nothing to do with the quality of the interest transferred. Although it is beyond the scope of this article to explore the problem in great detail, it would seem that the enactment of fair housing legislation,[9] and the appropriation of funds to construct additional public housing should have a meliorating effect on the total market.

Maintenance of leased premises and of common areas, adequacy of

---

[7] Persons interviewed in two Detroit projects were unhappy about living there. They revealed that police will not answer calls, doctors will not venture in, and merchants, upon learning of the address, will not extend credit.

[8] In the Detroit projects, private police, popularly called rent-a-cops, patrol all buildings; all grass plots are encircled by heavy chains, and even the advertising leaflet for the projects shows father and sons playing baseball in the parking lot, as there are no playgrounds.

[9] By 1964, eighteen states and thirty-four cities had enacted some form of fair housing laws. Weaver, *Foreword to* U.S. HOUSING AND HOME FINANCE AGENCY, FAIR HOUSING LAWS 3 (1964).

facilities for supplying utilities, and to some extent, privacy, are all the province of housing codes, whose enforcement and the problems attendant thereon have been exhaustively treated elsewhere.[10]

Duration, perhaps one of the most important considerations of the indigent tenant, is not subject to public regulation, except in one jurisdiction presently enforcing rent control legislation.[11]

Although some writers have expressed concern that the private law of landlord and tenant is not sufficiently developed to adequately protect the tenant,[12] at least one article discusses a number of remedies that should dispel some of these concerns.[13]

The specific private law problem is how to balance adequately the rights of landlord and tenant and to provide the impoverished tenant with rights of action which will make secure the interests set forth above. In the remaining pages an attempt will be made to outline two private law approaches for protecting further the rights of indigent tenants, the first through the courts, and the second in the legislature.

To achieve progress in the courts two case-law developments should prove useful. One development gives rise to a theory for imposing affirmative obligations on the landlord by implication, and the second involves the assimilation of a modified contract doctrine of substantial performance, applicable to the performance of both express and implied promises in the lease, replacing the harsh doctrine that covenants in a lease are independent. Although the opinions on which these developments are based are Michigan decisions, a brief perusal of cases noted in several of the standard treatises indicate that the analysis would hold in other jurisdictions as well.[14] Whether or not a particular court would accept such an approach on a case of first impression is another matter.

The legislative approach involves the enactment of a statutory lease which defines the minimum leasehold estate of the tenant, and balances the respective rights of both landlord and tenant.

---

[10] See, e.g., Note, *The Enforcement of Municipal Housing Codes*, 78 HARV. L. REV. 801 (1965).

[11] N.Y. UNCONSOL. LAWS §§ 8581-97 (McKinney Supp. 1965).

[12] *E.g.*, LeBlanc, *Landlord-Tenant Problems*, in CONFERENCE PROCEEDINGS, THE EXTENSIONS OF LEGAL SERVICES TO THE POOR 51 (U.S. Dep't of H.E.W. 1964); Lesar, *Landlord and Tenant Reform*, 35 N.Y.U.L. REV. 1279 (1960).

[13] Schoshinski, *Remedies of the Indigent Tenant: Proposal For Change*, 54 GEO. L.J. 519 (1966).

[14] See 6 WILLISTON, CONTRACTS §§ 890, 890A (3d ed. 1957) for a general contract approach to the interpretation of leases; 1 AMERICAN LAW OF PROPERTY § 3.45, at 267-68 nn.2, 7-12 (Casner ed. 1952), for illustrative cases on implied covenants. Compare 3A CORBIN, CONTRACTS § 686 (1960), where the theories of constructive eviction in leases and constructive conditions in other contracts are related.

I

TWO CASE-LAW DEVELOPMENTS IN THE TENANTS' FAVOR

A. Affirmative Obligations Imposed on the Landlord by Implication

As a general matter, parties to a contract establish reciprocal rights and duties through the accepted medium of arm's length bargaining. Thus, in the ideal circumstance, where the parties meet on equal terms to establish their obligations under the agreement, the prospective landlord offers the premises and certain services, and the prospective tenant offers to pay a price felt to be in accord with the going rate. When all terms have been agreed to by both sides, the exchange is concluded and the parties consider themselves bound. Of course, ideal circumstances are foreign to the poor tenant. He doesn't bargain with his landlord, for he cannot meet the landlord on anything approximating equal terms. Without bargaining strength he must accept the landlord's offer as to duration, price, and services. Yet it may be possible to create by implication obligations affecting the nature and quality of the tenant's interest.

From what sources will such duties stem? At least two can be clearly identified. The first source is the intent of the parties as it is manifest in the terms of the agreement and the circumstances surrounding its formation. It derives from the consensual nature of the arrangement and sounds in contract. The second source is the relationship which exists between the parties, in this case the relationship of landlord and tenant. Although the relationship is created by virtue of the parties' consent, its characterization as a source of duty is apart from its contractual foundations and sounds more in warranty.[15]

From the language of the contract one may infer that the parties intended more than they actually expressed. The limits of intent can be expanded by implication. One such expansion, based on a contractual analysis, is that the landlord intended and therefore impliedly promised that the premises would be fit for the purposes which the parties revealed in the agreement. In *Tyler v. Disbrow*,[16] the defendant had leased a dwelling house from plaintiff, covenanting that she had "received said demised premises in good order and condition,"[17] and that she would yield them up in as good condition. The defendant also promised to "keep said premises in a clean and healthy condition."[18]

---

[15] For a discussion of the history of warranty, and its origins in tort, see PROSSER, TORTS 651-57 (3d ed. 1964); Prosser, *The Implied Warranty of Merchantable Quality*, 27 MINN. L. REV. 117, 118-25 (1942).

[16] 40 Mich. 415 (1879).

[17] *Id.* at 417.

[18] *Ibid.*

Defendant took possession of the house, found that its sewers were not adequate to carry off waste, that refuse collected, and that the house was filled with "foul smells and stench."[19] Defendant tried unsuccessfully to remedy the defects and then attempted a surrender, which the plaintiff refused.

On appeal, a judgment for defendant in a suit for rent was affirmed, the court stating that it was "manifest from these [defendant's] covenants that the condition of the premises was a distinct consideration,"[20] and that "when the landlord rents his house with a distinct understanding that it is in good condition, that becomes a part of the consideration."[21] That the court had not conceived of the landlord's duty as arising from an express covenant was clear, for the court added that "the effect of the assertion could not be stronger if the covenant had been made by the lessor instead of the lessee."[22]

Here, the theory of the duty is pure contract, and the successful defense is predicated on a breach of a contractual duty.

The landlord-tenant relationship itself may give rise to obligations binding on the landlord, irrespective of the parties' failure to indicate any intent. The duty is conceived much like the duty in a negligence situation, but it is expressed in terms that sound in warranty. In *Leonard v. Armstrong*,[23] the defendant leased a house from plaintiff, and when it proved totally unfit for habitation for reasons running the gamut from openings in the walls to sewage in the basement, it was held on appeal that such conditions, stemming from defects in the construction of the house, rendered the premises untenantable and unfit for habitation, and hence the tenant was not compelled to remain on the premises and pay rent.[24] The issue was limited to the condition of the premises at the time the tenant took possession, and the court was satisfied that evidence had been permitted on that point only. It was held to be the duty of the landlord to put the premises in proper condition, a duty which the court appeared to assume existed as a natural concomitant of the relationship.

The court stated that the tenant "rented the premises for a dwelling for his family, *believing* as it appears, *that the premises were tenantable and fit for the purposes* for which he rented them."[25] It is suggested that the court was not requiring as an element of the defense that the tenant show reliance on some statement or other representation of the lessor

---

19 *Id.* at 416.
20 *Id.* at 417.
21 *Ibid.*
22 *Ibid.*
23 73 Mich. 577, 41 N.W. 695 (1889).
24 *Id.* at 581, 41 N.W. at 696.
25 *Ibid.* (Emphasis added.)

as would be the case in an action for fraud. Here the "reliance" required would appear to be nothing more than the general dependence of one party upon another when a particular relationship has been created. In the instant case, the lessor knew of the proposed use, since he rented the premises as a dwelling. The lessor was in a better position to know of the defects and to either repair or warn of their presence, whether he actually knew or not. The existence of the legally recognized relationship of landlord and tenant, and the factors of knowledge, control, and dependency which color that relationship, give rise to the particular consequence in which we are interested, the existence of an implied covenant of fitness for the purpose intended.[26]

The policy supporting implied obligations stems from the need to recognize affirmative duties, imposed on one party for the benefit of the other, which arise out of the nature of the relationship and the fact that one party must depend or rely on the other's superior knowledge, control, or ability to absorb certain risks.[27]

B. Limitations

1. Reliance on Contract Theory

The point being urged is that the sources of implied affirmative obligations in leasehold transactions are two: the parties' intent as manifest from the language and circumstances, and the existing landlord-tenant relationship. A failure to distinguish adequately between these two sources led to the confusion of theory and a denial of relief in the early English law.

In the second half of the 19th century implied covenants of fitness were not recognized. The reason was as stated by Baron Parke in *Hart v. Windsor*,[28] where he denied the defense of breach of implied covenant in a suit for rent where tenants had to vacate a dwelling house because of an infestation of bugs.

> The principles of the common law do not warrant such a position [that a lease contains an implied contract of fitness] and though, in the case of a dwelling house for habitation, there is no apparent injustice in inferring a contract of this nature, the same rule must apply to land taken for other purposes—for building upon, or for cultivation, and there would be no limit to the inconvenience which would ensue.[29]

---

[26] For another rationale for imposing implied obligations, see 3 CORBIN, CONTRACTS § 592 (1960 ed.), where the burden of a risk unanticipated by the contract is imposed on one party by implication.

[27] *But cf.* Pines v. Perssion, 14 Wis. 2d 590, 111 N.W.2d 409 (1961), for the statement of a different policy, more specifically directed to providing adequate housing than to balancing the obligations of parties to an agreement.

[28] 12 M.&W. 67, 152 Eng. Rep. 1114 (Ex. 1843).

[29] *Id.* at 88, 152 Eng. Rep. at 1122.

The careful reader will suggest that Baron Parke's confusion does not concern the source of duty but stems from his lumping together leases for dwellings with all leases of real property, and his unwillingness to admit that there are significant differences between the two which would warrant a different treatment so far as implied covenants are concerned. But the Baron went on to state that "it is much better to leave the parties in every case to protect their interests themselves, by proper stipulations, and if they really mean a lease to be void by reason of any unfitness in the subject for the purpose intended, they should express that meaning."[30] The rationale which he here suggests is that the tenant has adequate opportunity to inspect, and if he is not satisfied with what he sees or feels that added protections are necessary, then he may either look elsewhere for accommodations or provide adequate protections in the agreement.

To suggest that there would be no limits to a doctrine that recognized implied covenants in leases and that the tenant must be remitted to his contract rights is to deny the teachings of landmark decisions in the law of both landlord and tenant[31] and sale of goods,[32] where warranty-based relief was given for the failure to perform implied obligations arising out of the relationship. The Exchequer Court was not willing to recognize a developing source of affirmative duty,[33] although some of the lawyers

---

[30] *Ibid.*

[31] Smith v. Marrable, 11 M.&W. 5, 152 Eng. Rep. 693 (Ex. 1843); Collins v. Barrow, 1 M. & Rob. 112, 174 Eng. Rep. 38 (Ex. 1831); Salisbury v. Marshall, 4 Car. & P. 65, 172 Eng. Rep. 609 (N.P. 1829).

[32] Shepherd v. Kain, 5 B. & Ald. 240, 106 Eng. Rep. 1180 (K.B. 1821); Brown v. Edgington, 2 Man. & Gr. 279, 133 Eng. Rep. 751 (C.P. 1841).

[33] The refusal of the court in *Hart v. Windsor* to recognize warranty as a source of protection for the leaseholder may be subject to analysis in a somewhat broader context, that of "status" versus "contract." One might argue that the court was inclined to remit the parties to whatever mutual obligations they could devise in contract, rather than to acknowledge rights in the leaseholder by virtue of a status analogous to that of a purchaser of goods. This conclusion would be based on a rationale that the general movement in the law at the time was away from status and toward contract. *Cf.* MAINE, ANCIENT LAW 163-65 (1864 ed.). But this is an overly-broad generalization that fails to acknowledge one salient fact, the lessee is a two-status party. He is the holder of an interest in real property and a purchaser as well. Purchasers of goods in the late nineteenth century could rely on a fairly well developed scheme of warranty protection, a scheme which evolved in a time of rapid growth of manufacturing and of independent systems of distribution and marketing. See Kessler, *Protection of the Consumer Under Modern Sales Law*, 74 YALE L.J. 262, 266-72 (1964). At the same time the economic system of laissez-faire capitalism depended on freedom of contract (and freedom to restrain contract) to stimulate risk-taking and investment. Hence a litigant, if he were a property owner, purchaser, and contracting party, might find himself confronted by more than one prevailing legal theory and be unable to avail himself of the most favorable. An illustration of this problem is a "pure" land case, Sutton v. Temple, 12 M.&W. 52, 152 Eng. Rep. 1108 (Ex. 1843), where the tenant leased pasturage that was contaminated by an invisible but highly toxic substance. The court refused a defense of implied warranty in a suit for rent, and since ploughing the pasture would have constituted common law waste (ameliorating in this case) the best the tenant could hope for would be to stick a sublessee

were for they cited decided cases which established affirmative duties with acceptable limitations and argued that the circumstances in leases of houses were sufficiently analogous to those in the sale of goods that the court could apply the developing theories of warranty found there.[34] But the court, stuck on a theory of express contract and not willing to acknowledge any other source of duty, denied relief to the tenants and overruled the cases decided to that point in time which implied such covenants.[35]

The question is whether or not this attitude has survived and has had an impact on modern transactions in landlord and tenant. Clearly it has. Although one could not call the statutes prohibiting implied covenants in conveyances of leasehold interests modern,[36] they are still cited and have their origins in the "contract-only" thinking that convinced the English court that it should overrule or strictly limit its holdings in the implied covenant cases. This attitude is also the source of rulings in some state courts that if there are no words such as demise or grant in the lease, then no covenant of quiet enjoyment will be implied.[37] And, finally, this attitude is the reason why most courts find that there can be no implied covenant of fitness, for that is still the acknowledged general rule.[38] If concern is expressed by the court for an unwarranted expansion of the doctrine, counsel may refer to decisions which mention specific and limiting factors that work an exception to the general rule, without an attempt to formulate a new principle of law. For example, it has been held that the exception should apply only to short-term leases of premises fully furnished.[39] It has been suggested that knowledge of the use,[40] the fact that there is a housing shortage,[41] lack of opportunity to inspect,[42] latency of the defect,[43]

---

with the unfit grass, although his lessee could defend a suit for rent on the basis of fraud. *Caveat emptor!*

It would be inaccurate to suggest that the law is moving with measured step toward either a "status" or "contract" theory of jurisprudence. Perhaps a satisfactory hypothesis would be that status, or "rights in the air," is a pervasive concept, perhaps a fundamental one, and that it is in a constant state of flux, subject to erosions and accretions by contract, legislation, and judicial decision.

[34] Counsel for defendant based their arguments on the warranty theories which had been developing in the law of sales. 12 M.&W. at 71-78, 152 Eng. Rep. at 1116-18.

[35] *But cf.* the later decisions in Wilson v. Finch Hatton, 2 Ex. D. 336 (1877); and Collins v. Hopkins, [1923] 2 K.B. 617, where relief was granted on a theory of breach of implied covenant.

[36] *E.g.*, Mich. Stats Ann. § 26.524 (1953); N.Y. Real Prop. Law § 251; Wis. Stats. Ann. § 235.02 (1957).

[37] 1 American Law of Property § 3.47 n.3 (Casner ed. 1952).

[38] *Id.* at § 3.45 n.4.

[39] Ingalls v. Hobbs, 156 Mass. 348, 31 N.E. 286 (1892).

[40] Young v. Collett, 63 Mich. 331, 29 N.W. 850 (1886).

[41] Barnet, Landlord-Tenant Laws and the Slums (undated mimeograph on file in Research Section, Urban Law Program, University of Detroit School of Law).

[42] Schoshinski, *supra* note 13, at 521-22.

[43] *Ibid.*

and the like will justify finding the implied covenant of fitness. If these elements are controlling it makes little difference what the source of the duty is, for one could argue for such covenants in any lease on the basis of such factors. But by emphasizing the source of the duty the various classes of implied obligations can be increased. In addition to a duty to make the premises fit or a duty to repair,[44] the landlord may become obligated to notify of a change in owners or management, or to notify of a cancellation of fire insurance or of the existence of code violations.

2. Limitations Imposed by a Party

Another limitation on implied covenants is one imposed by a party to the agreement, wherein he limits, by provision in the lease, his liability to those terms expressed in the agreement. Whether the courts will hold such limitations binding on the tenant is a matter for some speculation, although no one would seriously insist that such disclaimers are dispositive of the landlord's liability for warranties implied as a matter of public policy. Thus it may be argued on behalf of the tenant that the public good requires that obligations be imposed by implication on the landlord and that any attempt to avoid them by disclaimer or limitation would be contrary to such policy.[45] A second approach is to argue that provisions inserted by the landlord to limit his duties are unconscionable and therefore void. Of course, the doctrine of unconscionability has developed in the law of sales, and has not matured to the point, even in that context, where one may anticipate a result with any great assurance. However, it is no great leap conceptually to accommodate the doctrine of unconscionability (or of overreaching in land transactions)[46] to the law of landlord and tenant. If the lessee is unfamiliar with legal terminology and lacks a basic understanding of the relationship of landlord and tenant, if the disclaimer is oppressive, and if the current housing situation and the tenant's financial condition are such that he had little choice in selecting accommodations, then the disclaimer or limitation may be held to be unconscionable.[47]

It should be clear that as a general matter the road to implied obliga-

---

[44] No such duty is established under the case law, but the obligation to make general repairs is imposed by statute. E.g., MICH. STATS. ANN. § 5.2843 (1958).

[45] See statements as to public policy and its effect on the validity of disclaimers in Henningsen v. Bloomfield Motors, Inc., 32 N.J. 358, 404, 161 A.2d 69, 95 (1960).

[46] Johnston Realty & Inv. Co. v. Grosvenor, 241 Mich. 321, 217 N.W. 20 (1928).

[47] A full discussion of unconscionable disclaimers as they are dealt with in the sales of goods appears in HAWKLAND, A TRANSACTIONAL GUIDE TO THE UNIFORM COMMERCIAL CODE § 1.190304 (1964); cf. UNIFORM COMMERCIAL CODE § 2-316, providing for disclaimer of implied warranties.

tions is not trouble free, but in the case of residential housing, the only significant obstacle would be the court's unwillingness to recognize the relationship itself as a source of implied obligation.

C. The Doctrine of Substantial Performance

The charge has been made that the law of landlord and tenant is bound conceptually to the old rules of real property conveyancing.[48] The courts, it is said, have failed to incorporate relevant doctrines from the law of contracts.[49] But on closer examination, one finds that the courts have been solving landlord and tenant problems with contracts analyses and that the courts are not entirely to blame for the failure to apply contracts rules in dwelling leases. The real problems lie elsewhere. First, most of the appellate decisions in the area of landlord and tenant have centered about commercial leases, for they are of significantly greater length and involve more money than the standard dwelling lease. Since there is considerably more at stake for the parties, they are more willing to contest at the appellate level. In these cases, counsel have effectively argued contract doctrines.[50]

The other problem is that in most jurisdictions the lawyer representing the poor client finds that his man is a defendant and that he must confront the statutes establishing the right of the landlord to summarily regain possession.[51] Whether the law of landlord and tenant has or has not assimilated relevant contract doctrines regarding the dependency of covenants is of little moment in the face of such a statute; whatever defenses the tenant may have by virtue of the landlord's failure to perform as promised cannot be pleaded. One can only show that the landlord has not met the requirements of the statute; if he has, the right to remain in possession is lost.[52] Of course this street is one-way for the landlord, too, as he may not maintain an action for rent.[53] But that is of little consolation to the tenant when his main interest is in establishing some degree of permanency in his housing arrangements.

Although the covenants in a lease are mutual promises, it has long been the rule that "in the absence of an expression to the contrary, these

---

[48] Levi, Focal Leverage Points in Problems Relating to Real Property, 66 COLUM. L. REV. 275 (1966).

[49] Lesar, Landlord and Tenant Reform, 35 N.Y.U.L. REV. 1279, 1281 (1960).

[50] See text accompanying notes 56-69 infra.

[51] E.g., MICH. STATS. ANN. § 27A.5634 (1962).

[52] Ibid. The only issues which may be considered in such a proceeding are: (1) whether the person seeking relief is entitled to possession, (2) whether a proper written demand for possession or payment of rent was made the required length of time before the complaint was made, and (3) whether rent is overdue. McSloy v. Ryan, 27 Mich. 110, 112 (1873).

[53] See, e.g., Gregor v. Old, 209 Mich. 43, 176 N.W. 580 (1920).

mutual promises are not mutually conditional and dependent."[54] This means in effect that the promises in a lease cannot also be constructive conditions precedent to the promisee's duty to perform. The failure of performance gives rise to a cause of action;[55] it does not permit the other to withhold his performance as well. This principle began to erode at an early date, and in the English case of *Smith v. Marrable*,[56] the court construed an implied covenant of fitness as a condition precedent to the tenant's duty to remain on the premises and pay rent. Although the English court later withdrew from this posture,[57] courts in the various American jurisdictions have not been hesitant to adopt that much of the doctrine that conditioned one party's performance on the other's having carried out his promise.[58] In Michigan the court early decided that the covenants in a lease, whether implied[59] or express,[60] were mutually dependent, although it did not always analyze the problem in the contractual language of nonperformance of conditions and failure of consideration,[61] but lapsed from time to time into the language of constructive eviction.[62]

Not every breach of promise is a total breach, and not every failure of performance will enable the other party to withhold his performance. Only when a party has substantially performed may he call forth the performance of another. This doctrine has been applied to leases in a form adopted to the circumstances of landlord and tenant. In *Walters v. Quality Biscuit Div.*,[63] the defendant-tenant moved from the premises prior to the end of the term, but continued paying rent. Thereafter, plaintiff's grantor, who owned the adjoining building and through whose premises

---

[54] 3A CORBIN, CONTRACTS § 686, at 238 (1960).

[55] 1 TIFFANY, REAL PROPERTY § 88, at 135 (3d ed. 1939).

[56] 11 M.&W. 6, 142 Eng. Rep. 693 (Ex. 1843); see Hart v. Windsor, 12 M.&W. 67, 152 Eng. Rep. 1114 (Ex. 1843), where Parke, B., states "I thought they [the cases supporting *Smith v. Marrable*] established the doctrine, not merely that there was an implied contract on the part of the lessor, that the house should be habitable, but an implied condition, that the lease should be void if it were not, and the tenant chose to quit." *Id.* at 87, 142 Eng. Rep. at 1122.

[57] Hart v. Windsor, *supra* note 56.

[58] *E.g.*, Medico-Dental Bldg. Co. v. Horton & Converse, 21 Cal. 2d 411, 132 P.2d 457 (1942); 6 WILLISTON, CONTRACTS § 890 (3d ed. 1962) and cases cited therein.

[59] Tyler v. Disbrow, 40 Mich. 415, 417 (1878): "[T]his consideration having failed, the lessee was justified in leaving, and in refusing to pay further rent."

[60] Stifter v. Hartman, 225 Mich. 101, 195 N.W. 673 (1923) (plaintiff failed to pay one-half expenses of phone and secretary, therefore defendant was justified in leaving shared premises).

[61] *E.g.*, Bostwick v. Losey, 67 Mich. 554, 558, 35 N.W. 246, 248 (1887) (plaintiff refused or neglected to repair flume and foundations of mill, and court held the consideration failed).

[62] See, *e.g.*, Lynder v. S. S. Kresge Co., 329 Mich. 359, 45 N.W.2d 319 (1951), where plaintiff did not block off entrance to leased store as promised, and court held defendant had been constructively evicted.

[63] 336 Mich. 214, 57 N.W.2d 503 (1953).

defendant's water pipes passed, shut off the flow. Defendant claimed constructive eviction and stopped paying rent. Plaintiff had a judgment for rent below, and on appeal the court affirmed, stating that "it is not every partial failure to comply with the terms of a contract by a party which will entitle the other party to abandon the contract at once."[64]

The breach was not intentional, and plaintiff made an immediate attempt to remedy the defect. He had, in effect, substantially performed his covenants, and the breach gave the defendant no more than a right of action for damages.

What is most significant in the opinion is the suggestion that substantial performance is measured in terms of the impairment of the beneficial use and enjoyment of the premises.[65] It would seem that where the use and occupation of the premises is the essence of the contract of leasing, if the failure of the landlord to meet his promised performance interferes with the tenant's use and enjoyment, and if the tenant can no longer use the premises for the activities in which he was engaged or about to engage at the time of the interference, then he may withhold his performance, treat the contract as no longer in effect, and declare his interest in the premises terminated.[66] His alternative, unless there is such an interference with the possessory interest as to amount to a repudiation,[67] is to treat the interference as a partial breach, sue, and tender performance.[68] The fact of the underlying conveyance may affect the contract rule, however, and it may be that even in the case of a total repudiation a suit to enjoin interference may be maintained if the tenant elects to treat the lease as remaining in force.[69]

D. Impact of the Summary Possession Statutes

In light of the statutes granting the landlord a right to summary possession, speculations about the tenant's alternatives in the event of the

---

[64] *Id.* at 220, 57 N.W.2d at 506, quoting from Rosenthal v. Triangle Dev. Co., 261 Mich. 462, 246 N.W. 182 (1933).

[65] "Neither may it be said that defendant was deprived, because of the shutting off of the water service, of any *beneficial use* that was enjoyed at the time, or of which it was in position to avail itself . . . ." *Id.* at 220, 57 N.W.2d at 506.

[66] The common law suspended the obligation to pay rent when the tenant was evicted, but the tenancy remained in force. 1 TIFFANY, REAL PROPERTY § 146 (3d ed. 1939). Hence to terminate the tenancy the lessee would have to rely on some theory of surrender by operation of law, see, *e.g.*, Hotel Marian Co. v. Walter Root, 77 Ore. 426, 150 Pac. 865 (1915), although periodic tenancies may not be subject to such surrender, 1 TIFFANY, *op. cit. supra* § 172, at 274.

[67] 4 CORBIN, CONTRACTS § 946, at 811-12 (1951).

[68] *Ibid.*

[69] See Grinnell Bros. v. Asiuliewicz, 241 Mich. 186, 216 N.W. 388 (1927), where landlord leased adjoining floor space to a meat market, and plaintiff music dealer sued to enjoin defendant's action. The court indicated it would have permitted vacation, but granted an injunction.

landlord's breach may be wholly academic. If the tenant withholds his rent payments or if he brings a suit to enjoin an interference with his possessory interest, he may be faced with a notice to vacate and a suit to regain possession.

In the case where the landlord's failure to perform meets the requirements for a constructive eviction, it would seem unfair to permit the landlord to sue to regain possession when the tenant subsequently withholds his rent. Where the landlord by his own acts has provoked the tenant into withholding rent, although the cases and statutes do not countenance the practice, the Detroit court hearing summary actions[70] will permit the tenant to show that the landlord has failed in his duty to maintain the premises, and if the tenant agrees to pay his rent within a certain time, the court will not always grant an order to dispossess.[71] This is an empty gesture for two reasons. First, the court has no power to issue an order to the landlord to remedy the defect, and second, the landlord need only wait until the beginning of the next period to give notice to terminate the tenancy.

There is one Michigan case to support the tenant's claim that the landlord cannot maintain a suit for possession where the landlord himself is at fault. In *Ravet v. Garelick*,[72] the court held that in the case of a partial eviction, an action under the statute for summary possession would not lie, since in that instance the whole of the rent is suspended, and there can be no action for nonpayment of rent where no rent is due.

When, to punish the tenant, the landlord gives notice to terminate the tenancy, the problem is more difficult. Although various grounds have been suggested for defending against a retaliatory eviction,[73] the problem of proving that notice has been given in retaliation would appear to be insurmountable once the landlord learns to give it without commenting on the reason.

The appropriate move would be to urge the legislature to amend the statute granting the right to summary possession, modifying it so that certain defenses may be pleaded. The statute should permit termination only for specific, extraordinary reasons,[74] and the plaintiff should be required to plead these as an element of his cause of action. In this way the impact of the statute would be lessened, and the tenant could have some assurance of permanency, conditioned on the performance of his obligations.

---

[70] Circuit Court Commissioners Court.

[71] Interview with Circuit Court Commissioner.

[72] 221 Mich. 70, 190 N.W. 637 (1922).

[73] Schoshinski, *Remedies of the Indigent Tenant: Proposal For Change*, 54 GEO. L.J. 519, 541 (1965).

[74] See text following note 102 *infra*.

II

A. Generally

One may speculate hopefully that the courts will adopt a sympathetic and helpful attitude toward the problems of the urban poor, accepting the theories and concepts urged upon them by counsel. The problems of poor tenants have heretofore been raised in limited circumstances, generally the prosecution of actions to regain possession from the tenant for nonpayment of rent or because of an unpermitted holding over, actions where the tenant is forever a defendant.

But one must be realistic and recognize that litigation is a slow method of effecting changes in the law, even when the need is urgent and the means are at hand. And of course the major stumbling block, the landlord's statutory right to summarily regain possession, effectively defeats the tenant's interest in maintaining a permanent home. That is perhaps his most important interest, for if the tenant must leave the premises either because of a judgment of eviction or as a part of his remedy of constructive eviction, any judgment for damages which he is fortunate enough to win is small consolation. Hence it may be necessary to turn to the legislature for adequate protections.

The perspective of a statute can be conceived in any number of ways. An attempt to redefine the landlord and tenant relationship, setting out the tenant's minimum estate, defining the rights and duties of the parties, and establishing conditions of performance, as in a restatement,[75] would be one possible, if monumental, approach.

Another approach would be to meet selected problems on a piecemeal basis, for example, by permitting rent withholding,[76] or by enacting a lien-repair law.[77] Yet another method would be to establish an administrative board, empowered to control the troublesome and oppressive private housing market. But an approach that deals with problems seriatim will forever be leaving something undone, and to depend on an unwieldy bureaucracy encumbered by the usual procedural red tape will merely add to the law's delay.

A more satisfactory legislative approach would be to set out, in a statute, a uniform standard dwelling lease, binding on the parties, which balances the rights of the parties and defines the tenant's possessory interest in terms of a minimum leasehold estate.

To affirm that the tenant holds an estate, as if the transaction were

---

[75] For a muted call for such a restatement, see 3A CORBIN, CONTRACTS 238 n.58 (1960).
[76] E.g., N.Y. REAL PROP. ACTIONS & PROC. LAW §§ 769-82.
[77] E.g., N.Y. MULTIPLE DWELLING LAW § 309.

one involving real property rather than rooms in a building, is a move away from what has been described as judicial recognition that a lease is no more than a promise of continuing permission to occupy the premises.[78] This is a reasonable extension of the doctrine of estates, for that doctrine has been held to apply to things other than land,[79] particularly where the subject matter has a relatively permanent existence.[80] Clearly the fee estate has been extended to units within a building,[81] and there is no reason why the leasehold cannot be similarly extended.[82]

The leasehold estate entails two characteristics that can be beneficial to the tenant. First, the leasehold is a possessory interest, that is, it carries the right to exclusive use and occupation.[83] Hence, the lessee has the right to maintain possession against the owner of the fee and third parties and to sue to restrain interferences with that possession. Second, time is a factor that measures the tenant's interest,[84] and since duration is a matter that may be fixed by consent of the parties, theoretically the tenant might agree with his landlord to extend the term, thereby assuring a greater degree of permanency.

The rub, of course, is that even if it is theoretically possible for the leaseholder to increase the incidents of his estate by contract, as a practical matter the landlord by contract can and does reduce those incidents so that the lessee has no more than a promise of a very limited right to occupy the rooms he rents. Hence an objective of the statute is to restore the estate concept by affirming a possessory interest in the tenant, and setting a minimum term. By setting out the landlord's obligations to protect the quality of the tenant's property interest and by prohibiting further agreements in derogation of that interest, it will be protected from erosion.

The landlord's interest, which can best be characterized as his investment or "endowment," must also be protected. Thus the contract aspects of the statute establish the parties' interests and their respective obligations in regard to those interests.

A significant problem is that of deciding which terms are important enough to be controlled by the statutory form. For the sake of simplicity the statute should be short. But a failure to include a troublesome term

---

[78] 6 WILLISTON, CONTRACTS 585 (3d ed. 1962).

[79] Regarding future estates in chattels, see SIMES, FUTURE INTERESTS 18-20 (1950).

[80] Cf. CRIBBET, PRINCIPLES OF PROPERTY 25-26 (1962).

[81] This is accomplished by the statutes which create horizontal real property regimes or condominia. E.g., CAL. CIV. CODE §§ 1350-59; IND. STATS. ANN. §§ 56-1201 to 56-1231 (Burns Supp. 1965); FLA. STATS. ANN. §§ 711.01-.23 (1963); MICH. STATS. ANN. §§ 26.50(1)-(30) (Supp. 1963).

[82] Cf. Shawmut Nat'l Bank v. City of Boston, 118 Mass. 125 (1875), which holds that a lease is not a conveyance of real property.

[83] 1 AMERICAN LAW OF PROPERTY § 3.38 (Casner ed. 1952).

[84] CRIBBET, op. cit. supra note 80, at 23.

might leave the tenant at a serious disadvantage. For example, if it were concluded that the matter of a security deposit were to be left to the parties' discretion, it would be possible for the landlord to require a forfeitable security deposit that would be in excess of the rent due for the statutory minimum term. The landlord would thereby gain a distinct advantage, holding a sum which he could declare forfeit, should he desire leverage in future disputes with his tenant. Obviously, however, the statute cannot be so long and involved that it determines the outcome in every possible situation, but it must be framed to include certain essential provisions, leaving formation of the remainder of the agreement to the parties and to the existing law.

It would also be necessary, as a preliminary matter, to relate the subject matter of the proposed bill to existing statutes. In response to pressure to change anachronistic common law rules, many states have modified by statute the doctrine of estates[85] and the rules of conveyancing,[86] and have redefined the liability of the tenant for rent when the buildings become untenantable[87] and the right of the landlord to maintain a suit for rent.[88] And they have of course established summary proceedings to recover possession.[89] The development of a statutory lease would require close attention to these acts to maintain uniformity of terminology and to avoid the creation of conflicts in the law.

The statute could not consist only of a standard form lease. A number of collateral matters would have to find expression, including such things as a definition of terminology and of the minimum estate; a limitation of the statute to the dwelling lease; an explanation of the lessor-lessee relationship to distinguish it from similar relationships to which the law has attached different consequences; and a determination of the ways in which the relationship can be created, extended, and terminated. Although the following paragraphs are not actual drafts of the sections of the proposed statute, they indicate what should be contained therein, accompanied by a brief discussion of some of the problems that may be encountered.

B. Provisions of the Lease

1. Purpose and Effect

Most statutes do not begin with a section devoted to purpose and effect, but in the case of model acts, or statutes which are innovative and intended to accomplish changes in existing law, such clauses are inserted

---

[85] E.g., MICH. STATS. ANN. §§ 26.1-.50 (Supp. 1963).
[86] E.g., MICH. STATS. ANN. §§ 26.521-.564 (Supp. 1963).
[87] E.g., MICH. STATS. ANN. § 26.1121 (1953).
[88] E.g., MICH. STATS. ANN. § 26.1101 (1953).
[89] E.g., MICH. STATS. ANN. § 27A.5634 (1962).

to indicate the reasons for which the statute was enacted and to encourage the courts to interpret liberally its provisions to effectuate the stated purposes. The purpose of the proposed act is two-fold: to recognize the estate interests of both parties, giving them adequate protection, and to achieve a fair and equitable balance between the rights and obligations of the lessor and lessee. It should also be stated in this section that the statute is limited in its application to leases of dwellings.

2. Definitions

A section setting forth definitions of the terminology used in the statute is standard where the subject matter and terminology are new, or where terms with common meanings are used in limited and specific senses, or where specific changes are being wrought. A reason for clarifying terms is to avoid confusion when the parties use statutory terms where they truly intend other consequences, such as the formation of a rooming agreement or a contract for hotel accommodations.

3. Defining The Tenant's Estate

The tenant's estate, in order to be recognized as a true leasehold, must have two characteristics. It must carry the right to exclusive use and occupation, that is, it must be possessory,[90] and it must have duration.[91] The time dimension is presently determined by the parties, or by the law according to the way in which rent is paid. Since the parties rarely discuss the term, the tenancy is almost always periodic, week-to-week or monthly. This arrangement is hardly permanent, and the statute should recognize a minimum initial term of sufficient duration so that the tenant enjoys some degree of permanency. One method is to bind both parties to a minimum initial term of four to six months duration, giving neither the right to terminate except for extraordinary reasons. Under these circumstances the tenant will have a greater liability than he now has, for he will be bound to pay for the full statutory period, although actual tender be in installments at thirty-day intervals. The hardship may not be too great, for the landlord and tenant will always be able to agree to a surrender. The landlord may be willing to consent to a surrender to free his premises for a tenant who can pay. The real problems lie with the poor tenant who has no money, but whose landlord would rather sue than seek another tenant, and with the individual newly arrived in the community who wants to rent for a period shorter than the minimum term before settling permanently elsewhere. To meet these objections, an alternative solution to binding both parties to a minimum term would be to

---

90 See text accompanying note 83 *supra*.
91 See text accompanying note 84 *supra*.

require the landlord to recognize a lengthy minimum term, yet permit the tenant to terminate as under the present law. In either case the estate concept has been preserved, but the character of the tenancy in terms of duration will be modified.

4. Defining the Lease

The theory is that whenever the transaction is a lease, the interest which the tenant receives will be denominated a leasehold estate as that estate is conceived by the statute. The question is, when can it be said that the transaction is a lease? Here again, the problem of statutory definition becomes acute. Since the need is for an objective standard, an appropriate place to search for it is in other statutes with standards analogous to the one required. A statute which comes immediately to mind is the housing code. In Michigan, a proposed housing code[92] provides a standard for defining the subject matter of the transaction such that every transaction involving the particular subject matter may be called a lease without doing an injustice to the actual intentions of the majority of landlords and tenants. The proposed code defines two kinds of housing units, dwelling units and rooming units, each of which has different characteristics, and each of which is treated differently under the statute. The dwelling unit is defined as one having sleeping, cooking, living, and sanitary facilities all within the unit.[93] Rooming units, on the other hand, have only sleeping and living facilities, with other facilities elsewhere in the structure or absent altogether.[94] If these standards are adopted, where a dwelling unit is hired for a term or from period to period and where the period is for a week or more, the law will presume that the transaction is a lease and therefore that the tenant has a leasehold estate in the premises. To establish the interest protected by the statute in this way has one adverse effect. A rooming unit cannot be the subject matter of a statutory lease, although at common law a room could be a proper subject for a lease. Of course, the roomer is clearly within his rights to bargain for a common law lease of the room, since the statute creates a lease only where the subject matter of the transaction is the dwelling unit.

If the bargaining method proves unsatisfactory for the impoverished person who wants the protections of the statute but cannot afford a "dwelling unit," the statute might be drawn so as to give any person the

---

[92] Mich. H. 2363, 73d Leg., 1st Sess. (1965).

[93] *Id.* at § 25(1). Some hotel suites would be included in this definition, and it would be necessary to qualify the definition of dwelling unit by adding the phrase "not including such units as are offered in the ordinary course of business by hotels, motels, and similar businesses serving transient clientele."

[94] *Id.* at § 60(3).

right to elect the statute when he takes a rooming unit. Of course, the land-lord would almost certainly reciprocate by raising the rent.

It is felt that no great injustice would be done by excluding rooming agreements from the scope of the statute, for they are the least permanent of all interests in residential housing at the common law, and to give such interests greater effect than that which they enjoyed at the common law might work a hardship on the owner of the premises and the roomer. This decision will protect transients and the businesses that cater to them from having to cope with a statute that offers unneeded protections.

5. *Creation by the Parties: Statute of Frauds*

If the agreement is oral or written, or if the tenant takes possession with the landlord's permission, the transaction should be subsumed under the statute, regardless of the nature of the tenancy which the parties intend to create. For example, the landlord may try to circumvent the statute by creating an oral lease for a term of a year or more. The lease would be void under the Statute of Frauds, and when the tenant took possession under the void lease, he would become a tenant at will[95] or from period to period.[96] Here the statute would apply to the tenancy created by operation of law and give the lessee a "term" for the minimum statutory period. The objective of the statute is to modify the law of landlord and tenant and recognize a uniform tenancy with minimum standards. Any transaction which creates a tenancy whose incidents exceed those estab-lished by the statute would not be caught by it.

So long as the premises come within the purview of the statute, and so long as rent, as defined by the statute, is paid or promised, the transac-tion will be denominated a lease.

The need for a payment or exchange of some kind, whether or not the parties call it rent, is necessary to bring the statute into operation. A basic, agreed exchange must take place. But as soon as there is consideration moving in both directions a condition precedent to the arising of the statutory lease has been fulfilled. A gift transaction would not suffice to bring the statute into play.

The statutory form must enable parties who wish to commit their agreements to writing to comply with the requirements of the Statute of Frauds. Few poor tenants will ever lease for a term of years; but since the statute will apply to all transactions, whether oral or written, where a dwelling is the subject matter, and since some persons lease apartments and houses for periods longer than a year, the statutory form must pro-

---

[95] Burby, Real Property 125-27 (3d ed. 1965).

[96] See Mich. Stats. Ann. § 26.1104 (1953); Barlum v. Berger, 125 Mich. 504, 84 N.W. 1070 (1901).

vide for compliance with the requirements of the Statute of Frauds. Meeting the Statute is stressed because the statutory lease is not itself a writing. The terms required by the Statute of Frauds are not supplied by the covenants in the form, but must be supplied by the parties by "filling in the blanks." Hence, space must be provided for such matters as the date, a description of the premises, the rent to be paid, and the names of the parties. And of course both parties should sign. One may hope that when the existence of a statutory form is known to them, indigents will be encouraged to demand a written lease, a move that will be beneficial should there ever be litigation in regard to "filled in" terms in the lease. Whether a writing will perform any educational service in teaching the tenant something about his rights in the transaction is questionable. The only real benefits may accrue when the tenant seeks out a lawyer to engage the landlord in court.

6. Terms Affecting the Parties' Performance

(a) *Covenants.*—The draftsman should set out in detail the promised performances, keeping in mind the statutory objective of securing the parties' "property" interests. The tenant's promise to pay rent and to maintain the premises in the condition in which he received them are the covenants of greatest importance to the landlord. The tenant should have the obligation to make tenantable repairs and those repairs made necessary by his own neglect.[97] On notice from the tenant the landlord should have the obligation to make all major repairs, fully and promptly. Such duties as are imposed on the landlord by the housing code, so long as they affect the nature and quality of the tenant's possessory interest, should be incorporated in the lease. It should also be the landlord's duty to put the premises in fit condition for occupancy at the commencement of the term, and his covenant to that effect should be set forth. Equally important is an express covenant of quiet enjoyment, for it offers wide protection against interference with the lessee's interest.

(b) *Mechanics of Performance and Remedies.*—One of the major problems in the mechanics of operation under a lease is that performances of the parties have not traditionally been conditioned one on the other. This is the claim and, although the cases demonstrate that this has not been the law in every instance for many years,[98] the problem still arises. Hence some provision in the lease should spell out, expressly, how the

---

[97] This requirement suggests the tenant's common law duty to repair, which is not an oppressive burden. See 1 AMERICAN LAW OF PROPERTY § 3.78, at 347 (Casner ed. 1952).

[98] See, *e.g.*, Medico-Dental Bldg. Co. v. Horton & Converse, 21 Cal. 2d 411, 132 P.2d 457 (1942); Walters v. Quality Biscuit Div., 336 Mich. 214, 57 N.W.2d 503 (1953); 6 WILLISTON, CONTRACTS § 890 (3d ed. 1962), and cases cited therein.

parties' performances are to be ordered. This may be done in the provision that establishes the duty or in a separate section that speaks to nothing but the mechanics of performance. Thus the problem of constructive conditions is avoided.

Establishing the order of performance and rights to withhold performance is no mean task, for although the performances of the two parties are presumably equal in value, the landlord, in effect, "does" more than the tenant in terms of the quantum of performance. Then, too, once the conveyance is made, a substantial part of the landlord's promised performance is executed. Although one may feel compelled to permit the tenant to withhold rent when the landlord fails in his promised performance, it may not be entirely fair to landlords as a class to do so, since the statute will apply to all dwelling leases, and not just those of slum property.

Since rent withholding or any other response will be conditioned on a failure of performance, the lease should spell out what will constitute substantial or less than substantial performance. And since the failure of a condition will in most instances be a failure of consideration, the response will be a remedy and should be set forth in that section.

The statutory lease is a contract, and those remedies with which the statutory lease is concerned are for breach of contract. Hence the statute will concern itself with such things as the right to withhold rent as an alternative remedy when there has been a failure of substantial performance,[99] payment of rent into escrow as a modified tender to keep the contract alive when the landlord has beached,[100] suits for damages for partial failure of consideration, and the like. Since the purpose of the contract is only to protect the underlying conveyance and the property interests created thereby, the remedies which accrue to a party by virtue of his status as the owner of an estate (for example, the right of a lessee to sue to enjoin an interference with quiet enjoyment)[101] are left unaltered by the statute and need not be mentioned by it.

It is of vital concern, however, to create a right in either party to terminate the minimum statutory term under certain circumstances. The landlord should not be forced to endure a tenant who will utterly destroy the premises, and by the same token the tenant should not be forced to

---

[99] In the absence of a statute rent withholding will generally result in eviction. For an examination of rent withholding as a viable remedy, see Comment, *Rent Withholding and the Improvement of Substandard Housing*, 53 CALIF. L. REV. 304 (1965).

[100] For the requirements of tender when the promised performance is a money payment, see 5 CORBIN, CONTRACTS § 1235 (1964 ed.). If a tender by payment into escrow is determined to be conditional, and therefore invalid, the statute would have to legitimize that arrangement.

[101] Grinnell Bros. v. Asiulewicz, 241 Mich. 186, 216 N.W. 388 (1927).

remain on the premises in the face of the landlord's manifest intent to make his stay as unpleasant as possible. For extraordinary reasons, then, the minimum term should be terminable by either party. When the tenant is committing waste or is creating a nuisance or other disturbance that could result in a claim of constructive eviction by other tenants, the landlord should have the right to regain possession. The matter of unpaid rent during the minimum term raises a more difficult problem. A failure to meet the requirement of timely payment of rent for one month, since it is actually an installment, may not be a total breach, although a continued failure to pay would be. The solution may lie in granting the landlord the right to begin an action for possession, and if the rent is tendered at trial, the relationship would remain in force.[102]

The tenant should clearly have the right to terminate for a substantial and continuing interference with his possessory interest. Both parties' remedies for breach of contract during the minimum term would be the same as under the general remedies section.

If such changes in the relationship are contemplated, the summary possession statute will have to be revised to correspond with the remedies section of the lease. For the statutory minimum term no such action should lie, except for the extraordinary reasons set forth in the lease. Once the minimum statutory period has ended, the landlord would no longer exercise the same free-wheeling right to regain possession which the statute now grants. A suit for possession based on nonpayment of rent could be met with the defense of substantial failure of consideration. A suit for possession based on termination could be defended on the basis of a failure to plead an extraordinary reason. In effect, the tenant would enjoy a term of unlimited duration, so long as he paid his rent and threatened no injury to the landlord's investment. But the tenant should not be bound to stay on the premises if he has a chance to improve his lot, and as to him the right to terminate on thirty days' notice should remain.

One anticipated difficulty is the matter of increased costs and the landlord's attempt to compensate for such increases by raising the rent. If the landlord is not permitted to terminate the tenancy after the expiration of the minimum initial term except for extraordinary reasons, the problem of controlling his conduct in the matter of rent increases becomes acute. Shorn of legal remedies to regain possession, the landlord will surely resort to economic pressures. Rather than broach the subject of price controls in the statute, it may be sufficient to permit the tenant to contest rent increases on the basis that they were made for a reason

---

[102] When rent is tendered and accepted in court the landlord's right to regain possession is not altered. Chiera v. McDonald, 121 Mich. 54, 79 N.W. 908 (1899).

other than the increased cost of doing business. The tenant need show only that the increase followed a complaint to the landlord or public authority about facilities, a suit against the landlord, participation in a tenant's council, the birth of a child to the tenant, and similar occurrences. If the statute provides that proof of such facts amounts to a prima facie case, the burden of going forward shifts to the landlord, and the tenant's battle is partly won.

CONCLUSION

The law of landlord and tenant is not so lacking in conceptual development that the indigent tenant must necessarily be denied redress in court. The heart of the matter is not entirely the shortcomings of the substantive law, rather it is a combination of related problems: the procedural anomaly of a statute which grants the right to regain possession but excludes otherwise acceptable defenses, the lack of tenant-plaintiffs and counsel to represent them, and hard-headed or recalcitrant judges whose sympathies lie with the landlords upon whom the poor descend to run their buildings into slums.

Current attempts to achieve satisfaction in the courts are meeting with some success, but success at the bar should be supplemented by a program of progressive legislation designed to overcome many of the seemingly insurmountable problems such as too-short duration and discrimination in tenant selection based on race and economic status. The suggested legislative approach of creating a uniform statutory lease proceeds on the theory that the legal incidents of leaseholding would be of benefit to indigent persons. It is acknowledged that these incidents may be reduced by contract when bargaining is free in the market. But contract can be used to secure these incidents, and protect the landlord's investment as well, for the statute requires that the parties accept the contract, regardless of bargaining strength. The draftsmen must be farsighted, however, for whatever changes are contemplated in the law to benefit the poor will have an effect on the entire law of landlord and tenant.

The odds against the legislature giving life to a statutory lease are high. There is an element of bargaining in legislative councils that makes all other bargaining pale by comparison, and if such a statute were introduced the superior lobbying strength of the real estate interests could well outstrip that of the organized poor. In the end the statute might reflect only the needs of property owners. But the uniform lease does provide protections for the landlord's interest, in fact, it balances protections for both parties' interests, and this may be enough to ensure passage in relatively unaltered form.

Should a wide ranging effort fail, one can adopt a piecemeal approach.

This method seems to be favored by legislators, since the smaller the steps by which one proceeds the fewer persons will take notice and complain. A legislative program, plus renewed efforts in the courts, should make an appreciable difference in the landlord-tenant relationships of the urban poor.

Juvenile Courts, Family Courts, and the Poor Man†

*Monrad G. Paulsen**

I

THE SETTING IN THE COURT

"IT IS A POOR MAN'S COURT." Martin Tolchin, a reporter for the New York Times, referred to the New York Family Court.[1] The judgment was correct when it was written in 1964 and it is correct today. For evidence we need look no further than the waiting rooms of that court and their population. Each morning a hundred stories of poverty are suggested by the faces and the personal effects of those who wait to appear before the judges. The cold atmosphere of the room only intensifies the feelings of helplessness, fear, and frustration which accompany poverty. "[C]ourtrooms are bare, toilet walls are defaced. The court's waiting rooms resemble those at hospital clinics. Negro and Puerto Rican families predominate, and many regard the trappings of justice with bitterness and suspicion."[2]

Impersonal attendants perform their duties with clipped routine, underscoring alienation. In the waiting rooms of the larger New York boroughs it is not unusual for fifty or sixty persons to be gathered. As each case is called the name of the respondent is shouted out in full voice by a court employee dressed like a police officer. The name of the youngster is likely to be sounded a second time if he does not leap forward immediately, lest a moment be wasted. Observers find it ironic to recall the words of the Illinois Family Court Act, which expressed the intended spirit of the New York law as well: "The children . . . as far as practicable . . . shall be treated not as criminals but as children in need of aid, encouragement and guidance."[3]

The courtrooms themselves are scarcely less disconcerting than the waiting rooms. In a busy court all sorts of court attendants and probation

---

† The material for this article was largely taken from the New York Family Court and from the author's personal observation in that court. It is submitted that most juvenile courts in large cities would leave similar impressions. The Family Court has jurisdiction over delinquency, neglect, support, adoption, paternity, and family offense matters, but not annulment, separation, or divorce.

* A.B., 1940, J.D., 1942, University of Chicago. Professor of Law, Columbia University.

[1] Tolchin, *Experts Wonder if Family Court is Doing its Job*, N.Y. Times, Jan. 18, 1964, p. 24, col. 3.

[2] *Ibid.*

[3] Ill. Laws 1953, § 1, at 1089.

370

officers come and go during a hearing. Respondents, I am certain, would be surprised to learn that the proceeding is a "private" hearing.

The very informality of a juvenile proceeding, designed to create an atmosphere of concern for the individual, may, according to the observations of Dr. Elliott Studt, create an image of the court as:

> [A] confused and confusing organization, in which it is difficult to know what to expect . . . .
>
> Because the official world has meant to be helpful by deemphasizing procedural aspects, there is often too little explanation about what is going on while the child and his parent are moved through a bewildering series of procedural steps.[4]

The Honorable Florence Kelley, Administrative Judge of the New York Family Court, put it: "No one is at home in this court."[5] A poor family brought before a juvenile court judge journeys into a foreign land. In New York City, the judge, a relatively well-paid member of the upper middle class, is a college graduate and the possessor of a law degree. He is, thus, separated by education and way of life from most of those who are paraded before him every day. The probation officer to whom a youngster may be assigned is also a college graduate. Though he may have been recruited from the same economic and social class as the youngster in his charge, he has by effort and energy risen from it. Even the court officers and clerks are better paid and, to some extent, better educated than most of those who come with their children. The poor are certainly not "at home" in this atmosphere with these people.

"No one is at home in this court." Few of the judges, probation officers, and court attendants are truly "at home" in their surroundings. At the end of the day most of them return to relatively stable families and middle-class life. The problems of communication which this estrangement creates are not widely understood and rarely confronted.

II

THE RESPONDENTS IN THE COURT

A. The Juvenile Court

Delinquent conduct is, of course, found among children of the upper and middle classes, but official rates of delinquency are higher among the poor. "Sociologists know that delinquency rates rise in disorganized neighborhoods, those without a stable culture, inhabited by socially and

---

4 Studt, *The Client's Image of the Juvenile Court*, in JUSTICE FOR THE CHILD 200 (Rosenheim ed. 1962).

5 A phrase from a conversation with Judge Kelley, Feb. 1, 1966.

economically disadvantaged groups. There are many such areas in New York City; their rates of delinquency and adolescent crime are high."[6] A map showing the distribution of delinquency in New York City (based on police records and Children's Court cases in 1958) reveals that the worst areas were three neighborhoods of great poverty: Harlem, the South Bronx, and the Bedford-Stuyvesant area of Brooklyn.[7]

Certainly in the great cities of the nation the overwhelming number of children processed through the juvenile court are the children of the poor. The upper and middle classes show surprising agility in keeping their delinquent children out of the court. In some cases we can be sure that a petition has not been filed against an offending middle-class youngster because restitution has been supplied to the victim of the child's misconduct. In other cases, the upper and middle-class youths have been shielded against juvenile court adjudications by their parents' ability to provide privately arranged corrective treatment. After an adjudication, a person of means can often arrange for the use of private facilities not available to the poor.

One imaginative researcher has called our attention to the fact that the very philosophy of the juvenile court with its emphasis on "saving" the child, on treatment rather than punishment, may itself be puzzling or, indeed, seem foolish to the young respondents.[8] Most youngsters raised on the street know that aggressive acts are followed by swift retribution. They not only know it, but they accept it as right. When a boy from the slums is ushered into the court because of unlawful conduct, he may think it strange to be confronted by officials moved by a philosophy of help rather than punishment. The scepticism of the youngster, it is fair to guess, colors his perception of the court's task. Measures designed to help or to provide treatment can very easily be perceived as punishment, simply because it is incredible to the juvenile that anything but punishment would follow the acts in which he was engaged. Perhaps, in the final analysis, this difficulty of communication is not so common because many courts are a good bit more punitive than the official theory admits.

Dr. Elliott Studt has a further point. She argues that today teenagers are bored, contemptuous, and impatient with the juvenile court because it is degrading for a teenager to be dealt with as a "child."

---

[6] Juvenile Delinquency Evaluation Project of the City of New York, Final Report No. II, Delinquency in the Great City 1 (1961).

[7] Id. at 13.

[8] See Younghusband, *The Dilemma of the Juvenile Court*, 33 Social Service Rev. 10, 14-17 (1959).

Teenagers are likely to see the court and its staff "as inept and essentially unable to deal with realities."[9] For example, she reports a comment about a probation officer: "I guess he tried to help. Mostly he lectured, I guess."[10] The juvenile court is also likely to be unpopular with parents because:

> [T]hese parents feel that the judge and his representative, the probation officer, have taken over in the name of the community the functions and responsibilities of parenthood . . . . Increased inadequacy, unnecessary dependency, a flagrant refusal to perform normal parental duties, and a hostile use of the court against the child are possible behavioral results.[11]

These views suggest that the aims of the court have misfired in relation to the respondents and their families. What the court attempts is sometimes frustrated by the very tools it uses.

FAILURES

The poor may be the principal customers of juvenile court services, but the operation of the court generally is not arranged for their convenience. In most cases the chief concern of those who administer the court is to meet the convenience of the judges and the staff. An enormous amount of time is wasted by the parents of children pulled into court. Little or no attempt is made to space appointments for court hearings. Everyone is told to come at 9:30 in the morning, and the reception rooms fill with employed mothers and fathers who lose more wages with each passing hour.

Waiting to appear in court is not only expensive for those the court must serve, but the waiting often proves to be futile. A case scheduled to be heard may not be ready and an adjournment will have to be ordered, with the consequent loss of another day's pay for parents. Children's courts in this country generally do not function with the equivalent of the prosecutor, someone who clearly carries the task of preparing the "state's case"—making certain that necessary witnesses are present on a given day and that those witnesses can establish the basis for juvenile court action. Postponement can be a disaster for a family of limited means, supported by an income of wages paid by the hour.

The fact that those who go to a juvenile court are generally the poor (in the big cities at least) transforms the court into a class institution, a fact which may inhibit its development and, indeed, may have an impact on all sorts of legislative choices. The following quotation is found in a confidential mimeographed report of an important study

---

[9] Studt, *supra* note 4, at 209.
[10] *Id.* at 210.
[11] *Id.* at 211.

group in one state considering the question whether child abuse cases should be reported to a department of social services or to the police. "According to statistics, many child abuse cases come from within families well-placed financially and of repute. In considering help to such families, reporting to the police, and taking court actions right away may not be appropriate."

B. The Family Court

If we speak not simply of children's cases in court, but of the adult cases in a famliy court which does not process divorce or annulment cases, the clear impression remains that the cases heard are those of the poor man. Certainly in New York City the entire Family Court possesses a proletarian flavor. In general, it is the daughters of the poor who bring filiation proceedings. Middle-class people, not deigning to spice their marital arguments with minor assaults, do not generally appear in the Family Offenses Term. Support orders not entered in connection with "matrimonial actions" (annulment, divorce, separation, or dissolution actions, which in New York are heard not in the Family Court but in the Supreme Court) are infrequently sought by persons of means.

In New York, the Family Court and the Surrogate's Court have concurrent jurisdiction over adoptions.[12] According to the original plan, this scheme was to end after two years, on September 1, 1964. From that date forward exclusive jurisdiction was to be lodged in the Family Court. The effective date for ending concurrent jurisdiction has been moved ahead from year to year. Several factors have been responsible for failure to place adoptions exclusively in the Family Court. The surrogates and their friends at the bar have resisted the move for selfish reasons; some persons have argued that the Family Court in New York City lacked facilities to handle the case load. Yet, in the background was another matter: a feeling that adoptive parents should not find it necessary to "rub elbows" with those who normally occupy the waiting room benches. Indeed, partly in order to meet this point, the newly organized "Adoption Term" in the New York Family Court is presently housed in a building quite apart from any other part of the court.

It is a common belief among New York social workers that the Family Court does not possess annulment, separation, or divorce jurisdiction because of notions related to class divisions. How would it be possible for the judges who preside over the delinquent, the neglected, and husbands who refuse to pay small support orders, to handle intelligently the complex separation agreements of the well-to-do?

---

[12] N.Y. FAMILY CT. ACT § 641.

III

THE JURISDICTION OF THE JUVENILE COURT

Jurisdictional provisions of a juvenile court act are likely to reach disproportionate numbers of the children of the poor. Juvenile courts throughout the United States may assert authority over "neglected" children. Poor children fall into the "neglect" category more frequently than the offspring of the well-to-do. Parents adjudged guilty of neglect are often self-centered persons, not truly interested in their children, who do not have the means to provide substitutes for ordinary care and affection. An alcoholic mother in a low income family failing to get her children off to school creates a problem of neglect. The alcoholic, suburbanite wife of a successful executive, on the other hand, may be able to avoid the issue by hiring a competent nurse. One suspects that many cases of the physical abuse of children are rooted in the despair occasioned by a lack of means to provide comfort and variety in living.

A statute which defines a neglected child as one who is without proper care because his parent or guardian "neglects or refuses to provide," may sometimes be applied to a youngster with parents who are paupers, not parents who refuse to share what they have. What one regards as proper care may, indeed, be a matter of dispute reflecting class and cultural differences.[13] Standards of child rearing adequate in one cultural setting may seem appalling in another. Neglect defined as raising a child in an environment which is "injurious or dangerous" may create a hazard for parents without means. Unhappily, the environment of the poor is often injurious and dangerous.

It is not suggested that juvenile courts do, in fact, take the children of the poor and give them to the rich. The sheer difficulty of finding new homes for neglected children is a powerful deterrent against pushing the definition of neglect to the limit. Yet the fact remains that a child of parents who are very poor stands in danger of a court-ordered separation from his parents to an extent which children of the middle and upper classes do not.

In defining juvenile delinquency, older juvenile court acts in the United States provide a description of life in the lower economic classes appropriate to a novel by Charles Dickens. The Illinois Juvenile Court Act of 1905 defined a delinquent child as any male under the age of 17 who breaks the law and who:

> knowingly associates with thieves, vicious or immoral persons; or who,

---

[13] See Chilman, *Child Rearing and Family Relationship Patterns of the Very Poor,* Welfare in Review, Jan. 1965, p. 9.

without just cause and without consent of its parents or custodian, absents itself from its home or place of abode, or who is growing up in idleness or crime; or who knowingly frequents a house of ill-repute; or who knowingly frequents any policy shop or place where any gaming device is operated; or who frequents any saloon or dram shop where intoxicating liquors are sold; or who patronizes or visits any public poolroom or bucket shop; or who wanders about the streets in the night time without being on any lawful business or occupation; or who habitually wanders about any railroad yards or tracks or jumps or attempts to jump onto any moving train; or enters any car or engine without lawful authority; or who habitually uses vile, obscene, vulgar, profane, or indecent language; or who is guilty of immoral conduct in any public place or about any schoolhouse.[14]

Children so described are hardly drawn from the choir of a fashionable Anglican congregation.

It is true that modern juvenile court acts generally do not contain such old-fashioned phrases and, further, it is true that these provisions have not often been invoked. Nevertheless, the phrases give us insight into the thinking of the founders of the juvenile court movement in respect to the kinds of children for which the court was created.

Jurisdictional formulations of delinquency often include vague phrases such as "engaging in conduct harmful to himself or others," "incorrigible," or "a child who is beyond the control of his parents or other custodian." Certainly such imprecise language has formed the basis for adjudications of delinquency in the case of Negro children engaged in civil rights demonstrations. One suspects that it can often be used generally against the children of the poor. Once more, such language may permit adjudications of delinquency for conduct related to cultural differences between economic classes.

Legislation does not choose the children who are actually brought into juvenile court. The decision whether to file a delinquency petition against a certain boy, a decision of considerable consequence to the youngster, is ordinarily within the province of the man on the beat. Therefore, an officer's opinion about the behavior of children in his neighborhood becomes an important matter. Indeed, where officers are generally stationed in the community is a factor affecting delinquency rates in so far as those rates are measured by arrests and court appearances. It is disturbing to read the finding of a study of police practices in Allegheny County, Pennsylvania, which asserts that defiance on the part of a youngster will lead to a juvenile court appearance more quickly than any other response.[15] "Such damage to the dignity of the police will

---

[14] Ill. Laws 1905, § 1, at 153.

[15] Goldman, The Differential Selection of Juvenile Offenders for Court Appearances, 1950 (unpublished thesis in Sociology Dep't, University of Chicago), cited in Handler, *The*

lead to court referral even in a minor case." Another study finds that boys who were:

> contrite, respectful and fearful had a greater chance of being released without citation or arrest than another who has committed the same offense, but was rude, obstinate, or even cool, i.e. interacted with the police as if the encounter were a routine event. Further, the youth's demeanor was often mentioned by police officers as the justification for arrest; appearance and stance as indicators of disrespect for conventional values became, for juveniles, a criteria for construing law violation.[16]

It is reasonable to believe that deprived youngsters, reared in an atmosphere mistrustful of law and lawmen, are likely to be seriously disadvantaged by such police attitudes.

IV

THE PROBLEMS OF COURTS FOR CHILDREN AND FAMILIES

Because juvenile courts and family courts serve large numbers of the poor, the poor experience, in full force, the troubles raised by the problems of those courts. Most of the charges made against these courts have spoken of untrained judges whose talents are not wisely used, of careless, slipshod procedure, and of ill-informed dispositional judgments together with inadequate facilities for care and treatment.

A. The Judges

Arguments for the creation of a specialized juvenile court or family court always bring out the point that the cases which come to these courts require a judge with special training and understanding. At the very least, the judge should be able to use expertly the social and psychological information which his staff gathers for him. Making the point real is still a dream in almost every court. By and large, special experience is lacking, politics still plays a major role in judicial selection, understanding and mutual confidence between the judges and the court staff are often absent. In many courts the judges are not specialists at all. In smaller communities juvenile court work will only be a small part of the judge's total caseload. In some city courts, district or circuit court judges rotate in and out of juvenile or family court assignments.

In New York City the family court judges change location from time to time, sitting, for example, two months in Manhattan after two months

---

Juvenile Court and the Adversary System: Problems of Function and Form, 1965 WIS. L. REV. 7, 18 n. 52.

[16] CENTER FOR THE STUDY OF LAW AND SOCIETY, ANNUAL REP. 1962-63, at 10 (University of California, Berkeley), cited in Handler, *supra* note 15, at 19 n.52.

in the Bronx. One of the most distinguished of the New York justices, the Honorable Justine Wise Polier, reported the results of some research which justified a harsh judgment of the practice. "Not infrequently a case was heard by as many as eight or ten judges before final disposition."[17] Judge Polier's research established that "a majority of the children have their cases disposed of by a judge who had not held the initial hearing and had not heard the case on the return of the social investigation during the second month."[18] This rotation system "minimizes the continuity and consistency needed in the handling of cases involving family relationships."[19] Each new judge confronted with any aspect of a pending juvenile case can only orient himself, as quickly as possible, from written papers without insight gained from personal contact. Furthermore, the probation staff, in attempting to deal with the problems of a single family, are confused and frustrated by the varying attitudes among the judges.

Judge Polier's research, directed to the Juvenile Term of the New York Family Court in Manhattan during 1961, established another striking fact. The twelve judges who sat in Juvenile Term during the year varied greatly in their rate of dismissing petitions alleging juvenile delinquency:

> Twelve judges rotated; each served four or five weeks. The rate of dismissal of children charged with delinquency varied from 2.2 per cent by one judge to 24.9 per cent by another judge; the average was 13.8 per cent. Where neglect was alleged, the rate of dismissal varied from 0.5 per cent to 23.1 per cent; the average was 3.3 per cent.[20]

The Children's Courts Project at the Columbia Law School will soon publish findings which establish the fact of disparity in adjudication rates even more dramatically. These findings suggest, like those of Judge Polier, that in a court founded on the notions that justice should regard the individual and that results should fit the particular respondent, an exceedingly important factor determining whether or not a youngster is adjudicated a juvenile delinquent is the person of the judge before whom he is called to appear. The "good news" of individualized justice becomes, in the phrase of my associate, Professor Louis Swartz, the "luck of the draw."

B. Procedure

For a long time observers of juvenile courts have complained that the judges consider hearsay, run their courts on too informal a basis,

---

17 POLIER, A VIEW FROM THE BENCH 12 (1964).
18 *Id.* at 13-14.
19 *Id.* at 12.
20 *Id.* at 2.

do not insist upon specific charges, fail to advise respondents or their parents of a right to counsel, and so forth. Fundamentally, the situations giving rise to these complaints occur because those who originated the juvenile court movement distrusted the adversary system. In juvenile court there were to be no adversaries, only friends of the child united in their desire to help him. The provision previously found in the 1953 Utah Code captured the prescription of the founders: "The court may conduct the hearing in an informal manner and may adopt any form of procedure in such cases which it deems best suited to ascertain the facts . . . ."[21]

Today's legislators, at least those in the most populous states, are impressed with the claims for a more formalized procedure and with the argument that the juvenile court benefits from broad scale participation of lawyers in the work of the court. The New York Family Court Act articulates a legislative finding "that counsel is often indispensable to a practical realization of a due process of law and may be helpful in making reasoned determinations of fact and proper orders of disposition."[22] To implement this finding the Act establishes a system of "law guardians" and emphasizes the right of respondents to retain counsel.[23]

The law guardians, attorneys admitted to practice law in the state of New York, are designated by the appellate division of the appropriate judicial department in three ways.[24] First, the appellate division may enter into an agreement with a legal aid society in a given county to provide law guardians for the family court. Second, the appellate division may designate a panel of law guardians for the family court in each county. Third, under a 1963 amendment, the appellate division may enter into an agreement with any qualified attorney or attorneys to serve as a law guardian for the family court in any county. This third way of providing law guardians makes it possible for the counties which do not have a legal aid society to benefit from specialized experience. Lawyers who appear in family court infrequently are not likely to be as useful as those who understand the court, its aims, procedures, and the workings of its staff.

In New York City there are about a dozen attorneys at work in Juvenile Term during every day that the Family Court sits. Over seventy-five per cent of the youngsters on delinquency petitions have lawyers appointed for them. The law guardian system in New York City is brought clearly to the attention of every child brought into court and his family.

---

21 Utah Laws 1931, ch. 29, § 24, at 60.
22 N.Y. FAMILY CT. ACT § 241.
23 Ibid.
24 N.Y. FAMILY CT. ACT § 243.

Indeed, it has been the practice in one of the boroughs to say to each child, "Is it acceptable to you that Mr. So and So act as your lawyer." To be without counsel takes an affirmative rejection of the offer.

Less and less frequently one hears the argument that alleged delinquents need not be represented by a lawyer at the crucial stages of a juvenile court hearing. There is argument about the proper role of a lawyer in children's court and about the stage at which the lawyer should participate, but most of the discussion ranges around these questions of detail.

The growing commitment to plans for involving lawyers in juvenile court cases is not, it seems to me, rooted in any widely accepted assertion of fact respecting the accuracy of determinations of guilt or innocence. Few argue that if a lawyer does not appear for the child, juvenile court judges often decide that one who has not offended is a delinquent. There is, of course, the point that lawyers can be helpful to make certain that the legal rules are followed at each stage of the proceeding, but the chief arguments for lawyer participation in the juvenile court are of a different sort.

A court without lawyers leaves only the judge to perform the triple role of prosecutor, defense lawyer, and impartial arbiter. These functions, necessary to a full hearing of both sides to a dispute, ought not to be joined. To Americans arguments about the facts forming a basis for a judicial decision ought to be submitted to a tribunal which tests evidence through cross-examination. In fact, in lawyerless juvenile court proceedings the judge cross-examines the witnesses; the very skill and energy which he brings to the task of pushing witnesses to tell the truth may present a frightening picture to a child looking to the judge for help in one of life's difficult moments.

Both at the point of intake and at a dispositional hearing an attorney may present arguments for the point of view which parents might assert, were they gifted with communication skills. Every juvenile court act requires that parents be notified of hearings, requirements which are thought so central that the court is without power to proceed if they are not satisfied. Why is so much importance attached to the notice requirement? Surely, the reason must be that the parents are expected to participate in some meaningful way. Yet any observer of a big city court knows how few parents come forward with argument and how ineptly those few go about it. A lawyer experienced in speaking up and making points clearly can be of enormous help to a vulnerable, poorly educated parent and to the youngster. Further the judge may find lawyers useful because, through them, they may be able better to explain to the parents the aims of the court and the purposes underlying a particular decision.

Judge Ketcham of the District of Columbia has made another point:

> First impressions, we all know, are most important—often indelible. A boy in community trouble for the first time feels very much alone. Whether justifiably or not, he sees school authorities, police and court officials as demanding, judgmental and often hostile. In some instances, even his parents appear to be critical and antagonistic. The court-appointed attorney will often be the first "outsider" to stand up for him. This can create a strong, new impression that the juvenile court law serves the boy, too, and is not just the agent of adult authority. The appointment of an attorney is, I believe, a more effective way of expressing concern than offering the boy cigarettes on his trip to the detention home.[25]

Judge Ketcham went on to argue that a respondent offered legal assistance at the expense of the community may perceive some of the community's concern for him. The presence of a vigorous lawyer "may renew in our children the respect for law, courts and the judicial process which is said to be on the decline."[26] Such points are hard to document but their appeal is undeniable. Indeed, if it is true that the poor perceive law as a hostile force and that disinherited youths look upon the world as a jungle, it is hard to reject the proposition that providing assistance at a crucial time will improve a disenchanted youngster's dismal vision of the world.

We may suspect that judges in the big cities, particularly in the north, find the presence of a lawyer for the respondent quite comfortable. As we have said, the gulf between the judge and the respondent is enormous. In particular, it seems probable that relatively well-paid, white judges, deciding difficult questions about Negro youngsters, do welcome the participation of "defense" counsel. It is easy to be misunderstood: A judge making a decision for the benefit of a youngster can easily be seen as making a decision motivated by racial prejudice. The dangers are somewhat reduced when the judge proceeds according to relatively formal rules in the presence of an advocate serving the respondent.

There are still other values which may come from the large scale employment of lawyers in juvenile court. Judge Ketcham also pointed out that the involvement of lawyers holds promise for the improvement of the juvenile court. If one encourages articulate lawyers to criticize and recommend improvements in the juvenile court system, the community may be alerted to the problems of the court, a development which may offset to some extent the lack of public attention implicit in the private character of the hearings.[27] Finally, the daily interchange between lawyers

---

[25] Ketcham, *Legal Renaissance in the Juvenile Court*, 60 Nw. U.L. Rev. 585, 595 (1965).
[26] *Ibid.*
[27] *Id.* at 596-97.

and social workers might result in a greater mutual understanding across professional lines.[28]

The main criticism of the law guardian system in New York is that it doesn't go far enough. Parents appearing in court on neglect petitions are not offered counsel. In those cases the law guardians represent the children but not the responding parents. Legal Aid assistance, offered as a general matter by the New York Legal Aid Society, is not available to the parents because Legal Aid regards itself as a single entity. The interest of the child and his parent may be in conflict, hence the Society cannot represent both. One cannot too strongly emphasize the need for lawyers in these cases. A neglect petition raises questions concerning the well-being and safety of a child, but it also raises questions respecting the happiness of respondent parents. In particular do parents need assistance in the great cities where there may be the sharpest differences between parents in the lower economic groups and the judge respecting a proper style of life. The author has witnessed an exceedingly sharp tongue-lashing given by a family court judge of conservative leanings to a Negro mother for providing a "bad example" for her daughter. The mother was living with a man, not her husband, a situation which had endured for nine years. The girl's father had deserted her mother some eleven years before, an event which the state of New York did not recognize as a ground for divorce. The woman was thunderstruck by the outburst and said nothing. The possible significance of the long, stable relationship and the reason for its irregular state were never presented to the judge. The judge might not have changed his mind, but certainly the woman had not the advantage of someone to speak for her and to explain the special circumstances of her case. She lacked an advocate, an advocate who conceivably could have prevented the loss of her child.

Free public counsel of the sort available in the juvenile court in New York is not readily available in the support parts of the Family Court. We need not again argue that an adversary procedure, set up to resolve situations of conflict, requires an advocate if the adversary procedure is to be successful.

C. A Unified Family Court Fragmented

The idea of a family court is born of the conviction that a single court ought to deal with the various problems of a single family, and of the belief that these problems require the assistance of well-trained experts for their resolution. An assault of a husband upon a wife, a running away by a child, the failure of a mother to prepare meals for her children all may be part of a single set of domestic problems. If the assailant is tried

---

[28] See *id.* at 598.

in the criminal court, the runaway is the subject of a delinquency case, and the mother brought in on neglect allegations, the family's troubles will be approached piecemeal and not reviewed in one place—in a single court.

To carry out the "family court idea" the New York Family Court was given jurisdiction over family offenses—neglect, delinquency, support, filiation, termination of parental rights, and conciliation.[29] The court is one and the power of the court is far-reaching, but the unity of the court has yielded to pressures for specialization and the realities of inadequate facilities.

While there are plans in New York City to erect a new family court building in Foley Square, the central location of the most important courts in Manhattan, at the moment the Family Court is scattered throughout the city. The Juvenile Term in Manhattan is separated, by many blocks, from the Support Term. In the four other boroughs these sections of the court meet in the same place. However, the Family Offenses Term meets at 80 Lafayette Street, the City Wide Filiation Term meets at 52 Chambers Street, and the Adoption Term meets at 235 West 23rd Street. Thus a given family problem might require a good bit of travel from one part of a single court to another.

Specialization not only tends to deprive families of some of the benefits which a family court promises, but specialization may undermine the reputation of those who must use the court. As Judge Sylvia Jaffin Liese has observed: "Why should we have a separate court in which a woman who walks in is immediately identified as an unmarried mother?"[30]

D. Disposition

The catalogue of complaints regarding dispositions in juvenile courts runs from charges of abuse of discretion to an absence of the institutions which might carry out wise judgments.

The flexible powers of the juvenile court have been misused in the south in connection with civil rights demonstrations.[31] The 1965 report of the U.S. Commission on Civil Rights reports that in Jackson, Mississippi, Americus, Georgia, and St. Augustine, Florida, juveniles who had been arrested in demonstrations "were threatened with imprisonment and, as a condition of exoneration or release, were forced to promise that they would not participate in future civil rights activities."[32]

---

[29] N.Y. FAMILY CT. ACT § 115.

[30] N.Y. Times, July 18, 1964, p. 24, col. 4.

[31] U.S. COMM'N ON CIVIL RIGHTS, LAW ENFORCEMENT, A REPORT ON EQUAL PROTECTION IN THE SOUTH 80-83 (1965).

[32] Id. at 80.

In Jackson, Mississippi, over one-half of the demonstrators arrested were juveniles. Release of the children to their parents was conditioned on the parents doing everything possible to prevent further participation in demonstrations.[33] In Americus, approximately 125 juveniles were arrested and about fifty were placed on probation on condition that they would not associate with certain civil rights leaders.[34]

Many juveniles in Americus were arrested for a long period of time and detained without bail or hearing.[35] The report tells the story of a fourteen-year-old Negro girl who was charged with assault with intent to kill, unlawful assembly, rioting, and aiding an attempt to escape. Bail was set at 12,000 dollars. She spent eighty-seven days in jail without a hearing.[36]

In St. Augustine the juvenile court judge sent a letter to Negro leaders stating that parents ought not permit children to take part in demonstrations, after which juveniles in picket lines were removed by the police. Four youngsters who refused to promise that they would refrain from demonstration activity spent six months in the county jail and reform schools until they were released in January 1964.[37]

In Maryland, juveniles who participated in a sit-in were committed to a state training school pending the hearing of an appeal from an adjudication of delinquency.[38] An appeal on this issue was unsuccessful because the Maryland High Court took the view that the trial court had not abused its discretion.[39] It is pleasant to record that after another appeal the adjudications of delinquency were reversed.[40] The adjudications, grounded on a "sit-in," and therefore an alleged criminal trespass, were held to be improper. Entering a theatre without tickets, lying on the theatre floor, and using profane language were, indeed, criminal activities; nevertheless, they were not a basis for a finding of delinquency under the Maryland law.[41] A determination of delinquency in Maryland requires an additional finding by the juvenile court judge that by reason of the offensive act the youngster is "in need of care or treatment . . . ."[42] The Maryland court said, "In the main the demonstrations in which they participated were conducted by adults who, although disorderly in many in-

---

33 *Ibid.*

34 *Id.* at 81.

35 *Ibid.*

36 *Id.* at 82.

37 *Id.* at 82-83.

38 *Ex parte* Cromwell, 232 Md. 305, 192 A.2d 775 (1963).

39 *Id.* at 309, 192 A.2d at 777.

40 In the Matter of Cromwell, 232 Md. 409, 194 A.2d 88 (1963).

41 *Id.* at 413, 194 A.2d at 90.

42 *Ibid.*

stances, were not engaged in acts involving moral turpitude."[43] The adult demonstrators had either been required to pay minimum fines or the cases had been dismissed. "Incarceration of these children beyond the immediate need for their protection could hardly be supported."[44]

Two cases from New York evidence failure at the level of disposition. In one case a judge failed to inform himself properly, in the other the legislators failed to provide the facility necessary for sensible obedience to their own command. The young respondent in the first of the cases had been adjudicated a juvenile delinquent and placed in a New York State Agricultural and Industrial Training School. Four days after the fact-finding hearing the juvenile had been brought, without his parents or the law guardian, before a judge of the Family Court in Buffalo, New York, for a dispositional hearing. The order committing him to the Training School, according to the Family Court Judge's notes, resulted from "written reports of no current investigation—see social history submitted in 1962"—nearly two years before the hearing. The disposition reached on the basis of this stale evidence was reversed;[45] nevertheless, it is significant that it occurred at all. In an area of the law where so few appeals are taken, one is warranted in suspecting that discovered errors are but a sample of the practice in uncontested cases.

In the State of New York, the youngster who is not able to respond to adult authority is not classified as a delinquent but as a "person in need of supervision." A person in need of supervision (or PINS) may not be "committed" to a training school, but must be "placed" in a facility which is appropriate to a PINS.

> The entire structure of the Family Court Act reflects a deliberate and calculated plan to place "persons in need of supervision" in authorized agencies for treatment and rehabilitation and not to commit them to penal institutions . . . .
> The enlightened method of treatment of persons in need of supervision should be encouraged.[46]

A case styled *In the Matter of Anonymous*[47] concerned a seventeen-year-old girl whose father had filed a petition alleging that she was a PINS, in that she kept late hours, lived in furnished rooms with two adult males, was suffering from syphilis for which she refused treatment, and refused to obey the lawful commands of her parents. There was no denial of the allegations.

---

[43] *Id.* at 414, 194 A.2d at 90.

[44] *Ibid.*

[45] In the Matter of Smith, 21 App. Div. 2d 737, 249 N.Y.S.2d 395 (1964).

[46] In the Matter of Anonymous, 43 Misc. 2d 213, 215, 250 N.Y.S.2d 395, 396 (Family Ct. 1964).

[47] *Supra* note 46.

For such a girl there are in the State of New York almost no facilities available. At that time, the state training schools could not be employed,[48] and no other agency would take her. She had stayed in Youth House for Girls, a center for temporary detention, for a long time. Judge Polier relied upon a report finding that the girl had "deteriorated as a result of overlong remands to temporary detention."[49] The State Department of Social Welfare had refused to accept the girl in its facilities. No voluntary agency was available and further remand in the temporary detention home would have been unthinkable. Judge Polier sadly came to the conclusion that she had "no alternative but to release her to the home from which she came."[50] She went on to write, "with concern and reluctance this Court finds that the girl in this case must be paroled to her parents in the absence of any facility for her treatment and rehabilitation."[51] The legislature had failed to set up the kind of institution required by its own legislation.

Not only is there a lack of placement facilities in New York for PINS, but placement facilities for certain neglected children are almost nonexistent. It is especially difficult to place neglected children of Puerto Rican and Negro backgrounds, with the result that these children are kept in temporary shelters for very long periods of time. Judge Polier's study of the New York Family Court as of April 30, 1963, found that 14.5 per cent of the Negroes in temporary shelter care had been kept there for over one year. No white child had been in temporary care for such a long time. Only fourteen per cent of white children had been in temporary care for over five months. In contrast, Judge Polier reported, "39.5 per cent of the neglected Negro children and twenty-two per cent of the Puerto Rican children remained in the shelters for six months or more on repeated court remands pending court disposition."[52] She affirmed that in New York there is only one significant shelter boarding home program for non-white neglected children involving long term placement.

"Caseloads in the juvenile term now defy any possibility of probation work."[53] The Polier study discovered that forty-nine New York City juvenile probation officers were carrying caseloads ranging from 117 to 256 children. With such caseloads probation officers can only consult the

---

[48] The New York legislature in 1965 amended the Family Court Act to allow placement of PINS in "authorized agencies," which includes state training schools. N.Y. FAMILY CT. ACT § 756.

[49] In the Matter of Anonymous, 43 Misc. 2d 213, 215, 250 N.Y.S.2d 395, 397 (Family Ct. 1964).

[50] Ibid.

[51] Ibid.

[52] POLIER, op. cit. supra note 17, at 26.

[53] Id. at 44.

Social Service Exchange, get a formal report from school, and hold an office interview with the child and one parent. There can be no attempt to study the causes of family problems or to work out a sophisticated plan of treatment.

The probation staff in New York City is not very well-trained. Typically the New York probation officer assigned to work with juveniles has a college degree, but it may represent work in a field quite foreign to social work. The officer may or may not have taken a few professional courses. Usually he has become a probation officer after serving for a number of years as a social investigator in the Welfare Department, thus meeting the experience qualifications of the New York City civil service. Typically, a person on the probation staff with a Master's Degree in social work is a case supervisor and thus one step removed from first-hand contact with the youngsters supposedly to be benefitted by being in the charge of a trained expert.

We perhaps need to be reminded about the shocking state of some of our institutions. A recent magazine article described the main characteristics of Junior Village, an institution for "dependent" or "neglected" children in Washington, D.C.[54] The author asserts that the City of "Washington is running a great factory of retardation and mental illness" because the Village is "too big, too crowded, and desperately understaffed, involuntarily inflicts severe—often permanent damage on small children."[55]

The crowded conditions of Junior Village reflect the fact that foster care is underdeveloped in the nation's capital. The number of homeless children has been rising, and the number of places to take care of them has not. The problem is particularly acute for Negroes; ninety-seven per cent of the children at Junior Village are Negroes.[56]

In the Village, mental retrogression occurs, it is charged, because the children are isolated "to a degree that would be impossible even in the most disorganized family."[57] The child is parted not only from his parents, but from his brothers and sisters, because the institution segregates children by age and sex. The children are further separated from the adult world by the eight-hour shift. The author argues, "One counselor gets him up in the morning, another puts him to bed at night, a third appears if he wakes in the night, and the following morning he sees a fourth face because the first counselor has a day off."[58] The birthdays of children are celebrated collectively, one a month, with a communal birthday cake.

---

[54] Anderson, *A Special Hell for Children in Washington*, Harpers, Nov. 1965, p. 51.
[55] *Id.* at 51-52.
[56] *Id.* at 55.
[57] *Id.* at 53.
[58] *Ibid.*

The damage to the children is often irreversible. Treatment in Junior Village leaves them impaired "in their ability to receive and return affection, to control their impulses, and to use their minds."[59] Ironically, it is expensive in terms of public money as well as in terms of the waste of human resources to keep a child in an institution. A child costs 300 dollars a month at Junior Village,[60] a handsome sum which few middle-class people are able to mount for their own children's needs.

E. Morals versus Conciliation in Family Court

Some of the poor do not share middle-class values about the regularity of family arrangements. "Common law" relationships often suffice. Whatever the economic or social position of the practice, a de facto family is much more important than a de jure relationship which no longer is maintained. Should minor assaults within a de facto family be transferred from a criminal court to a family court so that techniques of conciliation can be applied?

Under section 812 of the New York Family Court Act, transfers are to be made when the fighting occurs between spouses or "between members of the same household." This broad language led a District Judge in Nassau County to transfer an assault case to family court.

> At first blush it would seem strange that a court whose purpose, in large part, is restoration and preservation of marriages, should concern itself with crimes between persons who are living in a meretricious relationship. From a strictly moral or even legal point of view, it is difficult to see why such a matter should be considered fit for the conciliatory and rehabilitative procedures of the Family Court.
>
> Yet, if the jurisdiction were to be limited to legally constituted families, there was no need to add the word "or household" to the statute. The legislature must be presumed to have been aware of a fact that is common knowledge to every law enforcement and social agency and to every court in this state, namely: there are countless households where man and woman reside with their offspring in a domestic relationship on a permanent basis without being legally married. Such households are responsible for many of the most difficult social problems concerning such agencies on a daily, routine basis. They present behavior problems, support problems, mental and emotional problems. They concern the health, welfare and safety of children. They result in filiation proceedings, support proceedings and juvenile proceedings. In short, from a social point of view, this is a situation where the unique and flexible procedures and services available in the Family Court may possibly find a remedy. In some instances it may even be possible to arrange a legitimate marriage or at least furnish adequate counselling and protection.
>
> . . . .

---

[59] *Ibid.*
[60] *Id.* at 55.

It suffices to say that the relationship between this man and woman and the children residing with them is such as to constitute them a "household" as that term is generally used. They apparently eat, sleep and generally subsist as a single domestic unit depending on this defendant for support as its head. To hold otherwise from the mere fact that the man and woman are not legally married, would be to regard as meaningless surplusage the words "or household."[61]

A contrary view was taken by a Dutchess County judge. The facts differed from those in the prior instance in that here the man and woman had not "held themselves out" as husband and wife. Nevertheless, the language of the opinion suggests that this distinction would not be controlling for the judge who decided the case.

It is the public policy of this State not to place children in a situation which would impair their morals. Even if the parties held themselves out to be man and wife under an alleged common law marriage, which is not the case here, this relationship would not change the moral atmosphere generated by these people living together under one roof.

Assuming this court accepted jurisdiction, the most that we could do in order to help would be to effect a marital reconciliation, which is impossible in this situation. Actually, it would make the court a party, not only to an immoral relationship, but also, this court would be encouraging this relationship to continue.

The conciliation procedures cannot be utilized in this situation for there is no marriage to begin with.[62]

Should middle-class morality stand in the way of extending conciliation attempts to those who might benefit from the help? Surely state-provided conciliation procedures are appropriate to deal with domestic upheavals where children are involved in a de facto family of some permanence. Unless the community is prepared to remove the children of unmarried parents from the home, some effort should be made to make the environment physically and emotionally safe.

V

THE CRISIS IN THE JUVENILE COURT

The existence of a wide gap between the promise of the juvenile court and the reality has led to a sense of crisis among those working in the juvenile court field. Few today can regard a statement of Jane Addams' as anything but extraordinarily inaccurate in respect to the real situation obtaining in the juvenile courts of the United States:

There was almost a change in mores when the juvenile court was established. The child was brought before the judge with no one to prosecute him and none to defend him—the judge and all concerned were

---

[61] People v. Dugar, 37 Misc. 2d 652, 653-54, 235 N.Y.S.2d 152, 153-54 (Dist. Ct. 1962).
[62] Best v. Macklin, 46 Misc. 2d 622, 623, 260 N.Y.S.2d 219, 221 (Family Ct. 1965).

merely trying to find out what could be done on his behalf. The element of conflict was absolutely eliminated and with it all notions of punishment as such with its curiously belated connotations.[63]

The reformers had a faith in the scientific skills of psychologists, psychiatrists, and social workers. A Children's Bureau publication of 1929 characterized the new court: "The old courts relied upon the learning of lawyers; the new courts depend more upon psychiatrists and social workers . . . . Justice in the old courts was based on legal science; in the new courts it is based on social enginfeering."[64] Judge Julian Mack is the author of perhaps the most quoted statement about the task of the juvenile court: "The physical and mental condition of the child must be known . . . therefore . . . every child, before hearing, shall be subject to a thoroughly scientific psycho-physical examination."[65]

The operation of the court was to be presided over by a magistrate, educated, gifted, of almost saintly concern:

> The position of judge of a family court requires qualities of the highest order; Broadmindedness, executive ability, tact, knowledge of the law, knowledge of the principles governing social work, and knowledge of people. To these must often be added the ability to convince appropriating authorities and the general public that sufficient funds must be made available. These specifications are rarely filled.[66]

What has happened to these dreams? On the twenty-first of March, 1966, Mr. Justice Fortas delivered the first opinion of the Supreme Court of the United States relating to the juvenile courts. His words were not reassuring:

> While there can be no doubt of the original laudable purpose of juvenile courts, studies and critiques in recent years raise serious questions as to whether actual performance measures well enough against theoretical purpose to make tolerable the immunity of the process from the reach of constitutional guaranties applicable to adults.[67]

He went on to speak of the lack of

> personnel, facilities and *techniques to perform* adequately as representatives of the state in a *parens patriae* capacity . . . . There is evidence, in fact, that there may be grounds for concern that the child receives the worst of both worlds: that he gets neither the protections accorded

---

63 Quoted in Rosenheim, *Perennial Problems in the Juvenile Court*, in JUSTICE FOR THE CHILD 14 (Rosenheim ed. 1962).

64 U.S. DEP'T OF LABOR, CHILDREN'S BUREAU, THE CHILD, THE FAMILY AND THE COURT 21 (Pub. No. 193, 1929) (study by Flexner, Oppenheimer, and Lenroot).

65 BRECKENRIDGE & ABBOTT, THE DELINQUENT CHILD AND THE HOME 199 (1912).

66 U.S. DEP'T OF LABOR, *op. cit. supra* note 64, at 36.

67 Kent v. United States, 86 Sup. Ct. 1045, 1054 (1966).

to adults nor the solicitous care and regenerative treatment postulated for children.[68]

For the moment, at least, the Court did not insist on the full application of the Bill of Rights to juvenile cases; the lower court was reversed on the ground that the statutes applicable to the District of Columbia required the assistance of counsel at a hearing to determine whether a youngster should be transferred to the criminal court.

Mr. Justice Fortas wrote that *some* juvenile courts lack the personnel, facilities, and techniques to perform the parental tasks of government. Do *any* courts possess them? Can any courts which we are likely to see as existing institutions possess them?

Clearly, more resources more intelligently used can minimize some of the inconveniences and harms of the present system. Long-term, meaningless detentions in detention facilities can be avoided. Disposition of cases can be speeded up, educational opportunities can be extended. But what of the fundamental point of the reformers? *Do* we or *could* we have the tools for restructuring character by any program, however well-financed?

In 1920, a commentator observed that the juvenile court idea was designed to carry out "the duty of the state to give to the child who has made a slip another chance; to reclaim him, if possible, as a normal, useful member of society, and to shield him from the handicap and baneful atmosphere of criminal courts and jails."[69] How much of the goal is attainable? To some extent, surely, we can "shield him" from the harms and horrors of the criminal jail and the accusing atmosphere of a criminal courtroom. The juvenile court can give the child "who has made a slip" a second chance. We can rely on the warning which a child might take from an appearance in court to educate him a bit. The court mechanism gives us the means whereby the community can respond to a child's harmful conduct, can inform the youngster and other children that such conduct is not condoned, without at the same time taking harmful measures which might themselves create more trouble. The third task, the task to "reclaim him," is the troublesome one. We of course "reclaim" by giving a second chance and by preventing the harms the criminal law system can do, but can we in any other sense "reclaim" great numbers of children, and if so, by what techniques? The question and the challenge which we put to the reformers is precisely here. What are the means of change? Do they work? How expensive are they? How much is hope and how much is fact? The questions are put in no spirit of hostility. Those of us in the law who have

---

[68] *Ibid.* (Emphasis added.)

[69] Towne, *Shall the Age Jurisdiction of Juvenile Courts be Changed?*, 10 J. AMERICAN INSTITUTE CRIM. L. AND CRIM. 493, 497 (1920).

been concerned with juveniles and their court would like nothing better than to hear reassuring, affirmative answers.

Any answer which requires thousands of dollars of treatment for each offender of any serious degree is in practical effect a useless response. A recommendation of one hundred sessions of therapy does not give an item for mass production. We in 1966 seek with somewhat less assurance than in 1900 a hopeful answer to the question: What can the clinic do to change character? A useful answer will have to produce a correctional flivver—a useful, inexpensive, sturdy model (or line of models) which, because of its low cost, can be made available to all.

If we lack the means to perform miracles of human reclamation, should the juvenile court experiment be abandoned rather than merely modified by the introduction of more formal procedure derived from the criminal courts and by becoming somewhat less ready to undertake drastic intervention? In my view, such an abandonment would be quite wrong. An important reason why the juvenile court has survived is the grim prospect of the alternative. For example, in October 1965, a fourteen-year-old Colorado boy began serving a four to five year sentence in the state penitentiary on a rape charge growing out of an assault on a nine-year-old girl.[70] The maximum penalty for the offense was five years. The judge could have sent the boy to a reformatory where better facilities for rehabilitation were available. Nevertheless, the Colorado law permits the imposition of such severe punitive treatment.[71]

The young people who are brought to court, so many of them the children of the poor, would hardly benefit from being taken to a tribunal dealing with adult criminals. Juvenile courts, imperfect as they are, surely prevent some harm simply by doing less damage than the criminal courts would do to children in their middle teens. Acts done by teenagers may cause great damage, thus evoking cries of rage from the community. Often the juvenile courts, by an adjudication of delinquency, avoid harsh regimens of treatment. A great many youthful offenses are not significant indices of bad character. As to these, the juvenile court can reassure the community without destroying the life of the youngster by making an adjudication and thereafter leaving the youngster to treat himself.[72]

---

[70] Denver Post, Oct. 13, 1965, p. 8.

[71] See *id.*, Editorial, Oct. 19, p. 20.

[72] *Cf.* Note, *Juvenile Delinquents: The Police, State Courts, and Individualized Justice*, 79 HARV. L. REV. 775, 810 (1966): "If the system is maintained in the face of extremely limited treatment facilities and incompetent prediction methods, it might be well to establish a 'presumption' that a juvenile involved is more likely than not to reform himself as he matures. Considering the present number of police and intake 'settlements' and court 'continuances,' it may be said that such a 'presumption' is already in effect informally; but express recognition of the desirability of keeping the child out of treatment may have a good deal of value."

Poverty and the Law of Child Custody

*Herma Hill Kay** and *Irving Philips***

THE RELATIONSHIP OF A NATURAL PARENT or parent-surrogate to his children is a vital human relationship which has far-reaching implications for the growth and development of the child. It becomes the duty of the law to impinge upon the parent-child relationship at some of its critical points: divorce, separation, or death of the parents; delinquent behavior of the chvild; abuse or neglect of the child; and adoption of the child. In all these cases, the law has ultimately only one response to offer: It has the power to remove the child from his present home, whether that be with parents, foster parents, relatives, strangers, or an institution, and place him elsewhere either temporarily or for the duration of his minority. This power is typically exercised by a judge in a court hearing involving the general question of child custody, although the hearing itself may more particularly be concerned with a petition for divorce, adoption, guardianship, support, or a petition to make the child a ward or dependent child of the juvenile court.[1]

The general purpose of this article is to ask whether the law, in its approach to the child custody determination, hinders or advances the child's smooth progress toward social, emotional, psychological, and physical maturity. Our more specific purpose is to discuss the extent to which custody decisions are affected by poverty, including the problem of whether poverty itself creates new situations that may give rise—perhaps inappropriately—to custody decisions. Finally, we propose to raise again, hopefully from a different point of view, the general question of how custody decisions can reasonably be made.

I

THE LAW AND PRACTICE OF CHILD CUSTODY

The law of custody as developed in the opinions of appellate courts lends itself to vague, almost facile statement. Its English origins may be traced to feudal notions of parental authority over the child's services

* B.A., 1956, Southern Methodist University; J.D. 1959, University of Chicago. Professor of Law, University of California, Berkeley.

** B.A., 1943, Oberlin College; M.D., 1948, University of Illinois. Associate Clinical Professor of Psychiatry, University of California School of Medicine, San Francisco. Supervising Psychiatrist, Children's Service, The Langley-Porter Neuropsychiatric Institute.

[1] It has been remarked by a trial court judge experienced in family law matters that "the factors which judges consider in determining custody of children are generally the same in whatever legal form the question is presented." Weinman, *The Trial Judge Awards Custody*, 10 Law & Contemp. Prob. 721, 724 (1944).

and the wardship rights in his marriage and lands.[2] At common law, the father had an absolute right to the custody of his legitimate children;[3] the mother had no right even to visit her children without their father's consent.[4] The American colonies also recognized a paramount right to custody in the father, but statutes have been enacted in virtually all states that place the father and mother on an equal basis when they dispute custody between themselves.[5]

As a consequence of the historical emphasis on parental rights, many courts distinguish the right to custody of a natural parent from that asserted by all other persons, including close relatives. Thus, in the context of divorce and guardianship[6] cases, courts typically distinguish between disputes involving parent and nonparent contestants, and those involving only parents. In the former situation, many states recognize a so-called dominant parental right doctrine that requires a showing of parental unfitness before the child can be awarded to a nonparent.[7] The burden of proving a parent unfit is a heavy one; consequently, cases where a finding of unfitness is upheld on appeal tend to be illustrations of extreme behavior.[8]

---

[2] Sayre, *Awarding Custody of Children*, 9 U. CHI. L. REV. 672, 674-75 (1942); tenBroek, *California's Dual System of Family Law: Its Origin, Development, and Present Status*, 16 STAN. L. REV. 900, 925 (1964). For a statement of the modern English law, see Stone, *Parental Custody of Infants in English Law*, in SOCIETY OF INTERNATIONAL & COMPARATIVE LAW, SPECIAL PUBLICATIONS 10, at 18-22 (1966).

[3] Illegitimate children had no assured right of paternal custody at common law. Kay, *The Family and Kinship System of Illegitimate Children in California Law*, 67 AMERICAN ANTHROPOLOGIST 57, 58-59 (1965).

[4] 2 ARMSTRONG, CALIFORNIA FAMILY LAW 953 (1953). The mother's custodial right was not made equal to that of the father until 1925. Guardianship of Infants Act, 1925, 15 & 16 Geo. 5, c. 45.

[5] 2 ARMSTRONG, *op. cit. supra* note 4, at 954; MADDEN, PERSONS AND DOMESTIC RELATIONS 369-72 (1931).

[6] The question of guardianship of the mentally ill or mentally retarded child poses quite different problems. See Levy, *Protecting the Mentally Retarded: An Empirical Survey and Evaluation of the Establishment of State Guardianship in Minnesota*, 49 MINN. L. REV. 821 (1965).

[7] See ARMSTRONG, *op. cit. supra* note 4, at 993-1018 and cases there cited; MADDEN, *op. cit. supra* note 5, at 372-73; Bronson, *Custody on Appeal*, 10 LAW & CONTEMP. PROB. 737, 740-41 (1944); Foster & Freed, *Child Custody*, 39 N.Y.U.L. REV. 423, 425-27 (1964); Sayre, *supra* note 2, at 676-77; Simpson, *The Unfit Parent*, 39 U. DET. L.J. 347 (1962); tenBroek, *supra* note 2, at 919-27.

[8] A recent comprehensive survey of the appellate decisions summarized the profile of the unfit parent: "To determine when a parent is unfit, the courts consider several factors. . . . Among them are the moral character and emotional stability of the person who wishes custody of the child. A parent may, for example, be classified as unfit if he has been guilty of gross immorality or drunkenness, has been convicted of crime, has been cruel or violent towards members of the family, has been guilty of desertion, abandonment, or failure to support, has been mentally ill, or has stipulated or contracted for a relinquishment of custody.

In cases where each parent seeks custody of the child and no other person is involved, a finding of unfitness is unnecessary since neither parent enjoys as against the other a superior right to custody.[9] The typical divorce case presents this situation. In such cases, the overwhelmingly accepted legal position is that the award of custody should be made by considering "the best interests of the child,"[10] supplemented by a few simple rules of thumb such as the prevalent notion that young children should be placed with their mother.[11] Courts are said to place their reliance on the following factors in determining the best interests of the child:

> Among the factors considered by the courts are the social, spiritual, psychological, and economic conditions prevailing at the alternative environments. A child's physical and mental health is another factor which may dictate a custody award. . . .
>
> Other factors . . . have been the character of other persons in the home, educational and religious opportunities therein, and the type of home and neighborhood. . . .
>
> In addition, the courts may weigh assumed bonds of love and understanding between the child and the contesting parties, the length and intimacy of their association, and the wishes of the child. The ages of the child and the parties, the attachment of the child to his environment, and the amount of time available for his rearing, have also been deemed relevant. Other persuasive factors include a desire to keep siblings together rather than to split custody and a feeling on the part of the court in some cases that a given claim for custody is not bona fide but a maneuver in a power struggle between the adversaries. Finally there is a tendency to assume the local milieu is better for children than some foreign clime.[12]

These vague tests give virtually no guidance to the courts and satisfy none of the writers in the field. One particularly troublesome problem is the conflict between the tests themselves. Many a court has found itself

---

In such situations, there may exist both an element of parental unfitness and a danger of moral harm or bad example to the child." Foster & Freed, *supra* note 7, at 427-28. By "gross immorality" the authors apparently mean adultery. *Id.* at 429-31.

[9] See text accompanying note 5 *supra*.

[10] See ARMSTRONG, *op. cit. supra* note 4, at 960-92 and cases there cited; MADDEN, *op. cit. supra* note 5, at 376-77; tenBroek, *supra* note 2, at 915-19. This test also applies where all the contestants are nonparents, at least if they have the same degree of relationship to the child. Guardianship of Hall, 200 Cal. App. 2d 508, 19 Cal. Rptr. 426 (1962) (the contestants were the paternal grandparents and the maternal grandparents). See also CAL. PROB. CODE §§ 1405-07; CAL. CIV. CODE § 138(1).

[11] Foster & Freed, *supra* note 7, at 436; and cases there cited at note 64. This rule frequently finds its way into statutory expression. *E.g.*, CAL. CIV. CODE § 138(2).

[12] Foster & Freed, *supra* note 7, at 439-41. See also Comment, *The California Custody Decree*, 13 STAN. L. REV. 108, 110-11 (1960).

in the unhappy position of having to award a child to its parents despite a finding that the child's best interests would be served by a placement outside the parental home, because the parent could not be proved unfit. Such a case was *Stewart v. Stewart*,[13] decided by the California Supreme Court in 1953. The husband and wife had divorced in 1949, when their son was eight years old and their daughter was six. By agreement, neither parent sought custody; instead, the children were sent to live with their father's sister and her husband. The agreement, made part of the court's decree, provided that neither parent was to visit the children for three months after the entry of the interlocutory decree of divorce and that neither parent should ask for a modification of the decree, unless the custodians died, for one year. The mother remarried in 1950, and in 1952 asked for a modification of the decree to permit her to have sole custody of both children. The father did not ask for custody, but opposed the mother's petition and urged that the children be left with their aunt and uncle. The trial court denied the mother's petition, but failed to find that she was in any way unfit to have custody. The California Supreme Court noted in its opinion that a change of custody might entail serious emotional disturbances for the children,[14] but nevertheless thought itself forced by the dominant parental-right doctrine to reverse the trial court.

Many commentators believe that the dominant parental-right doctrine should be replaced by a broadened best-interests-of-the-child test so that the court's inquiry would focus on the needs of the child rather than the rights of the parents.[15] Apparently this proposal has a better chance of being accepted in cases like *Stewart* where the child has been living with the nonparents for a substantial period of time before the parent seeks to regain custody.[16]

Even if the best-interests test were to replace the parental-right approach, however, the hard problem of finding out what the best interests of the child require would not be solved. Thus, in a recent case that has attracted national attention,[17] the Supreme Court of Iowa upheld the Bannisters, maternal grandparents of a seven-year-old boy, in their refusal to return the child to his father. The father, Mr. Painter, had temporarily left his son, Mark, with the Bannisters following the sudden death of the child's mother and sister. Two years later, the father remarried and

---

13 41 Cal. 2d 447, 260 P.2d 44 (1953).

14 *Id.* at 453, 260 P.2d at 48.

15 *E.g.*, Foster & Freed, *supra* note 7, at 436-37; Foster & Freed, *Child Custody*, 39 N.Y.U.L. Rev. 615, 626-30 (1964); tenBroek, *supra* note 2, at 926-27. *But see* Sayre, *supra* note 2, at 677-85.

16 See Foster & Freed, *supra* note 7, at 436, and cases there cited at notes 60 and 61.

17 Painter v. Bannister, 140 N.W.2d 152 (1966) (Iowa). See Life, Nov. 4, 1966, pp. 101-02. A rehearing in *Painter* was denied on June 13, 1966.

he and his second wife were anxious to make a home for the boy in
California. The Bannisters, who had never approved of their daughter's
marriage to the father and who disapproved of his way of life, refused to
surrender the child. The father filed a petition for habeas corpus; the
lower court ordered the grandparents to return the boy, but the Iowa
Supreme Court reversed on appeal. There was no suggestion that the
father was unfit to have custody of his son; his second wife was considered
capable of providing able care for the child, and the mother's will had
nominated Mr. Painter as guardian of the child. Despite these favorable
factors, however, the court found that the best interests of the child
demanded that he be left with the grandparents. The court's evaluation
of the two homes indicated that:

> The Bannister home provides Mark with a stable, dependable, con-
> ventional, middle-class, middlewest background and an opportunity for
> a college education and profession, if he desires it. It provides a solid
> foundation and a secure atmosphere. In the Painter home, Mark
> would have more freedom of conduct and thought with an opportunity
> to develop his individual talents. It would be more exciting and chal-
> lenging in many respects, but romantic, impractical and unstable.[18]

Much was made of the testimony of Dr. Glenn R. Hawks, a child psychologist, to the effect that the boy "has already made an adjustment and sees
the Bannisters as his parental figures";[19] that any change of living arrangements at this point in his life would be detrimental to him;[20] and
that "the chances are very high (Mark) will go wrong if he is returned to
his father."[21] Accepting the psychologist's evaluation that the child's most
urgent immediate need was for security, the court made clear its belief
that "security and stability in the home are more important than intellectual stimulation in the proper development of a child."[22] This evaluation,
in the absence of supporting empirical studies, would appear to depend on
what kind of a child one hopes to produce: a decision that society normally
leaves to parents.

The Iowa Supreme Court in the *Painter* opinion displayed an unusual
willingness to substitute its assessment of the best interests of the child
for that of the trial court without sending the case back for a new hearing.
Many appellate courts do not attempt to discover from the transcript of
events at the trial level whether the court wrongly assessed the best
interests of the child. Thus, appellate courts have in effect discouraged

---

[18] Painter v. Bannister, *supra* note 17, at 154.
[19] *Id.* at 157.
[20] *Ibid.*
[21] *Ibid.*
[22] *Id.* at 156.

losing parties from appealing in all but the most flagrant cases by the uniform application of the rule that a trial court's custody decision will be reversed on appeal only when an abuse of discretion has occurred.[23] It may be doubted, however, whether trial courts, if left to the law's devices without special training or especially trained assistants, are in a better position to decide the custody issue than appellate courts. It is true that the trial judge has the advantage of seeing and hearing the witnesses, an advantage which should not be taken lightly. Even so, a trial judge's list of factors considered in deciding custody matters differs only slightly from those discovered by Foster and Freed in their study of the appellate cases.[24]

Finally, a word must be said about the modification of child custody decrees. Professor Foster has stated the law of modification in a paragraph: "Where modification is sought there must be a clear showing of a substantial change of circumstances since the time of the award under attack. In addition, it must be demonstrated that new circumstances require a change of custody in order to promote the best interests of the child."[25] Because a custody decision is never final, parties who will not accept defeat may engage in repeated modification hearings. Even if the local court makes plain that it will not listen patiently to repeated petitions, the parent of means may remove the child to another state, in defiance of the prior decree, there to begin again. The position of the custody decree in the conflict of laws is dangerously unsettled in view of the human emotions involved;[26] currently attempts are being made, albeit from different points of view, to work toward a sensible solution for the "interstate child."[27]

How, then, should the custody decision be made? On the one hand,

---

[23] Bronson, *supra* note 7, at 740; Stack v. Stack, 189 Cal. App. 2d 357, 372-73, 11 Cal. Rptr. 177, 188 (1961) (the court commented that appellate courts have "almost completely abdicated in this field in favor of the trial courts").

[24] *Compare* Weinman, *supra* note 1, at 734-35, *with* note 8 *supra*.

[25] Foster & Freed, *supra* note 15, at 623.

[26] The confusion has been created mainly by the United States Supreme Court's inability to agree upon a clear position as to the relationship between the Due Process and Full Faith and Credit Clauses of the Federal Constitution as those Clauses apply to child custody judgments. See Hazard, *May v. Anderson: Preamble to Family Law Chaos*, 45 VA. L. REV. 379 (1959).

[27] See, *e.g.*, the opinion for the Court by Traynor, J., in Sampsell v. Superior Court, 32 Cal. 2d 763, 197 P.2d 739 (1948); RESTATEMENT (SECOND) CONFLICT OF LAWS, § 117 (Tent. Draft No. 1, 1953); Currie, *Full Faith and Credit, Chiefly to Judgments: A Role for Congress*, in 1964 SUPREME COURT REVIEW 89, 109-118 (Kurland ed.); Ehrenzweig, *The Interstate Child and Uniform Legislation: A Plea for Extralitigious Proceedings*, 64 MICH. L. REV. 1 (1965); Ehrenzweig, *Interstate Recognition of Custody Decrees*, 51 MICH. L. REV. 345 (1953); Ratner, *Legislative Resolution of the Interstate Child Custody Problem: A Reply to Professor Currie and a Proposed Uniform Act*, 38 So. CAL. L. REV. 183 (1965).

parents are warned by a psychiatrist not to leave the decision to the courts;[28] on the other, courts are admonished by a Supreme Court Justice not to leave it to the parents.[29] As in so many other areas of family law where there is disagreement on the goals, the first steps are nevertheless agreed upon. Necessary reforms begin with special instruction in the law schools so that law students—future judges—can be made aware of the special skills needed for handling human problems.[30] In the absence of special training, the trial court judge must rely on others to place at his disposal the skills and insights of behavioral science that may render more precise and reliable the vague standards of the law.[31] How is this union of law and science to be accomplished? The traditional method, available to those who can afford it, is to call psychiatrists, psychologists, and social workers as expert witnesses. Such testimony is frequently helpful to the judge; but in too many cases the opposing side also has its psychiatrists, and the "battle of the experts" so long deplored in criminal law makes its appearance in the civil case. For example,[32] Mrs. X, a divorcee who was suffering from a severe emotional disorder, had recently been discharged from a private sanitarium. She was seeing a physician for continued psychiatric therapy. Custody of her children had been originally awarded to her, but changed to her husband. She retained liberal visitation rights. The children were being cared for by a housekeeper in the father's home. The father, a busy attorney, traveled a great deal and rarely had time to spend with the children. They complained that the mother often derided the father and insinuated to them that he was a homosexual. She, on the other hand, openly carried on affairs with various men while the children visited in her home. The mother decided that she wanted the children back and filed a petition for modification which was opposed by the father. She was supported by her own psychiatrist and two other psychiatrists who testified to her fitness to resume custody. Their evidence was supported by psychological tests indicating that the mother "had the ideal qualities for assuming custody of her children." The father produced evidence from a psychiatrist who had seen the mother while she was hospitalized and from another psychiatrist and a social worker who had

---

[28] DESPERT, CHILDREN OF DIVORCE 189-91 (1962).

[29] Ford v. Ford, 371 U.S. 187, 193 (1962) (Opinion for the Court by Mr. Justice Black).

[30] See Levy, *The Perilous Necessity: Nonlegal Materials in a Family Law Course*, 15 J. LEGAL ED. 413 (1963). Three casebooks now on the market combine legal and nonlegal materials for family law courses: FOOTE, LEVY & SANDER, CASES ON FAMILY LAW (temporary ed. 1966); GOLDSTEIN & KATZ, THE FAMILY AND THE LAW (1965); and HARPER & SKOLNICK, PROBLEMS OF THE FAMILY (Rev. ed. 1952).

[31] See Foster & Freed, *supra* note 7, at 441-42.

[32] Cases in this article which are not cited to a source are from the personal files of the authors.

seen the children. These witnesses told the court that the children needed their father and that the mother had a severe character disorder that would be disruptive to the continued growth of the children. The court, unable to decide the question on the basis of the conflicting testimony, requested an additional psychiatrist to evaluate the total family situation. Finally, the mother resolved the dilemma herself by becoming ill and having to be readmitted to the sanitarium.

One psychiatrist has recently suggested, as an alternative to the courtroom battle of experts, that the parents agree to divide custody between themselves, cooperating in making the necessary decisions, and leaving their differences to be resolved by an appointed committee consisting of "a pediatrician, a child psychiatrist or child analyst, an educator and/or an impartial lawyer or clergyman."[33] The committee would be assisted by a "trusted adult-ally outside the family circle with whom the child can talk in confidence"; the adult-ally would have "technical training and experience in the highly specialized art of listening to children," and would, as part of his function, "inform the committee of what the child thinks and feels, thus providing a sound basis for the committee's decisions."[34]

Assuming, as seems to be the case, that the committee's decision would be binding upon the parents unless a reviewing court determined that it would not serve the best interests of the child,[35] the proposal nevertheless appears to have serious drawbacks. Thus, no provision is made for the committee to understand the family's day-to-day problems, let alone their psychopathologies, to ensure expert knowledge on which to base decisions. Social acquaintance with the spouses prior to divorce would not serve this purpose adequately. Provision for consultation with the spouses after the divorce, even if acceptable to them, would probably render the device expensive enough to prevent most parents from attempting this solution. Finally, one should not assume easily that a committee is any more capable that an individual of remaining "impartial"[36] and free from the hostility that often characterizes divorced couples. Matters as complex as intrafamilial relations are not resolved by a committee.

A preferable approach is the establishment of family courts "staffed

---

[33] Kubie, *Provisions for the Care of Children of Divorced Parents: A New Legal Instrument*, 73 YALE L.J. 1197, 1198 (1964).

[34] *Id.* at 1199.

[35] Note, *Committee Decision of Child Custody Disputes and the Judicial Test of "Best Interests,"* 73 YALE L.J. 1201, 1204-05 (1964); Note, *Domestic Relations, New York Court Approves Use of Arbitration in Custody Disputes*, 33 FORDHAM L. REV. 726 (1965) (discussing Sheets v. Sheets, 22 App. Div. 2d 176, 254 N.Y.S.2d 320 (1964)).

[36] See Diamond, *The Fallacy of the Impartial Expert*, 3 ARCHIVES OF CRIMINAL PSYCHODYNAMICS 221 (1959).

with experts able to make a full-scale investigation and produce a report for the judge."[37] The true family court is commonly defined to have three major characteristics.[38] First, the court is headed by a specialist judge and has an integrated jurisdiction over all legal problems that confront the family in conflict. This characteristic means three things. It means that the family court should be a single court, if possible located in a single building. It can either be a special court or a court of general jurisdiction with specialized duties, such as the present juvenile and probate courts. It means also that the court should have a judge with a permanent, or at least lengthy, appointment to enable him to develop specialized skills in handling family problems. Finally, the specialized court should handle all legal problems of the family in conflict. Thus, it should handle:

> abandonment (of child, pregnant woman, spouse), abuse of child, adoption, alimony claims, annulment of marriage, assault and battery (intra-familial), bastardy, consent to marry, contributing (to delinquency, dependency, or neglect), custody of children, declaratory judgments, dependency of children, divorce, filiation proceedings, habeas corpus (intra-familial, husband and wife), juvenile delinquency, neglect of children, non-support (of child, parent, spouse), parent and child, partition of real estate (intra-familial), separate maintenance, visitation of children.[39]

The second major characteristic of the true family court is that it is assisted by a staff of specialists, trained in social work, psychology, psychiatry, and sociology. Information gathered about the court's "clients" would be kept in central files and be available to the court and its staff each time a family member appears in court. Finally, the true family court is a therapeutic institution: It exists for the purpose of providing help for families in trouble and employing the resources of the community to that end.

It remains only to be said that the family court, as thus described, is a movement rather than a reality. The court that comes closest to the three characteristics is the Domestic Relations Court of Toledo, Ohio,

---

[37] Foster & Freed, *supra* note 15, at 627.

[38] The text material on the family court is drawn from Kay, The Family Court, April 8, 1964, an unpublished address delivered in San Francisco and circulated in mimeograph form as Appendix C to *Hearings on Domestic Relations, A Synopsis of Testimony before the California Assembly Interim Committee on Judiciary, Subcommittee on Domestic Relations, Sacramento, California,* Aug. 13-14, 1964. See also Alexander, *The Therapeutic Approach,* in THE UNIVERSITY OF CHICAGO LAW SCHOOL CONFERENCE ON DIVORCE 51-54 (Conf. Series No. 9, 1952); DESPERT, CHILDREN OF DIVORCE 221-36 (1962); FLEXNER, OPPENHIEMER & LENROOT, THE CHILD, THE FAMILY, AND THE COURT, CHILDREN'S BUREAU PUBLICATION No. 193 (U.S. Dep't of Labor, 1939); Bodenheimer, *The Utah Marriage Counseling Experiment: An Account of Changes in Divorce Law and Procedure,* 7 UTAH L. REV. 443 (1961); *Symposium on the New York Family Court Act of 1962,* 12 BUFFALO L. REV. 409 (1963).

[39] Alexander, *The Family Court—An Obstacle Race?,* 19 U. PITT. L. REV. 602 (1958).

developed largely under the leadership of Judge Paul Alexander. Most of the other so-called family courts in this country, however, do not meet the definition here proposed. In the main they are either essentially juvenile courts to which special powers have been added but which lack jurisdiction over divorce such as the New York Family Court,[40] or they are divorce courts to which a reconciliation wing has been added but which lack jurisdiction over juveniles, such as the Los Angeles Court.[41]

II

CHILD CUSTODY AND THE POOR

An unspoken assumption of the discussion so far has been that when parents separate, they divorce; and that when they divorce, a court somewhere will award custody of the children. This assumption does not hold true for parents afflicted by poverty. Evidence has mounted swiftly that many parents lack funds to secure divorces and either separate by mutual agreement or one parent—usually the father—deserts the spouse and children.[42] Legal Aid Societies typically either refuse to process divorces in such cases or agree to do so only under conditions not imposed by private lawyers on their paying clients.[43] Spouses who have thus informally separated can establish new relationships only by illegal means. The number of families living together with one or both spouses married to others has become a serious problem in California. The concern of the

---

[40] Thus, the criticisms of the New York system contained in Professor Paulsen's article, *Juvenile Courts, Family Courts, and the Poor,* this symposium, do not apply to a true family court. Indeed, one of his major criticisms, that the New York court has become almost exclusively an institution of the poor, is directly related to the fact that the court does not handle divorce cases. Even though the upper and middle classes may be able to keep their delinquent children out of juvenile court, a court having divorce jurisdiction would process all classes. New York has recently enacted a new divorce bill (effective September 1, 1967) which broadens the grounds for divorce and provides for concilliation commissioners to decide whether marriage counselling is necessary, and for guardians to represent the interests of children involved in the divorce. Zion, *Divorce New York Style,* N.Y. Times, May 1, 1966, Sec. E., p. 6, col. 2. New York thus is apparently to have both a "Family Court" and a separate "Concilliation Court" to deal with family problems.

[41] Professor Foster has recently described and discussed the court systems which exist or were attempted in Ohio, Wisconsin, Utah, Maine, New Jersey, Los Angeles, Michigan, and New York. Foster, *Conciliation and Counseling in the Courts in Family Law Cases,* 41 N.Y.U.L. REV. 353 (1966). On May 11, 1966 Governor Brown appointed a Governor's Commission on the Family to consider the creation of Family Courts for California. San Francisco Chronicle, May 12, 1966, p. 8, col. 1.

[42] See, *e.g.,* Foster, *Common Law Divorce,* 46 MINN. L. REV. 43, 57-59 (1961). See generally Weyrauch, *Informal Marriage and Common Law Marriage,* in SEXUAL BEHAVIOR AND THE LAW 297 (Slovenko ed. 1965).

[43] Paulsen, *The Legal Needs of the Poor and Family Law,* in CONFERENCE PROCEEDINGS ON THE EXTENSION OF LEGAL SERVICES TO THE POOR 18-22 (U.S. Dep't of H.E.W. 1964). The conditions referred to are mandatory attempts at marital reconciliation through agency counseling.

State Department of Social Welfare was described in testimony before the California Assembly Interim Committee on Judiciary in 1964 by a representative of the Department:

> [W]e see a substantial number of people at the lower end of the economic scale for whom divorce action is a luxury beyond their financial means. They are no less prone to family breakdown than members of other economic classes but because they cannot afford the legal procedure of divorce, they must resort to the poor man's divorce, that is, separation or desertion. The real problem develops when, like people with conventional divorces, they decide to remarry and want to make the second marriage work. [After interruption for questions, Mr. Simmons returned to his text.] Forty-three per cent of AFDC [Aid to Families with Dependent Children] children born to parents who were not married to each other were actually members of such families in which the parents treated each other and their children in all respects as would a legally married couple. . . . We believe that some form of legal aid should be readily available to families where divorce is indicated on the basis of a social study and particularly to stabilize an existing second home and family for children.[44]

A. Offer-of-a-Free-Home Cases

The Department of Social Welfare, administrator of the AFDC program, encounters many other problems peculiar to the family law of the poor. One such problem formerly raised the child custody issue in a unique context. The States are required by the Federal Social Security Act to consider all income and resources available for the support of the child in determining his eligibility to receive aid.[45] The California Act, in addition, provides that children who live in institutions and receive a "bona fide offer of a proper home" are thereafter ineligible for further aid.[46] The State Social Welfare Board, in promulgating regulations for the administration of the program, interpreted the offer-of-a-free-home category to include offers made to all children receiving AFDC whether or not they lived in institutions.[47] Thus, the Regulations and the imple-

---

[44] CAL. ASSEMBLY INTERIM COMM. ON JUDICIARY, TRANSCRIPT OF PROCEEDINGS ON DOMESTIC RELATIONS 71, 92-92-93 (Los Angeles, Jan. 8-9, 1964). See also tenBroek, California's Dual System of Family Law: Its Origins, Development, and Present Status, 17 STAN. L. REV. 614, 617-21 (1965).

[45] 53 Stat. 1379 (1939), as amended, 42 U.S.C. 602(a)(7) (Supp. I, 1965).

[46] CAL. WELFARE & INST'NS CODE § 11264. The section is virtually identical to former § 1524, added in 1937.

[47] In one case, the appellant was represented by counsel who questioned the Board's statutory authority to extend the offer-of-a-free-home section to noninstitutionalized children, but the case was decided without passing on this question. See P., Feb. 25, 1955. (The cases are confidential, CAL. WELFARE & INST'NS CODE § 108-50, and are available only in the offices of the State Department of Social Welfare in Sacramento. Citations to Fair Hearing Appeals will therefore give only the applicant's initial and the date on which the appeal was heard before the Social Welfare Board.)

menting Handbook sections required workers to decide whether a bona fide offer of a free home made by a parent, relative, or other person should be considered as a resource in determining the child's future status as a needy child. Regulation C-316, which was superseded in 1963, provided that: "Decision as to the eligibility of a child who is offered a free home by a relative, other person, or agency, is to be made on the basis of the legal, social, emotional, and financial security for the child in the home offered as compared to his present home."[48] To be sure, if the worker's decision was that the offer must be considered as a resource available for the child's support, the resulting determination was merely that the child was ineligible for AFDC support in its present home; not that the child's custody must be transferred to the person making the offer.[49] Nevertheless, such a decision was obviously closely akin to a judicial assessment of whether the best interests of the child require its placement with the father or mother; and, indeed, a great many of the cases growing out of this Regulation were cases where the children were being maintained under the AFDC program in the home of the mother and the offer of a free home had been made by the father. Moreover, in many cases the practical economic effect of the termination of aid was the mother's inability to keep the child in her home.

Several important points are suggested by the offer-of-a-free-home cases that bear on the overall question of the supposed conflict between the use of public funds for private support and the right of individual recipients to be treated equally with nonrecipients.[50] Thus, in several cases legal custody was awarded to one parent prior to the application for AFDC. The child, being supported by public funds in the home of the custodial parent, was then offered a free home by the noncustodial parent. In such circumstances, the termination of aid to the custodial parent might nullify the court order without a modification hearing. Equal treatment of recipient and nonrecipient families would thus appear to require that the court's custody award be protected by continuing the grant of

---

[48] CAL. DEP'T OF SOCIAL WELFARE, MANUAL OF POLICIES AND PROCEDURES: AID TO FAMILIES WITH DEPENDENT CHILDREN, C-316 (No. 31-35, May 1, 1957) (superseded by Rev. 495, Nov. 1, 1962). As the text indicates, this regulation was superseded in 1963 by a new one, which effectively disposes of the issue. Present C-316 provides that "Except as provided in W & IC § 1524 [now § 11264, see note 46 *supra*] aid shall not be denied or discontinued for an otherwise eligible child who is offered a free home." During the years of its effectiveness, however, the old regulation C-316 and its predecessor, regulation C-390, accounted for approximately fifty Fair Hearing Appeals to the Social Welfare Board.

[49] This point was made in the CAL. DEP'T OF SOCIAL WELFARE, *op. cit. supra* note 48, and is reiterated in the Fair Hearing Appeals cases. *E.g.*, *A.*, Jan. 25, 1962; *T.*, March 20, 1958.

[50] See MCKEANY, THE ABSENT FATHER AND PUBLIC POLICY IN THE PROGRAM OF AID TO DEPENDENT CHILDREN 37-40 (1960); Reich, *Individual Rights and Social Welfare: The Emerging Legal Issues*, 74 YALE L.J. 1245 (1965).

public funds to enable the child to remain with the parent having legal custody. No such policy appears to have become official; the result of many of the appeals cases, however, enforced such a policy in practice. Thus, where the mother had legal custody and the children were supported in her home by AFDC, the Board tended to refuse to permit the withdrawal of funds to be used as a lever to force the mother to give up custody to the father,[51] even in the face of an indication that the mother's home might be considered unfit.[52] If, however, the father held legal custody and the children were supported by AFDC in the mother's home, the cases were in conflict. In several cases the grant was continued: in two, because the father had not "actually exercised" his legal right to custody;[53] in another, because his home was not immediately available for the child;[54] and, in another, apparently because the worker thought the child was better off in the mother's home.[55] In other cases, including one where the mother had deserted the family prior to reclaiming the children,[56] the father's right to custody was enforced by terminating the aid.[57]

In cases where the parents had separated without obtaining a legal custody award, or where they had never been legally married, the offer of a free home was evaluated from the general point of view of the best interests of the child. A sampling of the cases presenting this problem indicates that the factors considered were not substantially different from the factors said to motivate courts in awarding custody.[58] Thus, in one

---

[51] E.g., E., Nov. 15, 1962; J., Nov. 17, 1962 (mother had temporary custody); W., Sept. 23, 1960; S., April 23, 1954.

[52] D., May 25, 1961. (petition alleging unfitness of the home had been filed in the juvenile court, but no action had been taken).

[53] M., June 29, 1962. (record indicates that the father had asked the District Attorney to enforce his right to custody in September 1961); S., Feb. 25, 1955 (Although the father had legal custody, the boy was living with mother by agreement and Board did not wish to remove him from his high school where he was doing well and had many friends).

[54] A., Jan. 25, 1962.

[55] R., Aug. 26, 1960.

[56] J., Nov. 15, 1962.

[57] F., May 24, 1957; S., Oct. 21, 1955.

[58] See text accompanying notes 12, 24 supra. If the mother had the children in her home, AFDC was often continued to permit her to keep them, e.g., S., Sept. 22, 1961; S., Aug. 25, 1961, unless it clearly appeared that public policy would not be served by permitting the children to remain in her home, e.g., J., June 23, 1961 (mother had nine children by four different men; of the nine, three were in San Quentin and three others had juvenile records; father of the ten-year-old girl involved had married and apparently established a stable home). And see G., Oct. 18, 1956, where a Negro father had married a white woman and the Negro mother argued that racial mixing in the father's home would be bad for the children. The Board found that the evidence was insufficient to support the conclusion that the children "would have more adequate emotional and physical security" with the father than with the mother.

case[59] the father and mother had been divorced without obtaining a custody order and the two children of the marriage, together with another child whose paternity the father denied, lived with the mother. She established a "stable relationship" with another man and had four children by him. The father, meanwhile, had remarried and was earning approximately five hundred dollars per month. He and his second wife offered a free home to the oldest child, a girl aged ten. The mother, now living alone with the seven children, wished to keep the girl at home. Although a careful evaluation of the father's home indicated that it was "a good one in terms of love, understanding and emotional and financial security," the Board decided to continue the AFDC grant to support the girl in her mother's home. The decision was based on the girl's attachment to her mother, her express desire not to be separated from her brother and sister, and because "we cannot consider that the home offered is a suitable substitute for her present home or that the care reportedly available to her in the home of her father and stepmother . . . might adequately replace the emotional security that a mother can give her own children and which is essential to their well-being."[60]

The offer-of-a-free-home device presented opportunities for antagonistic family members to express their bitterness for each other by forcing custody evaluations which are not available in normal custody situations.[61] Thus, in one case,[62] a boy of seven had lived with his maternal grandmother since he was three months old, when she removed him from the prison hospital ward where he had been born. His mother was released from prison when the child was about two and a half years old; she lived with him and her mother until the boy was three. At that time the mother married and left to establish a home with her husband. The child was supported by AFDC in his mother's home for two months following her marriage; but his grandmother, unhappy because he was in his mother's home, offered to provide a free home for the boy. An evaluation determined that the grandmother's offer was a resource available for the child's support; AFDC to keep him in his mother's home was terminated and the boy returned to his grandmother. Some years later, the grandmother, now fifty-eight, in poor health, and partially blind, became unable to continue to support the boy and applied for AFDC; the mother thereupon countered with an offer to provide a free home. Investigation of the two homes disclosed that the grandmother lived in a small, two-room apartment

---

[59] *E.*, Sept. 27, 1957. See also *M.*, March 20, 1958; *H.*, Feb. 20, 1958; *T.*, Feb. 15, 1957 (grandmother versus father).

[60] *E.*, Sept. 27, 1957.

[61] Modification of a custody award is discussed in text accompanying note 25 *supra*.

[62] *T.*, March 20, 1958.

while the mother lived with her husband and their two children in a small house. The Board found that the long-term advantages offered to the boy by his mother and her husband, when coupled with the mother's preferential legal right to custody, indicated that the boy's best interests would be served by placement with the mother even though he would probably suffer a "temporary emotional trauma" at leaving his grandmother. Aid provided for his support in the grandmother's home was therefore discontinued.

Other unique problems were presented by fathers who agreed to provide a free home for their children only if the mother would consent to return as well; and by grandparents who agreed to provide for their grandchildren if the minor mother-daughter would return to the family home. Without exception in the fair hearing appeals, the Social Welfare Board properly refused to permit the withdrawal of AFDC funds to be used to force marital reconciliations.[63] Nor was the erring daughter required to return home, at least where she was within a year or so of attaining majority and where it was not entirely clear that her parents' offer was bona fide.[64] In one case, however, where the mother was sixteen and pregnant a second time, the Board obviously felt it improper to help her remain in "the home of an unmarried woman [her aunt] with dubious sources of unexplained and unreported income."[65]

There are indications in the Fair Hearing Appeals cases that the Staff and Social Welfare Board were uneasy with the offer-of-a-free-home cases. The determination, after all, was uncomfortably close to a child custody award for a program established to deal with child support. It is probably fair to assume that this discontent together with a critical review of the cases in the report of a California Senate Committee[66] investigating the role of the State Social Welfare Board, may have provided the necessary impetus for withdrawal of the Regulation.[67] The offer-of-a-free-home category of appeals cases, though now dormant, provides some important lessons in the workings of a public support program. In administrative law as in courtroom law it is probably fair to assume that the cases appealed are only a fraction of the cases heard; yet it cannot be assumed that the cases not appealed were all fairly or correctly decided.

---

[63] *H.*, Oct. 21, 1955; *P.*, Feb. 25, 1955; *cf. V.*, July 21, 1961 (mother and father were both married to others; county tried to force a reconciliation of the "common law marriage" but was overruled by the Board).

[64] *T.*, Dec. 21, 1956; *M.*, Dec. 21, 1956; *McC.*, March 26, 1954.

[65] *T.*, June 24, 1959.

[66] Sweet, The Role of the State Social Welfare Board in the Administration of the ANC Program in California 75-78 (1961) (Report to the Senate Fact Finding Committee on Labor and Welfare).

[67] For the text of the new regulation, see note 48 *supra.*

The appealed case often represents a sharp dissatisfaction with the proceedings below that can be used to illuminate other cases in which the disappointed client perhaps was not as determined to get justice or as convinced of the rightness of his position. Several such points are suggested in the offer-of-a-free-home appeals. Thus, in many of the cases, the county workers appeared convinced that the mother, having left her husband in Oklahoma, Louisiana, or Mississippi, turned her eyes to California's high welfare payments and decided to come to this state in order to qualify for relief. In one case, the local workers seemed to believe that the size of California's monthly payment had motivated the break-up: The mother, they claimed, "forsook her spouse for a monetary advantage, looking to the high ANC standards in California."[68] The fact that California requires a one-year residency period of all children not born in the state as a prerequisite to receiving aid[69] seems not to affect the county's suspicions of these migratory mothers. The offer-of-a-free-home regulations, with their emphasis on the child's financial security, could be used to send the child (and sometimes the mother) back to the state they had left. Thus it could become possible in a limited way for California to reinstate the wall of exclusion against the poor that the United States Supreme Court had destroyed in *Edwards v. California*,[70] all in the name of reuniting the family.

Another sore point touched on by many of the cases was the danger that the father's sudden desire to support the child in his own home may have been motivated by the efforts of the district attorney to compel him to support the child in the mother's home. For families living on a restricted budget, it may appear less costly to share the existing resources with a newcomer than to send a monthly payment to the mother. The situation brings out the bitter complaints typical of separated couples; the father suspects that the money he sends will not be spent on the children; the mother fears that the father's promises of support will not actually materialize. The Departmental Manual attempted to solve this problem by suggesting that the worker inquire whether the offer was made in good faith.[71] The infrequency with which the offers were made by persons not charged with the legal duty of supporting the child, however, raises doubts as to whether the county always fully explored the motivation for the offer.

A related point is the degree to which the person making the offer of a free home was motivated by the fact that the child may have reached an

---

[68] *S.*, Sept. 22, 1961.
[69] CAL. WELFARE & INST'NS CODE § 11252.
[70] 314 U.S. 160 (1941).
[71] CALIFORNIA DEP'T OF SOCIAL WELFARE, *op. cit. supra* note 48.

age at which he could be useful as a household helper or baby-sitter. A possible analogy to earlier devices for having children adopted to get them out of publicly-supported institutions[72] would be far-fetched; but nagging doubts as to whether the county evaluated the free home offers rigorously from the point of view of the best interests of the child are not easily laid to rest, particularly when several of the Board's decisions admonished the county for inadequate investigation of the offered home.

In short, the offer-of-a-free-home Regulation provided a vehicle in many cases for county attempts to lower the cost of the public support bill by means other than those designed to encourage "the employment and self-maintenance"[73] of the parents. Although the Board generally arrived at fair results in the cases that were appealed, the effectiveness of such decisions in controlling the county administrators was probably low. The withdrawal of the Regulation seems to have been the only meaningful way of reassuring the custodian that the Welfare authorities would no longer force the removal of children from the home because of the availability of a free home elsewhere.

B. Neglect

The custodian whose children are supported by AFDC may, however, have reason to fear that the welfare authorities will force the removal of the children on other grounds. Professor tenBroek has spoken of the tendency of the home visits of the welfare caseworker to raise "questions of fitness . . . with regard to . . . the suitability of the home for the rearing of the children, issues of morality, extra-marital relations, drinking, and the like."[74] Referral of child neglect cases from local welfare departments to probation departments may serve to reinforce the "inspection" aspects of the caseworker's visits in the minds of the recipients. Low budgets and inadequate staff have made extended casework services for welfare families impracticable except for a few experimental projects. A recent California study dealing with neglected children concludes that for the immediate future, the "referral of child neglect cases from the welfare departments to the probation departments will continue to be a common practice."[75] Such cases are not difficult to locate in the probation caseload of dependent and neglected children. Thus, in a recent case heard in a metropolitan juvenile court, the following testimony developed:

---

[72] See tenBroek, *California's Dual System of Family Law: Its Origin, Development, and Present Status*, 16 STAN. L. REV. 900, 955-61 (1964).

[73] CAL. WELFARE & INST'NS CODE § 11205.

[74] tenBroek, *supra* note 44 at 649.

[75] NATIONAL STUDY SERVICE, PLANNING FOR THE PROTECTION AND CARE OF NEGLECTED CHILDREN IN CALIFORNIA 39 (Final Report, Aug., 1965) [Hereinafter cited as NATIONAL STUDY SERVICE].

The household was composed of an eighteen-year-old mother and her three children, who ranged in age from two and a half years to eight months. Only the oldest child was supported by AFDC. The mother's husband, father of the two younger children, was absent on duty in the military service. The welfare caseworker, making an unannounced house visit, had found the mother absent from the home and the two older children alone in the house. Upon entering the house accompanied by a neighbor, the caseworker found the house "filthy," one child naked, and mouldy food in the refrigerator. She called the police and insisted that the children be taken into protective custody. The children were taken to the county reception center for dependent children, where they remained from Wednesday until Monday, when the detention hearing was held and they were released to the mother pending the juvenile court hearing. At this hearing, held a month later, the mother and father both appeared. The welfare worker testified that the house was "messy but not dirty" and that she had waited for about twenty or thirty minutes before removing the children. The mother's explanation of her absence was that she had been trying to find a baby-sitter to take care of the older children while she took the baby to see a doctor. She stated that she had never left the children alone before. The father defended his wife, pointing out that she had had a hard time trying to manage for eleven months while he had been in military service. He seemed bitter towards the worker's actions, and asked the court why, if the "welfare lady" really wanted to help his family, she hadn't offered to baby-sit for his wife instead of "calling the cops and bringing us to court?" Upon being told by the judge about the worker's responsibilities under the AFDC program, he stated that they had "gone off" welfare in order to avoid the home visits. He asked whether the court couldn't rely on him to take care of the family; having just ridded his family of the welfare worker, he obviously was not anxious to have her replaced by the probation officer. The court, however, accepted the Probation Department's recommendation that there be some supervision for the children. Accordingly, he made them dependent children of the court and placed them in the family home with provision for a further hearing in ten months.

Figures showing how many AFDC children are referred to probation departments of other protective service agencies as "neglected" children apparently are not available. A recent study in the Minneapolis-St. Paul area, however, indicates that "the educated, economically independent family is the rare exception among the neglect referrals."[76] A two-month

---

[76] Boehm, *The Community and the Social Agency Define Neglect*, 43 CHILD WELFARE 453, 459 (1964).

sample of neglect referrals disclosed that, although only three per cent of families in the general population were on public assistance, forty-two per cent of the neglect families were relief recipients.[77] The California study estimates that a "substantial" number of the 21,264 children who were referred to probation departments from all sources as possible dependent and neglected children during the twelve months ending June 30, 1964, are located in the AFDC caseload.[78] Referrals come to probation from the police, schools, local welfare agencies, private agencies, and individuals (parents, neighbors, and attorneys).[79] The probable causes of the referrals are many and varied. Alameda County gives the following breakdown of its 2,356 referrals for neglected and dependent children in 1964: unfit home situations (952 referrals); no supervision or control (601 referrals); no parent or guardian (356 referrals); parent ill or incapacitated (303 referrals); victims of rape or molestation (65 referrals); protective custody (49 referrals); child unhappy with home situation (20 referrals); and suicide attempts (10 referrals).[80]

A sampling of the cases recently before a metropolitan juvenile court indicates both the range of problems and the depressing sameness of the struggle to solve them with the resources at hand. One case involves three children all under ten years of age caught in the aftermath of divorce: their mother's second husband refused to have them in his home; their father's second wife, after keeping them for some time, was "no longer willing to care for them." The mother was ready to concede permanent legal custody to the father; but he was described as "weak" and under domination by his wife. The children were placed in a foster home; at last indication, the father and stepmother were willing to try it again. In another case, the children were found alone in the home in a condition described by the police officer who took them into custody as "without shoes, hair uncombed, clothing dirty, ragged, torn; unbathed, open sores." The house was covered with "dirt, debris, glass splinters on floor"; the kitchen disclosed a dishpan in stagnant water; a refrigerator empty and filthy; and a stove caked with grease. The father and mother agreed that the children should be placed in a foster home. The mother said she would try to find a job so that she could ultimately reclaim the children. In a third case, the mother and father, both under thirty-five, were unmarried.

---

[77] *Ibid.*

[78] NATIONAL STUDY SERVICE 8-12. It is known that 3,800 of the 20,189 children who had been declared dependent children of the court were being supervised in their own homes by the local welfare department because the family was receiving assistance of some kind. *Id.* at 44.

[79] *Id.* at 8-12.

[80] 1964 ALAMEDA COUNTY PROBATION DEPARTMENT, ANNUAL REPORT 3-4.

Both have attempted suicide. The child was removed from the home when she was eighteen months old because of the frequent drunken fights of the parents and because the mother left the child alone "more than once during the past six months" in violation of the child neglect standards of the California Probation Officers and the State Department of Social Welfare.[81] The parents agreed that they were unable to care for their daughter, and a foster home placement was arranged.

Despite the wide use of foster home placements in California,[82] these cases are not typical in using such placement in neglect cases. Of the 20,189 dependent children of the court being supervised by probation departments as of December 31, 1963, 11,000 were under supervision in their own homes and only 8,175 were in foster homes or the homes of relatives.[83] The problem of neglect is a specialized problem of child custody; perhaps it is fair to say that the problem is largely one of developing the resources and facilities needed to provide physical and emotional security to neglected children in their own homes. It is now becoming widely recognized that "because of the vital importance of a child's own parents, the primary efforts of any community should be to preserve them for him, to assist them in carrying their responsibilities successfully, and to prevent family breakdown."[84]

A special problem of neglect for poverty-stricken families appears to be that, because of the differences in socio-economic class attitudes toward parental competence, children may be removed from the home too soon.[85] Reinhart and Elmer, in their study of the abused child, noted that "in view of the gravity of the data at hand about a large proportion of the patients, it was anticipated that the follow-up study would reveal extreme pathology among the families. While this has been true of some family groups, a few others have shown warmth, good capacity for child-

---

[81] NATIONAL STUDY SERVICE 5-6.

[82] "It is estimated that there were approximately 21,000 children under agency supervision in licensed foster homes in California in June 1964." NATIONAL STUDY SERVICE 66. This figure does not include children placed directly by their parents. "It is estimated that the number so placed may be 10 per cent as many as placed by agencies." Id. at 66 n.30.

[83] NATIONAL STUDY SERVICE 44 (861 children were in institutions).

[84] Id. at 23.

[85] See Polier, The Invisible Legal Rights of the Poor, 12 CHILDREN 215, 218 (1965): "mothers in the aid to families with dependent children (AFDC) program receive on the average less than $1 a day for each child. If we find that the home is inadequate, that the mother is unable to cope with the problems of so many children, we remove the child to the home of a stranger or series of strangers, paying from public funds up to $7 a day for the child's care. If the child is removed to an institution, the institution is paid up to $14 a day. Finally, if the child becomes emotionally disturbed, payments from public funds may range from $10 to $25 a day. Thus, the further the child is removed from his family, the more we are ready to pay for his support."

rearing, and an unexpected degree of integration."[86] The allegation that the mother "has failed to provide a moral environment in that during the last six years, she has had six illegitimate pregnancies" may overlook qualities that make her a good mother to all the children. The important question is how such behavior influences the child's development,[87] since parental deficiencies may be balanced by parental strengths. At the same time, however, children should not be allowed to remain in homes under serious conditions of neglect merely because foster-care facilities are costly and inadequate.[88] The problem is how a caseworker can be trained to appraise family situations much different from those his own experience had led him to expect and in a way that will assume maximum protection for the child.

Even with the best casework services available, however, "the only way adequately to protect some children will be to remove them promptly from the care of their parents."[89] Here the placement problem becomes critical; perhaps more critical for the poverty families than for the well-to-do. A recent juvenile court case illustrates one aspect of the problem. a ten-year-old boy who had been supported by AFDC funds since birth was taken into protective custody following a beating by his stepfather. It was discovered that he had serious behavior problems that made foster placement inappropriate. Twenty institutions were approached as possible placements for the boy; none of them were available. He was rejected on a variety of grounds: He was either too young or too old; he did not meet the religious membership tests of some of the private institutions; he was too retarded for some, too bright for others. After six months of holding the boy at Juvenile Hall, the Probation Department was forced to report to the juvenile court that "there are currently no placement possibilities."

---

[86] Reinhart & Elmer, *The Abused Child*, A.M.A.J., April 27, 1964, pp. 358, 361.

[87] *Cf.* Ashwell v. Ashwell, 135 Cal. App. 2d 211, 286 P.2d 983 (1955), where the mother, her four children under six years of age, and her illegitimate baby were all living with the baby's father while waiting for her divorce to become final. The court, reversing the trial court's change of custody of the four children to their father, said: "It is proper to bear in mind, as these things are being considered, that in determining where custody of children shall lie the courts are not engaged in a disciplinary action to punish parents for their shortcomings as individuals nor to reward the unoffending parent for any wrong suffered by the sins of the other. . . . The prime question is, what is the effect upon the lives of the children and what will be the effect of a modified decree that disturbs their settled life and compels them to make adjustments to a life with strangers. In view of the tender ages of these children we think that the conduct of the mother as described in the testimony was at the time this change was ordered having no possible bad effect upon them. They were too young." *Id.* at 217, 286 P.2d at 987. But see Currin v. Currin, 125 Cal. App. 2d 644, 271 P.2d 61 (1954), where the court denied the mother custody in a situation where the mother's conduct was characterized as "indiscriminate, profligate and shameless." *Id.* at 650, 271 P.2d at 65.

[88] See Polier, *supra* note 85, at 219.

[89] NATIONAL STUDY SERVICE 23.

The Department nevertheless recommended against returning the boy to his home; the judge agreed that attempts at placement should be continued, but sent the boy home while the attempts were being pursued. Another case disclosed that a juvenile court in a neighboring state had deprived the mother of her two children, aged five and six, because she frequently beat them and left them unattended for prolonged periods. The children were placed in the custody of a maternal aunt and uncle and funds were supplied to help with their support. When the children were ten and eleven, the mother married a man recently paroled after serving a criminal sentence and asked that the children be returned to her home. Although her adjustment continued to be borderline, the children were returned to maintain the family home and because "the children need their mother." When the family moved to California, no records were forwarded and no supervision was maintained. When the children were twelve and thirteen, the younger, a girl, complained to her school counsellor that for the past two years she had been molested repeatedly by her stepfather. On further investigation, the boy reported that the stepfather had subjected him regularly to experiences of sodomy and fellatio. The juvenile court placed the children in a local foster home, and they were later permitted to return to their aunt and uncle. The original decision to return these children to their mother's home appears to have substantially contributed to the disruption of their lives.

Adoption, if viewed as a permanent solution to the placement problem, discloses sharp differences between white and nonwhite poverty groups. There seems no longer to be any doubt that minority-group children are not acceptable for adoption because of the practical impossibility of locating adoptive homes.[90] The lack of early protective services for these children is directly related to the adoption problem: California figures show that ninety per cent of all adoptive placements are made before the child is one year old.[91] The difficulties of placing the older child for adoption even under the best circumstances simply means that the problem is heightened for minority groups because their children are not made available for adoption at an early age.

Finally, the recent emergence of the "Battered Child Syndrome"[92] provides an aggravated microcosm in which the more general problems of the child custody law of the poor are reflected. Reports from the medical profession indicate that "many hold the sentiment that private patients

---

[90] *Id.* at 81-82; Polier, *supra* note 85, at 216-17.

[91] NATIONAL STUDY SERVICE 81.

[92] For an excellent beginning to a forthcoming comprehensive series of articles on this problem, see McCoid, *The Battered Child and Other Assaults Upon the Family: Part One,* 50 MINN. L. REV. 1 (1965).

should be managed differently from clinic patients. Pressure is strong to refer the latter to court almost in summary procedure, even before identifying information for family members can be obtained."[93] Often a physician will not report a private patient to police authorities, but will attempt to handle the situation himself. Children who receive private medical care are thus infrequently reported in the medical literature. The children of the poor, on the other hand, come to the attention of authorities through social welfare channels in which the reporting is done by welfare workers, police, and schools. This public scrutiny may result in more adequate protection for children of the poor: a sort of inverse discrimination. However, the reports even on poverty-stricken families tend to be limited to physical abuse. Psychological abuse is rarely a cause for the removal of a child from his home. Nevertheless, probation officers are pointing to a "Beverly Hills Syndrome," in which the child who is raised in economically favorable circumstances may be unwanted, uncared for, and rarely attended except by hired help. Problems of these children may become known to public authorities only through petty delinquencies such as alcoholism, promiscuity, motor vehicle violations, and property destruction.[94]

CONCLUSION

Child custody problems are not easily resolved. One of the primary duties of the law is to provide a procedure for handling custody matters so that the best available knowledge about the effect on a particular child of the dissolution of his family can be brought to bear on the solution of the problem. This task is not discharged by simply calling for equal treatment of the children of rich and poor families, for under the present law the rich child may fare as badly as the poor. The entire structure is in need of review.

Nor is it enough to place the entire effort behind proposals designed to keep families together, tempting though that goal may be. This is not an area in which success can be measured only in terms of the number of families who are reconciled. Some families should not stay together. For these families, the law must recognize that divorce is necessary and should be available to decently end the marriage, even for those unable to afford a lawyer. Divorce will not be abolished; and even if it were, family dissolution would not thereby be ended.[95] Moreover, as the anthro-

---

93 Reinhart & Elmer, *The Abused Child*, A.M.A.J., April 27, 1964, pp. 358, 359.

94 *The Beverly Hills Syndrome*, unpublished Proceedings of the Conference on Probation and the Law sponsored by the Department of Health and Welfare, State of California, San Francisco, April, 1963.

95 See Rheinstein, *Divorce and the Law in Germany: A Review*, 65 American J. of Sociology 489 (1960).

pologist Paul Bohannan has pointed out, divorce does not end family life: It ends only married life.[96] The divorced spouses are still parents and often they maintain an active kinship relation through the children, not only with each other but also with the children's new stepparents. Yet the law has rarely considered, let alone provided for, the family problems that follow after divorce.

As an integral part of divorce, a sensible custody plan must be worked out to prevent the spouses from using the children as battering-rams against each other. Much of the anguish that follows a bitter divorce could be averted if the law would use behavioral scientists in ways more in keeping with their experience and training.[97] Too often the psychiatrist called upon to aid the court in awarding custody is looked upon as an individual who gathers facts about the personal lives and emotional state of each parent to determine which is unfit or which will offer the best home. The determination is difficult if viewed in this perspective. The psychiatrist sees two parents in conflict who may be utilizing the custody determination as a means of retaliating against each other. If we perceive that custody disputes often result from conflict between parents who are originally hurt by the behavior of their mates and, in turn, convert this hurt into anger followed by retaliation, then the essential problem in such custody turmoils is to help each parent resolve aspects of his original conflict so that both will begin to work at what would be the best interests of the child rather than personal satisfaction. Reasonable parents in this situation who are acting unreasonably towards each other may be helped to resolve their differences about the child despite the divorce and allow an integrated solution to occur.

If providing short-term counseling for the parents within the court setting will help to attain this goal, then counseling should be provided at public expense through the establishment of family courts with experienced and trained personnel to offer help to the family after the divorce is granted and so long as the child is under the jurisdiction of the court. If sufficient time is allowed to begin work with each parent alone or together, the life of the child may be less disrupted by continued battles and repeated petitions for modification.

---

[96] Bohannan, Notes on the Ethnography of Divorce Among the American Middle Classes, Nov. 19, 1965 (Unpublished, read at the American Association of Anthropologists Meetings).

[97] See also Philips, *Mental Hygiene, Divorce and the Law*, 3 J. FAMILY L. 63, 70 (1963).

Guardianship or "Permanent Placement" of Children

*Hasseltine B. Taylor**

THOUSANDS OF CHILDREN are separated from their parents and living for long periods of time in foster care, in group homes, or in institutions.[1] Many of them are not free for adoption or have no adoptive parents in prospect. The need of many of them for permanent or long-term foster care has been pointed out.[2] For some of these children the formal and personal relationship of guardian and ward is believed by this writer to be appropriate not only from a legal standpoint but from a social standpoint as well. Such a status could contribute much to their emotional security and their identity in the home and the community.[3] The institution of guardian and ward is well established in legal history.[4]

The parents of some "children in need of parents"[5] may be unwilling to consent to their adoption. Yet their children have not been so completely abandoned or so seriously neglected as to be freed for adoption without their consent. Other parents may have delayed in reaching a decision to give the children in adoption until the children are too old to be in demand or to accept strangers easily in the place of parents. Some children are handicapped in ways that make licensed agencies hesitate to recommend them for adoption. Some are children belonging to minority groups in which little tradition of formal adoption exists. Despite the need for permanent homes many such children continue to live under temporary and unsatisfactory arrangements when they need and hunger for responsible, intimate, and durable relationships.

These children are receiving substitute care in various ways. Some are in the homes of relatives where the relatives, the parents, voluntary or governmental agencies support them. Others have been placed in foster homes selected and supervised by licensed child welfare agencies. In

---

* A.B., 1926, Louisiana State University; M.A., 1927, Columbia University; Ph.D., 1934, J.D., 1939, University of Chicago. Lecturer, University of California School of Social Welfare, Berkeley.

[1] JETER, CHILDREN, PROBLEMS AND SERVICES IN CHILD WELFARE PROGRAMS 76 (1963). The estimated number in temporary and long-term foster care rose between 1958 through March 1961 from 229,500 to 255,000. Kahn, *Child Welfare: Trends and Directions*, 41 CHILD WELFARE 459, 464 (1962).

[2] Smith, *Permanent or Long-Term Foster Family Care*, 43 CHILD WELFARE 192 (1964).

[3] Weissman, *Guardianship: Every Child's Right*, Annals, Sept. 1964, p. 134.

[4] 1 SCHOULER, DOMESTIC RELATIONS 907-24 (1921); TAYLOR, GUARDIAN AND WARD 9-30 (1934); WOERNER, THE AMERICAN LAW OF GUARDIANSHIP 39-77 (1897).

[5] MAAS & ENGLER, CHILDREN IN NEED OF PARENTS (1959).

California, many are in foster homes and institutions receiving state and county aid.

Child welfare agencies have made extended and organized efforts to develop foster family care and to create a demand for adoption of children but such agencies have given little attention to exploring the potential supply of legally appointable guardians or to the study of children for whom the relationship of guardian and ward might accord better with their needs than either adoption or substitute care in families, group homes, or in institutions. Permanent placement with minimum agency oversight is being suggested.[6]

Society supports agencies for child welfare and expects them to provide care for children whose parents cannot or will not provide it. However, the demand for care is greater than the supply. Geographical and social mobility have reduced the desire and obligation of relatives to care for children of their own blood. As more and more married women work out of the home, fewer find it possible to care for more than their own children and often need socially provided day care or other assistance in doing even that.[7] Some licensed adoption agencies have had to refuse to accept relinquishments for adoption from minority group parents for want of available adoptive-applicants. A great increase in illegitimate births has swelled the supply of children whose parents often wish to give them in adoption.[8] The individual child may find himself in a succession of temporary placements where he may suffer irreparable injury to his growth and development as an integrated person. Before serious crises develop in socially providing for child care, the alternative of guardianship, if tried, might open additional homes for children.

Parents, while living, are both the natural and legal guardians of their children unless they have relinquished them for adoption, have had their right to guardianship suspended by juvenile court guardianship, have been replaced by court-appointed guardians, or have had their rights terminated by judicial decree.[9] Parents, like strangers, must be appointed by the proper court to serve as guardians of their children's estates except where such estates are small. A court-appointed guardian of the person has the rights and responsibilities of a parent except for the duty

[6] Lewis, *Foster-Family Care: Has It Fulfilled Its Promise?*, Annals, Sept. 1964, p. 41; Smith, *supra* note 2, at 192-94.

[7] Barbey, *The Case for Day Care*, in HELPING THE FAMILY IN URBAN SOCIETY 89 (Delliquadri ed. 1963).

[8] It is estimated that 220,600 illegitimate births occurred in the United States in 1959. U.S. PUBLIC HEALTH SERVICE, DEP'T OF HEALTH, EDUCATION & WELFARE, VITAL STATISTICS IN THE UNITED STATES 1959 3-30 (1960).

[9] See generally FLEXNER, OPPENHEIMER & LENROOT, THE CHILD, THE FAMILY AND THE COURT (U.S. Children's Bureau Pub. No. 193, 1929).

to support the ward.[10] His office is terminable by resignation, removal for cause, or by successful assertion of the superior claim which a parent might be able to make to the child's guardianship. He is subject to the control of the court which appointed him. Yet children who are without parents or estates of their own are seldom related to a responsible adult in the relationship of guardian and ward.

Since the adoption of juvenile court laws, children who are brought to the attention of these courts and found dependent, neglected, or delinquent are made wards of the juvenile court. Whether left in the custody of their parents or placed in foster homes under the supervision of probation officers, committed to licensed institutions or to agencies for foster-home placement, they are wards of the court. Thus children whose parental guardianship or informal care does not fall conspicuously below the community's standard are not subject to court guardianship.

In recent decades attention has been called to the advantages of guardianship for minors without guardians and to the need for social services to be available to the courts in exercising jurisdiction over their appointment and more actively assuring their accountability.[11] The relationship of guardian and ward does not connote economic dependency on the part of the child. In fact, because of the failure of our law to require children to have guardians by nature or by appointment, it rather suggests that the child's own parents or someone who cared about him had planned for or sought the child's guardianship when parental care was lost by death or disability. It does not suggest that the child is or ever was "nobody's child," or a "social agency's child," or a "ward of the state."

The substitute parent when holding letters of guardianship enjoys the dignity of being in law as well as in fact a substitute parent subject only to the control of the court appointing him. He is not a foster parent whose role is contingent upon continuous supervision by a child welfare agency or juvenile court probation officer. His sense of responsibility for the child is probably stronger and the child's respect for him is probably greater when their relationship is a formal and settled one. If the guardian were selected by a child welfare agency, he would be familiar with the availability of social services when perplexed or wanting consultation. Where the child is receiving socially provided income, he, like a parent, could be held responsible for using it for the child's own needs and be as competent to report changes in the child's economic circumstances.

---

10 See 5 BANCROFT, PROBATE PRACTICE 159-239 (2d ed. 1950).

11 TAYLOR, GUARDIAN AND WARD (1934); WEISSMAN, GUARDIANSHIP: A WAY OF FULFILLING PUBLIC RESPONSIBILITY FOR CHILDREN (U.S. Children, Bureau Pub. No. 330, 1949); Breckinridge & Stanton, *The Law of Guardian and Ward with Special Reference to the Children of Veterans*, 17 SOCIAL SERVICE REV. 265 (1943).

Children without parents or estates are not likely to have a change in financial situation until they can achieve it by their own efforts. Should the unexpected occur through gift, inheritance, or receipt of damages for negligent injury, the appointed guardian of the person might or might not be the most suitable person to serve as guardian of the estate.

The child's welfare would probably be better served by living with a person in whom guardianship is vested than by being supervised in a home where authority is uncertainly divided.[12] It would be better served where the person having physical custody does not occupy a contingent role which may be visualized by the child and his associates as weighted on the side of domestic service instead of parenthood. The child could readily identify his relationship and explain the variance in surnames.[13]

Social agencies which would develop and encourage the use of the relationship of guardian and ward would be able to "close the case" after satisfactory placement had been achieved for appropriate children and letters of guardianship issued, as is done when an adoption decree is entered. All suspicion that an agency has an interest in maintaining high case loads, that it does not know when to let go of supervising homes, or that it is depriving a child of a personal guardian by sharing responsibility for the child's custody with a foster parent would be dispelled. After the guardian's appointment, a client relationship, if any, would be between the agency worker and the guardian, not the worker and the child. The child's needs might again bring him to the attention of a social agency or his guardian might resign or be removed and another would have to be appointed in his place.

It is believed that many persons for many reasons would find the role of guardian more attractive than that of adoptive parent on the one hand or foster parent on the other. The relationship of parent and child created by adoption carries with it the duty to support the child. Many suitable prospective guardians may not be economically secure or have enjoyed such security long enough to deliberately want to undertake such a responsibility. Others may feel that prior commitments or obligations are all that can be met comfortably. In some cases guardianship may provide a more satisfying emotional reward for both parties than adoption which is, regardless of legal effects, still a substitute for a natural relationship. A guardian can be enabled to support his ward by socially provided income without any

---

[12] See WOLINS, SELECTING FOSTER. PARENTS 15-33 (1963).

[13] Glover & Reid, *Unmet and Future Needs*, Annals, Sept. 1964, pp. 15-16 states: "It is thought that many Negro families as well as white, because of economic risks and responsibilities of adoption, will be interested in taking a young child into their homes on a permanent basis. Agencies will pay all expenses of the child's care; at the same time they will encourage the foster parents to assume as much responsibility as they are willing to take in other areas, even allowing them to give their names to the children."

suggestion of failure on his part. Such failure is often felt by parents when they cannot support their children. Guardianship of a child old enough to remember his parents or to cherish his own identity may serve the needs of the child and do so more comfortably for both. An adoptive parent, however sensitive he may be, occupies a role differently defined by society.

What appears to be lacking for this relationship to have the potential of another viable social resource for children in need of substitute parents is: (1) the extension of socially provided and reasonably assured income maintenance for children without other sources of income to children with guardians, and (2) conviction on the part of child welfare agencies and social workers that guardianship is worthy of exploration along with the possibilities of adoption or other forms of substitute care.

For these and other reasons which might be enumerated, the writer would like to see a demonstration project or projects undertaken by a public or voluntary child welfare agency and financed by funds authorized by section 526 of the Social Security Act as amended.[14] California offers particular opportunities for undertaking such a project because its Aid to Families with Dependent Children already extends to children in foster homes and institutions.[15] Such a demonstration project might supply a modicum of evidence in support of federal financial participation in state aid to needy children living with legally appointed guardians as well as children living with parents and specified relatives.

The Advisory Council on Public Assistance considered the extension of federal aid to the states for programs including children in foster homes.[16] It did not recommend this extension. Before Congress sees fit to enact such an expansion of coverage, the results of demonstration projects might influence Congress and state legislatures to make the lesser expansion—aid to needy children living with legally appointed guardians.

---

[14] 74 Stat. 997 (1960), as amended, 42 U.S.C. § 726 (1964). Under the Social Security Act of 1935 and its subsequent amendments federal grants-in-aid to states have been available for state programs providing money payments to dependent children living in their own homes or with specified relatives and social insurance benefits for children of primary beneficiaries have been available to many children. 70 Stat. 848 (1956), as amended, 42 U.S.C. § 601 (1964). In the absence of a surviving parent, children's benefits from the National OASDI program are paid to representative payees selected by and accountable to the administrative agency. Guardians are not required. The amendments of 1962 authorize state programs to use "restrictive payments" in a small percentage of the recipient families without loss of federal aid. 76 Stat. 188 (1962), 42 U.S.C. § 605 (1964). "Restrictive payments" are payments to persons other than the statutory caretaker (parent or relative) when the parent or relative caretaker demonstrates incapacity or unwillingness to use the aid for the child's needs.

[15] CAL. WELFARE & INST'NS CODE § 1500.1(b).

[16] Advisory Council on Public Assistance, *Report*, S. Doc. No. 93, 86th Cong., 2d Sess. 38 (1960).

Some states already provide for waiver of costs of guardianship proceedings where public aid is involved.[17]

Such a demonstration, if it supplied positive evidence supporting the hypothesis upon which such a proposal would be based, might result in greater use of Child Welfare Services by the court in appointing and supervising guardians of the persons of all children.[18] It might even bring reconsideration of the use of strangers as payees for minor and incompetent beneficiaries of social insurance and for children receiving Aid to Families with Dependent Children whose parent cannot be trusted with the grants. The essential distinction between modern public income maintenance programs and relief under the poor laws is that administrative authority is over programs only and does not extend to power over persons. This distinction should be preserved but is threatened by payments of aid to third parties selected by administrative agencies without a judicial finding that the parent has abused the trust.

Such a project would not demonstrate a substitute for adoption which is clearly superior wherever it is both possible and appropriate. It would not be intended to demonstrate even the value of every child having a guardian by nature or by appointment.[19] It could demonstrate with what ease or difficulty suitable persons willing to accept appointment by the court to this office could be found. It could throw light on whether a permanent home with a court appointed guardian is to be preferred to a permanent placement with minimal supervision of the placement agency. It is worth trying before there is a swing in fashion to group care.[20]

It may be that the great changes wrought in the structure of the family and of society and in the minds of men since the 18th Century have rendered the relationship of guardian and ward vestigial or even obsolete. Manifestations of the social interest in children so often advanced under the banner of the "rights of children" and projected in terms of their social importance as "human resources" grow apace. Yet there is a growing recognition that many are weary of alienation and want to embark upon "the quest for community."[21] Its stimulation is one of the purposes, or at least this is hoped to be one of the consequences of the Economic Opportunity Act of 1964. We cannot say as Lord Eldon did in the *Wellesley* case,[22] "It is not . . . from any want of jurisdiction that it does

---

[17] *E.g.*, CAL. GOV'T CODE § 6102.

[18] See WEISSMAN, *op. cit. supra* note 11, at 3.

[19] As recommended in SMITH, THE RIGHT TO LIFE 122-152 (1955), where the use of substitute payees is roundly condemned.

[20] Wolins, *Political Orientation, Social Reality, and Child Welfare*, 38 SOCIAL SERVICE REV. 429 (1964).

[21] NISBET, THE QUEST FOR COMMUNITY (1953).

[22] Wellesley v. Beaufort, 2 Russ. 1, 21, 38 Eng. Rep. 236, 243 (1827).

not act, but from a want of means to exercise its jurisdiction . . . ." Today in the United States, the means are available to permit the welfare of the child, not his estate, to determine the social and legal provisions made for him.

Family Law and Welfare Policies: The Case for "Dual Systems"

Thomas P. Lewis* and Robert J. Levy**

PROLOGUE

IN A RECENT CONFERENCE on "The Extension of Legal Services to the Poor" a speaker observed that some legal aid societies insist that a person seeking a divorce first submit to reconciliation procedures.[1] In the discussion that followed, a conferee insisted that a poor person should not be subject to a counseling requirement which the rich man could avoid with private counsel. Another suggested that counseling should be required of all who seek divorces irrespective of their economic status.[2]

It is becoming increasingly popular to analyze problems of the poor in this way—by drawing comparisons between the rich and the poor and cataloguing inequalities of one kind or another. The appeal for greater equality between rich and poor is a natural concomitant of the "Civil Rights Revolution" which can claim major judicial victories such as *Brown v. Board of Education*[3] and *Gideon v. Wainwright*[4] and major legislative-executive victories such as the Civil Rights Act of 1964[5] and, indirectly, the War on Poverty. Equality as the central theme for argument, description, or analysis dramatizes and highlights the status of the poor and carries a strong emotional appeal quite apart from any function it has as a legal command to action. Especially is this so today, for our society, which has always valued equality as an abstract ideal, shows an increasing willingness to conform its practices to its theories. Another factor contributing to the popularity of equality as a theme for argument is its apparent simplicity. Since equality is sought in the place of perceived inequality, the wisdom of rules or practices can be ignored; it is enough that one of two rules or practices be changed to conform to its counterpart. The conference session described above, for example, pro-

---

* A.B., 1959, LL.B., 1954, University of Kentucky; S.J.D., 1964, Harvard University. Professor of Law, University of Minnesota.

** A.B. 1952, Kenyon College; LL.B. 1957, University of Pennsylvania. Professor of Law, University of Minnesota.

[1] Paulsen, *The Legal Needs of the Poor and Family Law*, in CONFERENCE PROCEEDINGS ON THE EXTENSION OF LEGAL SERVICES TO THE POOR 18, 19 (U.S. Dep't of Health, Educ. & Welfare 1964).

[2] CONFERENCE PROCEEDINGS ON THE EXTENSION OF LEGAL SERVICES TO THE POOR 68 (U.S. Dep't of Health, Educ. & Welfare 1964).

[3] 347 U.S. 483 (1954).

[4] 372 U.S. 335 (1963).

[5] 78 Stat. 241 (1964) (codified in sections of 5 U.S.C., 28 U.S.C., and 42 U.S.C.).

duced two contradictory suggestions, each one equal to the task of ensuring "equality" of legal services.

But the simplicity of equality as a standard is often more apparent than real. The problem of "inequality" that concerned the conferees resulted from the fact that legal aid society policies might differ from those of a private practitioner available for hire by the rich. This problem is not limited to divorce remedies—that simply happened to be the subject under discussion. The reason assigned for attacking reconciliation procedures has equal force when applied to any divergence between the services of legal aid counsel and retained private counsel. If perfect equality is desired the only adequate remedy would be the provision of funds with which the poor might retain counsel of their own choosing. But this remedy creates additional problems of its own. It would not be a sensible allocation of resources to attempt to make legal services available to the supported group on demand. Whether individual retained counsel or group legal services are supplied, it is obvious that the lawyers involved or some agency will have to make judgments on the merits of the claims to be supported and pursued.[6] Since the wealthy make their own choices, at least a theoretical inequality would remain. The need to define the class to be provided funds for legal services presents a more difficult problem. Comparisons of legal services available according to economic status are usually drawn between the poor and the wealthy. The fact is, of course, that the bulk of our citizens are in neither category, but range across a wide spectrum between the extremes. It would very probably be impossible to define the benefited class and the claims to be funded in such a way as to avoid creating inequalities between members of the class and their fellow citizens on the next higher rung of the economic ladder. Resulting from a scheme premised on the eradication of inequality, these inequalities would be hard to justify.

None of this suggests that mandatory reconciliation procedures for legal aid clients are desirable or wise. There are differences of opinion on whether a family lawyer should explore available avenues of reconciliation before proceeding with a divorce action. A private practitioner may make his own choice of policies, accepting or rejecting clients who are unwilling to abide by them. A rejected client, of course, has the choice of seeking other counsel who will accept the case on his terms. Because a legal aid client does not have this kind of choice, it is perfectly clear that legal aid lawyers cannot be permitted in all respects to exercise the independence of the most independent private lawyer. Some policies of general application should be adopted by the societies concerning the

---

[6] The English have just grappled with this problem. See Iverson v. Iverson [1966] 1 All E.R. 258 (Prob.).

kinds of services they will offer, and their attorneys will have to be willing to live with those policies. It should be equally clear, however, that within the framework of general policies set by a legal aid society, the lawyers must be provided leeway for professional judgment if they are to be worthy of their calling.[7] Perhaps judgments about the worth of reconciliatory efforts in particular cases are the kind best left to the judgment of the lawyers involved, within the framework of any general policies established by the society. Whatever the outcome, legal aid societies should not be encouraged in the name of equality to provide the lowest common denominator of service available to the rich as a result of their ability to "shop" for counsel.

Equality is not a concept of fixed or easily identifiable value; its importance as well as its costs will vary with the circumstances to which it is applied. And these two variables—importance and cost—are not joined in a proportional relationship. If these characteristics are not borne in mind appeals to equality may be at best distracting, and at worst as full of false promise as the sweet singing of the sirens.

Equality is the touchstone of an important series of essays which provide the primary background for our topic—"America's Dual System of Family Law." Professor Jacobus tenBroek's major work, *California's Dual System of Family Law: Its Origins, Development, and Present Status*,[8] describes what he characterizes as two systems of family law, one for the poor and one for the rest of society. His purpose, especially in his discussion of the present status of California's family law,[9] is to draw attention to the inequality he believes to be inherent and inherently evil in the dual systems. Duality as sketched by Professor tenBroek has several sources, but by far the most prolific is the system of welfare laws and rules which regulate participation by the poor in governmental aid programs. This system is contrasted with the civil family law of California, that is, the rules of law which govern family relationships in the rest of society. For example, he notes that certain resources of a wife in California cannot be reached by a person who has furnished "necessaries" to the husband, but that these same resources will be counted by the state when it determines the need of the family unit for public assistance.[10] In the same vein, he complains that, while common law marriage is not recognized in California, the income of a man "assuming the

---

[7] See Sparer, *The Role of the Welfare Client's Lawyer*, 12 U.C.L.A.L. REV. 361, 377-80 (1965).

[8] (Pts. 1, 2), 16 STAN. L. REV. 257, 900 (1964), (pt. 3), 17 STAN. L. REV. 614 (1965) [hereinafter cited as tenBroek with appropriate volume and pages].

[9] tenBroek, 17 STAN. L. REV. 614.

[10] *Id.* at 623-24.

role of spouse" will be considered by the state in determining the financial eligibility of the children in the household for welfare benefits.[11] tenBroek's criticism of these and many other rules that govern the availability of welfare assistance is summarized in the following passage:

> Family Law in California is not single, uniform, and equal as to all families whatever their status, condition, or wealth. On the contrary, it is dual and distinguishes among families on the basis of poverty. It is therefore discriminatory as to the groups which are the principal victims of poverty: racial and ethnic minorities, the economically, socially, and educationally underprivileged, children of broken homes, the aged, the physically and mentally handicapped.[12]

Professor tenBroek's articles are a prodigious, informative effort, containing many thoughtful criticisms of an existing welfare system with which we agree. Yet we have found it difficult to apply his mode of analysis to problems of family law and the poor. In part I of this article we explain our principal difficulties with Professor tenBroek's methodology. In part II we formulate and apply more appropriate methods for analyzing family law doctrines and welfare policies.

I

THE DISTRACTING SEARCH FOR DUALITY

A. The Constitutional "Neutrality" of Indigence

The basic fault we find in Professor tenBroek's analysis is its designed capability of resolving important issues wholesale when a careful, particularistic analysis seems to be demanded. We believe this fault is traceable to conclusions drawn by tenBroek from assertions that poverty must be a constitutionally "neutral" factor. The constitutional under-pinning of his analysis appears more fully in the following passages:

> Although the recipients of public aid programs are still effectively outside the jurisdiction of the United States Constitution, a new spirit in constitutional law has given positive signs of its future potential. In two lines of decisions the Supreme Court has furthered the right to equal justice. In the first, it upheld the right of the poor to appeal decisions whenever others can do so, and to have writs and records supplied free. In the second, it held that all criminal defendants must have the aid of counsel, to be supplied free if they cannot afford to bear the costs. There can be no equal justice, the Court now holds, where the kind of trial a man gets depends on the amount of money he has. Welfare may take some departure and inspiration, too, from

---

[11] *Id.* at 620.
[12] tenBroek, 16 STAN. L. REV. at 978.

Brown v. Board of Educ., a decision in another contested arena of public services—that of education. The issue in that case was over the arbitrary criterion of race used as a basis of segregation of the public schools. *Is poverty a less arbitrary criterion when used as a basis of segregation in family law?* The unexcelled rhetoric of Mr. Justice Jackson in *Edwards v. California* . . . is directly in point:

> "Does 'indigence' as defined by the application of the California statute constitute a basis for restricting the freedom of a citizen, as crime or contagion warrants its restriction? We should say now, and in no uncertain terms, that a man's mere property status, without more, cannot be used by a state to test, qualify, or limit his rights as a citizen of the United States. 'Indigence' in itself is neither a source of rights nor a basis for denying them. The mere state of being without funds is a neutral fact— constitutionally an irrelevance, like race, creed, or color."
>
> . . . .
>
> When "the mere state of being without funds is a neutral fact— constitutionally an irrelevance"; when classifications based on poverty and handicap are measured by equal protection standards of constitutional purpose and proper classification; when constitutional rights cannot be sacrificed as a condition of granting public assistance; when law enforcement and penal intrusions into the law of welfare are fully restrained by the fourth, fifth, and fourteenth amendments; when free movement is recognized as a constitutional right forbidding residence restrictions in welfare; when the highest court in the land as well as the highest court in California see responsibility of relatives provisions as arbitrary and discriminatory taxation; when welfare categories and constitutional classifications coincide; when the granting and withholding of assistance and the variation of requirements among and between programs are subjected to due process and equal protection norms; when a presumption of competence and responsibility of clients becomes a welfare counterpart of the criminal law presumption of innocence—when these things happen, then indeed will the law of the poor feel the full impact of the pronouncement that *"separate"* is *"inherently unequal,"* generating among aid recipients "a feeling of inferiority as to their status in the community that may affect their hearts and minds in a way unlikely ever to be undone." Until that time, however, California's *separate, different, and unequal* system of family law of the poor will continue in force basically in the form in which [the Elizabethan poor laws] . . . gave it to England and the English-speaking world.[13]

Everyone must agree that "classifications based on poverty and handicap [should be] measured by equal protection standards of constitutional purpose and proper classification," and that "constitutional rights should not be sacrificed as a condition of granting public assistance." tenBroek's larger thesis, however, is reflected in the three pas-

---

[13] tenBroek, 17 STAN. L. REV. at 681-82. (Emphasis added.)

sages we have italicized above to the effect that "separate" is "inherently unequal," that poverty is always an arbitrary criterion for action in the same sense that race is, and hence, that dual systems of law, as he has characterized them, are inherently discriminatory.

In considering the soundness of these contentions, the full meaning of Mr. Justice Jackson's statement in *Edwards*,[14] quoted above, must be borne in mind. First, it must be remembered that Jackson's opinion was prompted by the majority holding in *Edwards* that the interstate movement of persons is "commerce." The whole of his opinion is dedicated to the proposition that interstate travel and taking up residence within a state are rights of national citizenship, protected from infringing state action by the fourteenth amendment. Most of Jackson's language is expressly directed to a consideration of the rights of national citizenship; all of it is uttered in that context. If Jackson meant that indigence must have no effect on one's claims to the rights of national citizenship, he was very likely correct. Since citizenship itself does not in any way depend on economic status, rights which inhere in citizenship should exist independently of the citizen's economic status.

The rights which inhere in national citizenship are not many, and it is probable Jackson intended his concept of neutrality to have a broader application than this. He says in a later passage that the possession of property must not be a pretext for unequal or exclusive civil rights. Application of his quoted language in this context is not difficult. Freedom of speech, freedom from unreasonable searches and seizures,[15] the privilege against self-incrimination, and the right to counsel,[16] for example, will not be granted or withheld on the basis of indigence. The economic status of an individual simply has no relevance to the purposes served by these rights and privileges. Beyond this kind of application, the validity of Jackson's rhetoric is more doubtful. If he meant that indigence is a neutral fact in the same sense that race or color would be regarded as a neutral fact in 1966, he was almost certainly wrong.

A truly neutral fact—one which is "constitutionally an irrelevance"—can be "neither a source of rights nor a basis for denying them." Race

---

14 Edwards v. California, 314 U.S. 160, 184-85 (1941).

15 "Midnight welfare searches" have not yet been ruled invalid, but no one would contend that application of the exclusionary rule announced in Mapp v. Ohio, 367 U.S. 643 (1961), could be made to turn on the economic status of a defendant.

16 It can be argued in one sense that the right to counsel established in Gideon v. Wainwright, 372 U.S. 335 (1963), depends upon a defendant's economic status. The sixth and fourteenth amendments guarantee the assistance of counsel to all defendants in "criminal prosecutions." If a defendant is unable to afford counsel government must provide counsel for him, but this right is based on the individual's status as a defendant in a criminal prosecution, not "indigence in itself."

and color very probably meet this test.[17] Indigence is not yet the source
of a right to demand benefits, supported by a correlative governmental
duty to provide them. But no one can doubt that government may
choose to create certain benefits and make them available only to the
indigent; too much governmental action is based on the essentially un-
challenged assumption that it may. At this point it might be contended
that reliance upon the neutral fact terminology is more limited—the
central concern is not with benefits but detriments, and poverty is a
neutral fact where detriments are to be imposed.

This argument oversimplifies in at least two ways the problems with
which this article is concerned. For one thing it assumes that the difference between benefits and detriments can be put to a litmus paper test.
Benign quotas, as their name implies, are presumably designed by well-
intentioned people desiring to help Negroes or other minorities, but reasonable men might differ in their characterization of the quotas as beneficial or detrimental.[18] In the same way, some schemes apparently designed
to benefit the poor arguably may be detrimental to them. Suppose a
school system develops a special curriculum for school districts containing large numbers of children from low-income families. Assuming
the purpose of this effort to be beneficial, its classification as beneficial or
detrimental nevertheless presents difficult questions. In any event, if
"neutrality" is a two-sided coin, we must at least recognize that power
must reside somewhere to decide which side of the coin is presented in
particular cases. This necessity is one very good reason for regarding
race and color as wholly neutral facts.

Secondly, once it is assumed that benefits can be granted on the basis
of indigence, another factor—governmental programs providing benefits—
must also be considered. Governmental spending programs are necessarily developed to accomplish purposes. Conditions must be established
to ensure that expenditures will be consistent with program goals. For
example, certain grants of public money might be tied to a vocational
training program. An individual desiring to participate in the program
will have to conform to the requirements of the program. Programs designed to assist dependent children must include minimum conditions to
ensure that the financial assistance reaches the needy children. In any
program developed to assist the indigent, "indigent" will have to be

---

[17] This is not to say necessarily that race can never influence the decision-making
process of government. See Fiss, *Racial Imbalance in the Public Schools—The Constitutional
Concepts*, 78 HARV. L. REV. 564, 574-83 (1965). The constitutional neutrality of race
has not been authoritatively established. See Kurland, *The Supreme Court 1963 Term—
Forward*, 78 HARV. L. REV. 143, 146-48 (1964).

[18] See Bittker, *The Case of the Checkerboard Ordinance: An Experiment in Race Relations*, 71 YALE L.J. 1387 (1962).

defined in terms of income as well as in terms of the unit of persons—individual or family—whose income is determinative. Ideally these rules or conditions will be developed to help secure the ends for which spending programs are designed; the rules will not be created simply to subject persons to particular treatment because they are indigent.

In addition to the conditions necessary to direct particular money towards particular ends, we know that programs designed for beneficial purposes often have unplanned, certainly undesired, latent consequences which require offsetting regulations.[19] For example, a negative income tax program based on total family income may encourage some young people to avoid formal marriage so that the "husband's" income will not lessen the family's total benefit. If the legislature decides that this encouragement should be removed in order to promote fairness to all, special rules will be required. Again, as in the case of purposive conditions, the needed rules will be responsive to problems connected with the spending program; they will not be designed simply to treat the indigent differently from the affluent.

These conditions and rules are the sources of much of the so-called "law of the poor." Because they are built into programs designed to benefit the poor and because their application does not turn on the existence of "indigence in itself," neither a benefits-detriments nor a "separate is inherently unequal" analysis is adequate to the task of formulating wise policy or sound answers to questions posed in constitutional terms.

B. Family Laws and Welfare Policies

The importance of recognizing that the great bulk of rules in welfare administration relate to governmental welfare programs and not to classifications based on "indigence in itself" cannot be overemphasized. Whether tenBroek's purpose in developing the theme of equality is to bring his case within the equal protection clause of the Constitution or simply to appeal to the philosophical ideal of equal justice under law—the like treatment of like cases—it is necessary to determine whether particular situations present "like" or different problems. This inquiry is missing (or supplied by assertion) in most of his analysis, an approach reflected in his characterization of the two systems of law to be compared as "dual systems of family law." Of course one system is the family law and the other, as evidenced by its source, is the welfare law of society. Labels are not necessarily meaningful, but the different sources of the law represented by our labels indicate the possibility that important differences of purpose may underlie specific rules in the two systems. A refusal to

---

[19] See BELL, AID TO DEPENDENT CHILDREN vii (1965).

inquire into this possibility results in an analysis that is more distracting than helpful to those who seek to evaluate particular rules and policies.

This is exemplified in tenBroek's discussion of "dual" concepts of property relations law between husband and wife. He sketches California's community property rules, noting that, while property "acquired by the labor or skill of either partner during the continuance of the partnership [marriage] belongs to both of them,"[20] each partner "may have property in which the other has no interest."[21] Describing the mutual obligations of support between husband and wife under the civil law, he writes:

> According to the Civil Code, the obligations of mutual respect, fidelity, and support which the marital partners assume are matters about which they "contract towards each other." The terms of the "contract" about support, however, are also established by the Civil Code. The obligations are mutual but not identical, those of the husband being the more comprehensive and also penally enforceable. Thus the husband must support the wife if he has "sufficient ability . . . or . . . is able to earn the means" to do so "unless by her misconduct he was justified in abandoning her." The wife must support the husband "when he has not deserted her . . . and he is unable, from infirmity, to support himself." In addition, the interspousal support obligation is stated in terms of a civil remedy for the third-person creditor who has met the need. Good faith suppliers to the wife of "articles necessary for her support" can "recover the reasonable value thereof from the husband." The earnings of the wife and some of her separate property are liable for the payment of debts contracted by the husband or by the wife for the necessaries of life furnished to them or either of them while they are living together. In contrast, property of the wife held by her at the time of the marriage or acquired afterward by devise, succession, or gift (other than by gift from husband), is not so liable.[22]

The family law of the poor is differentiated:

> As it emerges from the California Welfare and Institutions Code in implementive administrative material, the family law of the poor reflects a different conception of the marital rights and duties relating to property and support. Husband and wife are not seen as semi-independent partners, standing in a contractual relationship to each other, and maintaining distinct interests in community income and property; they are viewed rather as a single, integrated entity, having a single, undivided, and unseparated interest in a common pool of family resources derived from the income and property of both spouses. Withdrawals from the common pool might, indeed must, be made by both to meet the costs of living. The family law of the poor, by contrast with the civil family law, puts greater emphasis upon the community, less

---

[20] tenBroek, 17 STAN. L. REV. 622.

[21] *Id.* at 623.

[22] *Ibid.* (Footnote omitted.)

upon the individuals; greater emphasis upon meeting the needs of both spouses for support, less upon their individual rights to separate property and income.[23]

Thus California law regulates the obligations of support and property rights as between husband and wife, including the rights of third parties who furnish necessaries to one spouse or the other, but the rules change in detail when the state is the third party called upon to assist in the support of one of the spouses. For example, a third party supplier of necessaries to the husband can make no claim against property of the wife which she has brought to the marriage, but the state will look to such property as an available family resource in determining need for public assistance. Do these provisions create a dual system of family law or discrete systems of family law and welfare policies? Under the family law third parties supplying necessaries to a husband, poor or rich, have no claim against inherited property of the wife. Under the welfare law, government will consider the inherited property of the wife in determining the need of any husband who applies for public assistance. It is true that this latter rule will have no relevance for a husband who has no need for public assistance, but neither will the rule that makes assistance available on the basis of need. And a means test surely does not create an inherently discriminatory duality; as most rules of law, including these under discussion, it simply has inclusive and exclusive features. Consider the rules imposing liability on persons who negligently injure others. Persons who accidentally injure others are not liable simply because their situation is not covered by the rules. In deciding to treat a negligent person differently from a nonnegligent one, the state must not be arbitrary; but difference of treatment merely introduces a need to show an absence of arbitrariness, it does not carry its own proof of arbitrariness. The dual systems of law analysis stops just at the point when, for us, it has posed questions which need further analysis: What resources should be taken into account when the need of a family or a member of a family for governmental assistance is considered? Should government ignore the inherited wealth of a wife when considering the need of her husband for assistance by the rest of society? If it is determined that government should count a wife's inherited wealth as a family resource at the point when all of society is called upon to assist a family member—specifically the husband—does it follow that the family law should or must give to all husbands automatically and in all circumstances claims to the inherited wealth of the women they marry?

Since welfare policies must be developed in the context of an existing

---

[23] *Id.* at 624.

society and legal structure, it is apparent that family laws and notions held by society about family relationships and family life may have a quite important bearing on these policies. But the dual systems analysis often supplies the wrong clues to the precise relevance of the one system to the other. This shortcoming is borne out by analysis of two controversial welfare policies—those attaching important consequences to the presence of a "man in the house," and those creating or recognizing relative support obligations.

In discussing the welfare policy concerning the "man in the house" it will be convenient to refer to California's rule which is criticized by tenBroek. In the California Welfare and Institutions Code an obligation of support for a woman's children is imposed in terms upon a male living with the woman and assuming the role of spouse, if without his support the children would be needy and eligible for AFDC.[24] The courts have not yet interpreted this provision to mean more than that his income may be taken into account in determining the need of the family for purposes of public assistance.[25] A dual system of family law results because "while there are no common law husbands under the Civil Code . . . by illicit cohabitation with a man, the mother of needy children, under the law of the poor, acquires a community property interest in his income."[26] If the law simply discriminated between rich and poor, turning the application of the common law marriage doctrine on the economic status of the parties without more, tenBroek would have a strong case for condemning the resulting duality. But economic status alone is not the factor governing the application of the "man in the house" rule, and in any event, the "man in the house" rule is not a common law marriage doctrine. The comparison drawn by tenBroek comes down to a comparison between a man living with a mother who seeks public assistance for her children and a man living with a mother who does not need or seek such assistance. Neither man has a legal obligation to support the mother's children, and each is presumably free to sever the relationship, at the same time being subject to the woman's power to sever the relationship. Practically speaking the "community property interest" of the needy children's mother in her mate's income represents nothing more than the choice she must make when seeking AFDC between severing the relationship or maintaining the relationship and having his income counted as family resource. If he is unwilling to share his income to

---

[24] CAL. WELFARE & INST'NS CODE § 11351.

[25] People v. Owens, 231 Cal. App. 2d 691, 42 Cal. Rptr. 153 (1965); County of Kern v. Coley, 229 Cal. App. 2d 172, 40 Cal. Rptr. 53 (1964); People v. Rozell, 212 Cal. App. 2d 875, 28 Cal. Rptr. 478 (1963).

[26] tenBroek, 17 STAN. L. REV. 620.

the extent it reduces an AFDC allotment, she has a financial incentive to sever the relationship.

Under the family law of California no similar financial wedge threatens to part the unmarried couple. It is worth noticing, however, that the creation of one by the policymakers would satisfy objections based on duality. Still, there are reasons to believe this is not the crux of the problem. In the first place, it is difficult to conceive of the means by which nearly equal pressures could be brought to bear on men outside the context of public assistance. Since the relationship in either the welfare or nonwelfare context is only as permanent as the parties wish it to be, there is no reason to believe a mere rule of law creating an obligation of support would have significant effect. Secondly, there is no reason to believe that the couple seeking public assistance would derive any satisfaction from knowing that equality of position had been created as nearly as possible between them and others not seeking public assistance but otherwise similarly situated. Finally, and perhaps this follows from the first two observations, the "man in the house" rule ought to be judged on its merits before we accept any solution designed merely to create equivalence between welfare policy and particular family laws.

We believe that family laws, or family relationships, are relevant to an evaluation of the "man in the house" rule, but not the "family" or family law chosen for purposes of comparison by tenBroek. The "man in the house" rule is a derivative of society's organization around the married family. Because of this organization and because need is an essential test in most plans of public assistance, the income of a married father is necessarily considered in determining the need of his family for assistance. Usually the income of stepfathers is similarly considered. In the absence of a "man in the house" rule of some kind, different treatment would be accorded the income of some fathers and "stepfathers" resembling their married fellows in all respects except the existence or validity of a marriage ceremony between them and women with whom they are living. It is the availability of governmental assistance that makes this different treatment important enough to consider the need for an off-setting regulation. In short, the problem to which a "man in the house" rule ought to be addressed is one that springs from the creation of a welfare program geared to family units. It is in this context that the rule should be evaluated. In part II we consider the merits of a "man in the house" rule in this larger context.

A different kind of relationship between society's notions about the family and particular welfare policies is illustrated by rules creating relative support obligations. But again a dual systems analysis fails to disclose the relationship. For purposes of illustration, assume that the

state has a simple rule requiring financially able children to contribute
to the support of a needy parent who has applied for welfare benefits.
If this is the only rule of law in the jurisdiction establishing obligations
running from adult children to their parents, the children of self-sufficient
parents will have no obligation to their parents while the children of
poor parents may have an obligation. An argument can then be made
that there are two systems of family law.[27]

But nothing is gained by viewing the problem this way. There are
two classifying factors in the rule, the need of parents and the economic
status—the ability to contribute support—of the children. Since poor
children will have no obligation even if their parents are needy, while
well-to-do children will have an obligation, any discrimination on the
basis of the one factor favors the poor children. The other classifying
factor—the need of the parents—is surely a rational one, perhaps the
only rational one that could be used in light of the purpose of the rule.
Until the need of parents is established there is little reason for society to
be concerned about the obligations, if any, which children should have
toward their parents. And an application for public assistance, which
today is widely available, is not an irrational mechanism for determining
a parent's need. If the rule of relative support is unwise or unconstitutional, then, it must be because considerations other than discrimination
against the poor, as such, militate against the creation of obligations
running from adult children to their parents.

It is when rules of relative support are evaluated on their merits
that notions about family relationships become relevant. In fact, if there
is any support for schemes of relative responsibility, it will be found
in these notions. If we look for a moment at the laws of descent and
distribution, or at the definitions of "dependents" in many workmen's
compensation provisions governing death benefits, the role of family
relationship is quite apparent. For purposes of distributing a decedent's
property a distant relative will be selected as a beneficiary in preference
to the state or, needless to say, a stranger. A parent who was partially

---

27 As a matter of fact, both the civil family law and the "family law of the poor" in
California contain requirements that adult children help support their indigent parents. In
dealing with relative support problems, tenBroek analyzes a variety of relative support
rules on the basis of a variety of considerations, including due process, equal protection, and
social policy. His equal protection analysis is, for the most part, traditional in scope, taking
into account the rationality, if any, of a differentiation between the adult child or other
relative of an indigent person and the general public for purposes of attaching an obligation
to support the indigent person. He adds a "dual systems" analysis in which he characterizes
relative support laws as "laws of the poor" that discriminate against the poor. tenBroek, 17
STAN. L. REV. 644. Since we are dealing only with this aspect of the problem at this
time, we have tried to isolate it by using a simplified illustration.

supported by a decedent workman will in many states be entitled to a compensation benefit partially replacing the lost source of support. Similar treatment may not be accorded a nonrelative supported by a workman. Of course these laws do not deal with precisely the same problem as the one of designating the persons who should be obligated to support another person during his life. We expect the public at large to react differently to the intestacy laws that favor a nephew than to a rule that requires a nephew to support an indigent uncle. But it is still sensible to ask whether there are degrees of relationship that *should* be the basis of a support obligation. And the answer inevitably will depend, in part, on the attitudes that have evolved concerning the "family" with respect to other problems.

At the outset, we said that tenBroek's articles contain many "criticisms of an existing welfare system with which we agree." Our difficulty with his unifying theme does not lead us to disagree necessarily with other objections he registers or with certain remedies he proposes. Particular rules or policies as administered may be thoroughly objectionable for reasons unrelated to "dualism" as the concept is used by tenBroek. For example, in many relative support schemes, guidelines concerning amounts of contribution and the ability of children to contribute often are not clear, vesting dangerous discretion in welfare officials. Support obligations vary, often without rhyme or reason, according to the category of public assistance involved. Some programs of assistance, forced commitments of persons to mental institutions for example, are hardly distinguishable from many tax supported programs of institutional assistance or service. An adult child may be compelled, ironically, to support a parent who deserted him as a child. In an extensive analysis of California's crazy-quilt system of relative support obligations Professor tenBroek lays bare an imposing array of questionable policies and procedures.[28] Welfare policies and rules should be subjected to this kind of analysis. But we believe characterization of the rules as sources of dual systems distracts from the needed effort.

II

A DUALISTIC ANALYSIS OF FAMILY SUPPORT OBLIGATIONS—STEPFATHERS AND "THE MAN IN THE HOUSE"

By statute or administrative regulation, a number of states have attached "substitute parent" policies to their AFDC programs. The

---

[28] tenBroek, 17 STAN. L. REV. 629-46. His analysis includes an appraisal of Department of Mental Hygiene v. Kirchner, 60 Cal. 2d 716, 388 P.2d 720, 36 Cal. Rptr. 488 (1964), *vacated and remanded*, 380 U.S. 194, *decision on remand*, 62 Cal. 2d 586, 400 P.2d 321, 43 Cal. Rptr. 329 (1965), which held the relative support provisions in the state's mental illness programs unconstitutional under the state's equal protection clause.

typical provision denies benefits to any child whose mother is married to, or is maintaining a continuing family relationship with, a man whose income exceeds the relevant assistance eligibility standard.[29] We do not discuss provisions which deny benefits because of the mother's out of wedlock sexual behavior; such statutes raise issues comparable to other "suitable home" criteria.[30] Our concern is with stepfathers and with stable but informal (or invalid) family relationships. In the sections which follow, we explore the considerations which should be taken into account, first, in devising family law "substitute parent" support policies, and, second, in determining whether government financial assistance should be given to children whose families include a solvent "substitute parent."

A. Family Law

1. Stepfathers

Very few states impose child support obligations on stepfathers.[31] Almost universally, the legislature focuses on the natural father: He is required to support the child while the marriage subsists[32] and after the marriage has been terminated by divorce.[33] The mother often has a secondary obligation during and after the marriage.[34] The father is relieved of his support obligation only when he is completely divested of parental "rights" and "duties"—when another father adopts the child. It is not unlikely that the stepfather's exemption from support responsibility reflects ancient notions of the sanctity of blood ties and the indissolubility of marriage rather than any contemporary examination of the social values at stake. Yet statutory modifications will be difficult to accomplish. No legislator will enthusiastically depart from an historically determined doctrinal framework built upon an emotionally appealing, if simplistic, foundation: Since the natural father brought the children into the world, let him pay for them. Nonetheless, we have attempted a rational assessment and accommodation of the competing values. We believe that stepfathers should be encouraged to support their children. The need for legislation does not seem imperative, however, and a statute imposing a support obligation on stepfathers would produce a new series of difficult social and legal problems. We conclude, therefore, that the current doctrinal framework should be retained; stepfather support of the family

[29] See BELL, op. cit. supra note 19, at 76-92.

[30] Id. at 85-86. See also text accompanying note 83 infra.

[31] MADDEN, PERSONS AND DOMESTIC RELATIONS 390 (1931).

[32] See FOOTE, LEVY & SANDER, CASES ON FAMILY LAW 308 (1966).

[33] Id. at 918-24.

[34] See, e.g., OHIO REV. CODE ANN. § 3103.03 (Page 1960).

should be achieved by means of informal family processes rather than the compulsion of a statutory obligation.

It will be helpful, initially, to identify the several interests which must be taken into account in determining the scope of the stepfather's support responsibility. The child obviously has an important stake in the decision. His physical well being, his social and intellectual development, perhaps even his emotional stability, require continuing financial assistance. The child's mother should not have sole responsibility to provide for his needs—her earning capacity is limited; in any event, there is general agreement that the child benefits if the mother can choose not to work in order to devote her time and attention to him. The child also has an interest in the security provided by an intact and stable family; the child's need for these values is likely to be great, since he has been subjected to a severe emotional strain—his parents' divorce or his father's death—and to some period during which he has had to rely exclusively on his mother for care, protection, and discipline. In addition, the child who is no longer an infant may profit from a continued relationship with his natural father—if the relationship can be maintained without sacrificing other values. The natural father—even if he has remarried and acquired a new family—has a counterpart interest in maintaining a relationship with the child. At the same time, the natural father, especially if he has remarried, has an interest in shifting support responsibility to the stepfather. The stepfather's interests, on the other hand, may be inconsistent with the natural father's. Because the stepfather becomes the head of the new family, eliminating, or minimizing, the "parenting" role of the natural father would be to his advantage. The stepfather will probably be a better father for the child (he will certainly have less personal anxiety about his role and his authority) if the natural father cannot second-guess his decisions; and the stepfather can expect the child to adjust to the new family unit more quickly if he is the sole paternal decision-maker. The stepfather also has an interest in avoiding any permanent responsibilities to his wife's children if the marriage is a failure, unless he has voluntarily assumed them by adoption. Finally, the mother has an interest in maximizing her remarriage opportunities; when she has remarried, she shares the stepfather's interest in the new family's cohesiveness.[35]

---

[35] We are not concerned here with the stepfather's liability to third parties to whom the child may become obligated during the marriage. Merchants might be protected without enactment of a statutory support obligation. If the mother makes purchases for the child's benefit, the stepfather could be held liable either by applying the common law "necessaries" doctrine, MADDEN, *op. cit. supra* note 31, at 195, or by liberally interpreting a "family

Assigning priorities among these interests is much more difficult than describing them. Value choices have to be made without basic information about the behavior we are trying to influence; and we will have to rely on assumptions as to the likely effects of alternative policies. For example, a substantial number of California legislators argued that imposing a support obligation on the stepfather "would discourage men from marrying women with children and thus deter re-establishment of normal parental, family and home relationships for the children."[36] Yet there is no reliable evidence that prospective stepfathers would be deterred by a modification of current support doctrines. Indeed, unless the mother is receiving monthly payments from the natural father, many prospective stepfathers may believe that stepfathers now have a legal duty to support their stepchildren. We know that most divorced women re-marry[37] despite the fact that many natural fathers do not honor their support obligations.[38] The only hypothesis which seems warranted concerns behavior after the marriage takes place; although many stepfathers and mothers choose a standard of living in reliance upon the natural father's continuing support payments, most stepfathers will probably support their stepchildren no matter what the statutes require:

> Quite regardless of the presence or absence of legal liability, most stepfathers do support their stepchildren. As a practical matter, they can hardly avoid it. They all live under the common roof, view the

expense" statute: "statutes . . . declaring that the husband and wife shall be jointly liable for family expenses, such as necessary food, clothing, education of the children, etc." *Id.* at 200. If the child makes the purchase, although the stepfather may have no statutory duty, "if he voluntarily assumes the obligation of support, by receiving the children into his family and assuming to stand in loco parentis to the children, he is liable." *Id.* at 390. Finally, the stepfather's responsibility can be established by traditional agency principles. *Id.* at 391-92.

[36] tenBroek, *The Impact of Welfare Law Upon Family Law*, 42 CALIF. L. REV. 458, 479 (1954).

[37] In the age ranges of 25-35, when most women would have young children, the estimate of divorced women who remarry was well over ninety per cent. JACOBSON, AMERICAN MARRIAGE AND DIVORCE 85 (1959), cited in FOOTE, LEVY & SANDER, *op. cit. supra* note 32, at 773.

[38] FOOTE, LEVY & SANDER, *op. cit. supra* note 32, at 938, reporting data derived from KAPLAN, SUPPORT FROM ABSENT FATHERS OF CHILDREN RECEIVING ADC 1955, at 7, 15, 24-26 (U.S. Bureau of Public Assistance Rep. No. 41, 1960) (support awards in forty-two per cent of the families; support actually received in only about half of these cases, and in only 18.3% of total cases). These data relate to court awards of support rather than to separation agreements negotiated by the parties—a much more common method of settling financial affairs among middle and upper-class divorced couples. There is no information concerning the extent to which middle and upper-class natural fathers perform their decree or separation agreement obligations.

common television and the stepchildren cannot very well be driven from the table when the parents and other children are eating.[39]

The difficulties in accommodating the interests we have outlined are compounded because any support rule will have to be applied in a great variety of contexts. A statutory policy suited to poor natural fathers and rich stepfathers may look much less sensible if the natural father is the affluent one; a rule which reflects, and deals adequately with, the expectations and behavior of middle-class natural and substitute parents may not take adequate account of behavior patterns among lower-class families. The weight to be accorded any particular interest may vary with the several discrete family situations in which a stepfather figures: The mother may be widowed; the mother may be divorced, but the natural father may have disappeared, the natural father may take no interest in the child, or the child may be too young to have established a relationship with the natural father; or the mother may be divorced from a natural father who maintains (or wants to maintain) a continuing relationship with the child. Finally, a stepfather support obligation might be made concurrent with the natural father's duty or exclusive; his obligation could apply during his marriage to the mother or permanently. One of these variations, adopted because it is appropriate for one of the family situations, may be unwise or unacceptable for the others.

At first glance, a statutory stepfather support obligation seems to be a laudable and sensible goal. Family law policies should in part reflect existing family behavior patterns which are socially approved; since most stepfathers support their stepchildren, why should a small nonconforming minority be permitted to take advantage of a loophole in the statutory framework? In addition, family law doctrine should strive to coalesce the new family and encourage its continuity and permanence. Following a divorce, the mother almost always obtains custody of young children;[40] the natural father's interest in his child—usually minimal even immediately following the divorce—diminishes gradually over time.[41] Since the new family's cohesiveness would be fostered by minimizing the natural father's contacts, the stepfather should be encouraged to assume sole financial responsibility for the children. In short, the new family should be treated, to the extent possible, as if it were an integral and autonomous unit.

These family cohesiveness values can be fully realized, of course, only

---

[39] tenBroek, *supra* note 36, at 479.

[40] GOODE, AFTER DIVORCE 311-12 (1956) (close to ninety per cent of mothers obtain custody following divorce in the jurisdictions where data available).

[41] *Id.* at 315-16.

if the stepfather's support obligation is exclusive. If the natural father's support responsibility is to be terminated in order to minimize his contacts with the children, however, any possible loss to the child's financial interests must also be considered. If the mother is a widow the child's financial position cannot be damaged, and may be enhanced, by transposing the stepfather's customary behavior into a formal obligation. Even if the mother is divorced, the child may not lose very much: Following a divorce, the natural father's maintenance of support responsibility often runs a course parallel with his personal interest in the child.[42] Yet many natural fathers do maintain post-divorce financial responsibility for their children. An exclusive stepfather support rule would sacrifice the financial interests of these children; under current doctrines, the child has the advantage of the stepfather's informal support without losing the insurance policy which his natural father's income represents. To be sure, the child will probably be seriously penalized in only two situations: if the natural father's income is much greater that the stepfather's; or if the child's needs require large expenditures which are beyond the stepfather's means but not beyond the joint resources of the stepfather and the natural father.[43] Can we say, with any assurance, that the family cohesiveness values promoted by an exclusive stepfather support obligation justify requiring the child to take his financial chances with his stepfather in all cases? Without any data, it is easy to overestimate the extent to which the natural father's support responsibility may interfere with the new family's cohesiveness in those cases where the natural father does pay support. Since the natural father's payments directly or indirectly benefit the stepfather and mother as well as the child, continuing the natural father's obligation is not likely to disturb them. If the natural father simply pays support but takes no other interest, the child can probably be shielded from any hostility between his mother and natural father which financial controversies inevitably produce. The new family will be disrupted, then, when the natural father's contacts are personal rather than financial; yet an exclusive stepfather support obligation would not eliminate the contacts of a natural father who wants to maintain personal ties with his child.

A substantial body of statutory and judicial doctrine suggests that the natural father's interest in maintaining a personal relationship with

---

[42] See KAPLAN, *op. cit. supra* note 38, at 16 (almost ten per cent of husbands of ADC mothers imprisoned for criminal nonsupport).

[43] The child will only be penalized, of course, if the natural father will not contribute unless compelled to do so by a court order which relies on the natural father's statutory obligation. But these are the natural fathers (and the stepfathers) with whom a statutory obligation is designed to deal.

his child, despite the mother's remarriage and his own, is both important and socially approved. The noncustodian natural father has been permitted, even encouraged, to maintain a continuing relationship with the child. The natural father's visitation rights have been denied only under the most extraordinary circumstances.[44] Indeed, some courts have even refused to require support payments from the father if the mother willfully interferes with his visitation rights.[45] A common statutory provision requires the natural father's consent to an adoption of the child by the stepfather.[46] The natural father also retains some measure of his parental authority prerogatives.[47] It is certainly not socially desirable, even if it were politically possible,[48] to refuse to safeguard the natural father's affectional relationship with the child.

---

[44] Commonwealth ex rel. Lotz v. Lotz, 188 Pa. Super. 241, 244, 146 A.2d 362, 363-64 (1958), aff'd, 396 Pa. 287, 152 A.2d 663 (1959): "A parent has seldom been denied the right . . . . The cases in which visitation rights of a parent have been limited or denied have been those in which severe mental or moral deficiencies of the parent have constituted a real and grave threat to the welfare of the child. . . . The courts have granted visitation rights to parents even in those circumstances where the parent has ignored the children for a long period of time."

[45] Snellings v. Snellings, 272 Ala. 254, 130 So. 2d 363 (1961); Annot. 95 A.L.R.2d 118, 134-42 (1964). This seems to be the minority view unless the mother removes the children from the jurisdiction of the court. See FOOTE, LEVY & SANDER, op. cit. supra note 32, at 923-24.

[46] See, e.g., MINN. STAT. ANN. § 259.24(1) (Supp. 1965); In re Parks, 267 Minn. 468, 127 N.W.2d 548; Note, 49 MINN. L. REV. 128 (1964).

[47] To be sure, the stepfather is the child's effective custodian and for many purposes he exercises parental control; but a court usually retains jurisdiction to circumscribe the stepfather's discretion at the behest of the natural father, or even to terminate the stepfather's authority by returning the child to the natural father's custody. Consider a hypothetical case: Following the parents' divorce, the mother obtains custody of the child; she marries a Christian Scientist and announces that she has converted to the stepfather's faith; the natural father requests the court's aid to insure that the child will not be denied necessary medical care. It would be difficult to refuse the natural father some say as to the manner in which his child is being raised. The court might estop a natural father who has not taken a continuing interest in the child prior to the contest; the court might adopt a narrow "scope of review" in supervising the stepfather's authority. But these protective devices would not eliminate the natural father's ability to intervene. Cf. GOLDSTEIN & KATZ, THE FAMILY AND THE LAW 183-216 (1965). The commentators suggest that there is "a relation between the father's right to the cutody and services of his minor child, and his duty to support the child." MADDEN, op. cit. supra note 31, at 387. If the natural father's support payments are to be used for a particular purpose (for example, parochial school tuition), perhaps he should play a more substantial role in the decision-making process on that issue. But the contrary need not be true—if the father is not paying support because of circumstances beyond his control, his role should not be circumscribed. It seems proper to determine the natural father's ability to intervene in accordance with the scope of his continuing interest in the child—evaluating a number of factors including his performance of support obligations.

[48] The legislative commitment underlying the adoption statute referred to in note 46 supra suggests that the natural father's interest is both important and socially approved. The judges apparently concur. The Supreme Court of Minnesota, for example, recently

Yet preserving the relationship jeopardizes the cohesiveness of the new family unit. Visitation by the natural father frequently produces violent controversies. The natural father's contacts with the new family would be minimized, to be sure, if his visitation rights were protected without imposing a support obligation on him. But it is doubtful that providing an additional topic—the natural father's support payments— would contribute substantially to the frequency or unpleasantness of the quarrels. Moreover, the stepfather's interests and feelings must also be considered. It will not be easy for the stepfather to accept the idea that he is in all respects the child's father—whether or not he wants the role— despite the fact that the natural father can invade his family's privacy and can challenge his authority over the child.[49]

If the stepfather's obligation to support the child is to be exclusive, finally, his obligation should be made permanent. It hardly seems fair to require the natural father to plan his financial affairs to take account of the possibility that the mother's new marriage may end in divorce. It is true that the natural father's responsibility would theoretically be less onerous than it now is. Yet if the natural father remarries and acquires a family, there is no reason to penalize his second wife and family when

---

circumscribed the scope of a statute which authorized adoption without the consent of a natural parent "who has lost custody of the child through a divorce decree." MINN. STAT. ANN. § 259.24(1)(b) (Supp. 1965). Ordering dismissal of a stepparent's adoption petition, the court commented: "The correlative rights and duties inherent in the parent-child relationship are natural rights of such fundamental importance that it is generally held that parents should not be deprived of them 'except for grave and weighty reasons.' In an adoption proceeding, where an absolute severance of this relationship is sought, the consent provisions are designed to protect the natural rights of a parent to the custody, society, comfort, and services of the child. . . . [W]e believe that the legislature intended that more than the mere existence of custody in one divorced parent is required to dispense with the necessity of consent by the other parent. . . . [The statutory words] imply not only that custody must be granted exclusively to one parent but also that the right of the other parent thereto be lost, forfeited or extinguished . . . ." *In re* Parks, 267 Minn. 468, 475, 127 N.W.2d 548, 553 (1964). (Footnotes omitted.)

[49] These arguments suggest that the natural father's support obligation should be eliminated only in those situations in which there is a sufficient interest in the step-family's cohesiveness to warrant cutting off the natural father completely. For children who are very young when the mother remarries, such a rule might well be justified. This is not to suggest that such a policy would command enthusiastic legislative approval. See notes 46-48 *supra* and accompanying text.

Direct judicial enforcement of an exclusive stepfather support obligation may have unique disadvantages. Enforcement is likely to be necessary only against irresponsible stepfathers—those who might also be willing to forsake their families in order to evade a support order. In any event, family disputes which focus on the frequently delicate relationship between the stepfather and his wife's children will hardly be pleasant. If the natural father is available, it may be more sensible to pit the mother against him; in these disputes, at least, the stepfather and mother will not be adversaries.

his first wife does obtain another divorce.[50] And it would surely be inappropriate to establish a framework which might deprive the child of support from both his natural and surrogate parent. It would be more efficient and rational to apprise the stepfather that when he marries a divorced mother he incurs permanent responsibility for both mother and children. It is not at all clear, however, that it would be wise or politically possible to impose a permanent support obligation on stepfathers. If compelling the stepfather to support does in fact lessen remarriage opportunities for mothers, making the obligation permanent—in effect, disregarding the possible instability of the marriage—would maximize its deterrent effects. Many legislators who would have no objection to a stepfather support duty during the marriage would be unwilling to impose continuing responsibility on the stepfather for "someone else's kids" if he and the mother were to obtain a divorce.[51] Notions of the sanctity of blood ties have operated often enough to the stepfather's disadvantage—the cases in which the stepfather seeks the child's custody following the mother's death provide one good illustration[52]—and there is no reason to believe that judicial attitudes are likely to change. It does not seem unfair to apply these notions evenhandedly. In addition, since the mother has an interest in assuring continuity of support for her children, her not inconsiderable persuasive powers as a wife may be more

---

[50] This may happen under the current system, of course, especially if the court has reduced the natural father's support obligation when the mother remarried. But at least the natural father is on notice; and if he has some continuing obligation to his first family, he and his second wife will—or should—take his obligation into account in choosing a standard of living. There is some evidence, albeit inconclusive, that remarriages are less stable than first marriages. See FOOTE, LEVY & SANDER, *op. cit. supra* note 32, at 771 n.70.

[51] The English statute, imposing a support obligation on a parent for any "child of the family," enacts such a system. See Matrimonial Proceedings (Children) Act, 6&7 Eliz. 2, c. 40, pt. 1, § 1 (1958):

(1) Subject to the provisions of this section, section twenty-six of the Matrimonial Causes Act, 1950 (which enables the High Court to provide for the custody, maintenance and education of the children of the parties to matrimonial proceedings), shall apply in relation to a child of one party to the marriage (including an illegitimate or adopted child) who has been accepted as one of the family by the other party as it applies in relation to a child of both parties.

(2) In considering whether any and what provision should be made by virtue of the foregoing subsection for requiring any party to make any payment towards the maintenance or education of a child who is not his own, the court shall have regard to the extent, if any, to which that party had, on or after the acceptance of the child as one of the family, assumed responsibility for the child's maintenance and to the liability of any person other than a party to the marriage to maintain the child.

[52] See FOOTE, LEVY & SANDER, *op. cit. supra* note 32, at 853. See also Note, *Alternatives to "Parental Right" in Child Custody Disputes Involving Third Parties*, 73 YALE L.J. 151 (1963).

effective in accomplishing an adoption than a statutory support obligation would be. If the stepfather's failure to adopt can be attributed to the mother's hesitance, however, it does not seem fair to require him to provide post-divorce support for the child. In any event, the child can be protected to some extent without enacting an inflexible stepfather support provision: In most states the mother is entitled to support from her husband after a divorce, and the judge can informally take her children (and the natural father's circumstances) into account in determining the amount of alimony to which she is entitled.[53]

Imposing joint support obligations on both stepfather and natural father avoids some of the difficulties of an exclusive stepfather obligation. The stepfather's responsibility would not have to be permanent; and the child would not lose the benefits of two sources of support—at least while the mother's second marriage lasts. On the other hand, if the natural father is currently paying support, the system would have disadvantages as well. Some method would have to be devised to allocate responsibility between the natural father and stepfather. In the process, the child might come out the loser. Currently, the natural father's support payments are theoretically figured without regard to any benefits the stepfather provides the child. If the stepfather is legislatively recognized as a source of support for the child, his income will have to be taken into account in determining the amount of the natural father's payments. Of course, under present doctrines the court can reduce the natural father's decree obligation when the mother remarries;[54] but the pressures to reduce the natural father's support payments will inevitably be—indeed, should be—greater if the stepfather has a concurrent statutory support duty. If the natural father is taking an interest in the child as well as paying support, a formal stepfather support duty does not seem important enough to incur the costs of administering the system.

---

[53] For a recent case in which the court's separate maintenance award apparently took the wife's child by a previous marriage into account, see Johnson v. Davis, 140 N.W.2d 703 (N.D. 1966). The wife will probably obtain less money if the judge is disguising support payments in an alimony award. In community property states such as California, of course, upon divorce the wife generally has an immediate right to half of the assets which the husband has acquired with earnings during the marriage. During the marriage, however, the wife probably cannot obtain, in either common law or community property states, judicial aid in obtaining support from her husband. FOOTE, LEVY & SANDER, op. cit. supra note 32, at 303-13, 317-23.

[54] Cf., e.g., Commonwealth v. Camerson, 197 Pa. Super. 403, 179 A.2d 270 (1962) (release by custodian mother and stepfather of natural father's support obligation effective in absence of evidence that stepfather and mother cannot afford to support the child). See also Whybra v. Gustafson, 140 N.W.2d 760 (Ct. App. Mich. 1966) (support order against father of illegitimate child not an abuse of discretion, despite fact that amount was only half that proposed under uniform schedule used by judge as guide in divorce cases, because mother had married and child is now part of three-child household).

There is no reason to exacerbate already unedifying and unpleasant judicial controversies by adding issues such as the relative affluence of the natural father and the stepfather. It may not be possible to avoid bitterness between the mother and the natural father—bitterness which will have an effect on the child's contacts with the natural father. It hardly seems wise to insure the stepfather's active participation in the battle. To the extent that the natural father has reason to resent the stepfather, the child's relationship with the stepfather is likely to suffer. Since a great many natural fathers absent themselves and refuse to pay support,[55] the stepfather's obligation might be drafted to apply only when the natural father is either unable or refuses to pay support. Even this standard could produce serious problems of administration. The stepfather's liability would turn on the natural father's "abandonment" of the child, or on some equally vague standard for determining when the formal duty shifts. The issue would have to be relitigated in each support action brought against the stepfather; and the standard might encourage a bitter stepfather to make efforts to haul the natural father back into the controversy.

If we had some basis for predicting that stepfathers who do not now support their stepchildren during the marriage would do so if a formal support obligation were enacted, if we could say with assurance that enacting a joint support obligation would not modify present patterns of adjustment between stepfamilies and natural fathers because most natural fathers maintain neither personal nor financial interest in their children, there would be no reason not to impose a joint support obligation on the stepfather. But these inferences cannot be drawn at present; and, taking into account all the possible family contexts in which the rule would have to be applied, a stepfather support obligation might well produce more problems in some contexts than its value in the others justifies.[56] It may be wiser simply to rely upon the mother's interest in her children's financial security and her ability to persuade the stepfather to adopt the children.[57]

---

[55] See authorities cited in notes 38 and 42 *supra*.

[56] A stepfather support obligation is most clearly justified when the mother is widowed. The child's interests—financial as well as familial—would be served by encouraging the stepfather to adopt him. Since that is true, it does not make sense to make the status of stepfather too attractive. The stepfather is free to adopt the child, if the mother is willing, and no interests inconsistent with achieving maximum cohesiveness and permanence for the new family have to be protected. *But cf. In re* Guardianship of Woodward, 102 N.Y.S.2d 490 (Surr. Ct. 1951) (stepfather and paternal aunt established as joint personal guardians of wealthy child following mother's death; child's wealth derived from paternal grandparents; paternal grandparents and paternal aunt had contested stepfather's prior effort to adopt the child).

[57] The stepfather will usually be able to adopt if the natural father has "abandoned"

As we have already suggested, it is most difficult to accommodate all the conflicting interests, take account of the various contexts in which the issues may arise, and still formulate a sensible and flexible statutory support policy for stepfathers. We can be sure that a stepfather support statute would create new and difficult problems; since most stepfathers probably support the children during the marriage without a statutory duty, it does not seem unreasonable to prefer the status quo.

2. *"Men in the House"*

Stable, nonmarital family relationships present a different problem. Theoretically, a common law marriage,[58] despite the informality of its formation, is no different than the ceremonial variety; a common law husband has support obligations, his subsequent marriage without a divorce is bigamous, his wife is entitled to a widow's rights at his death.[59] In fact, however, the common law marriage doctrine makes sense only as a fictional, ex post facto method of preventing injustice to women and children who were members of a stable and viable family until some unforeseen event made proof of a valid marriage essential: The father dies or is killed, perhaps, and the mother or children file a wrongful death action, claim workmen's compensation benefits or the father's insurance policy, or seek social security benefits.[60] The man who might subsequently be considered a participant in a common law marriage is for all practical purposes free to leave his family whenever he wishes.[61] This is

---

the child. See authorities cited in note 46 *supra*. It is probably true that "abandonment" may be rigorously construed if the natural father appears to contest the adoption. *Cf.* authorities cited in note 52 *supra*. The only situations posing a serious problem are those in which the natural father has an interest in the child but no money, and the stepfather has money but is unwilling to support the child. We wonder whether such situations frequently occur.

[58] For a description and analysis of the concept, see Weyrauch, *Informal and Formal Marriage—An Appraisal of Trends in Family Organization*, 28 U. CHI. L. REV. 88 (1960). For a criticism of the doctrine, see Kirkpatrick, *Common-Law Marriages: Their Common Law Basis and Present Need*, 6 ST. LOUIS U.L.J. 30 (1960).

[59] See MADDEN, *op. cit. supra* note 31, at 39-40.

[60] See generally FOOTE, LEVY & SANDER, *op. cit. supra* note 32, at 272-94.

[61] It is true that the common law marriage issue may arise when the marriage is a going venture, *e.g.*, when one of the parties seeks separate maintenance, a divorce, or some other benefit of a legal marriage. See Colbert v. Colbert, 28 Cal. 2d 276, 169 P.2d 633 (1946) (separate maintenance action by common law wife who had divorced husband to evade rule prohibiting spouses to work in same agency; couple had continued to live together). Nonetheless, the great majority of appellate cases are of the type described in the text. It seems likely that if the issue is the common law husband's continuing support responsibility for his common law wife, the courts would at least require much more persuasive evidence of the "marriage." *Cf. Ex Parte* Threet, 160 Tex. 482, 333 S.W.2d 361 (1960). And the husband could always deny that he had performed the ritualistic formalities necessary to formation of a common law marriage.

certainly the most common method of dissolving even relatively stable "common law marriages":

> For many people at the lower end of the economic scale, divorce, the minimum cost of which in California is generally about 200 dollars is a luxury beyond their financial means. When poor families break down, the husband simply leaves. Desertion has become known as "the poor man's divorce."[62]

Under these circumstances, does it make any sense to impose a support obligation on such "husbands"? If the mother and father are not married, the paternity action permitted in most states will probably accomplish as much for the children as a support statute would;[63] if the parents' marriage is "void," either a legitimation statute or a paternity action statute will safeguard the children's right to support.[64] The problem, then, concerns only the "common law" husband who is not the children's father. Considering the difficulties of the task, imposition of a support obligation on such "men in the house" should not be undertaken.

Since such relationships will most frequently be found among poor families, the children will probably not be able to look to the natural father for support. If our major concern in these situations is the availability of welfare benefits, however, family law doctrines need not be modified.[65] Nor should we meddle with the system if the effort will be a waste of time: Some of the "husbands" served with complaints in support actions under these circumstances will undoubtedly "divorce" their spouses on the spot.[66] Equally important, framing a support policy for these situations would involve enormous practical and policy problems.

The legislature can extend ex post facto recognition to stable family relationships with little concern that the legislation will encourage their proliferation; nor does it seem likely that refusing ex post facto recogni-

---

[62] See tenBroek, 17 STAN. L. REV. 617. See also Foster, *Common Law Divorce*, 46 MINN. L. REV. 43 (1961).

[63] See FOOTE, LEVY & SANDER, *op. cit. supra* note 32, at 46-53.

[64] *Id.* at 32-34.

[65] In fact, utilizing family law doctrines to accomplish welfare purposes may be self-defeating. It is not unlikely that the demise of the common law marriage doctrine, see note 68 *infra*, is due in part to its frequent use in welfare contexts. See note 60 *supra* and accompanying text. Certainly employers who contribute to workmen's compensation funds have often lobbied for legislative abolition of the doctrine.

[66] *But cf.* Paulsen, *Juvenile Courts, Family Courts, and the Poor Man*, this symposium. If there is proof that the "man in the house" has exchanged *verba de praesenti* and met the other formalistic prerequisites of a common law marriage, and if a common law marriage is not only an ex post facto saving device but a marital status binding for all purposes, then imposing a support obligation might be appropriate. But see note 67 *infra* and accompanying text.

tion would deter very many people from forming stable, nonmarital relationships in the future. Yet a legislator may properly balk at providing a statutory support obligation lest it imply approval of such methods of family formation.[67] A support obligation can hardly be recognized in the states which have abolished the common law marriage doctrine.[68] Moreover, how could a fair support statute be drafted? It does not seem appropriate to require support from a casual paramour; and the prerequisites to liability—indicia of family status such as the stability of the relationship—would have to be phrased in the vaguest terms.[69] The most sensible course is to permit these informal families to resolve their financial problems by self-help.

B. · Welfare Policy

1. Stepfathers

In determining a child's eligibility for AFDC benefits, should the earnings of a stepfather be taken into account? The California statute,[70] and regulations in a number of other states,[71] make his income relevant. Dr. Bell commented:

> So long as the evidence genuinely supported the conclusioin that a man lived continuously in the home or was considered by the family to have the status of "father" and "husband," there may have been little logical basis for distinguishing such a family from those with two able-bodied legally married parents who were excluded until 1961 by Title IV of the Social Security Act, and also until the present time from numerous state and local general assistance programs, particularly in Southern states.[72]

We hold no brief for tying assistance benefits to rigid categories—permitting payment for physical but not for mental or emotional defect, or authorizing benefits when an incapacitated father is in the home but denying them if the father is simply unemployed. Yet it would be im-

---

[67] Cf. Schwartz, Book Review, 96 U. PA. L. REV. 914, 915-16 (1948). In any event, although it may be sensible for the legislature to extend to an informal family relationship which has in fact been permanent all the perquisites of a valid ceremonial marriage, the legislature need not treat the relationship as binding for all purposes. It may be wiser to permit couples who have begun a family relationship informally to terminate their relationship in the same fashion.

[68] Only about fifteen jurisdictions continue to recognize common law marriages. FOOTE, LEVY & SANDER, op. cit. supra note 32, at 270. A number of states which have abolished common law marriages continue to recognize one or more of the other ex post facto saving devices designed to prevent injustice to a participant in an invalid marriage. Id. at 278-94.

[69] If no support obligation is imposed upon stepfathers, of course, it would be much more difficult to justify a "man in the house" support obligation.

[70] CAL. WELFARE & INST'NS CODE § 11351.

[71] BELL, AID TO DEPENDENT CHILDREN 76 (1965).

[72] Id. at 86.

possible to obtain widespread support for an assistance program which ignored the earnings of a natural father. Indeed, only strongly felt notions of parental responsibility can explain the original ADC program's exclusion of a child whose "able-bodied" natural father is a member of the family.[73] These notions operate today. When the 1961 Social Security Act amendments broadened the program to include families with an unemployed father in the home,[74] "Congress imposed conditions designed to stimulate the employment or enhance the employability of that parent—that is, to eliminate his idleness and lack of visible means of support."[75] And the amendments permitted the states to continue pre-1961 policies.[76] It is perfectly natural that legislators would hesitate to adopt a program which might encourage lazy fathers to rely solely on the public to support their families—their concern is appropriate so long as it does not become an obsession. The Bureau of Public Assistance construed the original ADC provisions to permit exemption of the stepfather's income in determining a child's eligibility—apparently because a stepfather has no statutory obligation to support the child.[77] Yet if the Congress did not want to encourage lazy natural fathers, it should be equally opposed to encouraging lazy stepfathers. The issue, then, is whether stepfathers should be treated differently than are natural fathers when public funds are at stake.

There are practical reasons for taking the stepfather's income into account. If one factor to be considered in devising welfare programs is minimizing public expense without undermining the program's purposes —and, for better or worse, everyone seems to agree that cost minimization has been a factor[78]—the financially responsible stepfather cannot be ignored. Even if total program cost increments are irrelevant, sound welfare administration requires that the stepfather's solvency be considered. To the extent that the absolute number of beneficiaries can be minimized without unfairness, it may be possible to increase the rather

---

[73] BELL, op. cit. supra note 71, at 1–19, traces the history of the ADC program, and the "suitable home" policies which have been a part of it, to the Mothers' Pension programs of the 1920's. "The only families who were eligible [for a Mothers' Pension] in all states, though, were those whose fathers had been permanently eliminated by death, long-term imprisonment, or incurable insanity. In this way the twin headaches of nonsupporting fathers and immoral mothers were largely avoided." Id. at 9, See also id. at 80.

[74] 75 Stat. 75 (1961), as amended, 42 U.S.C. § 607 (1964).

[75] Rosenheim, Vagrancy Concepts in Welfare Law, 54 CALIF. L. REV. 511, 531-32 (1966).

[76] BELL, op. cit. supra note 71, at 86.

[77] BUREAU OF PUBLIC ASSISTANCE, SOCIAL SECURITY ADMINISTRATION, HANDBOOK OF PUBLIC ASSISTANCE ADMINISTRATION, PART IV, 3400-99 (Nov. 4, 1946), cited in BELL, op. cit. supra note 71, at 77 n.2. Dr. Bell suggests that the Bureau's rule was based upon the fact that the stepfather might have no duty to support the child. Ibid.

[78] E.g., BELL, op. cit. supra note 71, at 60-67; tenBroek, 17 STAN. L. REV. 676

paltry sums which beneficiaries now receive without additional appropriations. In addition, the incidental consequences of refusing to consider the stepfather's income may be unfortunate. If the mother is receiving benefits, the welfare department must seek recompense from the natural father;[79] if the natural father has established a new family, it may be socially more advantageous to permit the natural father to devote his funds to his new family so long as the stepfather is able to provide support. This is certainly true of families with marginal incomes. To be sure, the stepfather and mother may seek support from the natural father if AFDC benefits are cut off. But it is not unreasonable to assume that the mother and stepfather will pursue the natural father less relentlessly than the welfare department would.

More basic considerations also suggest that the stepfather's income should be counted in determining eligibility. One need not be bigoted—against the poor or other minority groups—to believe that welfare programs should encourage stepfathers to assume the support responsibilities which a natural father would be compelled to assume and which, as we have already indicated, many stepfathers voluntarily assume. A "substitute parent" rule will certainly encourage some stepfathers to support the children in their homes. On the other hand, a stepfather who can rely upon a monthly AFDC payment may not be as willing to devote his income to maintaining his wife's children. He might also be encouraged not to adopt the children, since his family's government bonus would then terminate. Indeed, there have been cases (in the welfare department records of at least one jurisdiction which did not at the time have a "substitute parent" rule) in which stepfathers have been urged not to adopt lest AFDC benefits be lost.[80] A "substitute parent" rule might encourage some stepfathers who obtain employment to divorce their wives; but are the divorce risks more substantial than the irresponsibility we encourage by exempting the stepfather? A "substitute parent" rule may encourage some stepfathers to stay unemployed; but is avoiding this disincentive more important than treating the stepfather's income as we would the natural father's income?

In short, any policy is likely to produce some undesirable side effects; the importance of the goal we seek must be weighed against the magni-

---

[79] For a description of the famous "NOLEO" amendment, Social Security Act Amendments of 1950, ch. 809, § 321, 64 Stat. 550, see BELL, *op. cit. supra* note 71, at 80. The amendment requires the welfare department to notify the responsible law enforcement official whenever aid is granted to a child who has been abandoned by his parent.

[80] One of the authors, in the course of a study of a state welfare department's investigations of "independent placement" adoptions, found several reports recommending that the court deny stepfather petitions because the children would lose their ADFC benefits if they were adopted.

tude of the undesirable consequences which inevitably accompany any method chosen to attain it. The only risk we take in approving a "substitute parent" rule is that a substantial number of marginal income stepfather families which are stable and providing a good and healthy environment for the child with a government income supplement would become unstable and less adequate for the children without the supplement. Obviously, we have not begun to explore the magnitude of this risk. There is probably agreement that benefits should not be given to wealthy stepfathers. We might indulge in the assumption that only poor step-families would seek benefits. Yet many stepfathers who do not need the money seek support payments from natural fathers who are in similar financial circumstances. Are the prospective benefits of making AFDC payments available to marginal income step-families worth the risk that some step-families which do not need the money will profit as well?[81] If the stepfather's income is not marginal, of course, the child may profit more in the long run if the stepfather is not discouraged from adopting him. In the absence of any reliable evidence as to the effects on family stability of either rule, we believe that the stepfather's income should be taken into account; the risks we have suggested do not seem sufficiently substantial to warrant eliminating a policy which encourages, even indirectly, financially able stepfathers to support their families.

2. "Men in the House"

The "man in the house" rule authorizes the welfare department to consider the income of a "male person assuming the role of spouse to the mother although not legally married to her"[82] in determining a child's eligibility for AFDC benefits. The rule has produced violent controversy. It seems likely, however, that much of the opposition has been occasioned by use of the rule to regulate the out-of-wedlock sexual behavior of AFDC mothers:

> [T]he "nonstable, nonlegal" union in Arkansas, the "male boarder" in Michigan, "Roger the Lodger" in Oregon, the "unrelated man living in the home" in Alabama were examples of a rather tenuous relation-

---

[81] Well-to-do stepfathers might feel too embarrased to claim welfare benefits. Or they might not want to submit to the caseworker supervision which is an inevitable concomitant of the grant. One might question whether it is sound to rely on these deterrents, at a time when so much is being heard about the "right" to benefits. See Handler, *Controlling Official Behavior in Welfare Administration*, this symposium. In any event, if stepfather families with marginal income may be unstable without a government financial increment, it is just as likely that natural father families, similarly situated, will be unstable. If stepfathers are to be helped, why not help natural fathers also? Of course, if the natural family breaks down, the natural father retains a formal support obligation; but that hardly provides security for the children. See authorities cited in note 38 *supra*.

[82] CAL. WELFARE & INST'NS CODE § 11351.

ship where there was no necessary presumption of a consistent or acknowledged relationship and evidence of the man's existence was sometimes so insubstantial or transient that he was dubbed the "phantom father" in one study.[83]

We are concerned only with the stable and openly acknowledged family relationships contemplated by the rules of the California Department of Social Welfare:

> a. He is in or around the home and is maintaining an intimate relationship with the mother, or is the father of one or more of the children, and
> b. He has assumed substantial financial responsibility for the ongoing expenses of the ANC family, and/or
> c. He has represented himself to the community in such a way as to appear in the relationship of husband and/or father.
> The existence of items a plus b and/or c creates a rebuttable presumption that the adult male has assumed the role of spouse.[84]

The rule recognizes (as does Professor tenBroek)[85] that in a society which includes many cultures and a substantial group of poverty-stricken individuals many perfectly stable informal families will inevitably be found. For some couples a "common law" understanding is a customary and acceptable alternative to a religious or civil ceremony. If welfare benefits are denied to families in which a legally married father's earnings are above the assistance level, is there any reason to treat the "common law" husband and father differently? In one of his earlier articles Professor tenBroek remarked:

> Viewed in welfare and financial terms, this family situation and the needs of the children would not be different if the man and woman were married according to all the conditions set down in the Civil Code. Yet if stepfather liability is not imposed [on common law stepfathers], the children are eligible for aid to needy children regardless of the man's income. A financial premium is consequently placed on the common law relationship, and inequity is sanctioned between common law and duly married stepfathers, and a line of distinction

---

83 BELL, *op. cit. supra* note 71, at 86.

84 tenBroek, 17 STAN. L. REV. 620, quoting CAL. AFDC MANUAL, Reg. § C-155. A disclaimer may be necessary. We would not imply approval of these factors as compared to others which might be phrased. We would not minimize the difficulty of the definitional task, nor the risks of maladministration of an appropriate standard—especially in those Southern states which seem to be pursuing improper goals. See BELL, *op. cit. supra* note 71, at 93-110. It may well be that more flexible safeguards than those presently available to the Federal Bureau of Family Services must be devised to protect against such risks. *Id.* at 186-94. But these are not arguments against *some* form of "man in the house" rule.

85 See tenBroek, 17 STAN. L. REV. 617, 619. See also People v. Shirley, 55 Cal. 2d 521, 525, 360 P.2d 33, 35, 11 Cal. Rptr. 537, 542 (1961).

is drawn between the two which has little bearing upon the financial program of aid to needy children.[86]

We do not want to be misunderstood. We are not urging a morality crusade. Rather, we see the rule simply as a method of eliminating an evasionary device. If a stepfather rule is adopted, a "man in the house" rule is a necessity—so that couples will not be encouraged to live together without marrying in order to continue the mother's AFDC benefits. The more inclusive rule is especially important in jurisdictions in which substantial populations feel little cultural compulsion to engage in ceremonial ("legal") marriage.[87]

The "man in the house" rule may accomplish what it was designed to accomplish—financially able "fathers" will remain in the home and will support the children.[88] We share Professor tenBroek's doubt, however, that in every case "it is reasonable to infer that a man assuming the role of spouse will contribute to the support of the mother and her needy child."[89] We also doubt the effectiveness of the circumscribed support obligation appended to the California "man in the house" rule: "[S]uch adult male person is bound to support, if able to do so, his wife's children if without support from such . . . adult male person they would be needy children eligible for aid under this chapter."[90] The only effective sanction will probably be the mother's threat: "Support me and the kids, or out you go!" If she does not threaten, and the children suffer, the community can intervene through the processes of the juvenile court.[91] If the mother makes use of her sanction because her AFDC benefits are at stake, the "man in the house" rule may have a "deterrent effect on stable common-law unions providing a two-parent home for the child by the withdrawal of the premium."[92] But the only men (who have or can obtain decent employment) likely to be influenced by the rule are: (1) those who would rather use their own income on themselves to the exclusion of their families, and (2) those who would be tempted to desert their families simply because the taxpayers' contribution to the

---

[86] tenBroek, *The Impact of Welfare Law Upon Family Law*, 42 CALIF. L. REV. 458, 483 (1954).

[87] "[C]ommon law marriage is an accepted custom among many Mexican families at the lower socio-economic level and is a legally recognized form of marriage in Mexico." tenBroek, 17 STAN. L. REV. 617.

[88] "The truth is that the rule was adopted not so much as a measure of contributions actually being made as it was a means of seeing to it that contributions were made." *Id.* at 657.

[89] *Id.* at 658 n.999.

[90] CAL. WELFARE & INST'NS CODE § 11351.

[91] See generally FOOTE, LEVY & SANDER, CASES ON FAMILY LAW 400-22 (1966).

[92] tenBroek, 17 STAN. L. REV. 658 n.999.

family's income is eliminated. We wonder whether it is socially useful to encourage the stability of such two-parent families. We do not know, it is true, that children will develop more favorably without a "father" than they will with a financially able "father" who refuses to support them. But we have no reason for believing the contrary. In any event, the only way to eliminate the deterrent effects of the rule would involve placing a "financial premium" on informal relationships. Since we must either encourage or discourage the stability of these families—we are not discussing immoral families, let us repeat, but families whose stability is based solely on the continuance of a governmental income increment— it does not seem improper to adopt the course suggested by middle-class notions of family support.

CONCLUSION

We will not be disappointed if our analyses of these family law and welfare policies produce disagreement. Indeed, rational doctrinal formulation is aided by presentation and vigorous defense of a variety of inconsistent—even contradictory—proposals. But the process will be helpful only if the arguments are on the merits. Demands for "equality" which disregard essential differences in the doctrines chosen for comparison will provide little guidance to legislators. The fourteenth amendment, although it obviously imposes limitations on legislative discretion, cannot be considered the sole repository of either family law or public welfare wisdom. The issues can be clarified and resolved more cogently if family law and welfare policies are differentiated and examined with care.

Dual Systems of Family Law: A Comment

Walter O. Weyrauch*

MUCH LEGAL REASONING seems to follow the model of a litigious, adversary context. The method has its proven merits as an intellectual tool facilitating discussion, even though at times issues are dichotomized and differences of opinion unduly stressed. While adopting this method, I shall try to provide a synthesis.

The article by Professors Thomas P. Lewis and Robert J. Levy, *Family Law and Welfare Policies—The Case for "Dual Systems,"* published in this symposium,[1] is difficult to evaluate for a reason that illustrates a recurrent problem of legal scholarship. The article was prompted by Professor Jacobus tenBroek's major effort, *California's Dual System of Family Law: Its Origin, Development, and Present Status,* which appeared in three installments in the *Stanford Law Review.*[2] As an inevitable consequence the comments of Lewis and Levy cannot be fully appreciated unless tenBroek's work is closely read, followed by a second reading of the Lewis and Levy paper. Most readers cannot be expected to engage in this circular process.

Ideally authors of critical essays should assume that only rarely will the original source be consulted in its totality. Perhaps an individual page reference will be checked. Even this may not be done by the reader, and the argumentation and comments of the critic are likely to be taken at face value. The critic is vested with a factual power over the subject matter, a situation that may inadvertently result in injustice. This imposes a responsibility on him, related to what may loosely be called "academic due process," to present his views in a fashion that incorporates the reasoning contained in the original source. Since incorporation by mere reference is not satisfactory, the original reasoning must somehow be made part of the critical essay, a very difficult task requiring close identifications. If the approach of the critic is essentially negative, he may face a contradictory, perhaps an impossible task. This is his dilemma.

Professors Lewis and Levy have made a diligent effort to do justice to Professor tenBroek's work. In an effort to enunciate his thoughts, they have inserted large quotes.[3] Perhaps even this is not quite satisfactory.

* Dr. Jur., 1951, University of Frankfort on the Main, Germany; LL.B., 1955, Georgetown University; LL.M., 1956, Harvard University; J.S.D., 1962, Yale University. Professor of Law, on leave, University of Florida, Gainesville; Visiting Research Lawyer, University of California, Berkeley, Space Sciences Laboratory, Social Sciences Project.

1 54 CALIF. L. REV. 748 (1966).

2 (pts. 1, 2), 16 STAN. L. REV. 257, 900 (1964); (pt. 3), 17 STAN. L. REV. 614 (1965) [hereinafter cited as tenBroek, with appropriate volume and page].

3 Lewis & Levy, *Family Law and Welfare Policies—The Case for "Dual Systems,"* 54 CALIF. L. REV. 751-52, 756-57 (1966).

The excerpts are taken from summarizing or concluding paragraphs, where tenBroek expresses his thoughts on a somewhat higher level of generalization.[4] Frequently the excerpts have an idealistic and visionary quality. Standing alone they lose much of their persuasive power because they do not have the support of the full article with its detailed substantiation.

Perhaps I should recapitulate what Professor tenBroek, as I see it, was attempting to do. He was trying to show by an exhaustive presentation of evidence that California has a dual system of family law, one law of the poor, distinct from the family law of the rest of the community— not necessarily only the rich, but all those in a more comfortable position.[5] Part of the significance of the study is its implication that other jurisdictions may have similar dual systems of law which regulate human conduct according to the class position of the participants. Yet by focusing on one jurisdiction, California, tenBroek has been able to penetrate the subject in greater depth than could normally be attempted.

The result of this dual system of law, according to Professor tenBroek, appears to be a separating wall in regard to almost any matter of concern for the family[6]—possession of property; support relations between husband, wife, and children; creation and dissolution of the family; custody of children; rights and duties of parents; and so on. In regard to the poor there appears to be less emphasis on rights, and fitness as a parent or even as a useful citizen is rarely presumed. The burden of proof is cast on the poor person, whatever the issue may be, to make a case in his favor. He is often subjected to official investigations, not infrequently to humiliation and harassment.[7] His plight is subject to exploitation for political purposes, for instance, during elections, because of the public concern for the spending and possible waste of tax moneys. The law of the poor appears to be largely a creation of the legislature and, by way of implementation, of the executive. Regulations of government agencies play an important role, as do actual practices of welfare workers and police which are often characterized by low visibility.[8]

The family law of the more fortunate, following Professor tenBroek's reasoning, is largely created and administered by the courts. The law

---

[4] tenBroek, 16 STAN. L. REV. at 978, 17 STAN. L. REV. at 623-24, 681-82.

[5] tenBroek, 16 STAN. L. REV. at 258.

[6] Emphasized throughout parts 2 and 3, 16 STAN. L. REV. 900; 17 STAN. L. REV. 614.

[7] tenBroek, 17 STAN. L. REV. at 662-75. See also Reich, *Midnight Welfare Searches and the Social Security Act*, 72 YALE L.J. 1347 (1963).

[8] tenBroek, 17 STAN. L. REV. at 614-17, 677. See also Goldstein, *Police Discretion Not to Invoke the Criminal Process: Low-Visibility Decisions in the Administration of Justice*, 69 YALE L.J. 543 (1960). As a consequence of the present situation the poor frequently are forced to exhaust administrative remedies before they get to the courts.

changes slowly here because of the conservative orientation of many judges, who are vested with substantial discretion.[9] Marriage is viewed as similar to a partnership between semi-independent parties, resulting in a network of legal relations often proprietary in nature.[10] The legislature appears to be basically uninterested. By contrast, the law of the poor is affected by continued tampering by the legislature and by pressure groups. It is a matter of persistent concern. Husband and wife are viewed as an integrated entity, having pooled resources for purposes of minimizing public aid.[11] Fiscal considerations are dominant and frequently enforced by conditions attached to welfare aid, designed to keep the costs of welfare programs low. The police power of the state appears to be used to secure the comfort and the wealth of those who are more fortunate against those who are in need and lack the time, power, and resources to pursue their legitimate aims.[12] All these propositions are not merely stated, but heavily substantiated, and the sources have to be read in conjunction with the propositions.

Professor tenBroek concludes by advocating basic changes. Following *Brown v. Board of Education*[13] he argues that separate treatment in respect to public services cannot result in equality, regardless of whether the criterion is race or a discriminatory differentiation between the poor and the more affluent. Race and poverty should be treated similarly for purposes of constitutional law,[14] especially since often the persons concerned are both members of ethnic minorities and indigent. tenBroek realizes that this is not necessarily the prevailing view of the moment, but he sees a hopeful trend because the problem of poverty is now discussed in terms of the fourteenth amendment's equal protection clause.[15]

Professors Lewis and Levy do not deny the existence of dual systems of law, but they try to make a case for them. Yet before I go into their

---

9 The discretion of the judges may be phrased in terms of a legal standard: for instance, "best interests of the child" and support "suitable to his circumstances." See tenBroek, 16 STAN. L. REV. at 915-27, 17 STAN. L. REV. at 646-48. Perhaps more important is the factual discretion which may result from the knowledge of trial judges that their decisions are not likely to be appealed. Even in case of appeal the parties have to overcome the reluctance of the higher courts to disturb the findings of judges "of first impression," who are viewed as being closer to the facts.

10 tenBroek, 17 STAN. L. REV. at 622-23.

11 *Id.* at 624-27.

12 *Id.* at 680.

13 347 U.S. 483 (1954). Other cases cited in support: Hardy v. United States, 375 U.S. 277 (1964); Gideon v. Wainwright, 372 U.S. 335 (1963); Griffin v. Illinois, 351 U.S. 12 (1956); Edwards v. California, 314 U.S. 160 (1941). See tenBroek, 16 STAN. L. REV. at 258, 17 STAN. L. REV. at 643-44, 681-82.

14 Referring to Mr. Justice Jackson in Edwards v. California, 314 U.S. 160, 184-85 (1941) (concurring opinion). See tenBroek, 17 STAN. L. REV. at 681-82.

15 *Id.* at 681.

analysis it may be helpful to compare the methodology of Professor tenBroek with that of his critics.

Professor tenBroek cites numerous statutes, court opinions, regulations, and opinions of attorney generals in support of his propositions, down to unpublished minutes of welfare boards and the annual reports of local district attorneys. He further engages in a historical analysis that traces the present legal situation in California to the Elizabethan poor law system of the sixteenth and early seventeenth centuries.[16] Throughout tenBroek's efforts one senses that he does not refer to law in the conventional way, distinguishing between the law and the facts. I am inclined to classify his work as empirical in nature, using legal references as data. Law appears as a fact, submitted in evidence for ultimate conclusions.[17] Lewis and Levy in comparison are not so much empirically oriented in their essay; they approach their topic in an analytical fashion. I do not mean to establish an artificial dichotomy between empirical and analytical methods, but merely wish to point out a difference in emphasis. In any event, reading both articles in conjunction one gets the feeling that their methodologies are somewhat incongruent, a factor that may impair communication.

Professors Lewis and Levy admit duality in law as described, but they find it distracting to emphasize equal protection problems in this context. Duality is viewed by them as a common phenomenon that results from many legal classifications. Lewis and Levy point out by way of illustration that we differentiate those who are negligent from those who accidentally injure others.[18] We also have to differentiate those who are in need from those who are not. Inevitably we define the indigent in terms of income and available resources. Some conditions for the spending of public funds must be established, as long as this does not undermine the purposes of welfare programs.[19] Lewis and Levy employ logical analysis to test the validity of the propositions that are put forward in tenBroek's article.

---

[16] tenBroek, 16 STAN. L. REV. at 257, 900. A historical description of the English dual system of family disorganization is contained in Mueller, *Inquiry Into the State of a Divorceless Society—Domestic Relations Law and Morals in England From 1660 to 1857*, 18 U. PITT. L. REV. 545 (1957).

[17] *Cf.* OLIVECRONA, LAW AS FACT 16-27 (1939). See also FULLER, THE MORALITY OF LAW 150 (1964). Much useful empirical research can be conducted in law libraries: for example, content analyses of legal sources. The work of the legal historian can be viewed under this perspective too.

[18] Lewis & Levy, *supra* note 3, at 757. What has been said in regard to Professor tenBroek's work applies similarly here. The reasoning of Professors Lewis and Levy can only be appreciated and understood fully if one reads the article in its totality. An individual illustration loses inevitably some of its persuasiveness by being paraphrased and removed from the context.

[19] *Id.* at 754-55, 775.

The world of facts is touched upon in a fashion that stresses notions of evidence and prevailing mores. Nothing is inherently wrong with a dual system of law and the resulting differences in treatment provided that the state is not arbitrary. The burden of proof should be on the one claiming arbitrariness and a violation of constitutional mandates.[20] Due regard should be given to legal policies in the light of commonly accepted notions of family life. Our society is built around the married family, and welfare programs are legitimately geared to this philosophy.[21]

Individual points are taken up by Professors Lewis and Levy to test the claimed arbitrariness of standards that may result in dual systems of family law and in a supposed inequality. If we had a proliferation of facts in tenBroek's article, we now face an imaginative effort to master the complexity of the problem by a point-by-point analysis. The authors introduce hypothetical situations to test whether there is discriminatory duality of substantive rules. Suppose that a particular jurisdiction has a rule that children who are financially able have to support their needy parents.[22] The rule has a number of consequences; for instance, children of the wealthy do not have to support their parents but children of poor parents may face such a burden. On the other hand, poor children have no support obligations, contrary to children who are financially able. The authors conclude that even though there may be duality, it is based on rational factors and thus not in violation of the equal protection clause. Some difference in treatment, if rational, is unavoidable and even desirable.

Professors Lewis and Levy stress that we lack reliable data about the impact of law on people. As a consequence we may have to rely on numerous assumptions.[23] Perhaps because of this difficulty the analysis is limited to stable family unions involving substitute parents. Should a stepfather or a "man in the house" be legally bound to support the children in the family, and should his financial status be considered in aid for dependent children programs? The answers given favor the prevailing legal situation.

Stepfathers are now immune from support obligations in most states, and legislators are unlikely to depart from ancient policies that the natural father is the one who should pay for his children.[24] Lewis and Levy point out many uncertainties and variables. We do not know whether a prospective support obligation of stepfathers may deter them from marriage; we

---

[20] *Id.* at 757, 780.

[21] *Id.* at 757-59, 765.

[22] *Id.* at 759-60.

[23] *Id.* at 759, 764-65.

[24] *Id.* at 762.

also do not know whether an exclusive support obligation of stepfathers promotes family cohesiveness.[25] We can hardly predict the consequences of a joint support obligation of both stepfathers and natural fathers, and we can only speculate on whether stepfathers who do not support their children would change their behavior under legal compulsion. However, since most stepfathers probably support the children in the family on a more or less voluntary basis, the *status quo* appears to be satisfactory.[26] Additional reasons speak against imposing support obligations on "men in the house" who are not natural fathers. If they are natural fathers paternity actions under existing law can be brought against them.[27]

In regard to whether the earnings of stepfathers and "men in the house" should continue to be taken into account for welfare benefits, Professors Lewis and Levy similarly favor the prevailing legal situation. Legislators cannot be expected to adopt a welfare program that encourages stepfathers to rely on public support of their families.[28] Furthermore, we do not know whether a substantial number of stepfather families with marginal income become unstable if welfare funds are withheld. In the absence of any reliable data we may prefer the prevailing practice which at least indirectly may encourage some financially able stepfathers to support their families.[29] The same reasoning applies even more to the "man in the house." It is possible that he may leave the mother if welfare funds are withheld because of his presence. But we do not know whether the children are better or worse off without such a "father." In the absence of evidence to the contrary, the authors see no reason in any of these instances to abandon prevailing courses suggested by middle-class notions.[30]

In analyzing the case for or against a dual system of family law it appears to me that we have not so much a confrontation of empirical data and of logic, but one of underlying value preferences. Professor tenBroek seems to favor social change because of basic injustices, perhaps at the cost of experimentation. Professors Lewis and Levy favor a more cautious approach, at least for the time being, because of insufficient evidence on many important factors relating to the family. Both positions are intrinsically valid, provided one recognizes them as based on different value perspectives. Even in this respect I wish to submit a caveat. Sometimes one gets the impression that the authors are not really far apart. They agree that many basic injustices are inherent in the present welfare laws.

---

[25] *Id.* at 764-66.
[26] *Id.* at 770-72.
[27] *Id.* at 772-74.
[28] *Id.* at 775.
[29] *Id.* at 776-77.
[30] *Id.* at 777-80.

Sometimes their language is similar. When tenBroek stresses that "a new spirit in constitutional law has given positive signs of its *future* potential,"[31] and Lewis and Levy counter that "indigence is *not yet* the source of a right to demand benefits, supported by a correlative governmental duty to provide them,"[32] one wonders whether at least some of the difference in opinion is related to a difference in style of thought.

A few reflections on the merits of the issue may be added. I tend to agree with Professor tenBroek that the present situation indicates sufficient evidence of damage. We need not go far. The Watts riots of August 1965 were a sudden and violent reaction against a felt injustice. The rioters of this Los Angeles Negro district directed themselves against police and social workers alike. Whether the riots were partly caused by inherent inequalities of dual systems of law or by failures of our welfare administration may be of minor concern. Similarly I consider the question academic whether the riots were caused by racial or economic factors, since it is hard to draw a distinction. Our law, as any legal system, to some extent has an ethnocentric orientation; in other words, it reflects and protects the value preferences of a dominant culture,[33] and whether we classify this culture in terms of race or of economics does not seem to make much difference for our purposes. Those who set the standards tend to view them as of universal application, even though in many instances segments of the population, ethnic minorities and the poor, may live according to somewhat different standards of conduct and achievement. Thus many of the commonly used phrases, "disrespect for law and order," "failure to live up to responsibilities," "lacking motivation," "low morals

---

[31] tenBroek, 17 STAN. L. REV. at 681. (Emphasis added.)

[32] Lewis & Levy, *supra* note 3, at 754. (Emphasis added.) Professor Charles A. Reich has described how close we are to changes in policy. Reich, *Individual Rights and Social Welfare: The Emerging Legal Issues*, 74 YALE L.J. 1245 (1965); Reich, *The New Property*, 73 YALE L.J. 733 (1964).

[33] I am trying to summarize here some of the thoughts contained in my essay, "Informal Marriage and Common Law Marriage," published in *Sexual Behavior and the Law* (Slovenko editor, 1965), at page 297, in particular under the heading "Impact of Caste and Class," pages 323-26. The permission of the editor, Professor Ralph Slovenko, and of the publisher, Charles C Thomas, is gratefully acknowledged.

Cultural factors may be eminently important in legal counseling and trial techniques, as I have suggested in FREEMAN, LEGAL INTERVIEWING AND COUNSELING 126, 131-32 (1964).

It is generally conceded that dual systems of law exist in regard to Negroes and whites in the South. See DAVIS, GARDNER & GARDNER, DEEP SOUTH—A SOCIAL ANTHROPOLOGICAL STUDY OF CASTE AND CLASS 483-538 (1941); MYRDAL, AN AMERICAN DILEMMA—THE NEGRO PROBLEM AND MODERN DEMOCRACY 523-69 (20th anniversary ed. 1962); *Breaching the White Wall of Southern Justice*, Time, April 15, 1966, p. 46. See also the statement of a high-ranking southern official: "The race prejudice is inherent in both races. The whites are the dominant race in this country, and of course control the handling of the prejudice." 1941-1942 FLA. ATTORNEY GENERAL'S BIENNIAL REP. 332-33. This social phenomenon, unpleasant as it is, is probably not limited to the South and to Negroes. It may apply in similar fashion to the poor and other outgroups.

and intelligence," may reflect ethnic preferences denying recognition to standards and conditions of living that vary from accepted norms.

The situation may at times acquire explosive elements because the deviating groups, even though heterogeneous in their make-up, are larger than commonly assumed. If one combines criteria of low income, low educational level, and substandard housing, about one-fourth to one-third of the total American population may be involved.[34] Furthermore, poverty and low social status do not necessarily coincide. Some members of ethnic minorities may be comfortably situated, yet share a sense of deprivation with the poor. Teamsters and longshoremen may have higher incomes than white-collar workers, yet the history of their labor organizations seems to indicate shared identifications with some outgroups. One also may consider segments of the American youth who, even though of middle-class origin, sometimes sympathize with the ways of the deprived and the poor. Add those who are marginal for other reasons or who are indifferent, and it may become somewhat speculative whether the prevailing mores are as stable and secure as assumed. A certain amount of socio-legal experimentation may be desirable even from the perspective of those who want to preserve our middle-class values.

On the other hand, the War on Poverty could conceivably have negative aspects if it were to evolve into a "war on poor people." Professor tenBroek points out the damaging effects that some past social crusades have had,[35] and Professors Lewis and Levy seem to feel that it is sometimes wise to permit lower-class families to resolve their problems by self-help under their own standards of conduct.[36] In this broader sense perhaps a case can be made for a dual system of law. However, we may have to

---

[34] According to the United States Census 30.9% of all American families had an annual income of less than $4,000 in 1959; 39,500,000 persons twenty-five years old and over did not go beyond the eighth grade of formal education in 1960; 26% of all housing units in the United States were deteriorating, dilapidated, or lacking plumbing facilities in 1960. BUREAU OF THE CENSUS, U.S. DEP'T OF COMMERCE, STATISTICAL ABSTRACT OF THE UNITED STATES 117, 333, 759 (83d ed. 1962).

Other estimates: Thirty-two million Americans live on the outskirts of poverty, 109 CONG. REC. 172 (1963) (State of the Union Message of President Kennedy); thirty-two to forty-five million citizens suffering from serious economic and social handicaps, 109 CONG. REC. 6452 (1963) (remarks of Senator Williams of New Jersey to the National Service Corps Act); forty to fifty million citizens live in poverty, HARRINGTON, THE OTHER AMERICA— POVERTY IN THE UNITED STATES 1, 175-91 (1962).

A recent Bureau of the Census study of South Los Angeles shows a declining purchasing power of the typical family and a sharp increase in the proportion of deteriorating and dilapidated housing units in the five years preceding the Watts riots. See *1960-65 Survey—A Study of the Decline of Watts*, San Francisco Chronicle, March 9, 1966, p. 6, col. 1.

[35] See authorities cited in note 7 *supra*. See also ALVES, CONFIDENTIALITY IN SOCIAL WORK 87-90 (1959).

[36] Lewis & Levy, *supra* note 3, at 774.

expand our definition of law for this purpose. Law should perhaps embody the normative behavior within the subcultures in question. The poor have created among themselves a law of their own. The family organization developed among the lower classes has elements conducive to social health.[37] Even though the practices do not necessarily conform to prevailing mores, they have assured survival under adverse circumstances.

In spite of its ethnocentric characteristics, our legal system has always recognized outgroup standards to some extent, often without openly admitting such recognition. Informal marriages, which frequently occur in the lower classes and ethnic minorities, have been sustained under theories of common law marriage, marriage by estoppel, prescription or ratification, putative marriage, *de facto* marriage, and so on. Not yet fully explored is the extent procedural devices have been used to reach substantive results: for instance, by application of presumptions of marriage in cases of prolonged cohabitation, or presumptions of no-marriage or of divorce in cases of factual marriage breakup.[38] Professors Lewis and Levy have validly suggested that it may be a good policy to permit couples who have entered into an informal marriage to terminate their relationship in the same informal fashion.[39] In many instances the normative behavior of the poor has been recognized by way of executive toleration, even though it is technically in violation of some legal prescription. These various methods result in a dual system of law that may have some positive aspects.

This comment cannot exhaust the full range of problems that are posed by dual systems of law. Whenever there is duality in law, we may have the possibility of conflicts, with all the legal implications. We may rethink the basic issues under the perspectives of systems science and operations research. A body of knowledge has been accumulated under these headings that may furnish novel insights. A systems approach was successfully applied during World War II in England and later on in the

---

[37] MYRDAL, *op. cit. supra* note 33, at 930-35. Professor Herma Hill Kay and Doctor Irving Phillips note that positive factors are easily overlooked because of the differences in class attitudes toward parental competence. Kay & Phillips, *Poverty and the Law of Child Custody*, 54 CALIF. L. REV. 717, 736-37 (1966).

On a more general level it is maintained by the Moynihan Report that the matricentric structure of the lower-class Negro family and the resulting dual system of family organization have been harmful: "[I]t is clearly a disadvantage for a minority group to be operating on one principle, while the great majority of the population, and the one with the most advantages to begin with, is operating on another." OFFICE OF POLICY PLANNING AND RESEARCH, U.S. DEP'T OF LABOR, THE NEGRO FAMILY—THE CASE FOR NATIONAL ACTION 29 (1965).

[38] I have described this in greater detail in my essay on informal marriage, *supra* note 33, at 318-23.

[39] Lewis & Levy, *supra* note 3, at 774 n.67.

United States to deal with military emergencies. After the War it proved to be useful in an industrial context. More recent developments concern the improvement of large-scale social systems.[40]

By independent inquiry, systems scientists have come close to the problems of dual systems of law, as can be seen from the following passage in Professor C. West Churchman's writings:

> Finally, when we come to social welfare, it is easy enough to point out that many of our policies simply attack the dignity of the human being by forcing him to comply with many kinds of regulations in order to attain support from society. If he claims support he is always subject to investigation because, according to those in power, many people try to claim support who do not deserve it. Compliance with the regulations forced by the state make the recipient of social welfare virtually admit that he is a less than adequate member of society.[41]

Needless to say that much current study in systems science is carried on without the benefit of legal consultants, just as legal research does not have the benefits of operations research. It is conceivable that a shift in emphasis stressing aspects of systems theory may be helpful in legal planning.

Another line of inquiry that can only be touched upon relates to double standards of morality. I realize that dual systems of law and double standards of morality do not fully coincide. Yet Professor tenBroek's article seems to bring double standards of this kind to our attention, because law supposedly is of universal quality, while in fact differentiations are made on the basis of economic conditions, ethnic factors, and so on. Even in regard to double standards of morality the problems appear to be complex. Eminent authorities have defended cultural patterns that result in

---

[40] See CHURCHMEN, ON THE ETHICS OF LARGE-SCALE SYSTEMS, PART I (Space Sciences Laboratory, University of California, Berkeley, Internal Working Paper No. 37, 1965); HOOS, THE APPLICATION OF SYSTEMS ANALYSIS TO SOCIAL PROBLEMS: THE CALIFORNIA EXPERIENCE (Space Sciences Laboratory, University of California, Berkeley, Internal Working Paper No. 32, 1965); 1 NATIONAL COMM'N ON TECHNOLOGY, AUTOMATION, AND ECONOMIC PROGRESS, REPORT, TECHNOLOGY AND THE AMERICAN ECONOMY 95-108 (1966); see also CHURCHMAN, ACKOFF & ARNOFF, INTRODUCTION TO OPERATIONS RESEARCH (1957).

The California studies referred to by Hoos have resulted in four reports—AEROJET-GENERAL CORP., CALIFORNIA WASTE MANAGEMENT STUDY—A REPORT TO THE STATE OF CALIFORNIA DEPARTMENT OF PUBLIC HEALTH (1965); LOCKHEED MISSILES & SPACE CO., CALIFORNIA STATEWIDE INFORMATION SYSTEM STUDY—FINAL REPORT (1965); NORTH AMERICAN AVIATION, INC., CALIFORNIA INTEGRATED TRANSPORTATION STUDY (1965); and SPACE-GENERAL CORP., A STUDY OF PREVENTION AND CONTROL OF CRIME AND DELINQUENCY—FINAL REPORT (1965). Perhaps the problem is now whether knowledge accumulated by the military and industry can be transferred to a social context.

[41] CHURCHMAN, ON THE ETHICS OF LARGE-SCALE SYSTEMS, PART I, ch. IV, at 6-7 (Space Sciences Laboratory, University of California, Berkeley, Internal Working Paper No. 37, 1965).

double standards. Margaret Mead has described valuable incidents of our perennial failure to live up to standards that perhaps are set too high.[42] Gustav Radbruch has expressed a similar thought in startling fashion. Double standards of morality, he has said, are characteristic of middle-class cultures, and they should not be viewed as inherently evil. They presuppose and are naturally allied to even stronger moral demands and commitments.[43] Be that as it may, the effectiveness of moral double standards probably depends somewhat on people being essentially unaware of them. When a double standard is articulated and thus brought to our attention, exposed as it were, it may become difficult to retain.

---

[42] MEAD, AND KEEP YOUR POWDER DRY—AN ANTHROPOLOGIST LOOKS AT AMERICA 10-11, 126-37 (new expanded ed. 1965).

[43] RADBRUCH, DER GEIST DES ENGLISCHEN RECHTS 12-13 (3d ed. 1956): "Feigned morality, if it is to make any sense, presupposes in a people an even stronger measure of genuine moral demands and commitments. The degree of hypocrisy is the best measure for the power of morality over a people." (This author's translation from the German language.)

Reimbursement of Counsel Fees and the Great Society†

In sorrow and in anger—and in hope

*Albert A. Ehrenzweig**

I

SORROW: THE LITTLE MAN'S PLIGHT

WHEN I CAME to this country twenty-seven years ago, I was penniless, did not speak English, had to support wife, children and parents, and was unable to use anything that I had learned and done as a judge and law teacher in my first life. And yet I was permitted and encouraged to rejoin my own profession for a life in freedom and dignity. I knew, I knew deep in my heart, that there was no other country in the world in which this could have happened.

Compared to this knowledge, it meant little that an American moving firm had cheated us out of our last belongings; and it was only a fleeting disappointment when I found out that I had no recourse in the courts of law. I was, of course, directed to a fine lawyer. "Sure," he said, "you have an airtight claim, and I shall take your case, but you will understand, I must have one hundred dollars as a retainer." I did *not* understand. Would he not get his fees from the defendant, as he would anywhere else in the world? I did not have the hundred dollars, and even if I had won, I would not have been made whole for I had to pay my own lawyer. Of course I did not sue. The little man had lost. A fleeting disappointment, true. But I then swore to myself that I would not forget the little man if I should ever cease to be one.

Twenty-seven years have gone by. But only now do I feel that I can, in good taste and good faith, take on the fight and attack an institution which, erroneously, is held in awe by the American legal profession as a sacred common law heritage: the power and, indeed, the right of the losing party in a civil suit to inflict on the winner not only the misery but

---

† Much of the following material appeared first in my paper, *Shall Counsel Fees Be Allowed?*, 26 CAL. S. B.J. 107 (1951). See also Potter & Cooper, *Attorney's Fees*, 14 TEX. B.J. 579 (1951), borrowing generously from that paper without citation. A recent article, Stoebuck, *Counsel Fees Included in Costs: A Logical Development*, 38 U. COLO. L. REV. 202 (1966), takes essentially the position advocated in this article, and includes a draft statute.

* Dr. Jur., 1928, Vienna, Austria; J.D., 1941, University of Chicago; LL.M., 1942, J.S.D., 1952, Columbia University. Walter Perry Johnson, Professor of Law, University of California, Berkeley; *Honorarprofessor* of Conflict of Laws, University of Vienna.

also the expense of enforcing his just claim. For I am convinced that my plea for the abolition of that power, made in sorrow and in anger and in hope, has an essential function in the War on Poverty to which every citizen wherever born, every lawyer wherever bred, has the right and duty to contribute.

Reform of criminal procedure has become the central problem of the law reform which is to serve the Great Society. It is of course crucially important for us to protect everybody as well as we can, against the hazards of criminal justice. But most of these hazards will forever remain. For mankind's helplessness in the face of crime and criminals, the persistence of mankind's retributive instincts warring with its curative reasoning and ideals will forever permit only alleviation of this innate tragedy.[1] On the other hand, that other phase of our administration of justice, civil procedure, being infinitely less burdened by psychological trauma and enigma, has proved capable of true reform elsewhere, and that reform is long overdue in this country. Strangely, terribly, intolerably, these United States, this citadel of democracy, which has taken it on itself to play the decisive role in building the Rule of Law throughout the world, has forgotten the little man in his struggle for civil justice.

This fact is incredible to those who, though subjects of foreign dictators, enjoy a truly democratic civil procedure. But lack of such a procedure in this country is, of course, not a sinister product of "capitalism." Rather it is the result of historical accident. That it has, nevertheless prevailed to this day, is due no doubt to the multifarious split in the laws of the several states, which has prevented them from partaking in the progress of civil procedure in other countries, socialist and capitalist alike. It will remain for a future generation of scholars and lawyers with greater leisure and peace of mind, without prejudice and with much self-denial, to approach this general problem. What I can do, what I feel I must do at this time, is to make an urgent plea for the immediate reform of *one* central facet of our civil procedure which, separable from the latter's body, can and must be destroyed as a pernicious historical relic—unknown in the rest of the world—the rule, I repeat, that the winning party in a law suit (with few and unimportant exceptions) cannot recover his counsel fees from the loser.

True, commercial civil litigation, with its finely honed tools of adversary proceedings between lawyers, has been developed in this country to a perfection not easily equalled elsewhere. And there is scant reason for redistributing the cost of such litigation among the equal partners. True, also, that that travesty of the little man's justice, the personal injury

---

[1] See Ehrenzweig, *A Psychoanalysis of the Insanity Plea*, 73 YALE L.J. 425 (1964).

suit, with its gamble, delay and expense, will have to await fundamental substantive reform which will replace this suit by new tools for the distribution of losses inevitably caused by modern mechanical enterprise.[2] And until this reform can be achieved against the continuing resistance of the "industries" of the "plaintiffs' bar" and of insurance, the contingent fee, that legitimate sibling of criminal champerty, will have to remain with us as an incurable symptom of an uncured disease. But the little man in his every day dealings with his contracts, his property,[3] his family,[4] and administrative agencies[5] can and must be helped at this time, not by the business of neighborhood referral or the charity of legal aid, but by a reform of our law of counsel fees.

Just a trifle, a little cog in the great wheel of justice? No, a festering cancer in the body of our law without whose excision our society will not be great. Big words, to be sure. I shall try to justify them first in angry terms of personal experience and then in terms of the teacher and lawyer, thus adding hope to sorrow and to anger.

II

ANGER: UNREASON AND HYPOCRISY

As early as forty years ago, the Massachusetts Judicial Council pleaded for reform,[6] asking: "On what principle of justice can a plaintiff wrongfully run down on a public highway recover his doctor's bill but not his lawyer's bill."[7] As long as thirty-eight years ago, Sir Arthur Goodhart urged a comparative and functional study of the problem.[8] Over and again public attention has been drawn to the intolerable consequences of our rule. Yet the American bar has remained satisfied with slogans calling for making its services available to the "poor" through patchwork measures such as referral services and legal aid.[9] Group services may be the next

---

[2] See EHRENZWEIG, NEGLIGENCE WITHOUT FAULT (1951); EHRENZWEIG, "FULL AID" INSURANCE (1954).

[3] See, e.g., Cohen, Law, Lawyers, and Property, 43 TEX. L. REV. 1072, 1079 (1965).

[4] See, e.g., Carlin & Howard, Legal Representation and Class Justice, 12 U.C.L.A.L. REV. 381, 413 (1965).

[5] See, e.g., Sparer, The Role of the Welfare Client's Lawyer, 12 U.C.L.A.L. REV. 361 (1965).

[6] See Judicial Council of Massachusetts, First Report, 11 MASS. L.Q. 1, 63-64 (1925).

[7] Id. at 64.

[8] Goodhart, Costs, 38 YALE L.J. 849 (1928).

[9] See the much-praised report of the A.B.A. Committee on Legal Aid and Indigent Defendants, 51 A.B.A.J. 398 (1965). See also, e.g., Westwood, Legal Aid on the March in the Nation's Capital, 51 A.B.A.J. 325 (1965). The problem is not limited to the "poor." See Note, Providing Legal Services for the Middle Class in Civil Matters: The Problem, the Duty, and a Solution, 26 U. PITT. L. REV. 811 (1965). Compare Fritz, How Lawyers Can Serve the Poor at Profit, 52 A.B.A.J. 448 (1966).

reluctant concession.[10] But even the War on Poverty stops short of the fundamental issue.[11] And everyone raising it, will run into a stone wall.

I have long had to harden myself against the argument of friends and colleagues that my alien scheme would offend the American sense of fairness. Many, many times I have made my defense as I shall restate it presently. Only once I tried to reach a greater audience. I spent several weeks in tedious research to show how the rest of the world felt about our rule and completed a paper with a great deal of documentation. It remained unnoticed and unanswered in the "Forum" section of the bar journal to which I submitted it.[12] I did not give up. In 1952, as chairman of a committee of the American Bar Association, I obtained the unanimous consent of my committee to a summary of my research and to a recommendation that a comparative study of the problem be undertaken[13]— only to have our report pigeonholed for almost ten years. To be sure, in 1963 a courageous successor, Mr. Benjamin Busch, encouraged by the then chairman and vice-chairman of the Section, not only sought to bring the report to renewed attention, but actually obtained comparative studies for four countries.[14] But here the matter rests and will rest unless and until those concerned with the War on Poverty take on the fight.

Why the stone wall? Why must we fight so bitterly for something that is a matter of course in the rest of the world? Is it not obvious that the little man can fight for his right only if he can hope that he and his lawyer will be made whole if he wins? As an American lawyer I know that the little man's only refuge, the small claims court, is unavailable in innumerable communities; and that where it exists, it is prevailingly a collection

---

10 See, *e.g.*, Tucker, *Brotherhood of Railroad Trainmen v. Virginia: A Call to Realism in Legal Ethics*, 14 J. Pub. L. 3 (1965); Schwartz, *Foreword: Group Legal Services in Perspective*, 12 U.C.L.A.L. Rev. 279 (1965).

11 See Shriver, *The OEO [Office of Economic Opportunity] and Legal Services*, 15 A.B.A.J. 1064 (1965).

12 Ehrenzweig, *supra* note †.

13 1953 Proceedings of Section of International and Comparative Law, A.B.A., 125 (1953). See also Avila, *Shall Counsel Fees Be Allowed*, 13 Cal. S. B.J. 42 (1942); Geller, *Unreasonable Refusal to Settle and Calendar Congestion—Suggested Remedy*, 1962 Proceedings of Section of International and Comparative Law, A.B.A. 134 (1963); Hornstein, *Legal Therapeutics: The "Salvage" Factor in Counsel Fee Awards*, 69 Harv. L. Rev. 658 (1956); Kuenzel, *The Attorney's Fee: Why Not A Cost Of Litigation*, 49 Iowa L. Rev. 75 (1963).

14 Baeck, *Imposition of Fees of Attorney of Prevailing Party Upon the Losing Party Under the Laws of Austria*, 1962 Proceedings of Section of International and Comparative Law, A.B.A. 119 (1963); Baeck, *Imposition of Legal Fees and Disbursements of Prevailing Party Upon the Losing Party—Under the Laws of Switzerland, id.* at 124; Dietz, *Payment of Court Costs by the Losing Party Under the Laws of Hungary, id.* at 131; Freed, *Payment of Court Costs by Losing Party in France, id.* at 126; Schima, *The Treatment of Costs and Fees of Procedure in the Austrian Law, id.* at 121.

agency, and presents otherwise the horrifying spectacle of a court without law, abandoned by the legal profession which, almost everywhere, is excluded from its precincts.[15] And as an American citizen I know that all the law now offers the little man, outside that second-rate court at some places and at some times, is charity. Legal aid, rather than legal right. If access to the court is said to be an inalienable right in the most rigid dictatorship, money then is the way to justice in the world's greatest democracy. But not only the little man is in jeopardy, the legal profession is hurting itself immeasurably by its doting on what it wrongly believes to be a hallowed tradition. From my experience as an Austrian judge I know that these hundreds of thousands of honest claims which now are either contemptuously disposed of by "law-less" magistrates as not worthy of the law's and the lawyer's attention, or condescendingly "aided" by the generosity of the profession and its apprentices, or simply suppressed by lack of machinery, all those hundreds of thousands of honest claims, if made recoverable by a reform of our system of counsel fees, would become the daily bread of a new proud profession of "little lawyers" serving the little man—as they do everywhere else in the world. And yet—the stone wall. Why?

How often have I heard my colleagues' chiding: "You simply have not grasped the American sense of fairness. It is bad enough to see one lose who in justice should have prevailed. To make him pay the winner's counsel would add injustice to injustice, would mean stepping on one who is down, and it would make honest men unwilling to go to court, be it as plaintiffs or as defendants."[16] But is it not obvious that this argument implies the cynical, and most certainly incorrect, belief that judges and juries are more often wrong than right? Indeed, as Arthur Goodhart has said pointedly in answer to this argument:[17] "If New Jersey justice is so much a matter of luck, it hardly seems worthwhile to have courts and lawyers; it would be cheaper, and certainly less dilatory, to spin a coin."[18]

---

[15] See Comment, 52 CALIF. L. REV. 876 (1964), and for a bibliography, LOUISELL & HAZARD, CASES ON PLEADING AND PROCEDURE 111 (1962).

[16] This reasoning is restated in Report of Committee on Comparative Procedure and Practice, 1962 PROCEEDINGS OF SECTION OF INTERNATIONAL AND COMPARATIVE LAW, A.B.A. 117, 118 (1963), as the "sincere . . . opinion of many practitioners" who maintain "that the right to sue without deterrence [sic] by the specter of the possibility of paying an adversary's legal fees is part of our democratic tradition and a bulwark of equality that reduces the differences in part between the wealthy and the poor and permits the less affluent to press for the redress of wrongs." See also a similar pseudo-historical statement in Conte v. Flota Mercante del Estado, 277 F.2d 664, 672 (2d Cir. 1960), relying on Goodhart, supra note 8, at 872-77. And see the most peculiar argument in JUDICIAL COUNCIL OF CALIFORNIA, 18TH BIENNIAL REPORT 65 (1961).

[17] See Satterthwaite, Increasing Costs to be Paid by the Losing Party, 46 N.J.L.J. 133 (1923).

[18] Goodhart, supra note 8, at 877. See also Goodhart, Legal Costs As a Subject for Comparative Law, 4 INT'L & COMP. L. BULL. 13 (1960).

Let us concede for the sake of argument that many court decisions should in justice have gone the other way, and that in those cases, if counsel fees were allowed, losing parties would be treated even more unjustly than they are now. But how can we ignore the fact that at the same time we would prevent that great majority of plaintiffs and defendants, who justly lose their cases, from getting away, as they do now, with unjustly burdening their prevailing opponents with the heavy expense of counsel fees? Only if our initial assumption is reversed and we must concede that litigants who should win, more often lose than win their cases, would our argument be incorrect.

Now, it could be argued, of course, that allowance to the victorious party of his counsel fees might, besides inflicting additional harm on losing litigants with meritorious claims, deter an additional number of such claims from even reaching the court—a result particularly undesirable in the ordinary, wholly unpredictable automobile accident case. But this argument, in the first place, is psychologically doubtful since, in view of the very unpredictability of jury assessments, additional uncertainty is unlikely to influence the parties' decision. And secondly, juries in making their assessments now probably quite generally take into account the plaintiff's counsel fees and would be likely to reduce their verdicts correspondingly if instructed as to plaintiff's right to recover his fees in addition to the sum assessed. On the other hand, the fact that allowance of counsel fees might deter a few skeptical defendants who fear that court or jury might fail to recognize their just defenses, would seem less objectionable than the present system under which many more, though confident that the law would properly decide in their favor, now refuse to defend suits in which they would ultimately, though relieved of paying an unjust claim, have to spend counsel fees far exceeding that claim. For similar reasons it cannot be argued that allowance of counsel fees would encourage frivolous plaintiffs who would no longer have to contemplate a possible consumption by counsel fees of their expected spoils. It seems likely that a greater number of such frivolous plaintiffs now only risking their own expense, would properly be deterred by the additional risk of having to pay their opponents' counsel fees. On the other hand, the prospect of recovery of counsel fees on meritorious claims would probably greatly increase the number of clients seeking lawyers' assistance. Be this as it may in the no-man's land of personal injury claims, these arguments are fully conclusive, I believe, for the little man's other claims which alone are the subject of my plea.

Suggestions aiming at a reform of the present law find strong support in the fact, stressed earlier, that this country now is probably alone in failing to allow counsel fees to the victorious litigant. True, the manner in which this allowance is made in other countries varies widely. In England, Canada, and other parts of the Commonwealth it is subject to the discretion of the court.[19] Elsewhere, statutory tariffs govern the assessment.[20] True also that under many systems parties will often choose separately to compensate their attorneys at a rate higher than that conceded by the statute or by the court. But most everywhere else in the world the chance of recovering counsel fees, however modest, from the losing opponent, is a strong inducement for the lawyer to take on a meritorious case without regard to his client's affluence and thus greatly to increase the number of those served by the legal profession.

Well accepted as allowance of counsel fees may be in other countries, we could not contemplate its adoption, however, without having first assured ourselves that the present American law of fees is not justifiable or even indispensable as the product of legal institutions or attitudes peculiar to this country. But I believe that I have won my case if I can prove that what continues to parade as a token of the American sense of fairness, is nothing but an historical accident. Once this is understood and accepted, we may cease to talk in sorrow and in anger—and have new hope for the future.

III

HOPE: HISTORY AND GOOD WILL

England, since time immemorial, has permitted the parties to recover their counsel fees from their losing opponents.[21] It seems beyond doubt that this principle was adopted in this country with the reception of English law. The Revised Statutes of New York of 1829 contain express provisions to this effect.[22] A Report of the Commissioners on Practice and Pleading of September 25, 1847, took it for granted that "the losing party, ought . . . as a general rule, to pay the expense of the litigation. He has caused a loss to his adversary unjustly, and should indemnify him for it. The debtor who refuses to pay, ought to make the creditor whole."[23] I have tried elsewhere to trace the legislative history leading to our present allegedly ancient rule,[24] and have submitted on the basis of that study that the rule is not founded on some age-old principle of the common law or a peculiar psychology of the American people; but that it is the result of a more or less accidental statutory history. Indeed, there are good reasons for assuming that what is now so often represented as a noble postulate

---

[19] The system is described in Goodhart, *supra* note 4, at 854-55.

[20] See authorities cited in note 14 *supra*.

[21] Goodhart, *supra* note 8, at 851-54.

[22] 2 N.Y. Rev. Stat., pt. III, ch. 10, § 9 (plaintiff), § 22 (defendant) (1829).

[23] COMMISSIONERS ON PRACTICE AND PROCEDURE, FIRST REPORT 206 (1848).

[24] Ehrenzweig, *supra* note †.

for restraint of the winner in a chance contest, is actually due to the simple fact that the New York legislature in 1848, in attempting to perpetuate what it considered a sound legal rule of recovery of attorneys' fees by the prevailing party, made the fatal mistake of fixing the amount recoverable in dollars and cents rather than in percentages of the amount recovered or claimed. It was this mistake probably that caused lawyers and courts, when rising living costs began to obscure the real purpose of the statutory amounts of "costs," gradually to forget the meaning of those amounts. And it was this process of gradual forgetting rather than a deepseated moral argument that has apparently caused the abolition of the prevailing party's right to the recovery of his counsel fees.

Once we have recognized this irrefutable fact, and once we share the opinion, supported by much domestic and foreign authority as well as common sense, that the present system denying counsel fees to the prevailing party is a serious threat to our administration of justice, the question of remedy becomes our main concern.

None of the existing schemes constitutes a wholly acceptable solution. The English system, partly adopted in this country by courts of equity[25] and generally in Alaska[26] and Nevada,[27] has been found wanting in view of its undesirable latitude of judicial discretion. Allowance of counsel fees in cases of bad faith, as practiced in Georgia,[28] though less uncertain, does not protect the prevailing party as such. And general recovery of fixed amounts, originally the law of the land, has been abandoned everywhere under the pressure of the devaluation of currency, while uniform percentages with or without maximum limit, as applied in San Francisco from 1866 to 1905[29] and, within narrow limits, in New York today,[30] have proved too rigid.

What the New York code commissioners suggested in 1848 still holds true: Counsel fees, to be justly recoverable by the prevailing party must be "graduated in part by the necessary labor performed, and in part by the amount in controversy."[31] Nothing else will do, neither the California rule applicable to suits for wages below three hundred dollars and providing

---

[25] See, *e.g.*, Williams v. MacDougall, 39 Cal. 80, 85 (1870). *But see* Miller v. Kehoe, 107 Cal. 340, 344, 40 Pac. 485, 486 (1895). See generally Macri v. Bremerton, 8 Wash. 2d 93, 111 P.2d 612 (1941).

[26] ALASKA STATS. ANN. § 9.60.010 (1962). The provision lodges discretion in the court to grant or withhold attorney fees as an item of costs. It is derived from Alaska Comp. Laws Ann. § 55-11-51, 52, 55 (1948), repealed, Alaska Stats. 1962, ch. 101. See United States v. Breeden, 110 F. Supp. 713 (D. Alaska 1953).

[27] NEV. REV. STAT. § 18.010 (1963).

[28] GA. CODE ANN. § 20-1404 (1965).

[29] Cal. Stats. 1865-66, ch. 91, § 6, repealed, Cal. Stats. 1905, ch. 331.

[30] N.Y. CIV. PRAC. LAWS & RULES § 8303 (1963, Supp. 1965).

[31] COMMISSIONERS ON PRACTICE AND PROCEDURE, *op. cit. supra* note 23, at 207.

for a straight twenty per cent fee without regard to the services performed,[32] nor the fixed sums[33] of the California Practice Act of 1851 which, though taking account of those services, had no relation to the amount in controversy.[34] But why not combine the two principles in one scheme of *percentage compensation for each service performed?* Would not the most natural solution be to restore the schedule of services under the Practice Act of 1851 and to substitute for the fixed amounts of that schedule percentages preserving their mutual relation? Further to follow precedent, the total of recovery should approximate the twenty per cent of the present rule applicable to suits for wages. In addition, it may be wise to grant the court limited discretion in penalizing parties suing or defending in obvious bad faith or taking procedural steps not reasonably necessary, and increasing the total of recovery in cases of extraordinary difficulty on the pattern of section 8303 of the New York Civil Practice Laws and Rules.[35] Both principles and details of such a plan would, of course, have to be subjected to much discussion among those who by professional experience and familiarity with local conditions are alone equipped to pass final judgment.

Is there hope? The Great Society is waiting.

---

[32] CAL. CODE CIV. PROC. § 1031.

[33] "Perhaps if the New York code of 1829, instead of providing for a fixed fee in every case, had allowed the successful party a reasonable counsel fee depending on the nature of the litigation, the [U.S.] system would have developed along the lines of the present English one." Goodhart, *supra* note 8, at 874. That the California legislature abolished the allowance in San Francisco of counsel fees to the prevailing party is probably due to a similar mistake of legislative technique, *i.e.*, the establishment in 1866 of a maximum fixed amount of one hundred dollars. Cal. Stats. 1865-66, ch. 91, § 60, repealed, Cal. Stats. 1905, ch. 331.

[34] Calif. Civ. Prac. Act §§ 494-514, Cal. Stats. 1851, ch. 5. The costs provisions were amended in a few minor details by Cal. Stats. 1853, ch. 178, §§ 8-11. Section 502 of the Civil Practice Act of 1851 did provide for a percentage recovery in certain actions, but the percentage was low (five per cent on the first one thousand dollars, two per cent thereafter) and allowances could in no event exceed five hundred dollars.

[35] N.Y. CIV. PRAC. LAWS & RULES § 8303 (1963, Supp. 1965).

The German System of Legal Aid:
An Alternate Approach†

*Philip A. Stohr**

WITH THE ENACTMENT of the Criminal Justice Act of 1964,[1] the right of the indigent criminal defendant to legal counsel in federal court proceedings is no longer dependent upon his means. Moreover, public defender and similar systems now employed in many of the states guarantee the same right to the indigent accused in the state courts.

Unfortunately, the plight of the *civil* litigant of modest or negligible financial means has not been affected by either of these developments. Aside from the often rather hit-and-miss assistance provided by existing legal aid programs, no provision has been made within the framework of the American legal system to afford counsel as a matter of right to the indigent involved in civil litigation, the consequences of which are frequently as profound for the individual as are those of many criminal proceedings.

The German *Armenrecht* (literally, law for the impoverished), implemented by some seventeen provisions of the German Code of Civil Procedure, represents an imaginative approach to the problem of the indigent's need for legal assistance in civil proceedings, and a brief consideration of its principal features may prove useful in the re-examination of our own legal aid system.

It should be made clear at the outset that the German system does not purport to guarantee legal counsel for the indigent in every type of civil proceeding. Appointment of an attorney is mandatory only with respect to the litigation in which representation by an attorney is a condition precedent to the bringing of a suit.[2] It is within the discretion

---

† Much of the research for this article was done in Germany under a grant from the Graduate Division of the University of California, Berkeley. The article relies heavily on information gained in the course of many interviews with judges, professors, and attorneys in Germany, which explains the absence in some cases of the usual citations of authority.

* B.A., 1960, Stanford University; LL.B., 1963, University of California, Berkeley. Member, California Bar.

[1] 78 Stat. 552, 18 U.S.C. § 3006A (1964).

[2] ZIVILPROZESSORDNUNG § 115(1)3 (Ger. 38th ed. Beck'sche 1965) [hereinafter all citations to the German Code of Civil Procedure (ZIVILPROZESSORDNUNG) will be cited to ZPO, followed by the relevant section. All citations are to the edition noted unless otherwise indicated]. Germany has two sets of courts of the first instance, the *Amstgerichte* and the *Landgerichte,* and in the latter, all litigants must be represented by counsel. The *Landgerichte* are very roughly analogous to California's superior courts (courts of general jurisdiction) as to their function. They are charged with jurisdiction over all monetary claims in excess

of the court whether counsel is assigned in other cases. When representation by counsel is not required by law, the courts are also authorized to appoint justice officials or student referendars (post-graduate law students) to serve as counsel. This latter provision has been criticized as an unjustified compromise of the basic precept underlying the *Armenrecht*; that is, appointment of able and competent counsel.[3]

Even in those cases in which representation by counsel is required by law, the financially disadvantaged party must meet two basic prerequisites before counsel will be appointed by the court. First, the individual must show to the satisfaction of the court that he would be unable to pay his own counsel fees without jeopardizing his ability to support his family and himself.[4] In practical terms, this requirement is nothing more than a consideration of the individual's income and the various demands upon it, as set forth by the *Armenrecht* applicant in a standard form supplied by the administrative office of the court. It is therefore difficult to cite any specific figure as the income level required for allowance of the applicant's petition for state-appointed counsel. The Code avoids an ironclad standard in favor of a definition capable of application to the variety of economic circumstances presented to the courts.[5]

In addition to this economic prerequisite, the applicant must meet a second requirement that the litigation he wishes to undertake, or his defense if an action has been filed against him, bears a reasonable chance of success and is not foolhardy and reckless.[6] The Code provides for a preliminary hearing at which the court may require the applicant to establish the plausibility of his case.[7] The applicable section also directs that the applicant's opponent should be heard at this preliminary hearing unless, for some particular reason, it would serve no purpose to hear his views. While the court may also require the filing of relevant documents or hear the testimony of nonparty witnesses, the Code makes it

---

of 1000 DM ($250) and are also the competent courts for all domestic relations litigation. KERN, GERICHTSVERFASSUNGSRECHT 187 (3d ed. 1959).

[3] Heindle, *Der Justizbeamte als Armenvertreter nach § 116 ZPO*, 13 NEUE JURISTICHE WOCHENSCHRIFT [hereinafter cited as NJW] 1749 (1960). Judge Heindl asserts in his critique that in the usual *Amtsgericht* proceeding—as indicated above, the amount in dispute is less than $250—it is a rare occurrence when a practicing attorney is assigned as counsel for the indigent litigant. In an interview with the writer, a Heidelberg *Amtsgericht* judge was equally critical of the frequency with which justice officials and law students are appointed to assist indigents.

[4] ZPO § 114(1).

[5] It should be noted that the Criminal Justice Act of 1964 features an equally flexible criterion, permitting the district court in its discretion to appoint counsel "if satisfied after appropriate inquiry that the defendant is financially unable to obtain counsel . . . ." 18 U.S.C. § 3006A(b) (1964).

[6] ZPO § 114(1).

[7] ZPO § 118a.

clear that the latter means of proof are to be employed only when the court cannot make its decision on the basis of the parties' own statements. As a rule, the courts do not require this additional proof. In interviews with two judges in Heidelberg, the writer gained the impression that in the usual case this preliminary hearing resembles the hearing of a general demurrer under California procedural law. Both judges stressed that the court should not have to look beyond the face of the complaint, aside from the amplifying remarks of the parties themselves. Some courts, however, have been criticized for converting this summary preliminary hearing into a proceeding resembling the main trial itself.[8] The 1961 report of a commission established to review the German Code of Civil Procedure and to study various proposals for its reform contains a recommendation that the Code be amended to eliminate the court's prerogative to hear witnesses at the preliminary hearings on the grounds it unnecessarily prolongs the proceedings.[9]

Until 1931 the law required the applicant to show only that his contemplated court action was not without some prospect of success. The law was amended in that year to provide in somewhat more positive terms that counsel would be appointed by the court if the applicant's case exhibited a "sufficient prospect of success."[10] This new phraseology apparently has not in practice subjected the applicant to a significantly more formidable burden of proof. According to one judge interviewed by the writer, the indigent's petition for counsel will be granted if his purported cause of action is not entirely without merit. The court's approval of the petition is tantamount to an acknowledgement that the allegations of the complaint may be true and sufficient to state a cause of action, even though the problem of proving their validity at the trial remains. As may be seen, this type of cursory examination of the applicant's complaint commits the matter in large measure to the discretion of the individual court.

The German courts generally apply the prospects-of-success test more leniently to the petition of the civil *defendant*. This is so for a number of reasons. Of primary importance, however, is the fact that the defendant is generally brought into the lawsuit involuntarily.[11] Accordingly, his defense is not viewed with the same scrutiny as is the original case brought by the plaintiff.

---

[8] Jacobs-Martini, *Das Armenrechtsprüfungsverfahren*, 6 NJW 246 (1953).

[9] DEUTSCHER BUNDES VERLAG, BERICHT DER KOMMISSION ZUR VORBEITUNG EINER REFORM DER ZIVILGERICHTSBARKEIT 268 (1961).

[10] Law of June 10, 1931, [1931] Reichsgesetzblatt 537 (Ger.).

[11] Judgment of Oct. 23, 1957, Oberlandesgericht Celle, 11 NJW 187 (1958) (Ger. Fed. Rep.).

An adjunct to the prerequisite that the petitioner's case bear some reasonable chance of successful prosecution is the provision that counsel will not be appointed and compensated by the state if his action is brought unnecessarily or frivolously.[12] The Code itself states that an action will be considered frivolous if a party of means in the same factual situation would not have brought an action at all or would have sued for only a portion of the relief sought in the indigent's complaint.[13] However, the concept of the frivolous lawsuit has been expanded in practice to encompass a number of situations in which the courts have sought to prevent misuse of the right to appointed counsel. One type of case falling into this category is that in which the petitioner's action is clearly superfluous with respect to the object he seeks to attain. Thus, appointment of counsel for an indigent was refused when he sought to recover a debt by means of a full-scale lawsuit when a summary remedy, equally effective and far less expensive and time-consuming, was available to him.[14] The courts will also reject a petition on this basis when it appears that the two parties in interest, one being of adequate financial means to bring his own lawsuit, conspire to bring a suit in the name of the other who is eligible for state-appointed counsel.

It should be noted that a finding by the court that a particular complaint is frivolous in the sense outlined above is not always tantamount to a complete rejection of the indigent's petition for counsel. In the case of the "superfluous" action, for example, a court will generally permit the petitioner to amend his complaint to seek relief by the more economical procedure. If, on the other hand, the indigent exhibits bad faith or in any way abuses his right to appointed counsel, as, for example, in a case of collusion with a party of means, the benefits of state-supported legal aid will be denied altogether.

The Code of Civil Procedure also authorizes revocation of the original order granting the *Armenrecht* petition in the event that one of the statutory prerequisites is found lacking at a later point in the proceedings.[15] The petition may also be revoked if the right of free counsel is abused. While some courts have held that the *Armenrecht* may be withdrawn retroactively in the case of an improvement of the petitioner's financial status to the point where he is able to pay his own counsel fees,[16] the weight of authority stands opposed to the retroactive applica-

---

[12] ZPO §§ 114(1), 115(1)(3).

[13] ZPO § 114(1).

[14] Judgment of July 2, 1955, Oberlandesgericht Stuttgart, 9 MONATSSCHRIFT FÜR DEUTSCHES RECHT [hereinafter cited as MDR] 556 (1955) (Ger. Fed. Rep.).

[15] ZPO § 121.

[16] *E.g.*, Judgment of Sept. 8, 1949, Oberlandesgericht Düsseldorf, 3 NJW 229 (1950) (Ger. Fed. Rep.).

tion of any order withdrawing legal aid.[17] Among the factors emphasized by those courts espousing the majority view is the adverse effect of a retroactive order upon the attorney who in good faith reliance on the original order has expended considerable time and effort on behalf of the indigent client.

Even as regards *prospective* application of the withdrawal order, the German courts have displayed considerable caution, in recognition of the fact that summary withdrawal under given circumstances can impose unjustified hardship on the litigant. Thus, it has been held that once having ruled that a petitioner's action bears a sufficient promise of success to warrant appointment of counsel, a court may not then withdraw the *Armenrecht* at some later stage in the proceedings solely upon the grounds that the court has revised its original estimate of the litigant's chances.[18] The soundness of this position is apparent. To hold otherwise would be to make the indigent's right to counsel contingent upon the vagaries of a particular court from one moment to the next. Another important factor discussed in the cases is the particular stage of the proceedings at which the court makes its determination that the litigant is no longer entitled to legal aid: For example, one court has stated categorically that aid may not be withdrawn in the final stages of an action.[19]

A singularly important feature of the German legal aid system is the provision of the Code of Civil Procedure which permits the state under certain circumstances to seek reimbursement from the indigent for the expense incurred in providing counsel.[20] Pursuant to the Code, the erstwhile indigent may be required to pay back the fees advanced by the state, either during or after termination of the lawsuit, if it is demonstrated to the satisfaction of the reviewing court that the litigant's financial position has improved to the point that he is able to pay his own fees without detriment to his support obligations. While the Code itself does not require actual improvement in the indigent's financial affairs, the weight of authority has adopted this interpretation,[21] generally on the grounds that an order requiring the litigant to reimburse the state

---

[17] ROSENBERG, LEHRBUCH DES DEUTSCHEN ZIVILPROZESSRECHTS 391 (9th ed. 1961), citing in particular the Judgment of Nov. 29, 1928, Kammergericht, 64 JURISTISCHE WOCHENSCHRIFT [hereinafter cited as JW] 802 (1928) (Ger.).

[18] Judgment of Nov. 5, 1959, Oberlandesgericht Cologne, 14 MDR 232 (1960) (Ger. Fed. Rep.)

[19] Judgment of Apr. 24, 1962, Oberlandesgericht Neustadt, 16 MDR 744 (1962) (Ger. Fed. Rep.).

[20] ZPO § 125.

[21] Lappe, *Die Voraussetzungen der Nachzahlungsverpflichtung gemäss § 125 ZPO*, 1958 RECHTSPFLEGER 137; BAUMBACH & LAUTERBACH, ZIVILPROZESSORDNUNG § 125, at 254 (27th ed. 1963); STEIN, JONAS & SCHÖNKE, ZIVILPROZESSORDNUNG § 125 (18th ed. 1953).

even though his economic circumstances had not changed significantly would constitute blatant disregard for his good faith reliance on the original order granting legal aid.

None of the parties to the lawsuit, including the appointed counsel, is authorized under the Code to petition for an order requiring repayment of fees. This watchdog function is entrusted instead to the administrative wing of the courts, although a party to the suit or even a member of the general public can suggest that the economic circumstances of a particular litigant bear further investigation.

It is regarded as sufficient that the indigent's improved financial situation existed at some point of time subsequent to the order granting legal aid, and the improved condition need not also exist at the time of the hearing upon the matter.[22] Accordingly, the indigent may not quickly squander a sum of money inherited during the course of the action and assert at the subsequent hearing that his indigent status remains unchanged.

Another issue in this area is the extent to which the courts may consider sums of money recovered by the indigent in the litigation itself in determining his ability to pay his own counsel fees. In those cases involving recovery of a sum earmarked to meet a particular need of the indigent, as for example in a personal injury suit, the courts have generally declined to include the money recovered among the indigent's available funds.[23] Some courts, however, have taken exception to any general rule excluding these sums from consideration in all cases and stress that each case must be examined on its facts to determine to what extent these monies can be applied towards reimbursement of the State without unduly prejudicing the indigent's return from his lawsuit. In the latter regard, these courts point out further that it is not the object of appointment of counsel by the State to place the indigent in a position more favorable than that of the nonindigent litigant, who in many instances must also resort to his recovery to pay legal fees.[24]

Much of this article has assumed that the indigent party is without counsel at the time he petitions the court for legal aid. In the actual practice of the German courts, this is not the case. To the contrary, the

---

[22] Lappe, *supra* note 21; Gaedeke, *Die Nachzahlungg anordnung aus* § *125 ZPO*, 65 JW 1634 (1929).

[23] See, *e.g.*, Judgment of Nov. 22, 1954, Oberlandesgericht Koblenz, 8 NJW 1116 (1955) (Ger. Fed. Rep.); Judgment of Oct. 31, 1955, Oberlandesgericht Hamm, 10 MDR 33 (1955) (Ger. Fed. Rep.).

[24] For an enlightening discussion of the various policy considerations bearing on this issue, see Judgment of Sept. 28, 1953, Oberlandesgericht Nurnberg, 4 Versicherungs-Recht 441 (1953) (Ger. Fed. Rep.).

indigent party in the great majority of cases has already contacted an attorney independent of the courts when the *Armenrecht* petition is presented.[25] The process of selection of attorneys to serve as appointed counsel in the minority of cases in which the indigent approaches the court without counsel is quite similar to the "list-at-large" procedure which prevails in the California courts with respect to the appointment of criminal defense counsel. At the time they are sworn, all German attorneys are asked if they would be willing to serve as *Armenrecht* counsel. The vast majority of the Bar offer their services in a spirit consistent with the duty imposed by the Attorney's Code.[26] A roster of the willing attorneys is prepared accordingly and the courts then proceed to select one name after another in the absence of peculiar facts or particularly difficult questions of law, in which case more experienced or specialized counsel is appointed.

The fees for appointed counsel do not compare favorably with the normal attorney's fees except in those cases involving relatively petty sums. Thus, in the case of a civil complaint for 1000 DM ($250), the statutory *Armenrecht* fee is 52 DM while the normal statutory fee is 54 DM. However, where 3000 DM ($750) are at stake, the fee for appointed counsel is set at 85 DM while the regular fee is 155 DM. The disparity between the two sets of fees increases markedly as the amount in dispute increases. For all cases in which 6000 DM or more are at issue, the *Armenrecht* fee is fixed at the arbitrary figure of 130 DM. In contrast, the normal fees continue to increase in direct relation to the amount at issue. Thus, the normal fee in an action for 60,000 DM is 730 DM. The appointed attorney would receive the set figure of 130 DM in the same suit.[27]

This discrepancy in fees is compensated for to some extent by a provision in the Code of Civil Procedure which authorizes the attorney to seek the difference between the *Armenrecht* fees and the normal statutory fees from the opposing party in the event that the indigent's case is successfully prosecuted.[28] Protection of the pecuniary interest of the appointed attorney is also the object of another Code section providing that any sum of money recovered from the indigent by virtue of a reimbursement order is to be divided equally as between the State and

---

25 Interview with Dr. Hans Hachenburg, retired presiding judge of the *Landgericht* Heidelberg, June 24, 1964.

26 BUNDESRECHTSANWALTSORDNUNG § 48(1)1 (Ger. 38th ed. Beck'sche 1965).

27 Comparative figures are drawn from BUNDESGEBÜHRENORDNUNG FÜR RECHTSANWÄLTE §§ 11 (appendix), 123 (Ger. 38th ed. Heinrich Schönfelder 1965).

28 ZPO § 124(1); see Ehrenzweig, *Counsel Fees and the Great Society*, this symposium.

the attorney if the order does not require repayment in full of both claims.[29]

Legal aid is also available at the appellate level under the German system. If the party desiring counsel for his appeal has previously sought and obtained legal aid in the first instance, the appellate court need not review his financial circumstances as a prerequisite to granting *Armenrecht*, although the courts generally do so if a substantial period of time has elapsed between the first instance proceedings and the appeal.[30] Similarly, the appellate court may not review the applicant's case with respect to its promise of successful defense on appeal when the indigent has prevailed in the first instance.[31]

On the basis of numerous conversations with German professors, judges, and attorneys, the writer is of the opinion that the *Armenrecht* has proved a workable and effective means of providing legal services for the impoverished. As might be expected, many of those interviewed directed criticism at the substantial discrepancy between the normal attorney fees and those paid the appointed counsel. This, however, is a remediable shortcoming, and does not affect the question of the overall soundness of the *Armenrecht* system.

The question remains, however, whether the *Armenrecht* system can be adapted to American conditions. While peculiar social conditions, in particular the geographical concentration and cultural isolation of the impoverished in our cities, may well render the concept of the neighborhood legal center the most effective program for the administration of legal aid in the United States, the referral system exemplified by the *Armenrecht* presents an alternative approach worthy of study and consideration. Granted the active and enthusiastic support of the local bar associations, there is no reason why a referral program could not operate as effectively in the context of the American legal system as it has in Germany, and it is to be hoped that this alternative will not be overlooked as scores of American communities prepare to implement new legal aid programs.

---

[29] ZPO § 126(3).

[30] ZPO § 119(2), as amplified in an interview with Dr. Hans Hachenburg, retired presiding judge of the *Landgericht* Heidelberg, July 1, 1964.

[31] ZPO § 119(2).

The Disabled and the Law of Welfare

Jacobus tenBroek* and Floyd W. Matson**

NOT ALL WHO ARE POOR are physically handicapped; not all who are handicapped are poor. But the two conditions—poverty and disability—are historically so intermeshed as to be often indistinguishable. Thus one of the primary meanings of the term "poor," according to the 1933 edition of the *Oxford English Dictionary*, is to be "out of health, unwell." Another is the state of being "in lean or feeble condition from ill feeding." Not only does poverty breed illness and disability; disability in turn begets poverty.

It has always been so. During the Middle Ages the institution of the "hospital" was in reality an almshouse or poorhouse, caring not just for the sick but for all the destitute.[1] In our day the same juxtaposition—or, rather, the same vicious circle—is apparent. Ferman, Kornbluh, and Haber point out that "United States National Health Survey statistics have shown that the poor get sick more frequently, take longer to recover, seek and receive less medical, dental, and hospital treatment, and suffer far more disabling consequences than persons with higher incomes."[2]

Throughout history the physically handicapped have been regarded as incompetent to aid themselves and therefore permanently dependent upon

---

* A.B., 1934, M.A., 1935, LL.B., 1938, J.S.D., 1940, University of California, Berkeley; S.J.D., 1947, Harvard University; D. Lit., 1956, Findlay College; LL.D., 1964, Parsons College. Member, 1950-1963, Chairman, 1960-1963, California State Social Welfare Board. Professor of Political Science, University of California, Berkeley.

** B.A., 1950, M.A., 1953, Ph.D., 1960, University of California, Berkeley. Professor of Political Science, University of Hawaii.

1 TIERNEY, MEDIEVAL POOR LAW: A SKETCH OF CANONICAL THEORY AND ITS APPLICATIONS IN ENGLAND 85-89 (1959). See also tenBroek, *California's Dual System of Family Law: Its Origin, Development, and Present Status*, 16 STAN. L. REV. 268 (1964).

2 POVERTY IN AMERICA 187 (Ferman, Kornbluh & Haber eds. 1965). Leon Keyserling notes: "Comparing men aged 45-64 who earn less than $2,000 a year with those earning $7,000 or more, the incidence of heart disease in the lower income group is almost three times as high; orthopedic impairments nearly four times as frequent; high blood pressure more than four times as common; arthritis and rheumatism nearly five times as prevalent; and the incidence of mental and nervous conditions and vision impairment more than six times as frequent." KEYSERLING, PROGRESS OR POVERTY 67 (1964). Herman Somers makes the statistics still more meaningful: "On an average day in 1963, more than five million persons, aged 14 to 64, were disabled—unable to work, attend school, keep house, or follow other normal activities. . . . We do not count the millions of others with chronic conditions who were partially limited in the amount of activity they could pursue." Somers, *Poverty and Income Maintenance for the Disabled*, in POVERTY IN AMERICA 240 (Gordon ed.) (1965). for earlier figures, see QUEEN & GRUENER, SOCIAL PATHOLOGY; OBSTACLES TO SOCIAL PARTICIPATION 119 (rev. ed. 1948); RUSK & TAYLOR, NEW HOPE FOR THE HANDICAPPED (1949); UNITED STATES PUBLIC HEALTH SERVICE, THE PREVALENCE AND CAUSES OF ORTHOPEDIC IMPAIRMENTS 1 (Bulletin, No. 4, 1935-36).

the charity of others—in short, as indigent beggars. In medieval and early modern times they were in fact the only "legitimate" beggars and were granted a special legal status as such.[3] This assumption of permanent helplessness persists today in the common consignment of the physically disabled to the category of "unemployables."[4] Whatever may be the justice or injustice of this assumption, it remains a fact that only a very small fraction—perhaps five or six per cent at most—of those with serious physical handicaps are gainfully employed in ordinary open occupations, with an additional two or three per cent at work in specially subsidized sheltered employment. In England, where generally comparable conditions prevail, and where an effective system of registering the blind makes possible the collection of employment and other data, 6,146 blind persons out of a total registration figure of 96,472 were occupied in open employment as of the end of 1963; 3,833 were in sheltered and home employment.[5]

The basic point emerges in the comment of an official of the Federal Bureau of Family Services, following a nationwide survey of recipients of Aid to the Permanently and Totally Disabled: "The study shows that these disabled recipients tend to follow the usual pattern of poverty. While their disabilities make them dependent upon public assistance for their livelihoods, lack of education and low job skills play a large part in preventing their rehabilitation to self-support."[6] In sum, the seriously dis-

---

[3] LEONARD, THE EARLY HISTORY OF ENGLISH POOR RELIEF 3 (1900); DE SCHWEINITZ, ENGLAND'S ROAD TO SOCIAL SECURITY: FROM THE STATUTE OF LABOURERS IN 1349 TO THE BEVERIDGE REPORT OF 1942, at 8 (1943).

[4] An expert on vocational rehabilitation recalls the depression period: "The U.S. Department of Labor in 1930, the American Federation of Labor, the U.S. Chamber of Commerce, the Brookings Institute and others constantly referred to 'unemployables,' but gave no explanation of what constitutes unemployability. It was assumed that the reduction of the labor market had restricted the opportunity for employment of a group of marginal people who (so the presentation ran) were less well equipped to secure and hold jobs because of physical defects. No attempt was made to analyze this group carefully and to determine the exact cause of their unemployability; nothing was done other than to impose on them the label of social misfits." KESSLER, REHABILITATION OF THE PHYSICALLY HANDICAPPED 17-18 (1947).

[5] MINISTRY OF HEALTH, REGISTER OF THE BLIND, NATIONAL STATISTICS 1963, at 2 (1964) (England and Wales). For the American blind, an official survey of the nationwide caseload of Aid to the Blind recipients has reported that under 8% of all recipients were "employed for pay" in 1962, and that of these about one-third were in sheltered work. Mugge, *Recipients of Aid to the Blind*, Welfare in Review, April 1965, p. 6; U.S. DEP'T OF HEALTH, EDUC. & WELFARE, STATE LETTER NO. 746, at Table 24 (July 2, 1964). Comparable figures for the State of California indicate that 96.5% of Aid to the Blind recipients between the ages of 20 and 49 are unemployed. CAL. DEP'T OF SOCIAL WELFARE, CALIFORNIA SOCIAL WELFARE PROGRAMS FOR THE BLIND: AN ANALYSIS 20 (March 1965).

[6] Fred H. Steininger, *A Vicious Circle: Poverty and Disability*, quoted in The Braille Monitor, Jan. 1965, p. 15.

abled person in our society is characteristically unemployed, underprivileged, unaccepted, and impoverished. In a word, he is poor.

For various reasons, certain groups and categories of the physically disabled are outside the purview of the present article. Among those to be excluded are: persons disabled as a by-product of active ongoing disease, whose disability is principally a matter of medical concern; children whose dependency and physical weakness is a matter of immaturity and presumably will pass; the aged, whose physical handicap is but one factor in a general and irreversible decline of powers; the temporarily disabled, as in the case of intoxication; the alcoholic and the drug addict, whose difficulties are psychosomatic or of emotional-mental origin.

This article is about the lame, the halt, and the blind—the ancient Biblical category broadly embracing those crippled or mutilated by accident or war, the congenitally defective and deformed, and those left paralyzed or impaired by disease that has run its course or has been arrested by medical attention. The forms of physical disability to be dealt with include, for example, the paralytic, those with serious defects, deformities, and amputations, the deaf, and the blind. Our emphasis will be upon the more serious types of disability, those for whom the problems of life and livelihood—and of other men's pride and prejudice—are most severe.

Failure to make necessary distinctions among the varieties of physical disability is common alike to popular and professional thought, with consequences often destructive to the effectiveness of social provisions intended for welfare and rehabilitation. Little more than half a century ago the typical American almshouse was described as embracing indiscriminately all of the following: "[T]he crippled and the sick; the insane; the blind; deaf mutes; feeble-minded and epileptic; people with all kinds of chronic diseases; . . . short term prisoners; thieves, no longer physically capable of crime; worn out prostitutes, etc."[7] The persisting tendency to lump together all those who appear "defective" is graphically exhibited in the following quotation from a current high school civics textbook: "The blind, the deaf, the dumb, the crippled, and the insane and feeble-minded are sometimes known collectively as the *defective*—people who are lacking some normal faculty or power. Such people often need to be placed in some special institution in order to receive proper attention."[8]

Over-inclusive classification of the physically disabled, in public law and programming, results among other things from routine pressures toward administrative simplification and convenience. In 1962, for

7 JOHNSON, THE ALMSHOUSE 57 (1911).
8 McCROCKLIN, BUILDING CITIZENSHIP 244 (1961).

example, a new optional title XVI was added to the public assistance provisions of the Social Security Act,[9] expressly to supersede the three separate titles governing respectively Old Age Assistance (title I),[10] Aid to the Blind (title X),[11] and Aid to the Permanently and Totally Disabled (title XIV).[12] Under the amendments, the states were invited to scrap these existing titles and the independent programs they governed, and to merge them under the single roof of the new collective category.[13] The issue raised by this administrative erasure of boundary lines has been whether the specialized services and distinctive character of each of the older titles—the outgrowth of long acquaintance with the peculiar characteristics of each of three clientele groups—would survive the exposure to uniform standards and uniform administration. The evidence to date, in those states which have opted for title XVI, is that more has been lost in program quality and effectiveness than has been gained in convenience and economy.[14]

Another version of the tendency to *overclassify*—to emphasize common denominators among disadvantaged groups at the expense of differences between them—is to be seen in the burgeoning subfield of sociology devoted to social pathology, and more specifically to the problem of "deviation" and "deviant groups." The concept of deviation represents a heuristic device to enable the identification of individuals or groups who depart significantly from "normal" patterns of behavior. Although in technical usage the term "deviant" has only statistical and nonevaluative meaning, most of the groups so identified, that is, criminals, delinquents, prostitutes, religious fanatics, addicts, etc., are also subject to widespread social disapproval and censure.

When a physically disabled group is added to the list of deviants, the tendency is to posit common abnormalities and behavioral (as well as statistical) aberrations. A case in point is Edwin M. Lemert's *Social Pathology*, published in 1951. Part Two of the book, entitled "Deviation

---

9 76 Stat. 197-205 (1962), as amended, 42 U.S.C. §§ 1381-85 (1964), as amended, 42 U.S.C. §§ 1382-83, 1385 (Supp. I, 1965).

10 49 Stat. 620-22 (1935), as amended, 42 U.S.C. §§ 301-06 (1964), as amended, 42 U.S.C. §§ 302-03, 306 (Supp. I, 1965).

11 49 Stat. 645-47 (1935), as amended, 42 U.S.C. §§ 1201-06 (1964), as amended, 42 U.S.C. §§ 1202-03, 1206 (Supp. I, 1965).

12 64 Stat. 555-58 (1950), as amended, 42 U.S.C. §§ 1351-55 (1964), as amended, 42 U.S.C. §§ 1352-53, 1355 (Supp. I, 1965).

13 Moreover, this course once embarked upon was irreversible; there could be no retreat from title XVI in the form of reactivation of the separate categories. Act of July 25, 1962, § 141(b), 76 Stat. 205.

14 See *Ohio Blind Fight Title XVI Threat*, The Braille Monitor, April 1965, p. 25; *Threat to Blind Welfare in Ohio*, The Braille Monitor, May 1965, pp. 44-45; *Three States Go Under*, The Blind American, Sept. 1963, pp. 4-6.

and Deviants," includes the following chapter headings: "Blindness and the Blind," "Radicalism and Radicals," "Prostitution and the Prostitute," "Crime and the Criminal," "Drunkenness and the Chronic Alcoholic," and "Mental Disorders." What is more remarkable even than this curious juxtaposition of unlike groups is the author's inclination to view the behavior of the blind as not only deviant but devious. Thus his chapter on blindness opens with these words: "Blindness is at once a dramatic and engaging handicap . . . ."[15] Subsequently he cites a newspaper report to illustrate "the relative ease with which the public may be manipulated by the blind."[16] His chapter concludes: "As long as the societal reaction toward the blind remains as it is, there will continue to be a sizable number of the blind who make a profession of dependency."[17] Elsewhere, following a summary account of two so-called "militant groups of the blind" in Minnesota, Lemert writes: "All these facts create interesting speculation. While the actions of the two groups may be regarded as the group equivalent of tantrum behaviour, they also raise a question as to what happens when the blind in a collective capacity desert their traditional roles of humility and agitate in an independent way like any other pressure group."[18]

The tendency to lump together all those who display a visible difference, either of appearance or behavior—as in the physical scale of "defectives" or the sociological scale of "deviants"—represents the survival in attenuated form of the cruder prejudices of primitive societies. We shall have more to say concerning the role of prejudicial public attitudes in later pages; here it is pertinent to call attention to the "indivisibility" of such negative reactions toward the disabled. In various earlier societies virtually any form of illness or defect marked its victim as a sinner. Thus no less

---

[15] LEMERT, SOCIAL PATHOLOGY 101 (1951).

[16] *Id.* at 141.

[17] *Id.* at 142.

[18] *Id.* at 107-08. For a different approach to the same phenomenon see the following quotation from Goffman describing the stereotyped adjustment of the "good deviant": "The nature of a 'good adjustment' requires that the stigmatized individual cheerfully and unselfconsciously accept himself as essentially the same as normals, while at the same time he voluntarily withholds himself from those situations in which normals find it difficult to give lip service to their similar acceptance of him. . . . It means that the unfairness and pain of having to carry a stigma will never be presented to . . . [normals]; it means that normals will not have to admit to themselves how limited their tactfulness and tolerance are; and it means that normals will remain relatively uncontaminated by intimate contact with the stigmatized, relatively unthreatened in their identity beliefs. . . . The stigmatized individual is asked to act so as to imply neither that his burden is heavy nor that bearing it has made him different from us. At the same time he must keep himself at that remove from us which ensures our painlessly being able to confirm his belief about him. . . . A *phantom acceptance* is thus allowed to provide the base for a *phantom normalcy*." Quoted in *Medical v. Rehabilitation Problems*, Rehabilitation Record, May-June 1965, p. 2.

than twelve physical blemishes are listed in the Bible as sufficient to disqualify a priest from officiating—among them "a blind man, or a lame, or
he that hath a flat nose, or anything superfluous, or a man that is broken-
footed, or brokenhanded, or crookbackt, or a dwarf, or that hath a blem-
ish in his eye, or be scurvy, or scabbed, or hath his bones broken . . . ."[19]

Psychologically, socially, and legally, the disabled throughout history
have enjoyed among themselves a peculiar "equality"; they have been
equally mistrusted, equally misunderstood, equally mistreated, and equally
impoverished.

The legal and constitutional status of the physically disabled—like
their status in society and in the economy—is a reflection of underlying
attitudes and assumptions concerning disability and of social policies based
upon those attitudes. For the most part it is the *cultural definition* of
disability, rather than the scientific or medical definition, which is instru-
mental in the ascription of capacities and incapacities, roles and rights,
status and security. Thus a meaningful distinction may be made between
"disability" and "handicap"—that is, between the *physical disability*,
measured in objective scientific terms and the *social handicap* imposed
upon the disabled by the cultural definition of their estate. "A disability
is a condition of impairment, physical or mental, having an objective aspect
that can usually be described by a physician. . . . A handicap is the
cumulative result of the obstacles which disability interposes between the
individual and his maximum functional level."[20]

Ideally these two concepts should be isomorphic; the "handicap" of
being blind, for example, should correspond to the visual and physical
limitations of blindness, without the superimposition of additional difficulties. In practice, however, the psychological and socio-economic handicap suffered by disabled persons far outweighs the actual physical
restrictions resulting from their impairment. Their dependent and segregated status is not an index merely of their physical condition; to an extent
only beginning to be recognized it is the product of cultural definition—an
assumptive framework of myths, stereotypes, aversive responses, and
outright prejudices, together with more rational and scientific evidence.

Of particular significance is the hypothesis advanced by numerous
investigators of the social psychology of physical handicap that negative
attitudes and practices toward the disabled resemble those commonly
attached to "underprivileged ethnic and religious minority groups."[21] One

---

19 VON HENTIG, THE CRIMINAL AND HIS VICTIM 16 n.35 (1948). Wright adds that the
later Talmudists extended the list of proscribed defects until it reached a total of 142.
WRIGHT, PHYSICAL DISABILITY—A PSYCHOLOGICAL APPROACH 259 (Murphy ed. 1960).

20 HAMILTON, COUNSELING THE HANDICAPPED IN THE REHABILITATION PROCESS 17 (1950).

21 WRIGHT, *op. cit. supra* note 19, at 14-15. See also CHEVIGNY & BRAVERMAN, THE AD-

study dealing systematically with this hypothesis confirmed that prejudicial attitudes toward blindness were significantly correlated with "anti-minority, anti-Negro and pro-authoritarian attitudes."[22]

It is not surprising that such prejudice against the disabled should find practical expression in discriminatory policies both legal and extralegal designed to "keep the handicapped in their place." Kessler describes the social handicap under which the disabled labor in emphatic terms:

> These attitudes that have made self-expression and adjustment more difficult can be expressed by the term psycho-social prejudice. It is an individual and collective reaction of hostility toward the crippled, the deformed, and the disabled, who are condemned as unproductive and useless burdens. This truculent attitude on the part of society is the greatest hurdle that the disabled person is called upon to surmount. ... The physically handicapped thus bears a double burden, his actual disability and the social restrictions it incurs .... The unwritten laws of primitive society that the crippled and disabled were to be sacrificed for the good of the group were carried over into the written laws of the ancients and for many centuries determined the treatment of disabled persons. Though public and private efforts have improved the status of the physically handicapped, the repugnance and distaste with which they have been regarded throughout history still prevail.[23]

However, along with this constellation of negative images surrounding disability goes another and different set of attitudes of more recent origin, nurtured alike by medical science and liberal humanitarianism, which gives emphasis to the normal capacities of the physically disabled and hence to their potential for full participation as equals in the social and economic life of the community. These two polar sets of attitudes, both of which are reflected in varying degree in legal and social provisions for the handicapped, may be designated respectively as *custodialism* and *integrationism*.

JUSTMENT OF THE BLIND 191-95 (1950); Dembo, Devaluation of the Physically Handicapped Person, 1953 (paper presented at American Psychological Association, Cleveland); Fielding, Attitudes and Aspects of Adjustment of the Orthopedically Handicapped Woman, 1950 (unpublished doctoral dissertation, Columbia University); PSYCHOLOGICAL ASPECTS OF PHYSICAL DISABILITY 18-32 (Garrett ed. 1952); SOMMERS, THE INFLUENCE OF PARENTAL ATTITUDES AND SOCIAL ENVIRONMENT ON THE PERSONALITY DEVELOPMENT OF THE ADOLESCENT BLIND (1944); Barker, *The Social Psychology of Physical Disability*, J. of Social Issues, Fall 1948, p. 28; Ladieu, Alder, & Dembo, *Studies in Adjustment to Visible Injuries: Social Acceptance of the Injured*, J. of Social Issues, Fall 1948, p. 55; Lewin, *Some Characteristics of the Socio-Psychological Life Space of the Epileptic Patient*, 10 HUMAN RELATIONS 249 (1957); Macgreagor, *Some Psycho-Social Problems Associated With Facial Deformities*, 16 AMERICAN SOCIOLOGICAL REV. 629 (1951); Mussen & Barker, *Attitudes Toward Cripples*, 39 J. OF ABNORMAL SOCIAL PSYCHOLOGY 351 (1944); Myerson, *Physical Disability as a Social Psychological Problem*, J. of Social Issues, Fall 1948, pp. 2, 6-10.

22 Cowen, Underberg & Verrillo, *The Development and Testing of an Attitude to Blindness Scale*, 48 J. OF SOCIAL PSYCHOLOGY 297, 304 (1958).

23 KESSLER, REHABILITATION OF THE PHYSICALLY HANDICAPPED 18-19 (1947).

The older custodial attitude is typically expressed in policies of segregation and shelter, of special treatment and separate institutions. The newer integrative approach focuses attention upon the needs of the disabled as those of normal and ordinary people caught at a physical and social disadvantage. The effect of custodialism is to magnify physical differences into qualitative distinctions; the effect of integrationism is to maximize similarity, normality, and equality as between the disabled and the able-bodied. The contrast between the two approaches is brought out in this analysis by an authority on education of the blind:

> In reviewing the way society has regarded and treated the blind during the history of the Western world, we can distinguish three phases. The blind were treated as liabilities, as wards, and as members in successive historical stages . . . . [In the Middle Ages] the blind were given the right to live and, beyond that, the right to be protected. The early church considered them as its special wards and throughout the middle ages they, together with children and the aged, were considered preferred receivers of charity. It is interesting to note that these groups are still singled out as special categories in the framework of social legislation in the United States and in other countries. . . .
>
> The third phase, that of the integration of the blind into society, began with the establishment of educational facilities for blind children. Since then many changes have occurred which justify our contention that we live in a period in which the integration of the blind into society is, although gradually, becoming a reality.[24]

The purpose of the present work is to determine the extent to which the law relating to the physically handicapped, originally formulated and developed on a firm foundation of custodialism, still embodies, implements, and encourages that concept today—or, on the other hand, the extent to which it expresses and reflects and catalyzes the transition now in progress from custodialism to integrationism. Our preliminary conclusion is that in this sphere, as in some others, the law lags seriously behind contemporary developments both in social theory and in growing public awareness of the actual potentialities of the physically disabled for full membership status in society. At the same time it should be recognized that the traditional legal structure no longer presents a solid front; significant cracks and fissures are developing here and there along the wall—portending, perhaps, a massive breakthrough yet to come.

I

THE SOCIAL SECURITY SYSTEM IN THE UNITED STATES

The two opposing conceptual frameworks regarding disability, which we have designated as custodialism and integrationism, appear to clash

---

[24] Lowenfeld, The Social Impact of Blindness Upon the Individual, August 1964 (paper read to the Assembly of the World Council for the Welfare of the Blind, New York).

like Milton's invisible armies throughout the broad range of legal policy and social custom affecting the physically handicapped. Nowhere is that conflict more acute, or the immediate issue more in doubt, than in the field of public welfare—and particularly in the national system of social security, made up of the federal and state programs of public assistance, social insurance, disability insurance, and unemployment insurance.

Today, a full generation after its enactment, the social security system is an established fact of our national life, a permanent institution all but universally accepted in its basic features and rationale. The program is now sufficiently mature and fixed in character to permit definite answers to inquiries concerning its long-range effects and purposes—specifically, with respect to the legal and institutional status of the physically disabled.

In effect the social security system makes not one but two separate and contradictory answers to such an inquiry. The two answers correspond to the deep cleavage within the system between the concepts embodied on the one hand in the social insurances—old age and survivors' insurance, unemployment compensation, and disability insurance—and on the other hand in the public assistance titles—aid to the aged, aid to the permanently and totally disabled, aid to families with dependent children, and aid to the needy blind. The first of these complexes was designed to embrace the common and recurring needs created by the complexities of our society and the uneven operation of our economic system. The second was intended mainly to fill the remaining gaps—to furnish relief for the uninsured residual groups.

In its entirety the social security system made sweeping changes in nearly every area of welfare, established the principle of national responsibility for the security of all citizens, and created a still-proliferating body of specific programs variously accommodating the needs of the disabled, the aged, and the unemployed—along with others threatened by what Franklin D. Roosevelt called "the misfortunes which cannot be wholly eliminated in this man-made world."[25] Three programs were directly aimed at the physically handicapped: the public assistance programs of aid to the permanently and totally disabled (title XIV) and aid to the blind (title X), and the contributory program of disability insurance.[26]

Both sides of the social security program—contributory insurance and noncontributory assistance—were products of the depression. "We can eliminate many of the factors that cause economic depressions," said President Roosevelt in presenting his proposal to Congress, "and we can

---

[25] H.R. Doc. No. 397, 73d Cong., 2d Sess. 2 (1934).

[26] For discussions of disability in relation to workmen's compensation, see CHEIT, INJURY AND RECOVERY IN THE COURSE OF EMPLOYMENT (1961); OCCUPATIONAL DISABILITY AND PUBLIC POLICY (Cheit & Gordon eds. 1963).

provide the means of mitigating their result. This plan for economic security is at once a measure of prevention and a method of alleviation."[27] However, it was the measure of prevention that was the favorite of the President and the Congress. The "method of alleviation," relief, was regarded as a more or less temporary stopgap, something of an embarrassment to all concerned, happily soon to be discarded like sackcloth as all Americans came to be covered by the more decent statutory clothing of the social insurances.

But after thirty years of existence the temporary method of alleviation has neither stopped functioning nor stopped the gaps in the social fabric; where a few such gaps have been filled, others not originally foreseen have emerged. Public assistance, like the poor whom it serves, it still very much with us. Whatever defects of character it possesses can no longer be excused, as in the past they have been, as the built-in obsolescence of a temporary structure scheduled for early slum clearance.

A brief comparison of the basic features of the two opposing faces of social security reveals the profound differences between them—differences which add up, in many respects, to the distance between custodialism and integrationism.

The social insurance part embodied whatever was new and modern about the social security system. First and most important, the planners intended its title to reveal its main characteristic: It was to be insurance. The covered person makes payments into the system on a regular basis and these are called premiums; when the specified contingency happens— death, old age, disability—the covered person or his dependents receive payments on a regular basis and these are called "insurance benefits," not aid, assistance, or relief. Since the covered person participates through his premium payments, he can claim the benefits as a matter of right; and since the premium payments are related to wages and work record, as a matter of earned right. The system being a system of insurance, based on premium payments and the right to benefits when the insurable event occurs, the amount of the benefit is fixed in advance, indeed, in the statute itself,[28] which in effect contains the terms of the insurance contract; the amount of the benefit is thereby made certain and predictable, rather than subject to administrative or social worker discretion and determinable after the event. Since the beneficiary is entitled to the benefit as a matter of earned contractual and statutory right upon the occurrence of a contingency, clearly identified in the insurance contract or statute and easily ascertainable as to its occurrence, it can immediately be seen that certain

---

[27] H.R. Doc. No. 83, 74th Cong., 1st Sess. (1935).

· [28] 49 Stat. 622-25 (1935), as amended, 42 U.S.C. §§ 401-25 (1964), as amended, 42 U.S.C. §§ 401-06, 409-11, 413, 415-18, 422-25 (Supp. I, 1965).

factors are completely irrelevant as conditions of eligibility or as determinants of the amount of the benefit: the beneficiary's financial situation
or other resources, whether he had savings or other income; proof of
need or any proof other than membership in the insured group and the
occurrence of the insurable event; the number, degree of consanguinity, or
opulence of his relatives; the location anywhere within the country of
his residence, the length of time he lived there or elsewhere, the presence of an intention to remain or to move about; his pattern of life, morals,
behavior, or general conduct.

True, this picture of the social insurances, created in the beginning and
steadily fostered ever since,[29] is not wholly or even largely borne out by
the actual provisions. The insurance principle is honored more in the
propaganda than in the reality. Half of the premium payment attributable
to each wage-earning beneficiary is not paid by the beneficiary at all but
by his employer.[30] The benefits do not bear a fixed ratio to the premiums,
by whomever paid. They are adjusted in favor of the low income groups
covered by the system,[31] of those whose period of coverage for one reason
or another is allowed to be shorter than the standard,[32] or those who, such

---

[29] Advisory Council on Social Security, *Recommendations for Social Security Legislation*,
S. Doc. No. 208, 80th Cong., 2d Sess. 1 (1948); Advisory Council on Social Security, *Report*,
S. Doc. No. 204, 80th Cong., 2d Sess. 1 (1948); Advisory Council on Social Security, *Final
Report*, S. Doc. No. 4, 76th Cong., 1st Sess. (1938); *Hearings on Social Security Before the
House Ways and Means Committee*, 76th Cong., 1st Sess. 4, 24 (1939); COMMITTEE ON
ECONOMIC SECURITY, REPORT, 74th Cong., 1st Sess. 4, 21, 26, 28 (1935); *Messages of Presi-
dents*, H.R. Doc. No. 81, 74th Cong., 1st Sess. (1935); H.R. Doc. No. 110, 76th Cong., 1st
Sess. (1939); H.R. Doc. No. 951, 76th Cong., 3d Sess. (1940); H.R. Doc. No. 594, 80th
Cong., 2d Sess. (1948); H.R. Doc. No. 676, 80th Cong., 2d Sess. (1948); SOCIAL SECURITY BD.,
SOCIAL SECURITY IN AMERICA 214 (1937); SOCIAL SECURITY BD., ANNUAL REPORT 14 (1936);
SOCIAL SECURITY BD., ANNUAL REPORT 12 (1937); SOCIAL SECURITY BD., ANNUAL REPORT 21,
23 (1938); SOCIAL SECURITY BD., ANNUAL REPORT 20 (1939); SOCIAL SECURITY BD., ANNUAL
REPORT 12 (1940); SOCIAL SECURITY BD., ANNUAL REPORT 28, 37, 40 (1941); SOCIAL SECURITY
BD., ANNUAL REPORT 18 (1942); SOCIAL SECURITY BD., ANNUAL REPORT 31 (1943); SOCIAL
SECURITY ADMINISTRATION, ANNUAL REPORT 18 (1947); SOCIAL SECURITY ADMINISTRATION,
ANNUAL REPORT 102 (1948); SOCIAL SECURITY ADMINISTRATION, ANNUAL REPORT 15, 79, 80
(1949); SOCIAL SECURITY ADMINISTRATION, ANNUAL REPORT 31, 33 (1950); SOCIAL SECURITY
ADMINISTRATION, ANNUAL REPORT 33 (1951); SOCIAL SECURITY ADMINISTRATION, ANNUAL
REPORT 29 (1952); U.S. DEP'T OF HEALTH, EDUC. & WELFARE, ANNUAL REPORT 14
(1953); U.S. DEP'T OF HEALTH, EDUC. & WELFARE, ANNUAL REPORT 24 (1956); U.S.
DEP'T OF HEALTH, EDUC. & WELFARE, ANNUAL REPORT 11 (1957); U.S. DEP'T OF HEALTH,
EDUC. & WELFARE, ANNUAL REPORT 12 (1960); U.S. DEP'T OF HEALTH, EDUC. & WELFARE,
ANNUAL REPORT 26, 28 (1961); U.S. DEP'T OF HEALTH, EDUC. & WELFARE, ANNUAL REPORT
25 (1962); U.S. DEP'T OF HEALTH, EDUC. & WELFARE, ANNUAL REPORT 5, 6 (1963); U.S.
DEP'T OF HEALTH, EDUC. & WELFARE, ANNUAL REPORT 6 (1964).

[30] INT. REV. CODE OF 1954, § 3111.

[31] Social Security Act § 203(a), 49 Stat. 623 (1935), as amended, 42 U.S.C. § 403(a)
(1964), as amended, 42 U.S.C. § 403(a) (Supp. I, 1965).

[32] Social Security Act § 214(a), added by 64 Stat. 492 (1950), as amended, 42 U.S.C.
§ 414(a) (1964).

as the disabled, are advantaged in various ways.[33] Benefit payments are made to dependents but premiums do not vary in the light of that fact but remain the same whether the primary beneficiary has dependents or not.[34] Benefit payments, moreover, are withheld or reduced if the primary beneficiary continues in substantial gainful employment in old age[35] or after disability.[36] Medical insurance benefits are provided to persons sixty-five years of age not hitherto enrolled "financed from premium payments by enrollees together with contributions from funds appropriated by the Federal Government."[37] As a result of these and other factors, there is only the most casual relationship between the benefits and premiums, premiums and wages, wages and past productive activity or work; and accordingly there is little foundation for the claim of benefits as a matter of earned right. The whole insurance concept thus becomes only a remote analogy rather than an operative reality. Though the earned right features of the social insurances is sharply undercut, still beneficiaries might logically claim benefits as a matter of statutory right based on the declaration "every individual . . . shall be entitled to an . . . insurance benefit" under specified circumstances.[38] Even this notion, however, was struck a rude blow by the United States Supreme Court in *Fleming v. Nestor*,[39] where an insured person was denied benefits under the Old Age and Survivors' Insurance program to which he had become entitled through

---

[33] Social Security Act § 214(b)(2), added by 64 Stat. 492 (1950), as amended, 42 U.S.C. § 414(a) (1964); Social Security Act § 216(i)(3)(B)(ii), added by 79 Stat. 413, 42 U.S.C. § 416(i)(3)(B)(ii) (Supp. I, 1965); Social Security Act § 223(c)(1)(B)(ii), added by 79 Stat. 413, 42 U.S.C. § 423(c)(1)(B)(ii) (Supp. I, 1965); Social Security Act § 223(c)(2)(B), added by 79 Stat. 413, 42 U.S.C. § 423(c)(2)(B) (Supp. I, 1965).

[34] Social Security Act § 202(b), 49 Stat. 623 (1935), as amended, 42 U.S.C. § 402(b) (1964), as amended, 42 U.S.C. § 402(b) (Supp. I, 1965) (wife's benefits); Social Security Act § 202(c), 49 Stat. 623 (1935), as amended, 42 U.S.C. § 402(c) (1964), as amended, 42 U.S.C. § 402(c) (Supp. I, 1965) (husband's benefits); Social Security Act § 202(d), 49 Stat. 623 (1935), as amended, 42 U.S.C. § 402(d) (1964), as amended, 42 U.S.C. § 402(d) (Supp. I, 1965) (child's benefits); Social Security Act § 202(e), 49 Stat. 623 (1935), as amended, 42 U.S.C. § 402(e) (1964), as amended, 42 U.S.C. § 402(e) (Supp. I, 1965) (widow's benefits); Social Security Act § 202(f), 49 Stat. 623 (1935), as amended, 42 U.S.C. § 402(f) (1964), as amended, 42 U.S.C. § 402(f) (Supp. I, 1965) (widower's benefits); Social Security Act § 202(g), 49 Stat. 623 (1935), as amended, 42 U.S.C. § 402(g) (1964), as amended, 42 U.S.C. § 402(g) (Supp. I, 1965) (mother's benefits); Social Security Act § 202(h), 49 Stat. 623 (1935), as amended, 42 U.S.C. § 402(h) (1964), as amended, 42 U.S.C. § 402(h) (Supp. I, 1965) (parent's benefits).

[35] Social Security Act § 203(b), 49 Stat. 623 (1935), as amended, 42 U.S.C. § 403(b) (1964).

[36] Social Security Act § 223(a), added by 70 Stat. 815 (1956), as amended, 42 U.S.C. § 423(a) (1964), as amended, 42 U.S.C. § 423(a) (Supp. I, 1965).

[37] 79 Stat. 301 (1965), as amended, 42 U.S.C. § 1395; (Supp. I, 1965).

[38] Social Security Act § 202(a), 49 Stat. 623 (1935), as amended, 42 U.S.C. § 402(a) (1964), as amended, 42 U.S.C. § 402(a) (Supp. I, 1965).

[39] 363 U.S. 602 (1960).

age and continuous payroll contributions. Speaking for the Court, which was divided five to four, Justice Harlan explicitly rejected the notion that social insurance benefits have the character of an earned right. "It is hardly profitable," said Justice Harlan, "to engage in conceptualizations regarding 'earned rights' and 'gratuities' . . . . To engraft upon the social security system a concept of 'accrued property rights' would deprive it of the flexibility and boldness in adjustment to ever-changing conditions which it demands."[40] The program instead was described as one "enacted pursuant to Congress' power to 'spend money in aid of the general welfare,' "[41]—one in which, accordingly, the contributions of employed persons were not on the order of premium payments into a trust fund, to be paid back to the insured upon maturity, but rather a tax to be used in public relief of the retired and disabled.

When all is said and done about stripping the social insurances of their supposed insurance attributes, this much remains, however, to be said: The beneficiary does make a financial contribution, whether correctly called a premium or a tax, which is regularly and observably deducted from his wages. From this he gains a feeling of personal involvement, the belief that his contribution is directly traceable to the benefit, and a strong sense that he has a right to it. Whatever may be the strictly logical and legal significance of the contribution, it is a political, social, and psychological fact of the utmost importance, both in terms of the continually increasing benefits and the willingness to pay for them, and in terms of a popular mass demand that the worst features of public assistance be avoided. Sustaining as far as possible the fiction of insurance thus has important consequences in the character of the system. And whether insurance or not, the system does provide a measure of protection to men against social hazards, hazards attendant upon the operation of the economy, hazards of industrial employment and unemployment in urbanized society—hazards beyond the control of the individual no matter how full he might be of all the middle-class virtues of character. Since the applicant's individual needs, merits, and qualities are irrelevant, and the conditions of eligibility are few and specific, administrative machinery and costs can be kept at a minimum.

It is quite otherwise with the theory and administration of the public assistance portions of the social security system. There, the pre-existing relief programs in the various states were caught up by the nation and deliberately incorporated into the new structure and means of financing. That pre-existing system consisted of the Elizabethan poor law as evolved in

---

[40] *Id.* at 610.
[41] *Id.* at 609.

Tudor England, transplanted to colonial America, and thereafter adapted and perpetuated.[42] Under this system aid could not be claimed as a right founded in a theory of prior contributions. It was to be made as a matter of governmental largesse and charity based on the need of the individual. Consequently governmental discretion as to the amount, character, and conditions of aid, and governmental machinery and technical apparatus brought to bear upon the assessment of individual need, are prime characteristics of the system of public assistance.

For the movement of countervailing forces in the direction of integrationism to become more than a token, broad recognition will be needed of the persisting residues of the poor law which remain embedded in the categories of public assistance. Specifically, these anachronistic features include: the means test; length-of-residence requirements; responsible relatives provisions; the custodial philosophy of casework; the conception of relief as a matter of charity rather than of right, with accompanying dependence on the police power and the law of crimes; and, cutting across all of these, the use of public welfare as a means of separately and discriminatorily categorizing the poor as a class apart.

II

THE MEANS TEST

If aid is to be granted on the basis of the need of the individual, how is that need to be determined? Is it to be by taking the average need of the members of the group to which the individual belongs and then allowing that as a fixed amount to all the members of the group? Is it to be by a series of presumed minimums or floors to relief for food, clothing, shelter, medical care, and the like? The answer of the Elizabethan poor law is that it is to be by the judgment of an administrator or social worker, acting within over-all budgetary limits and perhaps within major statutory guidelines, after investigating the situation of the individual. The formula describing this process is individual need individually determined. But the public will meet the needs of the individual, individually determined, only to the extent that the individual does not possess means of his own to meet them. The balancing of the individual's means against his needs has come to be called the means test. Traditionally applied in England from the origins of the poor law, utilized as an essential part of that law in the colonies, enacted by the state legislatures and carried out in administration in almost all of the states at the time of the adoption of the Social Security Act, the means test became an essential part of the administration of that

---

[42] Riesenfeld, *The Formative Era of American Public Assistance Law*, 43 CALIF. L. REV. 175 (1955); tenBroek, *California's Dual System of Family Law: Its Origin, Development, and Present Status*, 16 STAN. L. REV. 257, 900 (1964).

act, too. To make clear that this was so as against the few states which had established substantial modifications of the test,[43] the federal administration procured an amendment to the Social Security Act in 1939 explicitly imposing a requirement on the states that "in determining need, [they] take into consideration any other income and resources" that the individual applicant for aid might have.[44]

The official explanation of the requirement and of the test was provided by the Social Security administrators in President Truman's Memorandum of Disapproval, issued in 1948, of a provision passed unanimously by both houses of Congress exempting fifty dollars a month of earned income of blind aid recipients from consideration. "The aid to the blind program," said the Memorandum,

> in title X of the Social Security Act, like the other public assistance programs provided in that act, was designed and intended to provide financial assistance at a decent minimum of subsistence of those unable to provide for themselves. Necessarily, payments under these programs must be made on the basis of a finding as to the need of each individual for assistance, and for such a finding to be realistic and equitable to all alike it must be based on a consideration of each individual's earnings from employment and of any other resources available to him. To disregard an individual's income in determining the extent of his need for assistance negates the principle of providing assistance on the basis of need.[45]

Well-founded attacks upon the means test have been launched over the years from a variety of standpoints. Among other things, it is a mean test; it is demeaning to the dignity of the person; it withdraws from the recipient the management of his own affairs and invades the principle of the cash payment; it subjects the recipient to harassment and controls which weaken his resources of self-reliance, impede his rehabilitation, destroy his freedom, and perpetuate his dependence; it entails a degree of administrative discretion which opens the way to administrative abuse; it proliferates bureaucratic machinery, creates an army of welfare workers, and skyrockets the costs of administration. Individual determination of need has historically, and irresistibly, carried with it a punitive freight of moral and behavioral tests which reflect the impelling desire of the admin-

---

[43] *E.g.*, California, Illinois, and Pennsylvania. Cal. Stats. 1937, ch. 369, § 3084, at 1109; Pa. Laws 1937, No. 399, § 9(c), at 2055; ILL. STAT. ANN. ch. 23, § 703 (Smith-Hurd Supp. 1965). Pennsylvania and Missouri held out until 1950, when the federal Social Security Act was amended to let them in without complying with the administrative interpretation. 64 Stat. 554 (1950), 42 U.S.C. § 1202(a) (note) (1964); TENBROEK & MATSON, HOPE DEFERRED 93-95 (1959).

[44] Act of Aug. 10, 1939, ch. 666, § 701(b), 53 Stat. 1397, amending § 1002(a), ch. 531, 49 Stat. 645 (1935).

[45] President Truman, Memorandum of Disapproval, July 2, 1948.

istrators to keep the price down—and doubtless also reflect the ambivalent attitudes of welfare custodians whose quasi-parental relationship toward their dependent clients has been subjected to psychoanalytic scrutiny by Professor Bernard Diamond.[46] It is indeed possible that in some ideal world of mathematical abstraction, ruled only by Bentham's felicific calculus or Saint-Simon's universal gravity, the imposition of the means test would not carry with it all this pathological baggage; but in the real world of politics, prejudice, and power, the test of means is a symbol of meanness—a graphic exercise in the inhuman use of human beings.

The alternative to the means test within the framework of the existing system of social security is not far to seek logically, however hard it may be to achieve politically. Public assistance payments could be made to an individual as a part of a group. Four such groups exist ready made in the categorical aid programs: the aged, the blind, the permanently and totally disabled, families with dependent children. These are only illustrative. Once it is shown that a given person possesses the traits which make him a member of an aided group, his other individual characteristics are irrelevant. Thus upon proof of the attainment of the requisite age, or blindness, or permanent and total disability, nothing more would be required. All members of the group would then uniformly receive an equal grant, though payments might vary among the groups. The group characteristics would constitute the factor of individual eligibility and the amount of the payment would be fixed in the statute and aid would be received as a matter of statutory right. The amount of the grant should be sufficient to meet common human needs at socially determined standards of living.[47]

III

RESIDENCE REQUIREMENTS

To prevent the poor from wandering about the countryside, disturbing the peace and becoming rogues and vagabonds, to determine the unit of local government suitable for support of the needy individual and to fix responsibility on it, to keep administration local where knowledge of the individual and of available community resources exist—for all these reasons settlement rules have been established as a condition of eligibility for aid.[48] Once again this condition of eligibility goes back to Tudor

---

[46] Diamond, *Children of Leviathan: Psychoanalytic Speculations Concerning Welfare Law and Punitive Sanctions*, in this symposium.

[47] For a fuller discussion of this and other alternatives, see tenBroek & Wilson, *Public Assistance and Social Insurance—A Normative Evaluation*, 1 U.C.L.A.L. REV. 237 (1954).

[48] JORDAN, PHILANTHROPY IN ENGLAND 1480-1600, at 78-83 (1959); LEONARD, EARLY HISTORY OF ENGLISH POOR RELIEF 221 (1900); tenBroek, *California's Dual System of Family Law: Its Origin Development, and Present Status*, 16 STAN. L. REV. 259-65 (1964).

England, accompanies the poor laws to the New World, and, by the time of adoption of the Social Security Act, is embodied in a residence requirement of at least ten years in all but two of thirty states having pension plans for the blind and the aged.[49]

Given this all but universal custom and practice, it was natural for the states to seek to preserve their residential prerogatives when the time came to join the new program of public assistance under the Social Security Act. The states did so, in this instance, against the wishes of the Social Security Board, which as agent of the national will had no desire to preserve parochial barriers to national commingling and communion.[50] The Social Security Act itself, representing a compromise of the federal and the state interests, made only negative provision in the matter, prohibiting in its titles for the blind and the aged any residence requirement of longer than five years within the previous nine, including one year immediately preceding application;[51] for dependent children, the Act forbade a residence requirement of more than one year.[52]

Since the adoption of the Social Security Act, state residence requirements have had a curious history. In the aged and blind programs the requirements were substantially liberalized down to about 1950 and since that time have remained relatively static.[53] In the disabled program which began in 1950, the striking feature has been the preponderance of the one year requirement. The 1962 federal survey of the blind and disabled public assistance programs revealed the striking immobility of these

---

[49] SOCIAL SECURITY BD., SOCIAL SECURITY IN AMERICA, pt. 11, ch. vii (1937) (published for the Committee on Economic Security).

[50] SOCIAL SECURITY BD., ANNUAL REPORT 26-27 (1936); SOCIAL SECURITY BD., ANNUAL REPORT 37 (1937); Social Security Bd., Annual Report 107-08 (1938).

[51] Social Security Act §§ 2(b)(2), 1002(b)(1), 49 Stat. 620, 621, 645 (1935), 42 U.S.C. §§ 302(b)(2)(A), 1202(b)(1) (1964).

[52] Social Security Act § 402(b)(2), 49 Stat. 620, 628 (1935), 42 U.S.C. § 602(b)(2) (1964).

[53] Thus in 1941 in the aged program there were forty states with residence requirements at the federal maximum (five out of the last nine years), seven states with one year, no states without durational residence requirements. Advisory Council on Public Assistance, *Report on Public Assistance*, S. MISC. DOC. No. 93, 86th Cong., 2d Sess. (1960). In 1950, twenty-four states were at the federal maximum, twenty-two states required one year, and four states had no durational requirements. *Ibid.* In 1964, eighteen states were at the federal maximum, twenty-two required one year, and five had no durational requirements. U.S. DEP'T OF HEALTH, EDUC. & WELFARE, CHARACTERISTICS OF STATE PUBLIC ASSISTANCE PLANS UNDER THE SOCIAL SECURITY ACT (Pub. Ass. Rep. No. 50, 1964). In the blind program: In 1941, thirty-three states were at the federal maximum, seven states required one year, one state had no residence requirement, Advisory Council on Public Assistance, *supra;* in 1950, fourteen states were at the federal maximum, twenty-two states had a one-year requirement, seven states had no durational requirements, *ibid.;* in 1964, thirteen states were at the federal maximum, twenty-three required one year, and seven states had no durational requirements. U.S. DEP'T OF HEALTH, EDUC. & WELFARE, *op. cit. supra.*

groups: over sixty per cent were born in the state in which they are recipients and over eigthty per cent had lived in that state for at least ten years.[54] Following California's abolition of a durational residence requirement in the blind program in 1963[55] there has been no increase in the recipient rate except as to the identifiable group of blind persons already resident in the state but hitherto ineligible because of the five out of the last nine years residence requirement. Meanwhile numerous bills to abolish residence requirements in welfare have appeared in Congress with the blessing of the Department of Health, Education and Welfare along with such interested groups as the National Advisory Council on Public Assistance, the National Social Welfare Assembly, the American Legion, and the National Travelers Aid Society.[56] Although Congress has not as yet seen fit to knock down state barriers to free movement on the part of needy persons, such action is a logical and seemingly inescapable corollary to the amendments it passed in 1956 adding self-support and self-care to the list of purposes served by the public assistance programs.[57] The 1956 amendments registered the recognition of Congress that the human need of the disabled or blind individual to find his place as an active and contributing member of society is no less real or important than his animal need for food and shelter. It remains only for the lawmakers to recognize also that the effort to find one's place in society requires the possibility of moving freely within and throughout that society.

Little argument is needed any longer to affirm in principle the right of free movement for all persons in our society. Though not mentioned explicitly in the Constitution, it underlies and is an integral part of much that the Constitution guarantees and authorizes. It is presupposed by the system of personal rights which the Constitution is designed to protect. It seems particularly to be an aspect of the personal liberty guaranteed by the due process clauses of the fifth and fourteenth amendments. It is sheltered by concepts of the equal protection of the laws implicit in the fifth amendment and explicit in the fourteenth amendment. It is inseparably appurtenant to the ideas of national citizenship and federal union. It is encompassed within the national power of commerce and guaranteed by the idea of national commerce.

---

[54] U.S. DEP'T OF HEALTH, EDUC. & WELFARE, STATE LETTER No. 746, at Table 25 (July 2, 1964); *id.*, No. 747, at Table 21 July 2, 1964.

[55] Cal. Stats. 1963, ch. 510, §§ 11.8, 11.9.

[56] See, *e.g., Hearings on H.R. 10032 Before the House Committee on Ways and Means,* 87th Cong., 2d Sess. 437 (1962) (statement by N. H. Cruikshank, Director, Social Security Dep't, AFL-CIO). See also *id.* at 440 (statement by Dr. E. Winston, past President, APWA); *id.* at 331 (statement by R. E. Bondy, Director, NSWA).

[57] 70 Stat. 848 (1956), 42 U.S.C. §§ 301(a), 601(a), 1201(a), 1351(a) (1964).

But whether the "right to go and come at pleasure" is upheld on grounds of the commerce clause, as by the majority in *Edwards v. California*,[58] and *Heart of Atlanta Motel v. Unted States*,[59] or whether it is defended on grounds of the guarantees of the fourteenth amendment as by Justices Jackson[60] and Douglas[61] in the *Edwards* case and by Justice Douglas in *Heart of Atlanta Motel*,[62] it is seen by the courts as a basic right and given constitutional protection. Justice Goldberg, reviewing the congressional history of the fourteenth amendment in *Bell v. Maryland*,[63] pointed out: "The recurrent references to the right 'to go and come at pleasure' as being 'among the natural rights of free men' reflect the common understanding that the concepts of liberty and citizenship embraced the right to freedom of movement, the effective right to travel freely."[64]

The right of free movement consists of three major elements: the right to remain in and move about in one's home community; the right to leave one's home community unhindered, to travel to some other part of the country for temporary sojourn or for permanent residence; the right as a temporary sojourner or new resident in any community to stand upon an equal footing with the old residents at least as to essential rights and services.

True, the courts have not given equal emphasis to all of these constitutional sources, or all of these elements of the right. In *United States v. Guest*,[65] the United States Supreme Court sustained as within the federal jurisdiction an indictment under 18 U.S.C. section 241 alleging that the defendants, private citizens, "conspired to injure, oppress, threaten, and intimidate Negro citizens of the United States in the free exercise and enjoyment of 'the right to travel freely to and from the State of Georgia and use highway facilities and other instrumentalities of interstate commerce within the State of Georgia.' "[66] The Court held that the "right to travel from one State to another, and necessarily to use the highways and other instrumentalities of interstate commerce in doing so,"[67] is a "right

---

58 314 U.S. 160 (1941).

59 379 U.S. 241 (1964).

60 Edwards v. California, 379 U.S. 160, 181 (1941) (concurring opinion).

61 *Id.* at 177 (concurring opinion).

62 Heart of Atlanta Motel v. United States, 379 U.S. 241, 279 (1964) (concurring opinion).

63 378 U.S. 226 (1964).

64 *Id.* at 293 n.10 (concurring opinion). For more extensive treatment of the residence requirement, see Harvith, *The Constitutionality of Residence Tests for General and Categorical Assistance Programs*, in this symposium.

65 86 Sup. Ct. 1170 (1966).

66 *Id.* at 4326.

67 *Ibid.*

that the Constitution itself guarantees,"[68] occupying "a position fundamental to the concept of our Federal Union."[69] Since the right "finds
constitutional protection that is quite independent of the Fourteenth
Amendment,"[70] it is "secured against interference from any source whatever, whether governmental or private."[71]

Length of residence requirements are founded on a notion of locality
and community that belongs to an earlier period of history and geography.
In the time of Elizabeth I the hedges surrounding residence were the
natural, if prejudicial, concomitant of local economy and a parochial
society, in which all the salient burdens and responsibilities were concentrated in the locality. To be sure, it was the poor and the disabled
who felt that bitter truth and suffered the consequences—and whose
lives generally fulfilled the conditions of existence in Hobbes' state of
nature by being "solitary, poor, nasty, brutish, and short." By contrast the symbols of our present-day society are the freeway, the open
door, and the mainstream. With respect to matters which touch upon the
lives and interests of people everywhere in the land, the community is the
nation itself. Large-scale poverty, economic opportunity in an economically interdependent system, personal liberty, the right of free movement, the privileges and immunities of citizens of the United States,
equality of rights and opportunities, the heritage and indispensable conditions of a free people—what matters, if not these, intimately touch the
lives and interests of people everywhere in the land. One by one and
taken collectively they repudiate discriminatory restraints upon the
mobility of the poor, among which must be classed length of residence
requirements for public welfare aids and services. These restraints especially suffer the reproaches of the command of the equal protection of the
laws. That command cannot detect the difference between the needs of the
newcomer and the old-timer for food, clothing, shelter, and other necessities of life.[72]

IV

RESPONSIBILITY OF RELATIVES

In balancing the individual's means against his needs in the classic
process of the means test, all resources available to the individual are to be

---

[68] *Id.* at 4327 n.17.

[69] *Id.* at 4326.

[70] *Id.* at 4327 n.17.

[71] *Ibid.*

[72] "In our society, mobility of population is essential. Individuals should be free to move
where jobs are available and if, as a result of illness or other misfortune, they become needy,
they should not be denied assistance because they have crossed state or county lines. We
believe that residence and settlement provisions are socially unjustifiable." *Public Assistance,
A Report,* S. Doc. No. 204, 80th Cong., 2d Sess. (1948).

counted among his means. From the outset of the poor law one such available resource has been those relatives of the individual able to contribute to his support.[73] The responsibility imposed by law upon relatives to make such a contribution became in later centuries a general obligation at the common law[74] and in statutes and codes dealing with family relations,[75] but it was originally evolved as a device of the poor law system to reduce the cost to the public of relieving the poor.

In the contemporary public assistance programs of aid to the blind and aid to the permanently and totally disabled, as well as in those affecting the aged and dependent minors, the concept that public aid begins when the resources of relatives have been exhausted is still quite generally imposed, although it takes various forms in the statutes and administrative regulations.[76] In the early years of the Social Security Act, although the determination of relatives' responsibility was legally left to the states, the Federal Social Security Board brought its considerable weight to bear through admonitions that "administration of these aspects of state public assistance programs should not be such as to weaken the sense of family integrity on which children and the aged have always relied."[77] Still more specifically, it was declared that the need to be determined is that "which remains after legally responsible relatives of an aged [or blind] person have contributed to his support insofar as they are able."[78] As a result of the Board's pressure, several states which had previously prohibited the use of the resources of an applicant's family in determining his eligibility were forced to amend their laws or be held out of conformity.[79] In 1948 the federal officials reversed the Social Security Administration, and recommended that the states eliminate their provisions enforcing relatives' responsibility.[80] But this remnant of the poor law was not so easily dislodged from the statutes and administrative guidelines of the states; today, in one form or another, it is still on the books in most of them.

The relatives who are held responsible are a diverse assemblage of old

---

[73] 39 Eliz. 1, c. 3, § vii (1597); 43 Eliz. 1, c. 2, § vi (1601); tenBroek, *supra* note 45, at 282-89.

[74] *Id.* at 287-91.

[75] See, *e.g.*, CAL. CIV. CODE § 206; KY. REV. STATS. § 405.080 (1962).

[76] ALASKA STAT. § 47.25.580 (1962); DEL. CODE ANN. § 510 (Supp. 1964); ILL. STAT. ANN. ch. 23, § 112 (Smith-Hurd Supp. 1965); ME. REV. STAT. ANN. tit. 19, § 219 (1964); N.D. CENT. CODE ANN. § 50-24-03 (Supp. 1965); TEX. CIV. STAT. ANN. art. 695c, §§ 16-B-8(9), 20(5) (Vernon's Supp. 1965).

[77] SOCIAL SECURITY BD., ANNUAL REPORT 105 (1938).

[78] SOCIAL SECURITY BD., ANNUAL REPORT 43 (1937).

[79] See, *e.g.*, Mo. Laws 1939, at 739; Wash. Laws 1939, ch. 216, § 17, at 874.

[80] FEDERAL SECURITY AGENCY, BUREAU OF PUBLIC ASSISTANCE, PUBLIC ASSISTANCE GOALS FOR 1949, at 14 (1948).

and young, affluent and overburdened. For those public assistance recipients well along in years, the responsible relatives are their children,
now become adults with families of their own. On the other hand, for many
of the disabled and blind recipients, still comparatively young themselves,
the responsible relatives are parents advanced in years and often facing
their own problems of support in old age. In human terms the most
onerous aspect of the requirement is the role of the aid recipient. He is
confronted with the choice either of incurring family resentment by
accurate reporting of contributions or of failing to report the relatives'
reduced contribution and thereby reducing his income. Moreover, the
dependent status of the recipient upon other family members is officially
reinforced and sanctified rather than constructively attacked; neither the
independence of the disabled person nor the interdependence of the family
circle is well served by this tightening and policing of the bonds of kinship.[81]

V

WELFARE AS A SYSTEM OF CONTROL

At the heart of the system of public assistance, as indicated earlier, lies
the dogma of individual need individually determined, which finds practical expression in the device of the means test. In effect, under this policy,
it is the applicant who is tested and must be found wanting. It is not only
his means and resources but his character and background, his family
relationships and very style of life, which come under the scrutiny of the
welfare agency. Through an interminable succession of investigations
beginning with the application interview and culminating, but not ending,
in the issuance or withholding of the cash grant, the disabled client finds
himself confronted with a presumption not of innocence and eligibility but
of guilt and probable fraud. He is deprived from start to finish of what
Gordon W. Allport has termed "the right to be believed."[82] His answers
are checked; his claims of need tracked down; his resources identified and
counted against him; his relatives searched out and queried. Nor is this
surveillance a one-time-only procedure, briefly annoying but soon over
and done with; it is continuous and recurrent, ceasing only with the
client's death or his transfiguration into a state of self-sufficiency. For
the disabled recipient of aid, Big Brother is always watching.

Whatever modest degree of self-control and responsibility the disabled

---

[81] For a discussion of the constitutionality of the legal liability of relatives for the support
of welfare recipients in the present state of the law and the impact of California's landmark
decision in Department of Mental Hygiene v. Kirchner, 60 Cal. 2d 722, 388 P.2d 724, 36 Cal.
Rptr. 492 (1964), see tenBroek, *California's Dual System of Family Law: Its Origin, Development, and Present Status*, 17 Stan. L. Rev. 614, 638-46 (1965).

[82] Allport, Personality and Social Encounter 97 (1960).

person may have possessed before entering this web of bureaucracy and paternalism is soon wrested from him by the process of means test aid. It is the agency of welfare, not the recipient, who decides what life goals are to be followed, what ambitions may be entertained, what services are appropriate, what wants are to be recognized, what needs may be budgeted, and what funds allocated to each. In short, the recipient is told *what* he wants as well as how much he is wanting. In the velvet glove of public aid is an iron hand: If the recipient does not comply and conform, he may be removed from the rolls or have his budget reduced. The alternatives are obedience or starvation. The "concern of assistance with the whole range of income," as Karl de Schweinitz has observed, "always contains a threat to the freedom of the individual. Even when there is no conscious intent to dictate behavior to the beneficiary, the pervasive power of money dispensed under the means test may cause the slightest suggestion to have the effect of compulsion. 'Whose bread I eat, his song I sing.' "[83]

Reinforcing these tendencies of means test aid under public assistance —the chief effect of which is to perpetuate dependency and discourage initiative—is a cluster of attitudes among social workers supporting the professional inclination to "take whole responsibility for the whole client."[84] In part these attitudes reflect nineteenth-century pieties concerning the moral depravity and natural inferiority of the poor;[85] in part they embody ill-digested and outdated psychoanalytic concepts counseling passive adjustment on the part of the client-patient to an immutable social reality.[86] Whatever the sources of these attitudes, their consequences are unambiguous. Welfare clients, including the blind and the disabled, have been categorically judged incompetent to manage their lives and affairs. Uncooperative clients may find themselves labeled as "unstable defectives";[87] unmarried mothers can be seen as unable if not incapable of making their own independent decisions without casework services.[88] For blind clients, as a psychologist has coolly stated, "the only true answer

---

[83] DE SCHWEINITZ, PEOPLE AND PROCESS IN SOCIAL SECURITY 56-57 (1948).

[84] Keith-Lucas, *The Political Theory Implicit in Social Casework Theory*, 47 AM. POL. SCI. REV. 1090 (1953). See also Matson, *Social Welfare and Personal Liberty: The Problem of Casework*, 22 SOCIAL RESEARCH 253 (1955).

[85] "We think it as competent and as necessary for a State to provide precautionary measures against the moral pestilence of paupers, vagabonds, and possibly convicts, as it is to guard against the physical pestilence which may arise from unsound and infectious articles imported, or from a ship, the crew of which may be laboring under an infectious disease." New York v. Miln, 36 U.S. (11 Pet.) 357, 369 (1837).

[86] Matson, *supra* note 84.

[87] Overton, *Serving Families Who Don't Want Help*, 34 SOCIAL CASEWORK 304 (1953).

[88] Marcus, *Worker and Client Relationships*, 73 PROCEEDINGS OF THE NATIONAL CONFERENCE OF SOCIAL WORK 342 (1946).

lies in the unfortunate circumstance that the blind share with other neurotics the nonaggressive personality and the inability to participate fully in society."[89] The common denominator of such judgments is the pervasive if hidden assumption that the needy client of casework services is irrational, irresponsible, abnormal, and incompetent. In terms of policy and practice, the product of this assumption is a distinctive framework of protective shelter and benevolent custody—with no exit. Its name is public welfare.

VI

THE LAW OF CRIMES

Among the images of poverty bequeathed to us by the Statutes of Elizabeth was the invidious stereotype of the poor and disabled as all but invariably the victims of their own vices. The conceptual foundation for this unsentimental perspective on poverty has been well described by Tawney: "That the greatest of evils is idleness, that the poor are the victims, not of circumstances, but of their own 'idle, irregular and wicked courses,' that the truest charity is not to enervate them by relief, but so to reform their characters that relief may be unnecessary—such doctrines turned severity from a sin into a duty, and froze the impulse of natural pity with the assurance that, if indulged, it would perpetuate the suffering which it sought to allay."[90]

This concept of the characterological causation of poverty and dependency has not only a venerable history but a contemporary reality, in the context of what may fairly be called the "welfare law of crimes." For the corollary of the moralistic theory which holds poverty to be the result of personal wickedness and sin—hence a crime—is the punitive conception of welfare which converts it in effect into a law of crimes. In the eyes of that law there are no broad social problems of poverty or injustice to be solved but only individual wrongs to be righted, personal sins of commission to be expiated and corrected. And the proper corrective, in most cases, is some form of punishment.

The law of crimes has penetrated into the law and administration of social security in various ways and at various levels. Congress itself has taken a number of steps to assist this infiltration on both sides of the system. It has decreed, on the side of social insurance, that a person who commits treason may, as added punishment, be denied accrued benefits under the program; that one who has engaged in sedition may be similarly stripped; and so may those who have been deported on any of fourteen

---

[89] Cutsforth, *Personality and Social Adjustment Among the Blind*, in BLINDNESS 183 (Zahl ed. 1950).

[90] TAWNEY, RELIGION AND THE RISE OF CAPITALISM 221 (Penguin Books 1947).

different grounds.[91] Meanwhile, on the side of public assistance, Congress has augmented the influence of the law of crimes by adding to the federal statute a requirement that law enforcement officers must be notified in all cases of aid to needy children where there is an absence of a parent.[92]

At the state and local levels the penetration of the criminal law into public assistance has been seen in the proliferation of rules and practices bringing to bear the methods of the lie detector to determine truth, of the blood test to establish parentage, of the night call upon the homes of recipients to flush suspected partners, of the beating of park bushes and other public places to deter promiscuity—and in general of the formidable repressive weight of criminal investigation and police authority. This is not the place to recount in lurid detail the numerous events and episodes in which these methods of law enforcement have superseded the alternative methods of social case work and welfare administration.[93] But it is important to emphasize the fundamental contradiction in principle between the purposes of welfare law and those of the law of crimes. The human problems with which the programs of public assistance are most deeply concerned—problems of economic distress, of social pathology, of personal rehabilitation—require for their solution the utmost effort of sympathetic understanding and nonauthoritarian guidance of which skilled counselors and social workers are capable. But the assumptions and objectives of the law of crimes are not these. Its preliminary assumption is that persons in deprived circumstances are there through their own wilful or inherent fault; its objective is to eliminate the problem by suppression and punishment.

VII

TOWARD INTEGRATION: CONSTRUCTIVE FEATURES IN WELFARE

Thus far we have focused upon the custodializing features of public welfare programs for the disabled—features which treat them as a minority group permanently apart and permanently dependent: in other words, as "separate and unequal." To the extent that these prejudicial premises remain embedded in welfare law and administration, the legal and constitutional status of the physically handicapped individual resembles that of the American Negro prior to the equalitarian civil rights movement activated by *Brown v. Board of Education*[94] in 1954.

There is no single landmark event in the social history of the disabled

---

91 Social Security Act § 202(n), added by 68 Stat. 1083 (1954), as amended, 42 U.S.C. § 402(n) (1964).

92 Social Security Act § 402(a)(10), 49 Stat. 627 (1935), as amended, 42 U.S.C. § 602(a)(10) (1964).

93 For details see tenBroek, *supra* note 73, at 659-75.

94 347 U.S. 483 (1954`

comparable to the Supreme Court decision in the *Brown* case. There are, however, a number of episodes and actions in welfare which are similar in portent if not in scope. Doctrinally the most significant occurred in 1956 with the passage of amendments to the Social Security Act, contemplating a substantial revision of the public assistance programs away from poor relief toward social rehabilitation.[95] The specific expression of this new outlook was the addition of *self-support* and *self-care* to the list of official purposes to be served by the program.[96]

That change was a long time coming. In the two-score years between the original enactment of social security and the amendments of 1956, although recognition had grown steadily of the need for constructive revision and reform of the aid titles, there had been few overt actions toward that end. In 1950 Congress did succeed, against the opposition of federal administrators who had defeated a similar attempt two years earlier,[97] in passing a provision for the exemption of earned income up to a maximum of fifty dollars a month on the part of blind recipients of aid.[98] The constructive aspect of this liberalization of the means test was articulated in the Senate Finance Committee report accompanying the bill. The means test, said the committee, "stifles incentive and discourages the needy blind from becoming self-supporting and . . . therefore it should be replaced by a requirement that would assist blind individuals in becoming useful and productive members of their communities."[99] When the Social Security Board moved to cut down the full advantage of the fifty dollar exemption provision, Congress roused itself again two years later to pass an amendment providing that the states should not treat the exempt earnings of a blind aid recipient as an available resource to any member of his family seeking federally shared assistance.[100]

Again in 1954, in its "New Look" at welfare, the Eisenhower Administration wrought substantial changes in the nation's official programs of vocational rehabilitation under the Barden-LaFollette Act;[101] but for all its concern with the vocational and social reintegration of the disabled, the New Look scarcely perceived the potential relationship of public assistance to the goals of rehabilitation. Nevertheless by 1956 it was evident that new interpretations of the purposes of public aid were at hand. In presenting the Administration's proposals to the House Ways and

---

95 70 Stat. 848 (1956), 42 U.S.C. §§ 301, 601, 1201, 1351 (1964).

96 *Ibid.*

97 H.R. 6818, 80th Cong., 2d Sess. (1948) (defeated by pocket veto).

98 Social Security Amendments of 1950, ch. 809, § 341(c)(1), 64 Stat. 553.

99 S. REP. No. 1669, 81st Cong., 2d Sess. 56 (1950).

100 S. REP. No. 1806, 82d Cong., 2d Sess. 7 (1952).

101 68 Stat. 652 (1954), 29 U.S.C. §§ 31-42 (1964), as amended, 29 U.S.C. §§ 31-42 (Supp. I, 1965).

Means Committee in that year, Social Security Commissioner Charles I. Schottland announced that the time had arrived "for emphasis on the constructive aspects" of public assistance. Specifically recommending the addition of provisions for self-support and self-care, he said: "We should make clear to the states that this is a basic purpose of the program and one in which the federal government stands ready to share financially . . . ."[102]

As approved by Congress, the purpose declaration of the 1956 amendments included this phrase: "to promote the well-being of the Nation by encouraging the States to place greater emphasis on helping to strengthen family life and helping needy families and individuals to attain the maximum economic and personal independence of which they are capable . . . ."[103] The purpose clause of each of the public assistance titles was amended to read: "for the purpose of enabling each State to furnish financial assistance, as far as practicable under the conditions in such State, to needy individuals who are disabled [blind, aged] and of encouraging each State, as far as practicable under such conditions, to help such individuals attain" self-support or self-care, in the case of the disabled and blind, and self-care, in the case of the aged.[104]

The 1956 amendments thus introduced for each of the aided categories a new purpose defined in terms of the needs of that particular group. For the disabled and the blind, the need was seen to be for self-support and self-care; for these welfare clients, if not for others, the amendments wrought a basic change in principle concerning the extent and character of the needs to be met by public assistance. Previously the only needs recognized were physical and material: the demands of the organism for food, for shelter, for essential clothing, and for the preservation of life and health. Since 1956 the law embodies the clear awareness that, in our modern affluent society, the need for rehabilitation and self-support—for the dignity of independence, the pride of self-reliance, and the sense of personal achievement—is as genuine and almost as vital as the need of physical survival. If the opportunity for restoration to self-supporting independence is not a basic human need in psychological terms, it is today a basic *social* need. The 1956 amendments not only recognized the reality of that need but made it a responsibility of public welfare. That these high purposes have not been acted upon is not a reflection upon their viability but a revelation of the contradiction between their integrationist goals and the custodialism of means-test aid.

---

[102] *Hearings Before the House Committee on Ways and Means*, 84th Cong., 2d Sess. 3-10 (1956).

[103] 70 Stat. 846 (1956), 42 U.S.C. § 300(n) (1964).

[104] Social Security Amendments of 1956, ch. 836, § 311(a), 70 Stat. 848.

VIII

INCENTIVE EXEMPTIONS OF INCOME

The constructive start toward integration and independence made by the 1956 amendments has not been adequately supported by measures of direct action over the subsequent decade. In one respect, however, there has been definite progress: Rehabilitative provisions have emerged in both state and federal laws allowing disabled and other recipients to retain specified amounts of earnings and other resources useful in a plan for self-support.[105] Where successful, these measures help recipients to escape the relief rolls by encouraging rather than penalizing their first tentative and precarious efforts to bring in income.

As stated earlier, the first breakthrough for the principle of exempt income occurred in 1950 when Congress approved the fifty dollars exemption for blind aid recipients. A decade later the maximum was raised to eighty-five dollars per month, plus half of any income earned above that figure along with specified amounts of personal property and resources.[106] Until 1965 these allowable exemptions were mostly limited to the blind; now they have been extended in varying amounts to the other aid categories as well. As a result of the 1965 amendments, recipients of aid to the totally disabled gain an exemption, at the option of the state, of the first twenty dollars a month in earnings and one-half of the next sixty dollars.[107] Of equal or greater importance, any additional income and resources of a disabled person, without limit, can now be exempted where it is part of an approved plan to achieve self-support[108]—another integrating principle which was pioneered earlier for the needy blind.

IX

MOVES TOWARD A FLOOR OF PROTECTION

From various quarters in recent years has come a chorus of voices challenging the device of the means test and its underlying theory of "individual need individually determined." In their place the critics would put the principle of a floor to relief, a minimum grant of assistance to all who are in need, that is, *group* need *socially* determined. This principle, long advocated by interested organizations such as the National Federation of the Blind, has lately gained the support of the American Public

---

[105] 76 Stat. 197 (1962), as amended, 42 U.S.C. §§ 1201-06, 1351-55 (1964), as amended, 42 U.S.C. §§ 1201-06, 1351-55 (Supp. I, 1965).

[106] 74 Stat. 995 (1960), as amended, 42 U.S.C. § 1202(a)(8) (1964), as amended, 42 U.S.C. § 1202(a)(8) (Supp. I, 1965).

[107] 79 Stat. 418, 42 U.S.C. § 1382 (Supp. I, 1965).

[108] *Ibid.*

Welfare Association.[109] It has been advanced frequently in bills before Congress proposing reforms in public assistance; it has been notably galvanized by the war on poverty with its fresh approach to the human problems of deprivation; and it has even begun to look conservative alongside the dramatic proposals of such groups as the "*Ad Hoc* Committee on the Triple Revolution," calling for a guaranteed income to all Americans.[110] The idea of a common floor of protection for the needy is doubtless still far from implementation in the federal law; but it has made its way to the center of public discussion and legislative attention, and is unlikely to withdraw until its mission has been accomplished or accommodated.

Indeed the principle of a minimum floor to relief, below which the need of recipients is presumed and their income may not fall, has long been in effect in two state programs of aid to the blind—those of California and Nevada.[111]

X

CRACKS IN THE POOR LAW

The old edifice of poor relief, first constructed on the banks of the Thames three and a half centuries ago, then imported and rebuilt brick by brick on American soil, is still standing today. But it is a house divided. On one wall, through barred windows, it looks backward and holds fiercely to the ancestral ways. On the other side it faces present realities and looks to the future. Thus divided against itself, the structure of relief and welfare cannot indefinitely stand. The ancient requirements of residence and relatives' responsibility, in particular, are undergoing an attack which sooner or later must prove to be fatal. Eight states have seen fit to cut the bonds of residence for certain categories of welfare recipients;[112] all the major welfare agencies, including the Department of Health, Education and Welfare[113] are on record against them.

---

[109] American Public Welfare Ass'n, Statement Submitted to the Advisory Council on Public Welfare, San Francisco, California 7, August 1965.

[110] "We urge, therefore, that society, through its appropriate legal and governmental institutions, undertake an unqualified commitment to provide every individual and every family with an adequate income as a matter of right. . . . The unqualified right to an income would take the place of the patchwork of welfare measures—from unemployment insurance to relief—designed to ensure that no citizen or resident of the U.S. actually starves." The Triple Revolution, Memorandum on the *Ad Hoc* Committee on the Triple Revolution 10, April 1964 (printed by the Committee as a public service). A similar proposal for "a floor under the standard of life of every person in the community" is set forth in FRIEDMAN, CAPITALISM AND FREEDOM ch. xii (1962).

[111] CAL. WELFARE & INST'NS CODE §§ 12650, 13100; NEV. REV. STAT. § 426.420 (1953).

[112] California, Connecticut, Hawaii, Kentucky, Mississippi, New York, Rhode Island, and South Carolina. U.S. DEP'T OF HEALTH, EDUC. & WELFARE, PUBLIC ASSISTANCE REPORT No. 50 (1964).

[113] U.S. DEP'T OF HEALTH, EDUC. & WELFARE, REPORT 59 (1960), recommends reduction

This equalitarian and integrationist philosophy has given rise to another effort to blunt the edge of the poor law: namely, the movement to abolish state provisions regarding responsibility of relatives. California, in the vanguard of this movement, as of others in public welfare, has taken two steps: First, its legislature has abolished responsible-relatives provisions in public assistance for the blind and the disabled;[114] second, the state supreme court in *Department of Mental Hygiene v. Kirchner*[115] has extended the protection of the Constitution to those victimized by this residue of the poor law. The court held that care and treatment of the mentally ill in state institutions is a public responsibility, to be borne not by relatives but by the citizenry as a whole through a uniform system of taxation. "A statute," said the court, "obviously violates the equal protection clause if it selects one particular class of persons for a species of taxation and no rational basis supports such a classification. . . . Such a concept for the state's taking of a free man's property manifestly denies him equal protection of the law."[116]

This California Supreme Court decision, while addressed specifically to the responsibility of relatives of the mentally disturbed who are cared for in state institutions, involves a principle of much broader applicability —embracing all welfare recipients and their families. For the responsibility of the public to support mentally ill persons in state hospitals is not different from the responsibility it assumes when physically handicapped, or otherwise needy, persons are given public support in their own homes. Once the public has shouldered the responsibility, it can only be discharged through publicly apportioned taxation and cannot be shifted to private individuals, whether relatives or others. To do that is to impose upon a particular group a forbidden form of taxation—to appropriate their property in violation of the constitutional requirement of equal protection of the laws.

These various actions representing a small beginning of a change in public assistance have their counterpart in the social insurances. As with the social insurances generally, the trend in disability insurance is gradually to widen the scope of coverage and to reduce the barriers which still keep out large numbers of the physically handicapped. Thus the 1965 amendments liberalized eligibility requirements under the disability freeze in two directions: the previous stipulation of twenty quarters of mini-

---

to a maximum of one year. The Advisory Council on Public Assistance, Report, Dec. 31, 1959, also recommended this. The recommendation was listed without comment in DEP'T OF HEALTH, EDUC. & WELFARE, *supra* at 44.

[114] CAL. WELFARE & INST'NS CODE §§ 12600, 13600.

[115] 60 Cal. 2d 722, 388 P.2d 724, 36 Cal. Rptr. 492 (1964).

[116] *Id.* at 722-23, 388 P.2d at 724, 36 Cal. Rptr. at 492.

mum coverage under the program was reduced to six quarters for younger workers who are blind,[117] and older blind persons were granted eligibility even though they were engaged in some form of substantial gainful activity.[118] These small forward steps represented a compromise of more substantial reforms incorporated in legislation which had passed the Senate only to be cut down in the House-Senate conference committee.[119]

Beyond the social security system, in the wider context of social forces and political tides, there are further hopeful signs. One is implicit in the heralded "revolution in social work,"[120] which seeks to convert welfare clients from passive recipients into active participants in the process, by giving them structural representation in the making and administering of policies. This principle of partnership or "dialogue," given impetus recently by the community action programs of the Economic Opportunity Act,[121] was first brought to public attention through the militant campaign of federated blind groups in the 1950's for the right to organize and to be consulted in the administration of programs addressed to their welfare.[122] The dialogical principle also has found support in the "functionalist" school of casework theory which stresses a nondirective, client-centered relationship in the agency setting in contrast to the alleged custodialism of the rival "diagnostic" school.[123]

Another sign of changing attitudes toward welfare arises from what may be called the shock of recognition on the part of the planners and policy-makers, brought about by the unexpected persistence of the public assistance categories and their programs. When the social security system was first adopted thirty years ago, it was assumed that by 1965 old-age assistance would be swallowed up by old-age insurance, with much the same fate in store for the other assistance programs. On this assumption the aid programs were regarded as stopgaps and palliatives, intended to relieve the distress of poverty and disability but scarcely to solve the problem. Public assistance more or less frankly limited itself to dealing with the symptoms and left the causes for others to worry about.

---

[117] 79 Stat. 286, 42 U.S.C. § 416(i)(3)(B)(ii) (Supp. I, 1965).

[118] *Ibid.*

[119] H.R. 6675, 89th Cong., 1st Sess. (1965).

[120] Frank T. Riessman, The Revolution in Social Work: The New Nonprofessional, Trans-action, Nov.-Dec. 1964, pp. 12-17; Raab & Folk, *The Pattern of Dependent Poverty in California,* in Consultants' Reports to Welfare Study Commission, State of California, pt. 2, Jan. 1963.

[121] 78 Stat. 516, 42 U.S.C. §§ 2781-91 (1964), as amended, 42 U.S.C. §§ 2781-91 (Supp. I, 1965).

[122] *Hearings Before the House Committee on Education and Labor,* 86th Cong., 1st Sess. (1959).

[123] See Matson, *supra* note 84, at 267-71. See also the case for the case worker's role as that of "advocate" of the client-recipient advanced by Professor Scott Briar. Briar, *Welfare From Below: Recipients' Views of the Welfare System,* in this symposium.

But one of the most notable developments in thirty years of public assistance has been the failure of its categories to wither away. Instead, new categories and recipient groups have been added while the old have been strengthened. As the problems of welfare have persisted and grown, so has the concept of public assistance as a permanent long-range system with an independent rationale and a constructive function—serving vital needs which arise from socio-economic, no less than personal, causes and require to be met affirmatively on their own ground. It is this recognition which has found tentative expression in the new goals of self-support and self-care, in the principle of incentive exemptions of income and resources, and in the growing conception of public aid as a right rather than as an alms-taking privilege contingent upon the swearing of a pauper's oath.

But, for the integrative principle in welfare to prevail against the custodialism of old-fashioned poor relief, much more is needed by way of encouragement of the disabled client to make his way back to self-sufficiency and self-reliance. In this effort, public assistance must be directed toward opportunity as well as toward security—geared to employment and self-support as well as to relief. To the extent that public aid and welfare programs become fully committed to the goals of integrationism—that is, of economic opportunity, social equality, and personal dignity—to that extent they will justify the massive investment of funds and faith which the nation has put into them.

The Right to Live in the World:
The Disabled in the Law of Torts†

Jacobus tenBroek*

M OVEMENT, WE ARE TOLD, is a law of animal life. As to man, in any
event, nothing could be more essential to personality, social existence, economic opportunity—in short, to individual well-being and
integration into the life of the community—than the physical capacity,
the public approval, and the legal right to be abroad in the land.

Almost by definition, physical disability in many of its forms entails
difficulties in getting about, and this is so quite regardless of the particular surroundings. Such is the case of the cripple, the paraplegic, and
the legless. The word "halt" itself is a description of disability in terms
of limitation on mobility. Some difficulties in getting about arise out of
the conditions of the modern world in combination with the particular
disability, as in the case of the deaf person in traffic. However different
from what they are widely supposed to be, there are travel problems
inherent in blindness and these are to some extent increased, to some
extent diminished, by the structures and conditions of modern urban

---

† Author's Note: If the blind appear in these pages more than other disabled, it may be
because the author is blind and has a special interest in his kind. He thinks not, however.
The fact is that the blind individually and collectively are a very active group of the disabled,
if not the most active. If the National Federation of the Blind appears in these pages more
often than other organizations and agencies composed of the blind or dealing with their
problems, it may be because the author founded that organization in 1940, served as its
president for 21 years, and is still an active leader in it. He thinks not, however. The National Federation of the Blind is an aggressive, militant, activist organization of the blind
themselves which in a quarter of a century has achieved a great deal, legislatively and otherwise, and has always been in the thick of the fight. If the *Braille Monitor* is cited more often
than other magazines, it may be because the author is editor of that journal. He thinks not,
however. That journal specializes in information and coverage which have a special relevance
to the issues here discussed.

This article is amply flecked with footnotes, citing a wide range of formal materials. The
views expressed, the author believes, are verified by his personal experience as a disabled
individual far more than by all the footnote references put together.

The author wishes to acknowledge his indebtedness to the following persons for their
services as research assistants: Fay Stender, Robert Platt, Gary Shelton, Warren Deras, Barry.
McGough, Ken Cloke and Charles Miller; and to the Institute of Social Sciences of the
University of California, Berkeley and the National Federation of the Blind for making these
services available.

* A.B. 1934, M.A. 1935, LL.B. 1938, J.S.D. 1940, University of California, Berkeley;
S.J.D. 1947, Harvard University; D.Lit. 1956, Findley College; LL.D., 1964, Parsons College.
Member 1950-63, Chairman 1960-63, California State Social Welfare Board. Professor of
Political Science, University of California.

life and activities. In its 1962 survey of the characteristics of those receiving federal-state aid to the permanently and totally disabled, the Department of Health, Education and Welfare concluded that twenty-nine per cent are confined to the home because of physical or mental conditions, a conclusion apparently based on the responses of the recipients themselves rather than on medical evidence of physical capacity.[1] Of the roughly 85,000 aid-to-the-blind recipients, presumably the least active segment of the blind population, only 15.9 per cent are so confined.[2]

The actual physical limitations resulting from the disability more often than not play little role in determining whether the physically disabled are allowed to move about and be in public places. Rather, that judgment for the most part results from a variety of considerations related to public attitudes, attitudes which not infrequently are quite erroneous and misconceived. These include public imaginings about what the inherent physical limitations must be; public solicitude about the safety to be achieved by keeping the disabled out of harm's way; public feelings of protective care and custodial security; public doubts about why the disabled should want to be abroad anyway; and public aversion to the sight of them and the conspicuous reminder of their plight. For our purposes, there is no reason to judge these attitudes as to whether they do credit or discredit to the human head and heart. Our concern is with their existence and their consequences.

To what extent do the legal right, the public approval, and the physical capacity coincide? Does the law assure the physically disabled, to the degree that they are physically able to take advantage of it, the right to leave their institutions, asylums, and the houses of their relatives? Once they emerge, must they remain on the front porch, or do they have the right to be in public places, to go about in the streets, sidewalks, roads and highways, to ride upon trains, buses, airplanes, and taxi cabs, and to enter and to receive goods and services in hotels, restaurants, and other places of public accommodation? If so, under what conditions? What are the standards of care and conduct, of risk and liability, to which they are held and to which others are held with respect to them? Are the standards the same for them as for the able-bodied? Are there legal as well as physical adaptations; and to what extent and in what ways are these tied to concepts of custodialism or integrationism?

---

[1] U.S. Dep't of Health, Educ. & Welfare State Letter No. 747, Table 27, July 2, 1964.
[2] U.S. Dep't of Health, Educ. & Welfare, State Letter No. 746, Table 32, July 2, 1964. Roughly 40% travel with family members, friends, or paid guides; 13.3% with canes; 1% with dogs; 22.7% travel alone and without a cane. *Ibid.*

I

THE POLICY OF INTEGRATIONISM

A. Integrationism the Answer

It is the thesis of this paper that the answers to these questions to be returned by the courts, other agencies of government, and other public and private bodies should be controlled by a policy of integrationism—that is, a policy entitling the disabled to full participation in the life of the community and encouraging and enabling them to do so—that this policy is now, and for some time has been, the policy of the nation, declared as such by the legislatures of the states and by the Congress of the United States; and that the courts and others are thus bound to use that policy at least as guide, if not as mandate, in reaching their decisions, whatever may be their views as to its desirability or feasibility.

The policy of integrationism is implicitly and explicitly adopted by the nation and by all of the states in the set of laws, agencies and activities known as the Rehabilitation Program. Commenced in several of the states as long ago as 1918 and 1919,[3] and given national support by Congress in 1920,[4] that program has been enlarged in conception and increased in funding by successive legislative amendments,[5] by the impact of World War II, by pressures from organized groups of the disabled, and by a growing sense of its importance and potentialities.

At the head of the 1965 Rehabilitation Act Amendments stands this declaration: "The Secretary is authorized to make grants as provided in . . . this title for the purpose of assisting States in rehabilitating handicapped individuals so that they may prepare for and engage in gainful employment to the extent of their capabilities, thereby increasing not only their social and economic well-being but also the productive capacity of the Nation."[6] Specifically, the federal grants are to be made to these states to aid them in meeting the costs of rehabilitation services,[7] making innovations in those services,[8] expanding them by planning and initiating special services,[9] developing a comprehensive rehabilitation

---

[3] *E.g.* Gen. Acts of Mass. 1918, ch. 231, at 201-02; Cal. Stats. 1919, ch. 183, at 273-74; Laws of Ill. 1919, S.B. No. 449, at 534-37; Laws of Minn. 1919, ch. 365, at 389-90; New Stat. 1919, ch. 182, at 329; Laws of N.J. 1919, ch. 74, at 138-44. For a general history of vocational rehabilitation, see OBERMANN, A HISTORY OF VOCATIONAL REHABILITATION IN AMERICA (1965).

[4] 41 Stat. 735.

[5] 57 Stat. 374 (1943), 68 Stat. 652 (1954), 79 Stat. 1282 (1965).

[6] 79 Stat. 1282, 29 U.S.C. § 31 (Supp. I, 1965).

[7] 79 Stat. 1282, 1283, 29 U.S.C. §§ 31-33 (Supp. I, 1965).

[8] *Ibid.*

[9] 79 Stat. 1282, 1289, 29 U.S.C. § 34(a) (Supp. I, 1965).

plan in each of the states,[10] and for rehabilitation research,[11] demonstration,[12] and training projects.[13] The federal Vocational Rehabilitation Administration is authorized to conduct research and gather and disseminate information with respect to the abilities, aptitudes and capacities of handicapped individuals, development of their potentialities, and their utilization in gainful and suitable employment.[14] The 1965 Amendments also increase the appropriation for the earlier-created President's Committee on National Employ the Physically Handicapped Week[15] to carry out the function indicated by its title, to stimulate similar committees in the states, and to sponsor the annual event known as "Employ the Handicapped Week."[16] The purpose of the 1965 Amendments, said the House Committee on Education and Labor,[17] is "to provide the physically and mentally disabled persons of this Nation an improved and expanded program of services which will result in greater opportunities for them to more fully enter into the life of our country as active participating citizens."[18]

According to the 1964 annual report of the federal Vocational Rehabilitation Administration, in that year 119,000 disabled persons were rehabilitated through this program into productive activity and employment at an expenditure by states and nation of $133,000,000; 795 research and demonstration projects were conducted at a cost to the government of $15,179,000; and 447 teaching programs and 3,259 traineeships and research fellowships were granted at a cost of $16,-528,000.[19] Of the rehabilitated persons, over seventy per cent were unemployed when they entered the rehabilitation process, and most of the remainder had low earnings; about 16,000 were recipients of public assistance, and about 5,200 resided in tax-supported institutions.[20] With rehabilitation funds, scores of communities and organizations have been aided in the construction of comprehensive rehabilitation centers, special centers for specific disabilities, and clinics in connection with hospitals—all devoted to reducing and preventing dependency and thereby furthering the policy of integrationism.[21]

---

10 *Ibid.*
11 79 Stat. 1282, 1291, 29 U.S.C. § 37(a) (Supp. I, 1965).
12 *Ibid.*
13 *Ibid.*
14 *Ibid.*
15 Joint Resolution, 63 Stat. 409 (1949).
16 79 Stat. 1282, 1294, 29 U.S.C. § 38 (Supp. I, 1965).
17 H.R. REP. No. 432, 89 Cong., 1st Sess. (1965).
18 *Id.* at 2.
19 1964 U.S. DEP'T OF HEALTH, EDUC. & WELFARE ANN. REP. 327-29.
20 *Id.* at 329.
21 *Id.* at 330, 331.

All of the states receive grants-in-aid from the federal government under the vocational rehabilitation acts and necessarily commit themselves to the implicit and explicit policy of those acts of maximum integrationism for the disabled. In California, for example, an act coordinate to the national act has been in existence since 1919.[22] It currently vests state officials "with all necessary powers and authority to cooperate with the government of the United States"[23] and declares: "It is the public policy of the State of California to assist and encourage handicapped individuals to attain their maximum usefulness and self-sufficiency in order that they may make their full contribution to society."[24] Other state services and institutions such as the home-teacher-counselor service[25] and the Orientation Center for the Blind[26] espouse this policy with equal emphasis.

With this very same objective in mind, the public assistance titles of the Social Security Act have been amended: (1) to declare self-support one of the purposes of that act with respect to the blind and the permanently and totally disabled;[27] (2) to encourage the provision of services to help recipients attain or retain capability for self-support or self-care or likely to prevent or reduce dependency;[28] (3) to permit the blind and disabled to retain, without consequence to their aid eligibility or grant, other income and resources necessary to fulfill a plan for self-support;[29] (4) to exempt various amounts of earned income from consideration in determining the amount of the blind and disabled aid grants;[30] and, (5) to require that the states provide an incentive for employment giving consideration to any expenses reasonably attributable to the earning of income.[31] All of these amendments were designed to add new dimensions to the rehabilitative aspects of the public assistance programs.[32] From its beginning in 1954, the disability insurance program has contained a declaration that it is "the policy of the Congress that

---

22 Cal. Stats. 1919, ch. 183, CAL. EDUC. CODE, ch. 10.5.

23 CAL. EDUC. CODE § 6977.

24 CAL. EDUC. CODE § 6971.

25 CAL. EDUC. CODE § 6209.

26 CAL. EDUC. CODE § 6201-08.

27 70 Stat. 807, 849 (1956), 42 U.S.C. § 1201, 1351 (1964).

28 76 Stat. 172 (1962), 42 U.S.C. §§ 303, 1201, 1351 (1964).

29 49 Stat. 645 (1935), as amended, 42 U.S.C. §§ 1201-06 (1964), as amended by 79 Stat. 286, 42 U.S.C. §§ 1201-06 (Supp. I, 1965); 64 Stat. 555 (1950), as amended, 42 U.S.C. §§ 1351-55 (1964), as amended by 79 Stat. 286, 42 U.S.C. §§ 1202, 1382 (Supp. I, 1965); 76 Stat. 197 (1962), 42 U.S.C. §§ 1381-85 (1964).

30 79 Stat. 286, 418 (1965), 42 U.S.C. §§ 1201 (blind), 1351 (disabled) (Supp. I, 1965).

31 53 Stat. 1397 (1939), as amended, 42 U.S.C. § 1202 (Supp. I, 1965); 76 Stat. 172, 199 (1962), 42 U.S.C. § 1382 (1964).

32 S. REP. No. 1589, 87th Cong., 2d Sess. 2, 3, 17-18, 21 (1962); S. REP. No. 1856, 86th Cong., 2d Sess. 52 (1960); S. REP. No. 2133, 84th Cong., 2d Sess. 29 (1956).

disabled individuals applying for a determination of disability, and disabled individuals who are entitled to child's insurance benefits, shall be promptly referred" to the state rehabilitation agency, "for necessary vocational rehabilitation services, to the end that the maximum number of such individuals may be rehabilitated into productive activity."[33]

Rehabilitation reaches its point of culmination in remunerative employment and self-support through jobs in the common callings, industry, agriculture, independent businesses, and the professions. This congressional policy is implemented primarily through the obligation of rehabilitation counselors and other officials to assist disabled persons in finding such employment. Persuasion and demonstration are the accepted techniques. In some areas, however, there are and have been legal barriers to the employment of the disabled; elsewhere, private resistance has not yielded to persuasion and demonstration. Here the public commitment to the policy of integrationism has required legislative or judicial action. Legislative action has often been forthcoming, judicial action seldom. Congress has forbidden discrimination against the handicapped in the federal civil service.[34] A number of states, beginning with California in 1939,[35] have laid down a similar ban.[36] In addition some states have enacted special statutes prohibiting such discrimination with respect to teaching in the public schools,[37] social work,[38] physical therapy,[39] and the practice of chiropractic.[40]

Four other extensive legislative programs—the so-called architectural barriers statutes, the programs for the education of disabled children and youth in the regular public schools and colleges, the guide dog laws, and the white cane laws—are built upon an integrationist foundation and necessarily imply an integrationist objective. The architectural barriers statutes provide that public buildings and facilities hereafter constructed or remodeled shall be made "accessible to and functional for" the physically handicapped,[41] presupposing that the physically handicapped will make their way to such buildings and facilities and have occasion to be in them. The programs for the education of disabled students in the

---

33 68 Stat. 1052, 1082 (1954), 42 U.S.C. § 422 (1964).

34 22 Stat. 403 (1883), as amended, 5 U.S.C. § 633(2)9 (1964).

35 Cal. Stats., 1939, ch. 139, § 1 now contained in CAL. GOV'T CODE § 19701.

36 IDAHO CODE ANN. § 59-1025 (Supp. 1965); MO. STAT. ANN. § 36.180 (Supp. 1965); WIS. STAT. ANN. §§ 63.32, 63.33 (Supp. 1965); N.Y. CIV. SERV. LAW § 55 (Supp. 1965).

37 CAL. EDUC. CODE § 13125; MASS. GEN. LAWS ANN., ch. 71, § 38G (Supp. 1965); N.Y. EDUC. LAW § 3004; 24 PA. STAT. ANN. § 12-1209 (1959).

38 CAL. BUS. & PROF. CODE § 9030.

39 CAL. BUS. & PROF. CODE § 2631.

40 CAL. BUS. & PROF. CODE §§ 1000-8.1.

41 For a review of these statutes see text accompanying notes 102-31 *infra*.

public schools are supported by legislation opening the public schools to the blind and deaf, providing special tools, equipment, books, and supplementary teaching services, appropriating funds to enable blind students to hire sighted readers, and exempting scholarships from consideration in determining the amount of the blind aid grant.[42] Guide dog legislation strikes down restrictions on the use of the dog by the blind, and sometimes by other incapacitated persons, on common carriers, in public places and buildings, and in places of public accommodation.[43] The white cane laws are intended to make it safer for blind persons who travel with the aid of this device.[44] Congress in a Joint Resolution,[45] and the President in two Proclamations[46] setting aside a White Cane Safety Day, have emphasized that the cane is not only a useful travel aid but also a symbol of the independence and the social and economic integration of the blind.

From the foregoing, it is abundantly clear that integration of the disabled is the policy of the nation. This policy has been expressed by Congress and by the state legislatures, not once, but many times, and not merely with respect to a single, narrow area of human endeavor, but with respect to the whole broad range of social, economic, and educational activity backed up with numerous specially created agencies and instrumentalities of government, with affirmative assistance and negative prohibitions, and with vast expenditures of money amounting to hundreds of millions of dollars each year.

The basic question to which we seek an answer is this: How has this legislative policy of integrationism fared in the courts, and particularly in the law of torts? Has the law of torts been redirected and remolded according to the prescriptions of the policy? What redirecting and remolding do these prescriptions require?

B. Implications of Integrationism for the Law of Torts

According to the policy of integrationism, the disabled are not to be confined to their houses, asylums, and institutions—threatened, if they emerge, with not only social sanctions but legal sanctions as well, in the form of legal barriers, disadvantages, and inadequate protections. Nature may confine them to an iron lung, a bed, a wheel chair, straps, braces, or crutches, or to mouldering in health and idleness in chair-bound

---

[42] See, e.g., CAL. EDUC. CODE §§ 6821, 9354, 10651, 18060, 18060.2, 18102, 18103, 18106; CAL. WELFARE & INST'NS CODE §§ 12800, 18600-870.

[43] For a review of these statutes see text accompanying notes 69-102 infra.

[44] For a review of these statutes see text accompanying notes 360-411 infra.

[45] 78 Stat. 1003 (1964).

[46] 29 Fed. Reg. 14051 (1964); 30 Fed. Reg. 12931 (1965).

blindness. Mistaken public and family attitudes and the dependent law may not so confine them. Such confinement would in effect be a form of house arrest, which in the houses of the poor may not be noticeably different from outright imprisonment. Personal liberty, in this basic sense of the right not to be unjustly or causelessly confined, has been taken as a fundamental, natural, and social right in Chapter 39 of Magna Charta and the due process clauses of federal and state constitutions. If the disabled have the right to live in the world, they must have the right to make their way into it and therefore must be entitled to use the indispensable means of access, and to use them on terms that will make the original right effective. A right on such terms to the use of the streets, walks, roads and highways is a rock-bottom minimum. The right to gain access to the world in which they have a right to live must also include, as a part of the same rock-bottom minimum, the right to utilize the common thoroughfares by riding on common carriers. Upon descending from these, the disabled have a right of uninhibited and equal access to places of public accommodation to seek their ease, rest, sustenance, or recreation.[47]

II

THE RIGHT TO LIFE IN THE WORLD—THE ABLE-BODIED AND THE DISABLED

With respect to able-bodied groups and individuals, the basic rights of effective public access have been long established and newly vindi-

---

[47] Places of public accommodation are defined in some of the state acts in general terms; in others by specific listing. Utah's statute illustrates the former method: "All persons within the jurisdiction of this state are free and equal and are entitled to the full and equal accommodations, advantages, facilities, privileges, goods and services in all business establishments and in all places of public accommodation of every kind whatsoever . . . ." UTAH CODE ANN. § 13-7-1 to 13-7-4 (Supp. 1965); the ordinance of Rockville, Maryland, Ordinance 43-64, 1965, 9 Race Relations Rep. 1895 (1964-65), illustrates the exhaustive list method:

Section 13-2.02 . . . a. Any inn, hotel, motel or other establishment which provides lodging to transient or permanent guests;

b. Any restaurant, cafeteria, lunchroom, lunch-counter, soda fountain, or other facility principally engaged in selling food or beverages, whether alcoholic or not, for consumption on or off the premises, including, but not limited to, any such facility located on the premises of any retail establishment, or any gasoline station;

c. Any motion picture house, theater, concert hall, meeting hall, sports arena, stadium, recreation park, amusement park, picnic grounds, fair, circus, carnival, skating rink, swimming pool, tennis court, golf course, playground, bowling alley, gymnasium, shooting gallery, billiard or pool room, or any place used for common or public entertainment, exhibition, sports or recreational activity or other assembly;

d. Any retail store engaged in selling commodities of any type to the public;

e. Any service establishment serving the public, including but not limited to all hospitals, clinics, barber shops, beauty parlors, business or commercial services, repair services, or other services of any type offered to the public.

cated. They were safeguarded at the common law as to roads and streets, inns, other victualers, ferries, horseshoers, and carriers.[48] Three quarters of the states of the Union implicitly assume their general applicability while forbidding the discriminatory denial of them on the basis of race, creed, color, or ethnic origin.[49] Through the Civil Rights Act of 1875,[50] Congress sought to give them national protection. They were generally acknowledged, and, in part, expressly affirmed, by the United States Supreme Court in 1883 at the time the Civil Rights Act of 1875 was held not to be authorized by the fourteenth amendment.[51] In the debates upon the Civil Rights Act of 1964, these rights were loudly proclaimed.[52] The Senate Commerce Committee saw the denial of the right of equal access as an affront to human dignity,[53] the guarantee of the right as the "time honored means to freedom and liberty,"[54] and public accommodations themselves as existing "for the purpose of enhancing the individual freedom and liberty of human beings."[55] The House Judiciary Committee thought the right of equal access to public accommodations "so distinctive in nature that its denial constitutes a shocking refutation of a free society." "[T]he badge of citizenship . . . demands that establishments that do public business for private profit not discriminate . . . ."[56] President Lyndon Johnson in sponsoring enactment of the Civil Rights Act of 1964 declared "this is not merely an economic issue—or a social, political or international issue. It is a moral issue. . . . All members of the public should have equal access to facilities open to the public."[57] The United

---

48 Kisten v. Hildebrand, 48 Ky. (9 B. Mon.) 72 (1849) (dictum); Markham v. Brown, 8 N.H. 523 (1837); DeWolf v. Ford, 193 N.Y. 397, 86 N.E. 527 (1908); Hogan v. Nashville Interuban Ry., 131 Tenn. 244, 174 S.W. 1118 (1915) (dictum); Rex v. Irens, 7 C. & P. 213, 173 Eng. Rep. 94 (1835); Boss v. Lytton, 5 C. & P. 407, 24 E.C.L. 628 (K.B. 1832); Lane v. Cotton, 12 Mod. 472 (1701); White's case, 2 Dyer Rep. 158 (1558); De Termino Pascal, Keilway 50, Pl. 4 (1450); 3 BLACKSTONE, COMMENTARIES * 166; Hale, 1 HARG. LAW TRACTS 78 (1787).

49 See the list of thirty-two states supplied by Clark, J., in Heart of Atlanta Motel, Inc. v. United States, 379 U.S. 241, 259 (1964). For states not on Justice Clark's list see ARIZ. REV. STAT. ANN. §§ 41-1441, 41-1442 (Supp. 1965); Nev. Stat. 1965, ch. 332; UTAH CODE ANN. § 13-7-1 (Supp. 1965); Mo. ANN. STAT. § 314.010 (Supp. 1965).

5018 Stat. 335. That act forbade discrimination in "inns, public conveyances on land or water, theaters, or other places of public amusement . . . ."

51 The Civil Rights Cases, 109 U.S. 3, 24-25 (1883).

52 See, e.g., 110 CONG. REC. 12876 (1964) (Remarks of Senator Humphrey); id. at 1928 (Remarks of Rep. Joelson); id. at 1519-21 (Remarks of Rep. Celler); id. at 1538-40 (Remarks of Rep. Rodino); id. at 1540-42 (Remarks of Rep. Lindsay); id. at 1601-02 (Remarks of Rep. Mathias).

53 S. REP. No. 872, 88th Cong., 2d Sess. 18 (1964).

54 Id. at 22.

55 Ibid.

56 H.R. REP. No. 914, Part 2, 88th Cong., 1st Sess. 7 (1963).

57 State of the Union Message, 110 CONG. REC. 115 (1964).

States Supreme Court, in passing upon the constitutionality of that legislation, joined in the refrain that the denial of equal access was a social and moral wrong as well as a burden on commerce.[58] The act itself speaks of the entitlement of "all persons . . . to the full and equal enjoyment of the goods, services, facilities, privileges, advantages, and accommodations of any place of public accommodation."[59]

So the rights at stake are not merely procedural; nor are they comparative. They are substantive and belong to all men. Evocative reference to these, rather than a truly comparative conception, lies at the heart of the movement and legislation to gain access to public accommodations. The language is that of the equal protection clause of the fourteenth amendment and of the Civil Rights Act of 1866.[60] The vision, ardor, and simple principles are those of the Abolitionists.[61] The rhetoric is replete with moral reform, social justice, and natural rights. The sentences end with a prohibition against discrimination based on race, creed, color, ancestry, or national origin. But they begin with the declaration that "all persons are entitled to the full and equal enjoyment . . . of privileges . . . and accommodations."[62] The legislation in Arizona drives the point home.[63] An exception to the ban on discrimination based on the listed grounds, one would suppose, would permit discrimination on those grounds for particular purposes and presumably within narrow limits. Not so in Arizona. Assuming that a basic right of access is being guaranteed, the statute in that state provides that certain persons under certain conditions may be excluded. The excluded persons and conditions are unrelated to the forbidden grounds of discrimination. The persons are those who are of "lewd or immoral character," guilty of boisterous conduct or physical violence, under the influence of alcohol or narcotics, or who violate nondiscriminatory regulations of the place.[64] And not a blind man or a cripple is among them.

However much mingled with talk about burden on commerce, however much buttressed with common law precedents and founded in history, however much explicitly designed to strike down discriminations based on race, color, religion, national origin and sex, however much a product of the modern-day civil rights revolution, aimed principally at

---

[58] Heart of Atlanta Motel, Inc. v. United States, 379 U.S. 241, 257 (1964).

[59] 78 Stat. 241, 243, 42 U.S.C. § 2000(a) (1964).

[60] 14 Stat. 27.

[61] See TENBROEK, EQUAL UNDER LAW (1965); Graham, *The Early Anti-Slavery Backgrounds of the Fourteenth Amendment*, 1950 WIS. L. REV. 479, 610.

[62] *E.g.*, Civil Rights Act of 1964, 78 Stat. 241, 243, 42 U.S.C. § 2000(a) (1964); Nev. Stat. 1965, ch. 332, § 4; UTAH CODE ANN. §§ 13-7-1 to 13-7-3 (Supp. 1965).

[63] ARIZ. REV. STAT. ANN., ch. 27 (Supp. 1965).

[64] ARIZ. REV. STAT. ANN. § 41-1442(C) (Supp. 1965).

securing equal rights for colored persons, the statutes of the states in their present form, the Civil Rights Act of 1964, the congressional debates and proceedings upon it, and the judicial opinions validating its constitutionality—all, implicitly and explicitly, necessarily and unavoidably, are built upon a recognition of the absolute importance to the nation, community and individual, of persons having, holding, and enjoying rights of access to the community and to the public, quasi-public, and private instrumentalities necessary to make those rights effective.

Are humans to be denied human rights? Are persons after all not to be persons if they are physically disabled? Are members of the community to be robbed of their rights to live in the community, their certificates cancelled upon development or discovery of disability? These rhetorical questions, the hallmarks of crusade and reform throughout American history, have in our generation become the plea of the disabled as well. As with the black man, so with the blind. As with the Puerto Rican, so with the post-polio. As with the Indian, so with the indigent disabled.

Without legal redress in many areas, and with the frequency of arbitrary action, disabled persons have been turned away from trains, buses, and other common carriers, from lodgings of various sorts, from the rental of public and private housing, from bars, restaurants and places of public amusement, from banks to rent a safety deposit box, from other kinds of banks to give a pint of blood, and from gambling casinos in Nevada,[65] declared by statute as well as by common experience to be places in which the public is accommodated.[66]

In his widely used, much-quoted and, I think, justly celebrated text on the Law of Torts, Dean Prosser announces a remarkable proposition: "The man who is blind, or deaf, or lame, or is otherwise physically disabled, is entitled to live in the world. . . ."[67] Taken at its most literal level, surely this proposition proclaims a platitude. Obviously, we do not kill off our disabled, as the Greeks and Romans did their deformed babies. There is no campaign afoot in the land to extend euthanasia proposals from the incurably ill and the sufferers of unbearable pain to the halt, the lame, and the blind.

<hr>

[65] Nev. Stat. 1965, ch. 332, § 1.

[66] tenBroek, *Cross of Blindness*, 23 VITAL SPEECHES 732 (1957).

[67] PROSSER, TORTS § 32, at 155 (3d ed. 1964). Among the "otherwise physically disabled," Dean Prosser lists: bone condition, Wray v. Fairfield Amusement Co., 126 Conn. 221, 10 A.2d 600 (1940); crippled, lacking coordination on crutches, Goodman v. Norwalk Jewish Center, Inc., 145 Conn. 146, 139 A.2d 812 (1958); short stature, Mahan v. State, Use of Carr, 172 Md. 373, 191 Atl. 575 (1937); lame, Bianchetti v. Luce, 222 Mo. App. 282, 2 S.W.2d 129 (1927); club foot, Texas & N.O.R.R. v. Bean, 55 Tex. Civ. App. 341, 119 S.W. 328 (1909).

Read less literally, the right to live in the world is something more than the right to remain in it. Now Dean Prosser's proposition assumes something of the significance of one of Jefferson's self-evident truths—the inalienable right to life. In fact, Dean Prosser updates Thomas Jefferson: He moves from a noun to a verb—from the right to life to the right to live—and specifies, somewhat redundantly, that this shall be in the world. In the vernacular of the day, Dean Prosser is talking about the right "to live a little."

Taken in its broader sense, Dean Prosser's proposition is amply capable of accommodating the most enlightened social policy for the physically disabled in the law of torts and elsewhere. Properly understood, that proposition might be taken as a definitive statement of the goals, as a comprehensive formulation of the policy of integrationism.

Dean Prosser's grand pronouncement, however, while purporting to be drawn from the case law, and while seeming to express for the law of torts the legislatively established policy of the integration of the disabled, is in no sense an accurate summary of the law of torts as that law stands today. The judges either qualify or ignore Dean Prosser's pronouncement and the integrationist policy. In some areas, the pronouncement and the policy are completely rejected; in others, they are given only halting and partial credence; and in none are they fully and positively implemented by the courts. Dean Prosser himself immediately emasculates his proposition.[68] He applies it only to a narrow realm of street accidents. And even there, while freeing the disabled of negligence per se for being where they are, he hobbles them with the views of the able-bodied as to what their reasonable conduct should be. In these areas, the sum total of the law's beneficence to the disabled seeking a full-fledged right to live in the world can be easily and briefly summarized: The courts, prodding the tardy genius of the common law, have extended a variant of the reasonable man concept to those who injure the disabled on the streets, in traffic, and on common carriers. This constitutes a meager and inadequate accomplishment in the light of the integrationist purpose and the legislative declaration of policy. Unawareness of the policy and its applicability in various situations, rather than considered judgment, as to its social importance, practicability, or relevance in the law of torts, seems to be the principal reason for the widespread disregard of the policy.

A. The Rights of Dogs and the Rights of Men

The disabled are neither specifically included nor specifically excluded from the general public accommodations legislation. That legislation

---

[68] PROSSER, op. cit. supra note 67.

was extended at the time of passage to go beyond forbidding discrimination on a basis of race, color, and national origin, to cover discrimination based on religion[69] and, in employment, on sex.[70] During its passage through Congress, Congressman Dowdy offered an amendment to add age to the proscribed bases of discrimination.[71] The amendment was defeated by a vote of 123 to 94 after some members of the House had stated that they agreed with the substance and content of the motion, but thought the procedures set out in the act were not suited to the object sought.[72] The final act did, however, require that the Secretary of Labor make a "full and complete study of the factors which might tend to result in discrimination in employment because of age and of the consequences of such discrimination on the economy and individuals affected."[73] A proposal by the National Federation of the Blind to extend the protection of the act to the disabled did not reach the stage of formal introduction. The Civil Rights Act of 1964 does extend to "all persons" and does imply substantive rights. It is therefore possible, if not probable, that when we move away from the moment and the immediate cause of the legislation, the judges will bring the disabled within its shelter.

While state and national general public accommodations legislation has not expressly covered the disabled, that legislation has served as the model and source of specific public accommodations legislation for the blind in twenty-five states.[74] This has come about in a strange way. The blind have been led by the guide dogs not only into places of public accommodation but into the right to be there. It is not inaccurate to say that the basic right of all men to join their communities and to gain access to them by the normal means, including the use of public accommodations, has been gained by the blind in these twenty-five states as an

---

[69] Civil Rights Act of 1964, 78 Stat. 241, 243, 42 U.S.C. § 2000(a) (1964).

[70] 78 Stat. 241, 255, 42 U.S.C. § 2000(e)-2 (1964).

[71] 110 Cong. Rec. 2596 (1964).

[72] 110 Cong. Rec. 2599 (1964).

[73] 78 Stat. 241, 265, 42 U.S.C. § 2000(e)-14 (1964).

[74] Ark. Stat. §§ 78-211 to 78-213 (1957); Cal. Pen. Code § 643.5; Colo. Rev. Stat. Ann. § 115-12-9 (1953); Conn. Gen. Stat. Rev. § 22-346a (1958); Fla. Stat. § 413.08 (1963); Ga. Code Ann. §§ 79-601, 79-9901 (1964); Hawaii Rev. Laws §§ 109-20, 109-21 (1957); Idaho Code Ann. § 39-1604 (Supp. 1965); Ill. Ann. Stat. ch. 111 2/3, § 40a (Smith-Hurd 1954); Ind. Ann. Stat. §§ 16-212, 16-213 (Supp. 1964); Iowa Code Ann. §§ 351.30-351.32 (Supp. 1964); La. Rev. Stat. Ann. §§ 51, 52 (Supp. 1964); Maine Rev. Stat. Ann § 54 (Supp. 1963); Mass. Gen. Ann. Laws § 98A (1956); Mich. Stat. Ann. § 28.770(7/8) (1954); Mo. Ann. Stat. § 209.140 (1962); N.J. Stat. Ann. §§ 48:3-33, 48:3-34 (1940); N.M. Stat. Ann. § 47-1-7 (1953); N.Y. Pen. Law § 518; R.I. Gen. Laws Ann. §§ 39-2-16 to 39-2-17 (1956); Tenn. Code Ann. § 62-717 (Supp. 1965); Tex. Rev. Civ. Stat. art. 4596a, 889a (1948); Va. Code Ann. § 35-42.1 (Supp. 1964); Wash. Rev. Code §§ 49.60.216, 81.28.140 (1962); W. Va. Code Ann. §§ 2568(1), 2569 (1961).

incident to their reliance on the dogs and the need to have them exempted from restrictions with regard to pets. Whether the man takes the dog or the dog takes the man may be a question of some importance. There is quite a difference between saying, as California does, for example, that "any blind person"[75] is entitled to have the dog with him or, no "blind person . . . shall be denied admittance" though he has a guide dog with him;[76] and saying, on the other hand, as New Mexico does, that "no person shall debar a guide dog . . . in any place of public accommodation . . . provided such dog is safely muzzled and is under the control of the blind person."[77]

Whatever the relative roles of man and dog, the almost universal ban against dogs and other pets in places of public accommodation—a ban no doubt based on good reasons of public health, safety and convenience —had to be lifted in favor of the guide dog and its master if its services were to be available to him in getting about.[78] Since the exclusionary rule against pets is founded not only in practice and regulation but also in legislation, remedy had to be sought from the legislatures.[79] Organizations of the blind, individual guide dog owners, and the management of guide dog schools set to work, jointly and severally, to secure the statutes—which now exist in half the states of the Union—guaranteeing the right of the man to take the dog and the dog to take the man into public places and places of public accommodation.[80] In a very few statutes, such as that of Idaho, the right has been effected by simply making an exception to the prohibition that "no dog, cat or other animal shall be permitted in any eating place . . . ."[81] In most states, however, reliance

---

[75] CAL. PEN. CODE § 643.5(a).

[76] CAL. PEN. CODE § 643.5(b).

[77] N.M. STAT. ANN. § 47-1-7 (1954).

[78] For recent examples of the exclusion of a blind person and guide dog from a restaurant see Guide Dog v. Restaurant, N.Y. Times, Nov. 3, 1964, reprinted in Braille Monitor, Jan. 1965, p. 22; from public housing project see, New Orleans Housing Project Lifts Guide Dog Ban, Braille Monitor, Sept. 1965, p. 38.

[79] The only case reported concerning the guide dog statutes arose in Texas in 1945 (Boyd v. State, 148 Tex. Crim. 171, 186 S.W.2d 257) where the proprietor of a restaurant denied admission to a blind woman accompanied by a "seeing-eye" dog because of the dog. The proprietor was convicted of violating the Texas statute which relates primarily to carriers, but the conviction was reversed on appeal. The basis of the appellate court's action was the failure of the legislature to include facilities other than conveyances in the caption of the act as required by article III, § 35 of the Texas Constitution. The court, therefore, held § 2 of bill unconstitutional, but found the remaining sections severable.

[80] For general discussions of the use of guide dogs by blind persons, the training of dogs and masters, and the establishment of guide dog schools, see CHEVIGNY, MY EYES HAVE A COLD NOSE (1946); EUSTIS, THE SEEING EYE (1927); HARTWELL, DOGS AGAINST DARKNESS (1934); ZAHL, BLINDNESS, ch. 24 (1950).

[81] IDAHO CODE ANN. § 39-1604 (Supp. 1965). In 1965 Idaho adopted a guide dog statute based on that of California. IDAHO CODE ANN. § 18-5812-A (Supp. 1965).

is placed on the formulations in anti-race discrimination legislation which lie ready to guide draftsmanship and statutory classification and which suggest themselves as highly relevant and appropriate in the circumstances. The Massachusetts legislation follows the model more closely than many states, but it may be used to illustrate the point.

In Massachusetts, a trunk statute was adopted at the close of the Civil War in 1865.[82] At that time, color and race discrimination in "public places of amusement, public conveyance or public meeting"[83] was made an offense punishable by fine. The original provision has since been amended a number of times,[84] most recently and basically in 1950, by adding religion to the list of forbidden grounds of discrimination and by adding two sentences constituting the heart of the modern civil rights public accommodations formulation: "All persons shall have the right to the full and equal accommodations, advantages, facilities and privileges of any place of public accommodation, resort or amusement, subject only to the conditions and limitations established by law and applicable alike to all persons. This right is recognized and declared to be a civil right."[85] Before 1950 three other subsections had been added: one in 1941 forbidding race, color or nationality discriminations in employment on public works and in dispensing public welfare;[86] the second in 1943, making punishable as group libel publications intended maliciously to promote hatred of any group because of its race or color;[87] and the third, in 1938, declaring, under penal sanctions, "any blind person accompanied" by a guide dog, "properly and safely muzzled," to be "entitled to any and all accommodations, advantages, facilities and privileges of all public conveyances, public amusement and places of . . . public accommodations . . . to which persons not accompanied by dogs are entitled, subject only to the conditions and limitations applicable to all persons not accompanied by dogs . . . ."[88] Extra fare for the dog is not to be charged on public conveyances.

Again, the formulation employed in Georgia,[89] Indiana,[90] and Louisiana[91] is substantially the same: "Any person who by reason of loss or

---

[82] Mass. Acts & Resolves 1865, ch. 277, at 650.

[83] *Ibid.*

[84] Mass. Acts & Resolves 1866, ch. 252, at 242; Mass. Acts & Resolves 1885, ch. 316, at 774; Mass. Acts & Resolves 1893, ch. 43, at 1320; Mass. Acts & Resolves 1895, ch. 461, at 519.

[85] Mass. Gen. Laws Ann. ch. 272, § 98 (1959).

[86] Mass. Gen. Laws Ann. ch. 272, § 98B (1959).

[87] Mass. Gen. Laws Ann. ch. 272, § 98C (1959).

[88] Mass. Gen. Laws Ann. ch. 272, § 98A (1959).

[89] Ga. Code Ann. § 601 (Supp. 1964).

[90] Ind. Ann. Stat. § 16-212 (Supp. 1964).

[91] La. Rev. Stat. Ann. § 21:52 (Supp. 1964).

impairment of eyesight is accompanied by a dog . . . used as a leader or guide . . . is entitled to full and equal accommodations, advantages, facilities, and privileges of all public conveyances, hotels, lodging places, places of public accommodation, amusement or resort, and other places to which the general public is invited, and shall be entitled to be accompanied by such dog . . . subject only to the conditions and limitations applicable to persons not so accompanied . . . ."

Variations in detail in these statutes are numerous. They relate to: the mode of defining the blind persons or others entitled to the benefits of the act;[92] the public accommodations to which the act applies;[93] the presence or absence of restrictions on charging for the dog;[94] training, harnessing, leashing and muzzling the dog;[95] credentialing the master

---

[92] All the statutes require that the dog user be blind or partially blind, with the exception of Idaho, which permits guide dog trainers the same access to eating establishments as is afforded the blind user.

[93] Seventeen jurisdictions provide the dog-led blind with access to places of public accommodation in general and also to public conveyances (Arkansas, California, Connecticut, Georgia, Indiana, Iowa, Louisiana, Maine, Massachusetts, Michigan, Missouri, New Mexico, New York (except movie theatres), Rhode Island (except railroad cars other than chair cars on passenger trains), Tennessee, Texas, Washington). Five more provide access to public conveyances (Colorado, Hawaii, Illinois, New Jersey, West Virginia), two provide access only to eating places (Idaho, Virginia), and the remaining state, access to hotels and eating places (Florida). See note 74 *supra* for the applicable statutes.

[94] Sixteen jurisdictions have provisions prohibiting the exacting of additional charges because of the access afforded the guide dog (Arkansas, California, Connecticut, Georgia, Hawaii, Indiana, Iowa, Louisiana, Maine, Massachusetts, Missouri, New York, Rhode Island, Texas, Washington, West Virginia). In six states the prohibition is expressly applicable to both public places and public conveyances (Arkansas, California, Connecticut, Iowa, Missouri, Texas), expressly applicable to common carriers only in five states (Maine, Massachusetts, Rhode Island, Washington, West Virginia), impliedly applicable to public places and public conveyances in four states (Georgia, Indiana, Louisiana, New York), and impliedly applicable to carriers only in one state, Hawaii. See note 74 *supra* for the applicable statutes.

[95] Louisiana requires that both the dog and the master be trained at a "qualified dog guide school," such training to enable the master to use the particular dog as a guide. None of the states extends the statutory right to the "otherwise incapacitated" as is done in some white cane laws. See note 378 *infra* and accompanying text. Eleven states (Colorado, Connecticut, Georgia, Illinois, Maine, Massachusetts, Missouri, New Mexico, Texas, Washington, West Virginia) require that the dog guide be muzzled. The requirement is mandatory except in Maine, where the management of the facility to be charged may or may not so demand.

Seven states require harnessing (Arkansas, Connecticut, Iowa, Michigan, Tennessee, Washington, West Virginia). The language used in six of these is typified by the Arkansas provision which provides the right of access "when said dog guide is properly harnessed . . . ." The seventh state, Washington, requires harnessing only of "guide dogs" which are entitled to enter public places, as distinguished from "seeing eye" dogs, which can board public conveyances. Only one state, Idaho, provides that the dog need be leashed. A harness would seem to satisfy that requirement. Six states require expressly that the guide dog be under the control of the master (Colorado, Connecticut, Illinois, New Jersey, Rhode Island, Virginia). See note 74 *supra* for the applicable statutes.

and the dog;[96] custody of the dog in public places and conveyances;[97] exceptions to the operations of the act;[98] whether the benefit of the act is expressed in terms of a positively conferred right on the master and the dog or a negative limitation on the operators of places of public accommodation;[99] and the penalies which may be imposed for breach of

[96] Six states require the dog be "specially trained" (California, Idaho, Louisiana, Maine, Texas, Washington) of which two also require the user have credentials for the dog (Louisiana, Maine). Six states require the dog guide be properly credentialed (Connecticut, Louisiana, Maine, Michigan, Tennessee, West Virginia). Michigan requires the certifying school be approved by the Veteran's Administration and West Virginia requires the dog be identified by a certificate issued by "The Seeing Eye." Maine is silent as to the origin of the credential which may be required under the statute.

Connecticut and Maine require the credential be presented upon request of the agency to be charged under the statute. Louisiana provides the operation of the statute is inapplicable unless evidence of training is "furnished"—to whom or when is not indicated. Michigan and Tennessee require the blind person must first present for inspection the credentials on the dog, and West Virginia requires only that the blind person accompanied by a dog guide carry the prescribed certificate of identification, with no language requiring presentment upon demand or otherwise. See note 74 *supra* for the applicable statutes.

[97] Six states make express provisions regarding the custody of the admitted dog (Colorado, Connecticut, Illinois, New Jersey, Rhode Island, Virginia). Five of these grant the right of immediate custody to the master; the sixth, New Jersey, provides the master is to have custody, but subject to the rules and regulations prescribed by the Board of Public Utility. Texas and Washington also provide expressly for the custody of the dog aboard public conveyances; the former providing the carrier shall designate where the dog is to ride and the latter granting custody to the master. These two states have separate provisions for public places and common carriers, the custody in public places is impliedly granted the blind master.

Nineteen jurisdictions, including Texas and Washington, impliedly grant custody of the dog to the blind person while in places of public accommodation and/or public conveyances, with the exceptions as noted above (Arkansas, California, Florida, Georgia, Hawaii, Idaho, Indiana, Iowa, Louisiana, Maine, Massachusetts, Michigan, Missouri, New Mexico, New York, Tennessee, Texas, Washington, West Virginia). The implication arises from the language of the statute permitting access to the "accompanying" dog, or that allowing the user to "take" the dog with him. The implication is strongest in the three states (Georgia, Indiana, Louisiana), which prohibit the admitted dog from occupying a seat in public conveyances. See note 74 *supra* for the applicable statutes.

[98] Two states provide exceptions to the operation of their statutes where the admission of the dog guide would involve "danger." Hawaii provides the exception where the presence of the dog would endanger "other passengers"; New York provides the exception where such access would "tend to create a dangerous situation. . . ." The Hawaiian exception, while lacking specificity as to what danger is to be apprehended, does limit the range of the danger, while New York's exception is not so limited, the escape provision appears too vague to lend certainty to the statute. New York also excepts motion picture theatres from the scope of the statute. Rhode Island's statute excepts all railroad passenger cars other than chair cars, a loss of substantial significance. Hawaii also excepts the statute's applicability where the dog is unclean. While the statute does not specify the standard of uncleanliness essential to the exception, the exception does appear a reasonable one. See note 74 *supra* for the applicable statutes.

[99] Seventeen states confer a positive right (Arkansas, California, Connecticut, Florida, Georgia, Idaho, Indiana, Iowa, Louisiana, Maine, Massachusetts, Missouri, New Jersey, Rhode Island, Texas, Virginia, Washington); eleven impose a negative duty on the manage-

the act.[100]

Among all these variations in detail, however, the substantial formulation is generally the same: It is the formulation of the civil rights acts. The strengths and weaknesses of the formulation are the same in the one case as in the other for the meaning is the same. The terms are those of discrimination, that is, of classification and comparison. If other people similarly situated are entitled to the right, then the disabled are; and so are persons of minority race, color, and religion. The right may be denied to all if this is done on equal terms; that is, if the conditions and limitations are applicable to all, or, in other words, are made regardless of race, color, religion, disability, or being guided by a dog.

But the purpose of the legislation is a purpose with respect to which all people are similarly situated. The right of access to public accommodations and common carriers is a civil right. It is a basic right indispensable to participation in the community, a substantive right to which all are fully and equally entitled. The basic contradictions and reconciliations of procedural and comparative phraseology, on the one hand, and the fundamental substantive rights, on the other hand, implicit and explicit in the fourteenth amendment are here repeated.[101] Thus, while the guide dog statutes focus on the immediate problem of gaining access by persons with guide dogs and their right of access is declared to be the same as for those without dogs, and while, accordingly, no particular mention is made of the right of access of those without dogs, yet their right is presupposed, implicit and assumed and hence is incorporated within the benefits conferred by the act. The right of all blind persons,

ment of the facility (California, Colorado, Hawaii, Illinois, Michigan, New Mexico, New York, Rhode Island, Tennessee, Texas, Washington); and West Virginia imposes a positive duty on the management of the facility to give access to the dog-led blind. California and Rhode Island expressly confer a positive right on the dog-user and, in the same section, impose the correlative negative duty on the facility in express terms; Texas and Washington each have separate statutes for each of the two types of facilities. The Texas provisions are a conferral of a positive right on the blind with respect to public conveyances and an imposition of a negative duty on the management of the facility respecting public places. The Washington statutes are exactly opposite, the positive right relating to public places and the negative duty to public conveyances. See note 74 *supra* for the applicable statutes.

100 Nineteen states provide a penalty for the violation of the statutes (Arkansas, California, Connecticut, Florida, Georgia, Hawaii, Indiana, Iowa, Louisiana, Maine, Massachusetts, Michigan, Missouri, New Mexico, New York, Rhode Island, Tennessee, Texas, West Virginia) all of which are misdemeanors. It should be noted that the inclusion of a penalty provision does not necessarily relate to all provisions of the statute; hence Rhode Island's penalty provision is applicable only to the denial of the blind's right to be accompanied by the dog guide aboard public conveyances and elevators. See note 74 *supra* for the applicable statutes.

101 See HARRIS, THE QUEST FOR EQUALITY (1960); TENBROEK, EQUAL UNDER LAW (1965).

and more generally, of all disabled persons, to the use of public accommodations is therefore consequentially safeguarded by these acts.

Moreover, the existence of these acts in twenty-five states, with their explicit avowals and implicit assumptions, supported by the right of people generally to the use of public accommodations and common carriers, might reasonably be taken as a sufficient declaration of public policy and fundamental right to found judicial decisions in the other states vindicating the right of the disabled to full and equal access to these necessary instrumentalities of community life. Ultimately, indeed, such may be seen as a mandate of the equal protection clause of the fourteenth amendment.

B. Architectural Barriers

Guide dog legislation is intended to safeguard rights of access to and use of common carriers and public accommodations. The legislation seeks to accomplish the purpose by declaring the rights, in form at least on a comparative basis, and prohibiting the discriminatory denial or withdrawal of them. The legislation deals only with one group of the disabled: the blind, a group otherwise able-bodied and perfectly capable of mounting stairs and passing through narrow doorways once they find them. The formula employed in the guide dog legislation is inadequate on its face to deal with the general problem of architectural barriers. Architectural barriers are defined by the American Standards Association as features of "the common design and construction of buildings and facilities [that] cause problems for the physically handicapped that lessen the social and economic gains now evident in the rehabilitation of these individuals . . . [that] make it very difficult to project the physically handicapped into normal situations of education, recreation, and employment."[102] Simply declaring that the disabled, too, have rights of access and use and forbidding building operators to deny them would do little for the wheel chair-bound paraplegic physically denied access to and use of flights of stairs and narrow doorways. Moreover, prohibiting the installation of such barriers would not do the trick. A more constructive and affirmative approach is required. Buildings and facilities must be

---

[102] AMERICAN STANDARDS ASS'N, AMERICAN STANDARD SPECIFICATIONS FOR MAKING BUILDINGS AND FACILITIES ACCESSIBLE TO, AND USABLE BY, THE PHYSICALLY HANDICAPPED 3 (1961). For some of the growing literature on architectural barriers, see GOLDSMITH, DESIGNING FOR THE DISABLED (1963); id. at 226-36 (Bibliography); Nugent, Design of Buildings to Permit their Use by the Physically Handicapped, New Building Research, Fall, 1960, p. 51; Caniff, Architectural Barriers: A Personal Problem, 108 CONG. REC., app. 838 (1962).

erected according to a design taking account of the disabled and making buildings and facilities accessible to them and functional for them.

Specifications intended to do this were prepared by the American Standards Association in 1961.[103] They were developed in consultation with a large number of concerned government officials, private agencies with programs for the disabled, groups of the disabled themselves, and relevant business and professional associations. Principal sponsorship, however, came from the National Society for Crippled Children and Adults and the President's Committee on National Employ the Physically Handicapped Week. The specifications include: wide and suitably located parking places for the cars of the disabled;[104] at least one ground level or ramped entrance;[105] wide doors that can be opened with a single effort[106] and with enough neighboring level floor space for wheel chair maneuver;[107] single level stories or ramp-connected levels;[108] toilets, mirrors, towel dispensers,[109] drinking fountains,[110] and public telephones[111] of the proper height to be reached from wheel chairs; identifying features enabling the blind to find particular rooms;[112] auditory as well as visual signals;[113] open manholes, access panels, and excavations in the buildings and on the grounds barricaded at least eight feet from the hazard and warning devices used;[114] and, a prohibition on low-hanging or protruding door closers, signs, and fixtures.[115] The specifications are intended not only for public buildings and facilities, but for any buildings and facilities generally used by the public. They are applicable in remodeling present structures as well as in new construction.

While the specifications would seem a necessity for the disabled confined to wheel chairs and only less so for those on crutches and braces, they are also of importance for the estimated five million Americans with mobility impairments of other sorts. The Standards list among the direct beneficiaries those with "non-ambulatory disabilities," "semi-ambulatory disabilities," "sight disabilities," "hearing disabilities," "dis-

---

103 AMERICAN STANDARDS ASS'N, op. cit. supra note 102.
104 Id. at § 4.3.2.
105 Id. at § 4.1.
106 Id. at § 5.3.1.
107 Id. at § 5.3.2.
108 Id. at § 5.5.2.
109 Id. at § 5.6.
110 Id. at § 5.7.
111 Id. at § 5.8.
112 Id. at § 5.11.
113 Id. at § 5.12.
114 Id. at § 5.13.2.
115 Id. at §§ 5.13.3, 5.13.4.

abiltities of incoordination,"[116] and "those manifestations of the aging processes that significantly reduce mobility, flexibility, coordination, and perceptiveness. . . ."[117] The different and sometimes contradictory needs of these groups illustrate the fallacy of treating the disabled as a single homogeneous class for all purposes. Although all the disabled are helped by eliminating stairs, the crippled are helped far more than the deaf. Manholes, access panels and excavations are of greatest peril for the blind but are also hazardous for all. The deaf require visual signals which are of no use for the blind and vice versa for auditory signals. The paraplegic must have special toilet and washroom facilities and arrangements, while the blind couldn't care less where the mirror is located. For the persons in the wheel chair and the mobile cripple, a site is best developed which is level and without curbs and other abrupt changes. For the blind, large, level, open plazas and other areas around and among buildings, without discernible landmarks such as curbs and well-defined walks, can be traversed only by dead reckoning.

To secure acceptance of the specifications by architects, builders, owners, and operators, the National Society for Crippled Children and Adults and the President's Committee on National Employ the Physically Handicapped Week established steering committees in the various states. They, together with others, put on an active, national campaign. As a result, remarkable progress has been made in five years. Architectural barriers legislation has been adopted in twenty-one states.[118] A national commission on architectural barriers to the rehabilitation of the handicapped was established in 1965 in the Department of Health, Education, and Welfare to focus national attention on the problem and to advise, consult, study, and demonstrate.[119] The relevant professions, industries, unions, and other interests have been made acquainted with the

---

116 *Id.* at § 2.

117 *Id.* at § 2.6.

118 "Penn. Becomes 21st State To Pass Architectural Barriers Legislation." Performance, Dec. 1965, p. 3. Available statutes are: Calif. Assembly Concurrent Resolution No. 19 (1965 Reg. Sess.); Conn. Public Act No. 216 (Feb. 1965, Spec. Sess.); FLA. STAT. ch. 255.01, as amended by S.B. No. 109, ch. 65-493 (July 1, 1965); ILL. REV. STAT. ANN. ch. 111, § 11 (Smith-Hurd, Supp. 1965); IOWA CODE ANN. (Sen. File 352 Supp. 1965); MASS. GEN. LAWS ANN., ch. 149, § 44c (Supp. 1965); MINN. STAT. ANN. §§ 73.57-53.61 (Supp. 1965); MONT. REV. CODE ANN. §§ 69-3701 to 69-3719 (Supp. 1965); Neb. Sess. Laws 1965, ch. 430; N.H. REV. STAT. ANN. §§ 155.8-a, 8-b (Supp. 1965); N. MEX. STAT. ch. 67, § 16-18 (Supp. 1965); N.D. CODE ch. 48-02-18 (Supp. 1965); OHIO REV. CODE ANN. § 3781.111 (Supp. 1965); OKLA. STAT. ANN. tit. 61, § 11 (Supp. 1965); PA. STAT. ANN. §§ 1455.1-1455.4 (Supp. 1965); R.I. GEN. LAWS ANN. § 37-8-15 (Supp. 1965); S.C. CODE §§ 1-481 to 1-490 (Supp. 1965); WIS. STAT. ANN. §§ 101.305, 101.306 (Supp. 1965).

119 79 Stat. 1282, 29 U.S.C. §§ 31-33 (Supp. I, 1965).

nature of the problem of architectural barriers and the relatively simple and inexpensive design features required to reduce it.[120] The levels of attack have thus been private persuasion, official sponsorship, and, with respect to public buildings and facilities, legislative mandate.

The central feature of the state statutes is reliance on the work of the American Standards Association. Indeed, the principal divergence among the statutes is the extent to which they copy the specifications outright or incorporate them by reference. A fairly typical statute—and, having been passed in 1962, one of the earlier ones—is that of Massachusetts, which provides that public buildings "shall conform with the booklet entitled 'American standard specifications for making buildings and facilities accessible to, and usable by, the physically handicapped' approved by the American Standards Association, Incorporated on October thirty-first, nineteen hundred and sixty one."[121] Montana[122] and South Carolina,[123] on the other hand, practically enacted the booklet as it stood, even to the point of including explanatory footnotes. The state statutes differ among themselves as to the types of buildings and facilities covered, permissible exceptions, methods and agencies of enforcement, and a requirement for public hearing when administrative agencies are delegated authority to establish standards by way of regulations. Most of the statutes accept a variant of the formula used in Connecticut: "[A]ll buildings and facilities constructed, remodeled or repaired by the state or its agents or by any political subdivision of the state or its agents when state funds or state interest is involved."[124] Wisconsin applies its requirements to "any public buildings, including state-owned buildings or public housing projects . . . and mercantile buildings. . . ."[125] The excepting clause provided in the American Standard Specifications— "cases of practical difficulty, unnecessary hardship, or extreme differ-

---

[120] An example of voluntary compliance by those in charge of public buildings is that of the University of California which has approved a plan for all of its campuses to make them accessible to the disabled and usable by them. See, e.g., UNIVERSITY OF CALIFORNIA, BERKELEY, ARCHITECTS AND ENGINEERS MANUAL § 8.01, at 5-6 (1960); University of California, Building Design Considerations for Physically Handicapped Students, May 24, 1963. Indeed, with respect to at least one group of the disabled, the blind, there have been special facilities for at least the past twenty-five years on the Berkeley and Los Angeles campuses.

[121] Mass Acts & Resolves 1962, ch. 662.

[122] MONT. REV. CODE ANN. §§ 69-3701 to 69-3719 (Supp. 1965).

[123] S.C. CODE §§ 1-481 to 1-490 (Supp. 1965).

[124] Conn. Public Act No. 216 (Feb. 1965, Spec. Sess.).

[125] WIS. STAT. ANN. § 101.305 (Supp. 1965). Specifically excepts: apartment houses, convents and monasteries, jails or other places of detention, garages, hangers, hothouses, all buildings classified as hazardous occupancies, and state buildings specifically built for field service purposes, such as but not limited to conservation fire towers, fish hatcheries, tree nursery buildings and warehouses.

ences"[126]—is generally liberalized in the state statutes to require only "substantial conformity"[127] or conformity "in so far as feasible and financially reasonable."[128] Little is said in most of the statutes about enforcement. Usually the administrative officials responsible are identified but not much more.[129] Minnesota provides that construction or remodeling of public buildings owned by the state "shall not be hereafter commenced . . . until the plans and specifications . . . have been approved by the fire marshal."[130] Wisconsin's provision is specific and drastic: "The owner of any building who fails to meet the requirements of this section may be required to reconstruct the same by mandatory injunction in a circuit court suit brought by any interested person. Such person shall be reimbursed, if successful, for all costs and disbursements plus such actual attorney fees as may be allowed by the court."[131]

C. *The Struggle for the Streets*

"Public thoroughfares are for the beggar on his crutches as well as the millionaire in his limousine."[132] "The ordinary purpose of sidewalks and streets includes their use by the blind, the very young and the aged, the cripple and the infirm, and the pregnant woman. For such persons to use the streets is not contributory negligence."[133]

Once the disabled do appear in a public place where, as it is said, they have a right to be, what are the conditions of their presence? With what freedoms and liabilities do these phrases endow them? What are their responsibilities toward themselves, toward others, and of others toward them? Is the right to use the streets the same as the right of reasonably safe passage? If the disabled are liable for all acts or accidents proximately caused by their disability, if public bodies and able-bodied persons stand exactly in the same relationship to them as to

---

[126] AMERICAN STANDARDS ASS'N, *op. cit. supra* note 103, at § 1.2.

[127] N. MEX. STAT. § 67-16-18(B) (Supp. 1965).

[128] OKLA. STAT. ANN. tit. 61, § 11 (Supp. 1965). In Rhode Island the administrators need only "take into consideration standards promulgated by the American Standards Association . . . ." R.I. GEN. LAWS ANN. § 37-8-15 (Supp. 1965).

[129] *E.g.*, MONT. REV. CODE ANN. tit. 69-3719 (Supp. 1965); Neb. Sess. Laws 1965, ch. 430; N.H. REV. STAT. ANN. ch. 8-b (Supp. 1965). OKLA. STAT. ANN. tit. 61,512 (Supp. 1965); PA. STAT. ANN. tit. 71, § 1455.3 (Supp. 1965); S.C. CODE § 1-49 (Supp. 1965).

[130] MINN. STAT. ANN. ch. 73-60 (Supp. 1965).

[131] WIS. STAT. ANN. § 101.305(2) (Supp. 1965). For states requiring public hearings before issuance of standards see, *e.g.*, WIS. STAT. ANN. § 101.306 (Supp. 1965); Conn. Public Act. No. 216, § 2 (Feb. 1965, Spec. Sess.).

[132] Weinstein v. Wheeler, 127 Ore. 406, 413, 271 Pac. 733, 734 (1928), *rehearing denied*, 135 Ore. 518, 296 Pac. 1079 (1931).

[133] Garber v. City of Los Angeles, 226 Cal. App. 2d 349, 358, 38 Cal. Rptr. 157, 163 (1964), quoting David, *Municipality Liability in Tort in California*, 7 So. CAL. L. REV. 372, 452 (1934).

able-bodied persons, if, in other words, disability is not to be taken into consideration for these purposes so as positively to protect the disabled against major hazards if not minor harms—then the right to be in public places is best described by Shakespeare:

> And be these juggling fiends no more believed
> That palter with us in a double sense;
> That keep the word of promise to our ear,
> And break it to our hope.[134]

This would indeed be requiring the blind man to see at his peril, something that Oliver Wendell Holmes told us a long time ago is not to be done.[135] In these circumstances, every trip to the mailbox or store, every stroll in the sun, every congregation with one's neighbors, every catching of a bus to go to school or work—all the ordinary and routine transactions of daily life safely conducted by the rest of the community in public places as a matter of course—would be conducted by the disabled at great hazard; such great hazard in fact as to encourage, if not to make necessary, their custodialization. To live in the world presupposes progress toward a goal of integration.

The judicial answers to the questions posed above have come in the form of special substantive rules on the disabled collected under the rubric of the law of negligence. The courts and textwriters prefer to say that the standards are not special or different but one and the same for everybody.[136] It is the circumstances to which the standards apply that are special and different, a mode of expression giving a sense of rhetorical integrity. However, the differences are important, whether they are said to be in the standards, as in the case of children,[137] or in the circumstances to which the standards apply, as in the case of the disabled.[138]

Negligence first appeared as an independent tort or civil wrong for which the courts would allow an action for damages in the 19th century at a time when the industrial revolution, and particularly the develop-

---

134 MACBETH, Act V, scene viii, lines 19-23.

135 HOLMES, THE COMMON LAW 109 (1923 ed.).

136 Fenneman v. Holden, 75 Md. 1, 22 Atl. 1049 (1891); Jakubiec v. Hasty, 337 Mich. 205, 59 N.W.2d 385 (1953); Davis v. Feinstein, 370 Pa. 449, 88 A.2d 695 (1952); Fletcher v. City of Aberdeen, 54 Wash. 2d 174, 338 P.2d 743 (1959). 2 HARPER & JAMES, TORTS § 16.7 (1956); PROSSER, TORTS § 32, at 155 (3d ed. 1964); RESTATEMENT (SECOND), TORTS § 283c (1964); 38 AM. JUR. NEGLIGENCE § 210 (1941).

137 In 1841, in the case of Lynch v. Nurdin, L.R., 1 Q.B. 29 (1841), the Queens Bench laid down the basic doctrine in respect to the standard of care required of children—it was that of a reasonably prudent child of its years and development, not that of a reasonably prudent adult.

138 FLEMING, TORTS 249 (3d ed. 1965); 2 HARPER & JAMES, op. cit. supra note 136, § 16.7, at 923-24; PROSSER, op. cit. supra note 136, § 32, at 154-57; RESTATEMENT (SECOND), TORTS § 283c (1964).

ment of the railroads, was beginning to produce a heavy crop of accidental injuries to the person.[139] The law of negligence is still true to its origins and is dominated today by the same sorts of factors, multiplied a thousandfold by the accident-producing capacity of modern industry and urban life, and above all, by conditions of automobile traffic. Not only are these very factors the causes of a great deal of disability—though disease is still the major cause—but they constitute and give rise to new and ever-increasing hazards of life for those already disabled from whatever cause.

Summarizing the generally accepted doctrine, the second Restatement of the Law of Torts defines negligence as "conduct which falls below the standard established by law for the protection of others against unreasonable risk of harm."[140] The risk of harm is to be judged in the light of the likelihood that the harm will occur as well as its extent and severity. The risk, so judged, is then to be balanced against the character and importance of the conduct creating the risk and the feasibility and burden of providing protection against it.[141] The risk of harm is unreasonable if the first factors outweigh the second and the conduct which creates it is then said to be lacking in "due care." This is conduct in which the reasonable man of ordinary prudence does not engage. It is by this general formula, applied as the courts say to the special circumstances of the physically disabled, that the judges have sought to define the nature and scope of their right to live in the world. The judges pose as the critical question alike for those who create the risk and the disabled who run it: Would a reasonable man of ordinary prudence in like circumstances have done either?[142] It is only if the disabled plaintiff meets this standard of conduct and the defendant does not that the cost of injuries will be placed upon the latter. Otherwise, it will be allowed to lie where it falls.

If the disability is an element in the circumstances in which the disabled person finds himself, and if all elements in the circumstances are to be given their proper weight by the ordinarily prudent man in regulating his conduct, then a person's disability is to be taken into considera-

---

139 FLEMING, *op. cit. supra* note 138, at 107-08; 2 HARPER & JAMES, *op. cit. supra* note 136, § 12.3, at 751-52; PROSSER, *op. cit. supra* note 136, § 28, at 142-43.

140 RESTATEMENT (SECOND), TORTS § 282 (1964). See also FLEMING, *op. cit. supra* note 138, at 110; 2 HARPER & JAMES, *op. cit. supra* note 136, at §§ 16.1, 16.2; PROSSER, *op. cit. supra* note 136, at §§ 30, 31.

141 United States v. Carroll Towing Co., 159 F.2d 169 (2d Cir. 1947); Chicago, B. & Q. R.R. v. Krayenbuhl, 65 Neb. 889, 91 N.W. 880 (1902); PROSSER, *op. cit. supra* note 136, at 151-52; RESTATEMENT (SECOND), TORTS §§ 291-93 (1964).

142 PROSSER, *op. cit. supra* note 136, at 154; RESTATEMENT (SECOND), TORTS § 283 (1964).

tion in determining liability for injuries. In this proposition, English and American courts today unanimously agree.[143] Dean Prosser summarizes the conclusion by saying that the disabled person is entitled "to have allowance made by others for his disability"; and he in turn, must act reasonably "in the light of his knowledge of his infirmity . . . treated . . . merely as one of the circumstances under which he acts."[144] "Allowance made . . . for disability"; how, to what extent, in which circumstances, by whom? As to these issues, the courts are in strong disagreement. The disabled person, says Dean Prosser, "cannot be required to do the impossible by conforming to physical standards which he cannot meet."[145] Quite so! But if the right to live in the world consists only of exemption from this requirement, its proclamation may be a cruel hoax. To what requirements may they be subjected: to sally forth only in the care of an attendant? To use a dog as guide? To carry a cane, and if so, of any particular sort, and to be employed in any particular way? To travel only in familiar streets and places? Not to enter streets and places known to be defective or where work is being done? Not to enter streets and places possibly presenting particular traffic hazards? To proceed at his peril, because however carefully he may travel others need not anticipate his presence and take precautions accordingly?

The courts are divided as to the answers to each and every one of these questions; and the rhetoric is even more varied than the answers. The majority of courts say that it is not negligence per se for a blind man to walk the streets without a companion or attendant;[146] others that he may do so only in certain circumstances.[147] Some say that it is contributory negligence as a matter of law to travel without dog, cane, or

---

[143] E.g., Muse v. Page, 125 Conn. 219, 4 A.2d 329 (1939); Shields v. Consol. Gas Co., 193 App. Div. 86, 183 N.Y. Supp. 240 (Sup. Ct. 1920); Cook v. City of Winston-Salem, 241 N.C. 422, 85 S.E.2d 696 (1955); Weinstein v. Wheeler, 127 Ore. 406, 271 Pac. 733 (1928), *rehearing denied*, 135 Ore. 518, 296 Pac. 1079 (1931); Davis v. Feinstein, 370 Pa. 449, 88 A.2d 695 (1952); Smith v. Sneller, 345 Pa. 68, 26 A.2d 452 (1942); Fletcher v. City of Aberdeen, 54 Wash. 2d 174, 338 P.2d 743 (1959); Haley v. London Elec. Bd., [1965] A.C. 778 (1964).

[144] PROSSER, *op. cit. supra* note 136, § 32, at 155; FLEMING, *op. cit. supra* note 138, at 116-17, 162-63; 2 HARPER & JAMES, *op. cit. supra* note 136, § 16.7, at 920-21.

[145] PROSSER, *op. cit. supra* note 136, § 32, at 155. See also RESTATEMENT (SECOND), TORTS § 283c (1964).

[146] E.g., Town of Salem v. Goller, 76 Ind. 291, 292 (1881); Balcom v. City of Independence, 178 Iowa 685, 696, 160 N.W. 305, 310 (1916); Kaiser v. Hahn Bros., 126 Iowa, 561, 563, 102 N.W. 504, 505 (1905); Neff v. Town of Wellesley, 148 Mass. 487, 495, 20 N.E. 111, 113 (1889); Smith v. Wildes, 143 Mass. 556, 559, 10 N.E. 446, 448 (1887); Hestand v. Hamlin, 218 Mo. App. 122, 127, 262 S.W. 396, 397 (1924); Sleeper v. Sandown, 52 N.H. 244, 251 (1872); Davenport v. Ruckman, 37 N.Y. 568, 568-73 (1868); Fletcher v. City of Aberdeen, 54 Wash. 2d 174, 178, 338 P.2d 743, 745 (1959); Masterson v. Lennon, 115 Wash. 305, 308, 197 Pac. 38, 39 (1921).

[147] E.g., Florida Cent. R.R. v. Williams, 37 Fla. 406, 20 So. 558 (1896).

companion;[148] others, that the failure to use one or more of these travel aids presents a question for the jury as to whether due care was employed.[149] No courts say that a blind man may not, when taking the proper precautions, enter unfamiliar territory; most courts, however, emphasize the plaintiff's knowledge of the surroundings and the frequency of his presence.[150] Some say that the plaintiff's knowledge that the streets are or may be defective or dangerous creates a kind of assumption of risk;[151] others, that in the circumstances, the disabled person may proceed but must do so with due care in the light of his knowledge.[152] The latter rule is also applied by some courts to blind persons in railway depots, at railway street crossings, and like places of similar danger,[153] while others say that it is gross negligence for blind persons to be in such places alone.[154] Some courts say that the disabled may proceed upon the assumption that the streets and highways are kept in a reasonably safe condition, and that cities and abutting property owners must expect the disabled to be abroad in the land and accordingly must take precautions necessary to warn or otherwise protect them.[155] Others say that those who create, maintain, or tamper with the streets and public passageways are only under a duty to safeguard the able-bodied pedestrian.[156]

No courts have held or even darkly hinted that a blind man may rise

---

[148] *Id.* at 419-20, 20 So. at 561-62.

[149] Smith v. Sneller, 345 Pa. 68, 72, 26 A.2d 452, 454 (1942); Fraser v. Freedman, 87 Pa. Super. 454, 457 (1926).

[150] *E.g.*, Balcom v. City of Independence, 178 Iowa 685, 696, 160 N.W. 305, 309 (1916); Chesapeake & Potomac Tel. Co. v. Lysher, 107 Md. 237, 240, 68 Atl. 619, 621 (1908); Neff v. Town of Wellesley, 148 Mass. 487, 489, 20 N.E. 111 (1889); Smith v. Wildes, 143 Mass. 556, 559, 10 N.E. 446, 448 (1887); Hestand v. Hamlin, 218 Mo. App. 122, 127, 262 S.W. 396, 397 (1924); Sleeper v. Sandown, 52 N.H. 244, 252 (1872); Davenport v. Ruckman, 37 N.Y. 568, 573 (1868).

[151] *E.g.*, Garbanati v. City of Durango, 30 Colo. 358, 360, 70 Pac. 686 (1902); Cook v. City of Winston-Salem, 241 N.C. 422, 430, 85 S.E.2d 696, 701-02 (1955).

[152] *E.g.*, Hestand v. Hamlin, 218 Mo. App. 122, 128, 262 S.W. 396, 398 (1924); Marks' Adm'r v. Petersburg R. Co., 88 Va. 1, 13 S.E. 299 (1891).

[153] See, *e.g.*, Farley v. Norfolk & W. Ry., 14 F.2d 93 (4th Cir. 1926); Rosenthal v. Chicago & A.R.R., 255 Ill. 552, 556, 99 N.E. 672, 672-73 (1912); Lortz v. New York Cent. & H.R.R., 7 App. Div. 515, 522, 40 N.Y. Supp. 253, 257 (1896).

[154] Florida Cent. R.R. v. Williams, 37 Fla. 406, 419, 20 So. 558, 562 (1896).

[155] *E.g.*, Balcom v. City of Independence, 178 Iowa 685, 693, 160 N.W. 305, 308 (1916); Rock v. American Constr. Co., 120 La. 831-33, 45 So. 741-42 (1908); Sleeper v. Sandown, 52 N.H. 244, 245 (1872); Shields v. Consol. Gas Co., 193 App. Div. 86, 90, 183 N.Y. Supp. 240, 242-43 (1920); Davenport v. Ruckman, 37 N.Y. 568-73 (1868); Fletcher v. City of Aberdeen, 54 Wash. 2d 174, 179, 338 P.2d 743, 746 (1959); Masterson v. Lennon, 115 Wash. 305, 308, 197 Pac. 38, 39 (1921); Short v. City of Spokane, 41 Wash. 257, 261-62, 83 Pac. 183, 185 (1906); Haley v. London Elec. Bd., [1965] A.C. 778, 790 (1964).

[156] Hestand v. Hamlin, 218 Mo. App. 122, 127, 262 S.W. 396, 397 (1924); Carter v. Village of Nunda, 55 App. Div. 501, 504, 66 N.Y. Supp. 1059, 1061 (1900); Cook v. City of Winston-Salem, 241 N.C. 422, 428, 85 S.E.2d 696, 700 (1955).

in the morning, help get the children off to school, bid his wife goodby, and proceed along the streets and bus lines to his daily work, without dog, cane, or guide, if such is his habit or preference, now and then brushing a tree or kicking a curb, but, notwithstanding, proceeding with firm step and sure air, knowing that he is part of the public for whom the streets are built and maintained in reasonable safety, by the help of his taxes, and that he shares with others this part of the world in which he, too, has a right to live. He would then be doing what any reasonable, or prudent, or reasonably prudent blind man would do, and also what social policy must positively foster and judges in their developing common law must be alert to sustain.

What were these blind plaintiffs doing in the streets and highways when they were injured? The answer is very instructive. They were doing what other people do who live in the world. In the two leading Washington cases,[157] they were going to and from work as piano tuners; in Massachusetts, a piano tuner had stopped at a store, made a purchase, and was going on down the street;[158] in Pennsylvania, a door-to-door salesman of small household items was in course of canvassing houses;[159] in New York, a door-to-door salesman was returning home from the meat market down the street;[160] in London, a telephone operator was following his daily routine of going to work;[161] in City of Independence, Iowa, a businessman was on his usual path to and from the business part of town;[162] in New Hampshire, a farm hand was passing along a familiar road, "a good man to hire . . . for . . . chopping wood, felling trees, mowing, reaping, threshing grain, digging potatoes, planting and hoeing, although with difficulty the first time hoeing corn";[163] in Town of Spirit Lake, Iowa, the plaintiff was taking the only available walk to church;[164] in North Carolina, the plaintiff was making a Sunday afternoon visit to a friend;[165] in Vermont, the plaintiff, riding along on a jaunt in a wagon with another fellow and two women, got out on the public highway in the dark of night to urinate.[166] Moreover, almost all of these plaintiffs had one

---

157 Fletcher v. City of Aberdeen, 54 Wash. 2d 174, 338 P.2d 743 (1959); Masterson v. Lennon, 115 Wash. 305, 197 Pac. 38 (1921).

158 Smith v. Wildes, 143 Mass. 556, 10 N.E. 446 (1887).

159 Smith v. Sneller, 345 Pa. 68, 26 A.2d 452 (1942).

160 Shields v. Consol. Gas Co., 193 App. Div. 86, 183 N.Y. Supp. 240 (1920).

161 Haley v. London Elec. Bd., [1965] A.C. 778 (1964).

162 Balcom v. City of Independence, 178 Iowa 685, 160 N.W. 305 (1916).

163 Sleeper v. Sandown, 52 N.H. 244, 245 (1872).

164 Yeager v. Town of Spirit Lake, 115 Iowa 593, 88 N.W. 1095 (1902).

165 Cook v. City of Winston-Salem, 241 N.C. 422, 85 S.E.2d 696 (1955).

166 Glidden v. Town of Reading, 38 Vt. 52 (1865). In Missouri, the restaurant operator was walking to other parts of town for supplies as he usually did several times each day. Hestand v. Hamlin, 218 Mo. App. 122, 262 S.W. 396 (1924). In the Glenwood, Iowa case,

of the "common, well-known, compensatory devices for the blind . . . a cane, a seeing-eye dog, or a companion."[167]

The discussion in the cases has revolved around these principal topics: an analogy between the blind man in the daytime and the seeing man at night; the likelihood that the disabled will come by and be injured; contributory negligence of or the precautions taken or to be taken by the disabled person to prevent injury in the light of his disability; the practicability and cost to the city, contractor, or property owner of reducing the risk to reasonable proportions.

1. The Analogy

The early leading opinions dealing with the blind and the near-blind are preoccupied with an analogy built on sighted persons' conceptions of blindness: Blindness is shutting off the vision as by a blindfold or a perfectly dark night. This being so, and assuming the right of the blind to travel the streets at all, should not the law assimilate their daytime situation to that of the seeing man at night? In the early and much quoted New York case of *Davenport v. Ruckman*,[168] the court said:

> The streets and sidewalks are for the benefit of all conditions of people, and all have the right, in using them, to assume that they are in good condition, and to regulate their conduct upon that assumption. A person may walk or drive in the darkness of the night, relying upon the belief that the corporation has performed its duty and that the street or the walk is in safe condition. He walks by a faith justified by law . . . .[169]

This was the case of a person with some sight who, traveling along the walk in the daytime, had fallen into an unguarded cellarway. Four years later, the Supreme Court of New Hampshire dealt with the case of a totally blind person who, also traveling in the daytime, had fallen off a bridge fourteen to sixteen feet wide, the railing on one side of which was no longer present. It is immaterial, the plaintiff's attorney argued, "whether the accident happened for want of light or want of sight."[170]

---

the plaintiff "helps his wife in laundry work for their neighbors, and has on occasion received aid from the county . . . ." The court thought it could "fairly assume that he felt the hurt of his bruises . . . none the less keenly than he would had his balance in [the] bank been larger." Hill v. City of Glenwood, 124 Iowa 479, 485, 100 N.W. 522, 524 (1904). In Maryland, the man who sewed brooms was leaving the sheltered workshop at the Maryland School for the Blind and returning to his living quarters. Chesapeake & Potomac Tel. Co. v. Lysher, 107 Md. 237, 68 Atl. 619 (1908). In New York, the store owner was returning home from business, crossing a creek in a scow. Harris v. Uebelhoer, 75 N.Y. 169 (1878).

167 *E.g.*, Smith v. Sneller, 345 Pa. 68, 72, 26 A.2d 452, 454 (1942).
168 37 N.Y. 568 (1868).
169 *Id.* at 573.
170 Sleeper v. Sandown, 52 N.H. 244, 250 (1872).

Quite so, said the court: "Blindness of itself is not negligence. Nor [is] passing upon the highway with the sight of external things cut off by physical incapacity of vision . . . any more than passing upon the highway when the same things are wholly obscured by the darkness of night."[171] "[T]his plaintiff, although blind," the court added, "had the same right to assume the existence of a rail on each side that any traveller, passing either in the daytime or in the night-time would have. . . ."[172]

In the 1916 Iowa case, which has led the way for many states, the analogy of blindness to lack of light was given great weight in the case of a totally blind man who, again traveling in the daytime, fell into an unguarded seven-foot deep watermain ditch as he crossed the street.[173] The city was bound to make it safe for the sighted to pass at night when the sighted are blind. "[R]equiring a light for him who can see when there is a light proves that there is a duty to protect those who for any reason cannot see . . . ."[174]

While this analogy is basically weak in portraying as the same the travel problems of the blind and the sighted in the dark, it did prove a valuable starting point for the courts in seeing that the duty of the defendant is not confined to the able-bodied. Its logical, or perhaps more accurately, its psychological, role was thus historic in the process of imposing upon cities and abutting property owners an obligation to maintain the streets, highways, bridges and other public places in a condition safe for the disabled traveler—and this in an age when the courts were acutely concerned about keeping in hand judgments of plaintiff-minded juries in the interests of free enterprise and unencumbered industrial development.

While utilizing the analogy for this basic function, and moving, one feels, from humanitarian rather than policy considerations, the courts were not hindered by its difficulties or misled into many of its bypaths. If the daytime care the city owed the blind was the same as the night-time care it owed the sighted, then: providing a lamp should amply warn or illuminate; the use of compensatory travel aids would not be emphasized, unless perchance the sighted at night, in view of their unfortunate affliction, were to be required, on threat of contributory negligence, to use one of those well-known compensatory devices for men in want of light, such as a cane, a seeing-eye cat, or a blind attendant.[175]

171 *Id.* at 251.
172 *Id.* at 252.
173 Balcom v. City of Independence, 178 Iowa 685, 160 N.W. 305 (1916).
174 *Id.* at 691, 160 N.W. at 308.
175 Bussell v. City of Fort Dodge, 126 Iowa 308, 101 N.W. 1126 (1905).

At night the blind and the sighted would be put upon an identical footing.

The fact that lanterns placed about an excavation will not make the passage safe for a blind man, said the Iowa court is "adventitious." "Concede that there must be a light for those who have eyesight, when without the light the eyesight would be no protection, and it follows that there is a duty to guard those who cannot see, though a light be furnished, by guarding them with that which will be as much a protection to them as is the lamp to one whose inability to see is due to the darkness of the night."[176] So the differences do matter, too, and not just the similarities or supposed similarities.

The blind man must take his compensatory devices and cautions into the night, though the sighted are not expected to use them. Although the blind man in the road could not see, and, because the night was dark, could not be seen by the driver of a team bearing down on him, great emphasis was placed by the Vermont Supreme Court on his use of a cane in escaping from danger by safely finding the edge of the road and then falling into the ditch.[177] He had a right to assume, said the court, that the road was safe in its "surface, margin and muniments."[178] If plaintiff had been sighted, presumably he would have had the same right to a safe ditch but he would have been free to find it in whatever way a sighted man might in the light of all the circumstances. In another nighttime accident involving a blind man rowing across a creek, the New York court "assumed" that the creek was a public highway, "as much open to the use of a blind man as one having eyesight."[179] Whether sighted in the night or blind, a person "must be more cautious. He must bring about him greater guards, and go more slowly and tentatively than if he had his eyesight, or the light of day shone upon him."[180] Notwithstanding these firm declarations, the court in this case made much of the fact that the blind man had his sighted wife in the boat with him and that the night was clear. Neither enabled him to avoid a collision with a tug boat though both together had a lot to do with his avoiding the defense of contributory negligence.

Some courts have never accepted the basic conclusion about the extent of the defendant's duty, with or without the use of the analogy. In the 1955 case of *Cook v. City of Winston-Salem*,[181] the North Carolina Supreme Court held that the city and its contractors were under no duty

---

176 Balcom v. City of Independence, 178 Iowa 685, 691, 160 N.W. 305, 308 (1916).
177 Glidden v. Town of Reading, 38 Vt. 52, 53, 57 (1865).
178 *Id*. at 57.
179 Harris v. Uebelhoer, 75 N.Y. 169, 175 (1878).
180 *Ibid*.
181 241 N.C. 422, 85 S.E.2d 696 (1955).

to place a signal or guard at a dropoff from the path to the street resulting from an incompleted repaving operation *"during the daytime, when it was plainly visible."*[182]

2. *Likelihood of Harm*

Whether the risk of harm created by the conduct of the defendant is unreasonable depends in part on the likelihood that it will occur. If the likelihood is very slight, even though the potential harm be quite serious, the defendant is not charged with responsibility for safeguarding persons against it. This manner of stating the duty of the defendant, increasingly popular today, is not uniformly employed in the cases. Since there is a judicial tendency to describe the accident in terms of the actions of the plaintiff and to focus particularly on questions of contributory negligence, the courts often speak of the right of the plaintiff to proceed upon the assumption that the streets and highways will be maintained in a reasonably safe condition, leaving the duty of the defendant to maintain them implicit or expressed in a subordinate way.[183]

Another mode of stating the duty of the defendant is as the Iowa court did: The due care obligations of the plaintiff and the defendant are correlative. The blind man must use more precautions because he is blind; the city must act in the light of his right to be in the streets and in recognition of his disability.[184] The Iowa court also suggested a stricter standard: The wrongdoer need not anticipate the consequences of his actions; that they did in fact occur is sufficient. In this view, it would not matter that "no blind man had ever before used a walk in the town."[185] In any event, the particular plaintiff had used these very streets for ten years so the city could not claim ignorance of his presence. In 1905, the Washington Supreme Court approved this instruction: "The

---

[182] *Id.* at 428, 85 S.E.2d at 700.

[183] *E.g.*, Town of Salem v. Goller, 76 Ind. 291, 292 (1881); Smith v. Wildes, 143 Mass. 556, 559, 10 N.E. 446, 448 (1887); Sleeper v. Sandown, 52 N.H. 244, 251-53 (1872); Shields v. Consol. Gas Co., 193 App. Div. 86, 90, 183 N.Y. Supp. 240, 242-43 (1920); Harris v. Uebelhoer, 75 N.Y. 169, 174-77 (1878); Davenport v. Ruckman, 37 N.Y. 568, 573 (1868); Glidden v. Reading, 38 Vt. 52, 57 (1865).

The right of reliance on a safe street or highway antedates the cases announcing the right of the disabled to be upon the streets and highways. See, *e.g.*, Thompson v. Bridgewater, 24 Mass. (7 Pick.) 187 (1829). The first American cases dealing with the right of the blind were handed down in the 1860's. Winn v. City of Lowell, 83 Mass. 177, 189 (1861); Davenport v. Ruckman, 37 N.Y. 568, 573 (1868); Glidden v. Reading, 38 Vt. 52 (1865). An English court in Boss v. Litton, [1832] 5 C. & P. 407, 409, 24 E.C.L. 628, 630 (1831), first declared that "all persons, paralytic as well as others, had a right to walk in the road, and were entitled to the exercise of reasonable care on the part of persons driving carriages along it."

[184] Balcom v. City of Independence, 178 Iowa 685, 691-92, 160 N.W. 305, 308 (1916).

[185] *Id.* at 696, 160 N.W. at 309.

city is chargeable with knowledge that all classes of persons, including the healthy and diseased and lame, constantly travel its streets and sidewalks."[186] This doctrine was specifically applied to the blind in a later case.[187] Foreseeability is a term used by some courts to cover the presumption that the defendant is on notice that disabled persons are likely to happen along.[188]

The statement by an English author that "a century ago there was no rule either recognizing or refusing to recognize a duty of care toward blind pedestrians because they were rarely seen in the streets"[189] is inaccurate as to the facts in England and America and as to the law in America.[190] One century ago, two centuries ago, five centuries ago, the blind were notorious frequenters of the streets of the towns, carrying out their historic role, and often their privileged status, as beggars.[191] What was rare was a blind man moving about the streets for some other purpose, and especially for the regular activity of going to work as the plaintiff in *Haley v. London Elec. Bd.* was doing.[192] Indeed, the number of cases getting to appellate courts by and about the turn of the century involving blind or nearly blind plaintiffs is in many ways surprising. While some blind individuals were active and mobile, this course of conduct was not encouraged by governmental policy, by community attitudes, by the mores of the times, or by the public or private programs established for the benefit of the blind. Blind children attended segregated residential schools, if any, where classes and the activities of daily

---

186 Short v. City of Spokane, 41 Wash. 257, 262, 83 Pac. 183, 185 (1905).

187 Fletcher v. City of Aderdeen, 54 Wash. 2d 174, 338 P.2d 743 (1959). In Missouri it was held for a time that the city's duty to keep its sidewalks in repair only required it "to use ordinary care to maintain its streets in a reasonably safe condition for general traffic in all the usual and ordinary modes of travel." Bethel v. St. Joseph, 184 Mo. App. 388, 394, 171 S.W. 42, 44 (1914). See also Wilkerson v. City of Sedalia, 205 S.W. 877 (Mo. 1918). The Missouri Supreme Court overruled these cases in favor of the proposition that the duty of the city extended to providing reasonably safe streets for all classes of pedestrians including the disabled. Hunt v. St. Louis, 278 Mo. 213, 211 S.W. 673 (1919). See also Bianchetti v. Luce, 222 Mo. App. 282, 290, 2 S.W.2d 129, 133 (1928); Hanke v. St. Louis, 272 S.W. 933 (Mo. 1925).

188 Kennedy v. Cohn, 73 Pa. D. & C. 544, 548 (C.P. 1950); Clawson v. Walgreen Drug Co., 108 Utah 577, 583, 162 P.2d 759, 762 (1945); Haley v. London Elec. Bd., [1965] A.C. 778, 791 (1964).

189 Dias, *A Hole in the Road*, 73 THE LISTENER 292, 294 (1965).

190 See, *e.g.*, Winn v. City of Lowell, 83 Mass. (1 Allen) 177 (1861); Sleeper v. Sandown, 52 N.H. 244 (1872); Davenport v. Ruckman, 37 N.Y. 568 (1868).

191 tenBroek, *California's Welfare Law—Origins and Development*, 45 CALIF. L. REV. 241, 252 (1957); NUEVA RECOPILACIÓN, bk. I, tit. XII, law 15 (1567). See, *e.g.*, NOVISIMA RECOPILACIÓN, bk. VII, tit. XXXIX, law 8 (1805).

192 [1965] A.C. 778 (1964). See text accompanying notes 200-09 *infra*, for a discussion of this case.

life were all conducted within the confines of the institution.[193] In adult life, many of the blind were cared for and custodialized by their families or worked in sheltered shops attached to institutional living arrangements, often the residential school.[194] (Homes provided for the blind and almshouses cared for the aged.[195]) Yet even at this time, as we have just shown, some blind persons were abroad in the land and some courts were proclaiming their right to be there and imposing on public bodies the duty to protect them in the safe exercise of it.

Today the picture is quite different. Blind children and youths are attending public schools and colleges, making their way to and from them alone. Blind and otherwise disabled adults are encouraged in many ways to live active lives whether or not they are able to secure gainful employment: by financial aid programs which make this possible;[196] by case work services in the welfare system;[197] by home teacher programs throughout the country designed,[198] among other things, to teach blind persons to travel alone; by orientation and rehabilitation programs which regard mobility as a must.[199] The total number of blind people in a

---

[193] See generally FARRELL, THE STORY OF BLINDNESS (1956); FRAMPTON & KEARNEY, THE RESIDENTIAL SCHOOL (1953); FRENCH, FROM HOMER TO HELEN KELLER (1932); RICHARDS, SAMUEL GRIDLEY HOWE (1935); RICHARDS, LETTERS AND JOURNALS OF SAMUEL GRIDLEY HOWE (1909).

[194] See generally Chouinard, *Sheltered Workshops—Past and Present*, paper read at the Fifth Atlantic City Rehabilitation Conference, 1957; Chouinard & Garrett, *Workshops for the Disabled: A Vocational Rehabilitation Resource*, U.S. Dep't of Health, Educ. & Welfare, Office of Vocational Rehabilitation (Rehabilitation Services Ser. No. 371); FRENCH, *op. cit. supra* note 193. In Chesapeake & Pacific Tel. Co. v. Lysher, 107 Md. 237, 68 Atl. 619 (1908), the blind plaintiff when injured was leaving a sheltered shop located at the Maryland School for the Blind where he had worked for four years after graduating from the school. Samuel Gridley Howe, famed pioneer in education of the blind and other educational projects, started the first sheltered shop in the country in connection with the New England Asylum for the blind in 1840. The men who worked in it lived at the asylum until 1880. FARRELL, *op. cit. supra* note 193, at 68, 159-60.

[195] tenBroek, *California's Dual System of Family Law: Its Origin, Development, and Present Status*, 16 STAN. L. REV. 900, 931 (1964).

[196] 49 Stat. 645 (1935), as amended, 42 U.S.C. §§ 1201-06 (1964). See also CAL. WELFARE & INST'NS CODE §§ 13000-102 (California's Program for Aid to Potentially Self-Supporting Blind).

[197] 76 Stat. 186 (1962), 42 U.S.C. §§ 1201, 1351 (1964).

[198] See, e.g., CAL. EDUC. CODE § 6209.

[199] Over twenty public and private educational institutions throughout the country give mobility training. This does not include dog-guide centers, of which there are perhaps a dozen, or training offered by all residential schools or most resource classes in public schools. At least two groups are operating in California under grants from the Federal Department of Health, Education, and Welfare related to public schools—one in Alameda-Contra Costa County and one in Los Angeles County. There are many like projects country-wide. In two universities, West Michigan University located at Kalamazoo, Michigan, and Boston College in Boston, Massachusetts, mobility teacher training courses are offered. See also Rives, *The Blind and Today's Jobs*, Rehabilitation Record, March-April, 1965, p. 6.

community has increased with the general growth in population. But a far greater precentage of them than ever before is out in the community.

In the recent *Haley* case[200] decided by the Judicial Committee of the House of Lords, the foreseeability doctrine was thoroughly explored. Reliance was placed on common knowledge, government statistics, and the judicially noticeable fact that "we all are accustomed to meeting blind people walking alone with their white sticks on city pavements."[201] In the London area at the time there were 7,321 registered blind people, and in Great Britain as a whole, 107,000, or about 1 in every 500.[202] In the United States the figures are comparable.[203] Moreover, the growing use of the white cane has increased the visibility and conspicuousness of the blind part of the population. One would suppose that no court in the land would any longer hear a city, from the greatest metropolis to the least village, maintain that it could not be expected to anticipate that numbers of disabled persons, including blind, would pass that way, unattended, and in the free exercise of their right to be in the streets and highways. That the duty of providing suitable warning or protection might still not be imposed, as in North Carolina,[204] can rest only on a policy determination, and not on the defendant's claimed lack of knowledge. That policy determination is one contradicting the policy judgment of much of the rest of society.

The House of Lords in *Haley*[205] carefully avoided all policy questions and commitments. It merely insisted that the courts recognize the existing fact, a partial and grudging adaptation of the law to contemporary needs.[206] "No doubt there are many places open to the public," said Lord Reid, "where for one reason or another one would be surprised to see a blind person walking alone but a city pavement is not one of them. And a residential street cannot be different from any other. The blind people we meet must live somewhere and most of them probably left their homes unaccompanied."[207] Cities must be charged with this common knowledge and placed under a duty of warning or other protection. "If it be said that your Lordships are making new law," wrote Lord Evershed, "that is only because, whatever may have been the facts and circumstances reasonably to be contemplated a hundred years or more

---

200 Haley v. London Elec. Bd., [1965] A.C. 778 (1964).

201 *Id.* at 791.

202 *Id.* at 807.

203 Estimated at between 350,000 to 400,000. Hurlin, *Estimated Prevalence of Blindness in the United States and in Individual States*, 32 SIGHT SAVING REV. 4 (1962).

204 Cook v. City of Winston-Salem, 241 N.C. 422, 85 S.E.2d 696 (1955).

205 Haley v. London Elec. Bd., [1965] A.C. 778 (1964).

206 *Ibid*; see FLEMING, TORTS 162-63 (3d ed. 1965).

207 [1965] A.C. at 778, 791.

ago, at the present time it must be accepted as one of the facts of life that appreciable numbers of blind persons, having had the requisite training, are capable of using or use in fact public footpaths such as that in Charleton Church Lane and that accordingly their presence upon such footpaths cannot reasonably be disregarded or left out of account by those undertaking work of the character being in the present case done by the respondent board."[208] In overruling the 1950 leading case,[209] the Lords said they were merely distinguishing it and thereby allowed some dangerous doctrine to remain unrepudiated. The law, lagging far behind social developments, was merely catching up with what blind people were actually doing. The Lords were not implementing the public policy of integration, a policy which in large part accounted for so many blind people being in the streets and which made this decision necessary.

3. Contributory Negligence

Doctrines of contributory negligence are variously described as harsh, illogical, and disappearing.[210] Such doctrines have been particularly rife in the disabled cases. Here misconceptions as to the nature of disability have added to the general confusion and there is little evidence that these doctrines are disappearing. Some rhetorical regularity is being achieved as the courts gradually are eliminating talk of a higher standard of care imposed on the disabled person by reason of his disability,[211] and are speaking instead of a universal duty of ordinary care requiring the disabled person, by reason of his disability, to use greater efforts to avoid hazards, to take greater precautions, to be more keenly watchful by the fuller use of remaining senses, or otherwise to seek to compensate for his disability.[212] This rhetorical regularity, however, accomplishes no sub-

---

[208] Id. at 800-01.

[209] Pritchard v. Post Office, 114 J.P. 370 (C.A. 1950).

[210] FLEMING, op. cit. supra note 206, at 224-25; 2 HARPER & JAMES, TORTS § 22.3 (1956); PROSSER, TORTS § 64 (3d ed. 1964).

[211] See, e.g., Winn v. City of Lowell, 83 Mass. (1 Allen) 177, 180 (1861); Karl v. Juniata County, 206 Pa. 633, 637-38, 56 Atl. 78, 79 (1903).

[212] Garber v. City of Los Angeles, 226 Cal. App. 2d 349, 358, 38 Cal. Rptr. 157, 163 (1964); Muse v. Page, 125 Conn. 219, 223, 4 A.2d 329, 331 (1939); Balcom v. Independence, 178 Iowa 685, 692, 160 N.W. 305, 308 (1916); Kaiser v. Hahn Bros., 126 Iowa 561, 564, 102 N.W. 504, 506 (1905); Hill v. City of Glenwood, 124 Iowa 479, 481-82, 100 N.W. 522, 523 (1904); Gill v. Sable Hide & Fur Co., 223 Ky. 679, 680, 4 S.W.2d 676, 677 (1928); Chesapeake & Potomac Tel. Co. v. Lysher, 107 Md. 237, 241, 68 Atl. 619, 622 (1908); Keith v. Worcester Street Ry., 196 Mass. 478, 482-83, 82 N.E. 680-81 (1907); Neff v. Town of Wellesley, 148 Mass. 487, 495, 20 N.E. 111, 113 (1889); Sleeper v. Sandown, 52 N.H. 244, 251 (1872); Shields v. Consol. Gas Co., 193 App. Div. 86, 90, 183 N.Y. Supp. 240, 242 (1920); Carter v. Village of Nunda, 55 App. Div. 501, 504, 66 N.Y. Supp. 1059, 1061 (1900); Kennedy v. Cohn, 73 Pa. D. & C. 544, 552 (C.P. 1950); Clawson v. Walgreen Drug Co., 108 Utah 577, 584, 162 P.2d 759, 763 (1945); Masterson v. Lennon, 115 Wash. 305, 308, 197 Pac. 38, 39 (1921).

stantive change. Still to be decided in each case, in the light of the particular disability and other circumstances, is the question whether the individual plaintiff produced the requisite effort, precautions, watchfulness, or compensation. Whether described as a higher standard of care or as a standard of ordinary care applied to more difficult circumstances makes little difference in the end. The preponderant rule is that this question of requisite care is to be left to the jury or trier of fact. Two fairly recent cases, however, stand as leading authority for a different proposition.

In *Smith v. Sneller*[213] the Pennsylvania Supreme Court held a blind plaintiff guilty of contributory negligence as a matter of law who proceeded along the sidewalk without using one of the "common, well-known, compensatory devices for the blind, such as a cane, a 'seeing-eye' dog, or a companion."[214] In a follow-up case, the same court later held that once the blind person had the compensatory device it was then a question for the jury whether he was guilty of contributory negligence in its use.[215] In *Cook v. City of Winston-Salem*[216] the Supreme Court of North Carolina outdistanced even the Supreme Court of Pennsylvania, in an opinion that can only be regarded as more than 100 years behind the times, even though it adhered to the rhetorical regularities before mentioned. The blind plaintiff was declared guilty of contributory negligence in that he "failed to put forth a greater degree of effort than one not acting under any disabilities to attain due care for his own safety: that standard of care which the law has established for everybody" even though he was guided by a well-trained seeing-eye dog handled in the approved way and performing its function as trained.[217]

These cases raise the question as to the nature, adequacy, and proper use of the "common, well-known, compensatory devices for the blind" and their relationship to the law of contributory negligence. In the first place, one takes it for granted that the list of devices provided in the *Smith* case is illustrative and not necessarily exhaustive. Presumably, any or all of them could be discarded as outmoded if new and better devices were developed. Experimental efforts to this purpose have long been going on in the physics departments at the Massachusetts Institute of Technology and Haverford College, many blind-concerned agencies, and by numerous private individuals and companies. A central clearing and testing agency has been established at Massachusetts.

---

[213] 345 Pa. 68, 26 A.2d 452 (1942).
[214] *Id.* at 72, 26 A.2d at 454.
[215] Davis v. Feinstein, 370 Pa. 449, 452, 88 A.2d 695, 697 (1952).
[216] 241 N.C. 422, 85 S.E.2d 696 (1955).
[217] *Id.* at 431, 85 S.E.2d at 702.

Secondly, and more importantly, the situations presented in the cases we have been discussing, if no others, illustrate the limitations of the devices and the people who use them. The farm hand in New Hampshire fell off the unrailed side of a bridge though he "felt his way with his cane very carefully . . . ."[218] The piano tuner in Washington, using his cane in his habitual and customary way while traveling along the walk, "hit the pile of lumber with his cane at the narrow place in the sidewalk, stepped aside to avoid the lumber, and fell into the excavation . . ." on the other side of the walk.[219] The door-to-door salesman in New York carried a cane but, anticipating no danger, was not using it when he stepped off the curb and fell into the trench, which he could well have done even if he had first found the curb with his cane.[220] "[W]hen he approached the place where the rail was down," on the wooden walk elevated four feet over the street, the partially blind person in Colorado "commenced walking slowly, and felt about him with his cane very carefully, for the purpose of definitely locating the walk, but, notwithstanding these precautions, fell off."[221] Haley was using his cane which either went over or under the handle of the punner hammer placed athwart his path, the punner hammer then tripping him and proving a trap rather than a guard.[222] The door-to-door salesman in *Smith v. Sneller*[223] was not carrying a cane. He stepped on a two-foot-high pile of dirt bordering an unguarded trench across the sidewalk. The dirt gave way and he fell into the trench. This could easily have happened to a man with a cane despite the court's confident assertion that any one of the compensatory devices "probably would have been sufficient to prevent this accident."[224] Just how easily is illustrated by the follow-up Pennsylvania case where the blind plaintiff fell into an open cellarway though he "carried a white cane customarily employed by blind persons."[225] He was using his cane as a guide "moving it laterally in order to touch the walls of abutting buildings and keep on a straight course, and also tapping the ground before him . . . ."[226] The carouser by night in Vermont, in seeking the side of the highway, "put his cane before him with the point resting upon the ground, and in that manner felt his way

---

[218] Sleeper v. Sandown, 52 N.H. 244 (1872).

[219] Masterson v. Lennon, 115 Wash. 305, 307, 197 Pac. 38 (1921).

[220] Shields v. Consol. Gas Co., 193 App. Div. 86, 89, 183 N.Y. Supp. 240, 242 (1920).

[221] Garbanati v. City of Durango, 30 Colo. 358, 359, 70 Pac. 686 (1902).

[222] Haley v. London Elec. Bd., [1965] A.C. 778, 790 (1964).

[223] 345 Pa. 68, 71, 26 A.2d 452, 453 (1942).

[224] *Id.* at 72, 26 A.2d at 454.

[225] Davis v. Feinstein, 370 Pa. 449, 451, 88 A.2d 695, 696 (1952). See also Kennedy v. Cohn, 73 Pa. D. & C. 544, 546 (C.P. 1950).

[226] Davis v. Feinstein, *supra* note 225, at 452, 88 A.2d at 696.

before him, moving his cane about as he walked to find obstructions if there were any"; he felt the edge with his cane and then either stepped over or fell over into the ravine below.[227] The guide dog in North Carolina came to the edge of the drop-off and stopped as all good guide dogs should do. His master came down on the foot that was in the air and tumbled down the embankment.[228] The churchgoer in Spirit Lake, Iowa, was not saved from her accident by the fact that she was accompanied by her husband,[229] or the creek-crosser in New York by his wife.[230] All blind people are acquainted with the risk of traveling with an unfamiliar sighted companion who is so preoccupied with the problem of guiding him as to be inalert to ordinary hazards or unsure how to avoid them when observed.[231]

Among ordinary cane users and the so-called experts alike, there is a lively debate about the merits of various canes—should they be long or short, rigid or folding, metal, fiber glass, or wood, with curved or straight handles. Similar debate exists between the cane users and the dog users.[232] A blind person carrying two canes, one in each hand, tapping the ground before him with one, following the buildings and curb alongside with the other, still exposes his head as a ready target for every leaning ladder, protruding piece of scaffolding, or low-slung awning bar. An agile and adept blind person without any device may in any given case travel better than most blind persons with one. In this state of uncertainty, divided opinion and diverse experience, courts are unwise indeed to make any particular procedure so important as to declare contributory negligence per se the conduct of a blind person who does not use it.

In nineteen states,[233] questions of contributory negligence of the physi-

---

[227] Glidden v. Reading, 38 Vt. 52, 53 (1865).

[228] Cook v. City of Winston-Salem, 241 N.C. 422, 426, 85 S.E.2d 696, 699 (1955).

[229] Yeager v. Town of Spirit Lake, 115 Iowa 593, 597, 88 N.W. 1095, 1096 (1902).

[230] Harris v. Uebelhoer, 75 N.Y. 169, 170 (1878).

[231] In City of Rock Island v. Gingles, 217 Ill. 185, 75 N.E. 468 (1905), the only blind participant was a horse, who, at dusk, walked into a deep, unguarded trench in the street, drawing his sighted driver in after him. Though the horse had and was using one of those common, well-known, compensatory devices for blind horses, namely a sighted driver, he walked by a faith not justified by law.

[232] *A White Cane Debate: Liechty vs. Taylor,* The Braille Monitor, Mar. 1965, p. 16; *Guide Dog or White Cane: Which One,* The Braille Monitor, Mar. 1965, p. 29; *On Dogs: Ask the Man Who Owns One,* The Braille Monitor, May 1965, p. 4; *A Further Argument on the White Cane,* The Braille Monitor, July 1965, p. 14.

[233] ALASKA COMP. LAWS ANN. §§ 28.25.010-.040 (Supp. 1963); FLA. STAT. § 413.07 (1959); ILL. REV. STAT. ch. 95½, § 172a (1959); KAN. GEN. STAT. ANN. § 8-558 (1949); KY. REV. STAT. § 189.575 (Supp. 1962); LA. REV. STAT. § 32:217 (Supp. 1962); ME. REV. STAT. ANN. ch 22, §§ 132-35 (Supp. 1963); MISS. CODE ANN. § 8203.5 (1956); MO. ANN. STAT. §§ 304.080-110 (Supp. 1959); N.C. GEN. STAT. §§ 20-175 (1953); N.D. REV. CODE § 39-10-31

cally disabled in street and automobile accidents have now been settled by the so-called white cane laws, to be discussed in detail later.[234] In substance, those laws confer on the blind, and sometimes on otherwise disabled persons, positive rights in travel if they are carrying the white cane or are led by a guide dog. These laws in the nineteen states, preserve the pre-existing rights on streets and sidewalks and in traffic of blind persons without canes or dogs. The failure to have a cane or dog, it is declared, shall not be held to be contributory negligence or evidence thereof. In general, thus, in these nineteen states, blind persons without cane or dog may travel the streets and sidewalks without being flatly precluded from recovering for accidents, or, even without having their failure to use the travel aids considered at all as a factor in determining whether they were in the exercise of due care. This provision was incorporated in the white cane law of Pennsylvania,[235] enacted after the decisions in the *Fraser*[236] and *Smith*[237] cases and the rule in those cases making it negligence per se to travel without aids has therefore now been reversed by the legislature. To do just that was the intention of the drafters and sponsors of the white cane law in Pennsylvania. The provision is also incorporated in the white cane law of North Carolina[238] enacted prior to the decision of the North Carolina Supreme Court in *Cook v. City of Winston-Salem.*[239] Nevertheless, the provision and the statute were neither discussed nor applied by the court in rendering that decision. Since the blind pedestrian in that case was guided by a dog, the provision was not literally dispositive. Yet the provision and the other clauses of the white cane law can only be read to settle the case. They are designed to free the blind without travel aids of contributory negligence in ordinary street and sidewalk accidents and to free the blind with travel aids of contributory negligence in automobile accident cases. This design is frustrated and these laws are rendered meaningless by a decision which holds that the blind with travel aids (and presumably without them as well) are guilty of contributory negligence as a matter of law in ordinary street and sidewalk accident cases if they fail to see what

---

(Supp. 1957); PA. STAT. ANN. tit. 75, § 1039 (1960); R.I. GEN. LAWS ANN. §§ 31-18-13 to 31-18-16 (1956); S.C. CODE §§ 438-41 (Supp. 1962); S.D. CODE §§ 44.0318-1, 44.9932 (Supp. 1960); TEX. REV. CIV. STAT. ANN. art. 671e (1960); VT. STAT. ANN. tit. 23, § 1106 (1959); VA. CODE ANN. §§ 46.1-237 to 46.1-240 (1950); W. VA. CODE ANN. § 1721(373)(7) (Supp. 1961).

[234] See text accompanying notes 360-411 *infra*.
[235] PA. STAT. ANN. tit. 75, § 1039 (1960).
[236] Fraser v. Freedman, 87 Pa. Super. 454 (1926).
[237] Smith v. Sneller, 345 Pa. 68, 26 A.2d 452 (1942).
[238] N.C. Sess. Laws 1949, ch. 324, §§ 1-4.
[239] 241 N.C. 422, 85 S.E.2d 696 (1955).

is plainly visible to the seeing. In North Carolina, the white cane law is thus ignored by the supreme court and the blind are required to see.

4. Making the Risk Reasonable

The text-writers more than the courts talk about balancing the risk—that is, the likelihood of the harm occurring and its seriousness when it does—against the importance to the community of the defendant's activity and the feasibility and cost of taking preventive or protective action. Some of the cases, however, do talk in these terms in the field of our concern; and, in most no doubt, it is implicit. Just as, on the one hand, the judges do not consciously consider the importance and policy of the disabled being abroad, so, on the other, they automatically assume the importance and inevitability of trenches for sewers, water and gas pipes down streets and across sidewalks, cellarways and loading pits, street and sidewalk holes for telephone poles and watercocks, miscellaneous street and sidewalk defects without purpose, and obstructions and stumbling blocks left on the roads and walks. So far as the law of torts is concerned, these things are here to stay. No judge has ever so much as intimated that municipalities, street companies, plumbers, and abutting property owners should investigate alternative methods of conducting their activities. So the remaining question is the cost of preventive or protective measures and what they should be. Here again, the answer to this question is often assumed, though discussion of it is becoming more frequent.

In the blind cases, the issue has gradually narrowed to warning versus protection. When trenches, cellarways and holes are involved, must the defendant provide a barricade sufficient to stop and hold the blind pedestrian, or does he do enough if he supplies a contraption which would indicate to the pedestrian that danger lies ahead? No court in recent times has suggested that the defendant must station a workman at the spot. Two courts have taken a definite stand that an adequate warning was adequate.[240] Others leave the question of defendant's due care to the jury. In *Haley v. London Elec. Bd.*,[241] the Lords agreed that "In the exercise of reasonable care, local authorities and other public bodies are entitled to assume that if a blind man exercises his privilege of using a public footpath he will have been trained to protect himself from collisions by the use of his stick."[242] The guard is sufficient if it is of a nature such that the stick of a blind man properly being used would

---

[240] Masterson v. Lennon, 115 Wash. 304, 197 Pac. 38 (1921); Haley v. London Elec. Bd., [1965] A.C. 778 (1964).

[241] Haley v. London Elec. Bd., *supra* note 240.

[242] *Id.* at 799.

come into contact with it. It need not be so substantial that a blind man could not knock it over and "so be propelled into the excavation."[243] In their Lordships' informed opinion, "a light fence like a towel rail about two feet high,"[244] used by the post office department, will adequately serve this purpose. Their Lordships refused to overrule a case in which a blind woman, apparently not carrying a cane, walked into the Post Office light fence, pushed it ahead of her, fell into the hole beyond and was held guilty of contributory negligence.[245] Apparently, thus, in England, despite the talk about bringing the law up to date, the street-tampering defendant is entitled to assume that blind pedestrians will be trained in the use of a cane which they will carry, and that a light, moveable, rail fence will be detected by the cane user in time for him to stop. The holding of the *Haley* case goes no further than the facts of the case require; not nearly as far as the facts of life require. Only a minor fraction of the blind are trained and skillful in the use of the cane; a somewhat larger percentage, but still very small, use canes. What about the rest? Are they condemned to a life of ostracism? "One is entitled to expect of a blind person," said Lord Reid in the *Haley* case, "a high degree of skill and care because none but the most foolhardy would venture to go out alone without having that skill and exercising that care."[246] Many reasonable, prudent, blind people do just that. To do so is only as foolhardy as to choose to live in the world rather than become a vegetable in the back room of somebody else's home.

To speak of cost to the defendant in these situations is to speak of trifling sums, both in absolute terms and in the relation of money to social policy. To furnish barricades which would keep blind people out of trenches in the sidewalks and streets, said Lord Danning in the English court of appeals, would "be too great a tax on the ordinary businesses of life."[247] This has to be a figure of speech and not a serious financial calculation. The House of Lords in *Haley*, while accepting the principle of the court of appeals in this respect, yet found the necessary warning or protection devices to be very inexpensive.

In a 1920 Scottish case,[248] much quoted in *Haley*, consideration was given to financial factors. The blind cannot afford to hire attendants so they must be permitted on the streets without them.[249] The city allows them free passage on the tramway, indicating knowledge of their pres-

---

[243] *Id.* at 800.
[244] *Id.* at 790.
[245] Pritchard v. Post Office, 114 J.P. 360 (C.A. 1950).
[246] Haley v. London Elec. Bd., [1965] A.C. 778, 791 (1964).
[247] [1964] 2 Q.B. 121, 129 (1963).
[248] M'Kibbin v. Glasgow Corp., 57 Scottish L.R. 476 (1920).
[249] *Id.* at 593.

ence and their poverty.[250] No undue financial burden is placed on the city to guard watercock holes in the street. To require the city to pad the lampposts would be an undue burden.[251] All of this is to speak in absolute fiscal terms. It is to ignore the absolute fiscal cost, not to mention the incalculable social cost, of maintaining the blind in idleness. If all of the blind people capable of doing so were moved into the streets and into employment, more than enough money would be saved to pad all the lampposts, erect gold-plated padded barricades before every hole in the city, with enough left over to pay for a small war or two. The reason for not padding the lampposts is not financial. Nor is it the fact that they are common or ordinary street structures as the Scottish court said. It is that they are not very dangerous. They run up the cost of a blind man's band-aids but little more.

D. Oh, to be Carried by a Common Carrier

With respect to common carriers, a second area in which the law of torts takes note of the disabled, there are certain obvious contrasts with the streets, highways, and sidewalks. When proceeding on the latter, the pedestrian is the active agent, propelling himself along on his own volition, having some power of control as to his course, pace, and general procedure. The streets and sidewalks are a passive and submissive instrumentality, with relatively fixed locations, contours and general characteristics. When the pedestrian becomes a passenger, the situation is reversed. He has little control either of what happens to him or of the transport equipment, which, when set in motion, creates and constitutes its own dangers. The disabled share with others a passive role, their disability having next-to-nothing to do with whether they are killed in a plane crash, train wreck, but smash-up, or taxi collision. The disabled person comes into a situation of comparative disadvantage only when the transport facility is starting, stopping, or at rest, and he is getting off, or on, making a transfer, moving from carrier to station, or streetcar to curb.

Nor, in contrast with the situation on the streets, is there a problem of preventability, based on the practicability of protection by an inanimate device or the cost thereof. The employees of the carrier are on the spot, available to serve not only as a physical barricade when appropriate, but to provide mobile and positive help.[252] Whatever the legal duty, an established function of employees of carriers, in fact realized

---

[250] *Id.* at 594.

[251] *Id.* at 598.

[252] See generally 14 Am. Jur. 2d *Carriers* §§ 871-75 (furnishing adequate accommodations), §§ 876-80 (furnishing information to passengers), §§ 884-90 (stopping to receive and discharge passengers).

and discharged it is true in varying degrees, is that of service to the passenger: in giving direction, aiding him in getting on and off and in making connections, assisting with children, bundles, and luggage. In this context, also, responsibility is less dependent on questions of foreseeability, based on the likelihood that the disabled will come along and be injured. Responsibility is dependent on identifying the disabled among the passengers and adapting assistance to need.

The awareness of the carrier's employees of the presence among the passengers of disabled persons and their needs for assistance is discussed by the courts in terms of (1) actual notice given the employees by the disabled persons or others, and (2) constructive notice arising out of the fact that the disability in the given case is reasonably apparent, that is, observable by the ordinarily prudent employee.[253] Some courts will be satisfied with nothing less than actual knowledge on the part of the employee, however derived.[254] Those permitting constructive notice and relying on what the employees should have known in the circumstances, for the most part, leave a good deal to be desired in the standards of employee alertness demanded. They are certainly not those of 20/20 vision or comparable capacity to draw inferences. Courts have held that constructive notice of infirmity or disability and the need for assistance did not arise in the following situations: A 73-year-old woman, weighing about 180 to 200 pounds, slow and sluggish of movement, preparing to descend the steps of a railroad car;[255] and a woman with an observable limp produced by a wooden leg, even though an employee had assisted her up the train's stairs when she boarded.[256] It has also been held that blindness does not necessarily impart notice. Where a blind person got aboard a train alone, slept through his stop until the train began to pull away, and was then let off in the switchyard in the small hours of the morning where he wandered for well over an hour trying to find the station, and was struck by a switch engine, the company was found not

---

[253] See Central of Ga. Ry. v. Carlisle, 2 Ala. App. 514, 517, 56 So. 737, 738 (1911); Southern Pac. Co. v. Buntin, 54 Ariz. 180, 94 P.2d 639 (1939); Denver & R.G.R.R. v. Derry, 47 Colo. 584, 587, 108 Pac. 172, 173 (1910); Pullman Palace Car Co. v. Barker, 4 Colo. 344, 347, 34 Am. Rep. 89, 91 (1878); Mitchell v. Des Moines City Ry., 161 Iowa 100, 141 N.W. 43 (1913); Wilson v. Pennsylvania R.R., 306 Ky. 325, 326, 207 S.W.2d 755, 756 (1948); Louisville Ry. v. Wilder, 143 Ky. 436, 438, 136 S.W. 892, 893 (1911); Croom v. Chicago, M. & St. P. Ry., 52 Minn. 296, 53 N.W. 1128 (1893); Scott v. Union Pac. R. Co., 99 Neb. 97, 100, 155 N.W. 217, 218 (1915); Pierce v. Delaware L. & W.R. Co., 358 Pa. 403, 406, 57 A.2d 876, 877-878 (1948); Welsh v. Spokane & I. E. R. Co., 91 Wash. 260, 157 Pac. 679 (1916); Sullivan v. Seattle Elec. Co., 51 Wash. 71, 77, 97 Pac. 1109, 1112 (1908).

[254] Scott v. Union Pac. R.R., 99 Neb. 97, 100, 155 N.W. 217, 218 (1915); Sullivan v. Seattle Elec. Co., 51 Wash. 71, 77, 97 Pac. 1109, 1112 (1908).

[255] Wilson v. Pennsylvania R.R., 306 Ky. 325, 207 S.W.2d 755 (1948).

[256] Pierce v. Delaware L. & W.R. Co., 358 Pa. 403, 57 A.2d 876 (1948).

negligent for having failed to assist him to the depot. Sleepiness and blindness look the same.[257]

Though, as in the case of the streets, it is common knowledge to employees of common carriers, judges, and everybody else, supported if need be by government statistics, that disabled persons are in the habit of using common carriers unattended and that therefore they are likely to appear on any given carrier at any time, yet the majority of courts hold, today no less than in earlier times, that: carriers are for the able-bodied in the ordinary use of normal senses and limbs;[258] the employees are "not required to anticipate [special] wants or needs,"[259] are not under a duty "to be on the lookout to discover that any particular passenger needs special assistance,"[260] or "to observe the condition of the passengers" in order to see whether "they require such assistance";[261] employees need not "on their own initiative" render any special service,[262] such as helping to detrain a woman in feeble health who was carrying a sleeping child in one arm and a valise in the other.[263]

1. Duty of Care Owed by the Common Carrier to the Disabled Passenger

The duty which the carrier owes to disabled persons, once the employees are aware or should have been aware of their presence, is vari-

---

[257] Southern Pac. Co. v. Buntin, 54 Ariz. 180, 94 P.2d 639 (1939). Other cases in which the court found no constructive notice: a woman carrying a valise, a parasol, and a fan, accompanied by her husband, preparing to descend the steps of a railroad car, Central of Ga. Ry. v. Carlisle, 2 Ala. App. 514, 56 So. 737 (1911); a man with typhoid fever and resulting impaired reasoning and senses of sight and hearing, crossing tracks in the yard to catch a train and not yet having encountered any employee of the company, Scott v. Union Pac. R.R., 99 Neb. 97, 155 N.W. 217 (1915); a man who staggered when he boarded the train at Coeur d'Alene, Idaho, aided by a trainman who remarked to the conductor that he was "pretty full," but who did not stagger or otherwise evince intoxication when he detrained at Spokane, Wash. Welsh v. Spokane & I.E.R. Co., 91 Wash. 260, 157 Pac. 679 (1916).

[258] Sevier v. Vicksburg & Meridian R.R., 61 Miss. 8, 48 Am. Rep. 74 (1883).

[259] Illinois Cent. Ry. v. Cruse, 123 Ky., 463, 471, 96 S.W. 821, 823 (1906).

[260] Ibid; see Southern Ry. v. Hayne, 209 Ala. 186, 95 So. 879 (1923).

[261] Illinois Cent. Ry. v. Cruse, 123 Ky. 463, 471, 96 S.W. 821, 823 (1906).

[262] Ibid.

[263] Illinois Cent. Ry. v. Cruse, 123 Ky. 463, 96 S.W. 821 (1906). In 1939 the Supreme Court of Arizona said about the Cruse case: "The case, so far as we know, has never been seriously criticised, nor the doctrine laid down therein repudiated, and it has been quoted approvingly in many cases besides those above cited." Southern Pac. Co. v. Buntin, 54 Ariz. 180, 187, 94 P.2d 639, 643 (1939). See also Central of Ga. Ry. v. Carlisle, 2 Ala. App. 514, 517, 56 So. 737, 738 (1911); Pullman Palace Car Co. v. Barker, 4 Colo. 344, 347, 34 Am. Rep. 89, 91-92 (1878); Wilson v. Pennsylvania R.R., 306 Ky. 325, 326-27, 207 S.W.2d 755, 756 (1948); Scott v. Union Pac. R.R., 99 Neb. 97, 101, 155 N.W. 217, 218 (1915); Welsh v. Spokane & I.E.R. Co., 91 Wash. 260, 264-65, 157 Pac. 679, 680-81 (1913); Sullivan v. Seattle Elec. Co., 51 Wash. 71, 77-78, 97 Pac. 1109, 1112 (1908). Contra Louisville Ry. v. Wilder, 143 Ky. 436, 437, 136 S.W. 892, 893 (1911): The employees must "exercise . . . the highest degree of care" in discovering disabled persons.

ously stated as reasonable care and assistance in the circumstances,[264] special care and assistance,[265] or a high, higher, highest or extraordinary degree of care.[266] The variation does not seem particularly significant. All courts pretty well agree that the employees must render such assistance as is reasonably necessary for the safety of the disabled person considering the nature of his disability.[267] This standard was not attained: by a cab driver who shut the door on the thumb of a 65-year-old diabetic, with right leg cut off above the knee, standing at the side of the cab clutching the center post where the driver had left her after assisting her from a wheelchair;[268] by a street car conductor who stood idly by watching an 18-year-old girl on crutches, with one short and shriveled leg, make her way down the streetcar steps;[269] by the pullman porter who took hold of a blind passenger's elbows and assisted him up the first step to the platform and then allowed him to proceed up the steps "feeling his way along as best he could" until he found what seemed to him the proper opening, which instead of being the entrance to the car was "the end of the platform away from the door of the car . . . the same having been left open and not closed by a gate as was the usual custom at such times."[270] In the last case, the Colorado Supreme Court declared: "Putting it as mildly as the facts justify, we say . . . that the porter, knowing of plaintiff's blindness, was guilty of reprehensible negligence in suffering plaintiff to proceed up the platform steps without even cautioning him, or watching him, or guiding his movements."[271]

In comparison, a cab company was found not negligent where five blind people were entering the cab, the driver, in making room for one of them, asked a second to move from the back to the front seat, and a third shut the door on the fingers of the second.[272] The court said the

---

[264] Denver & R.G.R.R. v. Derry, 47 Colo. 584, 589, 108 Pac. 172, 174 (1910); Mitchell v. Des Moines City Ry., 161 Iowa 100, 108-09, 141 N.W. 43, 46-47 (1913); Singletary v. Atlantic Coast Line R. Co., 217 S.C. 212, 220, 60 S.E.2d 305, 308 (1950).

[265] Mitchell v. Des Moines City Ry., 161 Iowa 100, 109-10, 141 N.W. 43, 47 (1913); Illinois Cent. Ry. v. Cruse, 123 Ky. 463, 471, 96 S.W. 821, 823 (1906); Croom v. Chicago, M. & St. P. Ry., 52 Minn. 296, 298, 53 N.W. 1128, 1129 (1893); Welsh v. Spokane & I.E.R. Co., 91 Wash. 260, 264, 157 Pac. 679, 680 (1916).

[266] Southern Pac. Co. v. Buntin, 54 Ariz. 180, 185-86, 94 P.2d 639, 641 (1939); Pullman Palace Car Co. v. Barker, 4 Colo. 344, 347, 34 Am. Rep. 89, 91 (1878); Stallard v. Witherspoon, 306 S.W.2d 299, 301 (Ky. 1957); Fournier v. Central Taxi Cab Inc., 331 Mass. 248, 249, 118 N.E.2d 767, 769 (1954); Pierce v. Delaware L. & W.R. Co., 358 Pa. 403, 406, 57 A.2d 877, 879 (1948); Scott v. Union Pac. R.R., 99 Neb. 97, 99, 155 N.W. 217, 218 (1915).

[267] 2 HARPER & JAMES, TORTS § 16.14 (1956).

[268] Stallard v. Witherspoon, 306 S.W.2d 299 (Ky. 1957).

[269] Mitchell v. Des Moines City Ry., 161 Iowa 100, 141 N.W. 43 (1913).

[270] Denver & R.G.R.R. v. Derry, 47 Colo. 584, 587, 108 Pac. 172, 173-74 (1910).

[271] Id. at 590, 108 Pac. at 174.

[272] Fournier v. Central Taxi Cab, Inc., 331 Mass. 248, 118 N.E.2d 767 (1954).

company was not bound to protect disabled passengers against "highly improbable harm."[273]

In the case of accidents to pedestrians caused by defects, obstructions

---

[273] *Id.* at 249, 118 N.E.2d at 768 (1954). The duty common carriers owe to normal passengers is commonly phrased in terms of the highest degree of care, sometimes qualified by "consistent with the practical operation of the business." *Accord* Pullman Palace Car Co. v. Barker, 4 Colo. 344, 345, 34 Am. Rep. 89 (1878); McMahon v. New York, N.H., & H.R.R., 136 Conn. 372, 374, 71 A.2d 557, 558 (1950); Louisville Taxicab & Transfer Co. v. Smallwood, 311 Ky. 405, 408, 224 S.W.2d 450, 452 (1949); Griffin v. Louisville Taxicab & Transfer Co., 300 Ky. 279, 280, 188 S.W.2d 449, 450 (1945); Guinevan v. Checker Taxi Co., 289 Mass., 295, 297, 194 N.E. 100, 101 (1935); Scott v. Union Pac. R.R., 99 Neb. 97, 99, 155 N.W. 217, 218 (1915); Archer v. Pittsburgh Ry., 349 Pa. 547-48, 37 A.2d 539-40 (1944). Bennett v. Seattle Elec. Co., 56 Wash. 407, 411, 105 Pac. 825, 827 (1909). This doctrine was first laid down in this country by the United States Supreme Court in a case dealing with an overturned stagecoach where the carrier was said to undertake to transport persons safely "so far as human care and foresight can go . . . ." Stokes v. Saltonstall, 38 U.S. (13 Pet.) 181, 190 (1839). Harper and James point out that the reasonable care rule, announced by some courts, in guarding passengers against "the great potential dangers which attend rapid transit" is in effect the same as a high degree of care and that the difference between the two forms of statement "resolves itself into one merely of logomachy." 2 HARPER & JAMES, *op. cit. supra* note 267, § 16.14. Moreover, at the same time the courts speak of the highest degree of care, they sometimes declare that the carrier is not under any obligation to assist passengers in alighting, any help given is a matter of courtesy, the employees need merely call the station and stop long enough to provide reasonable opportunity for the passengers to leave the cars or board them. Central of Ga. Ry. v. Carlisle, 2 Ala. App. 514, 516, 56 So. 737, 738 (1911); Ill. Cent. Ry. v. Cruse, 123 Ky. 463, 96 S.W. 821 (1906); Steeg v. St. Paul City Ry., 50 Minn. 149, 151, 52 N.W. 393, 394 (1892); Yarnell v. Kansas City Ry., 113 Mo. 570, 576-77, 21 S.W. 1, 2 (1893). The high degree of care rule seems to be applied principally with respect to the operation of the equipment. Some courts hold that the carrier is bound to provide a suitable and safe place and means of boarding and alighting, and that whether these were provided and the assistance that should have been offered if they were not by the reasonably prudent employee are questions for the jury. *E.g.*, Mitchell v. Des Moines City Ry., 161 Iowa 100, 109, 141 N.W. 43, 47 (1913); Morarity v. Durham Traction Co., 154 N.C. 586, 588, 70 S.E. 938, 939 (1911). Employees in discharging their duties must take reasonable care not to injure passengers. Griffin v. Louisville Taxicab & Transfer Co., *supra* at 281, 188 S.W.2d at 450; Tefft v. Boston Elevated Ry., 285 Mass. 121, 188 N.E. 507 (1934); Benson v. Northland Transp. Co., 200 Minn. 445, 448, 274 N.W. 532, 533 (1937). For an analysis of the differences in boarding and alighting problems of taxis, buses, streetcars, and trains, see Southeastern Greyhound Lines v. Woods, 298 Ky. 773, 184 S.W.2d 93 (1944). The Kentucky court concluded that the rule that a carrier owes passengers the highest duty of care is too generally stated. Rather it should read: that the carrier has "the duty to exercise the highest degree of care, skill and diligence for the safety of the passenger as is required by the nature and risk of the undertaking, in view of the mode of conveyance and other circumstances involved, which may vary according to the immediate activity, instrumentality, time or place." *Id.* at 775-76, 184 S.W.2d at 95. "The modern trend is away from the artificial and perplexing categories of high and highest degree of care and toward the one standard for all cases of reasonable or ordinary care under the circumstances of the particular case." 14 AM. JUR. 2d *Carriers* § 916 (1964). For cases dealing with the duty of carriers to furnish suitable accommodations, including providing heat necessary for the health, comfort, and safety of passengers during the trip, see Silver v. New York Cent. R.R., 329 Mass. 14, 105 N.E.2d 923 (1925); Owen v. Rochester-Penfield Bus Co., 278 App. Div. 5, 103 N.Y.S.2d 137 (1951).

or excavations in the streets, the judicial focus of discussion is often the conduct of the pedestrian and whether he was duly careful in seeking to avoid harm to himself. In the common carrier cases, doubtless because of the nature of the business including its potential dangerousness in a number of ways, the courts are most often preoccupied with determining the character and extent of the duty of the defendant, and comparatively little is said about contributory negligence. The passenger is of course called upon to exercise due care for his own safety[274]—even required upon rare occasion to make "a more than ordinary diligent and attentive use" of his remaining senses[275]—but what that care is, in the circumstances of disability and the surroundings of various common carriers, is seldom analyzed. The situation is regarded as largely in the control of the carriers, and as very little in the control of the passengers. The passenger is under no duty to ask for needed services if his disability is apparent.[276] Contributory negligence would normally be hard to establish when the passenger was being assisted by the employee.[277] The principal areas left for possible contributory negligence are in the failure to request assistance when disability is not apparent or in not allowing employees a suitable chance to render the aid. The Supreme Court of South Carolina held that there was contributory negligence as a matter of law when a visibly deformed and crippled midget alighted from a train unaided.[278] He had not given the employees, said the court, "a reasonable opportunity" to help him.[279] It is pointed out in the American Law Reports that the carrier's conduct at times seems to give the disabled passenger a choice of two dangers: a danger of injury if he alights at once; a danger of injury if he is carried to some further point where there will be no one to aid him.[280] The passenger can hardly be charged with negligence if he decides to take his chances at once. In addition, the emergency doctrine is applicable in determining whether the choice was a reasonable

---

[274] See, *e.g.*, Yazoo & M.V.R. Co. v. Shaggs 181 Miss. 150, 179 So. 274 (1938); Singletary v. Atlantic Coast Line R. Co., 217 S.C. 212, 219, 60 S.E.2d 305, 308 (1950). The Washington Supreme Court said that the carrier owed the passenger, crazed with drink, "a duty commensurate with his condition. The corollary of this rule must be that his duty to care for his own safety should be measured by his condition as to sobriety." Bennett v. Seattle Elec. Co., 56 Wash. 407, 410, 105 Pac. 825, 827 (1909).

[275] Gonzales v. New York & Harlem R.R., 1 Jones & Spencer 57, 62 (N.Y. Sup. Ct. 1871); Anschel v. Pennsylvania R.R., 34 Pa. 123, 127, 29 A.2d 694, 697 (1943).

[276] Mitchell v. Des Moines City Ry., 161 Iowa 100, 108, 141 N.W. 43, 46 (1913): "Most people afflicted as she [plaintiff] was feel a delicacy in asking assistance or in urging upon the attention of strangers the fact that they are unfortunate and crippled."

[277] See cases cited in 14 AM. JUR. 2d *Carriers* § 1011 n.21 (1964).

[278] Singletary v. Atlantic Coast Line R. Co., 217 S.C. 212, 60 S.E.2d 305 (1950).

[279] *Id.* at 217, 60 S.E.2d at 308.

[280] Annot., 30 A.L.R.2d 334, 337 (1953).

one.[281] Moreover, it has been held that where the passenger's disability prevented him from discovering that the car was moving, he was not negligent per se in getting off.[282]

Noticeably absent from the common carrier cases is talk about some of the common, well-known, compensatory devices for the blind. Either the seeing-eye dog or the cane would be helpful in keeping the blind man from falling off the unguarded end of the train platform; but neither would be particularly helpful in finding a connecting train or in locating the station from the middle of the switchyard. The cane but not the dog would be helpful in descending train steps, locating the stool placed at the bottom, and determining the height of the steps. Doubtless the absence of judicial talk about these devices is due to the presence of the employee on the scene, regarded by courts as more useful and reliable than either of the other compensatory aids.

That the disabled who need them ought to be provided with attendants, as some courts have said,[283] leaves open the question: by whom? To require the impoverished disabled to supply them out of their own resources on penalty of not being able to travel on common carriers is simply one form of locking the disabled up in their houses and institutions. The government-sponsored arrangements[284] by which blind passengers may take a guide with them for the price of one ticket are a recognition of the poverty of the blind as well as their supposed need for guide services. They do not solve the problem of the blind person who is without a guide and who, because of the availability of these arrangements on almost all bus and railroad lines in the United States, is often told that he will not be permitted to get aboard unattended. The arrangements thus work in some cases to the disadvantage of the disabled traveler by giving support to the carriers in the free exercise of a supposed right not to accommodate them. Where services are abundantly available on the airlines, supplying the disabled passenger with many attendants, and only the blind person's poverty remains, the National Federation of the Blind has opposed the two-for-one concession authorized by bills currently pending before Congress.[285] As to poverty, the blind are not to be distinguished from others who are poor.[286]

---

281 *Ibid.*

282 Poak v. Pacific Elec. Ry., 177 Cal. 190, 170 Pac. 159 (1918).

283 *E.g.*, Croom v. Chicago M. & St. P. Ry., 52 Minn. 296, 53 N.W. 28 (1893).

284 See, *e.g.*, 44 Stat. 1247 (1927), 49 U.S.C. § 22(1) (1964); CAL. PUB. UTIL. CODE § 525; HAWAII REV. LAW § 109-22 (1957); KAN. GEN. STAT. ANN. § 66701 (1949); N.J. STAT. ANN. § 48:3-34 (1940).

285 H.R. 8068, 88th Cong., 1st Sess. (1964); National Federation of the Blind Resolution 64-09, Phoenix 1964.

286 Some smaller groups of the blind have favored these measures: The BVA Bulletin, Oct. 1964, Resolution No. 13.

The basis and extent of the duty of common carriers toward disabled passengers is set forth in the oft-quoted words of *Croom v. Chicago, M. & St. P. Ry.*:[287]

> Of course, a railroad company is not bound to turn its cars into nurseries or hospitals, or its employees into nurses. If a passenger, because of extreme youth or old age, or any mental or physical infirmities, is unable to take care of himself, he ought to be provided with an attendant to take care of him. But if the company voluntarily accepts a person as a passenger, without an attendant, whose inability to care for himself is apparent or made known to its servants, and renders special care and assistance necessary, the company is negligent if such assistance is not afforded. In such case it must exercise the degree of care commensurate with the responsibility which it has thus voluntarily assumed, and that care must be such as is reasonably necessary to insure the safety of the passenger, in view of his mental and physical condition. This is a duty required by law as well as the dictates of humanity.[288]

Thus, the basis of the duty is the voluntary and knowing acceptance of responsibility, making plain that common carriers are free to decline to carry disabled persons, at least those who "ought to be provided with an attendant to take care" of them.

The doctrine of the *Croom* case would seem, on its face, to infringe the common law command of equal and non-discriminatory access to the services and facilities of common carriers and to repudiate any general right on the part of the disabled to travel by this mode. The courts have taken the position that, first, the refusal of the carriers to transport disabled persons is based on proper classification and warrantable discrimination and therefore is not a violation of the common law command; and, second, that the disabled in general do not have a right to be carried by the common carriers, the cases sometimes cited for the proposition that they do being in fact the foundation of the doctrine of the *Croom* case.[289]

The common law command of equal and non-discriminatory access arises out of and is part of the notion that carriers are common, that is, that they hold themselves out to the public generally as in the business

---

[287] 52 Minn. 296, 53 N.W. 1128 (1893).

[288] *Id.* at 298, 53 N.W. 1129.

[289] See Williams v. Louisville & N.R., 150 Ala. 324, 43 So. 576 (1907); Yazoo & M. Valley R. v. Littleton, 177 Ark. 199, 5 S.W.2d 930 (1928); Illinois Cent. R. v. Allen, 121 Ky. 138, 89 S.W. 150 (1905); Illinois Cent. R. v. Smith, 85 Miss. 349, 37 So. 643 (1905); Zackery v. Mobile & O.R., 75 Miss. 746, 23 So. 434 (1898); Zackery v. Mobile & O.R., 74 Miss. 520, 21 So. 246 (1897); Sevier v. Vicksburg & M.R., 61 Miss. 8 (1883); Hogan v. Nashville Interurban Ry., 131 Tenn. 244, 174 S.W. 1118 (1915); Benson v. Tacoma Ry. & Power Co., 51 Wash. 216, 98 Pac. 605 (1908).

of transporting persons for hire.[290] The command is imposed by law, does not arise out of the contractual relation between the carrier and the passenger, is intended for the benefit of the traveling public and in many states is re-declared and strengthened by statute and constitutional provision.[291] But equal access, the courts hold, is provided when all who are similarly situated are admitted on the same terms and a ban against discrimination does not forbid distinctions among potential passengers that are warranted by the special relation of a particular class of persons to the function of the carrier or the act of transportation.[292] Thus they have held that carriers can refuse to receive persons who are objectionable, dangerous to the health, safety, or convenience of the other passengers: those "who desire to injure the company, notoriously bad, or justly suspicious persons, gross or immoral persons, drunken persons . . . those who refuse to obey the rules,"[293] those who are obnoxiously filthy,[294] or those who are affected with a contagious or repulsive disease.[295] To this motley crew, in view of the association in men's minds between these ill-assorted persons and problems, it was inevitable that the courts should add the physically disabled. To supply their need for attendants, would, in effect, convert the conveyance into a hospital and the carrier's employees into nurses.[296]

2. *The Right of the Disabled to be Transported on Common Carriers*

The leading cases on the right of the disabled to be carried by a common carrier open the door of the carrier only a crack to admit a few.[297] They hold that the carrier may not properly adopt a flat rule that

---

290 See, *e.g.*, Hogan v. Nashville Interurban Ry., *supra* note 289, at 254, 174 S.W. at 1120. See generally, 13 Am. Jur. 2d *Carriers* § 2 (1964).

291 See cases and statutes cited in 13 Am. Jur. 2d *Carriers* §§ 175, 181 (1964), 14 Am. Jur. 2d *Carriers* § 859 (1964).

292 *Ibid.*

293 Zachery v. Mobile & O.R. Co., 74 Miss. 520, 21 So. 246 (1897).

294 Atwater v. Delaware, L. & W.R. Co., 48 N.J.L. 55, 2 Atl. 803 (1886).

295 Pullman Car Co. v. Krauss, 145 Ala. 395, 40 So. 398 (1906); Bogard v. Illinois Cent. R., 144 Ky. 649, 139 S.W. 855 (1911); Atwater v. Delaware, L. & W.R., *supra* note 294.

296 Pullman Palace Car Co. v. Barker, 4 Colo. 344, 34 Am. Rep. 89 (1878); Croom v. Chicago, M. & St. P. Ry., 52 Minn. 296, 53 N.W. 1128 (1893).

297 In Pullman Palace Car Co. v. Barker, 4 Colo. 344, 34 Am. Rep. 89 (1878), the ill were declared to have the right. The statement was dictum however and the emphasis of the opinion was upon "the increased risk arising from conditions affecting their fitness to journey" resting upon their own shoulders where they are unknown to the carrier. *Id.* at 348, 34 Am. Rep. at 92. For the language casting doubt on the right in Colorado, see Denver & R.G.R.R. v. Derry, 47 Col. 584, 108 Pac. 172 (1910): "It may be that a railroad company is not bound to receive as a passenger one who is helpless or blind, or otherwise incapable of properly caring for himself, unless accompanied by a competent attendant." *Id.* at 588, 108 Pac. at 174. A 1911 Kentucky case, Louisville Ry. v. Wilder, 143 Ky. 436, 136 S.W. 892 (1911), declared the right in more encompassing terms: "[C]hildren . . . feeble, infirm, . . . aged

no sick, insane, imbecile, cripple, invalid, or blind person will be received by conductors, or sold tickets by agents, unless accompanied by some person charged with their care and comfort while traveling.[298] There was no disposition to question this rule as a wholesale invasion of the rights of a large class of people to live in the world, or to go about in it; no reference to the cases declaring the disabled have the same right as others to be upon the streets and highways, saying in effect that if they are able to get there they have a right to be there; no doubts about the proposition—indeed it was explicitly affirmed—that carriers may refuse to receive persons if they require "other care than that which the law requires the carrier to bestow upon all its passengers alike."[299] Moreover, the Mississippi court felt itself able to say what classes of persons require such "other care," though it faltered a little in vouchsafing information about the character of the additional care: "Primarily the affliction of blindness unfits every person for safe travel by railway, if unaccompanied."[300] Accordingly, the carrier might presume blind people unfit to travel alone, a presumption not to be regarded as "a hardship upon the persons afflicted with blindness or other disabling physical infirmity" but rather "as a safeguard thrown around them for their protection."[301] But since not every sick, crippled, infirm, or blind person requires additional care, the individual must be allowed to overcome this presumption against him if he can. This he can do by offering to the company's agent proof of his competence to travel alone. The company's flat rule of exclusion was thus to be traded for a presumption of the incompetence of the disabled, itself a rule of exclusion but not a flat one. This opened the door a crack to admit those adjudged by uninformed agents to be competent and who have the hardihood to insist on the point. In the social context of the day, the courts did not feel it necessary to find some rational justification for the closed-door policy which they and the carriers adopted; quite the contrary, they found it necessary to justify opening the door even the crack they did. Two reasons were given for doing so: fear that the less severely disabled—those only slightly sick or lacking a leg or arm—might be caught in the dragnet at

persons [and] persons who are encumbered with babies or bundles . . . . all these classes of persons have the right to use the car . . . ." *Id.* at 440, 136 S.W. at 894. Here again the statement is dictum. The question in the case was whether the carrier was negligent in starting the train before the plaintiff with a baby in her arms was seated.

[298] Illinois Cent. R. Co. v. Smith, 85 Miss. 349, 37 So. 643 (1905); Zackery v. Mobile & O.R. Co., 75 Miss. 746, 23 So. 434 (1898); Zackery v. Mobile & O.R. Co., 74 Miss. 520, 21 So. 246 (1897); Hogan v. Nashville Interurban Ry., 131 Tenn. 244, 174 S.W. 1118 (1915).

[299] Illinois Cent. R. Co. v. Smith, 85 Miss. 349, 356, 37 So. 643, 644 (1905).

[300] *Ibid.*

[301] *Ibid.*

the station door;[302] and the undesirability of placing an "unwarranted handicap on a class of men capable of being serviceable to society, and therefore on society itself."[303] The courts did not discuss why either serviceability to society or the right to live in it should be tested by the physical capacity to mount the train steps unaided or find one's way to a connecting carrier. They only thought it a proper test for those who could do these things unaided. To the best of our knowledge and belief this question was not put to Franklin Delano Roosevelt as he was assisted aboard a train to go to Washington to be inaugurated President of the United States.

The rule governing the right of the disabled to ride on common carriers, thus evolved by the courts around the turn of the century, constituted at that time a slight improvement on a harsher rule sought to be imposed by the railroads. While perhaps consistent with the prevailing social attitudes of that day, but certainly inconsistent with the rule long since developed by the courts regarding the right of the disabled to be on the streets and highways,[304] that rule is still invoked by the carriers today. In the summer of 1965, it was cited by an agent in Atlanta, Georgia, as justifying refusal to transport a blind person with normal ability to get about. It was widely circulated by the passenger agents' association as their answer to a flurry of protest from organizations of the blind.[305] "Rule 8(f). *Ticketing Infirm or Objectionable Passengers.*—No person, who because of mental, physical, or other disability, is incapable of caring for himself or herself, will be received as a passenger, *unless accompanied by a competent attendant,* and no contract for transportation or ticket purchased by or for such a person in contravention of this rule shall be valid."[306]

The objections to this rule which existed when it was formulated are still valid today and the changed times have added others. At least as to the physically disabled, it is wrong in principle. Services necessary for the use of their equipment and facilities should be provided by the carriers as part of the care which "the law requires the carrier to bestow upon all its passengers alike."[307] That this would compel them to convert their trains into hospitals and their employees into nurses is probably

---

302 Zackery v. Mobile & O.R. Co., 75 Miss. 746, 752, 23 So. 434, 435 (1898).

303 Hogan v. Nashville Interurban Ry., 131 Tenn. 244, 251-52, 174 S.W. 1118, 1120 (1915). The *Hogan* case involved a young paralytic who, using crutches, traveled by train daily to Vanderbilt University where he was a student and a teacher.

304 See text accompanying notes 132-67 *supra.*

305 Letter to R. Kletzing, president NFB, from Trans-Continental R.R. Passenger Ass'n, E. B. Padrick, Chairman, July 6, 1965.

306 *Ibid.*

307 Illinois Cent. R. Co. v. Smith, 85 Miss. 349, 356, 37 So. 643, 644 (1905).

colorful argument rather than fact. In any event, it speaks only to the cost; and the public should bear the cost of making effective such an important right. The argument about the necessity of Rule 8(f) is largely academic. In practice, services adequate to enable most disabled persons to travel, even though they might commonly be thought to require an attendant, are provided by the agents of the company or are available from porters and others on the premises. Equally important, the rule is misapplied by agents not generally knowledgeable about such things to exclude disabled persons who do not need an attendant. Arguments about cost, availability of existing services, and mis-administration, however, all must give way to the fact that the rule is in contravention of today's policy of integration of the disabled into the social and economic life of the community. That policy requires at least that the presumption of incompetence of the disabled should be exchanged for a presumption of competence, leaving the burden of disproof on the carrier; and that every disabled person who makes his way to the station should be put aboard with whatever help is necessary. In practice, this is what the large airlines do, without noticeable disaster to themselves or to the country. Architectural barriers in public conveyances should receive the same treatment as they do in public buildings and facilities.[308]

If the disabled are to live in the world, travel by common carrier is a necessary right—as necessary as is the right to use the streets, highways and sidewalks. Indeed, it may properly be regarded as aspect of the right to be upon the streets, highways, and walks. That the latter are public, while the common carriers are in some sense private, does not change the nature of the right or its necessity and harmony with basic social policy. People cannot live in the world, today, more than ever, without moving freely within communities and between communities. This involves not only walking or riding wheelchairs upon the sidewalks and streets, but also utilizing such means of transportation over them as are commonly available to others. The disabled are less able to use private cars driven by themselves, and are correspondingly more dependent on public transportation. The fact that common carriers are regulated and subsidized by the public, and are engaged in a common calling with historic common law implications of rights to equal access, does not create the claim of the disabled to live in the world and gain access to it through the use of common carriers. It does, however, add strength to that claim and make its denial even less tenable. Only when that right and its implications are fully understood by the courts, and avowed and implemented by them, will this branch of the law of torts

---

[308] See text accompanying notes 102-31 *supra*.

be brought into conformity with the demands of the second half of the twentieth century and its policy of the social and economic integration of the disabled.

The extent to which the existing rule of the carriers has been modified, if at all, by the guide dog statutes is not entirely clear. Those statutes in twenty-three[309] states expressly cover public conveyances, occasionally, as in California, detailing these as "common carriers, airplane, motor vehicle, railroad train, motor bus, street car, boat . . . ."[310] As noted earlier,[311] these statutes are generally addressed to the problem of gaining admittance for the dog, that is, of removing restrictions on its presence. In the case of public conveyances, they also seek to make plain that the master is not to be charged for the transportation of the dog,[312] and sometimes that the dog is not to occupy a seat.[313] The special question presented with respect to the carriers is whether the dog is to be treated as "a competent attendant" within the meaning of their rule; or whether the blind person adjudged by an agent to be incompetent is required to be accompanied by a competent human attendant in addition? The narrowest view of the statutes is that they do not enlarge the class of blind persons eligible to travel unattended and that the persons otherwise competent to travel alone may take their dogs with them. An intermediate view is that the statutes authorize all blind persons with dogs to travel, eliminating all questions of their competence. The broadest view is that the statutes presuppose a right of all persons to use common carriers, and, presupposing that right, they are designed to remove special obstacles placed in the way of blind persons having their dogs with them when exercising the right. The first view conforms to the literalism of the statutes. The third view conforms to the historic origins and purposes of the statutory formulation and the policy of integrationism. The second view does not particularly conform to either, but is the one that is followed in practice. Arguments between the agents of common car-

---

309 Arkansas, California, Colorado, Connecticut, Florida, Georgia, Hawaii, Illinois, Indiana, Iowa, Louisiana, Maine, Massachusetts, Michigan, Missouri, New Jersey, New Mexico, New York, Rhode Island, Tennessee, Texas, Washington, West Virginia. See note 74 *supra* for a listing of the applicable statutes.

310 CAL. PEN. CODE § 643.5.

311 See text accompanying notes 69-102 *supra.*

312 ARK. STAT. ANN. § 78-212 (Supp. 1957); CAL. PEN. CODE § 643.5; CONN. REV. STAT. § 22-346a (Supp. 1963); IDAHO CODE ANN. § 18-5812A (Supp. 1965). IOWA CODE ANN. § 351.30 (Supp. 1964); ME. REV. STAT. § 54 (Supp. 1963); MASS. STAT. ANN. § 98A (1956); MO. STAT. ANN. § 209.150 (1962); N.J. STAT. ANN. § 48:3-34 (1953); R.I. STAT. ANN. § 29-2-16 (1957); TEX. STAT. ANN. § 25-889a (1960); WASH. REV. CODE ANN. § 81.28.140 (1962); W. VA. CODE ANN. § 2568(1) (1961).

313 GA. CODE ANN. § 79-601 (1964); IND. STAT. ANN. § 16-212 (1964); LA. STAT. ANN. § 52 (Supp. 1964).

riers and the blind travelers focus on the right of the dog to go aboard; the right of the master is not disputed. Thus is human progress achieved. Since there are few guiding and no attendant functions the dog can perform in or about public conveyances, this is an ironic method of advancing human rights.

E. Automobiles

Automobile law is the third area in which the law of torts pays special attention to the disabled. The rules of negligence as they stood at the advent of the automobile have been applied generally to the new means of locomotion—true, not without some adaptation, selection, and difference of emphasis.

The starting point is the pre-existing right of people to use the streets and highways. They have this right whether afoot or in automobiles and they can exercise it without distinction as to time or place. Thus, pedestrians and drivers were early held to have an equal right not only to the use of the streets and highways but to be in any part of them at any time.[314] When using the streets and highways, pedestrians and drivers alike are under an obligation to proceed in a safe and careful fashion so as not to infringe the equal rights of others or to injure them. As always, due care is determined by the circumstances.[315]

Rules of the road have been developed by custom, statute and ordinance to make it possible for the hordes of pedestrians and drivers to use the roads and streets efficiently, with maximum satisfaction and minimum injury to all in the exercise of equal rights. Otherwise, automobiles would have to proceed at the pace of the slowest pedestrian. These rules generally provide that the pedestrian has the right of way in marked cross walks, at intersections, and on the side of the road. Drivers have the right of way elsewhere. Drivers and pedestrians alike must proceed with due care even when they have the right of way.[316] When they do not have the right of way, they may still proceed but must do so with care appropriate in the circumstances, including the circum-

---

[314] Apperson v. Lazro, 44 Ind. App. 186, 87 N.E. 97 (1909); McLaughlin v. Griffin, 155 Iowa 302, 135 N.W. 1107 (1912); Warruna v. Dick, 261 Pa. 602, 104 Atl. 749 (1918); Dougherty v. Davis, 51 Pa. Super. 229 (1912).

[315] Rush v. Lagomorsino, 196 Cal. 308, 237 Pac. 1066 (1925); Fahey v. Madden, 58 Cal. App. 537, 209 Pac. 41 (1923); Carpenter v. McKissick, 37 Idaho 729, 217 Pac. 1025 (1923); Stotts v. Taylor, 130 Kan. 158, 285 Pac. 571 (1930); Button v. Metz, 66 N.M. 485, 349 P.2d 1047 (1960); Feltner v. Bishop, 348 P.2d 548 (Wyo. 1960).

[316] CAL. VEHICLE CODE §§ 2.1950, 2.1954 (Supp. 1965). See also ILL. ANN. STAT., ch. 95½, § 172(c) (Supp. 1965); N.Y. VEHICLE & TRAFFIC LAW § 1154; TEXAS REV. CIV. STAT art. 6701d, § 79 (1960).

stance that others have the right of way.[317] In view of the apportionment of rights of way and alternate rights to use particular portions of the streets and highways, the equal character of the rights of pedestrians and drivers has gradually disappeared from the rhetoric of judicial opinions.

The disabled have the same right to the use of the streets and highways that other people do. When they exercise the right, they too must proceed with due care in the circumstances, including the circumstance of their disability. In 1909, an Indiana court, in a case involving an infirm and defectively sighted plaintiff who was run down by the defendant's automobile, held that the plaintiff had a right to be on the highway unattended and was bound to use only ordinary care when there.[318] The pedestrian and the car had the same right to the road and must not infringe each other's use.[319] Since the defendant had so infringed the right of the plaintiff by negligently failing to pay proper attention to his presence on the highway, judgment against him was sustained. In 1912, in a leading case[320] the Iowa Supreme Court, affirming a judgment for a plaintiff who was struck by the defendant's automobile, explicitly applied the rule in *Hill v. City of Glenwood*,[321] a 1904, blind plaintiff, defective sidewalk case. In the 1912 case, the plaintiff, who had been blind for five or six years and who was familiar with the streets of the town, walked along the main business street and waited to cross at the corner. He let a buggy go by, listened, heard nothing more, started across, and was struck. The court held that the plaintiff had done all he was required to do.[322]

As to contributory negligence in this area, the courts generally follow the line restated by the New Hampshire Supreme Court: "[T]he [reasonable man] standard has been flexible enough in the case of the aged and physically disabled persons to bend with the practical experiences of every day life. The law does not demand that the blind shall see, or the deaf shall hear, or that the aged shall maintain the traffic ability of the young."[323] The reasonable man standard does require that the dis-

---

317 CAL. VEHICLE CODE § 1951; NEW YORK VEHICLE & TRAFFIC LAW, §§ 1151, 1154; ILL. ANN. STAT. ch. 95½, §§ 170-175, especially § 172 (Supp. 1965); PA. STAT. ANN. tit. 75, § 1039 (1959); TEX. REV. CIV. STAT. art. 6701d, §§ 33-34, 82 (1960); N.C. GEN. STAT. § 20-174 (1937). See also Pearson & Dickerson Contractors v. Harrington, 60 Ariz. 354, 137 P.2d 381 (1943); Rhimer v. Davis, 126 Wash. 470, 218 Pac. 193 (1923).

318 Apperson v. Lazro, 44 Ind. App. 186, 87 N.E. 97 (1909).

319 *Id.* at 186, 88 N.E. at 100 (1909).

320 McLaughlin v. Griffin, 155 Iowa 302, 135 N.W. 1107 (1904).

321 124 Iowa 479, 100 N.W. 522 (1904).

322 McLaughlin v. Griffin, 155 Iowa 302, 135 N.W. 1107 (1904).

323 Bernard v. Russell, 103 N.H. 76, 77, 164 A.2d 577, 578 (1960).

abled make greater use of their remaining senses and faculties: that the blind listen more carefully, the deaf look more closely, and the aged or lame allow more space and time.

The distinctiveness of the problems of the deaf arises from the invisibility of their condition and hence the absence of notice to drivers. As a factor in travel accidents, especially those involving automobiles, deafness is almost automatically considered exclusively in terms of the standard of care of the deaf person or, in other words, of the negligence of the deaf plaintiff. The deaf pedestrian who puts himself in a place of danger by walking along a streetcar track must, on peril of being found contributorily negligent as a matter of law, look backward at suitable intervals as well as forward.[324] If he walks diagonally across the roadway on a clear but dark night, he must, at the same peril, be sufficiently watchful of his surroundings to discover that a car with lights aglow, moving at a lawful speed and on the proper side of the road, is approaching him from his right rear.[325] And if he should happen to stand in the middle of a country road just wide enough for one car, the jury might very well think that he should "take a position facing across the road instead of along it so that he could see both ways, or one way as well as the other, by merely turning his head."[326] On the other hand, the deaf pedestrian in making compensatory use of his eyes need not continually look in all directions but may fix his attention on the direction from which the next danger is to be anticipated.[327] He is entitled to assume, moreover, that drivers will not exceed the speed limit.[328] If the pedestrian was otherwise in a position of right the fact that hearing would have saved him will not relieve the defendant of liability.[329] A deaf pedestrian who, approaching the corner, stopped, waited for the light to change, and then proceeded to cross the street, was found not contributorily negligent either as a matter of law or as a matter of fact when he was struck by a fire truck responding to an alarm, moving north in a south-bound lane, with siren and bell sounding at intervals, the traffic on the block having been stopped.[330] The plaintiff, said the court, "used his eyes and did all that prudence and care would require under the circumstances. . . . [He] was entitled to assume that the green light gave him the right of

---

[324] Kerr v. Connecticut, 107 Conn. 304, 140 Atl. 751 (1928).

[325] Hizam v. Blackman, 103 Conn. 547, 131 Atl. 415 (1925).

[326] Hanson v. Matas, 212 Wis. 275, 279, 249 N.W. 505, 506 (1933).

[327] Robb v. Quaker City Cab Co., 283 Pa. 454, 129 Atl. 331 (1925).

[328] See, Covert v. Randall, 298 Mich. 38, 298 N.W. 396 (1941); Robb v. Quaker City Cab Co., *supra* note 327.

[329] Fink v. City of New York, 206 Misc. 79, 132 N.Y.S.2d 172 (Sup. Ct. 1954); *cf.* Wilson v. Freeman, 271 Mass. 438, 171 N.E. 469 (1930).

[330] Fink v. City of New York, *supra* note 329.

way. . . . [Plaintiff] is not to be penalized because of such affliction and not being able to hear siren and bell."[331]

Cases dealing with the contributory negligence of the lame are too few in number, scattered in jurisdiction, and some of them too old to be revealing of a judicial view of the special travel problems of this group. In a 1911 Arkansas case,[332] the appellate court held erroneous instructions to the jury that if the motorist ran into the pedestrian a prima facie case of the motorist's negligence was established. In holding, at this early stage of placing the automobile in its proper place in the law of torts, that negligence and contributory negligence were matters of fact, the court did not concern itself with the fact that the plaintiff was "a beggar on his crutches,"[333] except to say that such as he have the same right to the use of the streets as the man in his automobile. That the crutches gave notice to the motorist of the pedestrian's condition, and therefore of the care required of him in the circumstances, was not a subject of judicial comment.

The New Hampshire court, in a 1946 case,[334] held that the lame can only be required to do what they can do, and whether, with their limitation, they have exercised due care at an intersection is a question for the jury. In a 1954 Michigan case,[335] plaintiff, with a bad hip, and using a cane, was found contributorily negligent as a matter of law for failing to make "further observation in the direction of the approaching vehicle after proceeding into the lane of foreseeable danger. . . . Having discovered the oncoming vehicle, it is the pedestrian's duty to keep watch of its progress and to exercise reasonable care and caution to avoid being struck by it."[336] In Pennsylvania, with its fixation on contributory negligence, this rule was applied to a lame pedestrian with a cane who had not discovered the oncoming automobile in his careful observation before leaving the curb. The court held he must maintain a vigilant lookout all the way across.[337] In California, a cripple on crutches, crossing at an intersection and struck near the opposite curb, was held to have had a right to be where he was and to have exercised due care in the circumstances.[338] In that case, however, the plaintiff saw the defendant's car three or four blocks down the street and kept his eye on it all the

---

331 *Id*. at 80, 132 N.Y.S.2d at 173.

332 Millsap v. Brodgon, 97 Ark. 469, 134 S.W. 632 (1911).

333 *Id*. at 472, 134 S.W. at 633.

334 Bellemare v. Ford, 94 N.H. 38, 45 A.2d 882 (1946).

335 Heger v. Meissner, 340 Mich. 586, 66 N.W.2d 200 (1954).

336 *Id*. at 589, 66 N.W.2d at 222, citing Ludwig v. Hendricks, 235 Mich. 633, 638, 56 N.W.2d 409, 411 (1953).

337 Rucheski v. Wisswesser, 355 Pa. 400, 50 A.2d 291 (1947).

338 Florman v. Patzer, 133 Cal. App. 358, 24 P.2d 228 (1933).

way. But for the fact that the defendant was speeding, the plaintiff would have made it across.

In the case of the blind, relatively less emphasis is placed on the conduct of the pedestrian and more on that of the defendant: less on contributory negligence and more on the higher degree of care owed by the defendant.[339] The courts uniformly hold that the totally blind and the partially blind are entitled to rely upon the protection of traffic signals at intersections,[340] and that this is true whether they detect a change in the signal by the sound of a bell,[341] by notice from others that a light has changed,[342] or presumably by their realizing that other pedestrians are starting across and that cars have stopped. At intersections not controlled by traffic signals and when crossing streets elsewhere than at intersections, whether the blind or defectively sighted pedestrian was exercising due care in the circumstances is a question which the appellate courts direct be left to the jury.[343] The *American Law Reports* remarked upon the penalties of being partially blind as against being totally so.[344] Contributory negligence of the totally blind pedestrian, in being struck by a motor vehicle, is ordinarily left for the jury, and the jury usually brings in a verdict for the plaintiff which is then sustained by the court.[345] Not so with the partially blind. Their motor accident cases are also usually sent to the jury on the issues of negligence and contributory negligence, but the jury generally returns a verdict for the motorist which in turn the court usually sustains. If the *American Law Reports* has counted the cases correctly, and it is not entirely clear that it has with respect to the partially blind,[346] this may be a rule of life if not of law.

Though the disabled have the right to use the streets and highways and it is common knowledge that they exericse the right, yet the doctrine of foreseeability is seldom invoked in the automobile cases. A few early cases said that drivers must know what everybody else knows, that consequently they must expect that disabled persons will be among the pedestrians they approach and that they must proceed in a manner to

---

[339] Compare, however, Trumbley v. Moore, 151 Neb. 780, 39 N.W.2d 613 (1949), where a pedestrian with impaired vision was held contributorily negligent as a matter of law.

[340] *E.g.*, Griffith v. Slaybaugh, 29 F.2d 437 (D.C. Cir. 1928).

[341] Woods v. Greenblatt, 163 Wash. 433, 1 P.2d 880 (1931).

[342] Coco-Cola Bottling Co. v. Wheeler, 99 Ind. App. 502, 193 N.E. 385 (1935).

[343] See, *e.g.*, Muse v. Page, 125 Conn. 219, 4 A.2d 329 (1939); Bryant v. Emerson, 291 Mass. 227, 197 N.E. 2 (1935); Hefferon v. Reeves, 140 Minn. 505, 167 N.W. 423 (1918); Bernard v. Russell, 103 N.H. 76, 164 A.2d 577 (1960); Curry v. Gibson, 132 Ore. 283, 285 Pac. 242 (1930).

[344] Annot., 83 A.L.R.2d 769, § 3, at 775 (1962).

[345] *Ibid.*

[346] *Id.* at 776.

safeguard them against injury.[347] Other courts say, rather, that the driver has a right to proceed upon the assumption that all pedestrians in his path possess normal faculties and that they will exercise those faculties normally in the interests of their own safety.[348] Thus, while a person who digs a trench in a street is bound to anticipate that disabled persons will pass that way, and, accordingly, must put up adequate warning or guard,[349] that same trench-digger driving along the same street to work on the trench is not bound to anticipate the passage of those disabled persons, and hence need not drive his truck with precaution for their protection. At this point the rule of hazards in the street[350] is not applied to the driver of automobiles on the streets, although the basis for the rule would seem to exist in one case no less than in the other.

When the driver knows, or in the exercise of normal faculties should have known, that the pedestrian was disabled, he must exercise a high degree of care to avoid injuring him. The analogical origin and reasons are given by the Supreme Court of Louisiana: "The rule that motorists are held to unusual care, where children are concerned, applies also to adults, who, to the knowledge of the driver, possess some infirmity, such as deafness, or impaired sight, or who suffer from some temporary disability such as intoxication. The physical infirmity in one case, and the extreme youth in the other, affect the ability to sense impending danger and to exercise judgment in the emergency by the selection of proper means and observing the necessary precaution to avoid an accident."[351] In the leading case of *Weinstein v. Wheeler*,[352] the Oregon Supreme Court said that the driver "must use care commensurate with the danger" when he knows "or in the exercise of reasonable diligence ought to know" that the pedestrian is blind.[353] "It will not do to drive on under such circumstances and assume that one, who thus deprived of sight, will jump the right way."[354] The Oregon court at first said that the automobile must be brought to a stop but later modified this to the effect that the automobile must be stopped unless the exercise of due care will

---

347 See Warruna v. Dick, 261 Pa. 602, 104 A. 749 (1918); Doughtery v. Davis, 51 Pa. Super. 229 (1912).

348 *E.g.*, FLEMING, TORTS 249 (3d ed. 1965). Aydlette v. Keim, 232 N.C. 367, 61 S.E.2d 109 (1950).

349 Balcom v. City of Independence, 178 Iowa 685, 160 N.W. 305 (1916); Fletcher v. City of Aberdeen, 54 Wash. 174, 338 P.2d 743 (1959).

350 See text accompanying notes 173-74 *supra*.

351 Jacoby v. Gallaher, 10 La. App. 42, 46, 120 So. 888, 890 (1929).

352 127 Ore. 406, 271 Pac. 733 (1928).

353 *Id.* at 414, 271 Pac. at 733-34.

354 *Ibid.*

be satisfied with something less.[355] Whether such care was exercised in the circumstances is a question for the jury.

When should the driver know that the pedestrian is disabled? The crutches or wheelchair of the lame are obvious notice to him. Hearing aids, on the other hand, are very inconspicuous. Uncertain step and irregular progress are not obvious signs of blindness in the pedestrian although they may call for further observation by the motorist. The guide dog and the cane are important as devices of notice to the driver, whatever their usefullness as travel aids to the pedestrian. They are greatly emphasized by the courts and no doubt are very influential with juries.[356] Short of statutory command, however, the courts have not yet held that it is negligence as a matter of law for a driver to run into a blind man carrying a cane or guided by a dog. In *Cardis v. Roessel*[357] the Kansas City court of appeals came close to doing that. There the plaintiff, proceeding along the sidewalk at a steady pace, carrying a cane in the hand nearest the street, walked into the side of defendant's car which crossed the sidewalk in front of him to enter a gas station. Said the court in sustaining a jury verdict for plaintiff: Defendant "saw, or could have seen, if he had looked, that which was plainly visible; and it was his duty to look and see."[358] In effect, the court held that the jury is entitled to find that the defendant saw, or in the exercise of reasonable diligence, should have seen, the cane if the plaintiff carried it.[359]

F. White Cane Laws: The Struggle for the Streets Revisited

The rights of blind and partially blind persons in traffic are the subject of the so-called white cane laws. Generally, but with some significant and many minor variations, these statutes (1) free the blind and partially blind carrying a white cane or being guided by a dog of contributory negligence, whether as a matter of law or of fact, (2) make the driver who runs into them in effect negligent per se and frequently guilty of a crime, (3) eliminate questions about whether the driver had notice of the pedestrian's total or partial blindness, and (4) generally give the blind and partially blind a legal status in traffic, thus making effective their right to use the streets in urbanized and automobilized

---

[355] *Ibid.*

[356] See, *e.g.*, Cardis v. Roessel, 238 Mo. App. 1234, 186 S.W.2d 753 (1945); Curry v. Gibson, 132 Ore. 283, 285 Pac. 242 (1930).

[357] 238 Mo. App. 1234, 186 S.W.2d 753 (1945).

[358] *Id.* at 1239, 186 S.W.2d at 755.

[359] The case was submitted to the jury on the issue of humanitarian negligence under which it must be shown "that the plaintiff was in imminent and impending danger and oblivious thereof or unable to extricate himself, and that defendant saw and observed or could have seen and observed, plaintiff's said danger and his obliviousness or inextricability in sufficient time to have stopped, swerved, slowed, or warned." *Id.* at 1241, 186 S.W.2d at 756.

America. They substantially alter the law of negligence as it stood before the statutes, even in states where the courts extended the greatest protection to the disabled pedestrian.

However such laws have affected the legal status of the blind and partially blind, they have as a matter of fact greatly contributed to their safety. Knowledge that the white cane and dog are symbols of the blind is as yet far from universal but is becoming fairly well diffused. To the extent that this knowledge does exist, the cane and the dog provide effective notice and inspire efforts on the part of drivers to avoid their users and on the part of pedestrians and others to assist them.[360] The very reasons for the success of the white cane, ironically, are given by opponents of the statutes as arguments against them: They call attention to the blind and in fact make them a conspicuous class, advertising their helplessness, arousing public sympathy, and serving as a badge of their difference and limitations. According to this view, the more the knowledge of the significance of the white cane spreads, the worse the situation becomes for the blind.[361] The response of one blind man is that he would rather be conspicuous and alive than inconspicuous and dead. The organizations of the blind take the position, that far from being a badge of their separate, unequal and dependent status, the white cane is a symbol of the equality, independence and mobility of the blind.[362] The white cane has become the hall mark of the National Federation of the Blind.[363]

White cane campaigns are not confined to conveying word about the white cane laws. They are generally designed as well to inform the public about the social and economic conditions among the blind and the aspirations of the blind for full and useful lives. Such campaigns have long been organized around white cane days and white cane weeks sponsored by the National Federation of the Blind and by Lions Clubs. In 1964, the National Federation of the Blind secured a joint resolution by Congress asking the President to proclaim October 15 of each year as white cane safety day.[364] In his proclamations, the President has spoken not only of

---

360 When the New York legislature was considering enactment of a white cane law, a questionnaire on the merits of the proposal was distributed to chiefs of police, attorneys general, and safety officers in other states. A high proportion answered. The conclusion was that white cane laws, when properly publicized and administered, are a definite help to blind and sighted alike. *He Walks by Faith Justified by Law*, The Blind American, June 1961, p. 17; Liddle, *Mobility: A Survey, I, II, III*, The New Beacon, May, June, July 1964.

361 *A White Cane Debate: Leichty vs. Taylor*, The Braille Monitor, March 1965, p. 16; *Legal Victory for Blind Pedestrians*, The Braille Monitor, Dec. 1964, p. 1; Bartleson, *The White Cane*, The Braille Monitor, Dec. 1963, p. 10.

362 *He Walks by Faith Justified by Law, op. cit. supra* note 360.

363 Vice President Humphrey's address at the Twenty-fifth Annual Convention of the National Federation of the Blind, The Braille Monitor, Aug. 1965, p. 8.

364 78 Stat. 1003.

the travel significance of the white cane but of its significance as a symbol of the ability of the blind to live "normal productive lives."[365]

Though the use of the staff or cane as a travel aid by which the blind person feels his way and avoids obstructions and holes is doubtless very ancient, and though we know from the cases[366] that active blind persons have employed such a staff or cane in this country for over 100 years, the white cane as a device for giving notice to drivers and others that the user is blind is strictly modern, though by no means strictly American, and is related to the fabulous growth in the use of the automobile, the thickening of traffic conditions, and the skyrocketing of accidental injuries to pedestrians whether able-bodied or not. The white cane statutes began to be adopted by the states in the 1930's.[367] Their enactment is directly traceable to activities of organizations of the blind and to Lions Clubs.[368] Today, due to the continuing activities of these organizations, forty-nine states have white cane laws explicitly covering the blind and partially blind[369] and one covering the "incapacitated" pedestrian generally.[370]

---

[365] 29 Fed. Reg. 14051 (1964); 30 Fed. Reg. 12931 (1965).

[366] Balcom v. City of Independence, 178 Iowa 685, 160 N.W. 305 (1916); Sleeper v. Sandown, 52 N.H. 244, 250 (1872); Glidden v. Town of Reading, 38 Vt. 52, 53, 57 (1865).

[367] Cal. Stats. 1935, ch. 126, §§ 1-3 (1935); Idaho Code S.L. 1937, ch. 46, §§ 1-3, at 62; Mich. Stats. 1937, Act 10, at 13; Nev. Laws 1939, ch. 58, at 53; N.H. Laws 1939, ch. 65, § 1, at 56-57; N.J. Stats. 1939, ch. 274, § 1, at 696.

[368] William Taylor, a blind lawyer practicing in Media, Pennsylvania has been chairman of the National Federation of the Blind's White Cane Committee and an active leader in this work for over a quarter of a century.

[369] ALA. CODE ANN. tit. 36, § 58 (1940); ALASKA COMP. LAWS ANN. §§ 28.25.010-.040 (Supp. 1963); ARIZ. REV. STAT. ANN. § 28-798 (1955); ARK. STAT. ANN. §§ 75-631, 75-632 (1964); CAL. PEN. CODE §§ 643, 643a, 643b; COLO. REV. STAT. ANN. §§ 40-12-24 to 40-12-26 (1953); CONN. GEN. STATS. REV. § 211 (1949); DEL. CODE ANN. tit. 21, §§ 4144, 4150 (1964); FLA. STAT. ANN. § 413.07 (1955); GA. CODE ANN. § 68-1658 (1957); HAWAII REV. LAWS §§ 109-23 to 109-24 (Supp. 1963); IDAHO CODE ANN. §§ 18:5810-18:5812 (1947); ILL. ANN. STAT. ch. 95½, § 172a (Smith-Hurd 1957); IND. ANN. STAT. §§ 10-4925 to 10-4927 (1956); IOWA CODE §§ 321:332-321:334 (1962); KAN. GEN. STAT. ANN. § 8-558 (1949); KY. REV. STAT. § 189.575 (1962); LA. REV. STAT. § 32-217 (1962); ME. REV. STAT. ANN. ch. 22, § 132-35 (1963); MD. ANN. CODE art. 66½, § 194 (1957); MASS. LAWS ANN. ch. 90, § 14a (1949); MICH. STAT. ANN. § 28:770 (1954); MINN. STAT. ANN. § 169.202 (1960); MISS. CODE ANN. § 8203.5 (1942); MO. ANN. STAT. §§ 304.080-304.110 (1959); MONT. REV. CODES ANN. §§ 32.1143-32.1145 (1961); NEB. REV. STAT. §§ 28,478-28,480 (1956); NEV. REV. STAT. § 426.510 (1957); N.H. REV. STAT. ANN. § 263.58 (1963); N.J. STAT. ANN. § 4-37.1 (1961); N.M. STAT. ANN. § 64-18-65; N.Y. VEHICLE & TRAFFIC LAW § 1153; N.C. GEN. STAT. § 20-175 (1953); N.D. CODE ANN. tit. 39, § 39-10-31; OHIO REV. CODE ANN. §§ 4511.47, 4511.99E (1965); OKLA. STAT. ANN. tit. 7, § 11-13 (1951); ORE. REV. STAT. § 483.214 (1953); PA. STAT. ANN. tit. 75, § 1039 (1960); R.I. GEN. LAWS ANN. § 31-18-13 to 31-18-16 (1956); S.C. CODE § 44.0318-1, 44.9932 (1960); TENN. CODE ANN. §§ 59-880 to 59-881 (1955); TEX. REV. CIV. STAT. art. 6701e (1948); UTAH CODE ANN. § 41-6-80 (1960); VT. STAT. ANN. tit. 23, § 1106 (1959); VA. CODE ANN. §§ 46.1-237 to 46.1-240 (1950); WASH. REV. CODE §§ 46.60.260-.270 (1962); WIS. STAT. ANN. § 346.26 (1958); W. VA. CODE ANN. § 1721(373) (1961).

[370] WYO. STAT. ANN. § 31-163 (1957). The 1947 amendment which declared the cane

1. Jurisdictional Analysis of the White Cane Laws

A fairly typical white cane statute is that of Kentucky. It provides: "Whenever a pedestrian is crossing or attempting to cross a public street or highway, guided by a guide dog or carrying in a raised or extended position a cane or walking stick which is white in color or white in color and tipped with red, the driver of every vehicle approaching the intersection, or place where such pedestrian is attempting to cross, shall bring his vehicle to a full stop before arriving at such intersection or place of crossing, and before proceeding shall take such precautions as may be necessary to avoid injuring such pedestrian."[371] It is made unlawful for any person not totally or partially blind "or otherwise incapacitated" to carry such a cane or at least to do it in that position "while on any public street or highway."[372] The act is not to be construed as depriving totally or partially blind or "otherwise incapacitated persons" without a stick or dog of "the rights and privileges conferred by law upon pedestrians crossing streets or highways."[373] Nor is the failure of such persons to have a cane or dog "upon the streets, highways or sidewalks" to be "held to constitute nor be evidence of contributory negligence."[374] Violation is made punishable by a fine not to exceed twenty-five dollars.[375]

The provisions of the Kentucky statute as to: blindness or partial blindness; the otherwise incapacitated; the color of the cane; the position in which it is to be held; the alternative use of the dog; the duty of the driver; the crossing both of streets and highways; preservation of the rights of those without canes or dogs; declaration that they are not contributorily negligent; and the appending of a penal sanction, are all fairly common features in the white cane statutes.

In five states the benefits of the white cane statutes are extended only to those who are "blind."[376] Forty-three states extend protection to the wholly, totally or partially blind and the visually handicapped.[377] Fifteen

---

and dog using blind to be included in the class designated as "incapacitated" was subsequently repealed in 1955. Wyo. Sess. Laws 1955, ch. 225, § 70. It thus appears the wholly or partially blind in Wyoming may not be "incapacitated" within the meaning of the statute. There have been no cases so construing the statute.

[371] Ky. Rev. Stat. § 189.575(2) (1962).

[372] Ky. Rev. Stat. § 189.575(1) (1962).

[373] Ky. Rev. Stat. § 189.575(3) (1962).

[374] *Ibid.*

[375] Ky. Rev. Stat. § 189.990(1)(16) (1962).

[376] Arkansas, Illinois, Minnesota, Nebraska, New Jersey. See note 369 *supra* for the applicable statutes.

[377] Alabama, Alaska, Arizona ("blind or industrial blind," which uses 20/200 or peripheral vision defect standard) California, Colorado, Connecticut, Delaware, Florida, Georgia, Hawaii, Idaho, Indiana, Iowa, Kansas, Kentucky, Louisiana, Maine, Maryland, Massachusetts, Michigan, Mississippi, Missouri, Montana, Nevada, New Hampshire, New York, North Carolina, North Dakota, Ohio ("blind" is defined to include partially blind), Oklahoma,

states extend the protection of the white cane laws to those "otherwise incapacitated."[378] As these jurisdictions commonly specify that the protection of the statute shall extend to the "wholly or partially blind or otherwise incapacitated" the other disabilities embraced presumably are not of a visual character. Yet the other disabilities must be like blindness or partial blindness in that they involve traffic hazards which can be diminished by the use of the cane or dog.

The most popular device is the white cane, with or without a red tip, which is recognized in forty-one states.[379] Ten jurisdictions also recognize the use of metallic, chrome, aluminum or light-colored metal.[380] Only three states required the cane to be all white,[381] while five require the white cane have a red tip.[382] In eighteen states, the cane-using blind need only carry or use the cane to comply with the statutes' conditions[383] while twenty-six specify that the cane must be carried in the "raised or extended" position.[384] There are no cases construing this quite uncertain expression. Presumably the object of the requirement is to ensure that the cane is in such a position as to be visible to the approaching motorist or pedestrian. This object can be accomplished by the mere carrying or using of the long fiberglass white cane now coming into vogue. A few

Oregon ("blind" is defined to include partially blind), Pennsylvania, Rhode Island, South Carolina, South Dakota, Tennessee, Texas, Utah, Vermont, Virginia, Washington, West Virginia, Wisconsin. See note 369 *supra* for the applicable statutes.

[378] Alabama, Florida, Kansas, Kentucky, Louisiana, Maine, New York, North Dakota, South Carolina, South Dakota, Tennessee, Texas, Vermont, Virginia, West Virginia. See note 369 *supra* for applicable statutes.

[379] Alaska, California, Colorado, Connecticut, Delaware, Florida, Georgia, Hawaii, Idaho, Illinois, Iowa, Kansas, Kentucky, Louisiana, Maine, Maryland, Massachusetts, Michigan, Mississippi, Missouri, Montana, Nevada, New Hampshire, New Mexico, New York, North Carolina, North Dakota, Ohio, Oklahoma, Oregon, Pennsylvania, Rhode Island, South Carolina, South Dakota, Tennessee, Texas, Utah, Vermont, Virginia, West Virginia, Wisconsin. See note 369 *supra* for the applicable statutes.

[380] Alaska, Arkansas, Louisiana, Maine, Maryland, Mississippi, New York, Pennsylvania, Virginia, West Virginia. Not all types of canes are recognized by each of these states; each state listed does recognize one of the metallic type devices. See note 369 *supra* for the applicable statutes.

[381] Minnesota, Nebraska, Washington. See note 369 *supra* for the applicable statutes.

[382] Alabama, Arizona, Arkansas, Indiana, New Jersey. See note 369 *supra* for applicable statutes.

[383] Alabama, Arizona, Arkansas, California, Colorado, Connecticut, Georgia, Idaho, Illinois, Indiana, Iowa, Michigan, Montana, Nebraska, Nevada, New Jersey, Oklahoma, Utah. See note 369 *supra* for the applicable statutes.

[384] Alaska, Delaware, Florida, Kansas, Kentucky, Louisiana, Maine, Massachusetts, Mississippi, Missouri, New Hampshire, New Mexico, New York, North Dakota, Ohio, Oregon, Pennsylvania, Rhode Island, South Carolina, South Dakota, Tennessee, Texas, Vermont, Virginia, West Virginia, Wisconsin. See note 369 *supra* for the applicable statutes.

jurisdictions have altered the expression, substituting "at arm's length,"[385] "with arm extended,"[386] or carrying or using "an exposed cane."[387]

Thirty-seven states extend the protection of the white cane statutes to the user of the guide dog in the alternative.[388] States which permit the blind, the partially blind, and the otherwise incapacitated the use of the guide dog do not forbid its use by others,[389] unlike the common statutory practice with respect to the cane.

The duty imposed on the sighted pedestrian or motorist who approaches or comes in contact with the protected class of persons varies with the jurisdiction. Thirty-four states require the motorist to come to a full stop in all cases, and take such precautions as may be necessary to avoid accident or injury to the pedestrian.[390] Two of these states require the motorist to remain stationary until the pedestrian clears the roadway,[391] and Maryland requires the motorist, after stopping, to leave a clear path until the pedestrian is out of the street.[392] Virginia requires only that the motorist stop.[393] Eight states require the motorist to stop only when it is necessary to avoid accident or injury;[394] nine require the driver yield the right of way and/or take reasonable care to avoid injuring the protected pedestrian without specific mention of stopping.[395] Forty-one states impose the duty under the statute on the "approaching" motorist.[396]

---

[385] Maryland, North Carolina. See note 369 *supra* for the applicable statutes.

[386] Minnesota. See note 369 *supra* for the applicable statute.

[387] Hawaii. See note 369 *supra* for the applicable statute.

[388] Alabama, Alaska, Arizona, Arkansas, California, Florida, Hawaii, Illinois, Iowa, Kansas, Kentucky, Louisiana, Maine, Maryland, Massachusetts, Michigan, Mississippi, Missouri, Nebraska, New Hampshire, New Jersey, New Mexico, New York, North Carolina, North Dakota, Ohio, Oregon, Pennsylvania, Rhode Island, South Carolina, South Dakota, Tennessee, Texas, Utah, Vermont, Virginia, West Virginia. Of these, thirty-two require only the use of the "guide dog" or "seeing-eye dog" without more; the other five—Arkansas, Iowa, Michigan, New Hampshire, and Oregon—require the animal be "specially trained," harnessed, or in a particular position. See note 369 *supra* for the applicable statutes.

[389] See note 74 *supra* for applicable statutes.

[390] Arizona, California, Colorado, Florida, Georgia, Idaho, Illinois, Indiana, Iowa, Kansas, Kentucky, Maine, Maryland, Massachusetts, Michigan, Minnesota, Missouri, Montana, Nebraska, Nevada, New Hampshire, New Mexico, North Carolina, North Dakota, Oklahoma, Oregon, Rhode Island, South Carolina, South Dakota, Tennessee, Vermont, Virginia, Washington (inferentially), Wisconsin. See note 369 *supra* for the applicable statutes.

[391] Nebraska, North Carolina. See note 369 *supra* for the applicable statutes.

[392] MD. CODE ANN. art. 66½, § 194 (1957).

[393] VA. CODE § 46.1-237 (Supp. 1964).

[394] Alabama, Alaska, Louisiana, Mississippi, New York, Pennsylvania, Texas, West Virginia. See note 369 *supra* for the applicable statutes.

[395] Arkansas, Connecticut, Delaware, Hawaii, New Jersey, Ohio, Utah, Wisconsin, Wyoming. See note 369 *supra* for the applicable statutes.

[396] Alabama, Alaska, California, Colorado, Connecticut, Florida, Georgia, Hawaii, Idaho, Illinois, Indiana, Iowa, Kansas, Kentucky, Louisiana, Maine, Maryland, Massachusetts,

The duty imposed on the motorist to stop, take precaution, yield and the like is imposed on sighted pedestrians in nine states.[397]

Those states which require the driver to yield the right of way, or stop, or take reasonable care without specific reference to where or when, nevertheless require that deference be shown the disabled pedestrian, wherever he is found and within the space limitations prescribed by the particular statute. The specific mention of "approaching" adds nothing to the statutes, nor does the use of the term "upon observing." The motorist remains bound to that acuity of observation which graces the ubiquitous reasonable man, and so presumably will be charged with observing him whom he should have rather than him whom he did in fact. Similarly, the requirements of specific acts by the driver, such as sounding the horn and coming to a complete stop in all cases, do not provide greater protection to the disabled pedestrian than is secured by the duty of the driver to "take reasonable care." The driver is thus burdened with possible prosecution for the technical violation of a criminal statute, while his actions under the circumstances may well have been appropriate to the protection of the pedestrian from injury.

Three states provide that the driver must "immediately come to a full stop" when he "approaches within" a specified number of feet of the disabled pedestrian.[398] The distances specified are but three or ten feet, distances so short as to make it impossible for an automobile to stop or take other evasive action within them. If the driver need not anticipate the action commanded of him until he is within the distance mentioned, the only remaining question is the extent of the pedestrian's injuries; the driver's civil liability would apparently be strict liability, and his criminal liability cast in doubt because of the practical impossibility of compliance. Judges might reasonably interpret these statutes to require the driver to have come to a stop when he is three or ten feet from the pedestrian. Thus did Wisconsin solve this problem of draftsmanship: "An operator of a vehicle shall stop . . . before approaching closer than 10 feet . . . ."[399]

Thirty-six states provide that the protection of the statutes applies wherever the pedestrian seeks to cross the highway.[400] Thirteen states

Michigan, Mississippi, Missouri, Montana, Nebraska, Nevada, New Hampshire, New Mexico, New York, North Carolina, North Dakota, Ohio, Oregon, Pennsylvania, Rhode Island, South Carolina, South Dakota, Tennessee, Texas, Vermont, Virginia, West Virginia, Wisconsin. See note 369 *supra* for the applicable statutes.

[397] Alabama, Alaska, Arkansas, California, Colorado, Idaho, Indiana, Montana, Nevada. See note 369 *supra* for the applicable statutes.

[398] Georgia (three feet), Michigan (ten feet), Oklahoma (*knowingly* within three feet). See note 369 *supra* for the applicable statutes.

[399] WIS. STAT. ANN. § 346.26(1) (1958).

[400] Alabama, Arkansas, California, Colorado, Connecticut, Delaware, Florida, Georgia, Hawaii, Idaho, Illinois, Indiana, Iowa, Kansas, Kentucky, Maine, Massachusetts, Michigan,

restrict the protection to intersections and crosswalks.[401] Only five states deal with the intersection or crosswalk controlled by an officer or signal.[402] Presumably it would follow that in the remaining states where the disabled pedestrian is given the right of way without reference to places where there are signals or officers, the disabled pedestrian prevails over any claim built on the command of the officer or the right conferred by the light. Nevertheless, though the Texas statute makes no mention of the signal-controlled crossing, the courts in that state appear unwilling to permit the blind person to recover in a civil action where he entered the crossing against the light.[403]

Twenty-two states provide that their white cane statutes are not to be construed so as to deprive the disabled pedestrian without canes or dogs of rights to which they would otherwise be entitled; nor are they to be so construed that the failure of disabled pedestrians to use canes or dogs shall constitute contributory negligence or evidence thereof.[404] Two states provide only that the white cane statute is not to affect other rights outside the statute;[405] one state, Illinois, uses the contributory negligence disclaimer without reference to other rights,[406] and the remaining twenty-five states have no saving clause of either type. In these states, presumably, absence of a saving clause will not be construed to deprive disabled pedestrians of rights which were theirs before the statute or to affect the contributory negligence law otherwise applicable to disabled pedestrians without compensatory devices.

In thirty-eight states violations of the white cane statutes are made a

---

Montana, Nebraska, Nevada, New Hampshire, New Jersey, New Mexico, North Dakota, Ohio, Oklahoma, Oregon, Rhode Island, South Carolina, South Dakota, Tennessee, Utah, Vermont, Virginia, Wisconsin. See note 369 *supra* for the applicable statutes.

[401] Alaska, Arizona, Louisiana, Maryland, Minnesota, Mississippi, Missouri, New York, North Carolina, Pennsylvania, Texas, Washington, West Virginia. Alaska, Maryland, New York, North Carolina, Pennsylvania, Texas and West Virginia restrict the statutory applicability to "crosswalks or intersections"; Washington to crosswalks only; Arizona, Minnesota, Missouri, to intersections only, and Louisiana, and Mississippi use the term "at or near" crosswalks or intersections. See note 369 *supra* for the applicable statutes.

[402] Arkansas says that the special protection does not apply at crossing places controlled by a traffic signal; Maryland that they do not apply at crossings or intersections controlled by an officer or a signal; North Carolina, and Virginia that they do not apply when the crossing is manned but that they do apply when it is controlled by a signal; and New Jersey that traffic signals are not to affect the pedestrian's right. See note 369 *supra* for applicable statutes.

[403] Meacham v. Loving, 285 S.W.2d 936 (Tex. Sup. Ct. 1956).

[404] Alabama, Alaska, Arizona, Florida, Kansas, Kentucky, Louisiana, Maine, Massachusetts, Mississippi, Missouri, North Carolina, North Dakota, Pennsylvania, Rhode Island, South Carolina, South Dakota, Texas, Vermont, Virginia, West Virginia, Wisconsin. See note 369 *supra* for the applicable statutes.

[405] New Hampshire, Oregon. See note 369 *supra* for the applicable statutes.

[406] ILL. REV. STAT. ANN. ch. 95½, § 172A (Smith-Hurd 1957).

criminal offense, the penalty generally being a small fine or short term imprisonment.[407] In eleven states the only recourse against the driver is a civil action for damages.[408]

2. Critique and Suggested Reform

The saving clauses in the white cane statutes preserving the rights of the blind non-users of canes or dogs in traffic as they existed in the law before the adoption of the white cane statutes seem prudent and precautionary rather than strictly necessary. That those persons and their rights are not mentioned in the white cane statutes would be a weak and artificial basis of statutory construction upon which to deprive them of the minimum protection afforded them under pre-existing law. On the other hand, the provision that failure to use compensatory devices is not contributory negligence or evidence thereof is innovative and desirable. The reason is hard to find for penalizing the disabled who do not use such devices, for whatever cause—lack of knowledge about their existence or how to use them, embarrassment at becoming conspicuous, or a finding by the individual that the devices are not helpful to him. It seems particularly unjust to penalize those who have not had or do not have the opportunity to receive training in their use. The right to live in the world should not be made to depend on the use of these compensatory devices.

For the same reasons, the provisions in the Arkansas and Arizona white cane statutes requiring the blind to use these devices and making the requirement penalty enforceable should be repealed. If this objective is to be attained, it should be by educating the blind in the techniques of using the devices and in their values.[409]

---

407 Nineteen states provide that the violation of the statutory provisions is a misdemeanor, without specifying the penalty to be imposed upon conviction. Alabama, Arizona, California, Georgia, Idaho, Louisiana, Minnesota, Montana, Nebraska, Nevada, North Carolina, Ohio, Oklahoma, Pennsylvania, Rhode Island, South Carolina, South Dakota, Vermont, Virginia. Eleven states in addition to making the violation a misdemeanor, specify the permissible bounds of punishment which is limited to a fine. Arkansas, Colorado, Connecticut, Indiana, Iowa, Kentucky, Maryland, Massachusetts, North Dakota, Tennessee, Texas. Eight states, after declaring violations to be misdemeanors, provide for money fines and/or jail sentences as punishment. Alaska, Florida, Kansas, Maine, Michigan, Mississippi, Missouri, West Virginia. See note 369 *supra* for the applicable statutes.

408 Delaware, Hawaii, Illinois, New Hampshire, New Jersey, New Mexico, New York, Oregon, Utah, Washington, Wisconsin. See note 369 *supra* for the applicable statutes.

409 The Arizona statute, while penally requiring the blind person to use a compensatory device, at the same time declares such unaided travel not to be contributory negligence or evidence thereof. Thus, the blind pedestrian is criminally liable for his failure to take the prescribed action to protect his person while he is not disabled in the civil courts from recovering for the injuries which he suffers as a result of his breach of a legal duty. There are also some odd variances in draftsmanship. In Arkansas, cane users are given the right of way "travelling along or across the streets and highways"; it is only when "walking along the highways and streets" without a cane that blind travelers commit a misdemeanor.

The provision about the way in which the cane is to be held—that it must be in a raised and extended position—should be eliminated. It is not necessarily adapted to increasing the visibility of the cane by drivers, unnecessarily denies the use of the cane while crossing streets and highways as a travel aid in the ordinary way to avoid obstructions and trenches, and creates a certain danger for oncoming pedestrians on crowded streets.

The requirement that the driver stop before coming within a specified distance of the disabled pedestrian or that, without mentioning the distance, to come to a full stop immediately upon approaching the disabled pedestrian, has the advantage of laying down an objectively determinable standard and one which obviously contributes to the safety of the pedestrian. Some question might be raised, however, as to whether this requirement is too mechanical and exacts of the driver more than is necessary for the protection of the pedestrian.

Making the provisions of white cane statutes penally enforceable against drivers does not add significantly to the achievement of the objectives of those provisions. It is hard to imagine that the penal sanctions here have a deterrent effect. The act of running into a disabled pedestrian is not usually a matter of deliberation or design. When it is, more drastic sanctions are in order and are already provided elsewhere in the law. The white cane statutes deal with accidents: with reducing their number by notice to the driver of the physical condition of the pedestrian; with allocating the cost of them, when they do occur, to the drivers and thence to the insurance companies; and with implementing the right of the disabled to live in the world by giving them a right of way in traffic and minimizing, if not eliminating, the ordinary concepts of negligence law. As a practical matter, too, law enforcement agencies are very reluctant to prosecute. It was only after a vigorous campaign of pressure by an organization of the blind that the Berkeley Police Department and the Alameda County District Attorney's office finally proceeded with a prosecution in 1965, under California's white cane law, which is located in the Penal Code and declares breaches to be a misdemeanor,[410] of a motorist who had run down and killed a blind white cane user at an intersection. The judge, who tried the case without a jury and found the motorist guilty as charged, sentenced him to one hour's probation.[411]

In Arizona, the penal sanction applies to the blind pedestrian without compensatory device when he is walking on a street or highway." It is only at intersections that the blind cane user is given the right of way; and it is only while the disabled pedestrian is "on the highways that failure to use dog or cane may not" be held to constitute prima facie evidence of contributory negligence. See note 369 *supra* for the applicable statutes.

[410] CAL. PEN. CODE §§ 643, 643a, 643b.

[411] People v. McGlynn, No. C-8471, Municipal Ct. for the Berkeley-Albany Judicial Dist., July 15, 1965.

CONCLUSION

Writers on the law of torts tell us that tort law, always particularly responsive to changing social conditions, is now reaching a new stage in its development.[412] Originally concerned primarily with the protection of property and land, it came to focus, in the period of the industrial revolution, on other forms of property and on injuries to the person, shifting emphasis from the kind of interest infringed to the kind of conduct which created the injury.[413] Today, when millions of individuals are exposed to traffic, industrial, and many other kinds of accidents, which they are more or less powerless to prevent, individual responsibility for them based on the kind of conduct which brought them about is giving way to community responsibility based on the fact of harm. In accommodating to this change and in contributing to it, concepts of negligence have undergone a transformation; liability has been imposed on the industry the operations of which created the risk; private insurance carriers have assumed the burden and distributed the costs of liability; and social insurance has increasingly entered the field to protect men against hazards of old age, survivorship, unemployment, and disability—hazards over which the individual has little or no control.[414] Does the law of torts today in its dealings with the physically disabled reflect these broad social and legal changes, and especially, how does it stand with respect to the policy of integrating the disabled into the social, economic, and physical life of the community? This is the central question to be asked in reviewing many other fields affecting the disabled as well. Does the law of torts in its basic concepts and current application consciously reject that policy, treat it as a matter of indifference, passively acquiesce in it, or actively implement it? Among these alternatives, it is clear that the courts do not

---

[412] FLEMING, TORTS 108 (3d ed. 1965); 2 HARPER & JAMES, TORTS § 12.1 (1956); FRIEDMANN, LAW IN A CHANGING SOCIETY ch. 5 (1959).

[413] FRIEDMANN, op. cit. supra note 412.

[414] Ibid.; FLEMING, op. cit. supra note 412, at ch. 6; 2 HARPER & JAMES, op. cit. supra note 412, ch. 11-13; PROSSER, TORTS ch. 1, 4 (3d ed. 1964). Beyond current forms of liability insurance and the social insurance lies loss insurance. Professor Friedmann writes: "Especially in the main countries which have introduced compulsory liability insurance for motor car operators, the effective shift of liability from the driver to the insurance company has increasingly raised the question whether liability insurance should not be openly turned into loss insurance. Loss insurance means an abandonment of the principle of individual tort responsibility and frank substitution of compulsory insurance for loss incurred as a result of certain operations. Administration replaces to that extent civil litigation and an element of social insurance is injected into this sphere of private relationships . . . . There is increasing support for the idea that the social importance of traffic accidents justifies the transfer of this complex of legal relationships from the private to the public sphere. Insurance against traffic accidents in that conception becomes assimilated to insurance against industrial accidents which has for many years been separated in all common law countries from general tort liability and turned into a social insurance." FRIEDMANN, op. cit. supra note 412.

react positively to this policy, either by way of support or rejection. Indifference and acquiescence also do not accurately describe the judicial attitude. Unawareness is the precise characterization. In the cases, there is nothing like a systematic examination of the policy and its implications for the law of torts. One must scour hard to find an occasional reference to it.

Yet integration is the avowed policy of the land. However imperfectly and variously carried out, it is expressed in the self-care and self-support provisions of the Social Security Act;[415] the sprawling rehabilitation programs of the nation and states;[416] the orientation and rehabilitation centers now multiplying across the country; the programs for the education of the disabled in the public schools; the opening up, still quite incompletely in many areas, of state and federal civil service to the disabled on a non-discriminatory basis;[417] special statutes striking down artificial and arbitrary barriers to the employment of the disabled as teachers in the public schools;[418] and the increasing official and unofficial acceptance of disabled persons on a basis of their individual merits. In the past, the courts have been the dominant force in the creation of the substantive rules of conduct and liability. This has been true generally and specifically with respect to the physically disabled, and their rights to be abroad in the land. In fact, in earlier periods and in many jurisdictions, their rules on this subject embodied a policy in advance of the times. The legislature has now increasingly entered the field. Neither as a matter of the independent judicial role nor as a matter of independent judicial wisdom should the courts disregard the policy of integration thus declared by the legislature; rather decisional law should not only be brought into harmony with that policy but should give it active aid and comfort.

To recognize, as the House of Lords recently did in the *Haley* case,[419] and, as many American courts have done long since,[420] that social integration of the disabled is coming into practice and that considerable and ever-increasing numbers of the severely disabled are venturing into the community, and to adapt the law to that practice, is in a sense inevitable— and inevitably slow in some jurisdictions. But these judicial decisions are

---

415 79 Stat. 286, 42 U.S.C. 303, 1201, 1351 (Supp. I, 1965).

416 79 Stat. 1282, 29 U.S.C. § 31-45 (Supp. I, 1965).

417 *The Chavich Case—Outlook for Blind Teachers*, The Braille Monitor, Aug. 1965, p. 49.

418 CAL. EDUC. CODE § 13125; MASS. GEN. LAWS ANN. ch. 15, § 19a (Supp. 1965); N.Y. EDUC. LAW § 3004; PA. STAT. ANN. tit. 24, § 12-1209 (1962).

419 Haley v. London Elec. Bd., [1965] A.C. 778 (1964).

420 See Balcom v. City of Independence, 178 Iowa 685, 696, 160 N.W. 308, 1310 (1916); Sleeper v. Sandown, 52 N.H. 244, 251 (1872); Shields v. Consol. Gas Co., 193 App. Div. 86, 183 N.Y. Supp. 240 (1920); Masterson v. Lennon, 115 Wash. 305, 308, 197 Pac. 38, 39 (1921).

a response to the fact and not to the policy, to what is and not also to what ought to be. The demands of the policy are what now summon the spirit of reform and acknowledgement of the role of the legislature in the law of torts as it applies to the disabled.

Such reform would not necessarily entail casting aside the traditional framework of the law of negligence, though that might help. What is of utmost importance about carrying on the judicial analysis and discussion of the rights of the disabled to live in the world in the concepts and catch phrases of the law of negligence—unreasonable risk of harm, fault, due care, reasonable man of ordinary prudence, contributory negligence, greater caution, foreseeability—is not just that individual volition and personal conduct are stressed in areas in which they are no longer of paramount significance. The important point is that these concepts and phrases do not place in sharp relief the social policy at stake. Indeed, they come dangerously close actually to obstructing the view of that policy. The question to be asked is not whether the defendant created an unreasonable risk of harm, but whether he interfered with the effectuation of the policy of the social integration of the disabled; not whether the plaintiff conducted himself as a reasonable man of ordinary prudence acting in the light of all the circumstances, but whether he acted pursuant to his right to be a part of his community. Such a transformation of the forms and tests to be applied by the judges would not remove all legal limitations on the conduct of the disabled person. Other policies regarding what the English court of appeals called the ordinary transactions of life, such as those related to the need to dig trenches in the streets, would have to be given their necessary scope. The policy of integration, too, has its own built-in limitations: It cannot be pushed beyond the physical capacity of the disabled. But implementation of that policy does mean that many acts now regarded by those who are not disabled as unreasonable and foolhardy, but which nevertheless are within the disabled person's sense of the risks he must or would run to regain the life-bestowing benefits of the mainstream, would not be taken at his cost, or even at the cost of the trench-digger, but at the cost of the community.

The same result could be achieved also, it is recognized, within the traditional framework of tort law by reading the policy into the existing tests, by declaring reasonable that conduct of the disabled person which is in conformity with the policy, and unreasonable that conduct of the defendant which interferes with the policy. This method of reform fits in with the historic mode of the common law in adapting to changed social and economic conditions. By it, the reform can be accomplished gradually, without any appearance of discontinuity in the law, and within all the conservative safeguards of case-by-case trial. On the other hand, this method of reform tends to obscure, not only from everybody else, but from the judges themselves, the changes that are necessary and that are being made. It confuses the new direction by using the old signposts. The hands are less likely to be the hands of Esau if the voice is that of Jacob.

Basic determinants of decisions in the law of torts, are, textwriters agree, morality, admonition, compensation, imposition of costs on those who have a capacity to bear them, and the interest of furthering desirable activity without imposing disproportionate burdens on any individuals or groups.[421] Some of the overtones and some of the partially buried presuppositions of the reasonable man formula are moralistic and individualistic, deriving from the origins of modern negligence law in the industrial revolution and concomitant ethical, economic and political philosophy. In the era of unrestricted free enterprise, the law of torts moved toward the position that there could be no liability without fault and no fault without personal blameworthiness.[422] Dean Prosser emphasizes that personal fault has become, or is becoming, legal or social fault—"departure from the conduct required of a man by society for the protection of others"[423]—and that legal or social fault is giving way to the notion that the primary task is to decide which interest should prevail "even where no one is at fault."[424] But the turn of the century is still turning; and the process of discarding fault liability is far from complete. In considering what is desirable or possible social policy, great weight will always have to be given to the "ethical or moral sense of the community, its feeling of what is fair and just."[425] Today the integration policy is beginning to rest on such community feelings. But fault analysis is remarkably fruitless where there is no fault. Whether the disabled pedestrian or the city or its insurance carrier should bear the cost of an injury to the pedestrian resulting from a hazard in the street created by the city is a question of social policy, not of morality. Is the policy of integration of such social importance that it should outweigh the policy, also judged in terms of its social importance, of allowing public bodies which go about digging sewer ditches and opening other holes in the

---

421 2 HARPER & JAMES, op. cit. supra note 412, at § 11.5; PROSSER, op. cit. supra note 414, at § 4.

422 Professor Fleming writes that, in the era of the industrial revolution, "the axiom no liability without fault was quickly raised to a dogmatic postulate of justice, because it was best calculated to serve the interests of expanding industry and the rising middle class, in relieving them from the hampering burden of strict liability and conducing to that freedom of individual will and enterprise which was at the forefront of all contemporary aspirations." FLEMING, op. cit. supra note 412, at 108.

423 PROSSER, op. cit. supra note 414, at § 4.

424 Ibid.

425 2 HARPER & JAMES, op. cit. supra note 412, § 11.5, at 793.

street to do so without the burden, be it slight or great, of seeing to it that the disabled, among other people, will not be injured thereby.

Ideas of compensating the victim and admonishing the wrongdoer are basically linked to presuppositions about fault. The wrongdoer, that is the party who was at fault, must compensate the victim, that is, the party who was innocently going about his business, for the wrong done. Ideas of compensation, punishment, and prevention shade into each other. The admonitory objective of the law of torts today aims at reducing accidents by governing future conduct through the imposition of liability. This, however, is a one way street. It can have a deterrent impact only if liability is imposed on the defendant. The disabled prospective plaintiff does not wait to read the latest negligence decision before going out into the streets to mail a letter, catch a bus, or visit a friend. Even if he did do so and could understand it, the chances are good that he would reject it. The courts' notions of a reasonably prudent disabled person often do not agree with the notions of the reasonably prudent disabled person himself. He, for the most part, figures out what is convenient, possible, or safe for him, sometimes with the advice of experienced and knowledgeable persons, not infrequently on the basis of his own individual trial and error. On the other hand, it is the business of liability-conscious cities, insurance carriers, and construction and transportation companies, to keep abreast of the latest judicial decisions with an eye to altering their operations so as to avoid or reduce liabilities.

So with the distribution of the costs of accidents. The plaintiff generally cannot bear them personally and generally does not carry insurance against them. To the extent that he can bear them they may be ruinous. The defendant, on the other hand, a city, or a construction or transportation company, a store, business, or other place of public accommodation, can transmit the cost to a wider public by means of prices, rates, taxes or insurance. This also goes for the automobile driver, who, though he is only somewhat better off than the disabled pedestrian his car struck down, yet is usually covered by insurance. In the end, those who have the capacity to bear the costs must do so. Even aside from this principle of economic necessity, the cost of social policy should be borne by society. If the policy of integration is socially valuable, then it should be financed by the public generally, least of all by the necessitous disabled traveler.

Thus, while the individualistic, moralistic, fault bases of the reasonable man doctrines of the law of torts have no particular relevance to most aspects of the integration policy, and when they are invoked anyway, they are today tending more and more to give support to that policy, the admonitory, compensatory, and cost distribution aspects of the reasonable man doctrine—as in actual administration they tend to impose the liability on the defendant and the cost on the public—move in the general direction of supporting the policy of integration, though not necessarily consciously or for reasons that relate to the policy.

As a substitute for the policy of integration, or as a vehicle for effectuating it, the reasonable man standard suffers from another serious weakness. However much the courts may instruct juries that the reasonably prudent man is an idealized mortal, possessing human, not superhuman virtues, but no human or subhuman weaknesses or depravities; however often they may repeat that he is an abstraction not to be confused with any identifiable individual, and especially not with a judge or juror; and however much they may emphasize that he acts in the light of all of the circumstances and that he is physically disabled when the plaintiff is, the jurors are almost entirely able-bodied (blind people are excluded from jury service), and the judge has sound if somewhat aging limbs, fair enough eyesight, and, according to counsel, can hear everything but a good argument. The abstraction they conceive is unavoidably in their image and, in any event, will be applied through the filter of their experiences and make-up. Standing on good feet and legs, erect through the strength of taut muscles, peering through eyes approaching or receding from 20/20 visual acuity, the judge or juror, or their personified image, provide the blind, the deaf, the lame, and the otherwise physically disabled with a standard of reasonableness and prudence in the light of all of their circumstances, including some often quite erroneous imaginings about the nature of the particular disability. Created and applied from this disadvantage-point, the standard contains an inherent weakness which is not overcome by the occasional taking of testimony about the proper use of a cane or other aids and devices. The actions of the reasonably prudent man in like circumstances turn out to be not those taken by the reasonably prudent man actually in the circumstances, but those which a man not in those circumstances imagines he would take if he were in them. At the time of judgment, moreover, he is reasonably ignorant about what they are. In the sense intended by its author, the statement of Judge Hunt in *Davenport v. Ruckman* "that the blind have sources of knowledge not available to others"[426] is mere superstition. But in another sense, the statement contains a basic truth: Experience with disability is a more ready source of knowledge about the disability to those who have it than to those who do not.

The right to live in the world—to return to Dean Prosser's formulation of the problem and the proposition with which we began—entails at least a right of free and safe physical access to it through the use of

---

[426] 37 N.Y. 568 (1868).

streets and sidewalks, roads and highways, and the common modes of transportation, communication, and interchange. It includes as well full and equal access to places of public accommodation, places designed to accommodate men in the course of gaining access to the world.

The right to live in the world consists in part of the right to live out of it. The blind, the deaf, the lame, and the otherwise physically disabled, have the same right to privacy that others do; not only the right to rent a home or an apartment, public or private housing, but the right to live in it; the right to determine their living arrangements, the conduct of their lives; the right to select their mates, raise their families, and receive due protection in the safe and secure exercise of these rights. Some of the Englishmen whose houses were their castles, one may suppose, were physically disabled. At least Coke never said aught to the contrary. It was the ligeantia, not the visual acuity, which counted.

But the world in which the disabled, too, have a right to live is also on the streets, the highways and byways, in public buildings, and other public places, in the schools and colleges, in the public service and private callings, in the factories, shops and offices, in short, in all the places where men are, go, live, work, and play. The policy of the law, whether made by Congress or by the courts, whether carried out by executive or judicial action, whether implemented through the traditional formulas of the law of torts, the rhetoric of the policy of integration, or the human, natural, or inalienable rights of the Declaration of Independence, the Abolitionist Crusade, the thirteenth, fourteenth, and fifteenth amendments, and the civil rights revolution of today—the policy of the law should be by negative ban and positive fostering, to permit, enable and encourage men to be a part of their communities to the full extent of their physical capacities. The law of torts should link its labors to this conception.

It is no right of substance, it is no policy of integration, if the disabled are not entitled to this. It is no world with fewer appurtenances and access more narrowly defined. Without that right, that policy, that world, it is no living.

APPENDIX

MODEL WHITE CANE LAW

§ 1—It is the policy of this State to encourage and enable the blind, the visually handicapped, and the otherwise physically disabled to participate fully in the social and economic life of the State and to engage in remunerative employment.

§ 2—(a) The blind, the visually handicapped, and the otherwise physically disabled have the same right as the able-bodied to the full and free use of the streets, higways, sidewalks, walkways, public buildings, public facilities, and other public places. (b) The blind, the visually handicapped, and the otherwise physically disabled are entitled to full and equal accommodations, advantages, facilities, and privileges of all common carriers, airplanes, motor vehicles, railroad trains, motor buses, streetcars, boats or any other public conveyances or modes of transportation, hotels, lodging places, places of public accommodation, amusement or resort, and other places to which the general public is invited, subject only to the conditions and limitations established by law and applicable alike to all persons. (c) Every totally or partially blind person shall have the right to be accompanied by a guide dog, especially trained for the purpose, in any of the places listed in section 2(b) without being required to pay an extra charge for the guide dog; provided that he shall be liable for any damage done to the premises or facilities by such dog.

§ 3—The driver of a vehicle approaching a totally or partially blind pedestrian who is carrying a cane predominately white or metallic in color (with or without a red tip) or using a guide dog shall take all necessary precautions to avoid injury to such blind pedestrian, and any driver who fails to take such precautions shall be liable in damages for any injury caused such pedestrian; provided that a totally or partially blind pedestrian not carrying such a cane or using a guide dog in any of the places, accommodations or conveyances listed in section 2, shall have all of the rights and privileges conferred by law upon other persons, and the failure of a totally or partially blind pedestrian to carry such a cane or to use a guide dog in any such places, accommodations or conveyances shall not be held to constitute nor be evidence of contributory negligence.

§ 4—Any person or persons, firm or corporation, or the agent of any person or persons, firm or corporation who denies or interferes with admittance to or enjoyment of the public facilities enumerated in section 2 or otherwise interferes with the rights of a totally or partially blind or otherwise disabled person under section 2 shall be guilty of a misdemeanor.

§ 5—Each year, the Governor shall take suitable public notice of October 15 as White Cane Safety Day. He shall issue a proclamation in which:

(a) he comments upon the significance of the white cane;
(b) he calls upon the citizens of the State to observe the provisions of the White Cane Law and to take precautions necessary to the safety of the disabled;
(c) he reminds the citizens of the State of the policies with respect to the disabled herein declared and urges the citizens to cooperate in giving effect to them;
(d) he emphasizes the need of the citizens to be aware of the presence of disabled persons in the community and to keep safe and functional for the disabled the streets, highways, sidewalks, walkways, public buildings, public facilities, other public places, places of public accommodation, amusement and resort, and other places to which the public is invited, and to offer assistance to disabled persons upon appropriate occasions.

§ 6—It is the policy of this State that the blind, the visually handicapped, and the otherwise physically disabled shall be employed in the State Service, the service of the political subdivisions of the State, in the public schools, and in all other employment supported in whole or in part by public funds on the same terms and conditions as the able-bodied, unless it is shown that the particular disability prevents the performance of the work involved.

Mental Health Services for the Poor

Henry Weihofen*

MENTAL ILLNESS RANKS with heart disease and cancer as one of the
nation's three greatest health menaces. It is clearly the costliest.[1]
More hospital beds are occupied by mental patients than are required for
all other diseases combined.

Experts are convinced that mental illness is vastly more prevalent than
the statistics reveal, and that perhaps one person in ten in the United
States suffers from some form of mental illness.[2] Probably no more than
ten to twenty per cent of those needing treatment receive it.[3] The ones not
getting it are primarily the poor—because they cannot afford it and because they are skeptical and even hostile toward psychiatry and social
agencies generally.

One alarming circumstance is the extent of such illness and related
handicaps among our children and young people. The Department of
Health, Education, and Welfare estimates that some five million handicapped children and young people,[4] at least ten per cent of our school age
population, need special educational opportunities, of which there are few.
Three out of four retarded children today receive no special instruction

---

* Ph.B., 1926, J.D., 1928, J.S.D., 1930, University of Chicago. Professor of Law, University of New Mexico Law School.

[1] The noneconomic costs cannot be measured; the economic costs alone add up to
some 3.5 billion dollars a year. *New Directions Toward Community Health*, Blue Cross
Rep., July-Sept. 1964, pp. 10-13. See also FEIN, ECONOMICS OF MENTAL ILLNESS x-xii (Monograph Series No. 2, 1958) (report to the Staff Director, Joint Commission on Mental Illness
and Health); JOINT COMM'N ON MENTAL ILLNESS AND HEALTH, ACTION FOR MENTAL HEALTH,
FINAL REPORT 9-10 (1961); LINDMAN & McINTYRE, THE MENTALLY DISABLED AND THE LAW
1 (1961).

[2] This is the estimate made from facts compiled in 1961. NATIONAL COMM. AGAINST
MENTAL ILLNESS, WHAT ARE THE FACTS ABOUT MENTAL ILLNESS IN THE UNITED STATES?
1 (1961). Difficulties of getting agreement on a definition of mental illness and of finding
untreated cases have made for wide variations in estimates of prevalence. A recent study
conducted by the National Institute of Mental Health together with Group Health Association of Washington, D.C., based on a sample of more than 6,000 patients, concluded
that one in seven adults seen by a physician has a psychiatric ailment. Others have estimated
that as high a proportion as one-half of the patients treated by general practitioners have
predominantly psychiatric complaints or suffer from physical ills with psychiatric complications. See statement of Dr. S. Bernard Wortis in *Hearings Before House Committee on
Interstate and Foreign Commerce*, 83d Cong., 1st Sess., pt. 4, 1,034-35 (1953) (Causes,
Control and Remedies of the Principal Diseases of Mankind).

[3] NATIONAL COMM. AGAINST MENTAL ILLNESS, *op. cit. supra* note 2, at 1. Even this
estimate may be too high. See Scheff, *The Role of the Mentally Ill and the Dynamics of
Mental Disorder: A Research Framework*, 26 SOCIOMETRY 436, 440-41 (1963).

[4] Address by Wilbur J. Cohen, *A Day for Brighter Beginnings*, before the 16th Annual
Convention of the National Ass'n for Retarded Children, Sept. 29, 1965.

whatever.[5] They are left to shift for themselves in classrooms where they cannot compete. They are tomorrow's dropouts.

Half a million children of school age suffer from serious forms of mental illness, childhood schizophrenia, and other psychoses. Yet less than one per cent of these half million are getting adequate care.[6] Especially alarming is the high proportion of children and young people in the mentally-ill population. Of the 750,000 persons who in 1964 were served in out-patient psychiatric clinics, 300,000—or forty per cent—were under the age of twenty. Probably equally as many were placed on waiting lists of a year or more.[7] Delay in providing care for these young people may have tragic consequences for the nation that will never be set right later.

The incidence of mental illness is highest among low-income groups; and they receive the least attention.[8] Three-fourths of the mentally ill cannot afford treatment. One study indicated that of the children of families on welfare, thirty per cent have health problems, and nineteen per cent have emotional or behavior problems.[9] Wilbur J. Cohen, Under-Secretary of Health, Education, and Welfare, has estimated "that 50% or more of children with I.Q. scores between 70 and 80 come from disadvantaged homes."[10]

About eighty to ninety per cent of all mental retardates appear quite normal in the physical sense, but they function as mentally retarded. "These persons invariably derive from and have been reared in socially and economically disadvantaged environments. They are heavily represented in the slums of the metropolitan centers of the country and in depressed rural areas. Their greatest concentration is among minority groups residing in city slums."[11] Roots of this type of retardation are almost certainly to be found among the concomitants of deprived social and eco-

---

[5] *Ibid.*

[6] NATIONAL ASS'N FOR MENTAL HEALTH, THE NAMH PROGRAM: HOW WE SERVE 12 (1965).

[7] Estimate based on data for 1961-62 collected by the National Institute of Mental Health. U.S. DEP'T OF HEALTH, EDUC. & WELFARE, PILOT PROJECT IN TRIANING MENTAL HEALTH COUNSELORS 1 (1965).

[8] "At least in the United States, mental illness is more prevalent in the lower classes than in the upper; more severe there; less likely to be treated; and when treated, more likely to receive custodial or organic therapy than psychotherapy." BERELSON & STEINER, HUMAN BEHAVIOR: AN INVENTORY OF SCIENTIFIC FINDINGS 639 (1964).

[9] Westchester County Studies of Basic Causes of Poverty, Bull. of N.Y. State District Branches of the American Psychiatric Ass'n (Mar. 1965).

[10] Address by Wilbur J. Cohen, *A Day for Brighter Beginnings*, before the 16th Annual Convention of the National Ass'n for Retarded Children, Sept. 29, 1965.

[11] U.S. DEP'T OF HEALTH, EDUC. & WELFARE, PROCEEDINGS OF A CONFERENCE ON SPECIAL PROBLEMS IN VOCATIONAL REHABILITATION OF THE MENTALLY RETARDED, MADISON, WISCONSIN 16-17 (Rehabilitation Service Series No. 65, 1963).

nomic circumstances—poor or nonexistent pre-natal care, high rates of prematurity, and inadequate infant health supervision.[12]

In addition, this major group of the mentally retarded is exposed to all the influences that make for crime and delinquency, broken family relations, alcoholism, drug addiction, mental illness, and prostitution.[13] One misfortune reduces capacity to fend off others, so we have the hard-core, multi-problem families, in which we find mental illness, *and* crime, *and* alcoholism, and other ills. Any community mental health program is thus likely to become a poverty program, enmeshed in the problems of economic deprivation, unemployment or unemployability, and social disorganization.[14]

I

PROGRAM FOR THE FUTURE

A. Safeguards for Children

A large part of our school drop-out problem stems from mental retardation and mental illness. A study of 503 reported drop-outs from the Gary, Indiana school system in the year 1963-64 revealed that 59.7 per cent were retarded.[15] Another study showed that many drop-outs have definite internalized personality problems.[16]

Paradoxically, as school systems try to do more for retarded children, the drop-out rate rises. This is understandable. In the past, many school systems excluded children with a tested IQ of less than seventy. Such children therefore did not figure in the drop-out statistics. But even when given the help of special programs, low-IQ children are the most likely to drop out: Difficulty in learning to read and adjusting to the social patterns of the schoolroom may result in symptoms of withdrawal, schoolphobia, and rebellion, particularly in a school offering little or no individual counseling or special teaching. The strain of trying to keep up and the recognition of failure almost inevitably leads these unhappy children to adopt psychological and adaptive behavior to protect their egos. One such protective device is refusing schooling. Dropping out of school may literally preserve what mental health they have. But by doing so, they condemn themselves to the poverty and the feeling of worthlessness of the uneducated and untrained person. The vast size of the drop-out problem requires

---

12 *Ibid.*

13 PRESIDENT'S PANEL ON MENTAL RETARDATION, REPORT OF THE TASK FORCE ON LAW 10 (1963).

14 Pasamanick, Scarpitti, Lefton, Dinitz, Wernert & McPheeters, *Home vs Hospital Care for Schizophrenics*, 187 A.M.A.J. 177, 179 (1964).

15 Roser, *On Reducing Dropouts*, Fed. Probation, Dec. 1965, p. 49, at 51.

16 LICHTER, RAPIEN, SEIBERT & SKLANSKY, THE DROPOUTS (1962).

a heroic effort to stem the widening circle of this social blight. Needed are more pupil personnel services, work programs, family services, teachers with specialized skills, and more child guidance centers in the schools, with psychiatrists, psychologists, and social workers on the school staff.[17]

We cannot solve the heart-breaking problem of retardation and physical defects and handicaps by building bigger and better institutions. We must also improve the quality of human reproduction. No special training school, no braces or hearing aids or speech therapy can match nine safe months in the uterus of a healthy mother. Especially in some areas—the South and the charity hospitals of our cities—rates of premature births, fetal deaths, and neo-natal deaths are high and are rising, mainly among the indigent and nonwhite population. In Georgia from 1947 to 1960, although white premature births remained relatively level, nonwhite premature births rose from 68 per 1,000 live births to 130.[18]

Of 4.5 million live births expected in the United States this year, about 7.8 per cent are likely to be premature. About fifteen per cent of these "preemees" do not survive. Of those that do, about ten per cent will be so retarded mentally that they will need institutional care. At an average cost of two thousand dollars per year for each of these thirty thousand infants who will need institutional care, the *direct* cost of care for *this* year's class over their expected life span (fifty years) will be three billion dollars.[19] This amount does not include the costs of constructing the facilities or training the needed personnel.

This is the cost only for retardation due to prematurity. But prematurity is one cause of retardation for which we know ways to reduce the incidence—by better nutrition, prenatal care, and management of complicated pregnancies. Women who receive adequate pre-natal care are one-third as likely to give birth to premature babies as women who don't have such care. Very small premature babies are about ten times more likely to be mentally retarded than are children of normal birth. And a Johns Hopkins study showed that premature infants have two to three times as many physical defects and fifty per cent more illnesses than full-term infants.[20] Yet approximately thirty per cent of expectant mothers in the United States receive no prenatal care whatever.[21]

---

[17] See Roser, *supra* note 15, at 55.

[18] GA. DEP'T OF PUBLIC HEALTH, GA. VITAL STATISTICS, xvi (1961).

[19] A paper by Robert A. Aldrich, M.D., The Liquidation of the Problem Through Research and Training, read before the White House Conference on Mental Retardation, Sept. 18-20, 1963. See WHITE HOUSE CONFERENCE ON MENTAL RETARDATION, PROCEEDINGS 81, 82-83 (1963).

[20] PRESIDENT'S PANEL ON MENTAL RETARDATION, A PROPOSED PROGRAM FOR NATIONAL ACTION TO COMBAT MENTAL RETARDATION 51 (1962).

[21] NATIONAL ASS'N FOR RETARDED CHILDREN, THE MENTALLY RETARDED (undated).

Social-cultural factors adversely influencing the quality of births are prevalent among the indigent. A high percentage of them are functionally illiterate, and an even higher percentage are illegitimately pregnant.[22] All this points up the enormous sociological problem involved in giving indigent expectant mothers adequate ante-partum care.

We are in a vicious circle of indigency, unplanned parenthood, and poor reproductive quality. And the situation is getting worse. Dr. John D. Thompson of Emory University believes that within a decade it will deteriorate into utter chaos.[23] We know what the expected sharp increase in births will mean in terms of more schools, teachers, water, roads, and recreational facilities. But we haven't given much thought to the task of caring for the expectant mothers and trying to improve the quality of their infants.

Every American child should have the opportunity to be "created equal." We cannot, of course, assure every child good genes or loving, competent parents. "But it does not lie beyond the reach of justice to insist that no child be negligently born (without elementary pre and post-natal care) or negligently exposed after birth to surroundings, physical or social, that alter his chances for a rewarding maturity."[24]

B. The Need for New Techniques

The needs of the high-risk indigent group require special maternity-care programs and mental therapy techniques based on an adequate understanding of socio-cultural as well as medical factors. The poor live in a sub-culture. They typically do not understand mental troubles; they think of them as physical, as caused by such things as "bad blood," "a bump on the head," or "too much booze." They are disappointed if they don't get practical advice on how to solve their problems and run their lives. They expect pills and needles plus perhaps a little sympathy. They have no confidence in a "talking treatment." Hollingshead and Redlich in their classic study, *Social Class and Mental Illness*, found that less than two per cent of the lowest-class patients understood the aims or techniques of psychotherapy.[25] Freudian self-analysis is much too sophisticated. If

---

[22] An Emory University Hospital study of 250 expectant mothers found 17% functionally illiterate and 34% illegitimately pregnant. Thompson, *The Quality of Human Reproduction*, in WHITE HOUSE CONFERENCE ON MENTAL RETARDATION, PROCEEDINGS 85, 87 (1963).

[23] *Id.* at 88.

[24] PRESIDENT'S PANEL, *op. cit. supra* note 13, at 16.

[25] HOLLINGSHEAD & REDLICH, SOCIAL CLASS AND MENTAL ILLNESS: A COMMUNITY STUDY 339–41 (1958). See also Brill & Starrow, *Social Class and Psychiatric Treatment*, in MENTAL HEALTH OF THE POOR 74 (Riessman, Cohen & Pearl eds. 1964); Ruesch, *Social Factors in Therapy*, in PSYCHIATRIC TREATMENT 59 (1953).

treatment begins with the assumption that the indigent patient should gain "insight" into his own emotional psychological processes, his reaction is likely to be, "Don't give me a lot of talk; just tell me what to do to get well."

Lower class families often fail to recognize even serious mental disorder in a relative. He may have a lifelong history of hostility, suspicion, violence, and even bizarre behavior without his family's ever thinking of him as a "psychiatric case." To some extent this is true of people in all social classes but it is particularly true among the poor. They will attribute his conduct to meanness, laziness, or physical illness rather than to factors of psychogenic origin. This attitude is due not only to ignorance, but to a conscious or unconscious refusal to face an unpleasant fact. Just about the worst thing that can happen to a poor person is to be labelled "crazy," for such a label is all too likely to mean a life sentence in the state hospital. Psychiatry is a status symbol in Hollywood, but it means calamity and disgrace in Watts.

Even in communities where treatment is financially feasible, those members of the working class who need help may avoid it because of skepticism or hostility.[26] This, however, is becoming less true as a result of the spread of information about mental health programs and especially about the success of the new drugs and more intensive therapy that often enable patients to avoid long periods of hospitalization or even to remain in the community without hospitalization.

The patient who is involuntarily subjected to treatment is likely to resent and resist treatment, or at best passively to expect to be cured or cared for. Even the resentful patient, however, more often than not comes to recognize and admit that his stay in the hospital helped him; and he does cooperate by reporting to the after-care clinic and taking his drugs as prescribed. This is of course more likely if the treatment was humane and the physical facilities decently comfortable.

Because the illness so often comes to the attention of the authorities only through some crisis, commonly expressed in some anti-social way, the police are likely to be the first public representatives called. It is therefore important that they understand the nature of the person's behavior. If they do, he has a chance of being turned over to a psychiatric facility; if not, he is likely to be put through the penal mill.[27]

If the poor have not been eager to get psychiatric help, psychiatrists have not been eager to have them as patients.[28] Many of those who do try to work with low income patients fail, largely because they don't under-

---

[26] Gorman, *Psychiatry and Public Policy*, 122 AMERICAN J. OF PSYCHIATRY 55, 58 (1965).

[27] HOLLINGSHEAD & REDLICH, *op. cit. supra* note 25, at 184.

[28] *Id.* at 344.

stand the working class behavior style. Today, however, an appreciable number of psychiatrists are expanding from an exclusively private practice into "community psychiatry," devoted not so much to working with patients themselves as with other agencies, by educating, advising, and consulting with social workers, police, school counselors, probation officers, and others.

Because low income people often view mental illness in physical terms, they may be more willing to accept treatment from a general practitioner than from a psychiatrist. Special training should be designed to equip the G.P. with a practical therapy for the common man; this practical therapy would have to blur the distinction between mental and physical illness, be directive rather than nondirective, supportive, using tranquilizers, sedatives, stimulants, hormones, and vitamins—in the hope they will be helpful, either in fact or as placebos.

The treatment base should be near the client and should avoid the labyrinth of bureaucratic red tape—innumerable forms and many interviews. His first contact should be with someone with whom he can relate and talk. Perhaps the key is a neighborhood service center using non-professional people from the low income neighborhoods. In the South Bronx of New York City, Lincoln Hospital has set up three such centers, two of them in street-level store fronts. Each center is staffed with one or two mental health professionals, plus five to ten nonprofessionals picked from the neighborhood and given short intensive pre-employment training.[29]

If general community services such as schools, churches, and health facilities are good, there will be less need for specialized services. What the schools do, for example, affects the burden on specialized services for retarded or disturbed children.[30] The extent of community services, general and special, will affect admission and release policies of the residential institutions. If the schools have special classes for the retarded, if the community has sheltered workshops, training facilities, home-maker services, a day-care center, and special recreational programs, many persons can be kept at home and in the community instead of being committed to state institutions. Also, the institutions will be able to release more inmates than when there are no such supportive services.

What happens to institutionalized patients depends also on a number of other things. If the institution is supported in such a niggardly way that

---

[29] Riessman, *Strategy for Mental Health Centers*, in REPORT ON EXPANDING COMMUNITY MENTAL HEALTH SERVICES THROUGH COOPERATION WITH ORGANIZED LABOR, THE WORKER AND MENTAL HEALTH 26, 27 (1964). A grant to evaluate the impact and effectiveness of these centers was awarded by the National Institute of Mental Health in January 1966.

[30] PRESIDENT'S PANEL, *op. cit. supra* note 13, at 11; MENTAL HEALTH OF THE POOR viii (Riessman, Cohen & Pearl eds. 1964).

patients are used to do a substantial part of the work, the release rate is likely to be lower than if able-bodied patients did not do the hospital work. At one eastern state hospital, the use of state prisoners instead of hospital patients to do the hospital laundry work resulted in a remarkable rise in releases of patients.[31]

Whether the state can be sued in tort may also affect the kind of care provided in state institutions. The New York Court of Claims, in a recent decision[32] breaking new ground, upheld against demurrer a suit brought on behalf of an illegitimate infant born to a mentally deficient mother as the result of a rape by a fellow patient in a state mental institution. Liability of the state was rested on alleged negligent care and supervision of the mother.

Hollingshead and Redlich found that the kinds of care provided in psychiatric facilities vary directly with the socio-economic level of the patients. The private psychiatrist is most likely to be treating the more prosperous citizens. The state mental hospital is the major resource for the working class.[33] And it isn't primarily a matter of money. The poor are not prone to apply for out-patient treatment even in free psychiatric clinics. And when they do apply or become patients, they are treated differently, even in public clinics that purport to make no distinctions between paying and nonpaying patients. A recent study revealed that "not only were patients from upper social classes accepted for treatment more often, but their treatment was more apt to be given by a more senior or more experienced member of the staff than was the case with patients from lower social classes."[34]

Those who work with low income groups tell us that their psychological inaccessibility is not caused by any ingrained characteristic, but is due to suspicion and acculturated bias. Dr. Philip S. Wager, Chief of the Department of Psychiatry at the Southern California Permanente Medical Group in Los Angeles, said that with a proper approach, "within an hour or two the average working man is frank, far more frank than the middle class patient we see in Los Angeles, less intellectually defensive and able

---

31 Observations by the author made in connection with a study conducted at George Washington University under a grant from the National Institute of Mental Health. The study was completed in 1965. To date, no report has been published.

32 Williams v. State, 46 Misc. 2d 824, 260 N.Y.S.2d 953 (Ct. Cl. 1965), noted in 66 COLUM. L. REV. 127 (1966); cf. Zepeda v. Zepeda, 41 Ill. App. 2d 240, 190 N.E.2d 849 (1963), cert. denied, 379 U.S. 945 (1964).

33 HOLLINGSHEAD & REDLICH, op. cit. supra note 25, at 276-78.

34 Brill & Starrow, supra note 25, at 68. See also HOLLINGSHEAD & REDLICH, op. cit. supra note 25, at 192 (Psychiatrists "try to select what they call a good patient. We are not sure what attributes a good patient must have, but they include sensitivity, intelligence, social and intellectual standards similar to the psychiatrist's, a will to do one's best, a desire to improve one's personality and status in life, youth, attractiveness, and charm.").

to confide with direct expression of sincere emotion." And the authors of *Mental Health of the Poor* question the notion that psychotherapy is not suitable for blue-collar people: "The failure of psychotherapy with low income groups may be in large measure due to the insistence on a particular model of treatment, namely the psychodynamic, insight and reconstructive oriented approach."[35]

C. The Community Mental Health Movement

It is generally agreed that we should avoid as much as possible committing people to large state institutions. Isolating patients from family and friends is traumatizing and makes treatment more difficult. Treating patients in their community and preferably in their homes through the use of out-patient clinics and other local facilities is generally more effective: Treatment begins earlier and is more intensive.

If we had adequate local facilities, such as community centers and half-way houses, rehabilitation counselors, and vocational training, it has been estimated that one-third to one-half of all mental retardates could be released from institutions, made relatively self-sufficient, and the burden of their care removed from the taxpayers.[36] In a carefully controlled experiment in Louisville, Kentucky, a number of mentally ill patients who normally would have been hospitalized have been maintained in the local community more or less successfully.[37] The building of such community mental health centers has, during the past decade, become the goal of a nationwide movement to which the entire mental health field is committed, and Congress has appropriated funds to help the states establish such centers.[38] And they *are* being established. From 1955 to 1962, the number of patients served in out-patient clinics doubled—from 379,000 to

---

[35] MENTAL HEALTH OF THE POOR, *op. cit. supra* note 25, at vii.

[36] Shriver, *Mental Retardation: A 20th Century Challenge*, in WHITE HOUSE CONFERENCE ON MENTAL RETARDATION, PROCEEDINGS 21, 25 (1963).

[37] Pasamanick, Scarpitti, Lefton, Dinitz, Wernert & McPheeters, *supra* note 14, at 187.
A survey of the population of St. Elizabeths Hospital, Washington, D.C., conducted in 1961 determined that one-half the patients were releasable, if alternative facilities were available. Only 7% of these, however, were considered eligible for release to their own homes. Classification of Patients at Saint Elizabeths Hospital by Hypothetical Eligibility for Release (unpublished report 1963).

[38] In the Community Mental Health Centers Act of 1963, 77 Stat. 290 (1963), 42 U.S.C. §§ 2681-87 (1964), as amended, 42 U.S.C. §§ 2682-87 (Supp. I, 1965), Congress authorized $150 million in federal aid to the states for construction of comprehensive community mental health centers over three years, 1965-67. The federal share can range from one-third to two-thirds of the total cost. In 1965, Congress amended the act to authorize federal financial aid toward meeting the cost of technical and professional personnel serving such centers during the first 51 months any such center is in operation or during which new services are offered in existing centers. Grants can amount to 75% of eligible staff costs for the first 15 months, 60% in the first subsequent year, 45% of the next and 30% of the third and final year.

741,000. Few of these clinics thus far provide all the "five essential elements" of a center as defined by the Department of Health, Education, and Welfare (in-patient and out-patient services, part-time hospitalization, emergency services, and consultation and education services). But as projected, the program should within the next decade reduce the present mental hospital population of 530,000 by half.

General hospitals have also been adding psychiatric screening and treatment services. Today, more than one thousand general hospitals admit psychiatric patients.

San Mateo County, California, a suburban community in the San Francisco Bay Area, offers comprehensive mental health services in its Public Health Department. Nearly eight thousand patients get service each year through the adult clinic, child guidance clinic, in-patient therapeutic community (a thirty-bed open service in the general hospital), day hospital, rehabilitation service, nursery school for disturbed children, delinquent and offenders treatment, alcoholic rehabilitation unit, research and evaluation service, and the consultation service. The staff comprises seventy-four professional mental health workers plus twenty volunteer psychiatrists and psychologists in private practice. Needless to say, these services cost a lot of money—1.25 million dollars, or 2.50 dollars per capita, the highest in the nation. But the treatment cost per patient is far less than that in the state hospital, where the average is 6.00 dollars per day for three months, or about six hundred dollars per patient. The average total cost per patient treated in the San Mateo County General Hospital unit is only 216 dollars, even though the daily cost is twenty-seven dollars, because the average stay is but eight days. Out-patient care is even less. And because of this comprehensive mental health service, the county's state hospital admissions have remained static while admissions from four other Bay Area counties rose sixty-one per cent.

Other communities are also finding that a program of prevention through early detection and treatment in the home community makes long years in custodial hospitals unnecessary. Georgia, for example, found that of 1,800 mental patients treated in the psychiatric units of four general hospitals, only 126, or seven per cent, had to be sent to the state hospital. At the time of commitment it was estimated that sixty per cent would need long-term hospitalization.

Beginning with the Kennedy Administration, the federal government has undertaken a massive effort to encourage expansion of our mental health services. Under Medicare,[39] persons aged sixty-five get

---

[39] Health Insurance for the Aged Act, P.L. 89-97, 79 Stat. 290 (codified in scattered sections of 26, 42, and 45 U.S.C. (Supp. I, 1965), but see particularly 42 U.S.C. §§ 1395-96d (Supp. I, 1965)).

hospital benefits for up to ninety days for each spell of illness,[40] with the patient responsible for payment of an initial deductible of forty dollars[41] plus ten dollars a day for each day after sixty days.[42] In-patient services in a qualifying psychiatric hospital are included, but there is a lifetime limit of 190 days of covered services in psychiatric hospitals.[43] Psychiatric care received in a general hospital, however, does not count toward the 190-day lifetime limit.[44]

A 1965 amendment to the Social Security Act[45] authorizes federal aid of up to seventy-five per cent of the costs of comprehensive projects for diagnosing and treating children, particularly those of low income families. This amendment also authorizes federal funds to the states for needy aged residents of mental institutions.[46] These patients have long been excluded from receiving public assistance payments.

The Elementary and Secondary Education Act of 1965[47] will give a tremendous impetus to efforts at developing educational services for the retarded. Title I authorizes a three-year effort to encourage and support the creation, establishment, or improvement of special programs. This may include the construction of facilities to meet the needs of culturally deprived children from low income families, many of whom are diagnosed as mentally retarded but who actually only lack education.

Other amendments provide for expansion of vocational rehabilitation services,[48] a form of therapy more acceptable to the poor than Freudian analysis. With this encouragement, states are extending and improving rehabilitation services, especially for the severely disabled and other hard-to-rehabilitate cases. The 1965 amendments increased the federal participation from seventy-five to ninety per cent of cost during the first three years and seventy-five per cent for the next two years.[49] State vocational rehabilitation agencies are also encouraged to work with the more disabled public assistance cases and people in other hard-core dependency groups, such as young people rejected for the draft or the Job Corps, thus helping to return more people to self-help and employment. It is highly probable that the mental illness treatment program will have to become a part of a

---

40 79 Stat. 291, 42 U.S.C. § 1395d(a)(1) (Supp. I, 1965).
41 79 Stat. 293, 42 U.S.C. § 1395e(b)(1) (Supp. I, 1965).
42 79 Stat. 292, 42 U.S.C. § 1395e(a)(1) (Supp. I, 1965).
43 79 Stat. 292, 42 U.S.C. § 1395d(b)(3) (Supp. I, 1965).
44 See 79 Stat. 314, 42 U.S.C. § 1395x(c) (Supp. I, 1965).
45 79 Stat. 354, 42 U.S.C. § 729-1 (Supp. I, 1965).
46 79 Stat. 356, 360, 42 U.S.C. § 306(a) (Supp. I, 1965).
47 P.L. 89-10, 79 Stat. 27 (codified in scattered sections of 42 U.S.C. (Supp. I, 1965)).
48 79 Stat. 1282, 29 U.S.C. §§ 31-42 (Supp. I, 1965).
49 79 Stat. 1283, 42 U.S.C. § 33 (Supp. I, 1965).

nationwide group-practice medical care program; the economics of the situation demands it.[50] We have already moved in that direction. Medical and hospitalization benefits of group insurance policies and union contracts to cover mental illnesses are bringing psychiatric services to millions who never had them.[51] In the automobile and agricultural implements industry, recent agreements with the UAW provided mental illness insurance programs for nearly 2.5 million workers and dependents.[52] The program will pay for treatment by a private physician, clinic, or day-care program, and for forty-five days of continuous care in a hospital. The California Physicians' Service now provides psychiatric coverage for nearly 400,000 of its more than a million members.[53]

But even with facilities and services available, a community mental health program encounters special obstacles in servicing the poor. The Louisville experiment found that about ten per cent of the families refused to accept a patient back home, and an additional number would have preferred that the patient remain in the hospital until he was really better. Many of these families are economically deprived, and the patient represents an unwelcome burden. The home-care mental health program thus ties in directly to and needs the support of a program to alleviate poverty.

A demoralized and disorganized home environment imperils any home-care program. Returning a patient to such a home is like sending someone with a communicable physical disease into a home and neighborhood rife with the same disease. Home care can provide strengths and support to a patient that an institutional environment lacks, but home care in unfavorable conditions is probably worse than living alone or in a night hospital. To successfully reintegrate patients into an unfavorable family setting requires family counseling, an enriched program of homemaking services, job training, sheltered work shops, and frequent access to direct psychiatric services.

---

[50] Perlis, *Social Class in Mental Illness*, in REPORT ON EXPANDING COMMUNITY MENTAL HEALTH SERVICES THROUGH COOPERATION WITH ORGANIZED LABOR, THE WORKER AND MENTAL HEALTH 11, 13 (1964). Mr. Perlis is National Director of Community Services for the AFL-CIO.

[51] Most of the membership of Blue Cross Association is now covered at least to some extent for hospitalization for mental illness. *New Directions toward Community Mental Health*, Blue Cross Rep., July-Sept. 1964, pp. 14-18.

[52] Shoemaker, *Problems of Financing*, in THE WORKER AND MENTAL HEALTH, *op. cit. supra* note 50, at 40, 41-42.

Dr. Daniel Blain, past president of the American Psychiatric Association, is now heading a study of the impact of such pre-payment plans on mental health programs. The study is being financed by the National Institute of Mental Health and is being carried out jointly with the Research Institute of UAW.

[53] California State Dep't of Mental Hygiene, California Mental Health Progress, Oct. 1965.

D. The Need for Personnel

It takes no crystal ball to foresee that to provide all the needed psychiatric and related services, we shall need a vastly larger number of psychiatrists and other mental health professionals than we now have. Congress hopes that the Health Professional Educational Assistance Act of 1963[54] and the Nurse Training Act of 1964[55] will give us the necessary physicians and nurses from which mental health specialists can be had. Estimates are that the number of psychiatrists will increase from 18,593 in 1965 to 23,735 in 1970. Nurses will increase from 20,554 in 1965 to 25,690 in 1970.

But even such increases are not going to provide enough psychiatrists to do the job, especially since we are starting with a deficiency. New positions for psychiatrists are mushrooming in schools, colleges, churches, social agencies, courts, prisons, hospitals, and clinics. We face a tremendous increase in demands for intensive treatment for old people. The gap between demand and supply is rapidly widening.

As our mental hospitals develop better treatment methods, more patients will be released earlier. Many hospitals today discharge patients as soon as possible. But one out of three so released relapses[56] and has to be readmitted. One reason is the lack of follow-up medical care and social and vocational rehabilitation services after the patient is sent home. Such service costs only one-tenth of hospital care.[57] But we need the personnel to do it. We shall have to train nurses to follow patients into the community after discharge from the hospital. Psychiatric nursing personnel will be needed in a number of new areas, including day and night hospitals, out-patient clinics, mental health clinics, half-way houses, and follow-up visits in the home; and these psychiatric nurses will need new knowledge and skills, including some public health nursing skills and better knowledge of the community. We also need some 300,000 special education teachers for handicapped children.[58] We have perhaps 70,000, and many of these have minimal special training.[59]

New discoveries and new techniques can help combat certain forms of disorder, but they also require increased professional services. Thus the

---

[54] 77 Stat. 164 (1963), 42 U.S.C. §§ 292-92b, 292d-94e (1964), as amended, 42 U.S.C. §§ 292c-95g (Supp. I, 1965).

[55] 78 Stat. 908 (1964) (codified in scattered sections of 42 U.S.C., primarily at §§ 296-298b), as amended, 42 U.S.C. §§ 297b, 298b (Supp. I, 1965).

[56] NATIONAL ASS'N FOR MENTAL HEALTH, THE NAMH PROGRAM: HOW WE SERVE 16 (1965).

[57] Ibid.

[58] Address by Wilbur J. Cohen, A Day for Brighter Beginnings, before the 16th Annual Convention of the National Ass'n for Retarded Children, Sept. 29, 1965.

[59] Ibid.

best hope for combating phenylketonuria is early detection. But early detection of inborn errors of metabolism is difficult because the victims look normal. Legislation that would require testing for all such inborn errors might be a solution. But testing all new-born infants would require medical manpower.

We cannot begin to meet the demands for psychological and social help from all who need it.[60] We must find new sources of manpower, new ways to effectively use the professionally trained specialists we now have, and patterns of functioning that make the fullest use of the resources we have. For example, general practitioners may have to take over a bigger share of the job. Some hospitals are operating a post-graduate training course to teach GP's to recognize and diagnose early symptoms of mental illness.[61]

Dr. Lawrence S. Kubie, Director of Training at Sheppard and Enoch Pratt Hospital, has for years been crusading for a school of psychological medicine. It would grant a degree of Doctor of Psychological Medicine after six to eight years of college. The curriculum would include basic human biology, physiological and psychological growth processes, medical and psychiatric social work, sociology, education and learning theory, linguistics and communication theory, psychopharmacology, genetics, dynamic psychopathology, psychodiagnosis, and all forms of psychotherapy. "In one-half to two-thirds the time it takes to train a board-approved psychiatrist fully," Dr. Kubie has pointed out, "the same facilities could produce about twice as many well qualified diagnosticians and therapists. Each would finish earlier, and would have more years of useful professional life ahead of him. But we need a preliminary ten-year period for the special training of a cadre of new teachers."[62]

But even with heroic efforts to develop more efficient patterns of professional functioning, there aren't going to be enough professionals in any of the healing or behavioral professions. We are going to have to turn to nonprofessionals. Some experiments along this line are now going on. The National Institute of Mental Health began an experiment in 1960 to see whether educated housewives could be trained within two years to do limited psychotherapy. It was felt that women in their forties, with their children grown, could be trained to work therapeutically with patients. Such women, after managing their homes and raising their children, have

---

[60] Gorman, *Psychiatry and Public Policy*, 122 AMERICAN J. OF PSYCHIATRY 55, 59 (1965).

[61] Some of these programs are described in six papers. *Education of the Nonpsychiatrist Physician*, 122 AMERICAN J. OF PSYCHIATRY 485-508 (1965).

[62] SK & F Psychiatric Reporter, Sept.-Oct. 1965, pp. 4-5. See also Kubie, *A School of Psychological Medicine Within the Framework of a Medical School and University*, 39 J. MEDICAL EDUCATION 476 (1964).

had more life experience than the ordinary beginning professional worker. The experiment has been gratifyingly successful.[63]

In North Carolina and Tennessee, elementary school teachers are working with emotionally disturbed children in residential schools. The apparent success of the project suggests similar programs for other groups, such as the mentally retarded, the aged and senile, and even chronic psychotics.[64] Other such experiments are going on all over the country.

College students constitute another resource for personnel. The college Work-Study program has been a valuable source of mental health personnel.[65] VISTA (Volunteers in Service to America) workers in Georgia, North Carolina, and West Virginia, are working full time in slum areas, hospitals, schools, and institutions for the mentally ill and the mentally retarded.[66] Other mental health groups are recruiting and screening applicants for the Job Corps' Urban Centers for Women and other centers, to train unemployed young people to serve as mental hospital attendants and as laboratory technicians.[67]

Even if we had all the facilities and services needed, we would still face a special problem: how to get those who need these services to come and get them. In the old days, ward heelers took care of their people. Today we need a new kind of intervenor. Labor unions and veterans' organizations have recognized this, and have set up counselors and service representatives. A similar device being tried in several places is the "indigenous nonprofessional"—not the college-educated, middle-class housewife or the volunteer college student, but someone from the same neighborhood as the people he serves, often a member of the same minority group, sharing a common language, style, and interests. Thus a young man working with a recreation program for delinquents may be a former youthful offender.

The job of the indigenous nonprofessional is to be a link between the

---

[63] Dr. Lawrence S. Kubie, Director of Training at the Sheppard and Enoch Pratt Hospital, who participated in the experiment said, "It has been a heartening and exciting experience to see how a group of mature women, who have gone through the stresses and turmoils of bringing up their own families, with diverse college backgrounds but no prior technical training in psychological disciplines, could, in so short a time, become thoughtful, studious, perceptive, sensitive, and patient psychotherapeutic counselors. If anyone needed it, there would be no better proof that this opens up an important new way to attack the bottleneck caused by the shortage of trained workers in this field." Rioch, Elkes & Flint, *Pilot Project*, in U.S. DEP'T OF HEALTH, EDUC. & WELFARE, TRAINING MENTAL HEALTH COUNSELORS iv (1965).

[64] PROJECT RE-ED, A DEMONSTRATION PROJECT FOR THE REEDUCATION OF EMOTIONALLY DISTURBED CHILDREN (1963).

[65] Address by Senator Javits, *Mental Health and the War on Poverty*, at the annual meeting of the National Ass'n for Mental Health, New York, Nov. 18, 1965.

[66] *Ibid.*

[67] *Ibid.*

client and the community agencies, to serve as negotiator, investigator, expediter. He can also act as interpreter, explaining behavior that may puzzle or irritate agency staff or professional personnel, and explaining to clients agency procedures that may seem pointless and unsympathetic. He can thus help break the vicious cycle of misunderstanding, mistrust, and rejection that can so easily develop between the overworked staff and the desperate client.[68] The Neighborhood Youth Corps, through which high school dropouts are trained on the job with public institutions in their home towns, could be used for this purpose. Although this has been one of the more successful of the antipoverty programs, little has been done with the Corps in the field of mental illness.

E. Guardianship

A significant number of persons now sent to mental hospitals could remain home if provided with guardians and perhaps out-patient care. Some would not even need a guardian if they were given a little help in managing their affairs—perhaps nothing more than help in planning a budget plus a periodic check to see if they were following it. Others may need someone to accompany them when they cash their income checks and pay their rent, or to arrange for a near-by restaurant to help choose well-balanced and inexpensive meals, or to get a reliable contractor to make necessary repairs to the house. Possibly "indigenous non-professionals" could be used for such services. Others are incapable of making any important decisions or arrangements for themselves. For these, a more directive supervision is necessary if they are to be kept in the community rather than institutionalized.

In the modern welfare state, almost everyone has some income from social security benefits, public assistance payments, or pensions. The incompetent may need someone to manage this income, although he may be unable to pay court costs and fees for formal guardianship. Certain other changes have occurred in our society during this century that further suggest the need for a tax-supported device such as the public guardianship pioneered by Minnesota[69] and adopted to some extent in a few other states. People now live longer. But age tends to diminish one's capacity, physical and mental. Because our society is less rural and static than it was, families are less cohesive and there is less feeling of responsibility for the incompetent grandparent or other relative. The impersonality

---

68 PEARL & RIESSMAN, NEW CAREERS FOR THE POOR (1965); REIFF & RIESSMAN, THE INDIGENOUS NON-PROFESSIONAL (1965), originally published as a monograph, third in a series of reports by the National Institute of Labor Education (1964).

69 Levy, *Protecting the Mentally Retarded: An Empirical Survey and Evaluation of the Establishment of State Guardianship in Minnesota*, 49 MINN. L. REV. 821 (1965).

of modern life makes it difficult to find not only volunteer guardians, but also personal bondsmen. The individual man of substance who knew both the incompetent and the guardian and was willing to go on the guardian's bond has all but disappeared. Today, bonding is performed almost exclusively by commercial companies—who must charge for their service.

A few years ago Kentucky found that although its state hospitals had intensified their home and community placement programs, many patients could not be released because they had no relatives or friends interested in helping them. Most of them could be placed if they could qualify for public assistance; but they needed someone to act as guardian or committee. In a few counties public committees were available, but they charged five per cent for expenses. Operators of nursing homes or boarding homes into which patients could have been placed might have been appointed as guardians, but this would have created a conflict of interest. To meet the dilemma, the legislature in 1960 authorized the Department of Mental Health to be declared guardian for patients having no one else willing to serve.[70] The Director of the Guardianship Section is thus able to receive public assistance payments for patients after they leave the hospital, make payments to the home operators or to the patients themselves, and account to the court as required by law—all free of charge.

California, like a few other states, provides county Public Guardians.[71] The services are free, but are limited to patients in certain public institutions and recipients of public assistance. Although it does not solicit guardianship, the Los Angeles Public Guardian in 1962 served approximately 1,700 persons.[72] Most cases come either from the superior court after adjudication under Welfare and Institutions Code section 5076 or from the Bureau of Public Assistance.

Here, too, those in need of help may not seek it, nor even be aware that they need help, nor know where to find it. They may come to agency attention only as a result of some collateral crisis, such as physical illness, stroke, or an accident such as a broken hip. The immediate physical difficulty will often have mental complications. The protective service has a special responsibiilty to reach out to such persons, that is, to publicize its existence. "If persons are to seek help for themselves or others, they need to be assured of a place where the older person will receive the required attention. Persons who seek help for another need assurance that they will

[70] KY. REV. STAT. § 210.290 (Baldwin 1963).

[71] CAL. WELFARE & INST'NS CODE § 5076.

[72] Data collected by Professor William Cohen, U.C.L.A., for a study conducted at George Washington University under a grant from the National Institute of Mental Health. The study was completed in 1965. To date no report has been published.

not be expected to assume more responsibility than is commensurate with their relationship to him."[73]

Whether the appointed guardian is a relative, a commercial fiduciary, or a public guardian, a social caseworker should be available to advise the guardian and the court about available resources and to help in budgeting those resources. Often the condition that makes appointment of a guardian necessary entails a reduction in income or an increase in expense. Budgeting therefore may take on an importance it never had before, even when the person was mentally competent. Protective service might be more effectively rendered through an administrative agency than through a court. The agency could appoint, supervise, and terminate fiduciaryships for those requiring assistance in financial management. Such a venture would not be wholly novel. The Veterans Administration, the Bureau of Old Age, Survivors, and Disability Insurance of the Social Security Administration, and the Railroad Retirement Board have for years exercised judicial functions in designating recipients of benefits for incompetent beneficiaries. Their procedures and the experience under them could suggest ways to proceed. The VA, for example, tries to avoid the expense of judicial proceedings by designating someone as recipient for a veteran rated incompetent by the VA, rather than having a formal guardian appointed. The wife is the preferred person provided she is "qualified to administer the benefits payable and will agree to use the amounts paid for that purpose."[74]

Guardianship is a valuable device that has not been given much attention by the law or by social workers, and is probably not adequately appreciated. Resort to it will become urgent in the near future, especially for elderly incompetent persons.

II
LEGAL ASPECTS

A. Hospitalization and Incompetency Proceedings

When a poor person becomes mentally ill, he is more likely to be committed to a state hospital than to receive treatment in a local clinic or by a private psychiatrist. And the commitment procedure is almost certain to be summary and short. The same is true of incompetency proceedings. In New York, a fairly expensive incompetency proceeding called the sheriff's panel, carrying extensive procedural safeguards, is available for those who can afford it;[75] for others a much more summary proceeding is used.[76] In

---

[73] LEHMANN & MATHIASEN, GUARDIANSHIP AND PROTECTIVE SERVICES FOR OLDER PEOPLE 124 (1963).

[74] 38 C.F.R. §§ 13.55, 13.57 (Supp. 1965).

[75] N.Y. MENTAL HYGIENE LAW § 78.

[76] N.Y. MENTAL HYGIENE LAW § 76.

all states, commitment and incompetency cases are run through the courts in a minimum of time, on a minimum of evidence, and with essentially no hearing at all.[77]

Let me describe, for example, the Texas procedure. Texas has one of the most recent and most carefully drafted statutes in the country, the product of painstaking research financed by the Hogg Foundation and as carefully designed as any to preserve personal rights. It has, for example, a novel provision that no person may be indefinitely committed to a mental hospital without first having been sent there for a temporary stay of sixty days. At the hearing determining whether the person should be indefinitely hospitalized, the issue of incompetency may also be decided.

The Texas Mental Health Code[78] provides for a hearing and requires the appointment of an attorney *ad litem* to represent the person at the hearing. The statute, however, imposes no particular duties on the attorney. In at least one Texas city, these duties seem to consist of seeing that the papers are in order and that the notices were sent. Rarely does the attorney actively represent his client at the trial. The attorney receives ten dollars per case. The position is filled by rotation from a list of younger members of the bar—in this city the list is comprised of those who helped the judge in his campaign for office. At one hearing forty-one cases were heard in an hour and five minutes, an average of sixty-six seconds per case. All but one of the proposed patients were apparently temporary patients in the state hospital. All had signed waivers of jury trial. At the hearing, two doctors reported the weight, height, and color of hair and eyes of the patient (this for the form sent to the Department of Public Safety for action concerning drivers' licenses). The judge read the patient's name and the date of medical examination, and asked the doctors, "Is it your opinion and both of you that he is a mentally ill person and needs medical care and treatment for his own welfare and protection or the protection of others and is mentally incompetent?" The doctors answered, "Yes," and the next case was called. Only two of the forty patients actually appeared at the hearing.

The attorney *ad litem* earned four hundred dollars for sixty minutes of work plus travel time. He had no contact with his clients and had never seen nor heard from most of them. The Code contemplates that the issue

---

[77] Observations based on a study of nine communities throughout the United States. The study was conducted at George Washington University under a grant from the National Institute of Mental Health, and was completed in 1965. To date no report has been published.

[78] Tex. Rev. Civ. Stat. art. 5547-1 to 104 (Vernon's 1958), as amended, art. 5547-4 to 204 (Vernon's Supp. 1965), especially art. 5547-41 to 51, as amended, art .5547-47 to 49 (Vernon's Supp. 1965).

of incompetency be regarded as distinct from that of commitability,[79] but, as seen above, both are covered in one question and one answer.

In other states also, court-appointed counsel often play a passive role.[80] Privately retained lawyers are more likely to show diligence in learning the facts before the hearing. Though they may not take a belligerently opposing stance at the hearing, they will probably have taken pains to assure themselves that hospitalization is called for and that the client is being given fair treatment.

In most cases the need for guardianship or hospitalization is obvious. But in one case out of perhaps a hundred a summary procedure may work an injustice.[81] The problem is, of course, how to find that one case in a hundred without wasting time on unnecessary elaboration in the other ninety-nine. Most persons brought into court in hospitalization proceedings are without counsel. Most of them probably do not even see the necessity of counsel. They often do not have the financial resources to fight a governmental agency that may be recommending hospitalization. Corporations sometimes find it prudent to knuckle under rather than fight administrative orders. The poor, and particularly the mentally disabled poor, are even more easily regulated. Yet a lawyer, plus perhaps a psychiatrist, might not only successfully defend the case in court, but might see it dropped without getting to court.

In most states members of the family of a patient are legally obligated to pay all or part of the cost of hospital care if they have the financial means. The extent of means and the cost that the family is to bear is typically determined administratively. Many poor families do not protest this determination, even though the payments assessed may be very burdensome. In 1964 the California Supreme Court held that a statute imposing liability for the care of a mentally ill parent committed to a state hospital violated California's state constitutional guarantees of equal protection.[82] The court based its reasoning in part on "the social revolution which has been developing during the past half century," and which has "brought expanded recognition of the *parens patriae* principle . . . and other social responsibilities, including . . . public welfare programs to

---

[79] TEX. REV. CIV. STAT. art. 5547-51 (Vernon's 1958).

[80] See, *e.g.*, Cohen, *The Function of the Attorney and the Commitment of the Mentally Ill*, 44 TEXAS L. REV. 424, 448 n.108 (1966).

[81] SPECIAL COMM. TO STUDY COMMITMENT PROCEDURES OF THE ASS'N OF THE BAR OF THE CITY OF NEW YORK, MENTAL ILLNESS AND DUE PROCESS 189, 272 (1962).

[82] Department of Mental Hygiene v. Kirchner, 62 Cal. 2d 586, 400 P.2d 321, 43 Cal. Rptr. 329 (1965). A prior decision of the same court in this case, 60 Cal. 2d 716, 388 P.2d 720, 36 Cal. Rptr. 488 (1964), had on certiorari to the United States Supreme Court been remanded because the California court had not stated whether its holding was based on the equal protection clause of the fourteenth amendment or the California constitution, article I, §§ 11, 21, or both. 380 U.S. 194 (1960).

which all citizens are contributing through presumptively duly apportioned taxes."[83] The court concluded that "a statute obviously violates the equal protection clause if it selects one particular class of persons for a species of taxation and no rational basis supports such classification."[84]

In what promises to be a landmark decision, the Court of Appeals for the District of Columbia has held[85] that an aging person unable to care adequately for herself but not dangerous to others cannot be involuntarily kept in a mental hospital without full exploration of all possible alternatives available for her care in the community. A staff psychiatrist had testified that in his opinion she would not be a source of potential danger either to herself or others if released; the problem was only that she would be exposed to difficulties if left unattended. There would be no objection to release if she could have adequate attention under appropriate supervision, as in a nursing home. Her family, however, was not able to pay for such care or supervision. Her counsel therefore, on application for release on habeas corpus, argued that she was being deprived of her liberty not because of her mental condition but because of her poverty. The District statute provided for hospitalization or "any other alternative course of treatment which the court believes will be in the best interests of the person or of the public." The court's duty, it was said, is to consider whether the person and the public would be sufficiently protected if she were required to carry an identification card, so that she could be taken home if she wandered, or whether she should be required to accept public health nursing care, community mental health services or foster care, or whether welfare payments might finance private care. The burden, said the court, was not on the petitioner to show the availability of alternatives, but on the courts with the aid of community agencies to explore the possibilities.

---

[83] 60 Cal. 2d at 722, 388 P.2d at 723, 36 Cal. Rptr. at 491.

[84] *Id.* at 722, 388 P.2d at 724, 36 Cal. Rptr. at 492. Professor tenBroek has called the case "a landmark decision in the law of the poor," and one whose importance cannot be overestimated. tenBroek, *California's Dual System of Family Law: Its Origin, Development, and Present Status,* 17 STAN. L. REV. 614, 638-39 (1965).

An Arizona case has held that no right to appeal exists from an order of a juvenile court requiring parents to pay a specified amount for maintenance of their delinquent child in a state industrial school. The court did not reach the constitutional question of the validity of the statute subjecting parents to liability for such maintenance costs. Ginn v. Superior Court, 1 Ariz. App. 455, 404 P.2d 721 (1965).

Such portions of veterans' benefits as have been converted into permanent investments have been held subject to claims for reimbursement for amounts expended in institutional care of the veteran. District of Columbia v. Phillips, 347 F.2d 795 (D.C. Cir. 1965). The decision creates a problem for the committee or guardian of a mentally incompetent person: whether to spend all veterans' benefits received for the ward, or save and invest for emergencies with the result of subjecting such invested amounts to claims for maintenance.

[85] Lake v. Cameron, —— F.2d —— (1966).

Four members of the court dissented, saying that the majority's decision orders the court to perform functions which it is not equipped to carry out and which are normally reserved to social agencies. It is certainly true that it calls for major reforms in traditional methods of caring for the aged.

A related but narrower contention being argued with increasing frequency is that persons compulsorily institutionalized because they need treatment have the right to insist that they get the treatment which is the justification for their confinement. If the institution is not providing such treatment, the confinement is unjust and arguably unconstitutional.[86]

Little investigation seems to have been made of the extent to which state mental institutions are required to comply and do comply with standards applicable to similar operations conducted outside the institution. Thus, all states have industrial codes calling for certain safeguards for persons working in shops, mills, or manufacturing plants. Does the laundry at the state institution, for example, have to meet the same standards of safety and comfort that other laundries are required to maintain for their workers? Are the laundries and workshops in the institution subject to the general sanitary codes? What of laws concerning the dispensing of drugs? Certain drugs, such as the tranquilizers and barbiturates, are generally not allowed to be dispensed except by a registered nurse. In some (we do not know how many) state hospitals they are dispensed in great quantities without such restrictions. Is the medical service of the hospital accredited? The residents of a community can be counted on to show concern that their hospitals are accredited. But no one is likely to be equally concerned over the state hospital. The same is true of the staff. Are the hospital's physical therapists registered as such? Are they required to have the same qualifications as those practicing physical therapy outside the hospital?

Although institutions for the retarded are generally called schools, the

---

[86] Birnbaum, *The Right to Treatment*, 46 A.B.A.J. 499 (1960). Congress in enacting the present District of Columbia commitment law recognized a "moral obligation to afford adequate treatment to those hospitalized for mental illness." H.R. REP. No. 1833, 88th Cong., 2d Sess. 6 (1964). The act itself unequivocally provides that any person hospitalized in a public mental hospital shall "be entitled to medical and psychiatric care and treatment." D.C. CODE § 21-562 (Supp. 1966).

A New York court refused to order commitment of geriatric patients who were not actively psychotic or overtly mentally disturbed. Application for Certification, 20 Misc. 2d 866, 195 N.Y.S.2d 131 (Sup. Ct. 1959). The same court also refused to transfer to a mental hospital an elderly woman described as "confused, disoriented," with a very poor mental grasp and a diagnosis of chronic brain syndrome with senile brain disease. Application of Anonymous No. 13, 6 Misc. 2d 596, 159 N.Y.S.2d 842 (Sup. Ct. 1957). See also Brenner, *Denial of Due Process and Civil Rights to Aged Seniles Without Major Medical Impairment*, 34 N.Y. STATE B.J. 19, 21 (1962).

children in such institutions may, in comparison with normal children, receive inferior educational services. For example, the teachers may not meet the standards of qualification required for other teachers. Teacher-pupil ratios may be much more unfavorable. Are social security benefits to which institutionalized children are legally entitled being made available for their benefit? Are they getting equal benefits under the state's compulsory education laws, vocational rehabilitation acts, and federal and state provisions for aid to crippled children?

B. Protections in Criminal Cases

Any confession of a mentally retarded person obtained by police interrogation is likely to be nonvoluntary. Slight pressure—perhaps only suggestive questioning—may be frightening and coercive to a retarded person. Such a person is less likely than most to know his constitutional rights to remain silent and to consult an attorney. Even if told of these rights, he may not appreciate their significance. The retarded are vulnerable not only to threats and coercion but also to a show of friendliness. Some desire to please authority; if a confession will please, or will keep people from being angry with him, such a person may gladly confess, not appreciating the implications or consequences of his statements. Certainly, silence in the face of an accusation should not be taken as evidence of guilt: Lack of intelligence may make him unable to understand what is being asked or unable to understand quickly enough to formulate answers.

The President's Panel on Mental Retardation suggested that the police work out self-imposed standards for questioning the retarded; for example, a person suspected of being retarded would not be questioned unless his attorney, parent, or guardian was present.[87] But the courts also ought to review such confessions. Mental retardation might not have been apparent at the time of the police interrogation, and all too frequently unfair procedures have been used. The Supreme Court in recent years has recognized that mental retardation may diminish the ability to resist police pressure; it has held certain confessions involuntary and inadmissible in evidence.[88]

The test of competence to stand criminal trial is usually stated to be the ability to tell one's side of the story and to assist counsel. But competence to relate a story may not be the same as competence to withstand cross-examination. A mentally retarded witness, although telling the truth, may fail to give the impression of doing so, because he is easily confused

---

[87] PRESIDENT'S PANEL ON MENTAL RETARDATION, REPORT OF THE TASK FORCE ON LAW 34 (1963).

[88] Reck v. Pate, 367 U.S. 433 (1961); Culombe v. Connecticut, 367 U.S. 568 (1961); Fikes v. Alabama, 352 U.S. 191 (1957).

under pressure of effective cross-examination, with the result that he may be discredited in the eyes of the jury or even induced to testify untruthfully.

To help eliminate the inequality that lack of money creates, it has been proposed that in prosecutions in which mental condition is an issue, a defendant be furnished the assistance of a psychiatric expert. One federal court has held that due process of law requires that such assistance be provided in a felony prosecution.[89] Professor Larry A. Bear has said that "it is absolutely monstrous to allow the availability of a psychiatrist to assist the defense to depend upon the personal wealth of the defendant or his family. It is no answer to say that where the state provides an 'impartial' psychiatrist the defendant doesn't need one of his own. He is entitled to present any respectable psychiatric theory at his trial which might assist him in prevailing upon his plea, even though the 'impartial' expert may be prejudiced against it."[90] The Criminal Justice Act of 1964[91] now provides investigative, expert, and other services as well as the assistance of counsel, to indigent defendants in federal courts.[92] Little attention thus far seems to have been given to providing psychiatric expert services.[93] Mr. Justice Brennan has suggested that local branches of the American Psychiatric Association might be asked to provide free

---

[89] Bush v. McCollum, 231 F. Supp. 560 (N.D. Tex. 1964), aff'd, 344 F.2d 672 (5th Cir. 1965). See also United States ex rel. Smith v. Baldi, 192 F.2d 540 (3d Cir. 1951), in which three of the judges took the position that where there are grave indicia of mental disease and where it appears that counsel cannot properly prepare his client's case without the aid of a psychiatrist, refusal to provide psychiatric assistance in effect deprives the accused of benefit of counsel. The majority of the court, however, refused to accept the proposition that a defendant is constitutionally entitled to receive at public expense all the collateral assistance needed to make his defense.

[90] Bear, Reflections on the Problem of Formulating Pre-Trial Mental Examination Legislation in Criminal Cases, 34 REV. JUR. U.P.R. 307, 351 n.131 (1965). That "impartial" court-appointed experts may not in fact be impartial has been argued by other writers. Diamond, The Fallacy of the Impartial Witness, 1959 ARCHIVES OF CRIMINAL PSYCHODYNAMICS 221; Goldstein, The Psychiatrist and the Legal Process: The Proposals for an Impartial Expert and for Preventive Detention, 33 AMERICAN J. OF ORTHOPSYCHIATRY 123 (1963); Goldstein & Fine, The Indigent Accused, the Psychiatrist, and the Insanity Defense, 110 U. PA. L. REV. 1061 (1962); Hess & Thomas, Incompetency to Stand Trial: Procedures, Results, and Problems, 119 AMERICAN J. OF PSYCHIATRY 713 (1963); Koskoff, Unconscious Bias Sways Some Medical Experts, Va. Law Weekly Dicta, Feb. 19, 1959.

[91] 78 Stat. 552, 18 U.S.C. § 3006A (1964).

[92] Scotland also has since 1964 provided criminal legal aid to indigents, including payment not only of solicitors and counsel but also of necessary expert and other witnesses. Forensic Science Society Bull. No. 4, 1964, p. 4.

[93] See Report of the Judicial Conference of the United States on the Criminal Justice Act, Minutes of Meeting of Oct. 17, 1964, of the Committee to Implement the Criminal Justice Act of 1964, 36 F.R.D. 277, 374 (1965); Kutak, The Criminal Justice Act of 1964, 44 NEB. L. REV. 703, 737-40 (1965).

or low-cost psychiatric help to indigent defendants.[94] Such help might be crucial not only at the trial, but also when the court is considering what sentence to impose.

The people who land in prison are not generally the most dangerous criminals. They are the failures in crime. They fail for the same reasons they fail in noncriminal efforts; they are not bright, or they are too impulsive and lack foresight. Poverty may or may not have led them to commit crime, but once in prison, poverty will certainly work to keep them there. The man with no job or other assets justifying hope for success on parole is likely to serve the maximum sentence.

The statutory procedures of some states may discriminate against the criminal who has become insane while in prison. The New York procedure has recently been held by the United States Supreme Court to deny equal protection in that (1) it permits civil commitment at the expiration of a penal sentence without the jury review available to all other persons so committed, and (2) it permits commitment to a state hospital maintained by the Department of Correction and used primarily to house persons found insane while serving sentence, persons charged with crime but found mentally incompetent to stand trial, and persons acquitted of crime by reason of insanity, whereas other persons are committed to that institution only if after a judicial hearing they are found to be dangerously mentally ill.[95] The invidious discrimination here is against those convicted of crime, rather than against the poor as such. But convicts are generally poor.

The New York procedure also failed to provide for appointment of counsel, and the petitioner in the case had appeared at the hearing alone; but the Supreme Court did not discuss the issue.[96] The Supreme Court of Illinois, however, has held that even though commitment proceedings are civil in nature, a person sought to be committed at the expiration of sentence is entitled to have counsel appointed for him, unless he intelligently waives such right.[97]

---

[94] Brennan, *Law and Psychiatry Must Join in Defending Mentally Ill Criminals*, 49 A.B.A.J. 238, 242-43 (1963).

[95] Baxstrom v. Herold, 383 U.S. 107 (1966).

[96] In 1965, New York, under its Mental Hygiene Law, § 88, created a review commission. The presiding justice of each appellate division appoints a staff consisting of lawyers and civil service personnel to review admissions. The commission conducts a full investigation and makes a formal report to the judge holding the sanity hearing, who has discretion to appoint counsel if needed.

California added a provision to its Penal Code in 1961, providing that at any time after expiration of sentence the prisoner if retained in a mental hospital may petition for a hearing on the issue of his mental illness, in the manner provided for civil commitment. CAL. PEN. CODE § 2964. The judge may appoint an attorney or the public defender: if the prisoner is financially unable to employ counsel, counsel shall be appointed at his request. CAL. WELFARE & INST'NS CODE § 5565.

[97] People v. Breese, 34 Ill. 2d 61, 213 N.E.2d 500 (1966).

CONCLUSION

The poor need vastly expanded mental health services, especially local community health centers. To raise the money to build needed facilities and to find the personnel to staff them will be prodigious tasks, but even if we accomplish them, we shall still face the baffling problem of inducing the poor to use those services. The poor often do not recognize that they need help; even when they do, they may not know that services exist or how to obtain them. They are apathetic about finding out, or cynical, or hostile. That this attitude of defeat, bitterness, and despair has become so widespread throughout our nation is a damning indictment of our sins of the past. It should shame and goad us to more heroic efforts now.

Marriage and Legitimacy in Mexican Culture: Mexico and California†

Woodrow Borah* and Sherburne F. Cook**

T HE QUESTION of cultural transfer arises automatically when one deals with the social behavior of immigrants and their descendants to the first or second generation. It becomes unavoidable when one deals with an ethnic group refreshed by continuing immigration and living near enough to the country of origin to have continuing contact with it. Hence, inquiry into patterns of family union among Mexican-Americans in California requires lengthy study of such patterns among Mexicans in their own country. California, like the other southwestern states, has a relatively large minority of Mexican birth and descent. That minority (we shall call its members Mexican-Americans) tends to live at the lower end of the economic scale with most or all of the usual characteristics of poverty.[1] Its members therefore tend to need public assistance in larger proportion than other racial and ethnic groups except Negroes. Accordingly, their habits of family union and procreation become especially subject to inspection by members of the community who quickly discover a

---

† This study has been made possible through grants from the Institute of Social Sciences and the Center for Latin American Studies, Institute of International Studies, both at the University of California, Berkeley. We also make use of material obtained during periods as fellows of the John Simon Guggenheim Memorial Foundation and through filming by The Bancroft Library, University of California. For further materials on Mexico, we are indebted to assistance from the Dirección General de Estadística, Mexico City; the state governments of Oaxaca and Jalisco; and the Archbishop of Oaxaca, the Bishop of Huajuapan, and parish priests of the Mixteca Alta. For materials used in the second part of this study, we are especially indebted to N. R. Holcomb, former Director of the Santa Clara County Welfare Department, to his successor Frederick B. Gillett, and to the directors of the Santa Clara County Records Office and County Clerk's Office.

* A.B., 1935, M.A., 1936, University of California, Los Angeles. Professor of History, University of California, Berkeley.

** A.B., 1919, A.M., 1923, Ph.D., 1925, Harvard University. Professor Emeritus of Physiology, University of California, Berkeley.

1 The census of 1960 found 15.7 millions to be the total population of California, among whom there were 1.4 million people with Spanish surnames. Not all people with Spanish surnames are of Mexican origin or descent; on the other hand, many of the children of intermarriage with other groups would not have Spanish surnames. A reasonable estimate would be that people of Mexican birth and descent in California numbered over a million in 1960, or from seven to eight per cent of the total population. 1 U.S. BUREAU OF THE CENSUS, DEP'T OF COMMERCE, CENSUS OF POPULATION: 1960, pt. 6, at xiii, ix (1963). For information on the economic status of Mexican-Americans in the southwestern states, see Fogel, *Education and Income of Mexican-Americans in the Southwest* (University of California, Los Angeles. Graduate School of Business Administration. Division of Research. *Mexican-American Study Project, Advance Report 1*. November, 1965).

relatively high percentage of common law or informal family unions and a consequent higher percentage of illegitimate children. At this point there arises a series of questions of public policy that are often settled by default rather than by careful consideration by appropriate instrumentalities.[2] Such questions in the end will have to be considered somewhere. However, we shall not do so here. Our question is another: Is the higher percentage of informal family unions among Mexican-Americans a characteristic of poverty, shared with other poor groups? Or is it a carryover of patterns in Mexican culture? If the latter is true, the fact that certain other groups show similar behavior means only convergent behavior arising from different causes; that is, not all patients with fever have typhus.

"Marriage" we define as the association of a man and woman in a household for purposes of sexual intercourse, procreation, and such other cooperation as they may choose to give each other. Without a defining adjective, the term means legal marriage, one entered into by formal ceremonies and duly registered as required by law. The children of such unions are legitimate, that is, known as to both parents, entitled to support during minority from both and, if there is property, to a share in the inheritance. To change these relations requires express written instrument or court action. "Marriage" with such defining adjectives as "common law" or "informal" indicates that the family union has been entered into without all required formalities. The definition here is complicated because in Mexico such a union may have been blessed by the church but does not meet the statutory requirement of a civil ceremony. Children born to couples in informal union, however stable and long-term, are illegitimate, bastards in stark English. In most of our states and in most countries of the world, they are far less likely to be entitled to support from both parents during minority or to a share in property, especially that left by the father. Although during recent decades there have been changes in many jurisdictions in the rigorous medieval definitions, generally these definitions still hold true. They are especially true for people receiving public assistance (although inheritance is less likely to concern them) since the status of being a common law wife or illegitimate child may well affect the quality and extent of aid.

The study that we propose is neither easy nor simple. It requires examination both of Mexican law and custom, on the one hand, and of experience in California, on the other. For both territorial units, the topics

---

[2] They are: (1) Is it proper for welfare agencies to impose upon their clients a morality beyond that required by law of other sectors of the population? (2) To what extent should it be public policy that all groups within society must conform to a uniform pattern of morality, namely, what is often called middle-class morality? (3) Are the agencies administering public assistance the proper bodies for making and imposing such a decision?

to be covered are surprisingly little explored.[3] For Mexico, national statistics can be used since we are interested in the entire country, but to go behind the statistics or to look into formation of present patterns means a lengthy historical inquiry for which we must hunt for data. As for California, where we deal with a part of the population, the ordinary statistics do not contain the information desired. The man who would study the marital habits of Mexican-Americans must do his own digging. As a result, data for this study are far sparser than desirable. Another consequence is that the two parts of the study, both necessary if one is to look into possible cultural transfer, are based on different kinds of data and forced to follow the data into different though connected explorations. Part I of the study is a long historical examination of the formation of patterns of marriage and legitimacy in Mexico. It addresses itself to origins, earlier forms, and present-day characteristics. Part II is a study of characteristics found among Mexican-Americans in one part of California, namely Santa Clara County. It examines a small body of relatively current data. In structure and approach, it will be found different from most of Part I, but the two parts are linked and necessary. Each in turn, of course, has independent value.

I

MARRIAGE AND LEGITIMACY IN MEXICO

A. Spanish and Indian Antecedents

Mexico is a national state in territory conquered by the Spaniards from Indian tribes, many of which were of highly developed culture and political organization. Unlike the United States, the present-day Mexican population is descended in large proportion from the aboriginal inhabitants and in much smaller proportion from Spanish and European ancestors (with some Negro admixture).[4] But Mexico is Spanish-speaking and in its cultural heritage has been far more completely Europeanized than genetic proportions would indicate.[5] Accordingly, we must look to both a Spanish and an Indian heritage.

Mexico's Spanish heritage contained widely differing, indeed virtually irreconcilable, components of law and custom. Spanish law on marriage and legitimacy as it came to Mexico was essentially late Roman law. The law was restated by the church, which made two major changes.[6] One

---

[3] See, for example, how sparse is the bibliography for Mexico from the brief discussion in ITURRIAGE, LA ESTRUCTURA SOCIAL Y CULTURAL DE MÉXICO 12-23 (1951).

[4] BELTRÁN, LA POBLACIÓN NEGRA DE MÉXICO *passim* (1946); Borah, *Race and Class in Mexico*, 23 PACIFIC HISTORICAL REV. 337-39 (1954).

[5] CLINE, THE UNITED STATES AND MEXICO 24-87 (1953); Borah, *supra* note 4 at 337-39.

[6] See Gaynor, *Concubinage*, 4 CATHOLIC ENCYCLOPEDIA 207; articles on various aspects of marriage, 9 *id.* at 691-715; Jombart, *Concubinage*, 3 DICTIONNAIRE DE DROIT CANONIQUE

eliminated the Roman rule of easy divorce and remarriage, replacing it with a theological and philosophical interpretation which allowed annulment or separation but not divorce. The other discarded the harsh Roman rule refusing recognition to marriages between slaves or a slave and a free person, the church declaring both classes of unions, if permanent and subject to no other impediment, to be true Christian marriages. In Christianized form, the late Roman law was incorporated into the *Siete Partidas* of Alfonso X, the Learned, in the second half of the thirteenth century, restated in the *Nueva Recopilación de Castilla* of Philip II in 1567,[7] and remains the basis of Spanish marriage law today.[8] Legal marriage was monogamous, a formal union of man and woman of proper age and status. Aside from rank, freedom to enter into marriage meant that the parties were not bound by a previous and undissolved marriage, were not within forbidden degrees of consanguinity and spiritual relationship, and had not taken vows or holy orders. For twentieth-century people, the most unusual of these restrictions are probably those on spiritual relationship which applied the rules on incest to godparents and godchildren.[9] The ceremony of marriage was a religious sacrament, to be carried out by the church, although consummation was a private and essential act. Children born to a couple so united were automatically legitimate from birth. Potentially legitimate children were those born to a couple living together unmarried but who could be married if they wished. Such children automatically became legitimate if their parents married.[10] The rewards of marriage were high, for only legitimate children could inherit the surnames, titles, and property of their fathers. They alone were eligible for holy orders and higher posts in the church as well as for many posts of profit and preferment in civil life.[11] In keeping with the sacramental character of marriage, legitimacy and succession lay with church rather than civil courts.[12]

Along with this rigid legal category, there existed in folk custom in Spain a far freer practice that had its origin in prehistoric European custom[13] and was recognized in late Roman law. In the Roman Empire, a

---

1514-23 (1942); Naz, *Mariage en droit occidental*, 6 *id.* at 742-87; *Barraganía*, 7 ENCICLOPEDIA UNIVERSAL ILUSTRADA EUROPEO AMERICANO 894-96; *Matrimonio*, 33 *id.* at 1012-1137.

[7] The marginal annotations of Gregorio López to *Las Siete Partidas del Sabio Rey Don Alfonso el X* show the incorporation of the provisions on marriage, concubinage, and legitimacy in the Recopilación de Castilla. LAS SIETE PARTIDAS DEL SABIO REY DON ALFONSO EL X *passim* (1829-1831) [hereinafter cited as LAS SIETE PARTIDAS].

[8] On the current law of Spain, see *Matrimonio, supra* note 6, at 1098-1108.

[9] LAS SIETE PARTIDAS, Partida IV, Títulos II, VI-XIII.

[10] LAS SIETE PARTIDAS, Partida IV, Título XIII, Ley I.

[11] LAS SIETE PARTIDAS, Partida IV, Título XIII, Ley II, & Título XV, Ley IX.

[12] 1 GARCÍA GALLO, CURSO DE HISTORIA DEL DERECHO ESPAÑOL 310-11, 318-19 (1950).

[13] *Barraganía, supra* note 6, at 895.

single man and woman not prohibited by vows, marriage, holy orders, or relationship within a prohibited degree might join together without formality for a temporary or permanent union.[14] Frequently the woman was of lower social status than the man.[15] She was considered a quasi-wife with certain rights so long as the man did not marry another woman; the children, although not considered legitimate, were termed *naturales* to distinguish them from children begotten in more dubious relationships (*spurii*).[16] Although the early church frowned upon all temporary unions as an immoral pandering to the flesh, it recognized permanent unions as a true form of marriage even though the partners had not complied with ordinary legal forms and were not recognized as fully married by the civil law.[17] The efforts of the church were directed toward preventing priests and married men from taking partners or concubines and toward urging that partners in informal unions remain together for life. In medieval Spain, where the custom not only persisted but became widespread, it was called *barraganía*, and the woman a *barragana*.[18] So long as the partners were single and under no impediment that would have prevented marriage, they might live together at will, separate at will, or stay together for life. Their children were not legitimate but *hijos naturales*, bastards with the least stigma attached to the term. Local law and custom in many cities allowed limited rights of inheritance if the father had no legitimate children and had acquired no legal wife.[19] The status of *barraganas* is carefully regulated in the *Siete Partidas* with the wry comment that "Holy Church forbids that any Christian man have *barraganas*, for to live with them is mortal sin. But the wise men of old who made the laws permitted that some men might have them without civil penalty, for they held that it was a lesser evil to live with one woman than many, and that the paternity of the children would be more certain."[20] Any man not estopped by holy orders or state of marriage "may have a *barragana* without fear of civil penalty," runs the text, "provided that he take not a virgin nor a girl under twelve years nor a widow of honest life, and that all be done with good witness. And if a man wishes to take as *barragana* a widow or any other woman free from birth who is no longer virgin, at the time he does so, he should make public statement to that effect before respectable men. Should he receive her in other wise, there would be just doubt that she was his legal wife rather than his *barragana* . . . ."[21]

---

[14] Gaynor, *supra* note 6, at 207.

[15] *Ibid.*

[16] *Ibid.*

[17] *Ibid.*

[18] *Barraganía, supra* note 6, at 894-96.

[19] *Id.* at 895-96.

[20] Las Siete Partidas, Partida IV, Título XIV, opening statement (transl. by authors).

[21] Las Siete Partidas, Partida IV, Título XIV, Ley II (transl. by authors).

Much more objectionable to church and Spanish rulers was an extension of custom, also under the term *barraganía,* that permitted similar arrangements by priests and by married men. The practice became common with the breakdown of central power in the earlier Middle Ages and with the concomitant decline in centralized control of the western church and in church discipline. In the later Middle Ages the revitalized papacy and monarchs forbade such arrangements in persistent battle against customs which tolerated violation of celibacy by many of the clergy and de facto polygyny among many of the wealthy.[22]

The struggle of church and state against folk custom found expression in the remarkable categories of illegitimate children set forth in the *Siete Partidas:*[23]

Naturales—born to *barraganas;*
Fornezinos—born in adultery, from relations with a relative within the forbidden degrees, or to a nun;
Manzeres—born to prostitutes so that paternity is uncertain;
Spurii—born to *barraganas* living outside the man's house, that is, mistresses or women who may have relations with more than one man so that paternity is not certain;
Notos—born in wedlock but not the children of the husband.

The *hijos naturales* might be legitimated by grace of the civil rule,[24] by testament confirmed by the ruler,[25] by entering the illegitimate son in the service of a royal or noble court or a town in a public ceremony that meant a formal public declaration of paternity,[26] or, in the absence of legitimate sons, by public instrument.[27] Only the Pope might grant legiti-

---

[22] Ferdinand and Isabella, for example, in 1484 ordered that a married man of any class who kept a *barragana* should forfeit a fifth of his property and that a woman who lived with a married man or a man under church vows be punished. Konetzke, *Die Mestizen in der kolonialen Gesetzgebung: Zum Rassenproblem in spanischen Amerika,* 42 Archiv für Kulturgeschichte 131, 147 (1960) (citing the *Ordenanzas Reales de Castilla* of 1484). The punishment for women was stated at length in the standard instructions for *corregidores* (officials sent to supervise towns and cities for the crown). For the first offense, the woman was to be fined one mark of silver (eight ounces) and be exiled from the town for a year; for a second offense, she was to be fined one mark and be sent from the town for two years; for the third offense, the penalty was one mark of silver, another year of exile, and one hundred lashes. Los capitulos de corregidores de 1500, clause 47 (1963 ed.). The fine of one mark of silver became famous as the *marco del amancebado.*

An amusing account of the reception in the town of Talavera of a fourteenth-century order forbidding the keeping of *barraganas* by clergy and married men may be found in the *Cántica de los Clérigos de Talavera* in Libro de Buen Amor del Argobispo el Hita 166-67 (1962). As the poem remarks, if the order "pleased one, it grieved two thousand." *Ibid.*

[23] Las Siete Partidas, Partida IV, Título XV, Ley I.
[24] Las Siete Partidas, Partida IV, Título XV, Ley IV.
[25] Las Siete Partidas, Partida IV, Título XV, Ley VI.
[26] Las Siete Partidas, Partida IV, Título XV, Ley V.
[27] Las Siete Partidas, Partida IV, Título XV, Ley VII.

macy for the purposes of holy orders.[28] One further channel of grace for illegitimate children of all kinds lay in a general dispensation that permitted them to enter monastic orders.[29] As far as royal enactment then, illegitimate children of all kinds, and particularly those of lesser category than *hijos naturales*, suffered heavy disabilities. Folk practice and the negotiations of noble families obviously mitigated much of the effects of law in particular cases. The bastard of Charles V, Don Juan de Austria, for example, could command the Christian fleets at the Battle of Lepanto.[30]

Spanish law and custom thus contained widely differing views on marriage. It was a complex and contradictory heritage that the Spanish brought to the New World.

The heritage of Mexico in Indian rules of marriage and succession is more difficult to describe, even if we confine our discussion to the central part of the country, simply because there were many groups of varying practice which were in the process of being unified into one state. In this unification the Spanish merely carried on the work of the Aztecs and their predecessors in empire. Furthermore, although the pictographic system of writing in use at the time of the Spanish Conquest would have permitted the reduction of custom and precept to a code, there is no evidence to suggest that this was done. Our information is on custom and precept as it was reported by early Christian missionaries who questioned native informants.[31] Most of their reporting concerns the Nahuatl-speaking peoples centered around the Valley of Mexico, of whom the Aztecs are the best known, and reflects the interest of the missionaries. For example, we have a careful description of the formal preliminaries and ceremonies of marriage in an idealized description that probably deals with nobles and tells us little or nothing about unions of commoners and serfs.[32]

In general, there was formal marriage and determination of legitimacy for purposes of succession to office, title, or property, whether the people involved were royalty, nobles, or commoners.[33] Rules differed,

---

[28] LAS SIETE PARTIDAS, Partida IV, Título XV, Ley IV.

[29] Bernard, *Bâtard*, 2 DICTIONNAIRE DE DROIT CANONIQUE 251-62 (1937).

[30] See 13 ENCYC. BRITANNICA 94 (1963).

[31] See, *e.g.*, SAHAGÚN, HISTORIA GENERAL DE LAS COSAS DE NUEVA ESPAÑA (1945 ed.).

[32] *Id.* at 562-69.

[33] The description that follows is based on the following sources: VON REITZENSTEIN, LIEBE UND EHE IN OSTASIEN UND BEI DEN KULTURVÖLKERN ALTAMERIKAS 67-82, 101-04 (1910) (excellent summary of the older literature and chronicles); Spores, Cultural Continuity and Native Rule in the Mixteca Alta 1500-1600, March 1964 (unpublished thesis in Harvard General Library); Alfonso Caso, *La tenencia de la tierra entre los antiguos mexicanos*, Memoria de El Colegio Nacional México, No. 2, 1959, pp. 29-54; Carrasco, *El barrio y la regulación del matrimonio en un pueblo del Valle de México en el siglo XVI*, 17 REVISTA MEXICANA DE ESTUDIOS ANTROPOLÓGICOS 7-26 (1961); RICARD, LA "CONQUÊTE

however, for the various social strata and from region to region. Hereditary office, for example, might go to brothers rather than sons. In general, polygyny was common among nobles and rulers. It may well have been permitted to commoners, but we have no information on this point. Among the Mixtecos, living to the south of the Nahuatl area, the ruler of each of the city states and kingdoms had a principal wife, who had to be of royal descent through all traceable ancestors. Only children of the principal wife could inherit the realm. The other wives, although legitimate, were of inferior status, and their children became mere nobles. Other Indian groups were less rigid in their rules, but even among the Nahuatl-speaking groups of the Valley of Mexico it was common to invest a new dynasty with a claim to divine descent by having the new ruler beget his heir on a wife descended from the ancient Toltec rulers. The nobility, in general, chose their partners with some freedom and married in formal ceremonies. The marriage tie was protected by the death penalty for adultery. For commoners, marriage was far less elaborate in ceremony, with far less freedom of choice. The young men of the clan were paired off with young women, whom they might have chosen, but only with the consent or even at the command of the local rulers; the couples were then united in relatively simple ceremonies. Marriage was both endogamous and exogamous in relation to the *calpulli*, the local unit holding land in common and united by theoretical or actual descent from a common ancestor. How marriages could be dissolved we do not know, although the frequent shifts from one wife to another in the first generation of Christianity suggest that there was an easy way. Similarly, notwithstanding reports by Christian missionaries on the rigidity of punishment for adultery,[34] later practice in the first generation of Christian converts suggests that among commoners punishment was not invariable. For purposes of inheritance, birth in a union recognized by the community and further ratified by the registration of the offspring in the register of the *calpulli* was important for free commoners, for such registration carried with it the right to a share in communal land. For the rulers and nobility, formal marriage and recognition of proper descent of children were indispensable to ensure orderly inheritance. For serfs and slaves, about whom we know very little, some form of recognized succession by children must have been necessary to ensure the continued supply of labor and other services for the masters. The absence of detailed evidence makes any conclusion tentative, but

---

Spirituelie" du Mexique 134-41 (1933); *Decrees of First Mexican Provincial Church Council, 1555*, clause 8, in Llaguno, La Personalidad Jurídica del Indio y El III Concilio Provincial Mexicano 170 (1585); and Soustelle, La Vie Quotidienne des Aztèques à la Veille de la Conquête Espagnole 203-18 (1955).

34 *E.g.*, Motolinía, Memoriales 251-52 (1903 ed.).

such evidence as we have indicates that most of the Indian groups of central Mexico had customs of formal unions, whether temporary or permanent, and of formal registry of birth. As among all sedentary peoples, there was need to ensure orderly succession and to determine just who was entitled to what share. The Mexican Indians were thus better able than, say, nomads to receive an even more complicated system.

B. The Transfer of Spanish Law and Custom to Mexico

The Spanish conquest of Mexico in the early sixteenth century and consequent rapid Christianization of the Indians meant the imposition of Spanish law and custom on marriage and legitimacy.[35] But, just as the conquest set in motion far more than mere subjugation of the Indians, so the process of implantation was much more than mere overlay upon Indian customs or elimination of them and substitution of Spanish concepts. The Spanish migrated in numbers to the newly acquired realm of the Crown of Castille as, to a lesser extent, did other Europeans. The Europeans brought substantial numbers of Negro slaves, who were settled in the new European cities, on the coasts, and in the sugar regions on the temperate slopes of the central plateau. The immigration of Europeans and Negroes in itself meant a rapidly increasing non-Indian population, but the new groups also interbred with each other and with the Indians to produce an even more rapidly increasing population of mixed bloods. (Those of white and Indian mixture were called *mestizos* and those with any substantial trace of Negro genetic stock, *pardos*.) As a result, besides the substantial aboriginal population there formed another and rapidly increasing one of European law and behavior in the larger towns, the ports, mining camps, and on commerical farms, ranches, and plantations. Europeans, Negroes, and mixed bloods (unless they merged with the Indians, as did a few) belonged to European culture and were held responsible for the full observance of Spanish law. In the broadest use of the term, such people were *gente de razón*, people of reason or responsible people, as against the Indians, who were held to be in need of special guidance and protection. Thus Mexico during the colonial period consisted of two communities, one under special controls being brought to Spanish law and such of Spanish custom as church and state held proper, the other bringing with it and living automatically in the discordant mixture of law and folk practice that prevailed in Spain. The mixture may have become even more discordant through admixture of West African custom brought by slaves.

In dealing with the Indians, the Spanish had both to group them in a

---

[35] The following general discussion is based on SIMPSON, MANY MEXICOS 65-172 (3d ed. 1952).

polity acceptable to European concepts that would further the extraction of goods and services from them and to replace their heathen cults with Christianity. Christian marriage was an important part of the implantation of Christianity since acceptance of the Christian conceptions of family and legitimacy meant also acceptance of many of the complicated Christian ideas of morality. The missionary program for marriage was summarized by one of the royal secretaries in the first years of Spanish dominion:

> [The Indians] must be persuaded that men who marry may have only one wife, they being brought to understand that marriage is only with one woman while that woman lives and that the sons who are born to her are legitimate, that such sons and no others inherit their father's property. They are also to be informed of the meaning of spiritual relationships. They are not to have sexual intercourse with mothers, daughters, sisters, cousins, nor other relatives, for by doing so Christians incur penalty of death.[36]

The implementation of the program may be traced in the general course of conversion and in a series of special royal and church enactments which indicate the steady pressure and growing control of missionaries and civil administrators. In 1530, for example, the wife of Charles V, governing as Empress Regent, decreed that any Christian Indian, male or female, who married for a second time while the first spouse was alive, should be punished.[37] The terms of the decree left the unconverted free to continue their heathen ways. By 1551 the royal government could decree that no Indian, whether noble or commoner, should be permitted more than one wife even if he remained heathen.[38]

The regulations for enforced assimilation of the Indians into Christian polity in terms of marriage and legitimacy may be summarized briefly. As the royal instructions quoted above indicate, conversion automatically brought into force the rules of canon and civil law on monogamy, of prohibited degrees of blood and religious relationship, of requirements of age and freedom from vows, and of legitimacy and inheritance. In 1539 the full requirements of warnings, banns, and public proclamation, set forth in canon law and the rules of the Archbishopric of Seville, were ordered enforced in marriages of Indians.[39] Disputes over marriage and dissolution of union among Indians were to be handled by the church authorities,

---

[36] 4 ENCINAS, CEDULARIO INDIANO 269-70 (1945) (transl. by authors) [hereinafter cited as ENCINAS].

[37] RECOPILACIÓN DE LEYES DE LOS REYNOS DE LAS INDIAS, Libro VI, Título I, Ley IV (1841) [hereinafter cited as RECOPILACIÓN].

[38] RECOPILACIÓN, Libro VI, Título I, Ley V.

[39] *Decisions of Church Conference of 1539, Mexico City, April 27, 1539*, clauses 15-17, in 3 GARCÍA ICAZBALCETA, DON FRAY JUAN DE ZUMÁRRAGA 165-71 (1947).

but thereafter the parties might seek further hearing in any appropriate tribunal.[40] In other words, jurisdiction over Indians in such matters was vested in the ordinary ecclesiastical and civil courts.[41] In 1555 the First Mexican Provincial Church Council ordered that Indians, like Spaniards, do penance before the ceremony of marriage.[42] During the sixteenth century a standard system of parish registers was instituted for Indians and Spaniards alike. The First Mexican Provincial Church Council directed that baptism and marriages of Indians be recorded so that there might be a written record in case of doubt or dispute.[43] In 1585 the Third Mexican Provincial Church Council directed that parish registers of births, confirmations, marriages, and burials be kept for Indians as well as for Spaniards as required by the Council of Trent.[44] In general, practice in Mexico during the colonial period[45] down to the 1830's was to keep separate registers for Indians and for non-Indians.[46] Such registers and the priest's affidavits were the legally requisite evidence of legal marriage and legitimate descent. The parish records also acquired fiscal importance since they were used to verify counts of people in the towns liable to tribute and constituted an important means of preventing evasion.[47]

Freedom of choice in marriage was guaranteed by a series of regulations, the first of which was issued in the West Indies before the conquest of Mexico but automatically carried to the mainland.[48] Further regula-

---

[40] *Ibid.*

[41] *Ibid.*

[42] *Decrees of First Mexican Provincial Church Council, 1555*, clause 7, in LLAGUNO, *op. cit. supra* note 33, at 170.

[43] *Ibid; Decrees of the First Mexican Provincial Church Council, 1555*, clause 32, in CONCILIOS PROVINCIALES PRIMERO Y SEGUNDO, CELEBRADOS EN MÉXICO 88-89 (1769). The 1769 edition of Archbishop Lorenzana differs considerably from the text published by José A. Llaguno.

[44] CONCILIUM MEXICANUM PROVINCIALE III, Liber III, Titulum II, § II (1770).

[45] *Report of the Archbishop of Mexico to the King, Mexico City, October 24, 1815*, in Konetzke, *Documentos para la historia y crítica de los registros parroquiales*, 7 REVISTA DE INDIAS 581, 585 (1946).

[46] We found this in our inspection of parish records in the Mixteca Alta.

[47] RECOPILACIÓN, Libro I, Título XIII, Ley XXV (issued March 27, 1606). Our examination of parish registers showed clear evidence that in the tribute counts the registers were examined and each baptismal entry had to be accounted for by the presence of a new tributary at the appropriate age or by death or departure. Similarly the entries for deaths were used to verify deletions from the rolls of tributaries at the time of the counts.

[48] In 1514 the royal government ordered that Indians might marry freely with each other or with Spaniards without legal impediment. *Orders of Oct. 19, 1514, Valbuena*, and *Feb. 5, 1515, Valladolid, to Diego Colon*, in 4 ENCINAS at 271. The order entered the *Recopilación* as a general provision. RECOPILACIÓN, Libro VI, Título I, Ley II. The instruction was silent on impediment arising from difference in social degree, which, as in Spain, presumably continued to bar marriage between partners of too great disparity in rank. See the royal order issued at San Lorenzo, Oct. 24, 1775, and the pragmatic issued at El Prado, March 23, 1776, reprinted in 3 KONETZKE, COLECCIÓN DE DOCUMENTOS PARA LA HISTORIA DE LA FORMACIÓN SOCIAL DE

tions issued in Mexico by the church were aimed at breaking control of the Indian nobility over the marriages of commoners. Indians of proper ages and degrees of relationship for marriage were guaranteed freedom of choice and expressly protected from requiring permission of their caciques or from having partners chosen for them and forced upon them. The First Mexican Provincial Church Council ordered imprisonment for thirty days and such other penalties as the judge might assess for violation of its regulation.[49] The Third Church Council raised the penalty to automatic excommunication for anyone interfering with the free choice of partners to marriage.[50]

Spanish ideas were further implemented by new regulations forbidding sexual intercourse by partners within the prohibited degrees of relationship and by ordering punishment of informal unions in which one of the partners was already married or otherwise barred from legitimating the union by going through a church ceremony.[51] Presumably the reluctant tolerance accorded informal unions by partners who could have legitimated their union extended to mating among the Indians, but, as we shall see, church and lay authorities in Mexico were better able to enforce their will on the Indians and had excellent reasons for encouraging the celebration of full legal marriages. The penalties for violations of Spanish concepts of morality were the same for Indians as for Spaniards with the one major difference that fines and other monetary penalties could not be assessed against Indian offenders.[52]

In the course of the sixteenth century the Spanish concepts of legitimacy and inheritance through sons and daughters born in marriage were also imposed upon the Indians despite express injunctions that Indian custom be honored except where it was repugnant to natural law and Christian morality.[53] Inheritance by brothers rather than children and

---

HISPANOAMERICA 1493-1810, at 401-05, 406-13 (1962). As the text of the royal orders makes clear, they were merely a restatement of a principle that was supposed to have been enforced from time immemorial.

49 Decrees of First Mexican Provincial Church Council, 1555, clause 8, in LLAGUNO, op. cit. supra note 33, at 170.

50 CONCILIUM MEXICANUM PROVINCIALE III, Liber IV, Titulum I, § VIII (1770). The principle passed into civil law in the Ordinances of Philip III, Madrid, October 10, 1618, in RECOPILACIÓN, Libro VI, Título IX, Ley XXI.

51 Decrees of the First Mexican Provincial Church Council, 1555, clause 43, in CONCILIOS PROVINCIALES PRIMERO Y SEGUNDO, op. cit. supra note 43, at 104-05.

52 In accordance with this policy, the Spanish crown ordered as early as 1536 that the marco del amancebado should not be levied against Indians. Order of the Empress Regent for Charles V, Madrid, June 26, 1536, in 4 ENCINAS at 337, and in RECOPILACIÓN, Libro VII, Título VIII, Ley VI. See also the acceptance of this principle by the Mexican church in CONCILIUM MEXICANUM PROVINCIALE III, Liber V, Titulum IX, § 1 (1770).

53 RECOPILACIÓN, Libro II, Título I, Ley IV; id., Libro II, Título XV, Ley LXXXIII; id., Libro V, Título II, Ley XXII; Ballesteros, Los indios y sus litigios, según la Recopilación de 1680, 4 REVISTA DE INDIAS 618-21 (1945).

election of a successor within a single house of common male descent were hardly repugnant to either but disappeared in the course of the century as Spanish courts in Mexico repeatedly decided inheritance cases by reference to Spanish law and custom.[54] Substitution of Spanish law in this area of decision was virtually complete by 1580, that is, within a half century of the establishment of a formal high court in Mexico.[55] As part of the same sets of decisions, Spanish concepts of illegitimacy and the incapacity to inherit of children born outside of a registered church marriage were imposed by Spanish courts whenever matters of inheritance came under judicial inspection.[56]

The imposition of Spanish concepts upon the Indians went farther even than the acceptance of such ideas among the Spaniards themselves. The Indians as a subject race were much more within the power of Christian missionaries and lay authorities. The missionaries, in fact, dreamed of an organization of Indian life in which a docile people would be kept within Christian norms under their guidance with a minimum of interference by civil authorities or by Spaniards and other non-Indians.[57] In sympathy with some of these views, the Spanish crown assisted in trying to keep undesirable non-Indians, and indeed virtually all non-Indians, out of Indian communities. Unmarried Spaniards, mixed-bloods, and vagabonds were forbidden to tarry in Indian towns,[58] and even Spaniards on proper errands, such as travellers and merchants, were restricted to a stay of from two to three days unless they were assigned to the town for civil or religious duty.[59] The concern of the royal government for the Indians, we

[54] See authorities cited note 53 *supra*.

[55] *Ibid.*

[56] This paragraph is based upon our examination of suits over lands and inheritance of the titles and estates of Indian chiefs (*caciques*) in records within the Mexican national *archives* (Archivo General de la Nación), especially the *ramos* of *Tierras, Vinculos, Indios, Mercedes,* and *General de Parte*. In a suit in 1566-69 over the succession as *cacique* in Teposcolula, where the chief died without lineal heirs, the Spanish courts rejected the Mexican custom of choosing a new *cacique* from the ancestral line in Tilantongo and awarded succession, in accordance with Spanish ideas, to a collateral relative claiming through female relationship. The papers of the case are in 24 ARCHIVO GENERAL DE LA NACIÓN, TIERRAS, expediente 6. For a similar refusal to recognize native custom in 1562 for the area of Tlaxcala, see GIBSON, TLAXCALA IN THE SIXTEENTH CENTURY 74 (1952).

[57] PHELAN, THE MILLENNIAL KINGDOM OF THE FRANCISCANS IN THE NEW WORLD 42-74 (1956).

[58] RECOPILACIÓN, Libro VI, Título III, Leyes XXI-XXIII (the dates of the orders ranging from 1536 to 1646, the most important ones from 1536 to 1581). See also the *Instruction of May 2, 1563, Valladolid, to Luis de Velasco* (the new viceroy appointed to succeed Antonio de Mendoza) reprinted in 4 ENCINAS at 340-41. *But see* the *Order of the King to the Viceroy of New Spain, Tomar, May 8, 1581, ibid.* (providing that no Spaniard was to live among Indians unless of good life and behavior—a distinctly different idea).

[59] Travelers were restricted to the day they arrived, a day of rest, and departure on the third day. *Royal Order of November 20, 1536, Valladolid,* in RECOPILACIÓN, Libro VI,

need hardly add, far outran its ability to enforce such regulations. Far more effective than Spanish law in promoting Christian marriage and morality was a happy alliance between the desire of the missionaries to root out informal unions in all forms and the fiscal interests of the crown and Spaniards receiving support from tributes. For purposes of tribute levy upon the Indians, the fiscal unit was the married couple, who were held to pay a sum that by the early seventeenth century was fixed at slightly over two silver pesos (two dollars) a year. For a day laborer, the tax meant the wages of eight to twelve days a year. Unmarried women supported by their parents were exempt in most parts of Mexico. Unmarried men either paid half rate or, if they held no land, were exempt.[60] There was an obvious advantage to the fisc, and to Spaniards to whom it ceded its rights to tributes, in pairing off the Indians in formally married couples. As we shall see, pressure by priests and civil officials almost eliminated informal unions among the Indians and led to early marriages.[61] They were helped by native custom since the Indians were already used to being paired off by their chiefs. There was a very real concern for Christian morality, as well as fiscal advantage, in the pressure for formal marriage, as may be seen in the regulations that required Indian merchants not to remain away from their wives too long[62] and required Indians working in distant mines and textile establishments to see their wives often enough not to be led into relations with other women.[63]

Thus far we have dealt with the transfer of Spanish patterns to the Indians in Mexico. For the so-called *gente de razón* the transfer was automatic since they not only brought with them Spanish law in all its rigor, but also Spanish custom. The attempts of church and state to enforce

---

Título III, Ley XXIII. Merchants were allowed three days. *Royal Order of November 21, 1600, El Pardo*, in RECOPILACIÓN, Libro VI, Título III, Ley XXIV.

[60] MIRANDA, EL TRIBUTO INDIGENA EN LA NUEVA ESPAÑA DURANTE EL SIGLO XVI 139-43, 249-53 (1952). The usual tribute for a married pair was one silver peso and four and a half reales of ordinary tribute, the four and a half reales representing commutation to coin of the value of half a bushel of maize. In addition, in 1591-93 a special surtax of half a peso was added, called *servicio real*. That brought total tribute to two silver pesos and half a real. A small annual payment was made to the Indian community, ranging from one and a half to two reales. The silver peso was one ounce of silver, in effect our traditional dollar, and this was divided into eight reales, our "bits" in colloquial usage. *Ibid.*

[61] See, *e.g.*, *Letter of the King to the Viceroy of New Spain, July 5, 1578*, in 4 ENCINAS 322 (loss in tribute because of the failure of Indians to marry); *Order of the King to the President and Audiencia of Guatemala, Tomar, April 17, 1581*, in 4 ENCINAS 350 (ordering an end to forced marriages of women under canonical age for marriage). See also text preceding note 82 *infra*. The order to the authorities in Guatemala became general for Spanish America. See RECOPILACIÓN, Libro VI, Título I, Ley III.

[62] *Decrees of the First Mexican Provincial Church Council, 1555*, clause 71, in CONCILIOS PROVINCIALES PRIMERO Y SEGUNDO, *op. cit. supra* note 43, at 145-46.

[63] *Ordinances for Workshops (Obrajes), Mexico City, October 13, 1595*, clause 24, in 1 BELEÑA, RECOPILACIÓN SUMARIA DE TODOS LOS AUTOS ACORDADOS, pt. II, at 86 (1787).

Spanish and church law are evident in a long series of enactments. The Mexican provincial church councils reenacted a series of directives for enforcing official marital standards of morality.[64] The royal orders required enforcement of Spanish regulations against violations of public morality and ordered exaction of the *marco del amancebado* as in Spain, but in doubled amount to adjust for higher incomes and price levels in America.[65] A special series of problems which arose as migrating Spaniards declared themselves married and either changed spouses or merely shed them by migration brought forth repeated orders for the inspection of marriage credentials of Spanish couples migrating overseas[66] and rules that married men coming to any Spanish possession in the New World must either take their wives with them or have their wives' permission and post bond that they would return to Spain after a limited stay.[67] The need for repeating instructions[68] and the terms of renewal of orders suggest that enforcement was not rigorous. Mexico was a long remove in space and time from Spain, and the royal government in the colony was a relatively small number of officials who were dependent for compensation and enrichment upon fees and other direct, personal payments by the people they governed.

Spanish folk practice, of course, embodied a very different morality. Its acceptance of informal unions of single people without impediment to marriage could be and was tolerated by state and church although a zealous administrator or priest might take action against the partners for living in *pecado público*. But, whatever the official views, there also existed among the population of Spanish culture informal unions without regard to impediments, informal separations, and the acceptance of a double standard. As in much of Europe at the same time, the standard of conduct in the upper and middle classes enjoined chastity and legal marriage upon properly behaved women but valued sexual prowess and the keeping of mistresses by the men.[69] Among the lower classes the double standard

---

[64] See especially *Decrees of the First Mexican Provincial Church Council, 1555*, clauses 28-43, in CONCILIOS PROVINCIALES PRIMERO Y SEGUNDO, *op. cit. supra* note 43, at 98-105, and the long series of regulations reenacting the principal provisions of canon law, adopted by the Third Provincial Church Council, 1585, in CONCILIUM MEXICANUM PROVINCIALE III, Liber III, Titulum II, § II (1770).

[65] RECOPILACIÓN, Libro VII, Título VIII, Leyes IV, V.

[66] See *Decrees of Third Mexican Provincial Church Council, 1585*, clause 39, in CONCILIUM MEXICANUM PROVINCIALE III, Liber IV, Titulum I, § XII (1770).

[67] RECOPILACIÓN, Libro VII, Título III, Leyes I-IX; *id.*, Libro IX, Título XXVI, Ley XXIX; *id.*, Libro II, Título XVIII, Ley XXXIII; 2 JOSÉ DE AYALA, NOTAS A LA RECOPILACIÓN DE INDIAS 319 (1945).

[68] See, *e.g.*, the dates of repetition for RECOPILACIÓN, Libro VII, Título III, Ley I.

[69] GAGE, TRAVELS IN THE NEW WORLD 58-87 (Thompson ed. 1958); KONETZKE, DIE INDIANERKULTUREN ALTAMERIKAS UND DIE SPANISCH-PORTUGIESISCHE KOLONIALHERRSCHAFT 90-91 (1965); Konetzke, *supra* note 22, at 131-77.

tended to become a single one through acceptance of the same easy morality for women.[70] Racial mixing usually involved informal union rather than marriage.[71] Since marriage between an Indian woman and a Spaniard was generally regarded as a step down in the social scale for the Spaniard, much racial mixing came about through informal unions and casual pleasures.[72] Unions among Negroes and *pardos* (colored, in our usage) with other racial groups tended to be informal and casual for a number of reasons—a residue of West African customs of matrilineal reckoning of descent and the better political and economic position of women there,[73] the premium upon looser ties of union and mating inherent in the slave owners' desires for larger stock, the limitations in choice of partner inherent in slave status, and the premium existing in folk esteem on colored women as mistresses. Even by European terms of the time, Mexican society was considered morally lax.[74]

Although the gap between official morality and folk practice was wide, it was not completely unbridgeable. Legitimation was a prerogative reserved to the King acting through his Council of the Indies,[75] but that only meant that the cost of securing grace rose accordingly. It became a privilege of the wealthy handled according to schedule. One of the last schedules, issued in 1804, set a range according to the sin of the parents from 687½ to 4,125 silver pesos. These were the payments to the royal treasury and did not include the costs of petitioning at long remove and through a complex bureaucracy, a matter of thousands of pesos more.[76]

C. Colonial Patterns, 1600-1850

By the end of the sixteenth century, Spanish law and custom on marriage and legitimacy had been brought to Mexico with enough success

---

[70] See authorities cited note 69 *supra*.

[71] *Ibid.*

[72] *Ibid.*

[73] See generally RADCLIFFE-BROWN & FORDE, AFRICAN SYSTEMS OF KINSHIP AND MARRIAGE (1960); FEMMES D'AFRIQUE NOIRE (Paulme ed. 1960).

[74] See GAGE, *op. cit. supra* note 69, at 68, on the favoring of women of color as mistresses. On laxness of morals, one may form some judgment from the fact that two of the most frequent bases for prosecutions by the Mexican Inquisition were solicitation in the confessional by clergy and holding the view that simple fornication (i.e., without contravening degrees of relationship and other prohibitions) is not a serious sin. See the summaries of cases in TORIBIO MEDINA, HISTORIA DEL TRIBUNAL DEL SANTO OFICIO DE LA INQUISICIÓN EN MÉXICO *passim* (1905).

[75] RECOPILACIÓN, Libro II, Título XV, Ley CXX, incorporating a decree of Philip IV, Madrid, March 28, 1625.

[76] 3 KONETZKE, *op. cit. supra* note 48, at 781. The fees were: for a son or daughter to inherit, if both parents were single, 687½ pesos; for extraordinary legitimation in order to inherit the noble status of parents, the fathers being members of military orders and married, or clergy, 4,125 pesos; for other legitimations of the same class but the fathers being merely married men and the mothers single, 3,225 pesos.

that one may speak of colonial patterns, that is, Spanish ones with adaptations to Mexican conditions. These patterns lasted with relatively little further change through the rest of the colonial period and until the middle of the nineteenth century. During these two and a half centuries, the Spanish extended the effective zone of Spanish culture far to the north of their original conquests in central Mexico.[77] The patterns formed in central Mexico in the sixteenth century moved northward with the settlers and missionaries.[78] Within the entire zone of Spanish culture the Hispanized community tended to grow rapidly whereas the Indian segments, although increasing in absolute numbers, tended to become a smaller part of the total population.[79]

We have already described the general nature of the patterns of formal and informal union that obtained among the various racial groups. We now restate our description in terms of urban and rural and of subdivisions within those categories. Urban, for our purposes, meant Mexico City and the other Spanish settlements. The whites and *mestizos* of the Hispanized population were concentrated in them. Simultaneously they lived under the rule of Spanish law, church and civil, and adhered to Spanish folk practice. A double standard for men and women characterized the upper and middle classes. There was a relatively high percentage of concubinage or the keeping of mistresses and of free union. Colored women were especially prized as mistresses. Among the lower classes informal or free union was common and tended to be prominent in racial mixing. As the Indians of the suburbs, especially those around Mexico City, became used to Spanish dress and practice they also tended to take on Spanish practices in family union.[80] For one suburb of Mexico City, that of Guadalupe, we have a striking comment from the Dominican Thomas Gage, who visited it in 1625. He thought the population to be about two thousand Indians and a thousand *mestizos*. "These are of a mixed nature of Spaniards and Indians, for many poor Spaniards marry with Indian women, and others that marry them not but hate their husbands, find many tricks to convey away an innocent Uriah to enjoy his Bathsheba."[81] Nevertheless, although informal and irregular union was a prominent feature of custom in the Spanish cities, it should not be forgotten that most of the people did marry in accordance with church requirements and that Spanish law obtained in all the rigor of its requirements of formal marriage and legitimate birth for inheritance, the taking

---

[77] Sauer, *The Personality of Mexico*, 31 GEOGRAPHICAL REV. 353 (1941).

[78] *Ibid.*

[79] BORAH, NEW SPAIN'S CENTURY OF DEPRESSION 5-18 (1951).

[80] Borah, *Race and Class in Mexico*, 23 PACIFIC HISTORICAL REV. 331, 340 (1954); GAGE, *op. cit. supra* note 69, at 68-74.

[81] GAGE, *op. cit. supra* note 69, at 67.

of holy orders, and the holding of office. The stigma of illegitimacy might mean little among the lowest social groups, but among the middle and upper classes it had force.

Rural, for our purposes, must be divided into Indian and non-Indian. The Indian rural included large towns, which yet depended in great measure upon the cultivation of the surrounding fields for support. In general, Indian patterns of marriage were imposed through close control by the church, especially the parish priests, who tended to be the most important authority in the villages and towns, and by the fiscal pressure of royal administrators anxious to swell the tributes. Almost all Indians married early and in formal church ceremonies so that they furnished the maximum number of full tributary units. As a further result there were few or no illegitimate children although native pre-Conquest custom may have had an influence on this. We have examined the parish registers for perhaps half the parishes in the Mixteca Alta, a region of old Indian culture south of Mexico City in the State of Oaxaca. The extant registers usually begin some time during the seventeenth century and run to the present. We found that the Indians married early, that virtually all of them married, and that the baptismal registers show almost no illegitimate children. In the late eighteenth and early nineteenth centuries there was a very small number of illegitimate births, insignificant in terms of percentage, which were recorded mostly as *ninos expósitos*, foundlings left on the doorstep of the parish priest for him to baptize and provide for.[82] Local counts of population taken during those same years show also a few children living with unmarried women (*solteras*) and designated as younger siblings. The ages, in most instances, corroborated the designation rather than indicating an illegitimate child born to the *soltera*. As far as our evidence from the Mixteca (and other evidence from the census of 1777 discussed below) extends, church and state succeeded in imposing official morality upon the Indian population in an especially rigorous form. The more important agent was the church.

The non-Indian rural population came into being during the centuries after the conquest as the Spanish established ranches and farms in vacant country and near the Spanish cities. The virtual disappearance of the Indian population in the coastal zones led to replacement there by a new population of Spanish, mixed bloods, and Negroes, with the Negro mixtures a very important component. In all these rural areas the practice of the Hispanized community prevailed, and church and state were far less able to impose official morality. The colored population was con-

---

[82] The parish priest's share in tithes, first fruits, and so forth was theoretically a trust to provide for the poor as well as for his own needs. TIERNEY, MEDIEVAL POOR LAW: A SKETCH OF CANONICAL THEORY AND ITS APPLICATION IN ENGLAND 37-45 (1959).

sidered to be characterized by an especially high percentage of informal union, informal separation, and disregard for official morality.[83]

A quantitative test of the Mexican patterns of marriage and legitimacy during the colonial period is possible through analysis of the fragments that remain to us of the 1777 census for the Bishopric of Oaxaca[84] and also for a good deal of southern Veracruz and a small part of Tabasco.[85] It thus included a large Indian area of various tribal cultures; a good deal of non-Indian rural area on the Pacific and Caribbean coasts, with a relatively high proportion of colored population; and the City of Antéquera (today Oaxaca), a Hispanized urban center. Reports survive for over a third of the parishes with reasonable representation for the various Indian groups, both Pacific and Caribbean non-Indian coasts, and the complete return for the City of Antequera. As a sample for our purposes, the surviving returns are good.

Table 1 of the Appendix summarizes the material in the returns of 1777 for the Bishopric of Oaxaca relevant to test the statement of patterns that we have made. Table 1A gives the percentages by race of married men and unmarried men and women of eighteen years and over for all of the bishopric except the City of Antequera, which is treated separately since the inhabitants, though all Hispanized, were a jumble of races and racial mixtures. The census data clearly support the thesis that the Indians married early and in far greater proportion than did the other groups in the population. The colored population married at somewhat later ages and in lesser proportion. *Gente de razón*, here whites and *mestizos*, married at a later average age and to a somewhat lesser extent. The City of Antequera showed the same proportion of marriage as the *gente de razón* but a somewhat higher proportion of unmarried men and women. That percentage probably reflects immigration from rural areas.

Table 1B gives the average number of unmarried women (*solteras*) with children per thousand inhabitants in terms of the same division by race for the rural inhabitants and a single grouping for the City of Antequera. For the area outside of Antequera, the children were uniformly

---

83 GAGE, *op. cit. supra* note 69, at 68-70.

84 Three colonial censuses were taken, in 1742-48, 1777, and 1793. Almost all of the 1742-48 census has been lost except for summaries, which do not give adequate information on the categories of interest to us. *E.g.*, VILLASEÑOR Y SÁNCHEZ, THEATRO AMERICANO (1746-48) (totals for towns in terms of total numbers of family). Relatively large parts of the censuses of 1777 and 1793 have survived and are now being analyzed. The only part of them that has been reworked adequately from the original reports so that it gives information on such matters as marriage and informal union is the section of the census of 1777 for the Bishopric of Oaxaca. The census of 1777 was organized by bishoprics; the reporting agents were the parish priests.

85 Borah, *The Collection of Tithes in the Bishopric of Oaxaca During the Sixteenth Century*, 21 HISPANIC AMERICAN HISTORICAL REV. 386, 387 (1941).

reported as having been born to (*hijo de*) the unmarried women. For Antequera, reporting took two forms. One is the same as for the regions outside of Antequera; the other type shows a child of very young years listed as an orphan (*huérfano*) immediately following the name of an unmarried woman. In most instances the ages show a very young child and a women between the ages of eighteen and thirty. The former type of reporting is characteristic of the first part of the census for the city whereas the second is characteristic of the last part, with a middle part in which there is a transition from one to the other method. Clearly we are dealing here with a shift in the method of reporting. Although we have no concrete evidence, it is highly probable that the children designated as orphans were actually born to the women with whom they were listed. These data for Antequera are summarized in Table 1C. With respect to the areas of Antequera, the difference between Indians and rural non-Indians is striking in that the proportion of illegitimate Indian children is far less than that for either of the other two groups. With regard to the City of Antequera, if our interpretation of the recording is correct, there was a marked difference between rural non-Indians and the city.

Although the data for the Bishopric of Oaxaca alone cannot be deemed conclusive on this point, they indicate that there existed substantial differences between rural and urban Hispanic populations in customs of marriage and that the Hispanic rural population lay midway in its behavior between the Indians and the urban Hispanic. The data of Table 1 also indicate that the majority in all ethnic groups in the bishopric did get married by formal church ceremony.

The extent to which the data for the Bishopric of Oaxaca are representative of the rest of Mexico cannot be settled until the other remnants of the censuses of 1777 and 1793 are analyzed in the same way. Until then, about all that can be said is that nonquantitative material for the country as a whole suggests that, whatever the regional variation, the pattern was national.

D. The Move toward New Patterns: Legislation and Implementation Since 1855

The colonial patterns of marriage and legitimacy lasted with little modification until the middle of the nineteenth century. Independence from Spain, successfully declared in 1821, had slight effect at first since church and state continued to cooperate, and the colonial law was not changed. Whatever the disputes between liberals and conservatives or between pro and anti-clerical factions in the national and state capitals, the parish priests remained the recording officers for the only registers of births, marriages, and deaths—the parish books; a church ceremony remained the only legally recognized marriage giving rise to legitimate children; and cooperation of priests and local administrative officers maintained pressure upon the peasant population for observance of official and religious standards of morality. The urban population, especially the poorer segments, continued to show substantial deviation from official morality and substantial observance of custom.[86] The coming of independence, nevertheless, opened the country to the entrance of new ideas which by the middle of the nineteenth century led to new legislation and to institutional changes. Between 1853 and 1867, in the long series of Wars of the Reform, the cooperation of church and state came to an end, to be succeeded by periods of substantial hostility. The struggle which still continues, although in uneasy truce at the moment, has deeply affected patterns of marriage, informal union, and legitimacy in Mexico and for decades has seriously hampered efforts by the civil government to establish an accurate registry of vital statistics. If anything, the gap between statute and custom is wider today than in colonial times.

The pertinent changes and legislation may be summarized briefly by topic:

1. Abolition of the Jurisdiction of Ecclesiastical Tribunals in Civil Matters and Over Lay Persons

The reform government which came into office in Mexico after the famous Revolution of Ayutla on November 23, 1855, made the first move in the "Law of Administration of Justice and Organic Law for Courts of the Federation," known usually as the Ley Juárez after the then Minister of Justice.[87] The new Federal Constitution of 1857 accepted the principle in article 13: "In the Mexican Republic no person may be judged under private laws nor by special tribunals."[88] The Mexican state thus asserted exclusive jurisdiction over the population except for private jurisdiction of church tribunals over clergy.

---

[86] WILSON, MEXICO: ITS PEASANTS AND ITS PRIESTS 281-90 (1856); Gilmore, *The Condition of the Poor in Mexico, 1834*, 37 HISPANIC AMERICAN HISTORICAL REV. 213 (1957) (publishing a report by the British legation in Mexico City to the Foreign Office in answer to a circular inquiry).

[87] The pertinent sentences read "ecclesiastical tribunals shall cease to have competence in civil matters and shall continue to have jurisdiction over common crimes of the persons entitled to privilege of clergy until a law is enacted to regulate this point. . . . The provisions of this article are general for the entire Republic and the States cannot change or modify them." *Law of Administration of Justice and Organic Law for Courts of the Federation*, art. 42, in 7 DUBLÁN & LOZANO, LEGISLACIÓN MEXICANA 603 (1867-1913) (transl. by authors) [hereinafter cited as DUBLÁN & LOZANO].

[88] MEXICO CONST. tit. I, § I, art. 13 (1857) in 8 DUBLÁN & LOZANO 385-87 (transl. by authors). Military courts continue to have special jurisdiction over soldiers in actual service.

2. Separation of Church and State

The Constitution of 1857 at first did not provide unequivocally for separation of church and state. It merely omitted all reference to union of church and state and obliquely provided for freedom of religious belief.[89] During the long civil war, the reform government of Benito Juárez issued a series of decrees confiscating church property, denying civil recognition of church vows, removing cemeteries from church jurisdiction, and so on.[90] The changes were made part of the Constitution of 1857 through a series of amendments adopted on September 25, 1873,[91] and put into effect through an implementing act of Congress on December 14, 1874.[92] *Inter alia*, the amendments and act expressly provided for separation of church and state.[93]

3. Civil Registry

The civil registry is far more important in Mexico than in the United States because many of the statutory provisions on marriage and legitimacy are part of the statutes governing it.[94] The reformers of the 1850's planned to institute a more efficient system of recording vital statistics. The European experience had already demonstrated that reliance upon parish registers did not furnish comprehensive or reliable coverage.[95] The first "Organic Law of Civil Registry" of January 27, 1857, proposed a system that still envisaged the cooperation of church and state.[96] Although the law is notable only as a first effort since it was in effect for just a few months, certain provisions give interesting insights into the ideas of the time. Parents, godparents, or guardians abandoning children

---

[89] In Article 123: "The federal branches of government have exclusive jurisdiction for carrying out the measures provided by law in matters of religious cult and public [acts of religious] discipline." MEXICO CONST. tit. VI, art. 123, in 8 DUBLÁN & LOZANO 397 (transl. by authors).

[90] See 8 DUBLÁN & LOZANO 680-705.

[91] See 12 *id.* at 502-03.

[92] *Id.* at 683-88.

[93] *Id.* at 683 (art. 1).

[94] CÓDIGO CIVIL PARA EL DISTRITO Y TERRITORIOS FEDERALES, Titulo Cuarto (1965) [hereinafter cited as MEXICAN FEDERAL CIVIL CODE].

[95] The first plans for registry of vital statistics in the United Kingdom in the early nineteenth century tried to make the church registers the basis for registration. By the 1830's the attempt was given up as unworkable, and civil registration began in England in 1837. Birth, Death, and Marriage Registration Act, 1836, 6 & 7 Will. 4, c. 86; Krause, *The Changing Adequacy of English Registration, 1690-1837*, in POPULATION IN HISTORY 379 (Glass & Eversley eds. 1965). Even in Mexico the British legation did not consider that parish registers were a reliable system for obtaining vital statistics. See Gilmore, *supra* note 86. The British opinion was probably founded upon the registers in Mexico City. Those in the Mixteca Alta were kept with much greater care.

[96] See 8 DUBLÁN & LOZANO 364-65.

under seven years of age were to be punished according to the provisions of law then current;[97] those abandoning children from seven to ten years old were to be subject to a fine of from ten to three hundred pesos (at that time equivalent to our dollars) or by imprisonment of from one month to one year.[98] There was no mention of abandonment of children over ten.

This first law of civil registry was abrogated on March 30, 1858,[99] by a conservative government which forced the reform government out of Mexico City. From its refuge in Veracruz, the Juárez government issued a new "Organic Law of Civil Registry" on July 28, 1859.[100] The new law no longer envisaged cooperation with the church. Justices of the civil register in civil districts[101] were to keep the registers.[102] Only certified copies of the data in the civil registers were to be acceptable vital data for all legal purposes.[103] For all births the father was to make the declaration, or, if he did not, the doctor or midwife.[104] If the father did not choose to be registered, the mother alone was to be recorded. If both mother and father refused to be registered, the child was to be entered as born to unknown parents.[105] The rather bizarre provisions on foundlings of the law of January 27, 1857, were replaced by a simple injunction to bring them to the civil authorities for registry of birth and suitable provision for rearing.[106] The constitutional amendments of September 25, 1873, and the implementing act of Congress of December 14, 1874, also completed the establishment of the civil registry in Mexico.[107] The states were declared the proper entities to regulate the civil status of persons and to provide for the manner of performing and recording marriages and recording other vital statistics, subject to the proviso that the records of the civil register should be the only proof of civil status.[108] With some modifications the federal government incorporated the provisions of the Law of July 28, 1859, into the Civil Code of 1884 for federal matters and for the federal district and territories.[109] The states also enacted appropriate legislation

---

97 *Id.* at 370 (art. 58).

98 *Id.* at 370 (art. 59).

99 Text reproduced in García Cantu, *El Pensamiento de la Reacción Mexicana*, in HISTORIA DOCUMENTAL 1810-1962, at 493-94 (1965).

100 8 DUBLÁN & LOZANO 696.

101 *Id.* at 696-97 (arts. 1-4).

102 *Id.* at 697 (art. 4).

103 12 *id.* at 686 (art. 16).

104 8 *id.* at 699 (art. 19).

105 *Id.* at 699 (art. 20).

106 *Id.* at 699 (art. 21).

107 See notes 91, 92 *supra*.

108 12 DUBLÁN & LOZANO 686-87 (arts. 23, 24).

109 CÓDIGO CIVIL DEL DISTRITO FEDERAL Y TERRITORIO DE LA BAJA CALIFORNIA arts. 43-154 (1884).

for the civil registry, in most instances copying the federal legislation.[110] Since 1867 when the Juárez government returned in triumph to Mexico City, there has been a functioning civil register in all parts of Mexico, and, except in areas where riot and revolution have destroyed the records, there are continuous series.[111]

4. Civil Marriage

As part of the reform program, the government of Benito Juárez also issued the Law of July 23, 1859, on civil marriage.[112] Marriage was thenceforth declared to be a civil contract,[113] valid only if made and registered before the appropriate civil authorities[114] and subject solely to decisions of civil courts.[115] For unions after the date of the law, only the husband and wife of a civil ceremony had claim upon each other and only children born to such a marriage were legitimate in the eyes of civil law. The constitutional amendments of September 25, 1873, and implementing act of December 14, 1874, incorporated civil marriage into the constitution but provided that the states might regulate the manner of performing and recording marriages subject to the provisos that union entered into by free declaration of the parties should be the basis of civil marriage, that the union be monogamous, and that existing prohibitions on degrees of relationship not be changed.[116] The Federal Civil Code of 1884 made appropriate legislation for the federal district and territories and the states proceeded to enact their own laws, again usually copying the federal enactments.[117] A religious ceremony of marriage thus has no legal standing in Mexico, although once the civil ceremony has been performed, the couple are free to repeat their vows in any religious ceremony that they wish.[118] The nineteenth-century reform program, it should also be noted, provided for legal separation and annulment but not for divorce.[119]

---

110 CIVIL CODE FOR THE FEDERAL DISTRICT AND TERRITORIES OF MEXICO vi (Schoenrich transl. 1950) [hereinafter cited as SCHOENRICH].

111 Such is our conclusion after an examination of perhaps a third of the state archives. Since the records are kept in duplicate, it is usually possible to locate a surviving set in the local office of civil registry if the one in the state archive has vanished, and vice versa.

112 8 DUBLÁN & LOZANO 691.

113 Id. at 691 (arts. 1, 2).

114 Id. at 695 (art. 30).

115 12 id. at 686-87 (art. 25).

116 Id. at 686-87 (arts. 22-24).

117 CÓDIGO CIVIL DEL DISTRITO FEDERAL Y TERRITORIO DE LA BAJA CALIFORNIA arts. 109-30, 155-289 (1884).

118 Article 30 of the Law of July 23, 1859, expressly conceded this right. 8 DUBLÁN & LOZANO 691, 695.

119 Law of July 23, 1859, arts. 4, 8, in 8 DUBLÁN & LUZANO 691-92. In matters of divorce the major innovations were introduced in the Domestic Relations Law of 1917 and subsequently incorporated in the Federal Civil Code in 1928. SCHOENRICH vi.

The Mexican Revolution of 1910-17 and legislation since then have continued the changes instituted during the Wars of the Reform. The reform provisions have all been continued in the new Federal Constitution of 1917 and in subsequent legislation based on it.[120] The new Federal Civil Code of 1928 copied the clauses of the Civil Code of 1884.[121] In turn, the Civil Code of 1928 has been the model for most of the new state civil codes.[122] Such further changes as have been enacted provide for divorce,[123] authorize more liberal methods for legitimation of offspring,[124] and concede a limited and partial right of inheritance to the woman of an informal union if the couple have lived in monogamous relations for five years preceding the death of the man and if they have children by each other.[125] Prevailing federal civil law still continues a series of provisions that in some regards continue Spanish medieval legislation or accept French ideas. Only children born to parents married by civil ceremony recorded in the civil register are legitimate,[126] but children born to unwed parents become legitimate on the marriage[127] of the parents if they expressly state that such is their intention[128] or have already registered parenthood.[129] The officials of the civil register are forbidden to inquire into the paternity of the child registered as illegitimate, and, in general, investigation to determine paternity is rigidly limited.[130] The father of an illegitimate child need

---

[120] MEXICO CONST., tit. VII, art. 130 (1917), in LEYES FUNDAMENTALES DE MEXICO 1808-1964, at 875-77 (Tena Ramírez ed. 1964). The effect of the constitutional clause has been to restrain movements within some of the states to redefine matrimony more flexibly. The post-Revolutionary civil code of Tamaulipas, for instance, defined civil marriage for legal purposes as "the union, cohabitation, and continued sexual relation of a single man with a single woman." This definition was declared contrary to the federal constitution in a case before the Federal Supreme Court begun in 1947 and decided in 1954. The Supreme Court pointed out that the text of the Constitution of 1917 on civil marriage repeated that of the amendment of 1873 to the Constitution of 1857, and held that the change in definition of marriage therefore was limited to the intent of the Laws of the Reform, namely to remove marriage from the control of the church, but not otherwise to change the definition of the relationship. Virginia Reyes viuda de Hinojosa v. Tribunal Superior de Justicia del Estado de Tamaulipas, Sala Auxiliar de la Suprema Corte, July 10, 1954, No. D.876/951/2a, reprinted in 2 ROJINA VILLEGAS, DERECHO CIVIL MEXICANO pt. 1, at 459-65 (1959). The new civil code of Tamaulipas returns to the conventional definition. CÓDIGO CIVIL PARA EL E. L. Y S. DE TAMAULIPAS arts. 90-110 (1961).

[121] SCHOENRICH 11-61. The Schoenrich edition clearly indicates new articles and those in the Civil Code of 1884.

[122] Id. at vii.

[123] Id. at 55-69 (arts. 235-91).

[124] Id. at 82-88 (arts. 354-89).

[125] Id. at 327-28 (art. 1635).

[126] Id. at 79-80 (arts. 340-41).

[127] Id. at 82, 83 (arts. 354, 357).

[128] Id. at 82 (art. 355).

[129] Id. at 82-83 (art. 356).

[130] "The official of the civil registry and the witnesses who, according to article 58, are to be present at the act, are absolutely prohibited from making investigations as to paternity.

not recognize his child, but may do so. The mother, on the other hand, has no right to abandon the child; if she is not present at the registry and remains unknown, the child must be entered as the son of an unknown mother but a judicial investigation may be made into the identity of the mother.[131] An illegitimate child may inquire into the identity of his mother,[132] and, in certain instances, into the identity of his father, but only during the life of that parent.[133] In recording the birth of a child born of adulterous relations, the father, whether married or not, may recognize the child, but the mother, if married and living with her husband, may not do so unless her husband disowns the child and has judicial recognition of his repudiation.[134] A child born of incestuous relations may be recognized by both parents, and their names, but not the fact of incest, may be recorded.[135]

Mexican law today has within it possibilities for altering the normal rules of guardianship at registration which quickly become apparent when one finds a child registered as to the father but with mother unknown, or with both parents unknown but a grandparent or another adult presenting the child for registration and becoming guardian. The effect of the first kind of registration is to exclude the mother from any legal right to the child unless she is prepared to take the case to court; the effect of the second kind of registration is to relieve both parents of their legal obligation, but to provide for the child.[136]

Thus far we have described legislation. Compliance with the new legislation and implementation of the new system turned out to be a very different matter. The reformers of the mid-nineteenth century and subsequent legislators aimed at replacement of the old religious morality by an essentially similar civil morality[137] and at the establishment of a sophisticated system of registry. Their program had to be implemented by educating and so acquiring the cooperation of a population that in the nineteenth century was largely dispersed in small, rural settlements over

---

In the record there shall be stated only what the persons who present the child may declare, even though they may appear open to the suspicion of falsity; without prejudice to the punishment thereof in accordance with the provisions of the Penal Code." *Id.* at 19 (art. 69). *But see id.* at 87 (art. 382).

131 *Id.* at 17 (art. 60).

132 *Id.* at 87-88 (arts. 385-86).

133 *Id.* at 88 (art. 388).

134 *Id.* at 18 (arts. 62-63).

135 *Id.* at 18 (art. 64).

136 It was the finding of birth certificates with such notations in the state archive of Oaxaca that led us to further inquiries into Mexican law and custom.

137 This point is clearly evident in the provisions of the Law of July 23, 1859, on civil marriage, which merely transferred the regulations of canon law to civil law. Divorce continued to be forbidden and annulment and separation permitted in the terms of canon and Spanish law. See note 119 *supra*.

the countryside. The population, moreover, was overwhelmingly illiterate. A substantial segment of the people did not even speak Spanish.[138] Even today the Mexican population is to a great extent rural, and illiteracy is high in the countryside. Implementation of the program was further hampered by its anticlerical and liberal origin, for the victory of the Juárez government in 1867 did not secure the friendship and cooperation of church and conservatives. Although there have since been periods of truce, there have also been long periods of embittered relations and a fairly steady hostility to the assertion of civil jurisdiction. The church has not used its influence to support state regulations as it once did. The civil government, on the other hand, has attacked church influence and destroyed the power of the church to enforce its own morality but has not been able to obtain full acceptance of the substitutions it has enacted. Even as necessary an institution as the civil register was so tinged with liberalism and anticlericalism that Mexico in the years after 1867 had two rival systems of registration of vital statistics, the old church books, with religious but no civil value, and the official civil register. There was no legal bar to additional registry in the church book, provided the required entries were made in the civil ones, but substantial numbers of people used only the church books.[139] From the 1880's to 1910, during a period of truce in church-state relations, the new federal statistical services, under an unusually able director, Antonio Peñafiel, were able to bring about increasingly extensive recording of births, deaths, and marriages.[140] But it has taken much education and pressure to achieve substantial compliance with legal requirements for registry of vital statistics. Even today births are registered with surprising disregard for statutory deadlines.[141]

E. The Move toward New Patterns: Statistical Evidence

We try now to assess through examination of statistical evidence the impact of the great upheavals of 1853-67 and 1910-17 upon patterns of marriage and legitimacy in Mexico.

1. Proportions of Legitimate and Illegitimate Births in Two Mexican Regions for Various Years since 1870

Our first set of data give the percentages of illegitimate births to total

---

[138] DIRECCIÓN GENERAL DE ESTADÍSTICA, SECRETARÍA DE ECONOMÍA, ESTADÍSTICAS SOCIALES DEL PORFIRIATO: 1877-1910, at 119-21 (1956).

[139] Such was our conclusion upon examining both parish registers and civil registers in parts of Oaxaca for the period since 1870.

[140] The incompleteness of early registrations and the gradual improvement can be seen in the data on births, deaths, and marriages for the period 1877-1910. DIRECCIÓN GENERAL DE ESTADÍSTICA, op. cit. supra note 138, at 19-32.

[141] BENITEZ ZENTENO, ANALISIS DEMOGRÁFICO DE MEXICO 26-28 (1961); COLLVER, BIRTH RATES IN LATIN AMERICA 25-51, 138-42 (1965).

births recorded in two regions for selected years from 1870 to 1955.[142] The declarations of legitimacy or illegitimacy of the infants are those of the adults reporting the birth, usually one or both parents. Legally only an infant born to parents married in a civil ceremony recorded in the civil register is legitimate, although the officials of the civil register must accept without challenge the registrants' declaration.[143] The data for the two regions are summarized in Tables 2A and 2B. The first region (Table 2A) is the Mixteca Alta, an Indian peasant area in the State of Oaxaca. Church registers which we examined in approximately half the parishes for the seventeenth and eighteenth centuries and the nineteenth century down to 1855 or 1860 showed almost no illegitimate births, as measured by the lack of a formal church ceremony for the parents. The percentages in Table 2A show a sharp, steady rise in the proportion of illegitimate births as the generations married before 1867 ceased to bear children and new generations, which had to marry by civil ceremony to have legitimate offspring, became the procreators. Our samples show a peak in the years 1920-25, just after the Mexican Revolution, with illegitimate children forming 81.8 per cent of all registered births. For the District of Putla, the proportion of illegitimate to total births for those years was ninety-five per cent. The samples of data for later years show a drop in the proportion of illegitimate births, but as late as 1950-54 they constituted more than half of all births recorded and were running at a level approximately that of the years 1905-10. We cannot be sure when the peak in illegitimate births was reached, but it may have been at any time between 1915 and the early 1930's. The data for the Mixteca Alta indicate that the civil government has been unable to replace church marriage by civil marriage or to implant the new civil morality in the Mixteca. A large part, indeed a majority, of the adult population either continues to get married by church ceremony only or lives in informal union.[144] Caught between church and state, many Indians remained loyal to the church; others have turned to the old urban and Spanish folk practice, which has few legal formalities and runs up no legal or clerical fees.

Data for our second region are summarized in Table 2B. These are selections for a number of zones in the State of Jalisco to represent the distinctive climatic zones of the coast, the intermediate slopes rising to the plateau, the plateau itself, and the great urban aggregate of Guadalajara.

---

[142] In all instances, records for whole years were used and, if the archive had them, records for four consecutive years for each group. If such selection was not possible, records of whole years were found within the groups of years shown.

[143] See note 130 *supra.*

[144] See Table 3, *infra*, where the comparative data for the State of Oaxaca in 1960 are given.

Jalisco is a *mestizo* area of Hispanic settlement dating back to the middle of the sixteenth century. Except for the cities, notably Guadalajara, the state is of relatively uniform Hispanic peasant culture. Politically the state has been a stronghold of liberalism at times, but in the 1920's was also one of the centers of the Catholic Cristero movement of opposition to federal anticlerical measures. The data in this table show a very different pattern from the samples for the Mixteca Alta. We do not know what the percentage of illegitimate births was in the years immediately before 1870, but we may guess that Jalisco conformed to the pattern found in the Bishopric of Oaxaca in 1777 for rural *gente de razón*, that is, a somewhat higher percentage of informal union and illegitimacy than among the rural Indians but still a fairly low one compared to the percentages in Table 2A. Probably the percentages were not much different from the ones for 1880-84 in Table 2B. The data in Table 2B show little perceptible increase in the proportion of illegitimate births from 1880 to 1955. There are increases in the towns of the coast and in Guadalajara in the samples for 1921-25 and 1931-35, but samples for later years for the same towns show a drop to a relatively low level. We conclude that in Jalisco the population, urban and rural, accepted the changes in law and registry brought by the Wars of the Reform and has complied with the new provisions relatively well. Since its population is Hispanized *mestizo* or Hispanic, it has a distinctly higher level of literacy and economic well-being both in the countryside and in the towns than the Indian Mixteca Alta.

If Table 2B does not show significant change from the mid-nineteenth century to the present in proportions of illegitimate births, it does show enduring and significant zonal differences within the State of Jalisco. The towns of the coast consistently show the largest proportion of illegitimate births, followed in descending order by Guadalajara, the towns of the intermediate zone, and the plateau. For the towns of the district of Los Altos the values are even lower: Colotlán, 3.6 per cent; Arandas, 3.4 per cent; and Tepatitlán, 6.1 per cent. Los Altos was a Cristero stronghold in the 1920's. These differences are probably longer term and less related to political change than to patterns of settlement. The coastal zone of Jalisco shows resemblance to the pattern for *pardos* in the data of 1777 for the Bishopric of Oaxaca, and the patterns may reflect Negro settlement since in general coastal regions tend to have old Negro genetic stock that is now well absorbed. Similarly, the data for Guadalajara recall the 1777 results for the City of Antequera. As in the data from that census, however, the overwhelming proportion of the adults in all zones of Jalisco marry by legal ceremony and have legitimate offspring duly registered as such.

2. Present-Day Patterns of Marriage, Informal Union, Legitimacy, and Their Relation to Indian Sub-Cultures and Indices of Poverty

The national censuses of Mexico taken since the Revolution of 1910-17 have added a number of categories to their questionnaires and returns, which greatly assist our inquiry. In addition to questions on marriage by civil ceremony, church ceremony, or both, the census takers now ask whether adults live in informal union, called free union (*unión libre*) in the census, and ask further a series of questions on characteristics of poverty and well-being, for example, whether the families speak Spanish, eat wheat bread, sleep in beds rather than on mats, wear shoes, and are literate. In general, those of lower income tend to give negative answers. The questions on language and literacy were asked for censuses before the Revolution of 1910, whereas the other questions have been added since. One question—whether adults had dissolved a family union by informal decision—would have been most useful for our inquiry, but was asked only for the census of 1921.

For determining present-day patterns, we use data for the year 1960. We use only two indices of poverty in our analysis since speaking an Indian language and wearing sandals or going barefoot rather than wearing shoes give adequate evidence of the proportion and location of the population living in poverty. These data are presented in Table 3, arranged by existing states of the Mexican Union. All values are given in percentages rather than absolute numbers since we are interested only in comparisons.[145] All the correlations made are between parameters in values given for each state, the federal district, and the two federal territories, that is, thirty-two cases in all for each correlation.[146]

With respect to types of marital union, we have tabulated for each state the per cent of the following single and combined categories: (1) adults making no declaration of any kind (*no indicado*);[147] (2) people·

---

[145] These percentages, if not already set forth in the source, have been calculated from the actual magnitudes given. The basic numbers, of course, are available in the sources.

[146] For convenience, we shall call all territorial members of the Mexican Union, states, since the Mexican term *entidad federativa* has no simple English equivalent.

[147] Some question may be raised concerning the inclusion of the category *no indicado*. On first consideration, it might be thought that we are dealing here with people who were living in informal union rather than in legal or religious matrimony and who were unwilling to report that fact. However, the following points must be borne in mind: (1) The coefficient of variation (i.e., the Standard Deviation as percent of the mean) is 16.9, a relatively low value. The category of *no indicado*, therefore, appears as a relatively uniform percentage for each state with little relation either to the size or the location of that state. (2) The correlation of *no indicado* with percent of illegitimacy is nonsignificant ($r = +0.133$). (3) There is no improvement, and indeed no real change of any kind, in other correlations when *no indicado* is included. (4) Table 2.16 in the *Anuario Estadístico* is in two parts but

living in informal union (*unión libre*); (3) people married by civil ceremony only; (4) people married by religious ceremony only; (5) people
married both by civil and religious ceremony; (6) people living in informal union plus *no indicado*; (7) people living in informal union plus
those married by religious ceremony only plus *no indicado*; and (8)
people married by civil ceremony plus those married both by civil and
religious ceremony. The data for these categories refer only to males
sixteen years of age or older and females fourteen years of age or older,
in other words, people who have reached the minimum legal age for
marriage according to the Federal Civil Code[148] and almost all state civil
codes. We have omitted data on unmarried adults, widows and widowers,
and the divorced since those categories are irrelevant for our inquiry.

The correlations of the various categories are summarized in Table 4.
If we examine them, certain points emerge. The most important of these
is the extremely high positive correlation between the percentage of
people in a state living in *unión libre* or married by church ceremony only
and the percentage of illegitimacy. Since both these modes of union produce offspring who are legally illegitimate, the correspondence is not surprising. However, the extent of agreement between the two sets of data
is greater than perhaps might be anticipated. Indeed, if we divide all the
adults known to be, or probably, living in cohabitation into two groups,
one, those married legally (that is, married by civil ceremony only plus
those married both by civil and church ceremony), the other, those living
together in legally irregular or informal union (that is, those in *unión
libre* and those married by church ceremony only plus *no indicado*), we
find that each group has a correlation coefficient of 0.967 with the percentage of illegitimacy, the positive or negative sign of the coefficient
depending, of course, upon which component is being considered. The
validity of the Mexican marital data in the census returns is thereby
firmly established since such a high coefficient amounts to near certainty.
The correlation coefficient means further, of course, that each type of
union (*no indicado* excepted) produces a proportion of total births approximately equivalent to that type of union's proportion of the total
adults in all forms of family union. The children of casual coupling are
probably a small factor. These indications agree with an inference gleaned

---

is continuous, such that the category *no indicado* refers to all types of adults, widows and
widowers, unmarried, and divorced, as well as to people living together in marriage and
informal union, and undoubtedly includes individuals of all these categories. Hence it cannot
be equated with *unión libre* as such.

In spite of these objections, however, the group designated *no indicado* has been retained
in the total and in the calculation of correlations.

[148] MEXICAN FEDERAL CIVIL CODE art. 148. Municipal presidents (mayors) may grant a
dispensation as to age in serious and justified cases. *Ibid.*

from discussions with anthropologists that informal unions in Mexico tend to be stable.

In view of the extremely close similarity between each state's figures for matrimonial status and for legitimacy or illegitimacy of birth, it is unnecessary in making further tests to use both these factors. Since legitimacy or illegitimacy is a single parameter, uncomplicated by subordinate categories, it is preferable to use it alone in dealing with other variables.

Let us turn now to the geographical distribution of both legitimacy and type of marriage or union. The regional coincidence of the two characteristics is striking. The trend is readily apparent if we arrange the states according to (1) per cent of *unión libre* plus people married by religious ceremony only, and (2) per cent of illegitimacy. In both lists we have taken the percentages in decreasing order of magnitude and segregated three subgroups within each group: high, intermediate, and low. The results are given in Table 5.

In spite of small internal variations, the two lists are remarkably concordant, particularly at the extremes. There are indicated southern and northern foci of high percentages of *unión libre* and illegitimacy. The intermediate region is, of course, somewhat diffuse. It should be emphasized that we are probably dealing here with the results of numerous factors and an attempt at over-detailed analysis of the available data is likely to lead nowhere.

Nevertheless, the data do permit identification of some of the factors operating. To the extent possible, we have made the identification through the correlations in Table 4. With respect to urban-rural differences, states having a high proportion of rural population tend to have a high proportion of illegitimacy.[149] A more detailed and exact analysis on the basis of segregation of state data into urban and rural could be made, but for our purposes the correlation based on state totals is indicative, and there is no reason to suppose that more detailed analysis would lead to a very different result.

With respect to other indications of poverty, the correlations in Table 4 show that the proportion of illegitimacy has a significant positive relation with proportion of illiteracy and proportion of people who continue to speak or who know an Indian tongue. Similarly there is a strong negative correlation between proportion of illegitimacy and proportion of people who wear shoes. These correspondences combine to indicate the prevalence of *unión libre* and illegitimacy among the poorer, the rural, and the Indian segments of the Mexican population. Persons with all of

---

149 With or without the great urban concentration of Mexico City, the value of r is close to $+0.47$. This is somewhat beyond the one per cent level of probability and can be accepted as quite significant.

these characteristics are concentrated in the south of the country and along the West Coast. It is almost impossible to separate the Indian from the rural poor since in general Indians tend (in terms of adoption of new ways of European industrial and urbanized civilization) to be the more backward, as well as the more poverty-stricken, of the rural population.

3. Conditions Just Prior to The Revolution of 1910

For comparison of present patterns of marriage and legitimacy with those of the years immediately preceding the great upheaval of 1910-17, we have available data conveniently summarized in *Estadísticas Sociales del Porfiriato* 1877-1910.[150] For the Díaz period (1877-1910), there are no figures on *unión libre* since that category was recognized only after the Revolution of 1910, and then only for purposes of the national census. We can, however, compute the proportions of legitimate and illegitimate births.[151] The values for the earlier half of the Díaz period are obviously too low and reflect difficulties in persuading the Mexican population to enter births in the civil register. For the last years of the Díaz period, the values are far higher and undoubtedly indicate greatly improved registration. We use the values for 1900 and 1905 as most reliable. The percentages for 1900 and 1905 for each state are averaged and placed in Table 6.[152]

The proportion of illegitimate births to total births for Mexico as a whole was 42.23 per cent in 1900-05 and 25.04 per cent in 1959-61. Expressed as the mean of the state values, the proportion of illegitimate to total births fell from 39.25 per cent to 25.85 per cent. The value of t for the differences between the means is 2.815, which is just beyond the one per cent level of probability that is, the chance that the differences are due merely to random variation may be set at roughly one in a hundred. One may conclude, however, that this indication of considerable improvement in a period of sixty years is not so great a change after all. Two

---

[150] See Table 3 *infra*. We owe the compilation to the research staff built up at the Colegio de México for writing the history of Mexico since 1867 and to Moisés González Navarro, who supervised the selection and preparation of the volume. The data in which we are interested were taken from the *Anuarios Estadísticos* and the *Boletín Demográfico*, published by the Mexican federal statistical services for the last years of the Díaz regime.

[151] Table 15 in the *Estadísticas Sociales del Porfiriato* gives the totals by states of births registered for selected years from 1885 to 1910; table 16 gives the total of legitimate births registered for selected years from 1877 to 1905.

[152] A few adjustments were made to permit direct comparison with values for 1959-61; they are made necessary because of territorial changes since 1900. For example, the two values for Baja California had to be consolidated since the peninsula was a single federal territory before the Mexican Revolution. Quintana Roo, now a federal territory, was a part of the State of Yucatán until 1902. We have adjusted the entries so that the two sets of data are directly comparable.

entities, the federal district and the State of Michoacán, together account for much of the reduction in the proportion of illegitimate births. On the other hand, in Oaxaca and Veracruz high percentages of illegitimacy in 1900-05 showed little change by 1959-61.

With regard to the degree of change in the different states, it is possible to perform a fairly rapid test. Number the states from 1 to 30 in 1900-05, using the first place as the lowest in percentage of illegitimate births and the last place as the highest. Do the same for 1959-61. Then correlate according to relative position on the two scales. The coefficient or $r = +0.718$, an extremely significant value. Deletion of the federal district and Michoacán would raise this value considerably. It is clear, therefore, that with the two exceptions noted, the various states have maintained their relative standing very consistently. It is equally clear that except for these two states, the reduction in proportion of illegitimate births to the total has been only moderate, although a trend is evident.

Let us now consider one thing more. The data in Table 6, supplemented by reference to Table 5, enable us to test the validity of the results obtained in our examination of proportions of illegitimate births for selected years since 1870 for the Mixteca Alta and Jalisco. That examination disclosed that Indian areas had a consistently greater proportion of illegitimacy than Hispanized areas. If we examine the data in Table 6 in order to see how states with high proportions of Indian population conform to the pattern of the Mixteca Alta, we find that in general such states do show high proportions of illegitimate births both for the Díaz period and for recent years.[153]

---

153 The one such state which has reduced its proportion of illegitimate births very substantially is Michoacán—a tribute perhaps to the reforming zeal of its great cacique, Lázaro Cárdenas. It is also clear that there are two other major exceptions to the pattern of the Mixteca Alta. One is the State of Tlaxcala, which lies within the Nahuatl zone of central Mexico but shows consistently low percentages of illegitimate births and of unión libre plus marriage by church ceremony only. On the other hand, it shows a far higher percentage of illiteracy, in accordance with its character as an essentially rural and Indian state (although a Spanish-speaking one). It is also small and densely populated. We have no explanation and can only point out that Tlaxcala is aberrant.

The other exception is the lowland Maya region embraced in the two states of Yucatán and Campeche. Although they have relatively high percentages of illiteracy, both show consistently low proportions of the types of union which would produce illegitimate children and of such illegitimate birth. The two states have had a history that is considerably different from that of the rest of Mexico. They are lowland Maya—the highland Maya as in Chiapas show a different pattern more like that of the rest of Mexico—and in the nineteenth century were the scene of the devastating War of the Castes, an Indian revolt that nearly ended Mexican control of the peninsula. The two states for a century have had a highly commercialized agriculture producing sisal fiber for the world market, with consequent formation of large estates in the Díaz period and the creation of a substantial rural proletariat. See REED, THE CASTE WAR OF YUCATÁN (1964) (excellent and highly readable). See also the excellent study of the development of a rural proletariat held in debt peonage on the peninsula by

F. Conclusion to Part I

Let us now summarize and comment briefly upon this long historical and statistical inquiry. During the colonial period Mexico had, with some variation, the two basic patterns of family union that characterized Spain and indeed Europe: (1) an official system of morality, increasingly embodied in statute, that demanded formal marriages; (2) a folk pattern of custom that accepted informal and even temporary union. Church and royal pressure successfully imposed official morality upon the Indians; the Hispanized population, including Negroes and *pardos*, adhered to both patterns. The legal disabilities attaching to illegitimacy encouraged formal marriage among those groups with property or access to office; conversely, the folk pattern was more apt to prevail among the lowest social strata, who, having neither property nor hope of office, could view the stigma of illegitimacy with indifference. Such evidence as we have on proportions of formal marriages and illegitimate children in the population indicates that even among the Hispanized population the great majority of unions were by formal marriage.

Since 1855 the great reform movements that have convulsed Mexico have brought considerable change. In most of the Indian areas destruction of church influence led to substantially greater resort to the folk pattern of the Hispanized population. As the generations of Indians legally married by church ceremony ceased childbearing, the proportion of illegitimate to total births rose steadily. The Revolution of 1910 gave further impetus to this trend. In all probability, the high point of illegitimate births among the Indians was reached in the 1920's or early 1930's. Since then there has been a decrease. Our data on Jalisco indicate that after the reforms of the mid-nineteenth century the Hispanized population, which had a higher proportion of illegitimate births initially, showed far less rise or none. On the other hand, the Hispanized population participates in the decrease of recent years, which is country-wide.

The meaning of the changes since the 1850's becomes clearer if we remember that the requirement of civil marriage created a large new source of illegitimacy and that the conflict between church and state has encouraged reversion to informal union. Furthermore, despite two great movements of reform in slightly over a century, the Mexican codes have

---

Friedrich Katz. Katz, *Plantagenwirtschaft und Sklaverei: Der Sisalbau auf der Halbinsel Yucatán bis 1910*, 7 ZEITSCHRIFT FÜR GESCHICHTSWISSENSCHAFT 1002-27 (1959). Interestingly, the part of the peninsula which did not undergo this process, the area of rebel Indian retreat centered in what is now the Territory of Quintana Roo, shows a higher percentage than the two states of informal and merely church union with a resulting higher proportion of illegitimate births. All three jurisdictions show a rise since the Díaz period in the proportion of illegitimate births—contrary to the trend in the rest of the country. With the exceptions noted. the pattern of the Mixteca Alta is typical of the Indian areas of Mexico.

clung with but slight modification to the austere provisions of Spanish law denying to the children of informal unions rights to support and inheritance. Accordingly, the gap between statute and custom in family union and inheritance grew wider after 1855. Although we can cite only our own field research in Oaxaca and elsewhere as evidence for the statement, the gap leads often to direct defiance of statute. Obviously the woman and children of an informal union do not meekly surrender any property left upon death of the man even if by statute it should pass to other heirs or escheat to the state. They try to keep it and may count upon sympathy and cooperation from most of their neighbors. Only in 1928 did the Federal Civil Code adopt the article it now has giving a grudging and partial recognition of rights accruing to the woman and children of informal union. The states have lagged behind.[154]

Today irregular and informal union and consequent procreation of illegitimate children tend to be characteristic of the rural and the poor, both rural and urban, in Mexico. However, the relation is more complex than a direct cause and effect. The rural and the poor tend to be the last to receive new knowledge and new ways; they tend to cling to older practice after it has been abandoned by the upper and middle strata of the population. Our historical review suggests that such, rather than a vice attaching to poverty, is more probably the explanation in Mexico.

The slow decrease in the proportion of illegitimate births in recent decades does indicate widening acceptance of official morality. The causes are easily to be found in a series of economic and social factors: the spread of elementary schools since 1921 with consequent reduction in illiteracy, a slow but nonetheless real improvement in levels of popular consumption and well-being, and the movement of people to urban centers. The new urban and industrial culture which is spreading from Europe and the United States brings with it adherence to middle and upper-class standards of behavior that are much closer to official morality. One may speculate further that an ironic but effective force for imposing official morality is the need to prove existence of a stable family unit in order to qualify for low-cost public housing and the installment credit that brings such ardently desired goods as refrigerators and television sets.

---

[154] MEXICAN FEDERAL CIVIL CODE art. 1635. Schoenrich indicates that the article was adopted in the new code of 1928, which went into effect in 1932. SCHOENRICH vi-vii. Adoption by the states probably occurred upon adoption of relatively uniform codes based upon the federal one in the late 1950's. The States of Mexico and Tamaulipas, for example, copy the federal article. CÓDIGO CIVIL PARA EL E. L. Y S. DE TAMAULIPAS art. 1528 (1961); CÓDIGO CIVIL PARA EL E. L. Y S. DE MÉXICO art. 1464 (1961). However, the State of Oaxaca, which has a high rate of informal union and marriage by church only, with a consequent high rate of illegitimate births, has refused to adopt even the concession of the Federal Code. The *concubina* and her children have no rights of succession in default of a written instrument. CÓDIGO CIVIL PARA EL E. L. Y S. DE OAXACO arts. 1469-1504 (1961).

But this trend belongs to the immediate present and the future. The Mexicans now in California and those whose earlier immigration gave rise to Californians of Mexican descent were reared in the patterns of family union of some years or decades back. Our evidence has shown that they were reared in one or both of two patterns and that the north of Mexico, from which most of the immigrants have come, contains states of fairly high as well as states of low adherence to customary union and procreation of illegitimate children.

II

MARRIAGE AND LEGITIMACY AMONG MEXICANS IN CALIFORNIA: THE RECORDS OF SANTA CLARA COUNTY

We turn now to an examination of patterns of family union among Mexican-Americans in California. Until 1846 California was part of Mexico and conformed to Mexican patterns. After 1846 the small Mexican population was rapidly absorbed in a flood of migration from the east which made Anglo-American culture dominant in the state. Migration from Mexico into California continued, however, and in this century has brought large numbers. Except for political refugees, who are a small group numerically, the migrants are of lower class status. As we shall see, much of the migration into California of Mexicans and people of Mexican descent comes indirectly. Many first migrate to other states of our Southwest and from them to California. The children born in the Southwest to parents of Mexican birth obviously come to California with a background that is somewhat different from that of people coming directly from Mexico which, because of the concentration of Spanish-speaking population in the Southwest, is more likely to retain the conceptions of the older Mexican groups.

For this part of our study, we have had to depend upon data from one area, Santa Clara County, which has a relatively high proportion of Mexican-Americans and a low proportion of Negroes. Whether or not data from Santa Clara County are typical of the entire state is an important question that we cannot answer with certainty and one which the reader must bear in mind. At this point, all we can say is that our results are such that we judge them likely to be typical of the entire state.

Our data are drawn from two sources: (1) closed case histories of the County Welfare Department (consulted under necessary safeguards); and (2) the files of birth and marriage certificates kept at the County Records Office. From the Welfare Department, we have taken data both on Mexican-Americans (people of Mexican birth or descent) and, for purposes of comparison, on Anglo-Americans (white Americans, as far as possible of American parents). The tables give the number of people for each characteristic discussed. Inasmuch as all people in the welfare records are of an economically depressed group, the samples are subject to bias. The file of births is drawn necessarily from the entire population. That of marriages is selective since it includes only those couples who actually completed the marriage ceremony. It ignores extra-legal, common law, or casual unions. Thus, to a certain extent, it counterbalances the bias of the welfare records and provides information on that portion of the public in more favorable economic circumstances. Our sample on Mexican-Americans contains data on 840 marriages—substantially all those for persons with Spanish surnames registered between January 1, 1959, and August 1, 1960. A sample of an equal number of Anglo-American marriages was taken from the books for 1959 and 1960 as a series of consecutive groups of twenty-eight marriages each, spaced at regular intervals through nearly 2,000 pages.

A. Regional Origin

The Mexican-American population is ultimately derived from Mexico, but the actual immigration of persons may have been accomplished by more than one pathway. The origin of the existing population is referable to three places of birth: (1) California; (2) other states, particularly Texas, New Mexico, and Arizona; (3) Mexico. It is relevant to our study to consider whether, the Mexican-Americans recorded by the Welfare Department, on the one hand, and by the County Records Office, on the other, are drawn from similar sources.

From the Welfare Department files, we took data on those persons whose place of birth is stated, omitting minor children (most of whom were born in California) but including adult relatives of those persons actually seeking welfare assistance. It was also necessary to delete persons born before 1915 (almost all of whom were born in Mexico), in order to get a sample which would be comparable in age with the groups shown in the county records. These restrictions reduced to 347 the total number of Mexican-American welfare recipients studied.

Information from the County Records Office comes from the files on births and marriages. The birth certificates indicate the birthplace of the parents. Of the latter, there are 1,719 who have Spanish surnames. The marriage certificates give the age of the bride and groom as well as their birthplace. After removing those over forty-five years of age (that is, born before 1915) and those of full non-Mexican parentage, there are left 1,378 men and women.

Table 7 summarizes the data in terms of both absolute numbers and percentages for each source of information and for birth in each primary region. Inspection of the table leads to certain immediate conclusions.

First, the percentage of persons born in Mexico is relatively equal in the three samples, and therefore, people born in Mexico do not contribute disproportionately to the groups derived from the three sources of data. Second, there is a difference in proportionate contribution between Mexican-Americans born in California and those born in the Southwest. It appears, on inspection, that the birth and marriage records are sampling essentially the same population with respect to geographical origin, but that the persons studied from the welfare files have somewhat different geographical origins than subjects from the other two groups.[155] The Mexican-Americans in the welfare records tend on the whole to be migrants from other states, whereas those who appear in the marriage file have a higher proportion of native Californians.[156] The parents of newly born children (the subjects taken from birth certificates) are intermediate between the two other groups, as one would expect, for one group consists of those who are being legally married whereas the other group—the welfare aggregate—is both economically disadvantaged and contains many individuals in common law union.

B. Common Law Marriage (Informal Family Union)

Meaningful quantitative data concerning nonlegal forms of family union can be sought only from the files of the Welfare Department, where extensive information sheets and exhaustive case histories are preserved for each applicant. The files of marriage certificates at the County Records Office obviously tell nothing of extra-legal affairs. The birth records carefully and deliberately exclude any statement concerning parenthood or legitimacy. They do, however, indirectly provide a few items of useful information. We shall consider these before proceeding to the welfare data.

Although not required by law,[157] the form of the certificate and common practice call for an "informant," usually the mother, to sign the certificate of birth of the child. If the mother is unmarried, she frequently uses her maiden name, or that of her last husband if she is divorced. On

---

[155] These initial conclusions may be tested by calculating appropriate chi-squares. Thus if the numbers given in Table 7, part A, are treated as a 3 × 3 table with 9 cells the chi-square is 46.59, a value so great for 4 degrees of freedom as to dispel any doubt that the differences in place of origin as a whole are highly significant. If one starts with the figures obtained from birth certificates and compares them only with those from the marriage data in a 2 × 3 table, the chi-square is 4.62, a value at the 10 per cent level of probability, whereas a similar treatment of the figures from the birth certificates and the welfare data yields a chi-square of 32.42, or beyond the 1 per cent level of probability.

[156] This situation may be shown by computing chi-square for the absolute numbers of persons in all three groups who were born in California and in the American Southwest, omitting the natives of Mexico. Here the chi-square is 46.04, again a high value.

[157] See CAL. HEALTH & SAFETY CODE § 10125.

the other hand, if she has been cohabiting with a man, and the acquaintance is more than casual, she may use his name and imply that she is married. The mere appearance of the man's name on the certificate (with or without the title Mrs.) is therefore not certain evidence of a legal marriage. It may be presumed, although there is no way of proving it, that the children of many common law unions are thus endowed with pseudo-legitimacy.

A further disturbing factor, for statistical purposes, is the practice of sealing birth certificates. Frequently, for purposes of adoption or for other reasons, the birth certificate in the public file at the County Records Office is sealed off by a heavy sheet of paper. Roughly two per cent of the certificates are thus withdrawn from possible inclusion in the sample obtained for this study. For purposes of determining parents' age at the birth of their child or their ethnic origin, this removal probably makes no significant difference. For estimating the level of legitimacy, however, it may make a great deal of difference.

For what it is worth, it may be reported that out of approximately 1,050 birth certificates examined from the Mexican-American population and an equal number from the Anglo-American population, the former showed 4.67 per cent of the women using their maiden names, and the latter 0.95 per cent. This finding may or may not argue a greater tendency toward extra-legal unions among the Mexican-American population at large than among the Anglo-American.

Let us now consider the closed files of the Welfare Department. At this point comment is required concerning the validity of the available data. It has been argued with some justification that the file of a welfare department is an unsatisfactory source for comprehensive quantitative data pertaining to an intensive study of common law marriage *per se* and with reference to the circumstances attending the marriage as well as the factors contributing to it. This objection is based on the highly subjective, erratic, and sometimes very emotional aspects of a record taken by welfare personnel from applicants or recipients who are frequently apprehensive and distrustful.

It has also been argued, but with much less justification, that the simple enumeration of common law marriages is fatally unreliable. Admittedly we are not dealing with a signed, notarized marriage certificate. On the other hand we have at our disposal a massive body of verbal testimony. Every applicant when he first encounters the welfare organization must supply information in the way of personal and family history, which is transferred to what is called a Face Sheet. Special emphasis is placed upon the applicant's marital status, and if there is evidence of nonlegal cohabitation, the fact is so noted. Next follows the Social History, which consists of a précis of personal interviews conducted by case workers. Every visit, every conversation is recorded, sometimes in extraordinary detail with honesty and fidelity to fact. Frequently these histories run over dozens of closely typed pages and cover periods of many years. Finally, in the case of elderly or incapacitated persons, statements are secured from responsible adult relatives with respect to their own ability or inability to support the applicant for welfare aid. It takes time and patience, but a careful, impartial perusal of all these documents makes possible a decision as to whether a given couple was, or had been, living in legal or extra-legal matrimony. This is particularly true for unions entered into in the United States or those that are relatively recent. The one kind of declaration which probably contains much more error is that on unions formed in Mexico four to seven decades ago, especially when the information is provided by the children.

There are certain *ad hoc* tests which may be applied. Thus illegitimacy resulting from a casual relation in a hotel room can easily be identified as such and rejected as not representing a bona fide common law marriage. Conversely, cohabitation over several years with the birth of successive children can be identified as a genuine marital relationship of some sort. Further, if Mrs. X avers that she was married to Mr. X on a certain date at a certain town, it is highly probable that there was a legal marriage. Divorce and separation are also helpful in determining the type of original union, since conjugal difficulty very often is present in welfare cases. If there is, or was, a divorce and papers are displayed or if a divorce petition has been filed in a local court, then there must have been a legal marriage. If there has been an informal separation and serious effort is exerted by the welfare agency to heal the wounds, the probability is high that the couple had been legally married. But if the erring spouse is allowed to depart in peace, with little attempt to bring him or her back, then we probably are dealing with a common law union.

Thus by one device or another the task of determining whether a family union is legal or extra-legal is rendered much less difficult than might appear at first sight. At the same time, it must be conceded that a great deal of the information rests upon personal judgment and as such is subject to human error. The crucial question is whether such error is of sufficient magnitude to invalidate the basic results. We believe it is not. In the first place, cases with incomplete or inadequate data have been discarded. In the second place, any tendency on the part of the applicant to lie is often balanced by the perspicacity of the social worker and his ability to secure corroborative evidence from other persons such as relatives or friends. In the third place, and this is of fundamental importance, any tendency to prevaricate will create a bias in the direction of underestimating the extent of common law marriage. Consequently our values for the latter, if in error at all, are probably too low.

Our material is best presented as a series of brief summarizing statements with corresponding numerical tables where necessary.

1. Regional Origin of Mexican-Americans with Respect to Form of Union and Separation

We have already found that the Mexican-Americans appearing in the welfare records as a whole showed a relatively heavy preponderance of persons migrating to California from Texas and other Southwestern states. A segregation by age (those born before as opposed to those born after 1910) demonstrates a significantly greater number of the older people to have been born in Mexico, while most of the younger people were born in the United States. This situation is to be anticipated in any immigrant group, but it is complicated by the fact that many of the individuals now seeking welfare aid passed through or were born in the American Southwest prior to moving to California. Since the region of origin might be an important determinant of the type of marriage and also of separation among the Mexican-Americans in the files of the Welfare Department, this possibility requires investigation.

Among the Mexican-American women shown in the welfare files who were born in the United States, 27.7 per cent of the marriages for which there is reasonably secure evidence were by common law rather than by legal ceremony. Among the women born in Mexico 15.1 per cent of the marriages were by common law. This difference is barely significant statistically since the sample is small (See Table 8). The difference would seem to militate against cultural carry-over, but probably means no more than the likelihood that many of the common law marriages among the older women, most of whom were born in Mexico, were reported as legal marriages to the social workers in Santa Clara County. Many of the declarations were made by adult children.

Table 9 shows that birthplace is not a factor in determining whether a woman receiving welfare aid is still living with her husband or has been separated by death, divorce, or any other cause. On further breakdown, it is found that the women born in the United States demonstrate a greater number of separations by divorce or desertion, rather than by death, than do the women born in Mexico (See Table 9, part B). This situation may be in part referable to the greater marital stability among the members of the older age group, the majority of whom are Mexican born.

If an examination is made of the method of disunion among those who separate while still alive, a slightly stronger tendency is found (See Table 9, part C) for women born in the United States to seek legal divorce rather than tolerate informal separation or frank desertion. However, this differential is neither large enough nor based on an adequate sampling to be of much significance. Nevertheless, the possibility of an actual disparity is interesting, for it goes to the question of acculturation and might repay more extensive study with a larger sample. On the whole, place of birth does not appear to be a factor of much weight in determining the marital circumstances of Mexican-American women in the welfare files.

2. *Comparisons between Anglo and Mexican-American Women with Respect to Kind of Union and Separation*

(a) *Type of Marriage.*—With respect to selection of legal and common law union, there is a significant difference between the two ethnic groups (See Table 10). The Mexican-American welfare population shows 27.7 per cent common law marriages and 72.3 per cent legal, while the parallel figures for the Anglo-Americans are 6.2 and 93.8 per cent.[158]

The question may be asked whether internal differences exist among the Anglo-American population greater than those between that population as a whole and the Mexican-Americans. To answer this question, the Anglo-American welfare population sample was divided according to the states of origin of the women. The line ran roughly along the northern borders of Virginia, Tennessee, Missouri, Kansas, Colorado, and Arizona. Table 11 indicates a slight excess of common law marriages among those born in the South, but the difference is substantially nonsignificant. The Mexican-Americans from the welfare files therefore clearly show a greater tendency to common law union than do their Anglo-American counterparts.

(b) *Date of Birth and Type of Marriage.*—Although the Anglo and Mexican-Americans differ sharply in the relative proportion of common law to legal marriages, in both groups there is a much greater tendency for the younger women to resort to common law union (See Table 12). Indeed, a study of the first and second order interactions demonstrates that the two ethnic groups behave very similarly with respect to the effect of age on preference for common law rather than legal marriage.

(c) *Method of Separation.*—Of those who have been married, 59.7 per cent of the Anglo-American welfare applicants and 52.4 per cent of the Mexican-Americans have separated from their spouses due to all causes (See Table 13, part A). The difference is of little or no significance.

Among those women no longer living with their husbands 66.2 per cent

---

[158] The chi-square value for this distribution of attributes is 49.65, such a large value as to put beyond question the reality of a distinct difference between the two populations, in spite of the relatively small number of cases, and in spite of the errors which may have been introduced by the subjective method of gathering the basic data.

of the Anglo-Americans and 70.4 per cent of the Mexican-Americans separated otherwise than by death. This difference also is without significance (See Table 13, part B).

If we disregard the legality of the original union of those separating otherwise than by death, we find that 67.5 per cent of Anglo-American women separate by divorce rather than by informal separation. On the other hand, only 21.4 per cent of the Mexican-American women separating obtain formal divorces (See Table 13, part C). This is a highly significant difference.

It is of course evident that those groups living in informal union can separate only by desertion and never by divorce. For those legally married, however, the percentage of divorces among Anglo-American women, 79.1 per cent, much exceeds that among Mexican-American women, 49.0 per cent (See Table 13, part D). As a check upon possible variation among Anglo-American women from different regions with respect to this characteristic, women born in the North were compared with those born in the South. Table 13, part E, shows a slight differential in favor of divorce as opposed to desertion among northern women, but this disparity has only marginal significance.

Another way of assessing the behavior of Anglo-American as contrasted with Mexican-American women is by comparing the number still living in matrimony or separated by death, as one category, with the number separated by either divorce or desertion, as another category. Both categories were examined with reference to whether the original union was by common law or legal ceremony. Table 14 correlates three sets of variables: ethnic origin, type of union, and type of separation.

In the Anglo-American group, 36.4 per cent of those legally married separated by divorce or desertion, and 79.2 per cent of those united only by common law so separated. In the Mexican-American group, 22.8 per cent of the legal marriages and 71.6 per cent of the common law unions ended in divorce or desertion. A simple statistical analysis is shown in Table 14. The second order interaction, which here is an indicator of difference between ethnic groups, has a chi-square value which denotes complete nonsignificance. Thus the two groups do not diverge materially from each other in the behavior of those legally married as contrasted with those informally united. The conclusion is therefore justified that insofar as those reached by the Welfare Department are concerned, the strong tendency to separate is a feature of common law marriage as such, and is not associated with one ethnic group.

(d) *The Form of Marriage in the Population at Large.*—The file of marriage certificates at the Santa Clara County Records Office also yields information on the form of the marriage ceremony. It will be remembered that in Mexico, a couple may unite in formal marriage or by common law, called in Mexico *unión libre*. Those who embark upon formal matrimony, in turn, may follow one of three possible procedures: civil marriage, religious marriage, or both civil and religious. In California a couple must first secure a marriage license.[159] (Mexican law has an equivalent procedure.[160]) Thereafter the actual ceremony which ratifies the intention may be conducted by a judge or magistrate in a civil ceremony or by a clergyman in a religious ceremony.[161] The marriage certificate must show the signature and church affiliation of the officiating person.[162] For the sample under consideration, therefore, we know how the 840 native born, non-Mexican-American couples were married, and we have the same information concerning 840 couples of full or partial Mexican extraction.

Before the data are presented, it is worthwhile to stress certain facts which are actually common knowledge. The native born American population in California, from which our sample is drawn, is in the majority Protestant, although by no means overwhelmingly so. The indigenous population in Mexico is almost exclusively Roman Catholic. Thus the Census of 1960 gives the percentage of Catholics as approximately 96.5, and that of the Protestants as 1.7.[163]

Table 15 shows the distribution among the two ethnic groups of the three types of ceremony. The Anglo-American group follows the conventional pattern: roughly 70 per cent Protestant, 20 per cent Catholic, the remainder married by the judge. The Mexican-Americans are surprisingly different in two respects. First, one observes that nearly 15 per cent of the ceremonies, in the years 1959 and 1960, were performed by Protestant clergymen, as compared with 36 per cent by Catholic priests. Second, one notes that about one-half of the marriages were performed by the civil, not the church, authorities. Let it be stated again that these are the Mexican-Americans who are rejecting informal union in favor of legal matrimony.

What are the causes of this strong deviation from the religious traditions of their forefathers, but not yet full acceptance of conventional American behavior? One influence can be suggested. In Mexico, according to the 1960 census, a fifth of the population married by some kind of ceremony has been content with purely civil marriage; slightly more than two-thirds have been married both by civil and church rites.[164] The knowledge of the civil ceremony is thus widespread in the population.

---

159 CAL. CIV. CODE § 69.
160 MEXICAN FEDERAL CIVIL CODE arts. 101-103.
161 CAL. CIV. CODE § 70.
162 CAL. CIV. CODE § 73.
163 8 MÉXICO CENSO GENERAL DE POBLACIÓN: 1960, RESUMEN GENERAL, Table 18, at 282.
164 See Table 3 *infra*.

Hence the transition cannot have been difficult from this type of marriage in one country to the same thing in another, for the nearest approach in the United States to the Mexican civil ceremony is the rite performed by a judge. It is obvious, however, that cultural carry-over is only part of the explanation.

Apart from the effect of the tradition of civil marriage in Mexico, the examination of three other factors is permitted by the Santa Clara County data. These are: (1) divorce, (2) intermarriage, and (3) the age of the participants.

Remarriage of divorced persons is not usually permitted in the Roman Catholic church. Hence divorced Roman Catholics, if they desire to re-marry, must do so by civil ceremony or by a Protestant religious cere-mony. For the Anglo-American population, a further complication is that more than half are already Protestants for whom remarriage is possible in their own church. Finally, it must be borne in mind that the relative number of divorced persons in the Mexican-American group is much smaller at the outset than among the Anglo-Americans.

In view of these complexities, for the purpose of studying the effect of divorce on the type of marriage ceremony, it will be best to ignore the Catholic component entirely and compare directly the data for marriages by civil authority on the one hand, and by the Protestant clergy on the other. The absolute numbers are given in Table 16. It appears that never-married persons predominate heavily in all categories except those Anglo-Americans who were married judicially. This finding is somewhat unex-pected, since one might have predicted that divorced persons would have been relatively more numerous among the Mexican than among the Anglo-American fraction of the population.[165] On the basis of the figures in Table 16 it can be seen that Mexican-American divorced persons do not seek remarriage by judicial ceremony in preference to other methods and con-sequently that divorce is not a factor in building up the high level of court marriages among the Mexican-American population.

The ethnic background and family history of a couple may readily determine whether the wedding ceremony takes place before a judge or, if in a church, which church. Hence it is desirable to test the type of

---

[165] The difference seen in Table 16 may be further tested by the chi-square method. For Anglo-Americans the differences shown yield a chi-square value of 19.98, indicating a high level of significance. For Mexican-Americans the chi-square is 0.20—there is no significance. Approaching the problem from another direction, we may compare the relative number of the two groups who resort to judicial marriage after previous divorce. Chi-square is 34.94. Among those married by the Protestant clergy there is no significant difference. These results confirm the fact that many more divorced Anglo-Americans, in proportion to the numbers involved, prefer judicial marriage to a ceremony conducted by a clergyman. With the Mexican-Americans there is no particular distinction.

marriage with respect to whether the couple is of pure Mexican descent or whether one or more parents are non-Mexican. The data are given in Table 17. From inspection of the table, it appears that, relatively speaking, the civil courts married about as many couples of non-Mexican or mixed ancestry, in comparison with pure Mexican stock, as did the Catholic clergy. On the other hand, of those couples married by the Protestant clergy, a significantly greater proportion were of mixed origin, indeed more than twice as many. The reasons appear to lie in the probability that many, if not most, of the non-Mexican parents of the bride or groom are Protestants and exert considerable influence on the method of getting married. On the other hand, for those who prefer a judicial ceremony the religious affiliation of the parents seems to be of little consequence.

If one checks the number of very young brides in the two ethnic groups with reference to marriage by judicial or clerical ceremony regardless of church, one sees that more of the Mexican-American component has utilized the former method than has the Anglo-American component. The figures are in Table 18, where the distinction is drawn between those under eighteen years of age and those eighteen or older. With the Anglo-Americans there is no difference referable to age. With the Mexican-Americans there is a significant difference. Relatively more of the judicial ceremonies are performed with very young individuals. The over-all greater youthfulness of the Mexican-American brides may be an influence here. Furthermore, when females under sixteen or males under eighteen apply for a marriage license, it is required that special court permission be secured in order to obtain one.[166] When these licenses are granted, there may be some inclination on the part of the couple to be married in the same court that granted the license. On the whole, however, the numbers involved are not great and these factors cannot be of decisive influence in determining the form of the wedding ceremony.

After examination of those parameters which are subject to some degree of quantitative analysis, it is still necessary to explain the remarkable shift of that portion of the Mexican-American population which seeks legal marriage toward reliance upon civil rather than religious ceremony and upon Protestant in partial substitution for Catholic ceremony. Previous divorce or age of the participants will not significantly account for the phenomenon. Religious background of the parents comes closer to an explanation but is by no means a complete solution. Perhaps, basically, two factors must be reckoned with. One is the familiarity with civil marriage developed over decades in Mexico. The second is the influence of American Protestantism, which in turn manifests itself in two ways; the

---

[166] CAL. CIV. CODE § 56.

relative ease of marriage of divorced persons and the religious convictions of the parents.

If the Mexican tradition of civil marriage and American Protestantism help to provide the pathways along which marriage custom is moving, something else must furnish the driving force. The opinion may be advanced that this motivation is derived from the contemporary American environment through welfare agencies, church activities, majority public opinion, and many other elements. Despite a somewhat higher level of procreative activity which pervades all classes of Mexican-American society, there can have been no fundamental biological change within this segment of the population. Hence there are left only social forces, which are environmental rather than genetic.

If these considerations are valid with respect to type of legal matrimony, then it follows that common law marriage must be subject to the same pressures and these pressures are in the direction of the full transition from any form of extra-legal union to complete acceptance of some type of conventional ceremony. The problem has not yet been studied from the historical or developmental point of view, but we may guess that such a study would bring to light a recognizable and perhaps strong trend away from common law to legal marriage. This would be accompanied by a channelling of the Mexican-American population into the economically most feasible and the socially most acceptable modes of legal matrimony.

SUMMARY AND CONCLUSIONS

1. A comparison of birth, marriage, and welfare data for Mexican-Americans indicates that birth in Mexico does not constitute a factor influencing presence or absence in the welfare category or in the category of participants in legal marriage. Nevertheless, persons born in the American Southwest are more heavily represented in the welfare group than in that group which is recorded on marriage certificates.

2. In regard to type of matrimony, a study of common law marriage among women whose cases are on file at the Welfare Department indicates certain specific findings, as follows:

a. A comparison with Anglo-American women shows that common law marriage is far more frequent among Mexican-American women.

b. In both ethnic groups the older women have fewer common law marriages recorded than the younger.

c. Examination of welfare data shows that the strong tendency to separate by method other than divorce is inherent in the situation created by the informal union and is not peculiar to either ethnic group.

3. The file of marriage certificates demonstrates that there is a strong

preference by Mexican-American couples to marry either in a judicial or Protestant ceremony rather than in the Catholic church. This departure from Mexican religious tradition is referable neither to previous divorce nor youthful age on the part of those directly concerned. To a significant degree it is influenced by the religious affiliation of the parents of the Anglo-Americans, who, in mixed marriages, are likely to be non-Catholic.

4. The emergence of a new pattern governing the type of legal marriage among the Mexican-Americans is probably conditioned by several factors, such as familiarity with civil marriage in Mexico, frequent encounter with the Protestant churches in the case of mixed marriages, and a complex of social pressures exerted through the California environment, rather than through any modification of an intrinsic or biological nature. These considerations apply to common law as well as to formal marriage and are probably operating actively to reduce or eliminate the former type of union.

5. The data on Mexican-Americans in Santa Clara County show two differences in comparison with Anglo-Americans that may be related to the patterns of Mexican family union found in Part I of this study: the relatively high rate of common law marriage among the women who reach the Welfare Department and the strong tendency in legal marriages to resort to judicial rather than church ceremony. Common law union, of course, gives rise to illegitimate offspring. Can the differences be ascribed directly to cultural carry-over from Mexico to California? The answer must be equivocal: It is possible. An unequivocal answer requires examination of data from more counties, a survey of common law union among Mexican-Americans that extends beyond the people on welfare, and comparative examination of another major group of the poor, the Negroes. That comparative examination would have to look beyond the extent of informal unions to duration of such unions and the nature of family structure, especially the roles of the man and the woman in the home. The material in this article does support the hypothesis that Mexican-American behavior in family union is conditioned by cultural carry-over.

APPENDIX

TABLE 1
Selected Summaries of 1777 Census Data, Bishopric of Oaxaca

1 A

Married and Unmarried Persons of the Population as a Per cent

Race	Married Men	Unmarried Men and Women
Gente de Razón	16.2	16.5
Pardos	17.2	9.0
Indians	21.1	3.8
Antequera (Mixed)	16.1	19.4

1 B

Unmarried Women with Children per 1,000 Inhabitants

Race	Total Population in Returns (to nearest thousand)	Proportion
Gente de Razón	6,000	6.2
Pardos	13,000	5.6
Indians	188,000	0.95
Antequera (Mixed)	19,000	14.2

1 C

Probable Illegitimate Children in Antequera Census of 1777

Part of City	Females Undesignated as to Civil Status		Females Designated as *Solteras*	
	Children Designated as *Huérfanos*	Children Designated as *Hijos*	Children Designated as *Huérfanos*	Children Designated as *Hijos*
Rumbo de Arriba	141	2	21	1
Rumbo de Abajo	0	4	30	65

Total = 264
Population = 18,558
Cases per 1,000 Persons = 14.23 { Rumbo Arriba alone: 15.93 / Rumbo Abajo alone: 12.54

Note: Clergy and people in institutions are excluded from all sections of the Table.
Source: Archivo General de Indias, Seville, Sección de Audiencia de Méjico, Legajos 2589-91.

Notes to Table 1 C:
1. Observe the difference in designation of the females between the two *rumbos*.
2. In Rumbo de Abajo, Tandas 1-3 show for children 25 hijos, 30 huérfanos. Tandas 4-6 plus Consolación show 40 *hijos*, 0 *huérfanos*.
3. A great many, perhaps 100, equivocal cases are omitted. The figure 14.23, therefore, is conservative.

TABLE 2

2 A
Percentage of Registered Births Which Were Illegitimate
Mixteca Alta[a]

Years	Total Registered Births	Illegitimate Births (Per cent)
1870-1874	14,960	15.0
1888-1892	30,365	30.2
1905-1910	32,949	55.1
1920-1925	24,414	81.8[b]
1937-1947	19,140	56.8
1950-1954	39,823	52.7

Source: Registers of births in Archivo General del Estado, Oaxaca.
Notes:
a. The five districts are Coixtlahuaca, Nochixtlán, Teposcolula, Tlaxiaco, and Putla. Although the districts no longer exist as administrative entities under the Constitution of 1917, they continue to be used as groupings of *municipios* for archival and postal purposes.
b. For the district of Putla, the proportion was 95%.

2 B
Percentage of Registered Births Which Were Illegitimate
Jalisco

Years	Coastal Zone (4 towns)	Intermediate Zone (7 towns)	Plateau Zone (8 towns)	Total Jalisco exc. Guad.	Total Jalisco inc. Guad.	City of Guadalajara
1875						13.4
1880-1884	20.7	10.5	7.2	9.7	10.6	13.8
1890-1894	17.2	11.9	5.1	9.2	9.6	18.2
1904-1908	17.4	11.5	4.7	8.9	—	—
1915						12.7
1921-1925	21.5	11.9	5.5	11.3	12.3	19.6
1931-1935	26.8	14.4	5.3	11.4	13.9	34.4
1941-1945	19.3	11.7	4.9	9.5	10.5	17.0
1951-1955	17.2	10.3	5.8	9.1	10.1	15.6
Mean per cent	20.0	11.7	5.5	9.9	11.3	18.1
Per cent of Totals	20.1	11.8	5.5	10.8		17.7

Source: Registers of births in Archivo Municipal, Guadalajara and in the Archivo General del Estado, Guadalajara.

TABLE 3

3 A

Data on Forms of Marital Status, Illegitimacy, and Cultural Factors Forms of Marriage

Entity	Adults Living in Union Libre Per cent of Total	Adults in no indicato Per cent of Total	People in Formal Unions (Casados)			Per cent of Children Born Who Are Illegitimate 1959-1961	Per cent Illiterate	Per cent of Rural to Total Population	Per cent Speaking an Indian Language	Per cent of Population Who Wear Shoes
			Per cent by Civil Only of Casados	Per cent by Church Ceremony Only of Casados	Per cent of Casados by Civil & Church					
Country	15.02	5.16	20.56	11.57	67.87	25.04	37.78	49.30	10.39	60.24
Aguascalientes	4.47	4.49	4.33	2.12	93.55	9.46	27.06	40.32	0.37	75.83
Baja California	14.38	7.48	33.70	4.65	61.65	20.26	18.88	39.23	1.29	93.10
Baja Calif. T. Sur	13.48	6.11	22.74	10.78	66.48	33.30	20.50	63.41	0.45	81.31
Campeche	13.65	5.55	34.94	3.29	61.77	21.54	31.90	36.90	25.83	65.27
Coahuila	8.74	5.41	30.16	3.01	66.84	8.80	19.60	33.25	0.41	86.65
Colima	11.69	6.74	7.19	8.19	84.62	28.24	31.40	38.41	0.83	42.68
Chiapas	42.34	4.78	59.00	14.58	26.42	51.75	60.70	75.55	37.97	23.72
Chihuahua	10.38	6.21	21.73	5.17	73.10	14.17	25.08	42.86	4.05	82.77
Distrito Federal	12.07	4.89	21.32	5.96	72.72	14.24	16.58	4.20	1.10	91.37
Durango	10.98	5.22	14.26	9.74	76.00	20.16	24.83	64.52	0.91	68.20
Guanajuato	3.25	4.16	4.03	10.38	85.59	16.30	48.90	53.57	0.27	59.44
Guerrero	12.24	5.39	17.54	11.02	71.44	19.29	62.80	74.22	20.08	23.07
Hidalgo	30.05	4.80	26.04	21.32	52.64	50.60	56.00	77.58	28.07	36.20
Jalisco	4.98	6.21	4.80	4.93	90.27	9.79	34.82	41.50	0.49	57.86
México	8.48	5.34	13.50	19.89	66.61	24.16	42.60	61.38	10.82	55.39

TABLE 3 (Continued)

3 B
Data on Forms of Marital Status, Illegitimacy, and Cultural Factors

Entity	Per cent of Total Adults Living in Unión Libre	Per cent of Total Adults in no indicato	People in Formal Unions (Casados) Forms of Marriage			Per cent of Children Born Who Are Illegitimate 1959-1961	Per cent Illiteracy	Per cent of Rural to Total Population	Per cent Speaking an Indian Language	Per cent of Population Who Wear Shoes
			Per cent Civil Only of Casados	Per cent Church Ceremony Only of Casados	Per cent of Casados by Civil & Church					
Michoacán	5.19	4.04	6.33	9.95	83.72	13.79	49.10	59.39	3.78	55.72
Morelos	20.83	4.99	22.90	16.04	61.06	36.82	39.15	46.89	2.87	59.98
Nayarit	25.56	4.79	15.44	15.66	68.90	45.00	34.04	57.43	2.94	47.01
Nuevo León	6.23	5.81	29.42	2.30	68.28	5.43	19.29	29.65	0.25	87.06
Oaxaca	20.24	5.94	19.94	35.35	44.71	51.75	59.10	75.62	46.82	17.12
Puebla	16.14	4.04	16.10	21.10	62.80	35.45	49.76	60.79	17.74	35.52
Querétaro	3.88	4.53	4.03	5.78	90.19	10.00	57.10	71.83	4.11	40.47
Quintana Roo	22.00	5.25	31.12	11.63	57.25	26.77	35.50	68.00	60.75	61.84
San Luis Potosí	11.81	5.78	12.15	7.29	80.56	15.67	46.65	66.41	13.57	52.62
Sinaloa	32.64	6.11	46.70	7.32	45.98	46.50	33.95	61.81	0.84	57.03
Sonora	17.60	4.50	41.15	4.87	53.98	25.76	23.82	42.40	3.52	86.23
Tabasco	31.22	6.63	67.15	11.44	21.41	43.90	38.34	73.38	5.79	34.29
Tamaulipas	15.34	4.16	45.25	4.36	50.39	24.04	22.66	40.13	0.23	85.78
Tlaxcala	11.57	4.43	16.48	6.91	76.61	22.12	38.46	56.19	6.30	42.37
Veracruz	32.90	5.55	34.75	26.93	38.32	55.75	45.20	60.44	13.65	60.45
Yucatán	12.81	4.26	17.25	4.68	78.07	22.67	34.26	40.22	56.31	58.05

TABLE 3 (Continued)

3 C

Data on Forms of Marital Status, Illegitimacy, and Cultural Factors
Forms of Marriage

Entity	Per cent of Total Adults Living in Unión Libre	Per cent of Total Adults in no indicato	People in Formal Unions (Casados)			Per cent of Children Born Who Are Illegitimate 1959-1961	Per cent Illiteracy	Per cent of Rural to Total Population	Per cent Speaking an Indian Language	Per cent of Population Who Wear Shoes
			Per cent Civil Only of Casados	Per cent Church Ceremony Only of Casados	Per cent of Casados by Civil & Church					
Zacatecas	4.58	4.05	6.00	6.28	87.72	8.12	36.66	72.86	0.09	68.84
Mean	15.67	5.24	23.36	10.41	66.23	26.00	37.03	54.07	11.64	59.16
Mean exc. D. F.								56.70		

Sources: 8 México Censo General de Población: 1960, Resumen General, Tables 1, 17, 39; Anuario Estadístico de los Estados Unidos Mexicanos, Tables 2.15, 2.16, and 3.8 (1960-61).

TABLE 4
Summary of Correlations Relating to Matrimony and Legitimacy

Correlations Against Percentage of Illegitimate Children Born 1959-61	$r =$
A. Various Types of Union:	
1. *No Indicado*	+ 0.133
2. *Unión Libre*	+ 0.907
3. *Unión Libre* plus *No Indicato* (1 + 2)	+ 0.901
4. Married by Civil Ceremony Only	+ 0.376
5. Married by Religious Ceremony Only	+ 0.618
6. Married by Civil and Religious Ceremony	− 0.899
7. *Unión Libre* Plus Married by Religious Ceremony Only	+ 0.966
8. *Unión Libre* plus Married by Religious Ceremony Only plus *No Indicato* (1 + 2 + 5)	+ 0.967
9. Married by Civil Ceremony Only Plus Married by Civil and Religious Ceremonies (4 + 6)	− 0.967
B. Various Cultural Factors:	
1. Per cent Illiteracy	+ 0.393
2. Per cent Rural	
a. Omitting Federal District	+ 0.467
b. Including Federal District	+ 0.470
3. Per cent Speaking Indian Language	+ 0.359
4. Per cent Wearing Shoes	− 0.505

Note: The correlations are based upon the values for 32 states. For this number a value for *r* of less than 0.349 is non-significant, of 0.349 to 0.449 is significant, and of greater than 0.449 is very significant.

TABLE 5
Comparison of People Living in Irregular and Informal Union and Proportion of
Illegitimate Births

(*Unión Libre* plus Married by Religious Ceremony Only)

Per cent of *Unión Libre* and People Married by Religious Ceremony Only		Per cent of Illegitimate Births Average of 1959-1961	
50-30%		High	60-35%
Chiapas	50.05	Veracruz	55.75
Veracruz	49.48	Chiapas	51.75
Oaxaca	46.40	Oaxaca	51.75
Hidalgo	43.94	Hidalgo	50.60
Tabascc	38.35	Sinaloa	46.50
Sinaloa	37.02	Nayarit	45.00
Nayarit	36.47	Tabasco	43.90
Puebla	32.99	Morelos	36.82
Morelos	32.74	Puebla	35.45
Quintana Roo	30.71		
30-15%		Intermediate	35-18%
México	25.63	Baja Calif., Ter. Sur	33.30
Sonora	21.39	Colima	28.24
Guerrero	21.32	Quintana Roo	26.77
Tamaulipas	19.85	Sonora	25.76
Baja Calif., Ter. Sur	19.23	México	24.16
Durango	19.15	Tamaulipas	24.04
Colima	18.40	Yucatán	22.67
Baja California	17.96	Tlaxcala	22.12
San Luis Potosí	17.83	Campeche	21.54
Tlaxcala	17.37	Baja California	20.26
Distrito Federal	17.02	Durango	20.16
Yucatán	16.70	Guerrero	19.29
Campeche	16.31		
15%-5%		Low	18-5%
Chihuahua	14.69	Guanajuato	16.30
Michoacán	14.21	San Luis Potosí	15.67
Guanajuato	12.86	Distrito Federal	14.24
Coahuila	11.33	Chihuahua	14.17
Zacatecas	10.31	Michoacán	13.79
Jalisco	9.36	Querétaro	10.00
Querétaro	9.18	Jalisco	9.79
Nuevo León	8.25	Aguascalientes	9.46
Aguascalientes	6.46	Coahuila	8.80
		Zacatecas	8.12
		Nuevo León	5.43

Sources: Anuario Estadístico de los Estados Unidos Mexicanos 1960-1961, Tables 21.6 and
2.18.

TABLE 6
Illegitimate Births as Per cent of Total Births—1900-05 and 1959-61

State	1900-05 (Average of 2 years)	1959-61 (Average of 3 years)
Aguascalientes	14.73	9.46
Baja California, North & South	45.12	21.83
Campeche	15.97	21.54
Coahuila	10.42	8.80
Colima	47.62	28.24
Chiapas	73.15	51.75
Chihuahua	17.79	14.17
Distrito Federal	63.77	14.24
Durango	30.92	20.16
Guanajuato	47.50	16.30
Guerrero	29.72	19.29
Hidalgo	61.00	50.60
Jalisco	10.38	9.79
México	36.57	24.16
Michoacán	77.20	13.79
Morelos	53.80	36.82
Nayarit	53.10	45.00
Nuevo León	6.45	5.43
Oaxaca	66.65	51.75
Puebla	48.72	35.45
Querétaro	28.07	10.00
San Luis Potosí	24.37	15.67
Sinaloa	70.37	46.50
Sonora	46.72	25.76
Tabasco	46.20	43.90
Tamaulipas	31.20	24.04
Tlaxcala	23.62	22.12
Veracruz	62.55	55.75
Yucatán & Quintana Roo	17.50	22.91
Zacatecas	16.24	8.12
Total Country	42.23	25.04
Mean Percentage Values	39.25	25.78

Sources: Estadísticas Sociales del Porfiriato 1877-1910, Tables 15-16 of Section 1, at 19-21; Anuario Estadístico de los Estados Unidos Mexicanos 1960-1961, Table 3.8.

TABLE 7
Birthplace of Persons of Mexican Derivation

Source of Data	Born in California	Born in Southwestern States	Born in Mexico	Total
	A.—Absolute numbers			
Welfare	106	193	48	347
Birth Records	806	707	206	1,719
Marriage Records	686	514	178	1,378
Total	1,598	1,414	432	3,444
	B.—Percentages			
Welfare	30.57	55.60	13.83	100.00
Birth Records	46.90	41.14	11.96	100.00
Marriage Records	49.78	37.30	12.92	100.00
All Persons	46.38	41.08	12.54	100.00

Note: The three sources of data are the Welfare Department files and the birth and marriage records of the county.

TABLE 8
Place of Birth and Type of Marriage Among Mexican-American Women
Welfare Data

	Legal	Common Law	Per cent Common Law
Born in the United States	139	53	27.7
Born in Mexico	45	8	15.1
Per cent of total in Mexico	24.5	13.1	

TABLE 9
Place of Birth and Type of Marital Separation Among Mexican-American Women
Welfare Data

	A		
	Still living together	Not living together	Per cent not living together
Born in the United States	106	123	54.7
Born in Mexico	25	33	56.9
Per cent born in Mexico	19.1	21.2	
		chi-square = less than 1.0	

	B		
	Separated by death	Separated by all other causes	Per cent by other causes
Born in the United States	30	88	74.6
Born in Mexico	20	13	39.4
Per cent born in Mexico	40.0	12.6	
		chi-square = 12.88	

	C		
	Separated by divorce	Separated by desertion	Per cent by desertion
Born in the United States	31	57	64.9
Born in Mexico	2	11	84.6
Per cent born in Mexico	6.1	12.2	
		chi-square = 1.0	

TABLE 10
Type of Marriage in the Anglo and the Mexican-American Population
Welfare Data

	Legal	Common Law	Per cent Common Law
Anglo-American	302	20	6.2
Mexican-American	206	79	27.7
Per cent Mexican-Amer.	40.6	78.8	
		chi-square = 49.65	

TABLE 11
Differences Between Anglo-Americans Born in the South and Those Born in the North
Welfare Data

	North	South	Per cent in South
Legal	124	95	43.4
Common Law	7	13	65.0
Per cent common law	5.3	12.0	
		chi-square = 2.64	

TABLE 12
Date of Birth and Type of Marriage among Anglo and Mexican-American Women

A Anglo-American			B Mexican-American		
	Born 1870-1909	Born 1910-1949		Born 1870-1909	Born 1910-1949
Legal	123	179	Legal	55	151
Common law	1	19	Common law	9	70
Per cent			Per cent		
Common law	0.8	9.6	Common law	14.1	31.7

chi-square = 8.63   chi-square = 6.83
First order interaction = 13.05   First order interaction = 2.83
Second order interaction = 4.61
chi-square for second order interaction = 1.15 (non-significant)

TABLE 13
Separation among Anglo and Mexican-American Women

	A Anglo-American	Mexican-American		B Anglo-American	Mexican-American
Still Married	131	144	Death	66	47
No longer Married	195	159	Otherwise	129	112
Per cent no longer Married	59.7	52.4	Per cent not separated by death	66.2	70.4
	chi-square = 2.68; P = 0.11			chi-square = 0.56	

	C Total Separations other than by Death			D Separation of Legal Marriage by other than Death	
	Anglo-American	Mexican-American		Anglo-American	Mexican-American
Divorce	87	24	Divorce	87	24
Desertion	42	88	Desertion	23	25
Per cent divorced	67.5	21.4	Per cent divorced	79.1	49.0
	chi-square = 51.5			chi-square = 19.3	

	E Anglo-American	
	North	South
Divorce	31	24
Desertion	12	21
Per cent divorced	72.1	53.3
chi-square = 2.57		

TABLE 14

Tendency to Separate by Any Method from Legal or Common Law Marriages on the Part
of Anglo-American and Mexican-American Groups, that is, Those Still Living in
Matrimony or Separated by Death as Contrasted with Those Separated
by Divorce or Desertion

	Anglo-American				Mexican-American		
	Living together or separated by death	Divorced or deserted	Per cent divorced		Living together or separated by death	Divorced or deserted	Per cent divorced
Legal	192	110	36.4	Legal	166	49	22.8
Common				Common			
Law	5	19	79.2	Law	25	63	71.6

chi-square = 15.3　　　　　　　　　　　chi-square = 39.3
First order interaction = 6.63　　　　First order interaction = 8.54
Second order interaction = 1.29
chi-square for second order interaction = < 0.1, non-significant

TABLE 15

Division of Marriages for Anglo and Mexican-Americans According to Whether the
Ceremony was Performed by a Judge, a Catholic, or a Protestant Clergyman
From County Marriage Certificates

	Anglo-American			Mexican-American		
	Judicial	Catholic	Protestant	Judicial	Catholic	Protestant
Number	110	151	579	415	302	123
Per cent	13.1	18.0	68.9	49.5	35.9	14.7

TABLE 16

Remarriage of Divorced Persons by Courts and by Protestant Clergy

	Anglo-American		Mexican-American	
	Divorced	Never Married	Divorced	Never Married
Judicial	51	59	78	337
Protestant	144	435	26	97
Total	195	494	104	434

chi-square = 19.98　　　　　　　　chi-square = 0.20
Note: The term "divorced" means that one or both of the parties to a marriage had
been previously divorced.

TABLE 17

Marriages of Persons within the Mexican-American Group Who Were of Mixed Origin

	Mixed	Mexican
Judicial	129	286
Catholic	106	196
Protestant	83	40
Total	318	522

chi-square: Judicial and Catholic = 1.46
chi-square: Catholic and Protestant = 35.10
chi-square: Judicial and Protestant = 51.60

Note: The term "mixed" indicates that at least one of the four parents was of non-Mexican origin.

TABLE 18

Relative Number of Very Young Brides Married Judicially, or in Some Church, among the Anglo and Mexican-American Populations

	Anglo-American		Mexican-American	
	Married under 18 years	Married at 18 or over	Married under 18 years	Married at 18 or over
Judicial	17	93	111	304
Church	89	641	60	365
	chi-square = 0.65		chi-square = 19.88	

The Urban Law Program of the University of Detroit School of Law

Norman L. Miller and *James C. Daggitt***

THERE HAS RECENTLY BEEN a muttering of dissatisfaction on the part of many lawyers and legal educators which has steadily grown into a decidedly discomfiting rumble. In some cases it is the result of an awareness of the rigidity and pedantic, if not atrophic, qualities which exemplify the majority of curricula in the nation's law schools, both large and small; in other cases it has arisen because law schools seem to be preparing their students only for roles as desk lawyers, and closing their eyes to the urgency of new social and economic patterns which have begun to exert such insistent pressures that they can no longer be ignored.[1] More often than not, the two expressions are actually two different ways of looking at the same problem, namely, when will law schools recognize and reflect in changed curricula the changing needs of changing times?

In September 1965 the University of Detroit School of Law received a grant of 242,000 dollars from the Office of Economic Opportunity. The grant provides funds for a demonstration, research, and training program under Title II-A of the Economic Opportunity Act of 1964.[2]

Prior to receipt of this grant the law school reexamined its course of study, similar to that of practically all other U.S. law schools, and found it inconsistent with the realities of modern society, but, more particularly, based on a limited perspective of the role of the attorney in society. It was safely traditional, saleable, and consistent with the image that far too many lawyers have of the profession. It was also uncomfortably unsuited to our times and to the demands to be made on future lawyers.

---

* A.B., 1957, LL.B., 1960, University of Michigan; Cert. M.S., 1961, Wayne State University. Assistant Dean and Associate Professor of Law, Director of the Urban Law Program, University of Detroit School of Law.

** B.A., 1953 Amherst College; LL.B., 1964, University of Michigan. Member, D.C. Bar.

[1] See, *e.g.*, Reich, *Toward the Humanistic Study of Law*, 74 YALE L.J. 1402, 1406-07 (1965): "Many of the ills of legal education are symptomatic of the fact that it is primarily professional in orientation, although it should also be preparing students for lives of public service and scholarship. . . . [T]he most important reason for a new approach to the study of law is not simply to improve the present job of educating scholars, public servants, and practitioners as that job is now conceived. The ultimate justification for curricular revision, or rather the necessity, comes from the fact that the role of law in society has changed and is changing, and hence the role of lawyers must change. Law now permeates every activity. This trend is inevitable as society rapidly becomes more institutional and bureaucratic. Today's social problems necessarily become legal problems."

[2] 78 Stat. 508, 516, 42 U.S.C. §§ 2781-91 (1964).

I

THE URBAN COMMUNITY AND THE LAW

It appears eminently clear that American life patterns, public and private, personal and collective, will revolve around the urban community. These centers, containing millions of inhabitants, stretching hundreds of miles, will require the development of new legal relationships of an infinite variety. New concepts will be needed for urban governmental units creating ties of various kinds between the metropolitan center and the outlying suburban areas. No longer will there be simply a dependency on the center city's water supply, public transportation systems, and freeways. The immediate future will create dependencies on the complete range of planning and service expertise found in the center city which the outlying areas cannot afford or would be financially foolish to duplicate. Intelligent land use planning is essential.

It is also clear that city governments are beginning to challenge and, in many cases, to eclipse state governments in importance as a means through which federal programs may be effected. State capitals have not been particularly responsive or particularly sensitive to the needs of the large metropolitan areas within their borders. Cooperative city administrations are providing a more appealing local forum for the exercise of national policy. With the continually increasing urbanization of America's population, it is not surprising that the city should prove a more effective instrumentality for reaching the people.

There is a need to develop new legal concepts and attitudes in both public and private arenas. As the development of city-federal ventures continues, lawyers will create the units defining these relationships and their *modus operandi*. The development of cooperative and condominium housing requires lawyers to develop a new scheme of private rights and obligations. Attorneys representing private clients *must* keep up with the certain growth of public and administrative law. Better yet, they ought to participate in its development, to aid in its architecture. But to do this, the future lawyers must have an understanding of what and who will be involved in the urban centers of the future.

Urban law in both its public and private sectors is where law schools ought to be giving their attention now. But to do so requires an analysis, an understanding of the past and present. It requires, equally so, a fostering and nurturing of the idealism that first year students have that somehow manages to wither and decay as graduation approaches. One suspects that this disappearance of idealism results from a continuous three-year diet of case method instruction, unsensible and static rules of law, a realization of the inadequacies of the legal system and of the direct relationship between the quality of American legal service and the client's ability to pay.

Ought not law students also to be exposed to a developmental approach or method of legal studies? Have law schools forgotten that all their graduates do not become advocates of special interests?

The University of Detroit School of Law has chosen to enter the field of Urban Law. An examination of the legal problems of the urban poor brings the panorama of the entire urban society into focus. The lawyers serving the urban poor, the legal researchers accumulating law course materials dealing with the urban poor, preparing educational materials on legal topics for dissemination among the urban poor, or researching the legal problems which might be uniquely associated with the urban poor (public assistance law, landlord-tenant, government contracts, property, criminal law) of necessity must examine the entire life and structure of the metropolitan area. These are not problems in isolation. The legal nature of the urban political structure, its courts, and agencies must be known and understood.

II

THE DETROIT URBAN LAW PROGRAM

Situated as it is in the heart of the inner city of one of the country's great industrial areas, the University of Detroit School of Law is located in an area that might wryly be described as ideal for the study of the problems of urban poverty. From a window of the law school one can see both high-rise luxury apartments built on urban renewal land and skid-row ghettos. The concept of the Urban Law Program and the work toward its implementation have therefore a vital and intense immediacy.

The program involves four interrelated elements. The first is the restructuring of the law school curriculum and its extracurricular activities to focus on the legal problems of the poor as well as to deal with the legal issues arising out of urban situations. This will eventually include courses leading to graduate degrees in law, not previously offered.

The second element is the initiation of a community education program aimed at familiarizing the general community with the legal rights and services available to them.

The third component is a clinical experience for law students which will have the fourfold effect of making available additional legal help for the indigent, giving students invaluable practical opportunities to learn the operations of our legal system, exposing them to the daily problems of the urban poor, and bringing into the academic isolation of law school studies the concept of a legal intern program where practical application can be made of classroom knowledge.

The fourth element is a research program, not fully implemented at the time of writing, aimed at: (1) gathering information on the legal problems of the poor and the particular city in which they live; (2) legal research to provide the content for curriculum development and community education; (3) evaluation of the clinical program and study of the experience developed there; (4) study and drafting of legislation where appropriate; and (5) the development of an interdisciplinary approach to both urban law and the law school curriculum.

A number of new law courses have been proposed, and others have already been made part of the curriculum. Among those proposed are courses in public assistance law, urban property law, employee rights, and legal and social problems of juveniles in the urban community. Already instituted and part of the curriculum are a trial seminar, the academic companion of the clinical experience, aimed at giving the students the training they need to interview clients, prepare pleadings, and try cases, and an interdisciplinary law and poverty seminar. In the latter course, economists, sociologists, criminologists, psychologists, psychiatrists, and urban planners, among others, participate in the objectives of giving law students a thorough grounding in the many dimensions of the problems of urban life and the urban poor, and revealing the programs and assistance that other disciplines and the community have developed for the solution of nonlegal problems that will inevitably accompany the client of the future lawyer. Supplementary materials for the so-called traditional courses are also in preparation, designed to make the traditional courses more useful to the lawyer who intends to practice in the urban community.

As previously mentioned, plans are in process for introducing a Graduate Program in Urban Law. The field of urban law sorely needs specialists, both as practitioners and teachers. It takes years of practical experience to accumulate the specialized knowledge which can be acquired in a few well-conceived courses. With most law schools devoting so little time to courses relevant to urban practice, specialized education in this field must come at the graduate level. Such a program will culminate in an intensive internship for those who plan to become practitioners, including working as an attorney in the Urban Law Office or some other agency offering a similar experience. For those in the graduate program who wish to teach, a thesis requirement will be substituted for a part of the internship.

A law school which purports to be a law school for the urban community cannot confine its efforts to the select few who aspire to become lawyers. It also has an obligation to the total community it serves to instill in the members of the urban community an understanding of their rights and responsibilities under the law. The urban poor, in particular, often are abused by the legal process because they are ignorant of even the most elementary of its principles. They frequently submit to illegal acts and baseless legal claims because they do not realize the law provides the grounds and forum with which to resist.

This Community Education Program phase of the Urban Law Program has been extremely active and will undoubtedly become more so as the word spreads. Already, legal counseling and services have been sought by and given to tenants' councils, homeowners' groups, and the local Community Action Program of the Office of Economic Opportunity—called TAAP (Total Action Against Poverty) in Detroit. Students in the Program have lectured widely and often in junior and senior high schools, telling the young audiences of their legal rights and advising them, for example, what to do and what not to do in the case of an arrest.

The third phase of the Program, involving clinical experience for the law student has, to date, been the most vital and active part of the plan. The Urban Law Office of the University of Detroit was opened in November 1965 in a store front building one-half block from the law school. It is in an area which is also within walking distance of the courts and the jails, and close to some of the most depressed neighborhoods of the city. The Law Office, fully staffed, has three full-time attorneys, two neighborhood people working as investigators, a social worker, clerical staff, and between thirty and fifty participating students from the second and third year classes.

The place has a highly kinetic atmosphere, with a steady flow of people seeking and getting the help they need. If it is found that a client is able to pay legal fees, he is referred to a local lawyer on the Urban Law Office's reference list. If he does not have money for fees, he qualifies for help at the Urban Law Office. There are no restrictions on the types of cases handled.

The response to the Law Office has been so enthusiastic that there are more than seven hundred files now in the office. The effectiveness of the Law Office as a service to the urban poor remains to be seen and will not be known until a considerable amount of data can be gathered and evaluated over a period of time. There can be no doubt, however, that with such a response, there is a tremendous need for the services. Nor can there be much doubt that the young men and women who have participated as legal interns in the program have gained much from their experience, even in the few months that the Law Office has been open.

The fourth and final aspect of the program, the research aspect, is still in a highly formative state. Not until there has been time to collect and evaluate data will the research project make its major contribution to the Urban Law Program. The research section has, however, done considerable work in legislative drafting with regard to the proposed Michigan Housing Code of 1966.

CONCLUSION

That the problem of the emerging lawyer has become one of wide interest is manifestly shown by the widely different forums in which the problem has been discussed. From the article by Martin Mayer in the popular *Saturday Evening Post*[3] to a plethora of writings in law journals, similar ideas emerge: Law schools are not doing their job, law curricula are static, the product of most law schools is an individual primed mainly to take his place perhaps in the courtroom, or more likely only in the world of commerce. As Charles Reich has aptly stated:

> Until very recently the legal profession has narrowly limited its scope. Lawyers have traditionally concerned themselves with only one sector of the world in which law now operates, the sector of commerce. For most of them, day-to-day law has meant business law. Other problems have clustered around the business core, but these have also tended to be commercial in nature. Today, however, it is vitally necessary that lawyers actively participate in all of the areas of society in which law now plays a role. Their work may start with business, but it should range over criminal law, public housing, social welfare, unemployment, problems of the mentally ill, urban town and country planning, economic planning both local and national, civil rights, civil liberties, all forms of protest movements, and international law. In their private capacity they should be available to help all those individuals and groups who come in contact with law. They should learn to represent the various interest groups, constituencies and minorities in society— to help them develop points of view, speak for them, and interpret the world to them. That is the true scope of the practicing lawyer's calling.[4]

A large order? Indeed it is. But we feel that our Urban Law Program, both in its concept and in its execution, can answer that large order. The answer will arise out of the fact that the law school curriculum will, for the first time, give the law student direct experience with the problems of the urban community. A new dimension will be added by making, so to speak, the community a classroom. Perhaps in this way, the much quoted phrase of Oliver Wendell Holmes that "the life of the law has not been logic: it has been experience,"[5] will finally have an application in the life of our law students.

The rest remains to be written in the next few years. Our hopes, in addition to our aims, are high.

---

3 Mayer, *Justice, The Law and the Lawyer*, The Saturday Evening Post, Feb. 26, 1966, pp. 36, 72.

4 Reich, *supra* note 1, at 1407.

5 HOLMES, THE COMMON LAW 1 (Howe Ed. 1881).